The Chicago Manual of Style

The Chicago Manual of Style

SEVENTEENTH EDITION

The University of Chicago Press
CHICAGO AND LONDON

The University of Chicago Press, Chicago 60637
The University of Chicago Press, Ltd., London

First edition published 1906. Seventeenth edition 2017.
Printed in the United States of America

26 25 24 23 22 21 20 19 18 17   1 2 3 4 5

ISBN-13: 978-0-226-28705-8 (cloth)
DOI: https://doi.org/10.7208/cmos17

Library of Congress Cataloging-in-Publication Data

Title: The Chicago manual of style.
Description: Seventeenth edition. | Chicago ; London : The University of Chicago Press, 2017. | Includes bibliographical references and indexes.
Identifiers: LCCN 2017020712 | ISBN 9780226287058 (cloth : alk. paper)
Subjects: LCSH: Printing—Style manuals. | Authorship—Style manuals. | Authorship—Handbooks, manuals, etc. | Publishers and publishing—United States—Handbooks, manuals, etc.
Classification: LCC Z253 .U69 2017 | DDC 808/.0270973—dc23
LC record available at https://lccn.loc.gov/2017020712

♾ This paper meets the requirements of ANSI/NISO Z39.48-1992 (Permanence of Paper).

Contents

Part II · Style and Usage

Part III · Source Citations and Indexes

Preface

Since the publication of the eleventh edition of *The Chicago Manual of Style* in 1949, each new edition has been marked by a significant shift in publishing technologies, starting with the advent of phototypesetting in the 1950s, whereby text was rendered on photographic paper rather than as lines of metal type, the norm since the first edition. The introduction of computers and desktop publishing drove further changes until, starting in the early 1990s, the graphical internet changed everything once again.

Fast-forward to the seventeenth edition. Today, publishing generally relies on digital technologies (even for print), and more often than not the end product is available in your pocket, a development that had just started to take hold when the sixteenth edition was published. It is safe to say that most of us now have ready access, at any given moment and from practically anywhere we happen to be, not only to the classic novel *Moby-Dick* but also to the *Congressional Record* and a map of the human genome as well as the catalog of the Library of Congress and countless other databases. We can add to those practically anything else we might want (through a library or for a fee if necessary). At the same time, many of us are busy adding our own ideas to the conversation from the same devices that we use to enjoy this access to the ideas of others.

The seventeenth edition recognizes this shift in a number of ways. First, how we look for and find information influences what we choose to read. New coverage of metadata and keywords in chapters 1 and 2 recognizes the roles that authors and publishers play not only in making their work available but also in making sure it can be found by potential readers. This is complemented by significantly expanded coverage in chapter 4 of options for open-access publishing and distribution, which are also directly related to how readers engage with published sources. These and other discussions also recognize the needs of self-published authors and how they can benefit from close attention to procedures once followed mainly by traditional publishers.

The ways in which we read and conduct research and how we record and share our findings have also influenced coverage of source citations. Chapters 14 and 15 have been updated to include more detailed coverage related to identifying and citing sources consulted online, including tips for choosing the best form of link to cite, when and how to list a time stamp in addition to a date, and when to keep a permanent copy of a source. Expanded coverage of citation management applications recognizes that many writers document their sources automatically, often from the same platform used to consult the sources themselves. New coverage of social media demonstrates how to cite publicly accessible posts and comments as well as direct, private messages. Other newly added source types include live performances, app content (including video games), published standards, self-published books, and maps (including satellite data).

Dozens of changes throughout every chapter stem from the many ideas our readers have generously contributed through social media and our Q&A. For example, the new coverage on Hawaiian orthography in chapter 11 was inspired by reader requests. And the recognition in chapter 5 of the rising use of *they* as a gender-neutral singular pronoun referring to a specific person stems in part from discussions with our readers that go back to at least the fourteenth edition. Many crucial additions were suggested by our advisory board. These include coverage of PDF annotation tools and the more detailed checklist for electronic books in chapter 2, the discussion of electronic theses and dissertations in chapter 4, and coverage in chapters 1 and 14 related to journals that follow a continuous publishing model.

Broader changes affect the manual as a whole or specific chapters or subsections. Our extensive coverage of source citations for legal and public documents in chapter 14 has once again been updated to reflect the latest edition of *The Bluebook* (now in its twentieth edition). In general, paragraph titles and text have been revised with keyword searching in mind to make it easier to find specific content. And the bibliography has been thoroughly updated not only to include the latest resources but also to recognize the latest versions of older resources, including those that have moved exclusively online (as is the case for the continually updated unabridged dictionary from Merriam-Webster).

Meanwhile, the chapters on style and usage have been revised to include many refinements, clarifications, and additions. For example, chapter 5 has been expanded to cover sentence structure and syntax, including elliptical sentences, negation, expletives, and cleft sentences. Chapter 6 now includes coverage related to the use of commas with phrases and clauses in all positions in a sentence and clarifies the use of commas relative to quoted material, coverage that continues in chapter 13. Chapter 6 also includes new recommendations related to the use of nonbreaking and other types of spaces and the division of slashes and dashes at the ends of lines. Chapter 7 now recommends *email* (no hyphen) and *internet* (lowercase) in response to changes in usage and editorial preferences. Chapter 8 adds new guidelines for presenting

Korean names in text and for styling the names of operating systems, applications, and devices. Chapter 9 includes new examples featuring Chinese currency and bitcoins. Chapter 10 now sanctions using *US* as a noun (subject to editorial discretion). In these chapters and throughout the manual, examples have been updated to feature additional scenarios or to reflect the latest usage.

Once again, the recommendations in this manual have been guided by the principles that have been handed down through earlier editions, principles that have outlasted technological changes and cultural shifts. In writing, editing, and publishing, accuracy and attention to detail supported by clear, accessible prose never seem to go out of style. It is in support of these fundamental goals in the context of an evolving publishing landscape that this edition is offered.

On behalf of the University of Chicago Press
Russell David Harper
Spring 2017

Acknowledgments

The Chicago Manual of Style strives to codify the best practices of an institution and an industry. It thus requires the participation of many hands and many voices if it is to succeed. This edition has benefitted from the carefully crafted recommendations—some sweeping, some minor, all essential—of a host of publishing professionals. At the same time, those recommendations needed to be compared, vetted, and applied in a consistent manner and with a clear vision, a challenging task performed once again in exemplary fashion by this edition's principal reviser, Russell David Harper.

A preliminary outline as well as the entire penultimate draft of the manuscript was shaped by the guidance of an advisory board representing various communities of readers:

Shaye Areheart, Columbia Publishing Course
Richard Brown, Georgetown University Press
Marilyn Campbell, Rutgers University Press
Samuel Fanous, Bodleian Library
Barbara Flanagan, Macmillan Higher Education
William Germano, The Cooper Union for the Advancement of Science and Art
John E. Muenning, *New England Journal of Medicine*
Peter Olson, Sheridan Journal Services
Joshua Tallent, Firebrand Technologies

Freelance editor Joe Brown, John E. McIntyre of the *Baltimore Sun*, and Hope J. LeGro and Kathryn Owens of Georgetown University Press also offered numerous invaluable suggestions during the development process.

We would like to thank the many experts who advised us on our coverage of languages: Michael K. Bourdaghs, T. David Brent, Erik Carlson, Dennis Cokely, Thibaut d'Hubert, Ariela Finkelstein, Victor Friedman, Kathleen Hansell, Wadad Kadi, Elsi Kaiser, Ron Kekeha Solis, Kathryn Krug, John M. Lipski, Bruce Maylath, Christina von Nolcken, Lena Elisabeth Norrman, David A. Pharies, Thomas Shannon, Malynne Sternstein, Sem Sutter, Anna Szabolcsi, Jane Marie Todd, Marta Tonegutti, and Yuan Zhou. We are indebted to Diana Gillooly and Rick Schoen for their advice on mathematics; to Leslie Keros for her guidance on documentation; to Krista Coulson for her insights on digital publishing conventions; to Dean Blobaum for his recommendations on metadata; and to Michael Magoulias for his knowledge of journals publishing. We are also grateful to Susan Bielstein, Perry Cartwright, and Lisa Lucas for their review of copyright and permissions material; and to Ryden Anderson, Joseph Bizup, William T. FitzGerald, Ellen Gibson, Cheryl Iverson, and Angela Yokoe, who provided assistance on a variety of matters. We also owe a particular debt to Bryan A. Garner and William S. Strong for their authorship of whole chapters.

Within the University of Chicago Press, thanks go to David Morrow and Mary E. Laur, who oversaw the revision and publication process and advised on the many incarnations of the manuscript; to Michael Boudreau, Ruth Goring, Christie Henry, Carol Kasper, Michael Koplow, Devon Ritter, Carol Fisher Saller, Anita Samen, and Jill Shimabukuro for their essential role in shaping the manuscript; to Rossen Angelov, Matt Avery, and Debra Hebda for their leadership in developing the online edition; to Rachel Kelly, Bryanna Tartt, and Susan Zakin for their critical logistical support; and to Press director Garrett Kiely. Many other staff members contributed their knowledge and skills at various stages of the process: Carrie Adams, Skye Agnew, David Balsley, Adeetje Bouma, Michael Brehm, Owen Cook, Mary Corrado, Janet Deckenbach, Erin DeWitt, Elizabeth Ellingboe, Kelly Finefrock-Creed, Jenni Fry, Margaret Hivnor, Vinolia Huxley, Joe Jackson, Susan Karani, John C. Kessler, Ellen Kladky, James Lilly, Caterina MacLean, Anu Manila Mathew, Richard Martin, Timothy Mennel, Renaldo Migaldi, Scott Mitchell, Priya Nelson, Patricia O'Shea, Trevor Perri, Joseph G. Peterson, Randy Petilos, Mark Reschke, Jennifer Ringblom, Rose Rittenhouse, Lauren Salas, Christine Schwab, Joel Score, Amy Smith, Levi T. Stahl, Rachel Tenuta, Alan G. Thomas, Kyle Wagner, Ryo Yamaguchi, Serene Yang, Aiping Zhang, Langchi Zhu, and Yvonne Zipter. On behalf of the press, Christine Gever proofread the book, and Do Mi Stauber prepared the index.

On a final note, this edition, like its predecessor, is in many ways most indebted to Catharine Seybold and Bruce Young, who compiled the landmark twelfth edition of this manual as well as the thirteenth, to John Grossman, who compiled the fourteenth edition, and to Margaret Mahan, who was responsible for the fifteenth. In preparing this, the seventeenth edition of the manual, we have again striven to match their high standard for what has come to be known as "Chicago style."

The University of Chicago Press Staff
Spring 2017

I · The Publishing Process

1 · Books and Journals

Overview

1.1 **Scholarly publishing.** Books and journals have constituted the core of scholarly publishing for centuries. Book-length works in particular—given their breadth and variety—provide an overview of the anatomy of a scholarly work that, in conjunction with the discussion of journals and journal articles (see 1.77–116), can be usefully applied to many other types of published works.

1.2 **Publication format.** Almost all modern publishers have adopted an electronic workflow, from manuscript through publication. The published version can in turn be offered in a variety of formats, from printed and bound to online and other electronic formats. Many journal publishers have implemented a simultaneous print and electronic publishing model (see 1.77)—a model that has become the industry standard (though most readers now access journal content online). For books, though print has remained for many readers the format of choice, publishers now offer e-book versions of most of their books in addition to print as a matter of course. Moreover, many publishers, booksellers, and libraries depend almost entirely on an electronic workflow for making publications available to readers through online catalogs, search engines, bookshelf applications, and other means. This chapter focuses on the essential components of a book or a journal while taking into account the electronic workflow wherever it applies. For additional considerations related to electronic publication formats, see 1.117–25.

The Parts of a Book

Introduction

1.3 **Divisions and parts of a book—overview.** Books are traditionally organized into three major divisions: the front matter (also called preliminary matter, or prelims), the text, and the back matter (or end matter). These divisions are generally reflected in how items are grouped in the table of contents. The front matter presents information about a book's title, publisher, and copyright; it acknowledges debts to the work of others; it provides a way to navigate the structure of the book; and it introduces the book and sets its tone. The text proper comprises the narrative—including arguments, data, illustrations, and so forth—often divided into chapters and other meaningful sections. The back matter presents sources or source notes, appendixes, and other types of documentation supporting the text but outside its central focus or narrative. This section discusses the parts of a book according to the standard outline of these divisions and their components presented in 1.4.

1.4 **Divisions and parts of a book—outline.** The list that follows presents the traditional arrangement for the divisions and parts of a book, using lowercase roman numerals for pages in the front matter and arabic numerals for all the rest. Few books contain all these elements, and some books have components not listed here. Page numbers as well as indications of recto (right-hand page) or verso (left-hand page) may be applicable only to printed-and-bound books. Starting pages that cannot be assigned page numbers until after page makeup begin on the first available recto or, in some cases, the first available page, whether recto or verso (see also 1.5). Every page is counted in the page sequence, even those on which no number actually appears, such as the title and half-title pages, copyright page, and blank pages (see 1.6). Books published electronically typically retain the order or presentation of elements, especially for the main text. For endpapers, see 1.72.

Front matter	
Book half title	i
Series title, other works, frontispiece, or blank	ii
Title page	iii
Copyright page	iv
Dedication	v
Epigraph	v or vi
(Table of) Contents	v or vii
(List of) Illustrations	recto or verso
(List of) Tables	recto or verso
Foreword	recto
Preface	recto
Acknowledgments (if not part of preface)	recto
Introduction (if not part of text)	recto
Abbreviations (if not in back matter)	recto or verso
Chronology (if not in back matter)	recto
Text	
First text page (introduction or chapter 1)	1
or	
Second half title or first part title	1
Blank	2
First text page	3
Subsequent chapters	recto or verso

Conclusion	recto or verso
Epilogue or afterword	recto or verso
Back matter	
Acknowledgments (if not in front matter)	recto
Appendix (or first, if more than one)	recto
Subsequent appendixes	recto or verso
Chronology (if not in front matter)	recto
Abbreviations (if not in front matter)	recto
Glossary	recto
Notes (if not footnotes or chapter endnotes)	recto
Bibliography or References	recto
(List of) Contributors	recto
Illustration Credits (if not in captions or elsewhere)	recto
Index(es)	recto
About the author (if not on back cover or elsewhere)	recto

Pages and Page Numbers

1.5 **Book pages.** Publishers refer to the trimmed sheets of paper that you turn in a printed-and-bound book as leaves (or, especially in older books, folios, a term that can also refer to page or leaf numbers; see 1.6, 14.155). A page is one side of a leaf. The front of the leaf, the side that lies to the right in an open book, is called the recto. The back of the leaf, the side that lies to the left when the leaf is turned, is the verso. Rectos are always odd-numbered, versos always even-numbered. Electronic formats may or may not distinguish between recto and verso.

1.6 **Page numbers.** Printed books are paginated consecutively, and all pages except endpapers (see 1.72) are counted in the pagination, whether or not the numbers appear. The page number, or folio, is most commonly found at the top of the page, flush left verso, flush right recto. The folio may also be printed at the bottom of the page, and in that location it is called a drop folio. Drop folios usually appear either centered on each page or flush left verso and flush right recto. A page number that does not appear is sometimes referred to as a blind folio. *Not* paginated are pages that are inserted into printed books after pages have been made up—for example, color illustrations or photo galleries printed on a different type of paper (see 1.39). Reflowable electronic formats generally lack fixed page numbers, though many formats include location information to help orient readers in the text (see 1.123, 14.160).

1.7 **Roman numerals for front matter.** The front matter of a book is paginated with lowercase roman numerals (see 1.4). This traditional practice prevents renumbering the remainder of a book when, for example, a dedication page or additional acknowledgments are added at the last moment. By convention, no folio appears on blank pages or on "display" pages (i.e., such stand-alone pages as those for the half title, title, copyright, dedication, and epigraph), and a drop folio (or no folio) is used on the opening page of each succeeding section of the front matter (e.g., table of contents, foreword, preface).

1.8 **Arabic numbers for text and back matter.** The text, or the central part of a book, begins with arabic page 1. If the text is introduced by a second half title or opens with a part title, the half title or part title counts as page 1, its verso counts as page 2, and the first arabic number to appear is the drop folio 3 on the first page of text (see 1.46, 1.49). (Some publishers ignore the second half title in paginating their books, counting the first page of text as p. 1.) Page numbers generally do not appear on part titles, but if text appears on a part-title page (see 1.48), a drop folio may be used. Arabic numbering continues for the back matter. As in the front matter, the opening page of each chapter in the text and each section in the back matter carries either a drop folio or no page number. On pages containing only illustrations or tables, page numbers are sometimes omitted, except in the case of a long sequence of figures or tables. (When page numbers are retained, they are usually presented along with the running heads.) Page numbers are also omitted in the case of a blank page.

1.9 **Page numbers for multivolume works.** Pagination for works that run to more than one volume may depend on the index and the projected number of volumes. If an index to two volumes is to appear at the end of volume 2, consecutive pagination saves index entries from having to refer to volume as well as page number. In rare cases where back matter, such as an index, must be added to volume 1 later in the production process, lowercase roman folios may be used; these should continue the sequence from the front matter in that volume (including a final blank page)—if, for example, the last page of the front matter is xii, the back matter would start with page xiii. Multivolume works that run into the thousands of pages are usually paginated separately to avoid unwieldy page numbers. Index entries and other references to such works must include volume as well as page number. In either scenario—consecutive or separate pagination across volumes—the front matter in each volume begins anew with page i.

Running Heads

1.10 **Running heads defined.** Running heads—the headings at the tops of pages—function, like page numbers, as signposts. Especially useful in scholarly books and textbooks, they are sometimes omitted for practical or aesthetic reasons—in a novel or a book of poems, for example. Running heads are sometimes placed at the bottom of the page, where they are referred to as running feet, or, more rarely, in the left- and right-hand margins. In endnotes and other places where the information conveyed by these signposts is essential to readers, placement at the tops of pages is preferred. In this manual, *running head* is used for this element wherever it appears. For preparation of running-head copy, see 2.76. In electronic formats, running heads may be supplanted by other navigational features (see 1.123).

1.11 **Running heads for front matter.** Running heads are never used on display pages (half title, title, copyright, dedication, epigraph) or on the first page of the table of contents, preface, and so forth (see also 1.16). Any element in the front matter that runs more than one page usually carries running heads, and the same running head appears on verso and recto pages.

Verso	*Recto*
Contents	Contents
Preface	Preface

1.12 **Running heads for text.** Chapter openings and other display pages carry no running heads (see also 1.16). The choice of running heads for other text pages is governed chiefly by the structure and nature of the book. Among acceptable arrangements are the following:

Verso	*Recto*
Part title	Chapter title
Chapter number	Chapter title
Chapter title	Subhead
Chapter title	Chapter subtitle
Chapter title	Chapter title
Subhead	Subhead
Chapter author	Chapter title

Longer titles or heads may need to be shortened; see also 2.76. For a book without named chapters or other structural divisions (a novel, for example), the book title can be used for the running head on both verso and recto, or running heads can be omitted. In electronic formats, the title metadata may be used to supply the running heads by default (see also 1.75).

1.13 **Subheads as running heads.** When subheads in the text are used as running heads on recto pages and more than one subhead falls on a single page, the *last* one on the page is used as the running head. When subheads are used as running heads on versos, however, the *first* subhead on the page is used as the running head. (The principle is the same as for dictionary running heads.)

1.14 **Running heads for back matter.** Running heads for back matter follow the same pattern as those for front matter and text (but see 1.15). If there is an appendix, Appendix (or Appendix 1 or Appendix A, etc.) appears verso, the appendix title recto. If there is more than one index, the running heads must differentiate them (e.g., Index of Names, Index of Subjects).

1.15 **Running heads for endnotes.** The running heads for a section of notes in the back of the book should give the inclusive page numbers or (much less useful for readers but more expedient for the publisher) the chapter where the relevant note references are found in the text. If chapter numbers are used, it is essential that the running heads in the text also include chapter numbers (see 1.12). Thus, two facing running heads might read:

Verso	*Recto*
Notes to Pages 2–10	Notes to Pages 11–25
or	
Notes to Chapter One	Notes to Chapter Two

For a fuller explanation, see 14.47.

1.16 **Omission of running heads.** Besides display pages in the front matter (see 1.11), running heads are omitted on part titles, chapter openings, and any page containing only illustrations or tables. (For the omission of page numbers, see 1.7, 1.8.) Pages that include lines of text in addition to an illustration or table should include running heads. Running heads may also be included in long sequences of illustrations or tables to keep readers oriented.

Front Matter

TITLE PAGES

1.17 **Half title.** The half title (p. i in a printed book, no folio) normally consists only of the main title (less any subtitle) and is usually counted as the very first page in a printed-and-bound book. All other information—including author name, publisher, and edition—is omitted.

1.18 **Series title or frontispiece.** The verso following the half-title page (p. ii in a printed book) is usually blank. But if the book is part of a series, it may include the title and volume number of the series, the name of the general editor of the series, and sometimes the titles of previously published books in the series. (A series title may appear on the title page instead.) If the book is the published proceedings of a symposium, the title of the symposium and the date it was held and other relevant details may appear on page ii. Some publishers list an author's previous publications on page ii; Chicago generally lists these on the jacket or back cover (see 1.66). Alternatively, page ii might carry an illustration, called a frontispiece. If the frontispiece is printed on a different stock from the text, and thus is inserted separately, it will not constitute page ii, though it will still appear opposite the title page, which is normally page iii (see 1.19). Page ii might also be used for a title page across pages ii and iii.

1.19 **Title page.** The title page (p. iii or sometimes pp. ii and iii) includes the following elements:

- Full title of the book
- Subtitle, if any
- Name of the author, editor ("Edited by"), or translator ("Translated by")
- Edition number, for a new edition (see 1.25, 1.26)
- Name and location (city or cities) of publisher

No colon or other punctuation is needed between title and subtitle if they are differentiated by type size or style. The author's name should appear in the form preferred by the author or by which the author is generally known; Chicago usually omits any academic degrees or affiliations (but see 1.66). A publisher's logo may appear on the title page. Some publishers include the date of publication, which should correspond to the copyright date if possible (see 1.22). Self-publishers can follow this traditional arrangement as long as they publish under their own company name or imprint; if not, information about the publisher can be omitted (though some commercial self-publishing platforms may add their own imprints).

COPYRIGHT PAGE

1.20 **Components of a copyright page.** The Copyright Act of 1989 does not require that published works carry a copyright notice in order to secure copyright protection; nevertheless, most publishers continue to carry the notice to discourage infringement. The copyright notice is just one of several items typically included on the copyright page (p. iv). Books published by the University of Chicago Press include the following:

- Publisher's address
- Copyright notice—including, if applicable, copyright dates of previous editions and indication of copyright renewal or other changes, and followed by the statement "All rights reserved" and related language
- Publication date, including publishing history
- Country of printing
- Impression line, indicating number and year of current printing
- International Standard Book Number (ISBN) for each available format (e.g., cloth, paper, e-book)
- For continuously published resources, the International Standard Serial Number (ISSN), one for each available format, in addition to the ISBN
- A Digital Object Identifier (DOI), for books that have one
- For translations, indication of original-language title, publisher, and copyright
- Acknowledgments, permissions, and other credits, including acknowledgment of grants, if applicable and space permitting
- Cataloging-in-Publication (CIP) data
- Paper durability statement

For an example, see figure 1.1. Information included by other publishers may vary from this list. Self-published authors are encouraged to include, at a minimum, a copyright statement and a list of any assigned ISBNs, together with any other information that applies.

1.21 **Publisher's address.** The address of the publisher—and sometimes the addresses of overseas agents—is typically, though not always, given on the copyright page. An address may be abbreviated, consisting, for example, only of a city and perhaps a postal code. The URL for the publisher's home page may also be included. Self-published authors may want to include contact information to facilitate correspondence from readers.

The University of Chicago Press, Chicago 60637
The University of Chicago Press, Ltd., London
© 2017 by The University of Chicago
All rights reserved. No part of this book may be used or reproduced in any manner whatsoever without written permission, except in the case of brief quotations in critical articles and reviews. For more information, contact the University of Chicago Press, 1427 E. 60th St., Chicago, IL 60637.
Published 2017
Printed in the United States of America

26 25 24 23 22 21 20 19 18 17   1 2 3 4 5

ISBN-13: 978-0-226-26565-0 (cloth)
ISBN-13: 978-0-226-26579-7 (e-book)
DOI: https://doi.org/10.7208/chicago/9780226265797.001.0001

Library of Congress Cataloging-in-Publication Data

Names: O'Connell, Aaron B., 1973–
Title: Our latest longest war : losing hearts and minds in Afghanistan / edited by Aaron B. O'Connell.
Description: Chicago ; London : The University of Chicago Press, 2017. | Includes bibliographical references.
Identifiers: LCCN 2016034770 | ISBN 9780226265650 (cloth : alk. paper) | ISBN 9780226265797 (e-book)
Subjects: LCSH: Afghan War, 2001–
Classification: LCC DS371.412.O95 2017 | DDC 958.104/7—dc23
LC record available at https://lccn.loc.gov/2016034770

⊜ This paper meets the requirements of ANSI/NISO Z39.48-1992 (Permanence of Paper).

FIGURE 1.1. A typical copyright page, including copyright notice, impression date and number (denoting 2017 for the first impression), International Standard Book Number (ISBN) for each format, Digital Object Identifier (DOI), Library of Congress Cataloging-in-Publication (CIP) data, and paper durability statement. See 1.20.

The University of Chicago Press, Chicago 60637
The University of Chicago Press, Ltd., London

© 2008, 2014 by The University of Chicago
All rights reserved. First edition 2008.
Second edition 2014

Printed in the United States of America

23 22 21 20 19 18 17   3 4 5

FIGURE 1.2. Copyright notice of a second edition (2014), with impression line indicating that this edition was reprinted for the third time in 2017. See 1.23.

1.22 **Copyright notice.** The usual notice consists of three parts: the symbol ©, the first year the book is published, and the name of the copyright owner. This may be followed by the phrase "All rights reserved" (and any additional language required by the publisher) and a statement of publication date or publishing history (see 1.25, 4.41). (See fig. 1.1 for an example of Chicago's copyright notice.) The year of publication should correspond to the copyright date. If a book is physically available near the end of a year but not formally published until the beginning of the next, the later date is preferred as both copyright and publication date. Books published by the University of Chicago Press are usually copyrighted in the name of the university ("© 2017 by The University of Chicago"). Some authors, however, prefer to copyright their works in their own names ("© 2012 by Alison A. Author"), a preference discussed in 4.42. For information on copyright notices for journals, see 1.103; for a full discussion, see 4.39–46.

1.23 **Copyright dates of previous editions.** Each substantially new edition of a book (as distinct from a new impression, or reprinting, and not including paperback or electronic versions that do not constitute a new edition; see 1.26) gets a new copyright date, and the copyright dates of at least the most recent previous editions should appear in the copyright notice (see fig. 1.2). If the new edition is so extensive a revision that it virtually constitutes a new publication, previous copyright dates may be omitted. See also 1.25, 4.41.

1.24 **Copyright renewal or other changes.** The date of copyright renewal or a change in the name of the copyright owner is sometimes reflected in the copyright notice if the work is reprinted. Copyright renewal is shown in the following manner:

© 1963 by Maurice Sendak. © renewed 1991 by Maurice Sendak.

To indicate a change in copyright ownership (e.g., if copyright is assigned to the author or someone else after the initial copyright has been registered and printed in the first impression), the name of the new copyright owner is substituted for that of the previous owner. The copyright date remains the same unless the copyright has been renewed. Copyrights remain legally valid even if renewal or reassignment information cannot, for some reason, appear in a new edition or printing (see also 4.31–33).

1.25 **Publishing history.** The publishing history of a book, which usually follows the copyright notice, begins with the date (year) of original publication, followed by the number and date of any new edition. In books with a long publishing history, it is acceptable to present only the original edition and the latest edition in the publishing history. (A previous publisher's name need not be given unless the licensing agreement requires that it appear in the new edition.) Items in the publishing history may appear on separate lines; periods separate multiple items on the same line.

First edition published 1906. Seventeenth edition 2017.

Revised edition originally published 1999
University of Chicago Press edition 2010

1.26 **What constitutes a new edition?** *Edition* (as opposed to *impression*, or *printing*) is used in at least two senses. (1) A *new* edition may be defined as one in which a substantial change has been made in one or more of the essential elements of the work (e.g., text, notes, appendixes, or illustrations). As a general rule, at least 20 percent of a new edition should consist of new or revised material. A work that is republished with a new preface or afterword but is otherwise unchanged except for corrections of typographical errors is better described as a new impression or a reissue; the title page may include such words as "With a New Preface." (2) *Edition* may be used to designate a reissue in a different format—for example, a paperback, deluxe, or illustrated version, or an electronic version of a printed work—or under the imprint of a different publisher. Information about the new edition or format is usually included on the copyright page (see 1.25; see also 1.23). An edition other than the first is also designated on the title page: Second Edition, Third Edition, and so forth. Such phrases as "revised and expanded" are sometimes included on the title page but need not be, since the nature and extent of the revision are normally described in the prefatory material or on the cover.

1.27 **Country of printing.** The country in which a book is printed is usually identified on the copyright page (see fig. 1.1). In addition, if a book is printed in a country other than the country of publication, the jacket or cover must so state: for example, "Printed in China." This information may be removed for publication in electronic formats but need not be.

1.28 **Impression number and versioning.** A printing of a book, or impression, traditionally consists of a set number of books, generally in the hundreds or thousands, printed at one time. Each such impression, starting with the first, may be identified on the copyright page. Chicago uses a system that comprises a series of digits listed after the publishing history. The first group of numerals, reading from right to left, represents the last two digits of succeeding years, starting with the date of the most recent impression. These are followed by a series of numbers that indicate current and possible future impressions. See figures 1.1 and 1.2. Such a system was designed to spare printers from having to generate new text. Some publishers prefer to signal each impression more explicitly (e.g., Second printing, May 2020). Impression lines can be useful in the case of a book in which corrections have been made to an earlier printing; in this case, a new impression might be said to constitute a new *version* of a book (as opposed to a new *edition*; see 1.26). For books that are printed in smaller digital print runs or on demand and for e-books, the traditional system based on large offset print runs will not apply. Digital printing systems can be programmed to generate a date stamp and other identifiers, such as the city in which the copy was printed, to keep track of different versions of a book. For e-books, a unique identifier such as the ISBN or DOI can be used in combination with a last-modified date to track revisions, according to a system defined for the EPUB standard (see 1.118). An alternative system, modeled on identifiers for software programs (and specified by some self-publishing platforms), uses version numbers. For example, 1.0 might indicate the original version; 1.0.1 might indicate a minor revision and 1.1 a more significant revision; and 2.0 would indicate a new edition. Such information is included in a book's metadata (see 1.75); the last-modified date or version number may also be listed on

The University of Chicago Press, Chicago 60637
The University of Chicago Press, Ltd., London
© 2017 by The University of Chicago
All rights reserved. Published 2017.
Printed in the United States of America

26 25 24 23 22 21 20 19 18 17 1 2 3 4 5

ISBN-13: 978-0-226-41082-1 (cloth)
ISBN-13: 978-0-226-41096-8 (e-book)
DOI: https://doi.org/10.7208/chicago/9780226410968.001.0001

Originally published as *Séminaire: La peine de mort, Volume II (2000–2001)*
© 2015 Éditions Galilée

FIGURE 1.3. Part of the copyright page of a translation, including title and copyright of the original edition (as required by contract with the original publisher). See 1.29.

the copyright page or elsewhere. For information on evolving practices, consult the International Digital Publishing Forum.

1.29 **Original-language edition of a translation.** If a book is a translation from another language, the original title, publisher, and copyright information should be recorded on the copyright page (see fig. 1.3).

1.30 **Acknowledgments, permissions, and other credits.** The copyright page, if space permits, may include acknowledgments of previously published parts of a book, illustration credits, and permission to quote from copyrighted material (fig. 1.4), unless such acknowledgments appear elsewhere in the book—as in an acknowledgments section (see 1.41, 1.42) or in source notes (see 2.46, 14.54).

The illustration on the title page is a detail from a photograph of Nietzsche in Basel, ca. 1876. Photo Stiftung Weimarer Klassik. GSA 101/17.

For more on illustration credits, see 3.29–37. For a full discussion of permissions, see chapter 4. Some publishers also credit the designer of the cover or interior on the copyright page (see also 1.73).

1.31 **Acknowledgment of grants and subsidies.** Publishers should acknowledge grants of financial assistance toward publication on the copyright

The University of Chicago Press, Chicago 60637
The University of Chicago Press, Ltd., London
© 2017 by The University of Chicago
All rights reserved. No part of this book may be used or reproduced in any manner whatsoever without written permission, except in the case of brief quotations in critical articles and reviews. For more information, contact the University of Chicago Press, 1427 East 60th Street, Chicago, IL 60637.
Published 2017
Printed in the United States of America

26 25 24 23 22 21 20 19 18 17 1 2 3 4 5

ISBN-13: 978-0-226-07935-6 (cloth)
ISBN-13: 978-0-226-41177-4 (e-book)
DOI: https://doi.org/10.7208/chicago/9780226411774.001.0001

Portions of chapter 4 appeared as "A Colonial Cul de Sac: Plantation Life in Wartime Saint-Domingue, 1775–1782" in *Radical History Review* (Winter 2013) and are reprinted by permission of Duke University Press.

FIGURE 1.4. Part of a copyright page acknowledging earlier publication of content. See 1.30.

page. Acknowledgments requiring more space or greater prominence may appear elsewhere, in a separate section in the front or back matter. Wording and placement, including the use of any logo, should be as specified (or at least approved) by the grantors. Financial assistance made to authors is usually mentioned as part of the author's acknowledgments (see 1.41, 1.42).

1.32 **International Standard Book Number (ISBN).** An ISBN is assigned to each book by its publisher under a system set up in the late 1960s by the R. R. Bowker Company and the International Organization for Standardization (ISO). The ISBN uniquely identifies the book, thus facilitating order fulfillment and inventory tracking. In addition to appearing on the copyright page (see fig. 1.1), the ISBN should also be printed on the book jacket or cover (see 1.74). Each format or binding must have a separate ISBN (i.e., for hardcover, paperbound, e-book format, etc.), and, if practical, the copyright page should list them all (but only if they are to be published simultaneously). Additional information about the assignment and use of ISBNs may be obtained from Bowker, the ISBN Agency for the United States, or from the International ISBN Agency. These agencies also provide ISBNs and other resources to self-published authors, including information about copyright, bar codes, and related matters. Some books that are part of a monograph series may be assigned an ISSN (International Standard Serial Number) in addition to an ISBN; for more information, contact the US ISSN Center at the Library of Congress or the ISSN International Centre. (For the use of ISSNs in journal copyright statements, see 1.103.) See also 1.75.

1.33 **Digital Object Identifier (DOI).** Publishers that have registered their books with Crossref or one of the other international DOI registration agencies should list the DOI that refers to the book as a whole on the copyright page (see fig. 1.1). A DOI is a permanent identifier that can be used to find a book or other resource in any of its available formats, either as a link (in the form of a URL that begins https://doi.org/) or using a metadata search tool like the one available at Crossref.org. (Crossref recommends always presenting the DOI as a link.) Like an ISBN, the DOI should also appear on the book jacket or cover and should be included as part of a book's metadata (see 1.75). See also 14.8.

1.34 **Cataloging-in-Publication (CIP) data.** Since 1971 most US publishers have printed the Library of Congress Cataloging-in-Publication (CIP) data on the copyright pages of their books. CIP data is available for most books that are made available to libraries, including simultaneously published e-book versions of printed books. An example of CIP data may be found in figure 1.1. To apply for CIP data, and for up-to-date information about the program, consult the Library of Congress's online resources for publishers. Publishers who do not participate in the CIP program may still be eligible for cataloging by the Library of Congress through its Preassigned Control Number (PCN) program. Only US publishers are eligible for these programs. Similar cataloging programs are offered through Library and Archives Canada, the British Library (UK and Ireland), and the National Library of Australia. To date, books that have been self-published in the United States are not eligible for the CIP program through the Library of Congress but may be eligible for the PCN program. The CIP programs in Canada, the UK, Ireland, and Australia, on the other hand, do accept self-published works that meet certain eligibility requirements. Authors who want their works cataloged in national libraries can apply for these programs directly through the applicable library website, where they will also find any related requirements for depositing and registering their works (see also 4.47). Some self-publishing services will complete the necessary applications and fulfill any other requirements on the author's behalf.

1.35 **Paper durability and environmental statements.** Durability standards for paper have been established by the American National Standards Institute (ANSI), which since 1984 has issued statements to be included in books and other publications meeting these standards. In 1992 the standards were revised by the National Information Standards Organization (NISO) to extend to coated paper. (The International Organization for Standardization offers a similar standard, ISO 9706, available from the ISO catalog.) Under this revision, coated and uncoated papers that meet the standards for alkalinity, folding and tearing, and paper stock are authorized to carry the following notice, which should include the permanent paper sign (a circled infinity symbol):

> ♾ This paper meets the requirements of ANSI/NISO Z39.48-1992 (Permanence of Paper).

Some publishers are entitled to include logos or statements certifying that they meet certain requirements for recycled paper or paper that has been sourced or manufactured according to certain standards intended to minimize environmental impact. For more information, contact the Forest Stewardship Council. Additional resources include the US-based Green Press Initiative and the Canadian-based Canopy. Any statements related to paper durability or manufacturing standards for a print book may be removed for publication in electronic formats but need not be.

DEDICATION AND EPIGRAPH

1.36 **Dedication.** Choice of dedication—including whether to include one—is up to the author. It may be suggested, however, that the word *dedicated* is superfluous. Editors of contributed volumes do not customarily include a dedication unless it is jointly offered by all contributors. Nor do translators generally offer their own dedication unless it is made clear that the dedication is not that of the original author. The dedication usually appears by itself, preferably on page v.

1.37 **Epigraph and epigraph source.** An author may wish to include an epigraph—a quotation that is pertinent but not integral to the text—at the beginning of the book. If there is no dedication, the epigraph may be placed on page v (see 1.4); otherwise, it is usually placed on page vi, opposite the table of contents. Epigraphs are also occasionally used at chapter openings and, more rarely, at the beginnings of sections within chapters (see 1.49). The source of an epigraph is usually given on a line following the quotation, sometimes preceded by a dash (see 13.36). Only the author's name (in the case of a well-known author, only the last name) and, usually, the title of the work need appear; beyond this, it is customary not to annotate book epigraphs (but see 14.52).

TABLE OF CONTENTS AND LIST OF ILLUSTRATIONS OR TABLES

1.38 **Table of contents.** The table of contents for a printed work usually begins on page v or, if page v carries a dedication or an epigraph, page vii. It should include all preliminary material that follows it but exclude anything that precedes it. It should list the title and beginning page number of each section of the book: front matter, text divisions, and back matter, including the index (see fig. 1.5). If the book is divided into parts as well as chapters, the part titles appear in the contents, but their page numbers are omitted, unless the parts include separate introductions. Subheads within chapters are usually omitted from the table of contents, but if they provide valuable signposts for readers, they may be included (as in the print edition of this manual). In a volume consisting of chapters by different authors, the name of each author should be listed in the table of contents with the title of the chapter (as for chapters 4 and 5 in this manual). In a book containing illustrations that are printed together in a gallery or galleries (see 3.6), it is seldom necessary to list them separately in a list of illustrations. Their location may be noted at the end of the table of contents (e.g., "Illustrations follow pages 130 and 288"). A table of contents may be omitted for books without chapter or other divisions.

1.39 **List of illustrations or tables.** In a book with very few illustrations or tables or one with very many, all tied closely to the text, it is not essential to list them in the front matter. Multiauthor books, proceedings of symposia, and the like commonly do not carry lists of illustrations or tables. Where a list is appropriate (see 3.38), the list of illustrations (usually titled Illustrations but entered in the table of contents as List of Illustrations to avoid ambiguity) should match the table of contents in type size and general style. In books containing various kinds of illustrations, the list may be divided into sections headed, for example, Figures, Tables (see fig. 1.6), or Plates, Drawings, Maps. Page numbers are given for all illustrations printed with the text and counted in the pagination, even when the numbers do not actually appear on the text page. When a gallery of illustrations is printed on different stock and not counted in the pagination, its location is indicated by "Facing page 000" or "Following

Contents

FIGURE 1.5. Table of contents showing front matter, introduction, parts, chapters, back matter, and location of photo gallery. See 1.38.

ILLUSTRATIONS

FIGURES

. . . .

TABLES

FIGURE 1.6. Partial list of illustrations, with subheads. If the book contained no tables, the subhead "Figures" would be omitted. If it contained many tables, these would probably be listed on a new page under the heading "Tables." How best to list illustrations of various sorts depends as much on space as on logic. See 1.39.

page 000" in the list of illustrations (see fig. 1.7) or, more commonly, in the table of contents (fig. 1.5). A frontispiece, because of its prominent position at the front of the book, is not assigned a page number; its location is simply given as frontispiece. Titles given in lists of illustrations and tables may be shortened or otherwise adjusted (see 3.40). For treatment of titles, see 8.157–67.

Illustrations

Following page 46

FIGURE 1.7. Partial list of illustrations showing numbers, titles, and placement of unpaginated plates. (Compare fig. 1.5.) See 1.39.

FOREWORD, PREFACE AND ACKNOWLEDGMENTS, AND INTRODUCTION

1.40 **Foreword.** The term *foreword* should be reserved for prefatory remarks by someone other than the author—including those of an editor or compiler, especially if a work already includes an author's preface (see 1.41). The publisher may choose to mention the foreword on the title page (e.g., "With a Foreword by Conor Cruise O'Brien"). A foreword, which is set in the same size and style of type as the text, normally runs only a few pages, and its author's name usually appears at the end, following the text. The title or affiliation of the author of a foreword may be included along with the name, and a place and date may also be included. If a foreword runs to a substantial length, with or without a title of its own, its author's name may be given at the beginning instead of at the end. See also 1.43.

1.41 **Preface and acknowledgments.** The author's own statement about a work is usually called a preface. It is set in the same size and style of type as the text and includes reasons for undertaking the work, method of research (if this has some bearing on readers' understanding of the text), brief acknowledgments (but see 1.42), and sometimes permissions granted for the use of previously published material. A preface need not be signed; if there might be some doubt about who wrote it, however, or if an author wishes to sign the preface (sometimes just with initials), the signature normally appears at the end (see also 1.40). When a new preface is written for a new edition or for a reprinting of a book long out of print, it should precede the original preface. The original preface is then usually retitled Preface to the First Edition, and the new preface may be titled Preface to the Second Edition, Preface to the Paperback Edition, Preface 2017, or whatever fits. (Even in the absence of a new preface, the original preface may be retitled to avoid confusion.) In a book containing both an editor's preface and an author's preface, the editor's preface, which may be titled as such or retitled Editor's Foreword, comes first and should bear the editor's name at its conclusion.

1.42 **Separate acknowledgments.** If the author's acknowledgments are long, they may be put in a separate section following the preface; if a preface consists only of acknowledgments, its title should be changed to Acknowledgments. Acknowledgments may instead be put at the back of a book, preceding other back matter, a common practice especially for books targeted to the general reader. Acknowledgments that apply to all volumes of a multivolume work may be presented only in the first. See also 4.102–3.

1.43 **Introduction belonging to front matter.** Most introductions belong not in the front matter but at the beginning of the text, paginated with arabic numerals (see 1.47). Material about the book—its origins, for example—rather than about the subject matter should be included in the preface or in the acknowledgments (see 1.41). A substantial introduction by someone other than the author is usually included in the front matter, just before the main text, but if it is not more than three to five pages, it may more appropriately be called a foreword (see 1.40) and placed before the preface.

OTHER FRONT MATTER

1.44 **List of abbreviations.** Not every work that includes abbreviations needs a separate list of abbreviations with the terms or names they stand for. If many are used, or if a few are used frequently, a list is useful (see fig. 1.8); its location should always be given in the table of contents. If

Abbreviations

abl.	ablative	Lat.	Latin
ac.	accusative	Leon.	Leonese
act.	active	lit.	literally
adj.	adjective	m.	masculine
And.	Andalusian	Med.	Medieval
Ar.	Arabic	Mod.	Modern
Cast.	Castilian	Moz.	Mozarabic
Cat.	Catalan	n.	neuter
cf.	*confer* (compare)	nom.	nominative
conj.	conjugation	Occ.	Occitan
Cub.	Cuban	p.	person
dat.	dative	pas.	passive
decl.	declension	pl.	plural
Dom. Repub.	Dominican Republic	Port.	Portuguese
Eng.	English	sg.	singular
Equat. Guin.	Equatorial Guinea	Sp.	Spanish
ex.	example	var.	variant
f.	feminine	viz.	*videlicet* (namely)
Fr.	French	voc.	vocative
gen.	genitive		
Gr.	Greek		
irreg.	irregular		
It.	Italian		

FIGURE 1.8. A list of abbreviations. See 1.44.

abbreviations are used in the text or footnotes, the list may appear in the front matter. If they are used only in the back matter, the list should appear before the first element in which abbreviations are used, whether the appendixes, the endnotes, or the bibliography. A list of abbreviations is generally not a substitute for using the full form of a term at its first occurrence in the text (see 10.3). In the list, alphabetize terms by the abbreviation, not by the spelled-out form. See also 14.60.

1.45 **Publisher's, translator's, and editor's notes.** Notes on the text are usually treated typographically in the same way as a preface or foreword. A publisher's note—used rarely and only to state something that cannot be included elsewhere—should either precede or immediately follow the table of contents. A translator's note, like a foreword, should precede any element, such as a preface, that is by the original author. An explanation of an editor's method or a discussion of variant texts, often necessary in scholarly editions, may appear either in the front matter (usually as the last item there) or in the back matter (as an appendix or in place of one). Brief remarks about editorial method, however—such as noting that spelling and capitalization have been modernized—are often better incorporated into an editor's preface, if there is one.

Text

1.46 **Determining page 1.** The first page of the first chapter or the introduction (see 1.47) is usually counted as arabic page 1. Where the front matter is extensive, however, a second half title, identical to the one on page i, may be added before the text. The second half title should be counted as page 1, the first of the pages to be counted with an arabic page number (though the page number does not appear). The page following the second half title (its verso) is usually blank, though it may contain an illustration or an epigraph. A second half title is also useful when the book design specifies a double-page spread for chapter openings; in such a case, chapter 1 starts on page 2. If a book begins with a part title, the part title page is treated as arabic page 1 in the same manner as a second half title. See also 1.5, 1.6.

TEXT DIVISIONS

1.47 **Introduction belonging to main text.** Unlike the kind of introduction that may be included in the front matter (see 1.43), a text introduction is integral to the subject matter of the book and should not include acknowledgments or other material that belongs in the front or back matter. It is acceptable, however, to refer to the contents of the book ("In the first two chapters I discuss . . ."), though some authors and editors may prefer to limit such information to a preface. (These considerations do not apply in the case of a reprint or facsimile edition, where the front matter is furnished by a volume editor.) A text introduction carries arabic page numbers. A new introduction to a well-known work may be considered a text introduction even if it includes biographical or other material about the original author. If titled simply Introduction, it does not normally carry a chapter number and is usually considerably shorter than a chapter. Authors should consider adding a descriptive subtitle even to such shorter introductions, and an author who has titled chapter 1 Introduction should be encouraged to give the chapter a more evocative title.

1.48 **Division into parts.** Some books benefit from division into parts (see fig. 1.5). Each part usually carries a number and a title and should contain at least two chapters (an exception may be made for a part that includes only an introductory or concluding chapter). Chapters are numbered consecutively throughout the book; they do not begin with 1 in each part. Parts are sometimes called sections, though *section* is more commonly used for a subdivision within a chapter. Part titles that do not include introductions usually begin recto, followed by a blank verso and a recto chapter opening. If a part includes an introduction—usually short, titled or untitled—it may begin on a new recto following the part title, or on the verso of the part title, or on the part title itself. A text introduction to a book that is divided into parts precedes the part title to part 1 and needs no part title of its own. Likewise, a conclusion needs no part title, though in a book with parts it should begin recto to avoid appearing to belong only to the final part. No part title is needed before the back matter of a book divided into parts, though one may be useful before a series of appendixes or a notes section.

1.49 **Division into chapters—general.** Most nonfiction prose works are divided into numbered chapters of a more or less consistent length. Authors should aim for short, descriptive titles, which tend to give readers a better overview of a book's contents than longer, more whimsical titles. Each chapter normally starts on a new page, verso or recto, and its opening page should carry a drop folio (see 1.5, 1.6)—or sometimes no folio—and no running head (see 1.10–16). The first chapter ordinarily begins on a recto (but see 1.46). Chapter openings usually consist of the chapter number (*chapter* is often omitted), the chapter title, and the chapter subtitle, if any; together, these are referred to as the chapter display. Note reference numbers or symbols traditionally do not appear anywhere in the chapter display of printed books; accordingly, a note that refers to the chapter as a whole remains unnumbered and precedes the numbered notes (whether it appears on the first page of the chapter or in the endnotes). A chapter epigraph, sometimes considered part of the chapter display, may include a note reference, though traditionalists may prefer an unnumbered note. See also 14.52.

1.50 **Division into chapters—multiple authors.** In multiauthor books, the chapter author's name is usually given at the head of each chapter. An affiliation or other identifying information may be put in an unnumbered footnote on the first page of the chapter (see 14.55) or in a list of contributors (1.64). An unnumbered footnote may also be used to disclose the source of a chapter or other contribution that is being reprinted from an earlier publication. (For certain e-book formats that do not support footnotes as such, a source note or note about the author may need to appear immediately after, or be linked from, the chapter title or author's name.) When both the author's affiliation and the source of the contribution are given in the note, it is customary, but not essential, that the affiliation come first.

1.51 **Divisions for poetry.** In a book of previously unpublished poetry, each poem usually begins on a new page. Any part titles provided by the poet should then appear on separate pages (rectos) preceding the poems grouped under them. In a collection of previously published poems, more than one poem, or the end of one and the beginning of another, may appear on the same page.

1.52 **Divisions for letters and diaries.** Letters and diaries are usually presented in chronological order, so they are seldom amenable to division into chapters or parts. For diary entries, dates may be used as headings, and in published correspondence the names of senders or recipients of letters (or both) may serve as headings. The date of a letter may be included in the heading if it does not appear in the letter itself. Such headings in diaries and correspondence do not usually begin a new page.

1.53 **Conclusion.** The main text may end with a conclusion, in which the author typically makes some final statement about the subject presented and the implications of the study or poses questions inviting further investigation. A conclusion may assume the significance and proportions of a final chapter, with or without a chapter number; in such cases, authors should consider using a more descriptive title. A conclusion may begin either recto or verso, but for a book divided into parts it must begin recto so that it does not appear to belong to the final part only.

1.54 **Epilogue or afterword.** An epilogue or an afterword is a comparatively brief section that comments on the text, sometimes obliquely, or brings a narrative up to date. Such a section is sometimes added to a new edition of a book and may be written by a different author; in either case it is then usually called an afterword (cf. 1.40). An epilogue or afterword generally follows any conclusion and may begin either recto or verso, but for a book divided into parts or for an afterword added to a new edition, it should usually begin recto (see also 1.53); it is set in the same size and style of type as the rest of the text.

TEXT SUBDIVISIONS

1.55 **Subheads—wording.** Subheads within a chapter should be short and meaningful and, like chapter titles, parallel in structure and tone. The first sentence of text following a subhead should not refer syntactically to the subhead; words should be repeated where necessary. For example:

SECONDARY SPONGIOSA
The secondary spongiosa, a vaulted structure . . .
not
SECONDARY SPONGIOSA
This vaulted structure . . .

1.56 **Subhead levels and placement.** Many works require only one level of subhead throughout the text. Some, particularly scientific or technical works, require further subdivision. Where more than one level is used, the subheads are sometimes referred to as the A-level subhead (the first-level heading after the chapter title), B-level, C-level, and so on (or A-head, B-head, C-head, etc.). Only the most complicated works need more than three levels. The number of subhead levels required may vary from chapter to chapter. A lower-level subhead may follow an upper-level subhead with no intervening text, but when a section of text is subdivided, there should ideally be at least two subsections (e.g., two or more A-level subheads in a chapter or two or more B-level subheads under an A-level subhead). Occasionally, however, a single subdivision may be called for—for example, to emphasize a unique case or a special consideration. A single subdivision may also be needed for specialized sections like chapter endnotes (see 1.62). Subheads, which usually do not need to begin a new page, are generally set on a line separate from the following text, the levels differentiated by type style and placement. The lowest level, however, may be run in at the beginning of a paragraph, usually set in italics or boldface (as in the print edition of this manual) and followed by a period. It is then referred to as a run-in subhead (or run-in sidehead). Run-in heads are usually capitalized sentence-style (see 8.158).

1.57 **Numbered subheads.** Unless sections in a chapter are cited in cross-references elsewhere in the text, numbers are usually unnecessary with subheads. In general, subheads are more useful to a reader than section numbers alone. In scientific and technical works, however, the numbering of sections, subsections, and sometimes sub-subsections provides easy reference. There are various ways to number sections. The most common employs double or multiple (also called multilevel) numeration. In this system, sections are numbered within chapters, subsections within sections, and sub-subsections within subsections. The number of each division is preceded by the numbers of all higher divisions, and all division numbers are separated by periods, colons, or hyphens. Thus, for example, the numbers 4.8 and 4.12 signify, respectively, the eighth section and the twelfth section of chapter 4.[1] The series 4.12.3 signifies the third subsection in the twelfth section of chapter 4, and so on. The system employed by this manual is chapter number followed by paragraph number for easy cross-referencing. A system of multiple numeration may also be used for illustrations, tables, and mathematical equations (see, respectively, 3.11, 3.50, and 12.24–25).

1.58 **Ornamental or typographic breaks in text.** Where a break stronger than a paragraph but not as strong as a subhead is required, a set of asterisks or a type ornament, or simply a blank line, may be inserted between paragraphs. A blank line has the disadvantage that it may be missed if the break falls at the bottom of a page, a problem exacerbated by electronic formats with reflowable text. This quandary can be solved by differentiating the first few words of each paragraph that follows a break—for example, with small capitals. Whatever strategy is used to signal such a break, the same one should be used in each publication format.

Back Matter

1.59 **Appendixes.** An appendix may include explanations and elaborations that are not essential parts of the text but are helpful to a reader seeking further clarification, texts of documents, long lists, survey questionnaires, or sometimes even charts or tables. The appendix should not,

1. Multiple numeration using periods should not be confused with decimal fractions. Paragraph or section 4.9 may be followed by 4.10—quite unlike the decimal fraction system.

however, be a repository for odds and ends that the author could not work into the text. Relevant information that is too unwieldy or expensive to produce in print may be suitable for presentation on the publisher's website and under its aegis (a practice more common with journals). Appendixes usually follow the last book chapter, though an appendix may be included at the end of a chapter (introduced by an A-level subhead) if what it contains is essential to understanding the chapter. (In multiauthor books and in books that will be offered as individual chapters, any appendix must follow the chapter it pertains to.) When two or more appendixes are required, they should be designated by numbers (Appendix 1, Appendix 2, etc.) or letters (Appendix A, Appendix B, etc.), and each should be given a title as well. Appendixes may be set either in the same type size as the text proper or in smaller type.

1.60 **Chronology.** A chronological list of events may be useful in certain works. It may appear in the back matter under its own heading, but if it is essential to understanding the narrative, it is better placed in the front matter, immediately before the text. For an example, see figure 1.9.

1.61 **Glossary.** A glossary is a useful tool in a book containing many words in another language or other unfamiliar terms. Words to be defined should be arranged in alphabetical order, each on a separate line and followed by its definition. (The term may be followed by a period, a colon, or an em dash, or distinguished from the definition typographically, or both.) A glossary usually precedes the notes and bibliography or reference list but may follow the notes, especially if terms listed in the glossary appear in the notes. A glossary that consists mainly of terms that do not appear in the text may be included as an appendix. See also 2.23.

1.62 **Endnotes.** Endnotes, simply headed Notes, follow any appendix material and precede the bibliography or reference list (if there is one). Any notes to an appendix may be included with the endnotes and introduced by an appropriate subhead (Appendix). But if the appendix consists mainly of tables or other data, it may be best to keep the notes with the appendix (see 3.76–80). The notes to each chapter are introduced by a subhead indicating the chapter number and often the chapter title. The running heads to the endnotes should identify the text pages or chapters the notes apply to (see 1.15). Endnotes are normally set smaller than the text but larger than footnotes. Notes are usually placed at the ends of chapters in multiauthor books (see 14.43); such chapter endnotes are a requirement for books that will be offered as individual chapters. For unnumbered notes and notes keyed to line or page numbers, see 14.52, 14.53. For endnotes versus footnotes, see 14.43–48.

MADISON CHRONOLOGY

1787

27 May–17 September	JM attends Federal Convention at Philadelphia; takes notes on the debates
29 May	Virginia Plan presented
6 June	JM makes first major speech, containing analysis of factions and theory of extended republic
8 June	Defends "negative" (veto) on state laws
19 June	Delivers critique of New Jersey Plan
27 June–16 July	In debate on representation, JM advocates proportional representation for both branches of legislature
16 July	Compromise on representation adopted
26 July	Convention submits resolutions to Committee of Detail as basis for preparing draft constitution
6 August	Report of Committee of Detail delivered
7 August	JM advocates freehold suffrage
7 August–10 September	Convention debates, then amends, report of 6 August
31 August	JM appointed to Committee on Postponed Matters
8 September	Appointed to Committee of Style
17 September	Signs engrossed Constitution; Convention adjourns
ca. 21 September	Leaves Philadelphia for New York
24 September	Arrives in New York to attend Congress
26 September	Awarded Doctor of Laws degree in absentia by College of New Jersey

FIGURE 1.9. Opening page of a chronology. See 1.60. For date style, see 6.38.

1.63 **Bibliography or reference list.** Bibliographies and reference lists are normally set smaller than the text and in flush-and-hang style. A bibliography usually precedes the index and follows the notes, if any. In a multiauthor book or a book that will be offered in the form of individual chapters, a brief bibliography may be placed at the end of each chapter (see 14.62). For a discussion of the various kinds of bibliographies, see 14.64; for reference lists, see 15.10. For discographies and the like, which usually precede any bibliography or reference list but may instead be included as an appendix, see 14.262. For a full discussion and examples, see chapters 14 and 15.

1.64 **List of contributors.** A list of contributors may be appropriate for a work by many authors in which only the volume editor's name appears on the title page. The list (usually headed Contributors) may appear in the front matter, but the preferred location is in the back matter, immediately before the index. Names are arranged alphabetically by last name but not inverted ("Aiden A. Author," not "Author, Aiden A."). Brief biographical notes, affiliations, and contact information (if authorized by the contributor) may accompany the names. See figure 1.10. A work by only a handful of authors does not require a formal list of contributors if the authors' names appear on the title page and biographical data can be included elsewhere in the book (see 1.50, 1.66, 14.55).

1.65 **Index.** The index, or the first of several indexes, begins on a recto; subsequent indexes begin verso or recto. In a book with both name and subject indexes, the name index should precede the subject index. Indexes in printed books are normally set two columns to a page and in smaller type than the text. For a full discussion of indexes and indexing, see chapter 16.

1.66 **Biographical note.** A brief note on the author or authors (including any editors, compilers, and translators) lists previous publications and, if relevant, academic affiliation. When such a note does not appear in the back matter (usually as the final element; but see 1.67), it may appear in the front matter or, more commonly, on the back cover or on the inside flap of the dust jacket, according to the publisher's preference (see also 1.70, 1.71). If such biographical information appears in more than one place, the details, if not the wording, must be consistent. In a departure from earlier practice, Chicago now prefers to place biographical notes on the back cover or on the inside flap of the dust jacket rather than on the copyright page.

1.67 **Colophon.** The last page of a specially designed and produced book occasionally contains a colophon—an inscription including the facts of production. For an example, see the last page of the print edition of this manual. For another meaning of colophon, see 1.69.

1.68 **Errata.** In rare cases, errors severe enough to cause misunderstanding are detected in a finished book that has already been printed in significant numbers. If the copies have not yet been distributed, a separate page that lists errata may be supplied. An errata page prepared along with the rest of the text may be justified when all or part of a book consists of pages scanned from an earlier publication. It may be placed either at the end of the front matter or at the end of the book and should be listed in the table of contents. The following form may be adapted to suit the particulars:

Contributors

CARA BLUE ADAMS spent five years on the editorial staff of the *Southern Review*, where she served as managing editor and editor. Work she edited has appeared in national anthologies, including *The Best American Short Stories*, *The Best American Essays*, and the *PEN/O. Henry Prize Stories*. Her fiction and nonfiction have appeared in *Narrative*, the *Missouri Review*, the *Sun*, the *Kenyon Review*, and *Ploughshares*, and she has been named one of *Narrative*'s 15 Below 30 and given support from the Bread Loaf Writers' Conference, the Sewanee Writers' Conference, and the Virginia Center for the Creative Arts. She is assistant professor at Coastal Carolina University.

BRUCE ANDREWS is an experimental poet and performance writer, literary theorist, and music/sound designer for Sally Silvers & Dancers, and has just retired from thirty-eight years as a left-wing political science professor. Most recent of a dozen big books is *You Can't Have Everything... Where Would You Put It!*, followed by a chapbook, *Yessified (Sally's Edit)*, celebrating the Andrews Symposium and its expanded archive still online at http://www.fordhamenglish.com/bruce-andrews, with links to interviews, performance texts, poetry, collaborations, and critical essays on his work. Another online archive (and interactive project) materialized on April 1, 2014, as a curated twenty-five-hour "twitter sculpture" (Twitter .com @BruceAndrews25h), a 300-poem sequence.

ANDREI CODRESCU was born in Sibiu, Romania. He came to the United States at the age of nineteen, and has been writing poetry, essays, and novels. He is a commentator on NPR, an emeritus professor of English at Louisiana State University, and the editor of *Exquisite Corpse: A Journal of Books and Ideas*, in print from 1983 until 1996, then online from 1996 and ongoing at www.corpse.org. Codrescu won the Peabody Award for his film *Road Scholar*, and the Ovidius Prize for poetry. His recent books include *So Recently Rent a World: New and Selected Poems, 1968–2012*, *The Poetry Lesson*, and *Whatever Gets You through the Night: A Story of Sheherezade and the*

FIGURE 1.10. Partial list of contributors to an edited collection. See 1.64.

ERRATA

Page	*For*	*Read*
37, line 5	Peter W. Smith	John Q. Jones
182, line 15	is subject to	is not subject to
195, line 8	figure 3	figure 15
23, 214	Transpose captions of plates 2 and 51.	

Today it is more common for publishers to list such errata online, a practice especially suited to technical manuals. Publishers who make significant corrections to electronic versions of their books can include in the corrected version a notice and description of the changes (or a link to such documentation online); any readers who received the uncorrected version may need to be notified of the update. See also 1.28.

Covers and Jackets

1.69 **Clothbound covers.** The traditional clothbound hardcover book—so-called for the integument of cloth stretched over a cardboard cover—may include a paper dust jacket (see 1.71). Underneath the jacket, on the cloth itself, the spine is generally imprinted with the author's (or editor's) full name, or the last name only if space is tight; the title of the book (and any edition number); and the publisher's name. The subtitle is usually omitted. The publisher's name is often shortened or replaced by an emblem or device known as a colophon or logo. (For another meaning of colophon, see 1.67.) Considering a book as it stands upright on a shelf, spine copy on American publications is most commonly printed vertically (and read from the top down), but when space allows (as with longer books with wider spines), it may be printed horizontally (for easier reading on the shelf). The front panel may be blank, but it sometimes bears stamped or printed material, such as the title and author's name or the publisher's colophon or some other decoration. The back panel is usually blank, though a product code may be necessary for books with no jacket (see 1.74).

1.70 **Paperback covers.** The spine of paperback covers (and other flexible covers) usually carries the author's or editor's name, the publisher's name or colophon or both, and the title. The front cover carries the author's or editor's name, the title and (usually) the subtitle, and sometimes the name of a translator, a contributor of a foreword, an edition number, or the like. The back cover usually carries promotional copy, such as a description of the book or quotations from reviews or signed blurbs, a brief biographical statement about the author (see 1.66), the series title if the book is part of a series, and, sometimes, information about the publisher. (Some paperbacks include gatefolds, also called French flaps—extensions to the front and back covers that are folded into the book just like the dust jacket to a hardcover book; see 1.71.) See also 1.74.

1.71 **Dust jackets.** Hardcover books are often protected by a coated paper jacket (or dust jacket). In addition to the three parts to be found on the book cover itself, the jacket also has flaps that tuck inside the front and back covers. The front and spine carry the same kind of material as the front and spine of paperback covers (see 1.70). The material included on the back of a paperback cover is begun on the front flap of the hardcover jacket and completed on the back flap (where a biographical note on the author may appear; see 1.66). The back panel sometimes includes promotional copy from the publisher. See also 1.74. An alternative to the dust jacket is provided by the paper-over-board format (also called lithocase), which allows full-color images and type to appear directly on the hard outer cover—including on the inside front and back panels.

1.72 **Endpapers.** An endpaper is one of two folded sheets of paper appearing at the beginning and end of a hardcover book (or, more rarely, a book with a sturdy paperback or other flexible binding). Half of each sheet is glued against the inside of the cover, one to the front and one to the back; the base of each is then glued, at the fold (near the spine), to the first and last page of the book. Endpapers help secure a book within its covers. The free half of each sheet is called a flyleaf. Endpapers, sometimes colored, are usually of a heavier stock than the book pages, and they sometimes feature printed text or illustrations. Endpapers are not counted in a book's pagination.

1.73 **Credit lines for cover art.** If a credit line is required for artwork included on a jacket or cover, it normally appears on the back flap of the jacket or the back cover of a paperback or other book without a jacket. Credit for artwork on a paperback cover or on the actual cover (as opposed to the jacket) of a hardcover book may also appear inside the book, usually on the copyright page, since the cover is a permanent part of the bound book. See 3.29–37 for styling of credit lines.

1.74 **ISBN and bar codes on book covers.** In addition to the International Standard Book Number (ISBN; see 1.32), book covers need to include product and price codes (bar codes). These should appear at the foot of the back cover or dust jacket or any other protective case or wrapper. A detailed overview of the process and related resources can be found at the website of the US ISBN Agency, R. R. Bowker, or the International ISBN Agency.

Metadata, Abstracts, and Keywords

1.75 **Metadata for books.** Metadata (literally, data about data) consists of a set of core elements that can be used to describe any resource. Metadata for a book includes such elements as title and subtitle, author and author biography, edition, publisher, publication date, ISBN, price, bar code, and a description of the book's content. Some or all of these elements are usually printed on a book's cover or jacket. To facilitate the cataloging and selling of books, these and other metadata elements can be entered into a publisher's database according to a standard syntax such as XML-based ONIX. This structured information can be used to automate the content on a publisher's product pages. It can also be shared with libraries, booksellers, and the like to facilitate online search and discovery. Metadata is utilized by all parties involved in the publishing and supplying of books, and some metadata originates outside the publisher—for example, the CIP data created by the Library of Congress (see 1.34). The creation and maintenance of accurate and complete metadata is in fact an essential component of any modern publisher's workflow. (Authors who self-publish their books through a commercial service are usually required to supply and maintain basic metadata using the service's account management tools.) In addition to the elements mentioned above, metadata usually includes a cover image and information about formats—specifying, for instance, a hardcover book or a particular e-book format—as well as language, extent (e.g., page count or, for an audiobook, duration), subject headings (using a standard classification system such as BISAC in the United States or Thema internationally) and keywords, intended audience, availability, and other vital statistics. More detailed information and guidance is available from *The Metadata Handbook* (bibliog. 2.7) and from the Book Industry Study Group. See also 1.76.

1.76 **Abstracts and keywords for books.** Abstracts, long a feature of journal articles, are increasingly required for books. An abstract is a summary of a book's content written by the author and usually limited to a few hundred words or less. Publishers may require a summary of each chapter (including any introduction and conclusion) in addition to the abstract for the book as a whole. Authors should be advised to take care in writing abstracts; though they usually do not appear in the book itself (except in the sciences), abstracts often form the basis of a book's promotional copy or of the descriptive metadata shared with libraries and booksellers. Abstracts may be supplemented by keywords. A keyword is a word or phrase that identifies an important concept or name in the book. Publishers may ask authors to supply a set of keywords for each chapter as well as for the book as a whole. Keyword metadata supplements a book's other descriptive metadata to make it more visible to search engines. Authors who self-publish their books through a commercial service are typically given the option of entering a description and keywords along with the other metadata elements for their books. See also 1.75, 2.25.

The Parts of a Journal

Introduction

1.77 **Publication formats for journals.** The majority of scholarly journals are offered either in print and electronic formats or electronically only. Even the few remaining print-only journals generally rely on a mostly electronic workflow. Electronically published journals usually contain all the material included in any printed counterpart except, in some cases, advertising. Electronic journals typically present articles and other content in one of two ways (and often both): (1) as PDF files that correspond to the pages of the journal's print issues (if any); or (2) as full-text HTML suitable for viewing in a web browser and containing features and supplementary materials not available in the print edition (see 1.78, 1.114). Some journals also offer their content in EPUB or other e-book formats. (For definitions of *PDF*, *HTML*, *EPUB*, and related terms, see 1.118.)

1.78 **Noting differences between print and electronic versions.** Although a printed article should include all elements that are essential to understanding, interpreting, and documenting the text, many journals publish special materials electronically that are not available in the print version. These features—usually referred to collectively as supplementary data or supporting information—may include very large tables, supplemental reading lists, multimedia components, large data sets that can be exported to third-party software for analysis, or color versions of figures published in black and white in the printed journal; some of this material may constitute the basis of an online-only appendix (see also 1.114). In addition, some journals release unedited versions of manuscripts that have been accepted for publication (see 1.113). With the exception of these "in press" or "forthcoming" versions, any electronic-only articles, appendixes, and other features must be listed in the print version (either in the table of contents or on the first page of the applicable article), and differences between the print and electronic versions must be made apparent in the latter. See also 3.26.

1.79 **ISSNs and DOIs.** The issues of a journal are usually identified by volume number and date. The journal as a whole is identified by an International Standard Serial Number (ISSN); electronic journals are assigned a separate ISSN distinct from any counterpart for print. Journal articles are identified in three ways: (1) by page ranges, either print pages or e-pages; (2) by the Copyright Clearance Center code, which includes the ISSN and other information, including an article number (see 1.103); and (3) by Digital Object Identifiers (DOIs). A DOI is a unique, persistent identification string assigned to an article and sometimes to its components—including tables, figures, and multimedia objects that might be sold or packaged separately. (The metadata identifying such components must make it clear that they are part of a larger work; see also 1.92.) A DOI can form the basis of a persistent link when it is appended to https://doi.org/ (a practice recommended by the DOI registration agency Crossref for DOIs wherever they are listed). See also 14.8.

1.80 **Journal volumes and issues.** A volume of a journal usually comprises the issues published in a calendar year, though some journals (e.g., *Modern Philology*) prefer the academic year beginning in the autumn. The issues within a volume are typically numbered with arabic numerals, each new volume beginning with issue number 1. In some journals, however, the cover month, cover date, or season (Spring, Summer, etc., usually capitalized) is used in lieu of an issue number. In others, issue numbering does not start over with each volume, or the journal is numbered consecutively by issue only, with no volume number. For a journal published quarterly, a volume has four issues; for one published monthly, twelve issues. Some journals, however, publish two or more volumes in one year, depending on the frequency and length of issues.

Page Numbers and Running Heads

1.81 **Page numbers for journals.** Page numbers in a printed journal usually start with 1 in the volume's first issue and run continuously to the end of the volume. An issue always begins on a right-hand page (recto) and ends on a left-hand page (verso); thus the last page of an issue is an even number (though the preceding recto may be counted as the last page of content) and the first page an odd one. If issue 1 ends with page 264 (or 263, if the content ends on the preceding recto), then issue 2 starts on page 265. To help readers identify and cite articles, electronic journals with printed counterparts should list the page ranges that correspond to the printed version alongside information for the article wherever it appears (e.g., in the table of contents, at the head of the article itself, and in the citation data for the article). See figure 1.11. This should be done even for articles that are published in an electronic format that does not feature page breaks. Articles published electronically ahead of print may need to employ "dummy folios" (e.g., 000–000) until the print issue has been paginated. Articles that do not appear in the print version of a journal can use a separate page-numbering system (e.g., E1, E2, etc.), again running continuously to the end of the volume. See also 1.82.

1.82 **Page numbers for journals that use a continuous publishing model.** To facilitate publication and citation of articles independent of print issues, some journals have adopted a continuous publishing model, according to which each article is assigned a unique citation ID (which can be derived from the DOI for the article; see 1.79) rather than a traditional page range. PDF versions of articles are each paginated starting with the number 1, and individual pages can be cited according to citation ID number plus page number (e.g., 1234, p. 1; 1234, p. 2; etc.); such pagination is considered final and is used instead of the traditional pagination scheme in any print version of the journal. See also 14.174.

1.83 **Running heads or running feet in journals.** Running heads or feet typically bear the title of the journal (either spelled out or in abbreviated form); the author's surname or, for more than one author, a shortened version of the author list (such as Aldrich et al.); and the title of the article, usually shortened, or the name of the journal section (such as Brief Reports), or both. Arrangement of these pieces of information across rectos and versos varies among journals. For full-text, scrollable electronic articles, which will not have running heads per se, such information may be presented at the head of each article. Articles that have been downloaded for individual use typically show a URL and date of download in the header or footer of each page.

Covers, Front Matter, and Home Pages

1.84 **Journal covers.** A printed journal is usually bound in soft covers, like a paperback, and each issue generally uses the same overall design and color scheme. A journal's spine contains the title of the journal, the volume and issue numbers, and the date, month, or season and the year of publication. It may also note the beginning and ending page numbers

FIGURE 1.11. Partial table of contents for an issue of an online scholarly journal. Note that the page numbers, as in many scholarly journals, are sequential throughout a volume. See 1.81, 1.87.

of that issue. Each of the remaining four sides of the cover also contains important information, as follows:

- *Cover 1*, the front cover, displays the title of the journal; the volume and issue numbers; the date, month, or season and the year of the issue; the publisher's name; and sometimes the table of contents or an illustration. The title of a special issue, along with the name(s) of the editor(s) of the special issue, appears on cover 1. The front cover may be offered as an image on the home page for each issue.
- *Cover 2*, the inside front cover, usually contains the masthead with the names of the editor(s) and staff, the editorial board, the journal's International Standard Serial Number (ISSN), its dates or frequency of publication, subscription information, addresses for business and editorial correspondence, and the copyright line for the entire issue (see also 1.103). Cover 2 may also include information about postage; a statement about paper durability (see also 1.35); a statement about copying beyond fair use; information about obtaining back issues; mention of a submission fee, if that is part of the journal's practice; information about indexing of the journal's articles; a statement about advertising policy; a caption for any illustration that appears on cover 1; and the URL of the journal's home page. If the journal is sponsored by a scholarly society or other organization, cover 2 may supply the name and address of the society and the names of officers. Occasionally on cover 2 but more often in the front or back matter of each issue, there may be a statement of editorial policy for the journal indicating what kind of articles the journal publishes as well as information for contributors about how and in what form to submit a manuscript.
- *Cover 3*, the inside back cover, is often given over to advertising, or it may be used for information for contributors. If the table of contents begins on the back cover, it may be completed on cover 3.
- *Cover 4*, the back cover, carries the bar code for the journal issue in the lower right-hand corner. It may also carry the table of contents or titles of articles scheduled to appear in a forthcoming issue, or advertising. (If there is advertising on cover 4, the bar code may be put on cover 2 or cover 3.) If the table of contents begins on cover 1, it may be completed on cover 4.

1.85 **Journal front matter.** Many of the elements discussed in 1.84 can equally occur in the front matter, or preliminary ("prelim") pages. Some journals, because they have a sizable staff and a large number of editors on their advisory board, have space on cover 2 only for the masthead and advisory board editors; the other items then appear in the front matter.

1.86 **Journal home pages.** Most journal home pages include all materials typically found on the covers and in the front matter of a printed journal (see 1.84, 1.85), starting with such essential information as the volume number and date of the current issue and a table of contents with links to the latest articles. A statement of copyright, frequency of publication, and ISSN (print and electronic) should also be made available from a journal's home page. In addition, journal home pages may also provide (or provide links to) some or all of the following resources:

- A fuller description of the journal and its editorial policies and information about staff members
- Information about the history of the journal and, if applicable, the sponsoring society
- More extensive information for authors about preparation and submission of electronic text, tables, math, art, and other files (e.g., video files or large data sets)
- Links to other home pages (e.g., the publisher's home page, the sponsoring society's home page, other relevant societies' home pages, and databases or other online resources associated with the journal or the field)
- Individual and institutional subscription forms
- Site license agreement and registration forms
- Links to tables of contents for previous issues of the journal
- Lists of articles scheduled for upcoming issues, or links to articles published electronically ahead of upcoming issues
- A journal-specific or broader search engine
- Information about indexing and abstracting services
- Society meeting abstracts and information about upcoming meetings
- Society membership information and application forms
- Information about special services for subscribers (e.g., tables of contents distributed by email before publication in print)
- Links to related products or features (e.g., books, newsfeeds, blogs)
- Mail-to links for questions about manuscript submission and review, subscriptions, back issues, advertising, copyright and permissions, books and new media for review, passwords and other technical issues, and other topics

These resources are generally not associated with a particular issue of the journal but are simply updated as needed (but see 1.105).

1.87 **Journal table of contents.** The table of contents, usually headed Contents, appears in the front matter or on the cover(s) of the print issue (see 1.84) and is also available from a journal's home page. The table of contents should include the title of the journal (or, for a special issue, the title of a special issue and the names of its editors); the date, month, or season and the year of publication; the volume and issue numbers; and the titles of the articles in the issue along with the authors' names and the page range for each article (or, in print, the number on which each article begins). It may contain section titles, such as Reviews, or subheads for specific content areas. Additional items listed may include review articles, book reviews, book notes, commentaries, editorials, or other substantive items, and should include a list of articles published in electronic form only or direct readers to the journal's website for a list of those articles. The electronic table of contents, in addition to providing links to each format of each item in the list, will include links to article summaries, which usually include an abstract and other information that can be viewed without a subscription. See figure 1.11. Full articles that are freely available to the public should be labeled as such. Most journals also include options for downloading citations to individual articles (see also 14.5), either in the table of contents or with the articles themselves, or both.

1.88 **Information for journal contributors.** Information for potential contributors can vary in length from a sentence to several pages. Some journals also include a statement of editorial policy. These components—when they do not appear on cover 2 or cover 3 in a printed journal (see 1.84)—may appear in an issue's front or back matter. In many cases, the print journal will contain a brief version of these components and point the potential author to the electronic version for more details.

1.89 **Journal acknowledgments, announcements, and calls for papers.** Acknowledgments of reviewers, announcements of awards or conferences, and calls for papers are published periodically, and may appear in the preliminary pages or at the end of a journal issue. If the issue is a supplement or special issue on a single topic, perhaps representing the proceedings of a conference or symposium, the print issue may begin with a title page that contains the title of the supplement, the name(s) of any guest editor(s), information about the source of the articles, and sponsorship information, if any.

1.90 **Journal errata.** Journals periodically publish errata, which, in print issues, may appear in the front or the back matter. Electronic journals should provide two-way links from errata to the articles that contain the errors; in other words, the articles themselves should be updated to link to or otherwise indicate the relevant errata. The entries in the table of contents for the original articles should also contain links to the errata. Small errors in online articles that are corrected after the original publication date (e.g., broken images and typographical errors) are best accompanied by a note indicating the nature of the changes and when they were made. See also 1.112.

1.91 **Journal retractions.** Occasionally a journal will issue a retraction of a previously published article that has since been identified as unacceptable (e.g., for reasons of plagiarism or data falsification). The retraction should include the title of the retracted article, the full author list, the volume and issue in which the article appeared, and a brief explanation for the retraction (usually two or three sentences). The electronic version of the retraction should include a link to the retracted article; the article itself, which remains otherwise intact, should include a link to the retraction and a notice that it has been retracted.

Metadata, Abstracts, and Keywords

1.92 **Journal article metadata.** The majority of journal content is consumed in the form of individual articles retrieved by readers through internet or library searches. To facilitate this process, accurate and complete article metadata must be incorporated into the electronic records that a journal publisher shares with libraries and other content providers. Metadata for a journal article includes such elements as the title of the journal and ISSN, volume and issue number, author and author affiliations, article title, page range, publication date, and article DOI. Some of these data elements are printed in the journal issue or on its cover and are displayed along with the article online. Metadata for journals is typically recorded using a standard XML-based syntax and may be retrieved from a separate database or derived from the electronic markup of a journal's articles and other components. In addition to the items mentioned above, article metadata can include information about format (e.g., print, HTML, PDF, or e-book), language, content (including abstract and keywords), subject headings, access rights, sources of funding, and other pertinent details. Other types of metadata can help a publisher track the versions of a document through the proofreading and testing stages or facilitate linking of source citations in a reference list. For more information, including information about best practices, consult the Dublin Core Metadata Initiative, an organization responsible for developing standards related to electronic resource description. See also 1.93, 1.117.

1.93 **Journal article abstracts and keywords.** Many journals—in the sciences especially but also in the social sciences—publish abstracts along with their articles. These summaries, typically limited to a few hundred words or less, are usually supplied by the author and appear at the beginning of an article. Because abstracts are also generally made available as standalone items to allow subscribers and nonsubscribers alike to preview an article before they read or purchase it, they normally do not contain cited references or figure callouts or any other direct links to the article itself. The content of an abstract is extremely important because it can influence decisions made by researchers and other potential readers. Some journals have strict guidelines for what an abstract must include and how it should be structured—especially those that publish the results of original research. Abstracts are not usually required for letters, reviews, and other such materials (see 1.94). Abstracts are typically supplemented by keywords—words or phrases that are intended to increase the visibility of an article to search engines and to facilitate indexing (see 1.111). Though keywords normally repeat key terms found in the title, abstract, and text, synonyms or other variations may be added to anticipate search terms. Keyword metadata can be supplied by the author or derived from a controlled vocabulary such as the Medical Subject Headings (MeSH) used by the National Library of Medicine. See also 1.92.

Articles and Other Components

1.94 **Journal articles versus other components.** Journals consist principally of individual articles. Some journals also publish special kinds of articles—such as review essays, survey articles, or articles grouped as a symposium. Many articles include abstracts, which are considered part of the article (see 1.93). In addition to articles, journals may publish brief reports, letters to the editor, book reviews, book notes, announcements, calls for papers, errata, notes on contributors, and other ancillary materials.

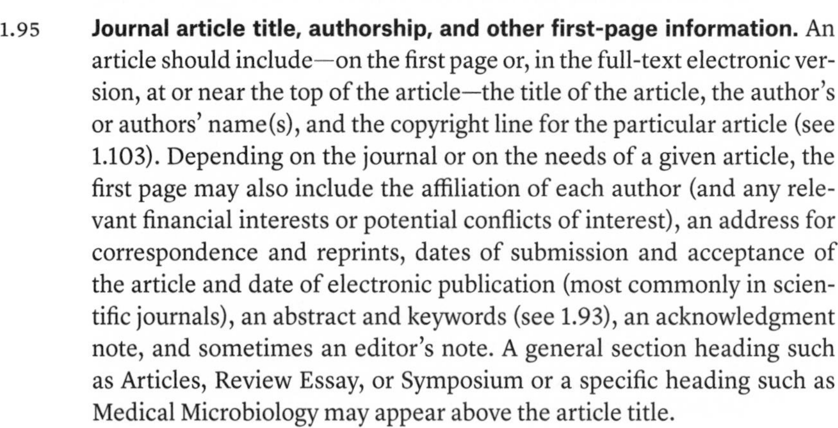

1.95 **Journal article title, authorship, and other first-page information.** An article should include—on the first page or, in the full-text electronic version, at or near the top of the article—the title of the article, the author's or authors' name(s), and the copyright line for the particular article (see 1.103). Depending on the journal or on the needs of a given article, the first page may also include the affiliation of each author (and any relevant financial interests or potential conflicts of interest), an address for correspondence and reprints, dates of submission and acceptance of the article and date of electronic publication (most commonly in scientific journals), an abstract and keywords (see 1.93), an acknowledgment note, and sometimes an editor's note. A general section heading such as Articles, Review Essay, or Symposium or a specific heading such as Medical Microbiology may appear above the article title.

1.96 **Cross-references and other links in journal articles.** Full-text electronic journal articles typically include links to elements within the document (e.g., tables and illustrations, reference list entries, and notes) and often also to outside resources such as the sources cited in the reference list and field-specific indexes or databases. They may also include links to supplementary materials not available in the print version (see 1.78). Articles are also typically accompanied by other linked items, including an article-specific list (or menu) that allows readers to move directly to other sections of the article (or to the PDF version) and a standard menu that allows them to move to the issue's table of contents, to the previous or next article in the issue, to the journal's home page, to search options and cited-by data, and to tools for citing and sharing the article. The display may also include thumbnail versions of the article's tables and illustrations.

1.97 **Journal article subheads.** An article, like a chapter in a book, may be divided into sections and subsections headed by subheads, sub-subheads, and so on (see 1.55–58). The number of subhead levels required may vary from article to article.

1.98 **Journal reviews.** Many journals include a book review section. Such sections, usually headed Reviews or Book Reviews, vary greatly in length from journal to journal. Within a section, each review carries a heading that lists information about the book being reviewed. The heading includes the author's name, the title of the book, place and date of publication, publisher's name, number of pages (including front matter), and price. If the book is part of a series, the series title may be given. Some journals include reviews of other journals or of films or other media. The name of the reviewer usually appears at the end of the review but occasionally follows the heading; alternatively, reviews are given a separate title in the manner of regular articles, and the name of the reviewer follows the title at the head of the review. Book notes use the same form of headings as book reviews, but the text is much shorter and reviewers may be listed by their initials. Some journals also publish a list of books or other materials received for review from publishers.

1.99 **Journal announcements.** Announcements include such items as notices of future conferences and symposia; calls for papers, award nominations, or research subjects; and employment opportunities.

1.100 **Journal contributors.** Basic information about contributors such as their professional affiliations typically appears with each article, usually at the head of the article or elsewhere on the first page. This information is also generally included as part of an article's metadata (see 1.92) and may be offered along with the abstract as part of an article's online summary. Some journals offer an index of past contributors to the journal as a whole. Journals may also feature a special section with additional information about contributors, such as their publications or fields of study.

1.101 **Letters to the editor.** Letters to the editor are typically treated as a minor component of a journal, published irregularly if at all, and sometimes only online. In some scientific journals, on the other hand, letters appear as a regular, prominent feature, often with replies, and may contain equations, tables, and figures.

1.102 **Journal editorials.** An editorial is not a regular feature in most academic journals but appears on a particular occasion. When there is a change of some sort—a new editor, modifications in editorial policy or style, features added or dropped, or graphic redesign of the journal (see 1.115)—an editorial announces and explains the change. A journal may provide an annual editorial summing up the year's activity. Some journals publish invited editorials, written by someone who is neither the journal's editor in chief nor a member of its editorial board, that comment on a particular article or group of articles. A special issue usually includes an introduction by the special issue's editor(s). The heading Editorial or Introduction is used, and the editor's name appears at the end of the piece.

1.103 **Journal copyright lines.** In addition to the copyright line that appears on cover 2, each substantive article or element in the journal normally carries its own copyright line. This usually appears at the bottom of the first page of the article, below any footnotes on that page, or, for full-text electronic articles, at the head of the article or some other prominent location. It contains three basic parts: (1) information on the current issue, including the title of the journal, the volume and issue numbers and date of publication, and the inclusive page numbers of the article; (2) the actual copyright notice, containing the copyright symbol, the year, and the name of the copyright owner (usually either the publisher or the sponsoring society); and (3) a series of numbers (the Copyright Clearance Center code) containing the journal's unique identification number (its International Standard Serial Number, or ISSN), the year, the volume and issue numbers, the article number (assigned by the publisher), and the per copy fee for photocopying, payable through the Copyright Clearance Center (CCC; see below).

The Journal of Modern History 86, no. 4 (December 2014): 743–779
© 2014 by The University of Chicago. 0022-2801/2014/8604-0001$10.00
All rights reserved.

For some journals, Chicago also includes a fourth element—the article's DOI (see 14.8); the DOI is always listed along with the full-text version of an article and its summary. Most but not all US journals use the CCC, which provides systems through which copyright owners can license the reproduction and distribution of materials in both print and electronic form. Its relations with equivalent agencies in other countries enable the CCC to collect fees for uses in those countries. Note that fees apply only to copyrighted material and not to articles in the public domain. See also 4.55–57, 4.97.

1.104 **Publication history for journal articles.** For all articles that are published electronically before they are published in print, the date of electronic publication should appear as part of the article's history, in both the print and the electronic versions, on the first page or otherwise near the head of the article. Some journals also include the date the article was received and the date it was accepted for publication. These dates provide important context for interpretation of the article; in the sciences, especially, what is known—or at least what has been reported—can change rapidly.

1.105 **Preserving the context of individual journal articles.** Publishers, libraries, and online aggregators typically offer journal content in the form of individual articles, letters, or reviews rather than in the context of the original issue as a whole. Publishers who seek to preserve the historical context of their back issues might consider making covers, front matter, and other ancillary materials from the original issue readily available along with the articles themselves. Such materials can provide important historical context about editors, sponsors, or even advertisers in the journal, all of which may be relevant in assessing the import of a work.

Tables and Illustrations

1.106 **Tables in journal articles.** Tables in electronic articles can be presented in multiple formats—for example, as an image of the typeset table, as a searchable hypertext version with links, or as a machine-readable version that allows readers to download the data and either repeat the analyses used in the article or use the data, perhaps in combination with data from other sources, for their own analyses. Table footnote citations can be linked to the table footnotes themselves; this is especially useful for navigation in very large tables. Links also allow readers to move freely from text to tables and back again, as well as from one table to another. Very large tables may be published in electronic form only; if there is also a print version of the article, both versions should make this difference explicit (see 1.78). For a full discussion of tables, see 3.47–88.

1.107 **Illustrations in journal articles.** An electronic article might display the same illustrations available in the print version of the article, though they may be presented in the text as thumbnail versions linked to larger, higher-resolution images. These images may contain additional navigational aids like the ones described for tables (see 1.106). A greater range of illustrations can be offered in electronic journals, which can include more illustrations than would be practical in print. Color can be used freely, without the costs associated with color printing (although color accuracy can vary considerably between display devices). High-resolution images can allow readers to see more detail, and electronic illustrations may include an audio component. Videos and animations allow readers to view movement and understand processes. Any differences between the content of the print and electronic versions should be noted explicitly in both formats (see 1.78, 3.26). For a full discussion of illustrations, see 3.3–46.

Source Citations

1.108 **Notes or author-date citations in journals.** One of the fundamental identifying marks of a journal is its documentation style—either notes (sometimes accompanied by a bibliography) or author-date citations. Notes, which still prevail in many humanities journals, may be footnotes or endnotes; if the latter, they appear at the end of the article, with the heading Notes. Author-date citations—used mostly by journals in science and the social sciences—consist of parenthetical text citations keyed to a reference list, which appears at the end of the article. For a discussion of Chicago's two preferred systems of documentation, see chapters 14 and 15. Some scientific journals use a system of numbered references cited in the text by reference number; depending on the system, the references are listed in alphabetical order or in the order cited in the text (see 14.3).

1.109 **Internal and external links to cited sources in journals.** In full-text electronic articles (and sometimes in enhanced PDF versions), text citations typically link to references, notes, or items in a bibliography, as the case may be, allowing readers to move from the text citation to the cited item and back to the text. Reference lists and bibliographies may in turn link to resources outside the article—for example, to cited articles or to an outside index or database (see 1.111).

Indexes

1.110 **Indexes to printed journal volumes.** At the end of a volume, some journals publish an index to the articles and other pieces published in that volume. The index appears in the volume's last issue. Names of authors, titles of articles, and titles and authors of books reviewed are indexed. More detailed subject indexes, on the other hand, are becoming rare. In the sciences especially, subject indexes have been superseded by searchable field-specific bibliographic databases (see 1.111).

1.111 **Electronic indexes and indexed searches.** Many journals have dispensed with subject indexes; readers have come to rely instead on indexed searches provided by the publisher or by a third-party bibliographic database or search engine to lead them to individual articles. In the sciences, journal subject indexes have been largely superseded by field-specific resources such as PubMed, the National Library of Medicine's bibliographic database of journal articles. PubMed allows readers to search the entire field of biomedicine for electronically indexed articles—with the help of a standard keyword vocabulary—rather than searching individual journals at a publisher's website. (Readers who reach an article through a database or search engine rather than by subscribing to the journal may need a subscription or otherwise pay to gain access to the full article.) See also 1.92, 1.93.

Version Control and Material Not Available in Print

1.112 **Journal article version of record.** Many journals consider the electronic version of an article to be the version of record; the print version, which should contain all elements that are essential to the article, may nevertheless include only a subset of the material available electronically. Whenever the electronic version is considered the version of record, it is extremely important to document any changes to the file after the electronic publication date. Release of electronic articles before they are published in print means that errors may turn up well before the print issue has been assembled; consequently, a print issue may include an erratum that concerns an article in the same issue. In this case, the erratum should state that the article is in the current issue and should specify the date of electronic publication. Some journals use a system like Crossref's CrossMark to track versions and any corrections or retractions. For more information on best practices related to version control for journal articles, consult *Journal Article Versions (JAV): Recommendations of the NISO/ALPSP JAV Technical Working Group*, published by the National Information Standards Organization (bibliog. 2.7). See also 1.90, 1.91.

1.113 **Preprints and "in press" articles and articles published ahead of print.** Manuscripts are sometimes released before publication: authors themselves may circulate drafts within a research community, or they may circulate versions submitted to a journal. They may post drafts on a preprint server—as is standard practice in the physics community—or on their own web pages. Some journals post "in press" or "forthcoming" articles on their website that have been accepted but not yet edited. These versions of an article are not to be confused with the final, edited electronic articles published in advance of the print issue (see 1.112). To facilitate publication of the latter, some journals in the sciences have adopted a continuous publishing model, according to which articles are published in final form individually, independent of any future print issue in which they may appear (see also 1.82).

1.114 **Supplemental journal content.** In addition to certain articles published ahead of print (see 1.113), journals often publish material not available in print or not applicable to print (e.g., multimedia components, large data sets); such material is usually referred to collectively as supplementary data or supporting information. Such supplemental content must be listed in any print version, and the electronic version must in turn make it clear that such material is available only online (see 1.78). At the same time, publishers must provide this content in a way that ensures its ongoing availability and accessibility, whether or not the electronic version is considered the version of record (see 1.112). By implementing standard practices for document structure and markup and for the inclusion and identification of supplemental media such as video and audio files, publishers can help ensure the permanence and accessibility of their material in libraries and other archives. Publishers should remain abreast of the latest standards for archival practices by consulting such groups as the International Organization for Standardization and the Digital Library Federation.

Design and Style

1.115 **Journal design.** A journal's design—physical, visual, and editorial—is determined when the journal is founded. At that time, a designer creates a design for the cover and the overall look of a journal and specifications for all of its regular features. Because the designer designs not for a specific text but for categories of text—article title, author's name, text, heads, subheads, and so on—the design of a journal should be simple and flexible as well as visually pleasing and easy to read. The design of the electronic version, which may be shared across journals offered via the same parent site, will have additional considerations based on the medium (see 1.117–25). It is the job of the manuscript editor and production personnel to fit the items for a particular issue into the overall design. A long-running journal may occasionally be redesigned typographically. More rarely in print but commonly in electronic formats, minor alterations in style may be introduced to accommodate changing technologies.

1.116 **Journal editorial style.** A journal's editorial style governs such things as when to use numerals or percent signs, how to treat abbreviations or special terms, and how to organize tables. Consistency of design and style contributes to a journal's identity; readers know what to expect, and the substantive contribution of each article stands out more sharply when typographical distractions are at a minimum.

Considerations for Electronic Formats

1.117 **Electronic workflows.** Most modern publishers use an electronic workflow as the basis of their publications, and many publishers, in turn, offer their publications in more than one format. To achieve such flexibility, a system of electronic markup may be used to describe the structure and components of a document such that it can be readily converted to any of a number of formats, from the printed page to an e-book format or for presentation in a web browser or as an app. Many publishers rely at least at some stage on XML (extensible markup language), a widely adopted standard initially developed to facilitate HTML presentations and now also used to facilitate EPUB, a standard e-book format. XML is also the basis of the Journal Article Tag Suite (JATS) published by the National Information Standards Organization (NISO) and used by many journal publishers. Publishers who do not use a standard set of tags can develop a customized workflow tailored to their requirements. In any electronic workflow, the primary function of markup is to identify the parts of a work—from titles and subheads to text and illustrations and other components (see also 2.81–83). Then, after conversion for publication, both the parts and the whole take on a new appearance and acquire new functions in different contexts depending on publication format. Considerations related to these differences are the subject of this section. (An extensive overview of publishing workflows and technologies, including a discussion of markup and related concepts, is offered as a supplement to the online edition of this manual.)

1.118 **Electronic publication formats.** Print, for centuries the basis of the publishing industry, has been joined in the last half century by a number of electronic formats, from plain-text ASCII files to full-featured web presentations and apps. Though plain text is technically sufficient for many purposes, the most common publishing formats support special characters, images, and other enhancements.

1. **PDF.** An abbreviation for *portable document format*, PDF is practically identical to print; in fact, it was designed as a means of preserving all the characteristics of a fixed layout and forms the basis of most modern printed publications. Though PDF essentially provides an image of the printed page, the text can be searchable and hyperlinks can be added for internal cross-references or to external resources. (PDF also supports embedded multimedia content, but to date few publishers have taken advantage of this.) PDF readers typically include tools for annotation, making it a suitable alternative to paper for proofreading or editing (see 2.133). PDF, offered by many journal publishers and used as the basis of some e-book formats, can also be included as a component of web publications and apps.
2. **E-book formats.** Book publishers especially have turned to e-book formats as a means of offering their content in a way that mimics many of the characteristics of the printed-and-bound book. PDF can be used as the basis of an e-book, but EPUB and a number of similar formats tailored to the specialized features of the software and devices that support them are more common. EPUB, short for *electronic publication*, is an open standard that defines the content and structure of e-books. Most e-book publications consist of reflowable text and images, though EPUB and some other e-book formats also support fixed-layout options. E-book formats include linked tables of contents and other navigational tools and are designed to be read one screen or "page" at a time. Software and devices for e-books typically support note-taking and bookmarking features and some multimedia content.
3. **HTML.** An abbreviation for *hypertext markup language*, HTML refers to a specific set of tags used to describe the text and graphics that are displayed in a web browser. Many journals offer full-text HTML versions of their articles in addition to or instead of PDF. Browser-based HTML is ideal for presenting multimedia content and complex tabular matter and for facilitating author and reader interaction as well as links to related content—all as part of the larger context of the publisher's or content provider's website (see 1.86). HTML is also especially suited to complex, extensively hyperlinked publications such as dictionaries and other reference works.
4. **Apps.** The term *app*, short for *application*, can be used to refer to any soft-

ware program, from a word processor to a web browser to the camera app on a mobile device. It can also refer to the software required to read a specific e-book format. For publishers, apps afford additional possibilities for offering content. Publishers of reference works or textbooks can develop app versions designed for the smaller screens and specialized hardware typical of mobile devices. Academic publishers, on the other hand, can tailor the electronic versions of their books and articles for compatibility with third-party bookshelf-style apps. Apps, together with web presentations, offer the widest range of possibilities for presenting content.

1.119 **Functional features in electronic formats.** The functional features available for different electronic formats vary not only according to what each format supports but also in how publishers implement them. For PDF and e-book formats, functional features are typically determined by the applications and devices used to read them. The features for web presentations and apps, on the other hand, are generally determined by the publisher. For a full-text HTML journal article, the available features are usually determined by an established website or app design and rarely vary from one issue to the next. But for a custom web presentation or app, functionality may have to be determined, designed, developed, and implemented from scratch. In this case, technical and editorial considerations overlap: functional features must be implemented and assessed with a clear understanding of the content and how the user will interact with that content. This is true to some degree of any electronic publication, as technologies change and even previously published content must be reevaluated in new contexts. Publishers must have a system in place for checking content in each environment in which it may be read (see 2.137–40).

1.120 **Navigation in electronic formats.** Navigation is the basis of any electronic publication, starting with search. Searchable PDF may be enhanced by publishers with linked tables of contents and other internal links, or by links to outside resources, but need not be. Any other navigational tools for PDF will depend on the software used to read it. Linked tables of contents are created as a matter of course for EPUB and similar e-book formats, which typically consist of a number of documents and images (i.e., the content of the book) "packaged" for delivery as a single set of files to be presented in a specific order according to a set of encoded instructions. Such navigation, then, is generally determined by the content and structure of the book itself, allowing publishers to streamline publication in e-book formats according to a strategy of consistent markup and file formats. Markup for e-books may also include internal links to notes and other cross-references and links to outside resources (but see 1.121). A web-based reference work or app, on the other hand, must take into account the fact that readers will typically consult smaller pieces of content and will expect to be able to shuttle through many parts of a work in a very short period of time and in no particular order. This generally involves a greater number of cross-references and hyperlinked items. Dictionaries, in fact, may be entirely hyperlinked, such that every word in every definition is linked to the entry for that term, and so on, providing endless pathways through a significant subset of a single language. Search is essential too. Readers expect to be able to search for and find any component of a work on the basis of a few key terms; any work that allows full-text searching will benefit from context-sensitive keyword indexing (see 16.7). Readers may also want to know where other readers are landing, through links to the most popular content or to cited-by statistics.

1.121 **Links in electronic formats.** There is no cost to following a hyperlink, provided there is a means of stepping back and forth between the link and the item it points to. But if there are too many links, or if they do not tend to lead to strongly related content—or, worse, if they fail—a publication risks irritating its readers. Beyond cross-references and linked tables of contents or other navigational items, a link can be directed to almost anything. Words might be linked to their definitions—either in a glossary or through a third-party dictionary. Authors' names might contain mail-to links or lead to their networking pages or to lists of their other works. URLs or other identifiers can be embedded in any piece of content. Some of these links, including links to dictionary definitions and outside searches for individual terms, may be a feature of a specific device or app. Publisher-created links, on the other hand, must be maintained and updated, often at significant cost. For this reason, links added to PDF and e-book formats are sometimes limited either to internal cross-references (which do not generally change) or to outside resources via a permanent identifier such as a DOI (see 14.8). The content of web-based works is generally more flexible, and some links can be checked or generated programmatically. For example, links to related titles or subjects can be generated by matching title or subject metadata against an evolving database each time a user calls up a specific piece of content. See also 2.34.

1.122 **Front or back matter in electronic formats.** PDF and most e-book formats will retain the traditional front matter of a printed publication, including the order in which it is presented. Readers of web-based publications, on the other hand, will want to be able to navigate primarily to the core content of the publication (and the content that it generates) rather than to ancillary elements such as prefaces, copyright information, or information about the publication or its authors. These elements can be demoted from their usual position in the front (or back) of a book and made accessible on the margins of the screen. Copyright information, however, should usually be included with each subdocument, and help and related documentation should also be available from any part of a publication. Much of the usual taxonomy for printed works—from copyright page to table of contents to preface, foreword, and introduction—will benefit from a different set of categories (i.e., home pages, "about us" links, site maps, help menus and other tools, search engines, etc.). The table of contents, however, especially in works that can be read in larger chunks—such as an online journal or this manual—may be a significant driver in the top-level navigation of a web-based publication. See also 1.125.

1.123 **Orienting the reader in electronic formats.** A primary advantage of a traditional printed-and-bound book or journal (or its PDF counterpart) is the presence of fixed page numbers. Page numbers give students and researchers a convenient means of making precise citations to the works they consult, allowing readers with access to the same book to retrace their steps (but without the benefit of searchable text). Printed publications also typically include running heads specific to chapter (or article), section, or other text division (see 1.10–16). Many e-books lack fixed page numbers because they allow for reflowable text and user-defined options for typeface and size. Instead, software and devices for e-books orient readers by means of location or screen numbers (and sometimes percentage relative to the work as a whole) and by bars that graphically represent a reader's position in the book and provide a means of shuttling between locations.[2] These navigational elements may appear in lieu of detailed running heads, or in addition to a simple running head displaying the title of the book (but see 2.76). For web-based publications and apps, readers can be oriented in a variety of ways independent of page numbers or running heads per se. Dictionaries and encyclopedias rely on a natural organizing principle: readers cite material *sub verbo*—or "under the word"—that is, by entry or entry title (14.232–34). Other types of publications broken into scrollable sections or subsections may benefit from hierarchical navigation based on a table of contents; section or paragraph numbering can be added as an aid to navigation and citation.

2. EPUB and some related formats support the inclusion of page number markers, and publishers who use the same workflow for their print books and e-books should consider including this metadata to allow readers of the e-book (depending on software and device) to locate page numbers referring to the printed book (see also 14.160).

Meanwhile, each page in a web-based publication or app can display the location in the current document relative to the section or chapter hierarchy and to the work or site as a whole (e.g., 1: Books and Journals » Chapter Contents » Considerations for Electronic Formats)—or provide a ready means of returning to the top-level navigation.

1.124 **Source citations in electronic formats.** A primary advantage of the electronic environment is the ability to link to and from in-text references and the items they refer to, solving the problem of footnotes versus endnotes that arises in printed books (see 14.43–48). A related advantage is the ability to link out to the cited resources themselves. Such links can be applied in any electronic format, from PDF to e-book to HTML (but see 1.121). On the other hand, in some electronic formats, linked-to items in the notes or in the bibliography or reference list may be presented apart from the context of the list as a whole, making such traditional bibliographic strategies as *ibid.* or the 3-em dash for repeated references impractical (see 14.34, 14.67).

1.125 **Indexes in electronic formats.** Traditional back-of-the-book indexes, like footnotes or endnotes, can benefit from the electronic environment by being hyperlinked to the text. For indexes that refer to printed page numbers, linking in e-book versions can be facilitated by the addition of page number or other markers defined for EPUB or other structured markup. A similar strategy can be used for web-based publications or apps. A more elegant but time-consuming and therefore costly approach involves doing away with the page number references and instead linking directly from the terms in the index to the corresponding location in the text. In the case of an index that refers to numbered paragraphs (as the one for this manual), linking an index is a relatively straightforward matter. See also 16.2, 16.13.

2 · Manuscript Preparation, Manuscript Editing, and Proofreading

Overview and Process Outline

2.1 **Overview—authors, manuscript editors, and proofreaders.** This chapter is divided into three parts. The first part (2.3–47) is addressed primarily to authors, conceived broadly to include compilers, translators, volume editors, editors of journals, and contributors to journals or books. It provides guidelines for preparing manuscripts that have been accepted for publication. The second part of the chapter (2.48–99) gives a detailed look at what happens to a manuscript once it has been submitted to a publisher. Specifically, the role of manuscript editors (also called copyeditors), whether on staff with a publisher or hired on a freelance basis, is discussed. The third part (2.100–140) deals with proofreading—essentially, the steps authors and publishers must take to ensure that their publications are ready to be presented to the public. The chapter uses the book as a model, though considerations for journals are included where applicable. (Journals usually post specific requirements and instructions that journal authors will need to consult.) Many of the recommendations will apply to other types of publications, including self-published works.

2.2 **Process outline—from approved manuscript to published work.** The following outline highlights the basic steps of the publication process from approved manuscript to published work. These steps are broadly modeled on a typical manuscript editing and proofreading schedule for a book-length work; the procedures for journals will vary. For a more detailed look at manuscript preparation, editing, and proofreading, see the discussions in the remainder of this chapter. For sample timetables for producing a book and a journal, see figures 2.1 and 2.2.

1. **Manuscript submission.** In addition to the final manuscript, the author submits to the publisher all artwork and any necessary permissions to reproduce illustrations or previously published material or to cite unpublished data or personal communications. See 2.3–6.
2. **Manuscript editing.** The manuscript editor suggests changes to the manuscript (and, where necessary, queries the author) and demarcates or checks the order and structure of the elements (e.g., illustrations, headings, text extracts). See 2.57–67, 2.69.
3. **Author review.** The author reviews the edited manuscript and answers any queries. All remaining changes and adjustments to the manuscript need to be indicated by the author at this stage. See 2.71, 2.88.
4. **Final manuscript.** The manuscript editor produces a final manuscript, incorporating the results of the author's review of the edited manuscript and, among other things, double-checking each element in the manuscript against

	Business days	Dates	
Transmittal	n/a	04/02/2015	**In editing three months**
Contract OK	n/a	04/02/2015	
Begin MS edit	5	04/09/2015	
MS to author	45	06/11/2015	
MS design in	15	07/02/2015	
MS from author	5	07/09/2015	
MS design OK	5	07/16/2015	
Final MS to production	5	07/23/2015	**In production six months**
Sample pages in	10	08/06/2015	
Sample pages OK	3	08/11/2015	
Pages in/to author	9	08/24/2015	
Pages and index MS from author	20	09/21/2015	
Pages and index MS to design	5	09/28/2015	
Pages to production	5	10/05/2015	
Pages to typesetter	1	10/06/2015	
Index MS to typesetter		10/06/2015	
Revised pages in	9	10/19/2015	
Index pages in		10/19/2015	
Mfg quotes requested		10/19/2015	
Mfg quotes received	5	10/26/2015	
Revised pages to typesetter		10/26/2015	
Index pages to typesetter		10/26/2015	
Estimate and release routing	2	10/28/2015	
Page revisions completed	8	11/09/2015	
Final lasers requested	5	11/16/2015	
Final lasers in	5	11/23/2015	
Final lasers OK	10	12/07/2015	
Estimate and release approved		10/30/2015	
Cover/dust jacket copy in/OK		11/13/2015	
Cover/dust jacket design in		07/23/2015	
Cover/dust jacket design OK		07/30/2015	
Cover mechanical in		11/30/2015	
Cover mechanical OK		12/07/2015	
Order date text/cover/dust jacket		12/14/2015	
Advances in		02/01/2016	
Books in warehouse	5	02/08/2016	

FIGURE 2.1. Sample design and production schedule for a book.

	Business days	JANUARY v1n1	APRIL v1n2	JULY v1n3	OCTOBER v1n4
MSS, running order, signed publication agreements, covers, prelim updates due in production		9/21	12/21	3/23	6/23
MSS converted / art processed / MSS to editors	5	9/28	12/29	3/30	6/30
Editing complete / MSS to typesetter	15	10/19	1/23	4/20	7/24
Page proofs typeset / proofs to authors	5	10/26	1/30	4/27	7/31
Corrections received from authors	3	10/31	2/2	5/2	8/3
PDFs annotated with editorial corrections, returned to typesetter for revised pages	10	11/14	2/16	5/16	8/17
Ahead-of-print articles posted / issue approved for pagination	5	11/21	2/23	5/23	8/24
Paginated issue from typesetter	5	11/30	3/2	5/31	8/31
Issue approved by editorial for print and post	5	12/7	3/9	6/7	9/8
Final issue materials delivered: print-ready PDFs from typesetter due to printer	1	12/8	3/10	6/8	9/11
Electronic deliverables due	5	12/14	3/16	6/14	9/15
Post electronic version and e-book	2	12/16	3/20	6/16	9/19
Mail print edition	10	12/22	3/24	6/22	9/25

FIGURE 2.2. Sample production schedule for a quarterly journal.

a design template for completeness, consistency, and proper markup. See 2.73–77.

5. **Proofreading and indexing.** Once the final manuscript has been converted for publication—for example, as a typeset and paginated book or journal article or the full text of an electronic publication (see 1.118)—it will need to be checked by the author and any additional proofreaders in at least one format (typically PDF or print, as *page proofs* or *proof*) for errors and inconsistencies. See 2.100–140. It is also at this stage that an index may be prepared and subsequently edited (see chapter 16; for journal indexes, see 1.110–11).

6. **Final revisions.** As the publisher makes sure all necessary corrections have been made, the index, if there is one, is proofread in its final format and corrected as needed (see 2.106). Book pages, especially, may go through several rounds of revision, though publishers usually set firm limits on changes beyond the first round of revisions. See 2.105.
7. **Prepress or final review.** For a printed-and-bound book, publishers usually review the typesetter's final files—either as an inexpensive printout or on-screen—before ink is committed to paper. Once the job is on the press, an initial set of folded-and-gathered sheets may be sent from the printer to the publisher for review before the job is finished (see 2.107). For electronic formats, a final version must be reviewed in each context in which it will be published before it is posted or distributed or otherwise made available to the public (see 2.137–40).
8. **Publication.** In the stages leading up to publication it is critically important to make all possible efforts to eliminate any errors or inconsistencies (typographical or otherwise) or other problems. The occasional error in a published work is inevitable, but even minor errors reflect badly on publishers and authors alike.

Manuscript Preparation Guidelines for Authors

Basic Manuscript Submission Requirements

2.3 **Manuscript submission checklist.** Before manuscript editing begins (see 2.48–99), an author should provide any of the elements in the list that follows that are to be included in the work. This list is modeled on the parts of a book (see 1.3–76). An author contributing to a journal should consult the journal's specific submission requirements.

- Title page
- Dedication
- Epigraph
- Table of contents
- List of illustrations
- List of tables
- Preface
- Acknowledgments
- Any other front matter
- All text matter, including introduction and part titles
- Notes
- Appendixes
- Glossary

- Bibliography or reference list
- Any other back matter
- All illustrations and all tables
- Illustration captions
- A list of special characters used in the manuscript
- Abstract(s) and keywords (see 1.76)
- All permissions, in writing, that may be required to reproduce illustrations or previously published material or to cite unpublished data or personal communications (see chapter 4)

All elements should be final and up to date—including any URLs cited in the work (see 14.6–18). The publisher usually furnishes the half-title page (see 1.17), the copyright page (see 1.20–35), and copy for the running heads (see 1.10–16, 2.76).

2.4 **Submitting the manuscript.** Publishers usually require the latest version of the electronic file(s) for the work, and authors are advised to make a secure backup of this final manuscript and to avoid making any further changes to it. Some publishers also require hard copy or PDF as a safeguard against any glitches in the electronic files—especially for book-length works or works with complex formatting or special typographical needs. To ensure that this copy is identical to the electronic files, any last-minute changes made to the electronic files before the manuscript is submitted must be reflected in the hard copy or PDF—either by means of a new printout or PDF or marked by hand (see also 2.5). Authors are advised to include a cover letter specifying the author's name, the title of the work, a total word count (rather than a page count), the electronic file names, and the software used. Any material (such as artwork) that cannot be included in electronic form must be noted and described. Conversely, any material that cannot be printed or supplied as PDF (such as videos, animations, or large data files that might be included in an electronic journal or web-based publication) must also be noted and described; for all such material, the software used, the number of items, their type(s), and the individual file names must be specified. For any additional instructions, authors should check with their publishers. For advice on manuscript formatting, see 2.7–25. For advice on preparing index manuscripts, see chapter 16. For paper-only manuscripts, see 2.6. For manuscripts consisting of previously published material, see 2.43.

2.5 **Making changes after a manuscript has been submitted.** Once an author has submitted a final manuscript to the publisher, the publisher is responsible for maintaining the version of record. An author who needs to make further changes after submitting the files must therefore alert the publisher immediately. Minor changes can usually be indicated later, on the edited document that the manuscript editor will send to the author for review (see 2.71, 2.88). For major changes, the author may need to send a revised manuscript to the publisher *before* editing begins. Authors should be advised, however, that many book publishers begin manuscript preparation immediately upon receipt and may not be able to accept a revised version after the original submission of the final manuscript. For journals, major changes are rarely permitted after an article has been accepted; schedules do not allow for them. Peer-reviewed articles that require major changes may also require additional review.

2.6 **Submitting a paper-only manuscript.** In the rare case of a typewritten manuscript, authors are typically required to submit two paper copies of the manuscript; they should keep a third copy for themselves. All copy must be double-spaced to leave sufficient room for pencil-editing marks between the lines. It is essential, moreover, that everything in a paper-only manuscript be legible. Anything added in handwriting before the manuscript is submitted to the publisher must be clearly written, in upper- and lowercase letters, directly above the line or in the margin. Avoid writing on the backs of pages in case the publisher photocopies the manuscript. Any correction longer than a short phrase should be provided as a separate document and inserted in the manuscript following the page to which it pertains—clearly labeled in both places to show where it should be inserted. Finally, to facilitate photocopying, use good-quality paper in a standard size—usually 8½ × 11 inches or A4 (210 × 297 mm). See also 2.43.

Manuscript Formatting

2.7 **Publishers' manuscript-preparation guidelines.** Many publishers have specific requirements or preferences regarding choice of software and typeface, as well as formats for submitting illustrations and tables along with the manuscript. These should be followed to the letter. Consistency and simplicity in all matters is essential. Authors should know that their manuscripts will almost always be converted into another software environment for publication and that, therefore, the consistency and accuracy of the content (i.e., the words themselves and the order in which they are presented) are more important than the style of presentation. As long as the basic structure of chapters and sections and the like is clear, a simple presentation is always preferable to an elaborately formatted manuscript. Authors who want a more explicit idea of what publishers look for in the format and structure of a manuscript would do well to consider the steps in a manuscript editor's typical cleanup routine (see 2.80).

2.8 **Line spacing.** Though authors may prefer to use less line spacing on the screen, publishers have customarily required that any printout be double-spaced—including all extracts and lists, footnotes or endnotes, bibliographies or reference lists, and any other material. The extra line spacing is crucial for manuscripts edited with pencil on paper; some publishers will choose to edit the paper copy and update the electronic files based on this edited copy. (Authors concerned about saving paper are encouraged to consult with their publishers about line-spacing requirements and any option for sending PDF instead of paper; see 2.4.) Avoid extra space or blank lines between paragraphs (see 2.12). If such a break is intended to appear in the printed version, indicate this explicitly with three asterisks set on a line by themselves (see also 1.58). If blank space rather than an ornament is preferred, specify this in a note to the publisher. For stanza breaks in poetry, see 2.20.

2.9 **Space between sentences or after colons.** One space or two? Like most publishers, Chicago advises leaving a single character space, not two spaces, between sentences and after colons used within a sentence, and this recommendation applies to both the manuscript and the published work. In fact, a well-structured electronic document will never include more than one consecutive character space. See also 2.12, 6.119–21.

2.10 **Justification and margins.** To avoid the appearance of inconsistent spacing between words and sentences, all text in a manuscript should be presented flush left (ragged right)—that is, lines should not be "justified" to the right margin. To leave enough room for handwritten queries, margins of at least one inch should appear on all four sides of the hard copy.

2.11 **Tabs versus indents.** Tabs are entered with the Tab key. Indents are applied using a word processor's indentation feature. Tabs can usually be identified on-screen by the right-pointing arrows that will appear in most word-processing programs when nonprinting characters are revealed; aside from the position of the text, indents are generally signaled on a graphical ruler or by a dialog box for paragraph formatting. (In word processing, a "paragraph" is any string of text that begins on a new line and is followed by a hard return, including not only the blocks of text traditionally referred to as paragraphs but also items in a list, headings, etc.) There are three basic types of indent:

- *First-line indent.* A first-line indent (also called a paragraph indent) is normally applied to each new paragraph of regular text. As its name suggests, only the first line is indented (from the left margin). A first-line indent can be applied either using a word processor's indentation feature or with a tab. Choose one method and use it consistently.
- *Left or right indent.* A left indent applies an equal indent relative to the left margin for each line in a paragraph, including the first line and any runover lines, and can be used to set off prose and poetry extracts. Never use tabs to achieve left indents. Indents from the right margin are usually not needed at the manuscript stage.
- *Hanging indent.* A hanging indent (also called flush-and-hang), in which every line but the first is indented from the left margin, is used for the items in a list, including a bibliography or reference list or an index. Never use tabs to achieve hanging indents.

In some cases, it will be necessary to use a first-line or hanging indent in combination with a left indent (as for a new paragraph in a block quotation or for a poetry extract; see 2.19, 2.20). For the purposes of the manuscript, the typical default value for tabs or indents can normally be used (usually half an inch). Avoid using two or more consecutive tabs. With the exception of a tab at the beginning of a new paragraph or a tab after a number or symbol in a vertical list (see 2.21), tabs should never appear within a paragraph.

2.12 **Paragraph format.** Each new paragraph should begin with a first-line indent, applied either with the Tab key or with your word processor's indentation feature (see 2.11); do *not* use the Space bar. Never use the Enter key or the Tab key in the middle of a paragraph; let the word processor determine the breaks at the ends of lines. Be sure to eliminate any extra character space or tab after the final punctuation at the end of a paragraph; the hard return should follow the punctuation immediately. When a paragraph is interrupted by a prose or poetry extract, list, equation, or the like, the text after the interruption begins flush left (i.e., with no first-line indent) unless it constitutes a new paragraph. For prose extracts, see 2.19; for poetry, see 2.20; for lists, see 2.21. See also 2.24.

2.13 **Hyphenation.** The hyphenation function on your word processor should be turned off. The only hyphens that should appear in the manuscript are hyphens that would appear regardless of where they appeared on the page (e.g., in compound forms). Do not worry if such a hyphen happens to fall at the end of a line or if the right-hand margin is extremely ragged. By the same token, do not attempt to manually break excessively long words (e.g., long URLs) with a hyphen. See also 2.96.

2.14 **Dashes.** For an em dash—one that indicates a break in a sentence like this—either use the em dash character on your word processor or type two hyphens (leave no space on either side). The 3-em dash, used in some bibliographies for a repeated author name, is usually best left to the manuscript editor; if it must be used, insert either three consecutive em dashes or six unspaced hyphens (see also 14.67). (For more on the em dash, see 6.85–92, 6.93–94.) Ensuring proper use of the en dash—a shorter dash that has special significance in certain types of compounds and in number ranges—is usually considered the manuscript editor's responsibility; authors can generally avoid the en dash and use hyphens instead. (For more on the en dash, see 6.78–84.)

2.15 **Italics, underline, and boldface.** Though underlining will generally be construed by publishers to mean italics, italics should be used instead wherever italics are intended. (In an electronically redlined manuscript, underlining may denote editorial changes; see 2.84 and fig. 2.4.) An author who intends underlining rather than italics to appear in certain instances in the published work must make these instances clear in a letter to the publisher (or a note to the manuscript editor). Use boldface only for words that must appear thus in the published version (but see 2.18).

2.16 **Special characters.** As far as your software allows, use the character that you intend rather than any keyboard substitute. For example, if you want a prime symbol, use the prime symbol from your word processor's list of special characters rather than an apostrophe. Since the advent of the Unicode standard for character encoding (see 11.2), many software environments include a wide array of special characters without the need for special fonts or other add-ons. Nonetheless, if you run up against a character that is not available to you, enclose a descriptive shorthand in angle brackets; for example, *<bhook>aci* might indicate that the publisher should render the Hausa word *ɓaci*. In either case, include a list of special characters used in your manuscript. See tables 11.1 and 11.2, which list some special characters and their names and hexadecimal code points for Unicode. Your list should show how each character is supposed to look; if a character is unavailable to you, copy the correct character from the applicable code chart from the Unicode website or elsewhere or draw it in by hand. If you plan to use a special font that may not support Unicode, consult your publisher first. For quotation marks and apostrophes, see 6.115, 6.117.

2.17 **Format for chapter titles and titles of other parts.** Titles for chapters and other parts of a manuscript usually begin on a new page. Use upper-

and lowercase letters rather than full capitals. The titles should match the entries in the table of contents. "Chapter 1," "Chapter 2," and so on should appear above the titles to numbered chapters. (For an overview of the parts of a book or a journal, see chapter 1.)

2.18 **Format for subheads.** Set each subhead on a new line, flush left. Each level of subhead must be clearly distinguished so that the different levels can be identified and carried over for publication. Levels can be distinguished by font size (e.g., larger for first-level subheads, smaller for second-level heads, etc.). A word processor's style palette can be useful in applying such distinctions and in managing subhead levels. (Authors are encouraged to consult their publishers' manuscript preparation guidelines for the preferred approach.) Use upper- and lowercase letters rather than full capitals. Chicago prefers headline-style capitalization for subheads (see 8.159), with no period added at the end. An exception is made for run-in heads, which are usually italicized and followed by a period and capitalized sentence-style (see 8.158). See also 1.56.

2.19 **Format for prose extracts.** Prose extracts (also called block quotations) should be indented from the left margin using your word processor's indentation feature, never with tabs. The first line should *not* have an additional paragraph indent. If there is more than one paragraph within the extract, however, each new paragraph should begin with an additional first-line paragraph indent, which can be added using the Tab key or your word processor's indentation feature. See 2.11. Use a hard return only at the end of the extract and after any paragraphs within the extract. Prose extracts should have the same line spacing as the surrounding text (see 2.8); they do not need to appear in a smaller font. The text that follows an extract should get a first-line indent only if it constitutes a new paragraph; if it continues the text that introduced the extract, it should start flush left (see 2.12). See also 13.22–24. For ellipses, see 13.50–58.

2.20 **Format for poetry extracts.** A poetry extract should be indented but *not* centered (even if it might appear centered in the printed version). Use your word processor's indentation feature to assign both a left indent and a hanging indent to each line. Let runover lines wrap to the next line normally; use a hard return at the end of each full line of poetry but never in the middle of a line, and do not use the Tab key to indent runovers. See 2.11. Runover lines must be clearly distinguished from indented lines of poetry. If certain lines of a poem are to receive a deeper indent than others, increase the left indent value accordingly. For poetry with unusual spacing or indentation, append a photocopy or scan of the original printed poem. Indicate a stanza break with an extra hard return. The source, if given after the extract, should appear in parentheses on a separate line, indented like the first line of the poem. (In the published version, the source may appear flush right.) Poetry extracts should have the same line spacing as the surrounding text (see 2.8); they do not need to appear in a smaller font. The text that follows a poetry extract should get a first-line indent only if it constitutes a new paragraph; if it continues the text that introduced the extract, it should start flush left (see 2.12). See also 13.25–29. For ellipses, see 13.57.

2.21 **Format for lists and outlines.** Items in an unnumbered list should be formatted using your word processor's indentation feature to assign both a left indent and a hanging indent. Let runover lines wrap to the next line normally; do not use the Tab key to indent runovers. See 2.11. In addition, in a numbered or lettered list (including a multilevel list or outline), each number or letter should normally be followed by a period or other punctuation and a tab. Bullets in a bulleted list are likewise followed by a tab. Alternatively, you may use your word processor's list and outline features, which will apply the necessary indents, tabs, and numbers, letters, punctuation, or symbols automatically. (These automatically generated numbers or letters or symbols may need to be converted to regular text to ensure compatibility with the software used for publication, a task that is normally considered to be the manuscript editor's or publisher's responsibility.) The text that follows a list should get a first-line indent only if it constitutes a new paragraph; if it continues the text that introduced the list, it should start flush left (see 2.12). See also 6.127–32.

2.22 **Format for footnotes and endnotes.** To take advantage of automatic renumbering, create notes that are linked to the text by using the footnote or endnote function on your word processor. The text of the notes should have the same line spacing as the rest of the manuscript; do not insert an extra hard return between notes (see also 2.8). Unless your publisher requests otherwise, in the manuscript notes may appear either as footnotes or as chapter or book endnotes (starting over at 1 for each chapter), regardless of how they are to appear in the published version. Do not mix footnotes and endnotes unless such a system is truly necessary (see 14.49). Avoid appending note references to chapter titles (see 1.49). Notes to tables should be numbered separately (see 2.31). For note form, see 14.24–60. For some considerations related to citation management software, see 14.5.

2.23 **Format for glossaries and lists of abbreviations.** Each entry in a glossary or list of abbreviations should begin on a new line, capitalized only if the term is capitalized in the text. Separate each term from the definition that follows with a period, a colon, or an em dash (choose one and use it consistently; see also 1.61, 2.14). In a glossary, begin the definition with a capital letter, as if it were a new sentence; in a list of abbreviations, the expanded term should be capitalized or lowercased as it would be in text. Unless all definitions consist of incomplete sentences, each glossary entry should end with a period. Any term or abbreviation that is consistently italicized in the text (not just on first use) should also be italicized in the glossary or list of abbreviations. (Abbreviations of consistently italicized terms should generally themselves be italicized; see also 14.60.) Entries should have the same line spacing as the rest of the manuscript (see 2.8) and may be formatted in flush-and-hang style or with ordinary first-line paragraph indents (see 2.11). Avoid multiple columns. See also 1.44 and 1.61.

2.24 **Format for bibliographies and reference lists.** Each entry in a bibliography or reference list should begin on a new line. Use your word processor's indentation feature to assign a hanging indent to each line. Never use the Tab key to indent runover lines. See 2.11. Use the same line spacing as for the rest of the manuscript (see 2.8). For capitalization, use of italics, and other matters of bibliographic style, see chapter 14. For some considerations related to citation management software, see 14.5.

2.25 **Format for abstracts and keywords.** Authors may be required to submit an abstract and keywords, not only for the book as a whole but for individual chapters as well. Abstracts and keywords are typically submitted as a separate file; some publishers provide a template. A book abstract normally consists of a single paragraph, not longer than 500 words, with no tables, lists, illustrations, or notes; chapter abstracts are usually somewhat shorter. (Publishers will often specify a word limit for each.) The book abstract should give a clear summary of the book's main arguments and conclusions. Chapter abstracts should give a clear overview of each chapter. Keywords, typically a set of five to ten key terms, accompany the book abstract, with additional sets for any chapter abstracts. Keywords are designed to enhance a book's visibility to search engines by repeating significant terms found in the abstract, though they can also include a synonym or other related term that users might be expected to enter in a search. Each keyword should consist of a single word (e.g., Olympics) or an accepted compound of no more than a few words (e.g., table tennis). Authors should take care in writing an abstract and choosing keywords; though they usually do not appear in the book itself (except in the sciences), they often form the basis of the promotional copy or descriptive metadata shared with libraries and booksellers. See also 1.76. Journal publishers usually have their own set of requirements for abstracts that authors can consult; see also 1.93.

Preparing Illustrations and Tables

2.26 **Formatting and submitting illustrations, captions, and tables.** Publishers usually prefer separate files for illustrations. Many publishers also prefer tables in separate files, but those created using a word processor may not need to be; consult your publisher. The approximate placement of illustrations or tables submitted as separate files should be called out in the text, keeping in mind that the exact locations of figures in a manuscript will be determined during typesetting (see 2.30). Captions for all illustrations should be furnished in a separate file; any list of illustrations should follow the table of contents (see 1.39). For a more detailed overview of illustrations and tables, see chapter 3.

2.27 **Submitting artwork.** Text figures that are to be supplied in digital format or reproduced by scanning a hard-copy original—such as paintings, maps, and photographic prints—should be furnished according to the publisher's specifications. Publishers often prefer to do their own scans. Glossy prints must be clearly labeled, usually on the back of the print or on a self-sticking label, in a manner that does not impair their quality (see 3.16). For further discussion, see 3.15–20.

2.28 **Numbering illustrations.** Illustrations may be consecutively numbered, or, in scientific and technical books, heavily illustrated books, and books with chapters by different authors, double numeration may be used. In double numeration, provide the chapter number, followed by a period, followed by the figure number (e.g., fig. 1.1, 1.2, 1.3, . . . , 2.1, 2.2, 2.3, . . . , etc.). In the event a figure is dropped or added, double numeration will simplify the work needed to renumber not just the illustrations but any applicable cross-references, especially in a heavily illustrated book. Illustrations are enumerated separately from tables. Plates to be grouped in a gallery are numbered separately from figures interspersed in the text (see 3.14). Even if numbers are not to appear with the illustrations in the published version, working numbers should be assigned for identification and should accompany the captions (see 3.13). For more details, see 3.8–14.

2.29 **Numbering tables.** Tables may be numbered consecutively throughout a book or, in a book with many tables or with chapters by different authors, double numeration may be used (e.g., table 1.1, 1.2, 1.3, . . . , 2.1,

2.2, 2.3, . . . , etc.). In a book with many tables, double numeration can simplify the task of renumbering in the event a table is dropped or added. Tables are enumerated separately from illustrations. Very simple tabular material (e.g., a two-column list) may be presented, unnumbered, along with the text. See also 3.50–51.

2.30 **Formatting text references and callouts to tables and illustrations.** A *text reference* is addressed to the reader ("see table 5," or "fig. 3.2") and will appear in the published version. A *callout* is an instruction, which will not appear in the published work, telling where a table or an illustration is to appear. In the manuscript, a callout should be enclosed in angle brackets or some other delimiter and placed on a separate line following the paragraph in which the table or illustration is first referred to ("<table 5 about here>"; "<fig. 3.2 about here>") or, if a later location is preferable, where the table or illustration is to appear. Tables and such illustrations as graphs and diagrams require both a text reference and a placement callout, unless they are to be grouped in a section separate from the regular text. Illustrations that are not referred to in the text still usually require placement callouts (see 3.8–14); unnumbered tables presented in the run of text do not require callouts (see 3.51).

2.31 **Formatting table notes and source notes.** Source notes appear at the foot of the table before any other notes. They are preceded by the word "Source" followed by a colon. Other notes to the table as a whole follow any source note and may be preceded by the word "Note" followed by a colon. Specific notes follow any other notes, and the notes to each table must be enumerated separately from any notes to the text (see 3.79). For a fuller discussion of notes to tables, see 3.76–80.

Cross-Checking the Manuscript

2.32 **Items to cross-check.** Before submitting a manuscript for publication, an author must cross-check all of its parts to avoid discrepancies. The following list includes major items to check:

- All titles and subtitles (introduction, parts, chapters, etc.) against table of contents
- Subheads against table of contents (if subheads are included there; see 1.38)
- Illustrations against their captions, text references, and callouts
- Illustration captions against list of illustrations
- Tables against their text references and callouts
- Table titles against list of tables

- All internal cross-references or hyperlinks (see also 2.35)
- All URLs and other external links
- All quotations against their original sources
- Notes against their text references
- Notes against bibliography (see chapter 14)
- Parenthetical text citations against reference list (see chapter 15)
- Abbreviations against list of abbreviations
- In a multiauthor work, authors' names in table of contents against chapter headings and list of contributors

2.33 **Checking quotations against original sources.** All quoted matter should be checked against the original sources, for both content and source citations, before a manuscript is submitted for publication. This authorial task is crucial because manuscript editors will not have access to all the sources that the author has used.

2.34 **Checking URLs and other external links.** Any URLs or other links to outside resources (e.g., database accession numbers)—including any mentioned in the text—should be double-checked just before a manuscript is submitted for publication. Those that no longer point to the intended source should be updated. At the same time, source citations that include links should be checked for completeness according to the guidelines in chapter 14; in most cases, readers should be able to find the resource with or without the link. See also 14.6–18.

2.35 **Checking cross-references.** All cross-references, whether to a chapter, a section, an appendix, or even a sentence of text, should be verified before a manuscript is submitted for publication. A chapter number or title may have been changed, or a passage deleted, after the original reference to it. Cross-references are best made to chapter or section numbers because these are known and can be entered at the manuscript stage. (Keep in mind, however, that references to whole chapters are often gratuitous and unhelpful; it's best to avoid peppering a manuscript with "see chapter 2 above" and "see chapter 4 below.") References to page numbers are generally discouraged because the pagination of a published work will not correspond to that of the manuscript, and the correct number will have to be supplied later in the process (usually by the author). Moreover, such cross-references may become meaningless in e-book versions that lack fixed page numbers (successful linking will require page number data from the printed version). Where absolutely necessary, use three zeros (e.g., "see p. 000") to signal the need to supply the final page number.

Preparing the Electronic Manuscript Files

2.36 **Publishers' guidelines for preparing and submitting electronic files.** For book-length projects, publishers may prefer to get separate electronic files for each of the various elements—front matter through table of contents, preface, chapters, appendixes, and so on (some of which will include embedded notes). Appropriately named separate files—especially for complex works—can help publishers get a sense of and deal with a book's component parts. Some authors (and editors), however, will prefer to work in a single file to facilitate searching and to take advantage of the outline views and other navigational tools available in modern word processors. Authors should always consult their publishers' manuscript preparation guidelines before submitting a final manuscript, whether for a book or for a journal article. Illustrations, which publishers handle separately from the text, should always be in separate files; tables created in an author's word-processing software may not need to be (see 2.26).

2.37 **Naming and saving the electronic files.** File names for a book should correspond more or less to the parts of the manuscript as listed in the table of contents (see 1.4). File names that include an author name and a descriptive label will help publishers keep track of them. For books with more than a few parts, use file names that will line up in book order in an alphanumerically sorted directory. The numerals added to the beginning of each of the following file names will facilitate this:

01 Jones contents
02 Jones preface
03 Jones chap01
04 Jones chap02
. . .
12 Jones biblio

File names usually also include extensions (e.g., .docx or .odf); whether or not these are visible, they should never be changed or deleted. A separate file for illustration captions might start with "00" (e.g., "00 Jones captions"). Electronic artwork files should usually be submitted as a separate group and named accordingly (e.g., "Jones fig 1.1," "Jones fig 1.2," etc.). File names for color illustrations may include the word *color*, especially if black-and-white illustrations have also been submitted. A complete list of all submitted files, including files for captions and illustrations, should accompany the manuscript. If PDF versions are required, these files should also be listed. If a hard copy is required, the manuscript should be arranged in the order specified in the table of contents.

2.38 **Numbering manuscript pages.** Each page of a manuscript, whether electronic or hard copy, must be numbered. Manuscripts submitted as multiple files need not be numbered consecutively from page 1 through to the end of the book. Instead, to ensure that no two pages in the manuscript are numbered the same, add descriptive page headers next to the page numbers in each file (e.g., "Introduction: 1," "Introduction: 2," etc.; "chapter 1: 1," "chapter 1: 2," etc.). Arabic numerals may be used for the front matter even though these pages may take on roman numerals in the published work. (It is typically the job of the manuscript editor to indicate where roman numerals will apply; see 2.75.) Manuscripts submitted as one file, on the other hand, can be numbered consecutively across the book starting with page 1 (see also 2.37). In a paper-only manuscript, pages added after the initial numbering may be numbered with *a* or *b* (e.g., 55, 55a, 55b).

2.39 **Removing comments and revision marks from the final files.** Authors should delete any comments embedded in their electronic manuscripts *before* submitting them for publication. This includes any text formatted as "hidden" and any comments inserted using the commenting feature in a word processor. Any outstanding queries should be addressed in a cover letter. Moreover, it is crucial that any revision marks (or "tracked changes") be removed before the manuscript is submitted—and that the final manuscript represent the very latest version. (Manuscript editors should always check for hidden text, comments, and revision marks and alert the author or publisher about any potential problems.)

2.40 **Backing up the final manuscript.** In addition to saving a separate electronic copy of each crucial stage of work on their manuscripts, authors are advised to save a backup copy of the version sent to the publisher for editing and publication. Prudence dictates retaining copies in at least two separate locations (e.g., on a computer hard drive and on a portable drive or with a secure file-hosting service). See also 2.5.

Preparing a Manuscript for a Multiauthor Book or Journal

2.41 **Volume editor's manuscript preparation responsibilities.** The specific responsibilities of the volume editor, contributors, and publisher (including manuscript editor) must be determined before a multiauthor manuscript is submitted. If there is more than one volume editor, the responsibilities of each must be spelled out. After ensuring that the contributors furnish their papers in a uniform style agreed to by all parties, the volume editor is usually responsible for the following:

- Getting manuscripts, including illustrations, from all contributors in a form acceptable to the publisher well before the date for submitting the volume
- Securing (or ensuring that the contributors have secured) written permission from copyright owners to reproduce material in copyrighted works published elsewhere, illustrations taken from another work, and the like (see chapter 4)
- Editing each contribution for sense and checking references and other documentation for uniformity of style (unless the publisher agrees to allow different documentation styles for separate chapters; see also 2.64), then sending edited manuscripts to the contributors for their approval before the volume is submitted to the publisher (an activity distinct from the manuscript editing that will be done later by the publisher)
- Providing a list of contributors with their affiliations and brief biographical notes to be included in the volume
- Providing a title page, table of contents, and any necessary prefatory material
- Sending the complete manuscript to the publisher in a form acceptable for publication (having first made sure that the manuscript includes only the latest version of each contributor's chapter)
- Adhering to the publisher's schedule, ensuring that contributors do likewise, keeping track of the contributors' whereabouts at all stages of publication, and assuming the responsibilities of any contributor who cannot fulfill them

Most if not all of these responsibilities also apply to journal editors.

2.42 **Additional responsibilities of the volume editor.** Depending on the arrangement with the publisher, the volume editor may also be responsible for the following:

- Sending a publishing agreement (provided by the publisher) to each contributor and returning the agreements, fully executed, to the publisher (see 4.58)
- Checking the edited manuscript and responding to all queries, or distributing the edited manuscript to the contributors and checking it after their review to ensure that all queries have been answered
- Proofreading the final version of the volume or delegating proofreading to the contributors and then checking their corrections
- Preparing the index

Compiling a Manuscript from Previously Published Material

2.43 **Preparing previously published material.** Manuscripts for an anthology or other work comprising previously published material are said to have been *compiled*. If the compiler retypes the original source or scans it using optical character recognition (OCR), the resulting text should be incorporated into a manuscript that follows the formatting requirements outlined in paragraphs 2.7–25. Manuscripts consisting of retyped text or text prepared with OCR must be proofread word for word against the original material *before* the final manuscript is submitted to the publisher for editing; in addition, publishers may request copies of the originals. If the original material is submitted on paper only, make sure the material is entirely legible (publishers may prefer legible single-sided photocopies or scans to pages from the original source). Unless there is ample space to insert corrections above the printed lines, any corrections should be written in the margins (see 2.119–33). See also 4.105.

2.44 **Permissible changes to previously published material.** The compiler of previously published material may make the following changes to the published material without editorial comment: notes may be renumbered; cross-references to parts of the original work that are no longer relevant may be deleted; obvious typographical errors and inadvertent grammatical slips may be silently corrected. See also 13.7–8. If wholesale changes have been made—for example, in spelling or capitalization conventions or notes style—the compiler should note such changes in a preface or elsewhere. For deletions indicated by ellipsis points, see 13.50–58.

2.45 **Footnotes or endnotes in previously published material.** Footnotes that appear as such in the original pages may be presented as footnotes or endnotes in the published version. If a compiler's or volume editor's notes are being added along with the original footnotes or endnotes, the new notes should be intermingled with but distinguished from the original notes (see 14.51); if the original material is being submitted to the publisher on paper only, it may be preferable to produce a separate electronic document for the notes.

2.46 **Source notes for previously published material.** Each selection of previously published material should be accompanied either by a headnote (a brief introduction preceding the selection) or by an unnumbered footnote on the first page of text. Include the source, the name of the copyright owner if the selection is in copyright (see chapter 4, esp. 4.2–49), and the original title if it has been changed. See also 14.54. If a selection has previously appeared in various places and different versions, the source note need not give the entire publishing history but must state which version is being reprinted.

2.47 **Reproducing previously published illustrations.** Compilers should contact their publisher about how to obtain illustrations from previously published material in a format suitable for printing. Photocopies of illustrations are not acceptable for reproduction. The compiler should procure glossy prints or the original publisher's scans. If these are unavailable, it may be possible to reproduce an illustration from the original publication.

Manuscript Editing

Principles of Manuscript Editing

2.48 **Levels of manuscript editing and who is responsible.** Manuscript editing, also called copyediting or line editing, requires attention to every word and mark of punctuation in a manuscript, a thorough knowledge of the style to be followed, and the ability to make quick, logical, and defensible decisions. It is undertaken by the publisher—either in-house or through the services of a freelance editor—when a manuscript has been accepted for publication. (Self-publishing authors, too, can benefit from the services of a professional editor.) It may include both mechanical editing (see 2.49) and substantive editing (see 2.50). It is distinct from developmental editing (not discussed in this manual), which more directly shapes the content of a work, the way material should be presented, the need for more or less documentation and how it should be handled, and so on. Since developmental editing may involve total rewriting or reorganization of a work, it should be done—if needed—*before* manuscript editing begins. For a comprehensive overview of the editing process, see *What Editors Do: The Art, Craft, and Business of Book Editing*, edited by Peter Ginna (bibliog. 2.1). For more on developmental editing, consult Scott Norton's *Developmental Editing: A Handbook for Freelancers, Authors, and Publishers* (bibliog. 2.1).

2.49 **Mechanical editing.** Mechanical editing involves the consistent application of a particular style to a written work—including text and documentation and any tables and illustrations. The central focus of part 2 in this manual, *style* is used here to refer to rules related to capitalization, spelling, hyphenation, and abbreviations; punctuation, including ellipsis points, parentheses, and quotation marks; and the way numbers are treated. Mechanical editing also includes attention to grammar, syntax, and usage. The rules set forth in a style manual like this one may be supplemented by a publisher's house style or the style of a particular discipline. Journal editors in particular follow a journal's established style, augmented by additional resources specific to the subject area. Books in a series or multivolume works should all follow one style consistently, as should separately authored chapters in a multiauthor book (but see 2.41). The style of any work, as well as occasional deviations from it, must be determined by author, editor, and publisher before editing begins. For substantive editing, see 2.50. See also 2.51, 2.55.

2.50 **Substantive editing.** Substantive editing deals with the organization and presentation of existing content. It involves rewriting to improve style or to eliminate ambiguity, reorganizing or tightening disorganized or loosely written sections, adjusting or recasting tables, and other remedial activities. (It should not be confused with developmental editing, a more drastic process; see 2.48.) In general, no substantive editing should be undertaken without agreement between publisher and editor, especially for book-length works; if major substantive work is needed, the author should be consulted and perhaps invited to approve a sample before the editing proceeds. A journal's manuscript editors, however, working on rigid schedules, may need to do substantive editing without prior consultation with authors if problems of organization, writing style, and presentation have not been addressed at earlier stages.

2.51 **Editorial discretion.** A light editorial hand is nearly always more effective than a heavy one. An experienced editor will recognize and not tamper with unusual figures of speech or idiomatic usage and will know when to make an editorial change and when simply to suggest it, whether to delete a repetition or an unnecessary recapitulation or simply to point it out to the author, and how to suggest tactfully that an expression may be inappropriate (or that an assertion might not be accurate). An author's own style should be respected, whether flamboyant or pedestrian. On the other hand, manuscript editors should be aware of any requirements of a publisher's house style, including any policies that are essential to the publisher—for example, those covering bias-free language (see 5.251–60). For communicating with the author and querying, see 2.68–72.

2.52 **Estimating editing time.** It is important to come up with a realistic estimate for how long the job of manuscript editing should take. This estimate (which is typically determined by the publisher and agreed to by the manuscript editor or, in the case of self-publishers, negotiated between author and manuscript editor) is important not only in ensuring the quality of the editor's work but in determining a reasonable fee as well as a schedule for completing the work. Most estimates start with the length of the manuscript. Because of inevitable variations in typefaces and margins and other formatting characteristics from one manuscript to another, the length is best determined by a word count rather than a page count (a word count can be derived from a page count for paper-only manuscripts). A 100,000-word book manuscript, edited by an experienced editor, might take seventy-five to one hundred hours of work before being sent to the author, plus ten to twenty additional hours after the author's review. This rough estimate may need to be adjusted to take into account any complexities in the text or documentation, the presence and characteristics of any tables and illustrations, and the degree of electronic formatting and markup that an editor will need to remove or impose (see 2.80). If in doubt, edit a small sample to serve as the basis of an estimate. An additional factor is of course the publication schedule, which may determine how many days are available for the editing stage or, in turn, may need to be adjusted depending on the estimate of editing time. Also pertinent is information about the author's availability to review the edited manuscript, amenability to being edited, propensity to revise, and so forth.

2.53 **Stages of manuscript editing.** Editors usually go through a manuscript three times—once to do the initial editing, easily the longest stage; a second time to review, refine, and sometimes correct the editing; and a third time after the author's review (see 2.72, 2.88). Editors working on electronic manuscripts may also be required to perform an initial, systematic cleanup (see 2.80)—though a publisher's manuscript editing or production department may perform such a cleanup before turning a manuscript over to an editor. Most editors begin the initial editing stage—sometimes in conjunction with the electronic cleanup—by looking through the entire document to assess the nature and scope of the work that will be required, to identify any matters that should be clarified with the author before editing begins, and to reduce the number of surprises that could cause delays if discovered later in the process. Then, some editors will prefer to edit the notes, bibliography, tables, figures, and other components separately from the text; others edit notes and other textual apparatus, or a part of it, along with the text. Whatever the procedure, all elements must be compared to ensure that the notes match their text references, citations correspond to the entries in the bibliography or reference list, tables correspond to any discussion of them in the text, and so on.

2.54 **Choosing a dictionary and other reference works.** A good dictionary is essential to a manuscript editor. Chicago recommends *Webster's Third New International Dictionary* and the latest edition of its chief abridgment, *Merriam-Webster's Collegiate Dictionary*; both are revised and updated online under the imprint of Merriam-Webster (see bibliog. 3.1). Editors also need reference works that furnish reliable spellings and identifications of persons, places, historical events, technical terminology, and the like. For some basic reference works, see section 4 of the bibliography. For a complete discussion of names and terms, see chapter 8. If a system of documentation other than Chicago is to be used, the applicable style manual should be at hand (see bibliog. 1.1).

2.55 **Keeping an editorial style sheet.** To ensure consistency, for each manuscript the editor must keep an alphabetical list of words or terms to be capitalized, italicized, hyphenated, spelled, or otherwise treated in any way unique to the manuscript. Changes that are made simply for consistency with house style need not be noted on the style sheet. It is enough to note, for example, "In all other respects, Chicago style is followed." (For paper-only manuscripts it is useful to add the page number of the first occurrence of each item.) Special punctuation, unusual diacritics, and other items should also be noted on the style sheet. Not only the author but also the publisher may need to refer to the style sheet at various stages of editing and production. See figure 2.3.

2.56 **Fact-checking.** In book publishing, the author is finally responsible for the accuracy of a work; most book publishers do not perform fact-checking in any systematic way or expect it of their manuscript editors unless specifically agreed upon up front. Nonetheless, obvious errors, including errors in mathematical calculations, should always be pointed out to the author, and questionable proper names, bibliographic references, and the like should be checked and any apparent irregularities queried. Editors need to be systematic about what they fact-check to avoid being distracted from the work at hand. It will sometimes be efficient to point out and correct obvious errors of fact that can be easily double-checked against reliable sources. For anything beyond that, however, fact-checking should be limited to what is needed to form an effective and judicious query to the author (see 2.69). For more information, consult Brooke Borel, *The Chicago Guide to Fact-Checking* (bibliog. 2.1).

action plans
antiracist

child welfare workers
co-citizen
Conservative Party (Norwegian)
Convention on Human Rights

first-person singular
ghetto-like
government

jinns (plur. of jinn)
King and Queen (per author's request)

Labor Party (Norwegian)
Labor government

minister of child and family affairs
Ministry of Child and Family Affairs

north (of Norway)
northerners
Norwegian Pakistanis

non-word

Parliament
pro-immigrant
pro-multicultural
Progress Party

situation analysis
Somali, Somalis
Students' Antiracist Movement

Third World

Ungdom mot vold (rom)

Western Europe

Youth Against Violence (Ungdom mot vold)

Mechanical matters
(1995:47–48) colon betw. year and pp.
Ellipses: three-dot method, not three-or-four
Quoted newspaper headlines: sentence style
"emphasis mine"

FIGURE 2.3. Manuscript editor's style sheet. When prepared for a pencil-edited manuscript, the style sheet usually indicates the page number for the first appearance of each item.

Editing Specific Parts of a Manuscript

2.57 **Editing front matter.** An editor should check any half title, title page, table of contents, and list of illustrations against the text and captions and against any applicable documentation included with the manuscript; discrepancies should be queried. If subheads are to be dropped from the table of contents, the author should be consulted (see also 1.38). For books, the editor should pay attention to the order of elements and may be asked to label the manuscript to ensure correct roman numeral pagination (see 1.7; see also 2.75). Publishers generally prepare the copyright page, though editors may be expected to review the author's biographical note and other elements (see 1.20; see also 1.66).

2.58 **Editing part titles and chapter or article titles.** The editor of a book manuscript should ensure that part and chapter titles and their subtitles, if any, are consistent with the text in spelling, hyphenation, and italics. Chicago recommends that all titles be in headline style unless a work is part of a series or journal that follows some other capitalization style (see 8.159). Part and chapter titles must be checked against the table of contents, and any discrepancy must be queried. Each title should be identified on the manuscript according to the publisher's requirements (for electronic manuscripts, see 2.81–83; for paper manuscripts, see 2.99). See also 1.47–54.

2.59 **Editing subheads.** Subheads should be checked for consistency with the text in spelling, hyphenation, and italics, and for parallel structure and tone. The text that immediately follows a subhead should be adjusted as needed for proper wording relative to the subhead (see 1.55). If there is more than one level of subhead, the hierarchy needs to be checked for sense and each level clearly identified (for electronic manuscripts, see 2.81–83; for paper manuscripts, see 2.99). If there are more than three levels of subhead, determine whether the lowest level can be eliminated. For electronic manuscripts, it may be wise to apply the appropriate markup for the different subhead levels based on the author's typographic distinctions at the outset, lest these distinctions be eliminated by any cleanup routine (see 2.80). If subheads are to appear in the table of contents, they must be cross-checked for consistency. Chicago recommends that all subheads be in headline style unless a work is part of a series or journal that follows some other capitalization style (see 8.159). But if an author has consistently used sentence style for subheads (see 8.158), that style should not be altered without consultation with the author and publisher, since it may be more appropriate in a particular work. If the majority of subheads consist of full sentences, sentence style may be preferred; no period is added except in the case of a run-in head (see 1.56). See also 1.55–58.

2.60 **Editing cross-references.** All references to tables, figures, appendixes, bibliographies, or other parts of a work should be checked by the manuscript editor. If the author, for example, mentions a statistic for 2017 and refers readers to table 4, which gives statistics only through 2016, the editor must point out the discrepancy. Place-names on a map that illustrate the text must be spelled as in the text. Cross-references to specific pages—the numbering of which is subject to change in the published version—should be minimized or eliminated. See also 2.35.

2.61 **Editing quotations and previously published material.** Aside from adjusting quotation marks and ellipsis points and the like to conform to house style (see 13.7–8), the editor must do nothing to quoted material unless the author is translating it from another language (or modernizing it), in which case it may be lightly edited (see 11.16); transcribed interviews or field notes may also be subject to editing (see 13.48, 13.49). Misspelled words and apparent transcription errors should be queried. An author who appears to have been careless in transcribing should be asked to recheck all quotations for accuracy, including punctuation. The editor should ensure that sources are given for all quoted material, whether following the quotation or in a note. In editing previously published material, especially if it has been abridged, the editor should read for sense to ensure that nothing is out of order or has been inadvertently omitted. Discrepancies should be queried. If the previously published material has been provided on paper only, any ambiguous end-of-line hyphens should be clarified (see 2.96). See also 2.43.

2.62 **Editing notes.** Each note must be checked against the text to ensure that its text reference is correct and in the right place and that any terms used in the note are treated the same way as in the text. When notes are to be printed as footnotes, the author may be asked to shorten an excessively long note or to incorporate some of the note into the text. Lists, tables, and figures should be placed not in footnotes but in the text or in an appendix. Manuscript editors may sometimes request an additional note to accommodate a needed source or citation. More frequently, in consultation with the author, they will combine notes or delete unneeded ones. See 14.56–60. An editor working on paper must take special care in renumbering notes. See also 2.63.

2.63 **Editing note citations, bibliographies, and reference lists.** Citations in notes, bibliographies, and reference lists must be carefully checked for documentation style (chapters 14 and 15; but see 2.64). Further, every subsequent reference to a work previously cited in the text or in a note must be given in the same form as the first reference or in the same shortened form (see 14.29–36). In a work containing a bibliography as well as notes, each citation in the notes should be checked against the bibliography and any discrepancy resolved or, if necessary, queried in both contexts so that the author can easily compare them (see 2.69). A bibliography need not include every work cited in the notes and may properly include some entries that are not cited. If author-date style is used, the editor will have checked all text citations against the reference list while editing the text and will have queried or resolved discrepancies. Bibliographies and reference lists should be checked for alphabetical order and, where applicable, for chronological order. For bibliographies, see 14.61–71; for reference lists and text citations, see 15.10–31. Many editors find it helpful to edit the bibliography or reference list before the text and notes. Editors working on-screen may need to make sure that the source citations and related text are free of any underlying codes generated by the author in creating or organizing them (see 14.5).

2.64 **Flexibility in style for source citations.** Imposing house style on notes prepared in another style can be immensely time-consuming and, if the existing form is consistent and clear to the reader, is often unnecessary. This is especially true of books, many of which are intended to stand alone. Before making sweeping changes, the manuscript editor should consult with the author or the publisher or both. In journal editing, on the other hand, such flexibility is generally not allowed. For the published journal, citations are often linked to the resources themselves; the creation of such links can be facilitated by a consistent, predictable format across articles.

2.65 **Editing illustrations and captions.** Wording in diagrams, charts, maps, and the like should generally conform to the spelling and capitalization used in captions or the text. Captions in turn must conform to the style of the text. Source information should be edited in consultation with the publisher and in conformance with any letters of permission. (If permissions are outstanding, the publisher, not the editor, should take up the matter with the author.) Illustrations may be added, dropped, or renumbered during editing; it is therefore essential to make a final check of all illustrations against their text references and callouts (see 2.30) and against the captions and list of illustrations to be sure that they match and that the illustrations show what they say they do. For details on preparing illustrations and captions, see 3.3–46. For checking credits, see 3.29–37.

2.66 **Editing tables.** Tables are usually best edited together, as a group, to ensure consistent style and presentation. Tables should also be checked for consistent numbering and correspondence with the text—including text references and placement callouts (see 2.30). For specific guidelines on editing tables, see 3.81–88.

2.67 **Editing indexes.** The schedule for editing an index—which, if it depends on page number locators rather than paragraph numbers, is almost never prepared before book or journal pages have been composed—must usually correspond to the schedule for reviewing corrections to proofs. For a more detailed discussion, including an index-editing checklist, see 16.132–34.

Communicating with Authors

2.68 **Contacting the author after an initial review of the manuscript.** Editors of book-length works are urged to contact their authors early on, after an initial review of the manuscript. This is especially important if an editor has questions or plans to make significant changes that, in the event the author proves not to be amenable, might take time and effort to undo. Likewise, to expedite production, a journal's manuscript editors may notify authors right away of any plans for systematic changes. Most authors are content to submit to a house style; those who are not may be willing to compromise. Unless usage is determined by journal or series style, the author's wishes should generally be respected. For a manuscript that requires extensive changes, it may be wise, if the schedule allows, to send a sample of the editing for the author's approval before proceeding (see 2.50).

2.69 **Writing author comments and queries.** Editors may generally impose a consistent style and correct errors without further comment—assuming these changes are apparent on the edited manuscript. Corrections to less obvious problems may warrant a comment. Comments should be concise, and they should avoid sounding casual, pedantic, condescending, or indignant; often, a simple "OK?" is enough. Comments that are not answerable by a yes or a no may be more specific: "Do you mean X or Y?" Examples of instances in which an editor might comment or query include the following:

- To note, on an electronic manuscript, that a particular global change has been corrected silently (i.e., without marking or tracking the change) after the first instance
- To point out a discrepancy, as between two spellings in a name, or between a source cited differently in the notes than in the bibliography
- To point out an apparent omission, such as a missing quotation mark or a missing source citation
- To point out a possible error in a quotation
- To point out repetition (e.g., "Repetition intentional?" or "Rephrased to avoid repetition; OK?")
- To ask for verification, as of a name or term whose spelling cannot be easily verified
- To ask for clarification where the text is ambiguous or garbled
- To point to the sources an editor has consulted in correcting errors of fact (but see 2.56)

For the mechanics of entering queries on a manuscript, see 2.87 (for electronic manuscripts) and 2.92 (for paper manuscripts).

2.70 **Writing a cover letter to the author.** The letter sent to the author with the edited manuscript, or sometimes separately, should include some or all of the following items (unless already communicated):

- An explanation of the nature and scope of the editing—for example, adjustment of spelling and punctuation to conform to house style (or to a particular style manual) and occasional rephrasing for clarity or to eliminate inadvertent repetition
- If the editing has been shown, an indication of how this has been done—that is, with change-tracking (redlining) software (see 2.84) or with pencil and paper (2.91)—and brief instructions for interpreting the marks
- Instructions as to how the author should respond to queries, veto any unwanted editing, and make any further adjustments to the edited manuscript (see 2.88, 2.91)
- A warning that the author's review of the edited manuscript constitutes the last opportunity to make any substantive changes, additions, or deletions and that quoted matter and citations should be checked if necessary
- A reminder to review the editing carefully, since even editors are fallible and the correction of any errors missed in editing and not caught until proofs may be deemed "author's alterations" and charged to the author (see 2.136)
- A reminder to retain a copy of the reviewed and corrected manuscript (to refer to at the proofreading stage)
- The deadline for return of the edited copy
- A brief discussion about the index, if any—whether the author is to prepare it, whether instructions are needed (see chapter 16), or whether a freelance indexer is to be engaged at the author's expense
- A request for confirmation of the author's contact information and availability for the rest of the publishing process

2.71 **Sending the edited manuscript to the author.** An electronically edited book manuscript—because of its length and, often, its complexity—may be sent to the author as hard copy (or as a PDF file that the author is asked to print out). The author reads and marks this printout as necessary, then returns it to the editor, who incorporates the author's marks into the electronic manuscript. The author may instead review the electronic manuscript (using the same word-processing software that the editor has used)—a procedure that saves printing and shipping costs. An editor working with an author in this manner needs to make sure the author does not make any undocumented changes—inadvertently or otherwise. (One strategy is to lock the document for editing such that any changes the author makes will be visibly tracked.) Alternatively, especially for article-length works, an author may be asked to review and annotate a PDF version of the edited manuscript on-screen (see 2.133). A pencil-edited manuscript should be scanned or photocopied before being sent to the author; likewise, authors are advised to photocopy or scan paper manuscripts with their handwritten comments before sending them back to the editor. Any manuscript that has been pencil edited—as well as electronically edited printouts that have been marked up by hand—is one of a kind; if lost, the work must be done over.

2.72 **Checking the author's review of the edited manuscript.** When the manuscript comes back from the author, the editor goes through it once again to see what the author has done, checking that all queries have been answered and editing any new material. (If the author has rewritten extensively, another editing pass and author review may be needed.) Except for style adjustments, the author's version should prevail; if that version is unacceptable for any reason, a compromise should be sought. As a part of this process, the editor updates the electronic files (see 2.89) or, if a manuscript is to be updated or typeset from a pencil-edited paper copy, clarifies or retypes the new material and crosses out the queries (see 2.92).

Preparing a Final Manuscript for Production

2.73 **Ensuring correct markup.** Ensuring correct markup for a manuscript entails double-checking that each of its component parts has been properly identified in the final, edited manuscript, according to whatever system of markup has been used at that stage. For a book, these parts will include title and table of contents, chapters and sections and subsections, individual subheads, paragraphs of text, extracts, lists, notes, illustrations and captions, tables, and so forth. (Journal articles and other smaller documents may include fewer component parts.) Character-level markup must also be checked. This includes the markup required for any numeral, symbol, letter, word, or phrase that might be differentiated from the surrounding text—for example, a word or phrase that might be italicized for emphasis or a cross-reference (like the ones at the end of this paragraph) that might be hyperlinked online. Checking markup is usually the manuscript editor's responsibility, at least initially. Manuscript editors are closest to the content and will be able to spot any missing or incorrectly identified elements, or items that are not accounted for in the publisher's design template or style sheets. Once a manuscript is in production, however, markup generally becomes the responsibility of the publisher's production department. (Self-published authors who do not engage the services of a manuscript editor or book designer will need to pay close attention to the details described in this section and to be aware of any formatting and submission guidelines provided by their self-publishing platform.) For electronic markup options, see 2.81–83; for paper manuscripts, see 2.99. For an overview of the parts of a book or a journal, see chapter 1.

2.74 **Type specifications and hand markup.** An editor may occasionally need to mark up the hard copy of a manuscript with appropriate type specifications at the first occurrence of the element they apply to. For example, in the margin next to the first block of regular text, "text: 10/12 Times Roman × 26" (meaning 10-point type with 12-point leading, each line 26 picas wide); and next to the first extract, "extract: 9/11 Times Roman; indent 2 pi from left." As long as all extracts have been identified as "ext," all first-level subheads as "A," and so forth, markup can be kept to a minimum. For more on hand markup, see 2.90–99.

2.75 **Ensuring correct pagination.** Publishers may require editors to indicate on the manuscript where roman page numbers are to end and arabic numbers begin—whether or not the number will actually appear (i.e., whether the folio is to be "expressed" or "blind"; see 1.46). Furthermore, if there is a part title and the first chapter begins on page 3, "arabic p. 3" will have to be specified at the chapter opening. The editor might also be required to specify whether subsequent elements are to begin on a recto or on a verso (see 1.4). Repagination of typeset, printed books is expensive; the editor should check that all elements—in the front matter, the text, and the back matter—are in their correct order and that the order is reflected in the table of contents. For journals, see 1.81.

2.76 **Preparing running heads.** The editor may be required to provide a list of suggested copy for running heads (or feet) (see 1.10–16). The list must clearly indicate which heads are to appear on versos (left-hand pages) and which on rectos (right-hand pages). To fit on a single line, usually containing the page number as well (see 1.6), a chapter or article title may have to be shortened for a running head but must include the key terms in the title. (In some cases, the key terms will be in the chapter subtitle.) For certain languages other than English, it is important to retain any word that governs the case ending of another word in the running head. The author's approval may be needed; if possible, the editor should send the running-head copy to the author along with the edited manuscript. Running-head copy normally accompanies the manuscript to the typesetter and should be included with the other electronic files. If the running heads are to reflect the content of particular pages (rather than chapters or sections), the exact copy must be determined after (or as) the pages are typeset. For example, running heads to notes that include page ranges can be determined only from the typeset pages (see 1.15). These are typically indicated by the publisher on the first proofreading copy. To accommodate the potential for running heads in electronic formats, short forms for chapter and other titles can be specified as part of the markup (e.g., as an "alt-title") and used for running heads where needed or for other purposes.

2.77 **A production checklist.** Manuscripts that are ready to be typeset or converted for publication are usually accompanied by a checklist of vital statistics that includes information about the project and how it is to be produced. Such a checklist, especially necessary for one-of-a-kind book-length works, might consist of the following information:

- Name of author(s) and title of work
- A list of component parts of the project: electronic files, printout, illustrations, and so forth
- Details about the software used to prepare the final manuscript and a list of file names
- An indication of how the electronic files have been marked up for production, a list of markup labels or styles, and any special instructions, including a list of any special characters or fonts
- A list of any material that is still to come
- An indication of how notes are to be set—for example, as footnotes, as chapter endnotes, or as endnotes to the book
- A list of elements to be included in the front matter, the text, and the end matter, and an indication of which elements must start recto (see 1.4)
- For book-length manuscripts, an indication of who will be receiving page proofs, and in what format (e.g., print or PDF)

The Mechanics of Electronic Editing

PREPARATION AND CLEANUP

2.78 **Saving the manuscript files and keeping backups.** It is best to save and back up a manuscript in stages, creating separate copies of each significant version. The author's original, unedited copy should be archived (i.e., saved without further changes), as should every significant stage of the editing process. Each major stage should be saved with a different name—for example, by appending "author's original," "clean unedited," "first edit," "to author," and so forth to the file name. For complex projects, use different directories (i.e., folders) for the different stages. Exercise caution when saving files and working on new versions: avoid saving over—or inadvertently working on—an earlier version of a file. During editing, open documents should be saved frequently. Some editors archive daily or weekly versions so that an earlier stage of the editing can be consulted if necessary. Another strategy is to use a file-hosting service that allows access to previously saved versions or deleted files. All saved versions should always be backed up to a second location as protection against loss.

2.79 **Manuscript cleanup tools.** Many publishers provide manuscript editors with a cleaned-up version of the author's electronic file(s)—formatted and ready to edit. The publisher usually specifies the required software and may expect the editor to use or apply a certain type of markup (see 2.81–83). (Publishers may instead give editors hard copy only, updating the electronic files from the pencil-edited copy as part of the production process; for paper editing, see 2.90–99.) Some editors, however, are required to clean up and format the author's electronic files themselves. Full-featured word processors provide a number of tools that can save time by automating certain tasks. At the very least, it is important to learn about search-and-replace options, including the use of pattern matching (with wildcards or regular expressions), and about macros, which can save keystrokes by replicating and repeating repetitive tasks (including tasks that involve searching and replacing). (Consult your word-processor's Help documentation for instructions and examples.) Some editors take advantage of third-party add-ins preloaded with cleanup macros, enhanced search-and-replace options, and other editing tools.

2.80 **Manuscript cleanup checklist.** Before editing the manuscript, the editor must be certain that the files represent the author's latest version (the presence of embedded revision marks may be a sign that this is not the case; see 2.39). The next step is to get the electronic files ready to edit—if the publisher has not done this already. The following checklist suggests a set of steps that can be adapted as necessary to become part of an editor's word-processing cleanup routine. Not all manuscripts will require each step, and the suggested order need not be adhered to. Some of the steps can be automated, but most of the checklist can also be accomplished manually—that is, applied on a case-by-case basis, as part of the first read-through (see 2.53). Always review—and be prepared to undo—any global change before saving a permanent version of a file.

Modify this checklist as needed to accord not only with the requirements of a specific manuscript but also with those of the publisher. Automatic redlining should usually be turned *off* during these steps (see 2.84).

1. Convert files for use in the editing software required by the publisher, if necessary.
2. To avoid having to apply this checklist more than once, consider combining separate files into a single electronic file. (Care must be taken to produce a complete manuscript, in the proper order and with no inadvertent deletions; always double-check the beginning and ending of each component and any notes thereto both when combining multiple files and when breaking a single file into smaller components.) Another option is to use macros that work across multiple files in a single directory (see 2.79).
3. If necessary, change the language settings of the manuscript and any subdocuments (e.g., from British English to American English, or vice versa). This will ensure, among other things, that the main dictionary gives appropriate suggestions.
4. Scroll through the whole manuscript (with the editing software set to display formatting and any markup—including marks for such "invisible" elements as spaces and hard returns), looking for and fixing any obvious conversion errors (e.g., with special characters) and formatting problems (e.g., hard returns in the middle of a paragraph), with reference to the original manuscript as necessary.
5. Identify any graphic elements and tables and handle appropriately—for example, moving figures or tables to separate files (see 2.26, 2.30).
6. Apply appropriate markup, as required, to any elements that are easy to identify at the outset but whose visual cues may be lost as the text is formatted. Look for chapter titles, subheads (and subhead levels), epigraphs, text and poetry extracts, extra line space (which may signal a stanza break in poetry or require an ornament or other device in text), and so forth. See also 2.81–83.
7. Delete or fix extraneous spaces and tabs, including instances of two or more consecutive spaces (between sentences or anywhere else) or spaces or tabs at the ends of paragraphs. Multiple spaces used to create first-line paragraph and other indents should be replaced either with tabs or with software-defined indents (be consistent).
8. Change instances of multiple hard returns to single hard returns.
9. Change underlining to italics. Some underlining, however, may be intended to represent true underscore—in, for example, a collection that transcribes handwritten letters; this should be preserved, with a note to the publisher explaining the exception. See also 6.2.
10. Fix quotation marks and apostrophes; make sure that apostrophes at the beginning of words are correct (e.g., ’em *not* ‘em for "them"). But first determine,

as applicable, that left and right single quotation marks have not been used by the author to stand in for breathing marks or other orthographic devices in transliterated languages (see chapter 11). See also 6.115, 6.117.

11. Fix commas and periods relative to quotation marks (see table 6.1).
12. Regularize em dashes and ellipses. For proper use of em dashes, see 6.85–92. For ellipses, see 13.50–58.
13. Replace hyphens between numerals with en dashes as appropriate. If you are using a macro to do this, it may be more efficient to let the macro run and to fix or add any exceptions during the first editing pass. For proper use of en dashes, see 6.78–84.
14. Convert footnotes to endnotes, or vice versa.
15. Delete any optional or conditional hyphens (i.e., software-dependent hyphens that allow words to break across the end of a line whether or not the hyphenation feature is turned on). Most word processors will allow you to search for these.
16. Find any lowercase els used as ones and any ohs (capital or lowercase) used as zeros—or vice versa—and fix. This can be done by using pattern matching to search for two-character combinations containing either an el or an oh next to an expression that will find any numeral (see also 2.79).
17. Fix any other global inconsistencies that might be amenable to pattern-matching strategies. For example, in a bibliography in which two- or three-letter initials in names have been closed up, you can search for and evaluate capital letter combinations and replace as necessary with the same combination plus a space (e.g., changing E.B. White to E. B. White).
18. Adjust line spacing, font, and margins as desired.

As a final step—assuming these steps have been applied before editing—save a copy of the resulting clean, unedited manuscript in case it becomes necessary to refer to it later (see 2.78).

ELECTRONIC MARKUP

2.81 **Generic markup for electronic manuscripts.** Each element of a manuscript—chapter display, subheads, text, prose extracts, poetry, notes, captions, and so forth—must be identified using consistent markup. The most basic (if least efficient) way to do this is with generic labels modeled on the descriptive identifiers used on pencil-edited manuscripts (see 2.99). Such labels are enclosed in angle brackets (< >), curly brackets ({ }), or some other delimiters such that they can be systematically identified and replaced for publication by formal typesetting markup. (This generic application of delimiters must not be mistaken for the tags used in formal markup languages such as XML.) Except for labels meant to be replaced with a character or string of characters, they are usually applied at the beginning and end of each element to which they apply. Publishers differ not only in what type of markup they recommend but also in what elements they mark up. Some require that every element be labeled, including body text; others regard body text as a default. Most do not require any markup for character-level formatting (e.g., italics, small capitals, boldface) because a word-processing software's built-in formatting attributes can be manipulated as necessary. Editors may need to invent markup for unusual elements. Consistency and accuracy are crucial. Moreover, editors must supply a complete list of markup with the manuscript. Some samples are as follows:

<cn> . . . </cn>	chapter number
<ct> . . . </ct>	chapter title
<a> . . . </a>	first-level subhead (A-head)
<b> . . . </b>	second-level subhead (B-head)
<ext> . . . </ext>	block quotation (prose extract)
<po> . . . </po>	poetry extract
<note-a> . . . </note-a>	first-level subhead in endnotes section
<tdotb>	t with dot below (i.e., when the Unicode character for ṭ is not available in the font being used to prepare the manuscript; see 11.2)
<! . . . !>	instruction to the typesetter—for example, to consult hard copy or page image for proper alignment or other formatting

The end "tags"—those that include a forward slash (/) and that indicate the end of a labeled element—may be unnecessary for elements that consist of a single paragraph. Consult the publisher's or typesetter's requirements. For using a word processor's built-in styles, see 2.82; for formal markup languages such as XML, see 2.83.

2.82 **Word-processing styles.** Manuscript editors may be expected to use a word-processing template loaded with paragraph and character styles defined for a book or article manuscript and supplied by the publisher. The advantage of such an approach is that manuscript editors (and authors, including self-published authors) can work in a familiar software environment while facilitating the more detailed markup required for publication in electronic formats. Word-processing styles are applied to each element of a manuscript, from chapter title to the title of a book in a reference list entry to the reference list entry itself. Each style carries a unique name and can be applied to any paragraph or string of characters within a paragraph. (A paragraph is any string of text followed by a single hard return.) Paragraph-level style names should be descriptive, corresponding to the type of element (e.g., "chapter number" or "A-head") rather than to its format or appearance. Character-level styles, by the same token, should specify the intent of the style rather than its format—for example, "emphasis" rather than "italic" or "exponent" rather than "superscript."[1] Appropriate font size, line spacing, italics, and other formatting attributes can and should be defined for each style in the manuscript to facilitate editing and author review. On the other hand, accuracy and consistency in applying styles is more important than any formatting in the manuscript. The publisher will map the styles to a design template for the printed work or to XML, which can be used to accommodate presentation in multiple formats, including print. If there are any text elements that do not lend themselves easily to the styles in a given template, it may be necessary to define new styles or to query the publisher. (Authors reviewing the edited manuscript should be advised not to modify styles.) An annotated list of styles should accompany the manuscript sent to production. See also 2.83.

2.83 **Formal markup languages.** A manuscript edited on paper or in a word processor may have to be converted and marked up at some point according to the rules defined for a formal markup language such as XML, especially if it is to be published as an e-book or as a web-presentation or app (see 1.117–25). Such a conversion can be facilitated during the editing stage by the use of word-processing styles (see 2.82). Styles are mapped to corresponding tags, and additional markup is added to delineate the structure of the manuscript, facilitate linking, and so forth. Each element, including each document or subdocument, is identified by a pair of opening and closing tags according to the rules of the particular markup language. Tags are nested; for example, the body of the document, enclosed between an opening and a closing tag, will include all sections and subsections of the document, and each of those parts in turn will be delimited by a pair of tags that identify the element and its place in the hierarchy. Tags are also used to delimit any element that may

1. Many publishers do not require editors to apply semantic markup for every character-level style, asking instead that they simply specify the intended format (e.g., italics or superscript). This approach, though easy to apply, has certain limitations. For example, readers using text-to-speech and related tools may not be able to fully appreciate the sense of the text if everything from an emphasized word to a term in a different language to a book title is marked simply as italic. Publishers concerned about providing accessible content for people with disabilities are encouraged to consult the guidelines offered by the Web Accessibility Initiative (WAI) of the World Wide Web Consortium (W3C) and, for EPUB (a standard format for e-books), the Accessibility Guidelines available from the International Digital Publishing Forum.

have a special function (such as a cross-reference that will be hyperlinked in electronic formats) or that will need to be differentiated from the surrounding text (such as an emphasized term or a book title). Such tagging is structural as well as semantic: each element is identified according to what it is rather than by how it is to be presented (but see 2.82, note 1). Details about presentation, including appearance and function, are specified in a style sheet for each format of publication. If editing takes place after conversion to a formal markup language, the editor usually helps to ensure that the tags have been applied correctly (see also 2.137–40). The successful implementation of such a workflow, on the other hand, requires significant technical expertise.

TRACKING CHANGES AND INSERTING QUERIES

2.84 **Tracking changes (redlining).** To show their work and thus facilitate the author's review, many editors use the change-tracking feature in their word processor to produce what is sometimes referred to as a redlined version (a name that invokes, in another medium, the editor's red pencil). The principle is simple: as long as the tracking feature is turned on, text that is added is underlined, <u>like this</u>; text that is deleted is struck through, ~~like this~~. (Added or deleted text can be displayed in a variety of other ways depending on software and settings.) Author queries are inserted using the word-processor's commenting feature (see 2.87). For a demonstration, see fig. 2.4. (Comments and changes usually appear in color by default; editors sending black-and-white printouts to their authors for review must take care that everything remains legible.) For any change that might be ambiguous or hard to interpret (e.g., a struck-through hyphenated term), it can be helpful to include an explanatory comment to the author at least at the first occurrence. By the same token, it is best to avoid making changes that might be missed; when in doubt, strike out the entire term and replace it by the corrected or preferred version. For example, to indicate a preference for the closed-up version of the name of the famous educator and writer, show ~~Du Bois~~<u>DuBois</u> rather than Du-Bois, the latter of which may be mistaken for a hyphenated term. See also 2.85. For marking changes on PDF files, see 2.133.

2.85 **Making silent changes (not tracking).** Whether to track all editing, mechanical as well as substantive, depends on a number of factors, including the editor's and publisher's preferences. In order to avoid irritating or distracting the author, some editors will prefer to track only the first instance of a global change (such as capitalization of a certain term) and alert the author to the change in a comment (see 2.87). Certain

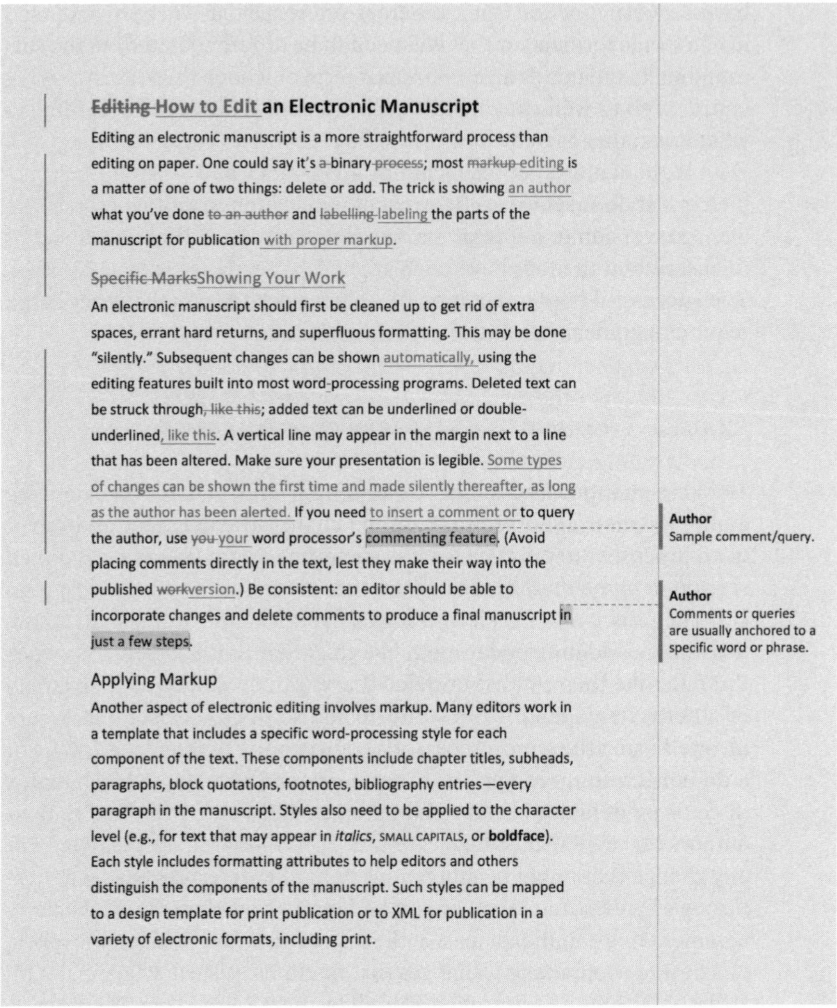

~~Editing~~ How to Edit an Electronic Manuscript

Editing an electronic manuscript is a more straightforward process than editing on paper. One could say it's ~~a~~ binary ~~process~~; most ~~markup~~ editing is a matter of one of two things: delete or add. The trick is showing an author what you've done ~~to an author~~ and ~~labelling~~ labeling the parts of the manuscript for publication with proper markup.

~~Specific Marks~~Showing Your Work

An electronic manuscript should first be cleaned up to get rid of extra spaces, errant hard returns, and superfluous formatting. This may be done "silently." Subsequent changes can be shown automatically, using the editing features built into most word-processing programs. Deleted text can be struck through~~, like this~~; added text can be underlined or double-underlined, like this. A vertical line may appear in the margin next to a line that has been altered. Make sure your presentation is legible. Some types of changes can be shown the first time and made silently thereafter, as long as the author has been alerted. If you need to insert a comment or to query the author, use ~~you~~ your word processor's commenting feature. (Avoid placing comments directly in the text, lest they make their way into the published ~~work~~version.) Be consistent: an editor should be able to incorporate changes and delete comments to produce a final manuscript in just a few steps.

Author
Sample comment/query.

Author
Comments or queries are usually anchored to a specific word or phrase.

Applying Markup

Another aspect of electronic editing involves markup. Many editors work in a template that includes a specific word-processing style for each component of the text. These components include chapter titles, subheads, paragraphs, block quotations, footnotes, bibliography entries—every paragraph in the manuscript. Styles also need to be applied to the character level (e.g., for text that may appear in *italics*, SMALL CAPITALS, or **boldface**). Each style includes formatting attributes to help editors and others distinguish the components of the manuscript. Such styles can be mapped to a design template for print publication or to XML for publication in a variety of electronic formats, including print.

FIGURE 2.4. A manuscript page illustrating the principles of on-screen revision marks (redlining) and author queries using Microsoft Word. Markup for headings, paragraphs, and text has been applied using Word's paragraph and character styles. See 2.82.

adjustments should almost never be shown—for example, changes to margins or a global application of "smart" quotation marks and apostrophes (see 6.115, 6.117). In general, most of the things listed in the cleanup checklist at 2.80 may be done silently. If a section of the manuscript such as a bibliography has been heavily edited, the editor may send a clean version of that section for the author to approve, with or without a version showing the edits for reference. But if changes have not been tracked for any reason, the editor must delineate for the author the nature of the editing either in a comment or in the cover letter with the edited manuscript (see 2.70).

2.86 **Document comparison software.** Document comparison software can highlight the differences between two versions of a document automatically. Best results are had with shorter documents in which the latest version is compared against an earlier version that has already been cleaned up and formatted (see 2.80). Comparing an edited document against the author's original manuscript may result in too many changes being reported, or worse, the results may be unintelligible. Editors should turn to document comparison software only in specific instances—for example, to make sure they are working on the latest version of a document. For communicating changes to the author, which usually requires a more predictable presentation in which some types of changes are made silently while others must be spelled out as clearly as possible, editors should track their changes as they edit (see 2.84).

2.87 **Inserting comments and queries.** Author queries should be inserted using the commenting feature available in most word processors. See fig. 2.4 for an example. Chicago no longer recommends using footnotes or bracketed text to insert queries. As a matter of principle, it is best to avoid adding content that is not intended for publication to the run of text. (Exceptions can be made for structural signposts such as image callouts or similar elements intended to be incorporated into the markup for the published version; see 2.30. Another exception is made by some publishers for embedded notes, which in certain applications do not support comments; alternatively, such comments may be placed in the text at the note reference marker.) See also 2.69.

2.88 **Author's review of the redlined manuscript.** Authors who review changes and queries online should be asked to use a compatible version of the software used to edit the manuscript. (Authors who cannot accommodate this request may have to review a printout instead or annotate a PDF file; see 2.71.) To guard against unwanted changes—inadvertent or otherwise—the editor may want to protect the manuscript with a password such that any changes the author makes will be visibly tracked. (Editors are advised to take care not to lose the password; it will be needed in order to unlock the files returned by the author and prepare the final manuscript.) Editors should include detailed instructions for making changes and adding or responding to queries. With password protection, authors can usually be asked simply to type any additions into the manuscript and delete any of the editor's changes or other unwanted text. For comments and replies to queries, however, authors should generally be advised to use the commenting feature lest any of their comments inadvertently make it into the text (see also 2.87).

2.89 **Accepting or rejecting tracked changes and deleting queries.** After the author has returned the redlined manuscript, the editor should go through each tracked change carefully and accept it or reject it, as the case may be, using the available word-processing tools. New material inserted by the author should be edited as necessary, and any other type of change should be checked for continuity with the surrounding text. It may be wise to read through each author comment or query first in order to spot any potential problems. After all comments and queries have been read and all changes have been incorporated, any remaining comments and queries should be deleted. Because of the potential for errors introduced at this stage, a spelling check should be run again as a final step. The final manuscript should have no remaining tracked changes or comments, with the exception of any comments intended for the publisher (though it may be better to send these in a cover letter).

The Mechanics of Editing on Paper

2.90 **Keeping a clean copy of paper manuscripts.** An editor working on paper should always keep a clean copy of the unedited manuscript to refer to—or as a backup in case any reediting is necessary. If the paper copy is a printout of an electronic manuscript, it is enough to archive a copy of the latter.

2.91 **Marking manuscripts on paper.** Editing a manuscript on paper—whether it is to be typeset from scratch or used to update the author's electronic manuscript—requires a technique similar to the one used for marking corrections on proofs (see 2.119–33). To allow for the more extensive changes typical of the editing stage, however, paper manuscripts are usually double-spaced so that editing can appear above the word or words it pertains to, rather than in the margin. (Manuscripts that consist of photocopies of tightly spaced previously published material are edited in the manner of page proofs.) All editorial changes should be made in a color that will reproduce clearly if the edited manuscript is photocopied or faxed, and the author should be asked to respond to the editing in a color distinct from that used by the editor. For marking queries, see 2.92. For a sample of a correctly marked manuscript, see figure 2.5.

How and Editor marks a Manuscript

PAPER MANUSCRIPTS are edited using marks that are not all that different than those used to correct proofs. A correction or an operational sign are, however inserted in a line of type, not in the margin as in proof reading. Editing marks are usually more expensive from those for proofreading, so any editors change must be in it's proper place and written clearly - even if the edited manuscript will only be used to update the electronic files.

Specific Marks

A caret shows where additional material is to be inserted. three lines under a lowercase letter tell the typesetter to make it a capital; 2 lines mean a small capital (A.D.); one line means italic; a wavy line means boldface; and a stroke through a Capital letter means lowercase. Unwanted underlinging is removed thus. A small circle around a comma indicates a period, A straight line between parts of a closed compound, or between two words accidentallyrun together, will request space between the two words-to be doubly sure, add a spacemark as well, two short parallel lines mean a hyphen is to be added between two words as in two=thirds of a welldone fish.

A circle around an abbrev. or numeral instructs the typesetter to spell it out, abbreviations ambiguous or not likely to be recognized by a type-setter should be spelled out by the editor (Biol.=Biology or Biological; gen.=gender, genetive, or genus) as should figures that might be spelled out more than one way (2500=twenty-five hundred or two thousand five-hundred). Dots under a crossed-out word or passage mean stet (let it stand). Hyphens apearing when dashes should be used-except double hyphens representing an em dash--should always be marked, otherwise a hyphen may be used between continuing numbers like 15-18 or may confusingly be used to set off parenthetical matter. Whenever it is ambiguous, or likely to confuse the typesetter an end-of= line hyphen should be underlined or crossed out so that the type- setter will know whether to retain the hyphen in the line or close up the word.

FIGURE 2.5. An example of a hand-marked manuscript page.

2.92 **Marking author queries on paper manuscripts.** In manuscripts edited on paper, queries are best written in the margin. When the author has responded, they can simply be crossed out. Chicago discourages the use of sticky notes for queries: they cannot be easily photocopied, and they may have to be detached in the process of updating the electronic files or (for paper-only manuscripts) typesetting the final pages (and thus may no longer be in place when the pencil-edited manuscript is sent back to the author with the proofs). For more extensive queries that require more space than the margin affords, a separate sheet, keyed by letter or symbol to a specific place in the manuscript, may be prepared.

2.93 **Three uses for circling.** Circling has three meanings on a manuscript. (1) Circling a number or an abbreviation in the text means that the element is to be spelled out. If a number can be spelled out in different ways, or if an abbreviation could possibly be misconstrued, the editor should write out the form required. (2) Circling a comma or a colon means that a period is to replace the comma or colon; when a period is inserted by hand, it should be circled so it will not be missed by whoever is updating or typesetting the manuscript. (3) Circling a marginal comment shows that the comment is not to be set in type (or incorporated into the manuscript) but is either a query to the author or an instruction for typesetting or updating the manuscript.

2.94 **Inserting, deleting, and substituting.** A regular caret (∧), used to indicate an insertion point for added text but also used to indicate subscripts (and, similarly, to indicate an added comma), should be carefully distinguished from an inverted caret (∨), used to mark superscripts, apostrophes, and the like. But, in general, do not use a caret to indicate added text that is being substituted for deleted text; simply cross out the deleted text and write the text to be substituted above it. See fig. 2.5.

2.95 **Adding, deleting, or transposing punctuation.** Special attention should be paid to punctuation when words are transposed or deleted; the new position of commas, periods, and the like must be clearly shown. Likewise, any punctuation at the beginning or end of text marked for transposition must be clearly marked for deletion or inclusion, as the case may be. More generally, any added or changed punctuation should be clearly marked—for example, by circling an added period, placing a caret over an added comma, or placing an inverted caret under added quotation marks. If necessary, write (and circle) "colon," "exclamation point," or whatever applies, either in the margin or close to the punctuation change.

2.96 **Marking dashes and hyphens.** Two hyphens with no space between or on either side clearly signal em dashes and need not be marked on a paper-only manuscript. Actual em dashes, which may be mistaken for en dashes in some typefaces, should be marked; 2- or 3-em dashes, even if consistently typed, should also be marked, as should en dashes, which might be mistaken for hyphens. Alternatively, a global instruction may be issued—for example, "all hyphens between inclusive numbers are to be set as en dashes." End-of-line hyphens should be marked to distinguish between soft (i.e., conditional or optional) and hard hyphens. Soft hyphens are those hyphens that are invoked only to break a word at the end of a line; hard hyphens are permanent (such as those in *cul-de-sac*) and must remain no matter where the hyphenated word or term appears. See also 2.13.

2.97 **Capitalizing, lowercasing, and marking for italics or boldface.** To indicate that a lowercase letter should be capitalized, triple underline it; to make it a small capital, double underline it. To lowercase a capital letter, run a slanted line through it. To mark for italics, underscore the word(s) to be italicized with a straight line; for boldface, make the underscoring wavy. For manuscripts that are to be typeset from scratch, there is usually no need to underline words that appear in italics in the manuscript, as long as the typesetter is instructed to italicize them. (Italics in some fonts are difficult to distinguish at a glance; underlining may reduce the incidence of missed italics.) If an author has used both underlining and italics, special instructions are needed (see 2.15). For mathematical copy, see 12.61–68.

2.98 **Marking paragraph indents, flush left or right, and vertical spacing.** Use a three-sided rectangular mark to indicate that text or other elements should be moved to the left (⊏) or to the right (⊐). A line may be drawn from the open side of the mark to the element to be moved (see fig. 2.5). To indicate paragraph indents, use the symbol ¶. To mark vertical space, use a rectangular mark that "points" up (⊓) or down (⊔); adjust the width to accommodate the element. To indicate a blank line, write "one-line #" and circle it. (In typographic usage the sign # means space, not number.)

2.99 **Marking the components of a paper manuscript.** The components of a paper manuscript—chapter number and title, subheads, prose extracts, poetry, and so forth—are marked with labels or descriptions that are circled and placed at the beginning of the element or in the margin next to it. For example, a circled "A" may be used to indicate a first-level subhead (see fig. 2.5). The handwritten labels are similar to the ones that can be used for generic markup in an electronic manuscript (see 2.81). See also 2.93.

Proofreading

Introduction

2.100 **What is proofreading?** Proofreading is the process of reading a text and scrutinizing all of its components to find errors and mark them for correction. Each major stage of a manuscript intended for publication—especially the final version the author submits to the publisher and, later, the copyedited version of the same—is generally reviewed in this way. Proofreading here, however, applies to the review of the manuscript *after* it has been converted to a format for publication but *before* it is published. Usually, this format consists of the typeset and paginated pages of a book or journal article (referred to as proofs or proof and read either on paper or as PDF) or the full text of a book or journal article intended for publication in one or more electronic formats other than PDF (see 1.118). Also subject to proofreading are covers and jackets or other packaging as well as the abstracts and other components that are published along with the work or as part of one or more electronic formats. For an illustration of how the stages described in this chapter fit into the overall publishing process for books and journals, see the outline at 2.2. For proofreaders' marks, see 2.119; for PDF markup, see 2.133. For proofing and testing electronic formats, see 2.137–40.

2.101 **Who should proofread?** For the majority of publications, authors are considered the primary proofreaders, and it is they who bear final responsibility for any errors in the published work. To help mitigate this responsibility, a professional proofreader may be hired by either the author or the publisher. (Self-publishing authors can also benefit from the services of a proofreader, whether or not they have also hired a professional editor.) Moreover, the manuscript editor and book designer and other publishing personnel are generally responsible for ensuring that the author's corrections (and those of any other proofreader) are successfully incorporated into the work before it gets published and that all related materials (promotional copy, website apparatus, etc.) are free of errors and inconsistencies.

2.102 **Proofreading schedule.** Since many people are involved in the production of a book, a few days' delay in returning proofs to the publisher or typesetter can cause a major delay in publication. When the time scheduled for proofreading appears to conflict with the demands of accuracy, or if any other problem arises that might affect the schedule, the proofreader should immediately confer with the publisher. For journals, where there is little room for delays of any kind, proofreading deadlines are generally nonnegotiable. See also 2.2.

Stages of Proof

2.103 **Keeping a record of each proofreading stage.** A record must be kept by the publisher of when each stage of proof has been corrected and by whom. For printed books, the best record for the first proofreading stage is a master set. The master set is either (a) a laser printout read and marked for corrections by the author and marked with additional corrections by the publisher and any others who have read or reviewed the master set or copies thereof, or (b) a PDF version of the same. Some publishers send a duplicate set of page proofs to the author and then transfer the author's corrections to the master set. For PDF, it is important to name the different iterations of the file appropriately and collate all corrections on the master file. At the next stage, revised proofs are usually reviewed by the publisher, who retains this new master set or file and a record of each additional round of corrections until the work has been published. (Each new round of corrections should be reflected in the file name for the PDF—e.g., by "rev01," "rev02," etc.) For electronic publications, the author and other proofreaders should each be required to sign off before a corrected version is delivered for further review. Likewise, for covers and jackets or other packaging, each person assigned to proofread should be required to sign off on the proofreading copy before a corrected version is routed for further review.

2.104 **First proofs and "galley" proofs.** The author and sometimes a designated proofreader read the first proofreading copy (*first proofs* or *first pages*), usually against the edited manuscript (see 2.110). For books, an index may be prepared from this first set of page proofs, either by the author or by a professional indexer (see chapter 16). For some complex book-length works, first proofs are issued in the form of "galleys." Strictly speaking, the term *galley proofs* is an anachronism, dating from the era when printers would arrange type into "galleys" from which long, narrow prints were prepared to proofread or edit type before the arduous task of composing it, by hand, into the form of book pages. Today, if a complex project presents a danger of extensive corrections at the page-proof stage, a publisher might request galley proofs (loosely paginated and with or without illustrations in place), since corrections to galleys will not entail having to redo page references in an index. These galleys are generated from the same electronic files as first proofs would be. (As an alternative to the galley stage, publishers might choose to undertake a proofreading of the final electronic manuscript.) The index is prepared not from the galleys, since pagination is not final, but from the "first" proofs that are issued at the next stage.

2.105 **Revised proofs.** After corrections to the first proofs have been made, the results must be checked for accuracy. This usually involves comparing *revised proofs* for all pages against the first pages (now known as "foul" proofs). These revised proofs should also be checked for any other differences between them and the first proofs and to make sure hyphenation errors or other page makeup problems have not been introduced. If the typesetter has circled or bracketed or otherwise indicated any changes to page makeup resulting from the corrections, the proofreader can check revised proofs more efficiently. Any corrections that have resulted in repagination may require adjustments to page references in the index. To maintain a proper record, nothing must be marked on the pages or in the PDF file for the foul proofs at this stage; any further corrections must be marked only on the revised printout or revised PDF. Any additional rounds of revision should be kept to a minimum.

2.106 **Index proofs.** Most indexes are prepared from the paginated first set of proofs (unless they reference paragraph numbers rather than page numbers, in which case they can be prepared from the final manuscript). Indexes must be proofread quickly, in the same time that the revisions to the first proofs are being checked. For the sake of efficiency, editors rather than authors usually proofread indexes. For a full discussion of indexes, see chapter 16.

2.107 **Prepress and press proofs.** For works that will be printed and bound, publishers usually review prepress proofs. Prepress proofs present an inexpensive image of what will come off the printing press—generated either from negative film or, more commonly, from electronic files. (The final typesetter's files—usually PDF—can generally be considered equivalent to prepress proofs.) These proofs—a "now or never" opportunity to look at what will be published, *before* ink is committed to paper—are normally checked for completeness of contents; page sequence; margins; location, sizing, position, and cropping (if any) of illustrations; and, for proofs made from film, any spots or smudges. For reasons of press schedule and expense, publishers will generally allow only the correction of grave errors at this stage, such as an incorrect title or a misspelled author's name. One additional look—at actual press sheets, folded and gathered into the proper page sequence (and called F&Gs)—is sometimes also granted book and journal publishers. (Press sheets that include full-color illustrations are occasionally sent to the publisher to approve before the entire work is printed.) By the time the publisher sees a complete set of F&Gs, copies of the work are off the press and may be in the bindery. Since any correction at this stage would involve reprinting an entire signature, the publisher may prefer to turn a blind eye. See also 1.68.

2.108 **Book cover and jacket proofs.** Whereas most publishers (and authors) will live, if not happily, with the inevitable typo inside a book, an error on the cover is a more serious matter. Proofs of die copy—author's name, title, publisher's imprint, and any other matter to be stamped on the spine or cover of a hardbound book—should be checked with extreme care. Likewise, proofs of jacket copy and paperback cover copy should be read and checked word for word (if not letter by letter), with special attention paid as follows:

- The cover should be consistent with the interior of the work in content and style. For example, the author's name and the title of the work—everywhere they appear, including cover, spine, and jacket flaps—must match those on the title page of the book (though the subtitle may be omitted from the cover or jacket). An author's full name is sometimes shortened in the running text of flap copy.
- Biographical material on the author should be checked against any biographical material inside the book, though the wording need not be identical.
- If the work is part of a series or a multivolume set, the series title or volume number must match its counterpart inside the book.
- The price (if it is to appear), the ISBN, and any necessary credit line for a photograph of the author or for artwork used on the cover or jacket must be verified.

Jacket and cover proofs and each stage of revisions thereto should be reviewed by everyone involved in the production of the book—including authors, editors, designers, and marketing personnel.

2.109 **Journal cover proofs.** Although the elements that appear on the covers of academic journals vary considerably, the following suggestions should apply to most journals: The front cover (called cover 1) must be checked carefully to ensure that elements that change with each issue, such as the volume and issue numbers and the month, date, or season of publication, are accurate and up to date. The spine must be similarly checked. If the contents of the issue are listed on cover 1, they must be checked against the interior to be sure that authors' names and article titles match exactly and, for journals that publish various types of articles, that articles have been listed in the correct section of the journal. If inclusive page numbers appear on the spine, these must be verified. The inside of the front cover (cover 2) often includes subscription prices and information on how to subscribe, names of editors and members of the editorial board, or copyright information; all such information must be checked. Covers 3 (inside of back cover) and 4 (back cover) may contain advertisements, instructions to authors on submitting articles, or a list of articles to appear in future issues. They all must be verified by the proofreader.

How to Proofread and What to Look For

2.110 **Proofreading against copy.** In proofreading parlance, *copy* refers to the edited manuscript. Proofs should be checked against the version of the manuscript that contains the author's final changes and responses to queries (see 2.72). In the event that the page proofs were typeset from a paper-only manuscript, the proofreader must read word for word against the edited manuscript, noting all punctuation, paragraphing, capitalization, italics, and so forth and ensuring that any handwritten editing has been correctly interpreted by the typesetter. Likewise, any element in an otherwise electronic manuscript that has been set from edited hard copy (e.g., math or tables) should be proofread carefully against the hard copy. Whether type has been set from electronic files or from paper, the proofreader must mark only the proofs, never the manuscript, which is now known as "dead" or "foul" copy. To assign responsibility for error correctly (see 2.135), the manuscript as earlier approved by the author must be kept intact. For checking revised proofs, see 2.105.

2.111 **Proofreading for spelling errors.** The proofreader should remain alert for the kinds of errors that are typically missed by computerized systems for checking spelling—from common typos such as *it's* where *its* is meant or *out* where *our* is meant, to more subtle errors like *lead* for *led* or *breath* for *breathe*, as well as other misspellings. The manuscript editor's style sheet (see 2.55) may be a useful reference. Note that a change to the spelling of a particular term should never be indicated globally; instead, each change must be marked throughout the proofs (if possible, the PDF should be searched to find and evaluate other instances of the term).

2.112 **Proofreading for word breaks.** End-of-line hyphenation should be checked, especially in proper names and terms in any language that may be outside the range of the dictionaries that automatically assign line breaks during typesetting. The first set of proofs is usually the first time that words have been divided, conditionally, at the ends of lines. Chicago recommends the word breaks given in *Merriam-Webster's Collegiate Dictionary* (see bibliog. 3.1). For words or names not listed in a dictionary, a liberal approach is advisable, since formal usage varies widely and any change requested may entail further breaks or create tight or loose lines (lines with too little or too much space between words). Such problems may be avoided if a list of nondictionary words and their preferred hyphenation (or an editor's style sheet if it includes this information) is submitted to the typesetter along with the manuscript. When it is a question of an intelligible but nonstandard word break for a line that would otherwise be too loose or too tight, the nonstandard break (such as the hyphenation of an already hyphenated term) may be preferred. No more than three succeeding lines should end in a hyphen (see 7.47). See also 2.13, 7.36–47. For dividing URLs at the ends of lines, see 7.46.

2.113 **Proofreading for typeface and font.** Each element in proofs—for example, chapter numbers and titles, subheads, text, extracts, figure captions—should be checked to ensure that it is presented in a consistent typeface and style in accordance with the design for the publication. Heads and subheads, in particular, should be checked for the typographic style assigned to their level (see 2.18, 2.59), and all set-off material (excerpts, poetry, equations, etc.) should be checked for font, size, and indentation. All material in italics, boldface, small capitals, or any font different from that of the surrounding text should be looked at to be sure the new font starts and stops as intended. Note that the conversion of manuscript files into other formats for publication can result in unexpected errors, such as the dropping or transmutation of a special character throughout the work or the inadvertent incorporation of a comment or other "invisible" electronic material into the text (see 2.87). For a systemic error, it may be preferable to indicate a single, or "global," instruction for making the change—to avoid cluttering the proofs with corrections of each instance. When a systemic problem is identified—especially one for a printed work that will affect pagination across more than a few pages and therefore the index—the publisher should be alerted immediately in case new first proofs are needed.

2.114 **Checking and proofreading page numbers and running heads.** Page numbers and running heads must be checked to ensure that they are present where they are supposed to be and absent where they are not (see 1.5–9, 1.10–16, 2.76), that the correct page number appears following a blank page, and that the typesetter has followed instructions as to what should appear on a recto, a verso, or a two-page spread. Running heads must be both proofread and checked for placement. For running heads to endnotes, the page numbers may need to be verified or supplied by checking the pages of text that correspond to the notes (see 1.15).

2.115 **Checking and proofreading illustrations and tables.** The proofreader must verify that all illustrations appear in the right location in the text, in the right size, right side up, not "flopped" (turned over left to right, resulting in a mirror image) or distorted, and with their own captions. Captions should be read as carefully as the text, and any locators should be checked to make sure they accurately refer to the parts or location of the illustrations to which they refer (see 3.24). Tables must be proofread both for content and for alignment. Where an illustration or a table (or more than one of either) occupies a full page, no running head or page number should appear (unless the page number appears as a drop folio); but if several full pages of illustrations or tables appear in sequence, the proofreader may request that page numbers (if they are absent), and sometimes running heads as well, be added to better orient readers (see 1.16). For a table presented as a two-page broadside, the proofreader should make sure it falls on facing pages (i.e., verso and recto; see also 3.87). If there are lists of illustrations and tables, all captions and titles should be checked against the lists, and page numbers must be verified or added.

2.116 **Proofreading for overall appearance.** For printed works, each page or, better, each pair of facing pages should be checked for length (see 2.117), vertical spacing, position of running heads and page numbers, and so forth. Conformity to the design specifications must be verified. Such apparent impairments as fuzzy type, incomplete letters, and blocks of type that appear lighter or darker than the surrounding text may be due to poor photocopying or a faulty printout. If in doubt, the proofreader may query "Type OK?" or "Too dark?" More than three consecutive lines that end with a hyphen or begin or end with the same word should be pointed out and, if possible, appropriate adjustments indicated. A page should not end with a subhead. Nor should a page begin with the last line of a paragraph unless it is full measure; a short line in this position is sometimes called a widow. A page can, however, end with the first line of a new paragraph, or what is sometimes referred to as an orphan. The last word in any paragraph must not be hyphenated unless at least four letters (in addition to any punctuation) are carried over to the final line. A word may break across a spread (verso to recto) but usually should not break at the end of a spread (recto to verso). To correct any of these occurrences, page length may be adjusted.

2.117 **Checking facing pages for text alignment.** Although facing pages of text must align, it is usually acceptable for both pages to run a line long or short to avoid widows (see 2.116) or to accommodate corrections. For example, if a correction on page 68 requires an added line, the typesetter may be asked to add space above a subhead on page 69 so that the two pages wind up the same length. Type can sometimes be rerun more loosely or more tightly to add (*save*) or eliminate (*lose*) a line.

2.118 **Proofreading for sense.** The proofreader must query—or correct, if possible—illogical, garbled, repeated, or missing text. Any rewriting, however, must be limited to the correction of fact or of gross syntactical error, since all source checking and substantive and stylistic changes should have been done at the editing stage. Changes that would alter page makeup across more than a couple of pages in printed works should be avoided, since repagination not only is expensive but, for books, can affect the index.

How to Mark Proofs

2.119 **Proofreaders' marks.** The marks explained in the following paragraphs and illustrated in figures 2.6 and 2.7 are commonly understood by typesetters and other publishing and printing personnel working in English. They can be used to mark up any kind of paper document, and they form the basis of the tools typically available for annotating PDF files (see 2.133). Even those who are obligated to annotate the PDF version (or transfer their marks from a printout to the PDF) will benefit from a thorough understanding of the principles discussed in this section.

2.120 **Where to mark proofs.** Corrections to proofs must always be written in the margin, left or right, next to the line concerned. A mark must also be placed in the text—a caret for an addition, a line through a letter or word to be deleted or replaced—to indicate where a correction is to be made. Never should a correction be written or marked only between the lines, where it could be missed. If a line requires two or more corrections, these should be marked in the margin in the order in which they occur, separated by vertical lines (see fig. 2.7). A guideline or an arrow should be used only when a correction cannot be written next to the line in which it occurs.

2.121 **Circling comments and instructions on proofs.** As with queries and instructions handwritten on a paper manuscript (see 2.93), verbal instructions written on proofs—such as "see attached typescript" or "ital" or "rom"—should be circled. Such circling indicates that these are instructions and that the words and abbreviations themselves should not be incorporated into the actual work.

Proofreaders' Marks

OPERATIONAL SIGNS

Delete

Close up; delete space

Delete and close up (use only when deleting letters *within* a word)

Let it stand

Insert space

Make space between words equal; make space between lines equal

Insert hair space

Letterspace

Begin new paragraph

Indent type one em from left or right

Move right

Move left

Center

Move up

Move down

Flush left

Flush right

Straighten type; align horizontally

Align vertically

Transpose

Spell out

TYPOGRAPHICAL SIGNS

Set in italic type

Set in roman type

Set in boldface type

Set in lowercase

Set in capital letters

Set in small capitals

Wrong font; set in correct type

Check type image; remove blemish

Insert here *or* make superscript

Insert here *or* make subscript

PUNCTUATION MARKS

Insert comma

Insert apostrophe *or* single quotation mark

Insert quotation marks

Insert period

Insert question mark

Insert semicolon

Insert colon

Insert hyphen

Insert em dash

Insert en dash

Insert parentheses

FIGURE 2.6. Proofreaders' marks.

Authors As Proofreaders

"I don't care what kind of type you used for my book," a myopic author once said to the publisher, but please print the proofs in large type. With current technology, such a request no longer sounds ridicul-ous to those familar with typesetting and printing.[1] Yet even today, type is not reset exept to correct errors. Proofreading is an Art and a craft. All authors should know the rudiiments thereof though no proof-reader expects them to be masters of it. Watch proof-reader expects them to be masters of it. Watch not only for misspelled or incorrect works (often a most illusive error but also for misplace dspaces, "unclosde" quotation marks and parenthesis, and imporper paragraphing; and learn to recognize the difference between an em dash—used to separate an interjectional part of a sentence—and an en dash used commonly between continuing numbers e.g., pp. 5–10; A.d. 1165-70) and the word dividing hyphen. Whatever is *underlined* in a MS. should of course, be italicized in print. Two lines drawn beneath letters or words indicate that these are to be reset in small capitals three lines indicate full capitals To find the errors overlooked by the proof-reader is the authors first problem in proof reading. The secrond prolem is to make corrections using the marks and symbols, devized by proffesional proof-readers, than any trained typesetter will understand. The third—and most difficult problem for authors proofreading their own works is to resist the temptation to rewrite in proofs.

Manuscript editor

1. With electronic typesetting systems, type can be reduced in size or enlarged.

FIGURE 2.7. Marked proofs.

2.122 **Communicating extensive changes on proofs.** Wherever the marks required to fix a line or two threaten to become illegible, cross out the whole passage and rewrite it correctly in the margin. If there is not enough room in the margin, make a separate document and include it with the proofs; the insertion point should be indicated in both places. To avoid repagination of print works, every effort must be made to match the word count of new material to that of the old. For material to be transposed from one page to another, circle or otherwise mark the passage and make a note in the margin; clearly mark the new location and make a note in that margin as well. Most types of global changes should be marked individually to ensure that each change is made correctly (see also 2.113).

2.123 **Making marks legible on proofs.** All corrections must be written clearly (such that they can be spotted at a glance) in upper- and lowercase letters. Red proof markings are often preferred for visibility, but any color will do as long as the proofreader's corrections are distinct from any made by the publisher or typesetter. Either a pen or a pencil may be used; in either case, the proofreader must be prepared to eradicate unwanted marks. Messy corrections may lead to further errors; indistinct corrections may be overlooked. If a small number of late-stage, hand-marked corrections to proofs must be transmitted to the typesetter electronically, the marks must be dark enough to scan or fax clearly, and they must not extend to the edges of the paper lest they be cut off on the recipient's copy.

2.124 **Marking copy for deletion on proofs.** To remove a letter, a word, or more, draw a diagonal line through a letter or a straight line through a word or phrase and write the delete mark (see fig. 2.6) in the margin. No part of the text should be obliterated, and a punctuation mark that is to be removed should be circled rather than crossed through, so that it is still visible. The form of the delete mark in the margin need not be exactly as shown in figure 2.6, but it should be made in such a way as not to be confused with a *d*, an *e*, or an *l*. The delete mark is used only when something is to be removed. When something is to be substituted for the deleted matter, only the substitution is written in the margin next to the line or lines that have been struck through. The mark for "delete and close up" should be used only when a letter or a hyphen is deleted from within a word or, in the case of longer deletions, when the material that remains is to be joined with no intervening space. See figure 2.7.

2.125 **Adding or deleting spaces on proofs.** All words in the same line should be separated by the same amount of space, though the spacing will vary from line to line in justified setting (where type is aligned along both the left and the right margins). When spaces within a line are unequal, insert carets in the problem areas of the text and write the equal-space mark (eq #) in the margin. To delete space between letters or words, use the close-up mark (see fig. 2.6) in the text as well as in the margin. To call for more space between words or letters, insert a vertical line in the text where the space is to be inserted and make a space mark (#) in the margin. The space mark is also used to show where more vertical space (or *leading*, a term derived from the lead that was used in hot-metal typesetting) is needed between lines. See also 2.98.

2.126 **Marking changes to paragraphing or indents on proofs.** To indicate a new paragraph, insert an L-shaped mark in the text to the left and partly under the word that is to begin a new paragraph and write the paragraph mark (¶) in the margin. To run two paragraphs together, draw a line in the text from the end of one paragraph to the beginning of the next and write "run in" in the margin. To indent a line one em space (see 6.120) from the left or right margin, draw a small square (□) to the left of the material to be indented and repeat the square in the margin. To indent two or more ems, draw a rectangle divided into two or more squares. To repeat the indents for more than one consecutive line, draw a line down from the square to the level of the baseline of the last affected line.

2.127 **Marking adjustments to position or alignment on proofs.** If a line of type, a title, an item in a table, or any other text appears too far to the left or right, use the marks for moving type right (⊐) or left (⊏). If text that is supposed to be centered appears not to be, use both marks (⊐⊏)—one on each side—to indicate centering. Use the marks for moving type up (⊓) or down (⊔) when something appears vertically out of place. All these marks must be inserted in the text as well as in the margin. To indicate that an indented line of type should start flush left (at the left-hand margin), insert a move-left (⊏) mark at the left of the first word in that line and write "fl" (flush left) in the margin, circled (see fig. 2.7). To indicate that an element should appear flush right—or that a line of type should be justified at the right margin—do the same thing but with the move-right (⊐) mark and marginal "fr" (flush right) or "justify." Finally, to indicate inaccurate alignment in tabular matter, use the mark for vertical alignment (||) or horizontal alignment (=), as the case may be. To apply any of these marks to more than one consecutive line (or column), make the mark long enough to encompass each affected line.

2.128 **Marking items to be transposed on proofs.** To move letters, words, or phrases from one place to another, circumscribe them in a way that precisely demarcates the items (including any punctuation) to be interchanged and write and circle "tr" (transpose) in the margin (see fig. 2.7).

For transposition of larger chunks of text or other elements, it may be best to draw a bracket or other mark around each item and include a circled instruction in the margin.

2.129 **Marking items to be spelled out on proofs.** When an abbreviation or numeral is to be spelled out, circle the item and write the spell-out mark (circled "sp") in the margin. If there is any ambiguity about the spelling, write the full word in the margin. See also 2.93.

2.130 **Using "stet" to revert corrections or deletions on proofs.** To undelete or restore something that has earlier been marked for deletion or correction, place a row of dots in the text under the material that is to remain, cross out the marginal mark or correction, and write "stet" ("let it stand")—or to avoid any ambiguity, "stet as set"—in the margin, circled.

2.131 **Marking changes to capitalization and font on proofs.** To lowercase a capital letter, draw a slash through the letter and write "lc" in the margin. To capitalize a lowercase letter, draw three lines under it and write "cap" in the margin. For small capital letters, draw two lines under the letters or words and write "sc" in the margin. For italics, draw a single line under the letter or words and write "ital" in the margin. To change italics to roman, circle the italicized letter or words and write "rom" in the margin. For boldface, draw a wavy line under the letter or words and write "bf" in the margin. To remove boldface, circle the boldface letter or words and write "not bf" in the margin. Remember to circle all marginal instructions (see 2.121). See also figs. 2.6 and 2.7.

2.132 **Marking changes to punctuation and accents on proofs.** To change a punctuation mark, circle it and write the correct mark in the margin. To add a mark, insert a caret and write the mark in the margin. Lest they be missed or misinterpreted, all punctuation marks in the margin should be clarified thus: a comma should have a caret over it; an apostrophe or a quotation mark should have an inverted caret under it; a parenthesis should have two short horizontal lines through it; a period should be circled; semicolons and colons should be followed by a short vertical line; question marks and exclamation points should be accompanied by the circled word "set"; and hyphens, en dashes, and em dashes should be differentiated by their appropriate symbols (see fig. 2.6). If an accent or a diacritical mark is missing or incorrect, the entire letter should be crossed out in the text and written in the margin with its correct accent; never must the accent alone appear in the margin. For clarity, the name of any unusual accent or diacritical mark (e.g., "breve") should also be written and circled in the margin (see 11.2).

2.133 **Proofreading tools for PDF.** The proofreading symbols and related markup developed for paper and pencil have been adapted for PDF readers by Adobe and others. The advantages of proofreading online—including searchable text and comments, typed annotations, automatic time and user stamps, no shipping costs, and quick turnaround—have influenced some publishers to incorporate PDF tools into their proofreading workflow. (Those who prefer to proofread on paper can still do so as long as they have access to a printer and are willing to transfer their marks to PDF later on.) With PDF proofreading tools, any annotation or other markup added to a page will automatically generate a corresponding item in a separate list that identifies the annotation by type and records the name of the reviser, the date and time the annotation was entered or last revised, the page number, and the text of the annotation, if any. Tools typically include options for striking out, inserting, or replacing text, adding highlighting or underscoring, inserting notes, and drawing lines and other shapes. As on paper, such markup overlays the text, leaving the original unchanged. It is important to avoid redundant markup (e.g., the use of one tool to draw a line through a word and a different tool to insert a correction in the same place); choose a single tool wherever possible, adding at most a virtual note to ensure that the intent of the markup is understood (e.g., "Correct spelling to 'felicidad' and put word in italics as shown"). All annotations should be apparent on the page, but the list can help ensure that none are missed. Whoever is responsible for making the changes can go systematically through the document and use the available tools to mark each item in the list as corrected (or not), further annotating any of the items as needed.

Double-Checking Proofs and Assigning Responsibility

2.134 **Double-checking proofs.** In addition to the tasks outlined in 2.110–18, the proofreader must perform the following checks, according to the needs of the particular work:

- Check article or chapter titles and, if necessary, subheads or other heads against the table of contents to ensure consistent wording, and verify or add beginning page numbers in the table of contents. Query—or delete, if necessary—any item listed in the table of contents that does not appear in the work.
- If footnotes are used, ensure that each footnote appears, or at least begins, on the page that includes its superscript reference number or symbol.
- Complete any cross-references (see 2.35).
- For a book, check the half title and the title page to be sure the title is correct and

the author's or volume editor's name is spelled right; verify that the information on the copyright page is accurate and complete.

- For a journal, check the covers, spine, and any front or back matter copy that is unique to the particular journal; with the previous year's volume at hand, check the elements that change with each issue, such as volume and issue numbers and date, month, or season of publication; ensure that the inclusive page numbers that appear on the spine are accurate; check front and back matter for any elements that may have changed, such as subscription prices or names of editors and members of the editorial board; ensure that copyright lines are included and accurate on all individual articles or other elements of the journal that carry them.

For additional checking required for electronic formats, see 2.137–40.

2.135 **Assigning responsibility for errors on proofs.** The proofreader may be asked to distinguish between errors introduced by the typesetting process, errors that were left uncorrected in the manuscript, and errors that were introduced during editorial cleanup after the author reviewed the editing. In such cases, corrections should be accompanied by abbreviations determined by the publisher or typesetter, such as PE (printer's error—the customary term for what is generally a typesetter's error), AA (author's alteration), EA (editor's alteration), and DA (designer's alteration). All such indications should be circled to prevent their being incorporated into the corrected proofs.

2.136 **Author's alterations (AAs) versus editor's alterations (EAs).** For books, a publisher's contract may allow an author to make, without penalty, alterations in proofs in terms of a percentage of the initial cost of the typesetting. Since the cost of corrections is very high relative to the cost of the original typesetting, an AA allowance of (for example) 5 percent does not mean that 5 percent of the proofs may be altered. An author may be asked to pay the cost of AAs beyond the AA allowance stipulated in the contract. Any rewriting or adding of new material by the author is considered an AA. Page numbers added to cross-references in proofs are also usually considered AAs. Corrections of errors uncaught or even introduced in editing are considered AAs if the author reviewed and approved the edited manuscript. Correction of an error introduced into the manuscript by the publisher after the author's review—made by the manuscript editor, for example, in entering the author's final adjustments—is an EA and not chargeable to the author. Supplying page numbers in lists of tables and illustrations and in running heads to notes constitutes an EA. For articles, consult the journal publisher.

Proofing and Testing Electronic Formats

2.137 **Checklist for proofing and testing electronic formats.** Every component of a publication must be checked and tested in its final format—from PDF to e-book formats to the full text of a web publication or app—*before* it gets published. In addition, the full text of publications offered in more than one format must be proofread word for word, according to the procedures outlined earlier in this chapter, in at least one. Elements appearing in one format and not another will also need to be proofread, and no element should be overlooked. This advice applies equally to any type of work, including self-published works. In addition to many of the tasks outlined in 2.110–18 and 2.134, a thorough check will include some or all of the following steps:

1. Look carefully at the layout to make sure that no elements are missing, that all elements are presented as intended, and that no markup added for another purpose (e.g., for a print version) adversely affects the electronic version.
2. Confirm that all special characters have been converted correctly (see 2.113; see also 11.2). Any character not available in Unicode and treated as a bit-mapped image must be checked for legibility and proper appearance.
3. Verify that all internal and external links and any other features intended to be clicked, tapped, swiped, or otherwise manipulated by the reader work as intended. For web publications and apps, a site map (i.e., a list or chart of all navigable pages) may facilitate this process.
4. Make sure that any illustrations and tables or other components outside the run of text are present and function and appear as desired.
5. Make sure that the content of each format matches exactly—if that is the intent—or varies as intended, and that any intended variation is noted explicitly in both versions (see 1.78).
6. Test for valid EPUB, HTML, or other markup using one of the tools offered for that purpose by the International Digital Publishing Forum, W3C, and others.
7. Proofread any recent changes in each format for spelling, sense, and proper integration into each new context.

Anyone responsible for proofing and testing electronic copy must look at every element of the publication systematically—preferably according to a more detailed checklist that will have been created during the development stages of the project or that applies to the latest procedures for publication in one or more formats. For a sample checklist for e-book formats, see figure 2.8.

EPUB QA CHECKLIST

GENERAL

Scroll/page through the entire book on at least one device, looking for missing content or content that is in the wrong location, missing page breaks, and other major formatting issues. Then test your EPUB file on devices for all of the retailers you will be targeting.

SPECIFIC

Metadata: The EPUB metadata should include, at a minimum, the title, author, language, and ISBN. Ensure that the title in the metadata matches the official title of the book as seen on the title page and front cover.

Linking: Check all URLs to make sure they link where intended. Check links for cross-references to chapters, figures, and the like. Check links to and from the table of contents.

Cover image: Ensure that the title matches the official title of the book as seen on the title page and in the metadata. Back covers are not normally included in e-books.

Copyright page: Check for the correct ISBN(s) for the e-book format(s). If there is an ISBN for print, make sure it is properly labeled: for example, "978-0-226-23410-6 (cloth)." Check any links to author and publisher websites.

Table of contents: Check the linking of each item in the TOC to ensure it points to the correct location in both HTML and navigation views. Also check any list of figures, tables, etc. Check that cover, table of contents, start page, and any other navigational landmarks work as specified.

Page numbers: Make sure page numbers have been embedded in the EPUB for books with a printed counterpart. Include the corresponding page list navigation element.

Headings: Check all part and chapter headings for proper size, alignment, and line spacing. Make sure hyphenation for headings has been disabled.

Embedded fonts: Test any embedded fonts at both small and large sizes. Glyphs should be legible on both E Ink and LCD displays. Make sure content also displays acceptably when the embedded fonts are turned off.

Special characters and Unicode: All special characters, including non-Latin text, symbols, and other nonstandard text, should be tested in the target reading systems, with and without embedded fonts turned on. Replace any non-Unicode fonts with Unicode text.

Character styles: Bold, italic, and other character styles should be checked for proper appearance. Small caps, especially, should be checked on each reading system. If you are concerned about accessibility or semantic markup, be sure to use the correct HTML and CSS code for those elements based on the context. Text colors may be used, but they should not be too light. Light text color may be unreadable on grayscale E Ink screens.

Block quotations and lists: Check block quotations, lists, and the like for acceptable layout. Check poetry for hanging indents and stanza breaks.

FIGURE 2.8. Sample checklist for a book prepared as an EPUB file. See also 2.137.

Notes: All notes should be linked in both directions. In reflowable formats, footnotes are usually converted to endnotes. If not, they should be placed after the paragraph or section, not in between words or sentences. Do notes with "ibid." appear out of context (e.g., in a pop-up)? Consider replacing with a short form of citation.

Bibliography: Check for proper formatting. If long URLs are included, it is best to left-justify the text of the whole bibliography to avoid large gaps between words.

Index: Retain any index from a printed counterpart, including all entries. Page number references should link to the proper location in the book. This can be either the print page number anchor or an anchor specific to that reference. References to figures, images, and tables should link directly to the element, not just to the page on which it appears. "See" and "see also" references should link to their targets in the index.

IMAGES:

- Check all images for quality and readability on target reading systems.
- Image resolution and file size should conform to retailer specs for each reading system.
- Images should be saved in an RGB color space, not CMYK.
- Use transparent backgrounds as applicable.
- Check captions for alignment; they should appear on the same page as the image whenever possible. Use CSS to scale images as necessary.

TABLES AND CHARTS:

- Tables should be coded in HTML, if at all possible, rather than presented as images.
- Check tables for legibility and to make sure content fits well on the screen when possible.
- Wherever possible, convert simple lists and the like to regular paragraph text, especially if they were presented in tabular format only to accommodate the printed page.
- Check charts and graphs for legibility. Charts that use color in meaningful ways should include explanations where needed for readers with grayscale screens.

AUDIO AND VIDEO CONTENT:

- Check retailer specs for multimedia content and encode/size as applicable.
- Include proper fallbacks (e.g., an image or an explanation that the media content is not supported in the reading system). If possible, include a link showing where the reader can access the media content online.
- Videos should always include a poster image.

FIGURE 2.8. (continued)

2.138 **Procedures for testing electronic formats.** Book publishers offering print and e-book formats or journal publishers following a standard print/PDF and full-text HTML workflow should have procedures in place for testing each new book or each new article and issue in each format. Because a consistent set of templates for markup can usually be applied to each new book or article, this testing is typically done just before publication—that is, *after* a manuscript has been finalized and converted for publication. Such testing should be done in the context of publication using a range of devices or apps that will be used to present the content and according to a checklist tailored to each format (see 2.137). A newly designed website or app, on the other hand, must usually be tested starting at an earlier stage—not just at the end and not only by a team of editors or proofreaders. By the time the content for a web-based publication or app has been finalized, the interface will usually have gone through several stages of editorial review to scrutinize basic design elements and navigational structure and to edit ancillary items such as error messages and label text (as on buttons). Some publications will also benefit from a beta test stage in which potential users are invited to report errors and suggest changes before the official release date. More specific testing routines should adhere to use-case documents (see 2.139). Testing after the release date will include editorial oversight of any new content generated by the publication, such as readers' comments. At all stages, procedures should be in place for regression testing—that is, testing that safeguards against unforeseen errors caused by the correction of other errors or by the introduction of new features or content or other changes.

2.139 **Documentation for testing electronic formats.** At the very least, publishers should have a master checklist in place for each publication format (see fig. 2.8); such checklists will usually suffice for e-book formats and for journal-publishing workflows that produce PDF or full-text HTML or both. Thorough testing of a web-based publication or app, on the other hand, should involve checking it against various documents that describe its intended functionality, behavior, and navigation. Several types of documents are typically created as part of a publication's development process. *Feature definition documents*, for example, provide detailed descriptions of how the various features of the website will function. Feature definition for a search engine would specify how search results are ordered and displayed on the page, how users are able to limit the search to certain kinds of results, how terms with diacritics are handled, and so forth. *Use-case documents* provide a more complete description of a feature's behavior, specifying exactly how the feature will respond to the user's every click, tap, or swipe. *Wire frames* or *design mockups* provide visual representations of the page's design and layout, and *user interface specifications* may provide additional guidelines. Finally, *test-case documents* provide step-by-step instructions on exactly how a given feature or page will be tested.

2.140 **Communicating changes across different formats.** Some journal publishers use an augmented PDF for the proofreading stage; this "content proof" reproduces the print version of an article or other component of the journal together with any content that will appear only in electronic formats. Authors and editors mark their changes directly on the PDF (see 2.133). In addition, the types of checklists and procedures discussed in 2.137 and 2.138 can be used as the basis of an error-reporting system for each electronic format tested in situ. The location of each reported error in each format should be made clear (e.g., through the use of a searchable phrase or by reference to a page number in the PDF, or both). Those involved in producing a web-based publication or app will need to follow a more elaborate and flexible system for tracking and implementing changes and stylistic decisions. A centralized database can facilitate reports from a range of different reviewers over an extended period of time. Procedures for using such a system should be developed (and fully documented) with the input of the web or app developers, designers, editors, proofreaders, and testers who will use it. In any single project, the entries in such a database—in conjunction with the documentation for testing described in 2.139—can serve as a contract between editors and the production team to ensure that each change, no matter how trivial, gets implemented properly.

3 · Illustrations and Tables

Overview

3.1 **Illustrations defined.** Illustrations, also called figures (and sometimes referred to as artwork or art), consist of images presented separately from the run of text. For the purposes of publication, such images usually consist of individual electronic files optimized for specific publication formats. Illustrations can reproduce anything from paintings, photographs, and line drawings to maps, charts, and examples from musical scores. This list is sometimes extended to include multimedia files presented in electronic publication formats. For a full discussion of illustrations—including guidelines on preparation, placement, numbering, and captioning, with examples drawn from University of Chicago Press publications—see 3.3–46.

3.2 **Tables defined.** A table is a more or less complex list presented as an array of vertical columns and horizontal rows. Like illustrations, tables are presented separately from the run of text. Tables are also related to illustrations in that both can be said to constitute a visual representation of data. Because they consist of alphanumeric text, however, tables are usually typeset along with the text rather than produced separately as images. For a full discussion of tables—including guidelines on preparation, placement, numbering, and editing, with examples drawn from University of Chicago Press publications—see 3.47–88.

Illustrations

Types of Illustrations and Their Parts

3.3 **Continuous tone versus halftone.** Continuous-tone art is any image such as a painting or a photograph that contains gradations of shading from light to dark—in black and white (grayscale) or color (see fig. 3.1). In order to duplicate continuous-tone images in offset printing, which uses one ink color (black) for black-and-white reproduction and four inks (cyan, magenta, yellow, and black—abbreviated CMYK) for color, a halftone reproduction must be produced (see fig. 3.2). A halftone breaks the image into an equally spaced array of dots that vary in size to create the illusion of continuous tone from dark to light. For both black-and-white halftone reproduction and illustrations to be reproduced in color, authors should consult their publisher's guidelines for preparing digital artwork. (Chicago offers such guidelines on its books and journals websites.) Color images produced digitally and intended for the screen are

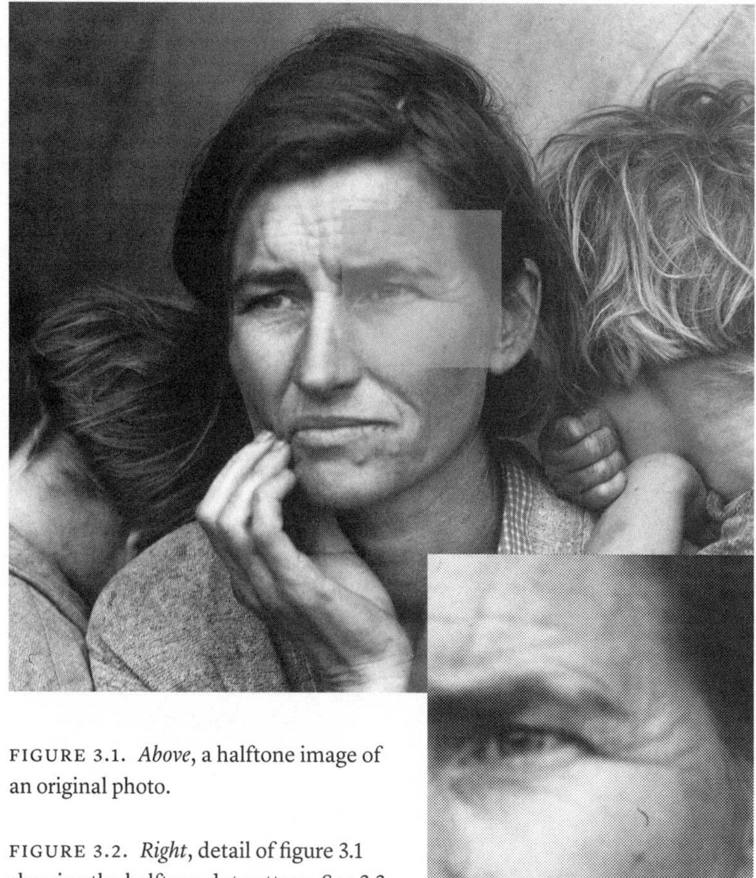

FIGURE 3.1. *Above*, a halftone image of an original photo.

FIGURE 3.2. *Right*, detail of figure 3.1 showing the halftone dot pattern. See 3.3.

rendered in pixels and in RGB (red, green, and blue) mode and need to be converted to CMYK for printing.

3.4 **Line art.** Artwork consisting of solid black on a white background, with no gray screens (i.e., shading)—such as a pen-and-ink drawing—is traditionally known as line art. See figures 3.3 and 3.4. Line art may be published in black and white or in color. Charts are usually created with software and rendered for publication as line art. (For more on charts, see 3.41–46.) Musical examples may be treated as line art and scanned if they are not typeset from scratch for publication—generally by specialists. See figure 3.5. Publishers can often reproduce computer-generated line art without having to remake it as long as it has been properly prepared; authors should obtain guidelines from the publisher. For the use

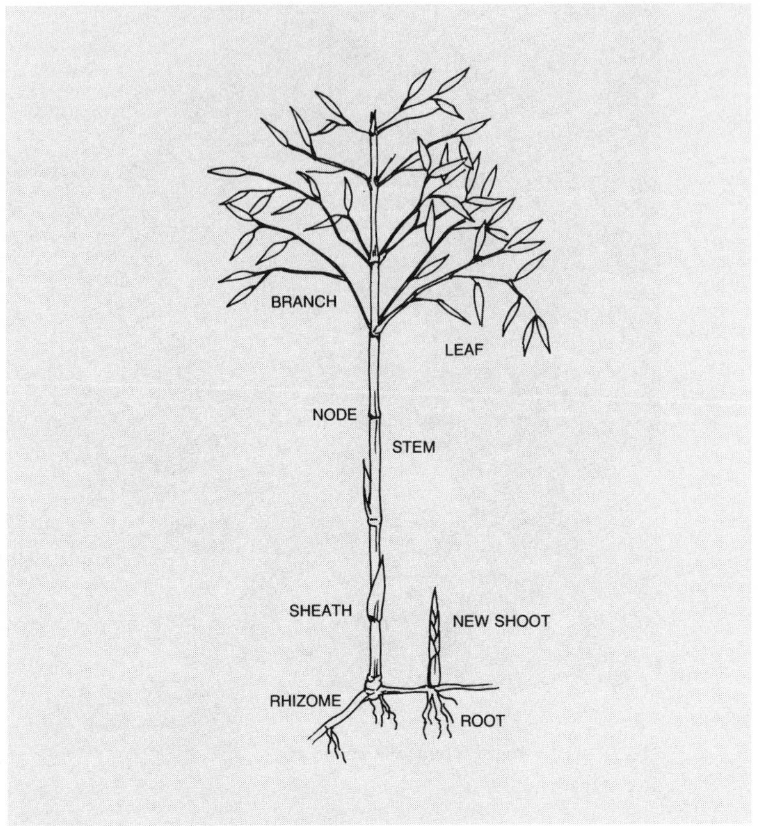

FIGURE 3.3. A line drawing with descriptive labels (see 3.4, 3.7). The surrounding text of the work from which this unnumbered and uncaptioned figure was drawn identifies the plant as a *Sinarundinaria* stem.

of shading in line art, see 3.19. For more on the conventions related to musical notation, see 7.70–75.

3.5 **Text figures and plates.** Illustrations—whether halftones or line art—that are interspersed in the text are referred to as text figures. (Occasionally, a special type of illustration, such as a map or a musical example, will be referred to in a work by type rather than by the generic term *figure*. See fig. 3.5.) The term *plate*, strictly speaking, refers to a full-page illustration that is printed separately, typically on coated paper; plates can appear individually between certain pages of text but are more often gathered into galleries (see 3.6). (In a work that contains both photographs and line art,

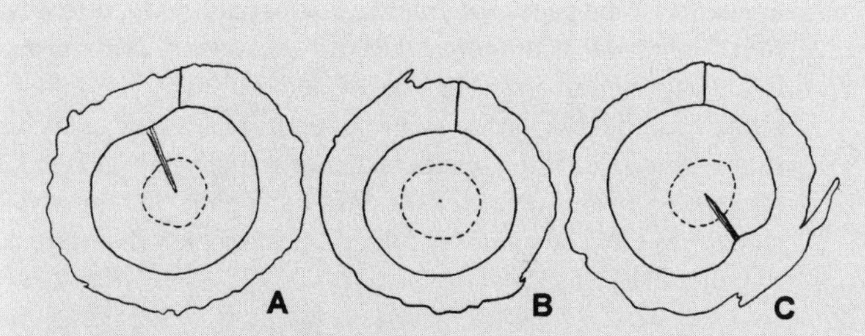

FIG. 3 Outline drawings of serial sections of parental root axis of *Carpinus caroliniana*. The vertical line at the top of each drawing represents the incision mentioned in "Materials and Methods." The outermost outline marks the surface of the axis, the next line inward marks the location of the vascular cambium, and the dotted line represents the terminus of the first season of growth. *A* and *C* are from sections that were 4 mm apart, each immediately adjacent to a branch root trace, with diminished secondary xylem accumulation toward the side with the branch root (cf. fig. 1*B* to understand the position of these sections relative to PBR). *B* represents a section between *A* and *C*, showing secondary xylem that is uniform in thickness around the parental axis.

FIGURE 3.4. A line drawing, including figure number and caption (see 3.4, 3.8–14, 3.21–28). The drawing's three parts, labeled with capital letters, are discussed in the caption (see 3.7).

FIGURE 3.5. Musical examples carry their captions above the illustration rather than below. Such examples can be reproduced photographically (e.g., from a published score) or typeset by specialists (see 3.4).

plate is sometimes used—a little loosely—for the former and *figure* for the latter.)

3.6 **Galleries.** A gallery is a section of a printed work devoted to illustrations—usually halftones. If printed on stock different from that used for the text, a gallery is not paginated; for example, an eight-page gallery could appear between pages 134 and 135. Such a gallery will typically consist of four, eight, twelve, or more pages (for purposes of printing and binding, it is always a number that can be divided by four). If the gallery is printed along with the text, on the same paper, its pages may be included in the numbering, even if the numbers do not actually appear (see 1.39). A gallery always begins on a recto (a right-hand page) and must fall between signatures (i.e., the groups of folded-and-gathered sheets that are bound together in a printed book).

3.7 **Captions, legends, keys, and labels.** The terms *caption* and *legend* are sometimes used interchangeably for the explanatory text that appears with an illustration—usually immediately below but sometimes above or to the side. (In a distinction rarely made today, the term *caption* once referred strictly to a phrasal title or a headline, whereas *legend* referred to the full-sentence explanation immediately following the caption. This manual uses *caption* to refer to both.) A *key* (also sometimes called a legend) appears within the illustration itself and not as part of the caption; it identifies the symbols used in a map or a chart. For more on captions, see 3.21–28. *Labels* are any descriptive terms that appear within an illustration. They may also be symbols (often letters) used to indicate an illustration's parts. See figures 3.3, 3.4, 3.6. See also 3.12, 3.44.

Placement and Numbering of Illustrations

3.8 **Placement of illustrations relative to text.** Unless illustrations are presented separately (as in a gallery; see 3.6, 3.14), each should appear as soon as possible after the first text reference to it. In an electronic work, a captioned thumbnail image linked to its larger counterpart(s) may appear after the paragraph in which the image is first referenced. In printed works, to accommodate page makeup, the image may precede the reference only if it appears on the same page or same two-page spread as the reference or if the text is too short to permit placing all figures and tables after their references. For illustrations that will be interspersed in the text, the author or (if the author has not done so) the editor must provide callouts that indicate in the manuscript the preferred location for each (see 2.30). (For illustrations that are to appear together in a printed gallery, placement callouts are usually unnecessary.) Note that a *callout* (e.g., "fig. 5 about here") is an instruction for typesetting or production and will not appear in the published work (for *text references*, which are addressed to readers, see 3.9). In electronic markup, a callout points to a specific source file. In a printed work, most illustrations will appear at

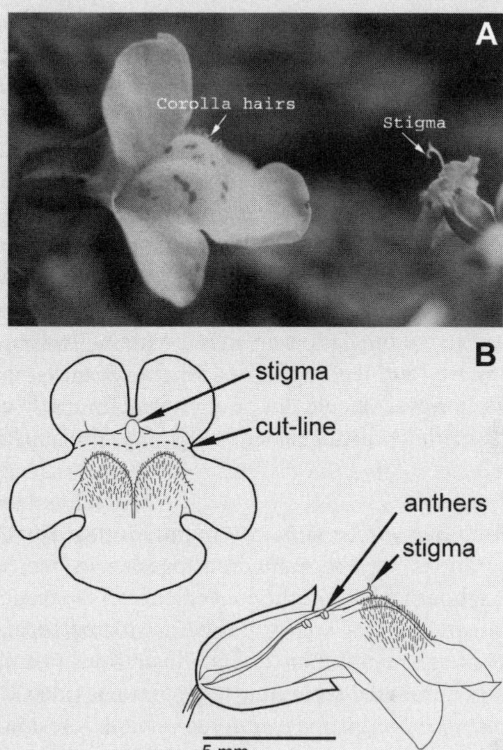

Fig. 1 Flower of *Mimulus guttatus*. *A*, Side-view photograph of two flowers illustrating the corolla hairs and stigma. The corolla and anthers have been pulled back to reveal the stigma and style on the left-hand flower. *B*, Line drawings of a front view and a side view. The cut line used in the phenotypic manipulation is illustrated in the front view. For the side view, the upper portion of the corolla has been removed to reveal the positions of the reproductive parts relative to the corolla hairs.

FIGURE 3.6. A figure consisting of a photograph and a line drawing, each with descriptive labels and identified by the letters *A* and *B*, respectively (see 3.12, 3.7).

either the top or the bottom of a page; in reflowable electronic formats, placement may vary with text size and other factors.

3.9 **Text references to numbered illustrations.** If there are more than a handful of illustrations in a work, they normally bear numbers (but see 3.13), and all text references to them should be by the numbers: "as figure 1 shows . . ."; "compare figures 4 and 5." If an electronic version of a work contains figures not available in a printed counterpart, any text references to these figures in the print version must make this clear (e.g., by adding "available online" after the reference; see also 1.78). An illustration should never be referred to in the text as "the photograph opposite" or "the graph on this page," for such placement may not be possible in the published version (but see 3.24). In text, the word *figure* is set in roman, lowercased, and spelled out except in parenthetical references, where the abbreviation *fig.* may be used. (In some publications, such terms are routinely capitalized whenever they appear with a number.) *Plate*, however, should not be abbreviated to *pl.* In captions, these terms are sometimes distinguished typographically from the rest of the caption (see 3.23).

3.10 **Continuous versus separate numbering of illustrations.** All types of illustrations may be numbered together in one continuous sequence throughout a work. For the convenience of the reader, a specific category of illustration may sometimes be numbered separately in book-length works (e.g., map 1, map 2, . . .); illustrations in a different medium are always numbered separately (e.g., video 1, video 2, . . .). In a work published in both print and electronic versions, illustrations should be numbered according to the same system and using the same numbers in both versions (see also 3.9, 1.78). For double numeration, see 3.11. For illustrations in a gallery, see 3.6, 3.14.

3.11 **Double numeration of illustrations.** In scientific and technical books, heavily illustrated books, and books with chapters by different authors, double numeration may be employed. Each illustration carries the number of the chapter followed by the illustration number, usually separated by a period. Thus, for example, figure 9.6 is the sixth figure in chapter 9. Should a chapter contain only one illustration, a double number would still be used (e.g., figure 10.1). Appendix figures may be numbered A.1, A.2, and so on, or, if there are several appendixes and each bears a letter, A.1, A.2, B.1, B.2, and so on. At the editing stage, double numeration makes it easier to handle multiple illustrations and, should any be added or removed, involves far less renumbering. It also makes it easier for readers to find a particular illustration. This manual uses double numer-

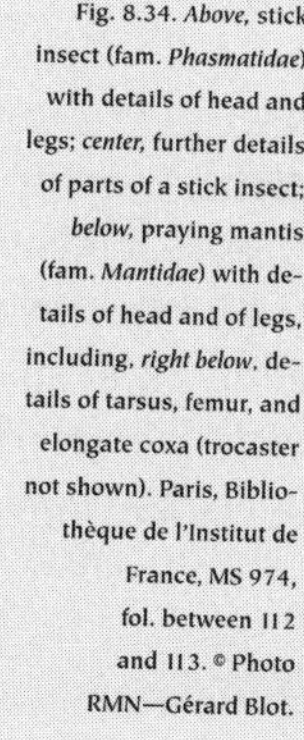

Fig. 8.34. *Above,* stick insect (fam. *Phasmatidae*) with details of head and legs; *center,* further details of parts of a stick insect; *below,* praying mantis (fam. *Mantidae*) with details of head and of legs, including, *right below,* details of tarsus, femur, and elongate coxa (trocaster not shown). Paris, Bibliothèque de l'Institut de France, MS 974, fol. between 112 and 113. © Photo RMN—Gérard Blot.

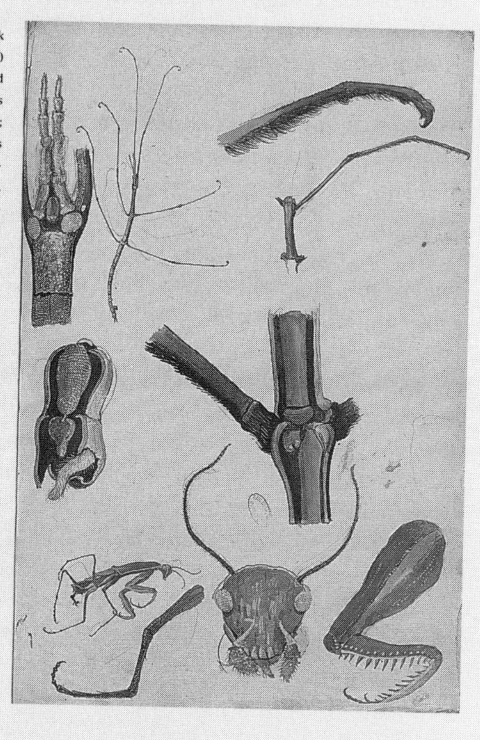

FIGURE 3.7. The relative position of each part in this composite figure is identified in the caption (see 3.24).

ation for illustrations and tables as well as for text paragraphs. See also 1.57.

3.12 **Identifying the parts of an illustration.** Chicago recommends the use of arabic numerals for illustrations of all kinds: "figure 12," "fig. 10.7." Where a figure consists of several parts, the parts may carry letters (*A*, *B*, *C*, etc.); a single caption, keying the letters to the parts, suffices (see figs. 3.4, 3.6). Text references may then refer, for example, to "fig. 10.7*C*" (note that the letters are usually italicized—with the number and when referred to alone). Parts may also be described according to their relative positions on a printed page (see fig. 3.7; see also 3.24); the relative positions must be maintained in an electronic version if the same description is to be used. (In the rare and undesirable event that a figure has to be added at a late stage to a work destined for print, when it is no longer feasible to renumber all the other figures, "fig. 10.7*A*" might refer to a figure inserted between figures 10.7 and 10.8.)

3.13 **Working numbers for unnumbered illustrations.** In some works, where illustrations are neither integral to the text nor specifically referred to, numbers are unnecessary. In the editing and production stages, however, all illustrations should carry working numbers, as should their captions, to ensure that they are correctly placed. Such working numbers should appear in illustration file names, on any photocopies, and in any placement callouts in the text (see 3.8).

3.14 **Numbering illustrations in a gallery.** When illustrations are gathered together in a gallery, they need not be numbered unless referred to in the text, although in the editing and production stages they should carry working numbers to ensure the correct order (see 3.13). If numbers are required and the work also contains illustrations interspersed in the text, two number sequences must be adopted. For example, text illustrations may be referred to as "figure 1" and so on and gallery illustrations as "plate 1" and so on.

Preparation of Artwork

3.15 **Submitting artwork to the publisher.** Authors preparing illustrations electronically must consult their publishers before submitting the files. Many publishers require hard copies or PDF along with artwork submitted in electronic form. (A still image may be required for an audiovisual file submitted as an enhancement to an electronic work.) A list of the software programs used to create the digital artwork should also be furnished, and the publisher should be made aware of any special fonts used in the construction of drawings, diagrams, maps, and so forth; the publisher may need the author to supply these fonts. See also 2.4, 2.36. Any author-supplied scans must be made in accordance with the publisher's guidelines, preferably by a professional graphic arts service; Chicago offers such guidelines on its books and journals websites. For color art intended for print, digital scans or photographs furnished by the lending institution or prepared by a professional prepress service are generally preferred. (Authors should check their contracts to ensure that color illustrations are permitted.) Images obtained from the internet—unless they have been specifically optimized for print—are usually not acceptable. Authors who plan to self-publish their works in print would do well to consult Chicago's detailed guidelines in addition to any guidelines provided by their self-publishing platform to get an idea of the steps required to ensure the best possible reproduction quality.

3.16 **Identifying artwork for the publisher.** Artwork submitted in electronic form should be saved in separate files with descriptive names that accurately identify each file (see also 2.37); these names should be included on any corresponding hard copies along with the numbers that correspond to the figure callouts in the manuscript. Original artwork submitted as hard copy (e.g., photographic prints) must be clearly identified by the author or, failing that, by the publisher, in a manner that does not harm the original. Each item should be numbered on the back in pencil, very gently, making sure no mark is visible on the other side. If the paper does not accept lead pencil, a removable self-sticking label should be used. To be avoided are ballpoint pens, grease pencils, felt-tip markers, staples, or paper clips. For numbering, see 3.8–14; for captions, see 3.21–28.

3.17 **Author's inventory of artwork.** Along with artwork, the author should supply a complete list of illustrations, noting any that are to appear in color, any sizing restrictions, any duplicates or extras, and any that are still to come. (Note, however, that for both books and journals, it is always expected and often mandatory that all illustrations be supplied at the time a manuscript is submitted; see 2.3.) If the work is to be published in print and electronic versions that will vary in the number of illustrations or in the use of color, that information must be noted in the inventory (see also 3.26).

3.18 **Publisher's inventory of artwork.** As soon as the illustrations arrive from the author, publishers should check each one against the author's inventory (see 3.17). If an illustration does not meet the publisher's resolution or file format requirements for digital art, or if a hard-copy photograph or transparent original is damaged or otherwise may not be reproducible, a replacement copy will need to be requested. (Missing illustrations will also need to be tracked down.) Each illustration should also be checked to be sure that it is properly numbered and labeled and that it corresponds correctly to each caption. (Authors should supply captions as a separate file; see 2.26.) Finally, publishers should check for any necessary permissions (see 4.75–94, 4.95–105).

3.19 **Cropping, scaling, and shading.** To make suggestions for reframing, or cropping, an image—that is, cutting it down to remove extraneous parts—

authors should either crop a digital copy or mark a printout or, for a hard-copy photograph or transparency, mark up a photocopy to avoid damaging the original. For images that need to be scaled, finished dimensions must be computed from the dimensions of the original. Authors need to be aware of this especially when preparing line art that contains labels or a key. The relations between font size, line weight (thickness, measured in points), and final printed size should be considered when drawings are created to ensure legibility. By scaling the image to its intended size and printing it out (or by using a photocopying machine), it is possible to get an idea of what the printed version will look like. Avoid hairline rules, which may disappear when printed. Likewise, avoid shading or color, which may print poorly when reduced; use stripes, spots, and other black-and-white fill patterns in charts to distinguish areas from plain black or white. (Many publishers now accept shading or color within properly prepared line art submitted electronically in specific formats; consult your publisher's manuscript submission guidelines before preparing final art.) See also 3.41–46.

3.20 **Artwork to be redrawn by the publisher.** In some cases, a publisher may agree to make corrections to or redraw line art (e.g., a line drawing or a chart) submitted for publication. (Authors should check with their publishers in advance.) Authors submitting such art should clearly mark any labels (words or symbols) to be altered or added on a photocopy or scan or, if there are more than a few, in a separate document, keyed to the illustration. Where possible, wording, abbreviations, and symbols should be consistent with those used in the text. By a similar token, capitalization should be reserved for those terms that would be capitalized in running text. All names on a map that is to be redrawn should be prepared as a separate list, in which countries, provinces, cities, rivers, and so forth are divided into separate groups, each group arranged alphabetically.

Captions

3.21 **Format and wording for captions.** A caption—the explanatory material that appears outside (usually below) an illustration—is distinct from a key and from a label, which appear within an illustration (see 3.7; see also 3.44). A caption may consist of a word or two, an incomplete or a complete sentence, several sentences, or a combination. No punctuation is needed after a caption consisting solely of an incomplete sentence. If one or more full sentences follow it, each (including the opening phrase) has closing punctuation. In a work in which most captions consist of full sentences, incomplete ones may be followed by a period for consistency. Captions should be capitalized in sentence style (see 8.158), but formal titles of works included in captions should be capitalized in headline style (see 3.22).

Wartime visit to Australia, winter 1940

The White Garden, reduced to its bare bones in early spring. The box hedges, which are still cut by hand, have to be carefully kept in scale with the small and complex garden as well as in keeping with the plants inside the "boxes."

3.22 **Formal titles in captions.** Titles of works should be presented according to the rules set forth in chapter 8 (see 8.156–201), whether standing alone or incorporated into a caption. Accordingly, most titles in English will appear in headline style (see 8.159), and many titles—including those for paintings, drawings, photographs, statues, and books—will be italicized; others will appear in roman type, enclosed in quotation marks (see 8.163). For titles in other languages, see 11.6–10. Generic titles, however (as in the last example below), are not usually capitalized.

Frontispiece of *Christian Prayers and Meditations* (London: John Daye, 1569), showing Queen Elizabeth at prayer in her private chapel. Reproduced by permission of the Archbishop of Canterbury and the Trustees of the Lambeth Palace Library.

The head of Venus—a detail from Botticelli's *Birth of Venus*.

Francis Bedford, *Stratford on Avon Church from the Avon*, 1860s. Albumen print of collodion negative, 18.8 × 28.0 cm. Rochester, International Museum of Photography at George Eastman House.

Friedrich Overbeck and Peter Cornelius, double portrait, pencil drawing, 1812. Formerly in the Collection Lehnsen, Scarsdale, New York.

3.23 **Separating illustration numbers from captions.** Illustration numbers should be distinct from the captions they introduce. A period after the number usually suffices (as in the first example below), and this is the format that authors should use in preparing their captions. Other treatments are sometimes used in the published version of a work. If the number is distinguished typographically—for example, by boldface—the period may not be necessary. Extra space may be added between the number and the caption to ensure legibility, as in the second example (which uses an em space; see 6.120). Whether *figure* is spelled out or abbreviated as *fig.* may be specified by journal style or, for books, may be up to the designer or editor or both.

Figure 3. Detailed stratigraphy and geochronology of the Dubawnt Supergroup.

PLATE 5 Palace of the Governors, Santa Fe, New Mexico. Undated photograph, circa 1900.

The word *figure* or *plate* is occasionally omitted—for example, in a book whose illustrations consist of a long series of continuously numbered photographs.

3.24 **Using locators in captions.** Italicize such terms as *top*, *bottom*, *left*, *right*, *above*, *below*, *left to right*, *clockwise from left*, or *inset* to identify elements within a single illustration or parts of a composite or, in print publications, an illustration that does not appear on the same page as the caption. If the term precedes the element it identifies, it should be followed by a comma or, if a list follows, a colon. When it appears in midsentence or follows the element, it may appear in parentheses. See figure 3.7.

Fig. 4. *Above left*, William Livingston; *above right*, Henry Brockholst Livingston; *below left*, John Jay; *below right*, Sarah Livingston Jay

Left to right: Madeleine K. Albright, Dennis Ross, Ehud Barak, and Yasir Arafat

Overleaf: The tall trees of the valley, planted by Russell Page, are reflected among the water lilies, *Nymphaea*, and pickerelweed, *Pontederia cordata.*

Figure 2. Schematic block diagram showing upper plate (*top*) and lower plate (*bottom*) of the Battle Lake thrust-tear fault system.

If the various parts of a figure have been assigned letters, these are used in a similar way, usually italicized (see also 3.12). Likewise, descriptive terms used to identify parts of a figure are usually italicized.

Figure 3. DNA sequence from a small region within the *PC* gene, showing the G→T transition at nucleotide 2229. The partial sequence of intron 13 is also shown. *A*, wild-type sequence; *B*, sequence from a PC-deficient Micmac homozygous for the mutation.

Figure 2. Duration of hospital stay for 22 patients colonized or infected with extended-spectrum β-lactamase-producing *Escherichia coli* isolates belonging to clonally related groups A (*gray bars*) and B (*white bars*). The black point represents

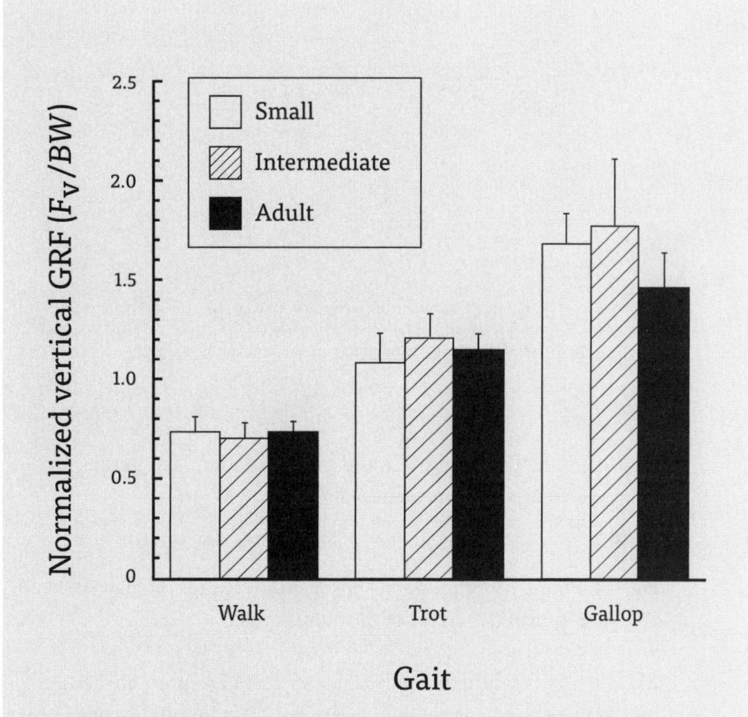

Figure 4. Normalized peak vertical forelimb GRFs versus gait. Normalized peak vertical forelimb GRFs for different gaits in the small, intermediate, and adult groups. Peak vertical forces (F_V) were normalized by dividing the forces by the body weight (*BW*) of the goat. Error bars represent ±1 sd.

FIGURE 3.8. A bar chart (also called a bar graph) with a key to the three types of bars (see 3.25). The caption includes the standard deviation (sd) for the T-shaped error bars. See also 3.41–46.

the date when the microorganism was isolated, and the asterisk indicates stay in the geriatric care hospital.

In the last example, the letters identify the study groups and not parts of the figure and are therefore not italicized.

3.25 **Identifying symbols or patterns used in figures.** When symbols or patterns are used in a map or chart, they must be identified either in a key within the figure or in the caption. See figures 3.8, 3.9. See also 3.24.

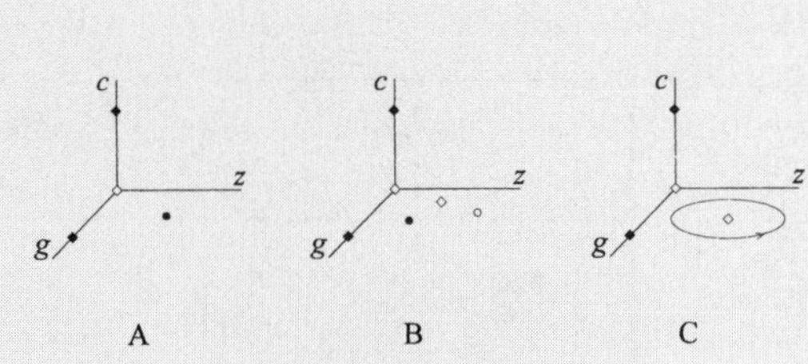

Figure 2: Attractors (*black circles, limit cycles*), saddles (*black squares, white squares*), and repellors (*white circles*) in the state space. *A*, *B*, and *C* refer to subregions [a], [b], and [c] of figure 1.

FIGURE 3.9. The symbols in this graph are identified in the caption. Compare figure 3.8 and the examples in 3.25. See also 3.41–46.

Fig. 9.4. Photosynthetic light response. Data are presented from shade-grown (■) and open-grown (□) culms of the current year.

or

Fig. 9.4. Photosynthetic light response. Data are presented from shade-grown (*filled squares*) and open-grown (*open squares*) culms of the current year.

3.26 **Identifying electronic enhancements in captions.** The caption to an illustration published in both print and electronic versions should add in the print version an indication of any electronic enhancement—such as color or video—available in the electronic version.

Figure 3. Egg candling showing embryonic development inside the egg. A color version of this figure is available online.

Video 1. Still photograph from a video (available in the online edition of the *American Naturalist*) depicting a juvenile gorilla sniffing, tasting, and discarding *Nauclea* fruits. Apes are often very choosy about the fruits they eat, which can result in many discarded food items at "magnet" resources that have been handled or tested by previous visitors. Video by Thomas Breuer (Max Planck Institute and Wildlife Conservation Society).

The electronic version should generally specify which features are not available in print—for example, in a list of an online journal article's contents, under a subheading "Enhancements" or "Electronic Supplements." See also 1.78.

3.27 **Including original dimensions in captions.** When a caption provides the dimensions of an original work of art, these follow the work's medium and are listed in order of height, width, and (if applicable) depth. This information need appear only if relevant to the text, unless the rights holder requests that it be included (see 3.32).

Oil on canvas, 45 × 38 cm
Bronze, 49 × 22 × 16 in.

See also the example in 3.22. Photomicrographs, in scientific publications, may include in their captions information about the degree of magnification (e.g., original magnification, ×400; *bar*, 100 μm).

3.28 **Illustration captions and accessibility.** Publishers concerned about providing content that is accessible to people with disabilities will want to consider adding appropriate text alternatives for illustrations in electronic formats. Properly marked-up text and captions will enhance accessibility; if an illustration is insufficiently described in either of these locations, alternative text will help readers who use text-to-speech and related tools understand the nature and content of the illustration. Editors or authors would ordinarily be in the best position to decide whether an illustration needs such text and how to write it, though not without recourse to detailed guidelines. For more information, consult the DIAGRAM Center, a Benetech literacy initiative; see also the Web Accessibility Initiative (WAI) of the World Wide Web Consortium (W3C) and, for EPUB, the Accessibility Guidelines provided by the International Digital Publishing Forum.

Credit Lines

3.29 **Sources and permissions.** A brief statement of the source of an illustration, known as a credit line, is usually appropriate and sometimes required by the owner of the illustration. Illustrative material under copyright, whether published or unpublished, usually requires permission from the copyright owner before it can be reproduced. You cannot simply snap a photo of your favorite Picasso and use it to illustrate your history of cubism; before attempting to reproduce the painting, you must write to obtain written permission, as well as a print of the work, from the museum or person that owns it. Nor may you use a photograph or other portrayal of an identifiable human subject without the consent of that person or someone acting on his or her behalf (e.g., by means of a model release form). Although it is the author's responsibility, not the publisher's, to obtain permissions, the publisher should be consulted about what needs permission and the best way to obtain it. For a fuller discussion of permissions, see 4.90, 4.95–105. For a work that will be published in electronic as well as printed form, see 4.64.

3.30 **Placement of credit lines.** A credit line usually appears at the end of a caption, sometimes in parentheses or in different type (or both). (A photographer's name occasionally appears in small type parallel to the bottom or side of a photograph.)

Fig. 37. The myth that all children love dinosaurs is contradicted by this nineteenth-century scene of a visit to the monsters at Crystal Palace. (Cartoon by John Leech. "Punch's Almanack for 1855," *Punch* 28 [1855]: 8. Photo courtesy of the Newberry Library, Chicago.)

If most or all of the illustrations in a work are from a single source, that fact may be stated in a note or, in the case of a book, in the preface or acknowledgments or on the copyright page. In a heavily illustrated book, all credits are sometimes listed together in the back matter (see 1.4) or, more rarely, in the front matter—sometimes as part of a list of illustrations (see 3.38–40). Note, however, that some permissions grantors stipulate placement of the credit with the illustration itself; others may charge a higher fee if the credit appears elsewhere.

3.31 **Crediting author as source of illustration.** Although illustrations created by the author do not need credit lines, such wording as "Photo by author" may be appropriate if other illustrations in the same work require credit. In works with more than one author, such wording may include the name of a particular author.

3.32 **Crediting material that requires permission.** Unless fair use applies (see 4.84–94), or unless blanket permission has been granted by means of a Creative Commons or similar license (see 3.34), an illustration reproduced from a published work under copyright always requires formal permission. In addition to author, title, publication details, and (occasionally) copyright date, the credit line should include any page or figure number. If the work being credited is listed in the bibliography or reference list, only a shortened form need appear in the credit line (see third example). For material acquired from a commercial agency, see 3.36. For proper citation style, see chapters 14 and 15.

Reproduced by permission from Mark Girouard, *Life in the English Country House: A Social and Architectural History* (New Haven, CT: Yale University Press, 1978), 162.

Reproduced by permission from George B. Schaller et al., *The Giant Pandas of Wolong* (Chicago: University of Chicago Press, 1985), 52. © 1985 by the University of Chicago.

Reprinted by permission from Cruze (2017, fig. 4).

Some permissions grantors request specific language in the credit line. In a work with many illustrations, such language in one or two credit lines may conflict with consistent usage in the rest. Editorial discretion should then be exercised; in giving full credit to the source, an editor may follow the spirit rather than the letter. (Where the grantor is intractable, it may be simpler to use the language requested.)

3.33 **Crediting commissioned material.** Work commissioned by the author—such as maps, photographs, drawings, or charts—is usually produced under a "work made for hire" contract (see 4.9–12). Even if no credit is required under such an arrangement, professional courtesy dictates mentioning the creator (unless the illustration is legibly signed and the signature reproduced).

Map by Kevin Hand
Photograph by Ted Lacey
Drawing by Barbara Smith

3.34 **Crediting material obtained free of charge.** For material that the author has obtained free and without restrictions on its use, the credit line may use the word *courtesy*.

Photograph courtesy of Ford Motor Company

Mies at the groundbreaking ceremony of the National Gallery, September 1965. Courtesy of Reinhard Friedrich.

Such material would include illustrations subject to certain Creative Commons licenses. For a discussion of such licenses, see 4.62.

3.35 **Crediting material in the public domain.** Illustrations from works in the public domain (see 4.19–33) may be reproduced without permission. For readers' information, however, a credit line is appropriate.

Illustration by Joseph Pennell for Henry James, *English Hours* (Boston, 1905), facing p. 82.

Reprinted from John D. Shortridge, *Italian Harpsichord-Building in the 16th and 17th Centuries*, US National Museum Bulletin 225 (Washington, DC, 1960).

3.36 **Crediting agency material.** Photographs of prints, drawings, paintings, and the like obtained from a commercial agency usually require a credit line.

Woodcut from Historical Pictures Service, Chicago
Photograph from Wide World Photos

3.37 **Crediting adapted material.** An author creating an illustration adjusted from, or using data from, another source should credit that source for reasons of professional courtesy and readers' information.

Figure 1.2. Weight increase of captive pandas during the first years of life. (Data from New York Zoological Park; National Zoological Park; Giron 1980.)

Adapted from Schwartz (2016, fig. 3.9).

Lists of Illustrations

3.38 **When to include a list of illustrations.** For book-length printed works, the criterion for when to include a list of illustrations is whether the illustrations are of intrinsic interest apart from the text they illustrate. A book on Roman architecture, illustrated by photographs of ancient buildings, would benefit from a list. Electronic works will often include a list as an aid to navigation. In a printed work, a list of illustrations, if included, usually follows the table of contents. A list of illustrations may occasionally double as a list of credits if these do not appear with the illustrations themselves (see 3.30). For guidelines and examples, see 1.39 and figures 1.6, 1.7.

3.39 **Listing illustrations from a gallery.** Illustrations that are to appear in printed galleries are not always listed separately. For example, in a book containing interspersed line art and two photo galleries, a line reading "Photographs follow pages 228 and 332" might be inserted after the detailed list of figures. If all the illustrations were in galleries, that line could appear at the end of the table of contents (see fig. 1.5). (All illustrations, including those in galleries, should be listed if integral to the text.)

3.40 **Shortening captions for a list of illustrations.** In the list of illustrations, long captions should be shortened to a single line (or two at the most).

The number at the end of each of the two entry examples indicates the page on which the illustration would be found.

[*Caption*] Fig. 18. The White Garden, reduced to its bare bones in early spring. The box hedges, which are still cut by hand, have to be carefully kept in scale with the small and complex garden as well as in keeping with the plants inside the "boxes."

[*Entry in list*] 18. The White Garden in early spring 43

[*Caption*] Plate 21. The tall trees of the valley, planted by Russell Page, are reflected among the water lilies, *Nymphaea*, and pickerelweed, *Pontederia cordata*.

[*Entry in list*] 21. Page's tall trees reflected among water lilies 75

Charts

3.41 **Charts defined.** A chart, also called a graph, is a device that presents data in a simple, comprehensible form—often along a set of *x* and *y* axes. A chart is considered line art and should be numbered and labeled as a figure (fig. 1, fig. 2, etc.). It should be used only if it summarizes the data more effectively than mere words can. While integral to the text, it should, like a table, make sense on its own terms. For guidance in chart design, consult Edward R. Tufte, *The Visual Display of Quantitative Information* (bibliog. 2.2). Charts intended for black-and-white reproduction should not be created in color. For an example of a typical chart, see figure 3.8. Figure 3.9—essentially a three-part graph—is a less typical example.

3.42 **Consistency among charts.** Where two or more charts are used within a work, especially if they deal with comparable material, they should follow a consistent style in graphics and typography. Whatever graphic device is used, elements of the same kind must always be represented in the same way. Different visual effects should be used only to distinguish one element from another, never just for variety.

3.43 **Axes and curves in graphs.** Both the *x* (horizontal) and the *y* (vertical) axes should be labeled (as in fig. 3.8); the axes serve a function similar to that of column heads and stubs in a table (see 3.52). The label on the *y* axis is read from the bottom up, though it may instead appear at the top of the axis. Curves are usually presented in graphically distinct forms—for example, one may be a continuous line, another a broken line. The elements in a bar chart or a pie chart that correspond to curves—the bars or the wedges—are also usually distinct. Use black and white for curves or fills rather than shading or color unless your publisher allows shading or color in appropriately prepared electronic files (see 3.19). All such elements should be labeled or else identified in a key or in the caption (see 3.7, 3.25).

3.44 **Chart titles and labels.** The title of a chart appears as part of the caption, immediately following the figure number, and is capitalized sentence-style (see 8.158). See 3.7; compare 3.54. Labels, the descriptive items within a chart, are normally lowercased (with the exception of proper nouns or other terms that would be capitalized in running text); if phrases, they may be capitalized sentence-style. Labels may be explained or discussed in a caption as needed (as in fig. 3.9).

3.45 **Abbreviations in labels.** Abbreviations and symbols may be used in labels as long as they are easily recognizable or explained in a key or in the caption. (The meaning of any abbreviation taken from the text should be clear from the figure alone in case the figure is reproduced in another context, apart from the text.) A form such as "US$millions" may be more appropriate for nonspecialized (or non-English-speaking) readers than "US$M," but the shorter form is acceptable if readers will find it clear and it is used consistently. Numbers and abbreviations are covered in chapters 9 and 10.

3.46 **Genealogical and pedigree charts.** Some charts show relationships between elements in a way that cannot be conveniently arranged along axes or into rows and columns. Charts that show family or genetic structure, in particular, may require a different visual arrangement that highlights multiple relationships. A genealogical chart (often referred to as a table), for example, attempts to show important relationships within a family or several families by means of branching and connecting lines. Figure 3.10 illustrates the complicated connection of Constantine the Great to Hilderic, King of the Vandals. These charts require careful planning to illustrate relationships with minimal crossing of lines or extraneous data and, for a printed work, to remain within a reproducible shape and size. Similar to the genealogical chart is the pedigree chart, used mainly in genealogical works. These fan-shaped diagrams illustrate the ancestry of a given person, typically detailing the two parents, four grandparents, eight great-grandparents, and sixteen great-great-grandparents. They may also show several generations of offspring from a single pair of ancestors and can be used to trace the inheritance of a trait or disorder.

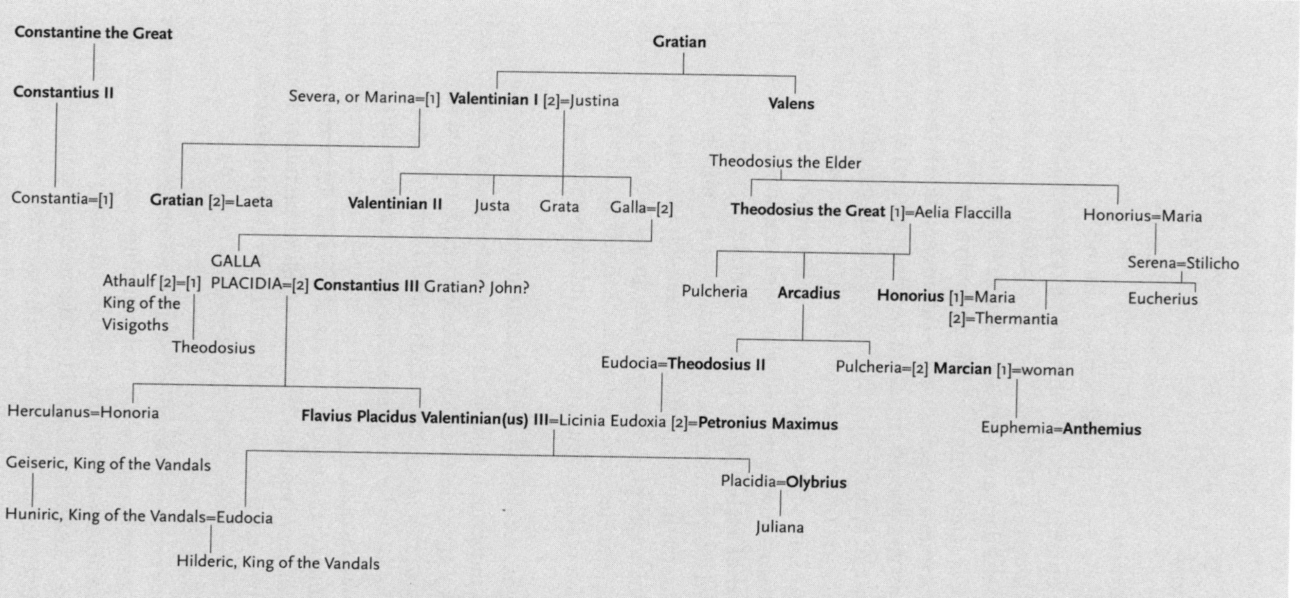

Fig. 18.5. The family of Galla Placidia Augusta. Stemmata are simplified; emperors are shown in boldface type.

FIGURE 3.10. A genealogical chart (see 3.46).

Tables

Introduction

3.47 **Table preparation.** This section describes and illustrates the basic elements of a table and accepted ways of editing, arranging, and typesetting these elements. No one table in this chapter should be taken as a prototype; all merely illustrate workable patterns and may be adapted according to the data and the potential users of the tables. Though most tables can be created using the table editor in a word processor, they are nonetheless expensive (i.e., time-consuming) both to typeset and to correct in proofs and should therefore be designed and constructed with care. It is wise to consult the publisher on the appropriate number, size, and physical form of any tables to be included in a work. A table should be as simple as the material allows and understandable on its own; even a reader unfamiliar with the material presented should be able to make general sense of a table. The text may highlight the main points in a table and summarize its message but should not duplicate the details. For excellent advice on table preparation, consult the *Publication Manual of the American Psychological Association* (bibliog. 1.1). For specific instructions on preparing the electronic files, consult your publisher. Chicago offers instructions for table preparation on its journals website.

3.48 **Use of tables.** A table offers an excellent means of presenting a large number of individual, similar facts so that they are easy to scan and compare. A simple table can give information that would require several paragraphs to present textually, and it can do so more clearly. Tables published online allow for the presentation of even more data, well beyond what may be practical in print. Tables are most appropriate for scientific, statistical, financial, and other technical material. In certain contexts—if, for example, exact values are not essential to an author's argument—a graph or a bar chart (see 3.41), or plain text, may more effectively present the data.

3.49 **Consistency among tables.** Because a prime virtue of tables is easy comparison, consistency in style is indispensable both within one table and among several. A consistent style for titles, column heads, abbreviations, and the like should be followed for all tables in a single work. Similarly, choices related to line spacing, indentation, fonts, rules, and other distinguishing features must be made uniformly for all tables in a work. Certain tables, however, may require rules or other devices not needed in other tables in the same work.

Table Numbering and Placement

3.50 **Table numbers and text references.** Tables should be numbered separately from any illustrations (table 1, table 2, etc.). In a book with many tables, or with chapters by different authors, double numeration by chapter is often used, as it is for illustrations (table 1.1, table 1.2, . . . , table 2.2, table 2.3, . . . , etc.; see 3.11). Every table should be cited in the text by the number rather than by location relative to the text, either directly or parenthetically (but see 3.51).

> The first column of table 2 displays the results of a model predicting the age trajectory of health, controlling for differences by cohort and excluding all other predictors.

> Ethnographic observation brought to light four analytically distinct but empirically interrelated types of worker response to the new regimes (see table 5.3).

Note that the word *table* is lowercased in text references. (In some publications, such terms are routinely capitalized whenever they appear with a number.) Table numbers follow the order in which the tables are to appear in the text, and first mentions should follow that order as well. (But where context demands a reference to a table in a subsequent chapter of a book, such wording as "A different set of variables is presented in chapter 5, table 10" may be appropriate.) Each table, even in a closely related set, should be given its own number (tables 14, 15, and 16, *rather than* tables 14A–C). For table numbers and titles, see 3.54.

3.51 **Placement of tables relative to the text.** A simple list or other tabular matter that requires no more than a few columns can usually be presented in the run of text and left unnumbered and untitled (see, e.g., the two-column list at 1.4 in this manual). A numbered table should appear as soon as possible after the first text reference to it. To accommodate page makeup, tables may break over one or more pages or be presented broadside across facing pages (see 3.86, 3.87). The author or (if the author has not done so) the editor must provide callouts that indicate in the manuscript the preferred location for each numbered table (see 2.30). Note that a *callout* (e.g., "table 3 about here") is an instruction for typesetting or production and will not appear in the published work (for *text references*, which are addressed to readers, see 3.50). In print, most tables that run to less than a page will appear at either the top or the bottom of a page. In electronic formats, tables may be marked up and presented with the run of text (sometimes as a thumbnail image that links to the full table). See also 3.8.

The Parts of a Table

3.52 **Table structure and use.** A table normally consists of rows and columns, which are analogous to the horizontal (x) and vertical (y) axes of a graph, respectively. The data in most tables include two sets of variables. One set of variables is defined in the top row of a table, in the column headings (see 3.56); the other set is defined along the far left-hand column of the table by the stub entries (see 3.59). If the data consist of dependent and independent variables, the independent variables are usually presented in the stub column, though this choice is sometimes limited by the physical dimensions of the table (see 3.86). The intersection between a row defined by a stub entry and a column defined by a column head is a cell (sometimes called a data cell). The anatomy of a basic table is presented in figure 3.11.

3.53 **Horizontal and vertical rules.** To produce a clear, professional-looking table, rules should be used sparingly. Many tables will require just three rules, all of them horizontal—one at the very top of the table, below the title and above the column heads; one just below the column heads; and one at the bottom of the table, along the bottom of the last row, above any notes to the table. Additional horizontal rules may be required to

TABLE 1. Table title

	Spanner head[a]		Spanner head	
Stub column head	Column head	Column head	Column head	Column head
Stub entry				
Stub subentry	0.00	0.00	0.00[b]	0.00
Stub subentry	0.00	0.00	0.00	0.00
Stub entry[c]				
Stub subentry	0.00	0.00	0.00	0.00
Stub subentry	0.00	0.00	0.00	0.00
Stub entry	0.00	0.00	0.00[b]	0.00

Note: General note to table. A general note might be used to explain how to interpret the data.

Source: A source note acknowledges the source of the data, if not the author's own.

[a] Note to the first spanner head.

[b] Note that applies to the data in two different data cells.

[c] Note to the second stub entry.

FIGURE 3.11. A five-column table modeling the basic parts of a table discussed in 3.52–69.

separate spanner heads from column heads (see 3.57) or to enclose cut-in heads (see 3.58). A rule above a row of totals is traditional but not essential (unless required by a journal or series style). See also 3.63. Vertical rules should be used sparingly—for example, when a table is doubled up (see 3.86) or as an aid to comprehension in an especially long or complex table (such as the twelve-page hyphenation guide at the end of chapter 7 of this manual; see 7.89).

3.54 **Table numbers and titles.** Table titles should be as succinct as possible and should not suggest any interpretation of the data. For example, a title such as "Grammar and punctuation errors at suburban schools" is preferable to "High degree of grammar and punctuation errors at suburban schools." Titles should be in noun form, and participles are preferred to relative clauses: for example, "Households subscribing to à la carte channels," not "Households that subscribe to à la carte channels." Table titles may be capitalized in sentence style (see 8.158), as in the examples in this chapter, or in the more traditional headline style (see 8.159), as long as one style prevails throughout the work. The title, which appears above the table, usually follows the number on the same line, separated by punctuation or by space and typographic distinction (as in the second example, which uses an em space; see 6.120). (Less commonly, the number appears on a line by itself, the title starting a new line.) The number is always preceded by the word *table.*

Table 6. Ratios of parental income coefficients to SAT score coefficients

Table 12 Fertilizer treatment effects on *Lythrum salicaria* and *Penthorum sedoides*

For table numbering and placement, see 3.50–51.

3.55 **Parenthetical information in table titles.** Important explanatory or statistical information is often included in parentheses in a title. Such material should be set in sentence style even if the main title is in headline style. More detailed information should go in a note to the table (see 3.78, 3.79).

Federal employees in the Progressive Era (total plus selected agencies)
Scan statistics S_L of varying lengths L for sib-pair data (broad diagnosis)
Gender as a factor in successful business transactions ($N = 4{,}400$)

For the use of *N* in statistical tables, see 3.85.

TABLE 2. Real-world magnitudes of the relationship between tort reform and death rates

Tort reform	Annual death rates (%)	Number of deaths in 2000	Deaths across all years
Cap on noneconomic damages	-3.54	-333	-5,242
Higher evidence standard for punitive damages	-2.57	-982	-11,798
Product liability reform	-3.83	-1,267	-16,841
Prejudgment interest reform	-4.88	-647	-9,060
Collateral source reform			
Offset awards	+4.71	+938	+14,160
Admit evidence	+2.43	+294	+4,468
Net effect		-1,998	-24,314

Note: Values presented are average changes. These computations are based on the coefficients from the primary regression (table 3) and the average annual populations and average annual death rates in the states that had each reform. The sums of the individual reforms differ by one from the net effects owing to rounding.

FIGURE 3.12. A four-column table with two levels of stub entries (*first column*). Note the parenthetical indication in the second column head, specifying percentages for the values in that column (see 3.56).

3.56 **Column heads.** Space being at a premium, column heads should be as brief as possible and are best capitalized sentence-style (as in all examples in this chapter). As long as their meaning is clear to readers, abbreviations may be used as needed. The first column (the stub) does not always require a head (see 3.59). In a work that includes a number of tables, column heads should be treated consistently. Like table titles, a column head may require an indication of the unit of measurement used or some other clarification of the data in the column. Such material, which may consist of a symbol or an abbreviation ($, %, km, *n*, and so on), should follow the column head in parentheses (see fig. 3.12). Parentheses may also be used in column heads when some of the data in the cells are in parentheses. For example, a column head might read "Children with positive results, % (no. positive/no. tested)," and a cell under this head could contain "27.3 (6/22)." If columns must be numbered for text reference, use arabic numerals in parentheses, centered immediately below the column head, above the rule separating the head from the column (see also 3.86).

3.57 **Spanner heads.** When a table demands column heads of two or more levels—when related columns require both a collective head and individual heads—spanner heads, or spanners (sometimes called decked heads), are used. A horizontal rule, called a spanner rule (or straddle), appears between the spanner and the column heads to show which columns the spanner applies to (see figs. 3.11, 3.13). For ease of reading, spanner heads should seldom exceed two levels.

3.58 **Cut-in heads.** Cut-in heads, spanning all columns but the first, may be used as subheads within a table. They usually appear between horizontal rules (see fig. 3.14), though extra vertical space above each head may be used instead. An exceptionally long table with one or more cut-in heads may be a candidate for division into two or more tables.

3.59 **Stub entries.** The left-hand column of a table, known as the stub, is usually a vertical listing of categories about which information is given in the corresponding columns to the right. If all the entries are of like kind, the stub usually carries a column head (e.g., "Tort reform" in fig. 3.12); even a general head such as "Characteristic" or "Variable" or "Year" aids readers. If the entries are self-explanatory (as in fig. 3.14), a head may be omitted from the stub; a head may also be omitted if the entries are too unlike (as in fig. 3.16). If the stub entries are words, they are capitalized sentence-style. Unless they are questions, they carry no end punctuation. They should be consistent in syntax: Authors, Publishers, Printers (*not* Authors, Publishing concerns, Operates print shop). Some tables do not include a stub (see 3.70).

3.60 **Stub entries with subheads.** Items in the stub may form a straight sequential list (e.g., all the states in the Union listed alphabetically) or a classified list (e.g., the states listed by geographic region, with a subhead for each region). The first word in a subentry as well as in a main entry is capitalized, to avoid confusion with runover lines. Subentries are further distinguished from main entries by being indented (as in fig. 3.12), or italics may be used for the main entries and roman for the subentries. A combination of italics and indents may also be used, especially if subsubentries are required. There is generally no need for colons following main entries, but a particular journal style may require them. See also 3.61.

3.61 **Runover lines in stub columns.** If there are no subentries, runover lines in stub entries should be indented (typically by one em in typeset copy). Only if there is extra space between rows should runovers be set flush left. If there are indented subentries, any runover lines must be more deeply indented than the lowest level of subentry (see fig. 3.12). Runovers from main entries and from subentries carry the same indent from

TABLE 3. Survey responses from patients who received intravenous (IV) prostanoids at center 1 in 2006

Question type and characteristic	No. (%) of patients, by prostanoid received		
	Epoprostenol (*n* = 48)	Treprostinil (*n* = 24)	*P*
IV catheter–related question			
Person responsible for care of IV catheter			
Patient	22 (47)	10 (43)	
Adult caregiver	23 (49)	13 (57)	
Both	2 (4)	0 (0)	.82
Catheter type			
Groshong	23 (50)	12 (50)	
Broviac	23 (50)	12 (50)	1.00
Catheter-dressing type			
Occlusive	27 (57)	15 (63)	
Nonocclusive	20 (43)	9 (38)	.68
Allowed >2 days between changes of dressing	14 (29)	7 (29)	1.00
Used sterile gloves when changing dressings	38 (79)	17 (71)	.43
Used mask when changing dressings	28 (58)	13 (54)	.74
Always washed hands before changing dressings	46 (96)	22 (92)	.60
Medication-related question			
Person responsible for medication preparation			
Patient	21 (45)	12 (52)	
Adult caregiver	24 (51)	10 (43)	
Both	2 (4)	1 (4)	.82
Used needleless device to access vial of medication or diluent[a]	4 (8)	5 (21)	.15
Cleaned top of vial of medication or diluenta with alcohol before use	45 (94)	24 (100)	.55
Always washed hands before medication preparation	46 (96)	22 (92)	.60
Miscellaneous question			
Used a swimming pool or hot tub	3 (6)	4 (17)	.18

[a] Refers to the treprostinil vial for patients who received treprostinil and to the diluent vial for patients who received epoprostenol.

FIGURE 3.13. A four-column table with a spanner head across the second and third columns, separated from the column heads by a horizontal rule (see 3.57). Note the three levels of stub entries (see 3.60). Note also that the spanner head specifies two units for each column—number and, in parentheses, percentage (see 3.56).

TABLE 4. Distribution of estimated school quality

	All schools	Rural	Urban
	OLS estimates[a]		
Mean	−.120	−.178	−.063
Minimum	−.72	−.72	−.30
Maximum	.33	.33	.18
	MLE estimates[b]		
Mean	−.063	−.101	−.025
Minimum	−.43	−.43	−.26
Maximum	.40	.40	.17

Note: School quality is measured as proportional deviations from Taha Hussein School.

[a] School-quality estimates from col. 1, table 1.

[b] School-quality estimates from col. 3, table 1.

FIGURE 3.14. A four-column table with two cut-in heads ("OLS estimates" and "MLE estimates") across three columns, separated by horizontal rules (see 3.58); a general note (see 3.78); and two lettered footnotes (see 3.79).

the left margin (in typeset copy, typically one em farther to the right than the indent for the lowest level of subentry). See also 6.120.

3.62 **Abbreviations in stub columns.** As in column heads (see 3.56), where space is at a premium, symbols or abbreviations ($, %, km, *n*, and so on) are acceptable in the stub. Ditto marks (" ") to indicate information that repeats from one row to the next are not, however, since they save no space and make work for readers. Any nonstandard abbreviations must be defined in a table footnote (see 3.79).

3.63 **Totals.** When the word *Total* appears at the foot of the stub, it is often indented more deeply than the greatest indent above (see fig. 3.21) or distinguished typographically (see fig. 3.15). See also 3.74, 3.75.

3.64 **Using leaders with stub entries.** Leaders—several spaced periods following a stub entry—are sometimes used in a table where the connection between the stub entries and the rows they apply to would otherwise be unclear. Some journals routinely use leaders in stubs (see fig. 3.16); books use them more rarely. Another practice—used routinely by some journals—is to apply shading to every other row.

TABLE 5. State expansion in the Progressive Era: Number of federal employees (total plus selected agencies)

Selected agencies	1909	1917	Increase (%)
Dept. of Agriculture	11,279	20,269	79.7
Interstate Commerce Commission	560	2,370	323.2
Dept. of Justice	3,198	4,512	41.1
Dept. of Commerce and Labor[a]	11,999	14,993	25.0
Dept. of the Navy[b]	3,390	6,420	89.4
Dept. of War[c]	22,292	30,870	38.5
Dept. of the Interior[d]	17,900	22,478	25.6
Federal Reserve Board	...	75	
Civil Service Commission	193	276	43.0
Federal Trade Commission	...	244	
Shipping Board	...	22	
Total			
DC and non-DC	342,159	497,867[e]	45.5
Excluding Post Office	136,799	198,199	44.9

Sources: Reports of the United States Civil Service Commission (Washington, DC: GPO): 1910, table 19; 1917, tables 9–10; 1919, p. vi; U.S. Department of Commerce, Bureau of the Census, *Statistical Abstract of the United States, 1917* (Washington, DC: GPO, 1918), table 392.

[a]The Departments of Commerce and Labor were combined until 1913. The Civil Service Commission continued to combine their employees in its subsequent reports through 1917. Separate employment figures for the Labor Department, taken from *The Anvil and the Plow: A History of the Department of Labor* (Washington, DC: GPO, 1963), appendix, table 6, show an essentially stable personnel level (2,000 in 1913, 2,037 in 1917). The bulk of employees (1,740) were attached to the Bureau of Immigration and Naturalization in 1917. The Bureau of Labor Statistics was second in importance, with 104. The Children's Bureau had 103, an increase of 88 from 1913; and the Conciliation Service had only 12, taken from the secretary's personal allotment. In the next two years of wartime, given new labor-market and conciliation functions, the departments' personnel would almost triple; however, the number fell back sharply in 1920.

[b]Exclusive of trade and labor employees.

[c]Excludes "ordinance and miscellaneous" categories.

[d]Includes Land, Pension, Indian, and Reclamation Services.

[e]Excludes Panama Canal workforce.

FIGURE 3.15. Four-column table with *Total* appearing in italics, to distinguish it from the stub entries above and below. Compare figure 3.21. See also 3.63. Also note the use of ellipsis dots for cells with no data; cells for which data is not applicable are blank. See 3.67.

3.65 **Table body and cells.** Strictly speaking, the table body includes all rows, columns, and heads. Nonetheless, it is often convenient to consider the body of a table as consisting of the points of intersection between the stub entries and the column headings—the real substance of the table. These intersections are called cells (or data cells). The fifth cell in the fourth column of the table in figure 3.12, for example, contains the datum

TABLE 6. Decisions on submitted manuscripts

			Time from receipt to decision							
			Less than 1 month		1–2 months		2–3 months		More than 3 months	
	2006	2005	2006	2005	2006	2005	2006	2005	2006	2005
Accepted										
Original manuscript accepted as submitted or with minor revisions. . .	0	2	0	0	0	0	0	1	0	1
Conditional acceptance of original manuscript; revised version accepted	0	0	0	0	0	0	0	0	0	0
Acceptance of resubmission of revised manuscript.	16	14	2	1	1	0	4	2	9	9
Rejected										
Original manuscript rejected with suggestion of resubmission	34	26	5	3	6	4	3	2	20	17
Original manuscript rejected without suggestion of resubmission	249	260	165	161	34	34	16	18	34	47
Rejection of resubmission of revised manuscript.	22	26	2	0	1	0	2	1	14	26
Total new submissions received	283	288								
Total resubmissions received.	38	41								
Manuscripts withdrawn	0	3								
Total submissions received	321	332	174	165	42	38	25	26	77	100
Percentage of total.	100	100	54	50	13	11	8	8	24	30

FIGURE 3.16. An eleven-column table with three levels of column heads, separated by spanner rules (see 3.57), and with leader dots from stub entries (see 3.64). Note also the two rows of totals; the rule above these rows is common but by no means required (see 3.63).

"+14,160." Though cells are usually occupied by data, they may be empty (see 3.67).

3.66 **Column data.** Whenever possible, columns should carry the same kinds of information. For instance, amounts of money should appear in one column, percentages in another, and information expressed in words in another (though two types of data can share the same column, as in the table in fig. 3.13; see 3.69). No column should contain identical information in all the cells; such information is better handled in a footnote.

3.67 **Empty cells.** If a column head does not apply to one of the entries in the stub, the cell should either be left blank or, better, filled in by an em dash (see 6.75) or three unspaced ellipsis dots (...). If a distinction is needed between "not applicable" and "no data available," a blank cell may be used for the former and an em dash or ellipsis dots for "no data" (see fig. 3.15). If this distinction is not clear from the text, a note may be added to the table. (Alternatively, the abbreviations *n/a* and *n.d.* may be used, with definitions given in a note.) A zero means literally that the quantity in a cell is zero (see figs. 3.13, 3.16).

3.68 **Matrixes.** A matrix is a tabular structure designed to show reciprocal relationships within a group of individuals, concepts, or whatever. In a matrix, the stub entries are identical to the column heads; therefore, the cells present two identical sets of intersections. The cells that would contain repeated data may be left blank if the relational order is not significant (see fig. 3.17); in some matrixes, the intersection of matching heads may be left blank or marked with an em dash or ellipsis dots (as in fig. 3.18). See also 3.67.

3.69 **Presenting multiple values in a single cell.** To allow for fewer columns, a single cell may contain two values, with one appearing in parentheses (see fig. 3.13). Such cases should be clarified in the column heading (see 3.56) or in a note.

Cell Alignment and Formatting

3.70 **Alignment of rows.** Each cell in a row aligns with the stub entry to which it belongs. If the stub entry occupies more than one line, the cell entry is normally aligned on the last line of the stub entry (see fig. 3.13). But if both the stub and one or more cells contain more than one line, the first lines are aligned throughout the body of the table. First lines are also aligned in a table where the content of each column is of the same

TABLE 7. Innovations in measures of Amgen operating performance and stock market returns: Correlation matrix for the variables

	Revenue	Net income	Operating cash flow	Free cash flow	S&P 500 return	CRSP return
Revenue	1.00					
Net income	.03	1.00				
Operating cash flow	−.07	.91	1.00			
Free cash flow	.09	.12	.04	1.00		
S&P 500 return	.05	.04	.22	.16	1.00	
CRSP return	.08	.00	.19	.16	.99	1.00

Note: For revenue, the innovation is defined as the log-first difference. For all the other operating variables, it is the arithmetic-first difference.

FIGURE 3.17. A seven-column matrix, in which the six column heads are identical to the six stub entries. Those cells that repeat order-independent relationships from other cells are left blank. See 3.68.

TABLE 8. Average Euclidean distances between populations, calculated from morphological data

Population	Chunliao	Lona	Yunshanchau	Tunchiu	Tenchu	Hohuanshan	Tatachia
Chunliao	...						
Lona	.57	...					
Yunshanchau	.75	1.25	...				
Tunchiu	.71	1.03	.78	...			
Tenchu	1.15	1.10	1.59	.97	...		
Hohuanshan	1.51	1.43	2.00	1.65	1.16	...	
Tatachia	1.85	2.03	2.17	1.69	1.24	1.55	...

FIGURE 3.18. An eight-column matrix. The intersections of like columns and stub entries are marked with ellipsis dots. See 3.68.

sort—in other words, where the first column is not a stub as described in 3.59 (see fig. 3.19). See also 3.71.

3.71 **Alignment of column heads.** Column heads that share a row align on the baseline; if any head occupies more than one line, all the heads in that row align on the last (lowest) line. Each column head except in the stub column is normally centered on the longest (i.e., widest) cell entry. If the longest entry is unusually long, adjustment may be necessary to give an appearance of balance. If centering does not work, align column heads

TABLE 9. Role-style differentiae in the Lewin, Lippitt, and White "group atmosphere" studies

Authoritarian	Democratic	Laissez-faire
All determination of policy by leader	All policies a matter of group discussion and decision, encouraged and assisted by the leader	Complete freedom for group or individual decision, with a minimum of leader participation
Techniques and activity steps dictated by the authority, one at a time, so that future steps were uncertain to a large degree	Activity perspective gained during discussion period. General steps to group goal sketched; when advice was needed, the leader suggested two or more alternative procedures from which choice could be made	Various materials supplied by leader, who made clear a willingness to supply technical information when asked. He took no other part in work discussion
Leader usually dictated the task and companion of each member	Members were free to work with whomever they chose, and division of tasks was left to the group	Complete nonparticipation of the leader
Leader tended to be "personal" in praise and criticism of each member's work; remained aloof from active group participation except when demonstrating	Leader was "objective" in praise and criticism and tried to be a regular group member in spirit without doing too much work	Leader did not comment on member activities unless questioned, did not attempt to appraise or regulate the course of events

FIGURE 3.19. Three-column table with no stub entries (see 3.59, 3.70).

and cells on the left. The stub head and entries are always aligned on the left.

3.72 **Alignment of numbers within columns.** Within a column, numbers without decimal points are usually aligned on the last digit, "ranged right" (see fig. 3.16). If the numbers include decimal points, they are typically aligned on the decimal point (see fig. 3.13). For quantities less than 1.0, zeros do not need to be added before the decimal in a table unless prescribed by a journal or series style (though they would usually be required in running text). See also 9.19. Where spaces rather than commas are used to separate groups of digits (see 9.55), alignment is made on the implicit comma. In all these arrangements, the column of numerals as a whole is usually centered within the column on the longest (i.e., widest)

TABLE 10. Descriptive statistics

Variable	Mean	Standard deviation
Cohort dummy		
1946	.128	.33
1947	.140	.35
1948	.145	.35
1949	.148	.35
1950	.145	.35
1951	.145	.35
1952	.148	.35
Education dummy		
Less than *baccalauréat*	.718	.45
Baccalauréat only	.096	.29
University diploma (*bac* + 2)	.074	.26
University degree	.111	.31
Years of higher education	1.440	2.47
Wage (log)	9.170	.49
Middle-class family background	.246	.43
N	26,371	26,371

Source: Labor Force Survey 1990, 1993, 1996, and 1999.

Note: Sample is male wage earners born between 1946 and 1952.

FIGURE 3.20. Three-column table in which values are aligned on the decimal point except for *N* values (*last row*); see 3.72.

numeral. A column including different kinds of numbers is best aligned on the ones that occur most frequently (as in the table in fig. 3.20, in which most of the values are aligned on the decimal point, but the values for *N* are centered; see also 3.85). Ellipses and em dashes are centered (see fig. 3.15).

3.73 **Alignment of columns consisting of words.** When a column consists of words, phrases, or sentences, appearance governs left-right alignment. If no runover lines are required, entries may be centered. Longer entries usually look better if they begin flush left. Runover lines may be indented or, if enough space is left between entries, aligned flush left with the first line (as in fig. 3.19).

3.74 **Format for totals, averages, and means.** Extra vertical space or short rules sometimes appear above totals at the foot of columns but may equally well be omitted. No rules, however, should appear above averages or means. Consistency must be maintained and, where applicable, journal or series style followed. The word *Total* in the stub is often

TABLE 11. Samples sizes across language versions, role groups, and years

	Role/group			
Language/year	Undergraduates	Postgraduates	Faculty	Subtotal
American				
2004	38,026	18,330	13,138	69,494
2005	53,954	17,015	12,669	83,638
2006	44,132	18,375	12,169	74,676
Subtotal	136,112	53,720	37,976	227,808
British				
2004	12,853	4,263	2,054	19,170
2005	26,140	7,774	1,900	35,814
2006	9,902	3,357	1,107	14,366
Subtotal	48,895	5,394	5,061	69,350
Total				297,158

FIGURE 3.21. Five-column table with subtotals and total (see 3.63, 3.74).

indented. Subtotals are similarly treated. See figure 3.21. See also 3.63, 3.75.

3.75 **When to use totals.** Totals and subtotals may be included or not, according to how useful they are to the presentation. When the percentages in a column are based on different *n*'s, a final percentage based on the total *N* may be informative and, if so, should be included (see 3.85). Note that rounding often causes a percentage total to be slightly more or less than 100. In such cases the actual value (e.g., 99% or 101%) should be given—if it is given at all—and a footnote should explain the apparent discrepancy. See also 3.63, 3.74.

Notes to Tables

3.76 **Order and placement of notes to tables.** Notes to a table are of four general kinds and, where two or more kinds are needed, should appear in this order: (1) source notes, (2) other notes applying to the whole table, (3) notes applying to specific parts of the table, and (4) notes on significance levels. Notes to a table always appear immediately below the table they belong to (i.e., as table footnotes) and must be numbered separately from the text notes. But if a multipage table contains no general notes and any specific notes pertain only to a single page, these notes may appear at the foot of the printed pages they apply to. In electronic formats, all notes are usually grouped at the bottom of the table (and specific notes may be linked to their references in the table).

3.77 **Acknowledging data in source notes to tables.** If data for a table are not the author's own but are taken from another source or other sources, professional courtesy requires that full acknowledgment be made in an unnumbered footnote. The note is introduced by *Source* or *Sources*, in italics and followed by a colon (see fig. 3.20), though other treatments are acceptable if consistently followed.

Sources: Data from Richard H. Adams Jr., "Remittances, Investment, and Rural Asset Accumulation in Pakistan," *Economic Development and Cultural Change* 47, no. 1 (1998): 155–73; David Bevan, Paul Collier, and Jan Gunning, *Peasants and Government: An Economic Analysis* (Oxford: Clarendon Press, 1989), 125–28.

If the sources are listed in the bibliography or reference list, a shortened form may be used:

Sources: Data from Adams (1998); Bevan, Collier, and Gunning (1989).

Unless fair use applies (see 4.84–94), a table reproduced without change from a published work under copyright requires formal permission. Credit should be given in a source note. See 3.32 for more information about styling credit lines, including examples. For more on source citations, see chapters 14 and 15.

3.78 **Notes applying to the whole table.** A note applying to the table as a whole follows any source note and is introduced by the word *Note*, in italics and followed by a colon, though other treatments are acceptable if consistently followed. See figures 3.11, 3.12, 3.14, 3.17, 3.20. If the substance of a general note can be expressed as a brief phrase, it may be added parenthetically to the title (for examples, see 3.55). Some publications, especially in the sciences, use headnotes, which immediately follow the title and expand on or qualify it; such a headnote is similar to the explanatory information in a figure caption (see 3.21).

3.79 **Notes to specific parts of a table.** For notes that apply to specific parts of a table, superior (superscript) letters, numbers, or symbols may be used; one system should be used consistently across all tables. Though superior letters are generally preferred, the choice may depend on context. Numerals may be preferred for tables whose data consist mainly of words or letters (e.g., tables 11.3, 11.4, and 11.5 in this manual), whereas symbols may be preferred for tables that include mathematical or chemical equations, where superior letters or numerals might be mistaken for exponents. Each table should have its own series of notes—beginning with *a* (usually in roman), 1, or *—separate from the text notes and the notes to other tables. The sequence runs from left to right, top to bottom, as in text. Unlike note reference numbers in text, however, the same letter, number, or symbol is used on two or more elements if the corresponding note applies to them. (A footnote reference attached to a column head is assumed to apply to the items in the column below it; a reference attached to a stub entry applies to that row.) The superior letter, number, or symbol is repeated at the foot of the table at the beginning of the corresponding note and may be followed by a space (if done so consistently) but never by a period. See figures 3.13, 3.14, 3.24. Where symbols are used, the sequence is as follows:

1. * (asterisk; but do not use if *p* values occur in the table; see 3.80)
2. † (dagger)
3. ‡ (double dagger)
4. § (section mark)
5. ‖ (parallels)
6. # (number sign, or pound)

When more symbols are needed, these may be doubled and tripled in the same sequence:

*, †, ‡, etc., **, ††, ‡‡, etc., ***, †††, ‡‡‡, and so on.

3.80 **Notes on significance levels.** If a table contains notes on significance levels (also called probability notes), asterisks may be used as reference marks. If two or three standard significance levels are noted, a single asterisk is used for the least significant level, two for the next higher, and three for the third. If values other than these three are given, however, footnote letters are preferable to asterisks, to avoid misleading the reader. In the note, the letter *p* (probability) is usually lowercase and in italics. Zeros are generally omitted before the decimal point. Probability notes follow all other notes (see fig. 3.22).

$^{*}p < .05$
$^{**}p < .01$
$^{***}p < .001$

These short notes may be set on the same line; if they are spaced, no intervening punctuation is needed, but if they are run together, they should

TABLE 12. Determinants of vote for McClellan in 1864

	Coefficient	SE	Odds ratio
Church seats held by			
Pietist sects (%)	−.454**	.117	.635
Liturgical sects (%)	.356*	.183	1.428
Labor force in manufacturing (%)	−.700**	.269	.497
Dummy = 1 if county above county mean for			
Personal property wealth	−.024	.040	.976
Real estate wealth	−.082*	.039	.921
Free population who are slave owners (%)	.159**	.025	1.172
Free population born in			
Ireland (%)	.009*	.004	1.010
Britain (%)	−.025**	.006	.975
Germany (%)	.013**	.003	1.013
Other foreign country (%)	−.011**	.004	.989
Logarithm of county population	−.053*	.026	.948
Dummy = 1 if region is			
Middle Atlantic	.506**	.062	1.659
East north central	.304**	.074	1.355
West north central	−.199**	.097	.820
Border	.115	.133	1.122
West	.110	.126	1.116
Constant	.374	.269	

Note: Results are from a weighted generalized least squares regression in which the dependent variable is $\log[M_i/(100 - M_i)]$, where M_i is the percentage of the vote cast for McClellan. County characteristics are county characteristics in 1860. N = 941 observations. Adjusted R^2 = .223. Our electoral data come from Clubb, Flanigan, and Zingale (2006). Our county characteristics are from Inter-university Consortium for Political and Social Research (2004), with the exception of the percentage born in a particular country, which we estimated from the 1860 census sample of Ruggles et al. (2004).

*$p < .05$

**$p < .01$

FIGURE 3.22. Four-column table with notes on significance, or probability, levels (p), following a general note (see 3.80).

be separated by semicolons. For more on p values, consult the *Publication Manual of the American Psychological Association* (bibliog. 1.1). Some journals capitalize p, and some give probability values in regular table footnotes.

Editing Tables

3.81 **Editing table content.** Tables should be edited for style—with special attention to matters of capitalization, spelling, punctuation, abbreviations, numbers, and use of symbols. They should be checked for internal consistency, consistency across multiple tables (e.g., to ensure uniform treatment of column heads and stub entries), and consistency with the style of the surrounding text. (The meaning of any abbreviation taken from the text should be clear from the table alone in case the table is reproduced in another context, apart from the text.) Any totals should be checked and discrepancies referred to the author for resolution. As in the text, footnote references must be checked against the footnotes, and the correct sequence of letters or symbols must be verified (see 3.79). Tables should be checked for relevance vis-à-vis the text, and they should be checked alongside each other for redundancy. A lay reader or a nontechnical editor should be able to make logical sense of a table, even if the material is highly technical.

3.82 **"Percent" versus "percentage."** Despite changing usage, Chicago continues to regard *percent* as an adverb ("per, or out of, each hundred," as in *10 percent of the class*)—or, less commonly, an adjective (*a 10 percent raise*)—and to use *percentage* as the noun form (*a significant percentage of her income*). The symbol %, however, may stand for either word. See also 3.84.

3.83 **Number ranges.** Anyone preparing or editing a table must ensure that number ranges do not overlap, that there are no gaps between them, and that they are as precise as the data require. It must be clear whether "up to" or "up to and including" is meant. Dollar amounts, for example, might be given as "less than $5, $5–$9, $10–$14, and $15–$19" (not "$1–$5, $5–$10," etc.). If greater precision is needed, they might be given as "$1.00–$4.99, $5.00–$9.99," and so forth. The symbols < and > must be used only to mean less than and more than. In a table including age ranges, >60 means "more than 60 years old" (*not* "60 and up," which would be represented by ≥60). For ≥ and ≤, insert correct symbols (do not use underline).

3.84 **Signs and symbols in tables.** In a column consisting exclusively of, for example, dollar amounts or percentages, the signs should be omitted from the cells and included in the column head (see 3.56 and figs. 3.12, 3.13) or, occasionally, in the stub entry (see fig. 3.22). Mathematical operational signs preceding quantities in a column of numbers are not necessarily aligned with other such signs but should appear immediately to the left of the numbers they belong to (see fig. 3.12).

3.85 **"N" versus "n."** An italic capital *N* is used in many statistical tables to stand for the total number of a group from which data are drawn (see fig. 3.20). An italic lowercase *n* stands for a portion of the total group

TABLE 13. Relative contents of odd isotopes for heavy elements

Element	Z	Y	Element	Z	Y
Sm	62	1.480	W	74	0.505
Gd	64	0.691	Os	76	0.811
Dy	66	0.930	Pt	78	1.160
Eb	68	0.759	Hg	80	0.500
Yb	70	0.601	Pb	82	0.550
Hf	72	0.440			

FIGURE 3.23. Three-column table doubled into two columns (see 3.86).

(see fig. 3.13). For example, if *N* refers to the total number of subjects (of both sexes) in a study, a lowercase *n* might be used when specifying the number of males and the number of females in the study.

3.86 **Adjusting and checking tables.** When preparing a table for publication, editors and compositors may need to adjust or check its format according to the following general guidelines:

1. *Adjusting long tables and wide tables.* Tables that are long and narrow with few columns but many rows, on the one hand, and very wide tables with many columns but few rows, on the other, may not work well—if at all—especially in print. The remedy for a long, skinny table is to double it up, running the table in two halves, side by side, with the column heads repeated over the second half. This approach can also allow a narrow but not necessarily long table to run the width of a page (see fig. 3.23). For a wide, shallow table, the remedy is to turn it around, making column heads of the stub items and stub items of the column heads; if the table turns out to be too narrow that way, it can then be doubled up. Some tables may need to be presented broadside (rotated ninety degrees counterclockwise and read left to right from the bottom to the top of a page); see figure 3.16. See also 3.52. For long tables, the editor may need to specify whether and where "continued" lines and repeated column heads are allowed (see 3.87) and where footnotes should appear (see 3.79).
2. *Adjusting oversize tables—other options.* If an oversize table cannot be accommodated in a printed work by the remedies suggested above, further editorial or typographic adjustments will be needed. Wording may be shortened or abbreviations used. Omitting the running head when a table takes a full page (see 1.16) allows more space for the table itself. A wide table may extend a little into the left margin if on a verso or the right margin if on a recto or, if it looks better, equally on both sides. For a particularly large table, the publisher may

TABLE 14. Timing of socialist entry into elections and of suffrage reforms

Country	(1)	(2)	(3)	(4)	(5)	(6)	(7)
Austria	1889	1897	1907	—	1919	—	—
Belgium	1885[a]	1894	1894	45.7	1948	38.4	22.2
Denmark	1878[a]	1884	1849	28.1[b]	1915	24.6	23.9
Finland	1899	1907	1906	22.0	1906	—	22.0
France	1879	1893	1876	36.5[c]	1946	33.9	24.9
Germany	1867	1871	1871	25.5	1919	34.2[d]	34.0[d]
Italy	1892[a]	—	1913	—	1945	—	—
Netherlands	1878	1888	1917	—	1917	—	—
Norway	1887	1903	1898	34.1	1913	27.7	28.8
Spain	1879	1910	1907	—	1933	—	—
Sweden	1889	1896	1907	28.9	1921	35.0	37.0
Switzerland	1887	1897	1848	—	—	—	—
United Kingdom	1893[a]	1892[e]	1918	—	1928	—	—

Note: Column headings are as follows: (1) Socialist Party formed; (2) first candidates elected to Parliament; (3) universal male suffrage; (4) workers as a proportion of the electorate in the first elections after universal male suffrage; (5) universal suffrage; (6) workers as a proportion of the electorate in the last election before extension of franchise to women; and (7) workers as a proportion of the electorate in the first election after the extension.

[a] Major socialist or workers' parties existed earlier and dissolved or were repressed.

[b] In 1884, approximate.

[c] In 1902.

[d] Under different borders.

[e] Keir Hardie elected.

FIGURE 3.24. Eight-column table with numbers replacing column heads to reduce width. The heads are defined in a general note to the table. Notes to specific parts of the table are indicated by superior (superscript) letters. See 3.86.

decide to reduce the type size or to publish the table in electronic form only, if that is an option. To reduce excessive width, two other measures (neither very convenient for readers) are worth considering: (1) numbers are used for column heads, and the text of the heads is relegated to footnotes, as illustrated in figure 3.24; or (2) column heads are turned on their sides so that they read up the printed page rather than across.

3. *Checking rules.* The editor should ensure that rules appear as needed and that spanner rules are the right length and are distinct from underlining (so that a rule and not italicized text appears in the typeset version). See 3.53, 3.57.
4. *Checking alignment of numbers and text.* Alignment of rows and columns must be clearly specified in the manuscript. Editors should check to make sure that numbers have been aligned properly (e.g., by decimal point) and that stub entries are aligned with and correspond to the rows to which they apply. See 3.70–75. Old-style numerals (like this: 1938), though elegant as page numbers

TABLE 15. Type of private capital flow (millions of US dollars)

	1992	1993	1994	1995	1996
			Asia		
China					
GDP	469,003	598,765	546,610	711,315	834,311
Current account	6,401	−11,609	6,908	1,618	7,243
Capital inflows	−250	23,474	32,645	38,674	39,966
Equity	7,922	24,266	34,208	36,185	39,981
Bank credits	4,008	2,146	3,786	8,405	10,625
Indonesia					
GDP	139,116	158,007	176,892	202,131	227,370
Current account	−2,780	−2,106	−2,792	−6,431	−7,663
Capital inflows	6,129	5,632	3,839	10,259	10,847
Equity	1,947	2,692	2,573	4,285	5,195
Bank credits	663	1,573	2,030	8,021	12,602
			Latin America		
Argentina					
GDP	228,990	257,842	281,925	279,613	297,460
Current account	−5,462	−7,672	−10,117	−2,768	−3,787
Capital inflows	7,373	9,827	9,279	574	7,033
Equity	4,630	4,038	3,954	4,589	7,375
Bank credits	1,152	9,945	1,139	2,587	959

TABLE 15 (*continued*)

	1992	1993	1994	1995	1996
			Latin America		
Brazil					
GDP	446,580	438,300	546,230	704,167	774,868
Current account	6,089	20	−1,153	−18,136	−23,602
Capital inflows	5,889	7,604	8,020	29,306	33,984
Equity	3,147	4,062	5,333	8,169	15,788
Bank credits	11,077	4,375	9,162	11,443	14,462
Chile					
GDP	41,882	44,474	50,920	65,215	69,218
Current account	−958	−2,554	−1,585	−1,398	−3,744
Capital inflows	3,134	2,996	5,294	2,488	6,781
Equity	876	1,326	2,580	1,959	4,090
Bank credits	2,192	804	1,108	1,100	1,808

FIGURE 3.25. Six-column table with repeated column heads and "continued" indication following a page break (see 3.87).

or in text that contains few numerals, should be avoided in tabular matter because they do not align horizontally as well as (and can be harder to read than) regular "lining" numerals (like this: 1938). (If old-style numerals must be used, a font that includes a fixed-width "tabular" version must be chosen to ensure that figures will align vertically within a column.)

5. *Checking running heads on full-page tables.* The editor should be sure that running heads are omitted on full-page and multipage tables (but see 1.16, 2.115).
6. *Checking typefaces and markup.* In a book that is not part of a series, the designer will set the typographic style for tables, as for the text and other elements. Journals follow their own established style for presentation and markup. Editors should make sure tables are edited in accord with the design, and formatting and markup for electronically prepared tables should be checked to make sure they have been consistently and correctly applied (see also 3.88). For a useful discussion of table design, see Richard Eckersley et al., *Glossary of Typesetting Terms* (bibliog. 2.7).

3.87 **Tables of more than one page ("continued" tables).** For a vertical table of more than one page, the column heads are repeated on each page. For a two-page broadside table—which should be presented on facing pages if at all possible—column heads need not be repeated; for broadside tables that run beyond two pages, column heads are repeated only on each new verso (see also 2.115). Where column heads are repeated, the table number and "continued" should also appear. See figure 3.25. For any table that is likely to run to more than one page, the editor should specify whether "continued" lines and repeated column heads will be needed and where footnotes should appear (usually at the end of the table as a whole; but see 3.76). The editor should also be sure that running heads are omitted on full-page and multipage tables (but see 1.16).

3.88 **Ensuring accessibility for tables.** Publishers concerned about providing content that is accessible to people with disabilities will want to ensure proper table markup for electronic formats. Such markup will enhance accessibility for readers who use text-to-speech and related tools (see 2.73, 2.137). Wherever possible, tables should be rendered as marked-up text rather than as images; if they must be rendered as images—or for an especially complex table—alternative text may be needed (see 3.28). For more information, consult the DIAGRAM Center, a Benetech literacy initiative; see also the Web Accessibility Initiative (WAI) of the World Wide Web Consortium (W3C) and, for EPUB, the Accessibility Guidelines provided by the International Digital Publishing Forum.

4 · Rights, Permissions, and Copyright Administration

WILLIAM S. STRONG

Overview

4.1 **The scope of this chapter.** The foundation on which the entire publishing industry rests is the law of copyright, and a basic knowledge of it is essential for both authors and editors. This chapter gives readers that basic knowledge: how copyright is acquired, how it is owned, what it protects, what rights it comprises, how long it lasts, how it is transferred from one person to another. Once that foundation is laid, the key elements of publishing contracts are discussed, as well as the licensing of rights (what publishers call the "rights and permissions" function). The treatment of rights and permissions includes some guidelines for "fair use." While every effort is made here to be accurate, copyright law is both wide and intricate, and this chapter makes no claim to be exhaustive. Also, this chapter should not be considered legal advice or substitute for a consultation with a knowledgeable attorney in any particular circumstance. (For more detailed treatment of specific issues, see the works listed in sec. 2.3 of the bibliography.)

Copyright Law and the Licensing of Rights

4.2 **Relevant law.** For most publishing purposes the relevant law is the Copyright Act of 1976 (Public Law 94-553), which took effect on January 1, 1978, and the various amendments enacted since then. The 1976 act was a sweeping revision, superseding previous federal law and eliminating (though not retroactively) the body of state law known as common-law copyright. It did not, however, make old learning obsolete. Because prior law continues to govern most pre-1978 works in one way or another, anyone involved with publishing should understand both the old and the new regimes. Both will affect publishing for decades to come. Note that the law discussed in this chapter is that of the United States. The United States and most other countries are members of the Berne Convention, the oldest international copyright treaty. While the Berne Convention and certain other treaties have fostered significant uniformity around the world, anyone dealing with copyrights should bear in mind that, conventions aside, the laws of other countries may contain significant differences from US law.

4.3 **How copyright comes into being.** Whenever a book or article, poem or lecture, database or drama comes into the world, it is automatically covered by copyright so long as it is "fixed" in some "tangible" form and embodies original expression. The term *tangible* applies to more than paper and traditional media; it includes things such as electronic memory. A copyrightable work is "fixed" as long as it is stored in some manner that is not purely transitory. Thus, an email message that is stored in the sender's computer is fixed and copyrightable, but an extemporaneous lecture that is broadcast without being recorded is not.

4.4 **Registration and notice not required.** Although it is advisable to register works with the United States Copyright Office, registration is not a prerequisite to legal protection. The practical reasons for registering are discussed in 4.50. Note that any work protected by US copyright can be registered. This includes not only works created or published in the United States but also those created or published in countries with which the United States has a copyright treaty. Copyright notice is no longer required but is recommended (see also 4.41–46).

4.5 **Original expression.** Copyright protects the original expression contained in a work. The term *expression* means the words, sounds, or images that an author uses to express an idea or convey information. Selection and arrangement of data or of preexisting materials—as in a database or anthology—constitutes expression, even without the addition of the compiler's own words. In any work, copyright protects the author's expression but not the underlying facts, ideas, or theories, no matter how novel those may be. That the expression be *original* for copyright purposes demands less than the term may suggest; the threshold is quite low. The law requires only a modicum of creativity: a simple abstract doodle may be protected. Where compilations of data are concerned, one may not copyright a simple telephone directory, no matter how much labor went into compiling it, but one may copyright such minimal intellectual effort as the selection and arrangement of entries in a price guide to used automobiles. What counts is not quality or novelty but only that the work be original with the author and not copied, consciously or unconsciously, from some other source. When a work includes some material that is not original, only the original material is protected. Thus, copyright in a new, annotated edition of an eighteenth-century book will cover only the annotations.

4.6 **Author the original owner.** Whoever is the author (a term not synonymous with *creator*, as will be seen) controls copyright at the outset and automatically possesses certain rights in the work. How these rights are owned, transferred, and administered is the focus of this chapter.

Varieties of Authorship

4.7 **Individual and joint authors.** For many types of works, the author is likely to be an individual. In scientific, technical, and medical publishing, especially in the realm of journals, a work will more likely than not involve the efforts of more than one author. Such works are typically joint works. As defined by the statute, a joint work is "a work prepared by two or more authors with the intention that their contributions be merged into inseparable or interdependent parts of a unitary whole."

4.8 **Collective works.** Works in which the independent contributions of two or more authors are combined are considered collective, rather than joint, works. Copyright in a collective work as such, which covers the selection and arrangement of materials, belongs to the compiler or editor and is separate from the copyright in each of the various components. Typical examples of collective works are newspapers, anthologies, journal issues, and edited volumes of contributed papers (see 4.58–59).

WORKS MADE FOR HIRE

4.9 **Employer as author.** Another type of authorship is work made for hire. The law regards the employer or other controlling party as the "author" of any such work and hence as the initial copyright owner. Some works are considered made for hire by definition; some can be treated as such by agreement.

4.10 **The three categories of work made for hire.** Present law defines much more stringently than pre-1978 law the conditions that must be met for a work to be considered made for hire. First, the work may be prepared within the scope of a person's employment. Common examples of this type of work made for hire include a story by a staff writer, or a photograph by a staff photographer, in a newspaper or weekly magazine, or marketing copy written by a company's paid staff. Second, a creative party *not* on the payroll will in certain instances be treated as an "employee" if that person is acting as the "agent" of another party. Determining agency is a difficult and somewhat ad hoc task, and involves considerations such as the control of one party over the other party's hours, assignments, and tools used in creating the work. The third type of work made for hire is the specially ordered or commissioned work that both hiring party and creator agree *in writing* to treat as such. This sort of arrangement is available for only a few narrowly defined types of work:

- Contributions to collective works, such as a book review commissioned for a journal
- Contributions to motion pictures or sound recordings
- Translations
- Instructional texts
- Tests
- Atlases
- Compilations of data or existing materials, such as anthologies and directories
- "Supplementary works" such as forewords, bibliographies, indexes, appendixes, textual notes, illustrations, and answer material for tests

A work that qualifies for such treatment will not be considered made for hire unless the written agreement between the commissioning party and the creative party expressly says so. The written agreement can be signed retroactively, although the safer practice is to obtain the parties' signatures before the work is created.

4.11 **Ineligible works.** It bears emphasizing that many kinds of works that could conceivably be commissioned do not qualify as works made for hire no matter what agreement may be made between writer and publisher. Monographs and novels, for example, are not eligible because they are not in any of the specific categories listed above. Thus, copyright in such a work remains with the writer unless expressly assigned. Although for most purposes an assignment of copyright from the author is indistinguishable in practical effect from a work-for-hire agreement, they have different implications for copyright duration (see 4.24) and termination (see 4.38).

4.12 **Joint authorship.** If any one of a group of coauthors is writing on a "for hire" basis, the resulting joint work will be treated as made for hire for copyright duration purposes (see 4.24), even though the other coauthor(s) might be independent and not writing "for hire." Thus, if an in-house researcher and an outside scholar collaborate on a paper, the copyright term given to that paper will be the work-for-hire term.

Rights of the Copyright Owner

4.13 **Rights of reproduction, distribution, and display.** The author of a work possesses, at the beginning, a bundle of rights that collectively make up copyright. They belong originally to the author, who can sell, rent, give away, will, or transfer them in some other way, individually or as a package, to whomever the author wishes. When a work is to be published, the author normally transfers some or all of these rights to the publisher, by formal agreement. Two of these rights are basic from the publisher's point of view: the right to make copies of the work (by printing or by digital reproduction, or both) and the right to distribute such copies to the public—in sum, to publish the work. In the case of online publishing, reproduction and distribution blend into the act of transmitting the work on demand to the reader's computer or other device. A third right—the right of public display—applies to online exploitation of works. A work is publicly displayed when made viewable online; if the user downloads or prints out the material concerned, distribution of a copy also occurs.

4.14 **Derivative work and performance rights.** A fourth and very important right is the right to make what the law terms derivative works—that is, works based on or derived from the original work, such as translations, abridgments, dramatizations, or other adaptations. A revised edition of a published work is generally different enough from the prior edition to qualify as a derivative work with a separate copyright. The fifth basic copyright right, the right of public performance, has only limited relevance for literary works as such; it applies, for example, when a poet gives a public reading of a poem. However, it has great significance for other works, such as motion pictures, that may spring from literary works.

4.15 **Moral rights; integrity of copyright management information.** In addition to the foregoing rights, the law gives the creators of certain works of fine art a so-called moral right against mutilation and misattribution. A dozen or more states have enacted legislation to roughly the same effect as the federal law but generally broader. This moral right, however, whether federal or state, has little effect on publishers (except perhaps while in possession of original artwork) and will not be addressed further here. Authors may also be able under common law to prevent the attribution to them of things that they did not write. In addition, federal law protects the integrity of "copyright management information." This information, for publications, consists of the following:

- The title and other information identifying the work, including the content of the copyright notice
- The name of, and other identifying information about, the author
- The name of, and other identifying information about, the copyright owner, including the content of the copyright notice
- Terms and conditions for use of the work
- Identifying numbers or symbols referring to such information or links to such information

Specifically, the law prevents intentional removal or alteration of copyright management information, or deliberate use of false copyright management information, if done with intent to induce, enable, facilitate, or conceal infringement.

4.16 **Trademark protection of titles and other elements.** Copying only the title of a work would likely not be considered a copyright infringement. But a title may acquire trademark protection under federal or state law or both. Book titles are harder to protect as trademarks than journal or lecture titles, because of judicial and administrative reluctance to give trademark protection to names that are used on only one specific product. Nevertheless, some book titles are clearly protectable; *Gone with the Wind* and *Winnie-the-Pooh* are titles that cannot be used without permission, at least so long as the books remain under copyright. And active franchising such as has occurred with both of those books will enable the trademark to survive long after that, although not in such a way as to prevent reproduction of the book itself, title and all. The same principles would apply to the names of characters or imaginary locales used in a work.

4.17 **Basic versus subsidiary rights.** Whoever controls the copyright in a work, whether author or publisher, may not only exercise those rights directly but also empower or authorize others to exercise them. If, for example, the author of a book has transferred the whole bundle of rights to a publishing house, the publishing house will itself exercise the basic rights of reproducing and distributing (i.e., publishing) the book. It will also be responsible for administering subsidiary rights. These rights (discussed in 4.64 and 4.65) usually involve exploiting markets in which the publishing house is not active. For example, rights for other languages, audio rights, and motion-picture rights involve specialized markets and require special expertise. For this reason, subsidiary rights are likely to be exercised by third parties under license from the publisher, although, if the publisher is part of a large media conglomerate, licensing is often intramural. Part of the publisher's responsibility to the author should be to see that subsidiary rights are exploited as effectively as possible. Licensing subsidiary rights also includes granting what the publishing industry calls *permissions*, a term that refers to such things as the licensing of photocopied or scanned materials for classroom use and allowing others to reproduce an original illustration from the book in a new work.

4.18 **Author retention of subsidiary rights.** Authors of "trade" books—fiction, biography, cookbooks, and other books for the general reader—are more likely than scholarly authors to be represented by agents and to retain some or all subsidiary rights. In such cases, subsidiary rights are licensed directly by the author (through his or her agent) to publishers in other countries, motion-picture producers, and the like. Typically, however, permissions are still handled by the publisher rather than the agent or author.

Copyright and the Public Domain

4.19 **Copyright duration before 1978.** Until January 1, 1978, a dual system of copyright existed in the United States. Common-law copyright, created by the individual states, protected works from the time of their creation until publication, however long that might be. A personal letter written in the eighteenth century but never published was protected as effectively as a 1977 doctoral thesis in the making. In neither case could the document be copied and distributed (that is, published) without the express permission of either the creator of the work or the creator's legal heirs. Statutory, or federal, copyright protected works at the moment of publication and for twenty-eight years thereafter, provided that a proper copyright notice appeared in the published work. See 4.39–46. Thereafter, copyright in the work could be renewed for another twenty-eight years if the original copyright claim had been registered with the United States Copyright Office (a division of the Library of Congress) and if a renewal claim was filed by the appropriate person(s) during the final year of the first term of copyright. Thus, in the normal course of things federal copyright in a work was intended to last for a total of fifty-six years from the date of publication, after which time the work went into the public domain—that is, it became public property and could be reproduced freely. See 4.22.

4.20 **Lengthening of copyright duration in 1978.** To enter the public domain is of course the ultimate fate of all copyrighted works. However, the elaborate system described in 4.19 was replaced as of 1978 by a unitary federal copyright of substantially greater length. Subsequent amendments have lengthened the term yet further and eliminated a number of formalities that used to be required. All these changes have made entering the public domain almost theoretical for works currently being created. As will be discussed below, other changes to the law have given many older works, particularly those originally published outside the United States, an unexpected reprieve (see 4.29).

4.21 **US government works.** Works created by employees of the US government in the course of their official duties are in the public domain. Works created by private parties under government contract, however, are eligible for copyright, although federal contracts often impose certain limitations on such copyright. Works by employees of state governments or governments of other countries are presumptively copyrightable, although state governments rarely attempt to enforce their copyrights.

4.22 **Uses of public-domain works.** Once in the public domain, a work is free for all to use. The use may be direct and simple; for example, Mark Twain's novels have now lost their copyrights and may be republished free of royalty. Or the public-domain works may be the compost from which new works, such as adaptations or other derivative works, spring in due course. Such new works are entitled to copyright, but their copyright is limited to the new material they contain. Determining whether a work has entered the public domain requires attention to complex rules. These are discussed at 4.26–30 and 4.39–46. The rules are also summarized in table 4.1.

DURATION OF COPYRIGHT FOR WORKS CREATED AFTER 1977

4.23 **"Life plus seventy."** Enacted in 1976 and effective on January 1, 1978, the present copyright law did away with the dual system of federal/common-law copyright. Present law is both simpler and more complex regarding copyright duration. It is simpler in that now one unified, federal system protects all works fixed in tangible form from the moment of fixation. It is more complex in that (i) terms of protection differ depending on authorship, and (ii) works existing before 1978 are subject to a variety of special rules. The paradigmatic copyright term, under the new law, is "life plus seventy"—that is, life of the author plus seventy years. (In the case of joint authors, the seventy years are added to the life of the last author to die.) As will be seen below, however, there are many exceptions to this rule.

4.24 **Works made for hire.** Since the owner of the copyright in a work made for hire is not the actual creator of the work (often, indeed, the copyright owner is a corporate entity), the law specifies a fixed term of years for the duration of copyright. This term is ninety-five years from the date of publication or 120 years from the date of creation, whichever is the shorter.

4.25 **Anonymous and pseudonymous works.** The regular rule for duration of copyright cannot be applied if an author publishes anonymously or under a pseudonym. The law prescribes the same fixed term of copyright

TABLE 4.1. Copyright duration

Date of creation/ publication	US or non-US work	Type of authorship	Term of protection
Created after 1977	Either	Single author—individual	Life plus 70 years
		Two or more individual authors	Life of last to die plus 70 years
		Work made for hire	95 years from first publication, or 120 years from creation, whichever expires first
		Pseudonymous	95 years from first publication, or 120 years from creation, unless identity is filed with Copyright Office
		Anonymous	95 years from first publication, or 120 years from creation, unless identity is filed with Copyright Office
Created before 1978 but not published before 2003	Either	Same as any of above	Same as corresponding term above
Created before 1978 but published after 1977 and before 2003	Either	Same as any of above	Same as corresponding term above or until December 31, 1947, whichever is later
Published or registered between January 1, 1964, and December 31, 1977	Either	Same as any of above	95 years from first publication
Published or registered between January 1, 1923, and December 31, 1963	US	Same as any of above	95 years from first publication, if copyright was renewed in 28th year, otherwise now in public domain
Published in the US between January 1, 1923, and December 31, 1963	Non-US	Same as any of above	95 years from first publication
Published abroad between January 1, 1923, and December 31, 1963	Non-US	Same as any of above	95 years from first publication[1]
Published anywhere before 1923	Either	Same as any of above	Public domain[1]

SOURCE: From William S. Strong, *The Copyright Book: A Practical Guide*, 6th ed. (Cambridge, MA: MIT Press). © 2014 Massachusetts Institute of Technology. Used with the kind permission of the publisher.

NOTE: The following special rules apply for special media; these rules supersede all the above except as noted. *Mask works*: 10 years from registration or from first commercial exploitation, whichever occurs first. *Architectural works*: Same as in chart above unless (i) constructed or published before 1990, in which case not under copyright, or (ii) created but neither constructed nor published before 1990, in which case same as in chart above but only if constructed before January 1, 2003, otherwise now in public domain. *Sound recordings made before February 15, 1972*: Protected by state antipiracy laws only, until February 15, 2067, after which date they will be in the public domain.

[1] This rule does not apply in the Ninth Circuit. There, non-US works published before 1978 do not start their US copyright term until publication in the United States.

for these works as for works made for hire—ninety-five years from the date of publication or 120 years from creation, whichever is the shorter. If after publication, however, such an author's name is revealed and recorded in the documents of the Copyright Office, the regular "life plus seventy" rule takes over, unless, of course, the work is made for hire.

DURATION OF COPYRIGHT FOR WORKS CREATED BEFORE 1978

4.26 **Pre-1978 unpublished works.** For unpublished works that were still under common-law copyright when the new law went into effect, there is a transitional rule. Such works are given the same copyright terms as post-1977 works, but in recognition of the fact that their authors might have died so long ago as to make life-plus-seventy meaningless, Congress added two provisos. First, such works were granted protection at least until December 31, 2002. Second, any such work that was ultimately published before December 31, 2002, is protected at least until December 31, 2047. Thus, these late-published works have a copyright term of not less than seventy years from the date the new law went into effect.

4.27 **Pre-1978 works published in the United States.** Works published in the United States before January 1, 1923, are now in the public domain. Works published during the years 1923 through 1963 have a copyright term of ninety-five years from the year of first publication if their copyrights were properly renewed in the twenty-eighth year after first publication. (The safest way to determine this is to commission a search of the Copyright Office records through a copyright attorney or a reputable search firm. Several university libraries have also made Copyright Office renewal records available online.) Works published from 1964 through 1977 will be protected without fail for ninety-five years from first publication, because renewal for such works is automatic. All the above assumes that these works were at all times published with proper copyright notice. For a discussion of copyright notice, see 4.39–46.

4.28 **New copyright for new editions.** When deciding whether a work may be republished without permission, bear in mind that each time a work is materially modified a new copyright comes into being, covering the new or revised material. Thus a seminal treatise published in 1920 is now in the public domain, but the author's revision published in 1934 may not be. One is free to republish the 1920 version, but that may be an empty privilege.

4.29 **Pre-1978 works published outside the United States.** The rules just described do not apply to works by non-US authors first published outside of the United States. Such works are generally protected in their own countries for the life of the author plus fifty or seventy years, depending on the country concerned. In the United States, such works automatically receive the same term of copyright as a pre-1978 US work, but without regard to whether proper copyright notice was used or whether copyright was renewed in the twenty-eighth year after publication. This is so because, effective January 1, 1996, Congress restored to copyright all such works that had forfeited copyright as a result of noncompliance with US notice and renewal requirements but that were still protected in their home country. Copyrights restored in this manner are subject to certain protections given to those who produced copies or derivative works before December 8, 1994, relying on the apparent forfeiture of copyright. Two points should be noted here, however. First, although it is generally assumed that a work published anywhere in the world before 1923 is now in the public domain in the United States, an anomalous decision in the Ninth Circuit Court of Appeals has held that works by non-US authors published abroad prior to 1923 may still be eligible for copyright protection in the United States, if no effort was made at the time to comply with US copyright law. This is out of sync with the rest of US copyright jurisprudence, but it remains the law in California and other states in the Ninth Circuit. Second, it should be noted that the US copyright term for non-US works, even after restoration, does not necessarily synchronize with the protection of those works outside the United States. If a French author of a work published in 1922 lived until 1970, the work would now be in the public domain in the United States but would remain under copyright in France through 2040. If the same author had published another work in 1923, that work would retain copyright in the United States through 2018, still twenty-two years less than in France. As this example shows, publishers who wish to reissue or otherwise make use of such public-domain works need to be aware that markets outside the United States may be foreclosed to them.

4.30 **Eligibility for restoration.** For purposes of the special restoration rules discussed in 4.29, a work is eligible if it was first published outside the United States and if at least one author was not a citizen of the US or domiciled in the US. The only substantial exception is for works published in the United States within thirty days after publication abroad, as had been done by some US publishers to get Berne Convention treatment "by the back door" before the United States became a member of Berne. Such works are not eligible for copyright restoration.

RENEWING COPYRIGHT IN PRE-1978 WORKS

4.31 **Benefits of renewal.** Although renewal of copyright for works published between 1964 and 1977 is now automatic, the law gives certain benefits to those who take the trouble to file actively for renewal. Filing for renewal fixes the ownership of the second-term copyright on the date of filing; automatic renewal vests ownership in whoever could have renewed on the *last day* of the first twenty-eight-year term. A renewal that has been actively obtained constitutes prima facie evidence of copyright and its ownership; the evidentiary value of an automatically renewed copyright is discretionary with the courts. Finally, and most importantly, if the renewal is allowed to happen automatically, existing derivative works can continue to be exploited for the second term of copyright, whereas active renewal gives the renewal-term owner—unless he or she signed a derivative work license explicitly covering the renewal term—the right to relicense derivative-work rights.

4.32 **Renewal by the author.** The author, if living, is the person entitled to file for renewal. Publishers who have obtained renewal-term rights from authors should continue to file for renewal on the author's behalf as they have traditionally done.

4.33 **Renewal if the author is deceased.** Whether renewal occurs by filing or automatically, if the author is not alive, the law allocates the copyright to his or her surviving spouse, children, or other heirs according to complex rules that will not be parsed here.

Assigning or Licensing Copyright

4.34 **Subdividing a copyright.** Copyright is often referred to as a "bundle" of rights. The basic components, as noted above, are the right to reproduce the work, the right to distribute copies of a work to the public, the right to make derivative works, and the rights to perform and display a work publicly. Each of these rights may be separately licensed or assigned. Furthermore, each of them may be carved up into smaller rights along lines of geography, time, or medium. Thus, for example, the right to publish a novel may be carved up so that Publisher A gets North American rights while Publisher B gets United Kingdom rights. A French translation license may be given to Librairie C for a ten-year fixed term. Or Publisher A may receive hardcover rights while Publisher B receives subsequent paperback rights. There is theoretically no end to the ways of subdividing a copyright, other than the limits of human ingenuity and the marketplace.

4.35 **Exclusive versus nonexclusive licenses.** Licenses may be exclusive or nonexclusive. Typically, anyone making a substantial investment in exploiting a license will insist on exclusive rights, whereas persons making ephemeral use at low marginal cost—a typical case being classroom photocopying—need no more than nonexclusive rights. An exclusive licensee is treated in general like an owner of copyright and has standing to sue any infringer of that right. A nonexclusive licensee holds something more like a personal privilege than a property interest, and cannot sue infringers or even, without the permission of the licensor, transfer the license to someone else. While most authorities believe that, by contrast, an exclusive licensee has the power to assign and sublicense the right concerned, a federal court opinion in mid-2002 cast doubt on that presumption. As a precaution, anyone drafting an exclusive license should expressly state that the license may be assigned and sublicensed at the discretion of the licensee.

4.36 **Goals of the parties to a license.** Many issues in license negotiation are common to all contracts: payment terms, duration, allocation of risk, remedies for default, and so on. But in drafting a copyright license, the parties need to be very careful to define clearly the scope of the license, taking into account possible evolution of technologies and markets. The goal of a licensor is to define the licensed right narrowly so as to preserve flexibility for future licensing. The licensee also wants flexibility and therefore seeks to define the licensed right broadly. Both sides, though, have a common interest in seeing that the license is clear and understandable. Drafting a license demands and deserves care and skill, as well as good communication between lawyers and their clients.

4.37 **Payment.** A license and the obligation to pay for that license are usually treated as reciprocal obligations, not mutually dependent ones. Thus the failure of a licensee to pay royalties does not automatically terminate the license and turn the licensee into an infringer. It gives the licensor a claim for contract damages, not a copyright infringement claim. Shrewd licensors will whenever possible reverse this presumption in their contracts, by stipulating that timely payment is a condition of the validity of the license; shrewd licensees will usually resist.

4.38 **Termination of transfers and licenses.** A copyright grant may contain express provisions for termination, triggered by such things as a book going out of print or its sales falling below X copies in a given time period (though the prevalence of ever-available digital editions and the growth of print-on-demand technology create challenges for anyone drafting an "out of print" clause these days). In addition, the statute itself gives individual authors the right to terminate licenses and assignments of copyright under certain conditions. Authors and their families may terminate any post-1977 copyright arrangement after thirty-five years, and a roughly comparable termination right applies to grants made before 1978. (The termination right is not applicable to works made for hire, and does not apply to agreements stipulating that a work is made for hire. See 4.10.) The mechanics of termination, including the determination of who has the right to terminate, are quite complicated and no more will be said here (for additional resources, see bibliog. 2.3).

Copyright Notice

4.39 **Changes to the rules.** No aspect of copyright has caused more grief than the rules of copyright notice. These rules have been responsible for most forfeitures of copyright. Largely a trap for the unwary, they were softened somewhat in 1978 and removed almost entirely in 1989. They were not without purpose or utility, but the rules prevented the United States from joining the Berne Convention, and in the end this and other disadvantages outweighed their utility.

4.40 **Three different regimes.** Congress could not easily dispense with the rules retroactively, however, and the resulting 1989 legislation means that we now operate simultaneously under three doctrines: (1) for works first published on or after March 1, 1989, no copyright notice is required; (2) for works first published in the United States between January 1, 1978, and February 28, 1989, copyright notice must have been used on all copies published before March 1, 1989, with the proviso that certain steps could be taken to redeem deficient notice (see 4.46); and (3) for US works first published before January 1, 1978, the copyright was almost certainly forfeited if the notice was not affixed to all copies; few excuses were or are available. (As noted above, non-US works have been retroactively exempted from these rules.) Notwithstanding the liberality of the new law, continued use of notice is strongly advised to deprive infringers of any possible defense of ignorance. The rules in 4.41–46 should therefore still be followed.

CONTENT OF NOTICE

4.41 **Three elements of the notice.** Under present law, as under the old law, the notice consists of three parts: (1) either the symbol © (preferred because it also suits the requirements of the Universal Copyright Convention), or the word *Copyright*, or the abbreviation *Copr.*; (2) the year of first publication; and (3) the name of the copyright owner. Many publishers also add the phrase "all rights reserved," and there is no harm in doing so, but the putative advantages of it (which were limited to Latin America) have all but vanished. (Other admonitions—e.g., "No part of this work may be reproduced in any manner without the express written consent of the publisher"—may be useful as No Trespassing signs but have no legal necessity or effect.) The year of first publication is not needed for greeting cards, postcards, stationery, and certain other works not germane to the publishing industry. Where a work is in its renewal term of copyright, it is customary, but not required, to include the year of renewal as well as the year of first publication. See also 1.20–35.

4.42 **Name used in the notice.** The name used in the notice should be the name of the author unless the author has assigned all rights to the publisher. However, it is not uncommon to see the publisher's name in the notice even when it does not own all rights. Conversely, authors sometimes insist on notice in their names even when they have assigned all rights. Such vagaries are regrettable but harmless, except where they mislead those seeking permission to use the copyrighted material.

4.43 **Placement of notice.** The copyright notice should be placed so as to give reasonable notice to the consumer. The old law was very specific about its location: for books, on either the title page or the page immediately following; and for journals and magazines, on the title page, the first page of text, or the front cover. Present law simply states that the notice should be so placed as "to give reasonable notice of the claim of copyright," but most publishers continue to place it in the traditional locations required by the old law. See also 1.84, 1.95, 1.103.

4.44 **United States government materials.** When a work consists "preponderantly" of materials created by the federal government, this must be stated in the notice. This may be done either positively (e.g., "Copyright is claimed only in the introduction, notes, appendixes, and index of the present work") or negatively (e.g., "Copyright is not claimed in 'Forest Management,' a publication of the United States government reprinted in the present volume"). Works produced by state or local governments or by governments of other countries are not per se in the public domain and are not subject to this notice provision.

4.45 **Notice on derivative works.** The new copyright in a derivative work entitles its publisher to use a new copyright notice with the current year date, and nothing requires that such notice delineate what is and is not covered by the copyright. This sometimes has the unfortunate by-product (not always unintended, let it be said) of making users think that the scope of copyright extends to the public-domain material. However, the better practice, at least where the derivative work is a revised edition, is to include the publication years of various editions. See 1.23.

4.46 **Correcting mistakes.** Under pre-1978 law, no mechanism was available to cure the effects of a defective notice: copyright was forfeited and that was that, unless the omission of notice was accidental and occurred in a very small number of copies. For publication between January 1, 1978, and March 1, 1989 (when the notice requirement was finally dropped altogether), a more lenient regime prevailed. A mistake in the owner's name, or a mistake by no more than a year in the date element of the notice, was largely excused. Any more serious mistake was treated as an omission of notice. Any omission of one or more of the necessary three elements would be excused if the omission was from a "relatively small" number of copies. If more extensive omission occurred, the copyright owner could still save the copyright from forfeiture by registering it (see 4.47–50) within five years after the defective publication and making a "reasonable effort" to add the notice to all copies distributed to the public after the omission was discovered. Very few cases have discussed what a "reasonable effort" is, and their explanations, being somewhat ad hoc, give limited guidance to anyone trying to determine whether a work in this category is still protected by copyright.

Deposit and Registration

4.47 **Deposit requirements.** In the United States, the law requires copyright owners to send copies of works published in print form to the Copyright Office for deposit and use in the Library of Congress. (At present, works published only online are exempt from mandatory deposit, although the Library of Congress may change the rules to require deposit upon request.) The copies must be sent within three months of publication. Although failure to make the required deposit does not forfeit the copyright, the copyright owner is subject to a fine for noncompliance if a specific request from the Library of Congress is ignored. Deposit of two copies of the "best edition" is required. If, for example, clothbound and paperback editions of a book are published simultaneously, the publisher should submit two copies of the cloth edition. If the work is a very expensive or limited edition, one may apply to the Library of Congress for permission to submit only one copy. When sending deposit copies to the Copyright Office, publishers usually have the copyright registered as well. In the case of printed materials, the deposit copies also serve the requirements for registration. For electronic publications, a single copy will suffice, and the Copyright Office makes several options available for this, which should be reviewed on its website. It should be noted that works published in other countries but distributed in the United States are subject to Library of Congress deposit requirements.

4.48 **Registration forms and fees.** To register a work the author or other claimant should ordinarily go online to the Copyright Office's interactive application form, available (with a reasonably good tutorial) from Copyright.gov. Paper forms can still be used, and must be used for group registrations, but they slow the registration process (never fast in the best of times, unfortunately) to a crawl. The Copyright Office offers all these forms and intelligible explanations of its registration rules, including its complex deposit requirements, on its website. The fees for registration vary depending on which process one uses. Publishers with large lists tend to keep funds on deposit at the Copyright Office and to charge their registration fees against their deposit accounts. Group registration is available for multiple photographs, unpublished works, and contributions to periodicals by a single author, as well as for certain serial publications. A single fee covers all items in the group being registered and, as noted above, the registration must be done using paper forms.

4.49 **Need for accuracy and candor.** It is important to answer all questions on the application accurately. Copyright owners have been sanctioned by courts for misleading the Copyright Office by, for example, failing to disclose that a work is based on preexisting materials. Statements on the application do not need to be exhaustive, but they must be correct and not evasive. However, in contrast to patent applications, there is no requirement for disclosure of adverse claims or any other information not specifically called for on the form.

4.50 **Benefits of registration.** Registration is not necessary to *obtain* a copyright (which exists in the work from the moment it is fixed in tangible form; see 4.3) or to ensure its validity. However, the prudent course is to register copyright because of the added protection registration affords. In cases of infringement, registration is a prerequisite to bringing suit unless the work was written by a non-US author and first published abroad. Registering at the time of publication avoids a scramble to register later if infringement is discovered. Moreover, if registration has been made within three months of publication, or before an infringement begins, the copyright owner, instead of going through the difficulties of proving actual damages, can sue for "statutory damages" (in effect, an award of damages based on equity rather than on proof of loss) and, most significantly, is eligible to be reimbursed for attorney's fees. Registration as a prerequisite to these remedies applies equally to works of US origin and works authored or published outside the US. Publishers fearing prepublication piracy of books in development should also consider the "preregistration" procedure on the website of the United States Copyright Office.

The Publishing Agreement

4.51 **Basic rights.** No publishing house may legally publish a copyrighted work unless it first acquires the basic rights to copy the work and distribute it to the public. Although in theory a publisher could proceed with no more than a nonexclusive license of these rights—and this is done in rare circumstances—for obvious reasons publishers generally insist on exclusive rights. In most instances these rights are acquired from the author by means of a contract called the publishing agreement.

New Books

4.52 **Basic book-contract provisions.** In book publishing the publisher typically draws up the contract for a new book, to be signed by both the publisher and the author or, in the case of a joint work, by all authors. In this contract the publisher and author agree to certain terms. The publisher undertakes to publish the book after acceptance of the manuscript and to pay the author for the rights conveyed. Usually, publishers pay book authors a stipulated royalty out of the proceeds, but in some cases a publisher will instead pay a lump-sum fee. The author, in addition to granting rights to the publisher, typically also gives certain warranties, including that the book does not infringe anyone else's copyright (see 4.72). The author usually agrees to correct and return the edited manuscript and proofs and to cooperate in future revisions of the work. Book-publishing agreements are generally fairly lengthy and detailed documents and include many other points of agreement. Among the common areas of negotiation are

- Royalty rates, including the points at which a royalty will rise, or escalate (e.g., X% on the first 10,000 copies, Y% on the next 20,000 copies, and Z% thereafter)
- Royalty advances and (for certain types of books, such as textbooks) expense allowances
- The standards for acceptance of the manuscript, with the publisher wanting to be able to terminate the agreement if the final submitted manuscript is not "satisfactory," and the author wanting to limit this discretion to editorial rather than business considerations, with an opportunity to cure editorial defects
- The period following acceptance within which the publisher must issue the work
- What rights, beyond print rights in the publisher's home territory (usually defined as either the US or North America) and digital rights, are granted to the publisher
- The nature and extent of the author's indemnification obligations should the book turn out to violate some third party's rights; where the publisher carries "media perils" insurance, these obligations are most often determined with reference to the insurance coverage
- The scope of the author's agreement not to write a competing work, defined by subject matter and audience
- What share of royalties the author receives for revised editions to which he or she does not contribute
- How rights revert to the author if the book goes out of print or ceases to sell (see 4.38)
- On what terms the author may audit the publisher's financial records to ensure full payment of royalties due

Finally, if a book is to be published under a Creative Commons license or according to an open-access arrangement—a growing sphere of publishing—the contract should specify exactly what rights the public is being given. These alternative publishing models are discussed in more detail at 4.61 and 4.62.

4.53 **Option clauses.** In former years publishing agreements often contained legally binding options on "the author's next book." These are no longer so common, but where a book is or might be part of a series or a set of related titles they are more common: for example, options for "the author's next book on the subject of X" or "the author's next book involving the character John Smith." Some publishers insist on a right of first review or first refusal, or a right to match outstanding offers on the author's next book.

4.54 **Other contracts.** In addition to contracts with the authors of new books, several other types of agreement are used in scholarly publishing for special kinds of works. Two of the common ones cover contributions to scholarly journals (see 4.55, 4.56, and fig. 4.1) and to edited compilations (see 4.58–59 and fig. 4.2).

THE UNIVERSITY OF CHICAGO PRESS
JOURNALS DIVISION
WWW.JOURNALS.UCHICAGO.EDU

PUBLICATION AGREEMENT
Journal Name

From: Firstname Lastname, Editor, *Journal Name* **To:**

Contribution:

The University of Chicago, on behalf of The University of Chicago Press ("the Press"), is pleased to consider for publication your contribution identified above ("the Contribution"), in its journal ("the Journal"), *Journal Name*.

In consideration of the publication of your Contribution, we ask you to assign the copyright to the Press, thus granting us all rights in the Contribution. The Press, in turn, grants to you as author several rights described herein and in the Guidelines for Journal Authors' Rights After Acceptance available on the website of the Press (as in effect from time to time, the "Guidelines"). The Press may amend the Guidelines at any time with or without notice to you, and your rights in the Contribution shall be governed by this agreement and the Guidelines in effect at the time of your proposed use. You will receive no monetary compensation from the Press for the assignment of copyright and publication of the Contribution. By signing below, you and the Press agree as follows:

Copyright Assignment:

The Press undertakes to publish the Contribution, subject to approval by the editor(s), in its Journal named above. In consideration of such publication, you hereby grant and assign to the Press the entire copyright in the Contribution, including any and all rights of whatever kind or nature now or hereafter protected by the copyright laws of the United States and of all foreign countries, in all languages and forms of communication. It is understood that the copyright to the Contribution has not been registered with the Library of Congress, but that in the event such registration has taken place you will promptly transfer the copyright registration to the Press. If the Contribution is deemed unacceptable for Publication, you will be notified and all rights will revert to you.

Grant of Rights to Author:

The University grants to you the following nonexclusive rights, subject to your giving proper credit to the original publication of the Contribution in the Journal, including reproducing the exact copyright notice as it appears in the Journal:

(i) to reprint the Contribution, in whole or in part, in any book, article, or other scholarly work of which you are the author or editor,
(ii) to use the Contribution for teaching purposes in your classes, including making multiple copies for all students, either as individual copies or as part of a printed course pack, provided that these are to be used solely for classes you teach,
(iii) to post a copy of the Contribution on your personal or institutional web server, provided that the server is noncommercial and there are no charges for access, and
(iv) to deposit a copy of the Contribution in a noncommercial data repository maintained by an institution of which you are a member, after the embargo period identified in the Guidelines and provided all relevant conditions described in the Guidelines have been met.

The rights granted in clauses (i) and (ii) above are intended to benefit the original creators of the Contribution only. Accordingly, if you claim ownership of or rights in the Contribution because it was created by your employee or as a work made for hire, as defined in the Copyright Act, the rights granted in clauses (i) and (ii) above shall not apply to you, and you must contact the Press for permission to make these uses.

Warranties and Indemnifications:

You warrant to the Press as follows:

(i) that the Contribution is your original work;
(ii) that it contains no matter which is defamatory or is otherwise unlawful or which invades rights of privacy or publicity or infringes any proprietary right (including copyright);
(iii) that you have the right to assign the copyright to the Press and that no portion of the copyright to the Contribution has been assigned previously; and
(iv) that the Contribution has not been published elsewhere in whole or in part (except as may be set out in a rider annexed hereto and signed by the Press) and that no agreement to publish is outstanding other than this agreement.

You agree to indemnify and hold the Press harmless against any claim arising from or related to the breach or inaccuracy of any of the warranties listed above.

Requirements for Publication:

You agree to prepare and revise the Contribution according to the instructions of the editor(s) and to meet all other requirements for publication communicated to you by the editor(s) or the Press. It is your responsibility to determine whether the Contribution includes material that requires written permission for publication in the Journal, including any material that is supplementary or ancillary to the Contribution; to obtain such permission, at your own expense, from the copyright owner; and to submit that permission to the editor(s) with the manuscript.

Please complete, sign, and date this agreement, and return it to the editor(s) by mail, fax, or email, retaining a copy for your files. An electronic signature may be used. You agree that an electronic signature shall be valid and binding for all purposes, and hereby waive any objection to use of an electronic version of this agreement as a substitute for the original for any legally recognized purpose. *All joint authors must sign, each on a separate form if necessary.*

AUTHOR SIGNATURE:

____

Name: ______________________ Date: __________
(Please print or type)

Address:
____
____
____

Telephone: ______________ Fax: ______________

Email: ______________________________

FOR THE UNIVERSITY OF CHICAGO:

Garrett Kiely
Director, The University of Chicago Press

Please return to:

Journal Name
Address line 1
Address line 2
City, ST 00000 USA
Fax: (###) ###-####
Email: xxx@xxx.xxx

For internal use only: MSID ______________ 01.16.2013

FIGURE 4.1. Agreement for publication of a journal article, currently in use by the University of Chicago Press. Here the author transfers all copyright rights to the publisher of the journal, and the publisher transfers back to the author the right to reprint the article in other scholarly contexts.

PUBLICATION AGREEMENT—ALTERNATE SIGNATURE FORM

Use this form only if you belong to one of the categories below. All other authors should sign the Publication Agreement. Return the completed form with the Publication Agreement by mail, fax, or email, retaining a copy for your files.

Contribution: ______________________________

US Government employees: Your signature below indicates that you were an employee of the United States Government at the time the Contribution was prepared and its preparation was undertaken as part of your official duties. Accordingly, you agree to the terms of the attached Publication Agreement with the exception of the section entitled Copyright Assignment, which does not apply to you.

Institution or Agency: ______________________________
(Please print or type)

Signature of author or agency representative: ______________________________

Name: ______________________ Date: ____________
(Please print or type)

Please note that in the case of a Contribution jointly authored by government employees and nongovernment employees, only the government employees should sign this form; all nongovernment authors should sign the Publication Agreement.

Work made for hire: Your signature below indicates that the Contribution was prepared as a "work made for hire" on your behalf and you are thereby entitled to grant and assign copyright as requested in the Publication Agreement. You understand that the rights granted in clause (i) and (ii) of the Grant of Rights to Author do not apply to you.

Employer: ______________________________
(Please print or type)

Signature of employer representative: ______________________________

Name: ______________________ Date: ____________
(Please print or type)

Title: ______________________
(Please print or type)

Author signing on behalf of joint author(s): Your signature below indicates that you have assigned copyright in the Contribution on behalf of the joint author(s) named below. You warrant that you have been granted by each such joint author the authority to act as his or her agent in this behalf and indemnify the Journal, its sponsor (if applicable), and the University of Chicago Press from any claim arising from the breach or inaccuracy of this warranty. It is your responsibility to communicate the terms of publication to each author named below.

Names of joint author(s): ______________________________
(Please print or type)

Your signature: ______________________________

Your name: ______________________ Date: ____________
(Please print or type)

For internal use only: MSID ______________ 01.16.2013

FIGURE 4.1. *(continued)*

PUBLICATION AGREEMENT

[Date]

[Name]
[Address line 1]
[Address line 2]
[Address line 3]

Books Division

Dear ___________:

The University of Chicago Press is pleased to undertake the publication of your essay or chapter ______________________ (the "Contribution") to be included in the volume now entitled ______________________, written/edited by __________________ (the "Work"). Accordingly, the following terms of publication are submitted for your consideration:

APPROVAL AND ACCEPTANCE: We mutually agree that publication of the Contribution is contingent upon its acceptance for publication by the Press and volume editor and upon the Work's approval by the Board of University Publications.

GRANT OF RIGHTS: By this Agreement, you grant us, the University of Chicago acting through its Press, all right, title, and interest in and to the Contribution in all languages and all other copyright interests throughout the world, in all media, and for all terms of protection that are now or hereafter available, including the continuing right to reprint (and to license third parties to reprint) the Contribution. We will secure copyright for the Contribution in the name of The University of Chicago.

However, you may include or adapt the Contribution for publication in any book of which you are the sole author without your being required to seek our formal permission. If you include or adapt the Contribution in such a book, we require that you provide routine credit and acknowledgment to our Work and to the Press as the original publisher. The acknowledgment with this subsequent use should also include the identical copyright notice as it appears in our publication.

WARRANTY: You warrant that the Contribution is original with you; that it contains no matter that is libelous or is otherwise unlawful or that invades individual privacy or infringes any proprietary right or any statutory copyright; and you agree to indemnify and hold the Press harmless against any claim or judgment to the contrary. Further, you warrant that you have the right to assign the copyright to The University of Chicago, and that no right protected by copyright to the Contribution has been previously assigned. It is understood that the copyright to the Contribution has not been registered with the United States Copyright Office, but in the event that such registration has taken place, you will promptly transfer the copyright to The University of Chicago.

THE UNIVERSITY OF CHICAGO PRESS

1427 EAST 60TH STREET, CHICAGO, ILLINOIS 60637 www.press.uchicago.edu

FIGURE 4.2. Agreement, or consent, for publication of an article or a chapter commissioned as a contribution to a collective work (see 4.58–59). Different forms of agreement are required for "works made for hire," such as translations, forewords, or indexes.

PREVIOUS PUBLICATION AND PERMISSION: You warrant that the Contribution has not been published elsewhere in whole or in part and that you have not given anyone else permission to publish or otherwise exploit any part of the Contribution (except as may be set out at the end of this Agreement and initialed by a representative of the Press). Should the Contribution contain any material that requires written permission to be included in the Contribution, you will obtain such permission at your own expense from the copyright proprietor using a Press-approved permission form.

SUBMISSION OF THE CONTRIBUTION: You will submit your final manuscript for the Contribution in electronic form according to Press guidelines. At the time you submit your final manuscript, you will also deliver (i) all figures, charts, graphs, and other illustrative material prepared according to our art and illustration submission requirements, and (ii) any permission agreements as required in the previous paragraph. You will submit all of these materials to the volume editor(s) unless it is mutually agreed that you will submit them directly to the Press.

COPYEDITING AND PROOFHANDLING: The Press will copyedit the Contribution, and the copyedited text will be reviewed by the volume editor(s), who will also bear responsibility for reading and correcting proofs.

COMPENSATION: As total compensation for your preparation of the Contribution and the above grant and assignment of rights, the Press will publish the Contribution and you will receive, upon publication, one free copy of the cloth or paperbound edition of the work (depending on the format of original publication), or 2 electronic editions. You may purchase additional copies of the Work for your own use at 40% discount from the then-prevailing list price. Following publication you may request the Press to provide you with an electronic copy of the print-ready file for your own chapter, for personal use, including posting to your own website, provided that there are no fees for access and the posting is not being made in conjunction with an effort to distribute copies of the Contribution in competition with the Press's publication.

If the foregoing terms are satisfactory, please sign and date this Agreement; return the Press's copy to __________________ immediately, retaining a copy for your files.

ACCEPTED AND APPROVED:	FOR THE UNIVERSITY OF CHICAGO:
______________________________	______________________________
[Name]	Garrett P. Kiely, Director The University of Chicago Press
______________________________ Date	
______________________________ Citizenship	
______________________________ Permanent address	

FIGURE 4.2. *(continued)*

Journal Articles

4.55 **Transfers of rights.** Contributors to a journal possess at the beginning exactly the same rights in their work as authors of books. Consequently, when an article has been accepted for publication in a scholarly journal, the publisher usually asks the author to sign a formal transfer of rights in the contribution. Where an article has multiple authors, many publishers now for the sake of simplicity ask only the lead author to sign, but require a representation that the lead author has the authority to bind all coauthors. In the absence of a written copyright transfer agreement, all that the publisher acquires is the privilege of distributing the contribution in the context of that journal. Contributors frequently do not know this and do not understand that without broad rights the publisher cannot license anthology, database, classroom photocopying, or other uses that spread the author's message. Explaining this will often overcome the author's reluctance to sign the transfer. In the agreement currently in use at the University of Chicago Press, the publisher returns to the contributor the right to reprint the article in other scholarly works (see fig. 4.1). Such a provision is fair to both sides and is to be encouraged. See also 4.66–68 regarding open-access policies applicable to certain kinds of journal articles.

4.56 **Less than full rights.** Some journal publishers, when an author refuses to transfer copyright in toto, ask instead for a license more closely tailored to their specific needs. Care must be taken in such cases to ensure that the contract covers all the subsidiary rights that the publisher may want to exercise or sublicense and that the publisher's rights are exclusive where they need to be. This is especially important for electronic database rights. The right to publish an article in a journal does not carry with it ipso facto the right to include that article in an electronic database. In general, the trend toward narrowing or customization of licenses from journal authors to their publishers imposes on publishers a need to keep careful records of what rights they have obtained in each article, so they do not grant subsidiary rights that they do not in fact control. See also 4.61.

4.57 **Journal editors.** The role of the journal editor must not be forgotten. Unless he or she is an employee or agent of the company or society that owns the journal, the editor has a separate copyright in each issue as a collective work. Journal publishers should make sure that ownership of that separate copyright is clearly agreed on.

Edited Compilations

4.58 **Edited books.** The agreement described for books in 4.52 is intended for books with one or a few authors. Another type of book, common in scholarly but not in trade publishing, is one in which the chapters are contributed by various authors commissioned by an editor. The editor, by selecting and arranging the contributions included in the work, adds another layer of authorship. As author of the collective work, the book as a whole, he or she should sign an agreement similar to the standard author agreement described above. A publisher may in some circumstances use an agreement of the same type for chapter contributors, especially if the contributors are to receive royalty shares. All such agreements, though, need to be modified to reflect the particular allocation of responsibilities between editor and contributors. Alternatively, in appropriate circumstances, publishers can use simpler forms (such as that in fig. 4.2), closer in style to journal author forms (see fig. 4.1). Finally, it is possible to use work-made-for-hire agreements for all these persons, although that is the least common solution. For symposia, see 4.59.

4.59 **Symposium proceedings.** Symposium proceedings, made up of papers by different authors, are sometimes published as special issues of journals and sometimes as stand-alone books. The editor of the proceedings, in either case, has a separate status as author because the proceedings, as a whole, are a collective work; hence, this editor should be contracted with in the same way as a book editor (see 4.58). If the proceedings are being published as a journal issue, the publisher needs to clarify who owns copyright in the editor's work and to secure from every contributor a contract more or less identical to that used for authors of articles published in regular issues of the journal concerned. If the proceedings are being published as a book, the editor should sign a standard book author agreement, modified as appropriate, and the contributors should sign separate forms covering their own papers (see fig. 4.2). Either the volume editor or the publisher will send these forms to all contributors. When these have been signed, they are returned to the publisher and filed with the contract for the volume.

Theses and Dissertations

4.60 **Copyright and graduate student work.** Most higher education institutions require that dissertations and some theses be submitted to an electronic repository, either institutional or commercial. Once the full text of a dissertation or thesis is published in such a repository, others may have access to the work. Authors of dissertations and theses usually retain the copyright to their work, however, and can register it with the US Copyright Office. Depending on institutional policies, authors may have the option to limit access to the work or to make it available freely online according to an open-access or Creative Commons model (see 4.61, 4.62). Papers published without open access are typically obtainable only through a commercial database or a library and sometimes are made available for sale in print form. Some institutions will waive the requirement to submit to a repository in certain circumstances or will allow authors to embargo their work, delaying public access for a specified period of time; typically, though, an abstract of an embargoed thesis or dissertation will still be publicly available through the repository. It is essential that authors of dissertations and theses understand the requirements of their institutions and also the implications of any publishing options available to them, as the ability for an author to reuse some or all of the work in subsequent books or journal articles may be limited by the terms under which the thesis or dissertation is made available. Regardless of how it is published, if a thesis or dissertation includes copyrighted material beyond the conventions of fair use (including in some cases material previously published by the author), the author must secure written permission from the copyright holder and should be prepared to submit permissions documentation with the paper. For more information, see *Copyright and Your Dissertation or Thesis: Ownership, Fair Use, and Your Rights and Responsibilities*, by Kenneth D. Crews (bibliog. 2.3).

Alternative Publishing Arrangements

4.61 **Open-access publishing models.** As a corollary to the open-source movement in the software industry, the trend in academic publishing has been toward various initiatives intended to increase access to copyrighted works by providing the full text of digital content for free. In publishing, this is known as open access, of which there are two basic types. The first is "green" open access, whereby an author retains or secures the right to deposit a version of the manuscript in an open-access repository, typically after a period of embargo. The NIH Public Access Policy, for example, mandates a form of green open access (see 4.68). Green open access typically entails little or no additional cost to the publisher, who nonetheless expects to cover publishing costs in the usual way (i.e., through subscriptions or sales and licensing of the published version). Under "gold" open access, by contrast, the author grants to the publisher the right to make the published version of the work immediately available on an open-access basis. This arrangement is typically made possible either through an institutional subsidy to the publisher or through page charges levied on authors but usually covered through subvention from their own institutions or from foundations. A variation on the gold model relies on library sales or other sources of revenue to provide a baseline amount that allows publishers to "unlock" an article or book for public access. Both green and gold forms of open access are typically accompanied by special licenses that remove certain permissions barriers (see 4.62). Although open access remains far more common in journal publishing, especially in the sciences, a number of academic book publishers have also begun to experiment with open access. For an overview of the subject, see Peter Suber, *Open Access* (bibliog. 2.3).

4.62 **Creative Commons licenses.** If academic publishing has been moving toward increased access to copyrighted content (see 4.61), a related movement seeks to remove barriers to reusing this content beyond what would be considered fair use. To this end, Creative Commons licenses offer a range of "open license" alternatives to standard "all rights reserved" copyright distribution. The six basic licenses, from least to most restrictive, are as follows:

Attribution (CC BY), whereby any member of the public is licensed to carry out unlimited free redistribution of copies of a work, including for commercial purposes, and to alter and otherwise create derivatives of that work. The only requirement it imposes on the licensee is that he or she give appropriate credit (hence the "by" in CC BY) to the author/copyright owner of the original work.

Attribution-ShareAlike (CC BY-SA)—similar to a CC BY license, except that any reuse must be licensed under identical terms (i.e., "shared alike," under a CC BY-SA license).

Attribution-NoDerivs (CC BY-ND)—similar to a CC BY license, except that the work cannot be altered or abridged (i.e., no derivatives).

Attribution-NonCommercial (CC BY-NC)—similar to a CC BY license, except that any reuse must be noncommercial.

Attribution-NonCommercial-ShareAlike (CC BY-NC-SA)—similar to a CC BY-NC license, except that any reuse must be licensed under the same terms (i.e., under a CC BY-NC-SA license).

Attribution-NonCommercial-NoDerivs (CC BY-NC-ND)—similar to a CC BY-NC license, except that no derivatives are allowed.

All these license forms may be found at the Creative Commons website. (There is also the option of adding on to one of these basic arrangements by means of a "CC+" license, in which the "+" customization is detailed on the publisher's website and made available by link.) While authors (particularly journal authors) may show enthusiasm for this model, publishers should approach it with caution. Thus, if an author of a journal article presses for the article to be published under a Creative Commons license (an open license, often CC BY, is encouraged or even required under some open-access agreements), the publisher in turn may wish to insist that the license include a "noncommercial" clause so that the article may not be published by commercial competitors. In publishing entire journal issues under a Creative Commons license, the publisher will normally also wish to include a "no derivatives" clause; otherwise it will have no control over how others rearrange and otherwise alter the collective work. And, as with any license, the publisher should be certain the author has the necessary clearances for any third-party material included in the work. A photographer, for example, may be willing to license electronic distribution of a photograph in the context of a particular journal in online form but balk at inclusion in an electronic version subject to a Creative Commons license. If a work is going to be distributed under a Creative Commons license, that should be disclosed to any licensor of material included in the work.

4.63 **Self-publishing agreements.** Authors who self-publish directly through a retail platform such as the ones offered by Amazon and Apple, or through a self-publishing aggregator that distributes to multiple retailers (and in some cases to libraries), are required to agree to one of the service's standard contracts before their works will be offered to the public. Under such contracts, the author generally retains copyright and gets to set the price of the work as long as it is within certain limits. Unlike contracts with traditional publishers, such contracts tend to be nonexclusive, allowing authors to sell their work through more than one platform (including on a personal website) and in other formats, including print, but some services offer exclusive options that promise special terms favorable to authors for specific formats. Authors usually cannot self-publish works that are under contract with a traditional publisher except in the rare case of a work for which the author has retained digital publishing rights. On the other hand, self-publishing a work does not necessarily preclude future publication of that work with a traditional publisher (authors can typically terminate a self-publishing agreement at any time), and self-publishing is always an option for works whose rights have reverted to the author.

Subsidiary Rights and Permissions

Handling Subsidiary Rights

4.64 **Categories of subsidiary rights.** Subsidiary rights are usually thought of as including the following categories, some applicable to all types of published works and others to books only:

Original-language rights outside the original publisher's territory, whereby a second publisher may be licensed to sell the book in its original version in the second publisher's own territory. Typically a US publisher will retain, and not license out, English-language rights in Canada or even all of North America. Licensed territories tend to be defined according to commonly recognized geographic regions (e.g., United Kingdom, British Commonwealth, Europe and the Middle East, or "rest of world"). If a license includes digital as well as print media, great care must be taken to ensure that the distributor honors only orders that can be traced by postal code or otherwise to the countries in its own territory.

Translation rights, whereby a publisher in another territory may be licensed to translate the work into another language and to exercise standard publisher's rights (reproduction, distribution, electronic display) in the translation. Note that copyright in the translation as a derivative work belongs as an initial matter to the translator or to the publisher of the translation, but the license can impose restrictions on the exercise of that copyright.

Serial rights, whereby a magazine or newspaper publisher may be licensed to publish the book or excerpts from it in a series of daily, weekly, or monthly installments. *First serial rights* refers to publication before the work has come out in book form, *second serial rights* to publication afterward.

Paperback rights, whereby a publisher is licensed to produce and sell a paperback version of the book. So-called quality, or trade, paperbacks are normally sold in bookstores, like clothbound books. Mass-market paperbacks are often marketed through newsstands and supermarkets, although many now find their way into bookstores. Where the publisher of the paperback is the original publisher, paperback rights are not subsidiary but primary, usually with their own royalty scale. Some books are published only in paper, with no previously published clothbound version; these are called original paperbacks.

Book-club rights, whereby a book club is given the right to distribute the book to its members for less than the regular trade price. Copies generally are sold to the book club in bulk at a steep discount.

Reprint rights, whereby another publisher is licensed to reprint the work, in whole or in part, in an anthology or some other collection or (usually if the work has gone out of print in English) in an inexpensive reprint edition. This category also includes licensing document-delivery companies to reproduce chapters of works on demand.

Rights to produce an edition in Braille or other format to ensure accessibility for people with disabilities. It should be noted, though, that under US copyright law various nonprofit organizations have the right to publish such editions without permission.

Dramatic rights, whereby a theatrical producer is given the right to produce a play or musical based on the work, or a movie producer or studio is given the right to make a motion picture based on the work. ("Live stage" and "motion picture" rights are often licensed separately.) A license is most obviously necessary where a work of fiction is concerned, but motion-picture producers will often license rights to biographies and other nonfiction works so as to ensure their ability to use material from the book concerned.

Audio rights, whereby the work is licensed for download or streaming in a digital audio format or for recording on compact disc or the like.

Electronic rights, whereby the work is licensed for sale in e-book format, for inclusion in a database, or for other electronic use. Where journals are concerned, the principal electronic subsidiary rights involve licensing the journal's content to aggregators and research services; see 4.65. (This sort of licensing also has some importance for scholarly books.) Where a book is concerned, if the publisher itself intends to issue the work in e-book or other electronic form, electronic rights should be considered not subsidiary rights but part of the publisher's basic publication right and subject to a primary royalty. Publishers should normally assign new ISBNs for the electronic versions of their works, just as they have always done when, for example, issuing a hardcover work in paperback form (see 1.32).

Enhanced electronic rights, whereby the text is enhanced with substantial hyperlinks, video data, and the like, creating a derivative work. If the originating publisher wishes to produce such a product and is for any reason not acquiring general derivative work rights in the contract, it should make sure specifically to obtain the right to enhance the electronic version of the work with such features.

Rights for scholarly use, whereby the publisher grants others permission to quote text or copy charts and other illustrations from the original.

Rights for educational use, whereby teachers are permitted to make copies of the work for their classes or to include excerpts from the work in course-specific anthologies ("course packs"). Until recently, photocopying was the standard medium for classroom use, but electronic reproduction is becoming more common and blurring some of the boundaries of subsidiary rights. Educational use may also involve, for instance, inclusion in electronic reserves in libraries or distribution over campus intranets.

Subsidiary rights in the context of journals also include microform (including microfilm and microfiche) and the right to create summaries of articles in so-called abstract form. Reproduction by document-delivery services is also particularly relevant to journals.

4.65 **Electronic-rights licensing.** The term *electronic rights* covers a wide range of possibilities, and the number is constantly growing. Among the users of electronic rights are aggregators, who make available online a large number of publications in a given field or fields; research services, both current and archival, that permit access to databases of publications, often by subscription; and services that allow library users to "borrow" electronic copies of works. The decision whether to license some or all of such uses is both an economic and a strategic one. The economic issue is whether the availability of a work through these services will augment or "cannibalize" the publisher's projected print sales. The strategic issue is even harder to quantify, involving the need to be on the cutting edge of publishing or, at least, not to be seen as a laggard in such matters. In entering into electronic-rights licenses, the publisher should satisfy itself that the delivery mechanism of the particular licensee has safeguards against excessive downloading or copying (as part of a strategy of what is known as digital rights management)—or that such downloading or copying is something the publisher can tolerate. The publisher will also generally want to ensure that an electronic license lasts only a few years, for the pace of change is such that all these issues need to be revisited frequently.

4.66 **Authors' electronic use of their own works.** Where books are concerned, the author seldom retains any right of electronic publication. In scholarly journals, on the other hand, the right of authors to make electronic use of their own works has become contentious. For example, publishers that have traditionally allowed their authors to make unlimited photocopies for their own students now face an analogous demand: that authors be permitted to post their works on campus websites. If the website is accessible only by password and only to members of the university, the risk of lost revenue is probably modest and probably less important than retaining the goodwill of the author. More problematic is the demand, increasingly frequent, that the author be permitted to post the article on his or her personal website, or on an open-access university website or other "institutional repository." Such dissemination has value, but it can also undercut revenue-generating activities such as licensing that help support the ongoing publication of scholarly work. Nevertheless, if there is a trend in this area, it lies in the direction of such open access.

4.67 **University licenses.** Several universities have adopted policies under which they presumptively receive nonexclusive licenses of journal articles written by their faculty, with the right to post those articles on the internet and to make and license "noncommercial" uses. (Commonly, faculty are permitted but not encouraged to opt out of this arrangement on a case-by-case basis.) Where this arrangement applies, a faculty author is supposed to present his or her publisher with an addendum to the publisher's standard contract, listing rights granted to the university. There are various forms of addenda in circulation; they can be problematic. One, for example, contains the following provision:

> Notwithstanding any terms in the Publication Agreement to the contrary, AUTHOR and PUBLISHER agree that in addition to any rights under copyright retained by Author in the Publication Agreement, Author retains: (i) the rights to reproduce, to distribute, to publicly perform, and to publicly display the Article in any medium for noncommercial purposes; (ii) the right to prepare derivative works from the Article; and (iii) the right to authorize others to make any noncommercial use of the Article so long as Author receives credit as author and the journal in which the Article has been published is cited as the source of first publication of the Article. For example, Author may make and distribute copies in the course of teaching and research and may post the Article on personal or institutional websites and in other open-access digital repositories.

Among its faults, this language (i) does not explicitly state what the author can, and cannot, do with derivative works that he or she creates; (ii) does not clarify whether what the author can distribute, display, and otherwise use is the author's own manuscript or the finished, published work; and (iii) does not prevent the author from licensing the article to a competing journal, if the latter is "noncommercial" (a word that has no commonly accepted legal meaning). Another problem is that only the publisher as copyright owner has the ability to police compliance with whatever "noncommercial" licenses the author or university may give—yet the publisher has no control over the licensing activity. Publishers would be well advised to develop their own addenda to use when presented with author requests for nonexclusive rights. Such addenda might give the author and his or her employer unlimited rights to use the article internally, the right to post manuscript versions of the article on the author's website, and the right to post a PDF or similar file of the final published version on the author's website after a decent interval of time.

4.68 **Public-access policies.** In a similar vein to the university policies addressed in the previous paragraph, some government agencies have implemented policies to provide public access to the results of their taxpayer-funded research and related activities. In the United States, the model for such a policy is the one adopted by the National Institutes of Health pursuant to congressional mandate. This policy requires submission, for posting on the National Library of Medicine's PubMed Central, of the final manuscripts of all peer-reviewed articles derived from NIH-funded research. Manuscripts are to be submitted upon final acceptance for publication—that is, after the entire peer review and editorial process is complete and the article is ready for publication. This policy, unlike the university policies discussed above, is not subject to any opt-out and cannot be altered by any addendum. (Publishers may, however, choose to substitute their own published versions of articles for such manuscripts.) Authors' contracts with their publishers must stipulate a time, no later than twelve months after the official date of publication, when their articles will be posted for public access. If publishers believe that licensing revenue will be directly affected once an article is available at no cost from PubMed Central, they will wish to push for the maximum delay (i.e., twelve months) on public posting. More than a dozen other US agencies or departments, including the National Science Foundation, the Centers for Disease Control and Prevention, and the Department of Energy, have since adopted similar public-access policies pursuant to a government-issued directive. Public-access policies have also been implemented by certain nongovernmental foundations, charities, and other such organizations. An example of these is the Wellcome Trust, an international charitable research foundation based in the United Kingdom.

4.69 **Economic considerations.** The list above by no means exhausts the various forms of subsidiary rights the publisher may handle, but it includes the major ones. Depending on the administrative structure of the publishing house and the importance and marketability of the work involved, various persons or departments may handle different aspects of subsidiary rights work—a special rights and permissions department, the sales or marketing department, the acquiring editor, or even the chief executive officer. When the publisher sells or licenses rights to others, money is paid, either in a lump sum or as a royalty, and these proceeds are normally split between the publisher and the author according to whatever terms are specified in the publishing contract. In a typical book-publishing agreement, the author receives at least 50 percent of such income and sometimes substantially more. Some publishers have tried to avoid paying the author so much by licensing at an artificially low royalty to a sister company or other affiliate, but such "sweetheart" arrangements are suspect and of doubtful legality. In general, licenses between related companies should be handled in the same way as those between unrelated companies unless the author agrees otherwise in advance.

Granting Permission

4.70 **Handling permission requests.** A publisher with a relatively large backlist of books and journals, such as the University of Chicago Press, may receive dozens of communications every day from people seeking to license material from its list. Some requests are for standard subsidiary rights licenses, as described above. Others are for permission to reproduce snippets of prose or verse, or an illustration or two, from a book or journal. Most publishers have a "rights and permissions" staff to handle these requests. Rights and permissions can be a major source of income but also a major item of expense. Strategies for streamlining the permissions function are discussed later in this chapter.

4.71 **The rights database.** One prerequisite to an efficient and legally safe rights and permissions program is a complete and accurate record of what rights the publisher has. This is especially sensitive where third-party materials such as illustrations are embedded in the material to be licensed. The publisher's rights database should also record any other conditions that might restrict the publisher's ability to license, such as a requirement that the author's approval be obtained.

The Author's Responsibilities

4.72 **Author's copyright warranties.** In signing a contract with a publisher, an author warrants (guarantees) that the work is original, that the author owns it, that no part of it has been previously published, that no other agreement to publish it or part of it is outstanding, and that any copyrighted material of other authors that is used in his or her work is used with permission. (The indemnification that backs up these and other warranties is, as noted in 4.52, often a subject of negotiation in publishing contracts.) Unless the publisher otherwise agrees, the burden falls on the author to ensure that permission is obtained, as discussed in 4.75–83, except where the author's use of the material is fair use, as discussed in 4.84–94.

4.73 **Other warranties.** The author should also warrant that the work does not libel anyone or infringe any person's right of privacy. If the work contains scientific formulas or practical advice, the author may also be asked to warrant that no instructions in the work will, if accurately followed, cause injury to anyone, although courts have so far balked (on First Amendment grounds) at imposing liability for injury on authors or publishers for inaccurate advice. Some publishers ask authors for a further warranty that any statement of fact in the work is indeed accurate, perhaps for fear of reputational risk more than of legal liability. Although the publisher is entitled to rely on authors' warranties, during the editorial process it behooves the publisher to be alert to possible exposure for defamation or invasion of privacy. With the caveat that these are complicated issues and beyond the scope of this book, as a generalization it may be said that defamation is the assertion of things that appear to be facts (not the assertion of opinions) about living people who can be identified from the text or context of the work, if those alleged facts would be likely to hold the subject up to scorn or ridicule in the relevant community. (There are countervailing considerations, such as whether the subject is a public figure, in which case the bar to liability is much higher than for private citizens.) With the same caveat, invasion of privacy takes several forms, but the most significant is the public disclosure of private facts about a living individual if the disclosure would be highly offensive to a reasonable person. If a publisher encounters material that appears to present risk on either count, the publisher should query the author on the matter, not merely rely on the author's warranty.

4.74 **The role of counsel.** Counsel versed in these areas of the law can be of help in reviewing passages about which the publisher has concern, determining, for example, whether permission is needed for the reproduction of certain material, or whether passages in a work are defamatory. It may be helpful for the publisher's counsel to have a direct line of communication with the author, so long as it is clear to all concerned that the lawyer represents the publisher, not the author. Counsel's suggestions for changes to the manuscript should be followed absent compelling considerations to the contrary.

Obtaining Permissions

4.75 **General principles for obtaining permissions.** Budget permitting, an author may wish to commission illustrations on a work-made-for-hire basis, using forms supplied by the publisher. With this exception, an author must obtain permission to use any copyrighted material created by others, unless the intended use is a "fair use" (see 4.84–94). Technically, permission need not be in writing, but it would be most unwise to rely on oral permission. No permission is required to quote from works of the United States government or works for which copyright has expired. See 4.26–30 for guidelines to determine whether copyright for old material has expired. Bear in mind that although the original text of a classic reprinted in a modern edition may be in the public domain, recent translations and abridgments, as well as editorial introductions, notes, and other apparatus, are protected by copyright. But whether permission is needed or not, the author should always, as a matter of good practice (and to avoid any possible charge of plagiarism), credit any sources used. See 4.100.

4.76 **Author's role in obtaining permissions.** Publishing agreements generally place on the author the responsibility to request any permission needed for the use of material owned by others. In the course of writing a book or article, the author should keep a record of all copyright owners whose permission may be necessary before the work is published. For a book containing many illustrations, long prose passages, or poetry, obtaining permissions may take weeks, even months. For example, the author may find that an American publisher holds rights only for distribution in the United States and Canada, and that European, British Commonwealth (ex Canada), and "rest of world" rights are held by one or more publishers across the Atlantic. The author, wishing worldwide distribution for the book (world rights), must then write to each of these requesting permission for use of the material. If the author of copyrighted material has died, or if the copyright owner has gone out of business, a voluminous correspondence may ensue before anyone authorized to grant permission can be found (see 4.82). The author should therefore begin requesting permissions as soon as a manuscript is accepted for publication. Most publishers wisely decline to start setting type for a book until all the author's permissions are in hand.[1]

4.77 **Interview and photo releases.** Although the copyright ownership of interviews is somewhat murky, prudence requires that the interviewee's permission be obtained for the use of any extract that exceeds the bounds of fair use. (Such permission is best obtained by a broad release at the time the interview occurs, whether in writing or on the sound recording made of the interview.) Photographs of living persons present another sort of challenge. The photographer unquestionably owns copyright in the image, but if that image is to be used on the cover of the book or in any marketing materials, the subject's release must be obtained. (Use of the image inside the book, to illustrate text, does not require such permission.)

4.78 **Author's own work.** The author should remember that permission is sometimes needed to reuse or even to revise his or her own work. If the author has already allowed a chapter or other significant part to appear in print elsewhere—as a journal article, for example—then written permission to reprint it, or to update or revise it, will need to be secured from the copyright owner of the other publication, unless the author secured the right of reuse in the contract with that earlier publisher. The law does not require that the prior publication be credited in the new publication, but it is a common courtesy to give credit on the copyright page of the book, in a footnote on the first page of the reprinted material, or in a special list of acknowledgments. The author's earlier contract may also require such credit. And if the first publisher owns copyright in the material, it may make credit a condition of permission to reprint. Also, if the first publisher owns copyright, the new publisher will need to flag its files so that subsequent permissions requests for that material are referred to the original copyright owner.

4.79 **Fees and record keeping.** Most publishing agreements stipulate that any fees to be paid will be the author's responsibility. (Textbooks are a rare exception; see 4.104.) When all permissions have been received, the author should send them, or copies of them, to the publisher, who will note and comply with any special provisions they contain. The publisher

1. It is possible to engage professional help in obtaining permissions for a large project. Specialists in this work are listed under "Consultants" in the annual publication *LMP* (*Literary Market Place*; see bibliog. 2.8). Note also that the allocation of responsibility described here may not apply in some cases, such as large-market college textbooks, for which the publisher may take on the permissions paperwork. See 4.104.

will file all permissions with the publishing contract, where they may be consulted in the event of future editions or of requests for permission to reprint from the work. The copyeditor will check the permissions against the manuscript to be sure all necessary credits have been given. See 1.30, 2.46, 4.102, 14.54.

4.80 **Permissions beyond the immediate use.** Many publishers, when giving permission to reprint material they control, will withhold the right to sublicense that material. In such a case the publisher of the later work will not be able to give third parties free and clear permission to use material in which content from the earlier work is embedded; they will have to go back to the original source. Some publishers will also limit their licenses to a single edition, sometimes even with a maximum print run stipulated, or to a specific time period such as five or seven years. Where this is so, the publisher receiving the permission will have to go back to the source for new permission, usually for an additional fee, for any new edition, paperback reprint, serialization, or whatever. Alternatively, the publisher granting permission can stipulate up front what fees are to be paid for further uses and permit the new publisher to secure such permission automatically on payment of the agreed-upon fee.

4.81 **Permissions for unpublished works.** Getting permission for unpublished material presents an entirely different problem. Instead of a publishing corporation or licensing agent, one must deal with the author or author's heirs, who may not be easily identified or found. If the writer is dead, it may be especially difficult to determine who controls the copyrights.

4.82 **The missing copyright owner.** The problem presented by unpublished works whose authors are dead is, in a larger sense, just an example of the problem of the missing copyright owner. Another typical example is the publisher that has gone out of business or at least is no longer doing business under a given imprint. This problem has come to be known as the "orphan works" problem and has been the subject of proposed legislation. The draft bills suggest practices that a publisher would do well to follow when considering use of an orphan work. The most important thing is to conduct a reasonable (and well-documented) effort to locate the copyright owner. The elements of a bona fide search will vary with the circumstances but would probably include a search of the Copyright Office records, an internet search, and queries to both private and public databases that might reasonably be expected to contain information as to the owner of the copyright. If such efforts yield no results, there is still some risk in going forward. Technically, use of the work might still be ruled an infringement of copyright should a copyright owner surface, but it is unlikely that any court would do more than require the payment of a reasonable permissions fee. Anyone proceeding with publication under these conditions should certainly be prepared to offer and pay a reasonable fee on receiving any objection from the rediscovered owner.

4.83 **Non-copyright restrictions on archives.** Authors who wish to include unpublished material in their works should be aware that private restrictions, unrelated to copyright, may limit its use. The keeper of a collection, usually a librarian or an archivist, is the best source of such information, including what permissions must be sought and from whom. Bear in mind that copyright in a manuscript is different from ownership of the paper on which it is written or typed. Most often a library or collector will own the physical object itself but not the right to reproduce it. Thus there may be two permissions required: one for access to the material and one for the right to copy. It is important not to mistake one for the other.

FAIR USE: QUOTING WITHOUT PERMISSION

4.84 **Overview of the legal doctrine of fair use.** The doctrine of fair use, which allows limited use of copyrighted work without permission, was originally developed by courts as an equitable limit on the absolute rights of copyright. Although incorporated into the new copyright law, the doctrine still does not attempt to define the exact limits of the fair use of copyrighted work. It does state, however, that in determining whether the use of a work in any particular case is fair, the factors to be considered must include the following:

1. The purpose and character of the use, including whether such use is of a commercial nature or is for nonprofit educational purposes
2. The nature of the copyrighted work
3. The amount and substantiality of the portion used in relation to the copyrighted work as a whole
4. The effect of the use on the potential market for, or value of, the copyrighted work

Essentially, the doctrine allows copying that would otherwise be infringement. For example, it allows authors to quote from other authors' work or to reproduce small amounts of graphic or pictorial material for purposes of review or criticism or to illustrate or buttress their own points. Authors invoking fair use should transcribe accurately and give credit to their sources. They should not quote in such a way as to make the author of the quoted passage seem to be saying something opposite to, or different from, what was intended.

4.85 **Validity of "rules of thumb."** Although the law lays out no boundaries or ironclad formulas for fair use, some publishers have their own rules of thumb. Such rules, of course, have no legal force: courts, not publishers, adjudicate fair use. The rules exist in part to give an overworked permissions department, which often cannot tell whether a proposed use of a quotation is actually fair, something to use as a yardstick. See also 4.94.

4.86 **A few general rules related to fair use.** Fair use is use that is fair—simply that. Uses that differ in purpose from the original, and uses that transform the copied material by changing its context or the way it is perceived, will always be judged more leniently than those that merely parallel or parrot the original. For example, substantial quotation of the original is acceptable in the context of a critique but may well not be acceptable if one is simply using the first author's words to reiterate the same argument or embellish one's own prose. Use of any literary work in its entirety—a poem, an essay, an article from a journal—is hardly ever acceptable. Use of less than the whole will be judged by whether the second author appears to be taking a free ride on the first author's labor. As a general rule, one should never quote more than a few contiguous paragraphs of prose or lines of poetry at a time or let the quotations, even if scattered, begin to overshadow the quoter's own material. Quotations or graphic reproductions should not be so substantial that they substitute for, or diminish the value of, the copyright owner's own publication. Proportion is more important than the absolute length of a quotation: quoting five hundred words from an essay of five thousand is likely to be riskier than quoting that amount from a work of fifty thousand. But an even smaller percentage can be an infringement if it constitutes the heart of the work being quoted.

4.87 **Epigraphs and interior monologues.** Quotation in the form of an epigraph does not fit neatly into any of the usual fair-use categories but is probably fair use by virtue of scholarly and artistic tradition. The same can be said of limited quotation of song lyrics, poetry, and the like in the context of an interior monologue or fictional narrative. Of course, this would not excuse the publication of a collection of epigraphs or lyrics without permission of the various authors being quoted.

4.88 **Fair use of unpublished works.** If the work to be quoted has never been published, the same considerations related to fair use apply. But if the author or the author's spouse or children are still living, some consideration should be given to their interest in controlling when the work is disclosed to the public.

4.89 **Paraphrasing.** Use that is not fair will not be excused by paraphrasing. Traditional copyright doctrine treats extensive paraphrase as merely disguised copying. Thus, fair-use analysis will be the same for both. Paraphrase of small quantities of material, on the other hand, may be so minimal that it does not constitute copying at all, so that fair-use analysis would never come into play.

4.90 **Pictorial and graphic materials.** A high level of uncertainty has historically plagued the question of fair use of pictorial and graphic materials. At the level of intuition, it seems that a monograph on Picasso should be free to reproduce details from his paintings in order, for example, to illustrate the critic's discussion of Picasso's brushwork. Reproducing the entire image in black and white may also be reasonably necessary to illustrate the author's analysis of Picasso's techniques of composition. Reproducing "thumbnail sketches" of images has been held to be a fair use since they are so small and of such poor resolution that they cannot reduce the commercial value of the original. However, justification wears thin when a painting is reproduced in vivid color occupying a full page; the result begins to compete with large-scale reproductions of artwork that have no scholarly purpose. Likewise, reproduction on the cover would in most cases count as commercial rather than scholarly use and justification under the other fair-use factors would thus have to be much more compelling. The same considerations apply, adjusted for the media concerned, to every other sort of pictorial material, including, for example, posters, street art, and film stills. A recent opinion from a leading federal court of appeals has provided a refreshingly generous reading of fair use where images are concerned. The case involved a book about the Grateful Dead, and held that the reproduction of entire concert posters in full color was fair use because the posters were "historical artifacts," used to provide a "visual context" for the text, and reproduced at a size far smaller than life, indeed at the "minimal image size and quality necessary to ensure the reader's recognition of the images as historical artifacts." These criteria, properly applied, should free up many a use that would otherwise be smothered by caution. For an overview of the subject, see the *Code of Best Practices in Fair Use for the Visual Arts*, published online by the College Art Association.

4.91 **Charts, tables, and graphs.** Reproduction of charts, tables, and graphs presents a difficult judgment call. An aggressive approach would justify copying a single such item on the ground that one chart is the pictorial equivalent of a few sentences. A more conservative approach would argue that a graph is a picture worth a thousand words and that reproducing it without permission is taking a free ride on the first author's work. This latter approach has the flaw of being too absolute in practice, for it is difficult under this rationale to imagine *any* fair use of such an image. Where the item in question represents a small portion of the original work and a small portion of the second work, the harm seems minimal, outweighed by the benefits of open communication. Certainly, reproduction of a single graph, table, or chart that simply presents data in a straightforward relationship, in contrast to reproduction of a graph or chart embellished with pictorial elements, should ordinarily be considered fair use. Indeed, some graphs that merely present facts with little or no expressive input—the equivalent, in two dimensions, of a mere list—may even be beyond the protection of copyright.

4.92 **Importance of attribution.** With all reuse of others' materials, it is important to identify the original as the source. This not only bolsters the claim of fair use but also helps avoid any accusation of plagiarism. Nothing elaborate is required; a standard footnote will suffice, or (in the case of a graph or table, for example) a simple legend that says "Source: [author, title, and date of earlier work]." Note that such a legend is not always clear: Does it mean that the data are taken from the original but reformatted by the second author or that the graph or table has itself been copied? If the latter, it is preferable to say "Reprinted from [author, title, and date of earlier work]" rather than merely "Source." See also 3.29–37, 3.77, 14.54.

4.93 **Unnecessary permissions.** Given the ad hoc nature of fair use and the absence of rules and guidelines, many publishers tend to seek permission if they have the slightest doubt whether a particular use is fair. This is unfortunate. Fair use is valuable to scholarship, and it should not be allowed to decay because scholars fail to employ it boldly. Furthermore, excessive permissions processing tends to slow down the gestation of worthwhile writings. Even if permission is sought and denied, that should not necessarily be treated as the end of the matter. The US Supreme Court has held that requesting permission should not be regarded as an admission that permission is needed. In other words, where permission is denied, or granted but for an unreasonable price, publishers and authors should consider whether a sound case might be made for fair use.

4.94 **Chicago's fair-use guidelines.** To reduce the expense of responding to permissions requests, and to reduce the friction in scholarly publishing that permissions handling can create, the University of Chicago Press posts guidelines on its website for what it considers to be fair use of excerpts from its own publications. These guidelines are intended to be generous and fair to all parties. Other publishers are encouraged to adopt them.

Requesting Permission

4.95 **Information required.** Would-be users can help reduce delay and miscommunication by submitting their requests for permission in the best possible form. All requests for permission to reprint should be sent to the copyright holder in writing and in duplicate. The request should contain the following explicit information:

1. The title of the original work and exact identification, with page numbers, of what is to be reprinted. Identification should include, in the case of a table or figure, its number and the page it appears on (e.g., fig. 6 on p. 43); in the case of a poem, the title and the page on which the poem appears; in the case of a prose passage, the opening and closing phrases in addition to the page numbers (e.g., "from 'The military genius of Frederick the Great' on p. 110 through 'until the onset of World War I' on p. 112"). The requester should be sure to cite the original source of the material, not any subsequent reprinting of it.
2. Information about the publication in which the author wishes to reproduce the material: title, approximate number of printed pages, form of publication (clothbound book, paperback book, e-book, journal, electronic journal), publisher, probable date of publication, approximate print run, and list price (if available).
3. The kind of rights requested. The most limited rights a user ought to accept are "nonexclusive world rights in the English language, for one edition." The best opening gambit would be "nonexclusive world rights in all languages and for all editions in print and other media, including the right to grant customary permissions requests but only where the licensed material is incorporated in [the requester's work]." The request for "the right to grant customary permissions" would, if granted, greatly simplify the downstream licensing of the new work. Unfortunately, such a right is not implicit in any nonexclusive license (see 4.35) and is seldom granted, and licensees of works in which earlier material is used end up needing to get multiple layers of permission.

Submitting a request in this form does not guarantee that the copyright owner will sign and return it—the owner may well have its own standard form that it returns to the requester—but it at least helps both parties by clearly defining what is under discussion. It is up to the copyright owner to state clearly what fee is demanded for the proposed use and what special conditions apply to the grant. When agreement on all terms is reached, the requester and the copyright owner should both retain copies of the final agreement, and a third copy (with original signature, if the process has been done on paper rather than electronically) should go to the publisher.

4.96 **Sample permissions letters.** The University of Chicago Press supplies authors or editors of books requiring many permissions with a model request letter (fig. 4.3) but suggests that they write on their own personal or (when appropriate) institutional letterhead. Every publisher would be well advised to adopt some variation of this practice as an aid to any authors not familiar with the permissions process.

4.97 **Digitizing and automating the permissions process.** The technologies of photocopying and electronic reproduction present a major institutional challenge to publishers. The volume of license requests under these headings exceeds the ability of traditional techniques to process them. Publishers have customarily processed such requests by hand, case by case, evaluating each request on its own merits and often tailoring a fee to the specific circumstances. Whether this approach can or should survive is an open question. The internet provides a powerful tool for handling requests rapidly and with little or no staff involvement. A properly designed website, coupled with the adoption of standard, publicly quoted fees, can create a highly efficient marketplace for copying, to the benefit of both the publisher and its customers. Authors seeking permission for use of other authors' work can obtain that permission immediately and can realistically budget for permissions fees in advance. The marketplace can be even more efficient when a royalty-rights organization such as the Copyright Clearance Center (see 1.103) enables users to obtain online permissions from multiple publishers through a single website. Whether these services become the standard, or inspire publishers to move their own rights and permissions work to the web, remains to be seen.

ILLUSTRATIONS

4.98 **Rights holders.** Permission to reproduce pictorial works used as illustrations in a book or journal article—as opposed to charts, graphs, or the like, which are usually created by the same author(s) as the text—will rarely be available from the publisher. A publisher who has used the pictorial work to illustrate text that someone is seeking to reprint may

Contracts & Subsidiary Rights

Books Division

To:

Reference:

Date:

I am writing to request permission to print the following material:

Author/Title/Date of publication:

Pages as they appear in your publication:

Other identifying information and remarks:

This material is to appear as originally published (any changes or deletions are noted on the reverse side of this letter) in the following work which the University of Chicago Press is presently preparing for publication:

Author (Editor)/Title:

Proposed date of publication:

Remarks:

I request nonexclusive world rights, including electronic rights, but only as part of my volume, in all languages, for all editions, and in all media. In addition, I ask permission for the Univ. of Chicago Press to include the illustrations in connection with advertising and promoting the book.

If you are the copyright holder, may I have your permission to reprint the above material in my book? If you do not indicate otherwise, I will use the usual scholarly form of acknowledgment, including publisher, author, title, etc.

If you are not the copyright holder, or if additional permission is needed for world rights from another source, please indicate so.

Thank you for your consideration of this request. A duplicate copy of this form is enclosed for your convenience.

Sincerely yours,

____

The above request is hereby approved on the conditions specified below, and on the understanding that full credit will be given to the source.

Date: ____________ Approved by: ________________________

THE UNIVERSITY OF CHICAGO PRESS

1427 EAST 60TH STREET, CHICAGO, ILLINOIS 60637 TEL: 773.702.7700 FAX: 773.702.2706

FIGURE 4.3. Suggestions for a letter seeking permission to reprint material in a scholarly book. Some of the information about the proposed book may be lacking when the author begins to request permissions, but as much information as possible should be supplied. Note that spaces are left so that the person addressed can use the letter itself for granting or denying the request or for referring the author elsewhere.

very well not have the right to sublicense use of the illustration. Even a publisher of, say, a collection of the artist's work may not have rights to the individual images. In such a case the permission seeker must deal with the owner of the object or the artist or both. Copyright ownership of artworks sold before 1978 is not always easy to determine, because before 1978 the law generally, but not always, assumed that so long as an original artwork remained unpublished, its copyright passed from hand to hand with ownership of the object itself. For post-1977 works, copyright belongs to the artist unless the artist has explicitly assigned it to someone else. But, even for such works, the person seeking permission to reproduce the artwork in a book or journal may, as a practical matter, need to deal with a museum that expects a fee for providing a reproduction, or allowing an author to make a photograph, of a work in its collection. Where the museum can deny permission to photograph the object, such a fee is the tariff one pays for physical access if nothing else. Where the museum is licensing its own reproduction or photograph of the work, it has less justification, for the law denies copyright to photographs that merely reproduce another two-dimensional image. Be that as it may, authors and publishers are generally loath to antagonize museums by challenging their positions.

4.99 **Stock agencies and image archives.** The only kind of pictorial work for which permissions are easily obtained is photographs, at least where the rights are administered by a stock agency or other commercial image archive. Such agencies have vast inventories of images and published and easy-to-understand fee structures. There are also websites that act as clearinghouses for photographic permissions.

4.100 **Information required.** A permission request for an illustration should be sent to the picture agency, museum, artist, or private individual controlling reproduction rights. Again, the request should be as specific as possible regarding the identity of what is to be reproduced, the form of publication in which it will appear, and the kind of rights requested. If the author making the request knows that the illustration will also be used elsewhere than in the text proper (such as on the jacket or in advertising), this fact should be noted.

4.101 **Fees.** Fees paid for reproducing material, especially illustrations procured from a stock-photo agency, usually cover one-time use only—in, say, the first edition of a book, or for a certain number of copies. If an illustration is also to be used on the jacket or in advertising, a separate and higher fee is customary. And if a book is reprinted as a paperback or goes into a second edition, another fee is usually charged. For obvious reasons, such arrangements are not optimal from the publisher's standpoint, and authors should try wherever possible to obtain permission covering all editions of their works in all media. Whether the publisher or the author should pay whatever additional fee is charged for cover use may be a matter for negotiation.

ACKNOWLEDGING SOURCES

4.102 **Credit lines.** Whether or not the use of others' material requires permission, an author should give the exact source of such material: in a note or internal reference in the text, in a source note to a table, or in a credit line under an illustration. Where formal permission has been granted, the author should, within reason, follow any special wording stipulated by the grantor. For a text passage complete in itself, such as a poem, or for a table, the full citation to the source may be followed by this simple acknowledgment:

Reprinted by permission of the publisher.

A credit line below an illustration may read, for example, as follows:

Courtesy of the Newberry Library, Chicago, Illinois.

For examples of various kinds of credit lines, see 3.29–37, 3.77, 14.54.

4.103 **Acknowledgments sections.** In a work that needs many permissions, acknowledgments are often grouped in a special acknowledgments section at the front or back of the work (see 1.42). Some citation of the source should still, however, be made on the page containing the relevant material.

FEES

4.104 **Responsibility for payment.** As noted above, publishing agreements generally make the author responsible for any fees charged for use of others' material. A publisher may agree to pay the fees and to deduct them from the author's royalties or—in rare instances—to split the fees with the author. If it appears that a book would be enhanced by illustrations not provided by the author, many publishing agreements enable the publisher to find the illustrations and (with the author's consent) charge any fees involved to the author's royalty account. One exception to these generalizations is school and college textbooks, where it is common for the publisher to provide a certain amount of its own funds to pay for illustrations.

4.105 **Anthologies.** A book made up entirely of other authors' copyrighted materials—stories, essays, poems, documents, selections from larger works—depends for its existence on permissions from the various copyright owners. The compiler of such a volume therefore should begin seeking permissions as soon as a contract for publication of the volume has been executed or a letter of intent has been received from the prospective publisher. Informal inquiries to copyright owners may be initiated before that time, but no sensible publisher of material to be anthologized is likely to grant permission for its use or to set fees without knowing the details of eventual publication. Once those details are known, the compiler must act quickly. Permission for a selection may be refused, or the fee charged may be so high that the compiler is forced to drop that selection and substitute another. And until all permissions have been received and all fees agreed on, the table of contents cannot be considered final.

II · Style and Usage

5 · Grammar and Usage

BRYAN A. GARNER

Grammar

Introduction

5.1 **The field of grammar.** In its usual sense, grammar is the set of rules governing how words are put together in sentences to communicate ideas—or the study of these rules. Native speakers of a language learn them unconsciously. The rules govern most constructions in any given language. The small minority of constructions that lie outside these rules fall mostly into the category of idiom and customary usage.

5.2 **Schools of grammatical thought.** There are many schools of grammatical thought—and differing vocabularies for describing grammar. Grammatical theories have been in upheaval in recent years. It seems that the more we learn, the less we know. As the illustrious editor in chief of the *Oxford English Dictionary* wrote in 1991: "An entirely adequate description of English grammar is still a distant target and at present seemingly an unreachable one, the complications being what they are."[1] In fact, the more detailed the grammar (it can run to many large volumes), the less likely it is to be of any practical use to most writers and speakers.

5.3 **Parts of speech.** As traditionally understood, grammar is both a science and an art. Often it has focused—as it does here—on parts of speech and their syntax. Each part of speech performs a particular function in a sentence or phrase. Traditional grammar has held that there are eight parts of speech: nouns, pronouns, adjectives, verbs, adverbs, prepositions, conjunctions, and interjections.[2] Somewhat surprisingly, modern grammarians cannot agree on precisely how many parts of speech there are in English. At least one grammarian says there are as few as three.[3] Another insists that there are "about fifteen," noting that "the precise number is still being debated."[4] This section deals with the traditional eight; each part of speech is treated below. The purpose here is to sketch some of the main lines of English grammar using traditional grammatical terms.

---

1. Robert W. Burchfield, *Unlocking the English Language* (New York: Hill and Wang, 1991), 22.
2. See Robert L. Allen, *English Grammars and English Grammar* (New York: Scribner, 1972), 7.
3. Ernest W. Gray, *A Brief Grammar of Modern Written English* (Cleveland: World, 1967), 70.
4. R. L. Trask, *Language: The Basics* (London: Routledge, 1995), 37.

Nouns

TRADITIONAL CLASSIFICATIONS

5.4 **Nouns generally.** A noun is a word that names something, whether abstract (intangible) or concrete (tangible). It may be a common noun (the name of a generic class or type of person, place, thing, process, activity, or condition) or a proper noun (the name of a specific person, place, or thing—hence capitalized). A concrete noun may be a count noun (if what it names can be counted—as with *horses* or *cars*) or a mass noun (if what it names is uncountable or collective—as with *information* or *salt*).

5.5 **Common nouns.** A common noun is the generic name of one item in a class or group {a chemical} {a river} {a pineapple}. It is not capitalized unless it begins a sentence or appears in a title. A common noun is usually used with a determiner—that is, an article or other word (e.g., *some*, *few*) that indicates the number and definiteness of the noun element {a loaf} {the day} {some person}. Common nouns may be analyzed into three subcategories: concrete nouns, abstract nouns, and collective nouns. A concrete noun is solid or real; it indicates something perceptible to the physical senses {a building} {the wind} {honey}. An abstract noun denotes something you cannot physically see, touch, taste, hear, or smell {joy} {expectation} {neurosis}. A collective noun—which can be viewed as a concrete noun but is often separately categorized—refers to a group or collection of people or things {a crowd of people} {a flock of birds} {a herd of rhinos}.

5.6 **Proper nouns.** A proper noun is the name of a specific person, place, or thing {John Doe} {Moscow} {the Hope Diamond}, or the title of a work {*Citizen Kane*}. Proper nouns may be singular {Mary} {London} or plural {the Great Lakes} {the Twin Cities}. A proper noun is always capitalized, regardless of how it is used—unless someone is purposely flouting the rules {k.d. lang}. A common noun may become a proper noun {Old Hickory} {the Big Easy}, and sometimes a proper noun may be used figuratively and informally, as if it were a common noun {like Moriarty, he is a Napoleon of crime [*Napoleon* here connotes an ingenious mastermind who is ambitious beyond limits]}. Proper nouns may be compounded when used as a unit to name something {the Waldorf-Astoria Hotel} {*Saturday Evening Post*}. Over time, some proper nouns (called *eponyms*) have developed common-noun counterparts, such as *sandwich* (from the Earl of Sandwich) and *china* (the porcelain, from the nation China). Articles and other determiners are used with proper nouns only when part of the noun is a common noun or the determiner provides emphasis {the Savoy Hotel} {Sam? I knew a Sam Hill once}.

5.7 **Mass nouns.** A mass noun (sometimes called a *noncount noun*) is one that denotes something uncountable, either because it is abstract {cowardice} {evidence} or because it refers to an aggregation of people or things taken as an indeterminate whole {luggage} {the bourgeoisie}. The key difference between mass nouns and collective nouns is that unlike collective nouns (which are count nouns), mass nouns almost never take indefinite articles and typically do not have plural forms (*a team*, but not *an evidence*; *two groups*, but not *two luggages*). A mass noun can stand alone {**music is** more popular than ever} or with a determiner other than an indefinite article (*some* music or *the* music but generally not *a* music). As the subject of a sentence, a mass noun typically takes a singular verb and pronoun {the **litigation is** so varied that **it** defies simple explanation}. Some mass nouns, however, are plural in form but are treated as grammatically singular {politics} {ethics} {physics} {news}. Others are always grammatically plural {manners} {scissors} {clothes}. But just as singular mass nouns don't take an indefinite article, plural mass nouns don't combine with numbers: you'd never say *three scissors* or *six manners*. Some that refer to concrete objects, such as *scissors* or *sunglasses*, can be enumerated by adding *pair of* {**a pair of** scissors} {**three pairs of** sunglasses}. Likewise, singular concrete mass nouns can usually be enumerated by adding a unit noun such as *piece* (with *of*) {**a piece of** cutlery} {**seven pieces of** stationery}. Both singular and plural mass nouns can take indefinite adjectives such as *any*, *less*, *much*, and *some* that express general quantity {what you need is **some courage**} {he doesn't have **any manners**}.

PROPERTIES OF NOUNS

5.8 **Properties of nouns.** Nouns have properties of case and number. Some traditional grammarians also consider gender and person to be properties of nouns.

5.9 **Noun case.** In English, only nouns and pronouns have case. *Case* denotes the relationship between a noun (or pronoun) and other words in a sentence. Grammarians disagree about the number of cases English nouns possess. Those who consider inflection (word form) the defining characteristic tend to say that there are two: common, which is the uninflected form, and genitive (or *possessive*), which is formed by adding *-'s* or just an apostrophe. But others argue that it's useful to distinguish how the common-case noun is being used in the sentence, whether it is playing a nominative role {the doctor is in} or an objective role {go see the doctor}. They also argue that the label we put on nouns according to their function should match those we use for *who* and for personal pronouns, most of which do change form in the nominative and objective cases (*who/whom*, *she/her*, etc.). See also 5.17–22.

5.10 **Noun number.** Number shows whether one object or more than one object is referred to, as with *clock* (singular) and *clocks* (plural).

5.11 **Noun gender.** English nouns have no true gender, as that property is understood in many other languages. For example, whether a noun refers to a masculine or feminine person or thing does not determine the form of the accompanying article as it does in French, German, Spanish, and many other languages. Still, some English words—almost exclusively nouns denoting people or animals—are inherently masculine {uncle} {rooster} {lad} or feminine {aunt} {hen} {lass} and take the gender-appropriate pronouns. But most English nouns are common in gender and may refer to either sex {relative} {chicken} {child}. Many words once considered strictly masculine—especially words associated with jobs and professions—have been accepted as common (or *indefinite*) in gender over time {author} {executor} {proprietor}. Similarly, many forms made feminine by the addition of a suffix {aviatrix} {poetess} have been essentially abandoned. See 5.251–60.

5.12 **Noun person.** A few grammarians attribute the property of person to nouns, distinguishing first person {I, Dan Walls, do swear that . . .}, second person {you, the professor, are key}, and third person {she, the arbiter, decides}. While those examples all use nouns in apposition to pronouns, that's not closely relevant to the question whether the nouns themselves have the property of person in any grammatical sense. But using that property in analyzing nouns does help to point out three things. First, as with grammatical case, one argument for the property of person is to keep the properties of nouns parallel to those of pronouns, even though English nouns do not change form at all in first, second, or third person as personal pronouns do. Second, person determines what form other words will take—here, the verbs. Third, the examples illustrate why attributing person to nouns requires a stretch of logic—if the pronouns were not present in the first two examples, the verb would be in the third person, even if Dan Walls were talking about himself and even if the speaker were addressing the professor.

PLURALS

5.13 **Plurals generally.** Because exceptions abound, a good dictionary or usage guide is essential for checking the standard plural form of a noun. But there are some basic rules for forming plurals, some of which are covered in chapter 7 (see 7.5–15). A few matters of agreement are treated in the paragraphs that follow.

5.14 **Plural form with singular sense.** Some nouns are plural in form but singular in use and meaning {good **news is** always welcome} {**economics is** a challenging subject} {**measles is** potentially deadly}. Also, a plural word used as a word is treated as a singular {**"mice" is** the plural of "mouse"} {**"sistren" is** an archaic plural}. Some traditional plurals, such as *data* and (to a lesser extent) *media*, have gradually acquired a mass-noun sense and are increasingly treated as singular. Although traditionalists stick to the plural uses {the **data are** inconclusive} {the **media are** largely misreporting the event}, the new singular uses—using the terms in a collective sense rather than as count nouns—exist alongside the older ones {the **data shows** the hypothesis to be correct} {the **media isn't** infallible}. (In the sciences, *data* is always plural.) In formal contexts, the most reliable approach is to retain the plural uses unless doing so makes you feel as if you're being artificial, stuffy, and pedantic. Consider using alternative words, such as *information* and *journalists*. Or simply choose the newer usage. But make your play and be consistent—vacillating will not win the admiration of readers and listeners.

5.15 **Plural-form proper nouns.** A plural geographical name is often treated as singular when the name refers to a single entity {the **United States is** a relatively young nation} {**Naples is** a very beautiful city}. But there are many exceptions {the **Alps have** never been totally impassable}. Names of companies, institutions, and similar entities are generally treated as collective nouns—and hence singular in American English, even when they are plural in form {**General Motors reports** that it will earn a profit} {**American Airlines has** moved its headquarters}. In British English, however, singular nouns that refer to individuals who work independently typically take plural verbs {**Manchester United have** won the FIFA Cup} {**England are** now leading in World Cup standings}.

5.16 **Tricky anomalies of the plural.** Not all English nouns show the usual singular-plural dichotomy. For example, mass nouns such as *furniture*, *spaghetti*, and *wheat* have only a singular form, and *oats*, *scissors*, and *slacks* (= pants) exist only as plurals. Some nouns look singular but are invariably plural {the **police were** just around the corner} {the **vermin**

seem impossible to eradicate}. Others look plural but are invariably singular {the **news is** good} {**linguistics is** my major}. Strangely enough, *person* forms two plurals—*persons* and *people*—but *people* also forms the plural *peoples* {the **peoples** of the world}.

CASE

5.17 **Function of case.** *Case* denotes the relationship between a noun or pronoun and other words in a sentence.

5.18 **Common case, nominative function.** The nominative (sometimes called the *subjective*) function denotes the person, place, or thing about which an assertion in a clause is made {the **governor** delivered a speech [*governor* is the subject]} {the **shops** are crowded because the holiday **season** has begun [*shops* and *season* are the subjects of their respective clauses]}. A noun serving a nominative function controls the verb and usually precedes it {the **troops** retreated in winter [*troops* is the subject]}, but through inversion it can appear almost anywhere in the sentence {high up in the tree sat a **leopard** [*leopard* is the subject]}. A noun or pronoun that follows a *be*-verb and refers to the same thing as the subject is called a *predicate nominative* {my show dogs are **Australian shepherds** [*Australian shepherds* is a predicate nominative]}. Generally, a sentence's predicate is the part that contains a verb and makes an assertion about the subject.

5.19 **Common case, objective function.** The objective (sometimes called the *accusative*) function denotes either (1) the person or thing acted on by a transitive verb in the active voice {the balloon carried a **pilot** and a **passenger** [*pilot* and *passenger* are objective: the direct objects of the verb *carried*]} or (2) the person or thing related to another element by a connective, such as a preposition {place the slide **under** the **microscope** [*microscope* is objective: the object of the preposition *under*]}. A noun in an objective function usually follows the verb {the queen consulted the **prime minister** [*queen* is nominative and *prime minister* is objective]}. But with an inverted construction, the object can appear elsewhere in the sentence {everything else was returned; the **jewelry** the **thieves** had already sold [*jewelry* is objective and *thieves* is nominative]}. A noun serving an objective function is never the subject of the following verb and usually does not control the number of the verb {an assembly of **strangers** was outside [the plural noun *strangers* is the object of the preposition *of*; the singular noun *assembly* is the subject of the sentence, so the verb *was* must also be singular]}.

5.20 **Genitive case.** The genitive case denotes (1) ownership, possession, or occupancy {the **architect's** drawing board} {**Arnie's** room}; (2) a relationship {the **philanthropist's** secretary}; (3) agency {the **company's** representative}; (4) description {a **summer's** day}; (5) the role of a subject {the **boy's** application [the boy applied]}; (6) the role of an object {the **prisoner's** release [someone released the prisoner]}; or (7) an idiomatic shorthand form of an *of*-phrase {**one hour's** delay [equal to *a delay of one hour*]}. The genitive case is also called the *possessive case*, but *possessive* is a misleadingly narrow term, given the seven different functions of this case—true possession, as ordinarily understood, being only one. For instance, the fourth function above is often called the descriptive possessive. This is a misnomer, however, because the form doesn't express actual possession but instead indicates that the noun is functioning as a descriptive adjective. The genitive is formed in different ways, depending on the noun or nouns and their use in a sentence. The genitive of a singular noun is formed by adding *-'s* {**driver's** seat} {**engineer's** opinion}. The genitive of a plural noun that ends in *-s* or *-es* is formed by adding an apostrophe {**parents'** house} {**foxes'** den}. The genitive of an irregular plural noun is formed by adding *-'s* {**women's** rights} {**mice's** cage}. The genitive of a compound noun is formed by adding the appropriate ending to the last word in the compound {**parents-in-law's** message}. All these *-'s* and *-s'* endings are called *inflected genitives*. See also 7.16–29.

5.21 **The "of"-genitive.** The preposition *of* may precede a noun or proper name to express relationship, agency, or possession. The choice between an inflected genitive and an *of*-construction depends mostly on style. Proper nouns and nouns denoting people or things of higher status usually take the inflected genitive {**Hilda's** adventures} {the **lion's** paw}. Compare *the perils of Penelope* with *the saucer of the chef*. Nouns denoting inanimate things can often readily take either the inflected form or the *of*-genitive {the **theater's** name} {the name **of the theater**}, but some sound right only in the *of*-genitive {the end **of everything**}. The *of*-genitive is also useful when a double genitive is called for—using both *of* and a possessive form {an idea **of Hill's**} {a friend **of my grandfather's**} (see also 7.26).

5.22 **Joint and separate genitives.** If two or more nouns share possession, the last noun takes the genitive ending. (This is called *joint* or *group possession.*) For example, *Peter and Harriet's correspondence* refers to the correspondence between Peter and Harriet. If two or more nouns possess something separately, each noun takes its own genitive ending. For example, *Peter's and Harriet's correspondence* refers to Peter's correspondence and also to Harriet's correspondence, presumably with all sorts of people. Joint possession is shown by a single apostrophe plus *-s* only when two nouns are used. If a noun and a pronoun are used to express joint possession, both the noun and the pronoun must show possession. For example, *Hilda and Eddie's vacation* becomes (when Eddie has already been mentioned) *Hilda's and his vacation* or (if Eddie is speaking in first person) *Hilda's and my vacation.*

APPOSITIVES

5.23 **Appositives—definition and use.** An appositive is a noun element that immediately follows another noun element in order to define or further identify it {George Washington, **our first president**, was born in Virginia [*our first president* is an appositive of the proper noun *George Washington*]}. An appositive is said to be "in apposition" with the word or phrase to which it refers. Commas frame an appositive unless it is restrictive {Robert Burns, **the poet**, wrote many songs about women named Mary [here, *poet* is a nonrestrictive appositive noun]} {**the poet** Robert Burns wrote many songs about women named Mary [*Robert Burns* restricts *poet* by precisely identifying which poet]}. A restrictive appositive cannot be removed from a sentence without obscuring the identity of the word or phrase that the appositive relates to. See also 6.28.

FUNCTIONAL VARIATIONS

5.24 **Nouns as adjectives.** Words that are ordinarily nouns sometimes function as other parts of speech, such as adjectives or verbs. A noun-to-adjective transition takes place when a noun modifies another noun {the **morning** newspaper} {a **state** legislature} {a **varsity** sport} (*morning*, *state*, and *varsity* function as adjectives). These are also termed *attributive nouns*. Note that they are typically singular in form (*car dealership*, not *cars dealership*). Occasionally the use of a noun as an adjective can produce ambiguity. For example, the phrase *fast results* can be read as meaning either "rapid results" or (less probably but possibly) "the outcome of a fast." Sometimes the noun and its adjectival form can be used interchangeably—e.g., *prostate cancer* and *prostatic cancer* both refer to cancer of the prostate gland. But sometimes the use of the noun instead of the adjective may alter the meaning—e.g., *a study group* is not necessarily *a studious group*. A preposition may be needed to indicate a noun's relationship to other sentence elements. But if the noun functions as an adjective, the preposition must be omitted; at times this can result in a vague phrase—e.g., *voter awareness* (awareness *of* voters or *by* them?). Context might suggest what preposition is implied, but a reader may have to deduce the writer's meaning.

5.25 **Nouns as verbs.** English nouns commonly pass into use as verbs; it has always been so. (The resulting verbs are called *denominal verbs.*) For example, in 1220 the noun *husband* meant "one who tills and cultivates the earth" {**the husband** has worked hard to produce this crop}. It became a verb meaning "to till, cultivate, and tend crops" around 1420 {you **must husband** your land thoughtfully}. New noun-to-verb transitions often occur in dialect or jargon. For example, the noun *mainstream* is used as a verb in passages such as *more school districts are mainstreaming pupils with special needs.* In formal prose, such recently transformed words should be used cautiously if at all.

5.26 **Adverbial functions.** Words that are ordinarily nouns occasionally function as adverbs {we rode **single file**} {Sam walked **home**}. This shift usually happens when a preposition is omitted {we rode **in a single file**} {Sam walked **to his home**}. Traditional grammarians have typically called such nouns-as-adverbs *adverbial objectives.* An adverbial objective often modifies an adjective rather than a verb {the team is **four members** strong}.

Pronouns

DEFINITION AND USES

5.27 **Pronouns defined.** A pronoun is a word used as a substitute for a noun or, sometimes, another pronoun. It is used in one of two ways. (1) A pronoun may substitute for an expressed noun or pronoun, especially to avoid needless repetition. For example, most of the nouns in the sentence *The father told the father's daughter that the father wanted the father's daughter to do some chores* can be replaced with pronouns (*his*, *he*, and *her*): *The father told his daughter that he wanted her to do some chores.* (2) A pronoun may also stand in the place of an understood noun. For example, if the person addressed has been identified elsewhere, the question *Susan, are you bringing your boots?* can be more simply stated as *Are you bringing your boots?* And in the sentence *It is too hot*, the indefinite *it* is understood to mean *the temperature* (*of something*). There are also a few word pairs, such as *each other*, *one another*, and *no one*, that function as pronouns. These are called *phrasal pronouns*.

5.28 **Antecedents of pronouns.** A pronoun typically refers to an antecedent—that is, an earlier noun, pronoun, phrase, or clause in the same or in a previous sentence. Pronouns with antecedents are called *anaphoric pronouns*. (*Anaphora* refers to the use of a word or phrase to refer to or replace one used earlier.) An antecedent may be explicit or implicit, but it should be clear. Miscues and ambiguity commonly arise from (1) a missing antecedent (as in *The clown's act with his dog made it a pleasure to watch*, where *it* is intended to refer to the circus, which is not explicitly mentioned in the context); (2) multiple possible antecedents (as in *Scott visited Eric after his discharge from the army*, where it is unclear who was discharged—Eric or Scott); and (3) multiple pronouns and antecedents in the same sentence (e.g., *When the bottle is empty or the baby stops drinking, it must be sterilized with hot water because if it drinks from a dirty bottle, it could become ill*—where one hopes that the hot-water sterilization is for the bottle).

5.29 **Adjective as antecedent.** A pronoun normally requires a noun or another pronoun as its antecedent. And because possessives function as adjectives, some writers have argued that possessives should not serve as antecedents of pronouns used in the nominative or objective case. But compare *Mr. Blain's background qualified him for the job* with *Mr. Blain had a background that qualified him for the job*. Not only is the identity of "him" perfectly clear in either construction, but the possessive in the first—a usage blessed by respected authorities—makes for a more economical sentence.

5.30 **Pronouns without antecedents.** Some pronouns do not require antecedents. The first-person pronouns *I* and *we* (as well as *me* and *us*) stand for the speaker or a group that includes the speaker, so they almost never have an antecedent. Similarly, the second-person pronoun *you* usually needs no antecedent {are **you** leaving?}, although one is sometimes supplied in direct address {Katrina, do **you** need something?}. Expletives such as *there* and *it* (some of which are pronouns) have no antecedents {**it** is time to go} {**this** is a fine mess} (see 5.239–41). And the relative pronoun *what* and the interrogative pronouns (*who*, *which*, *what*) never take an antecedent {**who** cares what I think?}. In colloquial usage, *they* often appears without an antecedent {**they** say she's a good golfer}, though skeptical listeners and readers may want to know who "they" are.

PROPERTIES OF PRONOUNS

5.31 **Four properties of pronouns.** A pronoun has four properties: number, person, gender, and case (see 5.17–22). A pronoun must agree with its antecedent in number, person, and gender. (This is called *pronoun-antecedent agreement.*) But only the third-person singular (*he, she, it*) is capable of indicating all three. Some pronouns can show only number—first-person singular and plural (*I, we*) and third-person plural. The second-person pronoun (*you*) indicates person only: it is no longer capable of showing singular or plural, since the form is the same for both in Modern English. First- and third-person personal pronouns (except *it*), *who*, and *whoever* can show nominative and objective case (*I, me*; *we, us*; *he, him*; *she, her*; *they, them*; *who, whom*; *whoever, whomever*); possessive pronouns represent the genitive case.

5.32 **Pronoun number and antecedent.** A pronoun's number is guided by that of its antecedent or referent—that is, a singular antecedent takes a singular pronoun of the same person as the antecedent, and a plural antecedent takes a plural pronoun of the same person as the antecedent {a **book** and **its** cover} {the **dogs** and **their** owner}. A collective noun takes a singular pronoun if the members are treated as a unit {the **audience** showed **its** appreciation} but a plural if they act individually {the **audience** rushed back to **their** seats}. A singular noun that is modified by two or more adjectives to denote different varieties, uses, or aspects of the object may take a plural pronoun {**British and American writing** differ in more ways than just **their** spelling [here, *writing* may be thought of as an elided noun after *British*]}. Two or more singular nouns or pronouns that are joined by *and* are taken jointly and referred to by a plural pronoun {the **boy and girl** left **their** bicycles outside}.

5.33 **Exceptions regarding pronoun number and antecedent.** There are several refinements to the rules stated in 5.32: (1) When two or more singular antecedents denote the same thing and are connected by *and*, the pronoun referring to the antecedents is singular {a **lawyer and role model** received **her** richly deserved recognition today}. (2) When two or more singular antecedents are connected by *and* and modified by *each*, *every*, or *no*, the pronoun referring to the antecedents is singular {**every college and university** encourages **its** students to succeed}. (3) When two or more singular antecedents are connected by *or*, *nor*, *either-or*, or *neither-nor*, they are treated separately and referred to by a singular pronoun {**neither the orange nor the peach** smells as sweet as **it** should}. (4) When two or more antecedents of different numbers are connected by *or* or *nor*, the pronoun's number agrees with that of the nearest (usually the last) antecedent. If possible, cast the sentence so that the plural antecedent comes last {neither the singer nor the **dancers** have asked for **their** paychecks}. (5) When two or more antecedents of different numbers are connected by *and*, they are referred to by a plural pronoun regardless of the antecedents' order {**the horses and the mule** kicked over **their** water trough}.

5.34 **Pronoun with multiple antecedents.** When a pronoun has two or more antecedents that differ from the pronoun in person, and the antecedents are connected by *and*, *or*, or *nor*, the pronoun must take the person of only one antecedent. The first person is preferred to the second, and the second person to the third. For example, if the antecedents are in the second and first person, the pronoun that follows is in the first person {**you or I** should get to work on **our** experiment [*our* is in the first person, as is the antecedent *I*]}. If the antecedents are in the second and third person, the pronoun that follows takes the second person {**you and she** can settle **your** dispute}. If the pronoun refers to only one of the connected nouns or pronouns, it takes the person of that noun {**you and Marian** have discussed **her** trip report}. At times the pronoun may refer to an antecedent that is not expressed in the same sentence; it takes the number of that antecedent, not of any connected noun or pronoun that precedes it {**neither they nor I** could do **his** work [*his* is referring to someone named in a preceding sentence]}.

5.35 **Pronoun case.** Sets of word forms by which a language differentiates the functions that a word performs in a sentence are called the word's *cases*. A pronoun that functions as the subject of a finite verb is in the nominative case {**they** went to town}. A personal pronoun in the possessive case is governed by the gender of the possessor {President Barack Obama took **his** advisers with him to Hawaii}. A pronoun that functions as the object of a verb or preposition is in the objective case {they gave **her** a farewell party} {they gave it to **him**}. A pronoun put after an intransitive verb or participle agrees in case with the preceding noun or pronoun referring to the same thing {it is **I**} (see 5.45). A pronoun used in an absolute construction is in the nominative: its case depends on no other word {**she** being disqualified, our best hope is gone}.

5.36 **Pronouns in apposition.** The case of a pronoun used in an appositive construction is determined by the function (subject or object) of the words with which it is in apposition {**we** three—Bruce, Felipe, and **I**—traveled to Augusta} {she asked **us**—Barbara, Sarah, and **me**—to move our cars}.

5.37 **Nominative case misused for objective.** The objective case governs personal pronouns used as direct objects of verbs {call **me** tomorrow}, indirect objects of verbs {write **me** a letter}, or objects of prepositions {makes sense to **me**}. One of the most persistent slips in English is to misuse the nominative case of a personal pronoun in a compound object:

POOR: The test would be simple for **you or I**.
BETTER: The test would be simple for **you or me**.

POOR: Read this and tell **Laura and I** what you think.
BETTER: Read this and tell **Laura and me** what you think.

The mistake may arise from overcorrecting a common error that young children are prone to—using the objective case for a personal pronoun in a compound subject, as in *Jim and me want to go swimming*. Such problems arise in compounds so exclusively that the foolproof way to check for them is to read the sentence with the personal pronoun alone: no one would mistake *The test would be simple for I* or *Read this and tell I what you think* for correct grammar.

CLASSES OF PRONOUNS

5.38 **Seven classes of pronouns.** There are seven classes of pronouns (the examples listed here do not include all forms of each):

personal (*I*, *you*, *he*, *she*, *it*, *we*, and *they*);
demonstrative (*that* and *this*);
reciprocal (*each other* and *one another*);
interrogative (*what*, *which*, and *who*);
relative (*that*, *what*, *which*, and *who*);
indefinite (*another*, *any*, *each*, *either*, and *none*); and
adjective (*any*, *each*, *that*, *this*, *what*, and *which*).

Many pronouns, except personal pronouns, may function as more than one type—e.g., *that* may be a demonstrative, relative, or adjective pronoun—depending on its use in a particular sentence.

PERSONAL PRONOUNS

5.39 **Form of personal pronouns.** A personal pronoun shows by its form whether it is referring to the speaker (first person), the person or thing spoken to (second person), or the person or thing spoken of (third person). Personal pronouns, in other words, convey the source, goal, and topic of an utterance. By their form they also display number, gender, and case.

5.40 **Identification of personal pronouns.** The first person is the speaker or speakers {**I** need some tea} {**we** heard the news}. The second person shows who is spoken to {**you** should write that essay tonight}. And the third person shows who or what is spoken of {**she** is at work} {**it** is in the glove compartment}. The first-person-singular pronoun *I* is always capitalized no matter where it appears in the sentence {if possible, **I** will send you an answer today}. All other pronouns are capitalized only at the beginning of a sentence, unless they are part of an honorific title {**Her** Majesty, the Queen of England}.

5.41 **Changes in form of personal pronouns.** Personal pronouns change form (or *decline*) according to person, number, and case. Apart from the second person, all personal pronouns show number by taking a singular or plural form. Although the second-person pronoun *you* is both singular and plural, it always takes a plural verb, even if only a single person or thing is addressed.

THE FORMS OF PERSONAL PRONOUNS

Singular Pronouns	*Nominative*	*Objective*	*Genitive*	*Reflexive*
First person	I	me	my, mine	myself
Second person	you	you	your, yours	yourself
Third person	he	him	his	himself
	she	her	her, hers	herself
	it	it	its	itself
Plural Pronouns				
First person	we	us	our, ours	ourselves
Second person	you	you	your, yours	yourselves
Third person	they	them	their, theirs	themselves

There are four essential rules about the nominative and objective cases. (1) If the pronoun is the subject of a clause, it is in the nominative case {**he** is vice president}. (2) If the pronoun is the object of a verb, it is objective {she thanked **him**}. (3) If a pronoun is the object of a preposition, it is objective {please keep this between **you** and **me**}. (4) If the pronoun is the subject of an infinitive, it is objective {Jim wanted **her** to sing}.

5.42 **Agreement of personal pronoun with noun.** A personal pronoun agrees with the noun for which it stands in both gender and number {**John** writes, and **he** will soon write well} {**Sheila** was there, but **she** couldn't hear what was said}.

5.43 **Personal pronouns and gender.** Only the third-person-singular pronouns directly express gender. In the nominative or objective case, the pronoun takes the antecedent noun's gender {the president is not in **her** office today; **she's** at a seminar}. In the genitive case, the pronoun always takes the gender of the possessor, not of the person or thing possessed {the woman loves **her** husband} {Thomas is visiting **his** sister} {the kitten pounced on **its** mother}. Some nouns may acquire gender through personification, a figure of speech that refers to a nonliving thing as if it were a person. Pronouns enhance personification when a feminine or masculine pronoun is used as if the antecedent represented a female or male person (as was traditionally done, for example, when a ship or other vessel was referred to with the pronoun *she* or *her*).

5.44 **Personal pronoun case.** Some special rules apply to personal pronouns. (1) If a pronoun is the subject of a clause, or follows a conjunction but precedes the verb, it must be in the nominative case {**she** owns a tan briefcase} {although Delia would like to travel, **she** can't afford to}. (2) If a pronoun is the object of a verb or preposition, it must be in the objective case {the rustic setting helped **him** relax} {that's a matter between **him** and **her**}. (3) If a prepositional phrase contains more than one object, all the objects must be in the objective case {will you send an invitation to **him** and **me**?}. (4) If a pronoun is the subject of an infinitive, it must be in the objective case {does Tina want **me** to leave?}.

5.45 **Personal pronoun after linking verb.** Strictly speaking, a pronoun serving as the complement of a *be*-verb or other linking verb should be in the nominative case {it was **she** who asked for a meeting}. In that construction, *she* functions as a predicate nominative; when a pronoun does this, it is termed an *attribute pronoun*. The same construction occurs when someone who answers a telephone call is asked, "May I speak to [answerer's name]?" The refined response is *This is he*, not *This is him*.

5.46 **Personal pronoun after "than" or "as-as."** The case of a pronoun following a comparative construction, typically at the end of a sentence, depends on who or what is being compared. In *My sister looks more like our father than I* [or *me*], for example, the proper pronoun depends on the meaning. If the question is whether the sister or the speaker looks more like their father, the pronoun should be nominative because it is the subject of an understood verb {my sister looks more like our father **than I do**}. But if the question is whether the father or the speaker looks more like the sister, the pronoun should be objective because it is the object of a preposition in an understood clause {my sister looks more like my father **than she looks like me**}. Whatever the writer's intent with the original sentence, and regardless of the pronoun used, the listener or reader can't be entirely certain about the meaning. It would be better to reword the sentence and avoid the elliptical construction.

5.47 **Special uses of personal pronouns.** Some personal pronouns have special uses. (1) *He*, *him*, and *his* have traditionally been used as pronouns of indeterminate gender equally applicable to a male or female person {if the finder returns my watch, **he** will receive a reward}. Because these pronouns are also masculine-specific, they have in recent years been regarded as sexist when used generically, and their indeterminate-gender use is declining (see 5.251–60). (2) *It* eliminates gender even if the noun's sex could be identified. Using *it* does not mean that the noun has no sex—only that the sex is unknown or unimportant {the baby is smiling at **its** mother} {the mockingbird is building **its** nest}. (3) *We*, *you*, and *they* can be used indefinitely—that is, without an antecedent—in the sense of "persons," "one," or "people in general." *We* is sometimes used by an individual who is speaking for a group {the council's representative declared, "**We** appreciate your concern"} {the magazine's editor wrote, "In our last issue, **we** covered the archaeological survey of Peru"}. This latter use is called "the editorial *we*." Some writers also use *we* to make their prose appear less personal and to draw in the reader or listener {from these results **we** can draw only one conclusion}. *You* can apply indefinitely to any person or all persons {if **you** read this book, **you** will learn how to influence people [*you* is indefinite—anyone who reads the book will learn]}. The same is true of *they* {**they** say that Stonehenge may have been a primitive calendar [those denoted by *they* are unidentified and perhaps unimportant to the point]}. (4) *It* also has several uses as an indefinite pronoun: (a) *it* may refer to a phrase, clause, sentence, or implied thought {he said that the website is down, but I don't believe **it** [without the pronoun *it*, the clause might be rewritten *I don't believe what he said*]}; (b) *it* can be the subject of a verb (usually a *be*-verb) without an antecedent noun {**it** was too far}, or an introductory word or expletive for a phrase or clause that follows the verb {**it** is possible that Jerry Paul is on vacation}; (c) *it* can be the grammatical subject in an expression about time, weather, distance, or the like {**it** is almost midnight} {**it** is beginning to snow}; and (d) *it* may be an expletive that anticipates the true grammatical subject or object {I find **it** hard to accept this situation}.

5.48 **Singular "they."** Normally, a singular antecedent requires a singular pronoun. But because *he* is no longer universally accepted as a generic pronoun referring to a person of unspecified gender, people commonly (in speech and in informal writing) substitute the third-person-plural pronouns *they*, *them*, *their*, and *themselves* (or the nonstandard singular *themself*). While this usage is accepted in those spheres, it is only lately showing signs of gaining acceptance in formal writing (see 5.256), where Chicago recommends avoiding its use (see 5.255).[5] When referring specifically to a person who does not identify with a gender-specific pronoun, however, *they* and its forms are often preferred. (*They* used in this sense was the American Dialect Society's Word of the Year for 2015.) Like singular *you*, singular *they* takes a plural verb. So when the context requires it, *they/them/their/theirs*, like *you/your/yours* (long used as both singular and plural forms), can be used to refer to one person {they have a degree in molecular biology} {their favorite color is blue}. And *themself* (like *yourself*) may be used to signal the singular antecedent (though some people will prefer *themselves*) {they blamed themself [or *themselves*]}. A number of other gender-neutral singular pronouns are in use, invented for that purpose; forms of these are usually singular and take singular verbs. In general, a person's stated preference for a specific pronoun should be respected. See also 5.251–60.

POSSESSIVE PRONOUNS

5.49 **Uses and forms of possessive pronouns.** The possessive pronouns, *my*, *our*, *your*, *his*, *her*, *its*, and *their*, are used as limiting adjectives to qualify nouns {**my** dictionary} {**your** cabin} {**his** diploma}. Despite their name, possessive pronouns function in a much broader series of relationships than mere possession {my professor} {your argument}. Each form has a corresponding absolute possessive pronoun (also called an *independent possessive*) that can stand alone without a noun: *mine*, *ours*, *yours*, *his*, *hers*, *its*, and *theirs*. The independent form does not require an explicit object: the thing possessed may be either an antecedent or something understood {this dictionary is **mine**} {this cabin of **yours** is nice} {where is **hers**?}. An independent possessive pronoun can also stand alone and be treated as a noun: it can be the subject or object of a verb {**hers** is on

5. The generic singular *they* was endorsed in 2015 by the editors of the *Washington Post*, though with a caveat to first try avoiding it if possible. Singular *they* is more likely to be accepted in British than in American English. See Bas Aarts, *Oxford Modern English Grammar* (Oxford: Oxford University Press, 2010), 5 ("the use of the plural pronoun *they* with a non-specific singular antecedent [is] sanctioned by widespread current usage").

the table} {pass me **yours**}, or the object of a preposition {put your coat with **theirs**}. When it is used with the preposition *of*, a double possessive is produced: *that letter of Sheila's* becomes *that letter of hers*. Such a construction is unobjectionable. Note that none of the possessive personal pronouns is spelled with an apostrophe.

5.50 **Possessive pronouns versus contractions.** The possessive forms of personal pronouns are *my*, *mine*, *our*, *ours*, *your*, *yours*, *his*, *her*, *hers*, *its*, and *their*, *theirs*. Again, none of them takes an apostrophe. Nor does the possessive form of *who* (*whose*). Apart from these exceptions, the apostrophe is a universal signal of the possessive in English, so it is a natural tendency (and a common error) to overlook the exceptions and insert an apostrophe in the pronoun forms that end in *-s* (or the sibilant *-se*). Aggravating that tendency is the fact that some of the words have homophones that are contractions—another form that is also signaled by apostrophes. The pronouns that don't sound like legitimate contractions seldom present problems, even if they do end in *-s* (*hers*, *yours*, *ours*). But several do require special attention, specifically *its* (the possessive of *it*) and *it's* ("it is"); *your* (the possessive of *you*) and *you're* ("you are"); *whose* (the possessive of *who*) and *who's* ("who is"); and the three homophones *their* (the possessive of *they*), *there* ("in that place" or "in that way"), and *they're* ("they are").

REFLEXIVE AND INTENSIVE PRONOUNS

5.51 **Basic uses of reflexive and intensive pronouns.** The words *myself*, *ourselves*, *yourself*, *yourselves*, *himself*, *herself*, *itself*, and *themselves* are used in two ways, and it's useful to distinguish between their functions as reflexive and intensive personal pronouns. Compare the intensive pronoun in *I burned the papers myself* (in which the object of *burned* is *papers*) with the reflexive pronoun in *I burned myself* (in which the object of *burned* is *myself*). Reflexive pronouns serve as objects that usually look back to the subject of a sentence or clause {the cat **scared itself**} {Gayla took it **on herself** to make the first move} {Ayoka **dressed herself** today} {don't **repeat yourself** [the subject of this imperative sentence is understood to be *you*]}. Intensive pronouns repeat the antecedent noun or pronoun to add emphasis {**I myself** don't care} {did you speak with the **manager herself**?} {**Kate herself** has won several writing awards} {did **you** knit that **yourself**?}. An intensive pronoun is used in apposition to its referent, so it's in the nominative case. A common problem occurs when the *-self* form does not serve either of those functions. For example, the first-person pronoun in a compound might be used as a subject:

POOR: **The staff and myself** thank you for your contribution.
BETTER: **The staff and I** thank you for your contribution.

Or it might be used as an object that does not refer to the subject:

POOR: Deliver the equipment to **my partner or myself.**
BETTER: Deliver the equipment to **my partner or me.**

DEMONSTRATIVE PRONOUNS

5.52 **Demonstrative pronouns defined.** A demonstrative pronoun (or, as it is sometimes called, a *deictic pronoun*) is one that points directly to its antecedent in the text: *this* or *that* for a singular antecedent {**this** is your desk} {**that** is my office}, and *these* or *those* for a plural antecedent {**these** have just arrived} {**those** need to be answered}. *This* and *these* point to objects that are near in space, time, or thought, while *that* and *those* point to objects that are somewhat remote in space, time, or thought. The antecedent of a demonstrative pronoun can be a noun, phrase, clause, sentence, or implied thought, as long as the antecedent is clear. *Kind* and *sort*, each referring to "one class," are often used with an adjectival *this* or *that* {**this kind** of magazine} {**that sort** of school}. The plural forms *kinds* and *sorts* are usually preferred with the plural demonstratives {**these kinds** of magazines} {**those sorts** of schools}. A demonstrative pronoun standing alone cannot refer to a human antecedent; it must be followed by a word denoting a person. For example: *I heard Mike's son playing. That child is talented.* In the second sentence, it would be erroneous to omit *child* or some such noun after *that.*

RECIPROCAL PRONOUNS

5.53 **Reciprocal pronouns generally.** *Each other* and *one another* are called *reciprocal pronouns* because they express a mutual relationship between elements {after much discussion, the two finally understood each other} {it's true that we love one another}. Compare the nuances of meaning that a reciprocal or plural reflexive pronoun creates in the same sentence: {after our hike, we all checked ourselves for ticks [each person inspected him- or herself]} {after our hike, we checked one another for ticks [each person inspected one or more of the others]}. Reciprocal pronouns can also take the inflected genitive *-'s* to express possession {we admired each other's watch}. In traditional usage, *each other* is reserved for two {she and I protected each other} and *one another* for more than two {all five of us watched out for one another}.

INTERROGATIVE PRONOUNS

5.54 **Interrogative pronouns defined.** An interrogative pronoun asks a question. The three interrogatives are *who*, *what*, and *which*. Only one, *who*, declines: *who* (nominative), *whom* (objective), *whose* (possessive) {**who** starred in *Casablanca*?} {to **whom** am I speaking?} {**whose** cologne smells so nice?}. In the nominative case, *who* is used in two ways: (1) as the subject of a verb {**who** washed the dishes today?} and (2) as a predicate nominative after a linking verb {it was **who**?}. In the objective case, *whom* is used in two ways: (1) as the object of a verb {**whom** did you see?} and (2) as the object of a preposition {for **whom** is this building named?}.

5.55 **Referent of interrogative pronouns.** To refer to a person, *who*, *what*, or *which* can be used. But they are not interchangeable. *Who* is universal or general: it asks for any one or more persons among a universe of people. The answer may potentially include any person, living or dead, present or absent {**who** wants to see that movie?} {**who** were your greatest inspirations?}. *Who* also asks for a particular person's identity {**who** is that person standing near the Emerald Buddha?}. *Which* and *what*, when followed by a noun denoting a person or persons, are usually selective or limited; they ask for a particular member of a group, and the answer is limited to the group addressed or referred to {**which** explorers visited China in the sixteenth century?} {**what** ice-skater is your favorite?}. To refer to a person, animal, or thing, either *which* or *what* may be used {**which** one of you did this?} {**what** kind of bird is that?}. When applied to a person, *what* often asks for the person's character, occupation, qualities, and the like {**what** do you think of our governor?}. When applied to a thing, *what* is broad and asks for any one thing, especially of a set {**what** is your quest?} {**what** is your favorite color?}.

RELATIVE PRONOUNS

5.56 **Relative pronouns defined.** A relative pronoun is one that introduces a dependent (or *relative*) clause and relates it to the independent clause. Relative pronouns in common use are *who*, *which*, *what*, and *that*. *Who* is the only relative pronoun that declines: *who* (nominative), *whom* (objective), *whose* (possessive) {the woman **who** presented the award} {a source **whom** he declined to name} {the writer **whose** book was a best seller}.

Who normally refers to a human being, but it can be used in the first, second, or third person. *Which* refers only to an animal or a thing. *What* refers only to a nonliving thing. *Which* and *what* are used only in the second and third person. *That* refers to a human, animal, or thing, and it can be used in the first, second, or third person. When a relative pronoun qualifies a noun element in the clause it introduces, it is sometimes called a *relative adjective*. See also 5.64.

5.57 **Gender, number, and case with relative pronouns.** A relative pronoun agrees with its antecedent in gender, person, and number. If a personal pronoun follows a relative pronoun, and both refer to the same antecedent in the independent clause, the personal pronoun takes the gender and number of that antecedent {I saw a farmer **who** was plowing **his** fields with **his** mule}. If the personal pronoun refers to a different antecedent from that of the relative pronoun, it takes the gender and number of that antecedent {I saw the boy and also the girl **who** pushed **him** down}. A personal pronoun does not govern the case of a relative pronoun. Hence an objective pronoun such as *me* may be the antecedent of the nominative pronoun *who*, although a construction formed in this way sounds increasingly archaic or even incorrect {she was referring to me, **who** never graduated from college} {it was we **whom** they objected to}. When a construction may be technically correct but sounds awkward or artificial {I, **who** am wronged, have a grievance}, the best course may be to use preventive grammar and find a different construction {I have been wronged; I have a grievance} {having been wronged, I have a grievance}.

5.58 **Positional nuances of relative pronouns.** A relative pronoun is in the nominative case when no subject comes between it and the verb {the professor **who** lectured was brilliant}. When one or more words intervene between the relative pronoun and the verb, the relative is governed by the following verb or by a verb or a preposition within the intervening clause {the person **whom** I called is no longer there} {it was John **who** they thought was in the bleachers}. When a relative pronoun is interrogative, it refers to the word or phrase containing the answer to the question for its consequent, which agrees in case with the interrogative {**whose** book is that? Joseph's}.

5.59 **Antecedent of relative pronouns.** Usually a relative pronoun's antecedent is a noun or pronoun in the independent clause on which the relative clause depends. For clarity, it should immediately precede the pronoun {the diadem **that** I told you about is in this gallery}. The antecedent may also be a noun phrase or a clause, but the result can sometimes be ambiguous: in *the bedroom of the villa, which was painted pink*, does the *which*-clause refer to the bedroom or to the villa? See 5.60.

5.60 **Remote relative clauses.** For clarity, pronouns must have unambiguous antecedents. A common problem with the relative pronouns *that*, *which*, and *who* arises if you separate the relative clause from the noun to which it refers. The longer the separation, the more pronounced the problem—especially when one or more unrelated nouns fall between the true antecedent and the clause. Consider *the guy down the street that runs through our neighborhood*: if the intent is for *that runs through our neighborhood* to refer to *the guy* rather than *the street*, the writer should reword the phrase to make that instantly clear to the reader.

POOR: Stress caused her to lose the **freedom** from fear of the future, **which she once enjoyed**.
BETTER: Stress caused her to lose **what she once enjoyed: freedom** from fear of the future.

POOR: After the news came out, the CEO fired **the aide**, a friend of the chairman, **who was the target** of the investigation.
BETTER: After the news came out, the CEO fired **the aide, who was the target** of the investigation and also a friend of the chairman.

5.61 **Omitted antecedent of relative pronoun.** If no antecedent noun is expressed, *what* can be used to mean *that which* {is this **what** you were looking for?}. But if there is an antecedent, use a different relative pronoun: *who* {where is the man **who** spoke?}, *that* (if the relative clause is restrictive, i.e., essential to the sentence's basic meaning) {where are the books **that** Jones told us about?}, or *which* (if the relative clause is nonrestrictive, i.e., could be deleted without affecting the sentence's basic meaning) {the sun, **which** is shining brightly, feels warm on my face}. See also 6.27.

5.62 **Relative pronoun and the antecedent "one."** A relative pronoun takes its number from its antecedent. That's easy enough when the antecedent is simply *one*. But if *one* is part of a noun phrase with a plural noun such as *one of the few* or *one of those*, the relative pronoun following takes the plural word as its antecedent—not *one*. Treat the pronoun as a plural and use a plural verb. For example, in *Lily is one of those people who are famous for being famous*, the plural verb *are* links a quality belonging to *those people*.

5.63 **Genitive forms for relative pronouns.** The forms *of whom* and *of which* are genitives {the child, the mother **of whom** we talked about, is in kindergarten} {this foal, the sire **of which** Belle owns, will be trained as a hunter-jumper}. These forms have an old-fashioned sound and can often be rephrased more naturally {the child **whose** mother we talked about is in kindergarten}. The relative *what* forms the genitive *of what* {a list **of what** we need}. The relative *that* forms the genitive *of that* (the preposition being placed at the end of the phrase) {no legend **that** we know **of**} or *of which* {no legend **of which** we know}.

5.64 **"Whose" and "of which."** The relatives *who* and *which* can both take *whose* as a possessive form (*whose* substitutes for *of which*) {a movie the conclusion **of which** is unforgettable} {a movie **whose** conclusion is unforgettable}. Some writers object to using *whose* as a replacement for *of which*, especially when the subject is not human, but the usage is centuries old and is widely accepted as preventing unnecessary awkwardness. Compare *the company whose stock rose faster* with *the company the stock of which rose faster*. Either form is acceptable, but the possessive *whose* is far smoother.

5.65 **Compound relative pronouns.** *Who*, *whom*, *what*, and *which* form compound relative pronouns by adding the suffix *-ever*. The compound relatives *whoever*, *whomever*, *whichever*, and *whatever* apply universally to any or all persons or things {**whatever** you do, let me know} {**whoever** needs to write a report about this book may borrow it}.

5.66 **"Who" versus "whom."** *Who* and *whoever* are nominative pronouns. Each can be used as a subject {**whoever** said that?} or as a predicate nominative {it was **who**?}. *Whom* and *whomever* are the objective forms, used as the object of a verb {you called **whom**?} or of a preposition {to **whom** are you referring?}. Three problems arise with determining the correct case. First, because the words are so often found in the inverted syntax of an interrogative sentence, their true function in the sentence can be hard to see without sorting the words into standard subject-verb-object syntax. In the following example, sorting the incorrect "I should say whom is calling" makes the case easier to determine:

POOR: **Whom** should I say is calling?
BETTER: **Who** should I say is calling?

Second, determining the proper case can be confusing when the pronoun serves a function (say, nominative) in a clause that itself serves a different function (say, objective) in the main sentence. The pronoun's function in its clause determines its case.

POOR: I'll talk to **whomever will listen.**
BETTER: I'll talk to **whoever will listen.**

POOR: **Whoever you choose** will suit me.
BETTER: **Whomever you choose** will suit me.

In the first example, the entire clause *whoever will listen* is the object of the preposition *to*. But in the clause itself, *whoever* serves as the subject, and that function determines its case. Similarly, in the second example *whomever* is the object of *choose* in the clause, so it technically ought to be in the objective case even though the clause itself serves as the subject of the sentence. Third, as the second example above shows, a further distraction can arise when the *who*-clause itself contains a nested clause, typically of attribution or identification (here, *you choose*).

INDEFINITE PRONOUNS

5.67 **Indefinite pronouns generally.** An indefinite pronoun is one that generally or indefinitely represents an object, usually one that has already been identified or doesn't need exact identification. The most common examples are *another*, *any*, *both*, *each*, *either*, *neither*, *none*, *one*, *other*, *some*, and *such*. There are also compound indefinite pronouns such as *anybody*, *anyone*, *anything*, *everybody*, *everyone*, *everything*, *nobody*, *no one*, *oneself*, *somebody*, and *someone*. *Each*, *either*, and *neither* are also called *distributive pronouns* because they separate the objects referred to from others referred to nearby. Indefinite pronouns have number. When an indefinite pronoun is the subject of a verb, it is usually singular {**everyone** is enjoying the dinner} {**everybody** takes notes during the first week}. But sometimes an indefinite pronoun carries a plural sense in informal prose {**nobody** could describe the music; they hadn't been listening to it} {**everyone** understood the risk, but they were lured by promises of big returns}. The forms of indefinite pronouns are not affected by gender or person, and the nominative and objective forms are the same. To form the possessive, the indefinite pronoun may take -*'s* {that is **no one's** fault} {is this **anyone's** jacket?} or the adverb *else* plus -*'s* {don't interfere with **anybody else's** business} {**no one else's** cups were broken}.

Adjectives

TYPES OF ADJECTIVES

5.68 **Adjectives defined.** An adjective is a word (more particularly, a type of word sometimes called an *adjunct*) modifying a noun or pronoun; it is often called a *describing word*. An adjective tells you what sort, how many, how large or small, whose, etc. It may modify an understood as well as an expressed noun {he is a **good** as well as a **wise** man [*man* is understood after *good*]}. An adjective may add a new idea to a noun or pronoun by describing it more definitely or fully {**red** wagon} {**human** error}. Or it may be limiting {**three** pigs} {**this** time}. Most adjectives derive from nouns, as *plentiful* derives from *plenty* or as *stylish* derives from *style*; some derive from verbs, roots, or other adjectives. Often a suffix creates the adjective. Among the suffixes that often distinguish adjectives are *-able* {manageable}, *-al* {mystical}, *-ary* {elementary}, *-ed* {hammered}, *-en* {wooden}, *-esque* {statuesque}, *-ful* {harmful}, *-ible* {inaccessible}, *-ic* {artistic}, *-ish* {foolish}, *-ive* {demonstrative}, *-less* {helpless}, *-like* {childlike}, *-ly* {ghostly}, *-ous* {perilous}, *-some* {lonesome}, and *-y* {sunny}. But many adjectives do not have distinctive endings and are recognizable only by their function {old} {tall} {brilliant}.

5.69 **Proper adjectives.** A proper adjective is one that, being or deriving from a proper name, always begins with a capital letter {a **New York** minute} {a **Cuban** cigar} {a **Canadian** dollar}. (But see 8.61.) A proper name used attributively is still capitalized, but it does not cause the noun it modifies to be capitalized. A place-name containing a comma—such as *Toronto, Ontario*, or *New Delhi, India*—should generally not be used as an adjective because a second comma may be considered obligatory {we met in a **Toronto, Ontario**, restaurant}. The comma after *Ontario* in that sentence is awkward. Compare the readability of *a New Delhi, India, marketplace* with *a New Delhi marketplace* or *a marketplace in New Delhi, India* (substituting a prepositional phrase for the proper adjective).

ARTICLES AS LIMITING ADJECTIVES

5.70 **Articles defined.** An article is a limiting adjective that precedes a noun or noun phrase and determines its use to indicate something definite (*the*) or indefinite (*a* or *an*). An article might stand alone or be used with other adjectives {**a** road} {**an** elaborate design} {**the** yellow-brick road}.

5.71 **Definite article.** A definite article points to a definite object that (1) is so well understood that it does not need description (e.g., *the package is here* is a shortened form of *the package that you expected is here*); (2) is a thing that is about to be described {**the** sights of Chicago}; or (3) is important {**the** grand prize}. The definite article belongs to nouns in the singular {**the** star} or the plural number {**the** stars}.

5.72 **Indefinite article.** An indefinite article points to a nonspecific object, thing, or person that is not distinguished from the other members of a class. The thing may be singular {**a** student at Princeton}, or uncountable {**a** multitude}, or generalized {**an** idea inspired by Milton's *Paradise Lost*}.

5.73 **Indefinite article in specific reference.** In a few usages, the indefinite article provides a specific reference {I saw **a great movie** last night} and the definite article a generic reference {**the Scots** are talking about independence [generalizing by nationality]}.

5.74 **Choosing "a" or "an."** With the indefinite article, the choice of *a* or *an* depends on the sound of the word it precedes. *A* precedes words with a consonant sound, including /y/, /h/, and /w/, no matter how the word is spelled {**a** eulogy} {**a** historic occasion} {**a** onetime pass}. *An* comes before words with a vowel sound {**an** insurance agent} {**an** *X-Files* episode} {**an** hour ago}. The same is true for abbreviations. If the first letter or syllable is sounded as a consonant, use *a* {**a** BTU calculation} {**a** PDF file}. If the first sound is a vowel, use *an* {**an** MBA degree} {**an** ATM}. See also 7.32–33, 10.9.

5.75 **Articles with coordinate nouns.** With a series of coordinate nouns, an article may appear before each noun, but it is not necessary {**the rosebush and hedge** need trimming}. If the things named make up a single idea, it's especially unnecessary to repeat the article {in the highest degree of dressage, **the horse and rider** appear to be one entity}. And if the named things are covered by one plural noun, the definite article should not be repeated {in the first and second years of college}. But if you want to distinguish concepts or add emphasis, then do repeat the article {**the time, the money**, and **the effort** were all wasted}.

5.76 **Effect of article on meaning.** Because articles have a demonstrative value, the meaning of a phrase may shift depending on the article used. For example, *an officer and gentleman escorted Princess Grace to her car* suggests (though ambiguously) that the escort was one man with two descriptive characteristics. But *an officer and a friend escorted Princess Grace to her car* suggests that two people acted as escorts. Similarly, *do you like the red and blue cloth?* suggests that the cloth contains both red and blue threads. But *do you like the red and the blue cloth?* suggests that two different fabrics are being discussed. The clearest way to express the idea that the cloth contains both red and blue is to hyphenate the phrase as a compound modifier: *red-and-blue cloth*; and with two kinds of cloth, the clear expression is either to repeat the word *cloth* (*the red cloth and the* *blue cloth*) or to use *cloth* with the first adjective rather than the second (*the red cloth and the blue*).

5.77 **Omitted article and zero article.** The absence of an article may alter a sentence's meaning—e.g., the meaning of *the news brought us little comfort* (we weren't comforted) changes if *a* is inserted before *little*: *the news brought us a little comfort* (we felt somewhat comforted). An article that is implied but omitted is called a *zero article*, common in idiomatic usage. For example, in the morning you may *make the bed*, but at night you *go to bed* (not *the bed*)—and notice *in the morning* versus *at night*. The zero article usually occurs in idiomatic references to time, illness, transportation, personal routines, and meals {by sunset} {has cancer} {travel by train} {go to bed} {make breakfast}.

5.78 **Article as pronoun substitute.** An article may sometimes substitute for a pronoun. For example, the blanks in *a patient who develops the described rash on __ hands should inform __ doctor* may be filled in with either a possessive pronoun or the definite article (*the*).

POSITION OF ADJECTIVES

5.79 **Basic rules for position of adjectives.** An adjective that modifies a noun element usually precedes it {perfect storm} {spectacular view} {a good bowl of soup}. Such an adjective is called an *attributive adjective*. An adjective may follow the noun element if the adjective (1) expresses special emphasis {reasons **innumerable**} {captains **courageous**}; (2) occurs in this position in standard usage {court-**martial**} {notary **public**}; (3) is a predicate adjective following a linking verb {I am **ready**}; (4) functions as an appositive set off by commas or dashes {the man, **tall and thin**, stood in the corner}; or (5) modifies a pronoun of a type usually followed by an adjective {anything good} {everything yellow} {nothing important} {something wicked}. (An adjective that follows its noun is termed a *postpositive adjective*.) Some adjectives are always in the predicate and never appear before what they modify {the city is **asleep**} {the door was **ajar**}. Others appear uniformly before the nouns they modify {**utter** nonsense} {a **mere** child}. Phrasal adjectives may precede or follow what they modify. When a modifying phrase follows the noun element it modifies, it is traditionally called an *adjective phrase*. See also 5.92.

5.80 **Adjective after possessive.** When a noun phrase includes a possessive noun, as in *children's shoes* or *the company's president*, the adjective follows the possessive {children's **athletic** shoes} {the company's **former** president} (unless the reference is to athletic children or a former company). The same is true of possessive pronouns {her red dress}.

5.81 **Adjective modifying pronoun.** When modifying a pronoun, an adjective usually follows the pronoun {the searchers found him **unconscious**} {some like it **hot**}, sometimes as a predicate adjective {it was **insensitive**} {who was so **jealous**?}. Occasionally, however, an adjective precedes the pronoun it modifies {**flustered**, he sat down} {they offered her the director position but, **uncertain**, she demurred}.

5.82 **Predicate adjective.** A predicate adjective is an adjective that follows a linking verb (see 5.101) but modifies the subject {the child is **afraid**} {the night became **colder**} {this tastes **delicious**} {I feel **bad**}. If an adjective in the predicate modifies a noun or pronoun in the predicate, it is not a predicate adjective. For example, in *the train will be late*, the adjective *late* modifies the subject *train*. But in *the train will be here at a late hour*, the adjective *late* modifies the noun *hour*, not the subject *train*. So even though it occurs in the predicate, it is not known as a *predicate adjective*, which by definition follows a linking verb.

5.83 **Date as adjective.** Dates are often used as descriptive adjectives, more often today than in years past. If a month-year or month-day date is used as an adjective, no hyphen or comma is needed {October 31 festivities} {December 2014 financial statement}. If a full month-day-year date is used, then a comma is sometimes considered necessary both before and after the year {the May 27, 2016, ceremonies}. But this construction is awkward because the adjective (which is forward looking) contains two commas (which are backward looking); the construction is therefore best avoided {commencement ceremonies on May 27, 2016}.

DEGREES OF ADJECTIVES

5.84 **Three degrees of adjectives.** An adjective is gradable into three degrees: the positive or absolute {hard}, the comparative {harder}, and the superlative {hardest}. A positive adjective simply expresses an object's quality without reference to any other thing {a big balloon} {bad news}.

5.85 **Comparative adjectives.** A comparative adjective expresses the relationship between a specified quality shared by two things, often to determine which has more or less of that quality {a cheaper ticket} {a happier ending}. The suffix *-er* usually signals the comparative form of a common adjective having one or two syllables {light–lighter} {merry–merrier}. These forms are called *synthetic comparatives*. A positive adjective with three or more syllables typically takes *more* (or *greater*, *less*, *fewer*, and so forth) instead of a suffix to form the comparative {intelligent–more intelligent} {purposeful–more purposeful}. These forms are called *periphrastic comparatives*. As noted, some adjectives with two syllables take the *-er* suffix {lazy–lazier} {narrow–narrower}, but most two-syllable adjectives take *more* {more hostile} {more careless}. A two-syllable adjective ending in *-er*, *-le*, *-ow*, *-ure*, or *-y* can typically use either the *-er* suffix or *more*.

5.86 **Superlative adjectives.** A superlative adjective expresses the relationship between at least three things and denotes an extreme of intensity or amount in a particular shared quality {the biggest house on the block} {the bitterest pill of all}. The suffix *-est* usually signals the superlative form of a common adjective having one or two syllables {lighter–lightest}. These forms are called *synthetic superlatives*. An adjective with three or more syllables takes *most* instead of a suffix to form the superlative {quarrelsome–most quarrelsome} {humorous–most humorous}. These forms are called *periphrastic superlatives*. Some adjectives with two syllables take the *-est* suffix {holy–holiest} {noble–noblest}, but most two-syllable adjectives take *most* {most fruitful} {most reckless}.

5.87 **Forming comparatives and superlatives.** A few rules govern the forming of a short regular adjective's comparative and superlative forms. (1) If the adjective is a monosyllable ending in a single vowel followed by a single consonant, the final consonant is doubled before the suffix is attached {red–redder–reddest}. (2) If the adjective ends in a silent *-e*, the *-e* is dropped before the suffix is added {polite–politer–politest}. (3) A participle used as an adjective requires *more* or *most* before the participle; no suffix is added to form the comparative or the superlative {this teleplay is **more boring** than the first one} {I am **most tired** on Fridays}. (4) A few one-syllable adjectives—*real*, *right*, and *wrong*—can take only *more* and *most*. Even then, these combinations occur only in informal speech. (5) *Eager*, *proper*, and *somber*, unlike many other two-syllable adjectives, also take only *more* and *most*; none can take a suffix. (6) A two-syllable adjective to which the negative prefix *un-* has been added can usually take either a suffix or *more* or *most*, even if the total number of syllables is three {unhappiest} {most unhappy}. (7) Many adjectives are irregular—there is no rule that guides their comparative and superlative forms {good–better–best} {less–lesser–least}. A good dictionary will show the forms of an irregular adjective. (8) An adjective can never take both a suffix and *more* or *most* (or *less*, *least*, etc.). This is a grammatical fault known as a *double comparative* (e.g., *more greener*) or a *double superlative* (e.g., *least greenest*). It is stigmatized as nonstandard.

5.88 **Equal and unequal comparisons.** A higher degree of comparison is signaled by a suffix (*-er* or *-est*) or by *more* or *most*. (See 5.85, 5.86.) A lower degree is shown by *less* (comparative) or *least* (superlative) {cold–less cold} {less cold–least cold}. Equivalence is shown by the use of the *as–as* construction {this is as old as that} and sometimes by *so*, but usually in the negative, where it signals a lower degree {that test was not so hard as the last one}.

5.89 **Noncomparable adjectives.** An adjective that by definition describes an absolute state or condition—e.g., *entire*, *impossible*, *pregnant*, *unique*—is called *noncomparable*. It cannot take a comparative suffix and cannot be coupled with a comparative term (*more*, *most*, *less*, *least*). Nor can it be intensified by a word such as *very*, *largely*, or *quite*. But on the rare occasion when a particular emphasis is needed, a good writer may depart from this rule and use a phrase such as *more perfect*, as the framers of the United States Constitution did in composing its preamble {We the People of the United States, in order to form a **more perfect** Union . . .}.

SPECIAL TYPES OF ADJECTIVES

5.90 **Participial adjectives.** A participial adjective is simply a verb's participle that modifies a noun or pronoun. It can be a present participle (verb ending in *-ing*) {the dining room} {a walking stick} {a rising star} or a past participle (usually a verb ending in *-ed*) {an endangered species} {a completed assignment} {a proven need}. Some past-participial forms have only this adjectival function, the past-participial verb having taken a different form {a shaven face} {a graven image}. A past participle functioning as an adjective may itself be modified with an adverb such as *quite* {a quite fatigued traveler}, *barely* {a barely concealed wince}, *little* {a little-known fact}, or an adverbial phrase such as *very much* {a very much distrusted public official}. If the past participle has gained a strong adjectival quality, *very* will do the job alone without the quantitative *much* {very tired} {very drunk}. But if the participial form seems more like a verb, *very* needs *much* to help it do the job {very much appreciated} {very much delayed}. A few past participles (such as *bored*, *interested*, *pleased*, *satisfied*) are in the middle of the spectrum between those having mostly adjectival qualities and those having mostly verbal qualities. With these few, the quantitative *much* is normally omitted. See also 5.110.

5.91 **Coordinate adjectives.** A coordinate adjective is one that appears in a sequence with one or more related adjectives to modify the same noun. Coordinate adjectives should be separated by commas or by *and* {skilled, experienced chess player} {nurturing and loving parent}. If one adjective modifies the noun and another adjective modifies the idea expressed by the combination of the first adjective and the noun, the adjectives are not considered coordinate and should not be separated by a comma. For example, *a lethargic soccer player* describes a soccer player who is lethargic. Likewise, phrases such as *white brick house* and *wrinkled canvas jacket* are unpunctuated because the adjectives are not coordinate: they have no logical connection in sense (a white house could be made of many different materials; so could a wrinkled jacket). The most useful test is this: if *and* would fit between the two adjectives, a comma is necessary.

5.92 **Phrasal adjectives.** A phrasal adjective (also called a *compound modifier*) is a phrase that functions as a unit to modify a noun. A phrasal adjective follows these basic rules: (1) Generally, if placed before a noun, the phrase should be hyphenated to avoid misdirecting the reader {dog-eat-dog competition}. There may be a considerable difference between the hyphenated and the unhyphenated forms: compare *small animal hospital* with *small-animal hospital.* (2) If a compound noun is an element of a phrasal adjective, the entire compound noun must be hyphenated to clarify the relationship among the words {time-clock-punching employees}. (3) If more than one phrasal adjective modifies a single noun, hyphenation becomes especially important {nineteenth-century song-and-dance numbers} {state-inspected assisted-living facility}. (4) If two phrasal adjectives end in a common element, the ending element should appear only with the second phrase, and a suspended hyphen should follow the unattached words to show that they are related to the ending element {middle- and upper-class operagoers}. (5) If the phrasal adjective denotes an amount or a duration, the plural should be dropped. For instance, *pregnancy lasts nine months* but is *a nine-month pregnancy*, and a shop *open 24 hours a day* has *a 24-hour-a-day schedule*. The plural is retained only for fractions {a two-thirds majority}. (6) If a phrasal adjective becomes awkward, the sentence should probably be recast. For example, *The news about the lower-than-expected third-quarter earnings disappointed investors* could become *The news about the third-quarter earnings, which were lower than expected, disappointed investors*. Or perhaps this: *Investors were disappointed by the third-quarter earnings, which were lower than expected*. See also 7.81–89.

5.93 **Exceptions for hyphenating phrasal adjectives.** There are exceptions to hyphenating phrasal adjectives: (1) If a phrasal adjective follows a linking verb, it is often unhyphenated—e.g., compare *a well-trained athlete* with *an athlete who is well trained.* (2) When a proper name begins a phrasal adjective, the name is not hyphenated {the Monty Python school of comedy}. (3) A two-word phrasal adjective that begins with an adverb ending in *-ly* is not hyphenated {a sharply worded reprimand} (but *a not-so-sharply-worded reprimand*). See also 7.84, 7.85.

5.94 **Adjectives as nouns.** An adjective-to-noun shift (sometimes called an *adnoun*) is relatively common in English. Some adjectives are well established as nouns and are perfectly suitable for most contexts. For example, *a postmortem examination* is often called *a postmortem*; *collectible objects* are *collectibles*; and *French people* are *the French.* Any but the most established among such nouns should be used only after careful consideration. If there's an alternative, it will almost certainly be better. For example, there is probably no good reason to use the adjective *collaborative* as a noun (i.e., as a shortened form of *collaborative enterprise*) when the perfectly good *collaboration* is available. See also 5.24–26.

5.95 **Adjectives as verbs.** Adjective-to-verb shifts are uncommon in English but occur once in a while, usually as jargon or slang {the cargo tanks were **inerted** by introducing carbon dioxide into them} {it would be silly to **low-key** the credit for this achievement}. They generally don't fit comfortably into formal prose.

5.96 **Other parts of speech functioning as adjectives.** Words that ordinarily function as other parts of speech, but sometimes as adjectives, include nouns (see 5.24), pronouns (see 5.49), and verbs (see 5.107).

Verbs

DEFINITIONS

5.97 **Verbs generally.** A verb shows the performance or occurrence of an action or the existence of a condition or a state of being, such as an emotion. A verb is the most essential part of speech—the only one that can express a full thought by itself (with the subject understood) {Run!} {Enjoy!} {Think!}. (One-word sentences such as *Why?* or *Yes* alone can express complete thoughts as well, but these are in fact elliptical sentences omitting a clause implied by context {Why [did she do that]?} {Yes[, you may borrow that book].}.)

5.98 **Transitive and intransitive verbs.** Depending on the presence or absence of an object, a verb is classified as transitive or intransitive. A transitive verb requires an object to express a complete thought; the verb indicates what action the subject exerts on the object. For example, *the cyclist hit a curb* states what the subject *cyclist* did to the object *curb*. (A few transitive verbs have what are called *cognate objects*, which are closely related etymologically to the verb {drink a drink} {build a building} {see the sights}.) An intransitive verb does not require an object to express a complete thought {the rescuer **jumped**}, although it may be followed by a prepositional phrase serving an adverbial function {the rescuer **jumped to the ground**}. Many verbs may be either transitive or intransitive, the different usages often distinguishing their meanings. For example, when used transitively, as in *the king's heir will succeed him*, the verb *succeed* means "to follow and take the place of"; when used intransitively, as in *the chemist will succeed in identifying the toxin*, it means "to accomplish a task." With some verbs, no such distinction is possible. For example, in *I will walk; you ride*, the verb *ride* is intransitive. In *I will walk; you ride your bike*, the verb *ride* is transitive, but its meaning is unchanged. A verb that is normally used transitively may sometimes be used intransitively to emphasize the verb and leave the object undefined or unknown {the patient eats poorly [*how well* the patient eats is more important than *what* the patient eats]}. The test for whether a given verb is transitive is to try it with various possible objects. For each sentence in which an object is plausible, the verb is being used transitively. If an object doesn't work idiomatically, the verb is being used intransitively.

5.99 **Ergative verbs.** Some verbs, called *ergative* or *ambitransitive verbs*, can be used transitively or intransitively {the impact **shattered** the windshield} {the windshield **shattered**}. The noun that serves as the object when the verb's use is transitive becomes the subject when the verb's use is intransitive. For example, with the noun *door* and the verb *open*, one can say *I opened the door* (transitive) or *the door opened* (intransitive). Many verbs can undergo ergative shifts {the torpedo **sank the boat**} {the **boat sank**}. For example, the verb *ship* was once exclusively transitive {the company **shipped the books** on January 16}, but in commercial usage it is now often intransitive {**the books shipped** on January 16}. Likewise, *grow* (generally an intransitive verb) was transitive only in horticultural contexts {the family **grew** several types of **crops**}, but commercial usage now makes it transitive in many other contexts {how to **grow your business**}. Careful writers and editors employ such usages cautiously if at all, preferring well-established idioms.

5.100 **Regular and irregular verbs.** The past-tense and past-participial forms of most English words are formed by appending *-ed* to the basic form {draft–drafted–drafted}. If the verb ends in *-e*, only a *-d* is appended {charge–charged–charged}. (Sometimes a final consonant is doubled.) These verbs are classified as *regular*, or *weak* (the latter is a term used in philology to classify forms of conjugation). But a few common verbs have maintained forms derived mostly from Old English roots {begin–began–begun} {bet–bet–bet} {bind–bound–bound} {bite–bit–bitten}. These verbs are called *irregular*, or *strong*. The various inflections of strong verbs defy simple classifications, but many past-tense and past-participial forms (1) change the vowel in the base verb (as *begin*), (2) keep the same form as the base verb (as *bet*), (3) share an irregular form (as *bind*), or (4) change endings (as *bite*). (The vowel change between cognate forms in category 1 is called an *ablaut*.) The verb *be* is highly irregular, with eight forms (*is*, *are*, *was*, *were*, *been*, *being*, *be*, and *am*). Because no system of useful classification is possible for irregular verbs, a reliable memory and a general dictionary are essential tools for using the correct forms consistently. Further complicating the spelling of irregular verbs is the fact that the form may vary according to the sense of the word. When used to mean "to offer a price," for example, *bid* keeps the same form in the past tense and past participle, but when it means "to offer a greeting," it forms *bade* (traditionally rhyming with *glad*) and *bidden*. The form may also depend on whether the verb is being used literally {wove a rug} or figuratively {weaved in traffic}. Finally, a few verbs that are considered regular have an alternative past tense and past participle that is formed by adding *-t* to the simple verb form {dream–dreamed} {dream–dreamt}. When these alternatives are available, American English tends to prefer the forms ending in *-ed* (e.g., *dreamed*, *learned*, *spelled*), while British English often prefers the forms ending in *-t* (*dreamt*, *learnt*, *spelt*).

5.101 **Linking verbs.** A linking verb (also called a *copula* or *connecting verb*) is one that links the subject to a closely related word in the predicate—a subjective complement. The linking verb itself does not take an object, because it expresses a state of being instead of an action {Mr. Block is **the chief executive officer**} {that snake is **venomous**} {his heart's desire is **to see his sister again**}. There are two kinds of linking verbs: *be*-verbs and intransitive verbs that are used in a weakened sense, such as *appear*, *become*, *feel*, *look*, *seem*, *smell*, and *taste*. The weakened intransitive verbs often have a figurative sense akin to that of *become*, as in *He fell heir to a large fortune* (he didn't physically fall on or into anything) or *The river ran dry* (a waterless river doesn't run—it has dried up). (See also 5.170.) Some verbs only occasionally function as linking verbs—among them *act* {act weird}, *get* {get fat}, *go* {go bald}, *grow* {grow weary}, *lie* {lie fallow}, *prove* {prove untenable}, *remain* {remain quiet}, *sit* {sit still}, *stay* {stay trim}, *turn* {turn gray}, and *wax* {wax eloquent}. Also, some passive-voice constructions contain linking verbs {this band **was judged** best in the contest} {she **was made** sales-force manager}. If a verb doesn't have a subjective complement, then it doesn't qualify as a linking verb in that particular construction. For instance, when a *be*-verb conveys the sense "to be situated" or "to exist," it is not a linking verb {Kansas City, Kansas, **is** across the river} {there **is** an unfilled receptionist position}. Likewise, if a verb such as *appear*, *feel*, *smell*, *sound*, or *taste* is followed by an adverbial modifier instead of a subjective complement {he **appeared in court**} or a direct object {the dog **smelled the scent**}, it isn't a linking verb.

5.102 **Phrasal verbs.** A phrasal verb is usually a verb plus a preposition (or particle), which serves as an adverb {settle down} {act up} {phase out}. A phrasal verb is not hyphenated, even though its equivalent noun or phrasal adjective might be—e.g., compare *to flare up* with *a flare-up*, and compare *to step up the pace* with *a stepped-up pace*. Three rules apply: (1) if the phrasal verb has a sense distinct from the component words, use the entire phrase—e.g., *hold up* means "to rob" or "to delay," and *get rid of* and *do away with* mean "to eliminate"; (2) avoid the phrasal verb if the verb alone conveys essentially the same meaning—e.g., *rest up* is equivalent to *rest*; and (3) don't compress the phrase into a one-word verb, especially if it has a corresponding one-word noun form—e.g., one *burns out* (phrasal verb) and suffers *burnout* (noun).

5.103 **Principal and auxiliary verbs.** Depending on its uses, a verb is classified as principal or auxiliary. A principal verb is one that can stand alone to express an act or state {he **jogs**} {I **dreamed** about Xanadu}. If combined with another verb, it expresses the combination's leading thought {a tiger **may roar**}. An auxiliary verb is used with a principal verb to form a verb phrase that indicates mood, tense, or voice {you **must study** for the exam!} {I **will go** to the store} {the show **was interrupted**}. The most commonly used auxiliaries are *be*, *can*, *do*, *have*, *may*, *must*, *ought*, *shall*, and *will*. For more on auxiliary verbs, see 5.144–53.

5.104 **Verb phrases.** The combination of an auxiliary verb with a principal verb is a verb phrase, such as *could happen*, *must go*, or *will be leaving*. When a verb phrase is modified by an adverb, the modifier typically goes directly after the first auxiliary verb, as in *could certainly happen*, *must always go*, and *will soon be leaving*. The idea that verb phrases should not be "split" in this way is quite mistaken (see 5.171). A verb phrase is negated when the negative adverb *not* is placed after the first auxiliary {we **have not** called him}. In an interrogative sentence, the first auxiliary begins the sentence and is followed by the subject {**must I** repeat that?} {**do you** want more?}. An interrogative can be negated by placement of *not* after the subject {**do you not** want more?}, but a contraction is often more natural {**don't you** want more?}. Most negative forms can be contracted {we do not–we don't} {I will not–I won't} {he has not–he hasn't} {she does not–she doesn't}, but *I am not* is contracted to *I'm not* (never *I amn't*). The corresponding interrogative form is *aren't I?* Sometimes the negative is emphasized if the auxiliary is contracted with the pronoun and the negative is left standing alone {he is not–he isn't–he's not} {we are not–we aren't–we're not} {they have not–they haven't–they've not}.

5.105 **Contractions.** Most types of writing benefit from the use of contractions. If used thoughtfully, contractions in prose sound natural and relaxed and make reading more enjoyable. *Be*-verbs and most of the auxiliary verbs are contracted when followed by *not*: *are not–aren't*, *was not–wasn't*, *cannot–can't*, *could not–couldn't*, *do not–don't*, and so on. A few, such as *ought not–oughtn't*, look or sound awkward and are best avoided. Pronouns can be contracted with auxiliaries, with forms of *have*, and with some *be*-verbs. Think before using one of the less common contractions, which often don't work well in prose, except perhaps in dialogue or quotations. Some examples are *I'd've* (I would have), *she'd've* (she would have), *it'd* (it would), *should've* (should have), *there're* (there are), *who're* (who are), and *would've* (would have). Also, some contracted forms can have more than one meaning. For instance, *there's* may be *there is* or *there has*, and *I'd* may be *I had* or *I would*. The particular meaning may not always be clear from the context.

INFINITIVES

5.106 **Infinitives defined.** An infinitive verb, also called the verb's *root* or *stem*, is a verb that in its principal uninflected form may be preceded by *to* {to dance} {to dive}. It is the basic form of the verb, the one listed in dictionary entries. The preposition *to* is sometimes called the *sign* of the infinitive {he tried **to open** the door}, and it is sometimes classed as an adverb. In the active voice, *to* is generally dropped when the infinitive follows an auxiliary verb {you must **flee**} and can be dropped after several verbs, such as *bid*, *dare*, *feel*, *hear*, *help*, *let*, *make*, *need*, and *see* {you dare **say** that to me?}. But when the infinitive follows one of these verbs in the passive voice, *to* should be retained {he cannot be heard **to deny** it} {they cannot be made **to listen**}. The *to* should also be retained after *ought* and *ought not* (see 5.149).

5.107 **Uses of the infinitive.** The infinitive has great versatility. It is sometimes called a *verbal noun* because it can function as part of a verb phrase {someone has **to tell** her} or a noun {**to walk** away now seems rash}. The infinitive also has limited uses as an adjective or an adverb. As a verb, it can take (1) a subject {we wanted **the lesson** to end}, (2) an object {try to throw **the javelin** higher}, (3) a predicate complement {want to race **home**?}, or (4) an adverbial modifier {you need to think **quickly** in chess}. As a noun, the infinitive can perform as (1) the subject of a finite verb {**to fly** is a lofty goal} or (2) the object of a transitive verb or participle {I want **to hire** a new assistant}. An infinitive may be governed by a verb {**cease to do** evil}, a noun {we all have **talents to be improved**}, an adjective {she is **eager to learn**}, a participle {they are **preparing to go**}, or a pronoun {let **him do** it}.

5.108 **Split infinitive.** Although from about 1850 to 1925 many grammarians stated otherwise, it is now widely acknowledged that adverbs sometimes justifiably separate the *to* from the principal verb {they expect **to more than double** their income next year}. See also 5.171.

5.109 **Dangling infinitive.** An infinitive phrase can be used, often loosely, to modify a verb—in which case the sentence must have a grammatical subject (or an unexpressed subject of an imperative) that could logically perform the action of the infinitive. If there is none, then the sentence may be confusing. For example, in *To repair your car properly, it must be sent to a mechanic*, the infinitive *repair* does not have a logical subject; the infinitive phrase *to repair your car* is left dangling. But if the sentence is rewritten as *To repair your car properly, you must take it to a mechanic*, the logical subject is *you*.

PARTICIPLES AND GERUNDS

5.110 **Participles generally.** A participle is a nonfinite verb that is not limited by person, number, or mood but does have tense. Two participles are formed from the verb stem: the present participle invariably ends in *-ing*, and the past participle usually ends in *-ed*. The present participle denotes the verb's action as being in progress or incomplete at the time expressed by the sentence's principal verb {**watching** intently for a mouse, the cat settled in to wait} {**hearing** his name, Jon turned to answer}. The past participle denotes the verb's action as being completed {**planted** in the spring} {**written** last year}.

5.111 **Participial phrases.** A participial phrase is made up of a participle plus any closely associated word or words, such as modifiers or complements. It can be used (1) as an adjective to modify a noun or pronoun {**nailed to the roof**, the slate stopped the leaks} {she pointed to the clerk **drooping**

behind the counter} or (2) as an absolute phrase {**generally speaking**, I prefer spicy dishes} {**they having arrived**, we went out on the lawn for our picnic}. For more on participial adjectives, see 5.90, 5.115.

5.112 **Gerunds.** A gerund is a present participle used as a noun. It is not limited by person, number, or mood. Being a noun, the gerund can be used as (1) the subject of a verb {**complaining** about it won't help}; (2) the object of a verb {I don't like your **cooking**}; (3) a predicate nominative or complement {his favorite pastime is **sleeping**}; or (4) the object of a preposition {reduce erosion by **terracing** the fields}. In some sentences, a gerund may substitute for an infinitive. Compare the use of the infinitive *to lie* as a noun {**to lie** is wrong} with the gerund *lying* {**lying** is wrong}.

5.113 **Distinguishing between participles and gerunds.** Because participles and gerunds both derive from verbs, the difference between them depends on their function. A participle is used as a modifier {the **running** water} or as part of a verb phrase {the meter **is running**}; it can be modified only by an adverb {the **swiftly** running water}. A gerund is used as a noun {**running is** great exercise}; it can be modified only by an adjective {**sporadic running and walking** makes for a great workout}.

5.114 **Fused participles.** As nouns, gerunds are modified by adjectives {**double-parking** is prohibited}, including possessive nouns and pronouns {**Critt's parking** can be hazardous to pedestrians}. By contrast, a present participle is always modified (if at all) by an adverb, whether the participle serves as a verb {**she's parking** the car **now**}, an adjective {I'll be looking for **a parking place**}, or an adverb {**finally parking**, we saw that the store had already closed}. It is traditionally considered a linguistic fault (a *fused participle*) to use a nonpossessive noun or pronoun with a gerund:

POOR: **Me painting** your fence depends on **you paying** me first.
BETTER: **My painting** your fence depends on **your paying** me first.

In the poor example, *me* looks like the subject of the sentence, but it doesn't agree with the verb *depends*. Instead, the subject is *painting*—a gerund, here seeming to be "modified" by *me*, a pronoun. In the predicate, *you* looks like the object of the preposition *on*, but the true object is the gerund *paying*. There are times, however, when the possessive is unidiomatic. You usually have no choice but to use a fused participle with a nonpersonal noun {we're not responsible for the jewelry having been mislaid}, a nonpersonal pronoun {we all insisted on something being done}, or a group of pronouns {the settlement depends on some of them agreeing to compromise}.

5.115 **Dangling participles.** Both participles and gerunds are subject to dangling. A participle that has no syntactic relationship with the nearest subject is called a *dangling participle* or just a *dangler*. In effect, the participle ceases to function as a modifier and functions as a kind of preposition. Often the sentence is illogical, ambiguous, or even incoherent, as in *Frequently used in early America, experts suggest that shaming is an effective punishment* (*used* does not modify the closest noun, *experts*; it modifies *shaming*), or *Being a thoughtful mother, I believe Meg gives her children good advice* (the writer at first seems to be attesting to his or her own thoughtfulness rather than Meg's). Recasting the sentence so that the misplaced modifier is associated with the correct noun is the only effective cure {**experts suggest that shaming**, often used in early America, is an effective punishment}. But rewording to avoid the participle or gerund may be preferable {I believe that **because Meg is a thoughtful mother, she** gives her children good advice}. Using passive voice in an independent clause can also produce a dangler. In *Finding that the questions were not ambiguous, the exam grades were not changed*, the participle *finding* "dangles" because there is no logical subject to do the finding. The sentence can be corrected by using active voice instead of passive, so that the participle precedes the noun it modifies {**finding that the questions were not ambiguous**, the **teacher** did not change the exam grades}. Quite often writers will use *it* or *there* as the subject of the independent clause after a participial phrase, thereby producing a dangler without a logical subject, as in *Reviewing the suggestions, it is clear that no consensus exists.* (A possible revision: *Our review of the suggestions shows that no consensus exists.*) Compare 5.116. See also 5.175.

5.116 **Dangling gerunds.** A dangling gerund can occur when a participle is the object of a preposition, where it functions as a noun rather than as a modifier. For example, *After finishing the research, the screenplay was easy to write* (who did the research and who wrote the screenplay?). The best way to correct a dangling gerund is to revise the sentence. The example above could be revised as *After Gero finished the research, the screenplay was easy to write*, or *After finishing the research, Gero found the screenplay easy to write*. Dangling gerunds can result in improbable statements. Consider *While driving to San Antonio, my phone ran out of power*. The phone wasn't at the wheel, so *driving* is a dangling gerund that shouldn't refer to *my phone*. Clarifying the subject of the gerund improves the sentence {**while I was driving to San Antonio**, my phone ran out of power}. Compare 5.115.

VOICE, MOOD, TENSE, PERSON, AND NUMBER

5.117 **Five properties of verbs.** A verb has five properties: voice, mood, tense, person, and number. Verbs are conjugated (inflected) to show these properties.

5.118 **Active and passive voice.** Voice shows whether the subject acts (active voice) or is acted on (passive voice)—that is, whether the subject performs or receives the action of the verb. Only transitive verbs are said to have voice. The clause *the judge levied a $50 fine* is in the active voice because the subject *judge* is acting. But *the tree's branch was broken by the storm* is in the passive voice because the subject *branch* does not break itself—it is acted on by the prepositional object *storm*. The passive voice is always formed by joining an inflected form of *to be* (or, in colloquial usage, *get*) with the verb's past participle. Compare *the ox pulls the cart* (active voice) with *the cart is pulled by the ox* (passive voice). As a matter of style, passive voice {the matter **will be given** careful consideration} is typically, though not always, inferior to active voice {**we will consider** the matter carefully}. The choice between active and passive voice may depend on which point of view is desired. For instance, *the mouse was caught by the cat* describes the mouse's experience, whereas *the cat caught the mouse* describes the cat's. What is important is to be able to identify passive voice reliably. Remember that the mere presence of a *be*-verb does not necessarily signal passive voice. For example, *he is thinking about his finances* isn't in the passive voice; it's just a *be*-verb plus a present participle.

5.119 **Progressive conjugation and voice.** If an inflected form of *be* is joined with a verb's present participle, a progressive conjugation results {the ox **is pulling** the cart}. If the verb is transitive, the progressive conjugation is in active voice because the subject is performing the action, not being acted on. But if both the principal verb and the auxiliary are *be*-verbs followed by a past participle {the cart is being pulled}, the result is a passive-voice construction.

5.120 **Verb mood.** Mood (or *mode*) indicates the manner in which the verb expresses an action or state of being. The three moods are indicative, imperative, and subjunctive.

5.121 **Indicative mood.** The indicative mood is the most common in English. It is used to express facts and opinions and to ask questions {amethysts cost very little} {the botanist lives in a garden cottage} {does that bush produce yellow roses?}.

5.122 **Imperative mood.** The imperative mood expresses commands {**go** away!}, direct requests {**bring** the tray in here}, and, sometimes, permission {**come** in!}. It is simply the verb's stem used to make a command, a request, an exclamation, or the like {**put** it here!} {**give** me a clue} {**help**!}. The subject of the verb, *you*, is understood even though the sentence might include a direct address {**give** me the magazine} {Cindy, **take** good care of yourself [*Cindy* is a direct address, not the subject]}. Use the imperative mood cautiously: in some contexts it could be too blunt or unintentionally rude. You can soften the imperative by using a word such as *please* {please **stop** at the store}. If that isn't satisfactory, you might recast the sentence in the indicative {**will you stop** at the store, please?}.

5.123 **Subjunctive mood.** Although the subjunctive mood no longer appears with much frequency, it is useful when you want to express an action or a state not as a reality but as a mental conception. Typically, the subjunctive expresses an action or state as doubtful, imagined, desired, conditional, hypothetical, or otherwise contrary to fact. Despite its decline, the subjunctive mood persists in stock expressions such as *perish the thought*, *heaven help us*, and *be that as it may*.

5.124 **Subjunctive versus indicative mood.** The subjunctive mood signals a statement contrary to fact {if I **were you**}, including wishes {if **I were** a rich man}, conjectures {oh, **were it** so}, demands {the landlord insists that **the dog go**}, and suggestions {I recommend that **she take** a vacation}. Three errors often crop up with these constructions. First, writers sometimes use an indicative verb form when the subjunctive form is needed:

POOR: If it **wasn't** for your help, I never would have found the place.
BETTER: If it **weren't** for your help, I never would have found the place.

Second, indicative-mood sentences sometimes resemble these subjunctive constructions but aren't statements contrary to fact:

POOR: I called to see **whether she were in**.
BETTER: I called to see **whether she was in**.

Third, one often sees *If I would have gone, I would . . .* , with two conditionals, instead of *If I had gone, I would . . .* (the better choice). Although the subjunctive mood is often signaled by *if*, not every *if* takes a subjunctive verb. When the action or state might be true but the writer does not know, the indicative is called for instead of the subjunctive {**if I am** right about this, please call} {**if Napoleon was** in fact poisoned with arsenic, historians will need to reevaluate his associates}.

5.125 **Present subjunctive mood.** The present-tense subjunctive mood is formed by using the base form of the verb, such as *be*. This form of subjunctive often appears in suggestions or requirements {he recommended **that we be ready** at a moment's notice} {we insist **that he retain control** of the accounting department}. The present-tense subjunctive is also expressed by using either *be* plus the simple-past form of the verb or a past-form auxiliary plus an infinitive {the chair proposed **that the company be acquired** by the employees through a stock-ownership plan} {today **would be convenient for me to search** for that missing file} {**might he take down** the decorations this afternoon?}. See also 5.123.

5.126 **Past subjunctive mood.** Despite its label, the past-tense subjunctive mood refers to something in the present or future but contrary to fact. It is formed using the verb's simple-past tense, except in the case of *be*, which becomes *were* regardless of the subject's number. For example, the declaration *if only I had a chance* expresses that the speaker has little or no chance. Similarly, *I wish I were safe at home* almost certainly means that the speaker is not at home and perhaps not safe—though it could also mean that the speaker is at home but quite unsafe. This past-tense-but-present-sense subjunctive typically appears in the form *if I* (*he*, *she*, *it*) *were* {if I were king} {if she were any different}. That is, the subjunctive mood ordinarily uses a past-tense verb (e.g., *were*) to connote uncertainty, impossibility, or unreality where the present or future indicative would otherwise be used. Compare *If I am threatened, I will quit* (indicative) with *If I were threatened, I would quit* (subjunctive), or *If the canary sings, I smile* (indicative) with *If the canary sang* (or *should sing*, or *were to sing*), *I would smile* (subjunctive).

5.127 **Past-perfect subjunctive mood.** Just as the past subjunctive uses a verb's simple-past-tense form to refer to the present or future, the past-perfect subjunctive uses a verb's past-perfect form to refer to the past. The past-perfect subjunctive typically appears in the form *if I* (*he*, *she*, *it*) *had been* {if he had been there} {if I had gone}. That is, the subjunctive mood ordinarily uses a past-perfect verb (e.g., *had been*) to connote uncertainty or impossibility where the past or past-perfect indicative would otherwise be used. Compare *If it arrived, it was not properly filed* (indicative) with *If it had arrived, it could have changed the course of history* (subjunctive).

5.128 **Verb tense.** Tense shows the time in which an act, state, or condition occurs or occurred. The three major divisions of time are present, past, and future (but see 5.131). Each division of time breaks down further into a perfect tense denoting a comparatively more remote time by indicating that the action has been completed: present perfect, past perfect, and future perfect. And all six of these tenses can be further divided to include a progressive tense (also called *imperfect* or *continuous*), in which the action continues.

5.129 **Present tense.** The present tense is the infinitive verb's stem, also called the *present indicative* {walk} {drink}. It primarily denotes acts, conditions, or states that occur in the present {the dog **howls**} {the air **is** cold} {the water **runs**}. It is also used (1) to express a habitual action or general truth {cats **prowl** nightly} {polluted water **is** a health threat}; (2) to refer to timeless facts, such as memorable persons and works of the past that are still extant or enduring {Julius Caesar **describes** his strategies in *The Gallic War*} {the Pompeiian mosaics **are** exquisite}; and (3) to narrate a fictional work's plot {the scene **takes** place aboard the *Titanic*}. The latter two uses are collectively referred to as the *historical-present tense*, and the third is especially important for those who write about literature. Characters in books, plays, and films *do* things—not *did* them. If you want to distinguish between present action and past action in literature, the present-perfect tense is helpful {Hamlet, who **has spoken** with his father's ghost, **reveals what he has learned** to no one but Horatio}. See also 5.132.

5.130 **Past indicative tense.** The past indicative denotes an act, state, or condition that occurred or existed at some explicit or implicit point in the past {the auction ended yesterday} {we returned the shawl}. For a regular verb, it is formed by adding *-ed* to its base form {jump–jumped} {spill–spilled}. If the verb ends in a silent *-e*, only a *-d* is added to form both the past tense and the past participle {bounce–bounced–bounced}. If it ends in *-y* preceded by a consonant, the *-y* changes to an *-i* before forming the past tense and past participle with *-ed* {hurry–hurried–hurried}. If it ends in a double consonant {block}, two vowels and a consonant {cook}, or a vowel other than *-e* {veto}, a regular verb forms the past tense and past participle by adding *-ed* to its simple form {block–blocked–blocked} {cook–cooked–cooked} {veto–vetoed–vetoed}. If the verb ends in a single vowel before a consonant, several rules apply in determining whether the consonant is doubled. It is always doubled in one-syllable words {pat–patted–patted}. In words of more than one syllable, the final consonant is doubled if it is part of the syllable that is stressed both before and after the inflection {prefer–preferred–preferred}, but not otherwise {travel–traveled–traveled}. In British English there is no such distinction: all such consonants are doubled. Irregular verbs form the past tense and past participle in various ways {give-gave-given} {stride-strode-stridden} {read-read-read}. See also 5.100.

5.131 **Future tense.** What is traditionally known as the *future tense* is formed by using *will* with a verb's stem form {will walk} {will drink}. It refers to an expected act, state, or condition {the artist **will design** a wall mural} {the restaurant **will open** soon}. *Shall* may be used instead of *will*, but in American English it typically appears only in first-person questions {**shall** we **go**?} and in statements of legal requirements {the debtor **shall pay** within 30 days}. In most contexts, *will* is preferred—or *must* with legal requirements. Most linguists are now convinced that, technically speaking, English has no future tense at all—that *will* is simply a modal verb that should be treated with all the others.[6] Yet the future tense remains a part of traditional grammar and is discussed here in the familiar way.

5.132 **Present-perfect tense.** The present-perfect tense is formed by using *have* or *has* with the principal verb's past participle {have walked} {has drunk}. It denotes an act, state, or condition that is now completed or continues up to the present {I **have put** away the clothes} {it **has been** a long day} {I will apologize, even if I **have done** nothing wrong}. The present perfect is distinguished from the past tense because it refers to (1) a time in the indefinite past {I **have played** golf there before} or (2) a past action that comes up to and touches the present {I **have played** cards for the last eighteen hours}. The past tense, by contrast, indicates a more specific or a more remote time in the past.

5.133 **Past-perfect tense.** The past-perfect (or *pluperfect*) tense is formed by using *had* with the principal verb's past participle {had walked} {had drunk}. It refers to an act, state, or condition that was completed before another specified or implicit past time or past action {the engineer **had driven** the train to the roundhouse before we arrived} {by the time we stopped to check the map, the rain **had begun** falling} {the movie **had** already **ended**}.

5.134 **Future-perfect tense.** The future-perfect tense is formed by using *will have* with the verb's past participle {will have walked} {will have drunk}. It refers to an act, state, or condition that is expected to be completed before some other future act or time {the entomologist **will have collected** sixty more specimens before the semester ends} {the court **will have adjourned** by five o'clock}.

6. See, e.g., R. L. Trask, *Language: The Basics* (London: Routledge, 1995), 58.

5.135 **Progressive tenses.** The progressive tenses, also known as *continuous tenses*, show action that progresses or continues. With active-voice verbs, all six basic tenses can be made progressive by using the appropriate *be*-verb and the present participle of the main verb, as so:

present progressive (*he is playing tennis*);
present-perfect progressive (*he has been playing tennis*);
past progressive (*he was playing tennis*);
past-perfect progressive (*he had been playing tennis*);
future progressive (*he will be playing tennis*); and
future-perfect progressive (*he will have been playing tennis*).

With the passive voice, the present- and past-progressive tenses are made by using the appropriate *be*-verb with the present participle *being*, plus the past participle of the main verb, as so:

present (*I am being dealt the cards*); and
past (*I was being dealt the cards*).

5.136 **Verb person.** A verb's person shows whether the act, state, or condition is that of (1) the person speaking (first person), (2) the person spoken to (second person), or (3) the person or thing spoken of (third person).

5.137 **Verb number.** The number of a verb must agree with the number of the noun or pronoun used with it. In other words, the verb must be singular or plural. Only the third-person present-indicative singular changes form to indicate number and person {I sketch} {you sketch} {she sketches} {they sketch}. The second-person verb is always plural in form, whether one person or more than one person is spoken to {**you are** a wonderful person} {**you are** wonderful people}.

5.138 **Agreement in person and number.** A finite verb agrees with its subject in person and number—which is to say that a singular subject takes a singular verb {the **solution works**}, while a plural subject takes a plural verb {the **solutions work**}. When a verb has two or more subjects connected by *and*, it agrees with them jointly and is plural {**Socrates and Plato were** wise}. When a verb has two or more subjects connected by *or* or *nor*, the verb agrees with the last-named subject {**Bob or his friends have** your key} {neither the **twins nor Jon is** prepared to leave}. When the subject is a collective noun conveying the idea of unity or multitude, the verb is singular {the **nation is** powerful}. When the subject is a collective noun conveying the idea of plurality, the verb is plural {the **faculty were** divided in their sentiments}. See also 5.15.

5.139 **Agreement of indefinite pronouns.** An indefinite pronoun such as *anybody*, *anyone*, *everybody*, *everyone*, *nobody*, *no one*, *somebody*, or *someone* routinely takes a singular verb {**everyone receives** credits for this course} {**somebody knows** where the car is}.

5.140 **Relative pronouns as subjects.** A relative pronoun used as the subject of a clause can be either singular or plural, depending on the pronoun's antecedent {a woman **who likes** skydiving} {people **who collect** books}. One of the trickiest constructions involves *one of those who* or *one of those that*:

POOR: She is one of those **employees who works** tirelessly.
BETTER: She is one of those **employees who work** tirelessly.

In this construction, the subject of the verb *work* is *who*, and the antecedent of *who* is *employees*, not *one*. You can see this easily if you reorder the syntax (without adding or subtracting a word): *Of those employees who work tirelessly, she is one*. See also 5.62.

5.141 **False attraction to predicate noun.** When the subject and a predicate noun differ in number, the subject governs the number of the verb {**mediocrity and complacency are the source** of his ire} {**the source** of his ire **is mediocrity and complacency**}. A plural predicate noun after a singular subject may mislead a writer into error by suggesting a plural verb. When this occurs, the simple correction of changing the number of the verb may make the sentence awkward, and the better approach then is to rework the sentence:

POOR: My **downfall are** sweets.
BETTER: My **downfall is** sweets.
BEST: **Sweets are** my downfall.

5.142 **Misleading connectives—"as well as," "along with," "together with," and the like.** Adding to a singular subject by using a phrasal connective such as *along with*, *as well as*, *in addition to*, *together with*, and the like does not make the subject plural. This type of distraction can be doubly misleading because the intervening material seems to create a compound subject, and the modifying prepositional phrase may itself contain one or more plural objects. If the singular verb sounds awkward in such a sentence, try the conjunction *and* instead:

POOR: The **bride** as well as her bridesmaids **were** dressed in mauve.
BETTER: The **bride** as well as her bridesmaids **was** dressed in mauve.
BEST: The **bride and her bridesmaids were** dressed in mauve.

5.143 **Agreement in first and second person.** A personal pronoun used as a subject requires the appropriate verb form according to the person of the pronoun:

I am	he is	I go	he goes
you are	she is	you go	she goes
we are	it is	we go	it goes
they are		they go	

Here comes the tricky point: pronouns joined by *or*, *either-or*, or *neither-nor* are traditionally said to take the verb form that agrees with the nearer subject {**either he or I am** in for a surprise} {**either you or he is** right} {**neither you nor I am** a plumber}. Because these constructions are admittedly awkward, speakers and writers typically find another way to express the thought {one of us is in for a surprise} {one of you is right} {neither of us is a plumber}.

AUXILIARY VERBS

5.144 **Auxiliary verbs generally.** An auxiliary verb (sometimes termed a *helping verb*) is a highly irregular verb used with one or more other verbs to form voice, tense, and mood. It always precedes the principal verb. The most common auxiliary verbs are explained in the following sections. See also 5.103.

5.145 **Modal auxiliaries.** A subset of auxiliary verbs, called *modal auxiliaries* or *modals*, are used to express ability, necessity, possibility, willingness, obligation, and the like {they **might** be there} {she **could be** leaving at this very moment}. They are so called because they indicate the principal verb's mood. All the verbs described below are modal auxiliaries except the last two: *do* and *have*.

5.146 **"Can" and "could."** *Can* uses only its stem form in the present indicative {I can} {it can} {they can}. In the past indicative, *can* becomes *could* for all persons {he **could see** better with glasses}. *Can* does not have an infinitive form (*to be able to* is substituted) or a present or past participle. (Such words lacking one or more inflected forms normal for their word class are traditionally called *defective*. Most modal auxiliaries are defective verbs.) When it denotes ability, capacity, or permission, *can* is always followed by an explicit or implicit bare infinitive as the principal verb {you **can carry** this trunk}. When used in the sense of permission, *can* is colloquial for *may* {**can** I **go** to the movies?}. *Can* also connotes actual possibility or common experience {storms **can be** severe in spring} {days **can pass** before a decision is announced}. *Could* is often used to talk about the past {she could hum a tune at six months of age} or to discuss someone's general ability at a given time {when he was eleven, he could drive a golf ball 250 yards}. But *could* is also used as a softer, less definite equivalent of *can* in reference to future events {we could travel to Cancun if you wanted to}. In this use, the meaning is close to "would be able to" {you could be promoted within six months if you'd just apply yourself!}.

5.147 **"May" and "might."** *May* denotes either permission {you may go to the movies} or possibility {I may go to the movies}. In negating permission, *may not* is sometimes displaced by the more intensive *must not*. Compare *You may not climb that tree* with *You must not climb that tree. May* most commonly connotes an uncertain possibility {you **may find** that assignment too difficult}, and it often becomes *might* {you **might find** that assignment too difficult}. Is there a connotative difference? Yes: *may* tends to express likelihood {we **may** get there on time}, while *might* expresses a stronger sense of doubt {we **might** get there on time—if the traffic clears}. *Might* can also express a contrary-to-fact hypothetical {we might have been able to make it if the traffic had been better}.

5.148 **"Must."** *Must* denotes a necessity that arises from someone's will {we **must obey** the rules}, from circumstances {you **must ask** what the next step is}, or from rule or obligation {all applications **must be** received by May 31 to be valid}. *Must* also connotes a logical conclusion {that **must be** the right answer} {that **must be** the house we're looking for} {it **must have been** Donna who phoned}. This auxiliary verb does not vary its form in either the present or past indicative. It does not have an infinitive form (*to have to* is substituted) or a present or past participle. Denoting obligation, necessity, or inference, *must* is always used with a bare infinitive {we **must finish** this design} {everyone **must eat**} {the movie **must be** over by now}.

5.149 **"Ought."** *Ought* denotes either what is reasonably expected of a person as a matter of duty {they **ought to fix** the fence} or what we guess or conclude is probable {they left at dawn, so they **ought to be** here soon}. It is more emphatic than *should* but less strong than *must*. This verb does not vary its form in either the present or past indicative. It has no infinitive form, or present or past participle. Denoting a duty or obligation, *ought* is always used with an infinitive, even in the negative {we **ought to invite** some friends} {the driver **ought not to have ignored** the signal}. *To* is occasionally omitted after *not* {you **ought not worry**}, but the better usage is to include it {you **ought not to worry**}. See also 5.106.

5.150 **"Should."** *Should*, the past-indicative form of *shall*, is used for all persons, and always with a principal verb {they **should be** at home} {**should** you **read** that newspaper?}. *Should* does not have an infinitive form or a present or past participle. *Should* often carries a sense of duty, compulsion, or expectation {I **should review** those financial-planning tips} {you **should clean** the garage today} {it **should be** ready by now}. Sometimes it carries a sense of inference {the package **should have been delivered** today}. And sometimes it conveys the speaker's attitude {how **should** I **know**?} {you **shouldn't have to deal** with that}. *Should* and *ought* are quite similar and often interchangeable in discussions of what is required, what is advisable, or what we think it is right for people either to do or to have done. *Should* is slightly less emphatic than *ought*, but it appears with greater frequency.

5.151 **"Will" and "would."** In its auxiliary uses, *will* uses only its stem form in the present indicative {she will} {they will}. In the past indicative, the only form for all persons is *would* {we **would go** fishing on Saturdays} {she **would say** that!}. *Will* often carries a sense of the future {she **will be** at her desk tomorrow} or, in the past form *would*, expresses a conditional statement {I **would recognize** the house **if** I saw it again}. It can also express certainty {I'm sure you will understand}; decisions and other types of volition {I really will work out more}; requests, orders, and offers {will you stop that!} {will you take $5 for it?}; or typical behavior {she will read for hours on end}.

5.152 **"Do."** The auxiliary verb *do* (sometimes called a *dummy auxiliary*) frequently creates emphatic verbs. It has two forms in the present indicative: *does* for the third-person singular and *do* for all other persons. In the past indicative, the only form for all persons is *did*. The past participle is *done*. As an auxiliary verb, *do* is used only in the present indicative {we **do plan** some charity work} and past indicative {**did** you **speak**?}. When the verb in an imperative statement is coupled with *not*, *do* also appears {**do not touch**!} {**don't be** an idiot!}. When denoting performance, *do* can also act as a principal verb {he **does** well in school} {they **do** good work}. *Do* can sometimes substitute for a verb, thereby avoiding repetition {Marion **dances** well, and **so do you**} {he **caught** fewer mistakes **than you did**}.

5.153 **"Have."** This verb has two forms in the present indicative: *has* for the third-person singular and *have* for all other persons. In the past indicative, the only form for all persons is *had*; the past participle is also *had*. When *have* functions as an auxiliary verb, the present or past indicative of *have* precedes the past participle of a verb to form that verb's present-perfect or past-perfect indicative mood {I **have looked** everywhere} {he **had looked** for a better rate}. When preceding an infinitive, *have* denotes obligation or necessity {I **have to finish** this paper tonight!}. *Had* plus *to* and an infinitive expresses the past form of *must* {I **had to leave** yesterday afternoon}. When denoting possession, action, or experience, *have* functions as a sentence's principal verb {she **has** a car and a boat} {you **have** a mosquito on your neck} {we'll **have** a party next week}. *Have* may also be used with *do* to express actual or figurative possession {**do** you **have** the time?} {**do** we **have** room?} {Vicky **did not have** her coat}.

"BE"-VERBS

5.154 **Forms of "be"-verbs.** The verb *be* has eight forms (*be*, *is*, *are*, *was*, *were*, *been*, *being*, and *am*) and has several special uses. First, it is sometimes a sentence's principal verb meaning "exist" {I think, therefore I **am**}. Second, it is more often used as an auxiliary verb {I **was** born in Lubbock}. When joined with a verb's present participle, it denotes continuing or progressive action {the train **is** coming} {the passenger **was** waiting}. When joined with a past participle, the verb becomes passive {a signal **was** given} {an earring **was** dropped} (see 5.118). Often this type of construction can be advantageously changed to active voice {he gave the signal} {she dropped her earring}. Third, *be* is the most common linking verb that connects the subject with something affirmed of the subject {truth **is** beauty} {we **are** the champions}. Occasionally a *be*-verb is used as part of an adjective {a rock star **wannabe** [want to be]} {a **would-be** hero} or noun {a **has-been**}.

5.155 **Conjugation of "be"-verbs.** *Be* is conjugated differently from other verbs. (1) The stem is not used in the present indicative form. Instead, *be* has three forms: for the first-person singular, *am*; for the third-person singular, *is*; and for all other persons, *are*. (2) The present participle is formed by adding *-ing* to the root *be* {being}. It is the same for all persons, but the present perfect requires also using *am*, *is*, or *are* {I **am being** stalked} {it **is being** reviewed} {you **are being** photographed}. (3) The past indicative has two forms: the first- and third-person singular use *was*; all other persons use *were* {she **was**} {we **were**}. (4) The past participle for all persons is *been* {I **have been**} {they **have been**}. (5) The imperative is the verb's stem {**be** yourself!}.

Adverbs

DEFINITION AND FORMATION

5.156 **Adverbs generally.** An adverb is a word (more particularly, an *adjunct*) that qualifies, limits, describes, or modifies a verb, an adjective, or another adverb {she studied **constantly** [*constantly* qualifies the verb *studied*]} {the juggler's act was **really** unusual [*really* qualifies the adjective *unusual*]} {the cyclist pedaled **very** swiftly [*very* qualifies the adverb *swiftly*]}. An adverb may also qualify a preposition, a conjunction, or an entire independent clause {the birds flew **right** over the lake [*right* qualifies the preposition *over*]} {this is **exactly** where I found it [*exactly* qualifies the conjunction *where*]} {**apparently** you forgot to check your references [*apparently* qualifies the rest of the clause]}. Some adverbs may modify an adjective {the bids differ by a **very** small amount} or an adverb {he moved along **very** quickly} but not a verb. (You can't say *He spoke very* or *She played very*.) Other adverbs of this sort—often called *intensifiers*—are *more*, *most*, *much*, *quite*, *rather*, *really*, *somewhat*, and *too* (see also 5.89). Grammarians have also traditionally used the term *adverb* as a catchall category to sweep in words that aren't readily put into other categories (such as *not*, *please*, and the infinitival *to* and the particle in a phrasal verb).

5.157 **Sentence adverbs.** An adverb that modifies an entire sentence is called a *sentence adverb* {**fortunately**, we've had rain this week} {**undoubtedly** he drove his car to the depot}. Sentence adverbs most commonly indicate doubt or emphasize a statement's certainty. Some common examples are *maybe*, *possibly*, and *however*.

5.158 **Adverbial suffixes.** Many adjectives have corresponding adverbs distinguished by the suffix *-ly* or, after most words ending in *-ic*, *-ally* {slow–slowly} {careful–carefully} {public–publicly} {pedantic–pedantically}. Most adjectives ending in *-y* preceded by a consonant change the *-y* to *-i* when the suffix is added, but some don't {happy–happily} {shy–shyly}. A few adjectives ending in *-e* drop the vowel {true–truly} {whole–wholly}. If an adjective ends in an *-le* that is sounded as part of a syllable, it is replaced with *-ly* {terrible–terribly} {simple–simply}. An adjective that ends in a double *-l* takes only a *-y* suffix {dull–dully}. Many adjectives ending in *-le* or *-ly* do not make appealing adverbs {juvenile–juvenilely} {silly–sillily}. If an *-ly* adverb looks clumsy (e.g., *ghastlily*, *uglily*), either rephrase the sentence or use a phrase {in a ghastly manner} {in an ugly way}. A few other suffixes are used for adverbs, especially in informal speech {he rides cowboy-style} {park your cars curbside}. A few nouns form adverbs by taking the ending *-ways* {side–sideways}, *-ward* {sky–skyward}, or *-wise* {clock–clockwise}. And adverbial suffixes are sometimes added to phrases {she replied matter-of-factly}. Finally, not every word ending in *-ly* is an adverb—some are adjectives {lovely} {curly}.

5.159 **Adverbs without suffixes.** Many common adverbs don't have an identifying suffix {almost} {never} {here} {now} {just} {seldom} {late} {near} {too}.

SIMPLE VERSUS COMPOUND ADVERBS

5.160 **Simple and flat adverbs.** A simple adverb is a single word that qualifies a single part of speech {hardly} {now} {deep}. A flat or bare adverb is one that has an *-ly* form but whose adjectival form may work equally well or even better, especially when used with an imperative in an informal context {drive slow} {hold on tight} {tell me quick}. Some flat adverbs are always used in their adjectival form {work fast} because the *-ly* has become obsolete (although it may linger in related words—e.g., *steadfast* and *steadfastly*). And the flat adverb may have a different meaning from the *-ly* adverb. Compare *I am working hard* with *I am hardly working.*

5.161 **Phrasal and compound adverbs.** A phrasal adverb consists of two or more words that function together as an adverb {in the meantime} {for a while} {here and there}. A compound adverb appears to be a single word but is a compound of several words {notwithstanding} {heretofore} {thereupon}. Compound adverbs should be used cautiously and sparingly because they tend to make the tone stuffy.

ADVERBIAL DEGREES

5.162 **Positive adverbs.** Like adjectives (see 5.84), adverbs have three degrees: the positive, the comparative, and the superlative. A positive adverb simply expresses a quality without reference to any other thing {the nurse spoke **softly**} {the choir sang **merrily**}.

5.163 **Comparative adverbs.** A comparative adverb compares the quality of a specified action done by two persons, groups, or things {Bitey worked **longer than Arachne**} {Rachel studied **more industriously than Edith**}. Most one-syllable adverbs that do not end in *-ly* form the comparative by taking the suffix *-er* {sooner} {harder}. These forms are called *synthetic comparatives.* Multisyllable adverbs usually form the comparative with *more* or *less* {the Shakespearean villain fenced **more ineptly** than the hero} {the patient is walking **less painfully** today}. These forms are called *periphrastic comparatives.* But there are exceptions for adverbs that end in *-ly* if the *-ly* is not a suffix {early–earlier}.

5.164 **Superlative adverbs.** A superlative adverb compares the quality of a specified action done by at least three persons, groups, or things {Sullie bowled **fastest** of all the cricketers} {of the three doctoral candidates, Dunya defended her dissertation the **most adamantly**}. In a loose sense, the superlative is sometimes used for emphasis rather than comparison {the pianist played **most skillfully**}. Most one-syllable adverbs that do not end in *-ly* form the superlative by taking the suffix *-est* {soonest} {hardest}. These forms are called *synthetic superlatives.* Multisyllable adverbs usually form the superlative with *most* or *least* {everyone's eyesight was acute, but I could see **most acutely**} {of all the people making choices, he chose **least wisely**}. These forms are called *periphrastic superlatives.* There are exceptions for adverbs that end in *-ly* if the *-ly* is not a suffix {early–earliest}.

5.165 **Irregular adverbs.** A few adverbs have irregular comparative and superlative forms {badly–worse–worst} {little–less–least}. A good dictionary is the best resource for finding an irregular adverb's forms of comparison.

5.166 **Noncomparable adverbs.** Many adverbs are noncomparable. Some, by their definitions, are absolute and cannot be compared {eternally} {never} {singly} {uniquely} {universally}. Most adverbs indicating time {now} {then}, position {on}, number {first} {finally}, or place {here} are also noncomparable.

POSITION OF ADVERBS

5.167 **Placement of adverbs.** To avoid miscues, an adverb should generally be placed as near as possible to the word it is intended to modify. For example, in *the marathoners submitted their applications to compete immediately*, what does *immediately* modify—*compete* or *submitted*? Placing the adverb with the word it modifies makes the meaning clear—e.g., *the marathoners immediately submitted their applications to compete.* A misplaced adverb can completely change a sentence's meaning. For example, *we nearly lost all our camping equipment* states that the equipment was saved; *we lost nearly all our camping equipment* states that almost everything was lost. An adverb's placement is also important because adverbs show time {we'll meet **again**}, place or source {put the flowers **here**} {**where** did you get that idea?}, manner {speak **softly**}, degree or extent {sales are **very** good} {**how** far is it to the British pub?}, reason {I don't know **why** Pat couldn't find the right answer}, consequence {we should **therefore** hasten to support her candidacy}, and number {**first**, we need to get our facts straight}. Adverbs can also express comments or observations {Vic was **undoubtedly** late} {Imani **clearly** recalled everything}.

5.168 **Adverbs that modify words other than verbs.** If an adverb qualifies an adjective, an adverb, a preposition, or a conjunction, it should immediately precede the word qualified {our vacation was **very short**} {the flight took **too long**} {your fence is **partly over** the property line} {leave **only when** the bell rings}. The adverb or adverbs modifying a single adjective, grouped with that adjective, are called an *adjective cluster* {a **classically trained** pianist}.

5.169 **Adverbs that modify intransitive verbs.** If an adverb qualifies an intransitive verb, it generally follows the verb {the students **sighed gloomily** when homework was assigned} {the owl **perched precariously** on a thin branch}. Some exceptions are *always*, *never*, *often*, *generally*, *rarely*, and *seldom*, which may precede the verb {mountaineers **seldom succeed** in climbing K2}.

5.170 **Adverbs and linking verbs.** Adverbs do not generally follow linking verbs (see 5.101), such as *be*-verbs, *appear*, *become*, *feel*, *hear*, *look*, *seem*, *smell*, and *taste*. These verbs connect a descriptive word with the clause's subject; the descriptive word after the verb applies to the subject, not the verb {he **seems** honest}. To determine whether a verb is a linking verb, consider whether the descriptive word describes the action or condition, or the subject. For example, *the sculptor feels badly* literally describes an impaired tactile sense (though that couldn't conceivably be the intended meaning). But *the sculptor feels bad* describes the sculptor as unwell or perhaps experiencing guilt (*bad* being not an adverb but a predicate adjective). Those adverbs that typically precede intransitive verbs (see 5.169), however, may modify linking verbs {she **quickly** became uncomfortable} {he **sometimes** seems dishonest}.

5.171 **Adverb within a verb phrase.** When an adverb qualifies a verb phrase, the normal place for the adverb is between the auxiliary verb and the principal verb {the administration **has consistently repudiated** this view} {the reports **will soon generate** controversy} {public opinion **is sharply**

divided}. (See 5.104.) Some adverbs may follow the principal verb {you must **go quietly**} {are you **asking rhetorically**?}. There has never been a rule against placing an adverbial modifier between the auxiliary verb and the principal verb in a verb phrase. In fact, it's typically preferable to put the adverb there {the heckler **was abruptly expelled**} {the bus **had been seriously damaged** in the crash}. Sometimes it is perfectly appropriate to split an infinitive with an adverb to add emphasis, clarify meaning, or produce a natural sound. (See 5.108.) A verb's infinitive or *to* form is split when an intervening word immediately follows *to* {to bravely assert}. If the adverb bears the emphasis in a phrase {to boldly go} {to strongly favor}, the split infinitive is justified and often even necessary. But if moving the adverb to the end of the phrase doesn't suggest a different meaning or impair the sound, then you have an acceptable way to avoid splitting the infinitive. Recasting a sentence just to eliminate a split infinitive or to avoid splitting the infinitive can alter the nuance or meaning of the sentence. For example, *it's best to always get up early* (*always* modifies *get up*) is not quite the same as *it's always best to get up early* (*always* modifies *best*). It can also make the phrasing sound unnatural—e.g., *it's best to get up early always.*

Prepositions

DEFINITION AND TYPES

5.172 **Prepositions generally.** A preposition is an uninflected function word or phrase linking a noun element (the preposition's object) with another part of the sentence to show the relationship between them. Prepositions express such notions as position (*about*, *above*, *below*, *on*, *under*), direction (*in*, *into*, *to*, *toward*), time (*after*, *before*, *during*, *until*), and source (*from*, *of*, *out of*). A preposition's object (sometimes termed an *oblique object*) is usually a noun, or else a pronoun in the objective case {**between** me and them}. Usually a preposition comes before its object, but there are exceptions. For example, a preposition used with the relative pronoun *that* (or with *that* understood) always follows the object {this is the moment (that) I've been waiting **for**}. It also frequently, but not always, follows the relative pronouns *which* {which alternative is your decision based **on**?} {this is the alternative **on which** my decision is based} and *whom* {there is a banker (whom) I must speak with} {I can't tell you **to whom** you should apply}. See also 5.180.

5.173 **Simple and compound prepositions.** Many prepositions are relatively straightforward. A simple preposition consists of a single monosyllabic word {as} {at} {by}. A compound preposition has two or more syllables; it may be made up of two or more words {into} {outside} {upon}.

5.174 **Phrasal prepositions.** A phrasal preposition, sometimes called a *complex preposition*, is two or more separate words used as a prepositional unit. These include *according to*, *because of*, *by means of*, *by reason of*, *by way of*, *contrary to*, *for the sake of*, *in accordance with*, *in addition to*, *in apposition with*, *in case of*, *in consideration of*, *in front of*, *in regard to*, *in respect to*, *in spite of*, *instead of*, *on account of*, *out of*, *with reference to*, *with regard to*, and *with respect to*. Many of these phrasal prepositions are symptoms of officialese, bureaucratese, or other types of verbose style. If a single-word preposition will do in context, use it. For example, if *about* will replace *with regard to* or *in connection with*, a judicious editor will inevitably prefer to use the simpler expression.

5.175 **Participial prepositions.** A participial preposition is a participial form that functions as a preposition (or sometimes as a subordinating conjunction). Examples are *assuming*, *barring*, *concerning*, *considering*, *during*, *notwithstanding*, *owing to*, *provided*, *regarding*, *respecting*, and *speaking of*. Unlike other participles, these words do not create danglers when they have no subject {**considering** the road conditions, the trip went quickly} {**regarding** Watergate, he had nothing to say}. See 5.115.

PREPOSITIONAL PHRASES

5.176 **Prepositional phrases generally.** A prepositional phrase consists of a preposition, its object, and any words that modify the object. A prepositional phrase can be used as a noun {**for James to change his mind** would be a miracle}, an adverb (also called an *adverbial phrase*) {we strolled **through the glade**}, or an adjective (also called an *adjectival phrase*) {we'd love to see the cathedrals **of Paris**}.

5.177 **Prepositional function.** Prepositions signal many kinds of relationships. For example, a preposition may express a spatial relationship {to} {from} {out of} {into}, time {at} {for} {throughout} {until}, cause {because of} {on account of}, means {like} {with} {by}, possession {without} {of}, exceptions {but for} {besides} {except}, support {with} {for}, opposition {against}, or concession {despite} {for all} {notwithstanding}.

5.178 **Placement of prepositional phrases.** A prepositional phrase with an adverbial or adjectival function should be as close as possible to the word it modifies to avoid awkwardness, ambiguity, or unintended meanings.

Compare *Is there a person with a small dog named Sandy here?* (is the person or the dog named Sandy?) with *Is there a person named Sandy here with a small dog?* Or compare *The woman with the Popular Front circulates petitions* with *The woman circulates petitions with the Popular Front.*

5.179 **Refinements on placement.** If a prepositional phrase equally modifies all the elements of a compound construction, the phrase follows the last element in the compound {the date, the place, and the budget **for the wedding** have been decided}. If the subject is singular and followed by a plural prepositional phrase, the predicate is singular—e.g., compare the predicate in *the man and his two daughters have arrived* with that in *the man with two daughters has arrived* and in *the man has arrived with his two daughters.*

5.180 **Ending a sentence with a preposition.** The traditional caveat of yesteryear against ending sentences or clauses with prepositions is an unnecessary and pedantic restriction. And it is wrong. As Winston Churchill is said to have put it sarcastically, "That is the type of arrant pedantry up with which I shall not put." A sentence that ends in a preposition may sound more natural than a sentence carefully constructed to avoid a final preposition. Compare, for example, *This is the case I told you about* with *This is the case about which I told you.* The "rule" prohibiting terminal prepositions was an ill-founded superstition based on a false analogy to Latin grammar. Today many grammarians use the dismissive term *pied-piping* for this phenomenon.

5.181 **Clashing prepositions.** If a phrasal verb {give in} precedes a prepositional phrase {in every argument}, the back-to-back prepositions, if they are the same, will clash {he gives in in every argument}. Recast the sentence when possible to avoid such juxtaposed prepositions—e.g., *rather than continue arguing, he always gives in,* or *in every argument, he gives in.* See also 6.55. For more on phrasal verbs, see 5.102.

5.182 **Elliptical prepositional phrases.** Sometimes a prepositional phrase is elliptical, being an independent expression without an antecedent. It often starts a clause and is normally detachable from the statement without affecting the meaning. Elliptical prepositional phrases include *for example, for instance, in any event, in a word, in the last analysis,* and *in the long run* {**in any event**, call me when you arrive}.

5.183 **Pronoun case in prepositional phrase.** If a pronoun appears in a prepositional phrase, the pronoun is usually in the objective case {with me} {alongside her} {between them} (see also 5.19, 5.35). But note that *than* may function as either a conjunction or a preposition {he's taller **than I [am]**} {he's taller **than me**}. In edited English, *taller than I* has predominated over *taller than me* in American English from its very beginnings, and in British English it predominated until the 1990s. Throughout the literary history of Modern English, *than me*, *than her*, etc. have been regarded as less polished (to say the least) than *than I*, *than she*, etc. That is to say, in formal registers *than* (like *as*) is considered a conjunction, not a preposition. But in spoken English, *than* and *as* are often treated as prepositions that take a pronoun in the objective case {you're better than me} {you're as well known as me}. A possessive pronoun may be used before the preposition's object {to my house}.

OTHER PREPOSITIONAL ISSUES

5.184 **Prepositions and functional variation.** Some words that function as prepositions may also function as other parts of speech. The distinguishing feature of a preposition is that it always has an object. A word such as *above*, *behind*, *below*, *by*, *down*, *in*, *off*, *on*, or *up* can be used as either an adverb or a preposition. When used as a preposition, it takes an object {let's slide **down the hill**}. When used as an adverb, it does not {we sat **down**}. Some conjunctions may serve as prepositions (e.g., *than* and *but*). Compare the prepositional *but* in *everyone but Fuzzy traveled abroad last summer* (*but* is used to mean "except") with the conjunctive *but* in *I like the cut but not the color* (*but* introduces a clause containing an implied separate action: *I don't like the color*).

5.185 **Use and misuse of "like."** *Like* is probably the least understood preposition. Its traditional function is adjectival, not adverbial, so that *like* governs nouns and noun phrases {teens often see themselves as star-crossed lovers **like Romeo and Juliet**}. As a preposition, *like* is followed by a noun or by a pronoun in the objective case {the person in that old portrait looks **like me**}. Increasingly today in ordinary speech, *like* displaces *as* or *as if* as a conjunction to connect clauses. For example, in *it happened just like I said it would happen*, traditional grammarians would want to replace *like* with *as*; and in *you're looking around like you've misplaced something*, *like* with *as if*. Because *as* and *as if* are conjunctions, they are followed by pronouns in the nominative case {do you work too hard, **as I** do?}. Although *like* as a conjunction has been considered nonstandard since the seventeenth century, today it is common in dialectal and colloquial usage {he ran **like** he was really scared}.

5.186 **Use and misuse of "only."** *Only* functions as an adjective, an adverb, and a conjunction, and it can modify any part of speech. It is probably poorly placed in sentences more often than any other word. *Only* emphasizes the word or phrase that immediately follows it. When *only* appears too early in the sentence, it has a deemphasizing effect; it can also alter the meaning of the sentence or produce ambiguity. Compare *I bought only tomatoes at the market* (I bought nothing else) with *I bought tomatoes only at the market* (I bought nothing other than tomatoes or I didn't buy tomatoes from any other place?). In idiomatic spoken English, *only* is placed before the verb, regardless of what it modifies: *I only bought tomatoes at the market*. This may be acceptable in speech because the speaker can use intonation to make the meaning clear. But since in writing there is no guidance from intonation, rigorous placement of *only* aids reader comprehension.

LIMITING PREPOSITIONAL PHRASES

5.187 **Avoiding overuse of prepositions.** Prepositions can easily be overused. Stylistically, a good ratio to strive for is one preposition for every ten to fifteen words. Five editorial methods can reduce the number of prepositions in a sentence.

5.188 **Cutting prepositional phrases.** If the surrounding prose's context permits, a prepositional phrase can be eliminated—e.g., *the most important ingredient in this recipe* could be reduced to *the most important ingredient* when it appears within a passage focused on a particular recipe.

5.189 **Cutting unnecessary prepositions.** A noun ending in *-ance*, *-ence*, *-ity*, *-ment*, *-sion*, or *-tion* is often formed from a verb {qualification–qualify} {performance–perform}. These nouns are sometimes called *nominalizations* or *zombie nouns*, and they often require additional words, especially prepositions (that is, *during her performance of the concerto* is essentially equivalent to *while she performed the concerto*, but it is somewhat more abstract and requires the preposition *of*). Using a verb instead of a nominalization often eliminates one or two prepositions. For example, *toward maximization of* becomes simply *to maximize*, so that *our efforts toward maximization of profits failed* might be edited down to *our efforts to maximize profits failed*.

5.190 **Replacing prepositional phrases with adverbs.** A strong adverb may replace a weaker prepositional phrase. For example, *the president spoke with force* is weak compared with *the president spoke forcefully*.

5.191 **Replacing prepositional phrases with genitives.** A genitive may replace a prepositional phrase, especially an *of*-genitive. For example, *I was dismayed by the complexity of the street map* essentially equals *The street map's complexity dismayed me*. See 5.20.

5.192 **Using active voice to eliminate prepositions.** Changing from the long passive voice (with *by* after the verb) to an active-voice construction always eliminates a preposition. For example, *the ship was sailed by an experienced crew* equals *an experienced crew sailed the ship*.

PREPOSITIONAL IDIOMS

5.193 **Idiomatic uses of prepositions.** Among the most persistent word-choice issues are those concerning prepositions. Which prepositions go with which words? You *fill* A *with* B but *instill* B *into* A; you *replace* A *with* B but *substitute* B *for* A; you *prefix* A *to* B but *preface* B *with* A; you *force* A *into* B but *enforce* B *on* A; finally, A *implies* B, so you *infer* B *from* A. And that's only the beginning of it.

5.194 **Shifts in prepositional idiom.** While prepositional idioms often give nonnative speakers of English nightmares, even native speakers of English may need to double-check them from time to time. Often the language undergoes some shifting. There may be a difference between traditional literary usage (*oblivious of*) and prevailing contemporary usage (*oblivious to*). Sometimes the writer may choose one or the other preposition for reasons of euphony. (Is it better, in a given context, to *ruminate on*, *about*, or *over* a specified problem?) Sometimes, too, the denotative and connotative differences can be striking: it's one thing to be *smitten with* another and quite a different thing to be *smitten by* another.

5.195 **List of words and the prepositions construed with them.** The list below contains the words that most often give writers trouble. Note that some of the words included here—such as verbs that can be used transitively {the tire abutted the curb} or words that can be used without further qualification {she refused to acquiesce} {his words were considered blasphemy}—do not always take prepositions.

abide (*vb.*): with ("stay"); by ("obey"); *none* (transitive)
abound (*vb.*): in, with [resources]
absolve (*vb.*): from [guilt]; of [obligation]
abut (*vb.*): on, against [land]; *none* (transitive)

accompanied (*adj.*): by (not *with*) [something *or* someone else]
accord (*vb.*): in, with [an opinion]; to [a person]
acquiesce (*vb.*): in [a decision]; to [pressure]
acquit (*vb.*): of (not *from*) [a charge]; *none* (transitive)
adept (*adj.*): at [an activity]; in [an art]
admit (*vb.*) ("acknowledge"): *none* (not *to*) (transitive)
admit (*vb.*) ("let in"): to, into
admit (*vb.*) ("allow"): of
anxious (*adj.*): about, over (preferably not *to*) [a concern]
badger (*vb.*): into [doing something]; about [a situation]
ban (*vb.*): from [a place]
ban (*n.*): on [a thing; an activity]; from [a place]
based (*adj.*): on (preferably not *upon*) [a premise]; in [a place; a field of study]; at [a place]
becoming (*adj.*): on, to [a person]; of [an office or position]
bestow (*vb.*): on (preferably not *upon*) [an honoree]
binding (*adj.*): on (preferably not *upon*) [a person]
blasphemy (*n.*): against [a religious tenet]
center (*vb.*): on, upon (not *around*) [a primary issue]
chafe (*vb.*): at [doing something]; under [an irritating authority]
coerce (*vb.*): into [doing something]
cohesion (*n.*): between, among [things; groups]
collude (*vb.*): with [a person to defraud another]
commiserate (*vb.*): with [a person]
compare (*vb.*): with (literal comparison); to (poetic or metaphorical comparison)
comply (*vb.*): with (not *to*) [a rule; an order]
confide (*vb.*): to, in [a person]
congruence (*n.*): with [a standard]
connive (*vb.*): at [a bad act]; with [another person]
consider (*vb.*): *none* (transitive); as [one of several possible aspects (*not* as a substitute for "to be")]; for [a position]
consist (*vb.*): of [components (said of concrete things)]; in [qualities (said of abstract things)]
contemporary (*adj.*): with [another event]
contemporary (*n.*): of [another person]
contiguous (*adj.*): with, to [another place]
contingent (*adj.*): on (preferably not *upon*)
contrast (*vb.*): to, with [a person or thing]
conversant (*adj.*): with, in [a field of study]
convict (*vb.*): of, for (not *in*)
depend (*vb.*): on (preferably not *upon*)
differ (*vb.*): from [a thing or quality]; with [a person]; about, over, on [an issue]

different (*adj.*): from (but when a dependent clause follows *different*, the conjunction *than* is a defensible substitute for *from what*: "movies today are different than they were in the fifties")

dissent (*n. & vb.*): from, against (preferably not *to* or *with*)

dissimilar (*adj.*): to (not *from*)

dissociate (*vb.*): from

enamored (*adj.*): of (not *with*)

equivalent (*adj.*): to, in (preferably not *with*)

excerpt (*n.*): from (not *of*)

forbid (*vb.*): to (formal); from (informal)

foreclose (*vb.*): on [mortgaged property]

hale (*vb.*): to, into [a place]; before [a magistrate]

hegemony (*n.*): over [rivals]; in [a region]

identical (*adj.*): with (preferred by purists), to [something else]

impatience (*n.*): with [a person]; with, at, about [a situation]

impose (*vb.*): on (preferably not *upon*) [a person]

inaugurate (*vb.*): as [an officer]; into [an office]

inculcate (*vb.*): into, in [a person]

independent (*adj.*): of (not *from*) [something else]

infringe (*vb.*): *none* (transitive); on (preferably not *upon*) [a right]

inhere (*vb.*): in (not *within*) [a person; a thing]

inquire (*vb.*): into [situations]; of [people]; after [people]

instill (*vb.*): in, into (not *with*) [a person]

juxtapose (*vb.*): to (not *with*)

mastery (*n.*): of [a skill or knowledge]; over [people]

militate (*vb.*): against [a harsher outcome]

mitigate (*vb.*): *none* (transitive)

oblivious (*adj.*): of (preferred), to [a danger; an opportunity]

off (*prep. & adv.*): *none* (not *of*)

predilection (*n.*): for [a preferred thing]

predominate (*vb.*) (not transitive): in, on, over [a field; rivals]

preferable (*adj.*): to (not *than*), over [an alternative]

pretext (*n.*): for [a true intention]

reconcile (*vb.*): with [a person]; to [a situation]

reticent (*adj.*): about [speaking; a topic]

sanction (*n.*): for [misbehavior]; of [a sponsoring body]; to [a person; an event]

shiver (*vb.*): from [cold]; at [something frightening]

stigmatize (*vb.*): *none* (transitive); as [dishonorable]

subscribe (*vb.*): to [a periodical or an opinion]; for [stock]

trade (*vb.*): for ("swap"); in ("sell"); with ("do business with"); at ("patronize"); in [certain goods]; on ("buy and sell at")

trust (*n.*): in [faith]; for ("beneficial trust")

undaunted (*adj.*): in [a task]; by [obstacles]

unequal (*adj.*): to [a challenge]; in [attributes]
used (*adj.*): to ("accustomed"); for ("applied to")
vexed (*adj.*): with [someone]; about, at [something]

Conjunctions

5.196 **Conjunctions defined.** A conjunction is a function word that connects sentences, clauses, or words within a clause {my daughter graduated from college in December, **and** my son will graduate from high school in May [*and* connects two sentences]} {I said hello, **but** no one answered [*but* connects two clauses]} {we're making progress slowly **but** surely [*but* joins two adverbs within a clause]}. In Standard English, conjunctions connect pronouns in the same case {he **and** she are colleagues} {the teacher encouraged her **and** me}. A pronoun following the conjunction *than* or *as* is normally in the nominative case even when the clause that follows is understood {you are wiser **than I** [am]} {you seem as pleased **as she** [does]}—except in informal or colloquial English {you are wiser than me}. In the latter instance, *than* can be read as a preposition (see 5.183).

5.197 **Simple versus compound conjunctions.** A conjunction may be simple, a single word such as *and*, *but*, *if*, *or*, or *though*. Most are derived from prepositions. Compound conjunctions are single words formed by combining two or more words. Most are relatively modern formations; they include words such as *although*, *because*, *nevertheless*, *notwithstanding*, and *unless*. Phrasal conjunctions are connectives made up of two or more separate words. Examples are *as though*, *inasmuch as*, *in case*, *provided that*, *so that*, and *supposing that*. The two main classes of conjunctions are coordinating and subordinating.

5.198 **Coordinating conjunctions.** Coordinating conjunctions join words or groups of words of equal grammatical rank, such as two nouns, two verbs, two phrases, or two clauses {are you speaking to him **or** to me?} {the results are disappointing **but** not discouraging}. Coordinating conjunctions are further broken down into copulative, adversative, disjunctive, and final. A coordinating conjunction may be either a single word or a correlative conjunction.

5.199 **Correlative conjunctions.** Correlative conjunctions are conjunctions used in pairs, often to join successive clauses that depend on each other to form a complete thought. Some examples of correlative conjunctions are *as–as*, *if–then*, *either–or*, *neither–nor*, *both–and*, *where–there*, *so–as*, and *not only–but also*. Correlative conjunctions must frame structurally identical or matching sentence parts {she wanted **both** to win the gold medal **and** to set a new record}; in other words, each member of the pair should immediately precede the same part of speech {they **not only read** the book **but also saw** the movie} {**if** the first **claim** is true, **then** the second **claim** must be false}.

5.200 **Subordinating conjunctions.** A subordinating conjunction connects clauses of unequal grammatical rank. The conjunction introduces a clause that is dependent on the independent clause {follow this road **until** you reach the highway} {that squirrel is friendly **because** people feed it} {Marcus promised **that** he would help}. A pure subordinating conjunction has no antecedent and is not a pronoun or an adverb {take a message **if** someone calls}.

5.201 **Special uses of subordinating conjunctions.** Subordinating conjunctions or conjunctive phrases often denote the following relationships: (1) *Comparison or degree*—e.g., *than* (if it follows comparative adverbs or adjectives, or if it follows *else*, *rather*, *other*, or *otherwise*), *as*, *else*, *otherwise*, *rather*, *as much as*, *as far as*, and *as well as* {is a raven less clever **than** a magpie?} {these amateur musicians play **as well as** professionals} {it's not true **as far as** I can discover}. (2) *Time*—e.g., *since*, *until*, *as long as*, *as soon as*, *before*, *after*, *when*, *as*, and *while* {**while** we waited, it began to snow} {the tire went flat **as** we were turning the corner} {we'll start the game **as soon as** everyone understands the rules} {the audience returned to the auditorium **after** the concert's resumption was announced}. (3) *Condition or assumption*—e.g., *if*, *though*, *unless*, *except*, *without*, and *once* {**once** you sign the agreement, we can begin remodeling the house} {your thesis must be presented next week **unless** you have a good reason to postpone it} {I'll go on this business trip **if** I can fly first class}. (4) *Reason or concession*—e.g., *as*, *inasmuch as*, *why*, *because*, *for*, *since*, *though*, *although*, and *albeit* {**since** you won't share the information, I can't help you} {Sir John decided to purchase the painting **although** it was very expensive} {she deserves credit **because** it was her idea}. (5) *Purpose or result*—e.g., *that*, *so that*, *in order that*, and *such that* {we dug up the yard **so that** a new water garden could be laid out} {he sang **so loudly that** he became hoarse}. (6) *Place*—e.g., *where* {I found a great restaurant **where** I didn't expect one to be}. (7) *Manner*—e.g., *as if* and *as though* {he swaggers around the office **as if** he were an executive}. (8) *Appositions*—e.g., *and*, *or*, *what*, and *that* {the buffalo, **or** American bison, was once nearly extinct}. (9) *Indirect questions*—e.g., *whether*, *why*, and *when* {he could not say **whether** we were going the right way}.

5.202 **Adverbial conjunctions.** An adverbial conjunction connects two clauses and also qualifies a verb {the valet has forgotten **where** Alvaro's car is parked [*where* qualifies the verb *is parked*]}. There are two types of adverbial conjunctions: relative and interrogative. A relative adverbial conjunction does the same job as any other adverbial conjunction, but it has an antecedent {do you recall that café **where** we first met? [*café* is the antecedent of *where*]}. An interrogative adverbial conjunction indirectly states a question {Barbara asked **when** we are supposed to leave [*when* poses the indirect question]}. Some common examples of conjunctive relative adverbs are *after*, *as*, *before*, *now*, *since*, *so*, *until*, *when*, and *where*. Interrogative adverbs are used to ask direct and indirect questions; the most common are *why*, *how*, *when*, *where*, and *what* {I don't see **how** you reached that conclusion}.

5.203 **Beginning a sentence with a conjunction.** There is a widespread belief—one with no historical or grammatical foundation—that it is an error to begin a sentence with a conjunction such as *and*, *but*, or *so*. In fact, a substantial percentage (often as many as 10 percent) of the sentences in first-rate writing begin with conjunctions. It has been so for centuries, and even the most conservative grammarians have followed this practice. Charles Allen Lloyd's words from 1938 fairly sum up the situation as it stands even today:

> Next to the groundless notion that it is incorrect to end an English sentence with a preposition, perhaps the most widespread of the many false beliefs about the use of our language is the equally groundless notion that it is incorrect to begin one with "but" or "and." As in the case of the superstition about the prepositional ending, no textbook supports it, but apparently about half of our teachers of English go out of their way to handicap their pupils by inculcating it. One cannot help wondering whether those who teach such a monstrous doctrine ever read any English themselves.[7]

Still, *but* as an adversative conjunction can occasionally be unclear at the beginning of a sentence. Evaluate the contrasting force of the *but* in question, and see whether the needed word is really *and*; if *and* can be substituted, then *but* is almost certainly the wrong word. Consider this example: *He went to school this morning. But he left his lunch box on the kitchen table.* Between those sentences is an elliptical idea, since the two actions are in no way contradictory. What is implied is something like

7. Charles Allen Lloyd, *We Who Speak English: And Our Ignorance of Our Mother Tongue* (New York: Thomas Y. Crowell, 1938), 19.

this: *He went to school, intending to have lunch there, but he left his lunch behind.* Because *and* would have made sense in the passage as originally stated, *but* is not the right word—the idea for the contrastive *but* should be explicit. To sum up, then, *but* is a perfectly proper way to open a sentence, but only if the idea it introduces truly contrasts with what precedes. For that matter, *but* is often an effective way of introducing a paragraph that develops an idea contrary to the one preceding it.

5.204 **Beginning a sentence with "however."** *However* has been used as a conjunctive adverb since the fourteenth century. Like other adverbs, it can be used at the beginning of a sentence. But *however* is more ponderous and has less impact than the simple *but*. As a matter of style, *however* is more effectively used within a sentence to emphasize the word or phrase that precedes it {The job seemed exciting at first. Soon, **however**, it turned out to be exceedingly dull.}. For purposes of euphony and flow, not of grammar, many highly accomplished writers shun the sentence-starting *however* as a contrasting word. Yet the word is fine in that position in the sense "in whatever way" (not followed by a comma) {however that may be, we've now made our decision}.

5.205 **Conjunctions and the number of a verb.** Coordinating and disjunctive conjunctions affect whether a verb should be plural or singular. Conjunctions such as *and* and *through* indicate that grouped sentence elements impart plurality, so a plural verb is correct {the best vacation **and** the worst vacation of my life **were** on cruises} {the first **through** seventh innings **were** scoreless}. But conjunctions such as *or* and *either–or* distinguish the elements and do not impart plurality, so the singular verb is used if the elements are singular {a squirrel **or** a chipmunk **raids** the bird feeder every day} {either William **or** Henry **dances** with Lady Hill}. Other types of conjunctions have no effect on the verb's number; for example, if *and* is used as a copulative conjunction, the verb that follows may be singular {Andrés's bicycle was new, **and** so **was** his helmet}. See also 7.8.

Interjections

5.206 **Interjections defined.** An interjection or exclamation is a word, phrase, or clause that denotes strong feeling {never again!} {you don't say!}. An interjection has little or no grammatical function in a sentence; it is used absolutely {**really**, I can't understand why you put up with the situation} {**oh no**, how am I going to fix the damage?} {**hey**, it's my turn next!}. It is frequently allowed to stand as a sentence by itself {**Oh**! I've lost my wallet!} {**Ouch**! I think my ankle is sprained!} {**Get out**!} {**Whoa**!}. Introductory words like *well* and *why* may also act as interjections when they are meaningless utterances {**well**, I tried my best} {**why**, I would never do that}. The punctuation offsetting the interjections distinguishes them. Compare the different meanings of *Well, I didn't know him* with *I didn't know him well*, and *Why, here you are!* with *I have no idea why you are here* and *Why? I have no idea*. See also 6.34, 6.35.

5.207 **Use of interjections.** Interjections are natural in speech {your order should be shipped, **oh**, in eight to ten days} and frequently used in dialogue (and formerly in poetry). As a midsentence interrupter, an interjection may direct attention to one's phrasing or reflect the writer's or speaker's attitude toward the subject, especially if the tone is informal or colloquial {because our business proposal was, **ahem**, poorly presented, our budget will not be increased this year}.

5.208 **Interjections and functional variation.** Because interjections are usually grammatically independent of the rest of the sentence, all other parts of speech may be used as interjections. A word that is classified as some other part of speech but used with the force of an interjection is called an *exclamatory noun*, *exclamatory adjective*, etc. Some examples are *good!* (adjective); *idiot!* (noun); *help!* (verb); *indeed!* (adverb); *me!* (pronoun); *and!* (conjunction); *quickly!* (adverb).

5.209 **Words that are exclusively interjections.** Some words are used only as interjections—for example, *ouch*, *whew*, *ugh*, *psst*, and *oops*.

Syntax

5.210 **Syntax defined.** *Syntax* is the collective term we use to denote all the rules governing how words are arranged into sentences. In an analytic language like English—one that, unlike a synthetic language, uses word order to show word relations (as opposed to inflections of various kinds)—syntax is particularly important in expressing meaning.

5.211 **Statements.** Most sentences are statements having a declarative structure in which (1) the clause contains a subject and (2) the subject precedes the verb. Sometimes in speech and informal writing, the subject is merely implied {[he] missed the ball} {[I] think I'll go to the store}. In a few negative idioms, the subject may follow part of the verb phrase {scarcely had we arrived when we had to return}.

5.212 **Questions.** Sentences that seek to elicit information are known as *questions*. They have an interrogative structure, which typically begins with a question word. There are three main types: (1) yes–no questions, which are intended to prompt an affirmative or negative response {will we be gone long?}; (2) *wh-* questions, so called because they characteristically start with *who*, *what*, *when*, *where*, *why*, *which*, or *how* (not quite a *wh-* word, but it counts) {which apples do you want?}; and (3) alternative questions, which prompt a response relating to options mentioned in the sentence {would you rather play golf or tennis?}.

5.213 **Some exceptional types of questions.** Four types of interrogative utterances aren't classifiable under the three categories given in 5.212. Two are yes–no questions. The first is the spoken sentence in which one's pitch rises at the end, in a questioning way—but the structure is that of a declarative sentence {he's going to Corpus Christi?}. To show vexation in such a question, the question mark may be paired with an exclamation point {she's going to Padre Island?!}. The second special type of yes–no question is the tag question, in which the interrogative inversion appears at the end of a statement {he has arrived, hasn't he?} {it's good, isn't it?}. A few tag questions are signaled by particular words without the interrogative inversion {it's raining, right?} {you're tired, eh?} {you want to go, yes?}. A third special type is the exclamatory question, in which the interrogative structure appears but when the statement is spoken, one's tone normally falls at the end {isn't it nice out here!} {how great is this!}. Finally, a rhetorical question is phrased in the interrogative structure but is meant as an emphatic or evocative statement, without the expectation of an answer {why should I care?} {who knows how long it might take?}.

5.214 **Directives.** A directive or imperative is a sentence that instructs somebody to do or not to do something. The word *command* is sometimes used as a synonym, but most grammarians consider the term *command* more appropriate for one of the eight main types of directives, all of which are in the imperative mood of the verb: (1) command {come here now!}; (2) prohibition {don't do that!}; (3) invitation {join us for dinner!}; (4) warning {watch out for rattlesnakes!}; (5) plea {stay here} {help!}; (6) request {put your book away}; (7) well-wishing {play well} {have a good time!}; and (8) advice {put on some insect repellent}.

5.215 **Exceptional directives.** Several directives depart from these common patterns, as when the subject is expressed {sit you down} {you stay there}; when they begin with *let* {let's have a picnic} {let us wait}; or when they begin with *do* {do help yourself}.

5.216 **Exclamations.** An exclamation expresses the extent to which a speaker is moved, aroused, impressed, or disgusted by something. It can take the form of a simple interjection {by golly!} {pishposh!}. Or it can follow a sentence structure consisting of *what* or *how* followed by a subject and verb {what an extraordinary novel this is!} {how well she writes!}. Exclamations are sometimes elliptically expressed {what finery!} {how pretty!} {how ugly!}. In formal, literary English, exclamations can be signaled by inverted word order {little did I expect such unfair treatment}.

The Four Traditional Types of Sentence Structures

5.217 **Simple sentence.** A simple sentence consists of a single independent clause with no dependent clause {no man is an island}. A sentence can be simple despite having internal compound constructions serving as subjects, main verbs, objects of prepositions, and others {time and tide wait for no man}.

5.218 **Compound sentence.** A compound sentence contains two independent clauses (called *coordinate clauses*) with no dependent clause {the rain was heavy, and my umbrella was not much help}. Grammarians are divided on the question whether one type of sentence should be labeled compound or simple: *She arrived early and stayed late.* Traditional grammarians have tended to call this a simple sentence with a compound predicate (where *arrived* and *stayed* are coordinate verbs). Transformational grammarians have tended to call it a compound sentence with an elided subject in the second clause {she arrived early[,] and [she] stayed late}.

5.219 **Complex sentence.** A complex sentence contains a single independent clause with one or more dependent clauses {I'll be home after I finish work}. Such a sentence may have only one dependent clause {she won **because she practiced so hard**}, or it may contain a variety of dependent clauses {the books **that were nominated** argued **that most behavioral differences among people aren't genetic in origin** [*that were nominated* is an adjective clause; *that most behavioral differences among people aren't genetic in origin* is a noun clause]}.

5.220 **Compound-complex sentence.** A compound-complex sentence contains multiple independent clauses and at least one dependent clause {it was a beautiful evening, so after we left work we went for a walk [*after we left work* is a dependent clause between two independent clauses]}. It differs from a complex sentence only in containing more than one independent clause. Like the independent clauses of a compound sentence, those of a compound-complex sentence are called *coordinate clauses*.

English Sentence Patterns

5.221 **Importance of word order.** English is known as an *analytic language*—one that depends largely on word order. (A *synthetic language*, such as Latin, depends largely on inflectional forms of words.) In the transition from Old English (AD 450–1100) to Middle English (1100–1500), the language lost most of its inflected forms—except those for pronouns (*I–me–mine* etc.). Nouns no longer have nominative and accusative cases. Instead, word order governs meaning. Consider this example: *Michael likes crystal. Michael* is the subject, *likes* the verb, and *crystal* the object. It's the basic subject-verb-object (SVO) pattern. We deduce the meaning from the position of the words: Michael is an admirer and perhaps a collector of fine glass. If we change it to *Crystal likes Michael*, the meaning is transformed because of the SVO order. We now infer that someone named Crystal thinks fondly about someone named Michael. The SVO pattern is highly significant: it governs the meaning of most English statements. Departures from it typically signal either unusual emphasis or the posing of a question (as opposed to the making of a statement).

5.222 **The basic SVO pattern.** Despite the seeming potential for monotony in having sentence after sentence using the same fundamental word order, English offers enough variety in vocabulary and in sentence elements that can function as subjects, verbs, and objects to keep things interesting. Consider these examples, all of which use the pattern but with interesting levels of sophistication:

Mary	likes	pomegranates.
S	V	O

The umpire we were talking about	rejected	our arguments.
S	V	O

The woman down the street	is selling	loaves of bread.
S	V	O

The obstacles that we face	create	opportunities.
S	V	O

How you think of yourself	affects	both	the way you approach
S	V		O

the problems of everyday life	and	the degree to which you're
O		O

perceived as being well adjusted.
O

5.223 **All seven syntactic patterns.** Syntactic patterns other than the SVO pattern are available, but they are limited to specific types that include two to four of these elements: subject (S), verb (V), [direct] object (O), indirect object (IO), complement (C), adverbial (A). Here are all seven basic clause patterns:

S + V: Sandy smiled.
S + V + O: Sandy hit the ball.
S + V + C: Sandy is eager.
S + V + A: Sandy plays well.
S + V + IO + O: Sandy gave Jerry the ball.
S + V + O + C: Sandy got her bag wet.
S + V + O + A: Sandy wrote her score on the card.

5.224 **Variations on syntactic order.** When clause elements appear in a different order, the inversion may indicate either a question {is Sandy all right? [V–S–C]} or a special kind of emphasis:

Yoda	my name	is!
C	S	V

Bully	you	say!
O	S	V

Inversions of this type achieve a special emphasis precisely because they depart from the normal sequence of sentence elements.

Clauses

5.225 **Clauses.** A *clause* is a grammatical unit that contains a subject, a finite verb, and any complements that the verb requires. An *independent clause* can stand alone as a sentence {José saw a squirrel}, while a *dependent clause* cannot stand alone because of the presence of a word by which it would normally be linked to an independent clause {**because he was hungry**, he sat down for a meal}. A dependent clause is usually introduced either by a relative pronoun (making it a relative clause) or by a subordinating conjunction, which establishes the semantic relationship between the independent clause and the dependent one. Combining related ideas by linking one or more dependent clauses to an independent one is called *subordination*, and the result is a complex sentence. Because a dependent clause is always subordinate to an independent clause for contextual meaning, it is also called a *subordinate clause*. A dependent clause commonly serves one of several functions: the direct object of a verb {everyone believed **that the note was genuine** [the *that*-clause is the direct object of *believed*]}; an adjectival clause modifying a noun element {he **who hesitates** is lost [*who hesitates* adjectivally modifies *he*]}; an adverbial clause modifying a verb or verb phrase {I bought the car **despite my father's warning not to** [the *despite*-clause modifies the verb *bought*]}.

5.226 **Relative clauses.** A relative clause is a subordinate clause that is introduced by a relative pronoun and modifies the noun element (or sentence or clause) it follows {the car **that you own**} {those **who follow his progress**} {they were ten minutes late to the opera, **which meant they couldn't enter until the end of the first act**}. In some relative clauses, called *contact clauses*, the relative pronoun is merely implied {all the people **you mention** have already registered [the relative pronoun *who* is implied in *people* [*whom*] *you mention*]}. Because the necessary connective is omitted, contact clauses are a type of elliptical clause—one often involving what is known as a *whiz-deletion* (so called because it so often amounts to the omission of *who is*).

5.227 **Appositive clauses.** A clause used in apposition to a noun element in the sentence is called an *appositive clause*. Though these are often (but not always) introduced with the same words that introduce relative clauses (*that*, *which*, *who*), the two differ in that a relative clause functions only within the sentence, while an appositive clause is self-contained: with its introductory relative pronoun removed, it could stand on its own as a grammatical sentence {we all heard the report **that the beloved broadcaster had died** [without *that*, the remaining appositive clause is grammatically complete: *the beloved broadcaster had died*]}.

5.228 **Conditional clauses.** A conditional clause (also called a *protasis*) is an adverbial clause, typically introduced by *if* or *unless* (or *should*, *although*, *though*, *despite*, or another subordinating conjunction), establishing the condition in a conditional sentence. Usually this is a direct condition, indicating that the main clause (also called the *apodosis*) is dependent on the condition being fulfilled. Sometimes, however, the clause may express an indirect condition {**if I recall correctly**, his assistant's name is Miljana}, alternative conditions {the party will be a success **whether or not it rains**}, or an open range of possibilities {**whatever you're doing**, it's working}. Most often, though, a conditional clause expresses a direct condition, which may be open (real or factual) or hypothetical (closed or unreal). An open condition leaves unanswered the question whether the condition will be fulfilled {**if you don't finish the work on time**, we'll have to reevaluate our arrangement}. A hypothetical condition, on the other hand, assumes that the condition has not been, is not, or is unlikely to be fulfilled {**if he had only remembered to wear a raincoat**, he wouldn't have ruined his new suit} {**if I had a hammer**, I could fix this creaky stair} {the transition would be much harder **if she left without giving notice**}.

Ellipsis

5.229 **Ellipsis generally.** A grammatical ellipsis (sometimes called an omission) occurs when part of a clause is left understood and the reader or listener is able to supply the missing words. (For the use of three dots to indicate text omitted from a direct quotation or for faltering or interrupted speech, see 13.50–58.) This "recovery" of omitted words is possible because of shared idiomatic knowledge, context, and what's called the *principle of recoverability* {he preferred chocolate, she vanilla [*preferred* is understood in the second clause]}. A sentence containing such an ellipsis is called an *elliptical sentence*. In colloquial speech, an ellipsis is useful to avoid repetition, shorten the message, and make it easier to understand. It's particularly appropriate for commands and exclamations, and especially when asking or answering a question whose complete answer would essentially repeat the question. For example:

Thank you. (I thank you.)
One lump or two? (Would you like one lump of sugar or two?)
Glad you like it! (I'm glad that you like it!)
Which is better? And why? (Which choice is better, and why is it better?)
[Can you tell me who built this house?] The Tucker family. (Yes, I can tell you. The Tucker family built this house.)

Negation

5.230 **Negation generally.** A statement may be expressed in positive or negative terms. Negation is the grammatical process of reversing the expression in a sentence. There are four common types: (1) using the negative particle *not* or *no*; (2) using negating pronouns such as *nobody*, *none*, *no one*, *nothing*, or negating adverbs such as *nowhere*, *never*, *neither*; (3) using the coordinating conjunctions *neither* and *nor* (or both of them as correlative conjunctions); (4) using words that are negative in meaning and function, such as *hardly* (= almost not), *scarcely* (= almost not), *barely* (= almost not), *few* (= not many; not much), *little* (= not much), *rarely* (= almost never), and *seldom* (= almost never)—or words having negative affixes such as *a-* {atypical}, *dis-* {disrobe}, *in-* {inimitable} (together with the assimilated forms *il-*, *im-*, and *ir-*), *non-* {nonemployee}, *un-* {untidy}, *-less* {careless}, and *-free* {hassle-free}.

5.231 **The word "not."** The simplest and most common form of negation involves using the particle *not*. Used with ordinary verbs and with auxiliary verbs, *not* typically negates a verb, an object, a phrase, or a clause. *Not* typically precedes whatever sentence element is being negated. To negate an ordinary verb in the present- or past-tense indicative mood, the verb is replaced by a compound of *do* or *did* plus *not* and a bare infinitive.

They sell newspapers in the hotel.
They do not sell newspapers in the hotel.

Kerri sings at the opera today.
Kerri does not sing at the opera today.

The waiter returned with our order.
The waiter did not return with our order.

Not usually immediately follows the principal verb or an auxiliary. If there are two or more verbs in the negative expression, *not* always follows the first of them.

I am happy.
I am not happy.

I should leave for work.
I should not leave for work.

I should leave for work, but I cannot find my glasses.

With participles, *not* precedes the participle {not given any warning, Josué nonchalantly opened the door} {not coming to any conclusions, the jury decided to suspend deliberations} {not having heard the news, Brett innocently asked how Tara was doing in school}. The subject is normally elided from the participial phrase. *Not* doesn't have to negate everything that follows it. It may be limited to the element immediately following {I discovered not a scientific breakthrough but a monstrous development}. A sentence containing *not* may be qualified by another element that limits the extent of the negation. The word's or clause's placement may significantly alter the scope of negation. For example:

He definitely did not accept the job offer.
[It is final: he rejected the job offer.]

He did not definitely accept the job offer.
[It is uncertain: he might still reject the offer.]

We have not eaten yet.
[We have not eaten, but we expect to eat at some time.]

Not can be contracted to *-n't* and appended to most auxiliary verbs without changing the form of the verb (e.g., *are not* → *aren't*, *would not* → *wouldn't*, *has not* → *hasn't*). The exceptions, involving *am*, *can*, *do*, *will*, and *shall*, are well known to native speakers of the language:

am → am not → [no contraction with negative: use *I'm not* etc.]
can → cannot → can't
will → will not → won't
shall → shall not → shan't

Shan't isn't used in American English except in jest; it still sometimes appears in British English.

5.232 **The word "no."** Unlike *not*, which can negate any element of a sentence, *no* negates only adjectives and nouns. When used with an adjective phrase, it might produce ambiguity. For example, in *we found no eggs*, it's clear that the speaker found nothing. But in *we found no fresh eggs for sale*, does the speaker mean they found no eggs at all, only eggs that weren't fresh, or eggs that were fresh but not for sale?

5.233 **Using pronouns and adverbs for negation.** Pronouns such as *nobody*, *none*, *no one*, and *nothing* and adverbs such as *nowhere* and *never* also result in negation. These words make it unnecessary to use *not*. They can help reduce the number of words and improve the flow of a sentence.

We did not see anyone in the audience.
We saw no one in the audience.

The children do not have anything to do.
The children have nothing to do.

You do not ever listen!
You never listen!

I cannot put the groceries anywhere.
There's nowhere to put the groceries.

5.234 **Using "neither" and "nor."** The correlative conjunctions *neither* and *nor* negate alternatives simultaneously. Traditionally, only pairs are framed by *neither-nor*, but writers and speakers sometimes use a *neither-nor-nor* construction, as in the last example below.

The dog and the cat are not friendly.
Neither pet is friendly.
Neither the dog nor the cat is friendly.

The radiator does not leak, and the water pump also does not leak.
Neither the radiator nor the water pump leaks.

Neither John nor Sally nor Brenda can attend the meeting.

In that last example, some writers include only the last *nor*. But again, a simple *neither-nor* construction isn't recommended with three or more elements, the sequence *neither-nor-nor* being preferable.

5.235 **Negative interrogative and imperative statements.** In a negative interrogative statement, the first auxiliary verb may be contracted with *not*: *Aren't you doing your homework tonight?* If it is not contracted, then *not* or *no* precedes the negated element {are you not doing your homework tonight?} {is there no satisfying you?}. Questions phrased with a negating word are called (unsurprisingly) *negative questions*; those without negation are *positive questions*. In an imperative statement, the negative particle always follows the imperative verb or is contracted with it {come no closer!} {don't talk back!}.

5.236 **Double negatives.** When a sentence contains two negatives, in Standard English they are usually thought to cancel each other out to make a mild positive {he didn't *not* say anything [he did say something]} {this isn't an uncommon problem [it's more or less common]}. In dialect, by contrast, the sentence is often meant to express an emphatic negative {he didn't say nothing [he said nothing at all]} {we're not going nowhere special [we're going somewhere, but it isn't special]}. Multiple negatives often lead to ambiguity. For example, in *I wouldn't be surprised if Dan doesn't find the hammer*, does the speaker expect Dan to find the hammer or not to find it? In general, though, multiple negation results in a cancellation of other negatives {we didn't say the children couldn't come along [we didn't forbid the children's coming]}.

5.237 **Other forms of negation.** A sentence can express negation even though it doesn't contain any plainly negative elements. Two common means of achieving this effect are using *but* in the sense "if not" and using *except* in the sense "but not" {what is a pampered dog *but* [= *if not*] a child in a fur suit?} {you may borrow the car *except* [= *but not*] when it is raining}.

5.238 **"Any" and "some" in negative statements.** When the negating particle is *not*, then *any-* words must be used with it, not *some-* words. *Any-* words include *any*, *anyone*, *anybody*, *anything*, and *anywhere*. *Some-* words include *some*, *someone*, *somebody*, *something*, and *somewhere*.

NOT THIS: I don't want to see somebody. [Unless the meaning is one particular person I'm not naming.]
BUT THIS: I don't want to see anybody.

NOT THIS: There aren't some seats left.
BUT THIS: There aren't any seats left.

Expletives

5.239 **Expletives generally.** Though *expletive* commonly denotes a swearword {expletive deleted}, in grammar *expletive* signifies a word that has no lexical meaning but serves a merely structural role in a sentence—as a noun element. The two most common expletives are *it* {it is true!} and *there* {there must be an answer}. An expletive *it* or *there* may be in the subject position, especially when the subject of a sentence is a clause {**it** is a rule that children must raise their hands to speak during class [**the rule** is that children must raise their hands to speak during class]} {**it** is better to stay here than to go there [**to stay here** is better than to go there]}. In this position, the expletive shifts the emphasis to the predicate containing the true subject. The sentence implies a "who" or "what" question that is answered by the subject. For example, *It is foolish to ignore facts* tells the reader "what" it is foolish to ignore and emphasizes "facts." An expletive *it* may also take the position of a direct object, especially when the real object is a clause or noun phrase {some people don't like **it** that stores are open for business on Thanksgiving [some people don't like **stores being open for business** on Thanksgiving]}. Using an expletive in this way can tighten a verb phrase and emphasize the object. Compare *it was taken for granted that our team would win* with *we took for granted that our team would win.*

5.240 **Expletive "it."** Whereas the pronoun *it* adds meaning to a sentence because it has an antecedent or else is the formal subject of a *be*-verb in the sense of "a person" or "a thing," an expletive *it* adds no meaning and takes the subject's or object's place when the subject or object shifts to the predicate: *It is not known what happened* can be restated as *What happened is not known.* Usually readers have no difficulty intuitively understanding whether they're encountering a pronoun *it* or an expletive *it.* But when the expletive and the pronoun appear close together, they may cause the reader to stumble {The much-anticipated feast was a disappointment; **it** was poorly cooked and presented. **It** is hard to believe that such a famous chef thought **it** would be edible, let alone delight gourmands.}. Avoid having several *its* in a passage clash in this way. Some other names for the expletive *it* are *ambient it*, *anticipatory it*, *dummy it*, *empty it*, *introductory it*, *nonreferential it*, and *prop it.*

5.241 **Expletive "there."** The word *there* is also frequently used as an expletive with *be* or an intransitive verb (especially a linking verb) followed by the subject {there are many different viewpoints presented in the students' essays} {there were several hundred members present at the conference}. An expletive *there* shouldn't be confused with *there* as an adverb of place. Compare *There seemed to be someone* with *Someone seemed to be there.*

Parallel Structure

5.242 **Parallel structure generally.** Parallel constructions—series of like sentence elements—are common in good writing. Compound structures may link words {win, lose, or draw}, phrases {government of the people, by the people, for the people}, dependent clauses {that all men are created equal; that they are endowed by their Creator with certain unalienable rights; that among these are life, liberty, and the pursuit of happiness}, or sentences {I came; I saw; I conquered}. Every element of a parallel series must be a functional match (word, phrase, clause, sentence) and serve the same grammatical function in the sentence (e.g., noun, verb, adjective, adverb). This syntactic linking of matching elements is called *coordination*. When linked items do not match, the syntax of the uncoordinated sentence breaks down:

POOR: She did volunteer work in the community kitchen, the homeless shelter, and taught free ESL classes offered by her church.

BETTER: She did volunteer work in the community kitchen, the homeless shelter, and her church, where she taught free ESL classes.

POOR: The candidate is a former county judge, state senator, and served two terms as attorney general.

BETTER: The candidate is a former county judge, state senator, and two-term attorney general.

In the second example, for instance, the subject, verb, and modifier (*the candidate is a former*) fit with the noun phrases *county judge* and *state senator*, but the third item in the series renders nonsense: *The candidate is a former served two terms as attorney general.* The first two elements in the series are nouns, while the third is a separate predicate. The corrected version makes each item in the series a noun element.

5.243 **Prepositions and parallel structure.** In a parallel series of prepositional phrases, repeat the preposition with every element unless they all use the same preposition. A common error occurs when a writer lets two or more of the phrases share a single preposition but inserts a different one with another element:

POOR: I looked for my lost keys in the sock drawer, the laundry hamper, the bathroom, and under the bed.

BETTER: I looked for my lost keys in the sock drawer, in the laundry hamper, in the bathroom, and under the bed.

If the series had not included *under the bed*, the preposition could have been used once to apply to all the objects: *I looked for my lost keys in the sock drawer, the laundry hamper, and the bathroom.*

5.244 **Paired joining terms and parallel structure.** Correlative conjunctions such as *either–or*, *neither–nor*, *both–and*, and *not only–but also* and some adverb pairs such as *where–there*, *as–so*, and *if–then* must join grammatically parallel sentence elements. It is a common error to mismatch elements framed by correlatives.

POOR: I'd like to either go into business for myself or else to write freelance travel articles.

BETTER: I'd like either to go into business for myself or else to write freelance travel articles.

POOR: Our guests not only ate all the turkey and dressing but both pumpkin pies as well.

BETTER: Our guests ate not only all the turkey and dressing but both pumpkin pies as well.

In the second example, the verb *ate*, when placed after the first correlative, attaches grammatically to *all the turkey* but not to *both pumpkin pies as well*. When moved outside the two phrases containing its direct objects, it attaches to both—and the phrasing becomes parallel.

5.245 **Auxiliary verbs and parallel structure.** If an auxiliary verb appears before a series of verb phrases, it must apply to all of them. A common error is to include one phrase that takes a different auxiliary verb:

POOR: The proposal would streamline the application process, speed up admission decisions, and has proved to save money when implemented by other schools.

BETTER: The proposal would streamline the application process, speed up admission decisions, and save money.

BETTER: The proposal would streamline the application process and speed up admission decisions. It has proved to save money when implemented by other schools.

The auxiliary verb *would* in that example renders the nonsensical *would has proved* when parsed with the third element of the predicate series. The first solution resolves that grammatical conflict, while the second breaks out the third into a separate sentence—which also avoids shifting from future tense to past tense in midsentence.

Cleft Sentences

5.246 **Cleft sentences defined.** A cleft sentence opens with a special type of subject clause (an *it*-clause, a *what*-clause, or a similar clause) that changes the focus by adding two or three words (such as *it*, *was*, and *who*; *there*, *are*, and *that*; or *what* and *was*) {it was the manager who handled the customer's complaint} {there are still some missing items that have to be accounted for} {what the campaign lacked was a vibrant slogan}.

Most often the sentence begins with an expletive *it* and a *be*-verb (the *it*-clause). The subject clause emphasizes new information that identifies a person, a place, a time, an object, a cause, etc. For example:

It was **Manuel** who met Adam in college. (The focus is on the actor.)
It was **Adam** whom Manuel met in college. (The focus is on the person that the actor met.)
It was **in college** that Manuel met Adam. (The focus is on the time or place when they met.)

The part of a cleft sentence beginning with the relative pronoun usually refers to information already given. Hence it may be reduced when the information that would be in the final clause is understood:

When did Manuel and Adam become acquainted?
It was in college (that they met).

5.247 **Types of cleft sentences.** A cleft sentence may be declarative {it is the quality of the work that concerns me} {there was an incident that led to the concert's postponement}. Or it may be interrogative {is it the quality of the work that you're concerned about?} {what was the incident that led to the concert's postponement?}. It may also be positive or negative. A positive cleft sentence states a truth. A negative cleft sentence uses simple negation (*not*, *no*) to state the contrary. Often the relative pronoun is elided in a whiz-deletion (as with the bracketed words below):

POSITIVE: **There are many** movies [**that** are] worth seeing this weekend.
NEGATIVE: **There are not many** movies [**that** are] worth seeing this weekend.
NEGATIVE: **There are no** movies [**that** are] worth seeing this weekend.

See also 5.226.

5.248 **Use of cleft sentences.** A cleft sentence is sometimes used for dramatic effect to signal a shift or a beginning, especially to create an interesting lead-in for a topic:

It was hours later that Burns discovered he'd left his wallet on the counter.
It was in 1912 that shipbuilders and legislators learned the cost of not providing ocean liners with adequate numbers of lifeboats.

In some contexts, a cleft sentence may imply a contrast or mistake. For instance, *It's not Joan who wants to be a social activist* implies that Joan is being distinguished from another person or that someone else has been mistakenly identified.

Word Usage

5.249 **Grammar versus usage.** The great mass of linguistic issues that writers and editors wrestle with don't really concern grammar at all—they concern usage: the collective habits of a language's native speakers. It's an arbitrary fact, but ultimately an important one, that *corollary* means one thing and *correlation* something else. Yet there seems to be an irresistible law of language that two words so similar in sound will inevitably be confused by otherwise literate users of language—a type of mistake called *catachresis*. Some confusions, such as the one just cited, are relatively new. Others, such as *lay* versus *lie* and *infer* versus *imply*, are much older.

Glossary of Problematic Words and Phrases

5.250 **Good usage versus common usage.** The best dictionaries are signaled by the imprints of Merriam-Webster, Webster's New World, American Heritage, Oxford University Press, and Random House. But one must use care and judgment in consulting *any* dictionary. The mere presence of a word in the dictionary's pages does not mean that the word is in all respects fit for print as Standard Written English. The dictionary merely describes how speakers of English have used the language; despite occasional usage notes, lexicographers generally disclaim any intent to guide writers and editors on the thorny points of English usage—apart from collecting evidence of what others do. So *infer* is recorded as meaning, in one of its senses, *imply*; *irregardless* as meaning *regardless*; *restauranteur* as meaning *restaurateur*; and on and on. That is why, in the publishing world, it is generally necessary to consult a style or usage guide, such as *Fowler's Modern English Usage* or my own *Garner's Modern English Usage*.

a; an. Use the indefinite article *a* before any word beginning with a consonant sound {a euphonious phrase} {a utopian dream}. Use *an* before any word beginning with a vowel sound {an officer} {an honorary degree}. The word *historical* and its variations cause missteps, but if the *h* in these words is pronounced, it takes an *a* {an hour-long talk at a historical society}. Likewise, an initialism (whose letters are sounded out) may be paired with one article, while an acronym (which is pronounced as a word) beginning with the same letter is paired with the other {an HTML website for a HUD program}.

ability; capability; capacity. *Ability* refers to a person's physical or mental power or skill to do something {the ability to ride a bicycle}. *Capability* refers more generally to power or ability to do something challenging {she has the capability to play soccer professionally} or to the quality of being able to use or be used in a certain way {a jet with long-distance-flight capability}. *Capacity* refers especially to a vessel's ability to hold or contain something {a high-capacity fuel tank}. Used figuratively, *capacity* refers especially to a person's physical or mental power to learn {an astounding capacity for mathematics}. It can also be used as a synonym for *ability* {capacity for love}, as a formal word for someone's job, position, or role {in an advisory capacity}, as a word denoting an amount that can be produced or dealt with {full capacity}, or as a means of denoting size or power {engine capacity}.

abjure; adjure. To *abjure* is to deny or renounce publicly, especially under oath {the defendant abjured the charge of murder} or to declare one's permanent abandonment of a place {abjure the realm}. To *adjure* is to charge someone to do something as if under oath {I adjure you to keep this secret} or to try earnestly to persuade {the executive committee adjured all the members to approve the plan}. Some writers misuse *adjure* for either *abhor* (= to detest) or *require* (= to mandate).

about; approximately. When idiomatically possible, use the adverb *about* instead of *approximately*. In the sciences, however, *approximately* is preferred {approximately 32 coding-sequence differences were identified}. Avoid coupling either word with another word of approximation, such as *guess* or *estimate*.

abstruse. See **obtuse**.

accept; except. To *accept* something is to receive it {accept this gift} or regard it as proper {accept the idea}. To *except* something is to exclude it or leave it out {club members will be excepted from the admission charge}, and to *except to* something is to object to it.

access, ***vb.*** The use of nouns as verbs has long been one of the most common ways that word-usage changes happen in English. Today, few people quibble with using *contact*, *debut*, or *host*, for example, as a verb. *Access* can be safely used as a verb when referring to computing {access a computer} {access the internet} {access a database}. Outside the digital world, though, it can be jarring and is best avoided.

accord; accordance. The first word means "agreement" {we are in accord on the treaty's meaning} {we have reached an accord}. The second word means "conformity" {the book was printed in accordance with modern industry standards}.

acquiesce. To *acquiesce* is to do what someone else wants or to passively allow something to happen. The connotation is usually acceptance without enthusiasm or even with opposition that is not acted on. The word traditionally takes the preposition *in* {the minority party acquiesced in the nomination}, although *to* is also accepted. *With* is not standard.

actual fact, in. Redundant. Try *actually* instead, or simply omit.

acuity; acumen. What is *acute* is sharp, and these two words apply to mental sharpness. *Acuity* most often refers to sharpness of perception—the ability to think, see, or hear clearly {visual acuity}. *Acumen* always refers to mental prowess, especially the ability to think quickly and make good judgments.

adduce; deduce; induce. To *adduce* is to give as a reason, offer as a proof, or cite as an example in order to prove that something is true {as evidence of reliability, she adduced her four years of steady volunteer work as a nurse's aide}. *Deduce* and *induce* are opposite processes. To *deduce* is to reason from general principles to specific conclusions, or to draw a specific conclusion from general knowledge {from these clues about who committed the crime, one deduces that the butler did it}. In a related logical sense, to *induce* is to form a general principle based on specific observations {after years of studying ravens, the researchers induced a few of their social habits}. In its more common uses, however, to *induce* is (1) to persuade someone to do something, especially something unwise {nothing could induce me to try that again}, or (2) to cause a particular physical response {induce labor} {induce vomiting}.

adequate; sufficient; enough. *Adequate* refers to the suitability of something in a particular circumstance {an adequate explanation} {adequate provisions}. *Sufficient* refers to an amount that is enough to meet a particular need (always with an abstract concept, a mass noun, or a plural) {sufficient water} {sufficient information} {sufficient cause} {sufficient resources}. *Enough*, the best word for everyday purposes, meaning "as much or as many as are needed or wanted," modifies both count nouns {enough people} and mass nouns {enough oil}.

adherence; adhesion. With a few exceptions, the first term is figurative, the second literal. Your *adherence* to the transportation code requires the *adhesion* of an inspection sticker to your windshield.

adjure. See **abjure.**

administrator. See **executor.**

admission; admittance. *Admission* is generally figurative, suggesting particularly the rights and privileges granted with permission to enter {the student won admission to a first-rate university} or the price paid for entry {admission is $10}. *Admittance* is more limited and more a matter of physical entry, but it too is tinged with the idea of permission {no admittance beyond this point}.

adopted; adoptive. *Adopted* applies to a child or dependent {adopted son}. It is incorrect when applied to the ones who do the adopting; instead, use *adoptive*, the more general adjective corresponding to *adopt* {adoptive parents}.

adverse; averse. Though etymologically related, these words have undergone differentiation. *Adverse* means either "strongly opposed" or "unfavorable" and typically refers to things (not people) {adverse relations between the nations complicated matters} {an adverse wind blew the ship off course}. *Averse* means "feeling negatively about" or "having a strong dislike or unwillingness," and it refers to people {he's averse to asking for directions}.

affect; effect. *Affect*, almost always a verb, means "to influence or do something that produces a change; to have an effect on" {the adverse publicity affected the election}. To *affect* can also mean "to pretend to have a particular feeling or manner" {affecting a Scottish accent}. (The noun *affect* has a specialized meaning in psychology: emotional expressiveness. Consult your dictionary.) *Effect*, usually a noun, means "an outcome, result" {the candidate's attempted explanations had no effect} or "a change caused by an event, action, occurrence, etc." {harmful effects of smoking}. But it may also be a verb meaning "to make happen, produce" {the goal had been to effect a major change in campus politics}.

affirmative, in the; in the negative. These are slightly pompous ways of saying *yes* and *no*. They result in part because people are unsure how to punctuate *yes* and *no*. The ordinary way is this: *he said yes* (without quotation marks around *yes*, and without a capital); *she said no* (ditto).

afflict. See **inflict.**

affront. See **effrontery.**

after having [+ past participle]. Though common, this phrasing is redundant. Try instead *after* [+ present participle]: change *after having passed the audition, she . . .* to *after passing the audition, she . . .* Or this: *having passed the audition, she . . .* See 5.110.

afterward, *adv.*; afterword, *n.* The first means "later"; the second means "an epilogue." On *afterward(s)*, see **toward.**

aggravate. Traditionally, *aggravate* most properly means "to intensify (something bad)" {aggravate an injury} {an aggravated crime}. If the sense is "to bother," try *annoy* or *irritate* or *exasperate* instead.

aid; aide. *Aid* can be a verb (= to help) or a noun (= assistance). *Aide* is a noun (= helper), as in *teacher's aide*; in military parlance, it denotes someone assigned to help a superior officer {general's aide}.

ain't. This contraction is famously dialectal—a word not to be used except either in the dialogue of a nonstandard speaker or in jest.

alibi. Avoid this as a synonym for *excuse*. The traditional sense is "the defense of having been elsewhere when a crime was committed."

all (of). Delete the *of* whenever possible {all the houses} {all my children}. The most common exception occurs when *all of* precedes a nonpossessive pronoun {all of us} {all of them}.

alleged. Traditional usage applies this participial adjective to things, especially acts {alleged burglary}, not to the actors accused of doing them {alleged burglar}. That distinction is still observed by some publications, but it has largely been abandoned. Although *allegedly* /ə-**lej**-əd-lee/ has four syllables, *alleged* has only two: /ə-**lejd**/.

all ready. See **already.**

all right. Two words. Avoid *alright*, which has long been regarded as nonstandard.

all together. See **altogether.**

allude; elude; illude. To *allude* is to hint at something indirectly {he alluded to the war by mentioning "our recent national unpleasantness"}. It's often loosely used where *refer* or *quote* would be better—that is, where there is a direct mention or quotation. To *elude* is to avoid capture {the fox eluded the hunters}. To *illude* (quite rare) is to deceive {your imagination might illude you}.

allusion; reference. An *allusion* is an indirect or casual mention or suggestion of something {the cockroach in this story is an allusion to Kafka}. A *reference* is a direct or formal mention {the references in this scholarly article have been meticulously documented}. See **reference.**

alongside. This term, meaning "at the side of," should not be followed by *of.*

a lot. Two words, not one.

already; all ready. The first refers to time {the movie has already started}; the second refers to preparation {are the actors all ready?}.

alright. See **all right.**

altar, ***n.***; **alter,** ***vb.*** An *altar* is a table or similar object used for sacramental purposes. To *alter* is to change.

alternate, ***adj. & n.***; **alternative,** ***adj. & n.*** *Alternate* implies (1) a substitute for another {we took the alternate route} or (2) every other or every second {alternate Saturdays}. *Alternative* implies availability as another, usually sounder choice or possibility {alternative fuel sources}. The noun uses are analogous {the awards committee named her as alternate} {we have no alternative}.

altogether; all together. *Altogether* means "wholly" or "entirely" {that story is altogether false}. *All together* refers to a unity of time or place {the family will be all together at Thanksgiving}.

amend; emend. The first is the general term, meaning "to change or add to something written or spoken" {the city amended its charter to abolish at-large council districts} or "to make better" {amend your behavior!}. The second means "to remove one or more mistakes from" (as of a text) {for the second printing, the author emended several typos that had reached print in the first}. The noun corresponding to *amend* is *amendment*; the one corresponding to *emend* is *emendation.*

amiable; amicable. Both mean "friendly," but *amiable* refers to people who are easy to like {an amiable waiter} and *amicable* to relationships that involve goodwill and a lack of quarreling {an amicable divorce}.

amid. See **between.**

among. See **between.**

amount; number. *Amount* is used with mass nouns {a decrease in the amount of pollution} {a small amount of money}. *Number* is used with count nouns {a growing number of dissidents} {the number of coins in your pocket}.

an. See **a.**

and. Popular belief to the contrary, this conjunction usefully begins sentences, typically outperforming *moreover*, *additionally*, *in addition*, *further*, and *fur-*

thermore. Yet it does not occur as a sentence-starter as often as *but*. See **but**; see also 5.203.

and/or. Avoid this Janus-faced term. It can often be replaced by *and* or *or* with no loss in meaning. Where it seems needed {take a sleeping pill and/or a warm drink}, try . . . *or* . . . , *or both* {take a sleeping pill or a warm drink, or both}. But think of other possibilities {take a sleeping pill, perhaps with a warm drink}.

anecdotal. This adjective corresponds to *anecdote*, but in one sense the words have opposite connotations. An anecdote is a story that is thought (but not known) to be true. But *anecdotal evidence* refers to accounts that are suspect because they are not rigorously verified.

angry. See **mad**.

anxious. Avoid it as a synonym for *eager*. The standard sense is "worried, nervous, distressed."

anyone; any one. The one-word *anyone* is a singular indefinite pronoun used in reference to no one in particular {anyone would know that}. The two-word phrase *any one* is a more emphatic form of *any*, referring to a single person or thing in a group {do you recognize any one of those boys?} {I don't know any one of those stories}.

anyplace. See **anywhere**.

anyway; anyways. The former is standard; the latter, traditionally considered dialectal, has made inroads into the speech of many otherwise educated people born since about 1980. But it remains nonstandard.

anywhere; any place. The first is preferred for an indefinite location {my keys could be anywhere}. But *any place* (two words) is narrower when you mean "any location" {they couldn't find any place to sit down and rest}. Avoid the informal one-word *anyplace*.

appertain. See **pertain**.

appraise; apprise. To *appraise* is to assess or put a value on something {the jeweler appraised the necklace}. To *apprise* is to inform or notify someone about something {keep me apprised of any developments}.

appreciate. Three senses: (1) to understand fully; (2) to increase in value; (3) to be grateful for (something). Sense 3 often results in verbose constructions; instead of *I would appreciate it if you would let me know*, try *I would appreciate your letting me know* or, more simply, *please let me know*.

apprise. See **appraise**.

approve; endorse. *Approve* implies positive thought or a positive attitude rather than action apart from consent. *Endorse* implies both a positive attitude and active support.

approve (of). *Approve* alone connotes official sanction or acceptance {the finance committee approved the proposed budget}. *Approve of* suggests thinking favorably about {she approved of her sister's new hairstyle}.

approximately. See **about**.

apt; likely. Both mean "fit, suitable," but *apt* is used for general tendencies or habits {the quarterback is apt to drop the football}. *Likely* expresses probability {because he didn't study, it's likely that he'll do poorly on the exam}. Although *likely* is traditional as a synonym of *probable*, many writers and editors object to its use as a synonym of *probably*. *Apt* has two other senses: (1) "exactly right for a given situation or purpose" {an apt remark} and (2) "quick to learn" {an apt pupil}.

area. Often a nearly meaningless filler word, as in *the area of partnering skills*. Try deleting *the area of*. In the sciences, however, its more literal meaning is often important and should be retained. See also **space.**

as far as. Almost always wordy. Avoid the nonstandard phrasing that uses *as far as* in place of *as for*—that is, avoid using *as far as* without the completing verb *is concerned* or *goes*. Even with the verb, though, this is usually a wordy construction. Compare *as far as change is concerned, it's welcome* with *as for change, it's welcome*.

as is. In reference to an acquisition, *as is* is framed in quotation marks and refers to the acceptance of something without guarantees or representations of quality {purchased "as is"}. The phrase *on an "as is" basis* is verbose.

as of yet. See **as yet.**

as per. This phrase, though common in the commercial world, has long been considered nonstandard. Instead of *as per your request*, write *as you requested* or (less good) *per your request*. The recent innovation *as per usual* for *as usual* is an illiteracy.

assault; battery. These are popularly given the same meaning. But in law *assault* refers to a threat that causes someone to reasonably fear physical violence, and *battery* refers to a violent or repugnant intentional physical contact with another person. In the strict legal sense, an assault doesn't involve touching; a battery does.

assemblage; assembly. An *assemblage* is an informal collection of people or things. An *assembly* is a group of people, especially decision makers, organized for a purpose {a national assembly}; a meeting {regular public assemblies}; or the process of putting together the parts of something {instructions for assembly}.

assent; consent. The meanings are similar, but *assent* connotes a more affirmative agreement after careful consideration; *consent* connotes mere allowance, or sometimes grudging acquiescence.

as such. This pronominal phrase always requires an antecedent for *such* {science is the organized search for truth and, as such, must be looked upon as an end in itself}. The phrase is now often loosely used as a synonym for *therefore*. Avoid this misusage {science seeks out truth in an organized way and, as such, must be looked upon as an end in itself}.

assumption; presumption. An *assumption* is not drawn from strong evidence; typically, it is a hypothesis that one accepts as true without definite proof {your assumption can be tested by looking at the public records}. A *presumption* implies a basis in evidence or at least experience; if uncontradicted, a *presumption* may support a decision {the legal presumption of innocence}.

assure. See **ensure.**

as to. This two-word preposition is best used only to begin a sentence that could begin with *on the question of* or *with regard to* {as to those checks, she didn't know where they came from}. Otherwise, use *about* or some other preposition.

as yet; as of yet. Stilted and redundant. Use *yet*, *still*, *so far*, or some other equivalent.

attain; obtain. To *attain* something is either to accomplish it through effort (e.g., a goal) {she soon attained a position of power} or to reach a particular age, size, level, etc. {the stock market attained a new high this morning}. To *obtain* something is to get it or gain possession of it {obtaining information}. In best usage, you *attain* a degree and *obtain* a diploma. It can be a fine distinction, and in common usage the words are often treated as synonyms.

at the present time; at this time; at present. These are turgid substitutes for *now*, *today*, *currently*, or even *nowadays* (a word of perfectly good literary standing). Of the three phrases, *at present* is least suggestive of bureaucratese.

at the time that; at the time when. Use the plain and simple *when* instead.

auger; augur. The spellings of these words can be tricky because they are pronounced the same /**aw**-gr/. The tool for boring is an *auger*. *Augur* means "a clairvoyant or seer" (noun) or "to foretell" (verb). *Augurs well* is an idiomatic equivalent of *bodes well*. The related noun *augury* refers to an indication of what will happen in the future.

avenge, *vb.*; revenge, *vb. & n.* *Avenge* connotes an exaction for a wrong {historically, family grudges were privately avenged}. The corresponding noun is *vengeance*. *Revenge* connotes the infliction of harm on another out of anger or resentment {the team is determined to revenge its humiliating loss in last year's championship game}. *Revenge* is much more commonly a noun {they didn't want justice—they wanted revenge}.

averse. See **adverse.**

avocation; vocation. An *avocation* is a hobby or pleasant pastime {stamp collecting is my weekend avocation}. A *vocation* is one's profession or, especially in a religious sense, one's calling {she had a true vocation and became a nun}.

awhile; a while. The one-word version is adverbial; it means "for a short time" {let's stop here awhile}. The two-word version is a noun phrase that follows the preposition *for* or *in* {she worked for a while before beginning graduate studies}.

backward(s). See **toward.**

bale; bail. The somewhat less common term is *bale* (= a bundle or to form into a bundle, as of hay or cotton). *Bail* is most often a verb (= to drain by scooping, as of getting water out of a boat using a pail); it is also a noun and verb regarding the posting of security to get out of jail pending further proceedings. *Bail* is also used informally to denote leaving quickly or escaping {the couple bailed from the party}. To *bail out* someone (a phrasal verb) is to get the person out of trouble.

based on. This phrase has two legitimate and two illegitimate uses. It may unimpeachably have verbal force (*base* being a transitive verb, as in *they based their position on military precedent*) or, in a passive sense, adjectival force (*based* being read as a past-participial adjective, as in *a sophisticated thriller based on a John le Carré novel*). Two uses, however, are traditionally considered slipshod. *Based on* should not have adverbial force (as in *Rates are adjusted annually, based on the 91-day Treasury bill*) or prepositional force (as a dangling participle, as in *Based on this information, we decided to stay*). Try other constructions {rates are adjusted annually on the basis of the 91-day Treasury bill} {with this information, we decided to stay}.

basis. Much overworked, this word most properly means "foundation; the facts, things, or ideas from which something can be developed." It often appears in the phrase *on a . . . basis* or some similar construction. When possible, substitute adverbs (*personally*, not *on a personal basis*) or simply state the time (*daily*, not *on a daily basis*). The plural is *bases* {the legislative bases are complicated}.

bated breath. So spelled—not *baited breath*. Someone who waits with *bated breath* is anxious or excited (literally "holding [abating] one's breath").

battery. See **assault**.

begging the question. This phrase traditionally denotes a logical fallacy of assuming as true what has yet to be proved—or adducing as proof for some proposition something that's every bit as much in need of proof as the first proposition. For example, someone might try to "prove" the validity of a certain religion by quoting from that religion's holy text. But the phrase gets misused in many ways—as (erroneously) meaning "prompting a question," "inviting an obvious question," "evading a question," and "ignoring a question."

behalf. *In behalf of* means "in the interest or for the benefit of" {the decision is in behalf of the patient}. *On behalf of* means "acting as agent or representative of" {on behalf of Mr. Scott, I would like to express heartfelt thanks}.

bemused. This word means "bewildered, distracted, or confused." It is not a synonym of *amused*.

benevolence; beneficence. *Benevolence* is the attribute of being disposed to kindness or capable of doing good {the priest's benevolence was plainly evident}. It applies most often to people but may also apply to things that are beneficial. *Beneficence* is a major act of kindness or the performance of good deeds generally {the villagers thanked him for his beneficence}. The first term denotes a quality, the second conduct.

beside; besides. *Beside* is a preposition of position, whether literal {beside the road} or figurative {beside the point}. *Besides* may be a preposition meaning "other than" {who's going besides us?} or an adverb meaning "also" or "anyway" {besides, who wants to know?}.

between; among; amid. *Between* indicates one-to-one relationships {between you and me}. *Among* indicates undefined or collective relationships {honor among thieves}. *Between* has long been recognized as being perfectly appropriate for more than two objects if multiple one-to-one relationships are understood from the context {trade between members of the European Union}. *Amid* is often used with mass nouns {amid talk of war}—though it can often be used with abstract nouns in the plural {resigned amid rumors of misconduct} {the investigation comes amid growing concerns}. *Among* is invariably used with plurals of count nouns {among the children}. Avoid *amidst* and *amongst*, especially in American English.

between you and me. This is the correct phrasing—not *between you and I*, which is a classic example of hypercorrection. Both pronouns function as objects of the preposition *between*. True, Shakespeare put the phrase *'tween you and I* in a character's mouth, but that was at a time when English grammar was much less settled than it came to be in the eighteenth century—and that usage was an outlier even in the Elizabethan era. Further, the sociolinguistic point that Shakespeare might have been making by having a character speak that phrase may well be lost in the mists of time.

bi-; semi-. Generally, *bi-* means "two" (*biweekly* means "every two weeks"), while *semi-* means "half" (*semiweekly* means "twice a week"). Because these prefixes are often confused with each other, writers should be explicit about the meaning.

biannual; semiannual; biennial. *Biannual* and *semiannual* both mean "twice a year" {these roses bloom biannually}. But *biennial* means "once every two years" or "every other year" {our legislature meets biennially}. To avoid confusion, write *semiannual* instead of *biannual*, and consider writing *once every two years* instead of *biennial*.

billion; trillion. The meanings can vary in different countries. In the United States, a *billion* is 1,000,000,000. In Great Britain, Canada, and Germany, a *billion* is traditionally a thousand times more than that (a million millions, or what Americans call a *trillion*)—though the American English sense now predominates even in British English. Further, in Great Britain a *trillion* is traditionally a million million millions, what Americans would call a *quintillion* (1,000,000,000,000,000,000). Although the American definitions are gaining acceptance, writers need to remember the historical geographic distinctions. See also 9.8.

blatant; flagrant. An act that is *blatant* is both bad and plain for all to see {a blatant error}. One that is *flagrant* is done brazenly as well as openly, often with a stronger suggestion of shocking illegality or immorality {a flagrant violation of the law}.

bombastic. A *bombastic* speech or essay is pompously long-winded and self-important but essentially empty of substance. The word has nothing to do with temper.

born; borne. *Born* is used only as an adjective {a born ruler} or in the fixed passive-voice verb *to be born* {the child was born into poverty}. *Borne* is the general past participle of *bear* {this donkey has borne many heavy loads} {she has borne three children}. It is also used to form compound terms {foodborne} {vectorborne}.

both-and. These correlative conjunctions should frame matching syntactic parts. Hence don't write *She is both a writer and she skis professionally*, but instead *She is both a writer and a professional skier.*

breach, ***n. & vb.*****; breech,** ***n.*** A *breach* is a gap in or violation of something {a breach of contract} or a serious disagreement {healing the breach between the nations}. To *breach* is to break, break open, or break through {breach the castle walls}. *Breech* refers to the lower or back part of something, especially the buttocks {a breech birth} or the part of a modern firearm where bullets are inserted {the rifle's breech}.

bring; take. The distinction may seem obvious, but the error is common. The simple question is, Where is the action directed? If it's toward you, use *bring* {bring home the bacon}. If it's away from you, use *take* {take out the trash}. You *take* (not *bring*) your car to the mechanic.

but. Popular belief to the contrary, this conjunction usefully begins contrasting sentences, typically with greater strength and speed than *however*. Avoid putting a comma after it. Cf. **and**; see also 5.203.

by means of. Often verbose. Use *by* or *with* if either one suffices.

by reason of. Use *because* or *because of* unless *by reason of* is part of an established phrase {by reason of insanity}.

cache; cachet. *Cache*, a count noun, refers either to a quantity of goods or valuables that have been stashed away or to a storage buffer within a computer. *Cachet*, generally a mass noun, refers most commonly to prestige or fetching appeal—or else a seal on a document or a commemorative design. *Cachet* sometimes appears, incorrectly, as *caché*.

can; could. *Can* means "to be able to" and expresses certainty {I can be there in five minutes}. *Could* is better for a sense of uncertainty or a conditional statement {could you stop at the cleaners today?} {if you send a deposit, we could hold your reservation}. See 5.146.

can; may. *Can* most traditionally applies to physical or mental ability {she can do calculations in her head} {the dog can leap over a six-foot fence}. In colloquial English, *can* also expresses a request for permission {can I go to the movies?}, but this usage is not recommended in formal contexts. *May* suggests possibility {the class may have a pop quiz tomorrow} or permission {you may borrow my car}. A denial of permission is properly phrased formally with *may not* {you may not borrow my credit card} or, less formally, with *cannot* or *can't* {you can't use the computer tonight}. See 5.146, 5.147.

cannon; canon. A *cannon* is an artillery weapon that fires metal balls or other missiles. A *canon* is (1) a general rule or principle, (2) an established criterion,

(3) the sum of a writer or composer's work, (4) the collective literature accepted by a scholastic discipline, (5) a piece of music in which a tune is started by one performer and is mimicked by each of the others, or (6) a Christian priest having special duties within a church or cathedral.

capability. See **ability.**

capacity. See **ability.**

capital; capitol. A *capital* is a seat of government (usually a city) {Jefferson City is the capital of Missouri}. A *capitol* is a building in which a legislature meets {the legislature opened its new session in the capitol today}.

carat; karat; caret. *Carat* measures the weight of a gemstone; *karat* measures the purity of gold. To remember the difference, think of *24K gold.* (In British English, the spelling *carat* serves in both senses.) *Caret* is a mark on a manuscript indicating where matter is to be inserted; borrowed from Latin in the seventeenth century, it literally means "(something) is lacking."

career; careen. The word *career*'s career as a verb meaning "to go full speed" may be about over, except in British English (in which the two verbs contend in what is still a tight race). In American English, its duties have been assumed by *careen* (traditionally, "to tip to one side while moving"), even though nothing in that verb's time-honored definition denotes high speed. So today in American English it's typically *careened down the hill* but in British English *careered down the hill.*

caret. See **carat.**

case. This multifaceted word is often a sign of verbal inflation, especially in its uses as a near-synonym of *situation.* For example, *in case* means "if"; *in most cases* means "usually"; *in every case* means "always." The word is justifiably used in law (in which a *case* is a lawsuit or judicial opinion) and in medicine (in which the word refers to an instance of a disease or disorder). By extension, it has analogous senses in social work, criminal detection, etc. Of course, the word can also denote a box or container {briefcase}, an argument or set of reasons {state your case}, or a grammatical word form.

cause célèbre. This word most strictly denotes a legal case, especially a prosecution, that draws great public interest. By extension, it refers to a notorious episode, event, or even person. It does not properly denote a person's pet cause. Though it retains its acute and grave accents, the phrase is now considered naturalized enough not to be italicized (except when called out as a phrase, as in the next sentence). Yet the plural retains its French form: *causes célèbres.*

censer; censor, *n.*; sensor. The correct spellings can be elusive. A *censer* is either a person who carries a container of burning incense or the container itself. A *censor* is a person who suppresses objectionable subject matter. A *sensor* is a mechanical or electronic device for discovering light, heat, movement, etc.

censor, *vb.*; censure, *vb.* To *censor* is to review books, films, letters, and the like to remove objectionable material—that is, to suppress {soldiers' letters are often censored in wartime}. To *censure* is to criticize strongly or disapprove, or to officially reprimand {the House of Representatives censured the president for the invasion} {in some countries the government *censors* the press; in the United States the press often *censures* the government}.

center around. Although this illogical phrasing does have apologists, stylists tend to use either *center on* or *revolve around*.

certainty; certitude. If you are absolutely sure about something, you display both *certainty* (firm conviction) and *certitude* (assurance of being certain). That fact you are sure about, however, is a *certainty* but not a *certitude*—the latter is a trait applied to people only.

chair; chairman; chairwoman; chairperson. *Chair* is widely regarded as the best gender-neutral choice. Since the mid-seventeenth century, *chair* has referred to an office of authority. See also 5.251–60.

childish; childlike. *Childlike* is used positively to connote innocence, eagerness, and freshness {a childlike smile}. *Childish* is pejorative; it connotes immaturity, silliness, and unreasonableness {childish ranting}.

chord; cord. *Chord* denotes (1) a group of harmonically consonant notes {major chords} {minor chords} or (2) a straight line joining the ends of an arc (sense 2 being a technical term in mathematics and engineering). *Cord* is the word denoting a thick string or rope {spinal cord} {umbilical cord} {vocal cord}, an enclosed wire that supplies electricity to an appliance or other equipment, or a quantity of firewood.

circumstances. Both *in the circumstances* and *under the circumstances* are acceptable, but *under* is now much more common in American English. *In* predominates in British English.

cite, *n.*; site. As a noun, *cite* is colloquial for *citation*, which refers to a source of information {a cite to *Encyclopaedia Britannica*}. A *site* is a place or location used for a particular purpose {building site} {website}. Cf. **sight**.

citizen; subject. In a governmental sense, these are near-synonyms that should be distinguished. A *citizen* owes allegiance to a nation whose sovereignty is a collective function of the people {a citizen of Germany}. A *subject* owes allegiance to an individual sovereign because the form of government is monarchical {a subject of the queen}.

class. This word denotes a category or group of things that are considered together because of their similarities {the class of woodwind instruments}. Properly, a *class* is never one type {the oboe is a type of woodwind} or one kind of thing {a drum is one kind of percussion instrument}.

classic; classical. *Classic* means "important, authoritative, outstanding" {*The Naked Night* is one of Ingmar Bergman's classic films}. *Classical* applies to a traditional set of values in literature, music, design, and other fields {classical Greek} {a classical composer} or to the definitive or earliest-characterized form {classical EEC syndrome}.

clean; cleanse. Although various cleaning agents are called "cleansers," *clean* displaced *cleanse* long ago in most of the word's literal senses. *Cleanse* retains the Old English root meaning "pure": its use today usually refers to spiritual or moral (or gastrointestinal) purification.

cleave. This verb was originally two different words, and that difference is reflected in the opposite meanings that *cleave* has: (1) to cut apart {to cleave meat} and (2) to cling together {standing in the rain, his clothes cleaving to his body}. (When a term is its own antonym, it is known as a *contronym*.) The conjugations are (1) *cleave*, *cleft* (or *clove*), *cleft* (or *cloven*); and (2) *cleave*, *cleaved*, *cleaved*.

clench; clinch. *Clench*, which connotes a physical action, normally involves a person's hands, teeth, jaw, or stomach {he clenched his hand into a fist}. *Clinch*, the more common term, has mostly figurative uses about finally achieving something after a struggle {clinched the title} {clinched the victory}. But there is an exception to the nonphysical uses of *clinch*: if two people *clinch*, they hold each other's arms tightly, as in boxing.

climactic; climatic. *Climactic* is the adjective corresponding to *climax* {during the movie's climactic scene, the projector broke}. *Climatic* corresponds to *climate* {the climatic conditions of northern New Mexico}.

clinch. See **clench.**

close proximity. Redundant. Write either *close* or *in proximity*.

closure; cloture. *Closure* denotes the temporary or permanent closing or final resolution of something. *Cloture* denotes the parliamentary procedure of closing debate and taking a vote on a legislative bill or other measure.

cohabit; cohabitate. *Cohabit* is the traditional verb for living with another person in a sexual relationship without being married. *Cohabitate*, a back-formation from *cohabitation*, is best avoided.

collaborate; corroborate. To *collaborate* is to cooperate on some undertaking, especially in the arts or sciences {the participants are collaborators}. To *corroborate* something is to back up its reliability with proof or evidence {the expert corroborated the witness's testimony}.

collegial; collegiate. *Collegial* answers to *colleague* {a healthy collegial work environment}; *collegiate* answers to *college* {collegiate sports}.

commendable; commendatory. What is done for a worthy cause is *commendable* {commendable dedication to helping the poor}. What expresses praise is *commendatory* {commendatory plaque}.

common; mutual. What is *common* is shared by two or more people {borne by different mothers but having a common father}. What is *mutual* is reciprocal or directly exchanged by and toward each other {mutual obligations}. Strictly, *friend in common* is better than *mutual friend* in reference to a third person who is a friend of two others.

commonweal; commonwealth. The *commonweal* is the public welfare. Traditionally, a *commonwealth* was a state established by public compact or by the consent of the people to promote the general good (commonweal), and where the people reserved supreme authority. In the United States, the word is synonymous with *state*, four of which are still called commonwealths: Kentucky, Massachusetts, Pennsylvania, and Virginia. The Commonwealth of Puerto Rico is also a US territory.

compare. To *compare with* is to discern both similarities and differences between things. To *compare to* is to liken things or to note primarily similarities between them, especially in the active voice {Are you comparing me to *him*? I hope not!}.

compelled; impelled. If you are *compelled* to do something, you have no choice in the matter {Nixon was compelled by the unanimous Supreme Court decision to turn over the tapes}. If you are *impelled* to do something, you still may not like it, but you are convinced that it must be done {the voter disliked some candidates but was impelled by the income-tax issue to vote a straight-party ticket}. Whereas *compel* connotes an outside force, *impel* connotes an inner drive.

compendious; voluminous. These are not synonyms, as many apparently believe. *Compendious* means "concise, abridged." *Voluminous*, literally "occupying many volumes," most commonly means "vast" or "extremely lengthy."

complacent; complaisant; compliant. To be *complacent* is to be content with oneself and one's life—with the suggestion that one may be smugly unwilling to improve or unprepared for future trouble. To be *complaisant* is to be easygoing and eager to please others. To be *compliant* is to be amenable to orders or to a regimen imposed by others.

compliment; complement. A *compliment* is a flattering or praising remark {a compliment on your skill}. A *complement* is something that completes or brings to perfection {the lace tablecloth was a complement to the antique silver}. The words are also verbs: to *compliment* is to praise, while to *complement* is to supplement adequately or to complete. In the grammatical sense, a *complement* is a word or phrase that follows the verb to complete the predicate. The corresponding adjectives are *complimentary*, meaning (1) "expressing praise" or (2) "given to someone free of charge"; and *complementary*, meaning (1) "going well together, despite differences," or (2) "consisting of two geometric angles that, added together, take up 90 degrees."

comprise; compose. Use with care. To *comprise* is "to consist of, to include" {the whole comprises the parts}. To *compose* is "to make up, to form the substance of something" {the parts compose the whole}. The phrase *is comprised of*, though increasingly common, remains nonstandard. Instead, try *is composed of* or *consists of*. See **include**.

concept; conception. Both words may refer to an abstract thought, but *conception* also means "the act of forming an abstract thought." Avoid using either word as a high-sounding equivalent of *idea*, *design*, *thought*, or *program*.

condole, *vb.*; console, *vb.* These are closely related but not identical. To *condole* *with* is to express sympathy to {community leaders condoled with the victims' families}. The corresponding noun is *condolence* {they expressed their condolences at the funeral}. To *console* is to comfort in a time of distress or disappointment {the players consoled their humiliated coach}. The corresponding noun is *consolation* {their kind words were small consolation}.

confidant; confidante; confident. A *confidant* is a close companion, someone (male or female) you confide in. *Confidante*, a feminine form, is a fading alternative spelling of *confidant* (used only in reference to a female confidant). It reflects French gender spellings. *Confident* is the adjective meaning "sure that something will happen in the way one wants or expects" or "sure that something is true."

congruous; congruent. Both terms mean "in harmony, in agreement." The first is seen most often in its negative form, *incongruous*, meaning "strange, unexpected, or unsuitable in a particular situation" {the modern house looks incongruous in this old neighborhood}. The second is used in math to describe triangles that are identical in their angles as well as in the length of their sides {congruent angles}.

connote; denote. To *connote* (in reference to language) is to convey a meaning beyond the basic one, especially through emotive nuance {the new gerund *parenting* and all that it connotes}. To *denote* (again in reference to language) is to specify the literal meaning of something {the phrase *freezing point* denotes 32 degrees Fahrenheit or 0 degrees Celsius}. Both words have figurative uses {all the joy that parenthood connotes} {a smile may not denote happiness}.

consent. See **assent.**

consequent; subsequent. The first denotes causation; the second does not. A *consequent* event always happens after the event that caused it, as does a *subsequent* event. But a *subsequent* event does not necessarily occur as a result of the first: it could be wholly unrelated but merely later in time.

consider. Add *as* only when you mean "to examine or discuss for a particular purpose" {handshaking considered as a means of spreading disease}. Otherwise, omit *as* {we consider him qualified}.

consist. There are two distinct phrases: *consist of* and *consist in*. The first, by far the more common one, applies to the physical components that make up a tangible thing {the computer-system package consists of software, the CPU, the monitor, and a printer}. The second refers to the essence of a thing, especially in abstract terms {moral government consists in rewarding the righteous and punishing the wicked}.

console. See **condole.**

contact, ***vb.*** If you mean *write* or *call* or *email*, say so. But *contact* is undeniably a brief way of referring to communication without specifying the means.

contagious; infectious. Both broadly describe a disease that is communicable.

But a *contagious* disease spreads by direct contact with an infected person or animal {rabies is a contagious disease}. An *infectious* disease is spread by germs on a contaminated object or element, such as earth or water {tetanus is infectious but not contagious}.

contemporary; contemporaneous. Both express coinciding time, but *contemporary* usually applies to people, and *contemporaneous* applies to things or actions. Because *contemporary* has the additional sense "modern," it is unsuitable for contexts involving multiple times. That is, a reference to *Roman, Byzantine, and contemporary belief systems* is ambiguous; change *contemporary* to *modern*.

contemptuous; contemptible. If you are *contemptuous*, you are feeling and showing that you think someone or something deserves no respect. If you are *contemptible*, others will have that attitude toward you.

content; contents. *Content* applies to the ideas, facts, or opinions in a written or oral presentation {the lecture's content was offensive to some who were present}. *Contents* usually denotes physical ingredients: the things that are inside a box, bag, room, or other container {the package's contents were difficult to discern by x-ray}. If the usage suggests many items, material or nonmaterial, *contents* is correct {table of contents} {the investigative report's contents}.

continual; continuous. What is *continual* may go on for a long time, but always there are brief interruptions, so that it can be characterized as intermittent or frequently repeated {continual nagging}. What is *continuous* never stops—it remains constant or uninterrupted {continuous flow of water}. A line that is continuous has no gaps or holes in it.

contravene; controvert. To *contravene* is to conflict with or violate (the law, a rule, etc.) {the higher speed limit contravenes our policy of encouraging fuel conservation}. To *controvert* is to challenge or contradict {the testimony controverts the witness's prior statement}.

convince. See **persuade**.

copyright, ***vb.*** This verb, meaning "to obtain the legal right to be the only producer or seller of a book, play, film, or other creative work for a specific length of time," is conjugated *copyright-copyrighted-copyrighted*. Note the spelling, which has nothing to do with *write*.

cord. See **chord**.

corollary; correlation. A *corollary* is either (1) a subsidiary proposition that follows from a proven mathematical proposition, often without requiring additional evidence to support it, or (2) a natural or incidental result of some action or occurrence. A *correlation* is a positive connection between things or phenomena. If used in the context of physics or statistics, it denotes the degree to which the observed interactions and variances are not attributable to chance alone.

corporal; corporeal. What is *corporal* relates in some way to the body {corporal punishment}; what is *corporeal* has a physical form that can be touched {not our spiritual but our corporeal existence}.

corps; core. A *corps* is a body of like workers, as in an army, with special duties and responsibilities {Marine Corps} {press corps}. It is often misspelled like its homophone, *core*, which denotes the central or most important part of something {the core of the problem} {the earth's core}.

correlation. See **corollary.**

corroborate. See **collaborate.**

could. See **can.**

couldn't care less. This is the standard phrasing. Avoid the illogical form *could care less.*

councillor; counselor. A *councillor* is one who sits on a council {city councillor}. A *counselor* is one whose job is to help and advise people with problems {personal counselor}. In British English, the spelling is *counsellor.*

couple. Using *couple* as an adjective has traditionally been regarded as nonstandard phrasing—though it is increasingly common as a casualism. Add *of* {we watched a couple of movies}. When referring to two people as a unit {married couple}, the noun *couple* takes either a singular or a plural verb {the couple is happy} {the couple are honeymooning in Ravello}. When the pronoun *they* follows *couple*—if a pronoun is used at all, it is normally plural—the plural verb is preferable {the couple were delighted by their friends' responses}.

court-martial. Two words joined by a hyphen, whether the phrase functions as a noun or as a verb. Because *martial* acts as an adjective meaning "military," the plural of the noun is *courts-martial.* The third-person-singular verb is *court-martials* {if the general court-martials him, he'll have much to answer for}. In American English, the inflected spellings of the verb are *court-martialed*, *court-martialing*; in British English, the spellings are *court-martialled*, *court-martialling.*

credible; creditable; credulous. *Credible* means "believable; deserving trust"; *creditable* means "praiseworthy; deserving approval"; *credulous* means "gullible; tending to believe whatever one is told—and therefore easily deceived." The most common error involving cognate forms of these words is in the malapropism *strains credulity.* If some form of that cliché must be used, it should read *strains credibility.*

crevice; crevasse. Size matters. A crack in the sidewalk is a *crevice* (accent on the first syllable) because it's narrow and typically not very deep; a fissure in a glacier or a dam is a *crevasse* (accent on the second syllable) because it's a deep open crack.

criminal. See **unlawful.**

criteria. This is the plural form of *criterion* (= a standard for judging): one *criterion*, two *criteria.* The double plural *criterias* is a solecism.

damp, *vb.*; dampen. Both words convey the sense "to moisten." *Damp* also means "to reduce with moisture" {damp the fire} or "to diminish vibration or oscillation of [a wire or voltage]" {damp the voltage}. In a figurative sense, *dampen* means "to make [a feeling, mood, activity, etc.] less intense or enjoyable" {dampen one's hopes}.

data. Though originally this word was a plural of *datum*, it is now commonly treated as a mass noun and coupled with a singular verb. In formal writing (and always in the sciences), use *data* as a plural. Whatever you do, though, use the term consistently within a single writing—either singular or (more formally) plural.

deadly; deathly. *Deadly* means "capable of causing death" {deadly snake venom} or "likely to cause as much harm as possible" {deadly enemies}. *Deathly* means "arousing thoughts of death or a dead body" {deathly silence}.

decide whether; decide if. See **determine whether.**

decimate. This word literally means "to kill every tenth person," a means of repression that goes back to Roman times. But the word has come to mean "to inflict heavy damage or destroy a large part of something," and this use has long been predominant. Avoid *decimate* when you are referring to complete destruction. That is, don't say that a city was *completely decimated.*

deduce. See **adduce.**

defamation; libel; slander. *Defamation* is the communication of a falsehood that damages someone's reputation. If it is recorded, especially in writing, it is *libel*; otherwise, it is *slander*.

definite; definitive. *Definite* means "clear, exact" {a definite yes}. *Definitive* means either "not subject to further revision in the near future" {we have a definitive agreement} or "of such high quality as to be unimprovable for a long time" {the definitive guide}.

delegate. See **relegate.**

deliberate, *adj.*; deliberative. As an adjective, *deliberate* means either "planned; carefully thought out" {a deliberate response} or "slow and steady" {deliberate progress}. *Deliberative* means "of, characterized by, or involving debate"; the word most often applies to an assembly {deliberative body} or a process {deliberative meetings}.

denote. See **connote.**

denounce; renounce. To *denounce* is either to criticize harshly, especially in public {they denounced the prisoner swap}, or to accuse, as by giving incriminating information about someone's illegal political activities to the authorities {denounced him to the police}. To *renounce* is either to relinquish or reject {renounced her citizenship} or to declare publicly that one no longer believes something or will no longer behave in some way {renounce violence}.

dependant, *n.*; dependent, *adj. & n.* In British English, the first is the preferable noun {he claimed three dependants on his tax return}; the second is the adjective {the family has become dependent on welfare}. But in American English, *dependent* is the usual form as both noun and adjective.

depend on. Although *upon* is best reduced to *on* in this phrase, no further reduction is idiomatic: *depend* demands an *on*. Hence don't write *That depends how we approach the problem* but rather *That depends on how we approach the problem.*

deprecate. In general, to *deprecate* is to strongly disapprove or criticize. But in the phrase *self-deprecating*—which began as a mistaken form of *self-depreciating* but is now standard—the sense of *deprecate* is "to belittle." In computing, *deprecate* serves as a warning: a *deprecated* feature or function is one that may be phased out of a future release of software, so users should begin looking for alternatives.

derisive; derisory. What is *derisive* ridicules as stupid or silly {derisive laughter}. What is *derisory* invites or deserves ridicule {that derisory "banana" hat}, especially when a laughably small amount of money is offered or given {my derisory paychecks}.

deserts; desserts. The first are deserved {he got his just deserts}, the second eaten {the many desserts on the menu}. *Just desserts* is a common misspelling (unless the meaning is "only postprandial sweets").

despite; in spite of. For brevity, prefer *despite.*

determine whether; determine if. The first phrasing is irreproachable style; the second is acceptable as a colloquialism. The same is true of *decide whether* versus *decide if.*

different. The phrasing *different from* is generally considered preferable to *different than* {this company is different from that one}, but sometimes the adverbial phrase *differently than* is all but required {she described the scene differently than he did}. In British English, *different to* is not uncommon—but it is distinctively British English, whereas *different from* is standard everywhere.

differ from; differ with. *Differ from* is the usual construction denoting a contrast {the two species differ from each other in subtle ways}. *Differ with* regards differences of opinion {the state's senators differ with each other on many issues}.

disburse; disperse. To *disburse* is to distribute money, especially from a large sum available for some specific purpose. To *disperse* is (1) to spread in various directions over a wide area {the clouds dispersed} or (2) to cause to go away in different directions {police dispersed the unruly crowd}.

disc. See **disk.**

discomfort; discomfit. *Discomfort* is a noun meaning "ill at ease." It can also be used as a verb meaning "to put ill at ease." But doing so often invites confusion with *discomfit*, which originally meant "to defeat utterly." Today it means "to thwart, confuse, annoy, or embarrass" {the ploy discomfited the opponent}. The distinction has become a fine one, since a *discomfited* person is also uncomfortable. *Discomfiture* is the corresponding noun.

discreet; discrete. *Discreet* means either "careful about not divulging secrets or upsetting others" {a discreet silence} or "showing modest taste; nonostentatious" {discreet jewelry}. *Discrete* means "separate, distinct, unconnected" {six discrete parts}.

discriminating, ***adj.*****; discriminatory.** The word *discrimination* can be used in either a negative or a positive sense, and these adjectives reflect that ambivalence. *Discriminatory* means "reflecting a biased, unfair treatment" {discriminatory employment policy}. *Discriminating* means "analytically refined, discerning, tasteful" {a discriminating palate}.

disinterested. This word should be reserved for the sense "not having a financial personal interest at stake and therefore able to judge a situation fairly; impartial." Avoid it as a replacement for *uninterested* (which means "unconcerned, bored").

disk; disc. *Disk* is the usual spelling {hard disk} {disk drive}. But *disc* is preferred in a few specialized applications {compact disc} {disc brakes} {disc harrow}—particularly where the object in question is circular and flat.

disorganized; unorganized. Both mean "not organized," but *disorganized* suggests (1) a group in disarray, either thrown into confusion or inherently unable to work together {the disorganized 1968 Democratic National Convention in Chicago}, or (2) a person who is exceedingly bad at arranging or planning things {disorganized students}.

disperse. See **disburse.**

distinctive; distinguished; distinguishable. A *distinctive* feature is something that makes a person (or place or thing) easy to recognize {U2's distinctive sound}. But it does not necessarily make that person *distinguished* (respected and admired) {the distinguished professor wears a distinctive red bow tie}. It does, however, make the person *distinguishable* (easy to see as being different from something else)—a term that does not carry the positive connotation of *distinguished*.

dive, ***vb.*** The preferred conjugation has traditionally been *dive-dived-dived*. The irregular form *dove*, though, has become the slightly predominant past-tense form in American English and should be accepted as standard: *dive-dove-dived*. Traditionalists will stick to the older inflection.

doctrinal; doctrinaire. *Doctrinal* means "of, relating to, or constituting a doctrine"; it is neutral in connotation {doctrinal differences}. *Doctrinaire* means "dogmatic," suggesting that the person described is stubborn and narrow-minded {a doctrinaire ideologue}.

doubtfully, ***adv.*** In recent years, this term has come into use as a sentence adverb functioning as a correlative of *hopefully* and as an antonym of *undoubtedly* {Will you be attending the party? Hopefully—but doubtfully. [That is, I hope I'll be able to go, but I doubt it.]}. Should you abstain from this usage in Standard Written English? No doubt.

doubtless, ***adv.*** Use this form (it's called a *flat adverb*)—not *doubtlessly*. See also 5.160.

doubt that; doubt whether; doubt if. *Doubt that* conveys a negative sense of strong skepticism or questioning {I doubt that you'll ever get your money back}. *Doubt whether* also conveys a sense of skepticism, though less strong {the official says that he doubts whether the company could survive}. *Doubt if* is a casual phrasing for *doubt that*.

drag. Conjugated *drag-dragged-dragged*. The past form *drug* is dialectal.

dream. Either *dreamed* (more typical in both American English and British English) or *dreamt* is acceptable for the past-tense and past-participial forms.

drink, ***vb.*** Correctly conjugated *drink-drank-drunk* {they had not drunk any fruit juice that day}.

drown, ***vb.*** Conjugated *drown-drowned-drowned*.

drunk, ***adj.*****; drunken.** *Drunk* describes a current state of intoxication {drunk driver}. (By contrast, a *drunk*—like a *drunkard*—is someone who is habitually intoxicated.) *Drunken* describes either a trait of habitual intoxication {drunken sot} or intoxicated people's behavior {a drunken brawl}.

dual; duel. *Dual* is an adjective meaning "having two parts or two of something" {dual exhaust}. A *duel* is a fight between two people, especially a formal and often deadly combat with pistols or swords.

due to. In strict traditional usage, *due to* should be interchangeable with *attributable to* {the erratic driving was due to some prescription drugs that the driver had taken} or *owed to* {thanks are due to all who helped}. When used adverbially, *due to* is often considered inferior to *because of* or *owing to*. So in the sentence *Due to the parents' negligence, the entire family suffered*, the better phrasing would be *Because of* [or *Owing to*] *the parents' negligence, the entire family suffered*.

due to the fact that. Use *because* instead.

dumb. This word means either "stupid" or "unable to speak." In the second sense, the adjective *mute* is clearer (and less offensive) for most modern readers. But on the noun use of *mute*, see **moot**.

dying; dyeing. *Dying* is the present participle of *die* (= to cease living); *dyeing* is the present participle of *dye* (= to color with a liquid).

each. As a noun serving as the subject of a clause, *each* takes a singular verb {each of them was present that day}. But when it serves as an emphatic appositive for a plural noun, the verb is plural {they each have their virtues} {the newspapers each sell for $3}.

each other; one another. Traditionalists use *each other* when two things or people are involved, *one another* when more than two are involved.

eatable. See **edible.**

economic; economical. *Economic* means "of, relating to, or involving large-scale finances" {federal economic policy}. *Economical* means "thrifty; financially efficient; cheap and not wasteful" {an economical purchase}.

edible; eatable. What is *edible* is fit for human consumption {edible flowers}. What is *eatable* is at least minimally palatable {the cake is slightly burned but still eatable}.

effect. See **affect.**

effete. Traditionally, it has meant "worn out, sterile" or "lacking power, character, or vitality." Today it is often used to mean "snobbish," "effeminate," or "unduly pampered." Because of its ambiguity, the word is best avoided altogether.

effrontery; affront. *Effrontery* is an act of shameless impudence or shocking audacity. An *affront* is a deliberate insult.

e.g. See **i.e.**

either. Like *neither*, this word takes a singular verb when it functions as subject {is either of the spouses present today?}.

elemental; elementary. Something that is *elemental* is an essential constituent {elemental ingredients} or a power of nature {elemental force}. Something that is *elementary* is basic, introductory, or easy {an elementary math problem}.

elicit; illicit. To *elicit* information or a reaction is to get it from someone, especially in challenging circumstances {to elicit responses}. Something *illicit* is disallowed by law or rule and usually also condemned generally by society {an illicit scheme}. Writers often mistakenly use the adjective *illicit* when they need the verb *elicit*.

elude. See **allude.**

embarrass. See **harass.**

emend. See **amend.**

emigrate. See **immigrate.**

eminent; imminent. What is *eminent* is famous, important, and respected {the eminent professor} or derives from high standing or authority {eminent domain}. What is *imminent* is looming, likely to happen soon, and almost always bad {imminent disaster}.

emoji; emoticon. An *emoji* (from the Japanese; pl. *emoji*) is a pictorial representation, or ideogram, that consists of a face, a hand gesture, or an object or symbol intended to express or suggest an emotion or attitude—or any number of ideas or things. An *emoticon* is a representation of a smiley face or other expressive gesture rendered as a combination of common keyboard characters—e.g., ;-).

emotive; emotional. The first means "arousing intense feeling" {emotive language calculated to persuade the jury}; the second means "of, relating to, or involving intense feelings" {an emotional response}.

empathy; sympathy. *Empathy* is the ability to understand other people's feelings and problems {tremendous empathy with others}. *Sympathy* is generally compassion and sorrow one feels for another's misfortunes, especially on a particular occasion {our sympathies are with you}—but it can also be support for a plan or idea {right-wing sympathies} or a mutual understanding and warmth arising from compatibility {there was no personal sympathy between them}.

endemic. See **epidemic.**

endorse. See **approve.**

enervate; innervate. These words are antonyms. To *enervate* is to weaken or drain of energy. To *innervate* is to stimulate or provide with energy.

enormity; enormousness. *Enormity* means "monstrousness, moral outrageousness, atrociousness" {the enormity of the Khmer Rouge's killings}. *Enormousness* means "hugeness" or "immensity" {the enormousness of Alaska}.

enough. See **adequate.**

enquire. See **inquire.**

ensure; insure; assure. *Ensure* is the general term meaning "to make sure that something will (or won't) happen." In best usage, *insure* is reserved for underwriting financial risk. So we *ensure* that we can get time off for a vacation, and we *insure* our car against an accident on the trip. We *ensure* events and *insure* things. But we *assure* people of things by telling them what's what, so that they won't worry. The important thing to remember is that we ensure occurrences and assure people.

enthused, ***adj.*** Use *enthusiastic* instead.

enumerable; innumerable. What's *enumerable* is countable and listable {the enumerable issues that we need on the agenda}. What's *innumerable* can't be counted, at least not practically {innumerable stars in the sky}. The second word is far more common. Because the two are pronounced so similarly, be wary of using them in speech.

envy. See **jealousy.**

epidemic; endemic; pandemic. An *epidemic* disease breaks out, spreads through a limited area (such as a state), and then subsides {an epidemic outbreak of measles}. (The word is frequently used as a noun {a measles epidemic}.) An *endemic* disease is perennially present within a region or population {malaria is endemic in parts of Africa}. (Note that *endemic* describes a disease and not a region: it is incorrect to say *this region is endemic for* [a disease].) A *pandemic* disease is prevalent over a large area, such as a nation or continent, or the entire world {the 1918–19 flu pandemic}.

equally as. This is typically faulty phrasing. Delete *as.*

et al. This is the abbreviated form of *et alii* ("and others")—the *others* being people, not things. Since *al.* is an abbreviation, the period is required—but note that no period follows the *et* (Latin for "and"). Cf. **etc.**

etc. This is the abbreviated form of *et cetera* ("and other things"); it should never be used in reference to people. *Etc.* implies that a list of things is too extensive to recite. But often writers seem to run out of thoughts and tack on *etc.* for no real purpose. Also, two redundancies often appear with this abbreviation: (1) *and etc.*, which is poor style because *et* means "and," and (2) *etc.* at the end of a list that begins with *for example*, *such as*, *e.g.*, and the like. Those terms properly introduce a short list of examples. Cf. **et al.**; see also 6.20.

event. The phrase *in the event that* is a verbose and formal way of saying *if.*

eventuality. This term often needlessly displaces more specific everyday words such as *event*, *result*, and *possibility*.

every day, ***adv.*****; everyday,** ***adj.*** The first is adverbial, the second adjectival. You may wear your *everyday* clothes *every day*.

every one; everyone. The two-word version is an emphatic way of saying "each" {every one of them was there}; the second is a pronoun equivalent to *everybody* {everyone was there}.

everywhere. This is the preferable word—not *everyplace*.

evoke; invoke. To *evoke* something is to bring it out {evoke laughter} or bring it to mind {evoke childhood memories}. *Invoke* has a number of senses, including to assert (something) as authority {invoke the Monroe Doctrine}, to appeal (to someone or a higher power) for help {invoke an ally to intervene}, and to conjure up {invoke spirits of the past}.

exceptional; exceptionable. What is *exceptional* is uncommon, superior, rare, or extraordinary {an exceptional talent}. What is *exceptionable* is objectionable or offensive {an exceptionable slur}.

executor; administrator. In a will, a person designates an *executor* to distribute the estate after death. When a person dies without a will or without specifying an executor, the court will appoint an *administrator* to do the same. The feminine forms *administratrix* and *executrix* are unnecessary and should be avoided.

explicit; implicit. If something is *explicit*, it is deliberately and clearly spelled out, as in the text of a well-drafted statute. If it is *implicit*, it is not specifically stated but is either suggested in the wording or necessary to effectuate the purpose. Avoid *implicit* to mean "complete, unmitigated."

fact that, the. This much-maligned phrase is not always avoidable. But hunt for a substitute before deciding to use it. Sometimes *that* alone suffices.

farther; further. The traditional distinction is to use *farther* for a physical distance {we drove farther north to see the autumn foliage} and *further* for a figurative distance {let's examine this further} {look no further}. Although it's a refinement of slight importance, connoisseurs will appreciate it.

faze; phase, ***vb.*** To *faze* is to disturb or disconcert {Jones isn't fazed by insults}. To *phase* (usually *phase in* or *phase out*) is to schedule or perform a plan, task, or the like in stages {phase in new procedures} {phase out the product lines that don't sell}. The negative adjective for "unaffected" is *unfazed*, not *unphased*.

feel. This verb is weak when used as a substitute for *think* or *believe*.

feel bad. Invariably, the needed phrase is *feel bad* (not *feel badly*). See 5.170.

fewer. See **less**.

fictional; fictitious; fictive. *Fictional* (from *fiction* as a literary genre) means "of, relating to, or involving imagination" {a fictional story}. *Fictitious* means "imaginary; counterfeit; false" {a fictitious name}. *Fictive* means "possessing the talent for imaginative creation" {fictive gift}; although it can also be a synonym for *fictional*, in that sense it is a needless variant. Also, anthropologists use *fictive* to describe relationships in which people are treated as family members despite having no bond of blood or marriage {fictive kin}.

finalize. Meaning "to bring to an end or finish the last part of," this word has often been associated with inflated jargon. Although its compactness may recommend it in some contexts, use *finish* when possible.

first. In enumerations, use *first*, *second*, *third*, and so on. Avoid the *-ly* forms.

fit. This verb is undergoing a shift. It has traditionally been conjugated *fit-fitted-fitted*, but today *fit-fit-fit* is prevalent in American English {when she tried on the dress, it fit quite well}. In the passive voice, however, *fitted* is still normal {the horse was fitted with a new harness}.

flagrant. See **blatant.**

flair. See **flare.**

flammable; inflammable. *Flammable* was invented in the early twentieth century as an alternative to the synonymous word *inflammable*, which some people misunderstood—dangerously—as meaning "not combustible." Today *flammable* is the standard term. Its antonym is *nonflammable.*

flare; flair. A *flare* is an unsteady and glaring light {an emergency flare} or a sudden outburst {a flare-up of fighting}. A *flair* is an outstanding talent {a flair for mathematics} or originality and stylishness {performed with flair}.

flaunt; flout. *Flaunt* means "to show off ostentatiously" {they flaunted their wealth}. *Flout* means "to openly disobey" {they flouted the rules}.

flounder; founder. Although the figurative sense of both verbs is "to go wrong," the literal senses evoke different images. To *flounder* is to struggle awkwardly, as though walking through deep mud {the professor glared while the unprepared student floundered around for an answer}. To *founder* (usually in reference to a boat or ship) is to sink or run aground {the ship foundered on the rocks}.

flout. See **flaunt.**

following. Avoid this word as an equivalent of *after*. Consider the possible miscue in *Following the presentation, there was a question-and-answer session. After* is both simpler and clearer.

forbear, ***vb.***; **forebear,** ***n.*** The terms are unrelated, but the spellings are frequently confused. To *forbear* is to refrain {he wanted to speak but decided to forbear [the conjugation is *forbear-forbore-forborne*]}. A *forebear* is an ancestor {the house was built by Murray's distant forebears}.

forego; forgo. To *forego* is to go before {the foregoing paragraph}. The word appears most commonly in the phrase *foregone conclusion.* To *forgo*, by contrast, is to do without or renounce {they decided to forgo that opportunity}.

foreword; preface. A book's *foreword* (not *forward*) is an introductory essay written by someone other than the book's author. An introductory essay written by the book's author is called a *preface*. See 1.40, 1.41, 1.43, 1.47.

forgo. See **forego.**

former; latter. In the best usage, these words apply only to pairs. The *former* is the first of two, the *latter* the second of two.

fortuitous; fortunate. *Fortuitous* means "happening by chance," usually (but not always) with a good result {the rotten tree could have fallen at any time; it was just fortuitous that the victims drove by when they did}. *Fortunate* means "lucky" {we were fortunate to win the raffle}. Today, unfortunately, *fortuitous* is poaching on the semantic turf of *fortunate*.

forward(s). See **toward**.

founder. See **flounder**.

free rein. So written—not *free reign*.

fulsome, ***adj.*** This word does not preferably mean "very full" but "too much, excessive to the point of being repulsive." Traditionally, a "fulsome speech" is one that is so overpacked with thanks or hyperbole as to sound insincere. The word's slipshod use arises most often in the cliché *fulsome praise*, which can suggest the opposite of what the writer probably intends.

further. See **farther**.

future, in the near. Use *soon* or *shortly* instead.

gauntlet; gantlet. Lexicographers and usage critics—especially American ones—have sought since the nineteenth century to make a distinction. Etymologically, the two words have different histories: throwing down the *gauntlet* (= glove) and running the *gantlope* (= ordeal). But *gauntlet* has taken over both meanings. The standard phrases have been *run the gauntlet* and *throw down the gauntlet* since about 1800—the former phrase by a 10-to-1 margin over the competing form *run the gantlet*. Efforts to separate the terms have run their grueling course.

gentleman. This word is a vulgarism when used as a synonym for *man*. When used in reference to a cultured, refined man, it is susceptible to some of the same objections as those leveled against *lady*. Use it cautiously. Cf. **lady**.

get. Though shunned by many writers as too casual, *get* often sounds more natural than *obtain* or *procure* {get a divorce}. It can also substitute for a stuffy *become* {get hurt}. The verb is conjugated *get-got-gotten* in American English and *get-got-got* in British English. *Get* is the only verb apart from *be*-verbs that, when coupled with a past participle, can create a passive-voice construction {get stolen} {get waylaid}.

gibe; jibe; jive. A *gibe* is a biting insult or taunt: *gibes* are figuratively thrown at their target {the angry crowd hurled gibes at the miscreant}. To *jibe* is to be in accord or to agree {the verdict didn't jibe with the judge's own view of the facts}. *Jive* can be either a noun (referring to swing music or to misleading talk that is transparently untrue) or a verb (meaning "to dance to such music" or "to try to mislead with lies").

gild. See **guild**.

go. This verb is conjugated *go-went-gone*. *Went* appears as a past participle only in dialect.

gourmet; gourmand. Both are aficionados of good food and drink. But a *gourmet* knows and appreciates the fine points of food and drink, whereas a *gourmand* tends toward gluttony.

graduate, ***vb.*** Whereas *graduate* means "to grant a diploma to or confer a degree on," *graduate from* means "to receive a diploma or degree from (a school, university, or other institution)." A school can *graduate* a student or a student can *graduate from* a school, but a student does not *graduate* a school—at least not in good usage.

grateful; gratified. To be *grateful* is to be thankful or appreciative. To be *gratified* is to be pleased, satisfied, or indulged.

grisly; grizzly. What is *grisly* is gruesome or horrible {grisly details}. What is *grizzly* is grayish {grizzly hair} or bearish {the North American grizzly bear}.

guild, *n.*; gild, *vb.* A *guild* is an organization of persons with a common interest or profession {a guild of goldsmiths}. To *gild* is to put a thin layer of gold on something {gild a picture frame}, sometimes in a figurative sense {gilding the lily}.

hail; hale. To *hail* is to salute or greet {hail, Caesar!}, to acclaim enthusiastically {hailed as the greatest novelist of her time}, or to shout as an attention-getter {hail a taxi}. To *hale* is to compel to go {haled into court}. *Hail* is also a noun denoting ice-pellet precipitation, or something like it {a hail of insults}. *Hale* is also an adjective describing someone who is physically sound and free from infirmities.

half (of). Delete the *of* whenever possible {half the furniture}. When *half* is followed by a singular noun, the verb is singular {half the state is solidly Democratic}; when it is followed by a plural noun, the verb is plural {half the people are Republicans}.

handful. If *handful* applies to a mass noun, use a singular verb {a handful of trouble is ahead}. But if *handful* applies to a plural count noun, use a plural verb {only a handful of walnut trees still line Main Street}.

hangar; hanger. One finds *hangars* (large buildings where aircraft are kept) at an airport {airplane hangars}. Everywhere else, one finds *hangers* {clothes hangers} {picture hangers}.

hanged; hung. *Hanged* is used as the past participle of *hang* only in its transitive form when referring to the killing (just or unjust) of a human being by suspending the person by the neck {criminals were hanged at Tyburn Hill}. But if death is not intended or likely, or if the person is suspended by a body part other than the neck, *hung* is correct {he was hung upside down as a cruel prank}. In most senses, of course, *hung* is the past form of *hang* {Abdul hung up his clothes}.

hanger. See **hangar**.

harass; embarrass. The first word has one *r*; the second has two. The pronunciation of *harass* also causes confusion. The dominant American pronunciation stresses the second syllable, while British English stresses the first.

harebrained. So spelled (after the timid, easily startled animal)—not *hairbrained*.

hark back. So written—preferably not *harken back* or *hearken back*.

healthy; healthful. Traditionally, a living thing that is *healthy* enjoys good health; something that is *healthful* promotes health {a healthful diet will keep you healthy}. But gradually *healthy* is taking over both senses.

help (to). Omit the *to* when possible {talking will help resolve the problem}.

he or she. To avoid sexist language, many writers use this alternative phrasing (in place of the generic *he*). Use it sparingly—preferably after exhausting all other, less obtrusive methods of achieving gender neutrality. In any event, *he or she* is much preferable to *he/she*, *s/he*, *(s)he*, and the like. See also 5.48, 5.255.

historic; historical. The shorter word refers to what is momentous in history {January 16, 1991, was a historic day in Kuwait}. *Historical*, meanwhile, refers simply to anything that pertains to or occurred in history {the historical record}. On the question whether to use *a* or *an* before *historic* and *historical*, see **a**.

hoard; horde. A *hoard* is a supply, usually secret and sometimes valuable. *Hoard* is also a verb meaning "to amass such a supply," especially when there is no need to do so. A *horde* was originally a tribe of Asian nomads; today a *horde* is a large crowd, especially one that moves in a noisy, uncontrolled way.

hoi polloi. This is a mildly disparaging phrase for "common people." It does not refer to elites, though some writers and speakers misuse it in this way (perhaps from false association with *hoity-toity*). It is a plural. Although *hoi* is Greek for "the," the phrase is commonly rendered *the hoi polloi* and has been at least since it was used by John Dryden in 1668.

holocaust. When capitalized, this word refers to the Nazi genocide of European Jews in World War II. When not capitalized, it refers (literally or figuratively) to extensive devastation caused by fire or to the systematic and malicious killings of human beings on a vast scale. Avoid any light or hyperbolic use of this word.

home in. This phrase is frequently misrendered *hone in*. (*Hone* means "to sharpen.") *Home in* refers to what homing pigeons and aerial bombs do; the meaning is "to come closer and closer to a target."

homicide. See **murder**.

hopefully. The old meaning of the word ("in a hopeful manner") seems unsustainable; the newer meaning ("I hope" or "it is to be hoped that"), as a sentence adverb, spread in the 1960s and 1970s and seems here to stay. But many careful writers still deplore the new meaning.

horde. See **hoard**.

humanitarian. This word means "involving the promotion of human welfare" {humanitarian philanthropy}. Avoid using it in a phrase such as *the worst humanitarian disaster in decades*, where it really means just "human."

hung. See **hanged**.

I; me. When you need a first-person pronoun, use one. It's not immodest to do so; it's superstitious not to. But be sure you get the right one {Sally and I are planning to go} {give John or me a call} {keep this between you and me}. See **between you and me**.

idyllic. An *idyll* is a short pastoral poem, and by extension *idyllic* means charming or picturesque. It is not synonymous with *ideal* (perfect).

i.e.; e.g. The first is the abbreviation for *id est* ("that is"); the second is the abbreviation for *exempli gratia* ("for example"). The English equivalents are preferable in formal prose, though sometimes the compactness of these two-character abbreviations makes them desirable. Always put a comma after either one. See also 6.20, 6.51.

if; whether. While *if* is conditional, *whether* introduces an alternative, often in the context of an indirect question. Use *whether* in two circumstances: (1) to introduce a noun clause: *he asked whether his tie was straight* (the alternatives are *yes* and *no*), and (2) when using *if* produces ambiguity. In the sentence *he asked if his tie was straight*, the literal meaning is "whenever his tie was straight, he asked"; the popular meaning "he wanted someone to tell him whether his tie did or didn't need straightening" may not be understood by all readers. More tellingly, *Call to let me know if you can come* means that you should call only if you're coming. *Call to let me know whether you can come* means that you should call regardless of whether the answer is yes or no. Avoid substituting *if* for *whether* unless your tone is intentionally informal or you are quoting someone. See **determine whether; whether.**

ilk. This noun commonly means "type" or "sort" in modern usage, and unobjectionably so today {of his ilk} {of that ilk}. The Scottish phrase *of that ilk* means "of the same name or place."

illegal. See **unlawful.**

illegible; unreadable. Handwriting or printing that is *illegible* is not clear enough to be read {illegible scrawlings}. Writing that is *unreadable* is so poorly composed as to be either incomprehensible or intolerably dull.

illicit. See **elicit; unlawful.**

illude. See **allude.**

immigrate; emigrate. To *immigrate* is to enter a country to live permanently, leaving a past home. To *emigrate* is to leave one country to live in another one. The cognate forms also demand attention. Someone who moves from Ireland to the United States is an *immigrant* here and an *emigrant* there. An *émigré* is also an *emigrant*, but especially one in political exile.

imminent. See **eminent.**

impact; impactful. Resist using *impact* as a verb. Try *affect* or *influence* instead. Besides being hyperbolic, *impact* is still considered a solecism by traditionalists (though it is gaining ground). Avoid *impactful*, which is jargon (replacements include *influential* and *powerful*). Cf. **access.**

impeachment. *Impeachment* is the legislative equivalent of an indictment, not a conviction. In the US federal system, the House of Representatives votes on impeachment, and the Senate votes on removal from office.

impelled. See **compelled.**

implicit. See **explicit.**

imply; infer. The writer or speaker *implies* (hints, suggests); the reader or listener *infers* (deduces). Writers and speakers often use *infer* as if it were synonymous with *imply*, but careful writers always distinguish between the two words. See **inference**.

important; importantly. In the phrase *more important(ly)*—usually at the outset of a sentence—traditionalists prefer the shorter form as an ellipsis of *what is more important*, normally with a comma following. But *more importantly* is now established as a sentence adverb—and it's unobjectionable.

impractical; impracticable. The first is the more general adjective, meaning "not sensible" or "unrealistic" {impractical planning that doesn't account for travel expenses}. The second means "impossible to carry out" {landing aircraft on that hole-ridden runway proved impracticable}. See also **practicable.**

in actual fact. See **actual fact, in.**

inasmuch as. *Because* or *since* is almost always a better choice. See **since.**

in behalf of. See **behalf.**

incidence; incident; instance. Be careful with the first of these words: it has to do with relative rates and ranges {the incidence of albinism within a given society}. Perhaps leave it to scientists and actuaries. An *incident* (= an event, occurrence, or happening) should be distinguished from an *instance* (= a case, example).

include; comprise. The basic difference between these near-synonyms is that *include* implies nonexclusivity {the collection includes 126 portraits [suggesting that there is much else in the collection]}, while *comprise* implies exclusivity {the collection comprises 126 silver spoons [suggesting that nothing else is part of the collection]}. Oddly, in patent law—and there alone—*comprise* carries a nonexclusive sense. See **comprise.**

in connection with. This is a vague, fuzzy phrase {she explained the financial consequences in connection with the transaction} {Ray liked everything in connection with golf} {Phipson was compensated in connection with its report}. Try replacing the phrase with *of*, *related to*, or *associated with* {she explained the financial consequences of the transaction}, *about* {Ray liked everything about golf}, or *for* {Phipson was compensated for its report}.

incredible; incredulous. *Incredible* properly means "too strange to be believed; difficult to believe." Colloquially, it is used to mean "astonishingly good" {it was an incredible trip}. *Incredulous* means "disbelieving, skeptical" {people are incredulous about the rising gas costs}.

inculcate; indoctrinate. One *inculcates* values *into* a child but *indoctrinates* the child *with* values. That is, *inculcate* always takes the preposition *into* and a value or values as its object {inculcate courage into soldiers}. *Indoctrinate* takes a person as its object {indoctrinate children with the habit of telling the truth}.

individual. Use this word to distinguish a single person from a group. When possible, use a more specific term, such as *person*, *adult*, *child*, *man*, or *woman*.

indoctrinate. See **inculcate.**

induce. See **adduce.**

in excess of. Try replacing this verbose phrase with *more than* or *over*. See **over.**

infectious. See **contagious.**

infer. See **imply.**

inference. Use the verb *draw*, not *make*, with *inference* {they drew the wrong inferences}. Otherwise readers may confuse *inference* with *implication*. See **imply.**

inflammable. See **flammable.**

inflict; afflict. Events, illnesses, punishments, etc. are *inflicted on* living things or entities {an abuser inflicts cruelty}. The sufferers are *afflicted with* or *by* disease, troubles, etc. {agricultural communities are afflicted with drought}.

ingenious; ingenuous. These words are similar in form but not in meaning. *Ingenious* describes what is intelligent, clever, and original {an ingenious invention}. *Ingenuous* describes a person who is candid, naive, and without dissimulation, or an action or statement with those qualities {a hurtful but ingenuous observation}.

innate; inherent. An *innate* characteristic is one that a living thing has from birth; it should be distinguished, then, from a talent or disposition that one acquires from training or experience. An *inherent* characteristic is also part of a thing's nature, but life is not implied. A rock, for example, has an inherent hardness.

innervate. See **enervate.**

innocent; not guilty. If you are *innocent*, you are without blame. If you are *not guilty*, you have been exonerated by a jury. Newspapers avoid the *not guilty* phrase, though, because the consequences of accidentally leaving off the *not* could be serious. See **pleaded.**

innumerable. See **enumerable.**

in order to; in order for. Often these expressions can be reduced to *to* and *for*. When that is so, and rhythm and euphony are preserved or even heightened, use *to* or *for*.

in proximity. See **close proximity.**

inquire. The normal spellings in American English and British English alike are *inquire* and *inquiry*. *Enquire* and *enquiry* are primarily British English variants.

in regard to. This is the phrase, not the nonstandard *in regards to*. But try a single-word substitute instead: *about*, *regarding*, *concerning*, etc.

insidious; invidious. What is *insidious* spreads gradually to cause damage—at first without being noticed {an insidious conspiracy}; what is *invidious* involves moral offensiveness and serious unpleasantness {invidious discrimination}.

in spite of. See **despite.**

instance. See **incidence.**

insure. See **ensure.**

intense; intensive. *Intense* means (1) "having a strong effect" {intense pressures}, (2) "involving a great deal of effort during a very short time" {intense concentration}, or (3) "having unduly strong feelings or a demeanor of exaggerated seriousness" {he's a bit too intense}. *Intense* is always preferred outside philosophical and scientific usages. But *intensive* should be retained in customary terms such as *labor-intensive* and *intensive care*.

intently; intensely. An act done *intently* is done purposefully and with concentration and determination. One that is done *intensely* is done with great power, passion, or emotion but not necessarily with deliberate intent.

inter; intern. *Inter* is a verb meaning "to bury (a dead person)"; the corresponding noun is *interment*. An *intern* is a student working temporarily to gain experience, especially in a profession. *Intern* is also a verb with two senses. As an intransitive verb, it means "to work as an intern" {interning at the US Senate}; the corresponding noun is *internship*. As a transitive verb, it means "to confine (a civilian) to a certain place or district without a criminal charge, especially in wartime or for political reasons"; the corresponding noun is *internment*.

in the affirmative. See **affirmative, in the.**

in the event that. See **event.**

in the near future. See **future, in the near.**

in the negative. See **affirmative, in the.**

inveigh; inveigle. To *inveigh* is to protest, usually against something {picketers inveighed against annexation}. To *inveigle* is to cajole or ensnare, especially by misleading {inveigling a friend to attend the party}.

invidious. See **insidious.**

invoke. See **evoke.**

irregardless. An error. Use *regardless* (or possibly *irrespective*).

it is I; it is me. Both are correct and acceptable. The first phrase, using the first-person predicate nominative, is strictly grammatical (and a little stuffy); the second is idiomatic (and relaxed), and it is often contracted to *it's me*. In third-person constructions, however, a greater stringency holds sway in good English {this is he} {it isn't she who has caused such misery}.

its; it's. *Its* is the possessive form of *it*; *it's* is the contraction for *it is* {it's a sad dog that scratches its fleas}.

jealousy; envy. *Jealousy* connotes feelings of resentment toward another, particularly in matters relating to an intimate relationship {sexual jealousy}. *Envy* refers to coveting another's advantages, possessions, or abilities {his transparent envy of others' successes}.

jibe; jive. See **gibe.**

karat. See **carat.**

kudos. Preferably pronounced /**k[y]oo**-dos/ (not /-dohz/), this word means "praise and admiration." It is singular, not plural. Hence avoid *kudo is* or *kudos are*.

lady. When used as a synonym for *woman*—indeed, when used anywhere but in the phrase *ladies and gentlemen*—this word will be considered objectionable by some readers who think that it refers to a patronizing stereotype. This is especially true when it is used for unprestigious jobs {cleaning lady} or as a condescending adjective {lady lawyer}. Some will insist on using it to describe a refined woman. If they've consulted this entry, they've been forewarned. Cf. **gentleman.**

last; lastly. As with *first*, *second*, etc., prefer *last* when introducing a final point of discussion—or (of course) *finally*.

latter. See **former.**

laudable; laudatory. *Laudable* means "praiseworthy, even if not fully successful" {a laudable effort}. *Laudatory* means "expressing praise" {laudatory phone calls}.

lay; lie. Admittedly, the traditional conjugations are more blurred than ever. Mastering them has proved difficult for people. Nevertheless, here goes. *Lay* is a transitive verb—that is, it demands a direct object {lay your pencils down}. It is inflected *lay-laid-laid* {I laid the book there yesterday} {these rumors have been laid to rest}. (The children's prayer *Now I lay me down to sleep* is a good mnemonic device for the transitive *lay*.) *Lie* is an intransitive verb—that is, it never takes a direct object {lie down and rest}. It is inflected *lie-lay-lain* {she lay down and rested} {he hasn't yet lain down in twenty-three hours}. In a doctor's office, you should be asked to *lie back* or *lie down*.

leach; leech. To *leach* is to percolate or to separate out solids in solution by percolation. A *leech* is a bloodsucker (whether literal or figurative). By extension of that noun, to *leech* is either to attach oneself to another as a leech does or to drain the resources of something.

lead. See **led.**

lease; let. Many Americans seem to think that *let* is colloquial and of modern origin. In fact, the word is three hundred years older than *lease* and just as proper. One distinction between the two words is that either the owner or the tenant can be said to *lease* property, but only the owner can be said to *let* it.

led. This is the correct spelling of the past tense and past participle of the verb *lead*. It is often misspelled *lead*, maybe in part because of the pronunciation of the metal *lead* and the past tense and past participle *read*, both of which rhyme with *led*.

leech. See **leach.**

lend, ***vb.***; **loan,** ***vb. & n.*** *Lend* is the correct term for letting someone use something with the understanding that it (or its equivalent) will be returned. The verb *loan* is standard especially when money is the subject of the transaction—but even then, *lend* appears somewhat more frequently in edited English. *Loan* is the noun corresponding to both *lend* and *loan*, vb. The past-tense and past-participial form of *lend* is *lent*.

less; fewer. Reserve *less* for singular mass nouns or amounts {less salt} {less soil} {less water}. Reserve *fewer* for plural count nouns {fewer calories} {fewer people} {fewer suggestions}.

lest. This is one of the few English words that invariably call for a verb in the subjunctive mood {he didn't want to drive lest he take a wrong turn} {he has turned down the volume lest he disturb his roommates}. The conjunction is somewhat more common in British English than in American English.

let. See **lease**.

libel. See **defamation**.

lie. See **lay**.

life-and-death; life-or-death. The problem of logic aside (life and death being mutually exclusive), the first phrase is the standard idiom {a life-and-death decision}.

light, ***vb.*** This verb can be inflected either *light-lit-lit* or *light-lighted-lighted*—and irreproachably so. The past-participial adjective tends to be *lighted* when not modified by an *-ly* adverb {a lighted building} {a well-lighted hall} but *lit* if an *-ly* adverb precedes {brightly lit sconces} {a nicely lit walkway}.

like; as. The use of *like* as a conjunction (as in the old jingle "tastes good like a cigarette should") has long been a contentious issue. Traditionally speaking, *like* is a preposition, not a conjunction equivalent to *as* {you're much like me [*me* is the object of the preposition *like*]} {do as I say [the conjunction *as* connects the imperative *do* with the independent clause *I say*]}. As a casualism, however, the conjunctive *like* has become especially common since the mid-twentieth century {nobody cares like I do} {it tastes good like a fine chocolate should}. In Standard Written English, a conjunctive *like* will still provoke frowns among some readers. But the objections are slowly dwindling. If you want your prose to be unimpeachable and heightened, stick to *as* and *as if* for conjunctive senses {as we've observed, man is a social animal} {it looks as if it might rain}. See also 5.185.

likely. See **apt**.

literally. This word means "actually; without exaggeration." It should not be used loosely in figurative senses, as in *they were literally glued to their seats* (unless glue had in fact been applied). Wherever guides have accepted this usage, they should be disregarded.

loan. See **lend**.

loathe, ***vb.*; loath,** ***adj.*** To *loathe* (the *th* pronounced as in *that*) something is to detest it intensely or to regard it with disgust {I loathe tabloid television}. Someone who is *loath* (the *th* pronounced as in *thing*) is reluctant or unwilling {Tracy seems loath to admit mistakes}.

lose; loose, ***vb.*; loosen.** To *lose* something is to be deprived of it. To *loose* something is to release it from fastenings or restraints. To *loosen* is to make less tight or to ease a restraint. *Loose* conveys the idea of complete release, whereas *loosen* refers to only a partial release.

lot. See **a lot**.

luxuriant; luxurious. The two terms are fairly often confused (an example of catachresis). What is *luxuriant* is lush and grows abundantly {a luxuriant head of hair}. What is *luxurious* is lavish, extravagant, and comfortable {a luxurious resort}.

mad; angry. Some people object to using *mad* to mean "angry" and would reserve it to mean "insane." But the first sense dates back seven hundred years and isn't likely to disappear. As common as it is in everyday use, though, it has been so stigmatized that most people avoid it in formal writing.

majority. This noun preferably denotes countable things {a majority of votes cast}, not uncountable ones {the majority of the time}. Use *most* whenever it fits. When referring to a preponderance of votes cast, *majority* takes a singular verb {her majority was 7 percent}. But referring to a predominant group of people or things, it can take either a singular verb {the majority in the House was soon swept away} or a plural one {the majority of the voters were against the proposal}. Typically, if a genitive with a plural object follows *majority*, the verb should be plural {a majority of music teachers prefer using the metronome}.

malevolent; maleficent. *Malevolent* describes an evil mind that wishes to harm others {with malevolent intent}. *Maleficent* is similar but describes desire by the miscreant for accomplishing evil {maleficent bullying}.

malodorous. See **odious.**

maltreatment. See **mistreatment.**

mankind. Consider *humankind* instead.

manslaughter. See **murder.**

mantle; mantel. A *mantle* is a long, loose garment like a cloak—almost always today being used in a metaphorical sense {assuming the mantle of a martyr}. A *mantel* is a wood or stone structure around a fireplace {family pictures on the mantel}.

masterful; masterly. *Masterful* describes a person who is dominating and imperious. *Masterly* describes a person who has mastered a craft, trade, or profession, or a product of such mastery; the word often means "authoritative" {a masterly analysis}. Because *masterly* does not readily make an adverb (*masterlily* being extremely awkward), try *in a masterly way*. See also 5.158.

may; can. See **can.**

may; might. *May* expresses what is possible, is factual, or could be factual {I may have turned off the stove, but I can't recall doing it}. *Might* suggests something that is uncertain, hypothetical, or contrary to fact {I might have won the marathon if I had entered}. See 5.147.

me. See **I.**

medal; meddle; metal; mettle. A *medal* is an award for merit; a *metal* is a type of substance, usually hard and heavy. To *meddle* is to interfere. And *mettle* is a person's character, courage, and determination to do something no matter how difficult.

media; mediums. In scientific contexts and in reference to mass communications, the plural of *medium* is predominantly *media* {some bacteria flourish in several types of media} {the media are reporting more medical news}. Although one frequently sees *media is*, the plural use is recommended. If *medium* refers to a spiritualist, the plural is *mediums* {several mediums have held séances here}.

memoranda; memorandums. Although both plural forms are correct, *memoranda* has predominated since the early nineteenth century. Don't use *memoranda* as if it were singular—the word is *memorandum* {this memorandum is} {these memoranda are}.

metal; mettle. See **medal.**

mete out. The phrase meaning "to distribute" or "to assign" is so spelled {mete out punishment}. *Meet out* is a common error, especially in the erroneous past tense *meeted out*.

might. See **may.**

militate. See **mitigate.**

minuscule. Something that is minuscule is "very small." Probably because of the spelling of the modern word *mini* (and the prefix of the same spelling, which is recorded only from 1936), it is often misspelled *miniscule*. In printing, *minuscules* are lowercase letters and *majuscules* are capital (uppercase) letters.

mistreatment; maltreatment. *Mistreatment* is the more general term. *Maltreatment* denotes a harsh form of mistreatment, involving abuse by rough or cruel handling.

mitigate; militate. To *mitigate* is to lessen or soften the effects of something unpleasant, harmful, or serious; *mitigating circumstances* lessen the seriousness of a crime. To *militate*, by contrast, is to have a marked effect on; the word is usually followed by *against* {his nearsightedness militated against his ambition to become a commercial pilot}. Avoid the mistaken phrase *mitigate against* for the correct *militate against*.

moot; mute. *Moot* (/moot/) means (traditionally) "debatable" {a moot point worth our attention} or (by modern extension) "having no practical significance" {a moot question that is of no account}. *Mute* (/m[y]oot/) means "silent, speechless"—and is often considered offensive when used as a noun {deaf-mute}.

more than. See **over.**

much; very. *Much* generally intensifies past-participial adjectives {much obliged} {much encouraged} and some comparatives {much more} {much worse} {much too soon}. *Very* intensifies adverbs and most adjectives {very carefully} {very bad}, including past-participial adjectives that have more adjectival than verbal force {very bored}. See 5.90.

murder; manslaughter; homicide. All three words denote the killing of one person by another. *Murder* and *manslaughter* are both unlawful killings, but *murder* is done maliciously and intentionally. *Homicide* includes killings that are not unlawful, such as by a police officer acting properly in the line of duty. *Homicide* also refers to a person who kills another.

mute. See **moot.**

mutual. See **common.**

myself. Avoid using *myself* as a pronoun in place of *I* or *me*—a quirk that arises most often after an *and* or *or*. Instead, use it reflexively {I did myself a favor} or emphatically {I myself have tried to get through that book!}. See also 5.51.

naturalist; naturist. *Naturalist* most often denotes a person who studies natural history, especially a field biologist or an amateur who observes and usually photographs, sketches, or writes about nature. *Naturist* denotes a nature worshipper or a nudist.

nauseous; nauseated. Whatever is *nauseous*, traditionally speaking, induces a feeling of nausea—it makes us feel sick to our stomachs. To feel sick is to be *nauseated*. Although the use of *nauseous* to mean *nauseated* may be too common to be called an error anymore, strictly speaking it is poor usage. Because of the ambiguity in *nauseous*, the wisest course may be to stick to the participial adjectives *nauseated* and *nauseating*.

necessary; necessitous. *Necessary* means "required under the circumstances" {the necessary arrangements}. *Necessitous* means "impoverished" {living in necessitous circumstances}.

neither. Four points. First, like *either*, this word when functioning as the subject of a clause takes a singular verb {neither of the subjects was given that medicine}. Second, a *neither-nor* construction should frame grammatically parallel expressions {neither the room's being too cold nor the heater's malfunction could justify his boorish reaction} (both noun elements). Third, a simple *neither-nor* construction should have only two elements {neither bricks nor stones}—though it's perfectly permissible to multiply *nor*s for emphasis {neither snow nor rain nor heat nor gloom of night}. Fourth, the word is acceptably pronounced either /**nee**-thər/ or /**nɪ**-thər/.

no. See **affirmative, in the.**

noisome. This word has nothing to do with *noise*. It means noxious, offensive, or foul-smelling {a noisome landfill}.

none. This word may take either a singular or a plural verb. A guideline: if it is followed by a singular noun, treat it as a singular {none of the building was painted}; if by a plural noun, treat it as a plural {none of the guests were here when I arrived}. But for special emphasis, it is quite proper (though possibly stilted) to use a singular verb when a plural noun follows {none of my suggestions was accepted}.

nonplussed. Traditionally meaning "surprised and confused" {she was nonplussed when he took off the mask}, this word is now frequently misused to mean "unfazed"—almost the opposite of its literary sense. Avoid this newer usage, and avoid the variant spelling *nonplused*. See **faze.**

notable; noticeable; noteworthy. *Notable* (= readily noticed) applies both to physical things and to qualities {notable sense of humor}. *Noticeable* means "detectable with the physical senses" {a noticeable limp}. *Noteworthy* means "remarkable; deserving attention" {a noteworthy act of kindness}.

not guilty. See **innocent.**

notwithstanding. One word. Less formal alternatives include *despite*, *although*, and *in spite of*. The word *notwithstanding* may precede or follow a noun {notwithstanding her bad health, she decided to run for office} {her bad health notwithstanding, she decided to run for office}.

number. See **amount**.

observance; observation. *Observance* means "obedience to a rule or custom" {the family's observance of Passover}. *Observation* means either "the watching of something" or "a remark based on watching or studying something" {a keen observation about the defense strategy}. Each term is sometimes used when the other would be the better word.

obtain. See **attain**.

obtuse; abstruse. *Obtuse* describes a person who can't understand; *abstruse* describes an idea that is hard to understand. A person who is *obtuse* is dull and, by extension, dull-witted. What is *abstruse* is incomprehensible or nearly so.

odious; odorous; odoriferous; malodorous. *Odious* means "hateful" or "extremely unpleasant" {odious Jim Crow laws}. It is not related to the other terms, but it is sometimes misused as if it were. *Odorous* means "detectable by smell (for better or worse)" {odorous gases}. *Odoriferous* means essentially the same thing: it has meant "fragrant" as often as it has meant "foul." *Malodorous* means "smelling quite bad." The mistaken form *odiferous* is often used as a jocular equivalent of *smelly*—but most dictionaries don't record it.

of. Avoid using this word needlessly after *all*, *off*, *inside*, and *outside*. Also, prefer *June 2015* over *June of 2015*. To improve your style, try removing every *of*-phrase that you reasonably can.

off. Never put *of* after this word {we got off the bus}.

officious. A person who is *officious* is aggressively nosy and meddlesome—and overeager to tell people what to do. The word has nothing to do with *officer* and should not be confused with *official*.

on; upon. Prefer *on* to *upon* unless introducing an event or condition {put that on the shelf, please} {upon the job's completion, you'll get paid}. For more about *on*, see **onto**.

on behalf of. See **behalf**.

one another. See **each other**.

oneself. One word—not *one's self*.

onto; on to; on. When is *on* a preposition, and when an adverb? The sense of the sentence should tell, but the distinction can be subtle. *Onto* implies a movement, so it has an adverbial flavor even though it is a preposition {the gymnast jumped onto the bars}. When *on* is part of the verb phrase, it is an adverb and *to* is the preposition {the gymnast held on to the bars}. One trick is to mentally say "up" before *on*: if the sentence still makes sense, then *onto* is probably the right choice {she leaped onto the capstone}. Alone, *on* does not imply motion {the gymnast is good on the parallel bars}.

oppress; repress. *Oppress*, meaning "to persecute or tyrannize," is more negative than *repress*, meaning "to restrain or subordinate."

or. If this conjunction joins singular nouns functioning as subjects, the verb should be singular {cash or online payment is acceptable}.

oral. See **verbal.**

oration. See **peroration.**

ordinance; ordnance. An *ordinance* is a municipal regulation or an authoritative decree. *Ordnance* is military armament, especially artillery but also weapons and ammunition generally.

orient; orientate. To *orient* is to get one's bearings (literally, "to find east") {it took the new employee a few days to get oriented to the firm's suite}. Unless used in the sense "to face or turn to the east," *orientate* is a poor variation to be avoided.

ought; should. Both express a sense of duty, but *ought* is stronger. Unlike *should*, *ought* requires a fully expressed infinitive, even in the negative {you ought not to see the movie}. Don't omit the *to*—as many otherwise well-educated speakers and writers have begun doing in recent years. See 5.149, 5.150.

outside. In spatial references, no *of* is necessary—or desirable—after this word unless it is used as a noun {outside the shop} {the outside of the building}. But *outside of* is acceptable as a colloquialism meaning "except for" or "aside from."

over. As an equivalent of *more than*, this word is perfectly good idiomatic English.

overly. Avoid this word, which is not considered the best usage. Try *over-* as a prefix {overprotective} or *unduly* {unduly protective}.

pair. This is a singular form, the plural being *pairs* {three pairs of shoes}. Yet *pair* may take either a singular verb {this pair of sunglasses was on the table} or a plural one {the pair were inseparable from the moment they met}.

palette; palate; pallet. An artist's *palette* is either the board that an artist uses for mixing colors or (collectively) the colors used by a particular artist or available in a computer program. Your *palate* is the roof of your mouth specifically or your taste in food generally. A *pallet* is a low, usually wooden platform for storing and transporting goods in commerce, or a crude bed consisting of a bag filled with straw.

pandemic. See **epidemic.**

parameters. Though it may sound elegant or scientific, this word is usually just pretentious when it is used in nontechnical contexts. Stick to *boundaries*, *limits*, *guidelines*, *grounds*, *elements*, or some other word.

partake in; partake of. To *partake in* is to participate in {the new student refused to partake in class discussions}. To *partake of* is either to get a part of {partake of the banquet} or to have a quality, at least to some extent {this assault partakes of revenge}.

partly; partially. Both words convey the sense "to some extent; in part" {partly responsible}. *Partly* is preferred in that sense. But *partially* has the additional senses of "incompletely" {partially cooked} and "unfairly; in a way that shows bias toward one side" {he treats his friends partially}.

past; passed. *Past* can be an adjective {past events} (often postpositive {times past}), a noun {remember the past}, a preposition {go past the school}, or an adverb {time flew past}. *Passed* is the past tense and past participle of the verb *pass* {we passed the school} {as time passed}.

pastime. This word combines *pass* (not *past*) and *time*. It is spelled with a single *s* and a single *t*.

peaceable; peaceful. A *peaceable* person or nation is inclined to avoid strife {peaceable kingdom}. A *peaceful* person, place, or event is serene, tranquil, and calm {a peaceful day free from demands}.

peak; peek; pique. These three sometimes get switched through writerly blunders. A *peak* is an apex, a *peek* is a quick or illicit glance, and a fit of *pique* is an episode of peevishness and wounded vanity. To *pique* is to annoy or arouse: an article *piques* (not *peaks*) one's interest.

pedal; peddle. *Pedal* is a noun, verb, or adjective relating to the pedal extremity, or foot. As a noun, it denotes a device that is operated by the foot and does some work, such as powering a bicycle or changing the sound of a piano. As a verb, it means to use such a device. As an adjective, it means "of or concerning such a device or its use." *Peddle* is a verb meaning either "to try to sell goods to people by traveling from place to place" or "to sell questionable goods to people"—questionable because they may be illegal, harmful, or low quality {peddling magazine subscriptions door to door}.

peek. See **peak.**

pendant, *n.*; pendent, *adj.* A *pendant* is an item of dangling jewelry, especially one worn around the neck. What is *pendent* is hanging or suspended from something.

penultimate. This adjective means "next to last" {the penultimate paragraph in the précis}. Many people have started misusing it as a fancy equivalent of *ultimate*. The word *antepenultimate* means "the next to the next-to-last."

people; persons. The traditional view is that *persons* is used for smaller numbers {three persons} and *people* with larger ones {millions of people}. But today most people use *people* even for small groups {only three people were there}.

peroration; oration. A *peroration*, strictly speaking, is the conclusion of an *oration* (speech). Careful writers avoid using *peroration* to refer to a rousing speech or piece of writing.

perpetuate; perpetrate. To *perpetuate* something is to sustain it or prolong it indefinitely {perpetuate the species}. To *perpetrate* is to commit or perform an act, especially one that is illegal or morally wrong {perpetrate a crime}.

personally. Three points. First, use this word only when someone does something that would normally be done through an agent {the president personally signed this invitation} or to limit other considerations {Jean was affected by the decision but was not personally involved in it}. Second, *personally* is redundant when it modifies a verb that necessarily requires the person's presence, as in *The senator personally shook hands with the constituents.* Third, *personally* shouldn't appear with *I* when one is stating an opinion; it weakens the statement and doesn't reduce the speaker's liability for the opinion. The only exception arises if a person is required to advance someone else's view but holds a different personal opinion {in the chamber I voted to lower taxes because of the constituencies I represented; but I personally believed that taxes should have been increased}.

persons. See **people.**

persuade; convince. *Persuade* is associated with actions {persuade him to buy a suit}. *Convince* is associated with beliefs or understandings {she convinced the auditor of her honesty}. The phrase *persuade to (do)* has traditionally been considered better than *convince to (do)*—the latter having become common in American English in the 1950s. But either verb will take a *that*-clause {the committee was persuaded that an all-night session was necessary} {my three-year-old is convinced that Santa Claus exists}.

pertain; appertain. *Pertain to*, the more common term, means "to relate directly to" {the clause pertains to assignment of risk}. *Appertain to* means "to belong to or concern something as a matter of form or function" {the defendant's rights appertain to the Fifth Amendment}.

peruse. This term, which means "to read with great care" (*not* "to read quickly" or "to scan") should not be used as a fancy substitute for *read.*

phase. See **faze.**

phenomenon. This is the singular {the phenomenon of texting}, the plural being *phenomena* {cultural phenomena}.

pique. See **peak.**

pitiable; pitiful. To be *pitiable* is to be worthy of pity. To be *pitiful* is either to be very poor in quality or to be so sad or unfortunate as to make people feel sympathy.

pleaded; pled. The first is the standard past-tense and past-participial form {he pleaded guilty} {they have pleaded with their families}. Avoid *pled.*

plethora. This noun denotes an excess, surfeit, or overabundance. Avoid it as a mere equivalent of "abundance."

populace; populous. The *populace* is the population of a country as a whole. A *populous* place is densely populated.

pore. To *pore over* something written is to read it intently {they pored over every word in the report}. Some writers confuse this word with *pour.*

practicable; possible; practical. These terms differ in shading. What is *practicable* is capable of being done; it's feasible. What is *possible* might be capable of happening or being done, but there is some doubt. What is *practical* is fit for actual use or in a particular situation. See also **impractical.**

precede; proceed. To *precede* is to happen before or to go before in some sequence, usually time. It also means "to outrank" or "to surpass" in some measure such as importance, but this sense is usually conveyed with the noun *precedence* {the board's vote takes precedence over the staff's recommendation}. The word is often misspelled *preceed.* To *proceed* is to go on, whether beginning, continuing, or resuming.

precipitate, *adj.*; precipitous. What is *precipitate* occurs suddenly or rashly, without proper consideration; it describes demands, actions, or movements. What is *precipitous* is dangerously steep; it describes cliffs and inclines.

precondition. Try *condition* or *prerequisite* instead.

predominant, *adj.*; predominate, *vb.* Like *dominant*, *predominant* is an adjective {a predominant point of view}. Like *dominate*, *predominate* is a verb {a point of view that predominates throughout the state}. Using *predominate* as an adjective is nonstandard.

preface. See **foreword**.

prejudice, *vb.* Although *prejudice* is a perfectly normal English noun to denote an all-too-common trait, the corresponding verb is a legalism. For a plain-English equivalent, use *harm* or *hurt*. But the past-participial adjective *prejudiced* is perfectly normal in the sense "biased; harboring strong and often unfair feelings against."

preliminary to. Make it *before*, *in preparing for*, or some other natural phrasing.

prescribe. See **proscribe**.

presently. This word is ambiguous. Write *now* or *soon*, whichever you really mean.

presumption. See **assumption**.

preventive. Although the corrupt form *preventative* is fairly common, the strictly correct form is *preventive.*

previous to. Make it *before.*

principle; principal. A *principle* is a natural, moral, or legal rule {the principle of free speech}. The corresponding adjective is *principled* {a principled decision}. A *principal* is a person of high authority or prominence {a school principal} or an initial deposit of money {principal and interest}. *Principal* is also an adjective meaning "most important." Hence a *principal* role is a primary one.

prior to. Make it *before* or *until.*

proceed. See **precede**.

process of, in the. You can almost always delete this phrase without affecting the meaning.

propaganda. This is a singular noun denoting information that, being false or misleading, is used by a government or political group to influence people {propaganda was everywhere}. The plural is *propagandas.*

prophesy; prophecy. *Prophesy* is the verb meaning "to say what will happen in the future, especially by using supernatural or magical knowledge" {the doomsayers prophesied a market boom despite the bad news}. *Prophecy* is the noun denoting a prediction, especially one made by someone claiming to have supernatural or magical powers {their prophecies did not materialize}. *Prophesize* is an erroneous form.

proscribe; prescribe. To *proscribe* something is to prohibit it {legislation that proscribes drinking while driving}. To *prescribe* is to say officially what must be done in a particular situation {Henry VIII prescribed the order of succession to include three of his children} or to specify a medical remedy {the doctor prescribed anti-inflammatory pills and certain exercises}.

protuberance. So spelled. Perhaps because *protrude* means "to stick out," writers want to spell *protuberance* (= something that bulges out) with an extra *r* (after the *t*). But the words are from different roots.

proved; proven. *Proved* is the preferred past participle for the verb *prove* {it was proved to be true}. Use *proven* only as an adjective {a proven success}.

proximity. See **close proximity**.

purposely; purposefully. What is done *purposely* is done deliberately or intentionally—"on purpose." What is done *purposefully* is done with a certain goal or a clear aim in mind. An action may be done *purposely* without any particular interest in a specific result—that is, not *purposefully*.

question whether; question of whether; question as to whether. The first phrasing is traditionally considered best. The others are phraseologically inferior. See **as to.**

quick(ly). *Quickly* is the general adverb. But *quick* is properly used as an adverb in the idiomatic phrases *get rich quick* and *come quick*. See also 5.160.

quote; quotation. Traditionally a verb, *quote* is often used as an equivalent of *quotation* in speech and informal writing. Also, there is a tendency for writers (especially journalists) to think of *quotes* as contemporary remarks usable in their writing and of *quotations* as being wisdom of the ages expressed pithily.

rack; wrack. The spelling *rack* is complex: it accounts for nine different nouns and seven different verbs. Indeed, it is standard in all familiar senses {racking his brain} {racked with guilt} {nerve-racking} {rack and ruin}. *Wrack* is the standard spelling only for the noun meaning "seaweed, kelp."

raise; raze. To *raise* is to elevate, move upward, enhance, bring up, etc. {we raised some money}. To *raze* is to demolish, level to the ground, remove, etc. {they razed the building}.

reason. Two points. First, as to *reason why*, although some object to the supposed redundancy of this phrase, it is centuries old and perfectly acceptable English. *Reason that* is not always an adequate substitute {can you give reasons why *that* is preferable to *which* as a restrictive relative pronoun?}. Second, *reason . . . is because* is not good usage—*reason . . . is that* being preferred {the reason we returned on July 2 is that we wanted to avoid hordes of tourists}.

recur; reoccur. To *recur* is to happen again and again {his knee problems recurred throughout the rest of the year}, to return to in one's attention or memory {she recurred to her war experiences throughout our visit}, or to come back to one's attention or memory {the idea recurred to him throughout the night}. To *reoccur* is merely to happen again {the leak reoccurred during the second big rain}.

reek. See **wreak.**

reference; referral. A *reference* is a source of information, a person to provide information, an authority for some assertion, or a strong allusion to something. It's also an attributive adjective {reference book}. It's not universally accepted as a transitive verb. *Referral* is a narrower term denoting the practice or an instance of (1) directing someone to another person who can help, especially a professional or a specialist, or (2) relegating some matter to another body for a recommendation or resolution.

refrain; restrain. To *refrain* is to restrain yourself or to keep from doing something; it is typically an act of self-discipline. Other people *restrain* you by stopping you from doing something, especially by using physical force {if you don't refrain from the disorderly conduct, the police will restrain you}. Yet it is possible to restrain oneself by controlling one's own emotions or behavior—and doing so is known as *self-restraint.*

refute, ***vb.*** To *refute* is to prove that a statement or an idea is wrong—not merely to deny or rebut.

regardless. See **irregardless.**

regrettable; regretful. What is *regrettable* is unfortunate or unpleasant enough to make one wish that things were otherwise. A person who is *regretful* feels sorry or disappointed about something done or lost. The adverb *regrettably*, not *regretfully*, is the synonym of *unfortunately*.

rein; reign. A *rein* (usually plural) controls a horse; it is the right word in idioms such as *take the reins*, *give free rein*, and, as a verb, *rein in*. A *reign* is a state of or term of dominion, especially that of a monarch but by extension also dominance in some field. This is the right word in idioms such as *reign of terror* and, as a verb, *reign supreme*.

relegate; delegate. To *relegate* is to assign a lesser position than before {the officer was relegated to desk duty pending an investigation}. To *delegate* is to authorize a subordinate to act in one's behalf {Congress delegated environmental regulation to the EPA} or to choose someone to do a particular job or to represent an organization or group {she was delegated to find a suitable hotel for the event}.

reluctant. See **reticent.**

renounce. See **denounce.**

reoccur. See **recur.**

repellent; repulsive. *Repellent* and *repulsive* both denote the character of driving others away. But *repulsive* has strong connotations of being so disgusting as to make one feel sick.

repetitive; repetitious. Both mean "occurring over and over." But whereas *re-*

petitive is fairly neutral in connotation, *repetitious* has taken on the nuance of tediousness that induces boredom.

repress. See **oppress.**

repulsive. See **repellent.**

restive; restful. *Restive* means "so dissatisfied or bored with a situation as to be impatient for change." *Restful* means "peaceful, quiet, and conducive to relaxation."

restrain. See **refrain.**

reticent. Avoid using this word as a synonym for *reluctant*. It means "unwilling to talk about what one feels or knows; taciturn" {when asked about the incident, the congressional representative became uncharacteristically reticent}.

revenge. See **avenge.**

rob; steal. Both verbs mean "to wrongfully take [something from another person]." But *rob* also includes a threat or act of harming, usually but not always to the person being robbed.

role; roll. A *role* is an acting part {the role of Hamlet} or the way in which someone or something is involved in an activity or situation, especially in reference to influence {the role that money plays as an incentive}. *Roll* has many meanings, including a roster {guest roll}; something made or done by rolling {roll of the dice}; and something in the shape of a cylinder or sphere, whether literally {dinner roll} or figuratively {bankroll}. *Roll* can also be a verb meaning to rotate {roll over!}, to wrap [something] {roll up the leftovers}, or to move forward {the cart rolled down the hill}.

run the gauntlet. See **gauntlet.**

sacrilegious. This is the correct spelling. There is a tendency by some to switch the *i* and *e* on either side of the *l*, but in fact the word is related to *sacrilege*, not *religion* or *religious*.

seasonal; seasonable. *Seasonal* means either "happening as expected or needed during a particular time of year" {snow skiing is a seasonal hobby} or "relating to the seasons or a season" {the seasonal aisle stays stocked most of the year, starting with Valentine's Day gifts in January}. *Seasonable* means "timely" {seasonable motions for continuance} or "fitting the time of year" {it was unseasonably cold for July}.

self-deprecating. See **deprecate.**

semi-. See **bi-.**

semiannual. See **biannual.**

sensor. See **censer.**

sensual; sensuous. What is *sensual* involves indulgence of the physical senses—especially sexual gratification. What is *sensuous* usually applies to aesthetic enjoyment; it is primarily hack writers who imbue the word with salacious connotations.

sewer; sewage; sewerage. *Sewer* denotes a wastewater pipe or passage. *Sewage* denotes the waste carried through such a pipe or passage. *Sewerage* denotes the sewer system as a whole, including treatment plants and other facilities, and the function of the disposal of sewage and wastewater in general.

shall. This word is complicated. The reality is that *shall* is little used in everyday contexts outside British English—not in North America but also not in Australia, Ireland, or Scotland. In legal contexts, it frequently appears in statutes, rules, and contracts, supposedly in a mandatory sense but actually quite ambiguously. It is perhaps the most widely litigated word in the law—with wildly varying results in its multifarious interpretations. Legal drafters are therefore often advised to avoid it altogether in favor of *must*, *is*, *will*, *may*, and other words or phrases among which *shall*'s various meanings can be allocated.[8] See also 5.131.

shear; sheer. *Shear* is the noun or verb relating to (1) the cutting tool or (2) a force affecting movement, such as a crosswind or the slipping of plates in an earthquake. *Sheer* is most often an adjective meaning (1) "semitransparent" {a sheer curtain}, (2) "nothing but" {sheer madness}, or (3) "almost vertical" {a sheer cliff}.

shine. When this verb is intransitive, it means "to give or make light"; the past tense is *shone* {the stars shone dimly}. When it is transitive, it means "to cause to shine"; the past tense is *shined* {the caterer shined the silver}.

should. See **ought.**

sight; site. A *sight* may be something worth seeing {the sights of London} or a device to aid the eye {the sight of a gun}, among other things. A *site* is a place, whether physical {a mall will be built on this site} or electronic {website}. The figurative expression meaning "to focus on a goal" is *to set one's sights*. Cf. **cite.**

simplistic. This word, meaning "oversimplified," has derogatory connotations. Don't confuse it with *simple*.

since. This word may relate either to time {since last winter} or to causation {since I'm a golfer, I know what "double bogey" means}. Some writers erroneously believe that the word relates exclusively to time. But the causal *since* was a part of the English language before Chaucer wrote in the fourteenth century, and it is useful as a slightly milder way of expressing causation than *because*. Still, if there is any possibility of confusion with the temporal sense, use *because*.

sink. Inflected *sink-sank-sunk*. Avoid using *sunk* as a simple past, as in *the ship sunk*.

site. See **cite; sight.**

slander. See **defamation.**

slew; slough; slue. As a noun, *slew* (/sloo/) is an informal word equivalent to *many* or *lots* {you have a slew of cattle}. It is sometimes misspelled *slough* (a legitimate noun meaning "a grimy swamp," pronounced either /sloo/ or

8. See Garner, *Legal Writing in Plain English*, 2nd ed. (Chicago: University of Chicago Press, 2013), 125–28; *Garner's Dictionary of Legal Usage*, 3rd ed. (New York: Oxford University Press, 2011), 952–55 (collecting many authorities).

/slow/). The phrase *slough of despond* (from Bunyan's *Pilgrim's Progress* [1678]) means "a state of depression or sadness from which one cannot easily lift oneself." This term is etymologically different from *slough* (/sləf/), meaning "to discard" {slough off dry skin}. As a present-tense verb, to *slew* is to turn or slide violently or suddenly in a different direction—or to make a vehicle do so {the car keeps slewing sideways}. In American English, a variant spelling of this verb is *slue*. As a past-tense verb, *slew* corresponds to the present-tense *slay* {Cain slew Abel}.

slow. This word, like *slowly*, may be an adverb. Generally, prefer *slowly* {go slowly}. But in colloquial usage *slow* is often used after the verb in a pithy statement, especially an injunction {go slow!} {take it slow}. See also 5.160.

slue. See **slew.**

sneak. This verb is conjugated as a regular verb: *sneak-sneaked-sneaked*. Reserve *snuck* for dialect and tongue-in-cheek usages.

space. As a figurative noun, this word has become a voguish equivalent of *area* {though not initially interested in journalism, he has decided to move into that space}. Although (or perhaps because) this usage is au courant, avoid it. See also **area.**

spit. If used to mean "to expectorate," the verb is inflected *spit-spat-spit* {he spat a curse} {he has spit many a curse}. But if used to mean "to skewer," it's *spit-spitted-spitted* {the hens have been spitted for broiling}.

stanch. See **staunch.**

stationary; stationery. *Stationary* describes a state of immobility or of staying in one place {if it's stationary, paint it}. *Stationery* denotes writing materials, especially paper for writing letters, usually with matching envelopes {love letters written on perfumed stationery}. To remember the two, try associating the *-er* in *stationery* with the *-er* in *paper*; or remember that a *stationer* is someone who sells the stuff.

staunch; stanch. *Staunch* is an adjective meaning "ardent and faithful" {a staunch Red Sox supporter}. *Stanch* is the American English verb meaning "to stop the flow"; it is almost always used in regard to bleeding, literally or metaphorically {after New Hampshire the campaign hemorrhaged; only a big win in South Carolina could stanch the bleeding}. In British English, however, *staunching the flow* is the standard wording.

steal. See **rob.**

strait; straight. A *strait* (often pl.) is (1), literally, a narrow channel connecting two large bodies of water separated by two areas of land {Strait of Magellan} or (2), figuratively, a difficult position {dire straits}. This is the word used in compound terms with the sense of constriction {straitlaced} {straitjacket}. *Straight* is most often an adjective meaning unbent, steady, sober, candid, honest, or heterosexual.

strata, ***n.*** This is the plural for *stratum*. Keep it plural {Fussell identified nine discrete strata in American society}. Avoid the double plural *stratas*.

strategy; tactics. A *strategy* is a long-term plan for achieving a goal. A *tactic* is a shorter-term method for achieving an immediate but limited success. A strategy might involve several tactics. By the way, although *strategy* is so spelled, *stratagem* has an *a* in the middle syllable.

subject. See **citizen.**

subsequent. See **consequent.**

such. This word, when used to replace *this* or *that*—as in "such building was later condemned"—is symptomatic of legalese. *Such* is actually no more precise than *the*, *this*, *that*, *these*, or *those*. It's perfectly acceptable, however, to use *such* with a mass noun or plural noun when the meaning is "of that type" or "of this kind" {such impudence galled the rest of the family} {such vitriolic exchanges became commonplace in the following years}. See also **as such.**

sufficient. See **adequate.**

supersede. The root of this word derives from *sedeo*, the Latin word for "to sit, to be established," not *cedo*, meaning "to yield." Hence the spelling varies from the root in words such as *concede*, *recede*, and *secede*. Avoid the variant *supercede*.

sympathy. See **empathy.**

systematic; systemic. *Systematic* means "according to a plan or system, organized methodically, or arranged in a system." *Systemic*, meaning "affecting the whole of something," is limited in use to physiological systems {a systemic disease affecting several organs} or, by extension, other systems that may be likened to the body {systemic problems within the corporate hierarchy}.

tactics. See **strategy.**

take. See **bring.**

tantalizing; titillating. A *tantalizing* thing torments us because we want it badly yet it is always just out of reach. A *titillating* thing tickles us pleasantly, literally or figuratively, and the word often carries sexual connotations.

text, ***vb.*** Inflected *text-texted-texted*, as a regular verb. Avoid using the uninflected *text* for the past-tense forms.

that; which. These are both relative pronouns (see 5.56–66). In polished American prose, *that* is used restrictively to narrow a category or identify a particular item being talked about {any building that is taller must be outside the state}; *which* is used nonrestrictively—not to narrow a class or identify a particular item but to add something about an item already identified {alongside the officer trotted a toy poodle, which is hardly a typical police dog}. *Which* is best used restrictively only when it is preceded by a preposition {the situation in which we find ourselves}. Nonrestrictively, it is almost always preceded by a comma, a parenthesis, or a dash. (In British English, writers and editors seldom observe the distinction between the two words.) Is it a useful distinction? Yes. The language inarguably benefits from having a terminological as well as a punctuational means of telling a restrictive from a nonrestrictive relative pronoun, punctuation often being ill-heeded. Is it acceptable to use *that* in reference to people? Is *friends that arrive early* an acceptable alternative to *friends who arrive early*? The answer is yes. *Person that* has long been considered good idiomatic English. Even so, *person who* is nearly three times as common as *person that* in edited English. See also 6.27.

there; their; they're. *There* denotes a place or direction {stay there}. *Their* is the possessive pronoun {all their good wishes}. *They're* is a contraction of *they are* {they're calling now}.

therefore; therefor. The words have different senses. *Therefore*, the common word, means "as a result; for that reason" {the evidence of guilt was slight; therefore, the jury acquitted the defendant}. *Therefor*, a legalism, means "for it" or "for them" {he took the unworn shirt back to the store and received a refund therefor}.

thus. This is the adverb—not *thusly*. Use *thus* (it's called a *flat adverb*). See 5.160.

till. This is a perfectly good preposition and conjunction {open till 10 p.m.}. It is not a contraction of *until* and should not be written *'til*.

timbre; timber. *Timbre* is a musical term meaning "tonal quality of the sound made by a particular musical instrument or voice." *Timber* is the correct spelling in all other uses, which relate to trees or wood.

titillating. See **tantalizing**.

tolerance; toleration. *Tolerance* is the habitual quality of being *tolerant*—that is, willing to allow people to say, believe, or do what they want without criticism or punishment. *Toleration* is a particular instance of being *tolerant*.

torpid. See **turbid**.

tortious; tortuous; torturous. What is *tortious* relates to torts (civil wrongs) or to acts that give rise to legal claims for torts {tortious interference with a contract}. What is *tortuous* is full of twists and turns and therefore makes travel difficult {a tortuous path through the woods}. What is *torturous* involves severe physical and mental suffering {a torturous exam}.

toward; towards. The preferred form in American English is *toward*: this has been so since about 1900. In British English, *towards* predominates. The same is true for other directional words, such as *upward*, *downward*, *forward*, and *backward*, as well as *afterward*. The use of *afterwards* and *backwards* as adverbs is neither rare nor incorrect (and is preferred in British English). For the sake of consistency, many American editors prefer the shorter forms without the final *s*.

transcript; transcription. A *transcript* is either a written record, as of a trial or a radio program, or an official record of a student's classes and grades. *Transcription* is the act or process of creating a transcript.

transpire, ***vb.*** Although its traditional sense is "to come to be known" {it transpired that he had paid bribes}, *transpire* more commonly today means "happen" or "occur" {what transpired when I was away?}. In that newer sense, *transpire* still carries a vague odor of jargon and pretentiousness. But that is disappearing.

trillion. See **billion.**

triumphal; triumphant. Things are *triumphal* (done or made to celebrate a victory) {a triumphal arch}. But only people feel *triumphant* (displaying pleasure and pride as a result of a victory or success) {a triumphant Caesar returned to Rome}.

turbid; turgid; torpid. *Turbid* water or liquid is thick and opaque from churned-up mud or detritus {a turbid pond}; by extension, *turbid* means "unclear, confused, or disturbed" {a turbid argument}. *Turgid* means "swollen," and by extension "pompous and bombastic" {turgid prose}. *Torpid* means "idle, lazy, and sleepy" {a torpid economy}.

ultimate. See **penultimate.**

unexceptional; unexceptionable. The first means "not very good; no better than average." The second means "not open to objection."

uninterested. See **disinterested.**

unique. Reserve this word for the sense "one of a kind." Avoid it in the sense "special, unusual." Phrases such as *very unique, more unique, somewhat unique,* and so on—in which a degree is attributed to *unique*—aren't the best usage. See also 5.89.

unlawful; illegal; illicit; criminal. This list is in ascending order of negative connotation. An *unlawful* act may even be morally innocent (for example, letting a parking meter expire). But an *illegal* act is something that society formally condemns, and an *illicit* act calls to mind moral degeneracy {illicit drug use}. Unlike *criminal,* the first three terms can apply to civil wrongs.

unorganized. See **disorganized.**

unreadable. See **illegible.**

upon. See **on.**

upward(s). See **toward.**

use; utilize. *Use* is usually the best choice for simplicity. *Utilize* is most often an overblown alternative of *use,* but it is occasionally the better choice when the distinct sense is "to use to best effect" {how to utilize our staff most effectively}.

venal; venial. A person who is *venal* is mercenary or open to bribery—willing to use power and influence dishonestly in return for money {a venal government official}; a thing that is *venal* is purchasable {venal livestock}. A *venial* fault or sin is trivial enough to be pardonable or excusable {a venial offense} {a venial error}.

verbal; oral. If something is put into words, it is *verbal.* Technically, *verbal* covers both written and spoken utterance. If you wish to specify that something was conveyed through speech, use *oral.*

very. See **much.**

vocation. See **avocation.**

voluminous. See **compendious.**

waive; wave. To *waive* is to relinquish claim to or not to insist on enforcing. To *wave* is to move to and fro.

wangle. See **wrangle.**

whether. Generally, use *whether* alone—not with the words *or not* tacked on {they didn't know whether to go}. The *or not* is necessary only when you mean to convey the idea "regardless of whether" {we'll finish on time whether or not it rains}. On the distinction between *whether* and *if,* see **if.**

which. See **that.**

while. *While* may substitute for *although* or *whereas,* especially if a conversational tone is desired {while many readers may disagree, the scientific community has overwhelmingly adopted the conclusions here presented}. Yet because *while* can denote either time or contrast, the word is occasionally ambiguous; when a real ambiguity exists, *although* or *whereas* is the better choice.

who; whom. Here are the traditional rules: *who* is a nominative pronoun used as (1) the subject of a finite verb {it was Jim who bought the coffee today} or (2) a predicate nominative when it follows a linking verb {that's who}. *Whom* is an objective pronoun that may appear as (1) the object of a verb {I learned nothing about the man whom I saw} or (2) the object of a preposition {the woman to whom I owe my life}. Today there are two countervailing trends: first, there's a decided tendency to use *who* colloquially in most contexts; second, among those insecure about their grammar, there's a tendency to overcorrect oneself and use *whom* when *who* would be correct. Writers and editors of formal prose often resist the first of these; everyone should resist the second. See also 5.66.

whoever; whomever. Avoid the second unless you are certain of your grammar {give this book to whoever wants it} {I cook for whomever I love}. If you are uncertain why these examples are correct, use *anyone who* or (as in the second example) *anyone.*

who's; whose. The first is a contraction {who's on first?}, the second a possessive {whose life is it, anyway?}. Unlike *who* and *whom, whose* may refer to things as well as people {the Commerce Department, whose bailiwick includes intellectual property}. See 5.64.

workers' compensation. This is the preferred name for workplace accident-insurance plans, not *workmen's compensation.* Notice that *workers* is always plural. When used as a phrasal adjective, it is hyphenated {workers'-compensation system}.

wrack. See **rack.**

wrangle; wangle. To *wrangle* is to argue, especially angrily over a long period {still wrangling over their parents' estate}. To *wangle* is to get something or arrange for something to happen by cleverness, manipulation, or trickery {wangle a couple of last-minute tickets}.

wreak; reek. *Wreak* means (1) "to cause a great deal of harm or many problems" {to wreak havoc on the administration} or (2) "to punish someone in revenge" {to wreak vengeance on his erstwhile friends}. The past tense is *wreaked*, not *wrought*. (The latter is an archaic form of the past tense and past participle of *work*.) *Reek* can be a verb meaning "to stink" or a noun meaning "stench."

wrong; wrongful. These terms are not interchangeable. *Wrong* has two senses: (1) "immoral, unlawful" {it's wrong to bully smaller children} and (2) "improper, incorrect, unsatisfactory" {many of the math answers are wrong}. *Wrongful* likewise has two senses: (1) "unjust, unfair" {wrongful conduct} and (2) "unsanctioned by law; having no legal right" {it was a wrongful demand on the estate}.

yes. See **affirmative, in the.**

your; you're. *Your* is the possessive form of *you* {your class}. *You're* is the contraction for *you are* {you're welcome}.

Bias-Free Language

5.251 **Maintaining credibility.** Discussions of bias-free language—language that is neither sexist nor suggestive of other conscious or subconscious prejudices—have a way of descending quickly into politics. But there is a way to avoid the political quagmire: if we focus solely on maintaining credibility with a wide readership, the argument for eliminating bias from our writing becomes much simpler. Biased language that is not central to the meaning of the work distracts many readers and makes the work less credible to them. Few texts warrant a deliberate display of linguistic biases. Nor is it ideal, however, to call attention to a supposed absence of linguistic biases, since this will also distract readers and weaken credibility.

5.252 **Gender bias.** Consider the issue of gender-neutral language. On the one hand, many reasonable readers find it unacceptable to use the generic masculine pronoun (*he* in reference to no one in particular). On the other hand, it is unacceptable to many readers (often different readers) either to resort to nontraditional gimmicks to avoid the generic masculine (by using *he/she* or *s/he*, for example) or to use *they* as a kind of singular pronoun (but see 5.48). Either approach sacrifices credibility with some readers.

5.253 **Other biases.** The same is true of other types of biases, such as slighting allusions or stereotypes based on characteristics such as race, ethnicity, disability, religion, sexual orientation, transgender status, or birth or family status. Careful writers avoid language that reasonable readers might find offensive or distracting—unless the biased language is central to the meaning of the writing.

5.254 **Bias and the editor's responsibility.** A careful editor points out to authors any biased terms or approaches in the work (knowing, of course, that the bias may have been unintentional), suggests alternatives, and ensures that any biased language that is retained is retained by choice. Although some publishers prefer to avoid certain terms or specific usages in all cases, Chicago's editors do not maintain a list of words or usages considered unacceptable. Rather, they adhere to the reasoning presented here and apply it to individual cases. What you should strive for—if you want readers to focus on your ideas and not on the political subtext—is a style that doesn't even hint at the issue. So unless you're involved in a debate about, for example, sexism, you'll probably want a style, on the one hand, that no reasonable person could call sexist and, on the other hand, that never contorts language to be nonsexist.

5.255 **Techniques for achieving gender neutrality.** Achieving gender neutrality for generic references to people often involves rewording. Nine methods are suggested below because no single method will work for every writer or in every context. Choose the combination of methods that works best in the context you've created.

1. Omit the pronoun. Sometimes a personal pronoun is not really necessary. For instance, in *the programmer should update the records when data is transferred to her by the head office*, if there is only one programmer, the pronoun phrase *to her* can be omitted: *the programmer should update the records when data is transferred by the head office*. Note that the shorter sentence is tighter as well as gender-free.
2. Repeat the noun. If a noun and its pronoun are separated by many words, try repeating the noun. For instance, *a writer should be careful not to needlessly antagonize readers, because her credibility would otherwise suffer* becomes *a writer should be careful not to needlessly antagonize readers, because the writer's credibility would otherwise suffer*. Take care not to overuse this technique. Repeating a noun too frequently will irritate readers. If you have to repeat a noun more than twice in a sentence or repeat it too soon, you should probably rewrite the sentence.
3. Use a plural antecedent. By using a plural antecedent, you eliminate the need for a singular pronoun. For instance, *a contestant must conduct himself with dignity at all times* becomes *contestants must conduct themselves with dignity at all times*. The method may cause a slight change in connotation. In the example, a duty becomes a collective responsibility rather than an individual one.
4. Use an article instead of a pronoun. Try replacing the singular personal pronoun with a definite or indefinite article. Quite often you'll find that the effect on the sentence's meaning is negligible. For instance, *A student accused of cheating must actively waive his right to have his guidance counselor present*

becomes *A student accused of cheating must actively waive the right to have a guidance counselor present.*

5. Use the neutral singular pronoun *one*. Try replacing the gender-specific personal pronoun with the gender-neutral singular pronoun *one*. For instance, *an actor in New York is likely to earn more than he is in Paducah* becomes *an actor in New York is likely to earn more than one in Paducah.*
6. Use the relative pronoun *who*. This technique works best when it replaces a personal pronoun that follows *if*. It also requires revising the sentence slightly. For instance, *employers presume that if an applicant can't write well, he won't be a good employee* becomes *employers presume that an applicant who can't write well won't be a good employee.*
7. Use the imperative mood. The imperative eliminates the need for an explicit pronoun. Although its usefulness is limited in some types of writing, you may find that it avoids prolixity and more forcefully addresses the target audience. For instance, *a lifeguard must keep a close watch over children while he is monitoring the pool* becomes *keep a close watch over children while monitoring the pool.*
8. In moderation, use *he or she*. Although it is an easy fix, the phrase *he or she* should be used sparingly, preferably only when no other technique is satisfactory. For instance, *"abstractitis" is Ernest Gowers's term for writing that is so abstract and obtuse (hence abstruse) that the writer does not even know what he is trying to say* becomes *"abstractitis" is Ernest Gowers's term for writing that is so abstract and obtuse (hence abstruse) that the writer does not even know what he or she is trying to say.* If you find you need to repeat the pronouns in the same sentence, don't. Revise the sentence instead.
9. Revise the sentence. If no other technique produces a sentence that reads well, rewrite the sentence so that personal pronouns aren't needed. The amount of revision will vary. For instance, *if a boy or girl misbehaves, his or her privileges will be revoked* might become *if someone misbehaves, that person's privileges will be revoked.* And *a person who decides not to admit he lied will be considered honest until someone exposes his lie* might become *a person who denies lying will be considered honest until the lie is exposed.*

See also 5.256.

5.256 **Gender-neutral singular pronouns.** Traditionally, the only gender-neutral third-person singular personal pronoun in English is *it*, which doesn't refer to humans (with very limited exceptions). Clumsy artifices such as *s/he* and *(wo)man* or artificial genderless pronouns have been tried—for many years—with no success. They won't succeed. And those who use them invite credibility problems. Indefinite pronouns such as *anybody* and *someone* don't always satisfy the need for a gender-neutral alternative because they are traditionally regarded as singular antecedents that call for a third-person singular pronoun. Many people substitute the plural *they* and *their* for the singular *he* or *she*. *They* and *their* have become common in informal usage, but neither is considered fully acceptable in formal writing, though they are steadily gaining ground. For now, unless you are given guidelines to the contrary, be wary of using these forms in a singular sense. This advice, like the techniques for achieving gender neutrality discussed in 5.255, applies mainly to generic references, where the identity of the person is unknown or unimportant. For references to a specific person, the choice of pronoun may depend on the individual. Some people identify not with a gender-specific pronoun but instead with the pronoun *they* and its forms or some other gender-neutral singular pronoun; any such preference should generally be respected. See 5.48.

5.257 **Problematic gender-specific suffixes.** The trend in American English is toward eliminating sex-specific suffixes. Words with feminine suffixes such as *-ess* and *-ette* are easily replaced with the suffix-free forms, which are increasingly accepted as applying to both men and women. For example, *author* and *testator* are preferable to *authoress* and *testatrix*. Compounds with *-man* are more problematic. The word *person* rarely functions well in such a compound; *chairperson* and *anchorperson* sound more pompous and wooden than the simpler (and correct) *chair* or *anchor*. Unless a word is established (such as *salesperson*, which dates from 1901), don't automatically substitute *-person* for *-man*. English has many alternatives that are not necessarily newly coined, including *police officer* (first recorded in 1797), *firefighter* (1903), and *mail carrier* (1788).

5.258 **Necessary gender-specific language.** It isn't always necessary or desirable to use gender-neutral terms and phrasings. If you're writing about something that clearly concerns only one sex (e.g., *women's studies*; *men's golf championship*) or an inherently single-sex institution (e.g., a sorority; a Masonic lodge), trying to use gender-neutral language may lead to absurd prose {be solicitous of a pregnant daughter's comfort; he or she will need your support}.

5.259 **Sex-specific labels as adjectives.** When gender is relevant, it's acceptable to use the noun *woman* as a modifier {woman judge}. In recent decades, *woman* has been rapidly replacing *lady* in such constructions. The adjective *female* is also often used unobjectionably. In isolated contexts it may strike some readers as being dismissive or derogatory (perhaps because it's a biological term used for animals as well as humans), but when parallel references to both sexes are required, the adjectives *male* and *female* are typically the most serviceable choices {the police force has 834 male and 635 female officers}.

5.260 **Avoiding other biased language.** Comments that betray a writer's conscious or unconscious biases or ignorance may cause readers to lose respect for the writer and interpret the writer's words in ways that were never intended. In general, emphasize the person, not a characteristic. A characteristic is a label. It should preferably be used as an adjective, not as a noun. Instead of referring to someone as, for instance, *a Catholic* or *a deaf-mute*, put the person first by writing *a Catholic man* or *he is Catholic*, and *a deaf-and-mute child* or *the child is deaf and mute*. Avoid irrelevant references to personal characteristics such as sex, race, ethnicity, disability, age, religion, sexual orientation, transgender status, or social standing. Such pointless references may affect a reader's perception of you or the person you are writing about or both. They may also invoke a reader's biases and cloud your meaning. When it is important to mention a characteristic because it will help the reader develop a picture of the person you are writing about, use care. For instance, in the sentence *Shirley Chisholm was probably the finest African American woman member of the House of Representatives that New York has ever had*, the phrase *African American woman* may imply to some readers that Chisholm was a great representative "for a woman" but may be surpassed by many or all men, that she stands out only among African American members of Congress, or that it is unusual for a woman or an African American to hold high office. But in *Shirley Chisholm was the first African American woman to be elected to Congress and one of New York's all-time best representatives*, the purpose of the phrase *African American woman* is not likely to be misunderstood.

6 · Punctuation

Overview

6.1 **The role of punctuation and the scope of this chapter.** Punctuation should be governed by its function, which in ordinary text is to promote ease of reading by clarifying relationships within and between sentences. This function, although it allows for a degree of subjectivity, should in turn be governed by the consistent application of some basic principles lest the subjective element obscure meaning. The principles set forth in this chapter are based on a logical application of traditional practice in the United States. Some of the more significant exceptions have been noted where they apply. For the special requirements of languages other than English, mathematics, source citations (including bibliographies), indexes, and more, see the appropriate chapters in this manual or consult the index.

Punctuation in Relation to Surrounding Text

6.2 **Punctuation and italics.** All punctuation marks should appear in the same font—roman or italic—as the main or surrounding text, except for punctuation that belongs to a title in a different font (usually italics). So, for example, the word *and*, which in this sentence is in italics, is followed by a comma in roman type; the comma, strictly speaking, does not belong to *and*, which is italicized because it is a word used as a word (see 7.63). Depending on typeface, it may be difficult to tell whether a comma is in italics or not (to say nothing of periods); for other marks it will be more evident. Readers of this manual online may be able to view the source code for italic text, and all those who prepare manuscripts or publications in electronic formats will need to pay attention to this level of detail (see 2.80; see also 2.81–83). In the first four examples that follow, the punctuation marks next to italic text belong with the surrounding sentence and are therefore presented in roman. In the last two examples, the three punctuation marks that belong with the italic titles—the exclamation mark following "Help," the colon following "Sublime," and the comma following "Code"—are in italics (the comma following "Beauty" is in roman).

For light amusement he turns to the *Principia Mathematica*!

How can they be sure that the temperature was in fact *rising*?

The letters *a*, *b*, and *c* are often invoked as being fundamental.

There are two primary audiences for *The Chicago Manual of Style*: perfectionists and humorists.

but

The Beatles' *Help!* was released long before the heyday of the music video.

After reading *Geek Sublime: The Beauty of Code, the Code of Beauty*, she was inspired to write a program that generates poetry from prose.

For parentheses and brackets, see 6.5; for quotation marks, see 6.6. For a different approach, see 6.4.

6.3 **Punctuation and boldface or color.** The choice of boldface (or, by extension, type in a different color), unlike that of italics (see 6.2), is sometimes an aesthetic rather than a purely logical decision. Punctuation marks following boldface or color should be dealt with case by case, depending on how the boldface is used. In the first example, the period following "line spacing" belongs with the boldface glossary term and is therefore set in bold; the period following "leading" is part of the surrounding sentence and is therefore *not* set in bold. In the middle two examples, the punctuation next to the boldface terms belongs with them, like the first period in the first example. In the final example, the question mark belongs to the surrounding sentence and not to the boldface word (see 7.79).

line spacing. See **leading**.

Figure 6. Title page from an apocryphal *Second Poetics*.

For sale: a 2005 Subaru Legacy and two gently used sleeping bags.

Will the installation remain stalled until I choose **I accept**?

6.4 **Punctuation and font—aesthetic considerations.** According to a more traditional system, periods, commas, colons, and semicolons should appear in the same font as the word, letter, character, or symbol immediately preceding them if different from that of the main or surrounding text. In the third and fourth examples in 6.2, the commas following *a* and *b* and the colon following the title of this manual would be italic, as would the comma following the book title in the last example (i.e., after *Beauty*). A question mark or exclamation point, however, would appear in the same font as the immediately preceding word only if it belonged to that word, as in the title *Help!* in 6.2. This system, once preferred by Chicago and still preferred by some as more aesthetically pleasing, should be reserved—if it must be used—for publications destined for print only. In electronic publications, where typeface may be determined by content as well as appearance (e.g., a book title might be tagged as such, separate from any surrounding punctuation), the more logical system described in 6.2 should be preferred. See also 2.82, note 1.

6.5 **Parentheses and brackets in relation to surrounding text.** Parentheses and brackets should appear in the same font—roman or italic—as the surrounding text, not in that of the material they enclose. This system, though it may occasionally cause typefitting problems when a slanting italic letter touches a nonslanting roman parenthesis or bracket, has two main virtues: it is easy to use, and it has long been practiced. For printed works, a thin space or a hair space may need to be added between overlapping characters (see 6.120). For electronic works, where type display will vary depending on hardware and software, no such adjustments should normally be made.

> The Asian long-horned beetle (*Anoplophora glabripennis*) attacks maples.
> The letter stated that my check had been "recieved [*sic*] with thanks."

When a phrase in parentheses or brackets appears on a line by itself, however, the parentheses or brackets are usually in the same font as the phrase.

[continued on page 72]

6.6 **Quotation marks in relation to surrounding text.** Like parentheses and brackets (see 6.5), quotation marks should appear in the same font—roman or italic—as the surrounding text, which may or may not match that of the material they enclose. In the first two examples, the quotation marks are in roman; in the third example, they have been italicized as part of the italic title.

> The approach to the runway was, they reported, "*extremely dangerous*" (italics in original).
> "*Hamlet* and the Pre-Jazz Hipster Persona" is the fourth article in a series on literature and fashionable existentialism.
> I just finished reading *Sennacherib's "Palace without Rival" at Nineveh*, by John Malcolm Russell.

As with parentheses and brackets, when a sentence or phrase in quotation marks appears on a line by itself, the quotation marks are usually in the same font as the sentence or phrase. See also 13.62.

6.7 **Punctuation and space—one space or two?** In typeset matter, one space, not two, should be used between two sentences—whether the first ends in a period, a question mark, an exclamation point, or a closing quotation mark or parenthesis. By the same token, one space, not two, should follow a colon. When a particular design layout calls for more space between two elements—for example, between a figure number and a caption—the design should specify the exact amount of space (e.g., em space). See also 6.119–21.

6.8 **Punctuation with URLs and email addresses.** Sentences that include an email address or a uniform resource identifier such as a URL should be punctuated normally. Though angle brackets or other "wrappers" are standard in some applications, these are generally unnecessary in normal prose (see 6.104). Readers of print sources should assume that any punctuation at the end of an email address or URL belongs to the sentence. By the same logic, any hypertext markup for electronic formats should exclude the surrounding punctuation. For dividing an email address or a URL at the end of a line, see 7.46.

Chicago's online forum, which can be found at http://www.chicagomanualofstyle.org, continues to attract much constructive commentary.

Write to me at grammar88@parsed-out.edu.

Punctuation in Relation to Closing Quotation Marks

6.9 **Periods and commas in relation to closing quotation marks.** Periods and commas precede closing quotation marks, whether double or single. (An apostrophe at the end of a word should never be confused with a closing single quotation mark; see 6.118.) This is a traditional style, in use in the United States well before the first edition of this manual (1906). For an exception, see 7.79. See also table 6.1.

He described what he heard as a "short, sharp shock."

"Thus conscience does make cowards of us all," she replied.

TABLE 6.1. Punctuation relative to closing quotation marks and parentheses or brackets

Closing mark	Double or single quotation marks*	Parentheses or brackets†
Period	Inside	Inside or outside; see 6.13
Comma	Inside	Outside
Semicolon	Outside	Outside
Colon	Outside	Outside
Question mark or exclamation point	Inside or outside; see 6.10	Inside or outside; see 6.70, 6.74
Em dash	Inside or outside; see 6.87	Outside

*See also 6.9, 6.70, 6.74.

†See also 6.18, 6.98, 6.101, 6.103.

In an alternative system, sometimes called British style (as described in the *New Oxford Style Manual*; see bibliog. 1.1), single quotation marks are used, and only those punctuation points that appeared in the original material are included within the quotation marks; all others follow the closing quotation marks. (Exceptions to the rule are widespread: for example, periods are routinely placed inside any quotation that begins with a capital letter and forms a grammatically complete sentence.) Double quotation marks are reserved for quotations within quotations. This system or a variation (like the one prescribed by *Scientific Style and Format*, bibliog. 1.1) may be appropriate in works of textual criticism or in computer coding and other technical or scientific settings. See also 13.7–8, 13.30–31.

6.10 **Other punctuation in relation to closing quotation marks.** Colons and semicolons—unlike periods and commas—follow closing quotation marks; question marks and exclamation points follow closing quotation marks unless they belong within the quoted matter. (This rule applies the logic that is often absent from the traditional US style described in 6.9.) See also table 6.1.

Take, for example, the first line of "Filling Station": "Oh, but it is dirty!"
I can't believe you don't know "Filling Station"!
I was invited to recite the lyrics to "Sympathy for the Devil"; instead I read from the op-ed page of the *New York Times*.
Which of Shakespeare's characters said, "All the world's a stage"?
"Timber!"
"What's the rush?" she wondered.

6.11 **Single quotation marks next to double quotation marks.** When single quotation marks are nested within double quotation marks, and two of the marks appear next to each other, a space between the two marks, though not strictly required, aids legibility. For print publications, typesetters may place a thin space or a hair space between the two marks (as in the print edition of this manual). In electronic environments (including manuscripts submitted for publication), a nonbreaking space can be used (as in the online edition of this manual); such a space will prevent the second mark from becoming stranded at the beginning of a new line. See also 6.120, 13.30. In the example that follows, note that the period precedes the single quotation mark (see also 6.9).

"Admit it," she said. "You haven't read 'The Simple Art of Murder.' "

Periods

6.12 **Use of the period.** A period marks the end of a declarative or an imperative sentence. In some contexts, a period is referred to as a dot (as in a URL) or a point (as in decimals). In British usage, a period is called a full stop. Between sentences, it is followed by a single space (see 2.9, 6.7, 6.119). A period may also follow a word or phrase standing alone, as in the third example. For the many other uses of the period, consult the index.

The two faced each other in silence.
Wait here.
My answer? Never.

6.13 **Periods in relation to parentheses and brackets.** When an entire independent sentence is enclosed in parentheses or square brackets, the period belongs inside the closing parenthesis or bracket. When matter in parentheses or brackets, even a grammatically complete sentence, is included within another sentence, the period belongs outside (but see also 6.98). Avoid enclosing more than one complete sentence within another sentence. In the third example, two periods are required—one for the abbreviation *etc.* and one for the sentence as a whole, outside the parentheses (see also 6.14, 6.123). For periods relative to quotation marks, see 6.9.

Fiorelli insisted on rewriting the paragraph. (His newfound ability to type was both a blessing and a curse.)
Felipe had left an angry message for Isadora on the mantel (she noticed it while glancing in the mirror).
His chilly demeanor gave him an affinity for the noble gases (helium, neon, etc.).
There were many groundbreaking moments in *All in the Family*. (The one featuring "the kiss," with Sammy Davis Jr., springs to mind.)
"All the evidence pointed to the second location [the Lászlós' studio]."

6.14 **When to omit a period.** Unless it ends in an abbreviation or other expression that normally requires a period, no period should follow a display line (i.e., chapter title, subhead, or similar heading), a running head, a column head in a table, a phrase used as a caption (but see 3.21), a dateline in correspondence, a signature, or an address. (Likewise, a comma is sometimes omitted for aesthetic reasons at the end of a line set in display type; see 8.165.) A run-in subhead at the beginning of a paragraph, however, is followed by a period (see 1.56). When an expression that ends in a period (e.g., an abbreviation) falls at the end of a sentence, no additional period follows (see 6.123; but see 6.13). For use or omission of the period in lists and outline style, see 6.127–32. For punctuation with URLs and email addresses, see 6.8.

6.15 **Periods in ellipses.** An ellipsis—a series of three periods, or dots (sometimes referred to as suspension points)—may be used to indicate an omission in quoted material; for a full discussion of this use, see 13.50–58. An ellipsis may also be used to indicate faltering speech or an incomplete sentence or thought (see 13.41, 13.55). For the use of ellipses in languages other than English, see 11.19, 11.32, 11.49, 11.65, 11.102. For the use of the em dash to indicate a sudden break or interruption, see 6.87.

Commas

6.16 **Use of the comma.** The comma, aside from its technical uses in scientific, bibliographical, and other contexts, indicates the smallest break in sentence structure. It usually denotes a slight pause. In formal prose, however, logical considerations come first. Effective use of the comma involves good judgment, with the goal being ease of reading.

6.17 **Commas in pairs.** Whenever a comma is placed before an element to set it off from the surrounding text (such as "1920" or "Minnesota" in the first two examples below), a second comma is required if the phrase or sentence continues beyond the element being set off. This principle applies to many of the uses for commas described in this section. An exception is made for commas within the title of a work (third example); such commas are considered to be independent of the surrounding sentence.

August 18, 1920, was a good day for American women.
Sledding in Duluth, Minnesota, is facilitated by that city's hills and frigid winters.
but
Look Homeward, Angel was not the working title of Wolfe's manuscript.

6.18 **Commas relative to parentheses and brackets.** When the context calls for a comma at the end of material in parentheses or brackets, the comma should follow the closing parenthesis or bracket. A comma never precedes a closing parenthesis. (For its rare appearance before an opening parenthesis, see the examples in 6.129.) Rarely, a comma may appear inside and immediately before a closing bracket as part of an editorial interpolation (as in the last example; see also 13.59).

After several drummers had tried out for the part (the last having destroyed the kit), the band decided that a drum machine was their steadiest option.

Her delivery, especially when she would turn to address the audience (almost as if to spot a long-lost friend), was universally praised.

"Conrad told his assistant [Martin], who was clearly exhausted, to rest."

"The contents of the vault included fennel seeds, tweezers, [straight-edged razors,] and empty Coca-Cola cans."

Series and the Serial Comma

6.19 **Serial commas.** Items in a series are normally separated by commas (but see 6.60). When a conjunction joins the last two elements in a series of three or more, a comma—known as the serial or series comma or the Oxford comma—should appear before the conjunction. Chicago strongly recommends this widely practiced usage, blessed by Fowler and other authorities (see bibliog. 1.2), since it prevents ambiguity. If the last element consists of a pair joined by *and*, the pair should still be preceded by a serial comma and the first *and* (as in the last two examples below).

She posted pictures of her parents, the president, and the vice president.

Before heading out the door, he took note of the typical outlines of sweet gum, ginkgo, and elm leaves.

I want no ifs, ands, or buts.

Paul put the kettle on, Don fetched the teapot, and I made tea.

Their wartime rations included cabbage, turnips, and bread and butter.

Ahmed was configuring updates, Jean was installing new hardware, and Alan was running errands and furnishing food.

If the sentence continues beyond the series, add a comma only if one is required by the syntax of the surrounding sentence.

Apples, plums, and grapes can all be used to make wine.

but

Apples, plums, and grapes, available at most large grocery stores, can all be used to make wine.

In the rare case where the serial comma does not prevent ambiguity, it may be necessary to reword. In the following example, the repetition of *and* makes it clear that Lady Gaga is not the writer's mother (and see the examples at the end of this paragraph). In the second example, "Lady Gaga" might be read as an appositive (see 6.28).

I thanked my mother and Lady Gaga and Madonna.
not
I thanked my mother, Lady Gaga, and Madonna.

Note that the phrase *as well as* cannot substitute for *and* in a series of items.

The team fielded one Mazda, two Corvettes, and three Bugattis, as well as a battered Plymouth Belvedere.
not
The team fielded one Mazda, two Corvettes, three Bugattis, as well as a battered Plymouth Belvedere.

In a series whose elements are all joined by conjunctions, no commas are needed unless the elements are long and delimiters would be helpful.

Would you prefer Mendelssohn or Schumann or Liszt?
You can turn left at the second fountain and right when you reach the temple, or left at the third fountain and left again at the statue of Venus, or in whatever direction Google sends you.

6.20 **Commas with "etc." and "et al."** The abbreviation *etc.* (*et cetera*, literally "and others of the same kind") and such equivalents as *and so forth* and *and the like* are preceded by a comma; they are followed by a comma only if required by the surrounding text. This small departure from the recommendation in previous editions treats such terms as equivalent to the final element in a series (see 6.19). (According to a more traditional usage, such terms were often set off by two commas.) In formal prose, Chicago prefers to limit the abbreviation *etc.* to parentheses, notes, and tabular matter. See also 5.250 under *etc.*

The map was far from complete (lacking many of the streets, alleys, etc. seen in earlier iterations).
The philosopher's population studies, classic textbooks, stray notes, and so forth were found in the attic.
but
For a discussion or periods, commas, and the like, see chapter 6.

The abbreviation *et al.* (*et alia* [neut.], *et alii* [masc.], or *et aliae* [fem.], literally "and others"), whether used in regular text or (more often) in bibliographical references, should be treated like *etc.* If *et al.* follows a single item, however (e.g., "Jones et al."), it requires no preceding comma. (Nor is a preceding comma required in the rare case that *etc.* follows a single item.) Note that neither *etc.* nor *et al.* is italicized in normal prose (see the first example above).

6.21 **Omitting serial commas before ampersands.** When an ampersand is used instead of the word *and* (as in company names), the serial comma is omitted.

Winken, Blinken & Nod is a purveyor of nightwear.

See also 14.88, 14.135.

Commas with Independent Clauses

6.22 **Commas with independent clauses joined by coordinating conjunctions.** When independent clauses are joined by *and*, *but*, *or*, *so*, *yet*, or any other coordinating conjunction, a comma usually precedes the conjunction. If the clauses are very short and closely connected, the comma may be omitted (as in the last two examples) unless the clauses are part of a series. These recommendations apply equally to imperative sentences, in which the subject (*you*) is omitted but understood (as in the fifth and last examples). (For the use of a semicolon between independent clauses, see 6.56.)

We activated the alarm, but the intruder was already inside.
All watches display the time, and some of them do so accurately.
Do we want to foster creativity, or are we interested only in our intellectual property?
The bus never came, so we took a taxi.
Wait for me at the bottom of the hill on Buffalo Street, or walk up to Eddy Street and meet me next to the Yield sign.
Donald cooked, Sally poured the wine, and Maddie and Cammie offered hors d'oeuvres.
but
Electra played the guitar and Tambora sang.
Raise your right hand and repeat after me.

6.23 **Commas with compound predicates.** A comma is not normally used to separate a two-part compound predicate joined by a coordinating conjunction (cf. 6.22). (A compound predicate occurs when a subject that is shared by two or more clauses is not repeated after the first clause.) A comma may occasionally be needed, however, to prevent a misreading (as in the fourth example).

He printed out a week's worth of crossword puzzles and arranged them on his clipboard.
Kelleher tried to contact the mayor but was informed that she had stopped accepting unsolicited calls.
He stood up and opened his mouth but failed to remember his question.
but
She recognized the man who entered the room, and gasped.

When *then* is used as a shorthand for *and then*, a comma usually precedes the adverb. (See also 6.57.)

She filled in the last square in Sunday's puzzle, then yawned.
but
She filled in the last square in Sunday's puzzle and then yawned.

Compound predicates of three or more parts treated as a series are punctuated accordingly (see 6.19).

She scrubbed the floors, washed the dishes, and finished her essay on twenty-first-century labor-saving technologies.

Commas with Dependent Clauses

6.24 **Commas with introductory dependent clauses.** When a dependent clause precedes the main, independent clause, it should be followed by a comma. A dependent clause is generally introduced by a subordinating conjunction such as *if*, *because*, or *when* (see 5.200, 5.201).

If you accept our conditions, we shall agree to the proposal.
Until we have seen the light, we cannot guarantee a safe exit from the tunnel.
Whether you agree with her or not, she has a point.

Compare 6.25.

6.25 **Commas with dependent clauses following the main clause.** A dependent clause that follows a main, independent clause should *not* be preceded by a comma if it is restrictive—that is, essential to fully understanding the meaning of the main clause (see also 6.27). For instance, in the first example below, it is not necessarily true that "we will agree to the proposal"; the dependent *if* clause adds essential information.

We will agree to the proposal if you accept our conditions.
Paul sighed when he heard the news.
He wasn't running because he was afraid; he was running because he was late.

If the dependent clause is merely supplementary or parenthetical (i.e., nonrestrictive, or not essential to the meaning of the main clause), it should be preceded by a comma. Such distinctions are occasionally tenuous. In the fourth example below, the meaning—and whether the subject is running or not—depends almost entirely on the presence of the comma (compare with the third example above). If in doubt, rephrase.

I'd like the *tom yum*, if you don't mind.
At last she arrived, when the food was cold.
She has a point, whether you agree with her or not.
He wasn't running, because he was afraid of the dark.
or
Because he was afraid of the dark, he wasn't running.

Compare 6.24.

6.26 **Commas with intervening dependent clauses (two consecutive conjunctions).** When a dependent clause intervenes between two other clauses joined by a coordinating conjunction, causing the coordinating and subordinating conjunctions to appear next to each other (e.g., *and if*, *but if*), the conjunctions need not be separated by a comma. See also 6.22, 6.24.

Burton examined the documents for over an hour, and if Smedley had not intervened, the forgery would have been revealed.
She claimed to have seen the whole film, but when we pressed her for details, she failed to recall the name of Rhett and Scarlett's only child.

By a similar logic, when a dependent clause intervenes between an independent clause and a dependent clause introduced by a subordinating conjunction, no comma is needed between the two subordinating conjunctions (e.g., *that if*).

They decided that if it rained, they would reschedule the game.

Strictly speaking, it would not be wrong to add a comma between the conjunctions in any of the examples above. Such usage, which would extend the logic of commas in pairs (see 6.17), may be preferred in certain cases for emphasis or clarity. See also 6.32.

Commas with Relative Clauses, Appositives, and Descriptive Phrases

6.27 **Commas with relative clauses—"that" versus "which."** A clause is said to be restrictive (or defining) if it provides information that is essential to understanding the intended meaning of the rest of the sentence. Restrictive relative clauses are usually introduced by *that* (or by *who/whom/whose*) and are never set off by commas from the rest of the sentence. The pronouns *that* and *who* or *whom* may occasionally be omitted (but need not be) if the sentence is just as clear without them, as in the second and fourth examples (before "I" [*that*] and "we" [*whom*], respectively).

The manuscript that the editors submitted to the publisher was well formatted.
The book I have just finished is due back tomorrow; the others can wait.
I prefer to share the road with drivers who focus on the road rather than on what they happen to be reading.
The drivers we hire to make deliveries must have good driving records.
The author whose work I admire the most is generally the one whose books I have most recently read.

A clause is said to be nonrestrictive (or nondefining or parenthetical) if it could be omitted without obscuring the identity of the noun to which it refers or otherwise changing the intended meaning of the rest of the sentence. Nonrestrictive relative clauses are usually introduced by *which* (or *who/whom/whose*) and are set off from the rest of the sentence by commas.

The final manuscript, which was well formatted, was submitted to the publisher on time.
Ulysses, which I finished early this morning, is due back on June 16.
I prefer to share the road with illiterate drivers, who are unlikely to read books while driving.
Boris Pasternak, whose most famous creation was a doctor, wrote what is probably the best novel about the Russian Revolution.

Although *which* can be substituted for *that* in a restrictive clause (a common practice in British English), many writers preserve the distinction between restrictive *that* (with no commas) and nonrestrictive *which* (with commas). See also 5.250 under *that; which.*

6.28 **Commas with appositives.** A word, abbreviation, phrase, or clause that is placed in apposition to a noun (i.e., providing an explanatory equivalent) is normally set off by commas if it is nonrestrictive—that is, if it can be omitted without obscuring the identity of the noun to which it refers.

K. Lester's only collection of poems, *An Apocryphal Miscellany*, first appeared as a series of mimeographs. (The collection has been identified as his only one; the title provides additional rather than essential information.)

This year's poet laureate, K. Lester, spoke first. (There is only one laureate this year.)

Ursula's husband, Jan, is also a writer. (Ursula has only one husband.)

Ursula's son, Clifford, had been a student of Norman Maclean's. (Ursula has only one son.)

If, however, the word or phrase is restrictive—that is, it provides (or may provide) essential information about the noun (or nouns) to which it refers—no commas should appear.

O'Neill's play *The Hairy Ape* was being revived. (O'Neill wrote a number of plays; the title identifies the one being revived.)

The renowned poet and historian K. Lester scheduled a six-city tour for April. (K. Lester is not the world's only renowned poet and historian.)

Caligula's sister Drusilla has been the subject of much speculation. (Caligula had three sisters.)

The playwright's son Julio was there. (Whether the playwright has sons in addition to Julio is not known.)

Though the possessive may be used with a restrictive appositive (e.g., Caligula's sister Drusilla's son), avoid such a construction with a nonrestrictive appositive. Instead, reword as needed.

The motorcycle belonging to Ursula's mother, Hulga, was a Harley.

not

Ursula's mother's, Hulga's, motorcycle was a Harley.

See also 5.23, 6.27.

6.29 **Commas with descriptive phrases.** A descriptive phrase that is restrictive—that is, essential to the meaning (and often the identity) of the noun it belongs to—should not be set off by commas. A nonrestrictive phrase, however, should be enclosed in commas (or, if at the end of a sentence, preceded by a comma). In the first example, the descriptive phrase ("with the guitar over her shoulder") is essential information that identifies which woman is the mother. In the second example, the identity of the person who turned to the drummer ("My mother") is clear; the fact that she has a guitar over her shoulder is not essential information. See also 6.27.

The woman with the guitar over her shoulder is my mother.
My mother, with her guitar over her shoulder, turned to the drummer and gave the signal to begin.

Commas with Participial and Adverbial Phrases

6.30 **Commas with participial phrases.** An introductory participial phrase is normally set off from the rest of the sentence by a comma.

Exhilarated by her morning workout, she headed for the ocean.
Having forgotten his lines, the actor was forced to ad-lib.

When such a phrase occurs in the middle of a sentence, it should be set off by commas unless it is used restrictively, providing essential information about the main clause (see also 6.29).

The actor, having forgotten his lines, was forced to ad-lib.
but
Actors forgetting their lines may be forced to ad-lib. (The phrase "forgetting their lines" specifies which actors may be forced to ad-lib.)

Likewise, a comma sets off such a phrase at the end of a sentence unless the phrase is used restrictively.

She headed for the ocean, exhilarated by her morning workout.
The actor was forced to ad-lib, having forgotten his lines.
but
She always headed for the ocean exhilarated by her morning workout. (It is *not* true that she always headed for the ocean; it *is* true that she always headed for the ocean in a state of exhilaration from her morning workout.)

A comma should *not* be used if the participial phrase modifies the subject of a sentence by means of a linking verb (see 5.101), even if the sentence is inverted.

Running along behind the wagon was the archduke himself!

6.31 **Commas with adverbial phrases.** Although an introductory adverbial phrase can usually be followed by a comma, it need not be unless misreading is likely. Shorter adverbial phrases are less likely to merit a comma than longer ones.

On the other hand, his vices could be considered virtues.
With three consecutive swings, Jackson made history.
In 1931 Henrietta turned fifty.
but
Before eating, the members of the committee met in the assembly room.
To Anthony, Blake remained an enigma.

When such a phrase occurs in the middle of a sentence, it is normally set off by commas (cf. 6.29).

Jackson, with three consecutive swings, made history.
His vices, on the other hand, could be considered virtues.

At the end of a sentence, a comma is necessary only when the phrase is used in a nonrestrictive sense, providing information that is not essential to the meaning of the rest of the sentence.

Jackson made history with three consecutive swings.
Henrietta turned fifty in 1931.
but
Henrietta turned fifty a decade later, in 1931.

A comma should *not* be used to set off an adverbial phrase that introduces an inverted sentence.

Before the footlights stood one of the most notorious rakes of the twenty-first century.

6.32 **Commas with a participial or adverbial phrase plus a conjunction.** When a participial or adverbial phrase immediately follows a coordinating conjunction, the use of commas depends on whether the conjunction joins two independent sentences. If the conjunction is simply a part of the predicate or joins a compound predicate, the first comma follows the conjunction (see also 6.23).

We were extremely tired and, in light of our binge the night before, anxious to go home.

The Packers trailed at halftime but, buoyed by Rodgers's arm, stormed back to win.

If the conjunction joins two independent clauses, however, the comma precedes the conjunction (see also 6.22).

We were elated, but realizing that the day was almost over, we decided to go to bed.

Strictly speaking, it would not be wrong to add a second comma after *but* in the last example. Such usage, which would extend the logic of commas in pairs (see 6.17), may be preferred in certain cases for emphasis or clarity. See also 6.26.

Commas with Introductory Words and Phrases

6.33 **Commas with introductory phrases.** Whether to use a comma to set off an introductory phrase can depend on the type of phrase, its relationship to the rest of the sentence, and its length. For participial phrases, see 6.30. For adverbial phrases, see 6.31. Some cases involving specific words are discussed below (6.34 and 6.35). For dependent clauses, see 6.24.

6.34 **Commas with an introductory "yes," "no," or the like.** A comma should follow an introductory *yes*, *no*, *OK*, *well*, and the like, except in certain instances more likely to be encountered in informal prose or dialogue.

Yes, it is true that 78 percent of the subjects ate 50 percent more than they reported.
No, neither scenario improved the subjects' accuracy.
OK, I'll try the quinoa.
Well then, we shall have to take a vote.
but
No you will not!

6.35 **Commas with an introductory "oh" or "ah."** A comma usually follows an exclamatory *oh* or *ah* unless it is followed by an exclamation mark (or a dash) or forms part of a phrase (e.g., "oh boy," "ah yes"). No comma follows a vocative *oh* or (mainly poetic and largely archaic) *O*. See also 7.31.

Oh, you're right!
Ah, here we are at last!
Oh no! Ah yes! Oh yeah?
My oh my!
Oh mighty king!
"O wild West Wind . . ."

Commas with Two or More Adjectives Preceding a Noun

6.36 **Commas with coordinate adjectives.** As a general rule, when a noun is preceded by two or more adjectives that could, without affecting the meaning, be joined by *and*, the adjectives are separated by commas. Such adjectives, which are called coordinate adjectives, can also usually be reversed in order and still make sense. If, on the other hand, the adjectives are not coordinate—that is, if one or more of the adjectives are essential to (i.e., form a unit with) the noun being modified—no commas are used. See also 5.91.

Shelly had proved a faithful, sincere friend. (Shelly's friendship has proved faithful *and* sincere.)

It is going to be a long, hot, exhausting summer. (The summer is going to be long *and* hot *and* exhausting.)

but

She has many faithful friends.

He has rejected traditional religious affiliations.

She opted for an inexpensive quartz watch.

6.37 **Commas with repeated adjectives.** When an adjective is repeated before a noun, a comma normally appears between the pair.

Many, many people have enjoyed the book.

Commas with Dates and Addresses

6.38 **Commas with dates.** In the month-day-year style of dates, commas must be used to set off the year—a traditional usage that not only applies the logic of commas in pairs (see 6.17) but also serves to separate the numerals for day and year. By a similar logic, when the day of the week is given, it is separated from the month and day by a comma. Commas are usually unnecessary, however, between the name for the day and the ordinal in references where the month is not expressed (see also 9.31). Commas are also unnecessary where month and year only are given, or where a named day (such as a holiday) is given with a year. For dates used adjectivally, see 5.83. See also 9.29–36.

The performance took place on February 2, 2006, at the State Theatre in Ithaca.

The hearing was scheduled for Friday, August 11, 2017.

Monday, May 5, was a holiday; Tuesday the sixth was not.

Her license expires sometime in April 2021.
On Thanksgiving Day 1998 they celebrated their seventy-fifth anniversary.

In the day-month-year system—useful in material that requires many full dates (and standard in British English)—no commas are needed to set off the year. For the year-month-day (ISO) date style, see 9.36.

The accused gradually came to accept the verdict. (See his journal entries of 6 October 2015 and 4 January 2017.)

6.39 **Commas with addresses.** Commas are used to set off the individual elements in addresses or place-names that are run in to the text (see also 6.17). In a mailing address, commas should be used sparingly, mainly to set off the separate lines of the address, but also to separate city and state or province (but not the postal code), apartment numbers, and the like. If in doubt about the accuracy of an address, consult the applicable postal service. (Preferred postal usage will be tailored for use on address labels and may consist of all capital letters and spare punctuation, a style that need not be emulated in regular text and related contexts.) For place-names used adjectivally, see 5.69.

A printout was sent to the author at 743 Olga Drive NE, Ashtabula, OH 44044, on May 2.
Queries can be sent to the author at 123 Main St., Apt. 10, Montreal, QC H3Z 2Y7.
Waukegan, Illinois, is not far from the Wisconsin border.
The plane landed in Kampala, Uganda, that evening.

Some institutional names include place-names set off by commas. When such a name appears in the middle of a clause, a second comma is required to set off the place-name. See also 6.81.

California State University, Northridge, has an enrollment of . . .
but
The University of Wisconsin–Madison has an enrollment of . . .

Commas with Quotations and Questions

6.40 **Commas with quotations.** An independent clause quoted in the form of dialogue or from text and introduced with *said*, *replied*, *asked*, *wrote*, and the like (including variations of such terms) is usually introduced with a comma (but see 6.65, 13.16). This traditional usage considers the grammar and syntax of the quoted material to be separate from the text that introduces it.

It was Thoreau who wrote, "One generation abandons the enterprises of another like stranded vessels."
She replied, "I hope you aren't referring to us."

Commas are required regardless of the position of the explanatory text relative to the quotation (but see 6.125).

"I hope," she replied, "you aren't referring to us."
"I hope you aren't referring to us," she replied.

If, however, such a quotation is introduced by *that*, *whether*, *if*, or a similar conjunction (see 5.200), no comma is normally needed.

Was it Stevenson who said that "the cruelest lies are often told in silence"?
He wondered whether "to think is to live."

For the location of a comma in relation to closing quotation marks, see 6.9. For quoted titles and expressions, see 6.41; for questions, see 6.42. For words such as *yes* and *no*, see 13.40. For a more detailed discussion and illustration of the use or omission of commas before and after quoted material, including dialogue, see 13.13–17, 13.50–58, and the examples throughout chapter 13.

6.41 **Commas with quoted or italicized titles and expressions.** Titles or expressions set off from the surrounding text with quotation marks or italics are usually treated like noun forms; commas are used or omitted as they would be with any other noun.

His favorite story in Joyce's *Dubliners* is "Counterparts."
She recites the poem "One Art" every night before bed.
Of her many favorites, "One Art" is the one she knows best.

A common mistake is to use a comma before a title or expression whenever it follows a noun that describes it (e.g., *story*, *novel*, or *poem*). In fact, the rule for appositives applies: the title or expression is set off by commas only if it is nonrestrictive—that is, if it can be omitted without obscuring the identity of the noun (i.e., *story*, *novel*, etc.) to which it refers (see 6.28). In the first example below, the quoted or italicized titles identify *which* poem by Bishop (she wrote many) and *which* novel by Weiner (she has published more than one); in the third example, the quoted words tell us *which* motto appears over the door. In the second and fourth examples, *which* story (the last one in the collection) and *which* proverb (Tom's favorite) have already been identified.

Elizabeth Bishop's poem "One Art" was featured in Jennifer Weiner's novel *In Her Shoes* and read by Cameron Diaz in the movie adaptation of the book.
In the collection's last story, "Negocios," Junot Díaz gives us a portrait of Papi.
The motto "All for one and one for all" appears over the door.
Tom's favorite proverb, "A rolling stone gathers no moss," proved wrong.

For quotations marks versus italics for the titles of works, see 8.163. See also 7.62.

6.42 **Commas with questions.** A direct question is sometimes included within a sentence but not enclosed in quotation marks. Such a question is usually introduced by a comma (unless it comes at the beginning of a sentence) and begins with a capital letter. This slight departure from earlier editions of the manual recognizes that such a question is analogous to (and can be treated like) a direct quotation (see 6.40; see also 6.65).

She wondered, What am I doing?
Legislators had to be asking themselves, Can the fund be used for the current emergency, or must it remain dedicated to its original purpose?

If the question ends before the end of the sentence, no comma is required after the question mark (see also 6.125).

What am I doing? she wondered.

If the result seems awkward, rephrase as an indirect question. An indirect question does not require a question mark, nor does it need to be set off with a comma. Indirect questions are never capitalized (except at the beginning of a sentence). See also 6.69.

She wondered what she was doing.
The question of how to tell her was on everyone's mind.
Ursula wondered why her watch had stopped ticking.
Where to find a reliable clock is the question of the hour.

Commas in Personal and Corporate Names

6.43 **Commas with "Jr.," "Sr.," and the like.** Commas are not required with *Jr.* and *Sr.*, and they are never used to set off *II*, *III*, and the like when these are used as part of a name. In an inverted name, however (as in an index; see 16.41), a comma is required before such an element, which comes last.

John Doe Sr. continues to cast a shadow over his son.
Jason Deer III has turned over stewardship of the family business to his cousin.
but
Doe, John, Sr.
Deer, Jason, III

If a comma is used to set off *Jr.* or *Sr.*, a second comma is normally required in the middle of a sentence (see 6.17); rephrase as needed to avoid the possessive.

the speech made by John Doe, Sr. (*not* John Doe, Sr.'s, speech)

6.44 **Commas with "Inc.," "Ltd.," and the like.** Commas are not required with *Inc.*, *Ltd.*, and such as part of a company's name. A particular company may use such commas in its corporate documentation; articles and books about such companies, however, should generally opt for a consistent style rather than make exceptions for particular cases.

QuartzMove Inc. was just one such company named in the suit.

If a comma is used to set off the abbreviation, a second comma is normally required in the middle of a sentence (see 6.17); rephrase as needed to avoid the possessive. See also 6.43.

Commas with Antithetical Elements

6.45 **Commas with "not" phrases.** When a phrase beginning with *not* is interjected in order to clarify a particular noun, commas should be used to set off the phrase. See also 6.46.

We hoped the mayor herself, not her assistant, would attend the meeting.
They want you, not him.

6.46 **Commas with "not . . . but," "not only . . . but also," and the like.** With an interjected phrase of the type *not . . . but* or *not only . . . but also*, commas are usually unnecessary.

Works of art are created not by inspiration but by persistence.
Being almost perfectly ambidextrous, she wore not one watch but two.
They marched to Washington not only armed with petitions and determined to get their senators' attention but also hoping to demonstrate their solidarity with one another.

If, however, such a phrase seems to require special emphasis or clarification (usually a matter of editorial judgment), commas may be used to set off the *not* phrase. Alternatively, a dash may be used in place of the first comma, in which case a second comma usually becomes unnecessary.

She was in the habit of placing her orders months ahead of the competition—not only as a matter of personal pride but also to bolster her credibility as an early adopter.

6.47 **Commas with "the more," "the less," and so on.** A comma is customarily used between clauses of *the more . . . the more* type. Shorter phrases of that type, however, rarely merit commas.

The more I discover about the workings of mechanical movements, the less I seem to care about the holy grail of perfectly accurate timekeeping.
but
The more the merrier.

Other Uses of the Comma

6.48 **Commas with parenthetical elements.** If only a slight break is intended, commas may be used to set off a parenthetical element inserted into a sentence as an explanation or comment. Such elements are occasionally awkward, especially if they are inserted between an adjective and the noun it modifies; in such cases, rewording may help.

All the test participants, in spite of our initial fears, recovered.
The Hooligan Report was, to say the least, a bombshell.
Most children fail to consider the history behind new technologies, if they think of it at all.
She was the fastest, not to mention the strongest, runner on her team.
or, better,
She was the fastest runner on her team, not to mention the strongest.

If a stronger break is needed or if there are commas within the parenthetical element, em dashes (6.85) or parentheses (6.95) should be used instead of commas.

6.49 **Commas with "however," "therefore," "indeed," and the like.** Commas—sometimes paired with semicolons (see 6.57)—are traditionally used to set off conjunctive adverbs such as *however*, *therefore*, and *indeed*. When the adverb is essential to the meaning of the clause, or if the emphasis is on the adverb itself, commas are usually unnecessary (as in the last two examples).

A truly efficient gasoline-powered engine remains, however, a pipe dream.
Indeed, not one test subject accurately predicted the amount of soup in the bowl.
but
If you cheat and are therefore disqualified, you may also risk losing your scholarship.
That was indeed the outcome of the study.

6.50 **Commas with "such as" and "including."** The principles delineated in 6.29 apply also to phrases introduced by *such as* or *including*. Nonrestrictive phrases introduced by these terms are set off by commas (because they are not essential to the meaning or identity of the noun they modify). When such phrases are restrictive (i.e., essential to the meaning or identity of the noun), commas are not used.

The entire band, including the matutinal lead singer, overslept the noon rehearsal.
Some words, such as *matutinal* and *onomatopoetic*, are best avoided in everyday speech.
but
Words such as *matutinal* and *onomatopoetic* are best avoided in everyday speech.

6.51 **Commas with "that is," "namely," "for example," and the like.** Expressions of the type *that is* are traditionally followed by a comma. They are best preceded by an em dash or a semicolon rather than a comma, or the entire phrase they introduce may be enclosed in parentheses or em dashes.

There are simple alternatives to the stigmatized plastic shopping bag—namely, reusable cloth bags and foldable carts.
The committee (that is, its more influential members) wanted to drop the matter.
Keesler managed to change the subject; that is, he introduced a tangential issue.
Bones from various small animals—for example, a squirrel, a cat, a pigeon, and a muskrat—were found in the doctor's cabinet.

When *or* is used in a sense analogous to *that is* (to mean "in other words"), the phrase it introduces is usually set off by commas.

The compass stand, or binnacle, must be situated within the helmsman's field of vision.

Note that in formal writing, Chicago prefers to confine the abbreviations *i.e.* ("that is") and *e.g.* ("for example") to parentheses or notes, where they are followed by a comma.

> The most noticeable difference between male and female ginkgo trees (i.e., the presence of berries in the latter) is also the species' most controversial feature.

6.52 **Commas with "too" and "either."** The adverbs *too* and *either* used in the sense of "also" generally need not be preceded by a comma.

> I had my cake and ate it too.
> Anders likes Beethoven; his sister does too.
> The airport lacked charging stations; there were no comfortable chairs either.

When *too* comes in the middle of the sentence or clause, however, a comma aids comprehension.

> She, too, decided against the early showing.

See also 6.31.

6.53 **Commas with direct address.** A comma is used to set off names or words used in direct address.

> Ms. Jones, please come in.
> James, your order is ready.
> Hello, Ms. Philips.
> Hi, Pratchi. Please sit down.
> Take that, you devil.
> Kiss me, you fool!
> Are you listening, class?
> It's time to go, Marta.
> I am not here, my friends, to discuss personalities.

In correspondence, a comma typically follows the greeting, though a colon may be used instead (especially in formal correspondence; see 6.66).

> Dear Lucien, . . .

If the greeting itself consists of a direct address, two marks of punctuation are needed (i.e., the comma in the direct address and the colon or comma following the greeting). (The first mark is often left out in casual correspondence.)

Greetings, Board Members: . . .
Hi, Karel, . . .

6.54 **Commas to indicate elision.** A comma is often used to indicate the omission of a word or words readily understood from the context.

In Illinois there are seventeen such schools; in Ohio, twenty; in Indiana, thirteen.
Thousands rushed to serve him in victory; in defeat, none.

The comma may be omitted if the elliptical construction is clear without it.

One student excels at composition, another at mathematics, and the third at sports.
Jasper missed her and she him.

6.55 **Commas between homonyms.** For ease of reading and subject to editorial discretion, two words that are spelled alike but have different functions may be separated by a comma if such clarification seems desirable.

Let us march in, in twos.
Whatever is, is good.
but
"It depends on what *means* means."

Semicolons

6.56 **Use of the semicolon.** In regular prose, a semicolon is most commonly used between two independent clauses not joined by a conjunction to signal a closer connection between them than a period would. (For the similar use of a colon, see 6.61.)

She spent much of her free time immersed in the ocean; no mere water-*resistant* watch would do.
Though a gifted writer, Miqueas has never bothered to master the semicolon; he insists that half a colon is no colon at all.

For the use of the semicolon in index entries, see 16.96, 16.17. For its use in parenthetical text citations, see 15.30. For its use with a second subtitle of a work, see 14.90.

6.57 **Semicolons with "however," "therefore," "indeed," and the like.** Certain adverbs, when they are used to join two independent clauses, should be preceded by a semicolon rather than a comma. These conjunctive adverbs include *however*, *thus*, *hence*, *indeed*, *accordingly*, *besides*, and *therefore* (see also 6.58). A comma usually follows the adverb but may be omitted if the sentence seems just as effective without it (see also 6.31).

The accuracy of Jesse's watch was never in question; besides, he was an expert at intuiting the time of day from the position of the sun and stars.
Kallista was determined not to miss anything on her voyage; accordingly, she made an appointment with her ophthalmologist.
The trumpet player developed a painful cold sore; therefore plans for a third show were scrapped.

The adverb *then* is often seen between independent clauses as shorthand for *and then*, preceded by a comma. This usage is perfectly acceptable, and it is more or less obligatory in the imperative (as in the first example below); some writers, however, may prefer to use a semicolon, which is strictly correct.

Touch and hold the icon, then drag it to the trash.
First we went out for shiitake burgers, then we enjoyed vegan sundaes.
or
First we went out for shiitake burgers; then we enjoyed vegan sundaes.
but
First we went out for shiitake burgers, and then we enjoyed vegan sundaes.

See also 6.22, 6.23.

6.58 **Semicolons with "that is," "for example," "namely," and the like.** A semicolon may be used before an expression such as *that is*, *for example*, or *namely* when it introduces an independent clause. For an example, see 6.51. See also 6.57.

6.59 **Semicolons before a conjunction.** Normally, an independent clause introduced by a coordinating conjunction is preceded by a comma (see 6.22). In formal prose, a semicolon may be used instead—either to effect a stronger separation between clauses or when the second independent clause has internal punctuation. Another option is to use a period instead of a semicolon; see 5.203.

Frobisher had always assured his grandson that the house would be his; yet there was no provision for this bequest in his will.
Garrett had insisted on remixing the track; but the engineer's demands for over-

time pay, together with the band's reluctance, persuaded him to accept the original mix.

or

Garrett had insisted on remixing the track. But the engineer's demands . . .

6.60 **Semicolons in a complex series.** When items in a series themselves contain internal punctuation, separating the items with semicolons can aid clarity. If ambiguity seems unlikely, commas may be used instead (see 6.19). See also 6.129. Note that when a sentence continues beyond a series (as in the third example), no additional semicolon is required.

The membership of the international commission was as follows: France, 4; Germany, 5; Great Britain, 1; Italy, 3; United States, 7.

The defendant, in an attempt to mitigate his sentence, pleaded that he had recently, on doctor's orders, gone off his medications; that his car—which, incidentally, he had won in the late 1970s on *Let's Make a Deal*—had spontaneously caught fire; and that he had not eaten for several days.

Marilynn, Sunita, and Jared, research assistants; Carlos, programming consultant; and Carol, audiovisual editor, provided support and prepared these materials for publication.

but

She decided to buy three watches—an atomic watch for travel within the United States, a solar-powered, water-resistant quartz for international travel, and an expensive self-winding model for special occasions.

Colons

6.61 **Use of the colon.** A colon introduces an element or a series of elements illustrating or amplifying what has preceded the colon. Between independent clauses it functions much like a semicolon (see 6.56), and in some cases either mark may work as well as the other; use a colon sparingly, however, and *only* to emphasize that the second clause illustrates or amplifies the first. (The colon usually conveys or reinforces the sense of "as follows"; see also 6.64.) The colon may sometimes be used instead of a period to introduce a series of related sentences (as in the third example below).

The watch came with a choice of three bands: stainless steel, plastic, or leather.

They even relied on a chronological analogy: just as the Year II had overshadowed 1789, so the October Revolution had eclipsed that of February.

Yolanda faced a conundrum: She could finish the soup, pretending not to care that what she had thought until a moment ago was a vegetable broth was in fact made from chicken. She could feign satiety and thank the host for a good meal. Or she could use this opportunity to assert her preference for a vegan diet.

For use of the em dash instead of a colon, see 6.85. For colons in ratios, see 9.58. For the use of colons with subtitles, see 14.89. For the use of colons in indexes, see 16.95. For other uses of the colon—in source citations, URLs, mathematical expressions, and other settings—consult the index or search the online edition of this manual.

6.62 **Space after colon.** In typeset matter, no more than one space should follow a colon. Further, in some settings—as in a source citation between a volume and page number with no intervening date or issue number (see 14.116, 14.177), a biblical citation (see 14.239), or a ratio (see 9.58)—*no* space should follow a colon. See also 6.7.

6.63 **Lowercase or capital letter after a colon.** When a colon is used within a sentence, as in the first two examples in 6.61, the first word following the colon is lowercased unless it is a proper noun. When a colon introduces two or more sentences (as in the third example in 6.61) or when it introduces speech in dialogue or a quotation or question (see 6.65), the first word following it is capitalized.

6.64 **Colons with "as follows" and other introductory phrases.** A colon is normally used after *as follows*, *the following*, and similar expressions. (For lists, see 6.127–32.)

The steps are as follows: first, make grooves for the seeds; second, sprinkle the seeds; third, push the earth back over the grooves; fourth, water generously.

Kenzie's results yield the following hypotheses: First, . . . Second, . . . Third, . . .

On the other hand, a colon is not normally used after *namely*, *for example*, and similar expressions; these are usually followed by a comma instead (see 6.51).

6.65 **Colons to introduce quotations or questions.** A colon is often used to introduce speech in dialogue.

Michael: The incident has already been reported.
Timothy: Then, sir, all is lost!

A colon may also be used to introduce a quotation or a direct but unquoted question, especially where the introduction constitutes a grammatically complete sentence.

The author begins by challenging nature itself: "The trees were tall, but I was taller."
The question occurred to her at once: What if I can't do this?

For quotations or questions introduced with *said*, *replied*, *asked*, *wrote*, and the like, where a comma is normally used (see 6.40, 6.42), a colon may be used occasionally for emphasis or to set up a block quotation. See also 13.13–17.

6.66 **Colons in formal communication.** At the beginning of a speech or a formal communication, a colon usually follows the identification of those addressed. For use of a comma in direct address, see 6.53.

Ladies and Gentlemen:
To Whom It May Concern:
Dear Credit and Collections Manager:

6.67 **Some common misuses of colons.** Many writers assume—wrongly—that a colon is always needed before a series or a list. In fact, if a colon intervenes in what would otherwise constitute a grammatical sentence—even if the introduction appears on a separate line, as in a list (see 6.127–32)—there is a good chance it is being used inappropriately. A colon, for example, should *not* be used before a series that serves as the object of a verb. When in doubt, apply this test: to merit a colon, the words that introduce a series or list must themselves constitute a grammatically complete sentence.

The menagerie included cats, pigeons, newts, and deer ticks.
not
The menagerie included: cats, pigeons, newts, and deer ticks.

An exception may be made when a word or phrase introduces a series or list and the verb is elided or otherwise understood. In such cases a colon is usually required.

Pros: accuracy and water resistance. Cons: cheap-looking exterior, . . . (The pros included accuracy and water resistance. Among its cons were a cheap-looking exterior, . . .)

Question Marks

6.68 **Use of the question mark.** The question mark, as its name suggests, is used to indicate a direct question. It may also be used to indicate editorial doubt or (occasionally) to express surprise, disbelief, or uncertainty at the end of a declarative or imperative sentence. See also 6.72, 6.122, 6.124, 14.132.

Who will represent the poor?
Thomas Kraftig (1610?–66) was the subject of the final essay.
This is your reply?

6.69 **Direct and indirect questions.** A question mark is used to mark the end of a direct but unquoted question within a sentence. This usage is no different from that of a directly quoted question (see 6.125). See also 6.42.

Is it worth the risk? he wondered.

An indirect question never takes a question mark.

He wondered whether it was worth the risk.
How the two could be reconciled was the question on everyone's mind.

When a question within a sentence consists of a single word, such as *who*, *when*, *how*, or *why*, a question mark may be omitted, and the word is sometimes italicized.

She asked herself why.
The question was no longer *how* but *when*.

A polite request disguised as a question does not always require a question mark. Such formulations can usually be reduced to the imperative.

Will the audience please rise.
Would you kindly respond by March 1.
or
Please respond by March 1.
but
Would you mind telling me your age?

6.70 **Question marks in relation to surrounding text and punctuation.** A question mark should be placed inside quotation marks, parentheses, or brackets only when it is part of (i.e., applies to) the quoted or parenthetical matter. See also 6.10, 6.125.

The ambassador asked, "Has the Marine Corps been alerted?"
"Is it worth the risk?" he asked.

Why was Farragut trembling when he said, "I'm here to open an inquiry"?
The man in the gray flannel suit (had we met before?) winked at me.
Why did she tell him only on the morning of his departure (March 18)?
"What do you suppose he had in mind," inquired Newman, "when he said, 'You are all greater fools than I thought'?"

Exclamation Points

6.71 **Use of the exclamation point.** An exclamation point (which should be used sparingly to be effective) marks an outcry or an emphatic or ironic comment. See also 6.122, 6.124.

Heads up!
According to one model, Miami will remain above sea level until at least 2100. We should all be so lucky!

6.72 **Exclamation rather than question.** A sentence in the form of a direct question may be marked as rhetorical by the use of an exclamation point in place of a question mark (see also 6.126).

How could you possibly believe that!
When will I ever learn!

6.73 **Exclamation point as editorial protest or amusement.** Writers and editors should be aware that an exclamation point added in brackets to quoted matter to indicate editorial protest or amusement risks being interpreted as contemptuous or arrogant. Unless such a sentiment is intended, this device should be avoided. Nor is it a substitute for the Latin expression *sic* (thus), which should be reserved to indicate an error in the source that might otherwise be taken as an error of transcription (see 13.61).

6.74 **Exclamation points in relation to surrounding punctuation.** An exclamation point should be placed inside quotation marks, parentheses, or brackets only when it is part of the quoted or parenthetical matter. See also 6.10, 6.125.

The performer walked off the stage amid cries of "Brava!"
She actually believes the seller's claim that the MP3 sounds "as good as the uncompressed original"!
Alex Ramirez (I could have had a stroke!) repeated the whole story.

Hyphens and Dashes

6.75 **Hyphens and dashes compared.** Hyphens and the various dashes all have their specific appearance (shown below) and uses (discussed in the following paragraphs). The hyphen, the en dash, and the em dash are the most commonly used. Though the differences can sometimes be subtle—especially in the case of an en dash versus a hyphen—correct use of the different types is a sign of editorial precision and care. See also 2.13, 2.14, 2.96.

hyphen -   en dash –   em dash —   2-em dash ⸺   3-em dash ———

Hyphens

6.76 **Hyphens in compound words.** The use of the hyphen in compound words and names and in word division is discussed in 5.92 and in chapter 7, especially 7.36–47 and 7.81–89. See also 6.80.

6.77 **Hyphens as separators.** A hyphen is used to separate numbers that are not inclusive, such as telephone numbers (see 9.57), social security numbers, and ISBNs. (For hyphens with dates, see 9.36.) It is also used to separate letters when a word is spelled out letter by letter, as in dialogue or in reference to American Sign Language (see 11.125–35).

1-800-621-2376
978-0-226-15906-5 (ISBN)
"My name is Phyllis; that's p-h-y-l-l-i-s."
A proficient signer can fingerspell C-O-L-O-R-A-D-O in less than two seconds.

For hyphens in URLs and email addresses, see 7.46.

En Dashes

6.78 **En dash as "to."** The principal use of the en dash is to connect numbers and, less often, words. With continuing numbers—such as dates, times, and page numbers—it signifies *up to and including* (or *through*). For the sake of parallel construction, the word *to* or *through* (or *until*), never the en dash, should be used if the word *from* precedes the first element in such a pair; similarly, *and* should be used if *between* precedes the first element.

The years 1993–2000 were heady ones for the computer literate.
For source citations and indexing, see chapters 14–16.
In Genesis 6:13–21 we find God's instructions to Noah.
Join us on Thursday, 11:30 a.m.–4:00 p.m., to celebrate the New Year.
I have blocked out December 2016–March 2017 to complete my manuscript.
Her articles appeared in *Postwar Journal* (3 November 1945–4 February 1946).
but
She was in college from 2012 to 2016 (*not* from 2012–16).
He usually naps between 11:30 a.m. and 1:30 p.m. (*not* between 11:30 a.m.–1:30 p.m.)

In other contexts, such as with scores and directions, the en dash signifies, more simply, *to*.

The London–Paris train leaves at two o'clock.
On November 20, 1966, Green Bay defeated Chicago, 13–6.
The legislature voted 101–13 to adopt the resolution.

For more on dates and times, see 9.29–36, 9.37–40. For more on number ranges, see 9.60–64. See also 6.107.

6.79 **En dash with an unfinished number range.** An en dash may be used to indicate a number range that is ongoing—for example, to indicate the dates of a serial publication or to give the birth date of a living person. No space intervenes between the en dash and any mark of punctuation that follows.

The History of Cartography (1987–) is a multivolume work published by Chicago.
Jack Stag (1950–) *or* Jack Stag (b. 1950)

6.80 **En dashes with compound adjectives.** The en dash can be used in place of a hyphen in a compound adjective when one of its elements consists of an open compound or when both elements consist of hyphenated compounds (see 7.82). Whereas a hyphen joins exactly two words, the en dash is intended to signal a link across more than two. Because this editorial nicety will almost certainly go unnoticed by the majority of readers, it should be used sparingly, when a more elegant solution is unavailable. As the first two examples illustrate, the distinction is most helpful with proper compounds, whose limits are made clear within the larger context by capitalization. The relationship in the third example depends to some small degree on an en dash that many readers will perceive as a hyphen connecting *music* and *influenced*. The relationships in the fourth example are less awkwardly conveyed with a comma.

the post–World War II years
Chuck Berry–style lyrics
country music–influenced lyrics (*or* lyrics influenced by country music)
a quasi-public–quasi-judicial body (*or, better,* a quasi-public, quasi-judicial body)

A single word or prefix should be joined to a hyphenated compound by another hyphen rather than an en dash; if the result is awkward, reword.

non-English-speaking peoples
a two-thirds-full cup (*or, better,* a cup that is two-thirds full)

An abbreviated compound is treated as a single word, so a hyphen, not an en dash, is used in such phrases as "US-Canadian relations" (Chicago's sense of the en dash does not extend to *between*).

6.81 **En dashes with campus locations.** Some universities that have more than one campus use an en dash to link the campus location to the name of the university. Usage varies widely; when in doubt, follow the stated preference of the institution. See also 6.39.

the University of Wisconsin–Madison
the University of Wisconsin–Milwaukee
but
the University of California, San Diego
the State University of New York at Buffalo
the University of Massachusetts Amherst; UMass Amherst

6.82 **En dashes and line breaks.** In printed publications, line breaks should generally be made after an en dash but not before, in the manner of hyphens. If possible, avoid carrying over a single character to the next line, as in a number range or score. In reflowable electronic formats, it is usually best to let the software determine such breaks. See also 7.36–47.

6.83 **En dash as em dash.** In British usage, an en dash (with space before and after) is usually preferred to the em dash as punctuation in running text, a practice that is followed by some non-British publications as well (see 6.85).

6.84 **En dash as minus sign.** The en dash is sometimes used as a minus sign, but minus signs and en dashes are distinct characters (defined by the Unicode standard as U+2212 and U+2013, respectively; see 11.2, 12.9). Both the characters themselves and the spacing around them may differ; moreover, substituting any character for another may hinder searches in electronic publications. Thus it is best to use the correct character, especially in mathematical copy.

Em Dashes

6.85 **Em dashes instead of commas, parentheses, or colons.** The em dash, often simply called the dash, is the most commonly used and most versatile of the dashes. (In British usage, spaced en dashes are used in place of em dashes; see 6.83.) Em dashes are used to set off an amplifying or explanatory element and in that sense can function as an alternative to parentheses (second and third examples), commas (fourth and fifth examples), or a colon (first example)—especially when an abrupt break in thought is called for.

It was a revival of the most potent image in modern democracy—the revolutionary idea.
The influence of three impressionists—Monet, Sisley, and Degas—is obvious in her work.
The chancellor—he had been awake half the night—came down in an angry mood.
She outlined the strategy—a strategy that would, she hoped, secure the peace.
My friends—that is, my former friends—ganged up on me.

To avoid confusion, the em dash should never be used within or immediately following another element set off by an em dash (or pair of em dashes). Use parentheses or commas instead.

The Whipplesworth conference—which had already been interrupted by three demonstrations (the last bordering on violence)—was adjourned promptly.
or
The Whipplesworth conference—which had already been interrupted by three demonstrations, the last bordering on violence—was adjourned promptly.

6.86 **Em dash between noun and pronoun.** An em dash is occasionally used to set off an introductory noun, or a series of nouns, from a pronoun that refers back to the noun or nouns and introduces the main clause.

Consensus—that was the will-o'-the-wisp he doggedly pursued.
Broken promises, petty rivalries, and false rumors—such were the obstacles she encountered.

6.87 **Em dashes for sudden breaks or interruptions.** An em dash or a pair of em dashes may indicate a sudden break in thought or sentence structure or an interruption in dialogue. (Where a faltering rather than sudden break is intended, an ellipsis may be used; see 6.15.)

> "Will he—can he—obtain the necessary signatures?" asked Mill.

> "Well, I don't know," I began tentatively. "I thought I might—"
> "Might what?" she demanded.

If the break belongs to the surrounding sentence rather than to the quoted material, the em dashes must appear outside the quotation marks.

> "Someday he's going to hit one of those long shots, and"—his voice turned huffy—"I won't be there to see it."

6.88 **Em dashes with "that is," "namely," "for example," and similar expressions.** An em dash may be used before expressions such as *that is* or *namely*. For examples, see 6.51; see also 6.58.

6.89 **Em dashes with other punctuation.** In modern usage, a question mark or an exclamation point—but never a comma, a colon, or a semicolon—may precede an em dash. A period may precede an em dash if it is part of an abbreviation (see also 14.51).

> Without further warning—but what could we have done to dissuade her?—she left the plant, determined to stop the union in its tracks.
> Only if—heaven forbid!—you lose your passport should you call home.
> No one—at least not before 11:42 p.m.—could have predicted the outcome.

If the context calls for an em dash where a comma would ordinarily separate a dependent clause from an independent clause, the comma is omitted. Likewise, if an em dash is used at the end of quoted material to indicate an interruption, the comma can be safely omitted before the words that identify the speaker (see also 6.125).

> Because the data had not been fully analyzed—let alone collated—the publication of the report was delayed.
> "I assure you, we shall never—" Sylvia began, but Mark cut her short.

6.90 **Em dashes and line breaks.** In printed publications, line breaks should generally be made after an em dash but not before, in the manner of hyphens. In the case of a closing quotation mark (or any other mark of punctuation) immediately following the dash, however, the quotation mark and dash must not be broken at the end of a line (see also 6.87,

6.89). In reflowable electronic formats, it is usually best to let the software determine such breaks. See also 7.36–47.

6.91 **Em dashes in lieu of quotation marks.** Em dashes are occasionally used instead of quotation marks to set off dialogue (à la writers in some European languages). Each speech starts a new paragraph. No space follows the dash.

—Will he obtain the necessary signatures?
—Of course he will!

6.92 **Em dashes in lists, indexes, and tables.** In informal settings, em dashes are sometimes used in the manner of bullet points in a vertical list (see 6.130). Such usage is best avoided in formal prose, though em dashes may sometimes be used in a similar manner to organize subentries in an index (see 16.27). In tables, an em dash may be used for an otherwise blank or empty data cell (see 3.67).

2-Em and 3-Em Dashes

6.93 **2-em dash.** A 2-em dash represents a missing word or part of a word, either omitted to disguise a name (or occasionally an expletive) or else missing from or illegible in quoted or reprinted material. When a whole word is missing, space appears on both sides of the dash. When only part of a word is missing, no space appears between the dash and the existing part (or parts) of the word; when the dash represents the end of a word, a space follows it (unless a period or other punctuation immediately follows). See also 7.66, 13.59.

"The region gives its ⸺ to the language spoken there."
Admiral N⸺ and Lady R⸺ were among the guests.
David H⸺h [Hirsch?] voted aye.

Although a 2-em dash sometimes represents material to be supplied, it should not be confused with a blank line to be filled in, which should normally appear as an underscore (e.g., ___).

6.94 **3-em dash.** In a bibliography, a 3-em dash followed by a period represents the same author(s) or editor(s) named in the preceding entry. Such usage, because it can obscure important information, is best applied by the publisher or manuscript editor rather than by the author. See also 14.67–71, 15.17–20.

Chaudhuri, Amit. *Odysseus Abroad*. New York: Alfred A. Knopf, 2015.
———. *A Strange and Sublime Address*. London: Minerva, 1992.

Parentheses

6.95 **Use of parentheses.** Parentheses—stronger than a comma and similar to the dash—are used to set off material from the surrounding text. Like dashes but unlike commas, parentheses can set off text that has no grammatical relationship to the rest of the sentence.

He suspected that the noble gases (helium, neon, etc.) could produce a similar effect.

Intelligence tests (e.g., the Stanford-Binet) are no longer widely used.

Our final sample (collected under difficult conditions) contained an impurity.

Wexford's analysis (see chapter 3) is more to the point.

Dichtung und Wahrheit (also known as *Wahrheit und Dichtung*) has been translated as *Poetry and Truth* (or, as at least one edition has it, *Truth and Fiction*).

The disagreement between Johns and Evans (its origins have been discussed elsewhere) ultimately destroyed the organization.

For the use of parentheses as delimiters for letters or numbers in a list or outline, see 6.129, 6.132. For parenthetical references to a list of works cited, see 15.21–31. For parenthetical references following quoted material, see 13.64–72. For parentheses in notes and bibliographies, see chapter 14. For parentheses in mathematics, see chapter 12, especially 12.26–35. For roman versus italic type, see 6.5.

6.96 **Parentheses for glosses or translations.** Parentheses are used to enclose glosses of unfamiliar terms or translations from other languages—or, if the term is given in English, to enclose the original word. In quoted matter, brackets should be used (see 6.99). See also 7.53, 11.9.

A drop folio (a page number printed at the foot of a page) is useful on the opening page of a chapter.

The term you should use for 1,000,000,000 is *mil millones* (billion), not *billón* (trillion).

German has two terms for eating—one for the way humans eat (*essen*) and another for the way animals eat (*fressen*).

6.97 **Parentheses within parentheses.** Although the use of parentheses within parentheses (usually for bibliographic purposes) is permitted in some publications—especially in law—Chicago prefers brackets within parentheses (see 6.101). (British style is to use parentheses within parentheses.) For parentheses in mathematics, see 12.26.

6.98 **Parentheses with other punctuation.** An opening parenthesis should be preceded by a comma or a semicolon only in an enumeration (see 6.129); a closing parenthesis should never be preceded by a comma, a semicolon, or a colon. A question mark, an exclamation point, and closing quotation marks precede a closing parenthesis if they belong to the parenthetical matter; they follow it if they belong to the surrounding sentence. A period precedes the closing parenthesis if the entire sentence is in parentheses; otherwise it follows. (Avoid enclosing more than one sentence within another sentence; see 6.13.) Parentheses may appear back to back (with a space in between) if they enclose entirely unrelated material; sometimes, however, such material can be enclosed in a single set of parentheses, usually separated by a semicolon. See also table 6.1. For parentheses in documentation, see chapters 14 and 15.

Having entered (on tiptoe), we sat down on the nearest seats we could find.

Come on in (quietly, please!) and take a seat.

If *parenthesis* is Greek for the act of inserting, is it redundant to insert something in parentheses (i.e., in English)?

On display were the watchmakers' five latest creations (all of which Shellahan coveted).

Five new watches were on display. (Shellahan fancied the battery-powered quartz model.)

Strabo is probably referring to instruction (διδασκαλία) (Jones et al. 2017).

Brackets and Braces

6.99 **Use of square brackets.** Square brackets (often simply called brackets) are used mainly to enclose material—usually added by someone other than the original writer—that does not form a part of the surrounding text. Specifically, in quoted matter, reprints, anthologies, and other non-original material, brackets enclose editorial interpolations, explanations, translations of terms from other languages, or corrections. Sometimes the bracketed material replaces rather than amplifies the original word or words. For brackets in mathematical copy, see 12.26. See also 13.59–63.

"They [the free-silver Democrats] asserted that the ratio could be maintained."

"Many CF [cystic fibrosis] patients have been helped by the new therapy."

Satire, Jebb tells us, "is the only [form] that has a continuous development." [This was written before the discovery of the Driscoll manuscript.—Ed.]

If quoted matter already includes brackets of its own, the editor should so state in the source citation (e.g., "brackets in the original"); see 13.62 for an analogous situation with italics.

6.100 **Square brackets in translated text.** In a translated work, square brackets are sometimes used to enclose a word or phrase in the original language. (Translators should use this device sparingly.) If quoted matter already includes brackets of its own, the editor should so state in a note or elsewhere (see also 6.99).

The differences between society [*Gesellschaft*] and community [*Gemeinschaft*] will now be analyzed.

6.101 **Square brackets for parentheses within parentheses.** Chicago prefers square brackets as parentheses within parentheses, usually for bibliographic purposes. For mathematical groupings, see 12.26.

(For further discussion see Richardson's excellent analysis [1999] and Danneberger's survey [2000].)

6.102 **Square brackets in phonetics.** Square brackets may be used to enclose a phonetic transcription.

The verb *entretenir* [ãtrətnir], like *keep*, is used in many idioms.

6.103 **Square brackets with other punctuation.** For brackets with other punctuation, most of the same principles apply as for parentheses (see 6.98). For their use in enclosing editorial interpolations, however, the appearance of other punctuation and its position relative to the brackets may depend on the source. In the first example, the comma after "Dear Jacob" is part of the missing greeting that the editor is interpolating. In most cases, however, material added in brackets should be treated as if it were in parentheses. See also 14.145.

The original letter, the transcription of which was incomplete, probably read as follows: "[Dear Jacob,] It's been seventy years since I last set eyes on you [. . .]"

The report was unambiguous: "The scholars fled Ithaca [New York] and drove south."

not

The report was unambiguous: "The scholars fled Ithaca[, New York,] and drove south."

6.104 **Angle brackets and braces.** The term *angle brackets* is used here to denote the mathematical symbols for less than (<) and greater than (>) paired to work as delimiters (<. . .>). (True mathematical angle brackets, ⟨ and ⟩, not readily available in most typefaces, are reserved for mathematical notation; see, for example, 12.55.) Angle brackets are most often used to enclose tags in XML and related markup languages (see 2.83). By extension, some manuscript editors opt for angle brackets—unlikely to appear elsewhere in a typical word-processed manuscript—to enclose generic instructions for typesetting (see 2.81). Although angle brackets are sometimes used to set off URLs and email addresses (e.g., in message headers in email applications), Chicago discourages this practice for regular prose. Angle brackets are also occasionally used instead of brackets in textual studies to indicate missing or illegible material (see 6.99). Braces, {}, also called curly brackets, provide yet another option for enclosing data and are used in various ways in certain programming languages. They are also used in mathematical and other specialized writing (see, e.g., 12.28). Braces are not interchangeable with parentheses or brackets. See the example phrases throughout chapter 5 for one possible use of braces.

Slashes

6.105 **Other names for the slash.** The slash (/)—also known as virgule, solidus, slant, or forward slash, to distinguish it from a backward slash, or backslash (\)—has various distinct uses. For a discussion of the niceties associated with the various terms, see Richard Eckersley et al., *Glossary of Typesetting Terms* (bibliog. 2.7).

6.106 **Slashes to signify alternatives.** A slash most commonly signifies alternatives. In certain contexts it is a convenient (if somewhat informal) shorthand for *or*. It is also used for alternative spellings or names. Where one or more of the terms separated by slashes is an open compound, a space before and after the slash can make the text more legible.

he/she	Hercules/Heracles
his/her	Margaret/Meg/Maggie
and/or	World War I / First World War

Occasionally a slash can include the sense of *and*—while still also conveying a sense of alternatives (but see 6.107). (Note that in most cases a hyphen is the better choice for *and*—e.g., "mother-daughter friendship.")

an insertion/deletion mutation (a mutation with insertions or deletions or both)
an MD/PhD program (a program that offers one or both of these degrees)
a Jekyll/Hyde personality (a personality that includes the two alternating traits)

6.107 **Slashes with two-year spans.** A slash is sometimes used in dates instead of an en dash (see 6.78), or even in combination with an en dash, to indicate the last part of one year and the first part of the next. See also 9.64.

The winter of 1966/67 was especially severe.
Enrollment has increased between 1998/99 and 2001/2.
The fiscal years 2005/6–2009/10 were encouraging in one or two respects.

6.108 **Slashes with dates.** Slashes (or periods or hyphens) are used informally in all-numeral dates (e.g., 3/10/02), but this device should be avoided in formal writing and wherever clarity is essential (in the United States the month usually comes first, but elsewhere it is more common for the day to come first). If an all-numeral format must be used, use the ISO standard date format (year, month, day, in the form YYYY-MM-DD; see 9.36).

6.109 **Slashes in abbreviations.** A slash may stand as shorthand for *per*, as in "110 km/sec," "$450/week," or, in certain abbreviations, in lieu of periods, as in "c/o" (in care of) or "n/a" (not applicable; see also 3.67).

6.110 **Slashes as fraction bars.** A slash can be used to mean "divided by" when a fraction bar is inappropriate or impractical. When available, single-glyph fractions may be used (e.g., ½ *rather than* 1/2). See also 12.45.

6.111 **Slashes to show line breaks in quoted poetry.** When two or more lines of poetry are quoted in regular text, slashes with space on each side are used to show line breaks. See also 13.29.

"Thou hast not missed one thought that could be fit, / And all that was improper dost omit."

6.112 **Slashes in URLs and other paths.** Slashes are used in URLs and other paths to separate directories and file names. Spaces are never used in such contexts. In typeset paths, a line break may occur before a slash but not between two slashes (see 7.46). Some operating systems use backward slashes (or backslashes, \) or colons rather than, or in addition to, slashes. See also 14.17.

http://www.chicagomanualofstyle.org/help.html

6.113 **Slashes and line breaks.** In printed publications, where slashes are used to signify alternative terms, a line break should be made after the slash, never before. If possible, avoid carrying over a single character to the next line, as in an expression signifying a two-year span. Fractions should not be broken at the end of a line. If a slash is used to show where a line break occurs in poetry, a break can be made either after or before the slash. For URLs, a line break should be made before the slash (see 7.46). In reflowable electronic formats, it is usually best to let the software decide such breaks.

Quotation Marks

6.114 **Quotation marks relative to other punctuation and text.** For the location of closing quotation marks in relation to other punctuation, see 6.9–11. For the use of quotation marks with a comma, see 6.40; with a colon, 6.65; with a question mark, 6.70; with an exclamation point, 6.74. For a full discussion of quotation marks with dialogue and quoted matter, see 13.9–10, 13.13–17, 13.30–38. For the use of quotation marks with single words or phrases to signal some special usage, see 7.57, 7.60, 7.63. For quotation marks in French, see 11.29, 11.30; in German, 11.41; in Italian, 11.47; in Spanish, 11.63. For quotation marks with titles of certain types of works, see the examples in chapter 8.

6.115 **"Smart" quotation marks.** Published works should use directional (or "smart") quotation marks, sometimes called typographer's or "curly" quotation marks. These marks, which are available in any modern word processor, generally match the surrounding typeface. For a variety of reasons, including the limitations of typewriter-based keyboards and of certain software programs, these marks are often rendered incorrectly. Care must be taken that the proper mark—left or right, as the case may be—has been used in each instance. All software includes a "default" quotation mark ("); in published prose this unidirectional mark, though far more portable than typographer's marks, signals a lack of typographical sophistication. Proper directional characters should also be used for single quotation marks (‘’). The hexadecimal code points for Unicode are as follows: left double quotation mark (“), U+201C; right double quotation mark (”), U+201D; left single quotation mark (‘), U+2018; right single quotation mark or apostrophe (’), U+2019 (see 11.2). See also 6.117.

Apostrophes

6.116 **Use of the apostrophe.** The apostrophe has three main uses: to indicate the possessive case, to stand in for missing letters or numerals, and—in rare instances—to form the plural of certain expressions. For more on the possessive case, see 7.16–29, 5.20. For contractions, see 7.30. For plurals, see 7.5–15—especially 7.15.

6.117 **"Smart" apostrophes.** Published works should use directional (or "smart") apostrophes. In most typefaces, this mark will appear as a raised (but not inverted) comma. The apostrophe is the same character as the right single quotation mark (defined for Unicode as U+2019; see 6.115). Owing to the limitations of conventional keyboards and many software programs, the apostrophe continues to be one of the most abused marks in punctuation. There are two common pitfalls: using the "default" unidirectional mark ('), on the one hand, and using the left single quotation mark, on the other. The latter usage in particular should always be construed as an error. Some software programs automatically turn a typed apostrophe at the beginning of a word into a left single quotation mark; authors and editors need to be vigilant in overriding such automation to produce the correct mark, and typesetters need to take care not to introduce errors of their own. (If necessary, consult your software's help documentation or special characters menu.)

We spent the ’90s (*not* ‘90s) in thrall to our gadgets.
Where’d you get ’em (*not* ‘em)?
I love rock ’n’ roll (*not* rock ‘n’ roll).

6.118 **Apostrophes relative to other punctuation.** An apostrophe (’) is considered part of the word (or number) in which it appears. An apostrophe should not be confused with a single closing quotation mark; when a word ends in an apostrophe, no period or comma should intervene between the word and the apostrophe.

The last car in the lot was the Smiths’.

Spaces

6.119 **Use of the space.** The spaces that occur in running text are not punctuation per se, but they play a similar if more fundamental role. The primary use of the space is as a separator—for example, between words and sentences (see 6.7) or between a numeral and a unit of measure (see 10.49). Spaces come in different widths (see 6.120), and nonbreaking spaces can be used to control breaks at the end of a line (see 6.121). For other uses of the space, consult the index.

6.120 **Spaces with different widths.** The regular type of space that is added to a line of text with the Space bar is the one used in almost all contexts (it is the space that occurs between the words and sentences in this paragraph and almost everywhere else in this manual). This type of space varies in width when a line is justified to the left and right margins. In addition, there are a number of spaces with fixed widths, based on the spaces that typesetters have been using for centuries. En spaces and em spaces are wider than the regular space and match the width of en dashes and em dashes in a particular font (see 6.75). Em spaces in particular are sometimes used as a design element, as between a figure number and caption (see 3.23). A thin space or a hair space may be used between contiguous single and double quotation marks (see 6.11). These fixed-width spaces are usually appropriate only in professionally typeset material intended for print or PDF. Though each is defined for Unicode (see 11.2), they may not be supported by a given device or application and should therefore be used with caution (if at all) in electronic publication formats (cf. 6.121). For tabs and indents, see 2.11.

6.121 **Nonbreaking spaces.** A regular nonbreaking space, readily available in word processors and page-layout programs, can be used to prevent certain elements that contain spaces from breaking over a line. These include the spaced ellipses preferred by Chicago (see 13.50) and numerals that use spaces rather than commas as separators (see 9.55, 9.56). Nonbreaking spaces can also be used to prevent a numeral from being separated from an abbreviated unit of measure (e.g., 11.5 km) or to prevent a break between initials in a name like E. B. White. The nonbreaking space is defined for Unicode (as the "no-break space," U+00A0; see also 11.2) and is widely supported in electronic publication formats. This space, like the Space bar space, varies in width when a line is justified to the left and right margins. Especially for printed formats, spaces of different fixed widths are sometimes used for specific contexts and defined not to break over the line (see 6.120).

Multiple Punctuation Marks

6.122 **Likely combinations for multiple punctuation marks.** The use of more than one mark of punctuation at the same location usually involves quotation marks, em dashes, parentheses, or brackets in combination with periods, commas, colons, semicolons, question marks, or exclamation points. For quotation marks see 6.9–11, 6.40, 6.65, 6.70, 6.74. For em dashes see 6.89, 6.94. For parentheses and brackets see 6.85, 6.97, 6.98, 6.101, 6.103, 6.129. For ellipses see 13.50–58. See also table 6.1.

6.123 **Abbreviation-ending periods with other punctuation.** When an abbreviation or other expression that ends with a period occurs at the end a sentence, no additional period follows (see 6.14). Of course, when any other mark of punctuation is needed immediately after the period, both the period and the additional mark appear (see also 6.9, 6.13).

The study was funded by Mulvehill & Co.
Johnson et al., in *How to Survive*, describe such an ordeal.

6.124 **Periods with question marks or exclamation points.** A period (aside from an abbreviating period; see 6.123) never accompanies a question mark or an exclamation point. The latter two marks, being stronger, take precedence over the period. This principle continues to apply when the question mark or exclamation point is part of the title of a work, as in the final example (cf. 6.125).

Their first question was a hard one: "Who is willing to trade oil for water?"
What did she mean when she said, "The foot now wears a different shoe"?
She owned two copies of *Will You Please Be Quiet, Please?*

6.125 **Commas with question marks or exclamation points.** When a question mark or exclamation point appears at the end of a quotation where a comma would normally appear, the comma is omitted (as in the first example below; see also 6.42). When, however, the title of a work ends in a question mark or exclamation point, a comma should also appear if the grammar of the sentence would normally call for one. This usage recognizes not only the syntactic independence of titles but also the potential for clearer sentence structure—especially apparent in the final example, where the comma after *Help!* separates it from the following title. (The occasional awkward result may require rewording.) Compare 6.124. See also 14.96.

"Are you a doctor?" asked Mahmoud.
but
"Are You a Doctor?," the fifth story in *Will You Please Be Quiet, Please?*, treats modern love.

All the band's soundtrack albums—*A Hard Day's Night*, *Help!*, *Yellow Submarine*, and *Magical Mystery Tour*—were popular.

6.126 **Question mark with exclamation point.** In the rare case of a question or exclamation ending with a title or quotation that ends in a question mark or exclamation point, include both marks only if they are different and the sentence punctuation seems essential.

Have you seen *Help!*?
Who shouted, "Long live the king!"?
I just love *Who's Afraid of Virginia Woolf?*!
but
Who starred opposite Richard Burton in *Who's Afraid of Virginia Woolf?*
Who wrote "Are You a Doctor?"
Where were you when you asked, "Why so blue?"

The question mark is sometimes used in combination with the exclamation point to express excitement or disbelief, a practice that is best avoided in formal prose; see also 6.72.

Lists and Outline Style

6.127 **Lists and outlines—general principles.** Items in a list should consist of parallel elements. Unless introductory numerals or letters serve a purpose—to indicate the order in which tasks should be done, to suggest chronology or relative importance among the items, to facilitate text references, or, in a run-in list, to clearly separate the items—they may be omitted. Where similar lists are fairly close together, consistent treatment is essential. Note that the advice in this section applies primarily to lists that occur in the text. For lists of illustrations and tables, see 1.39; for lists of abbreviations, see 1.44; for glossaries, see 1.61; for indexes, see chapter 16.

6.128 **Run-in versus vertical lists.** Lists may be either run in to the text or set vertically. Short, simple lists are usually better run in, especially if the introductory text and the items in the list together form a sentence (see 6.129). Lists that require typographic prominence, that are relatively long, or that contain multiple levels (see 6.132) should be set vertically.

6.129 **Run-in lists.** If numerals or letters are used to mark the divisions in a run-in list, enclose them in parentheses. If letters are used, they are sometimes italicized (within roman parentheses; see 6.5). If the introductory material forms a grammatically complete sentence, a colon should precede the first parenthesis (see also 6.61, 6.64, 6.67). The items are separated by commas unless any of the items requires internal commas, in which case all the items will usually need to be separated by semicolons (see 6.60). When each item in a list consists of a complete sentence or several sentences, the list is best set vertically (see 6.130).

The qualifications are as follows: a doctorate in physics, five years' experience in a national laboratory, and an ability to communicate technical matter to a lay audience.

Compose three sentences to illustrate analogous uses of (1) commas, (2) em dashes, and (3) parentheses.

For the duration of the experiment, the dieters were instructed to avoid (a) meat, (b) bottled drinks, (c) packaged foods, and (d) nicotine.

Data are available on three groups of counsel: (1) the public defender of Cook County, (2) the member attorneys of the Chicago Bar Association's Defense of Prisoners Committee, and (3) all other attorneys.

You are advised to pack the following items: (*a*) warm, sturdy outer clothing and enough underwear to last ten days; (*b*) two pairs of boots, two pairs of sneakers, and plenty of socks; and (*c*) three durable paperback novels.

6.130 **Vertical lists—capitalization, punctuation, and format.** A vertical list is best introduced by a grammatically complete sentence, followed by a colon (but see 6.131). There are two basic types of lists: (1) unordered, in which the items are introduced by a bullet or other such marker or by nothing at all, and (2) ordered, in which items are introduced by numbers or letters. If the list is unordered, and unless the items consist of complete sentences, each item carries no end punctuation and each can usually begin lowercase (except for proper nouns). For lists whose items require more prominence, capitalization may instead be preferred; choose one approach and follow it consistently. If items run over to one or more new lines, the runover lines are usually assigned a hanging indent (see 2.11). (An alternative to indenting runover lines is to insert extra space between the items.)

Your application must include the following documents:

a full résumé
three letters of recommendation
all your diplomas, from high school to graduate school
a brief essay indicating why you want the position and why you consider yourself qualified for it
two forms of identification

To avoid long, skinny lists, short items may be arranged in two or more columns.

An administrative facility can be judged by eight measures:

image	quality
security	functional organization
access	design efficiency
flexibility	environmental systems

Each of these measures is discussed below.

If the items are numbered (i.e., the list is ordered; see also 6.127), a period follows the numeral. It is customary to capitalize items in a numbered list even if the items do not consist of complete sentences (but see 6.131). Closing punctuation is used only if items consist of complete sentences. For the use of roman numerals and letters, see 6.132.

Compose three sentences:

1. To illustrate the use of commas in dates
2. To distinguish the use of semicolons from the use of periods
3. To illustrate the use of parentheses within dashes

In a numbered list, runover lines are aligned with the first word following the numeral; a tab usually separates the number from the text of the list (see also 2.21).

To change the date display from "31" to "1" on the day following the last day of a thirty-day month, the following steps are recommended:

1. Pull the stem out past the date-setting position to the time-setting position.
2. Make a mental note of the exact minute (but see step 4).
3. Turn the stem repeatedly in a clockwise direction through twenty-four hours.
4. If you are able to consult the correct time, adjust the minute hand accordingly and press the stem all the way in on the exact second. If you are not able to consult the correct time, settle on a minute or so past the time noted in step 2.

Bulleted lists are usually formatted in the same way as numbered lists.

Use the Control Panel to make changes to your computer:

- To uninstall or repair a program or to change how it runs, go to Programs, and then choose Programs and Features.
- To adjust the resolution displayed by your monitor, go to Appearance and Personalization, and then choose Display. (Lowering the resolution will increase the size of images on the screen.)

- To add a language other than English or to change handwriting options, go to Clock, Language, and Region, and then choose Language.

If none of the items in a bulleted list consist of complete sentences, however, each item can usually begin lowercase (except for proper nouns). For bulleted lists whose items require more prominence, capitalization may instead be preferred (as throughout this manual); choose one approach and follow it consistently.

The style sheet allows for two types of lists:
- ordered lists, marked with numbers or letters
- unordered lists, marked by bullets or other ornaments (or unmarked)

Sometimes list format may not be the best choice. For example, when items in a list consist of very long sentences, or of several sentences, and the list itself does not require typographic prominence, the items may be formatted like regular paragraphs of text, each paragraph beginning with a number (and formatted with a first-line paragraph indent) and punctuated as normal prose (see also 2.12).

6.131 **Vertical lists punctuated as a sentence.** If the items in a vertical list complete a sentence begun in the introductory text, semicolons or commas may be used between the items, and a period should follow the final item. (If the items include internal punctuation, semicolons are preferred; see also 6.60.) Each item begins with a lowercase letter, even if the list is a numbered list (cf. 6.130). A conjunction (*and* or *or*) before the final item is optional. Such lists, often better run in to the text, should be set vertically only if the context demands that they be highlighted.

Reporting for the Development Committee, Jobson reported that
1. a fundraising campaign director was being sought;
2. the salary for this director, about $175,000 a year, would be paid out of campaign funds; and
3. the fundraising campaign would be launched in the spring of 2017.

In the case of an unnumbered or bulleted list, the punctuation and capitalization would remain the same as in the example above.

6.132 **Vertical lists with multiple levels (outlines).** Where items in a numbered list are subdivided (i.e., into a multilevel list, also called an outline), both numerals and letters may be used. Any runover lines should be aligned with the first word following the numeral or letter; a tab usually separates the number or letter from the text of the list (see also 2.21).

Applicants will be tested for their skills in the following areas:

1. Punctuation
   a. Using commas appropriately
   b. Deleting unnecessary quotation marks
   c. Distinguishing colons from semicolons
2. Spelling
   a. Using a dictionary appropriately
   b. Recognizing homonyms
   c. Hyphenating correctly
3. Syntax
   a. Matching verb to subject
   b. Recognizing and eliminating misplaced modifiers
   c. Distinguishing phrases from clauses while singing the "Conjunction Junction" song

In the following example, note that the numerals and letters denoting the top three levels are set off by periods and those for the lower four by single or double parentheses, thus distinguishing all seven levels by punctuation as well as indentation. Note also that numerals of more than one digit are aligned vertically on the last digit.

I. Historical introduction
II. Dentition in various groups of vertebrates
    A. Reptilia
        1. Histology and development of reptilian teeth
        2. Survey of forms
    B. Mammalia
        1. Histology and development of mammalian teeth
        2. Survey of forms
            a) Primates
                (1) Lemuroidea
                (2) Anthropoidea
                    (a) Platyrrhini
                    (b) Catarrhini
                        i) Cercopithecidae
                        ii) Pongidae
            b) Carnivora
                (1) Creodonta
                (2) Fissipedia
                    (a) Ailuroidea
                    (b) Arctoidea
                (3) Pinnipedia
            c) Etc. . . .

In a list with fewer levels, one might dispense with capital roman numerals and capital letters and instead begin with arabic numerals. What is important is that readers see at a glance the level to which each item belongs. Note that each division and subdivision should normally contain at least two items.

7 · Spelling, Distinctive Treatment of Words, and Compounds

Overview

7.1 **Recommended dictionaries.** For general matters of spelling, Chicago recommends the dictionaries published by Merriam-Webster—specifically, *Webster's Third New International Dictionary* (or its ongoing online-only revision) and the latest edition of its chief abridgment, *Merriam-Webster's Collegiate Dictionary* (regularly updated online and referred to below as *Webster's*). If more than one spelling is given, or more than one form of the plural (see 7.6), Chicago normally opts for the first form listed (even for equal variants), thus aiding consistency. If, as occasionally happens, the *Collegiate* disagrees with the *Third International*, the *Collegiate* (or its online counterpart) should be followed, since it represents newer lexical research. For further definitions or alternative spellings, refer to another standard dictionary such as the *American Heritage Dictionary of the English Language*. At least for spelling, one source should be used consistently throughout a single work. (For full bibliographic information on these and other English dictionaries, including Canadian, British, and Australian references, see bibliog. 3.1.)

7.2 **Spellings peculiar to particular disciplines.** Where a variant spelling carries a special connotation within a discipline, the author's preference should be respected. For example, "archeology," though it is listed as an equal variant of "archaeology" in *Webster's*, is the spelling insisted on by certain specialists. In the absence of such a preference, Chicago prefers the first-listed "archaeology." (*Webster's* separates equal variants by *or*; secondary variants are preceded by *also*.)

7.3 **Non-US spelling.** In English-language works by non-US authors that are edited and produced in the United States, editors at Chicago generally change spelling used in other English-speaking countries to American spelling (e.g., *colour* to *color*, *analyse* to *analyze*). Since consistency is more easily maintained by this practice, few authors object. In quoted material, however, spelling is left unchanged (see 13.7).

7.4 **Supplementing the dictionary.** Much of this chapter is devoted to matters not easily found in most dictionaries: how to form the plural and possessive forms of certain nouns and compounds; how to break words at the end of a printed line, especially those that are not listed in the dictionary; when to use capitals, italics, or quotation marks for distinctive treatment of words and phrases; and, perhaps most important but placed at the end of the chapter for easy reference (7.89), when to use hyphens with compound words, prefixes, and suffixes.

Plurals

7.5 **Standard plural forms.** Most nouns form their plural by adding *s* or—if they end in *ch*, *j*, *s*, *sh*, *x*, or *z*—by adding *es*. Most English speakers will not need help with such plural forms as *thumbs*, *churches*, *fixes*, or *boys*, and these are not listed in standard dictionary entries, including those in *Webster's Collegiate*. (All inflected forms are listed in *Webster's Third New International*, and *Webster's* and other dictionaries published online generally accommodate the correct plural forms in their search engines.) Most dictionaries do, however, give plural forms for words ending in *y* that change to *ies* (*baby* etc.); for words ending in *o* (*ratio*, *potato*, etc.); for certain words of Latin or Greek origin such as *crocus*, *datum*, or *alumna*; and for all words with irregular plurals (*child*, *leaf*, etc.).

7.6 **Alternative plural forms.** Where *Webster's* gives two forms of the plural—whether as primary and secondary variants, like *zeros* and *zeroes*, or as equal variants, like *millennia* and *millenniums*—Chicago normally opts for the first. In some cases, however, different forms of the plural are used for different purposes. A book may have two *indexes* and a mathematical expression two *indices*, as indicated in the *Webster's* entry for *index*.

7.7 **Plurals of compound nouns.** *Webster's* gives the plural form of most compounds that are tricky (*fathers-in-law*, *coups d'état*, *courts-martial*, *chefs d'oeuvre*, etc.). For those not listed, common sense can usually provide the answer.

bachelors of science   masters of arts   spheres of influence   child laborers

7.8 **Plurals for centuries.** The plural is normally used to refer to more than one century with ordinals (or other modifiers) joined by *and*; the plural is also used for ranges expressed with *through*. For ranges expressed with *to* or for alternatives expressed with *or* or *nor*, use the singular. Also use the singular in compound modifiers (as in the last example; see also 7.88).

the eighteenth and early nineteenth centuries
in the fifth through eighth centuries
but
from the twentieth to the twenty-first century
as of the fifth or sixth century
eighteenth- and nineteenth-century technologies

7.9 **Plurals of proper nouns.** Names of persons and other capitalized nouns normally form the plural by adding *s* or *es*. Exceptions, including the last example, are generally listed in *Webster's* (see also 7.10).

Tom, Dick, and Harry; *pl.* Toms, Dicks, and Harrys
the Jones family, *pl.* the Joneses
the Martinez family, *pl.* the Martinezes
the Bruno family, *pl.* the Brunos
Sunday, *pl.* Sundays
Germany, *pl.* Germanys
Pakistani, *pl.* Pakistanis
but
Romany, *pl.* Romanies

An apostrophe is never used to form the plural of a family name: "The Jeffersons live here" (*not* "Jefferson's"). For the apostrophe in the possessive form of proper nouns, see 7.17.

7.10 **Plural form for Native American group names.** For the plurals of names of Native American groups, Chicago now defers to the first-listed form in *Webster's*, in the absence of any overriding preference of the author or publisher. For names not found there, check an up-to-date encyclopedia or other trusted resource or, unless the author or publisher has a preference, opt for consistency with other such names mentioned in the text. See also 7.2.

the Hopi of northeastern Arizona
the Iroquoian language spoken by the Cherokee
the languages of the Iroquois

7.11 **Singular form used for the plural.** Names ending in an unpronounced *s* or *x* are best left in the singular form.

the seventeen Louis of France
the two Dumas, father and son
two Charlevoix (*or, better,* two towns called Charlevoix)
The class included three Margaux (*but* two Felixes)

7.12 **Plural form of italicized words.** If an italicized term such as the title of a newspaper or book or a word used as a word must be written in the plural, the *s* is normally set in roman. A title already in plural form, however, may be left unchanged. In case of doubt, avoid the plural by rephrasing.

two *Chicago Tribune*s and three *Milwaukee Journal Sentinel*s
several *Madame Bovary*s (*or, better,* several copies of *Madame Bovary*)
too many *sic*s
but
four *New York Times*

The plural endings to italicized words in another language should also be set in italics.

Blume, Blumen	*cheval, chevaux*	*señor, señores*

7.13 **Plural form for words in quotation marks.** The plural of a word or phrase in quotation marks may be formed in the usual way (without an apostrophe). If the result is awkward, reword. Chicago discourages a plural ending following a closing quotation mark.

How many more "To be continueds" (*not* "To be continued"s) can we expect?
or, better,
How many more times can we expect to see "To be continued"?

7.14 **Plurals of noun coinages.** Words and hyphenated phrases that are not nouns but are used as nouns usually form the plural by adding *s* or *es*. (If in doubt, consult an unabridged dictionary like *Webster's Third New International*, which indicates the preferred inflected forms for most nouns, including all of the examples below.)

ifs and buts	thank-yous
dos and don'ts	maybes
threes and fours	yeses and nos

7.15 **Plurals for letters, abbreviations, and numerals.** Capital letters used as words, numerals used as nouns, and abbreviations usually form the plural by adding *s*. To aid comprehension, lowercase letters form the plural with an apostrophe and an *s* (compare "two *a*s in *llama*" with "two *a*'s in *llama*"). For some exceptions beyond those listed in the last three examples, see 10.42; see also 10.52 (for the International System). For the omission of periods in abbreviations like "BS," "MA," and "PhD," see 10.4. See also 7.63–69.

the three Rs	URLs	*but*
x's and *y*'s	BSs, MAs, PhDs	p. (page), pp. (pages)
the 1990s	vols.	n. (note), nn. (notes)
IRAs	eds.	MS (manuscript), MSS (manuscripts)

Possessives

The General Rule

7.16 **Possessive form of most nouns.** The possessive of most *singular* nouns is formed by adding an apostrophe and an *s*. The possessive of *plural* nouns (except for a few irregular plurals, like *children*, that do not end in *s*) is formed by adding an apostrophe only. For the few exceptions to these principles, see 7.20–22. See also 5.20.

the horse's mouth a bass's stripes puppies' paws children's literature
a herd of sheep's mysterious disappearance

7.17 **Possessive of proper nouns, abbreviations, and numbers.** The general rule stated at 7.16 extends to the possessives of proper nouns, including names ending in *s*, *x*, or *z*, in both their singular and plural forms, as well as abbreviations and numbers.

Singular forms

Kansas's legislature	Tacitus's *Histories*
Chicago's lakefront	Borges's library
Marx's theories	Dickens's novels
Jesus's adherents	Malraux's masterpiece
Berlioz's works	Josquin des Prez's motets

Plural forms

the Lincolns' marriage
the Williamses' new house
the Martinezes' daughter
dinner at the Browns' (*that is, at the Browns' place*)

Abbreviations and numbers

FDR's legacy Apollo 11's fiftieth anniversary
HP Inc.'s latest offerings

Avoid forming the possessive of an abbreviation that is followed by a spelled-out form in parentheses (or vice versa).

the long history of IBM (International Business Machines)
not
IBM's (International Business Machines') long history

7.18 **Possessive of words and names ending in unpronounced "s."** Words and names ending in an unpronounced *s* form the possessive in the usual way—with the addition of an apostrophe and an *s* (which, when such forms are spoken, is usually pronounced).

Descartes's three dreams
the marquis's mother
François's efforts to learn English
Vaucouleurs's assistance to Joan of Arc
Albert Camus's novels

7.19 **Possessive of names like "Euripides."** Classical proper names of two or more syllables that end in an *eez* sound form the possessive in the usual way (though when these forms are spoken, the additional *s* is generally not pronounced).

Euripides's tragedies the Ganges's source Xerxes's armies

Exceptions to the General Rule

7.20 **Possessive of nouns plural in form, singular in meaning.** When the singular form of a noun ending in *s* is the same as the plural (i.e., the plural is uninflected), the possessives of both are formed by the addition of an apostrophe only. If ambiguity threatens, use *of* to avoid the possessive.

politics' true meaning
economics' forerunners
this species' first record (*or, better,* the first record of this species)

The same rule applies when the name of a place or an organization or a publication (or the last element in the name) is a plural form ending in *s*, such as *the United States*, even though the entity is singular.

the United States' role in international law
Highland Hills' late mayor
Callaway Gardens' former curator
the National Academy of Sciences' new policy

7.21 **"For . . . sake" expressions.** For the sake of euphony, a few *for . . . sake* expressions used with a singular noun that ends in an *s* end in an apostrophe alone, omitting the additional *s*.

for goodness' sake   for righteousness' sake

Aside from these traditional formulations, however, the possessive in *for . . . sake* expressions may be formed in the normal way.

for expedience's sake
for appearance's sake (*or* for appearances' sake [plural possessive] *or* for the sake of appearance [*or* appearances])
for Jesus's sake

7.22 **An alternative practice for words ending in "s."** Some writers and publishers prefer the system, formerly more common, of simply omitting the possessive *s* on all words ending in *s*—hence "Dylan Thomas' poetry," "Etta James' singing," and "that business' main concern." Though easy to apply and economical, such usage disregards pronunciation in the majority of cases and is therefore not recommended by Chicago.

Particularities of the Possessive

7.23 **Joint versus separate possession.** Closely linked nouns are considered a single unit in forming the possessive when the thing being "possessed" is the same for both; only the second element takes the possessive form.

my aunt and uncle's house
Gilbert and Sullivan's *Iolanthe*
Minneapolis and Saint Paul's transportation system

When the things possessed are discrete, both nouns take the possessive form.

my aunt's and uncle's medical profiles
Dylan's and Jagger's hairlines
New York's and Chicago's transportation systems
Gilbert's or Sullivan's mustache

7.24 **Compound possessives.** In compound nouns and noun phrases, the final element usually takes the possessive form, even in the plural.

student assistants' time cards
my daughter-in-law's address
my sons-in-law's addresses

7.25 **Possessive to mean "of."** Analogous to possessives, and formed like them, are certain expressions that would otherwise include *of*. (Such usage is one of the genitive forms discussed in 5.20.) In the first example below, the literal meaning is "in three days of time." If the result seems ambiguous or awkward, reword.

in three days' time (*or* in three days)
an hour's delay (*or* a one-hour delay)
six months' leave of absence (*or* a six-month leave of absence)

7.26 **Double possessive.** According to a usage that is sometimes referred to as the double possessive or double genitive (see 5.21), a possessive form may be preceded by *of* where *one of several* is implied. Where the meaning is not literally possessive, however, the possessive form should not be used.

a friend of Dick's (*or* a friend of his)
but
a student of Kierkegaard

7.27 **Possessive versus attributive forms for groups.** Although terms denoting group ownership or participation sometimes appear without an apostrophe (i.e., as an attributive rather than a possessive noun), Chicago dispenses with the apostrophe only in proper names (often corporate names) that do not officially include one. In a few established cases, a singular noun can be used attributively; if in doubt, choose the plural possessive. (Irregular plurals such as *children* and *women* must always be in the possessive.)

children's rights (*or* child rights)
farmers' market
women's soccer team
boys' clubs
veterans' organizations
players' unions
taxpayers' associations (*or* taxpayer associations)
consumers' group (*or* consumer group)
but
Publishers Weekly
Diners Club
Department of Veterans Affairs

In some cases, the distinction between attributive and possessive is subtle. Of the following two examples, only the first connotes actual possession.

the Lakers' game plan (the team's game plan)
but
the Lakers game (the game featuring the team)

When in doubt, opt for the possessive.

7.28 **Possessive with gerund.** A noun followed by a gerund (see 5.112) may take the possessive form in some contexts. This practice, usually limited to proper names and personal nouns or pronouns, should be used with caution. For an excellent discussion, see "Possessive with Gerund," in *Fowler's Modern English Usage* (bibliog. 1.2). The possessive is most commonly used when the gerund rather than the noun that precedes it can be considered to be the subject of a clause, as in the first four examples below. In the fifth example, *Fathers* is clearly the subject of the sentence and *assuming* is a participle (verb form) rather than a gerund (noun form); the possessive would therefore be incorrect.

Fathers' assuming the care of children has changed the traditional household economy.
We all agreed that Jerod's running away from the tigers had been the right thing to do.
Our finding a solution depends on the nature of the problem.
Eleanor's revealing her secret (*or* Eleanor's revelation) resulted in a lawsuit.
but
Fathers assuming the care of children often need to consult mothers for advice.

When the noun or pronoun follows a preposition, the possessive is usually optional.

She was worried about her daughter (*or* daughter's) going there alone.
I won't stand for him (*or* his) being denigrated.
The problem of authors (*or* authors') finding the right publisher can be solved.

7.29 **Possessive with italicized or quoted terms.** As with plurals (see 7.12), when an italicized term appears in roman text, the apostrophe and *s* should be set in roman. When the last element is plural in form, add only an apostrophe, in roman (see 7.20). Chicago discourages, however, attempting to form the possessive of a term enclosed in quotation marks (a practice that is seen in some periodical publications where most titles are quoted rather than italicized).

the *Atlantic Monthly*'s editor
the *New York Times*' new fashion editor
Gone with the Wind's admirers
but
admirers of "Ode on a Grecian Urn"

Contractions and Interjections

7.30 **Contractions.** In contractions, an apostrophe normally replaces omitted letters. Some contractions, such as *won't* or *ain't*, are formed irregularly. Colloquialisms such as *gonna* or *wanna* take no apostrophe (there being no obvious place for one). *Webster's* lists many common contractions, along with alternative spellings and, where appropriate, plurals. Note that an apostrophe—the equivalent of a right single quotation mark (' *not* ')—is always used to form a contraction (see 6.117).

singin'   gov't   'tis (*not* 'tis)   dos and don'ts   rock 'n' roll

Contractions that end in a period (e.g., *Dr.*) are generally referred to as abbreviations (see 10.2).

7.31 **Interjections.** As with contractions, *Webster's* lists such interjections as *ugh*, *er*, *um*, and *sh*. For those not found in the dictionary—or where a different emphasis is required—plausible spellings should be sought in literature or invented.

atchoo!   shhh!

The interjection *oh* is not to be confused with the vocative *O* (largely obsolete), which is always capitalized; *oh* is capitalized only at the beginning of a sentence. See also 6.35.

Where, oh where, have you been?
Oh! It's you!
but
"Thine arm, O Lord, in days of old . . ."

"A" and "An"

7.32 **"A" and "an" before "h."** The indefinite article *a*, not *an*, is used in English before words beginning with a pronounced *h*. (British English differs from American English in not pronouncing the *h* is many cases; when in doubt, check a standard dictionary.) See also 5.74.

a hotel a historical study
but
an honor an heir

7.33 **"A" and "an" before abbreviations, symbols, and numerals.** Before an abbreviation, a symbol, or a numeral, the use of *a* or *an* depends on (or, conversely, determines) how the term is pronounced. In the first example below, "MS" would be pronounced *em ess*; in the second, it would be pronounced *manuscript*. In the last two examples, "007" would be pronounced *oh oh seven* and *double oh seven*, respectively.

an MS treatment (a treatment for multiple sclerosis)
a MS in the National Library
an NBC anchor
a CBS anchor
a URL
an @ sign
an 800 number
an 007 field (in a library catalog)
a 007-style agent

Ligatures

7.34 **When not to use ligatures.** The ligatures æ (*a* + *e*) and œ (*o* + *e*) should not be used in Latin or transliterated Greek words. Nor should they be used in words adopted into English from Latin, Greek, or French (and thus to be found in English dictionaries). Compare 7.35.

aesthetics
Encyclopaedia Britannica (contrary to corporate usage)
oedipal
a trompe l'oeil mural
a tray of hors d'oeuvres
Emily Dickinson's oeuvre

7.35 **When ligatures should be used.** The ligature æ (*a* + *e*) is needed for spelling Old English words in an Old English context. And the ligature œ (*o*

+ *e*) is needed for spelling French words in a French context. (See also 11.21.) Compare 7.34.

Ælfric   es hæl   le nœud gordien   *Œuvres complètes*

Word Division

7.36 **Dictionary word division.** The advice in this section applies only to published works and mainly to print or PDF (and not to reflowable electronic formats); word breaks should not be applied at the manuscript stage (see 2.13). For end-of-line word breaks, as for spelling and plural forms, Chicago turns to *Webster's* as its primary guide. The dots between syllables in *Webster's* indicate where breaks may be made; in words of three or more syllables, there is usually a choice of breaks. The paragraphs in this section are intended merely to supplement, not to replace, the dictionary's system of word division—for example, by suggesting preferred breaks where more than one might be possible. These recommendations are also intended to serve as a guide for determining appropriate hyphenation settings in page-layout applications. Most such programs automate hyphenation relative to a standard dictionary but allow users to define certain rules (e.g., to specify the minimum number of characters to carry to a new line or the maximum number of consecutive lines that can end in a hyphen) and to make exceptions (e.g., for specific words). For division of non-English words (other than those that are included in an English-language dictionary), see chapter 11. For end-of-line breaks relative to en and em dashes, see 6.82, 6.90; for slashes, see 6.113.

7.37 **Word divisions that should be avoided.** Single-syllable words, including verb forms such as *aimed* and *helped*, are never divided. Since at least two letters must appear before a break, such words as *again*, *enough*, and *unite* also cannot be divided. And at least three letters must appear after a break, so divisions that carry only two letters over to the next line, even where indicated by *Webster's*, are usually also avoided (but see 6.82, 6.113).

women (*rather than* wom-en)
losses (*rather than* loss-es)
sur-prises (*rather than* surpris-es)

In languages other than English, however, it may be not only permissible but customary to carry two-letter word endings to the next line (see, e.g., 11.33, 11.34, 11.42, 11.43, 11.50, 11.51, 11.66, 11.67).

7.38 **Dividing according to pronunciation.** In the usage preferred by Chicago and reflected in *Webster's*, most words are divided according to how the break will affect pronunciation rather than according to derivation.

knowl-edge (*not* know-ledge)
democ-racy *or* de-mocracy (*not* demo-cracy)

Special attention should be paid to breaks in certain words with multiple meanings and pronunciations, such as *proj-ect* (noun) and *pro-ject* (verb), which automatic hyphenation may not properly account for.

7.39 **Dividing after a vowel.** Unless a resulting break affects pronunciation, words are best divided after a vowel. When a vowel forms a syllable in the middle of a word, it should remain on the first line if possible. Diphthongs are treated as single vowels (e.g., the *eu* in *aneurysm*).

criti-cism (*rather than* crit-icism)
liga-ture (*rather than* lig-ature)
an-tipodes *or* antipo-des (*rather than* antip-odes)
aneu-rysm (*rather than* an-eurysm)

7.40 **Dividing compounds, prefixes, and suffixes.** Hyphenated or closed compounds and words with prefixes or suffixes are best divided at the natural breaks.

poverty- / stricken (*rather than* pov- / erty-stricken)
thanks-giving (*rather than* thanksgiv-ing)
dis-pleasure (*rather than* displea-sure)
re-inforce (*rather than* rein-force)

7.41 **Dividing words ending in "ing."** Most gerunds and present participles may be divided before the *ing*. When the final consonant before the *ing* is doubled, however, the break occurs between the consonants. For words ending in *ling*, check the dictionary.

certify-ing giv-ing dab-bing run-ning fiz-zling bris-tling

7.42 **Dividing proper nouns and personal names.** Proper nouns of more than one element, especially personal names, should be broken, if possible, between the elements rather than within any of the elements. If a break within a name is needed, consult the dictionary. Many proper nouns appear, with suggested divisions, in the listings of biographical and geographical names in *Webster's Collegiate*. For fuller treatment, consult the online revision of *Webster's Third New International* (bibliog. 3.1). Those that cannot be found in a dictionary should be broken (or left unbroken) according to the guidelines elsewhere in this section. If pronunciation is not known or easily guessed, the break should usually follow a vowel.

Alek-sis
Heitor Villa- / Lobos (*or, better,* Heitor / Villa-Lobos)
Ana-stasia

A personal name that includes initials should be broken after the initials. A break before a number or *Jr.* or *Sr.* should be avoided. A nonbreaking space can prevent such breaks (see 6.121).

Frederick L. / Anderson
M. F. K. / Fisher
Elizabeth II (*or, if necessary,* Eliza- / beth II)

7.43 **Dividing numerals.** Large numbers expressed as numerals are best left intact. To avoid a break, reword the sentence. If a break must be made, however, it should come only after a comma and never after a single digit. See also 12.23.

1,365,- / 000,000 *or* 1,365,000,- / 000

7.44 **Dividing numerals with abbreviated units of measure.** A numeral used with an abbreviated unit of measure is best left intact; either the numeral should be carried over to the next line or the abbreviation should be moved up. A nonbreaking space can prevent such breaks (see 6.121). (Numerals used with spelled-out units of measure, which tend to form longer expressions, may be broken across a line as needed.)

345 m   24 kg   55 BCE   6:35 p.m.

7.45 **Division in run-in lists.** A number or letter, such as (3) or (c), used in a run-in list (see 6.129) should not be separated from the beginning of what follows it. If it occurs at the end of a line, it should be carried over to the next line. A nonbreaking space can prevent such breaks (see 6.121).

7.46 **Dividing URLs and email addresses.** In printed works, it is often necessary to break an email address or a uniform resource identifier such as a URL at the end of a line. Such a break should be made between elements if at all possible: *after* a colon or a double slash; *before or after* an equals sign or an ampersand; or *before* a single slash, a period, or any other punctuation or symbol. To avoid confusion, an address that contains a hyphen should be broken before the hyphen rather than after (so that the hyphen begins a new line); by a similar logic, a hyphen should never be added to break an email address or URL. If a particularly long element must be broken to avoid a seriously loose or tight line, it can be broken between words or syllables according to the guidelines offered elsewhere in this section. Editors, proofreaders, and compositors should use their discretion in applying these recommendations, aiming for a balance between readability and aesthetics. See also 6.8, 14.18.

http://
www.chicagomanualofstyle.org/
or
http://www
.chicagomanualofstyle.org/
or
http://www.chicago
manualofstyle.org/

Authors should not break URLs in their manuscripts (see 2.13).

7.47 **Hyphenation and appearance.** For aesthetic reasons, no more than three succeeding lines should be allowed to end in hyphens. (Such hyphens are sometimes referred to as a hyphen stack or ladder.) And though hyphens are necessary far more often in justified text, word breaks may be needed in material with a ragged right-hand margin to avoid exceedingly uneven lines. (In manuscript preparation, however, hyphenation should never be applied; see 2.13.) In reflowable electronic publication formats, end-of-line hyphenation may be applied automatically by a particular application or device; such hyphenation can sometimes be suppressed for aesthetic reasons (as for chapter titles and other headings).

Italics, Capitals, and Quotation Marks

7.48 **Setting off proper names and titles of works.** With the exception of musical and computer terminology, most of the recommendations in this section are related to the distinctive treatment of letters, words, and phrases as such. For the use of italics, capitals, and quotation marks to indicate or set off proper nouns and titles of works, see chapter 8.

7.49 **Italics and markup.** Italics (or, more rarely, boldface) have been used for centuries as the default means of setting off text from the surrounding (usually roman) context. Italics as such are used for emphasis, key terms or terms in another language, words used as words, titles of works, and so on. For electronic publication formats, semantic markup can be added that specifies the nature of the term and not just how it will be presented on the screen. Among other advantages, such markup has the potential to enhance accessibility for readers—for example, by determining how a word will be vocalized by text-to-speech applications. Publishers concerned about providing accessible content are encouraged to consult the guidelines offered by the Web Accessibility Initiative (WAI) of the World Wide Web Consortium (W3C) and, for EPUB (a standard format for e-books), the Accessibility Guidelines available from the International Digital Publishing Forum. See also 2.81–83.

Emphasis

7.50 **Italics for emphasis.** Use *italics* for emphasis only as an occasional adjunct to efficient sentence structure. Overused, italics quickly lose their force. Seldom should as much as a sentence be italicized for emphasis, and never a whole passage. In the first example below, the last three words, though clearly emphatic, do not require italics because of their dramatic position at the end of the sentence.

> The damaging evidence was offered not by the arresting officer, not by the injured plaintiff, but by the boy's own mother.

On the other hand, the emphasis in the following example depends on the italics:

> It *was* Leo!

7.51 **Boldface or underscore for emphasis.** Occasionally, **boldface** or <u>underscore</u> (also called underlining) is used for emphasis. In formal prose, especially in print, italics are usually more appropriate (see 7.50). See also 7.56, 7.79.

7.52 **Capitals for emphasis.** Initial capitals, once used to lend importance to certain words, are now used only ironically (but see 8.94).

> "OK, so I'm a Bad Mother," admitted Mary cheerfully.

Capitalizing an entire word or phrase for emphasis is rarely appropriate in formal prose. If capitals are wanted—in dialogue or in representing newspaper headlines, for example—small caps rather than full capitals look more graceful. Note that "capitalizing" a word means setting only the initial letter as a capital. Capitalizing a whole word, LIKE THIS, is known as "setting in full caps" (or "all caps"). Setting a word in small capitals—or "small caps"—results in THIS STYLE. (For the use of small capitals in representing terms in American Sign Language, see 11.125–35.) See also 10.8.

"Be careful—WATCH OUT!" she yelled.
We could not believe the headline: POLAR ICE CAP RETURNS.

Words from Other Languages

7.53 **Unfamiliar words and phrases from other languages.** Use italics for isolated words and phrases from another language unless they appear in *Webster's* or another standard English-language dictionary (see 7.54). If a word from another language becomes familiar through repeated use throughout a work, it need be italicized only on its first occurrence. If it appears only rarely, however, italics may be retained.

Her love for *fútbol* and *telenovelas* set her apart from her bookish peers.
The word he used, *Kaffeetasse* (coffee cup), was just accurate enough to gain the desired result.

This rule does not extend to proper nouns, which can generally appear in roman type (except for titles of books and the like). For further discussion and examples, including the treatment of translated terms, see 11.3–5. For capitalization in other languages, see 11.18.

7.54 **Roman for familiar words from other languages.** Words and phrases from another language that are familiar to most readers and listed in *Webster's* should appear in roman (*not* italics) if used in an English context, and they should be spelled as in *Webster's*. German nouns, if in *Webster's*, are lowercased (but see 11.39). See also 7.55.

pasha	a priori	the kaiser
weltanschauung	recherché	de novo
in vitro	bourgeois	eros and agape

but
He never missed a chance to *épater les bourgeois*.

If a familiar term, such as *mise en scène*, should occur in the same context as a less familiar one, such as *mise en bouteille* (not listed in *Webster's*), either both or neither should be italicized, so as to maintain internal consistency. See also 7.53.

7.55 **Roman for Latin words and abbreviations.** Commonly used Latin words and abbreviations should not be italicized.

ibid. et al. ca. passim

Because of its peculiar use in quoted matter, *sic* is best italicized.

"mindful of what has been done here by we [*sic*] as agents of principle"

Highlighting Key Terms and Expressions

7.56 **Italics or boldface for key terms.** Key terms in a particular context are often italicized on their first occurrence. Thereafter they are best set in roman.

The two chief tactics of this group, *obstructionism* and *misinformation*, require careful analysis.

Occasionally, boldface may be used for key terms, as in a textbook or to highlight terms that also appear in a glossary; such usage should be noted in the text. See also 7.79.

7.57 **"Scare quotes."** Quotation marks are often used to alert readers that a term is used in a nonstandard (or slang), ironic, or other special sense. Such scare quotes imply "This is not my term" or "This is not how the term is usually applied." Like any such device, scare quotes lose their force and irritate readers if overused. See also 7.59, 7.60.

My rotary simulation app allows me to "dial" phone numbers again.
"Child protection" sometimes fails to protect.

7.58 **Mixing single and double quotation marks.** In works of philosophy or other specialized contexts, single and double quotation marks are sometimes used to signal different things. For example, single quotation marks might be used for special terms and double quotation marks for their definitions. Chicago discourages such a practice, preferring a mix of italics, quotation marks, and parentheses instead.

7.59 **"So-called."** A word or phrase preceded by *so-called* need not be enclosed in quotation marks. The expression itself indicates irony or doubt. If, however, it is necessary to call attention to only one part of a phrase, quotation marks may be helpful.

So-called child protection sometimes fails to protect.
Her so-called mentor induced her to embezzle from the company.
but
These days, so-called "running" shoes are more likely to be seen on the feet of walkers.

7.60 **Common expressions and figures of speech.** Quotation marks are rarely needed for common expressions or figures of speech (including slang). They should normally be reserved for phrases borrowed verbatim from another context or terms used ironically (see 7.57).

Myths of paradise lost are common in folklore.
I grew up in a one-horse town.
Only techies will appreciate this joke.
but
Though she was a lifetime subscriber to the *Journal of Infectious Diseases*, she was not one to ask "for whom the bell tolls."

7.61 **Signs and notices.** Specific wording of common short signs or notices is capitalized headline-style in running text (see 8.159). A longer notice is better treated as a quotation.

The door was marked Authorized Personnel Only.
She encountered the usual Thank You for Not Smoking signs.
We were disturbed by the notice "Shoes and shirt required of patrons but not of personnel."

7.62 **Mottoes.** Mottoes may be treated the same way as signs (see 7.61). If the wording is in another language, it is usually italicized and only the first word capitalized. See also 7.53, 6.41.

The flag bore the motto Don't Tread on Me.
My old college has the motto *Souvent me souviens.*
The motto "All for one and one for all" appears over the door.

Words as Words and Letters as Letters

7.63 **Words and phrases used as words.** When a word or term is not used functionally but is referred to as the word or term itself, it is either italicized or enclosed in quotation marks. Proper nouns used as words, as in the third example, are usually set in roman (see also 7.64).

The term *critical mass* is more often used metaphorically than literally.
What is meant by *neurobotics*?
You rarely see the term iPhone with a capital *i*.

Although italics are the traditional choice, quotation marks may be more appropriate in certain contexts. In the first example below, italics set off the Spanish term, and quotation marks are used for the English (see also 7.53). In the second example, quotation marks help to convey the idea of speech.

The Spanish verbs *ser* and *estar* are both rendered by "to be."
Many people say "I" even when "me" would be more correct.

7.64 **Letters as letters.** Individual letters and combinations of letters of the Latin alphabet are usually italicized.

the letter *q*
a lowercase *n*
a capital *W*
The plural is usually formed in English by adding *s* or *es*.
He signed the document with an *X*.
I need a word with two *e*'s and three *s*'s.

Roman type, however, is traditionally used in two common expressions (see also 7.15).

Mind your p's and q's! dotting the i's and crossing the t's

Roman type is always used for phonetic symbols. For details, consult Geoffrey K. Pullum and William A. Ladusaw, *Phonetic Symbol Guide* (bibliog. 5).

7.65 **Scholastic grades.** Letters used to denote grades are usually capitalized and set in roman type. No apostrophe is required in the plural (see also 7.15).

She finished with three As, one B, and two Cs.

7.66 **Letters standing for names.** A letter used in place of a name is usually capitalized and set in roman type. If it bears no relation to an actual name, it is not followed by a period.

Let us assume that A sues B for breach of contract . . .

If a single initial is used to abbreviate an actual name, it is usually followed by a period; if used to conceal a name, it may be followed by a 2-em dash and no period (see 6.93). If no punctuation follows the dash, it must be followed by a space.

Professor D. will be making his entrance shortly.
Senator K—— and Representative L—— were in attendance.

If two or more initials are used as an abbreviation for an entire name, no periods are needed. See also 8.4, 10.12.

Kennedy and Johnson soon became known as JFK and LBJ.

7.67 **Letters as shapes.** Letters that are used to represent shapes are capitalized and set in roman type (an S curve, an L-shaped room). (Using a sans serif font in a serif context, as is sometimes done, does not necessarily aid comprehension and, unless the sans serif perfectly complements the serif, tends to look clumsy.)

7.68 **Names of letters.** When legibility cannot be counted on, editors and proofreaders occasionally need to name letters ("a cue, not a gee"). The name of a letter, as distinct from the letter itself, is usually set in roman type, without quotation marks. The following standard spellings are drawn from *Webster's Collegiate*. With vowels, which are not named in standard dictionaries, it may be best to give an example ("*a* as in *apple*"). (For the names of special characters, see chapter 11, esp. tables 11.1 and 11.2.)

b	bee	*k*	kay	*s*	ess
c	cee	*l*	el	*t*	tee
d	dee	*m*	em	*v*	vee
f	ef	*n*	en	*w*	double-u
g	gee	*p*	pee	*x*	ex
h	aitch	*q*	cue	*y*	wye
j	jay	*r*	ar	*z*	zee

7.69 **Rhyme schemes.** Lowercase italic letters, with no space between, are used to indicate rhyme schemes or similar patterns.

The Shakespearean sonnet's rhyme scheme is *abab*, *cdcd*, *efef*, *gg*.

Music: Some Typographic Conventions

7.70 **Suggested references for music publishing.** Music publishing is too specialized to be more than touched on here. Authors and editors requiring detailed guidelines may refer to D. Kern Holoman, *Writing about Music* (bibliog. 1.1). For an illustration of typeset music, see figure 3.5. For styling the titles of musical works, see 8.193–97. For a more general reference work, consult *The New Grove Dictionary of Music and Musicians* and the other Grove musical dictionaries, available from Oxford Music Online (bibliog. 5).

7.71 **Musical pitches.** Letters standing for musical pitches (which in turn are used to identify keys, chords, and so on) are usually set as roman capitals. The terms *sharp*, *flat*, and *natural*, if spelled out, are set in roman type and preceded by a hyphen. Editors unfamiliar with musicological conventions should proceed with caution. In the context of harmony, for example, some authors may regard a hyphenated "C-major triad" as being based on the note rather than the key of C. See also 7.74.

middle C
the key of G major
the D-major triad *or* D major triad
an F augmented triad (an augmented triad on the note F)
G-sharp *or* G♯
the key of B-flat minor *or* B♭ minor
Beethoven's E-flat Major Symphony (the *Eroica*)
an E string

A series of pitches are joined by en dashes.

The initial F–G–F–B♭

7.72 **Octaves.** In technical works, various systems are used to designate octave register. Those systems that group pitches by octaves begin each ascending octave on C. In one widely used system, pitches in the octave below middle C are designated by lowercase letters: c, c♯, d, . . . , a♯, b. Octaves from middle C up are designated with lowercase letters bearing superscript numbers or primes: c^1, c^2, and so on, or c′, c″, and so on. Lower octaves are designated, in descending order, by capital letters and capital letters with subscript numbers: C, C_1, C_2. Because of the many systems and their variants in current use, readers should be alerted to the system employed (e.g., by an indication early in the text of the symbol used for middle C). Technical works on the modern piano usually designate all pitches with capital letters and subscripts, from A_1 at the bottom of the keyboard to C_{88} at the top. Scientific works on music usually designate octaves by capital letters and subscripts beginning with C_0 (middle C = C_4). When pitches are otherwise specified, none of these systems is necessary.

middle C   A 440   the soprano's high C

To indicate simultaneously sounding pitches (as in chords), the pitches are listed from lowest to highest and are sometimes joined by plus signs.

C + E + G

7.73 **Chords.** In the analysis of harmony, chords are designated by roman numerals indicating what degree of the scale the chord is based on.

V (a chord based on the fifth, or dominant, degree of the scale)
V^7 (dominant seventh chord)
iii (a chord based on the third, or mediant, degree of the scale)

Harmonic progressions are indicated by capital roman numerals separated by en dashes: IV–I–V–I. While roman numerals for all chords suffice for basic descriptions of chordal movement, in more technical writing, minor chords are distinguished by lowercase roman numerals, and other distinctions in chord quality and content are shown by additional symbols and arabic numerals.

7.74 **"Major" and "minor."** In some works on musical subjects where many keys are mentioned, capital letters are used for major keys and lowercase for minor. If this practice is followed, the words *major* and *minor* are usually omitted.

7.75 **Dynamics.** Terms indicating dynamics are usually given in lowercase, often italicized: *piano*, *mezzo forte*, and so on. Where space allows, the spelled-out form is preferred in both text and musical examples. Symbols for these terms are rendered in lowercase boldface italics with no periods: ***p***, ***mf***, and so on. "Editorial" dynamics—those added to a composer's original by an editor—are sometimes distinguished by another font or by parentheses or brackets.

Computer Terms

7.76 **Application-specific versus generic usage.** Typographic conventions for expressing the names of particular keys, menus, commands, and the like vary not only across devices, operating systems, and applications (also called programs or apps) but also across successive iterations of each. In general, any specific reference to a named component or function should follow the usage that appears with the device or software itself. Likewise, the names for recognized standards should follow accepted usage. References to generic components or functions—or to specific components or functions discussed in a generic sense—often require no special treatment. For more comprehensive coverage, see the style guides published by Microsoft and Apple (bibliog. 1.1) or consult a user's guide or similar documentation for a specific context. For the treatment of proper names for software and devices, see 8.155.

7.77 **Capitalization for keys, menu items, and file formats.** The basic alphabet keys as well as all named keys are capitalized even if they are lowercased on a particular keyboard. Named menu items and labels for toolbars, tabs, buttons, icons, and the like are usually spelled and capitalized as in a particular application or operating system or on a particular device. Abbreviations for file formats are rendered in full capitals unless expressed as extensions (see also 10.49). Items or actions that are not specifically labeled can usually be treated generically.

The function key F2 has no connection with the keys F and 2.
The Option key on a Mac is similar to the Alt key on a typical PC.
One purpose of the Return key (or, on a PC, Enter) is to insert a hard return.
To activate Caps Lock, double-tap Shift (the arrow key).
To show your work in Word, use Track Changes.
Airplane Mode can be toggled on and off using the airplane icon in the Control Center.
Choosing Cut from the Edit menu is an alternative to pressing Ctrl+X.
Save the file as a PNG or a GIF, not as a JPEG.
but
The extensions .html and .htm are both used for HTML files.

7.78 **Keyboard combinations and shortcuts.** To indicate that different keys are to be pressed simultaneously (as in a keyboard shortcut), use the plus sign or the hyphen without a space on either side. The choice of plus or hyphen may depend on the operating system; in the examples below, the plus sign is used for examples from Microsoft Windows and the hyphen for Apple's OS. Spell out *Shift*, *Hyphen*, and *Space*—and anything else that might otherwise be ambiguous. (The capital *S* in the second and third examples does *not* indicate that the Shift key should be pressed as part of the combination.)

To insert a double dagger, press Option-Shift-7; on a PC, press Alt+0135 (on the numeric keypad).
To save, press Ctrl+S.
To save, press Command-S.
If the screen freezes, press Ctrl+Alt+Delete.
To empty the trash without a prompt, press Option-Shift-Command-Delete.

7.79 **Setting off file names and words to be typed or selected.** In most contexts, a combination of quotation marks and capitalization will be sufficient for setting off file names and words to be typed or selected or that otherwise require user interaction or input. References to named items that use headline-style capitalization do not usually require quotation marks (see 8.159); items that use sentence-style capitalization usually do (see 8.158). For file names or words or other strings to be typed, quotation marks can be used; any punctuation that belongs to the surrounding sentence should appear *outside* the quotation marks (see also 6.9).

To list your music by album title, tap More, then tap Albums.
To start page numbering on the second page, choose the Layout tab from the Page Setup dialog box and select the checkbox labeled "Different first page."
If your server uses "index.html" as its default file name, the name of your own default file cannot be "index.htm".
To change the directory to your desktop, type "cd Desktop".

When a greater prominence than capitalization or quotation marks is desired, a different type treatment may be used to highlight or set off elements. A single treatment may be applied across different types of elements, or different treatments may be used to signal different things. For example, boldface or italics could be used for menu items and the like, and a fixed-width (monospaced) font such as Courier could signal items to be typed and directory paths, file names, variables, and other strings. Any punctuation that follows such text should appear in the font of the surrounding text; see also 6.2, 6.3. Any quotation marks, single or double, belonging to text in a fixed-width font should be of the default, nondirectional kind (cf. 6.115).

To insert a thorn, choose **Symbol** from the **Insert** tab, then enter **00FE** in the **Character code** field.
Click **Save As**; name your file `appendix A, draft`.
To set the value, type `$var = "1"`. (*not* `"1"`)
Type `c:\KindleGen\kindlegen`, followed by a space and the file name(s) for your book content.

For additional guidance, consult the latest style guides from Microsoft and Apple (bibliog. 1.1).

7.80 **Terms like "web" and "internet."** Terms related to the internet are capitalized only if they are trademarked as such or otherwise constitute the proper name of an organization or the like. Generic terms that are capitalized as part of a proper name may be lowercased when used alone or in combination (see also 8.68). For treatment of the names of keys, menu items, and file formats, see 7.77. For terms such as *email*, see 7.89.

hypertext transfer protocol (HTTP); a transfer protocol; hypertext
internet protocol (IP); the internet; net neutrality; intranet
Wi-Fi (a trademark); wireless network; Ethernet (a trademark); cellular (or mobile) networks; NFC (near-field communication)
the World Wide Web Consortium (W3C); the World Wide Web; the web; website; web page
the Open Source Initiative (the corporation); open-source platforms

Compounds and Hyphenation

7.81 **To hyphenate or not to hyphenate.** Far and away the most common spelling questions for writers and editors concern compound terms—whether to spell as two words, hyphenate, or close up as a single word. Prefixes (and occasionally suffixes) can be troublesome also. The first place to look for answers is the dictionary. This section, including the hyphenation guide in 7.89, offers guidelines for spelling compounds not necessarily found in the dictionary (though some of the examples are drawn from *Webster's*) and for treatment of compounds according to their grammatical function (as nouns, adjectives, or adverbs) and their position in a sentence. See also 5.92.

7.82 **Compounds defined.** An open compound is spelled as two or more words (*high school*, *lowest common denominator*). A hyphenated compound is spelled with one or more hyphens (*mass-produced*, *kilowatt-hour*, *non-English-speaking*). A closed (or solid) compound is spelled as a single word (*birthrate*, *smartphone*). A permanent compound is one that has been accepted into the general vocabulary and can be found in the dictionary (like all but one of the examples in this paragraph thus far). A temporary compound is a new combination created for some specific, often onetime purpose (*dictionary-wielding*, *impeachment hound*); such compounds, though some eventually become permanent, are not normally found in the dictionary. Not strictly compounds but often discussed with them are words formed with prefixes (*antigrammarian*, *postmodern*); these are dealt with in section 4 of 7.89. (For examples of combining forms—a type of prefix in which a word like *electric* is modified to form a combination like *electromagnetic*—see section 2 of 7.89, under *combining forms*.)

7.83 **The trend toward closed compounds.** With frequent use, open or hyphenated compounds tend to become closed (*on line* to *on-line* to *online*). In some cases, one term will become closed (*birthrate*) while a closely related term remains open (*death rate*). When in doubt, opt for an open compound.

7.84 **Hyphens and readability.** A hyphen can make for easier reading by showing structure and, often, pronunciation. Words that might otherwise be misread, such as *re-creation* or *co-op*, should be hyphenated. Hyphens can also eliminate ambiguity. For example, the hyphen in *much-needed clothing* shows that the clothing is greatly needed rather than abundant and needed. Where no ambiguity could result, as in *public welfare administration* or *graduate student housing*, hyphenation is unnecessary.

7.85 **Compound modifiers before or after a noun.** When compound modifiers (also called phrasal adjectives) such as *high-profile* or *book-length* precede a noun, hyphenation usually lends clarity. With the exception of proper nouns (such as *United States*) and compounds formed by an adverb ending in *ly* plus an adjective (see 7.86), it is never incorrect to hyphenate adjectival compounds before a noun. When such compounds *follow* the noun they modify, hyphenation is usually unnecessary, even for adjectival compounds that are hyphenated in *Webster's* (such as *well-read* or *ill-humored*).

7.86 **Adverbs ending in "ly."** Compounds formed by an adverb ending in *ly* plus an adjective or participle (such as *largely irrelevant* or *smartly dressed*) are not hyphenated either before or after a noun, since ambiguity is virtually impossible. (The *ly* ending with adverbs signals to the reader that the next word will be another modifier, not a noun.)

7.87 **Multiple hyphens.** Multiple hyphens are usually appropriate for such phrases as *an over-the-counter drug* or *a winner-take-all contest*. If, however, the compound modifier consists of an adjective that itself modifies a compound, additional hyphens may not be necessary. The expressions *late nineteenth-century literature* and *early twentieth-century growth* are clear without a second hyphen. (Similar expressions formed with *mid*—which Chicago classifies as a prefix—do not follow this pattern; see 7.89, section 4, under *mid*.) See also 7.89, section 3, under *century*.

7.88 **Suspended hyphens.** When the second part of a hyphenated expression is omitted, the suspended hyphen is retained, followed by a space (or, in a series, by a comma).

fifteen- and twenty-year mortgages
Chicago- or Milwaukee-bound passengers
five-, ten-, and twenty-dollar bills
but
a five-by-eight-foot rug (a single entity)
a three-to-five-year gap (a single range)

Omission of the second part of a solid compound follows the same pattern.

both over- and underfed cats
but
overfed and overworked mules (*not* overfed and -worked mules)

7.89 **Hyphenation guide.** In general, Chicago prefers a spare hyphenation style: if no suitable example or analogy can be found either in this section (7.81–89) or in the dictionary, hyphens should be added only if doing so will prevent a misreading or otherwise significantly aid comprehension. Each of the four sections of the following table is arranged alphabetically (by first column). The first section deals with compounds according to category; the second section, with compounds according to parts of speech. The third section lists examples for specific terms. The fourth section lists common prefixes, most of which join to another word to form one unhyphenated word; note especially the hyphenated exceptions. (Compounds formed with suffixes—e.g., *nationhood*, *penniless*—are almost always closed.)

Category/specific term	*Examples*	*Summary of rule*
1. COMPOUNDS ACCORDING TO CATEGORY		
age terms	a *three-year-old* a *five-year-old* child a *fifty-five-year-old* woman a test for *nine-to-ten-year-olds* a group of *ten-* and *eleven-year-olds* but *seven years old* *eighteen years of age*	Hyphenated in both noun and adjective forms (except as in the last two examples); note the space after the first hyphen in the fifth but not the fourth example (see 7.88). The examples apply equally to ages expressed as numerals.
chemical terms	*sodium chloride* *sodium chloride* solution	Open in both noun and adjective forms.
colors	*emerald-green* tie *reddish-brown* flagstone *blue-green* algae *snow-white* dress *black-and-white* print but his tie is *emerald green* the stone is *reddish brown* the water is *blue green* the clouds are *snow white* the truth isn't *black and white*	Hyphenated before but not after a noun.
compass points and directions	*northeast* *southwest* *east-northeast* a *north–south street* *the street runs north–south*	Closed in noun, adjective, and adverb forms unless three directions are combined, in which case a hyphen is used after the first. When *from . . . to* is implied, an en dash is used (see 6.78).
ethnic terms. See **proper nouns and adjectives relating to geography or nationality** in section 2.		
foreign phrases. See **non-English phrases**		
fractions, compounds formed with	a *half hour* a *half-hour* session a *quarter mile* a *quarter-mile* run an *eighth note*	Noun form open; adjective form hyphenated. See also **number** entries in this section and **half** in section 3.

Category / specific term	*Examples*	*Summary of rule*
1. COMPOUNDS ACCORDING TO CATEGORY (continued)		
fractions, simple	*one-half* *two-thirds* *three-quarters* *one twenty-fifth* *one and three-quarters* a *two-thirds* majority *three-quarters* done a *one twenty-fifth* share	Hyphenated in noun, adjective, and adverb forms, except when second element is already hyphenated. See also **number + noun** and 9.14.
money	a *five-cent* raise *sixty-four-million-dollar* question a deal worth *thirty million dollars* *multimillion-dollar* deal but *$30 million* loan a *$50–$60 million* loss	For amounts with spelled-out units, hyphenate before a noun but leave open after; where units are expressed as symbols, leave open in all positions, except between number ranges. See also **number + abbreviation** and 9.20–25, 9.60.
non-English phrases	an *a priori* argument a *Sturm und Drang* drama *in vitro* fertilization a *tête-à-tête* approach	Open unless hyphens appear in the original language.
number + abbreviation	the *33 m* distance a *2 kg* weight a *3 ft. high* wall a *7 lb., 8 oz.* baby	Always open. See also **number + noun.**
number + noun	a *hundred-meter* race a *250-page* book a *fifty-year* project a *three-inch-high* statuette it's *three inches high* a *one-and-a-half-inch* hem *one and a half inches* a *seven-pound, eight-ounce* baby a *six-foot-two* [or *six-foot, two-inch*] adult *six feet two* [or *six feet, two inches* tall] *five-to-ten-minute* intervals (a single range) but *five- or ten-minute* intervals (two values)	Hyphenated before a noun, otherwise open. Note the space after the first number in the last example (see 7.88). See also **number + abbreviation** and 9.13.

Category/specific term	*Examples*	*Summary of rule*
1. COMPOUNDS ACCORDING TO CATEGORY (continued)		
number + ***percent***	*50 percent* a *10 percent* raise a *30–40 percent* increase	Noun and adjective forms always open, except between number ranges. See also 9.18, 9.60.
number, ordinal, + noun	*third-floor* apartment *103rd-floor* view on the *third floor* *fifth-place* contestant *twenty-first-row* seats in the *twenty-first row*	Hyphenated before a noun, otherwise open (but see **numbers, spelled out**). See also **century** in section 3.
number, ordinal, + superlative	a *second-best* decision *third-largest* town *fourth-to-last* contestant he arrived *fourth to last*	Hyphenated before a noun, otherwise open.
numbers, spelled out	*twenty-eight* *three hundred* *nineteen forty-five* *five hundred fifty-two* contestants *twenty-eighth* *three hundredth* *five hundred fifty-second* contestant	Twenty-one through ninety-nine hyphenated; others open. Applies equally to cardinals and ordinals. See also **fractions, simple**.
relationships. See **foster**, **grand**, **in-law**, and **step** in section 3.		
time	at *three thirty* the *three-thirty* train a *four o'clock* train the *5:00 p.m.* news	Usually open; forms such as "three thirty," "four twenty," etc. are hyphenated before the noun.
2. COMPOUNDS ACCORDING TO PARTS OF SPEECH		
adjective + noun	*small-state* senators a *high-quality* alkylate a *middle-class* neighborhood the neighborhood is *middle class*	Hyphenated before but not after a noun.
adjective + participle	*tight-lipped* person *high-jumping* grasshoppers *open-ended* question the question was *open ended*	Hyphenated before but not after a noun.

Category / specific term	*Examples*	*Summary of rule*
2. COMPOUNDS ACCORDING TO PARTS OF SPEECH (continued)		
adverb ending in *ly* + participle or adjective	a *highly paid* ragpicker a *fully open* society he was *mildly amusing*	Open whether before or after a noun.
adverb not ending in *ly* + participle or adjective	a *much-needed* addition it was *much needed* a very *well-read* child *little-understood* rules a *too-easy* answer the *best-known* author the *highest-ranking* officer the *worst-paid* job a *lesser-paid* colleague the *most efficient* method a *less prolific* artist a *more thorough* exam a *rather boring* play the *most skilled* workers (most in number) but the *most-skilled* workers (most in skill) a *very much needed* addition	Hyphenated before but not after a noun; certain compounds, including those with *more*, *most*, *less*, *least*, and *very*, can usually be left open unless ambiguity threatens. When the adverb rather than the compound as a whole is modified by another adverb, the entire expression is open.
combining forms	*electrocardiogram* *socioeconomic* *politico-scientific* studies the *practico-inert*	Usually closed if permanent, hyphenated if temporary. See 7.82.
gerund + noun	*running shoes* *cooking class* *running-shoe* store	Noun form open; adjective form hyphenated. See also **noun + gerund**.
noun + adjective	*computer-literate* accountants *HIV-positive* men the stadium is *fan friendly* she is *HIV positive*	Hyphenated before a noun; usually open after a noun.
noun + gerund	*mountain climbing* a *mountain-climbing* enthusiast *time-clock-punching* employees a *Nobel Prize–winning* chemist (see 6.80) *decision-making* *head-hunting* *bookkeeping* *caregiving* *copyediting*	Noun form usually open; adjective form hyphenated before a noun. Some permanent compounds hyphenated or closed (see 7.82).

Category/specific term	*Examples*	*Summary of rule*
2. COMPOUNDS ACCORDING TO PARTS OF SPEECH (continued)		
noun + noun, single function (first noun modifies second noun)	*student nurse* *restaurant owner* *directory path* *tenure track* *tenure-track* position *home-rule* governance *shipbuilder* *gunrunner* *copyeditor*	Noun form open; adjective form hyphenated before a noun. Some permanent compounds closed (see 7.82).
noun + noun, two functions (both nouns equal)	*writer-director* *philosopher-king* *city-state* *city-state* governance	Both noun and adjective forms always hyphenated.
noun + numeral or enumerator	*type A* a *type A* executive *type 2* diabetes *size 12* slacks a *page 1* headline	Both noun and adjective forms always open.
noun + participle	a *Wagner-burdened* repertoire *flower-filled* garden the garden was *flower filled* but the room was *air-conditioned*	Hyphenated before a noun, otherwise open unless verb form hyphenated in *Webster's* (see also **phrases, verbal**).
participle + noun	*chopped-liver* pâté *cutting-edge* methods their approach was *cutting edge*	Adjective form hyphenated before but not after a noun.
participle + *up*, *out*, and similar adverbs	*dressed-up* children *burned-out* buildings *ironed-on* decal we were *dressed up* that decal is *ironed on* we *ironed on* the decal	Adjective form hyphenated before but not after a noun. Verb form always open.
phrases, adjectival	an *over-the-counter* drug a *matter-of-fact* reply an *up-to-date* solution sold *over the counter* her tone was *matter of fact* his equipment was *up to date*	Hyphenated before a noun; usually open after a noun.
phrases, noun	*stick-in-the-mud* *jack-of-all-trades* a *flash in the pan*	Hyphenated or open as listed in *Webster's*. If not in the dictionary, open.

Category / specific term	*Examples*	*Summary of rule*
2. COMPOUNDS ACCORDING TO PARTS OF SPEECH (continued)		
phrases, verbal	*babysit* *handcraft* *air-condition* *fast-talk* *strong-arm* *sucker punch*	Closed, hyphenated, or open as listed in *Webster's*. If not in the dictionary, leave open.
proper nouns and adjectives relating to geography or nationality	*African Americans* *African American* president a *Chinese American* *French Canadians* *South Asian Americans* the *Scotch Irish* the *North Central* region *Middle Eastern* countries but *Sino-Tibetan* languages the *Franco-Prussian* War the *US-Canada* border *Anglo-American* cooperation *Anglo-Americans*	Open in both noun and adjective forms, unless the first term is a prefix or unless *between* is implied. See also 8.39.
3. COMPOUNDS FORMED WITH SPECIFIC TERMS		
ache	*toothache* *stomachache*	Always closed.
all	*all out* *all along* *all over* an *all-out* effort an *all-American* player the book is *all-encompassing* but we were *all in* [tired]	Adverbial phrases open; adjectival phrases usually hyphenated both before and after a noun.
book	*reference book* *coupon book* *checkbook* *cookbook*	Closed or open as listed in *Webster's*. If not in the dictionary, open.
borne	*waterborne* *food-borne* *mosquito-borne*	Closed if listed as such in *Webster's*. If not in *Webster's*, hyphenated.

Category / specific term	*Examples*	*Summary of rule*
3. COMPOUNDS FORMED WITH SPECIFIC TERMS (continued)		
century	the *twenty-first century* *fourteenth-century* monastery *twenty-first-century* history a *mid-eighteenth-century* poet *late nineteenth-century* photographs her style was *nineteenth century*	Noun forms always open; adjectival compounds hyphenated before but not after a noun. See also **old** (below), **mid** (in section 4), and 7.87, 9.32.
cross	a *cross section* a *cross-reference* *cross-referenced* *cross-grained* *cross-country* *crossbow* *crossover*	Many compounds formed with *cross* are in *Webster's* (as those listed here). If not in *Webster's*, leave noun forms open; hyphenate adjective, adverb, and verb forms.
e	*email* *e-book* *e-commerce* *eBay*	Hyphenated except for *email* (a departure from previous editions) and certain proper nouns. See also 8.154.
elect	*president-elect* *vice president elect* *mayor-elect* *county assessor elect*	Hyphenated unless the name of the office consists of an open compound. See also **vice**.
ever	*ever-ready* help *ever-recurring* problem *everlasting* he was *ever eager*	Usually hyphenated before but not after a noun; some permanent compounds closed.
ex	*ex-partner* *ex-marine* *ex–corporate executive*	Hyphenated, but use en dash if *ex-* precedes an open compound (see 6.80).
fold	*fourfold* *hundredfold* but *twenty-five-fold* *150-fold*	Hyphenated with hyphenated forms of spelled-out numbers or with numerals; otherwise closed.
foster	*foster mother* *foster parents* a *foster-family* background	Noun forms open; adjective forms hyphenated.
free	*toll-free* number *accident-free* driver the number is *toll-free* the driver is *accident-free*	Compounds formed with *free* as second element are hyphenated both before and after a noun.

Category / specific term	*Examples*	*Summary of rule*
3. COMPOUNDS FORMED WITH SPECIFIC TERMS (continued)		
full	*full-length* mirror the mirror is *full length* three *bags full* a *suitcase full*	Hyphenated before a noun, otherwise open. Use *ful* only in such permanent compounds as *cupful*, *handful*.
general	*attorney general* *postmaster general* *lieutenants general*	Always open; in plural forms, *general* remains singular.
grand, great-grand	*grandfather* *granddaughter* *great-grandmother* *great-great-grandson*	*Grand* compounds closed; *great* compounds hyphenated.
half	*half-asleep* *half-finished* a *half sister* a *half hour* a *half-hour* session *halfway* *halfhearted* we *half expected* to fly	Adjective forms hyphenated before and after the noun; noun and verb forms open. Some permanent compounds closed, whether nouns, adjectives, or adverbs. Check *Webster's*. See also **fractions** in section 1.
house	*schoolhouse* *courthouse* *safe house* *rest house*	Closed or open as listed in *Webster's*. If not in the dictionary, open.
in-law	*sister-in-law* *parents-in-law*	All compounds hyphenated; only the first element takes a plural form.
like	*catlike* *childlike* *Christlike* *bell-like* a *penitentiary-like* institution	Closed if listed as such in *Webster's*. If not in *Webster's*, hyphenated; compounds retain the hyphen both before and after a noun.
mid. See section 4.		
near	in the *near term* a *near accident* a *near-term* proposal a *near-dead* language	Noun forms open; adjective forms hyphenated.
odd	a *hundred-odd* manuscripts *350-odd* books	Always hyphenated.

Category / specific term	*Examples*	*Summary of rule*
3. COMPOUNDS FORMED WITH SPECIFIC TERMS (continued)		
old	a *three-year-old* a *105-year-old* woman a *decade-old* union a *centuries-old* debate a child who is *three years old* the debate is *centuries old*	Noun forms hyphenated. Adjective forms hyphenated before a noun, open after. See also **age terms** in section 1.
on	*online* *onstage* *ongoing* *on-screen* *on-site*	Sometimes closed, sometimes hyphenated. Check *Webster's* and hyphenate if term is not listed. See also 7.83.
percent. See **number + *percent*** in section 1.		
pseudo. See section 4.		
quasi	a *quasi corporation* a *quasi-public* corporation *quasi-judicial* *quasiperiodic* *quasicrystal*	Noun form usually open; adjective form usually hyphenated. A handful of permanent compounds are listed in *Webster's*.
self	*self-restraint* *self-realization* *self-sustaining* *self-conscious* the behavior is *self-destructive* *selfless* *unselfconscious*	Both noun and adjective forms hyphenated, except where *self* is followed by a suffix or preceded by *un*.
step	*stepbrother* *stepparent* *step-granddaughter* *step-great-granddaughter*	Always closed except with *grand* and *great*.
style	dined *family-style* *1920s-style* dancing danced *1920s-style* *Chicago-style* hyphenation according to *Chicago style* *headline-style* capitalization capitalized *headline-style* use *headline style*	Adjective and adverb forms hyphenated; noun form usually open.

Category / specific term	*Examples*	*Summary of rule*
3. COMPOUNDS FORMED WITH SPECIFIC TERMS (continued)		
vice	*vice-consul* *vice-chancellor* *vice president* *vice-presidential* duties a speech that was *vice presidential* *vice admiral* *viceroy*	Adjective forms hyphenated before the noun; noun forms sometimes hyphenated, sometimes open, occasionally closed. Check *Webster's* and hyphenate if term is not listed.
web	a *website* a *web page* *web-related* matters	Noun form open or closed, as shown; if term is not in any dictionary, opt for open. Adjective form hyphenated. See also 7.80.
wide	*worldwide* *citywide* *Chicago-wide* the canvass was *university-wide*	Closed if listed as such in *Webster's*. If not in *Webster's*, hyphenated; compounds retain the hyphen both before and after a noun.
4. WORDS FORMED WITH PREFIXES		
Compounds formed with prefixes are normally closed, whether they are nouns, verbs, adjectives, or adverbs. A hyphen should appear, however, (1) before a capitalized word or a numeral, such as *sub-Saharan*, *pre-1950*; (2) before a compound term, such as *non-self-sustaining*, *pre–Vietnam War* (before an open compound, an en dash is used; see 6.80); (3) to separate two *i*'s, two *a*'s, and other combinations of letters or syllables that might cause misreading, such as *anti-intellectual*, *extra-alkaline*, *pro-life*; (4) to separate the repeated terms in a double prefix, such as *sub-subentry*; (5) when a prefix or combining form stands alone, such as *over- and underused*, *macro- and microeconomics*. The spellings shown below conform largely to *Merriam-Webster's Collegiate Dictionary*. Compounds formed with combining forms not listed here, such as *auto*, *tri*, and *para*, follow the same pattern.		
ante	antebellum, antenatal, antediluvian	
anti	antihypertensive, antihero, *but* anti-inflammatory, anti-Hitlerian	
bi	binomial, bivalent, bisexual	
bio	bioecology, biophysical, biosociology	
cis	cisgender, cissexual, cisatlantic, *but* cis-Victorian, *cis*-2-pentene (*cis* in italics), cis male (*cis* as adjective)	
co	coequal, coauthor, coeditor, coordinate, cooperation, coworker, *but* co-op, co-opt	
counter	counterclockwise, counterrevolution	
cyber	cyberspace, cyberstore	

4. WORDS FORMED WITH PREFIXES (continued)	
de	decompress, deconstruct, deontological, *but* de-emphasize, de-stress
extra	extramural, extrafine, *but* extra-administrative
hyper	hypertension, hyperactive, hypertext
infra	infrasonic, infrastructure
inter	interorganizational, interfaith
intra	intrazonal, intramural, *but* intra-arterial
macro	macroeconomics, macromolecular
mega	megavitamin, megamall, *but* mega-annoyance
meta	metalanguage, metaethical, *but* meta-analysis (not the same as *metanalysis*)
micro	microeconomics, micromethodical
mid	midthirties, a midcareer event, midcentury, *but* mid-July, the mid-1990s, the mid-twentieth century, mid-twentieth-century history
mini	minivan, minimarket
multi	multiauthor, multiconductor, *but* multi-institutional
neo	neonate, neoorthodox, Neoplatonism, neo-Nazi (*neo* lowercase or capital and hyphenated as in dictionary; lowercase and hyphenate if not in dictionary)
non	nonviolent, nonevent, nonnegotiable, *but* non-beer-drinking
over	overmagnified, overshoes, overconscientious
post	postdoctoral, postmodernism, posttraumatic, *but* post-Vietnam, post–World War II (see 6.80)
pre	premodern, preregistration, prewar, preempt, *but* pre-Columbian, Pre-Raphaelite (*pre* lowercase or capital as in dictionary; lowercase if term is not in dictionary)
pro	proindustrial, promarket, *but* pro-life, pro-Canadian
proto	protolanguage, protogalaxy, protomartyr
pseudo	pseudotechnocrat, pseudomodern, *but* pseudo-Tudor
re	reedit, reunify, reproposition, *but* re-cover, re-creation (as distinct from *recover*, *recreation*)
semi	semiopaque, semiconductor, *but* semi-invalid
sub	subbasement, subzero, subcutaneous
super	superannuated, supervirtuoso, superpowerful

4. WORDS FORMED WITH PREFIXES (continued)	
supra	supranational, suprarenal, supraorbital, *but* supra-American
trans	transgender, transsexual, transmembrane, transcontinental, transatlantic, *but* trans-American, *trans*-2-pentene (*trans* in italics), trans fat (*trans* as adjective)
ultra	ultrasophisticated, ultraorganized, ultraevangelical
un	unfunded, unneutered, *but* un-English, un-unionized
under	underemployed, underrate, undercount

8 · Names, Terms, and Titles of Works

Overview

8.1 **Chicago's preference for lowercase.** Proper nouns are usually capitalized, as are some of the terms derived from or associated with proper nouns. For the latter, Chicago's preference is for sparing use of capitals—what is sometimes referred to as a "down style." Although *Brussels* (the Belgian city) is capitalized, Chicago prefers *brussels sprouts*—which are not necessarily from Brussels (see 8.61). Likewise, *President Taft* is capitalized, but *the president* is not (see 8.19–33). (In certain nonacademic contexts—e.g., a press release—such terms as *president* may be capitalized.) The term "down style" may also refer to sentence-style capitalization for titles of works (see 8.158); in most contexts, Chicago prefers headline-style capitalization (sometimes called "up style"; see 8.159).

8.2 **Italics and quotation marks for titles and other terms.** Chicago prefers italics to set off the titles of major or freestanding works such as books, journals, movies, and paintings. This practice extends to cover the names of ships and other craft, species names, and legal cases. Quotation marks are usually reserved for the titles of subsections of larger works—including chapter and article titles and the titles of poems in a collection. Some titles—for example, of a book series or a website, under which any number of works or documents may be collected—are neither italicized nor placed in quotation marks. For more on the titles of works, including matters of capitalization and punctuation, see 8.156–201. For the use of italics and quotation marks to highlight or set off certain letters, words, or phrases, see 7.48–69.

Personal Names

General Principles

8.3 **Personal names—additional resources.** For names of well-known deceased persons, Chicago generally prefers the spellings in the biographical entries of *Merriam-Webster's Collegiate Dictionary* (referred to below as *Webster's*), which are incorporated into the regularly updated online version (see bibliog. 3.1), or, for names not found there, *Encyclopaedia Britannica* (bibliog. 4.3). For living persons, consult either *Webster's* or *Britannica* or, for names not found there, *Who's Who* or *Who's Who in America*, among other resources. (See bibliog. 4.1 for these and other useful works.) Where different spellings appear in different sources (e.g., W. E. B. DuBois versus W. E. B. Du Bois), the writer or editor must make a choice and stick with it. Names of known and lesser-known persons not in the standard references can usually be checked and cross-checked at any number of reputable online resources (e.g., for authors' names, library catalogs or booksellers). The name of a living person should, wherever possible, correspond to that person's preferred usage.

8.4 **Capitalization of personal names.** Names and initials of persons, real or fictitious, are capitalized. A space should be used between any initials, except when initials are used alone. See also 7.66, 10.12.

Jane Doe	P. D. James	Malcolm X
George S. McGovern	M. F. K. Fisher	LBJ

Unconventional spellings strongly preferred by the bearer of the name or pen name (e.g., bell hooks) should usually be respected in appropriate contexts (library catalogs generally capitalize all such names). E. E. Cummings can be safely capitalized; it was one of his publishers, not he himself, who lowercased his name. Most editors will draw the line at beginning a sentence with a lowercased name and choose either to rewrite or to capitalize the first letter for the occasion. When a personal name includes a lowercase particle, the particle is capitalized if it begins a sentence or a note (but see 14.21; see also 8.5).

8.5 **Names with particles.** Many names include particles such as *de*, *d'*, *de la*, *el*, *von*, *van*, and *ten*. Practice with regard to capitalizing and spacing the particles varies widely, and confirmation should be sought in a biographical dictionary or other authoritative source. When the surname is used alone, the particle is usually (but not always) retained, capitalized or lowercased and spaced as in the full name (though always capitalized when beginning a sentence or a note; see also 8.4). *Le*, *La*, and *L'* are always capitalized when not preceded by *de*; *the*, which sometimes appears with the English form of a Native American name, can be lowercased unless it begins a sentence or a note. See also 8.7, 8.8, 8.9, 8.10, 8.11, 8.14, 8.34.

Alfonse D'Amato; D'Amato
Diana DeGette; DeGette
Walter de la Mare; de la Mare
Paul de Man; de Man
Thomas De Quincey; De Quincey
Page duBois; duBois
W. E. B. DuBois; DuBois (but see 8.3)
Daphne du Maurier; du Maurier
Robert M. La Follette Sr.; La Follette
John Le Carré; Le Carré
Pierre-Charles L'Enfant; L'Enfant
Farouk El-Baz; El-Baz
Abraham Ten Broeck; Ten Broeck
the Prophet (Tenskwatawa)
Robert van Gulik; van Gulik
Stephen Van Rensselaer; Van Rensselaer
Wernher von Braun; von Braun

8.6 **Hyphenated and extended names.** A hyphenated last name or a last name that consists of two or more elements should usually retain each element. (In the case of someone who is generally known by a shorter form, that form may be used, but only after the fuller form has been established.) For names of prominent or historical figures, *Webster's* and other reliable alphabetical listings usually indicate where the last name begins.

Victoria Sackville-West; Sackville-West
Ralph Vaughan Williams; Vaughan Williams (*not* Williams)
Ludwig Mies van der Rohe; Mies van der Rohe (*not* van der Rohe); Mies
but
John Hope Franklin; Franklin
Charlotte Perkins Gilman; Gilman

For unhyphenated compound names of lesser-known persons for whom proper usage cannot be determined, use only the last element (including any particle[s]; see 8.5). But see 8.11.

Non-English Names in an English Context

8.7 **French names.** The particles *de* and *d'* are lowercased (except at the beginning of a sentence). When the last name is used alone, *de* (but not *d'*) is often dropped. Its occasional retention, in *de Gaulle*, for example, is suggested by tradition rather than logic. (When a name begins with closed-up *de*, such as *Debussy*, the *d* is always capitalized.)

Jean d'Alembert; d'Alembert
Alfred de Musset; Musset
Alexis de Tocqueville; Tocqueville
but
Charles de Gaulle; de Gaulle

When *de la* precedes a name, *la* is usually capitalized and is always retained when the last name is used alone. The contraction *du* is usually lowercased in a full name but is retained and capitalized when the last name is used alone. (When a name begins with closed-up *Du*, such as *Dupont*, the *d* is always capitalized.)

Jean de La Fontaine; La Fontaine
René-Robert Cavelier de La Salle; La Salle
Philippe du Puy de Clinchamps; Du Puy de Clinchamps

When the article *le* accompanies a name, it is capitalized with or without the first name.

Gustave Le Bon; Le Bon

Initials standing for a hyphenated given name are usually hyphenated.

Jean-Paul Sartre; J.-P. Sartre; Sartre

There is considerable variation in French usage; the guidelines and examples above merely represent the most common forms.

8.8 **German and Portuguese names.** In the original languages, particles in German and Portuguese names are lowercased and are usually dropped when the last name is used alone. But in English contexts, if another form is widely known, it may be used instead.

Alexander von Humboldt; Humboldt
Maximilian von Spee; Spee
Heinrich Friedrich Karl vom und zum Stein; Stein
Ludwig van Beethoven; Beethoven
Agostinho da Silva; Silva
but
Vasco da Gama; da Gama

8.9 **Italian names.** Particles in Italian names are most often uppercased and retained when the last name is used alone.

Gabriele D'Annunzio; D'Annunzio
Lorenzo Da Ponte; Da Ponte
Luca Della Robbia; Della Robbia

In many older aristocratic names, however, the particle is traditionally lowercased and dropped when the last name is used alone.

Beatrice d'Este; Este   Lorenzo de' Medici; Medici

8.10 **Dutch names.** In English usage, the particles *van*, *van den*, *ter*, and the like are lowercased when full names are given but usually capitalized when only the last name is used.

Johannes van Keulen; Van Keulen
Pieter van den Keere; Van den Keere

Vincent van Gogh; Van Gogh
Gerard ter Borch; Ter Borch

8.11 **Spanish names.** Many Spanish names are composed of both the father's and the mother's family names, usually in that order, sometimes joined by *y* (and). When the given name is omitted, persons with such names are usually referred to by both family names but sometimes by only one (usually, but not always, the first of the two family names), according to their own preference (or, sometimes, to established usage). It is never incorrect to use both.

José Ortega y Gasset; Ortega y Gasset *or* Ortega
Pascual Ortiz Rubio; Ortiz Rubio *or* Ortiz
Federico García Lorca; García Lorca (popularly known as Lorca)

Spanish family names that include an article, a preposition, or both are treated in the same way as analogous French names.

Tomás de Torquemada; Torquemada
Manuel de Falla; Falla
Bartolomé de Las Casas; Las Casas
Gonzalo Fernández de Oviedo; Fernández de Oviedo

Traditionally, a married woman replaced her mother's family name with her husband's (first) family name, sometimes preceded by *de*. If, for example, María Carmen Mendoza Salinas married Juan Alberto Peña Montalvo, she could change her legal name to María Carmen Mendoza (de) Peña or, if the husband was well known by both family names, to María Carmen Mendoza (de) Peña Montalvo. Many women in Spanish-speaking countries, however, no longer take their husband's family name. For alphabetizing, see 16.84.

8.12 **Russian names.** Russian family names, as well as patronymics (the name preceding the family name and derived from the name of the father), sometimes take different endings for male and female members of the family. For example, Lenin's real name was Vladimir Ilyich Ulyanov (given name, patronymic, family name); his sister Maria was Maria Ilyinichna Ulyanova. In Russian sources (and, by extension, their English translations), often only the given name and patronymic are used; in such instances the patronymic should not be confused either for a middle name or for the family name.

8.13 **Hungarian names.** In Hungarian practice, the family name precedes the given name—for example, Molnár Ferenc, Kodály Zoltán. In English contexts, however, such names are usually inverted—Ferenc Molnár, Zoltán Kodály. In some cases, the family name includes an initial—for example, É. Kiss Katalin. When such a name is inverted for English contexts (i.e., to become Katalin É. Kiss), the initial should not be confused for a middle initial. When such a name is inverted, as for an index, it is properly listed under the initial (see 16.78).

8.14 **Arabic names.** Surnames of Arabic origin (which are strictly surnames rather than family names) are often prefixed by such elements as *Abu*, *Abd*, *Ibn*, *al*, or *el*. Since these are integral parts of a name, just as *Mc* or *Fitz* forms a part of certain names, they should usually not be dropped when the surname is used alone. Capitalization of such elements varies widely, but terms joined with a hyphen may usually be lowercased. See also 11.79, 11.80, 16.75.

Syed Abu Zafar Nadvi; Abu Zafar Nadvi
Abdul Aziz Ibn Saud; Ibn Saud
Tawfiq al-Hakim; al-Hakim
but
Anwar el-Sadat; Sadat (as commonly known)

Names of rulers of older times, however, are often shortened to the first part of the name rather than the second.

Harun al-Rashid; Harun (al-Rashid, "Rightly Guided," was Harun's *laqab*, a descriptive name he took on his accession to the caliphate)

8.15 **Chinese names.** In Chinese practice, the family name comes before the given name. (This practice should be followed in English contexts with names of Chinese persons but not with those of persons of Chinese origin whose names have been anglicized.) For use of the Pinyin and Wade-Giles systems of transliteration, see 11.82–90.

Chiang Kai-shek; Chiang (Wade-Giles)
Mao Tse-tung; Mao (Wade-Giles)
Li Bai; Li (Pinyin)
Du Fu; Du (Pinyin)
but
Anthony Yu; Yu
Tang Tsou; Tsou

8.16 **Japanese names.** In Japanese usage, the family name precedes the given name. Japanese names are frequently westernized, however, by authors writing in English or persons of Japanese origin living in the West.

Yoshida Shigeru; Yoshida
Kanda Nobuo; Kanda
but
Akira Kurosawa; Kurosawa
Shinzō Abe; Abe

8.17 **Korean names.** In Korean usage, the family name precedes the given name, and this is how it is usually presented even in English-language contexts. Persons of Korean origin living in the West, however, often invert this order.

Kim Dae-jung; Kim
Oh Jung-hee; Oh
but
Chang-rae Lee; Lee

8.18 **Other Asian names.** In some Asian countries, people are usually known by their given name rather than by a surname or family name. The Indonesian writer Pramoedya Ananta Toer, for example, is referred to in short form as Pramoedya (not as Toer). For further examples, see 16.76, 16.80, 16.85, 16.86. If in doubt, use the full form of a name in all references or consult an expert or consult the usage in a reputable source that discusses the person in question.

Titles and Offices

8.19 **Titles and offices—the general rule.** Civil, military, religious, and professional titles are capitalized when they immediately precede a personal name and are thus used as part of the name (traditionally replacing the title holder's first name). In formal prose and other generic text, titles are normally lowercased when following a name or used in place of a name (but see 8.20). For abbreviated forms, see 10.11–26.

Abraham Lincoln, president of the United States (*or* President Abraham Lincoln of the United States); President Lincoln; the president
General Bradley; the general
Cardinal Newman; the cardinal
Governors Ige and Brown; the governors

Although a full name may be used with a capitalized title (e.g., President Abraham Lincoln)—and though it is perfectly correct to do so—some writers choose to avoid using the title before a full name in formal prose, especially with civil, corporate, and academic titles (see 8.22, 8.27, 8.28). (For titles used in apposition to a name, see 8.21.) Note also that once a title has been given, it need not be repeated each time a person's name is mentioned.

Elizabeth Warren, senator from Massachusetts (*or* Senator Elizabeth Warren of Massachusetts); Senator Warren; Warren; the senator

8.20 **Exceptions to the general rule for titles and offices.** In promotional or ceremonial contexts such as a displayed list of donors in the front matter of a book or a list of corporate officers in an annual report, titles are usually capitalized even when following a personal name. Exceptions may also be called for in other contexts for reasons of courtesy or diplomacy.

Maria Martinez, Director of International Sales

A title used alone, in place of a personal name, is capitalized only in such contexts as a toast or a formal introduction, or when used in direct address (see also 6.53, 8.36).

Ladies and Gentlemen, the Prime Minister.
I would have done it, Captain, but the ship was sinking.
Thank you, Mr. President.

8.21 **Titles used in apposition.** When a title is used in apposition before a personal name—that is, not alone and as part of the name but as an equivalent to it, usually preceded by *the* or by a modifier—it is considered not a title but rather a descriptive phrase and is therefore lowercased.

the empress Elisabeth of Austria (*but* Empress Elisabeth of Austria)
German chancellor Angela Merkel (*but* Chancellor Merkel)
the Argentinian-born pope Francis
former president Carter
former presidents Reagan and Ford
the then secretary of state Hillary Clinton

8.22 **Civil titles.** Much of the usage below is contradicted by the official literature typically generated by political offices, where capitalization of a title in any position is the norm (see 8.20). In formal prose, however, civil titles are capitalized only when used as part of the name (except as noted). See also 10.13.

the president; George Washington, first president of the United States; President Washington; the presidency; presidential; the Washington administration; Washington; Benigno Aquino III, president of the Philippines; President Aquino; Aquino
the vice president; John Adams, vice president of the United States; Vice President Adams; vice presidential duties
the secretary of state; John Kerry, secretary of state; Secretary of State Kerry *or* Secretary Kerry
the senator; the senator from New York; New York senator Kirsten E. Gillibrand (see 8.21); Senator Gillibrand; Senators Gillibrand and Schumer; Senator Mikulski, Democrat from Maryland (*or* D-MD)
the representative; the congressman; the congresswoman; Robin Kelly, representative from Illinois *or* congresswoman from Illinois; Congresswoman Kelly *or* Rep. Robin Kelly (D-IL); Kay Granger, representative from Texas; Congresswoman Granger; the congresswoman *or* the representative; Representatives Kelly and Granger
the Speaker; Paul Ryan, Speaker of the House of Representatives; Speaker Ryan (*Speaker* is best capitalized in all contexts to avoid conflation with generic speakers)
the chief justice; John G. Roberts Jr., chief justice of the United States; Chief Justice Roberts (see also 8.64)
the associate justice; Elena Kagan, associate justice; Justice Kagan; Justices Kagan and Sotomayor
the chief judge; Timothy C. Evans, chief judge; Judge Evans
the ambassador; Matthew W. Barzun, ambassador to the Court of St. James's *or* ambassador to the United Kingdom; Ambassador Barzun
the governor; Earl Ray Tomblin, governor of the state of West Virginia; Governor Tomblin
the mayor; Rahm Emanuel, mayor of Chicago; Mayor Emanuel
the state senator; Teresa Fedor, Ohio state senator; the Honorable Teresa Fedor
the state representative (same pattern as state senator)
the governor general of Canada; the Right Honourable David Johnston
the minister of finance (*or* finance minister); Arun Jaitley, finance minister of India; Jaitley
the prime minister; the Right Honourable Pierre Elliott Trudeau, former prime minister of Canada; Theresa May, the British prime minister
the premier (of a Canadian province); the Honourable Brad Wall
the member of Parliament (UK and Canada); Jane Doe, member of Parliament, *or, more commonly,* Jane Doe, MP; Jane Doe, the member for West Hamage

the chief whip; Jackson Mphikwa Mthembu, chief whip of the African National Congress; Mthembu
the foreign secretary (UK); the foreign minister (other nations); the British foreign secretary; the German foreign minister
the chancellor; Angela Merkel, chancellor of Germany; Chancellor Merkel
the chancellor of the exchequer (UK); George Osborne; Chancellor Osborne
the Lord Privy Seal (UK; always capitalized)

For use of *the Honorable* and similar terms of respect, see 8.33, 10.18.

8.23 **Titles of sovereigns and other rulers.** Most titles of sovereigns and other rulers are lowercased when used alone. See also 8.32.

King Abdullah II; the king of Jordan
Queen Elizabeth; Elizabeth II; the queen (in a British Commonwealth context, the Queen)
the Holy Roman emperor
Nero, emperor of Rome; the Roman emperor
Hamad bin Isa al-Khalifa, king of Bahrain; King Hamad
the shah of Iran
the sharif of Mecca
the paramount chief of Basutoland
Wilhelm II, emperor of Germany; Kaiser Wilhelm II; the kaiser
the führer (Adolf Hitler)
Il Duce (used only of Benito Mussolini; both *i* and *d* capitalized)

8.24 **Military titles.** As is the case with civil titles, military titles are routinely capitalized in the literature of the organization or government with which they are associated. Nonetheless, in formal prose, most such titles are capitalized only when used as part of a person's name. Occasional exceptions may be made if ambiguity threatens. See also 10.13.

the general; General Ulysses S. Grant, commander in chief of the Union army; General Grant; the commander in chief
the general of the army; Omar N. Bradley, general of the army; General Bradley
the admiral; Chester W. Nimitz, fleet admiral; Admiral Nimitz, commander in chief of the Pacific Fleet
the chairman; Joseph F. Dunford Jr., chairman of the Joint Chiefs of Staff; General Dunford
the captain; Captain Frances LeClaire, company commander
the sergeant; Sergeant Carleton C. Singer; a noncommissioned officer (NCO)
the warrant officer; Warrant Officer John Carmichael
the chief petty officer; Chief Petty Officer Tannenbaum

the private; Private T. C. Alhambra
the British general; General Sir Guy Carleton, British commander in New York City; General Carleton

For abbreviations, often used when a title precedes a name and appropriate in material in which many military titles appear, see 10.15.

8.25 **Quasi-military titles.** Titles and ranks used in organizations such as the police, the merchant marine, or the Salvation Army are treated the same way as military titles.

the chief of police; Frederick Day, Parkdale chief of police; Chief Day
the warden; Jane Simmons, warden of the state penitentiary; Warden Simmons

8.26 **Religious titles.** Religious titles are treated much like civil and military titles (see 8.22, 8.24).

the rabbi; Rabbi Avraham Yitzhak ha-Kohen Kuk; the rabbinate
the cantor *or* hazan; Deborah Bard, cantor; Cantor Bard
the sheikh; Sheikh Ibrahim el-Zakzaky
the imam; Imam Shamil
the ayatollah; Ayatollah Khomeini
the Dalai Lama (traditionally capitalized); *but* previous dalai lamas
the sadhu; the guru; the shaman
the pope; Pope Francis; the papacy; papal
the cardinal; John Cardinal Dew (in formal contexts) *or* Cardinal John Dew; Cardinal Dew; the sacred college of cardinals
the patriarch; Cyrillus Lucaris, patriarch of Constantinople; the patriarchate
the archbishop; the archbishop of Canterbury; Archbishop Williams (*or, in this case,* Dr. Williams)
the bishop; the bishop of Toledo; Bishop Donnelly; bishopric; diocese
the minister; the Reverend Shirley Stoops-Frantz
the rector; the Reverend James Williams (see also 10.18, 8.33)

8.27 **Corporate and organizational titles.** Titles of persons holding offices such as those listed below are rarely used as part of a name. If a short form is required, either the generic term or simply a personal name suffices.

the chief executive officer; Pat Beldos, chief executive officer of Caterham Industries; the CEO
the director; Gabriel Dotto, director of the Michigan State University Press

the school superintendent; Janice Bayder, superintendent of Coriander Township High School District
the secretary-treasurer; Georgina Fido, secretary-treasurer of the Kenilworth Kennel Society

8.28 **Academic titles.** Academic titles generally follow the pattern for civil titles (see 8.22).

the professor; Françoise Meltzer, professor of comparative literature; Professor Meltzer
the chair; Mark Payne, chair of the Department of Classics; Professor Payne (but see 8.30)
the provost; Eric D. Isaacs, provost of the University of Chicago; Isaacs
the president; Robert J. Zimmer, president of the University of Chicago; Zimmer *or* President Zimmer
the dean; John W. Boyer, dean of the College at the University of Chicago (*the College* is an official division of the University of Chicago); Dean Boyer
named professorships; Wendy Doniger, Mircea Eliade Distinguished Service Professor of the History of Religions in the Divinity School; Professor Doniger; Anthony Grafton, Dodge Professor of History, Princeton University; Professor Grafton
the professor emeritus (masc.); the professor emerita (fem.); professors emeriti (masc. or masc. and fem.); professors emeritae (fem.); Professor Emerita Neugarten (note that *emeritus* and *emerita* are honorary designations and do not simply mean "retired")

8.29 **Other academic designations.** Terms denoting student status are lowercased.

freshman *or* first-year student   sophomore   junior   senior

Names of degrees, fellowships, and the like are lowercased when referred to generically. See also 10.21.

a master's degree; a doctorate; a fellowship; master of business administration (MBA)

8.30 **Descriptive titles.** When preceding a name, generic titles that describe a person's role or occupation—such as *philosopher* or *historian*—should be lowercased and treated as if in apposition (see 8.21). Compare 8.28.

the historian William McNeill (*not* Historian McNeill)

8.31 **Civic and academic honors.** Titles denoting civic or academic honors are capitalized when following a personal name. For awards, see 8.83; for abbreviations, see 10.22.

Roberta Bondar, Fellow of the Royal Society of Canada; the fellows

8.32 **Titles of nobility.** Unlike most of the titles mentioned in the previous paragraphs, titles of nobility do not denote offices (such as that of a president or an admiral). Whether inherited or conferred, they form an integral and, with rare exceptions, permanent part of a person's name and are therefore usually capitalized. The generic element in a title, however (duke, earl, etc.), is lowercased when used alone as a short form of the name. (In British usage, the generic term used alone remains capitalized in the case of royal dukes but not in the case of nonroyal dukes; in North American usage, such niceties may be disregarded.) For further advice, consult *The Times Style and Usage Guide* (bibliog. 1.1), and for a comprehensive listing, consult the latest edition of *Burke's Peerage, Baronetage, and Knightage* (bibliog. 4.1). See also 8.23.

the prince; Prince Charles; the Prince of Wales
the duke; the duchess; the Duke and Duchess of Windsor
the marquess; the Marquess of Bath; Lord Bath
the marchioness; the Marchioness of Bath; Lady Bath
the earl; the Earl of Shaftesbury; Lord Shaftesbury; Anthony Ashley Cooper, 7th (*or* seventh) Earl of Shaftesbury; previous earls of Shaftesbury
the countess (wife of an earl); the Countess of Shaftesbury; Lady Shaftesbury
the viscount; Viscount Eccles; Lord Eccles
Baroness Thatcher; Lady Thatcher
Dame Judi Dench; Dame Judi (*not* Dame Dench)
the baron; Lord Rutland
the baronet; the knight; Sir Paul McCartney; Sir Paul (*not* Sir McCartney)
Lady So-and-So [husband's last name] (wife of a marquess, earl, baron, or baronet)
Lady Olivia So-and-So (daughter of a duke, marquess, or earl); Lady Olivia
the Honourable Jessica So-and-So (daughter of a baron)
the duc de Guise (lowercased in accordance with French usage); François de Lorraine, duc de Guise
the count; Count Helmuth von Moltke *or* Graf Helmuth von Moltke; the Count of Toulouse *or* the comte de Toulouse

Note that marquesses, earls, viscounts, barons, and baronesses are addressed, and referred to after first mention, as Lord or Lady So-and-So, at least in British usage. The following entry, drawn from *Burke's Peerage,*

Baronetage, and Knightage, illustrates the complexities of British noble nomenclature:

The 5th Marquess of Salisbury (Sir Robert Arthur James Gascoyne-Cecil, K.G., P.C.), Earl of Salisbury, Wilts; Viscount Cranborne, Dorset, and Baron Cecil of Essendon, Rutland; co-heir to the Barony of Ogle

8.33 **Honorifics.** Honorific titles and respectful forms of address are capitalized in any context. For the use of many such terms in formal correspondence, see "Forms of Address," a comprehensive listing at the back of the print edition of *Merriam-Webster's Collegiate Dictionary*. For abbreviations, see 10.18. See also 8.26.

the Honorable Angus Stanley King Jr. (US senator, member of Congress, etc.)
the Right Honourable Justin Trudeau (Canadian prime minister)
the First Gentleman; the First Lady
the Queen Mother
Pandit Nehru
Mahatma Gandhi
Her (His, Your) Majesty; His (Her, Your) Royal Highness
the Most Reverend William S. Skylstad (Roman Catholic bishop)
Your (Her, His) Excellency
Mr. President; Madam President
Madam Speaker
Your Honor
but
sir, ma'am
my lord, my lady

Epithets, Kinship Names, and Personifications

8.34 **Epithets (or nicknames) and bynames.** A descriptive or characterizing word or phrase used as part of, or instead of, a person's name is capitalized. A *the* used as part of such a name is not capitalized (except, e.g., at the beginning of a sentence).

the Great Emancipator (Abraham Lincoln)
the Sun King (Louis XIV)
the Wizard of Menlo Park (Thomas Edison)
Stonewall Jackson
Old Hickory (Andrew Jackson)
the Young Pretender (Charles Edward Stuart)

the Great Commoner (William Jennings Bryan)
Catherine the Great
Babe Ruth
the Swedish Nightingale (Jenny Lind)
Ivan the Terrible

When used in addition to a name, an epithet is enclosed in quotation marks and placed either within or after the name. Parentheses are unnecessary.

George Herman "Babe" Ruth
Jenny Lind, "the Swedish Nightingale"
Ivan IV, "the Terrible"

8.35 **Epithets as names of characters.** In references to works of drama or fiction, epithets or generic titles used in place of names are normally capitalized.

John Barrymore performed brilliantly as Chief Executioner.
Alice encounters the Red Queen and the Mad Hatter.

8.36 **Kinship names and the like.** Kinship names are lowercased unless they immediately precede a personal name or are used alone, in place of a personal name. Used in apposition, however, such names are lowercased (see 8.21). This usage extends to certain words that express a similar type of relationship. See also 8.20.

my father and mother
the Brontë sisters
Let's write to Aunt Maud.
I believe Grandmother's middle name was Marie.
Please, Dad, let's go.
my daughter's coach
Ask Coach Wilson.
You can count on me, Coach.
but
She adores her aunt Maud.

Kinship terms used in connection with religious offices or callings are treated similarly.

The note referred to a certain Brother Thomas, one of the brothers from the Franciscan monastery.

8.37 **Personifications.** The poetic device of giving abstractions the attributes of persons, and hence capitalizing them, is rare in today's writing. The use of capitals for such a purpose is best confined to quoted material.

"The Night is Mother of the Day, / The Winter of the Spring, / And ever upon old Decay / The greenest mosses cling." (John Greenleaf Whittier)
but
In springtime, nature is at its best.
It was a battle between head and heart; reason finally won.

Ethnic, Socioeconomic, and Other Groups

8.38 **Ethnic and national groups and associated adjectives.** Names of ethnic and national groups are capitalized. Adjectives associated with these names are also capitalized. For hyphenation or its absence, see 8.39. Note that terms such as *black* and *white*, when referring to ethnicity, are usually lowercased unless a particular author or publisher prefers otherwise.

Aboriginal peoples; Aboriginals (*or* Aborigines); an Aboriginal; Aboriginal art
African Americans; African American culture
American Indians; an American Indian (see text below)
Arabs; Arabian
Asians; Asian influence in the West; an Asian American
the British; a British person *or, colloquially,* a Britisher, a Brit
Caucasians; a Caucasian
Chicanos; a Chicano; a Chicana
European Americans
the French; a Frenchman; a Frenchwoman; French Canadians
Hispanics; a Hispanic
the Hopi; a Hopi; Hopi customs (see also 7.10)
Inuit; Inuit sculpture
Italian Americans; an Italian American neighborhood
Jews; a Jew; Jewish ethnicity (see also 8.96)
Latinos; a Latino; a Latina; Latino immigration
Métis; Métis history and culture
Native Americans; Native American poetry (see text below)
New Zealanders; New Zealand immigration
Pygmies; a Pygmy; Pygmy peoples
Romanies; a Romany; the Romany people
but
black people; blacks; people of color
white people; whites

Many among those who trace their roots to the Aboriginal peoples of the Americas prefer *American Indians* to *Native Americans*, and in certain historical works *Indians* may be more appropriate. Canadians often speak of *First Peoples* (and of *First Nations*) when not referring to specific groups by name.

8.39 **Compound nationalities.** Whether terms such as *African American*, *Italian American*, *Chinese American*, and the like should be spelled open or hyphenated has been the subject of considerable controversy. But since the hyphen does not aid comprehension in such terms as those mentioned above, it may be omitted unless a particular author or publisher prefers the hyphen. See also the table at 7.89, section 2, under *proper nouns and adjectives relating to geography or nationality*.

8.40 **Class.** Terms denoting socioeconomic classes or groups are lowercased.

the middle class; a middle-class neighborhood
the upper-middle class; an upper-middle-class family
the 1 percent
blue-collar workers
the aristocracy
the proletariat
homeless people

8.41 **Sexual orientation and gender identity.** Terms that refer to individuals or groups according to sexual orientation or gender identity or expression are lowercased. For pronoun use with individuals who do not identify with a gender-specific pronoun, see 5.48.

lesbians; lesbian history
gay men
transgender women; transgender men

8.42 **Generation.** Terms denoting generations are usually lowercased. Following *Webster's* and many other sources, however, lettered *Generations X*, *Y*, and *Z* are capitalized.

the me generation
baby boomer(s); boomers; baby busters
the MTV generation
the millennials
but
Generation X, Generation Y, Generation Z

8.43 **Physical characteristics.** Terms describing groups or individuals according to a physical characteristic or a disability are usually lowercased.

wheelchair users	blind persons	deaf children

Some writers capitalize *deaf* when referring to people who identify themselves as members of the distinct linguistic and cultural group whose primary language is ASL—the Deaf community—and lowercase it when referring to people who have a hearing loss or to those deaf people who prefer oral methods of communication. See also 11.125.

Names of Places

8.44 **Names of places—additional resources.** For the spelling of place-names, consult the geographical listings in *Merriam-Webster's Collegiate Dictionary* (bibliog. 3.1) or *Encyclopaedia Britannica* (bibliog. 4.3) or, for names not listed there, the United States Board on Geographic Names or one of the other resources listed in the bibliography (bibliog. 4.2). Since names of countries and cities often change, frequently updated online resources should be preferred over print for modern place-names. For country names, the US Central Intelligence Agency's *World Factbook* is a good place to start (bibliog. 4.2). For historical works, writers and editors should attempt to use the form of names appropriate to the period under discussion.

Parts of the World

8.45 **Continents, countries, cities, oceans, and such.** Entities that appear on maps are always capitalized, as are adjectives and nouns derived from them. An initial *the* as part of a name is lowercased in running text, except in the rare case of an initial *the* in the name of a city.

Asia; Asian	South China Sea
Ireland; Irish	the North Pole
California; Californian	the Netherlands; Dutch
Chicago; Chicagoan	*but*
Atlantic Ocean; Atlantic	The Hague

8.46 **Points of the compass.** Compass points and terms derived from them are lowercased if they simply indicate direction or location. But see 8.47.

pointing toward the north; a north wind; a northern climate
to fly east; an eastward move; in the southwest of France; southwesterly

8.47 **Regions of the world and national regions.** Terms that denote regions of the world or of a particular country are often capitalized, as are a few of the adjectives and nouns derived from such terms. The following examples illustrate not only the principles sketched in 8.1 but also variations based on context and usage. For terms not included here or for which no suitable analogy can be made, consult *Webster's* or an encyclopedia: if an otherwise generic term is not listed there (either capitalized or, for dictionary entries, with the indication *capitalized* next to the applicable subentry), opt for lowercase. Note that exceptions based on specific regional, political, or historical contexts are inevitable (a few that are generally applicable are included below) and that an author's strong preference should usually be respected. See also 8.46.

the Swiss Alps; the Australian Alps; the Alps; an Alpine village (if in the European or Australian Alps); Alpine skiing; *but* alpine pastures in the Rockies (see also 8.53)
Antarctica; the Antarctic Circle; the Antarctic Continent
the Arctic; the Arctic Circle; Arctic waters; a mass of Arctic air (*but* lowercased when used metaphorically, as in "an arctic stare"; see 8.61)
Central America, Central American countries; central Asia; central Illinois; central France; central Europe (*but* Central Europe when referring to the political division of World War I)
the continental United States; the continent of Europe; *but* on the Continent (used to denote mainland Europe); Continental cuisine; *but* continental breakfast
the East, eastern, an easterner (referring to the eastern part of the United States or other country); the Eastern Seaboard (*or* Atlantic Seaboard), East Coast (referring to the eastern United States); eastern Massachusetts (*but* East Tennessee); the East, the Far East, Eastern (referring to the Orient and Asian culture); the Middle East (*or, formerly more common,* the Near East), Middle Eastern (referring to Iran, Iraq, etc.); the Eastern Hemisphere; eastern Europe (*but* Eastern Europe when referring to the post–World War II division of Europe); east, eastern, eastward, to the east (directions)
the equator; equatorial climate; the Equatorial Current; Equatorial Guinea (formerly Spanish Guinea); the forty-second parallel north (of the equator)
the Great Plains; the northern plains; the plains (*but* Plains Indians)
the Midwest, midwestern, a midwesterner (as of the United States); the middle of Texas (*but* Middle Tennessee)
the North, northern, a northerner (of a country); the North, Northern, Northerner (in American Civil War contexts); northern Ohio (*but* Northern California); North Africa, North African countries, in northern Africa; North America, North American, the North American continent; the North Atlantic,

a northern Atlantic route; the Northern Hemisphere; the Far North; north, northern, northward, to the north (directions)

the Northeast, the Northwest, northwestern, northeastern, a northwesterner, a northeasterner (as of the United States); the Pacific Northwest; the Northwest Passage

the poles; the North Pole; the North Polar ice cap; the South Pole; polar regions (*see also* Antarctica; the Arctic)

the South, southern, a southerner (of a country); the South, Southern, a Southerner (in American Civil War contexts); the Deep South; southern Minnesota (*but* Southern California); the South of France (region); Southeast Asia; South Africa, South African (referring to the Republic of South Africa); southern Africa (referring to the southern part of the continent); south, southern, southward, to the south (directions)

the Southeast, the Southwest, southeastern, southwestern, a southeasterner, a southwesterner (as of the United States)

the tropics, tropical; the Tropic of Cancer; the Neotropics, Neotropical (of the New World biogeographical region); the subtropics, subtropical

the Upper Peninsula (of Michigan); the upper reaches of the Thames

the West, western, a westerner (of a country); the West Coast; western Arizona (*but* West Tennessee); the West, Western (referring to the culture of the Occident, or Europe and the Western Hemisphere; *but* westernize); west, western, westward, to the west (directions)

8.48 **Popular place-names or epithets.** Popular names of places, or epithets, are usually capitalized. Quotation marks are not needed. Some of the following examples may be used of more than one place. None should be used in contexts where they will not be readily understood. See also 8.34.

Back Bay
the Badger State
the Badlands
the Bay Area
the Beltway
the Bible Belt
the Big Island
the Cape
City of Light
the Delta
the East End
the Eastern Shore
the Eternal City
the Fertile Crescent
the Gaza Strip
the Gulf
the Holy City
the Jewish Quarter
the Lake District
the Left Bank
the Loop (Chicago)
Midtown (Manhattan)
the Old World
the Panhandle
the Promised Land
the Rust Belt
Silicon Valley
Skid Row
the South Seas
the South Side
the Sun Belt
the Twin Cities
the Upper West Side
the Village (Greenwich Village)
the West End
the Wild West
the Windy City

Certain terms considered political rather than geographical need not be capitalized. Some editorial discretion is advisable, however. In reference to Soviet-era global politics, for example, the following terms might be suitably capitalized:

the iron curtain *or* Iron Curtain   the third world *or* Third World

8.49 **Urban areas.** Generic terms used for parts of urban areas are not capitalized.

the business district
the inner city
the metropolitan area; the greater Chicago metropolitan area; Chicagoland
the tristate area
but
Greater London (an official administrative region)

On the other hand, a work that treats a specific local culture may choose to favor an established local usage (e.g., Greater Boston).

8.50 **Real versus metaphorical names.** *Mecca* is capitalized when referring to the Islamic holy city, as is *Utopia* when referring to Thomas More's imaginary country. Both are lowercased when used metaphorically. See also 8.61.

Stratford-upon-Avon is a mecca for Shakespeare enthusiasts.
She is trying to create a utopia for her children.

Political Divisions

8.51 **Political divisions—capitalization.** Words denoting political divisions—from *empire*, *republic*, and *state* down to *ward* and *precinct*—are capitalized when they follow a name and are used as an accepted part of the name. When preceding the name, such terms are usually capitalized in names of countries but lowercased in entities below the national level (but see 8.52). Used alone, they are usually lowercased, though reasonable exceptions based on specific regional, political, or historical contexts should be respected. See also 9.46.

the Ottoman Empire; the empire
the British Commonwealth; Commonwealth nations; the Commonwealth (*but* a commonwealth)

the United States; the republic; the Union (Civil War era); the Confederacy (Civil War era)
the United Kingdom; Great Britain; Britain (*not* the kingdom)
the Russian Federation (formerly the Union of Soviet Socialist Republics; the Soviet Union); Russia; the federation
the Republic of South Africa (formerly the Union of South Africa); South Africa; the republic
the Fifth Republic (France)
the Republic of Indonesia; the republic
the Republic of Lithuania; the republic
the Federal Democratic Republic of Ethiopia; the republic; the State of the Gambella Peoples; the state
the Commonwealth of Australia; the commonwealth; the state of New South Wales; the Australian Capital Territory
the Commonwealth of Puerto Rico
Washington State; the state of Washington
the New England states
the province of Ontario
Jiangxi Province
Massachusetts Bay Colony; the colony at Massachusetts Bay
the British colonies; the thirteen colonies
the Indiana Territory; the territory of Indiana
the Northwest Territory; the Old Northwest
the Western Reserve
Lake County; the county of Lake; the county; county Kildare (Irish usage)
New York City; the city of New York
the City (the old city of London, now the financial district, always capitalized)
Shields Township; the township
the Eleventh Congressional District; the congressional district
the Fifth Ward; the ward
the Sixth Precinct; the precinct

A generic term that is capitalized as part of the name of an official body remains capitalized when it is used in the plural to refer to two or more names and applies to both.

Lake and Cook Counties
the Republics of Indonesia and South Africa

8.52 **Governmental entities.** In contexts where a specific governmental body rather than the place is meant, the words *state*, *city*, and the like are usually capitalized when used as part of the full name of the body. See also 8.51.

She works for the Village of Forest Park.
That is a City of Chicago ordinance.
but
Residents of the village of Forest Park enjoy easy access to the city of Chicago.

Topographical Divisions

8.53 **Mountains, rivers, and the like.** Names of mountains, rivers, oceans, islands, and so forth are capitalized. The generic term (*mountain* etc.) is also capitalized when used as part of the name. In the plural, it is capitalized when it is part of a single name (Hawaiian Islands) and when it is used with two or more names, whether beginning with the generic term (Mounts Washington and Rainier) or when the generic term comes second and applies to two or more names (e.g., the Illinois and the Chicago Rivers).

Walden Pond
Silver Lake
Lake Michigan; Lakes Michigan and Erie; the Great Lakes
the Illinois River; the Illinois and the Chicago Rivers
the Nile River valley; the Nile valley; the Nile delta; the Mississippi River valley; the Mississippi delta (where *river* forms part of the proper names but *valley* and *delta* do not; see also 8.54)
the Bering Strait
the Mediterranean Sea; the Mediterranean
the Pacific Ocean; the Pacific and the Atlantic Oceans
the Great Barrier Reef
the Hawaiian Islands; Hawaii; *but* the island of Hawaii (the Big Island)
the Windward Islands; the Windwards
the Iberian Peninsula
Cape Verde
the Black Forest
Stone Mountain
Mount Washington; Mount Rainier; Mounts Washington and Rainier
the Rocky Mountains; the Rockies (see also 8.47)
Death Valley; the Valley of Kings
the Continental Divide
the Horn of Africa; the Horn (to avoid confusion with a different kind of horn)
the Indian subcontinent (a descriptive rather than proper geographical name)

8.54 **Generic terms for geographic entities.** When a generic term is used descriptively (or in apposition; see 8.21) rather than as part of a name, or when used alone, it is lowercased.

the Amazon basin
along the Pacific coast (*but* the West Coast; see 8.47)
the California desert
the river Thames
the Hudson River valley

8.55 **Non-English terms for geographic entities.** When a generic term from a language other than English forms part of a geographic name, the equivalent English term should not be included. See also 11.4.

the Rio Grande (*not* the Rio Grande River)
Fujiyama (*not* Mount Fujiyama)
Mauna Loa (*not* Mount Mauna Loa)
the Sierra Nevada (*not* the Sierra Nevada Mountains)

Public Places and Major Structures

8.56 **Thoroughfares and the like.** The names of streets, avenues, squares, parks, and so forth are capitalized. The generic term is lowercased when used alone but capitalized when used as part of a plural name.

Broadway
Fifty-Fifth Street; Fifty-Seventh and Fifty-Fifth Streets
Hyde Park Boulevard; the boulevard
Interstate 80; I-80; an interstate highway; the interstate
the Ishtar Gate; the gate
Jackson Park; the park
London Bridge; the bridge
the Mall (in London)
Park Lane
Pennsylvania Avenue; Carnegie and Euclid Avenues
Piccadilly Circus
the Spanish Steps; the steps
Tiananmen Square; the square
US Route 66; Routes 1 and 2; a state route

See also 9.50–52.

8.57 **Buildings and monuments.** The names of buildings and monuments are generally capitalized. The generic term is usually lowercased when used alone but capitalized when used as part of a plural name (as in the fifth example).

the Babri Mosque; the mosque
the Berlin Wall; the wall
Buckingham Fountain; the fountain
the Capitol (where the US Congress meets, *as distinct from* the capital city)
the Chrysler Building; the building; the Empire State and Chrysler Buildings
the Houses of Parliament
the Jefferson Memorial; the memorial
the Leaning Tower of Pisa
the Pyramids (*but* the Egyptian pyramids)
Shedd Aquarium; the aquarium
the Stone of Scone
Symphony Center; the center
Tribune Tower; the tower
the Washington Monument; the monument
Westminster Abbey; the abbey
the White House

Though major works of art are generally italicized (see 8.198), some massive works of sculpture are regarded primarily as monuments and therefore not italicized.

the Statue of Liberty; the statue
Mount Rushmore National Memorial; Mount Rushmore
the Colossus of Rhodes; the colossus

8.58 **Rooms, offices, and such.** Official names of rooms, offices, and the like are capitalized.

the Empire Room (*but* room 421)
the Amelia Earhart Suite (*but* suite 219)
the Lincoln Bedroom
the Oval Office
the West Wing of the White House

8.59 **Non-English names for places and structures.** Non-English names of thoroughfares and buildings are not italicized and may be preceded by English *the* if the definite article would appear in the original language. See also 11.4.

the Champs-Elysées
the Bibliothèque nationale
the Bois de Boulogne
Unter den Linden (never preceded by *the*)
the Marktstrasse
the Piazza delle Terme

Words Derived from Proper Names

8.60 **When to capitalize words derived from proper names.** Adjectives derived from personal names are normally capitalized. Those in common use may be found in *Webster's*, sometimes in the biographical names section (e.g., Aristotelian, Jamesian, Machiavellian, Shakespearean). If not in the dictionary, adjectives can sometimes be coined by adding *ian* (to a name ending in a consonant) or *an* (to a name ending in *e* or *i*)—or, failing these, *esque*. As with Foucault and Shaw, the final consonant sometimes undergoes a transformation as an aid to pronunciation. If a name does not seem to lend itself to any such coinage, it is best avoided. See also 8.61, 8.79.

Baudelaire; Baudelairean
Bayes; Bayesian
Dickens; Dickensian
Foucault; Foucauldian
Jordan; Jordanesque (à la Michael Jordan)
Kafka; Kafkaesque
Marx; Marxist
Mendel; Mendelian
Rabelais; Rabelaisian
Sartre; Sartrean
Shaw; Shavian

8.61 **When to lowercase words derived from proper names.** Personal, national, or geographical names, and words derived from such names, are often lowercased when used with a *nonliteral* meaning. For example, the cheese known as "gruyère" takes its name from a district in Switzerland but is not necessarily from there; "swiss cheese" (lowercase *s*) is a cheese that resembles Swiss emmentaler (which derives its name from the Emme River valley). Although some of the terms in this paragraph and the examples that follow are capitalized in *Webster's*, Chicago prefers to lowercase them in their nonliteral use. See also 8.79.

anglicize
arabic numerals
arctics (boots)
bohemian
bordeaux
brie
brussels sprouts
burgundy
champagne
cheddar
delphic
diesel engine
dutch oven
epicure

frankfurter
french dressing
french fries
french windows
gruyère
herculean
homeric
india ink
italicize
italic type
jeremiad
lombardy poplar
manila envelope
morocco leather
pasteurize
pharisaic
philistine, philistinism
platonic (but see 8.79)
quixotic
roman numerals
roman type
scotch (*but* Scotch whisky, a product of Scotland)
stilton
swiss cheese (not made in Switzerland)
venetian blinds
vulcanize
wiener

Names of Organizations

Governmental Bodies

8.62 **Legislative and deliberative bodies.** The full names of legislative and deliberative bodies, departments, bureaus, and offices are capitalized (but see 8.65). Adjectives derived from them are usually lowercased, as are many of the generic names for such bodies when used alone (as on subsequent mentions). For generic names used alone but not listed here, opt for lowercase. For administrative bodies, see 8.63; for judicial bodies, see 8.64. See also 11.4.

the United Nations General Assembly; the UN General Assembly; the assembly
the League of Nations; the league
the United Nations Security Council; the Security Council; the council
the United States Congress; the US Congress; the 115th Congress; Congress; 115th Cong.; congressional (see also 9.45)
the United States Senate; the Senate; senatorial; the upper house of Congress
the House of Representatives; the House; the lower house of Congress
the Electoral College
the Committee on Foreign Affairs; the Foreign Affairs Committee; the committee
the Illinois General Assembly; the assembly; the Illinois legislature; the state senate
the Chicago City Council; the city council
the British Parliament (*or* UK Parliament); Parliament; an early parliament; parliamentary; the House of Commons; the Commons; the House of Lords; the Lords

the Crown (the British monarchy); Crown lands
the Privy Council (*but* a Privy Counsellor)
the Parliament of Canada; Parliament; the Senate (upper house); the House of Commons (lower house)
the Legislative Assembly of British Columbia; the National Assembly of Quebec *or* Assemblée nationale du Québec
the Oireachtas (Irish parliament); Seanad Éireann (Irish upper house); Dáil Éireann (Irish lower house)
the Assemblée nationale *or* the National Assembly (present-day France); the (French) Senate; the parliamentary system; the Parlement de Paris (historical)
the States General *or* Estates General (France and Netherlands, historical)
the Cortes Generales; the Cortes (Spain); Cortes Españolas (Franco era)
the Cámara de Diputados (the lower house of Mexico's congress)
the Bundestag (German parliament); the Bundesrat (German upper house); the Reichstag (imperial Germany)
the House of People's Representatives; the House of Federation; the Council of Ministers (Ethiopia)
the Dewan Perwakilan Rakyat *or* the House of Representatives; the Majelis Permusyawaratan Rakyat *or* People's Consultative Assembly (Indonesia)
the European Parliament; the Parliament

8.63 **Administrative bodies.** The full names of administrative bodies are capitalized. Adjectives derived from them are usually lowercased, as are many of the generic names for such bodies when used alone. See also 8.62.

the United States Census Bureau; census forms; the census of 2000
the Centers for Disease Control and Prevention; the CDC (abbreviation did not change when "and Prevention" was added to name)
the Department of the Interior; the Interior
the Department of State; the State Department; the department; departmental
the Department of the Treasury; the Treasury
the Eunice Kennedy Shriver National Institute of Child Health and Human Development; the NICHD
the Federal Bureau of Investigation; the bureau; the FBI
the Federal Reserve System; the Federal Reserve Board; the Federal Reserve
the United States Foreign Service; Foreign Service Officer; officer in the Foreign Service
the National Institutes of Health; the NIH; the National Institute of Mental Health; the NIMH
the Occupational Safety and Health Administration; OSHA
the Office of Human Resources; Human Resources

the Peace Corps
the United States Postal Service; the Postal Service; the post office
the Illinois State Board of Education; the board of education
the Ithaca City School District; the school district; the district

8.64 **Judicial bodies.** The full name of a court, often including a place-name, is capitalized. Subsequent references to a court (or district court, supreme court, etc.) are lowercased, except for the phrase "Supreme Court" at the national level.

the United States (*or* US) Supreme Court; the Supreme Court; *but* the court
the United States Court of Appeals for the Seventh Circuit; the court of appeals
the Arizona Supreme Court; the supreme court; the supreme courts of Arizona and New Mexico
the District Court for the Southern District of New York; the district court
the Court of Common Pleas (Ohio); the court
the Circuit Court of Lake County, Family Division (Illinois); family court
the Supreme Court of Canada; the Supreme Court; the court
the Birmingham Crown Court; Dawlish Magistrates' Court (England)
the Federal Supreme Court (Ethiopia)

States, counties, and cities vary in the way they name their courts. For example, *court of appeals* in New York State and Maryland is equivalent to *supreme court* in other states; and such terms as *district court*, *circuit court*, *superior court*, and *court of common pleas* are used for similar court systems in different states. Generic names should therefore be used only after the full name or jurisdiction has been stated.

8.65 **Government entities that are lowercased.** Certain generic terms associated with governmental bodies are lowercased. Compare 8.51.

administration; the Carter administration
brain trust
cabinet (*but* the Kitchen Cabinet in the Jackson administration)
city hall (the municipal government and the building)
civil service
court (a royal court)
executive, legislative, or judicial branch
federal; the federal government; federal agencies
government
monarchy
parlement (French; *but* the Parlement of Paris)

parliament, parliamentary (*but* Parliament, usually not preceded by *the*, in the United Kingdom)
state; church and state; state powers

Political and Economic Organizations and Movements

8.66 **Organizations, parties, alliances, and so forth.** Official names of national and international organizations, alliances, and political movements and parties are capitalized (e.g., "the Labor Party in Israel"). Words like *party*, *union*, and *movement* are capitalized when they are part of the name of an organization. Terms identifying formal members of or adherents to such groups are also usually capitalized (e.g., "a Socialist"; "a Republican"). Names of the systems of thought and references to the adherents to such systems, however, are often lowercased (e.g., "an eighteenth-century precursor of socialism"; "a communist at heart"). Nonliteral or metaphorical references are also lowercased (e.g., "fascist parenting techniques"; "nazi tendencies"). For consistency, however—as in a work about communism in which the philosophy and its adherents, the political party, and party members and adherents are discussed—capitalizing the philosophy, together with the organization and its adherents, in both noun and adjective forms, will prevent editorial headaches.

the African National Congress party (*party* is not part of the official name); the ANC
Arab Socialist Baʿth Party; the Baʿth Party; the party; Baʿthists
Bahujan Samaj Party; the BSP
Bolshevik(s); the Bolshevik (*or* Bolshevist) movement; bolshevism *or* Bolshevism (see text above)
Chartist; Chartism
the Communist Party (*but* communist parties); the party; Communist(s); Communist countries; communism *or* Communism (see text above)
the Democratic Party; the party; Democrat(s) (party members or adherents); democracy; democratic nations
the Entente Cordiale (signed 1904); the Entente; *but* an entente cordiale
the Ethiopian Somali Democratic League; the league; the party
the European Union; the EU; the Common Market
the Fascist Party; Fascist(s); fascism *or* Fascism (see text above)
the Federalist Party; Federalist(s) (US history); federalism *or* Federalism (see text above)
the Free-Soil Party; Free-Soiler(s)
the General Agreement on Tariffs and Trade; GATT
the Green Party; the party; Green(s); the Green movement

the Hanseatic League; Hansa; a Hanseatic city
the Holy Alliance
the Know-Nothing Party; Know-Nothing(s)
the Labour Party; Labourite(s) (members of the British party)
the League of Arab States; the Arab League; the league
the Libertarian Party; Libertarian(s); libertarianism *or* Libertarianism (see text above)
Loyalist(s) (American Revolution; Spanish Civil War)
Marxism-Leninism; Marxist-Leninist(s)
the National Socialist Party; National Socialism; the Nazi Party; Nazi(s); Nazism
the North American Free Trade Agreement; NAFTA
the North Atlantic Treaty Organization; NATO
the Organisation for Economic Co-operation and Development; the OECD; the organization
the Popular Front; the Front; *but* a popular front
the Populist Party; Populist(s); populism *or* Populism (see text above)
the Progressive Party; Progressive movement; Progressive(s); progressivism *or* Progressivism (see text above)
the Quadruple Alliance; the alliance
the Rashtriya Janata Dal; the RJD (National People's Party)
the Republican Party; the party; the GOP (Grand Old Party); Republican(s) (party members or adherents); republicanism; a republican form of government
the Social Democratic Party; the party; Social Democrat(s)
the Socialist Party (*but* socialist parties); the party; Socialist(s) (party members or adherents); socialism *or* Socialism (see text above)
the United Democratic Movement; the movement
the World Health Organization; WHO

8.67 **Adherents of unofficial political groups and movements.** Names for adherents of political groups or movements other than recognized parties are usually lowercased.

anarchist(s)
centrist(s)
independent(s)
moderate(s)
mugwump(s)
opposition (*but* the Opposition, in British and Canadian contexts, referring to the party out of power)
but
the Left; members of the left wing; left-winger(s); on the left
the Right; members of the right wing; right-winger(s); on the right
the Far Left

the Far Right
the radical Right
the Tea Party; Tea Partiers (modeled on names for established parties)

Institutions and Companies

8.68 **Institutions and companies—capitalization.** The full names of institutions, groups, and companies and the names of their departments, and often the shortened forms of such names (e.g., the Art Institute), are capitalized. A *the* preceding a name, even when part of the official title, is lowercased in running text. Such generic terms as *company* and *university* are usually lowercased when used alone (though they are routinely capitalized in promotional materials, business documents, and the like).

the University of Chicago; the university; the University of Chicago and Harvard University; Northwestern and Princeton Universities; the University of Wisconsin–Madison (see also 6.81)
the Department of History; the department; the Law School
the University of Chicago Press; the press
the Board of Trustees of the University of Chicago; the board of trustees; the board
the Art Institute of Chicago; the Art Institute
the Beach Boys; the Beatles; the Grateful Dead, the Dead; the Who (*but* Tha Eastsidaz)
Captain Beefheart and His Magic Band; the band
the Cleveland Orchestra; the orchestra
the General Foods Corporation; General Foods; the corporation
the Green Bay Packers; the Packers
the Hudson's Bay Company; the company
the Illinois Central Railroad; the Illinois Central; the railroad
the Library of Congress; the library
the Manuscripts Division of the library
the Museum of Modern Art; MOMA; the museum
the New School (see also 8.69)
the New York Stock Exchange; the stock exchange
Skidmore, Owings & Merrill; SOM; the architectural firm
the Smithsonian Institution; the Smithsonian
Miguel Juarez Middle School; the middle school

8.69 **Corporate names with unusual capitalization.** Corporate names that appear in all lowercase in logotype and other promotional settings can often be capitalized in the usual way. A copyright or "About Us" statement on a corporate website can be helpful in determining a usage that might be suitable for regular text. Words that would normally be lowercase in headline-style capitalization can usually be lowercased (see 8.159). Spellings that begin lowercase but include a capital letter are usually appropriate for running text, even at the beginning of a sentence, as are names with additional internal capitals (see 8.154). A preference for all uppercase should be respected. If a company appears to prefer all lowercase even in running text, an initial capital can be applied as a matter of editorial expediency.

Intel (*not* intel)
Adidas (*not* adidas)
AT&T (*not* at&t)
Ebrary (*not* ebrary)
Parsons the New School for Design (lowercase *the*, contrary to corporate usage)
but
GlaxoSmithKline
HarperCollins
RAND Corporation
eBay

Associations

8.70 **Associations, unions, and the like.** The full names of associations, societies, unions, meetings, and conferences, and often the shortened forms of such names, are capitalized. A *the* preceding a name, even when part of the official title, is lowercased in running text. Such generic terms as *society* and *union* are usually lowercased when used alone.

the Congress of Industrial Organizations; CIO; the union
Girl Scouts of the United States of America; a Girl Scout; a Scout
the Independent Order of Odd Fellows; IOOF; an Odd Fellow
Industrial Workers of the World; IWW; the Wobblies
the International Olympic Committee; the IOC; the committee
the League of Women Voters; the league
the National Conference for Community and Justice; the conference
the National Organization for Women; NOW; the organization
the New-York Historical Society (the hyphen is part of the official name of the society); the society
the 130th Annual Meeting of the American Historical Association; the annual meeting of the association

the Quadrangle Club; the club
the Textile Workers Union of America; the union

On the other hand, a substantive title given to a single meeting, conference, speech, or discussion is enclosed in quotation marks. For lecture series, see 8.87.

"Inside the Mind of a Master Procrastinator," a TED talk by Tim Urban posted in March 2016.

Historical and Cultural Terms

Periods

8.71 **Numerical designations for periods.** A numerical designation for a period is usually lowercased; however, certain periods may be treated as proper nouns (in which both the numerical designation and the term for the period are capitalized) to avoid any confusion with the generic meaning of the same term (see also 8.51). For the use of numerals, see 9.33, 9.45.

the twenty-first century
the nineteen hundreds
the nineties
the quattrocento
the second millennium BCE
but
the Eighteenth Dynasty (Egypt)

8.72 **Descriptive designations for periods.** A descriptive designation of a period is usually lowercased, except for proper names or to avoid ambiguity with a generic term. For traditionally capitalized forms, see 8.73.

ancient Greece
the antebellum period
antiquity
the baroque period
the colonial period
a golden age
the Hellenistic period
imperial Rome
modern history
the Romantic period (see also 8.79)
the Shang dynasty (considered an era rather than a political division; see 8.51)
the Victorian era

8.73 **Traditional period names.** Some names of periods are capitalized, either by tradition or to avoid ambiguity. See also 8.75.

the Augustan Age
the Common Era
the Counter-Reformation
the Dark Ages
the Enlightenment
the Gay Nineties
the Gilded Age
the Grand Siècle
the High Middle Ages (*but* the early Middle Ages, the late Middle Ages)
the High Renaissance
the Jazz Age
the Mauve Decade
the Middle Ages (*but* the medieval era)
the Old Kingdom (ancient Egypt)
the Old Regime (*but* the ancien régime)
the Progressive Era
the Reformation
the Renaissance
the Restoration
the Roaring Twenties

8.74 **Cultural periods.** Names of prehistoric cultural periods are capitalized. For geological periods, see 8.134–36.

the Bronze Age
the Ice Age
the Iron Age
the Stone Age

Similar terms for modern periods are often lowercased (but see 8.73).

the age of reason
the age of steam
the information age
the nuclear age

Events

8.75 **Historical events and programs.** Names of many major historical events and programs are conventionally capitalized. Others, more recent or known by their generic descriptions, are often lowercased but may be capitalized to prevent ambiguity. If in doubt, opt for lowercase. For wars and battles, see 8.113–14; for religious events, 8.108; for acts and treaties, 8.80.

the Arab Spring
Black Lives Matter
Boston Tea Party
the Boxer Rebellion
the Cold War (*but* a cold war, used generically)
the Cultural Revolution
the Great Chicago Fire; the Chicago fire; the fire of 1871
the Great Depression; the Depression
the Great Fire of London; the Great Fire
the Great Plague; the Plague (*but* plague [the disease])
(President Johnson's) Great Society
the Industrial Revolution
the Long March
the May 18 Democratic Uprising (*or* Gwangju Uprising)
the New Deal
Occupy Wall Street; the Occupy movement
Prohibition
Reconstruction
the Reign of Terror; the Terror
the South Sea Bubble
the War on Poverty
but
the baby boom
the Black September attacks
the civil rights movement
the crash of 1929
the Dreyfus affair
the gold rush
the Moroccan crises
the Tiananmen Square protests
the war on terror

8.76 **Speeches.** Titles of a select few speeches are traditionally capitalized. Others are usually lowercased (but see 8.188).

Washington's Farewell Address
the Gettysburg Address
the annual State of the Union address
Franklin Roosevelt's second inaugural address
the Checkers speech
Martin Luther King Jr.'s "I Have a Dream" speech

8.77 **Meteorological and other natural phenomena.** Named hurricanes and other tropical cyclones are capitalized, as are many other named meteorological phenomena. If in doubt, consult a dictionary or encyclopedia. Natural phenomena identified generically by a place-name or a year are usually lowercased.

Cyclone Becky; the 2007 cyclone
Hurricane Katrina; the 2005 hurricane
El Niño
the Northridge earthquake of 1994
the Arctic polar vortex

Use the pronoun *it*, not *he* or *she*, when referring to named storms, hurricanes, and the like (notwithstanding the practice of using male and female proper names to refer to such events).

8.78 **Sporting events.** The full names of major sporting events are capitalized.

the Kentucky Derby; the derby
the NBA Finals; the finals
the Olympic Games; the Olympics; the Winter Olympics
the World Cup

Cultural Movements and Styles

8.79 **Movements and styles—capitalization.** Nouns and adjectives designating cultural styles, movements, and schools—artistic, architectural, musical, and so forth—and their adherents are capitalized if derived from proper nouns. (Words such as *school* and *movement* remain lowercased.) Others may be lowercased, though a few (e.g., Beat, Cynic, Scholastic, New Criticism) are capitalized to distinguish them from the generic words used in everyday speech. Some of the terms lowercased below may appropriately be capitalized in certain works if done consistently—especially those that include the designation "often capitalized" in *Webster's*. (But if, for example, *impressionism* is capitalized in a work about art, other art movements must also be capitalized—which could result in an undesirable profusion of capitals.) For religious movements, see 8.97. See also 8.60.

abstract expressionism
Aristotelian
art deco
art nouveau
baroque
Beat movement; the Beats (*but* beatnik)
Beaux-Arts (derived from École des Beaux-Arts)
British Invasion
camp
Cartesian
Chicago school (of architecture, of economics, of literary criticism)
classicism, classical
conceptualism
cubism
Cynicism; Cynic
Dadaism; Dada
deconstruction
Doric
Epicurean (see text below)
existentialism
fauvism
formalism
Gothic (*but* gothic fiction)
Gregorian chant
Hellenism
Hudson River school
humanism
idealism
imagism
impressionism
Keynesianism
mannerism
miracle play
modernism
mysticism; mystic
naturalism
neoclassicism; neoclassical
Neoplatonism
New Criticism
nominalism
op art
Peripatetic (see text below)
philosophe (French)
Platonism
pop art
postimpressionism
postmodernism
Pre-Raphaelite
Reaganomics
realism
rococo
Romanesque
Romanticism; Romantic
Scholasticism; Scholastic; Schoolmen
scientific rationalism
Sophist (see text below)
Stoicism; Stoic (see text below)
structuralism
Sturm und Drang (*but* storm and stress)
surrealism
symbolism
theater of the absurd
transcendentalism

Some words capitalized when used in reference to a school of thought are lowercased when used metaphorically.

epicurean tastes
peripatetic families
she's a sophist, not a logician
a stoic attitude

Acts, Treaties, and Government Programs

8.80 **Formal names of acts, treaties, and so forth.** Formal or accepted titles of pacts, plans, policies, treaties, acts, programs, and similar documents or agreements are capitalized. Incomplete or generic forms are usually lowercased. For citing the published text of a bill or law, see 14.282, 14.283.

the Articles of Confederation
the Bill of Rights
the Brady law
the Constitution of the United States; the United States (*or* US) Constitution; the Constitution (usually capitalized in reference to the US Constitution); Article VI; the article (see also 9.28)
the Illinois Constitution; the constitution
the Constitution Act, 1982 (Canada)
the Corn Laws (Great Britain)
the Declaration of Independence
the due process clause
the Equal Rights Amendment (usually capitalized though not ratified); ERA; *but* an equal rights amendment
the Family and Medical Leave Act of 1993; FMLA; the 1993 act
the Fifteenth Amendment (to the US Constitution); the Smith Amendment; the amendment
the Food Stamp Act of 1964; food stamps
the Hawley-Smoot (*or* Smoot-Hawley) Tariff Act; the tariff act
Head Start
impeachment; the first and second articles of impeachment
the Kyoto Protocol; the protocol
the Marshall Plan
the Mayflower Compact; the compact
Medicare (lowercase in Canada); Medicaid
the Monroe Doctrine; the doctrine
the Munich agreement (1938); Munich
the New Economic Policy; NEP (Soviet Union)
the Open Door policy
the Peace of Utrecht
the Reform Bills; the Reform Bill of 1832 (Great Britain)
the Social Security Act; Social Security (*or, generically,* social security)
Temporary Assistance for Needy Families; TANF
Title VII *or* Title 7
Treaty for the Renunciation of War, *known as* the Pact of Paris *or* the Kellogg-Briand Pact; the pact

the Treaty of Versailles; the treaty
the Treaty on European Union (official name); the Maastricht treaty (informal name)
the Wilmot Proviso

8.81 **Generic terms for pending legislation.** Informal, purely descriptive references to pending legislation are lowercased.

The anti-injunction bill was introduced on Tuesday. (See also the table at 7.89, section 4.)

Legal Cases

8.82 **Legal cases mentioned in text.** The names of legal cases are italicized when mentioned in text. The abbreviation *v.* (versus) occasionally appears in roman, but Chicago recommends italics. In footnotes, legal dictionaries, and contexts where numerous legal cases appear, they are sometimes set in roman. For legal citation style, see 14.269–305.

Bloomfield Village Drain Dist. v. Keefe *Miranda v. Arizona*

In discussion, a case name may be shortened.

the *Miranda* case (or simply *Miranda*)

Awards

8.83 **Capitalization for names of awards and prizes.** Names of awards and prizes are capitalized, but some generic terms used with the names are lowercased. For military awards, see 8.115.

the 2017 Nobel Prize in Physiology or Medicine; a Nobel Prize winner; a Nobel Prize–winning physiologist (see 6.80); a Nobel Peace Prize; the Nobel Prize in Literature
the 2017 Pulitzer Prize for Commentary (*but* a Pulitzer in journalism)
an Academy Award; the Academy Award for Best Picture; an Oscar
an Emmy Award for Outstanding Supporting Actor in a Comedy Series; she has three Emmys
a Webby Award; the Webbys; the Webby Award for Activism (Web); a Webby
the Presidential Medal of Freedom

a Guggenheim Fellowship (*but* a Guggenheim grant)
an International Music Scholarship
National Merit Scholarship awards; Merit Scholarships; Merit Scholar

Oaths and Pledges

8.84 **Formal oaths and pledges.** Formal oaths and pledges are usually lowercased.

the oath of citizenship
the Hippocratic oath
the presidential oath of office
marriage vows
but
the Pledge of Allegiance

Academic Subjects, Courses of Study, and Lecture Series

8.85 **Academic subjects.** Academic subjects are not capitalized unless they form part of a department name or an official course name (see 8.86) or are themselves proper nouns (e.g., English, Latin).

She has published widely in the history of religions.
They have a wide variety of courses in gender studies.
He is majoring in comparative literature.
She is pursuing graduate studies in philosophy of science.
but
Jones is chair of the Committee on Comparative Literature.

8.86 **Courses of study.** Official names of courses of study are capitalized.

I am signing up for Archaeology 101.
A popular course at the Graham School of General Studies is Basic Manuscript Editing.
but
His ballroom dancing classes have failed to civilize him.

8.87 **Lectures.** Names of lecture series are capitalized. Titles for individual lectures are capitalized and usually enclosed in quotation marks. See also 8.70.

This year's Robinson Memorial Lectures were devoted to the nursing profession. The first lecture, "How Nightingale Got Her Way," was a sellout.

Calendar and Time Designations

8.88 **Days of the week, months, and seasons.** Names of days and months are capitalized. The four seasons are lowercased (except when used to denote an issue of a journal; see 14.171). For centuries and decades, see 8.71.

Tuesday	spring	the vernal (*or* spring) equinox
November	fall	the winter solstice

8.89 **Holidays.** The names of secular and religious holidays or officially designated days or seasons are capitalized.

All Fools' Day
Christmas Day
Earth Day
Election Day
Father's Day
the Fourth of July, the Fourth
Good Friday
Halloween
Hanukkah
Holy Week
Inauguration Day
Independence Day
Kwanzaa
Labor Day
Lent
Lincoln's Birthday
Martin Luther King Jr. Day
Memorial Day
Mother's Day
National Poetry Month
New Year's Day
New Year's Eve
Passover
Presidents' Day
Ramadan
Remembrance Day (Canada)
Rosh Hashanah
Saint Patrick's Day
Thanksgiving Day
Veterans Day
Yom Kippur
Yuletide
but
D-day
a bank holiday

8.90 **Time and time zones.** When spelled out, designations of time and time zones are lowercased (except for proper nouns). Abbreviations are capitalized. See also 9.37–40, 10.41.

eastern standard time; EST
central daylight time; CDT
mountain standard time; MST
Pacific daylight time; PDT
Greenwich mean time; GMT
daylight saving time; DST

Religious Names and Terms

Deities and Revered Persons

8.91 **Deities.** Names of deities, whether in monotheistic or polytheistic religions, are capitalized.

Allah	Jehovah
Astarte	Mithra
Freyja	Satan (*but* the devil)
God	Serapis
Itzamna	Yahweh

Some writers follow a pious convention of not fully spelling out the name of a deity (e.g., *G-d*). This convention should be respected when it is practical to do so.

8.92 **Alternative names.** Alternative or descriptive names for God as supreme being are capitalized. See also 8.93.

Adonai
the Almighty
the Deity
the Holy Ghost *or* the Holy Spirit *or* the Paraclete
the Lord
Providence
the Supreme Being
the Trinity

8.93 **Prophets and the like.** Designations of prophets, apostles, saints, and other revered persons are often capitalized.

the Buddha
the prophet Isaiah
Jesus; Christ; the Good Shepherd; the Son (*or* son) of man
John the Baptist
the Messiah
Muhammad; the Prophet
Saint John; the Beloved Apostle
the Virgin Mary; the Blessed Virgin; Mother of God
but
the apostles

the patriarchs
the psalmist

8.94 **Platonic ideas.** Words for transcendent ideas in the Platonic sense, especially when used in a religious context, are often capitalized. See also 7.52.

Good; Beauty; Truth; the One

8.95 **Pronouns referring to religious figures.** Pronouns referring to God or Jesus are not capitalized unless a particular author or publisher prefers otherwise. (Note that they are lowercased in most English translations of the Bible.)

They prayed to God that he would deliver them.
Jesus and his disciples

Religious Groups

8.96 **Major religions.** Names of major religions are capitalized, as are their adherents and adjectives derived from them.

Buddhism; Buddhist
Christianity; Christian; Christendom (see also 8.98)
Confucianism; Confucian
Hinduism; Hindu
Islam; Islamic; Muslim
Judaism; Jew; Jewry; Jewish
Shinto; Shintoism; Shintoist
Taoism; Taoist; Taoistic
but
atheism
agnosticism

8.97 **Denominations, sects, orders, and religious movements.** Like the names of major religions, names of denominations, communions, sects, orders, and religious movements are capitalized, as are their adherents and adjectives derived from them. See also 8.99.

the Amish; Amish communities
Anglicanism; the Anglican Communion (*see also* Episcopal Church)

Baptists; a Baptist church; the Baptist General Convention; the Southern Baptist Convention
Catholicism (*see* Roman Catholicism)
Christian Science; Church of Christ, Scientist; Christian Scientist
the Church of England (*but* an Anglican church)
the Church of Ireland
Community of Christ
Conservative Judaism; a Conservative Jew
Dissenter (lowercased when used in a nonsectarian context)
Druidism; Druid (sometimes lowercased)
Eastern Orthodox churches; the Eastern Church (*but* an Eastern Orthodox church)
the Episcopal Church; an Episcopal church; an Episcopalian
the Episcopal Church of Scotland
Essenes; an Essene
Gnosticism; Gnostic
Hasidism; Hasid (singular); Hasidim (plural); Hasidic
Jehovah's Witnesses
Jesuit(s); the Society of Jesus; Jesuitic(al) (lowercased when used pejoratively)
Methodism; the United Methodist Church (*but* a United Methodist church); Wesleyan
Mormonism; Mormon; the Church of Jesus Christ of Latter-day Saints
Nonconformism; Nonconformist (lowercased when used in a nonsectarian context)
Old Catholics; an Old Catholic church
the Order of Preachers; the Dominican order; a Dominican
Orthodox Judaism; an Orthodox Jew
Orthodoxy; the (Greek, Serbian, etc.) Orthodox Church (*but* a Greek Orthodox church)
Protestantism; Protestant (lowercased when used in a nonsectarian context)
Puritanism; Puritan (lowercased when used in a nonsectarian context)
Quakerism; Quaker; the Religious Society of Friends; a Friend
Reform Judaism; a Reform Jew
Roman Catholicism; the Roman Catholic Church (*but* a Roman Catholic church)
Satanism; Satanist
Seventh-day Adventist; Adventist; Adventism
Shiism; Shia; Shiite
Sufism; Sufi
Sunnism; Sunni; Sunnite
Theosophy; Theosophist; the Theosophical Society
Vedanta
Wicca; Wiccan
Zen; Zen Buddhism

8.98 **"Church" as institution.** When used to refer to the institution of religion or of a particular religion, *church* is usually lowercased unless a particular author or publisher prefers otherwise.

church and state	the church in the twenty-first century
the early church	the church fathers

Church is capitalized when part of the formal name of a denomination (e.g., the United Methodist Church; see other examples in 8.97) or congregation (e.g., the Church of St. Thomas the Apostle).

8.99 **Generic versus religious terms.** Many terms that are lowercased when used generically, such as *animism*, *fundamentalism*, or *spiritualism*, may be capitalized when used as the name of a specific religion or a sect.

a popular medium in turn-of-the-century Spiritualist circles
but
liberal versus fundamentalist Christians

8.100 **Religious jurisdictions.** The names of official divisions within organized religions are capitalized. The generic terms used alone are lowercased.

the Archdiocese of Chicago; the archdiocese
the Eastern Diocese of the Armenian Church
the Fifty-Seventh Street Meeting; the (Quaker) meeting
the Holy See
the Missouri Synod; the synod

8.101 **Places of worship.** The names of the buildings in which religious congregations meet are capitalized. The generic terms used alone are lowercased.

Babri Mosque; the mosque
Bethany Evangelical Lutheran Church; the church
Temple Emanuel; the temple; the synagogue
Nichiren Buddhist Temple; the temple

8.102 **Councils, synods, and the like.** The accepted names of historic councils and the official names of modern counterparts are capitalized.

the Council of Chalcedon (*or* the Fourth Ecumenical Council)
the General Convention (Episcopal)

the Second Vatican Council; Vatican II
the Synod of Whitby

Religious Writings

8.103 **Scriptures.** Names of scriptures and other highly revered works are capitalized but not usually italicized (except when used in the title of a published work).

the Bhagavad Gita (*or* Bhagavad Gītā)
the Bible (*but* biblical)
the Book of Common Prayer
the Dead Sea Scrolls
the Hebrew Bible
Koran; Koranic (*or* Qur'an; Qur'anic)
the Mahabharata (*or* Mahābhārata)
Mishnah; Mishnaic
Sunna
Talmud; Talmudic
Tao Te Ching
Tripitaka
the Upanishads
the Vedas; Vedic
but
sutra(s)

8.104 **Other names and versions for bibles.** Other names and versions of the Hebrew and Christian bibles are usually capitalized but not italicized.

the Authorized Version *or* the King James Version
the Breeches (*or* Geneva) Bible
Codex Sinaiticus
Complutensian Polyglot Bible
the Douay (*or* Rheims-Douay) Version
the Holy Bible
Holy Writ (sometimes used figuratively)
the New English Bible
the New Jerusalem Bible
the New Revised Standard Version
Peshitta
the Psalter (*but* a psalter)

the Septuagint
the Vulgate
but
scripture(s); scriptural

8.105 **Books of the Bible.** The names of books of the Bible are capitalized but never italicized. The word *book* is usually lowercased, and the words *gospel* and *epistle* are usually capitalized. But in a work in which all three terms are used with some frequency, they may all be treated alike, either lowercased or capitalized. See also 9.26, 10.44–48.

Genesis; the book of Genesis
Job; the book of Job
2 Chronicles; Second Chronicles; the second book of Chronicles
Psalms (*but* a psalm)
John; the Gospel according to John
Acts; the Acts of the Apostles
1 Corinthians; the First Epistle to the Corinthians

8.106 **Sections of the Bible.** Names of sections of the Bible are usually capitalized but not italicized.

the Hebrew scriptures *or* the Old Testament
the Christian scriptures *or* the New Testament
the Apocrypha; Apocryphal (*or, generically,* apocryphal)
the Epistles; the pastoral Epistles
the Gospels; the synoptic Gospels
the Pentateuch *or* the Torah; Pentateuchal
Hagiographa *or* Ketuvim; hagiographic

8.107 **Prayers, creeds, and such.** Named prayers, canticles, creeds, and such, as well as scriptural terms of special importance, are usually capitalized. Parables and miracles are usually lowercased.

the Decalogue; the Ten Commandments; the first commandment
Kaddish; to say Kaddish
the Lord's Prayer; the Our Father
Luther's Ninety-Five Theses
the Nicene Creed; the creed
Salat al-Fajr
the Sermon on the Mount
the Shema

but
the doxology
the miracle of the loaves and fishes
the parable of the prodigal son
the star of Bethlehem

Religious Events, Concepts, Services, and Objects

8.108 **Religious events and concepts.** Religious events and concepts of major theological importance are often capitalized. Used generically, such terms are lowercased.

the Creation
the Crucifixion
the Diaspora
the Exodus
the Fall
the Hegira
the Second Coming
but
Most religions have creation myths.
For the Romans, crucifixion was a common form of execution.

Doctrines and principles are usually lowercased.

atonement dharma original sin resurrection

8.109 **Heaven, hell, and so on.** Terms for divine dwelling places, ideal states, places of divine punishment, and the like are usually lowercased (though they are often capitalized in a purely religious context). See also 8.50.

heaven
hell
limbo
nirvana
outer darkness
paradise
the pearly gates
purgatory
but
Eden
Elysium
Hades
Olympus

8.110 **Services and rites.** Names of services and rites are usually lowercased (though they may be capitalized in strictly religious contexts; if in doubt, consult *Webster's*).

baptism	morning prayer; matins
bar mitzvah	the seder
bat mitzvah	the sun dance
confirmation	vespers

Terms denoting the Eucharistic sacrament, however, are traditionally capitalized, though certain terms may be lowercased in nonreligious contexts or when used generically.

the Eucharist
Holy Communion
High Mass; Low Mass; attend Mass; *but* an afternoon mass

8.111 **Objects.** Objects of religious use or significance are usually lowercased, especially in nonreligious contexts.

altar	mandala	sacred pipe
ark	mezuzah	sanctuary
chalice and paten	rosary	stations of the cross

Military Terms

Forces and Troops

8.112 **Armies, battalions, and such.** Titles of armies, navies, air forces, fleets, regiments, battalions, companies, corps, and so forth are capitalized. Unofficial but well-known names, such as Green Berets, are also capitalized. Words such as *army* and *navy* are lowercased when standing alone, when used collectively in the plural, or when not part of an official title. Many of the lowercased terms below are routinely capitalized in official or promotional contexts (see 8.19). See also 9.47.

the Allies (World Wars I and II); the Allied forces
American Expeditionary Force; the AEF
Army Corps of Engineers; the corps
Army of Northern Virginia; the army
Army of the Potomac
Army Special Forces
the Axis powers (World War II)
Canadian Army (a branch of the Canadian Forces)
Canadian Forces *or* Canadian Armed Forces
the Central powers (World War I)

Combined Chiefs of Staff (World War II)
Confederate army (American Civil War)
Continental navy (American Revolution)
Eighth Air Force; the air force
Fifth Army; the army
First Battalion, 178th Infantry; the battalion; the 178th
French Foreign Legion
Green Berets
Joint Chiefs of Staff
the Luftwaffe; the German air force
National Guard
Pacific Fleet (US, World War II)
Red Army (Russian, World War II); Russian army
the Resistance; the French Resistance; a resistance movement
Rough Riders
Royal Air Force; RAF; British air force
Royal Canadian Air Force (a branch of the Canadian Forces)
Royal Canadian Mounted Police; the Mounties; a Mountie
Royal Canadian Navy (a branch of the Canadian Forces)
Royal Navy; the British navy
Royal Scots Fusiliers; the fusiliers
Seventh Fleet; the fleet
Thirty-Third Infantry Division; the Thirty-Third Division; the division
Union army (American Civil War)
United States (*or* US) Army; the army
United States Army Signal Corps; the Signal Corps *or* the signal corps
United States Coast Guard; the Coast Guard *or* the coast guard
United States Marine Corps; the Marine Corps *or* the marine corps; the US Marines; a marine
United States Navy; the navy

Wars, Revolutions, Battles, and Campaigns

8.113 **Wars and revolutions.** Names of most major wars and revolutions are capitalized. The generic terms are usually lowercased when used alone. More recent, unresolved conflicts can usually be lowercased.

American Civil War; the War between the States
American Revolution; American War of Independence; the revolution (sometimes capitalized); the Revolutionary War
Crusades; the Sixth Crusade; a crusader
French Revolution; the Revolution of 1789; the Revolution (usually capitalized

to distinguish the Revolution of 1789 from the revolutions in 1830 and 1848); revolutionary France
Great Sioux War; the Sioux war
Iran-Iraq War
Iraq War
Korean War; the war
Mexican Revolution; the revolution
Napoleonic Wars
Norman Conquest; the conquest of England
Persian Gulf War *or* Gulf War
the revolution(s) of 1848
Russian Revolution; the revolution
Seven Years' War
Shays's Rebellion
Six-Day War
Spanish-American War
Spanish Civil War
Vietnam War
War of 1812
Whiskey Rebellion
World War I; the First World War; the Great War; the war
World War II; the Second World War; World Wars I and II; the First and Second World Wars; the two world wars
but
the South Sudanese civil war; the civil war in South Sudan
the Ukrainian unrest

8.114 **Battles and campaigns.** Some of the names of major battles and campaigns that have entered the general lexicon are capitalized. In other, more generic descriptions, only proper names are capitalized. For names not included here, consult an encyclopedia.

Battle of Britain
Battle of Bunker Hill; Bunker Hill; the battle
Battle of the Bulge (*or* Battle of the Ardennes)
battle of Vimy Ridge
the Blitz
European theater of operations; ETO
Mexican border campaign
Operation Devil Siphon
third battle of Ypres
Vicksburg Campaign
western front (World War I)

Military Awards

8.115 **Medals and awards.** Specific names of medals and awards are capitalized. For civil awards, see 8.83.

Croix de Guerre (sometimes lowercased)
Distinguished Flying Cross; DFC
Distinguished Service Order; DSO
Medal of Honor (US congressional award); the medal
Purple Heart
Silver Star
Victoria Cross; VC

Names of Ships and Other Vehicles

8.116 **Ships and other named vessels.** Names of specific ships and other vessels are both capitalized and italicized. Note that when such abbreviations as USS (United States ship) or HMS (Her [or His] Majesty's ship) precede a name, the word *ship* or other vessel type should not be used. The abbreviations themselves are not italicized. For much useful information, consult Eric Wertheim, *The Naval Institute Guide to Combat Fleets of the World* (bibliog. 5).

Mars global surveyor; Mars polar lander; *Phoenix* Mars lander; *Phoenix*
the space shuttle *Discovery*
the *Spirit of St. Louis*
HMS *Frolic*; the British ship *Frolic*
SS *United States*; the *United States*
USS *SC-530*; the US ship *SC-530*

Every US Navy ship is assigned a hull number (according to a system formally implemented in 1920), consisting of a combination of letters (indicating the type of ship) and a serial number. Where necessary to avoid confusion between vessels of the same name—in a work on naval history, for example—the numbers should be included at first mention. Smaller ships such as landing craft and submarine chasers are individually numbered but not named.

USS *Enterprise* (CVN-65) was already on its way to the Red Sea.

8.117 **Other vehicle names.** Names of makes and classes of aircraft, models of automobiles and other vehicles, names of trains or train runs, and names of space programs are capitalized but not italicized.

Acela Express	Concorde	Project Apollo
Boeing 787 Dreamliner	Metroliner	Subaru Forester

8.118 **Pronouns referring to vessels.** When a pronoun is used to refer to a vessel, the neuter *it* or *its* (rather than *she* or *her*) is preferred. See also 5.43, 8.77.

Scientific Terminology

Scientific Names of Plants and Animals

8.119 **Scientific style—additional resources.** The following paragraphs offer only general guidelines. Writers or editors requiring detailed guidance should consult *Scientific Style and Format* (bibliog. 1.1). The ultimate authorities are the *International Code of Nomenclature for Algae, Fungi, and Plants* (*ICN*), whose guidelines are followed in the botanical examples below, and the *International Code of Zoological Nomenclature* (*ICZN*) (see bibliog. 5). Note that some fields, such as virology, have slightly different rules. Writers and editors should try to follow the standards established within those fields.

8.120 **Genus and specific epithet.** Whether in lists or in running text, the Latin names of species of plants and animals are italicized. Each *binomial* contains a genus name (or *generic name*), which is capitalized, and a species name (also called *specific name* or *specific epithet*), which is lowercased (even if it is a proper adjective). Do not confuse these names with phyla, orders, and such, which are not italicized; see 8.126.

The Pleistocene saber-toothed cats all belonged to the genus *Smilodon*.
Many species names, such as *Rosa caroliniana* and *Styrax californica*, reflect the locale of the first specimens described.
The pike, *Esox lucius*, is valued for food as well as sport.
For the grass snake *Natrix natrix*, longevity in captivity is ten years.
Certain lizard taxa, such as *Basiliscus* and *Crotaphytus*, are bipedal specialists.

8.121 **Abbreviation of genus name.** After the first use the genus name may be abbreviated to a single capital letter. If two or more species of the same genus are listed together, the abbreviation may be doubled (to indicate the plural) before the first species, though repeating the abbreviation with each species is more common. But if species of different genera beginning with the same letter are discussed in the same context, abbreviations may not be appropriate.

Two methods allow us to estimate the maximum speeds obtained by *Callisaurus draconoides* in the field. Irschick and Jayne (1998) found that stride durations of both *C. draconoides* and *Uma scoparia* do not change dramatically after the fifth stride during accelerations from a standstill.

The "quaking" of the aspen, *Populus tremuloides*, is due to the construction of the petiole; an analogous phenomenon has been noted in the cottonwood, *P. deltoides*.

Among popular species of the genus *Cyclamen* are *CC. coum*, *hederifolium*, and *persicum* . . . [or, more commonly, *C. coum*, *C. hederifolium*, and *C. persicum* . . .]

Studies of *Corylus avellana* and *Corokia cotoneaster* . . . ; in further studies it was noted that *Corylus avellana* and *Corokia cotoneaster* . . .

8.122 **Subspecies and varieties.** A subspecific zoological name or epithet, when used, follows the binomial species name and is also italicized. If the two names are the same, the first one may be abbreviated.

Noctilio labialis labialis (or *Noctilio l. labialis*) *Trogon collaris puella*

In horticultural usage, the abbreviations "subsp." (or "ssp."), "var.," and "f." (none of them italicized) are inserted before the subspecific epithet or variety or form name. See also 8.123.

Buxus microphylla var. *japonica*
Hydrangea anomala subsp. *petiolaris*
Rhododendron arboreum f. *album*

8.123 **Unspecified species and varieties.** The abbreviations "sp." and "var.," when used without a following element, indicate that the species or variety is unknown or unspecified. The plural "spp." is used to refer to a group of species. The abbreviations are *not* italicized.

Rhododendron spp. *Rosa rugosa* var. *Viola* sp.

8.124 **Author names.** The name of the person who proposed a specific epithet is sometimes added, often abbreviated, and never italicized. A capital *L.* stands for Linnaeus; *Mill.* stands for Miller.

Diaemus youngi cypselinus Thomas
Euchistenes hartii (Thomas)
Felis leo Scop.
Molossus coibensis J. A. Allen
Quercus alba L.
Linaria spuria (L.) Mill.

The parentheses in the second example, from zoology, mean that Thomas originally described the species *E. hartii* but referred it to a different genus. In botanical usage, the name of the person who referred it to the new genus is added after the parentheses, as in the last example.

8.125 **Plant hybrids.** The crossing of two species is indicated by a multiplication sign (×; *not* the letter *x*) between the two species names, with space on each side. Many older primary plant hybrids are indicated by a multiplication sign immediately before the specific epithet of the hybrid, with space only before it.

Magnolia denudata × *M. liliiflora* (crossing of species)
Magnolia ×*soulangeana* (hybrid name)

8.126 **Higher divisions.** Divisions higher than genus—phylum, class, order, and family—are capitalized but *not* italicized. (The terms *order*, *family*, and so on are not capitalized.) Intermediate groupings are treated similarly.

Chordata (phylum)
Chondrichthyes (class)
Monotremata (order)
Ruminantia (suborder)
Hominidae (family)
Felinae (subfamily)
Selachii (term used of various groups of cartilaginous fishes)
The new species *Gleichenia glauca* provides further details about the history of Gleicheniaceae.

8.127 **English derivatives.** English words derived from the taxonomic system are lowercased and treated as English words.

carnivore(s) (from the order Carnivora)
hominid(s) (from the family Hominidae)
irid(s) (from the family Iridaceae)
feline(s) (from subfamily Felinae)
astilbe(s) (from the genus *Astilbe*)
mastodon(s) (from the genus *Mastodon*)

Vernacular Names of Plants and Animals

8.128 **Plants and animals—additional resources.** For the correct capitalization and spelling of common names of plants and animals, consult a dictionary or the authoritative guides to nomenclature, the *ICN* and the *ICZN*, mentioned in 8.119. In general, Chicago recommends capitalizing only proper nouns and adjectives, as in the following examples, which conform to *Merriam-Webster's Collegiate Dictionary*:

Dutchman's-breeches
jack-in-the-pulpit
mayapple
Cooper's hawk
rhesus monkey
Rocky Mountain sheep

8.129 **Domestic animals and horticultural categories.** Either a dictionary or the guides to nomenclature *ICZN* and *ICN* should be consulted for the proper spelling of breeds of domestic animals and broad horticultural categories.

German shorthaired pointer
Hereford
Maine coon *or* coon cat
Thoroughbred horse (*but* purebred dog)
Rhode Island Red
boysenberry
rambler rose

8.130 **Horticultural cultivars.** Many horticultural cultivars (cultivated varieties) have fanciful names that must be respected since they may be registered trademarks.

the Peace rose
a Queen of the Market aster

In some horticultural publications, such names are enclosed in single quotation marks; any following punctuation is placed *after* the closing quotation mark. If the English name follows the Latin name, there is no intervening punctuation. For examples of this usage, consult any issue of the magazine *Horticulture* (bibliog. 5).

The hybrid *Agastache* 'Apricot Sunrise', best grown in zone 6, mingles with sheaves of cape fuchsia (*Phygelius* 'Salmon Leap').

Genetic Terms

8.131 **Genetic nomenclature—additional resources.** Only the most basic guidelines can be offered here. Writers or editors working in the field of genetics should consult the *AMA Manual of Style* or *Scientific Style and Format* (both in bibliog. 1.1) and online databases including the HGNC (HUGO Gene Nomenclature Committee) database of human gene names and the Mouse Genome Database (both in bibliog. 5).

8.132 **Genes.** Names of genes, or gene symbols, including any arabic numerals that form a part of such symbols, are usually italicized. (Italicization helps differentiate genes from entities with similar names.) Symbols for genes contain no Greek characters or roman numerals. Human gene symbols are set in full capitals, as are the gene symbols for other primates. Mouse and rat gene symbols are usually spelled with an initial capital. Gene nomenclature systems for other organisms (yeast, fruit flies, nematodes, plants, fish) vary. Symbols for proteins, also called gene products and often derived from the symbols of the corresponding genes, are set in roman.

Human genes

BRCA1
GPC3
IGH@ (the symbol @ indicates a family or cluster)
SNRPN

Mouse genes

Cmv1
Fgfl2
Rom1
Wnt1
NLP3 (gene symbol); NLP3p (encoded protein; note *p* suffix)
GIF (gene symbol); GIF (gastric intrinsic factor)

Only a very few gene symbols contain hyphens.

HLA-DRB1, for human leukocyte antigen D-related β chain 1

8.133 **Enzymes.** Enzyme names consist of a string of italic and roman characters. The first three letters, which represent the name of the organism (usually a bacterium) from which the enzyme has been isolated, are italicized. The roman numeral that follows represents the series number. Sometimes an upper- or lowercase roman letter or an arabic numeral (or both), representing the strain of bacterium, intervenes between the name and series number.

*Ava*I *Bam*HI *Cla*I *Eco*RI *Hind*III *Sau*3AI

Geological Terms

8.134 **Geological terms—additional resources.** The following paragraphs offer only the most general guidelines. Writers or editors working in geological studies should consult US Geological Survey, *Suggestions to Authors of the Reports of the United States Geological Survey*, and *Scientific Style and Format* (both listed in bibliog. 1.1).

8.135 **Formal versus generic geological terms.** Formal geological terms are capitalized in both noun and adjective forms; terms used generically are not. The generic terms *eon*, *era*, and the like are lowercased or omitted immediately following a formal name. Eons are divided into eras, eras into periods, periods into epochs, and epochs into stages. The term *ice age* is best lowercased in scientific contexts because of the uncertainty surrounding any formal use of the term (cf. *Little Ice Age*); but see 8.74.

the Archean (eon)
the Mesoproterozoic (era)
the Tertiary period of the Cenozoic (era)
the Paleocene (epoch)
Pleistocene-Holocene transition
the second interglacial stage *or* II interglacial
Illinoian glaciation

The modifiers *early*, *middle*, or *late* are capitalized when used formally but lowercased when used informally.

Early Archean	*but*
Middle Cambrian	early Middle Cambrian
Late Quaternary	in late Pleistocene times

8.136 **Stratigraphy.** Formal stratigraphic names are capitalized. For prehistoric cultural terms, see 8.74.

Fleur de Lys Supergroup	Niobrara Member
Ramey Ridge Complex	Morrison Formation

Astronomical Terms

8.137 **Astronomical terms—additional resources.** The following paragraphs offer only the most general guidelines. Writers or editors working in astronomy or astrophysics should consult *Scientific Style and Format* (bibliog. 1.1) and the website of the International Astronomical Union.

8.138 **Celestial bodies.** The names of galaxies, constellations, stars, planets, and such are capitalized. For *earth*, *sun*, and *moon*, see 8.140, 8.141.

Aldebaran
Alpha Centauri *or* α Centauri
the Big Dipper *or* Ursa Major *or* the Great Bear
Cassiopeia's Chair
the Crab Nebula
85 Pegasi
the Magellanic Clouds
the Milky Way
the North Star *or* Polaris, polestar
Saturn
but
Halley's comet
the solar system

8.139 **Catalog names for celestial objects.** Celestial objects listed in well-known catalogs are designated by the catalog name, often abbreviated, and a number.

Bond 619   Lalande 5761   Lynds 1251 *or* L1251   NGC 6165

8.140 **"Earth."** In nontechnical contexts, the word *earth*, in the sense of our planet, is usually lowercased when preceded by *the* or in such idioms as "down to earth" or "move heaven and earth." When used as the proper name of our planet, especially in context with other planets, it is capitalized and *the* is usually omitted.

Some still believe the earth is flat.
The gender accorded to the moon, the sun, and the earth varies in different mythologies.
Where on earth have you been?
The astronauts have returned successfully to Earth.
Does Mars, like Earth, have an atmosphere?

8.141 **"Sun" and "moon."** The words *sun* and *moon* are usually lowercased in nontechnical contexts and always lowercased in the plural.

The moon circles the earth, as the earth circles the sun.
Some planets have several moons.

Some publications in the fields of astronomy and related sciences, however, routinely capitalize these words when used as proper nouns. (See also 8.138.)

8.142 **Descriptive terms.** Merely descriptive terms applied to celestial objects or phenomena are not capitalized.

aurora borealis *or* northern lights
gegenschein
interstellar dust
the rings of Saturn

Medical Terms

8.143 **Medical terms—additional resources.** The following paragraphs offer only the most general guidelines. Medical writers or editors should consult the *AMA Manual of Style* or *Scientific Style and Format* (both in bibliog. 1.1).

8.144 **Diseases, procedures, and such.** Names of diseases, syndromes, diagnostic procedures, anatomical parts, and the like are lowercased, except for proper names forming part of the term. Acronyms and initialisms are capitalized.

acquired immunodeficiency syndrome *or* AIDS
Alzheimer disease (see below)
computed tomography *or* CT
Down syndrome (see below)
finger-nose test
islets of Langerhans
non-Hodgkin lymphoma (see below)
ultrasound; ultrasonography

The possessive forms *Alzheimer's*, *Down's*, *Hodgkin's*, and the like, though less common in medical literature, may be preferred in a general context. For x-rays and radiation, see 8.151.

8.145 **Infections.** Names of infectious organisms are treated like other specific names (see 8.119–27). Common forms of such names and the names of conditions based on such names are neither italicized nor capitalized, except in the case of a proper noun.

Microorganisms of the genus *Streptococcus* are present in the blood of persons with streptococcal infection.

The larvae of *Trichinella spiralis* are responsible for the disease trichinosis.

The Ebola virus (which refers to the species *Zaire ebolavirus*) derives its name from the Ebola River.

8.146 **Drugs.** Generic names of drugs, which should be used wherever possible in preference to brand names, are lowercased. Brand names must be capitalized; they are often enclosed in parentheses after the first use of the generic name. For guidance, consult the *AMA Manual of Style* and *Scientific Style and Format* (bibliog. 1.1) and *USP Dictionary of USAN and International Drug Names* (bibliog. 3.3). For brand names and trademarks, see 8.153.

The patient takes weekly injections of interferon beta-1a (Avonex) to control his multiple sclerosis.

Physical and Chemical Terms

8.147 **Physical and chemical terms—additional resources.** The following paragraphs offer only the most general guidelines for nontechnical editors. Writers or editors working in physics should consult AIP Publishing's online author resources (bibliog. 1.1) or, among other journals, *Physical Review Letters* (bibliog. 5); those working in chemistry should consult *The ACS Style Guide* (bibliog. 1.1).

8.148 **Laws and theories.** Though usage varies widely, Chicago recommends that names of laws, theories, and the like be lowercased, except for proper names attached to them.

Avogadro's hypothesis (*or* Avogadro's law)
the big bang theory
Boyle's law
(Einstein's) general theory of relativity
Newton's first law

8.149 **Chemical names and symbols.** Names of chemical elements and compounds are lowercased when written out. Symbols, however, are capitalized and set without periods; the number of atoms in a molecule appears as a subscript. For a list of symbols for the elements, including atomic numbers, see 10.63.

ozone; O_3
sodium chloride; NaCl
sulfuric acid; H_2SO_4
tungsten carbide; WC

8.150 **Mass number.** In formal chemical literature, the mass number appears as a superscript to the left of the symbol. In work intended for a general audience, however, it may follow the symbol, after a hyphen, in full size.

^{14}C (formal style); C-14 *or* carbon-14 (informal style)
^{238}U (formal style); U-238 *or* uranium-238 (informal style)

8.151 **Radiations.** Terms for electromagnetic radiations may be spelled as follows:

β-ray (noun or adjective) *or* beta ray (in nonscientific contexts, noun or adjective)
γ-ray (noun or adjective) *or* gamma ray (in nonscientific contexts, noun or adjective)
x-ray (noun, verb, or adjective)
cosmic ray (noun); cosmic-ray (adjective)
ultraviolet ray (noun); ultraviolet-ray (adjective)

Note that the verb *to x-ray*, though acceptable in a general context, is not normally used in scholarly medical literature, where writers would more likely speak of obtaining an x-ray image, or a radiograph, of something, or of subjecting something to x-ray analysis.

8.152 **Metric units.** Although the spellings *meter*, *liter*, and so on are widely used in the United States, some American business, government, or professional organizations have adopted the European spellings (*metre*, *litre*, etc.). Chicago's publications show a preference for the traditional American spellings. For abbreviations used in the International System of Units, see 10.51–59.

Brand Names and Trademarks

8.153 **Trademarks.** Brand names that are trademarks—often so indicated in dictionaries—should be capitalized if they must be used. A better choice is to substitute a generic term when available. Although the symbols ® and ™ (for registered and unregistered trademarks, respectively) often accompany trademark names on product packaging and in promotional material, there is no legal requirement to use these symbols, and they should be omitted wherever possible. (If one of these symbols must be used at the end of a product name, it should appear before any period, comma, or other mark of punctuation.) Note also that some companies encourage the use of both the proper and the generic term in reference to their products ("Kleenex facial tissue," not just "Kleenex") and discourage turning product names into verbs, but these restrictions, while they may be followed in corporate documentation, are not legally binding. (In fact, *Webster's* includes entries for lowercase verbs *google*, *photoshop*, and *xerox*.) See also 8.155.

Bufferin; buffered aspirin
Coca-Cola; cola
Google; search engine; search
Jacuzzi; whirlpool bath
Kleenex; (facial) tissue
Levi's; jeans
Photoshop; image-editing software
Ping-Pong; table tennis
Post-it Note; sticky note
Pyrex; heat-resistant glassware
Scrabble
Sharpie; permanent marker
Vaseline; petroleum jelly
Xerox; photocopier; copy

More information about registered trademarks can be found on the websites of the US Patent and Trademark Office and the International Trademark Association.

8.154 **Brand names or trademarks with an initial lowercase letter.** Brand names or trademarks spelled with a lowercase initial letter followed by a capital letter need not be capitalized at the beginning of a sentence or heading; the existing capital letter is sufficient to signal that these are proper nouns. Likewise, names that begin with a capital letter and include additional capitals in the middle of the word should be left unchanged. (In either scenario, such capital letters are sometimes referred to as intercaps or midcaps.) Chicago draws the line, however, at names in all lowercase; in order to signal that such a term is in fact a proper noun, an initial capital should be applied even midsentence (as for *Mini* in the last example; see also 8.69, 8.155).

iTunes is both an app and a media service.
Does your iPhone have an AccuWeather app?
PowerPoint has become virtually synonymous with presentation software.
but
The Mac Mini is a good solution for cluttered workspaces.

In text that is set in all capitals, such distinctions are usually overridden (e.g., POWERPOINT); with a mix of capitals and small capitals, they are preserved (e.g., iPHONE).

Software and Devices

8.155 **Names for applications, operating systems, and devices.** References to specific applications (also called programs or apps) and the operating systems and devices they run on are set in roman type without quotation marks (but see 8.190); capitalization can usually reflect the usage displayed by the software or the device itself. If in doubt, consult a help menu or a user's guide. Occasionally, an apparent preference for lowercase can be overridden (as in the first example below; see also 8.154). Generic references can be treated as ordinary text.

OS X; Macintosh; Mac Mini (contrary to corporate usage); Mac
Windows 10; HP desktop computer; notebook computer; PC
Microsoft Word; Apple Pages for Mac; LibreOffice Writer; Google Docs; word processor
iOS 10; iPhone; the Maps app for iOS 10; the Sleep/Wake button
Firefox; a browser; the Firefox app for Android
the Messenger app for Android; Apple's Messages app; a messaging app
Kindle; the Kindle app for Apple devices; Android's Kindle app
The iPhone's Clock app includes a stopwatch, a countdown timer, and an alarm.
Does your phone have a clock app?
I prefer the *New Yorker*'s iPhone app to the printed magazine.
Use your word-processing program to track changes and insert comments.

For typographic conventions for the names of particular keys, menus, commands, and the like, see 7.76–80.

Titles of Works

8.156 **Treatment of titles in text and notes—overview.** The following guidelines apply primarily to titles as they are mentioned or cited in text or notes. They apply to titles of books, journals, newspapers, and websites as well as to shorter works (stories, poems, articles, etc.), divisions of longer works (parts, chapters, sections), unpublished works (lectures etc.), plays and films, radio and television programs, musical works, and artworks. For details on citing titles in bibliographies and reference lists, see chapters 14 and 15. For the treatment of titles in languages other than English, see 11.6–10.

Capitalization, Punctuation, and Italics

8.157 **Capitalization of titles of works—general principles.** Titles mentioned or cited in text or notes are usually capitalized headline-style (see 8.159). For aesthetic purposes, titles appearing on the cover or title page or at the head of an article or chapter may deviate from Chicago's rules for the capitalization of titles. For capitalization of non-English titles, see 11.6. For the use of quotation marks versus italics, see 8.163.

8.158 **Principles and examples of sentence-style capitalization.** In sentence-style capitalization, only the first word in a title, the first word in a subtitle, and any proper names are capitalized. This style or some variant of it is commonly used in library catalogs and in the reference lists of some journals (see 15.13) and is the style recommended for most titles from other languages (see 11.6). It is also useful for some types of subheads (see 2.18), including those that include terms (such as species names) that require their own internal capitalization (but note that the specific epithet remains lowercase in headline style; see 8.159, rule 7). See also 8.162.

The house of Rothschild: The world's banker, 1849–1999
Crossing *Magnolia denudata* with *M. liliiflora* to create a new hybrid: A success story

8.159 **Principles of headline-style capitalization.** The conventions of headline style are governed mainly by emphasis and grammar. The following rules, though occasionally arbitrary, are intended primarily to facilitate the consistent styling of titles mentioned or cited in text and notes:

1. Capitalize the first and last words in titles and subtitles (but see rule 7), and capitalize all other major words (nouns, pronouns, verbs, adjectives, adverbs, and some conjunctions—but see rule 4).
2. Lowercase the articles *the*, *a*, and *an*.
3. Lowercase prepositions, regardless of length, except when they are used adverbially or adjectivally (*up* in *Look Up*, *down* in *Turn Down*, *on* in *The On Button*, *to* in *Come To*, etc.) or when they compose part of a Latin expression used adjectivally or adverbially (*De Facto*, *In Vitro*, etc.).
4. Lowercase the common coordinating conjunctions *and*, *but*, *for*, *or*, and *nor*.
5. Lowercase *to* not only as a preposition (rule 3) but also as part of an infinitive (*to Run*, *to Hide*, etc.), and lowercase *as* in any grammatical function.
6. Lowercase the part of a proper name that would be lowercased in text, such as *de* or *von*.

7. Lowercase the second part of a species name, such as *fulvescens* in *Acipenser fulvescens*, even if it is the last word in a title or subtitle.

For examples, see 8.160. For hyphenated compounds in titles, see 8.161.

8.160 **Examples of headline-style capitalization.** The following examples illustrate the numbered rules in 8.159. All of them demonstrate the first rule; the numbers in parentheses refer to rules 2–7.

Mnemonics That Work Are Better Than Rules That Do Not
Singing While You Work
A Little Learning Is a Dangerous Thing (2)
Four Theories concerning the Gospel according to Matthew (2, 3)
Taking Down Names, Spelling Them Out, and Typing Them Up (3, 4)
Tired but Happy (4)
The Editor as Anonymous Assistant (5)
From *Homo erectus* to *Homo sapiens*: A Brief History (3, 7)
Defenders of da Vinci Fail the Test: The Name Is Leonardo (2, 3, 6)
Sitting on the Floor in an Empty Room (2, 3), *but* Turn On, Tune In, and Enjoy (3, 4)
Ten Hectares per Capita, *but* Landownership and Per Capita Income (3)
Progress in In Vitro Fertilization (3)

8.161 **Hyphenated compounds in headline-style titles.** The following rules apply to hyphenated terms appearing in a title capitalized in headline style. For rules of hyphenation, see 7.81–89.

1. Always capitalize the first element.
2. Capitalize any subsequent elements unless they are articles, prepositions, coordinating conjunctions (*and*, *but*, *for*, *or*, *nor*), or such modifiers as *flat* or *sharp* following musical key symbols.
3. If the first element is merely a prefix or combining form that could not stand by itself as a word (*anti*, *pre*, etc.), do not capitalize the second element unless it is a proper noun or proper adjective.
4. Capitalize the second element in a hyphenated spelled-out number (*twenty-one* or *twenty-first*, etc.) or hyphenated simple fraction (*two-thirds* in *two-thirds majority*).

The examples that follow demonstrate the numbered rules (all the examples demonstrate the first rule; the numbers in parentheses refer to rules 2–4).

Under-the-Counter Transactions and Out-of-Fashion Initiatives (2)
Bed-and-Breakfast Options in Upstate New York (2)
Record-Breaking Borrowings from Medium-Sized Libraries (2)
Cross-Stitching for Beginners (2)
A History of the Chicago Lying-In Hospital (2; "In" functions as an adverb, not a preposition)
The E-flat Concerto (2)
Self-Sustaining Reactions (2)
Anti-intellectual Pursuits (3)
Why Solar Is the Future of E-books (3)
A Two-Thirds Majority of Non-English-Speaking Representatives (3, 4)
Ninety-Fifth Avenue Blues (4)
Atari's Twenty-First-Century Adherents (4)

Under another, simplified practice that is not recommended by Chicago, only the first element and any subsequent element that is a proper noun or adjective are capitalized.

8.162 **Titles containing quotations.** When a direct quotation of a sentence or an independent clause is used as a title, headline-style capitalization may be imposed, even for longer quotations. See also 14.94.

"We All Live More like Brutes Than like Humans": Labor and Capital in the Gold Rush

8.163 **Italics versus quotation marks for titles.** The choice of italics or quotation marks for a title of a work cited in text or notes is determined by the type of work. Titles of books and periodicals are italicized (see 8.168); titles of articles, chapters, and other shorter works are set in roman and enclosed in quotation marks (see 8.177).

Many editors use *The Chicago Manual of Style.*
Refer to the article titled "A Comparison of MLA and APA Style."

For treatment of book series and editions, see 8.176; for poems and plays, see 8.181–84; for fairy tales and nursery rhymes, see 8.185; for pamphlets and forms, see 8.186–87; for unpublished works, see 8.188; for movies, television, radio, and podcasts, see 8.189; for video games, see 8.190; for websites and blogs, see 8.191–92; for musical works, see 8.193–97; for works of art and exhibitions, see 8.198–201. For titles from other languages, see 11.6–10.

8.164 **Subtitle capitalization.** A subtitle, whether in sentence-style or headline-style capitalization, always begins with a capital letter. Although on a title page or in a chapter heading a subtitle is often distinguished from a title by a different typeface, when referred to it is separated from the title by a colon. When an em dash rather than a colon is used, what follows the em dash is not normally considered to be a subtitle, and the first word is not necessarily capitalized. See also 14.90.

"Manuals of Style: Guidelines, Not Strangleholds" (headline style)
Tapetum character states: Analytical keys (sentence style)
but
Chicago—a Metropolitan Smorgasbord

8.165 **Permissible changes to titles.** When a title is referred to in text or notes or listed in a bibliography or reference list, its original spelling (including non-Latin letters such as π or γ) and hyphenation should be preserved, regardless of the style used in the surrounding text. Capitalization may be changed to headline style (8.159) or sentence style (8.158), as applicable. As a matter of editorial discretion, an ampersand (&) may be changed to *and*, or, more rarely, a numeral may be spelled out (see 14.88). On title pages, commas are sometimes omitted from the ends of lines for aesthetic reasons. When such a title is referred to, such commas should be added, including any comma omitted before a date that appears on a line by itself at the end of a title or subtitle. (Serial commas should be added only if it is clear that they are used in the work itself; see 6.19.) If title and subtitle on a title page are distinguished by typeface alone, a colon must be added when referring to the full title. A dash in the original should be retained; however, a semicolon between title and subtitle may usually be changed to a colon. (For two subtitles in the original, see 14.90. For older titles, see 14.97.) The following examples illustrate the way titles and subtitles are normally punctuated and capitalized in running text, notes, and bibliographies using headline capitalization. The first three are books, the fourth an article.

Disease, Pain, and Sacrifice: Toward a Psychology of Suffering
Melodrama Unveiled: American Theater and Culture, 1800–1850
Browning's Roman Murder Story: A Reading of "The Ring and the Book"
"Milton Friedman's *Capitalism and Freedom*—a Best-Seller for Chicago"

For titles within titles (as in the third and fourth examples above), see 8.173, 8.177. For double titles connected by *or*, see 8.167.

8.166 **Titles in relation to surrounding text.** A title, which is considered to be a singular noun, always takes a singular verb. Moreover, any punctuation that is part of the title should not affect the punctuation of the surrounding text (with the exception of a sentence-ending period, which should be omitted after a title ending in a question mark or exclamation point; see 6.124). See also 6.28, 6.125, 8.174.

The Waves is not a typical novel. (singular verb in spite of plural in title)
Her role in *Play It Again, Sam* confirmed her stature. (no comma after *Sam*)
Three stories she never mentioned were "Are You a Doctor?," "The Library of Babel," and "The Diamond as Big as the Ritz." (comma after first title in spite of the question mark)

8.167 **Double titles connected by "or."** Old-fashioned double titles (or titles and subtitles) connected by *or* have traditionally been punctuated in a variety of ways. When referring to such titles, prefer the punctuation on the title page or at the head of the original source. In the absence of such punctuation (e.g., when the title is distinguished from the subtitle by typography alone), or when the source is not available to consult, prefer the simpler form shown in the first example (see also 8.165). This small departure from advice in earlier editions of this manual recognizes the importance of balancing editorial expediency with fidelity to original sources. See also 14.91.

The Tempest, or The Enchanted Island
but
Moby-Dick; or, The Whale

Books and Periodicals

8.168 **Treatment of book and periodical titles.** When mentioned in text, notes, or bibliography, the titles and subtitles of books and periodicals are italicized and capitalized headline-style (see 8.159), though some publications may require sentence style for reference lists (see 8.158, 15.13). A book title cited in full in the notes or bibliography may be shortened in text (e.g., a subtitle may be omitted). For short titles in notes, see 14.30.

8.169 **An initial "a," "an," or "the" in book titles.** An initial *a*, *an*, or *the* in running text may be dropped from a book title if it does not fit the surrounding syntax. When in doubt, or if the article seems indispensable, it should be retained.

Fielding, in his introduction to *The History of Tom Jones, a Foundling*, announces himself as a professional author.
Fielding's *History of Tom Jones* . . .
That dreadful *Old Curiosity Shop* character, Quilp . . .
but
In *The Old Curiosity Shop*, Dickens . . .
In L'Amour's *The Quick and the Dead* . . .

8.170 **An initial "the" in periodical titles.** When newspapers and other periodicals are mentioned in text, an initial *the*, even if part of the title on the masthead, is usually lowercased (unless it begins a sentence) and not italicized. Most newspapers and many journals (and, by analogy with journals, some magazines) are referred to with a definite article whether or not it might be considered part of the official title; treating the definite article as part of the surrounding text facilitates consistency in discussions that mention a variety of periodical titles. In the examples below, *The* is included on the masthead or cover of all but the *Los Angeles Times*, the *Chicago Tribune*, and the *Journal of Labor Economics* (an article never appears with *Forbes*). As with book titles, use of the definite article will depend on the syntax of the surrounding sentence (see 8.169).

I read the *Los Angeles Times* on my phone and the *Chicago Tribune* on my computer, but I prefer the paper edition of the *New York Times*.
She reads the *Journal of Labor Economics* at work and the *American Naturalist* at home.
Do you get your information from the *Wall Street Journal* or *Forbes*?
The *New Yorker*'s cartoons generally have nothing to do with the surrounding text.
but
I'm a *New Yorker* fan for the cartoons alone.
Her *Wall Street Journal* subscription expired last month.

Some editors may prefer to retain an initial *The* with the titles of periodicals that otherwise consist of a single word (but not with a title that is actually a short form). This practice should be used consistently, and only with titles that include the article.

Have you read *The Week* this week? How about *The Believer*?
Would you believe *The Onion*?
I saw it in *The Times* (referring to the British publication).
but
I read *Harper's* mainly for its puzzles.
Does the *Times* (referring to the *New York Times*) publish a crossword?

Because it may govern the inflection of the following word, non-English titles retain the article in the original language—but only if it is an official part of the title (see also 11.27).

We read *Le Monde* and *Die Zeit* while traveling in Europe.
but
Did you see the review in the *Frankfurter Allgemeine*?

In citation form, an initial *the* is dropped from periodical titles (except for those, if any, for which the *The* has been incorporated into the title in the text; see above); for languages other than English, articles are retained (see 14.193, 14.194).

8.171 **"Magazine" and other descriptive terms.** A word like *magazine*, *journal*, or *review* should be italicized only when it forms part of the official title of a particular periodical. When such a word functions as an added descriptive term, it is treated as part of the surrounding text. See also 8.170.

I read it both in *Time* magazine and in the *Wall Street Journal.*
but
His article was reprinted in the *New York Times Magazine.*

8.172 **Periodical titles in awards, buildings, and so forth.** When the title of a newspaper or periodical is part of the name of a building, organization, prize, or the like, it is not italicized.

Los Angeles Times Book Prize   Chicago Defender Charities   Tribune Tower

8.173 **Italicized terms and titles within titles.** Any term within an italicized title that would itself be italicized in running text—such as a word from another language, a genus name, or the name of a ship—should be set in roman type (*reverse italics*). See also 8.116, 8.120, 8.165, 14.95.

From Tyrannosaurus rex *to King Kong: Large Creatures in Fact and Fiction*
The Big E: The Story of the USS Enterprise

A title of a work within another title, however, should remain in italics and be enclosed in quotation marks. See also 14.94.

A Key to Whitehead's "Process and Reality"

8.174 **Title not interchangeable with subject.** The title of a work should not be used to stand for the subject of a work.

Dostoevsky wrote a book about crime and punishment (*not* . . . about *Crime and Punishment*).
Edward Wasiolek's book on Dostoevsky's *Crime and Punishment* is titled *"Crime and Punishment" and the Critics*. (See also 8.173.)
In their book *The Craft of Translation*, Biguenet and Schulte . . . (*not* In discussing *The Craft of Translation*, Biguenet and Schulte . . .)

8.175 **Titles of multivolume works.** Titles of multivolume books are treated in the same manner as titles of single-volume works, as are named titles of individual volumes. The word *volume* may be abbreviated in parentheses and notes; it is capitalized (and never abbreviated) only if part of the title. For treatment of multivolume works in bibliographies and reference lists, see 14.116–22. See also 8.176.

The Day of the Scorpion, volume 2 of *The Raj Quartet*
Art in an Age of Counterrevolution, 1815–1848 (vol. 3, *A Social History of Modern Art*)
the fourth volume of the landmark eleventh edition of *Encyclopaedia Britannica*

8.176 **Titles of series and editions.** Titles of book series and editions are capitalized but not italicized. The words *series* and *edition* are capitalized only if part of the title. See also 14.123–26.

the Loeb Classical Library
a Modern Library edition
Late Editions: Cultural Studies for the End of the Century
the Crime and Justice series
a book in the Heritage of Sociology Series

Numbered or named editions of a specific publication (as in a cited source) are usually not part of a title and are set in roman and lowercase (if in doubt, consult a library catalog). See also 14.113.

Black's Law Dictionary, 10th ed.
Kuhn, *The Structure of Scientific Revolutions*, 50th anniversary ed.
but
Hayek, *The Constitution of Liberty: The Definitive Edition*

Articles in Periodicals and Parts of a Book

8.177 **Articles, stories, chapters, and so on.** Titles of articles and features in periodicals and newspapers, chapter and part titles, titles of short stories or essays, and individual selections in books are set in roman type and enclosed in quotation marks.

John S. Ellis's article "Reconciling the Celt" appeared in the *Journal of British Studies.*
In chapter 3 of *The Footnote*, "How the Historian Found His Muse," Anthony Grafton . . .
"Tom Outland's Story," by Willa Cather . . .

Book titles and other normally italicized terms remain italicized within an article title. A term quoted in the original title is enclosed in single quotation marks (since it is already within double quotation marks). See also 14.94.

The article "Schiller's 'Ode to Joy' in Beethoven's Ninth Symphony" received unexpected attention.
Neuberger's "Sergei Eisenstein's *Ivan the Terrible* as History" calls the filmmaker's approach to history "serious and nuanced."

Titles of regular departments or columns in periodicals are set in roman with no quotation marks (see also 14.190, 14.195).

In this week's Talk of the Town, Lizzie Widdicombe features . . .

8.178 **Collected works.** When two or more works originally published as separate books are included in a single volume, often as part of an author's collected works, they are best italicized rather than placed in quotation marks.

The introduction to the *Critique of Pure Reason* in Kant's *Collected Works* . . .

8.179 **Terms like "foreword," "preface," and so on.** Such generic terms as *foreword*, *preface*, *acknowledgments*, *introduction*, *appendix*, *bibliography*, *glossary*, and *index*, whether used in cross-references or in reference to another work, are lowercased and set in roman type.

The author states in her preface that . . .
For further documentation, see the appendix.
Full details are given in the bibliography.
The book contains a glossary, a subject index, and an index of names.

8.180 **Numbered chapters, parts, and so on.** The words *chapter*, *part*, *appendix*, *table*, *figure*, and the like are lowercased and spelled out in text (though sometimes abbreviated in parenthetical references). Numbers can usually be given in arabic numerals, regardless of how they appear in the original. (Subject to editorial discretion, an exception is sometimes made for references within a work to other parts of the same work numbered with roman numerals; for other exceptions, see 9.26, 9.28.) If letters are used, they may be upper- or lowercase (following the original) and are sometimes put in parentheses. See also 3.9, 3.50.

This matter is discussed in chapters 4 and 5.
The Latin text appears in appendix B.
The range is presented numerically in table 4.2 and diagrammed in figure 4.1.
These connections are illustrated in table A3.
Turn to section 5(a) for further examples.

Poems and Plays

8.181 **Titles of poems.** Titles of most poems are set in roman type and enclosed in quotation marks. A very long poetic work, especially one constituting a book, is italicized and not enclosed in quotation marks.

Robert Frost's poem "The Housekeeper" in his collection *North of Boston*
Dante's *Inferno*

8.182 **Poems referred to by first line.** Poems referred to by first line rather than by title are capitalized sentence-style, even if the first word is lowercased in the original, but any words capitalized in the original should remain capitalized. See also 8.158, 16.145.

E. E. Cummings, in "My father moved through dooms of love," . . . ("my" is lowercased in the original)
"Shall I compare thee to a Summer's day?"

8.183 **Titles of plays.** Titles of plays, regardless of the length of the play, are italicized.

Shaw's *Arms and the Man*, in volume 2 of his *Plays: Pleasant and Unpleasant*

8.184 **Divisions of plays or poems.** Words denoting parts of long poems or acts and scenes of plays are usually lowercased, neither italicized nor enclosed in quotation marks. Numbers are arabic, regardless of the original.

canto 2   stanza 5   act 3, scene 2

Fairy Tales and Nursery Rhymes

8.185 **Titles of folktales, fables, nursery rhymes, and the like.** Folktales, fables, fairy tales, nursery rhymes, and the like are usually treated in the manner of shorter poems and set in roman type and enclosed in quotation marks. Italics should be used to refer to fairy tales published as books, plays, and the like.

"Aladdin" is arguably the most well-known tale in *A Thousand and One Nights.*

"Rumpelstiltskin" originally appeared in the Grimm brothers' *Children's and Household Tales.*

Everybody knows at least one verse of "Jack and Jill."

Ella Enchanted is a retelling by Gail Carson Levine of "Cinderella."

The opera *Hansel and Gretel* (*Hänsel und Gretel*) is based on the fairy tale of the same name.

Pamphlets, Reports, and Forms

8.186 **Titles of pamphlets and reports.** Titles of pamphlets, reports, and similar freestanding publications are, like books, italicized when mentioned or cited in text or notes (see also 8.168, 14.220).

Payne's *Common Sense*, first published anonymously . . .

Young Adult Migration: 2007–2009 to 2010–2012, a report published in 2015 as part of the US Census Bureau's American Community Survey . . .

8.187 **Titles of forms.** Government, departmental, and other titled or numbered forms can usually be capitalized according to the usage in the form itself; wording should follow the usage in the document itself but may be shortened if necessary.

Form 1040-ES, Estimated Tax for Individuals (*or* 1040-ES)

DHS TRIP Traveler Inquiry Form (*or* DHS TRIP)

United States Census 2010; the Census (*but* a census form)

Unpublished Works

8.188 **Titles of unpublished works.** Titles of unpublished works—theses, dissertations, manuscripts in collections, unpublished transcripts of speeches, and so on—are set in roman type, capitalized as titles, and enclosed in quotation marks. Titles of manuscript collections take no quotation marks. The title of a not-yet-published book that is under contract may be italicized, but the word *forthcoming* (or *in press* or some other equivalent term), in parentheses, must follow the title. For speeches, see 8.76. See also 15.45.

In a master's thesis, "Charles Valentin Alkan and His Pianoforte Works," . . .
"A Canal Boat Journey, 1857," an anonymous manuscript in the Library of Congress Manuscripts Division, describes . . .
Letters and other material may be found in the Collis P. Huntington Papers at the George Arents Library of Syracuse University.
Gianfranco's *Fourth Millennium* (forthcoming) continues this line of research.

Movies, Television, Radio, and Podcasts

8.189 **Titles for movies, television, radio, and podcasts.** Titles of movies (or films) and movie series and of television, radio, and podcast programs and series are italicized. A single episode in a television, radio, or podcast series is set in roman and enclosed in quotation marks. Sequels should be numbered as in the source itself; if in doubt, prefer arabic numerals (see also 9.43). The names of networks, channels, streaming services, and the like are set in roman.

Gone with the Wind
The Godfather, Part II (see also 9.43)
The Hunger Games; *The Hunger Games: Mockingjay—Part 1*; the *Hunger Games* film series
Sesame Street on PBS
The Ten O'Clock News, WGBH's long-running program
"The Alibi," the first episode in the podcast *Serial*, a *This American Life* spin-off
NPR's *Ask Me Another*, a podcast hosted by Ophira Eisenberg
Performance Today, hosted by Fred Child and produced by American Public Media; broadcast by Minnesota Public Radio and others and also available as a podcast
"Thirsty Bird," the first episode in the second season of the Netflix series *Orange Is the New Black*
Season 5, episode 4, of the *Masterpiece* series *Downton Abbey*, originally broadcast on ITV (UK) and PBS (US) and also available from Amazon Video
but
the ten o'clock news

Video Games

8.190 **Titles of video games.** Though video games are technically software applications, or apps (see 8.155), they may be treated like movies, a usage that recognizes the narrative and audiovisual similarities between the two art forms. Older video games—despite being technically simpler than the majority of today's apps—are treated in the same way. (Note that this usage does not apply to other types of games, which are set in roman rather than italics and capitalized only if trademarked: e.g., Monopoly *but* poker.) See also 8.189.

Pong
Ms. Pac-Man
Tetris
Angry Birds; the *Angry Birds* app
Nintendo's *Mario Bros.*; *Mario Kart Wii*; *Mario Kart 7* for Nintendo 3DS
Call of Duty; *Call of Duty 2*; *Call of Duty: Modern Warfare 3*; the *Call of Duty* series
The Sims 4; *The Sims*, a series that debuted in 2000

Websites and Blogs

8.191 **Titles of websites and web pages.** Titles of websites mentioned or cited in text or notes are normally set in roman, headline-style, without quotation marks. An initial *The* should be lowercased except at the beginning of a sentence. Titled sections, pages, or special features on a website should be placed in quotation marks. Titles of the types of works discussed elsewhere in this chapter (i.e., books, journals, etc.) should usually be treated the same whether they are published in print or online. But in a departure from the recommendations in the previous edition, the title of a website that does not have (and never had) a printed counterpart, even if it is analogous to a traditionally printed work, can be treated like the titles of other websites, subject to editorial discretion. (When in doubt, treat the source as if there is no printed counterpart.) See also 14.205–10.

Project Gutenberg; Jane Austen's *Emma*, available as an audiobook from Project Gutenberg
the Internet Movie Database; IMDb (note lowercase *b*); IMDb's page for *Live and Let Die*; "Roger Moore (I)"; the page for early Bond portrayer Roger Moore
Google; Google Maps; the "Maps Help Center"
Facebook, Twitter, Instagram, and other social-networking sites; the Facebook app (see 8.155)

Wikipedia; Wikipedia's "Let It Be" entry; Wikipedia's entry on the Beatles' album *Let It Be*

but

The Chicago Manual of Style Online; the online edition of *The Chicago Manual of Style*; "Chicago Style Q&A"; "New Questions and Answers"

Encyclopaedia Britannica Online; the online version of *Encyclopaedia Britannica*

the *Oxford English Dictionary Online*; the *OED Online*; the online version of the *Oxford English Dictionary*

the *Onion* (but see 8.170)

Many websites either do not have a formal title or do not have a title that distinguishes it as a website. These can usually be identified according to the entity responsible for the site along with a description of the site and, in some cases, a short form of the URL. For example, http://www.apple.com/ might be referred to in running text as Apple.com.

The website for Apple Inc.; Apple.com

Microsoft's website; Microsoft.com

the website for the University of Chicago Press, Books Division

8.192 **Blogs and blog posts.** Titles of named blogs (and video blogs), like the titles of journals and other periodicals (see 8.163), can usually be italicized. An initial "the" can be treated as part of the title (an exception may be made for news blogs whose titles are styled like those of newspapers; see 8.170). Titles of blog posts should be placed in quotation marks (untitled posts should be referred to by date). See also 14.205–10.

Sinosphere: Dispatches from China; "Q. and A.: Chang-rae Lee on His Tale of Migrants from an Environmentally Ruined China," by Edward Wong, in *Sinosphere*, a blog about China in the *New York Times*

Wasted Food; "Vancouver Hoovers Up Food Waste," in *Wasted Food*, a blog by Jonathan Bloom

"Surprise of the Day: Hungry Great White Shark Steals Fisherman's Catch," in *I Can Has Cheezburger?*, a video blog known for its "Lolcats"

the *Huffington Post*; "Why the 99 Percent Keeps Losing," by Robert Kuttner

In many cases, the distinction between a blog and a website (not to mention social-networking service or app) will be blurry (as in the case of the *Huffington Post*). When in doubt, treat the source like a website (see 8.191). For podcasts, see 8.189.

Musical Works

8.193 **Musical works—additional resources.** The following paragraphs are intended only as general guidance for citing musical works. Writers or editors working with highly musicological material should consult D. Kern Holoman, *Writing about Music* (bibliog. 1.1). For a more general reference work, consult *The New Grove Dictionary of Music and Musicians* and the other Grove musical dictionaries, available from Oxford Music Online (bibliog. 5). For typographic conventions used in musicology, see 7.70–75.

8.194 **Operas, songs, and the like.** Titles of operas, oratorios, tone poems, and other long musical compositions are italicized and given standard title capitalization. Titles of songs and other shorter musical compositions are set in roman and enclosed in quotation marks, capitalized in the same way as poems (see 8.181, 8.182).

"La vendetta, oh, la vendetta" from *The Marriage of Figaro*
the "Anvil Chorus" from Verdi's *Il Trovatore*
Handel's *Messiah*
Rhapsody in Blue
Finlandia
"All You Need Is Love" (a song by the Beatles)
"So What" (a composition by Miles Davis)
"The Star-Spangled Banner"
"Oh, What a Beautiful Mornin'" from *Oklahoma!*
"Wohin?" from *Die schöne Müllerin*

8.195 **Instrumental works.** Many instrumental works are known by their generic names—*symphony*, *quartet*, *nocturne*, and so on—and often a number or key or both. Such names are capitalized but not italicized. A descriptive title, however, is usually italicized if referring to a full work, set in roman and in quotation marks if referring to a section of a work. The abbreviation *no.* (number; plural *nos.*) is set in roman and usually lowercased. (For letters indicating keys, see 7.71.)

B-flat Nocturne; Chopin's nocturnes
the Menuetto from the First Symphony; the third movement
Concerto no. 2 for Piano and Orchestra; the second movement, Allegro appassionato, from Brahms's Second Piano Concerto; two piano concertos
Bartók's Concerto for Orchestra (or *Concerto for Orchestra*)

Bach's Mass in B Minor
Hungarian Rhapsody no. 12; the Twelfth Hungarian Rhapsody
Charles Ives's Piano Sonata no. 2 (*Concord, Mass., 1840–60*); the *Concord* Sonata
Symphony no. 6 in F Major (*Pastoral*); the Sixth Symphony; the *Pastoral* Symphony; the *Pastoral*
Air with Variations ("The Harmonious Blacksmith") from Handel's Suite no. 5 in E
Elliott Carter's String Quartet no. 5 and his *Figment* for cello
Augusta Read Thomas's Triple Concerto (*Night's Midsummer Blaze*)

8.196 **Opus numbers.** The abbreviation *op.* (opus; plural *opp.* or *opera*) is set in roman and usually lowercased. An abbreviation designating a catalog of a particular composer's works is always capitalized (e.g., BWV [Bach-Werke-Verzeichnis]; D. [Deutsch] for Schubert; K. [Köchel] for Mozart; WoO [Werke ohne Opuszahl], assigned by scholars to certain unnumbered works). When *op.* or a catalog number is used restrictively (see 6.29), no comma precedes it.

Sonata in E-flat, op. 31, no. 3; Sonata op. 31
Fantasy in C Minor, K. 475; Fantasy K. 475

8.197 **Recordings.** The official title of an album (and sometimes a title under which it has come to be known) is italicized; that of the performer or ensemble is set in roman. Individual items on the album—songs, movements, and the like—are treated as illustrated in the paragraphs above. See also 14.263.

On *The Art of the Trumpet*, the New York Trumpet Ensemble plays . . .
The single "Revolution" should not be confused with "Revolution 1," an earlier take of the song that appeared on *The Beatles* (a.k.a. *The White Album*).
Miles Davis's *Kind of Blue* is one of the most influential jazz records ever made.
His Majestie's Clerkes' *Hear My Prayer: Choral Music of the English Romantics* includes Vaughan Williams's Mass in G Minor.

Works of Art and Exhibitions

8.198 **Paintings, photographs, statues, and such.** Titles of paintings, drawings, photographs, statues, and other works of art are italicized, whether the titles are original, added by someone other than the artist, or translated. The names of works of antiquity (whose creators are often unknown) are usually set in roman. See also 8.57.

Rothko's *Orange Yellow Orange*
Leonardo da Vinci's *Mona Lisa* and *The Last Supper*
North Dome, one of Ansel Adams's photographs of Kings River Canyon
Hogarth's series of drawings *The Rake's Progress*
Michelangelo's *David*
the Winged Victory
the Venus de Milo

8.199 **Maps.** Maps can often be referred to in text with generic descriptive titles. If a map is known by a formal title rather than a generic description, use italics. See also 11.9.

a fifteenth-century reconstruction of Ptolemy's world map (ca. AD 150)
the *Yu ji tu* (Map of the tracks of Yu), from 1136
the *Tabula Hungariae*, Lázár's map of Hungary
Arno Peters's projection of the world map; the Peters projection map
Google Maps, satellite view of metropolitan Los Angeles

Maps as illustrations require captions and credit lines as discussed in chapter 3. To cite a map included in a book, see 14.158. To cite a standalone map, see 14.237.

8.200 **Cartoons.** Titles of regularly appearing cartoons or comic strips are italicized.

The Far Side *Doonesbury* *Rudy Park* *Dilbert*

8.201 **Exhibitions and such.** Titles of world's fairs and other large-scale exhibitions and fairs are capitalized but not italicized. Smaller exhibitions (e.g., at museums) and the titles of exhibition catalogs (often one and the same) are italicized.

the Great Exhibition of the Works of All Nations; the Great Exhibition of 1851; London's Crystal Palace Exhibition; the exhibition
the World's Columbian Exposition
the Century-of-Progress Expositions (included more than one fair)
the New York World's Fair
but
A remarkable exhibition, *Motor Cycles*, was mounted at the Guggenheim Museum.
We saw the exhibition *Ansel Adams at 100* when visiting the Museum of Modern Art.
We decided to buy the catalog *Ansel Adams at 100*, by John Szarkowski.

9 · Numbers

Overview

9.1 **Overview and additional resources.** This chapter summarizes some of the conventions Chicago observes in handling numbers, especially in making the choice between spelling them out and using numerals. Such a choice should be governed by various factors, including whether the number is large or small, whether it is an approximation or an exact quantity, what kind of entity it stands for, and what context it appears in. Sometimes the goal of consistency must give way to readability (e.g., at the beginning of a sentence; see 9.5). The guidelines in this chapter apply mainly to general works and to scholarly works in the humanities and social sciences, where numeric quantities are relatively infrequent. But even in scientific and other technical contexts, numerals can never totally replace spelled-out numbers. For more detailed treatment of numbers in technical contexts, consult *Scientific Style and Format* (bibliog. 1.1). See also 9.13–17.

Numerals versus Words

General Principles

9.2 **Chicago's general rule—zero through one hundred.** In nontechnical contexts, Chicago advises spelling out whole numbers from zero through one hundred and certain round multiples of those numbers (see 9.4).

Thirty-two children from eleven families were packed into eight vintage Beetles.
Many people think that seventy is too young to retire.
The property is held on a ninety-nine-year lease.
According to a recent appraisal, my house is 103 years old.
The three new parking lots will provide space for 540 more cars.
The population of our village now stands at 5,893.

Most of the rest of this chapter deals with exceptions and special cases. For hyphens used with spelled-out numbers, see 7.89, section 1. For some additional considerations, consult the index, under *numbers*. For numerals in direct discourse, see 13.44. For an alternative rule, see 9.3.

9.3 **An alternative rule—zero through nine.** Many publications, including those in scientific or journalistic contexts, follow the simple rule of spelling out only single-digit numbers and using numerals for all others (but see 9.7). Most of the exceptions to the general rule (9.2) also apply to this alternative rule. Round multiples of hundreds, thousands, and hundred thousands, however, are typically expressed as numerals when the alternative rule is in force (cf. 9.4).

9.4 **Hundreds, thousands, and hundred thousands.** The whole numbers one through one hundred followed by *hundred*, *thousand*, or *hundred thousand* are usually spelled out (except in the sciences or with monetary amounts)—whether used exactly or as approximations. See also 9.8, 9.24.

Most provincial theaters were designed to accommodate large audiences—from about seven hundred spectators in a small city like Lorient to as many as two thousand in Lyon and Marseille.
A millennium is a period of one thousand years.
The population of our city is more than two hundred thousand.
Some forty-seven thousand persons attended the fair.
but
The official attendance at this year's fair was 47,122.

In a context with many large numbers—especially if round numbers occur alongside numerals that are not round—it may be best to opt for numerals for all such numbers. See also 9.7.

9.5 **Number beginning a sentence.** When a number begins a sentence, it is always spelled out. To avoid awkwardness, a sentence can often be recast. In the first example, some writers prefer the form *one hundred and ten*; Chicago's preference is to omit the *and*.

One hundred ten candidates were accepted.
or
In all, 110 candidates were accepted.

If a year must begin a sentence, spell it out; it is usually preferable, however, to reword. Avoid *and* in such expressions as *two thousand one*, *two thousand ten*, *two thousand fifty*, and the like (see also 9.29).

Nineteen thirty-seven was marked, among other things, by the publication of the eleventh edition of Bartlett's *Familiar Quotations*.
or, better,
The year 1937 . . .

If a number beginning a sentence is followed by another number of the same category, spell out only the first or reword.

One hundred eighty of the 214 candidates had law degrees; the remaining 34 were doctoral candidates in fish immunology.

or, better,

Of the 214 candidates, 180 had law degrees; the remaining 34 were doctoral candidates in fish immunology.

9.6 **Ordinals.** The general rule applies to ordinal as well as cardinal numbers. Note that Chicago prefers, for example, *122nd* and *123rd* (with an *n* and an *r*) over *122d* and *123d*. The latter, however, are common especially in legal style (see 14.269–305). The letters in ordinal numbers should *not* appear as superscripts (e.g., 122nd, *not* 122nd).

Gwen stole second base in the top half of the first inning.
The restaurant on the forty-fifth floor has a splendid view of the city.
She found herself in 125th position out of 360.
The 122nd and 123rd days of the strike were marked by a rash of defections.
The ten thousandth child to be born at Mercy Hospital was named Mercy.

In the expression "*n*th degree," Chicago style is to italicize the *n* (see also 7.64).

9.7 **Consistency and flexibility.** Where many numbers occur within a paragraph or a series of paragraphs, maintain consistency in the immediate context. If according to a given rule you must use numerals for one of the numbers in a given category, use them for all in that category. (An exception should be made at the beginning of a sentence; see 9.5.) In the same sentence or paragraph, however, items in one category may be given as numerals and items in another spelled out. According to the general rule, in the first example, the numerals 50, 3, and 4 would normally be spelled out (see 9.2); in the second and third examples, 30,000 and 2,000, respectively, would normally be spelled out (see 9.4; see also 9.8). According to the alternative rule, in the fourth and fifth examples, 9 and 1, respectively, would normally be spelled out (see 9.3).

General Rule

A mixture of buildings—one of 103 stories, five of more than 50, and a dozen of only 3 or 4—has been suggested for the area.

In the second half of the nineteenth century, Chicago's population exploded, from just under 30,000 in 1850 to nearly 1.7 million by 1900.

Between 1,950 and 2,000 people attended the concert.

Alternative Rule

Though most of the test subjects were between 13 and 18, two were 11 and one was 9.

The movie lasted 1 hour and 36 minutes, a typical length for a romantic comedy.

An exception to either rule may also be made to avoid a thickly clustered group of spelled-out numbers, regardless of category. And in some cases, an exception may be applied not only to a paragraph or passage of text but to a work as a whole. If, for example, a book includes many mentions of ages, all ages might be given as numerals. For numerals in direct discourse, see 13.44.

Large Numbers

9.8 **Millions, billions, and so forth.** Whole numbers used in combination with *million*, *billion*, and so forth usually follow the general rule (see 9.2). See also 9.4. For monetary amounts, see 9.20–25; for the use of superscripts in scientific contexts, see 9.9.

The city had grown from three million in 1960 to fourteen million in 1990.

The survey was administered to more than half of the city's 220 million inhabitants.

The population of the United States recently surpassed three hundred million.

To express fractional quantities in the millions or more, a mixture of numerals and spelled-out numbers is used. In the second example below, the number fourteen is expressed as a numeral for the sake of consistency (see 9.7).

By the end of the fourteenth century, the population of Britain had probably reached 2.3 million.

According to some scientists, the universe is between 13.5 and 14 billion years old.

Note that *billion* in some countries (including, until recently, Great Britain) means a million million (a trillion in American usage), not, as in American usage, a thousand million; in this alternate system, the prefix *bi-* indicates twelve zeros (rather than the American nine), or twice the number of zeros in one million. Likewise, *trillion* indicates eighteen zeros (rather than the American twelve), *quadrillion* twenty-four (rather than the American fifteen), and so on. Editors working with material by writers who may not be familiar with English usage for these terms may need to query how they are used. See 5.250 under *billion; trillion*.

9.9 **Powers of ten.** Large round numbers may be expressed in powers of ten, especially in scientific writing. This system is known as scientific notation. For further examples, consult *Scientific Style and Format* (bibliog. 1.1).

$10^2 = 100$	$10^9 = 1{,}000{,}000{,}000$
$10^3 = 1{,}000$	$10^{12} = 1{,}000{,}000{,}000{,}000$
$10^6 = 1{,}000{,}000$	$5.34 \times 10^8 = 534{,}000{,}000$

Inversely, very small numbers may be expressed in negative powers of ten.

$10^{-2} = 0.01$	$10^{-9} = 0.000000001$
$10^{-3} = 0.001$	$10^{-12} = 0.000000000001$
$10^{-6} = 0.000001$	$5.34 \times 10^{-8} = 0.0000000534$

9.10 **"Mega-," "giga-," "tera-," and so forth.** According to the International System of Units (*Système international d'unités*, abbreviated internationally as SI), very large quantities may be indicated in some contexts by the use of the prefixes *mega-* (million), *giga-* (billion), *tera-* (trillion), and so on, as part of the unit of measure. Inversely, very small numbers may be expressed by *milli-* (thousandth), *micro-* (millionth), *nano-* (billionth), and so on. These expressions are often formed with symbols (e.g., *M*, for *mega-*, as in MB, *megabytes*). In astrophysical contexts, the abbreviations *Myr* and *Gyr*, standing for megayear (one million years) and gigayear (one billion years), are sometimes used. See also 9.9. For a complete list of SI prefixes, see 10.56. See also 9.11.

3 terahertz = 3×10^{12} hertz   7 Gyr = 7×10^9 years

9.11 **Binary systems.** Bases other than ten are common especially in computing, where numbers are usually expressed with bases that are powers of two (e.g., binary, octal, or hexadecimal). When such numbers are used, the base if other than ten should be indicated. Abbreviations *b* (binary), *o* (octal), and *h* (hexadecimal) may precede the number with no intervening space. Alternatively, the base can be expressed as a subscript. In the following example, the four-digit base-ten number is expressed without a comma, following SI usage (but see 9.56):

b11110010001 = 1937   *or* $11110010001_2 = 1937_{10}$

Note that terms such as *megabyte*, when used as binary multiples, are approximations—a megabyte was originally equal to 1,048,576 bytes.

Current SI usage dictates that such prefixes refer to positive powers of ten (where a megabyte is equal to 1,000,000 bytes). If binary multiples must be referred to, the first two letters of the prefix plus *bi* should be used (*kibibyte*, *mebibyte*, *gibibyte*, etc.).

9.12 **Use of "dex."** The term *dex* is sometimes used in scientific notation as shorthand for *decimal exponent*.

Errors of 3 dex (i.e., 10^3) can lead to dangerous misconceptions.

Physical Quantities

9.13 **Physical quantities in general contexts.** In nontechnical material, physical quantities such as distances, lengths, areas, and so on are usually treated according to the general rule (see 9.2). See also 9.15.

Within fifteen minutes the temperature dropped twenty degrees.
The train approached at seventy-five miles an hour.
Some students live more than fifteen kilometers from the school.
Three-by-five-inch index cards are now seldom used in index preparation.
She is five feet nine (*or, more colloquially,* five foot nine *or* five nine).

It is occasionally acceptable to depart from the general rule for certain types of quantities that are commonly (or more conveniently) expressed as numerals; such a departure, subject to editorial discretion, must be consistently applied for like quantities across a work. See also 9.7. For the absence of the hyphen in the second example below, see 7.89, section 2, under *noun + numeral or enumerator*.

a 40-watt bulb
a size 14 dress
a 32-inch inseam
a fuel efficiency of 80 miles per gallon (or 3 liters per 100 kilometers)

9.14 **Simple fractions.** Simple fractions are spelled out. For the sake of readability and to lend an appearance of consistency, they are hyphenated in noun, adjective, and adverb forms. In the rare event that individual parts of a quantity are emphasized, however, as in the last example, the expression is unhyphenated. See also 7.89, section 1, under *fractions, simple*. For decimal fractions, see 9.19.

She has read three-fourths of the book.
Four-fifths of the students are boycotting the class.
I do not want all of your material; two-thirds is quite enough.
A two-thirds majority is required.
but
We divided the cake into four quarters; I took three quarters, and my brother one.

9.15 **Whole numbers plus fractions.** Quantities consisting of whole numbers and simple fractions may be spelled out if short but are often better expressed in numerals (especially if a symbol for the fraction is available, as in the examples here). For decimal fractions, see 9.19. For fractions in mathematical text, see 12.45. See also 9.17, 10.66.

We walked for three and one-quarter (*or* three and a quarter) miles.
I need 6⅞ yards of the silk fabric.
Lester is exactly 3 feet 5¼ inches tall.
Letters are usually printed on 8½″ × 11″ paper.

9.16 **Numbers with abbreviations and symbols.** If an abbreviation or a symbol is used for the unit of measure, the quantity is always expressed by a numeral. Such usage is standard in mathematical, statistical, technical, and scientific text, where physical quantities and units of time are expressed in numerals, whether whole numbers or fractions, and almost always followed by an abbreviated form of the unit (see also 10.49–68). Note that hyphens are never used between the numeral and the abbreviation or symbol, even when they are in adjectival form (see 7.89, section 1, under *number + abbreviation*). In the last example (which can express inches and feet or minutes and seconds, respectively), note the use of symbols for prime and double prime, which are *not* equivalent to the apostrophe and quotation mark. A space is normally used between the numeral and the unit of measure, except in a few cases—for example, with degree, percent, and prime symbols (but see 10.58). See also 7.44.

50 km (kilometers); a 50 km race
21 ha (hectares)
4.5 L (liters)
85 g (grams)
240 V (volts)
10°C, 10.5°C
3′6″

A unit of measurement used *without* a numeral should always be spelled out, even in scientific contexts.

We took the measurements in kilojoules (*not* kJ).

9.17 **Units for repeated quantities.** For expressions including two or more quantities, the abbreviation or symbol is repeated if it is closed up to the number but not if it is separated. See also 10.49. For the use of spaces with SI units and abbreviations or symbols, see 10.58.

35%–50%   3°C–7°C   6¾″ × 9″   2 × 5 cm

Percentages and Decimal Fractions

9.18 **Percentages.** Except at the beginning of a sentence, percentages are usually expressed in numerals. In nontechnical contexts, the word *percent* is generally used; in scientific and statistical copy, the symbol % is more common.

Fewer than 3 percent of the employees used public transportation.
With 90–95 percent of the work complete, we can relax.
A 75 percent likelihood of winning is worth the effort.
Her five-year certificate of deposit carries an interest rate of 5.9 percent.
Only 20% of the ants were observed to react to the stimulus.
The treatment resulted in a 20%–25% increase in reports of night blindness. (See also 9.17.)
but
Thirty-nine percent identified the "big bang" as the origin of the universe; 48 percent said they believed in human evolution. (See also 9.7.)

Note that *percent*, an adverb, is not interchangeable with the noun *percentage* (1 percent is a very small percentage). Note also that no space appears between the numeral and the symbol %.

9.19 **Decimal fractions and use of the zero.** Large or complex fractions are expressed as numeric decimal fractions (cf. 9.14). When a quantity equals less than 1.00, a zero normally appears before the decimal point as an aid to readability, particularly in scientific contexts and especially if quantities greater than 1.00 appear in the same context. Note that a unit of measure with a quantity of less than one is generally treated as if it were plural (see 10.65, 10.53). See also 9.55, 9.58.

a mean of 0.73
the ratio 0.85
In Cyprus, there were 0.96 females for every male in the general population; in the sixty-five-and-over age group, the number was 1.30.

In contexts where decimal quantities must be 1.00 or less, as in probabilities, batting averages, and the like, or between −1.00 and 1.00, as in correlation coefficients, a zero is typically omitted before the decimal point. For zeros with decimal points in tables, see 3.72.

$p < .05$ $R = .10$ Ty Cobb's career batting average was .367.

By a similar token, the zero is routinely omitted from firearm calibers expressed as fractions of an inch.

They found and confiscated a .38 police special and a .22-caliber single-shot rifle.

Money

9.20 **Words versus monetary symbols and numerals.** Isolated references to amounts of money are spelled out for whole numbers of one hundred or less, in accordance with the general principle presented in 9.2. See also 9.3.

seventy-five cents = 75¢ fifteen dollars = $15 seventy-five pounds = £75

Whole amounts expressed numerically should include zeros and a decimal point only when they appear in the same context with fractional amounts (see also 9.19). Note the singular verb in the second example.

Children can ride for seventy-five cents.
The eighty-three dollars was quickly spent.
The instructor charged €125 per lesson.
Prices ranged from $0.95 up to $10.00.

For larger amounts, see 9.24.

9.21 **Non-US currencies using the dollar symbol.** In contexts where the symbol $ may refer to non-US currencies, these currencies should be clearly identified.

three hundred Canadian dollars = C$300 *or* Can$300
$749 in New Zealand dollars = NZ$749
If you subtract A$15.69 from US$25, . . .
ninety-eight Mexican pesos = Mex$98

In more formal usage, the International Organization for Standardization's three-letter currency codes (e.g., USD for United States dollars, CAD for Canadian dollars, NZD for New Zealand dollars, AUD for Australian dollars, and MXN for Mexican pesos) may be more appropriate. See also 9.23. For a complete list, consult ISO 4217, available from the ISO website. See also *Scientific Style and Format* or the *Style Manual* from the US Government Publishing Office (bibliog. 1.1). Where the context makes clear what currency is meant, the dollar sign alone is enough.

9.22 **British currency.** The basic unit of British currency is the pound, or pound sterling, for which the symbol is *£*. One-hundredth of a pound is a penny (plural *pence*), abbreviated as *p* (no period).

fifteen pounds = £15   fifty pence = 50p   £4.75, £5.00, and £5.25

Until the decimalization of British currency in 1971, the pound was divided into shillings (s.) and pence (d.).

Ten pounds, fifteen shillings, and sixpence = £10 15s. 6d.
twopence halfpenny = 2½d.

9.23 **Other currencies.** Most other currencies are handled the same way as US currency, with a decimal point between the main unit and subunits (e.g., EUR 10.75). When letters rather than symbols are used, a space separates the letter(s) from the numeral.

forty euros (*or, in European Union documents,* 40 euro) = €40 (*or* EUR 40)
95 (euro) cents (*or, in European Union documents,* 95 cent)
725 yen = ¥725 (*or* JPY 725)
100 yuan renminbi (*or* 100 yuan) = ¥100 *or* RMB 100 (*or* CNY 100)
65.50 Swiss francs = SF 65.50 (*or* CHF 65.50)
12.5 bitcoins = BTC 12.5 (*or* XBT 12.5)

Before adoption of the euro, monetary symbols included *F* (French franc), *DM* (deutsche mark), and *Lit* (Italian lira), among others. The International Organization for Standardization defines three-letter codes (including EUR) for most countries; these may be more appropriate in formal or technical contexts. See also 9.21.

9.24 **Large monetary amounts.** Sums of money of more than one hundred dollars are normally expressed by numerals or, for numbers of a million or more, by a mixture of numerals and spelled-out numbers, even for whole numbers (cf. 9.4, 9.8).

An offer of $1,000 once seemed high; we eventually agreed to pay more than fifteen times that amount.
Most of the homes that went into foreclosure were valued at more than $95,000.
She signed a ten-year, $250 million contract.
The military requested an additional $7.3 billion.
The marquess sold his ancestral home for £25 million.

In certain financial contexts, thousands are sometimes represented by *K*.

Three-bedroom condominiums are priced at $350K.

9.25 **Currency with dates.** In contexts where the value of a currency in any particular year is relevant to the discussion, the date may be inserted in parentheses, without intervening space, after the currency symbol. When letters alone are used, spaces intervene before and after the parentheses (see also 9.21, 9.23).

US$(1992)2.47
£(2002)15,050
but
USD (1992) 2.47

Numbered Divisions in Publications and Other Documents

9.26 **Page numbers, chapter numbers, and so forth.** Numbers referring to pages, chapters, parts, volumes, and other divisions of a book, as well as numbers referring to illustrations or tables, are set as numerals. Pages of the front matter are usually in lowercase roman numerals; those for the rest of the book are in arabic numerals (see 1.5–9). For the use of en dashes with number ranges, see 6.78. For documentation style, see chapters 14 and 15. See also 8.180.

The preface will be found on pages vii–xiv and the introduction on pages 1–35.
See part 3, especially chapters 9 and 10, for further discussion; see also volume 2, table 15 and figures 7–9.
Upon completion of step 3, on page 37, the reader is asked to consult appendix B, table 7.

Biblical references are given in numerals only; chapter and verse are separated by a colon with no space following it. For abbreviations, see 10.44–48.

Acts 27:1
Exodus 20:3–17
Psalm 121; Psalms 146–50
2 Corinthians 11:29–30
Gen. 47:12

9.27 **Volume, issue, and page numbers for periodicals.** References to volumes, issues, and pages of a journal are usually made, in that order, with arabic numerals; the words *volume* and *page* are usually omitted. See also 14.164–204.

Their article appeared in *Modern Philology* 112, no. 3 (2015): 554–68.

9.28 **Numbered divisions in legal instruments.** Arabic or roman numerals are commonly used to distinguish divisions within legal instruments and other documents. When in doubt about a reference to a legal document, prefer arabic numerals or, if possible, consult the document itself for guidance. A mixture of arabic and roman numerals sometimes distinguishes smaller from larger divisions. For legal style in source citations, see 14.269–305.

They have filed for Chapter 11 protection from creditors.
Proposition 20 will be voted on next week.
A search of Title IX (of the Education Amendments of 1972) turns up no mention of athletics.
Do you have a 401(k)?
In paragraph 14(vi) of the bylaws, . . .
According to the Constitution of the United States, article 2, section 4 (*or* Article II, Section 4), . . .
but
the Fifth Amendment (*or* Amendment V)

Dates

9.29 **The year used alone.** Years are expressed in numerals unless they stand at the beginning of a sentence (see 9.5), in which case rewording may be a better option. For eras, see 9.34.

We all know what happened in 1776.
Records for solar eclipses go back at least as far as 3000 BCE.
Twenty twenty (*or* Two thousand twenty) should be a good year for clairvoyants.
or, better,
The year 2020 should be a good year for clairvoyants.

9.30 **The year abbreviated.** In informal contexts, the first two digits of a particular year are often replaced by an apostrophe (not an opening single quotation mark). See also 6.117.

the spirit of ’76 (*not* ‘76)   the class of ’06

9.31 **Month and day.** When specific dates are expressed, cardinal numbers are used, although these may be pronounced as ordinals. For the month-day-year date form versus the day-month-year form, see 9.35; see also 6.38.

August 12, 2014, was a sad day for film buffs.
The *Watchmaker's Digest* (11 November 2011) praised the new model's precision.

When a day is mentioned without the month or year, the number is usually spelled out in ordinal form.

On November 5, McManus declared victory. By the twenty-fifth, most of his supporters had deserted him.

9.32 **Centuries.** Particular centuries referred to as such are spelled out and lowercased. For the use of the singular versus the plural, see 7.8. See also 7.15, 9.34.

the twenty-first century
the eighth and ninth centuries
from the ninth to the eleventh century
but
the 1800s (the nineteenth century)

Note that expressions such as "turn of the twenty-first century" are potentially ambiguous; prefer "turn of the century," and only where the context makes the period absolutely clear.

9.33 **Decades.** Decades are either expressed in numerals or spelled out (as long as the century is clear) and lowercased. Chicago calls for no apostrophe to appear between the year and the *s* (see 7.15).

the 1940s and 1950s (*or, less formally,* the 1940s and ’50s)
or
the forties and fifties

Note that the first decade of any century cannot be treated in the same way as other decades. "The 2000s," for example, could easily be taken to refer to the whole of the twenty-first century. To refer to the second decade (i.e., without writing "second decade"), prefer numerals (e.g., 1910s); the expression "the teens" should be avoided, at least in formal contexts.

the first decade of the twenty-first century (*or* the years 2000–2009)
the second decade of the twenty-first century *or* the 2010s (*or* the years 2010–19)

Note that some consider the first decade of, for example, the twenty-first century to consist of the years 2001–10; the second, 2011–20; and so on. Chicago defers to the preference of its authors in this matter. See also 8.71, 9.64.

9.34 **Eras.** Era designations, at least in the Western world, are usually expressed in one of two ways: either CE ("of the Common Era") and BCE ("before the Common Era"), or AD (*anno Domini*, "in the year of the Lord") and BC ("before Christ"). Other forms include AH (*anno Hegirae*, "in the year of [Muhammad's] Hegira," or *anno Hebraico*, "in the Hebrew year"); AUC (*ab urbe condita*, "from the founding of the city [Rome]"); and—for archaeological purposes—BP ("before the present"). Note that the Latin abbreviations AD and AH precede the year number, whereas the others follow it. Choice of the era designation depends on tradition, academic discipline, or personal preference. These abbreviations often appear in small capitals, sometimes with periods following each letter. For consistency with the guidelines in chapter 10, Chicago recommends full capitals and no periods; see also 10.38.

Herod Antipas (21 BCE–39 CE) was tetrarch of Galilee from 4 BCE until his death.
Britain was invaded successfully in 55 BC and AD 1066.
The First Dynasty appears to have lasted from 4400 BP to 4250 BP in radiocarbon years.
Mubarak published his survey at Cairo in 1886 (AH 1306).
The campsite seems to have been in use by about 13,500 BP.
Rome, from its founding in the eighth century BCE, . . .

Note that the second half of a pair of inclusive dates used with BCE or BC, where the higher number comes first, should be given in full to avoid confusion (e.g., "350–345 BCE"). See also 9.64.

9.35 **All-numeral dates and other brief forms.** For practical reasons, all-numeral styles of writing dates (e.g., 5/10/99 or 5.10.99) should not be used in formal writing (except with certain dates that may be known that way: e.g., 9/11, for September 11, 2001). Whereas in American usage the first numeral refers to the month and the second to the day, in much of the rest of the world it is the other way around. When quoting letters or other material dated, say, 5/10/03, a writer must first ascertain and then make it clear to readers whether May 10 or October 5 is meant (not to mention 1903 or 2003). In text, therefore, the full date should always be spelled out (see 9.31). In documentation and in tables, if numerous dates occur, months may be abbreviated, and the day-month-year form, requiring no punctuation, may be neater (e.g., 5 Oct 2003). See also 10.39. For ISO style, see 9.36.

9.36 **ISO style for dates.** The International Organization for Standardization (ISO) recommends an all-numeral style consisting of year-month-day (i.e., from largest component to smallest), hyphenated. The year is given in full, and the month or day, if one digit only, is preceded by a zero. Thus July 14, 2018, would appear as 2018-07-14. Among other advantages, this style allows dates to be sorted correctly in an electronic spreadsheet and other applications. See also 9.40.

Time of Day

9.37 **Numerals versus words for time of day.** Times of day in even, half, and quarter hours are usually spelled out in text. With *o'clock*, the number is always spelled out. In the third example, the *a* before *quarter* is optional.

Her day begins at five o'clock in the morning.
The meeting continued until half past three.
He left the office at a quarter of four (*or* a quarter to four).
We will resume at ten thirty.
Cinderella almost forgot that she should leave the ball before midnight. (See also 9.38.)

Numerals are used when exact times are emphasized. Chicago recommends lowercase a.m. (*ante meridiem*) and p.m. (*post meridiem*), though these sometimes appear in small capitals, with or without periods. (Note that the abbreviations *a.m.* and *p.m.* should not be used with *morning*, *afternoon*, *evening*, *night*, or *o'clock*.)

The first train leaves at 5:22 a.m. and the last at 11:00 p.m.
She caught the 6:20 p.m. flight.

Please attend a meeting in Grand Rapids, Michigan, on December 5 at 10:30 a.m. (EST).

For more on time zones, see 10.41.

9.38 **Noon and midnight.** Except in the twenty-four-hour system (see 9.39), numbers should never be used to express noon or midnight (except, informally, in an expression like *twelve o'clock at night*). Although noon can be expressed as 12:00 m. (m. = *meridies*), very few use that form. And the term 12:00 p.m. is ambiguous, if not illogical. In the second example below, note the double date for clarity.

The meeting began at 9:45 a.m. and was adjourned by noon.
Rodriguez was born at midnight, August 21–22.

9.39 **The twenty-four-hour system.** In the twenty-four-hour system of expressing time (used in military and scientific contexts and considered regular usage in many countries outside the United States, English-speaking Canada, and several other regions that still use the twelve-hour system), four digits always appear, often with no punctuation between hours and minutes. In settings where *hours* is not used, or where the time may be confused with a year, a colon may be used (as in the twelve-hour system). See also 9.40.

12:00 = noon
00:00 *or* 24:00 = midnight (24:00 generally refers to the end of a given day)
00:01 = 12:01 a.m.
14:38 = 2:38 p.m.
At 1500 hours (*or* 1500h) we started off on our mission.
General quarters sounded at 0415.

9.40 **ISO style for time of day.** The International Organization for Standardization (ISO) recommends the twenty-four-hour system (see 9.39), with or without colons, with the addition of seconds following minutes; fractions of a second follow a period. To avoid ambiguity, colons should be used between hours and minutes and between minutes and seconds in running text and similar contexts. This format may be preceded by an ISO-style date (see 9.36). (Note that when the time of day is spelled out, a comma between minutes and seconds denotes *and*; cf. 6.38.)

09:27:08.6 = 27 minutes, 8.6 seconds after 9:00 a.m.
2018-07-14 16:09:41.3 = July 14, 2018, at 9 minutes, 41.3 seconds after 4:00 p.m.

Numbers with Proper Names and Titles

9.41 **Numerals for monarchs, popes, and so forth.** Sovereigns, emperors, popes, and Orthodox patriarchs with the same name are differentiated by numerals, traditionally roman.

Elizabeth II Benedict XVI

In continental European practice, the numeral is sometimes followed by a period (e.g., Wilhelm II.) or a superscript (e.g., François Ier) indicating that the number is an ordinal. In an English context, the roman numeral alone should appear. See also 11.27.

9.42 **Numerals with personal names.** Some personal names are followed by a roman numeral or an arabic ordinal numeral. No punctuation precedes the numeral unless the name is inverted (as in an index entry). For *Jr.*, see 6.43.

Adlai E. Stevenson III
Michael F. Johnson 2nd
but
Stevenson, Adlai E., III

9.43 **Numbers for sequels.** Numerals are often used to designate the sequel to a novel or a movie or to differentiate two chapter titles dealing with the same subject matter. When quoting such titles, follow the usage—roman or arabic (or spelled out)—reflected in the source itself. (For the use of *sic*, see 13.61.)

The Godfather; *The Godfather, Part II*; *The Godfather, Part III*
Jaws; *Jaws 2*; *Jaws 3-D*
Dumb and Dumber To [*sic*]
chapter 9, "Alligator Studies in the Everglades—I"
chapter 10, "Alligator Studies in the Everglades—II"

9.44 **Vehicle and vessel numbers.** Boats and the like differentiated by a number usually take a roman numeral, spacecraft an arabic numeral. See also 8.116–18.

Bluebird III *Mariner 9*

9.45 **Numbers for successive governments.** Ordinal numbers designating successive dynasties, governments, and other governing bodies are spelled out if one hundred or less. See also 8.51, 8.62, 8.71.

Eighteenth Dynasty
Fifth Republic
Second Continental Congress
Second International
Ninety-Seventh United States Congress
115th Congress

9.46 **Numbered political and judicial divisions.** Ordinal numbers designating political or judicial divisions are spelled out if one hundred or less. See also 8.51.

Fifth Ward Twelfth Congressional District Tenth Circuit 101st Precinct

9.47 **Numbered military units.** Ordinal numbers designating military units are spelled out if one hundred or less. See also 8.112.

Fifth Army
Fourth Infantry Division
First Corps Support Command
101st Airborne Division

9.48 **Numbered places of worship.** Ordinal numbers that are part of the names of places of worship are spelled out.

Fourth Presbyterian Church Twenty-First Church of Christ, Scientist

9.49 **Unions and lodges.** Numbers designating local branches of labor unions and fraternal lodges are usually expressed in arabic numerals after the name. Commas can usually be omitted.

Chicago Typographical Union No. 16
American Legion Post 21
United Auto Workers Local 890

Addresses and Thoroughfares

9.50 **Numbered highways.** State, federal, and interstate highways are designated by arabic numerals. Names for state routes vary from state to state. See also 8.56.

US Route 41 (*or* US 41)
Interstate 90 (*or* I-90)
Illinois Route 50 (*or* Illinois 50; IL 50); Route 50
M6 motorway (England)

9.51 **Numbered streets.** Names of numbered streets, avenues, and so forth are usually spelled out if one hundred or less. For the use of *N*, *E*, *SW*, and the like, see 10.34. See also 8.56.

First Avenue   Ninety-Fifth Street   122nd Street

9.52 **Building and apartment numbers.** Building numbers, in arabic numerals, precede the street name. For preferred forms of mailing addresses, consult the applicable postal service; for readability and to conform to the style of the surrounding text, however, usage may differ slightly from what might be appropriate for a mailing label or the like. See also 6.39, 10.34.

They lived in Oak Park, at 1155 South Euclid Avenue, for almost ten years.
She now lives in unit 114A, 150 Ninth Avenue, with an unrivaled view of the city.
Our office is at 1427 East Sixtieth Street, Chicago, Illinois.
Please mail a copy of the German-language edition to 1427 E. 60th St., Chicago, IL 60637.

When a building is referred to in running text by its address, the number is often spelled out.

One Thousand Lake Shore Drive   One IBM Plaza

Plurals and Punctuation of Numbers

9.53 **Plural numbers.** Spelled-out numbers form their plurals as other nouns do (see 7.5).

The contestants were in their twenties and thirties.
The family was at sixes and sevens.

Numerals form their plurals by adding *s*. No apostrophe is needed (see also 7.15).

Among the scores were two 240s and three 238s.
Jazz forms that were developed in the 1920s became popular in the 1930s.

9.54 **Comma between digits.** In a style followed in most general contexts in the United States and most other English-speaking parts of the world, for numerals of one thousand or more, commas are used between groups of three digits, counting from the right. Commas are *not* used for figures to the right of the decimal marker.

1,512 32,987 4,000,500 *but* 0.32987

Nor are commas used in page numbers, line numbers (e.g., in poetry and plays), addresses, and years (though years of five digits or more do include the comma). See also 9.34.

Punctuation conventions can be found on page 1535 of the tenth edition.
Our business office is at 11030 South Langley Avenue.
Human artifacts dating from between 35,000 BP and 5000 BP have been found there.

In scientific writing, commas are often omitted from four-digit numbers. See also 9.56.

9.55 **The decimal marker.** According to the predominant usage in the United States and elsewhere, where commas are used between groups of three digits for numerals of one thousand or more (see 9.54), a period is used as the decimal marker (and called a decimal point).

33,333.33

In many other countries, including France (and French-speaking Canada), Germany, Italy, and Russia, the decimal marker is represented by a comma. Where this is the case, a thin, fixed space, not a comma, separates groups of three digits. (In electronic publications, a regular nonbreaking space may be used; see 6.121.)

33 333,33

This practice reflects SI usage, which allows either the comma or the decimal point as a decimal marker (see 9.56). English-speaking Canadians increasingly follow SI usage, using spaces rather than commas to separate groups of digits (while retaining the decimal point). In US publications, US style should be followed, except in direct quotations and except where SI style is required. See also 10.58.

9.56 **Space between digits (SI number style).** In the International System of Units (SI units), thin, fixed spaces rather than commas are normally used to mark off groups of three digits, both to the left and to the right of the decimal marker. (In electronic publications, a regular nonbreaking space may be used; see 6.121.) No space is used for groups of only four digits either to the left or to the right of the decimal marker (except in table columns that also include numbers having five or more digits, where it is needed for alignment). To mark the decimal, either a decimal point or a comma may be used, according to what is customary in a given context or region (the examples that follow show the decimal point). See also 9.55, 9.54.

3 426 869 0.000 007 2501.4865 (*or* 2 501.486 5)

For more on SI units, see Ambler Thompson and Barry N. Taylor, *Guide for the Use of the International System of Units (SI)*, and *The International System of Units (SI)*, a brochure published in English and French by the Bureau International des Poids et Mesures (see bibliog. 2.4).

9.57 **Telephone numbers.** In the United States and Canada, telephone numbers consist of the prefix 1 (also called the trunk prefix), an area code (also called the trunk code), and a seven-digit number consisting of a three-digit exchange prefix followed by a four-digit line number. When written, the seven-digit number is conventionally separated by a hyphen; to signal that it may be optional for local calls, the area code is often placed in parentheses. The prefix 1, the same for all numbers (and not always necessary to place a call), can usually be omitted. (Its appearance with toll-free numbers beginning with 800 and the like is customary but not mandatory.) An extension follows the number, separated by a comma.

(000) 000-0000 *or* (1-000) 000-0000
(000) 000-0000, ext. 0000

An alternative style, which recognizes the increasing need to use the area code even for local calls, drops the parentheses. Either style is acceptable, as long as it is used consistently. (On the other hand, the use of periods or other punctuation as separators in place of hyphens is generally not recommended.)

000-000-0000 *or* 1-000-000-0000

For international numbers, use spaces rather than hyphens as separators. A plus symbol, which stands in for the international prefix (e.g., 011 for international calls from the United States or Canada), is placed immediately before the country code (e.g., 52 for Mexico, 66 for Thailand, or 44 for the United Kingdom) with no intervening space. Because their meaning may not be clear, parentheses should not be used for international numbers (e.g., to enclose a national access code that is not needed for international calls).

+52 55 0000 0000 (for a number in Mexico City, Mexico)
+66 2 000 0000 (for a number in Bangkok, Thailand)
+44 20 0000 0000 (for a number in London, UK)
not
+44 (0) 20 0000 0000

If the international prefix must be expressed, it precedes the country code and is separated from it by a space (e.g., for a call initiated from the United States or Canada, 011 44 20 . . .). A US or Canadian number written for an international audience follows a similar pattern (the country code for both is 1).

+1 607 000 0000 (for a number in New York State)

Spaces or hyphens as separators are the norm within most countries; however, the use of parentheses and number groupings varies widely, not only across countries but also within countries, and for landline versus mobile numbers. For more guidance, consult the latest standard from the International Telecommunication Union (bibliog. 5) or, for more specific advice, a local or international directory.

9.58 **Ratios.** Ratios composed of whole numbers may generally be expressed using *to* and spelled out in ordinary text according to one of the rules stated at 9.2 and 9.3. In contexts where numerals are preferred, a colon may be used as a shorthand for *to*, with no space on either side.

a three-to-one ratio
a 13-to-2 ratio (see 9.3; see also 9.7)
or
a 13:2 ratio

In some contexts, ratios may be expressed as decimal fractions, in the manner of percentages (see 9.19).

9.59 **Numbered lists and outline style.** For the use of numerals (arabic and roman) and letters to distinguish items in lists, see 6.127–32.

Inclusive Numbers

9.60 **The en dash for inclusive numbers.** An en dash used between two numbers implies *up to and including*, or *through*.

Please refer to pages 75–110.
Here are the figures for 2000–2009.
Campers were divided into age groups 5–7, 8–10, 11–13, and 14–16.

The en dash should not be used if *from* or *between* is used before the first of a pair of numbers; instead, *from* should be followed by *to* or *through* (or *until*), and *between* should be followed by *and*.

from 75 to 110 (*not* from 75–110)
from 1898 to 1903
from January 1, 1898, through December 31, 1903
between about 150 and 200

Inclusive spelled-out numbers should be joined by *to*, not by an en dash.

participants aged forty-five to forty-nine years
sixty-to-seventy-year-olds

For more on the use of the en dash, see 6.78–84. See also 7.89, section 1, under *age terms*.

9.61 **Abbreviating, or condensing, inclusive numbers.** Inclusive numbers are abbreviated according to the principles illustrated below (the examples show page numbers, which do not require commas). This system, used by Chicago in essentially this form since the first edition of this manual, is efficient and unambiguous. See also 9.62, 9.60, 14.148.

First number	*Second number*	*Examples*
Less than 100	Use all digits	3–10 71–72 96–117
100 or multiples of 100	Use all digits	100–104 1100–1113
101 through 109, 201 through 209, etc.	Use changed part only	101–8 808–33 1103–4

110 through 199, 210 through 299, etc.	Use two digits unless more are needed to include all changed parts	321–28 498–532 1087–89 1496–500 11564–615 12991–3001

To avoid ambiguity, inclusive roman numerals are always given in full.

xxv–xxviii   cvi–cix

9.62 **Alternative systems for inclusive numbers.** A foolproof system is to give the full form of numbers everywhere (e.g., 234–235, 25039–25041). Another practice, more economical, is to include in the second number only the changed part of the first (e.g., 234–5, 25000–1). Chicago, however, prefers the system presented in 9.61.

9.63 **Inclusive numbers with commas.** When inclusive numbers with commas are abbreviated, and only numbers in the hundreds place and below change, the rules described in 9.61 should apply. If a change extends to the thousands place or beyond, it is best to repeat all digits.

6,000–6,018   12,473–79   1,247,689–710   1,247,689–1,248,125

9.64 **Inclusive years.** Inclusive years may be abbreviated following the pattern illustrated in 9.61. When the century changes, however, or when the sequence is BCE, BC, or BP (diminishing numbers), all digits must be presented. See also 9.34.

1897–1901
the war of 1914–18
fiscal year 2017–18 (*or* 2017/18; see 6.107); FY 2017–18
the winter of 2000–2001
in 1504–5
327–321 BCE (seven years, inclusively)
327–21 BCE (307 years, inclusively)
115 BC–AD 10
15,000–14,000 BP

In book titles it is customary but not obligatory to repeat all digits; when a title is mentioned or cited, the form of the original should be respected (see also 8.165).

TABLE 9.1. Roman and arabic numerals

Arabic	Roman	Arabic	Roman	Arabic	Roman
1	I	17	XVII	200	CC
2	II	18	XVIII	300	CCC
3	III	19	XIX	400	CD
4	IV	20	XX	500	D
5	V	21	XXI	600	DC
6	VI	22	XXII	700	DCC
7	VII	23	XXIII	800	DCCC
8	VIII	24	XXIV	900	CM
9	IX	30	XXX	1,000	M
10	X	40	XL	2,000	MM
11	XI	50	L	3,000	MMM
12	XII	60	LX	4,000	MV̄
13	XIII	70	LXX	5,000	V̄
14	XIV	80	LXXX	10,000	X̄
15	XV	90	XC	100,000	C̄
16	XVI	100	C	1,000,000	M̄

Roman Numerals

9.65 **Roman numerals—general principles.** Table 9.1 shows the formation of roman numerals with their arabic equivalents. The general principle is that a smaller letter before a larger one subtracts from its value, and a smaller letter after a larger one adds to it; a bar over a letter multiplies its value by one thousand. Roman numerals may also be written in lowercase letters (i, ii, iii, iv, etc.). In older sources, a final *i* was often made like a *j* (vij, viij), and sometimes a *v* appeared as a *u* (uj); citations to roman numeral page numbers in older works should follow the original usage.

9.66 **The advent of subtrahends (back counters).** The use of subtrahends (back counters) was introduced during the Renaissance. Note that IIII, not IV, still appears on some clock faces. The Romans would have expressed the year 1999, for example, as MDCCCCLXXXXVIIII. A more modern form, approved by the US government and accepted (if reluctantly) by classical scholars, is MCMXCIX (*not* MIM, considered a barbarism).

9.67 **Chicago's preference for arabic rather than roman numerals.** Chicago uses arabic numerals in many situations where roman numerals were formerly common, as in references to volume numbers of books and journals or chapters of books (see 9.27). Most of the exceptions are treated elsewhere, as follows: for the use of roman numerals in the front matter of books, see 1.4, 1.7, 9.26; in legal instruments, 9.28; with the names of monarchs, prelates, and such, 9.41; with personal names, 9.42; in titles of sequels, 9.43; with names of certain vessels, 9.44; and in outline style, 6.132.

10 · Abbreviations

Overview

10.1 **Abbreviations—additional resources.** This chapter provides guidance for using abbreviations and symbols in general and scholarly writing. It also offers some guidance in technical work, especially for the generalist editor confronted with unfamiliar terms. For abbreviations not listed here, Chicago recommends *Merriam-Webster's Collegiate Dictionary* (bibliog. 3.1) and the multivolume *Acronyms, Initialisms & Abbreviations Dictionary* (bibliog. 4.7). Authors and editors of technical material will need to refer to more specialized manuals, starting with *Scientific Style and Format* (bibliog. 1.1).

10.2 **Acronyms, initialisms, contractions.** The word *acronym* refers to terms based on the initial letters of their various elements and read as single words (AIDS, laser, NASA, scuba); *initialism* refers to terms read as a series of letters (IRS, NBA, XML); and *contraction* refers to abbreviations that include the first and last letters of the full word (Mr., amt.). (For the type of contractions normally formed with apostrophes, see 7.30.) These definitions are not perfect. For example, sometimes a letter in an initialism is formed not, as the term might imply, from an initial letter, but rather from its initial sound (as the *X* in XML, for extensible markup language) or from the application of a number (W3C, for World Wide Web Consortium). Furthermore, an acronym and an initialism are occasionally combined (JPEG), and the line between initialism and acronym is not always clear (FAQ, which can be pronounced either as a word or as a series of letters). In this chapter the umbrella term *abbreviation* will be used for all three, as well as for shortened (i.e., abbreviated) forms (ibid., vol., prof., etc.), except where greater specificity is required. (Occasionally, a *symbol* abbreviates a term, as in © for *copyright*. On the other hand, abbreviations for units are often referred to as symbols in SI usage; see 10.51–59.)

10.3 **When to use abbreviations.** Outside the area of science and technology, abbreviations and symbols are most appropriate in tabular matter, notes, bibliographies, and parenthetical references. A number of expressions are almost always abbreviated, even in regular prose, and may be used without first spelling them out. Many of these will be listed as main entries with pronunciation (labeled as nouns rather than as abbreviations) in the latest edition of *Webster's* (e.g., ATM, DIY, DNA, GPS, HMO, HTML, IQ, JPEG, laser, Ms., NASA). Others, though in more or less common use (CGI, FDA, HVAC, MLA), should generally be spelled out at first occurrence—at least in formal text—as a courtesy to those readers who might not easily recognize them. The use of less familiar abbreviations should be limited to terms that occur frequently enough to warrant abbreviation—roughly five times or more within an article or chapter—and the terms must be spelled out on their first occurrence. The abbreviation usually follows immediately, in parentheses, but it may be introduced in other ways (see examples). Such an abbreviation should not be offered only once, never to be used again, except as an alternative form that may be better known to some readers.

Among recent recommendations of the Federal Aviation Administration (FAA) are . . .
According to the weak law of large numbers (WLLN) . . .
The National Aeronautics and Space Administration was founded in 1958. Since its inception, NASA has . . .
The benefits of ERISA (Employee Retirement Income Security Act) are familiar to many.
The debate over genetically modified organisms, or GMOs, is by no means limited to the United States.

Writers and editors should monitor the number of different abbreviations used in a document; readers trying to keep track of a large number of abbreviations, especially unfamiliar ones, will benefit from a list of abbreviations (see 1.44, 2.23). In a work with few abbreviations and no list, when an abbreviation reappears after a long interval in which it is not used, it may be helpful to repeat the spelled-out name as a reminder. For rules concerning the plural form of various abbreviations, see 7.15. For abbreviations preceded by *a*, *an*, or *the*, see 7.33, 10.9. For abbreviations in charts or tables, see 3.45, 3.62, 3.81.

10.4 **Periods with abbreviations.** In using periods with abbreviations, Chicago recommends the following general guidelines in nontechnical settings. For the use of space between elements, see 10.5.

1. Use periods with abbreviations that end in a lowercase letter: p. (page), vol., e.g., i.e., etc., a.k.a., a.m., p.m., Ms., Dr., et al. (*et* is not an abbreviation; *al.* is). An exception may be made for the few academic degrees that end in a lowercase letter (e.g., DLitt, DMin); see 10.21 and rule 3.
2. Use periods for initials standing for given names: E. B. White; do not use periods for an entire name replaced by initials: JFK.
3. Use no periods with abbreviations that include two or more capital letters, even if the abbreviation also includes lowercase letters: VP, CEO, MA, MD, PhD, UK, US, NY, IL (*but see rule 4*).
4. In publications using traditional state abbreviations, use periods to abbreviate

United States and its states and territories: U.S., N.Y., Ill. Note, however, that Chicago recommends using the two-letter postal codes (and therefore *US*) wherever abbreviations are used; see 10.27. For Canadian provinces and territories, see 10.28. See also 14.274.

Note that the British and the French (among others) omit periods from contractions (Dr, assn, Mme). Note also that a slash is occasionally used instead of periods (as in *c/o* or *n/a*) but more often denotes *per* (see 6.109). Units of measure in nontechnical settings are usually spelled out. In scientific usage, periods are generally omitted for abbreviated units of measure and other technical terms (see 10.49–68).

10.5 **Abbreviations and spaces.** No space is left between the letters of initialisms and acronyms, whether lowercase or in capitals. Space is usually left between abbreviated words, unless an abbreviated word is used in combination with a single-letter abbreviation. For personal names, see 10.12.

RN	Gov. Gen.	*but*
C-SPAN	Mng. Ed.	S.Dak. (but see 10.27)
YMCA	Dist. Atty.	S.Sgt.

10.6 **Capitals versus lowercase for acronyms and initialisms.** Initialisms tend to appear in all capital letters, even when they are not derived from proper nouns (HIV, VP, LCD). With frequent use, however, acronyms—especially those of five or more letters—will sometimes become lowercase (scuba); those that are derived from proper nouns will retain an initial capital (Unicef). (In British usage, it is common to retain an initial capital even for acronyms derived from generic terms.) Chicago generally prefers the all-capital form (e.g., UNICEF), unless the term is listed otherwise in *Webster's*. In the sciences, however, it is common to encounter forms with a mix of lowercase and capital letters or in all lowercase (e.g., mRNA, IgG, bp); where such forms are considered standard, they should generally be respected.

NAFTA (*not* Nafta)

Note that the words in a spelled-out version of an acronym or initialism are capitalized only if they are considered to be proper nouns (as in the official name of an organization or a trademark); otherwise, they should generally be lowercased, even when they appear alongside the abbreviated form.

North American Free Trade Agreement (NAFTA)
KFC (Kentucky Fried Chicken)
transmission-control protocol/internet protocol (TCP/IP)
OCD (obsessive-compulsive disorder)

10.7 **Italic versus roman type for abbreviations.** Chicago italicizes abbreviations only if they stand for a term that would be italicized if spelled out—the title of a book or periodical, for example. Common Latin abbreviations are set in roman (see also 7.55).

OED (*Oxford English Dictionary*)
JAMA (*Journal of the American Medical Association*)
ibid. etc. e.g. i.e.

10.8 **Small versus full-size capitals for acronyms and initialisms.** Some designs call for small capitals rather than full-size capitals for acronyms and initialisms (e.g., NASA rather than NASA). Though such usage may be considered desirable for a work that includes many acronyms and initialisms, Chicago does not generally recommend it. If small capitals must be used, the decision of what to mark should be made by the editor, who should apply small capitals on the final manuscript (e.g., using a word processor's small-capitals feature). In general, small capitals should be limited to acronyms or initialisms mentioned in running text. Avoid applying small capitals to such items as two-letter postal codes in notes or bibliographies or to roman numerals (e.g., following a personal name). It should be noted that small capitals are not treated in the same way across all software applications and markup systems; small capitals should therefore be checked after conversion for publication to make sure they have not reverted to lowercase or full capitals (see also 2.81–83). See also 10.38, 10.41. For the use of small capitals for emphasis, see 7.52.

10.9 **"A," "an," or "the" preceding an abbreviation.** When an abbreviation follows an indefinite article, the choice of *a* or *an* is determined by the way the abbreviation would be read aloud. Acronyms are read as words and are rarely preceded by *a*, *an*, or *the* ("member nations of NATO"), except when used adjectivally ("a NATO initiative"; "the NATO meeting"). See 10.2; see also 7.33.

an HMO
a UFO
a NATO member

a LOOM parade
an AA meeting
a AA battery (pronounced *double A*)
an NAACP convention
an NBA coach
an HIV test
an MS symptom (a symptom of multiple sclerosis)
but
a MS by . . . (would be read as *a manuscript by* . . .)

Initialisms, which are read as a series of letters, are often preceded by a definite article ("member nations of the EU"). Whether to include the article may depend on established usage. For example, one would refer to the NBA and the NAACP, on the one hand, but to W3C, PBS, and NATO, on the other—though all these organizations include the definite article in spelled-out form. If no established usage can be determined, use the definite article if it would be used with the spelled-out form. Some terms, such as DIY (do it yourself), do not ordinarily require a definite article in spelled-out form and therefore do not require one as an initialism.

10.10 **Abbreviations containing ampersands.** No space is left on either side of an ampersand used within an initialism. See also 10.24.

R&D   Texas A&M

Names and Titles

Personal Names, Titles, and Degrees

10.11 **Abbreviations for personal names.** Normally, abbreviations should not be used for given names. A signature, however, should be transcribed as the person wrote it.

Benj. Franklin   Geo. D. Fuller   Ch. Virolleaud

10.12 **Initials in personal names.** Initials standing for given names are followed by a period and a space. A period is normally used even if the middle initial does not stand for a name (as in Harry S. Truman).

Roger W. Shugg   P. D. James   M. F. K. Fisher

If an entire name is abbreviated, spaces and periods can usually be omitted.

FDR (Franklin Delano Roosevelt)
MJ (Michael Jordan)
JLo (Jennifer Lopez)
but
J.Lo (the title of Lopez's 2001 album)

10.13 **Abbreviating titles before names.** Many civil or military titles preceding a full name may be abbreviated. When preceding a surname alone, however, they should be spelled out. See also 8.19.

Rep. Dan Lipinski; Representative Lipinski
Sen. Kirsten E. Gillibrand; Senator Gillibrand
Vice Adm. Carol M. Pottenger; Vice Admiral Pottenger

10.14 **Abbreviations for civil titles.** The following abbreviations, among others, may precede a full name where space is tight:

Ald.	Atty. Gen.	Insp. Gen.	Prof.
Assoc. Prof.	Fr. (father)	Judge Adv. Gen.	Sr. (sister)
Asst. Prof.	Gov.	Pres.	Supt.

10.15 **Abbreviations for military titles.** The US military omits periods in the official abbreviated forms of its ranks. The abbreviations for a given title may vary across branches. The army, for example, uses *SSG* for *staff sergeant*; the air force and marines prefer *SSgt*. (In the examples below, such variants are not presented.) In general contexts, however, including military history, traditional abbreviations—which tend not to vary across the armed forces—are preferred. The following very selective list merely illustrates the difference between military usage and traditional forms. Where no traditional abbreviation is appropriate before a name, use the full form.

ADM	Adm.	GEN	Gen.
A1C	Airman First Class	LT	Lt.
BG	Brig. Gen.	1LT	1st Lt.
CDR	Cdr.	2LT	2nd Lt.
COL	Col.	LG	Lt. Gen.
CPT	Capt.	LTC	Lt. Col.
CWO	Chief Warrant Officer	MAJ	Maj.

MG	Maj. Gen.	SGT	Sgt.
MSG	M.Sgt. (master sergeant)	SSG	S.Sgt. (staff sergeant)
PO	Petty Officer	WO	Warrant Officer

For the latest official forms of rank insignia, consult the website of the US Department of Defense. In addition, there are many reference books containing more detailed lists of abbreviations and terms, some of which are published regularly. See, for example, Timothy Zurick, *Army Dictionary and Desk Reference* (bibliog. 5). For Canadian military ranks and abbreviations, start with the website of the National Defence and the Canadian Armed Forces. For the United Kingdom, consult the websites of the various forces. See also 8.112.

10.16 **Abbreviations for social titles.** Social titles are always abbreviated, whether preceding the full name or the surname only. The spelled-out forms *Mister* or *Doctor* might be used without a name—as in direct address (see also 8.20).

Ms.	Mr.	*but*
Mrs.	Mx.	Thank you, Doctor.
Messrs.	Dr. Jekyll	

Social titles are routinely omitted in most prose, though a few periodicals in particular persist in using them. When an academic degree or professional designation follows a name, such titles are always omitted.

Jennifer James, MD (*not* Dr. Jennifer James, MD)

Similarly, the now somewhat archaic abbreviation *Esq.* (Esquire) is used only after a full name and never when *Mr.*, *Dr.*, or the like precedes the name.

10.17 **Abbreviations for French social titles.** Note the presence or absence of periods after the following abbreviations for French social titles (which can be used with either a full name or a surname only). *Mme* and *Mlle* are considered contractions (see 10.2) and therefore do not take a period. This usage should be observed when such forms appear untranslated in English-language settings.

M. MM. Mme Mlle

When *Monsieur*, *Messieurs*, *Madame*, or *Mademoiselle* is used without a name, in direct address, it is spelled out (and, in French usage, generally lowercased).

10.18 **Abbreviations for "Reverend" and "Honorable."** The abbreviations *Rev.* and *Hon.* are traditionally used before a full name when *the* does not precede the title. With *the*, such titles should be spelled out.

Rev. Sam Portaro; the Reverend Sam Portaro
Hon. Henry M. Brown; the Honorable Henry M. Brown

With a last name only, such titles are normally omitted. The construction "Reverend So-and-So," however, is common, especially in informal prose or speech.

Rev. Jane Schaefer; Schaefer (*or* Reverend Schaefer)
the Honorable Patricia Birkholz; Birkholz

10.19 **Abbreviations for "Junior," "Senior," and the like.** The abbreviations *Jr.* and *Sr.*, as well as roman or arabic numerals such as *III* or *3rd* after a person's name, are part of the name and so are retained in connection with any titles or honorifics. Note that these abbreviations are used only with the full name, never with the surname only. See also 6.43, 9.42.

Jordan Balfence Jr. spoke first. After Mr. Balfence relinquished the podium, . . .
Zayd Zephyr III, MBA, spoke last. In closing, Mr. Zephyr reiterated . . .

In some contexts—for example, a biography that includes frequent mentions of a father and son who share the same name—it may be appropriate to use *Jr.* or *Sr.* or the like with a first name alone.

Henry Jr., in his later years (and despite the publication of *The Golden Bowl* and other masterpieces), was never again to enjoy the kind of wealth that Henry Sr. had once taught him to take for granted.

10.20 **Abbreviations for the names of saints.** The word *Saint* is often abbreviated (*St.*, pl. *SS.*) before the name of a Christian saint; it should normally be spelled out in formal prose but need not be if space is at a premium. The choice for one or the other should be implemented consistently.

Saint (*or* St.) Teresa
Saints (*or* SS.) Francis of Paola and Francis of Sales

When *Saint* or *St.* forms part of a personal name, the bearer's usage is followed. See also 10.30.

Augustus Saint-Gaudens   Muriel St. Clare Byrne

10.21 **Abbreviations for academic degrees.** Chicago recommends omitting periods in abbreviations of academic degrees (BA, DDS, etc.) unless they are required for reasons of tradition or consistency with, for example, a journal's established style. In the following list of some of the more common degrees, periods are shown only where uncertainty might arise as to their placement. Spelled-out terms, often capitalized in institutional settings (and on business cards and other promotional items), should be lowercased in normal prose. See also 8.29.

AB	artium baccalaureus (bachelor of arts)
AM	artium magister (master of arts)
BA	bachelor of arts
BD	bachelor of divinity
BFA	bachelor of fine arts
BM	bachelor of music
BS	bachelor of science
DB	divinitatis baccalaureus (bachelor of divinity)
DD	divinitatis doctor (doctor of divinity)
DDS	doctor of dental surgery
DLitt *or* DLit	doctor litterarum (doctor of letters; doctor of literature)
DMD	dentariae medicinae doctor (doctor of dental medicine)
DMin	doctor of ministry
DO	doctor of osteopathy *or* osteopathic physician
DVM	doctor of veterinary medicine
EdM	educationis magister (master of education)
JD	juris doctor (doctor of law)
LHD	litterarum humaniorum doctor (doctor of humanities)
LittD	litterarum doctor (doctor of letters)
LLB (LL.B.)	legum baccalaureus (bachelor of laws)
LLD (LL.D.)	legum doctor (doctor of laws)
LLM (LL.M.)	legum magister (master of laws)
MA	master of arts
MBA	master of business administration
MD	medicinae doctor (doctor of medicine)
MDiv	master of divinity
MFA	master of fine arts
MS	master of science
MSN	master of science in nursing
MSW	master of social welfare *or* master of social work
PhB	philosophiae baccalaureus (bachelor of philosophy)
PhD	philosophiae doctor (doctor of philosophy)
PhG	graduate in pharmacy
SB	scientiae baccalaureus (bachelor of science)

SM	scientiae magister (master of science)
STB	sacrae theologiae baccalaureus (bachelor of sacred theology)

These designations are set off by commas when they follow a personal name.

Ariel Z. Lee, JD, attended the University of Chicago Law School.

10.22 **Abbreviations for professional, religious, and other designations.** Abbreviations for many other designations, professional and otherwise, follow the pattern of academic degrees (see 10.21), for which Chicago recommends dispensing with periods. Spelled-out terms, often capitalized in institutional settings, are lowercase unless they designate the proper name of an organization.

CNM	certified nurse midwife
FAIA	fellow of the American Institute of Architects
FRS	fellow of the Royal Society
JP	justice of the peace
LPN	licensed practical nurse
MP	member of Parliament
OFM	Order of Friars Minor
OP	Ordo Praedicatorum (Order of Preachers)
RN	registered nurse
SJ	Society of Jesus

These designations, like academic degrees, are set off by commas when they follow a personal name.

Joan Hotimlanska, LPN, will be working on the second floor.

Companies and Other Organizations

10.23 **Commonly used generic abbreviations for firms and companies.** All of the abbreviations in the following list may be found in *Webster's* and other standard dictionaries. Use periods, or not, according to the recommendations in 10.4. See also 10.69.

Assoc.	Inc.
Bros.	LLC (limited liability company)
Co.	LLP (limited liability partnership)
Corp.	LP (limited partnership)

Ltd.	RR (railroad)
Mfg.	Rwy. *or* Ry. (railway)
PLC (public limited company)	

In certain languages other than English, periods are omitted from abbreviations if they are contractions (see 10.2).

Cia (Sp. *compañia*)   Cie (Fr. *compagnie*)

10.24 **Abbreviations and ampersands in company names.** Abbreviations and ampersands are appropriate in notes, bibliographies, tabular matter, and the like. See also 14.135.

Ginn & Co.   JPMorgan Chase & Co.   Moss Bros.   RAND Corp.

In running text, company names are best given in their full forms. It should be noted, however, that some full forms include ampersands and abbreviations. If in doubt, especially with reference to contemporary firms, look up the company name at a corporate website or other authoritative source. Such elements as *Inc.*, *& Co.*, and *LLC* may be omitted unless relevant to the context.

Johnson & Johnson was founded in 1886.
JPMorgan Chase operates in more than sixty countries.
AT&T Corporation was once known as the American Telephone and Telegraph Company.

Abbreviations for companies and other organizations that use initialisms as described in 10.4, rule 3, generally appear without periods; the occasional exception may be made in the case of a clear and established preference (as in the band name R.E.M.).

10.25 **Abbreviations for media companies.** Abbreviations for media companies often take the form of call letters used for broadcasting. These are always capitalized and do not take periods.

ABC   CBS   HBO   KFTV   MTV   NBC   TBS   WFMT   WTTW

10.26 **Abbreviations for associations and the like.** Both in running text (preferably after being spelled out on first occurrence) and in tabular matter, notes, and so forth, the names of many agencies and organizations, governmental and otherwise, are commonly abbreviated. Whether acronyms or initialisms (see 10.2), such abbreviations appear in full capitals and without periods. For *a*, *an*, or *the* with abbreviations, see 10.9.

AAUP	EU (European Union)	WHO
AFL-CIO	HMO (*pl.* HMOs)	WTO (*formerly* GATT)
EPA		

Geographical Terms

10.27 **Abbreviations for US states and territories.** In running text, the names of states, territories, and possessions of the United States should always be spelled out when standing alone and preferably (except for DC) when following the name of a city: for example, "Lake Bluff, Illinois, was incorporated in 1895." In bibliographies, tabular matter, lists, and mailing addresses, they are usually abbreviated. In all such contexts, Chicago prefers the two-letter postal codes to the conventional abbreviations. Note that if traditional abbreviations must be used, some terms may not be subject to abbreviation. See also 10.4.

AK	Alaska *or* Alas.	LA	La.
AL	Ala.	MA	Mass.
AR	Ark.	MD	Md.
AS	American Samoa	ME	Maine
AZ	Ariz.	MH	Marshall Islands
CA	Calif.	MI	Mich.
CO	Colo.	MN	Minn.
CT	Conn.	MO	Mo.
DC	D.C.	MP	Northern Mariana Islands
DE	Del.	MS	Miss.
FL	Fla.	MT	Mont.
FM	Federated States of Micronesia	NC	N.C.
		ND	N.Dak.
GA	Ga.	NE	Neb. *or* Nebr.
GU	Guam	NH	N.H.
HI	Hawaii	NJ	N.J.
IA	Iowa	NM	N.Mex.
ID	Idaho	NV	Nev.
IL	Ill.	NY	N.Y.
IN	Ind.	OH	Ohio
KS	Kans.	OK	Okla.
KY	Ky.	OR	Ore. *or* Oreg.

PA	Pa.	UT	Utah
PR	P.R. *or* Puerto Rico	VA	Va.
PW	Palau	VI	V.I. *or* Virgin Islands
RI	R.I.	VT	Vt.
SC	S.C.	WA	Wash.
SD	S.Dak.	WI	Wis. *or* Wisc.
TN	Tenn.	WV	W.Va.
TX	Tex.	WY	Wyo.

10.28 **Abbreviations for Canadian provinces and territories.** Canadian provinces and territories are normally spelled out in text (e.g., "Kingston, Ontario, is worth a visit") but may be abbreviated in bibliographies and the like—using the two-letter postal abbreviations, which have the advantage of applying to both the English and French forms.

AB	Alberta
BC	British Columbia *or* Colombie-Britannique
MB	Manitoba
NB	New Brunswick *or* Nouveau-Brunswick
NL	Newfoundland and Labrador *or* Terre-Neuve-et-Labrador
NS	Nova Scotia *or* Nouvelle-Écosse
NT	Northwest Territories *or* Territoires du Nord-Ouest
NU	Nunavut
ON	Ontario
PE	Prince Edward Island *or* Île-du-Prince-Édouard
QC	Quebec *or* Québec
SK	Saskatchewan
YT	Yukon

10.29 **Comma with city plus state abbreviation.** When following the name of a city, the names of states, provinces, and territories are enclosed in commas, whether they are spelled out (as in running text) or abbreviated (as in tabular matter or lists). In an exception to the rule, no comma appears between the postal code and a zip code. See also 6.39, 6.17.

Bedford, PA, and Jamestown, NY
but
Send the package to J. Sprocket, 3359 Fob Dr., Quartz, IL 60000.

10.30 **Abbreviations for place-names with "Fort," "Mount," and "Saint."** Generic terms as elements of geographic names are usually spelled out in formal prose (and in mailing addresses) but can be abbreviated where space is at a premium or to reflect predominant usage. *San* and *Santa* (e.g., San Diego, Santa Barbara) are never abbreviated. For French placenames with *Saint*, see 11.26.

Fort (Ft.) Myers
Mount (Mt.) Airy
Port (Pt.) Arthur
Saint (St.) Louis
Saint (St.) Paul

Names of Countries

10.31 **Abbreviating country names.** Names of countries are usually spelled out in text but may be abbreviated in tabular matter, lists, and the like. Use discretion in forming the abbreviations; for tables, make sure they are defined in a note to the table if there is any possibility of confusion (see 3.76–80). The examples below reflect entries in standard dictionaries (all are listed in *Webster's*, with the exception of *Swed.*, which is listed in *American Heritage*).

Fr. Ger. Isr. It. Neth. Russ. Sp. Swed.

Certain initialisms, on the other hand, may be appropriate in regular text, especially after the full form has been established (see 10.2, 10.3). For more on *US*, see 10.32.

UAE (United Arab Emirates)
US
UK
GDR (the former German Democratic Republic, or East Germany) *or* DDR (Deutsche Demokratische Republik)
FRG (the former Federal Republic of Germany) *or* BRD (Bundesrepublik Deutschland)
USSR (the former Union of Soviet Socialist Republics)

In certain technical applications, it may be advisable to use either the two-letter or three-letter standard abbreviations based on the English names of countries as defined by the International Organization for Standardization (ISO 3166-1, alpha-2 and alpha-3, respectively). For these lists, consult the ISO website.

10.32 **"US" versus "United States."** Where necessary, initialisms for country names can be used in running text according to the guidelines set forth in 10.3 (see also 10.31). Note that, as a matter of editorial tradition, this manual has long advised spelling out *United States* as a noun, reserving *US* for the adjective form only (where it is preferred) and for tabular matter and the like. In a departure, Chicago now permits the use of *US* as a noun, subject to editorial discretion and provided the meaning is clear from context.

US dollars
US involvement in China
China's involvement in the United States
or
China's involvement in the US

See also 10.4.

Addresses

10.33 **Mailing addresses—postal versus standard abbreviations.** Standard abbreviations preferred by the US Postal Service (first column) are in all caps and do not use periods; these forms are most appropriate for mailing addresses. In tabular matter and the like, Chicago prefers the form of abbreviations presented in the second column. For those not listed here, consult a dictionary. For standard postal abbreviations, consult the USPS or other regional postal service. In running text, spell out rather than abbreviate. See also 10.34.

AVE	Ave.	PO BOX	PO Box
BLDG	Bldg.	RD	Rd.
CT	Ct.	RM	Rm.
DR	Dr.	RTE	Rte.
EXPY	Expy.	SQ	Sq.
HWY	Hwy.	ST	St.
LN	Ln.	STE	Ste. (*or* Suite)
PKWY	Pkwy.	TER	Ter. (*or* Terr.)
PL	Pl.		

10.34 **Abbreviations for compass points in mailing addresses.** Single-letter compass points accompanying a street name are normally followed by a period; two-letter compass points are not. (The US Postal Service does not use periods for either; see 10.33; see also 10.4.) Note that when used in an address, the abbreviations *NE*, *NW*, *SE*, and *SW* remain abbreviated even in running text (there is no comma before them when they follow a street name). The *N* in the third example is a street name and not a compass point.

1060 E. Prospect Ave. (*or, in running text,* 1060 East Prospect Avenue)
456 NW Lane St. (*or, in running text,* 456 NW Lane Street)
I stayed in a building on N Street SW, close to the city center.

A compass point that is the name (or part of the name) of a street or a place-name must never be abbreviated (e.g., South Ave., Northwest Hwy., South Shore Dr., West Bend, East Orange). For the use of numerals in addresses, see 9.51, 9.52.

Compass Points, Latitude, and Longitude

10.35 **Abbreviations for compass points.** Points of the compass may be abbreviated as follows, without periods (but see 10.34). In formal, nontechnical text, however, these terms are usually spelled out.

N, E, S, W, NE, SE, SW, NW, NNE, ENE, ESE, etc.
N by NE, NE by N, NE by E, etc.

10.36 **Abbreviations for "latitude" and "longitude."** In nontechnical contexts, the words *latitude* and *longitude* are never abbreviated in running text or when standing alone.

longitude 90° west   the polar latitudes

Global positioning coordinates are expressed in a variety of ways (though latitude is always given first). Some systems use a minus sign (or hyphen) to indicate south or west. Others use decimal minutes. The following three coordinates are equivalent. The comma is often omitted.

36 25.217, −44 23.017   N 36°25′13″, W 44°23′01″   N 36 25.217, W 44 23.017

In technical work, the abbreviations *lat* and *long*, usually without periods, may be used when part of a coordinate. They can sometimes be dropped, since the compass point identifies the coordinate.

lat 42°15′09″ N, long 89°17′45″ W
lat 45°16′17″ S, long 116°40′18″ E
The chart showed shoal water at 19°29′59″ N, 107°45′36″ W.

Note that primes (′) and double primes (″), *not* quotation marks, are used. For greater detail, consult *Scientific Style and Format* (bibliog. 1.1).

Designations of Time

10.37 **Other discussions related to time.** For units of time (seconds, minutes, etc.), see 10.68. For numerical designations of dates and times of day, see 9.30, 9.33, 9.35, 9.37–40.

10.38 **Abbreviations for chronological eras.** The following abbreviations are used in running text and elsewhere to designate chronological eras. Although these have traditionally appeared in small capitals (with or without periods), Chicago recommends full capitals without periods, in keeping with the general guidelines in this chapter (see 10.4; see also 10.8). The first four precede the year number; the others follow it. See also 9.34.

AD	anno Domini (in the year of [our] Lord)
AH	anno Hegirae (in the year of the Hegira); anno Hebraico (in the Hebrew year)
AM	anno mundi (in the year of the world) (not to be confused with ante meridiem; see 10.41)
AS	anno salutis (in the year of salvation)
AUC	ab urbe condita (from the founding of the city [Rome, in 753 BCE])
BC	before Christ
BCE	before the Common Era
BP	before the present
CE	Common Era
MYA	million years ago
YBP	years before the present

10.39 **Abbreviations for months.** Where space restrictions require that the names of months be abbreviated, one of the following systems is often used. The second and third, which take no periods, are used respectively in computer systems and indexes of periodical literature. In formal prose, Chicago prefers the first.

Jan.	Jan	Ja	July	Jul	Jl
Feb.	Feb	F	Aug.	Aug	Ag
Mar.	Mar	Mr	Sept.	Sep	S
Apr.	Apr	Ap	Oct.	Oct	O
May	May	My	Nov.	Nov	N
June	Jun	Je	Dec.	Dec	D

10.40 **Abbreviations for days of the week.** Where space restrictions require that days of the week be abbreviated, one of the following systems is often used. The second (common in computer code) and third use no periods. In formal prose, Chicago recommends the first.

Sun.	Sun	Su	Thurs.	Thu	Th
Mon.	Mon	M	Fri.	Fri	F
Tues.	Tue	Tu	Sat.	Sat	Sa
Wed.	Wed	W			

10.41 **Abbreviations for time of day.** The following abbreviations are used in text and elsewhere to indicate time of day. Though these sometimes appear in small capitals (with or without periods), Chicago prefers the lowercase form, with periods, as being the most immediately intelligible. For further explanation and examples, see 9.37, 9.39. See also 10.4.

a.m. *ante meridiem* (before noon)
m. *meridies* (noon [rarely used])
p.m. *post meridiem* (after noon)

The abbreviations *a.m.* and *p.m.* should not be used with *morning*, *afternoon*, *evening*, *night*, or *o'clock*. (See also 7.89, section 1, under *time*.)

10:30 a.m. *or* ten thirty in the morning
11:00 p.m. *or* eleven o'clock at night

Time zones, where needed, are usually given in parentheses—for example, 4:45 p.m. (CST).

GMT	Greenwich mean time	MST	mountain standard time
EST	eastern standard time	MDT	mountain daylight time
EDT	eastern daylight time	PST	Pacific standard time
CST	central standard time	PDT	Pacific daylight time
CDT	central daylight time		

It should be noted that Greenwich mean time has long been superseded by the nearly identical coordinated universal time (UTC) as the basis of international time. References to GMT, however, remain widespread not only in the United Kingdom but also in the United States and Canada and elsewhere.

Scholarly Abbreviations

10.42 **Scholarly abbreviations.** Scholarly abbreviations and symbols such as those listed in this section are typically found in bibliographic references, glossaries, and other scholarly apparatus. Some of them are no longer widely used and are listed here mainly as an aid to interpreting older texts. In formal prose, Chicago prefers to confine such abbreviations to parentheses or notes. Some can stand for several terms; only the terms likely to be encountered in scholarly works (mainly in the humanities) and serious nonfiction are included here. The choice between different abbreviations for one term (e.g., *L.* and *Lat.* for *Latin*) depends on the writer's preference, context, readership, and other factors; if in doubt, choose the longer form. Note that Latin abbreviations are normally set in roman. Note also that *ab*, *ad*, *et*, and other Latin terms that are complete words take no periods. See also 7.55, 10.4. For terms used more commonly in science and technology, see 10.49.

abbr.	abbreviated, -ion
ab init.	*ab initio*, from the beginning
abl.	ablative
abr.	abridged, abridgment
acc.	accusative
act.	active
add.	addendum
ad inf.	*ad infinitum*
ad init.	*ad initium*, at the beginning
ad int.	*ad interim*, in the intervening time
adj.	adjective
ad lib.	*ad libitum*, at will (often used without a period)
ad loc.	*ad locum*, at the place
adv.	adverb
aet. *or* aetat.	*aetatis*, aged
AFr.	Anglo-French
AN	Anglo-Norman
anon.	anonymous (see 14.79)
app.	appendix
arch.	archaic
art.	article
AS	Anglo-Saxon
b.	born; brother
Bd.	*Band* (Ger.), volume
bib.	Bible, biblical
bibl.	*bibliotheca*, library
bibliog.	bibliography, -er, -ical
biog.	biography, -er, -ical
biol.	biology, -ist, -ical

bk.	book
c.	century; chapter (in law citations)
c. *or* cop.	copyright (see 10.43)
ca. *or* c.	*circa*, about, approximately (*ca.* preferred for greater clarity)
Cantab.	*Cantabrigiensis*, of Cambridge
cet. par.	*ceteris paribus*, other things being equal
cf.	*confer*, compare ("see, by way of comparison"; should not be used when *see* alone is meant)
chap. *or* ch.	chapter
col.	color (best spelled out); column
colloq.	colloquial, -ly, -ism
comp.	compiler (*pl.* comps.), compiled by
compar.	comparative
con.	*contra*, against
conj.	conjunction; conjugation
cons.	consonant
constr.	construction
cont.	continued
contr.	contraction
corr.	corrected
cp.	compare (rarely used; *cf.* is far more common)
d.	died; daughter
Dan.	Danish
dat.	dative
def.	definite; definition
dept.	department
deriv.	derivative
d. h.	*das heißt* (or *das heisst*), namely (used only in German text; note the space between initials)
d. i.	*das ist*, that is (used only in German text; note the space between initials)
dial.	dialect
dict.	dictionary
dim.	diminutive
diss.	dissertation
dist.	district
div.	division; divorced
do.	ditto
dram. pers.	*dramatis personae*
Dr. u. Vrl.	*Druck und Verlag*, printer and publisher
DV	*Deo volente*, God willing; Douay Version (see 10.48)
ea.	each

ed. — editor (*pl.* eds.), edition, edited by (never add *by* after *ed.*: either "ed. Jane Doe" or "edited by Jane Doe"; use *eds.* only after, never before, the names of two or more editors; see examples throughout chapter 14)
EE — Early English
e.g. — *exempli gratia*, for example (not to be confused with *i.e.*)
ellipt. — elliptical, -ly
ency. *or* encyc. — encyclopedia
eng. — engineer, -ing
Eng. — English
engr. — engraved, -ing
enl. — enlarged
eq. — equation (*pl.* eqq. *or* eqs.; see also 10.43)
esp. — especially
et al. — *et alii* (or *et alia*), and others (normally used of persons; no period after *et*)
etc. — *et cetera*, and so forth (normally used of things)
et seq. — *et sequentes*, and the following
ex. — example (*pl.* exx. *or* exs.)
f. *or* fem. — feminine; female
f. — *für* (Ger.), for
fasc. — fascicle
ff. — and following (see 14.149)
fig. — figure
fl. — *floruit*, flourished (used with a date to indicate the productive years of a historical figure whose birth and death dates are unknown)
fol. — folio
Fr. — French
fr. — from
frag. — fragment
fut. — future
f.v. — *folio verso*, on the back of the page
Gael. — Gaelic
gen. — genitive; genus
geog. — geography, -er, -ical
geol. — geology, -ist, -ical
geom. — geometry, -ical
Ger. *or* G. — German
ger. — gerund
Gk. — Greek
hist. — history, -ian, -ical

HQ	headquarters
ibid.	*ibidem*, in the same place (see 14.34)
id.	*idem*, the same (see 14.35)
i.e.	*id est*, that is (not to be confused with *e.g.*)
IE	Indo-European
ill.	illustrated, -ion, -or
imp. *or* imper.	imperative
incl.	including
indef.	indefinite
indic.	indicative
inf.	*infra*, below (best spelled out)
infin.	infinitive
in pr.	*in principio*, in the beginning
inst.	instant (this month); institute, -ion
instr.	instrumental
interj.	interjection
intrans.	intransitive
introd. *or* intro.	introduction
irreg.	irregular
It.	Italian
L.	Latin; left (in stage directions)
l.	left; line (*pl.* ll., but best spelled out to avoid confusion with numerals 1 and 11)
lang.	language
Lat. *or* L.	Latin
lit.	literally
loc.	locative
loc. cit.	*loco citato*, in the place cited (best avoided; see 14.36)
loq.	*loquitur*, he or she speaks
m.	male; married; measure (*pl.* mm.)
m. *or* masc.	masculine
marg.	margin, -al
math.	mathematics, -ical
MHG	Middle High German
mimeo.	mimeograph, -ed
misc.	miscellaneous
MM	Maelzel's metronome
m.m.	*mutatis mutandis*, necessary changes being made
Mod.E.	Modern English
MS (*pl.* MSS)	*manuscriptum* (pl. *manuscripta*), manuscript
mus.	museum; music, -al
n.	*natus*, born; note, footnote (*pl.* nn.); noun

nat.	national; natural
NB, n.b.	*nota bene*, take careful note (capitals are illogical but often used for emphasis)
n.d.	no date; not determined
neg.	negative
neut.	neuter
no. (*pl.* nos.)	number
nom.	nominative
non obs.	*non obstante*, notwithstanding
non seq.	*non sequitur*, it does not follow
n.p.	no place; no publisher; no page
n.s.	new series
NS	New Style (dates)
ob.	*obiit*, died
obs.	obsolete
occas.	occasional, -ly
OE	Old English
OFr.	Old French
OHG	Old High German
ON	Old Norse
op. cit.	*opere citato*, in the work cited (best avoided; see 14.36)
o.s.	old series
OS	Old Style (dates)
Oxon.	*Oxoniensis*, of Oxford
p.	page (*pl.* pp.); past (*also* pa.)
para. *or* par.	paragraph (see 10.43)
pass.	passive
pa. t.	past tense
path.	pathology, -ist, -ical
perf.	perfect
perh.	perhaps
pers.	person, -al
pers. comm.	personal communication
pl.	plate (best avoided; see 3.9); plural
posth.	posthumous, -ly
p.p.	past participle
ppl.	participle
PPS	*post postscriptum*, a later postscript
prep.	preposition
pres.	present
pron.	pronoun
pro tem.	*pro tempore*, for the time being (often used without a period)

prox.	*proximo*, next month
PS	*postscriptum*, postscript
pt.	part
pub.	publication, publisher, published by
QED	*quod erat demonstrandum*, which was to be demonstrated
quar. *or* quart.	quarter, -ly
q.v.	*quod vide*, which see (used only in a cross-reference *after* the term referred to; cf. *s.v.*)
R.	*rex*, king; *regina*, queen; right (in stage directions)
r.	right; recto; reigned
refl.	reflexive
repr.	reprint, -ed
rev.	review; revised, revised by, revision (never add *by* after *rev.*: either "rev. Jane Doe" or "revised by Jane Doe")
RIP	*requiescat in pace*, may he or she rest in peace
s.	son; substantive, -ival
s.a.	*sine anno*, without year; *sub anno*, under the year
sc.	scene; *scilicet*, namely; *sculpsit*, carved by
Sc. *or* Scot.	Scottish
s.d.	*sine die*, without setting a day for reconvening; stage direction
sd.	sound
sec.	section (see 10.43); *secundum*, according to
ser.	series
s.h.	speech heading
sing. *or* sg.	singular
s.l.	*sine loco*, without place (of publication)
s.n.	*sine nomine*, without name (of publisher)
sociol.	sociology, -ist, -ical
Sp.	Spanish
s.p.	speech prefix
st.	stanza
subj.	subject, -ive; subjunctive
subst. *or* s.	substantive, -al
sup.	*supra*, above
superl.	superlative
supp. *or* suppl.	supplement
s.v. (*pl.* s.vv.)	*sub verbo*, *sub voce*, under the word (used in a cross-reference *before* the term referred to; cf. *q.v.*)
syn.	synonym, -ous
t.	*tome* (Fr.), *tomo* (Sp.), volume
techn.	technical, -ly
theol.	theology, -ian, -ical

t.p. title page
trans. translated by, translator(s) (never add *by* after *trans.*: either "trans. Jane Doe" or "translated by Jane Doe"); transitive
treas. treasurer
TS typescript
ult. *ultimatus*, ultimate, last; *ultimo*, last month
univ. university
usw. *und so weiter*, and so forth (equivalent to *etc.*; used only in German text)
ut sup. *ut supra*, as above
v. verse (*pl.* vv.); verso; versus; *vide*, see
v. *or* vb. verb
v.i. *verbum intransitivum*, intransitive verb; *vide infra*, see below
viz. *videlicet*, namely
voc. vocative
vol. volume
vs. *or* v. versus (in legal contexts use *v.*)
v.t. *verbum transitivum*, transitive verb
yr. year; your

10.43 **A few scholarly symbols.** The symbols below often appear in bibliographies and other scholarly apparatus rather than their equivalent abbreviations (see 10.42).

© copyright
= equals, the same as (for examples, see 10.46)
¶ (*pl.* ¶¶) paragraph
§ (*pl.* §§) section

Biblical Abbreviations

10.44 **Biblical abbreviations—an overview.** In running text, books of the Bible are generally spelled out. See also 9.26.

The opening chapters of Ephesians constitute a sermon on love.
Jeremiah, chapters 42–44, records the flight of the Jews to Egypt.
According to Genesis 1:27, God created man in his own image.

In parenthetical citations or in notes, or where many such references appear in the text, abbreviations are appropriate.

My concordance lists five instances of the word *nourish*: Gen. 47:12, Ruth 4:15, Isa. 44:14, Acts 7:21, and 1 Tim. 4:6.

For authoritative guidance in many biblical areas not covered here, consult *The SBL Handbook of Style* (bibliog. 1.1). For citing scriptural references in notes and bibliographies, see 14.238–41.

10.45 **Abbreviations for the Old Testament.** These are the traditional abbreviations and commonly used shorter forms for books of the Old Testament. (Note that the shorter forms have no periods.) The listing is alphabetical, both for easier reference and because the order varies slightly in different versions of the Bible. Alternative names for the same books are indicated by an equals sign (see 10.43). For the New Testament, see 10.47.

Amos *or* Am	Amos
1 Chron. *or* 1 Chr	1 Chronicles
2 Chron. *or* 2 Chr	2 Chronicles
Dan. *or* Dn	Daniel
Deut. *or* Dt	Deuteronomy
Eccles. *or* Eccl	Ecclesiastes
Esther *or* Est	Esther
Exod. *or* Ex	Exodus
Ezek. *or* Ez	Ezekiel
Ezra *or* Ezr	Ezra
Gen. *or* Gn	Genesis
Hab. *or* Hb	Habakkuk
Hag. *or* Hg	Haggai
Hosea *or* Hos	Hosea
Isa. *or* Is	Isaiah
Jer. *or* Jer	Jeremiah
Job *or* Jb	Job
Joel *or* Jl	Joel
Jon. *or* Jon	Jonah
Josh. *or* Jo	Joshua
Judg. *or* Jgs	Judges
1 Kings *or* 1 Kgs	1 Kings
2 Kings *or* 2 Kgs	2 Kings
Lam. *or* Lam	Lamentations
Lev. *or* Lv	Leviticus
Mal. *or* Mal	Malachi
Mic. *or* Mi	Micah
Nah. *or* Na	Nahum
Neh. *or* Neh	Nehemiah
Num. *or* Nm	Numbers
Obad. *or* Ob	Obadiah

Prov. *or* Prv	Proverbs
Ps. (*pl.* Pss.) *or* Ps (*pl.* Pss)	Psalms
Ruth *or* Ru	Ruth
1 Sam. *or* 1 Sm	1 Samuel
2 Sam. *or* 2 Sm	2 Samuel
Song of Sol. *or* Sg	Song of Solomon (= Song of Songs)
Zech. *or* Zec	Zechariah
Zeph. *or* Zep	Zephaniah

10.46 **Abbreviations for the Apocrypha.** The books of the Apocrypha are accepted in Roman Catholic versions of the Bible, though not in Jewish and Protestant versions. Some are not complete in themselves but are continuations of books listed in 10.45. These are the traditional abbreviations and commonly used shorter forms. (Note that the shorter forms have no periods.) Alternative names for the same books are indicated by an equals sign (see 10.43). Where no abbreviation is given, the full form should be used.

Bar. *or* Bar	Baruch
Ecclus.	Ecclesiasticus (= Sirach)
1 Esd.	1 Esdras
2 Esd.	2 Esdras
Jth. *or* Jdt	Judith
1 Macc. *or* 1 Mc	1 Maccabees
2 Macc. *or* 2 Mc	2 Maccabees
Pr. of Man.	Prayer of Manasses (= Manasseh)
Sir. *or* Sir	Sirach (= Ecclesiasticus)
Sus.	Susanna
Tob. *or* Tb	Tobit
Ws	Wisdom (= Wisdom of Solomon)
Wisd. of Sol.	Wisdom of Solomon (= Wisdom)

10.47 **Abbreviations for the New Testament.** These are the traditional abbreviations and commonly used shorter forms for books of the New Testament. (Note that the shorter forms have no periods.) The listing is alphabetical, both for easier reference and because the order varies slightly in different versions of the Bible. Alternative names for the same books are indicated by an equals sign (see 10.43). For the Old Testament, see 10.45.

Acts	Acts of the Apostles
Apoc.	Apocalypse (= Revelation)
Col. *or* Col	Colossians

1 Cor. *or* 1 Cor	1 Corinthians
2 Cor. *or* 2 Cor	2 Corinthians
Eph. *or* Eph	Ephesians
Gal. *or* Gal	Galatians
Heb. *or* Heb	Hebrews
James *or* Jas	James
John *or* Jn	John (Gospel)
1 John *or* 1 Jn	1 John (Epistle)
2 John *or* 2 Jn	2 John (Epistle)
3 John *or* 3 Jn	3 John (Epistle)
Jude	Jude
Luke *or* Lk	Luke
Mark *or* Mk	Mark
Matt. *or* Mt	Matthew
1 Pet. *or* 1 Pt	1 Peter
2 Pet. *or* 2 Pt	2 Peter
Phil. *or* Phil	Philippians
Philem. *or* Phlm	Philemon
Rev. *or* Rv	Revelation (= Apocalypse)
Rom. *or* Rom	Romans
1 Thess. *or* 1 Thes	1 Thessalonians
2 Thess. *or* 2 Thes	2 Thessalonians
1 Tim. *or* 1 Tm	1 Timothy
2 Tim. *or* 2 Tm	2 Timothy
Titus *or* Ti	Titus

10.48 **Abbreviations for versions and sections of the Bible.** Versions and sections of the Bible are usually abbreviated in the form of initialisms, especially when they consist of more than one word.

Apoc.	Apocrypha
ARV	American Revised Version
ASV	American Standard Version
AT	American Translation
AV	Authorized (King James) Version
CEV	Contemporary English Version
DV	Douay Version
ERV	English Revised Version
EV	English version(s)
HB	Hebrew Bible
JB	Jerusalem Bible
LXX	Septuagint
MT	Masoretic Text

NAB	New American Bible
NEB	New English Bible
NJB	New Jerusalem Bible
NRSV	New Revised Standard Version
NT	New Testament
OT	Old Testament
RSV	Revised Standard Version
RV	Revised Version
Syr.	Syriac
Vulg.	Vulgate
WEB	World English Bible

Technology and Science

10.49 **Miscellaneous technical abbreviations.** The following list, which cannot aim to be comprehensive, includes some abbreviations used in various branches of the physical and biological sciences and in technical writing. Some, such as *PC* and *DVD*, are also in wide general use. Abbreviations used in highly specialized areas have generally been omitted, as have most adjectival forms. Many of the abbreviations for units are identical to or compatible with those used in the International System of Units, or SI (see 10.51–59). Periods are omitted in any context (compare 10.4). The capitalization given below, based largely on current usage, sometimes departs from that used in *Merriam-Webster's Collegiate Dictionary* (see bibliog. 3.1). The first letter of abbreviations derived from proper names (e.g., A [ampere], V, Wb, and the *C* in °C) are usually capitalized (though the spelled-out term is lowercased—unless, like Celsius, it forms a unit name with another term, as in "degree[s] Celsius"), as are the prefix letters for *mega-* (M), *giga-* (G), *tera-* (T), and so on (see 10.56). Plurals do not add an *s* (10 A, 5 ha). With few exceptions (mainly abbreviations with degree symbols), a space usually appears between a numeral and an abbreviation (22 m *but* 36°C); see also 10.58. For units with repeated quantities, see 9.17. For statistical abbreviations, see 10.50. For traditional US units of measure, see 10.64–68. See also 9.16.

A	ampere; adenine (in genetic code)
Å	angstrom
ac	alternating current
AF	audio frequency
Ah	ampere-hour
AM	amplitude modulation
ASCII	American Standard Code for Information Interchange

atm	atmosphere, -ic
av *or* avdp	avoirdupois
bar	bar (no abbreviation)
BD	Blu-ray Disc
Bé *or* °Bé	degree Baumé
bhp	brake horsepower
BMI	body mass index
bp	boiling point; base pair
bps	bits per second
Bps	bytes per second
Bq	becquerel
Btu	British thermal unit
C	coulomb; cytosine (in genetic code)
°C	degree Celsius
cal	calorie
Cal	kilocalorie (in nonscientific contexts; *see also* kcal)
cc	cubic centimeter (in clinical contexts; *see also* cm^3)
cd	candela
CD	compact disc
cgs	centimeter-gram-second system (SI)
Ci	curie
cm	centimeter
cM	centimorgan
cm^3	cubic centimeter (in scientific contexts; *see also* cc)
cp	candlepower
CP	chemically pure
cps *or* c/s	cycles per second
CPU	central processing unit
cu	cubic
d	day; deuteron
Da	dalton
dB	decibel
dc	direct current
DNS	domain name system
DOI	Digital Object Identifier (DOI is a registered trademark)
DOS	disk operating system
dpi	dots per inch
DVD	digital versatile (*or* video) disc
dyn	dyne
emf	electromotive force
erg	erg (no abbreviation)
eV	electron volt
F	farad

°F	degree Fahrenheit
FM	frequency modulation
fp	freezing point
fps	frames per second; feet per second
FTP	file transfer protocol
g	gram; gas
G	guanine (in genetic code)
Gb	gigabit
GB	gigabyte
Gbps	gigabits per second
GeV	10^9 electron volts
GIF	graphic interchange format
GIS	geographic information system
GPS	global positioning system
Gy	gigayear; gray (joule per kilogram)
H	henry (*pl.* henries)
h	hour; helion
ha	hectare
hp	horsepower
HTML	hypertext markup language
HTTP	hypertext transfer protocol
Hz	hertz
IP	internet protocol
IR	infrared
IU	international unit
J	joule
JPEG	*from* Joint Photographic Experts Group (file format)
K	kelvin (no degree symbol); kilobyte (in commercial contexts)
kat	katal
kb	kilobar (DNA); kilobase (RNA)
kb *or* kbit	kilobit
KB *or* K	kilobyte
Kbps	kilobits per second
kc	kilocycle
kcal	kilocalorie (in scientific contexts; *see also* Cal)
KE	kinetic energy
kg	kilogram
kHz	kilohertz
kJ	kilojoule
km	kilometer
kmh *or* kmph	kilometers per hour
kn	knot (nautical mph)
kW	kilowatt

kWh	kilowatt-hour
L	liter (capitalized to avoid confusion with numeral 1)
lm	lumen
lx	lux
m	meter
M	molar; metal
Mb	megabase; megabit
MB	megabyte
Mbps	megabits per second
Mc	megacycle
mCi	millicurie
MeV	million electron volts
mg	milligram
MIDI	musical instrument digital interface
mks	meter-kilogram-second system (SI)
mL	milliliter
mol	mole
mp	melting point
MPEG	*from* Moving Pictures Experts Group (file format)
mpg	miles per gallon
mph	miles per hour
MP3	*from* MPEG-1 Audio Layer 3 (file format)
MP4	*from* MPEG-4 Part 14 (file format)
ms	millisecond
N	newton; number (often italic; see also 10.50)
neg	negative
nm	nanometer; nautical mile
Ω	ohm
OCR	optical character recognition
OS	operating system
Pa	pascal
pc	parsec
PC	personal computer
PDF	portable document format
PE	potential energy
pF	picofarad
pH	negative log of hydrogen ion concentration (measure of acidity)
PNG	*from* portable network graphics (file format)
pos	positive
ppb	parts per billion
ppm	parts per million
ppt	parts per trillion; precipitate
R	electrical resistance

°R	degree Réaumur
rad	radian
RAM	random-access memory
RF	radio frequency
ROM	read-only memory
rpm *or* r/min	revolutions per minute
s	second
S	siemens
SGML	standard generalized markup language
soln	solution
sp gr	specific gravity
sq	square
sr	steradian
std	standard
STP	standard temperature and pressure
Sv	sievert
t	metric ton (10^3 kg); triton (nucleus of tritium)
T	tesla; thymine (in genetic code)
Tb	terabit
TB	terabyte
Tbps	terabits per second
TCP/IP	transmission-control protocol/internet protocol
temp	temperature
U	uracil (in genetic code)
UCS	universal character set
URI	uniform resource identifier
URL	uniform resource locator
USB	universal serial bus
UV	ultraviolet
V	volt
W	watt
Wb	weber
wt	weight
w/v	weight per volume
w/w	weight per weight
XML	extensible markup language
y	year
Z	atomic number (often italic)

10.50 **Statistical abbreviations.** The following abbreviations are used in statistical material, especially in tables. They are often italicized. See also 12.57, 12.58, and table 12.3.

ANCOVA	analysis of covariance
ANOVA	analysis of variance
CI	confidence interval
CL	confidence limit
CLT	central limit theorem
df, DF, *or* dof	degrees of freedom
GLIM	generalized linear model
HR	hazard ratio
IQR	interquartile range
LS	least squares
MLE	maximum likelihood estimate
MS	mean square
N	number (of population or sample)
n	number (of sample or subsample)
ns	not (statistically) significant
OLS	ordinary least squares
OR	odds ratio
p	probability
r	bivariate correlation coefficient
R	multivariate correlation coefficient
R^2	coefficient of determination
RMS	root mean square
sd *or* SD	standard deviation
se *or* SE	standard error
sem *or* SEM	standard error of the mean
SS	sum of squares
SSE	error sum of squares
SST	total sum of squares
WLLN	weak law of large numbers
$\bar{x}$ or $\bar{X}$	mean value
χ^2	chi-square distribution

The International System of Units

10.51 **SI units—overview.** The International System of Units (Système international d'unités, abbreviated internationally as SI) is an expanded version of the metric system. It is in general use among the world's scientists and in many other areas. The following paragraphs discuss only the basics. For the latest official guidelines, consult *The International System of Units*, a brochure published in French and English by the Bureau International des Poids et Mesures and available online. For further guidance, see

Ambler Thompson and Barry N. Taylor, *Guide for the Use of the International System of Units* (bibliog. 2.4); and *Scientific Style and Format* (bibliog. 1.1).

10.52 **SI units—form.** No periods are used after any of the SI symbols for units, and the same symbols are used for both the singular and the plural. Most symbols are lowercased; exceptions are those that stand for units derived from proper names (e.g., A, for *ampere*) and those that must be distinguished from similar lowercased forms. All units are lowercased in their spelled-out form except for terms like Celsius (which follows the word "degree" in its unit name; see also 10.49). See also 10.53.

10.53 **Plurals for SI units.** Though abbreviations for SI units are the same for plural and singular forms, the noun forms for such units would generally be written out or pronounced in the plural (e.g., 3 m = three meters; *but* a three-meter span). The only exception is for a quantity of exactly 1; for quantities such as 0.5 m or 1.6 m, the unit would generally be read as if it were plural (zero point five meters; one point six meters). See also 9.19, 10.65.

10.54 **SI base units.** There are seven fundamental, or base, SI units. Note that although *weight* and *mass* are usually measured in the same units, they are not interchangeable. Weight is a force due to gravity that depends on an object's mass. Note also that no degree sign is used with the symbol K. See also 10.55.

Quantity	*Unit*	*Symbol*
length	meter	m
mass	kilogram	kg
time	second	s
electric current	ampere	A
thermodynamic temperature	kelvin	K
amount of substance	mole	mol
luminous intensity	candela	cd

Not to be confused with the symbols for base *units* are the corresponding symbols for base *quantities*. These symbols, which represent variable quantities, appear in italic type (e.g., *l*, length; *m*, mass; *t*, time).

10.55 **Kilogram versus gram as SI base unit.** Although for historical reasons the kilogram rather than the gram was chosen as the base unit, prefixes are applied to the term *gram*—megagram (Mg), milligram (mg), nanogram (ng), and so forth. See also 10.56.

10.56 **SI prefixes.** Prefixes, representing a power of ten, are added to the name of a base unit, a derived unit, or an accepted non-SI unit (see 10.57, 10.59) to allow notation of very large or very small numerical values. The units so formed are called multiples and submultiples of SI units. For example, a kilometer, or km, is equal to a thousand meters (or 10^3 m), and a millisecond, or ms, is equal to one-thousandth of a second (or 10^{-3} s). The following prefixes, with their symbols, are used in the international system. Note that in three cases the final vowel of an SI prefix is omitted: kΩ, kilohm (*not* kiloohm); MΩ, megohm (*not* megaohm); ha, hectare (*not* hectoare).

Factor	*Prefix*	*Symbol*	*Factor*	*Prefix*	*Symbol*
10^{24}	yotta	Y	10^{-1}	deci	d
10^{21}	zetta	Z	10^{-2}	centi	c
10^{18}	exa	E	10^{-3}	milli	m
10^{15}	peta	P	10^{-6}	micro	μ
10^{12}	tera	T	10^{-9}	nano	n
10^{9}	giga	G	10^{-12}	pico	p
10^{6}	mega	M	10^{-15}	femto	f
10^{3}	kilo	k	10^{-18}	atto	a
10^{2}	hecto	h	10^{-21}	zepto	z
10^{1}	deka	da	10^{-24}	yocto	y

These prefixes should not be used to indicate powers of two (as in the field of electrical technology, or computing). If binary multiples must be used, the first two letters of the SI prefixes must be followed by *bi*, to form *kibi-* (Ki), *mebi-* (Mi), *gibi-* (Gi), *tebi-* (Ti), *pebi-* (Pi), and *exbi-* (Ei). See also 9.11.

10.57 **Units derived from SI base units.** Derived units are expressed algebraically in terms of base units or other derived units.

Derived unit	*In terms of SI base units*
square meter	m^2
cubic meter	m^3
meter per second	m/s
meter per second squared	m/s^2
kilogram per cubic meter	kg/m^3

Certain derived units have special names and symbols. Several of the most common—hertz (Hz), volt (V), watt (W), and so forth—are listed in

10.49. These are used in algebraic expressions to denote further derived units. A few are listed below.

Derived unit	*Symbol*	*In terms of SI base units*
joule per kelvin	J/K	$m^2\ kg\ s^{-2}\ K^{-1}$
newton meter	N m *or* N · m	$m^2\ kg\ s^{-2}$
newton per meter	N/m	$kg\ s^{-2}$

A derived unit can often be expressed in different ways. For example, the weber may be expressed either as Wb or, in another context, in terms of the volt second (V s *or* V · s).

10.58 **SI units and abbreviations—spacing.** Only numbers between 0.1 and 1,000 should be used to express the quantity of any SI unit. Thus 12,000 meters is expressed as 12 km (not 12 000 m), and 0.003 cubic centimeters as 3 mm^3 (not 0.003 cm^3). (For the use of spaces rather than commas between groups of digits in SI units, see 9.56.) In SI usage as in general usage, a space usually appears between the numeral and any abbreviation or symbol. Contrary to general usage, however, SI usage also stipulates a space before a percentage sign (%) or before a degree symbol used for temperature (compare the advice in the introduction to the table at 10.49). In expressions of degrees, minutes, and seconds, SI usage shows (but does not stipulate) a space between quantities. Many publications do not observe these exceptions, and Chicago does not require them in its publications.

SI style	*Chicago style*
22 °C	22°C
22° 14′ 33″	22°14′33″
0.5 %	0.5% (see also 9.18)

10.59 **Non-SI units accepted for use.** Certain widely used units such as liter (L, capitalized to avoid confusion with the numeral 1), metric ton (t), and hour (h) are not officially part of the international system but are accepted for use within the system.

Astronomy

10.60 **Astronomical abbreviations—additional resources.** Astronomers and astrophysicists employ the International System of Units (see 10.51–59) supplemented with special terminology and abbreviations. The paragraphs in this section offer a minimum of examples for the generalist.

Additional guidelines may be found at the website of the International Astronomical Union.

10.61 **Celestial coordinates.** Right ascension, abbreviated RA or α, is given in hours, minutes, and seconds (abbreviations set as superscripts) of sidereal time. Declination, abbreviated δ, is given in degrees, minutes, and seconds (using the degree symbol, prime, and double prime) of arc north (marked + or left unmarked) or south (marked −) of the celestial equator. Note the abbreviations (set as superscripts) and symbols used.

$14^{h}6^{m}7^{s}$ −49°8′22″

Decimal fractions of the basic units are indicated as shown.

$14^{h}6^{m}7^{s}.2$ +34°.26

10.62 **Some other astronomical abbreviations.** A few of the more commonly used astronomical abbreviations are listed here. A more extensive list is available in *Scientific Style and Format* (bibliog. 1).

AU *or* ua	astronomical unit (mean earth–sun distance)
lt-yr	light-year (9.46×10^{12} km)
pc	parsec (parallax second: 3.084×10^{13} km)
kpc	10^{3} pc
Mpc	10^{6} pc
UT	universal time (see also 10.41)

Chemical Elements

10.63 **Naming conventions for chemical elements.** The International Union of Pure and Applied Chemistry (IUPAC) is the recognized body that formally approves element names. Each element bears a number (reflecting the number of protons in its nucleus) as well as a name—as in "element 106," also known as seaborgium. This number is an important identifier in cases where formal names are in dispute; between 1995 and 1997, for example, the American Chemical Society and IUPAC adopted different names for some of the same elements. The differences were reconciled, and the list that follows reflects names and symbols approved by IUPAC. Names for undiscovered or unconfirmed elements are provisionally assigned using Latin for the digits of their atomic number (e.g., *ununoctium*, one-one-eight, for element 118, which was confirmed in 2015 and named *oganesson* the following year). The elements in the following list are arranged in alphabetical order by common name. If the symbol is based on a term other than the common name—for example, Sb (*stibium*) for antimony—the term is added in parentheses. Although the names of elements are always lowercased, the symbols all have an initial capital. No periods are used. In specialized works, the abbreviations commonly appear in text as well as in tables, notes, and so forth. See also 8.149, 8.150.

89	Ac	actinium
13	Al	aluminum (US), aluminium (IUPAC)
95	Am	americium
51	Sb	antimony (*stibium*)
18	Ar	argon
33	As	arsenic
85	At	astatine
56	Ba	barium
97	Bk	berkelium
4	Be	beryllium
83	Bi	bismuth
107	Bh	bohrium
5	B	boron
35	Br	bromine
48	Cd	cadmium
20	Ca	calcium
98	Cf	californium
6	C	carbon
58	Ce	cerium
55	Cs	cesium (US), caesium (IUPAC)
17	Cl	chlorine
24	Cr	chromium
27	Co	cobalt
112	Cn	copernicium
29	Cu	copper
96	Cm	curium
110	Ds	darmstadtium
105	Db	dubnium
66	Dy	dysprosium
99	Es	einsteinium
68	Er	erbium
63	Eu	europium
100	Fm	fermium
114	Fl	flerovium
9	F	fluorine
87	Fr	francium
64	Gd	gadolinium
31	Ga	gallium
32	Ge	germanium
79	Au	gold (*aurum*)
72	Hf	hafnium
108	Hs	hassium
2	He	helium
67	Ho	holmium
1	H	hydrogen
49	In	indium
53	I	iodine
77	Ir	iridium
26	Fe	iron (*ferrum*)
36	Kr	krypton
57	La	lanthanum
103	Lr	lawrencium
82	Pb	lead (*plumbum*)
3	Li	lithium
116	Lv	livermorium
71	Lu	lutetium
12	Mg	magnesium
25	Mn	manganese
109	Mt	meitnerium
101	Md	mendelevium
80	Hg	mercury (*hydrargyrum*)
42	Mo	molybdenum
115	Mc	moscovium
60	Nd	neodymium
10	Ne	neon
93	Np	neptunium
28	Ni	nickel
113	Nh	nihonium

41	Nb	niobium	106	Sg	seaborgium
7	N	nitrogen	34	Se	selenium
102	No	nobelium	14	Si	silicon
118	Og	oganesson	47	Ag	silver (*argentum*)
76	Os	osmium	11	Na	sodium (*natrium*)
8	O	oxygen	38	Sr	strontium
46	Pd	palladium	16	S	sulfur
15	P	phosphorus	73	Ta	tantalum
78	Pt	platinum	43	Tc	technetium
94	Pu	plutonium	52	Te	tellurium
84	Po	polonium	117	Ts	tennessine
19	K	potassium (*kalium*)	65	Tb	terbium
59	Pr	praseodymium	81	Tl	thallium
61	Pm	promethium	90	Th	thorium
91	Pa	protactinium	69	Tm	thulium
88	Ra	radium	50	Sn	tin (*stannum*)
86	Rn	radon	22	Ti	titanium
75	Re	rhenium	74	W	tungsten (*wolfram*)
45	Rh	rhodium	92	U	uranium
111	Rg	roentgenium	23	V	vanadium
37	Rb	rubidium	54	Xe	xenon
44	Ru	ruthenium	70	Yb	ytterbium
104	Rf	rutherfordium	39	Y	yttrium
62	Sm	samarium	30	Zn	zinc
21	Sc	scandium	40	Zr	zirconium

US Measure

10.64 **Periods with abbreviations of US measure.** In the rare instances in which abbreviations for US units of measure are used in scientific copy, they are usually set without periods; in nonscientific contexts, periods are customary. See also 10.4.

10.65 **Plural forms for abbreviations of US measure.** Abbreviations of US units of measure, like their scientific counterparts, are identical in the singular and the plural (but see 10.68).

10 yd.   5 lb.   8 sq. mi.

Note that the unit of measure in such expressions as 0.5 yd. and 1.5 yd. is generally pronounced as if it were plural (i.e., point five yards; one point five yards); the singular is reserved for measures of exactly one. See also 10.53.

10.66 **US abbreviations for length, area, and volume.** In the following examples, note that the proper symbols for foot and inch are prime (′) and double prime (″), *not* the single (’) and double (”) quotation marks:

Length		*Area*		*Volume*	
in. *or* ″	inch	sq. in.	square inch	cu. in.	cubic inch
ft. *or* ′	foot	sq. ft.	square foot	cu. ft.	cubic foot
yd.	yard	sq. yd.	square yard	cu. yd.	cubic yard
rd.	rod	sq. rd.	square rod		
mi.	mile	sq. mi.	square mile		

As in expressions of latitude and longitude (see 10.35), there is no space in such expressions as the following (for a height or length of *6 ft., 1 in.*):

6′1″

Exponents are sometimes used with abbreviations to designate area or volume, but only when no ambiguity can occur.

425 ft.^{2} (= 425 sq. ft. *not* 425 ft. by 425 ft.) 638 ft.^{3} (= 638 cu. ft.)

10.67 **US abbreviations for weight and capacity.** The US system comprises three systems of weight and mass: avoirdupois (the common system), troy (used mainly by jewelers), and apothecaries’ measure. Although confusion is unlikely, an abbreviation can, if necessary, be referred to the appropriate system thus: lb. av., lb. t., lb. ap. Also, the systems of capacity measure used in the United States and the British Commonwealth differ (an American pint being more than three ounces smaller than a British pint, for example), but the same abbreviations are used.

Weight or mass		*Dry measure*	
gr.	grain	pt.	pint
s.	scruple	qt.	quart
dr.	dram	pk.	peck
dwt.	pennyweight	bu.	bushel
oz.	ounce		
lb. *or* #	pound		
cwt.	hundredweight		
tn.	ton		

Liquid measure

min. *or* ♍	minim
fl. Dr. *or* f. ʒ	fluid dram
fl. oz. *or* f. ℥	fluid ounce
gi.	gill
pt.	pint
qt.	quart
gal.	gallon
bbl.	barrel

As with length and so forth, abbreviations do not change in the plural.

12 gal.   3 pt.

10.68 **US and general abbreviations for time.** The following abbreviations, though not limited to the US system of measure, are used mainly in nontechnical contexts:

sec.	second	h. *or* hr.	hour	mo.	month
min.	minute	d. *or* day	day	yr.	year

In nontechnical writing, the plurals of these abbreviations, unlike those of length, area, weight, and the like, are often formed by adding an *s*.

5 secs.   12 hrs. *or* 12 h.   15 yrs.

Business and Commerce

10.69 **Commercial abbreviations—some examples.** As for many other abbreviations in nonscientific contexts, periods for abbreviations of commercial terms are normally used in lowercased forms (see 10.4). See also 10.42–43, 10.64–68. For company names, see 10.23.

acct.	account, -ant
agt.	agent
a.k.a.	also known as
amt.	amount
AP	amounts payable
APR	annual percentage rate
AR	amounts receivable
ASAP	as soon as possible

att.	attached, -ment
attn.	attention
a.v. *or* AV	ad valorem
bal.	balance
bbl.	barrel(s)
bcc	blind carbon copy *or* blind copy, -ies
bdl. *or* bdle.	bundle
bl.	bale(s)
BS	bill of sale
bu.	bushel(s)
c. *or* ct.	cent
cc	carbon copy *or* copy, -ies
c.l. *or* CL	carload
c/o	in care of
COD	cash on delivery
COGS	cost of goods sold
COLA	cost-of-living adjustment
CPI	consumer price index
CPM	cost per thousand (*mille*)
cr.	credit, -or
ctn.	carton
cttee. *or* comm.	committee
d/b/a	doing business as
dis.	discount
dist.	district
distr.	distributor, -ion
DJIA	Dow Jones Industrial Average
doz.	dozen
dr.	debtor
dstn.	destination
ea.	each
EEO	equal employment opportunity
EOE	equal opportunity employer
EOM	end of month
exec.	executive
f.a.s. *or* FAS	free alongside ship
f.o.b. *or* FOB	free on board
FY	fiscal year
GAAP	generally accepted accounting principles
GL	general ledger
GM	general manager; genetically modified
gro.	gross
inst.	instant (this month)

inv.	invoice
IPO	initial public offering
JIT	just in time
LBO	leveraged buyout
LCL	less-than-carload lot
LIFO	last in, first out
M and A *or* M&A	mergers and acquisitions
mdse.	merchandise
mfg.	manufacturing
mfr.	manufacturer
mgmt.	management
mgr.	manager
MO	mail order; money order
msg.	message
mtg.	meeting
mtge.	mortgage
NA *or* n/a	not applicable; not available
NGO	nongovernmental organization
nt. wt.	net weight
OJT	on-the-job training
OS	operating system; out of stock
OTC	over the counter
P and H *or* P&H	postage and handling
pd.	paid
pkg.	package
POE	port of embarkation; port of entry
POP	point of purchase
POS	point of sale; point of service
PP	parcel post
ppd.	postpaid; prepaid
pr.	pair
QA	quality assurance
Q&A	question and answer
QC	quality control
qtr.	quarter
qty.	quantity
®	registered trademark (see 8.153)
recd. *or* rec'd	received
S and H *or* S&H	shipping and handling
SM	unregistered service mark
std.	standard
TBA	to be announced
TBD	to be determined

™	unregistered trademark (see 8.153)
treas.	treasurer, -y
ult.	ultimo (last month)
VAT	value-added tax
whsle.	wholesale

11 · Languages Other than English

Overview

11.1 **Scope and organization.** This chapter provides guidelines for presenting text from languages other than English in English-language contexts. These guidelines are general: authors or editors working with languages in which they are not expert should seek additional guidance from someone who is. More than two dozen languages are covered, with those languages that commonly appear and those that present complex problems being considered most fully. The chapter begins with the treatment of words and phrases, titles of works, and quotations, the principles of which apply to most of the languages discussed (see 11.3–17). It then addresses languages using the Latin alphabet, transliterated (or romanized) languages, classical Greek, Old English and Middle English, and American Sign Language. Individual languages or groups of languages are presented in alphabetical order within their particular sections. (For the treatment of personal names, see 8.7–18.)

11.2 **Unicode.** Many of the letters and symbols required by the world's languages are included in a widely used standard for character encoding called Unicode. The Unicode standard (published by the Unicode Consortium; bibliog. 2.7) is widely supported by modern operating systems and browsers and many other applications (including word processors) and is required by such standards as XML and EPUB. Unicode assigns a unique identifying hexadecimal number (or code point) and description to tens of thousands of characters. Even fonts with Unicode character mapping, however, typically support only a subset of the Unicode character set. For this reason, it is desirable to determine at the outset which characters will be needed for a publication. Table 11.1 lists special characters, with Unicode numbers and abbreviated descriptions, needed for each of the languages treated in this chapter that use the Latin alphabet. Table 11.2 lists special characters that may be needed for certain transliterated languages. For Russian (Cyrillic) and Greek characters, see tables 11.3, 11.4, and 11.5. Unicode numbers mentioned in text should be prefixed by U+ (e.g., U+00E0 for *à*).

General Principles

Words and Phrases from Other Languages

11.3 **Non-English words and phrases in an English context.** Italics are used for isolated words and phrases from another language, especially if they are not listed in a standard English-language dictionary like *Merriam-Webster's Collegiate* (see 7.1) or are likely to be unfamiliar to readers (see also 7.54). (For proper nouns, see 11.4.) If such a word or phrase becomes familiar through repeated use throughout a work, it need be italicized only on its first occurrence. If it appears only rarely, however, italics may be retained.

The *grève du zèle* is not a true strike but a nitpicking obeying of work rules.

She preferred to think of it optimistically as a *sueño reparador*—rather than, as in English, a sleep that was merely restful.

Unless the term appears in a standard English-language dictionary and is being used as such, observe the capitalization conventions of the original language. In the following examples, the German word for computer (which is the same as the English word) is capitalized because it is a noun, and the French adjective *française* is lowercase even though it would be capitalized in English (as "French"). See also 11.18.

The German word for computer is *Computer*. The French word is *ordinateur*. In Spanish, the word is either *computadora* or *ordenador*, depending on region or context.

We were prepared to learn the nuances of *la langue française*.

The plurals of non-English words should be formed as in the original language (see also 7.12).

We were sent off with some beautiful *Blumen* (not *Blumes* [italic ess] and not *Blume*s [roman ess]).

An entire sentence or a passage of two or more sentences in another language is usually set in roman and, unless it is set as a block quotation or extract (see 13.9–29), enclosed in quotation marks (see 11.11).

11.4 **Non-English proper nouns in an English context.** With the exception of titles of books and the like, proper nouns from other languages are generally *not* italicized, even on first mention (cf. 11.3). This usage extends to named places and structures, institutions and companies, brand names, and other categories as discussed in chapter 8. (For titles of works, see 11.6–10.) Capitalization should follow predominant usage in the original language. In some cases, this may entail observing a preference for capitalization that runs counter to the conventions for generic text. If the editor is unfamiliar with the language, an expert, or the author, should be consulted; when in doubt, opt for sentence-style capitalization (see

8.158). See also 11.18. An initial *the* may be used if the definite article would appear in the original language.

She won the Premio Nadal for her second novel, *Viento del norte*.
Mexico City's Ángel de la Independencia is known familiarly as "El Ángel."
The Real Academia Española was founded in 1713.
A history of the Comédie-Française has just appeared.
The Académie française dates to the reign of Louis XIII.
I prefer the Bibliothèque nationale by day and the Bois de Boulogne by night.
He is a member of the Société d'entraide des membres de l'ordre national de la Légion d'honneur.
Leghorn—in Italian, Livorno—is a port in Tuscany.
When he asked her to meet him along Unter den Linden, she was amused by the consecutive prepositions—one in English and one in German, just like them.

Translations of proper nouns from other languages should be capitalized headline-style (see 8.159).

He is a member of the Mutual Aid Society for Members of the National Order of the Legion of Honor.

Original (or transliterated) names of proper nouns presented as glosses should not be italicized (but see 11.5).

The number of cases adjudicated by the Supreme People's Court of the People's Republic of China (Zhonghua renmin gongheguo zuigao renmin fayuan) has increased sharply.

11.5 **Translations of terms from other languages.** A translation following a word, phrase, or title from another language is enclosed in parentheses or quotation marks. See also 6.96, 11.3, 11.4, 11.9, 14.99.

The word she wanted was *pécher* (to sin), not *pêcher* (to fish).
The Prakrit word *majjao*, "the tomcat," may be a dialect version of either of two Sanskrit words: *madjaro*, "my lover," or *marjaro*, "the cat" (from the verb *mrij*, "to wash," because the cat constantly washes itself).
A group of German expressionists known as Die Brücke (The Bridge) were influential in the decade leading up to the First World War.
Leonardo Fioravanti's *Compendio de i secreti rationali* (Compendium of rational secrets) became a best seller.

If a non-English word other than a proper noun is presented as a parenthetical gloss, it should be presented in italics as in running text (but see 11.4).

He said that to fish (*pêcher*) was to sin (*pécher*).

For quotations from other languages, see 11.11–17.

Titles of Works from Other Languages

11.6 **Capitalization of titles from other languages.** For titles of works from other languages, whether these appear in text, notes, or bibliographies, Chicago recommends a simple rule: capitalize only the words that would be capitalized in normal prose—the first word of the title and subtitle and all proper nouns or any term that would be capitalized under the conventions of the original language. That is, use *sentence style* (see 8.158). This rule applies equally to titles using the Latin alphabet and to transliterated titles. For examples, see 14.98. For special considerations related to German capitalization, see 11.39. For variations in French, see 11.27.

11.7 **Punctuation of titles from other languages.** When a non-English title is included in an English-language context, the following changes are permissible: a period (or, more rarely, a semicolon) between title and subtitle may be changed to a colon (and the first word of the subtitle may be capitalized); guillemets (« ») or other non-English styles for quotation marks may be changed to regular quotation marks (“ ” or ‘ ’); and any space between a word and a mark of punctuation that follows may be eliminated. Commas should not be inserted (even in a series or before dates) or deleted, nor should any other mark of punctuation be added or deleted. See also 8.165.

11.8 **Italic versus roman type for titles from other languages.** Titles of works in languages that use the Latin alphabet (including transliterated titles) are set in italic or roman type according to the principles set forth in 8.156–201—for example, books and periodicals in italic; poems and other short works in roman.

Stendhal’s *Le rouge et le noir* was required reading in my senior year.
We picked up a copy of the *Neue Zürcher Zeitung* to read on the train.
She published her article in the *Annales de démographie historique*.
Strains of the German carol “Es ist ein’ Ros’ entsprungen” reached our ears.
Miguel Hernández’s poem “Casida del sediento” has been translated as “Lament of the Thirsting Man.”

11.9 **Non-English titles with English translation.** When the title of a work in another language is mentioned in text, an English gloss may follow in parentheses (see 6.96). If the translation has not been published, the English should be capitalized sentence-style (as in the first example below; see 8.158) and should appear neither in italics nor within quotation marks. A published translation, however, is capitalized headline-style (as in the second and third examples; see 8.159) and appears in italics or quotation marks depending on the type of work (see 8.156–201). Some editorial discretion may be required, especially if the translation is incorporated into running text (as in the third example). For translations of non-English titles in notes and bibliographies, see 14.99. See also 11.10.

Leonardo Fioravanti's *Compendio de i secreti rationali* (Compendium of rational secrets) became a best seller.

Proust's *À la recherche du temps perdu* (*Remembrance of Things Past*) was the subject of her dissertation.

but

La ciudad y los perros, which literally means "the city and the dogs," was published in English under the title *The Time of the Hero*.

11.10 **Original-language title of work versus translation.** Readership and context will determine whether to use the original or the translated title of a non-English work mentioned in running text. In a general work, titles that are widely known in their English translation could be cited in English first, with the original following in parentheses; in some cases, the original can be omitted entirely. Some authors prefer to cite all non-English titles in an English form, whether or not they have appeared in English translation. As long as the documentation clarifies what has been published in English and what has not, translated titles standing in for the original may be capitalized headline-style and treated like other English-language titles (see 8.159, 8.163). See also 11.9.

"The West" in the title of the Chinese classic *Journey to the West* (*Xī yóu jì*) refers mainly to the Indian subcontinent.

Molière's comedy *The Miser* may have drawn on an obscure late-medieval French treatise, *The Evils of Greed*, recently discovered in an abandoned château.

Quotations from Other Languages

11.11 **Typographic style of quotations from other languages.** Quotations from a language other than English that are incorporated into an English text are normally treated like quotations in English, set in roman type and run in or set off as block quotations according to their length. (For a complete discussion of quotations, see chapter 13.) They are punctuated as in the original except that quotation marks can usually replace guillemets (or their equivalents), and punctuation relative to quotation marks and spacing relative to punctuation are adjusted to conform to the surrounding text (see 11.19). For isolated words and phrases, see 11.3. For excerpts from the original language following an English translation, see 11.12.

The narrator's "treinta o cuarenta molinos de viento" become Quixote's "treinta, o pocos más, desaforados gigantes," a numerical correspondence that lets the reader trust, at the very least, the hero's basic grasp of reality.

If em dashes rather than quotation marks are used for dialogue in the original (see 11.31, 11.47, 11.64, 11.101), they should be retained in a block quotation but may be replaced by quotation marks if only a phrase or sentence is quoted in running text.

11.12 **Translations relative to quotations.** A translation may follow the original in parentheses—or, as in 11.13, the original may follow a translation. Quotation marks need not be repeated for the parenthetical translation (or parenthetical original, as the case may be); any internal quotation marks, however, should be included (as in the second example). See also 6.96, 11.5. If a long sentence or more than one sentence appears in parentheses or brackets, as in the second example, closing punctuation of the original and the translation should remain distinct.

A line from Goethe, "Wer nie sein Brot mit Tränen aß" (Who never ate his bread with tears), comes to mind.

À vrai dire, Abélard n'avoue pas un tel rationalisme: "je ne veux pas être si philosophe, écrit-il, que je résiste à Paul, ni si aristotélicien que je me sépare du Christ." (As a matter of fact, Abelard admits no such rationalism. "I do not wish to be so much of a philosopher," he writes, "that I resist Paul, nor so much of an Aristotelian that I separate myself from Christ.")

Whether to provide translations of quoted passages depends on the linguistic abilities of the intended audience. For example, in a work to be read by classicists, Latin or Greek sources may be quoted freely in the original. Or in a literary study of, say, Goethe, quotations from Goethe's work may be given in the original German only. For a wider readership, translations should be furnished.

11.13 **Source of quotation plus translation.** When both a source and a translation are required in text, the source may be placed in parentheses, with the original (or translation, as the case may be) following, separated by a semicolon. The following example quotes a thirteenth-century author writing in Middle Dutch. See also 13.68–69.

> Hadewijch insists that the most perfect faith is "unfaith," which endlessly stokes desire and endlessly demands love from God. "Unfaith never allows desire to rest in any faith but always distrusts her, [feeling] that she is not loved enough" (letter 8:39; Ende ontrowe en laet gegherten niewers ghedueren in gheenre trowen, sine mestrout hare altoes, datse niet ghenoech ghemint en es).

If adding a translation or the original in text creates too much clutter, it may be placed in a note, in which case it is enclosed in quotation marks but not in parentheses or brackets. If the parenthetical passage in the second example in 11.12 were to appear in text without the French, as either a run-in or a block quotation, a note could read as follows:

> 1. "À vrai dire, Abélard n'avoue pas un tel rationalisme: 'je ne veux pas être si philosophe, écrit-il, que je résiste à Paul, ni si aristotélicien que je me sépare du Christ.'"

See also 13.30.

11.14 **Crediting the translation of a quoted passage.** When quoting a passage from a language that requires a translation, authors should use a published English translation if one is available and give credit to the source of that translation, including the title of the translation, the translator's name, relevant bibliographic details, and page number (see 14.99). Authors providing their own translations should so state, in parentheses following the translation, in a note, or in the prefatory material—for example, "my translation" or "Unless otherwise noted, all translations are my own." If an individual other than the author provided the translations, that person should be credited in a similar manner, but by name. See also 11.9.

11.15 **Adjusting translated quotations.** An author using a published translation may occasionally need to adjust a word or two; "translation modified" or some such wording must then be added in parentheses or in a note (see also 13.62). In addition, it is recommended that such modifications be indicated by square brackets (see 13.59, 13.60). These devices should be used sparingly. If a published translation is unsuitable for the author's purpose, it should be abandoned and all quoted passages newly translated.

11.16 **Editing translated quotations.** Quotations from published translations can be modified only with respect to the permissible changes described in 13.7. In new translations furnished by the author, however, capitalization, punctuation, spelling, and idiom may be adjusted for consistency with the surrounding text.

11.17 **The sin of retranslation.** Never should a passage from a work originally published in English (or any other language, for that matter) be retranslated from a version that has been translated into another language. For example, an author quoting from a German study of Blackstone's *Commentaries* that quotes from Blackstone in German must track down the original Blackstone passages in English and reproduce them. If unable to locate the original, the author must resort to paraphrase.

Languages Using the Latin Alphabet

11.18 **Capitalization—English versus other languages.** Capitalization is applied to more classes of words in English than in any other Western language (but see 8.1). Most of the other languages discussed in this chapter follow a simpler set of rules. Except where stated to the contrary, the language in question is assumed to lowercase all adjectives (except those used as proper nouns), all pronouns, months, and days of the week. In addition, capitals are used more sparingly than in English for names of offices, institutions, and so on. Translated terms, however, are subject to Chicago's recommendations for capitalization of names and terms (see chapter 8). For personal names, see 8.7–18.

11.19 **Punctuation—original language versus English context.** The remarks in this chapter related to punctuation point out the more obvious departures from what is familiar to readers of English. For the purposes of illustration, quotation marks in the style of the original language have been preserved in the examples; however, spacing relative to these and other punctuation marks has been adjusted to conform to the typographic style of this manual. In quotations from other languages (and in translations), regular English-style quotation marks can usually replace the guillemets or whatever is used in the original (with the placement of periods and commas adjusted as needed; see 6.9–11). Dashes used to mark dialogue, however, should be preserved in block quotations presented in the original language. See 11.11. Another exception is the punctuation at the beginning of Spanish questions and exclamations (see 11.62), which should be preserved for quotations in Spanish (but omitted when the passage is translated).

11.20 **Word division for languages other than English.** Though conventions for dividing words at the ends of lines vary widely, the following general rules apply to non-English languages as well as to English: (1) Single-syllable words should never be broken. (2) No words should be broken after one letter, nor should a single letter be carried over to another line (see also 7.37). (3) Hyphenated words and solid compounds should be broken at the hyphen or between elements, if at all possible. See also 7.40; for proper nouns, see 7.42. Specific rules for some of the languages covered in this chapter appear in the relevant sections below.

11.21 **Special characters in the Latin alphabet.** Words, phrases, or titles from another language that occur in an English-language work must include any special characters that appear in the original language. Those languages that use the Latin alphabet may include letters with accents and other diacritical marks, ligatures, and, in some cases, alphabetical forms that do not normally occur in English. Table 11.1 lists the special characters that might be required for each language treated in this section. Most authors will have access to Unicode-compliant software (see 11.2) and will therefore be able to reproduce each of these characters without the addition of any specialized fonts. Authors should nonetheless supply a list of special characters used within a manuscript (see 2.16) to ensure the correct conversion to a particular font required for publication or, for electronic projects, to ensure compatibility across systems that may not support Unicode. If type is to be reproduced from an author's hard copy, marginal clarifications may be needed for handwritten accents or special characters. In either case, use table 11.1 to correctly identify the character by name and Unicode number (e.g., for *Đ* or *đ*, indicate "D with stroke [U+0110]" or "d with stroke [U+0111]"). For diacritical marks used in transliteration, see 11.74.

11.22 **International Phonetic Alphabet (IPA).** Phonetic symbols using IPA notation are based on the Latin alphabet and are defined for Unicode (see 11.2). For the latest version of the IPA alphabet, consult the website of the International Phonetic Association. For additional information on the subject of phonetics, including treatment of other systems of notation, consult Geoffrey K. Pullum and William A. Ladusaw, *Phonetic Symbol Guide* (bibliog. 5).

TABLE 11.1. Special characters (and Unicode numbers) for languages using the Latin alphabet

Character (and Unicode number)	Description	Languages that use it
„ (201E), “ (201C)	double low-9 quotation mark, left double quotation mark	German
« (00AB), » (00BB)	double angle quotation marks (guillemets)	French, German (reversed), Italian, Spanish
‘ (2018)	‘okina (represented by left single quotation mark)	Hawaiian
À (00C0), à (00E0)	A/a with grave	French, Italian, Portuguese
Á (00C1), á (00E1)	A/a with acute	Czech, Hungarian, Icelandic, Portuguese, Spanish
Â (00C2), â (00E2)	A/a with circumflex	French, Moldovan, Portuguese, Romanian, Turkish
Ã (00C3), ã (00E3)	A/a with tilde	Portuguese
Ä (00C4), ä (00E4)	A/a with diaeresis	Finnish, German, Swedish, Turkmen
Å (00C5), å (00E5)	A/a with ring above	Finnish, Danish, Norwegian, Swedish
Ā (0100), ā (0101)	A/a with macron	Hawaiian, Latin
Ă (0102), ă (0103)	A/a with breve	Latin, Moldovan, Romanian
Ą (0104), ą (0105)	A/a with ogonek	Polish
Æ (00C6), æ (00E6)	ligature Æ/æ	Danish, Icelandic, Norwegian, Old English and Middle English
Ɓ (0181), ɓ (0253)	B/b with hook	Hausa
Ç (00C7), ç (00E7)	C/c with cedilla	Albanian, Azeri, French, Portuguese, Turkish, Turkmen
Ć (0106), ć (0107)	C/c with acute	Bosnian, Croatian, Montenegrin, Polish, Serbian
Č (010C), č (010D)	C/c with caron (haček)	Bosnian, Croatian, Czech, Montenegrin, Serbian
Ð (00D0), ð (00F0)	eth	Old English and Middle English, Icelandic
Ď (010E), ď (010F)	D/d with caron (haček)	Czech
Đ (0110), đ (0111)	D/d with stroke	Bosnian, Croatian, Montenegrin, Serbian
Ɗ (018A), ɗ (0257)	D/d with hook	Hausa
È (00C8), è (00E8)	E/e with grave	French, Italian, Portuguese
É (00C9), é (00E9)	E/e with acute	Czech, French, Hungarian, Icelandic, Italian, Portuguese, Spanish
Ê (00CA), ê (00EA)	E/e with circumflex	French, Portuguese
Ë (00CB), ë (00EB)	E/e with diaeresis	Albanian, French
Ē (0112), ē (0113)	E/e with macron	Hawaiian, Latin
Ĕ (0114), ĕ (0115)	E/e with breve	Latin
Ę (0118), ę (0119)	E/e with ogonek	Polish
Ě (011A), ě (011B)	E/e with caron (haček)	Czech
Ȝ (021C), ȝ (021D)	yogh	Old English and Middle English
Ə (018F), ə (0259)	schwa	Azeri
Ğ (011E), ğ (011F)	G/g with breve	Azeri, Turkish
Ì (00CC), ì (00EC)	I/i with grave	Italian, Portuguese

(continued)

TABLE 11.1. *(continued)*

Character (and Unicode number)	Description	Languages that use it
Í (00CD), í (00ED)	I/i with acute	Czech, Hungarian, Icelandic, Portuguese, Spanish
Î (00CE), î (00EE)	I/i with circumflex	French, Moldovan, Romanian, Turkish
Ï (00CF), ï (00EF)	I/i with diaeresis	French, Portuguese
Ī (012A), ī (012B)	I/i with macron	Hawaiian, Latin
Ĭ (012C), ĭ (012D)	I/i with breve	Latin
İ (0130)	I with dot above	Azeri, Turkish
ı (0131)	dotless i	Azeri, Turkish
Ƙ (0198), ƙ (0199)	K/k with hook	Hausa
Ł (0141), ł (0142)	L/l with stroke	Polish
Ñ (00D1), ñ (00F1)	N/n with tilde	Spanish
Ń (0143), ń (0144)	N/n with acute	Polish
Ň (0147), ň (0148)	N/n with caron (haček)	Czech, Turkmen
Ò (00D2), ò (00F2)	O/o with grave	Italian, Portuguese
Ó (00D3), ó (00F3)	O/o with acute	Czech, Hungarian, Icelandic, Polish, Portuguese, Spanish
Ô (00D4), ô (00F4)	O/o with circumflex	French, Portuguese
Õ (00D5), õ (00F5)	O/o with tilde	Portuguese
Ö (00D6), ö (00F6)	O/o with diaeresis	Azeri, Finnish, German, Hungarian, Icelandic, Swedish, Turkish, Turkmen
Ø (00D8), ø (00F8)	O/o with stroke	Danish, Norwegian
Ō (014C), ō (014D)	O/o with macron	Hawaiian, Latin
Ŏ (014E), ŏ (014F)	O/o with breve	Latin
Ő (0150), ő (0151)	O/o with double acute	Hungarian
Œ (0152), œ (0153)	ligature Œ/œ	French
Ř (0158), ř (0159)	R/r with caron (haček)	Czech
Ś (015A), ś (015B)	S/s with acute	Polish, Montenegrin
Ş (015E), ş (015F)	S/s with cedilla	Azeri, Turkish, Turkmen
Ș (0218), ș (0219)	S/s with comma below	Moldovan, Romanian
Š (0160), š (0161)	S/s with caron (haček)	Bosnian, Croatian, Czech, Montenegrin, Serbian
ß (00DF)	sharp S (eszett)	German
Ț (021A), ț (021B)	T/t with comma below	Moldovan, Romanian
Ť (0164), ť (0165)	T/t with caron (haček)	Czech
Þ (00DE), þ (00FE)	thorn	Old English and Middle English, Icelandic
Ù (00D9), ù (00F9)	U/u with grave	French, Italian, Portuguese
Ú (00DA), ú (00FA)	U/u with acute	Czech, Hungarian, Icelandic, Portuguese, Spanish
Û (00DB), û (00FB)	U/u with circumflex	French, Turkish
Ü (00DC), ü (00FC)	U/u with diaeresis	Azeri, French, German, Hungarian, Portuguese, Spanish, Turkish, Turkmen
Ů (016E), ů (016F)	U/u with ring above	Czech
Ū (016A), ū (016B)	U/u with macron	Hawaiian, Latin
Ŭ (016C), ŭ (016D)	U/u with breve	Latin
Ű (0170), ű (0171)	U/u with double acute	Hungarian
Ý (00DD), ý (00FD)	Y/y with acute	Czech, Icelandic, Turkmen

TABLE 11.1. (*continued*)

Character (and Unicode number)	Description	Languages that use it
Ƴ (01B3), ƴ (01B4)	Y/y with hook	Hausa
Ź (0179), ź (017A)	Z/z with acute	Polish, Montenegrin
Ż (017B), ż (017C)	Z/z with dot above	Polish
Ž (017D), ž (017E)	Z/z with caron (haček)	Bosnian, Croatian, Czech, Montenegrin, Serbian, Turkmen

African Languages

11.23 **African capitalization and punctuation.** Most African languages—with the exception, most notably, of Arabic (see 11.76–81)—use the Latin alphabet and follow English capitalization and punctuation. The most widespread of these is Swahili, spoken by many different ethnic groups in eastern and central Africa. Hausa, Fulfulde, Yoruba, Igbo, Wolof, and Bambara are also spoken by millions, largely in western Africa; the same is true for Kikongo (or Kongo) and Lingala in the Congo-Zaire region and of Amharic and Somali in the Horn of Africa region. Amharic and other Ethiopian Semitic languages such as Tigrinya use the Geʿez alphabet, not covered here. Xhosa and other "click" languages spoken in southern Africa do not follow English capitalization. The names of African languages themselves vary widely from ethnic group to ethnic group and from region to region. It is now standard practice to capitalize the names of African languages in the traditional way—for example, Kiswahili rather than KiSwahili or KISwahili. Xhosa speakers refer to and spell their language "isiXhosa" but "Isixhosa" (sometimes "Isizhosa") is also found in English-language publications.

11.24 **African special characters.** Swahili uses no additional letters or diacritics. Among the more than two thousand other African languages, however, many rely on diacritics and phonetic symbols to stand for sounds that cannot be represented by letters or combinations of letters. Hausa, which is spoken by millions of people across western Africa, requires the following special characters (see also table 11.1):

Ɓɓ, Ɗɗ, Ƙƙ, Ƴƴ

In Nigeria, both the upper- and the lowercase *y* with a "hook" are represented instead with an apostrophe (*'Y'y*). Additional diacritics, too numerous to be listed here, may be needed in other African languages.

Languages such as French, Portuguese, and Arabic that are used in Africa are addressed in separate sections in this chapter.

French

11.25 **French—additional resources.** As is the case with many languages, there is considerable variation in French publications with respect to capitalization and punctuation. For excellent advice, with frequent reference to the Académie française and numerous examples from literature, consult the latest edition of *Le bon usage*, known to many by the name of its original editor, Maurice Grevisse (bibliog. 5). Further guidance may be had at the website of the Académie française.

11.26 **French capitalization.** Generic words denoting roadways, squares, and the like are lowercased, whether used alone or with a specific name as part of an address. Only the proper name is capitalized.

le boulevard Saint-Germain
la place de l'Opéra
13, rue des Beaux-Arts

In most geographical names, the generic word is lowercased and the modifying word capitalized.

la mer Rouge   le pic du Midi

Names of buildings are usually capitalized.

l'Hôtel des Invalides   le Palais du Louvre

In names of organizations and institutions, only the first substantive and any preceding modifier are capitalized, but not the preceding article (except at the beginning of a sentence).

l'Académie française   la Légion d'honneur   le Grand Théâtre de Québec

In hyphenated names, both elements are capitalized.

la Comédie-Française   la Haute-Loire

Names of religious groups are usually lowercased.

un chrétien des juifs

In names of saints, the word *saint* is lowercased. But when a saint's name is used as part of a place-name or the name of a church or other institution, *saint* is capitalized and hyphenated to the following element.

le supplice de saint Pierre *but* l'église de Saint-Pierre

Adjectives formed from proper nouns are usually lowercased.

une imagination baudelairienne

See also 11.18.

11.27 **Titles of French works.** French publications vary in the way they capitalize titles of works. In general, Chicago recommends sentence-style capitalization (see 8.158), the rule followed by Grevisse, *Le bon usage* (see 11.6, 11.25). Note that a superscript ordinal letter should remain in the superior position, as in the last example (cf. 14.88). An exception may be made for the French newspaper *Le Monde*, which always appears thus.

L'Apollon de Bellac: Pièce en un acte	*Le père Goriot*
L'assommoir	*Paris au XXe siècle*
L'exil et le royaume	but
Les Rougon-Macquart	*Le Monde*

According to an alternative practice advocated by the Académie française and others (and exemplified by the title *Le Monde*), for titles beginning with a definite article (*Le*, *La*, *L'*, *Les*), the article and the first substantive (noun or noun form) and any intervening modifier are capitalized (e.g., *La Grande Illusion*). Titles that begin with a modifier are treated in the same way, with the modifier and first substantive capitalized (e.g., *Mauvais Sang*); any other titles, including those beginning with an indefinite article (*Un*, *Une*) are capitalized sentence-style (e.g., "Un cœur simple"). This style, if adopted for French titles, should be used consistently. For punctuation in titles, see 11.7.

11.28 **Spacing with French punctuation.** In French typeset material, fixed thin spaces generally occur before colons, semicolons, question marks, and exclamation marks; between guillemets (« ») and the text they enclose (see 11.29); and after an em dash used to introduce dialogue (see 11.31). In electronic documents, fixed (i.e., nonbreaking) spaces can be used to avoid stranding a mark at the beginning of a line or, in the case of an opening guillemet, at the end (see 6.121). In an English context, the typographic conventions of the publication as a whole can be observed, and such spacing need not be duplicated. (If for any reason French spacing is required, however, it must be followed consistently and according to French practice for all marks.) See also 11.19.

11.29 **French use of guillemets.** For quotation marks, the French use guillemets (« »), often with a fixed thin space (or, especially in electronic documents, a regular nonbreaking space; see 6.121) to separate the guillemets from the quoted matter. If such guillemets are retained in an English context, as for a quotation in French (but see 11.19), they can usually be spaced like regular quotation marks (see also 11.28). Such tags as *écrit-il* or *dit-elle* are often inserted within the quoted matter without additional guillemets. Only punctuation belonging to the quoted matter is placed within the closing guillemets; other punctuation follows them.

«Mission accomplie?» a-t-il demandé.

En ce sens, «avec» signifie «au moyen de».

À vrai dire, Abélard n'avoue pas un tel rationalisme: «je ne veux pas être si philosophe, écrit-il, que je résiste à Paul, ni si aristotélicien que je me sépare du Christ».

As in English (see 13.32), when a quotation (other than a block quotation) continues for more than one paragraph, opening guillemets appear at the beginning of each additional paragraph; closing guillemets appear only at the end of the last paragraph. See also 11.30.

11.30 **Quotation marks in French.** For quotations within quotations, double (or sometimes single) quotation marks are used. Formerly, additional guillemets were used, with opening guillemets repeated on each runover line. (Note that when guillemets are used, if the two quotations end simultaneously, only one set of closing guillemets appears.) See also 11.29.

«Comment peux-tu dire, "Montre-nous le père"?»

Regular quotation marks are sometimes seen in French contexts in lieu of guillemets—especially in email correspondence and other electronic settings. This usage is considered informal.

11.31 **French dialogue.** In dialogue, guillemets are often replaced by em dashes. In French publications, the dash is usually followed by a thin space; in English publications, the space is not necessary (see 11.28).

Such dashes are used before each successive speech but are not repeated at the end of a speech. To set off a quotation within a speech, guillemets may be used. See also 11.29.

—Vous viendrez aussitôt que possible? a-t-il demandé.
—Tout de suite.
—Bien. Bonne chance!

—Tu connais sans doute la parole «De l'abondance du cœur la bouche parle».
—Non, je ne la connais pas.

11.32 **French ellipses.** The French often use an ellipsis to indicate an interruption or break in thought. An ellipsis is also sometimes used in lieu of *and so forth*. In French practice, an ellipsis consists of three unspaced dots closed up to the word they follow (*like* this... *rather than* this . . .); in English contexts, they may be spaced in the manner recommended elsewhere in this manual (see 13.50–58) and shown in the examples below. See also 11.19.

«Ce n'est pas que je n'aime plus l'Algérie . . . mon Dieu! un ciel! des arbres! . . . et le reste! . . . Toutefois, sept ans de discipline . . .»

To indicate omissions, the French use unspaced ellipses enclosed in brackets, with thin spaces between the brackets and the dots. In English contexts, spaced periods may be used (but with no space between the brackets and the periods they enclose; see 13.58).

«Oh, dit-elle avec un mépris écrasant, des changements intellectuels! [. . .]»
Les deux amis se réunissaient souvent chez Luc [. . .].

11.33 **French word division—vowels.** In French, a word is divided after a vowel wherever possible. One-letter syllables at the ends or beginnings of lines should be avoided (see 11.20).

ache-ter (*not* a-cheter)   in-di-vi-si-bi-li-té   tri-age

Two or more vowels forming a single sound, or diphthong, are never broken.

écri-vain   fouet-ter   Gau-guin   éloi-gner   vieux

11.34 **French word division—consonants.** A division is normally made between two adjacent consonants, whether the same or different.

der-riè-re   Mal-raux   *but*
feuil-le-ter   ob-jet   qua-tre
ba-lan-cer   par-ler   ta-bleau

Groups of three adjacent consonants are normally divided after the first.

es-prit   res-plen-dir

11.35 **French words containing apostrophes.** Division should never be made immediately after an apostrophe.

jus-qu'au   au-jour-d'hui

11.36 **French words best left undivided.** Since there are as many syllables in French as there are vowels or diphthongs (even if some are unsounded except in poetry), the French break words that appear to English speakers to be of only one syllable (e.g., *fui-te*, *guer-re*, *sor-tent*). French practice also permits division after one letter (e.g., *é-tait*). In English-language publications, however, such breaks should be avoided, since they may confuse readers not fluent in French. Words of four or fewer letters should in any case be left undivided. See also 7.37.

11.37 **French accents and ligatures.** French employs the following special characters (see also table 11.1):

À à, Â â, Ç ç, É é, È è, Ê ê, Ë ë, Î î, Ï ï, Ô ô, Œ œ, Ù ù, Û û, Ü ü

Although French publishers have often omitted accents on capital letters (especially *A*) and may set the ligature *Œ* as two separate letters (*OE*), all the special characters needed for French—including capitalized forms—are widely available, and they should be retained wherever needed in English-language contexts. This practice, advocated by the Académie française, is especially helpful to readers who may not be familiar with French typographic usage.

German

11.38 **The new German orthography.** The new rules for German orthography (including spelling and capitalization) adopted in 1998 and made mandatory for schools and public documents in 2005 (subject to certain revisions) have been controversial. Some publications have continued to follow traditional rules, or a combination of house style and traditional rules, whereas others have adopted the new rules. Some book publishers honor the preference of their authors and, by a similar token, do not update spelling when reprinting older works. Material quoted from German should therefore reflect the spelling in the source. For principles and details of the new orthography, consult the latest edition of *Duden: Die deutsche Rechtschreibung* (bibliog. 5). The recommendations and examples in this section reflect the new orthography.

11.39 **German capitalization.** In German, all nouns and words used as nouns are capitalized, whether in ordinary sentences or in titles of works (see 11.6).

ein Haus	Deutsch (the German language)
die Weltanschauung	eine Deutsche (a German woman)
das Sein	etwas Schönes

Adjectives derived from proper names are generally lowercased. Exceptions include invariable adjectives ending in *er* (often referring to a city or region) and adjectives that themselves are part of a proper name. For further exceptions, consult *Duden* (see 11.38).

die deutsche Literatur
nordamerikanische Sprachen
die platonischen Dialoge
but
eine berühmte Berliner Straße
der Nahe Osten
der Deutsch-Französische Krieg

The pronouns *Sie*, *Ihr*, and *Ihnen*, as polite second-person forms, are capitalized. As third-person pronouns they are lowercased. The familiar second-person forms *du*, *dich*, *dein*, *ihr*, *euch*, and so on—once routinely capitalized—are now lowercased.

11.40 **German apostrophes.** An apostrophe is used to denote the colloquial omission of *e*.

wie geht's	was gibt's	hab' ich

Although an apostrophe rarely appears before a genitive *s*, an apostrophe is used to denote the omission of the *s* after proper names ending in an *s* sound (*ce*, *s*, *ss*, *ß*, *tz*, *x*, or *z*) or in a silent *s*, *x*, or *z*.

Alice' Geburtstag	Cixous' Theaterstücke
Jaspers' Philosophie	Leibniz' Meinung

11.41 **German quotation marks.** In German, quotations usually take reversed guillemets (» «); split-level inverted quotation marks („ “); or, in Switzerland, regular guillemets (see 11.29). Other punctuation is placed outside the closing quotation marks unless it belongs to the quoted matter.

Eros bedeutet für sie primär »zusammen-sein mit« und nicht »anschauen«.
Denn: „An die Pferde“, hieß es: „Aufgesessen!“

11.42 **German word division—vowels.** In German, division is made after a vowel wherever possible. See also 11.20.

Fa-brik hü-ten Bu-ße

Two vowels forming a single sound, or diphthong, are never broken.

Lau-ne blei-ben

Further, a break should never be made after a single vowel at the beginning or end of a word (*aber*, *Ofen*, *Treue*).

11.43 **German word division—consonants.** Two or more adjacent consonants, whether the same or different, are divided before the last one unless they belong to different parts of a compound (see also 11.20).

klir-ren	Meis-ter
Was-ser	*but*
Verwand-te	Morgen-stern

The consonant combinations *ch*, *ck*, *ph*, *sch*, and *th* are not divided unless they belong to separate syllables. (Until the 1998 spelling change, *st* was subject to this rule. The combination *ck*, on the other hand, used to be changed at the end of a line to *kk* and divided between the *k*'s.)

Mäd-chen	*but*
Zu-cker	Klapp-hut
Philo-so-phie	Häus-chen
rau-schen	

11.44 **German word division—compounds.** Compound words should be divided between their component elements whenever possible (see also 11.20).

Meeres-ufer	Rasier-apparat
mit-einander	Tür-angel

11.45 **German special characters.** For setting German in roman type (the old Gothic or Fraktur type having long been out of use), the eszett, or sharp *s* (*ß*), and three umlauted vowels are needed (see also table 11.1).

Ä ä, Ö ö, ß, Ü ü

Although umlauted vowels are occasionally represented by omitting the accent and adding an *e* (*ae*, *Oe*, etc.), the availability of umlauted characters in text-editing software makes such a practice unnecessary. The eszett (*ß*), also widely available, must not be confused with, or replaced by, the Greek beta (β). In the new spelling it is replaced by *ss* in certain words. Consult a German dictionary published after 1998. In German-speaking areas of Switzerland, the eszett is rarely used.

Italian

11.46 **Italian capitalization.** In Italian, a title preceding a proper name is normally lowercased.

il commendatore Ugo Emiliano	la signora Rossi

In commercial correspondence, the formal second-person pronouns are capitalized in both their nominative forms, *Lei* (singular) and *Voi* (plural), and their objective forms, *La* (accusative singular), *Le* (dative singular), and *Vi* (accusative and dative plural). The older singular and plural forms *Ella* (*Le*, *La*) and *Loro* (*Loro*, *Loro*) are handled the same way. These pronouns are capitalized even in combined forms.

Posso pregarLa di farmi una cortesia?
Vorrei darLe una spiegazione.

See also 11.6, 11.18. For a fuller treatment of this and other matters of style, consult Roberto Lesina, *Il nuovo manuale di stile* (bibliog. 5).

11.47 **Italian quotations and dialogue.** Italian uses guillemets (« ») to denote quoted matter, but usually without the space between guillemets and quoted text that appears in many French publications. Regular quotation marks (double or single) are also frequently used in Italian—sometimes as scare quotes (see 7.57) in the same text in which guillemets are used for quotations. Note that periods and commas are correctly placed *after* the closing guillemet or quotation mark.

> «Cosa pensi del fatto che io possa diventare "un qualcosa di imperial regio"? Questo non è proprio possibile».

In dialogue, em dashes are sometimes used, as in French. The dash is used before each successive speech. Unlike in French, however, another dash is used at the end of the speech if other matter follows in the same paragraph. The spaces that typically surround the dashes in Italian texts need not be used in English contexts (see 11.19).

> —Avremo la neve,—annunziò la vecchia.
> —E domani?—chiese Alfredo, voltandosi di scatto dalla finestra.

11.48 **Italian apostrophes.** An apostrophe is used to indicate the omission of one or more letters. A space should appear after an apostrophe that follows a vowel; after an apostrophe that follows a consonant, however, *no* space should appear.

> po' duro   de' malevoli   l'onda   all'aura

11.49 **Italian ellipses.** Italian, like French (see 11.32), uses ellipses to indicate interruptions or breaks in thought. To indicate omitted material, the dots are enclosed in brackets. Though Italian typography usually calls for unspaced dots, in English publications Chicago recommends spaced periods wherever ellipses occur (see 13.50–58). See also 11.19.

> Voglio . . . quattro milioni.   Davvero? [. . .] Non ci avevo pensato.

11.50 **Italian word division—vowels.** In Italian, division is made after a vowel wherever possible. One-letter syllables at the ends or beginnings of lines should be avoided (see 11.20).

> acro-po-li (*not* a-cropoli)   mi-se-ra-bi-le   ta-vo-li-no

Consecutive vowels are rarely divided, and two vowels forming a single sound, or diphthong, are never divided.

miei pia-ga Gio-van-ni Giu-sep-pe pau-sa gio-iel-lo

11.51 **Italian word division—consonants.** Certain consonant groups must never be broken: *ch*, *gh*, *gli*, *gn*, *qu*, *sc*, and *r* or *l* preceded by any consonant other than itself.

ac-qua-rio	la-ghi	pa-dre	ri-flet-te-re
fi-glio	na-sce	rau-che	so-gna-re

Three groups of consonants, however, may be divided: double consonants; the group *cqu*; and any group beginning with *l*, *m*, *n*, or *r*.

bab-bo	ac-qua	cam-po	den-tro
af-fre-schi	cal-do	com-pra	par-te

11.52 **Italian word division—words containing apostrophes.** Division should never be made immediately after an apostrophe (but see 11.48).

dal-l'accusa del-l'or-ga-no quel-l'uomo un'ar-te l'i-dea

11.53 **Italian special characters.** In Italian, the following special characters are required (see also table 11.1):

À à, È è, É é, Ì ì, Ò ò, Ù ù

Although the grave accent on capitalized vowels is sometimes dropped, in stressed final syllables it must be retained to avoid confusion.

CANTÒ (he sang) CANTO (I sing) PAPÀ (daddy) PAPA (pope)

Especially in older works, an apostrophe is sometimes seen with a capital letter in place of the accent on a stressed final (or single) vowel. In direct quotations, such usage should be retained.

E' (it is) E (and) PAPA' (daddy)

Latin

11.54 **Latin capitalization—titles of works.** Titles of ancient and medieval Latin works should usually be capitalized in sentence style—that is, only the first word in the title and subtitle, proper nouns, and proper adjectives are capitalized (see 8.158).

De bello Gallico *De viris illustribus* *Cur Deus homo?*

Renaissance and modern works or works in English with Latin titles, on the other hand, can usually be capitalized headline-style (see 8.159). (If there is any doubt about the era to which the title belongs, opt for sentence style.)

Novum Organum *Religio Medici*

See also 11.6.

11.55 **Latin word division—syllables.** A Latin word has as many syllables as it has vowels or diphthongs (*ae*, *au*, *ei*, *eu*, *oe*, *ui*, and, in archaic Latin, *ai*, *oi*, *ou*) and should be divided between syllables (see also 11.20).

na-tu-ra cae-li-co-la in-no-cu-us

11.56 **Latin word division—single consonants.** When a single consonant occurs between two vowels, the word is divided before the consonant unless it is an *x*. Note that *i* and *u* sometimes act as consonants (and, when they do, are sometimes written as *j* and *v*).

Cae-sar me-ri-di-es in-iu-ri-or (*or* in-ju-ri-or) *but* lex-is

11.57 **Latin word division—multiple consonants.** When two or more consonants come together, the word is divided before the last consonant, except for the combinations noted below.

om-nis cunc-tus

The combinations *ch*, *gu*, *ph*, *qu*, and *th* are treated as single consonants and thus never separated.

co-phi-nus lin-gua ae-qua-lis

The following consonant groups are never broken: *bl*, *br*, *chl*, *chr*, *cl*, *cr*, *dl*, *dr*, *gl*, *gr*, *phl*, *phr*, *pl*, *pr*, *thl*, *thr*, *tl*, and *tr*.

pan-chres-tus li-bris ex-em-pla pa-tris

11.58 **Latin word division—compounds.** Compound words are divided between parts; within each part the rules detailed elsewhere in this section apply. The commonest type of compound word begins with a preposition or a prefix (e.g., *ab-*, *ad-*, *in-*, *re[d]-*).

ab-rum-po   ad-est   red-eo   trans-igo

11.59 **Latin special characters.** Latin requires no special characters for setting ordinary copy. Elementary texts, however, usually mark the long vowels with a macron and, occasionally, the short vowels with a breve, as follows. (See also table 11.1.)

Ā ā, Ă ă, Ē ē, Ĕ ĕ, Ī ī, Ĭ ĭ, Ō ō, Ŏ ŏ, Ū ū, Ŭ ŭ

Spanish

11.60 **Spanish—additional resources.** There is considerable variation in Spanish-language publications throughout the world with respect to capitalization, punctuation, and other matters. For further guidance, consult the extensive resources available from the Real Academia Española, including such essential guides as the *Diccionario panhispánico de dudas* and the *Ortografía de la lengua española* (bibliog. 5).

11.61 **Spanish capitalization.** In Spanish, a title preceding a proper name is normally lowercased. When abbreviated, however, titles are capitalized.

el señor Jaime López   *but*
la señora Lucía Moyado de Barba   el Sr. López
doña Perfecta

Nouns as well as adjectives denoting membership in nations are lowercased, but names of countries are capitalized.

los mexicanos   la lengua española   Inglaterra

Names of organizations and institutions, historical events, buildings, streets, and the like are usually capitalized (see also 8.159).

Real Academia Español
Universidad Nacional Autónoma de México
Plaza del Dos de Mayo

See also 11.4, 11.6, 11.18.

11.62 **Spanish question marks and exclamation points.** A question or an exclamation in Spanish is preceded by an inverted question mark or exclamation point and followed by a regular mark.

¿Qué pasa, amigo? ¡Olvídalo en ese caso!

If a vocative or dependent construction precedes a question or exclamation, it is written as follows:

Amigo, ¿qué pasa? En ese caso, ¡olvídalo!

Because the opening marks are integral to Spanish punctuation, they should be retained even when Spanish is being quoted in an English context (see 11.19).

11.63 **Spanish guillemets and quotation marks.** Spanish traditionally uses guillemets (« ») as quotation marks. Only punctuation belonging to the quoted matter is placed within the closing guillemets; other punctuation follows them. Within a quotation, em dashes may be used to set off words identifying the speaker. In Spanish publications, the opening dash is usually *preceded* by a space; the closing dash is then *followed* by a space unless immediately followed by punctuation. In English contexts, such spaces need not be used (see also 11.19). (For quotations within quotations, regular quotation marks are used, as in French; see 11.30.)

«Vino el negocio a tanto—comenta Suárez—, que ya andaban muchos tomados por el diablo».

In lexical studies, it is typical to see single quotation marks used for glosses, with no punctuation preceding the gloss (cf. 11.5).

Muchos adverbios se forman añadiendo *-ly* al adjetivo: *courteous* 'cortés', *courteously* 'cortésmente', *bold* 'atrevido', *boldly* 'atrevidamente'.

Increasingly, Spanish-language publications use regular quotation marks rather than guillemets for all quotations. Where this is the case, the rules for punctuation marks relative to the quotation marks are the same as they are for guillemets (but see 11.11).

11.64 **Spanish dialogue.** In dialogue, an em dash (or, less frequently, a guillemet) introduces each successive speech. Any other matter that follows the quoted speech in the same paragraph is generally preceded by a dash or a comma. See also 11.63.

—Esto es el arca de Noé, afirmó el estanciero.
—¿Por qué estas aquí todavía?—preguntó Juana alarmada.

11.65 **Spanish ellipses.** In Spanish, as in French (see 11.32), ellipses are used to indicate interruptions or breaks in thought. In Spanish publications, these dots are generally unspaced; in English contexts, they may be spaced as recommended elsewhere in this manual (see 13.50–58). To indicate omitted material, the dots are enclosed in brackets. See also 11.19.

Hemos comenzado la vida juntos . . . quizá la terminaremos juntos también . . .

La personalidad más importante del siglo XIX es Domingo Faustino Sarmiento [. . .], llamado el hombre representante del intelecto sudamericano. [. . .] El gaucho [. . .] servía de tema para poemas, novelas, cuentos y dramas.

11.66 **Spanish word division—vowels.** In Spanish, division is made after a vowel whenever possible. See also 11.20.

ca-ra-co-les mu-jer re-cla-mo se-ño-ri-ta

Two or more vowels that form a single syllable (a diphthong or a triphthong) may not be divided.

cam-bias fue-go miau tie-ne viu-da

If adjacent vowels belong to separate syllables, however, they are divided between syllables.

ba-úl cre-er pa-ís te-a-tro

11.67 **Spanish word division—consonants.** If two adjacent consonants form a combination that would generally not occur at the beginning of a Spanish word, the break is made between them.

ac-cio-nis-ta ad-ver-ten-cia al-cal-de an-cho efec-to is-leño

The consonant groups *bl*, *br*, *cl*, *cr*, *dr*, *fl*, *fr*, *gl*, *gr*, *pl*, *pr*, and *tr*—all pairs that can occur at the beginning of Spanish words—are inseparable (unless each belongs to a different element of a compound, as in *sub-lu-nar*; see 11.68, 11.20).

ci-fra	li-bro	no-ble	re-gla
co-pla	ma-dre	pa-tria	se-cre-to
im-po-si-ble	ne-gro	re-fle-jo	te-cla
le-pra			

Groups of three consonants not ending with one of the inseparable pairs listed above always have an *s* in the middle. They are divided after the *s*.

cons-pi-rar   cons-ta   ins-tan-te   obs-cu-ro   obs-tan-te

Spanish *ch* and *ll* were long considered single characters, alphabetized as such, and never divided. The Spanish Royal Academy has now declared that these combinations are to be alphabetized as two-letter groups, and new publications have adopted this convention. Along with *rr*, however, they still cannot be divided, since they represent single sounds. For details, consult Real Academia Española, *Ortografía de la lengua española* (bibliog. 5).

ci-ga-rri-llo   mu-cha-cho

11.68 **Dividing Spanish compounds.** Compound words are often but not always divided between their component parts.

des-igual	mal-es-tar	semi-es-fe-ra	sub-lu-nar
in-útil	trans-al-pi-no	bien-aven-tu-ra-do	sub-ra-yar

but

no-so-tros (no longer considered a compound by Spanish speakers)

11.69 **Spanish special characters.** Spanish employs the following special characters (see also table 11.1):

Áá, Éé, Íí, Ññ, Óó, Úú, Üü

Other Languages Using the Latin Alphabet

11.70 **Special considerations for other languages using the Latin alphabet.** In addition to the languages covered elsewhere in this section, there are dozens of other languages that use the Latin alphabet. Special considerations for a number of them are listed below. For the special characters required for each of these languages, see table 11.1. See also 11.6, 11.18.

Albanian. Since 1972, Albanian has had a single, unified orthography, based on a standard originally adopted in 1909. Writers and editors working with older texts may need to take historical context into account and determine whether a spelling is conditioned by the specific time when it was used or whether it is preferable to follow the current norm.

Croatian and Bosnian. The former Serbo-Croatian language used both Latin and Cyrillic alphabets. The modern Bosnian and Croatian standard languages use only the Latin version of that same alphabet. Although the substitution of *dj* for *đ* is sometimes seen (e.g., in informal correspondence), standard orthographic practice in all the successor languages of Serbo-Croatian distinguishes these two consistently. See also Serbian and Montenegrin.

Czech, a Slavic language written in the Latin alphabet, uses many diacritical marks to indicate sounds not represented by this alphabet, as shown in table 11.1. Note that the lowercase *d* and *t* with caron (the single glyphs *ď* and *ť*, respectively) are often seen with an apostrophe instead.

Danish. The polite second-person pronouns *De*, *Dem*, and *Deres* (increasingly rare, and not to be confused with the third-person pronouns *de*, *dem*, and *deres*) and the familiar *I* are capitalized in Danish. Until the middle of the twentieth century, common nouns were capitalized, as in German.

Dutch. For the capitalization of particles with personal names, see 8.10. Proper adjectives (as well as nouns) are capitalized as in English. When a word beginning with the diphthong *ij* is capitalized, both letters are capitals: *IJsland*. When a single letter begins a sentence, it is lowercased, but the next word is capitalized: *'k Heb niet . . .*

Finnish. Because Swedish is the second official language in Finland, the Finnish alphabet taught in schools and the standard keyboard used in Finland include the Swedish *a* with ring above (see table 11.1).

Hawaiian. The Hawaiian alphabet was developed in the nineteenth century from the Latin alphabet. In addition to the five vowels with macrons listed in table 11.1, Hawaiian uses the *ʻokina*, a glottal stop represented by a left single quotation mark (U+2018)—for example, in the place-name *Hawaiʻi*. See also 6.115.[1]

Hungarian uses a wide variety of accented vowels, as shown in table 11.1.

Icelandic includes the consonants *Ðð* (eth) and *Þþ* (thorn), which were also used in Old and Middle English (see 11.122–24). (The eth, which never begins a word, is capitalized only in contexts where all capitals are used.) In addition to featuring an acute-accented version of each regular vowel (including *Ýý*), Icelandic includes the vowels *Ææ* and *Öö*.

1. A modifier letter turned comma (U+02BB) may be used instead of a left single quotation mark to represent the *ʻokina* and is preferred by some authors and publishers as a means of differentiating the glottal stop from the common mark of punctuation. In many typefaces, however, the two glyphs have an identical appearance.

Norwegian. The polite second-person pronouns *De*, *Dem*, and *Deres* (increasingly rare, and not to be confused with the third-person pronouns *de*, *dem*, and *deres*) are capitalized in Norwegian. Until the middle of the twentieth century, common nouns were capitalized, as in German.

Polish. In formal address the second-person plural pronoun *Państwo* (you) is capitalized, as are related forms: *Czekam na Twój przyjazd* (I await your arrival); *Pozdrawiam Cię!* (Greetings to you!). Division of Polish words is similar to that of transliterated Russian (see 11.98–108). Division normally follows syllabic structure (e.g., *kom-pli-ka-cja*; *sta-ro-pol-ski*). Note that the conjunction *i* (and) should never appear at the end of a line but must be carried over to the beginning of the next.

Portuguese. Titles and nouns or adjectives denoting nationality are capitalized as in Spanish (see 11.61). Accented capitals, sometimes dropped in Portuguese running text, should always be used when Portuguese is presented in an English context.

Romanian and Moldovan are now both written using the same Latin orthography. Note that *Șș* and *Țț*—Latin *Ss* and *Tt* with comma below—often appear instead with a cedilla, though the comma is correct. *Ââ* and *Îî* represent identical sounds but have different etymological origins. The use of *Ââ* has been restricted, eliminated, and reinstated in whole or in part during various orthographic reforms. Writers and editors, therefore, should take care to determine whether a spelling is conditioned by the specific time when it was used or whether it is preferable to follow the current norm.

Serbian and Montenegrin. The former Serbo-Croatian language used both Latin and Cyrillic alphabets. In the modern Montenegrin standard language, both versions of that alphabet are official. In the modern Serbian standard language, the Cyrillic version of that same alphabet is official, though the Latin alphabet is also used, as regulated by law. Note that although the substitution of *dj* for *đ* is sometimes seen (e.g., in informal correspondence), standard orthographic practice in all the successor languages of Serbo-Croatian distinguishes these two consistently. In addition to the letters needed for Serbian, two extra letters are required for Montenegrin: *Śś* and *Źź* (see table 11.1). See also Croatian and Bosnian.

Swedish. In Swedish, the second-person pronouns *Ni* and *Er*, traditionally capitalized in correspondence, are now lowercased in all contexts.

Turkish and Azeri. Modern Turkish has undergone a number of orthographic reforms since the original change to the Latin alphabet in 1928. Differences in the spellings of a name or word can therefore depend on the time period. Writers and editors should take care to determine whether a spelling is conditioned by the specific time when it was used or whether it is preferable to follow the current norm. In Turkish, as in English, the names of months and days of the week are capitalized. The Azeri (Azerbaijani) standard alphabet in use since 1992 is identical to the Turkish alphabet except for the presence of Əə, *Qq*, and *Xx* (lacking in Turkish), and the absence of vowels with circumflex. Conventions for capitalization and spelling are similar to those for Turkish. Note that in both languages, the letter *i* retains its dot when capitalized.

Turkmen and Uzbek. Turkmenistan has successfully transitioned from a Cyrillic to a Latin alphabet. In Uzbekistan the transition is still ongoing. Uzbek requires no special characters aside from the left single quotation mark in the letters *O‘o‘* and *G‘g‘* (not shown in table 11.1).

Languages Usually Transliterated (or Romanized)

11.71 **Transliteration.** In nonspecialized works it is customary to transliterate—that is, convert to the Latin alphabet, or romanize—words or phrases from languages that do not use the Latin alphabet. For discussion and illustration of scores of alphabets, see Peter T. Daniels and William Bright, eds., *The World's Writing Systems* (bibliog. 5). For alphabetic conversion, the most comprehensive resource is the Library of Congress publication *ALA-LC Romanization Tables* (bibliog. 5), available online. Do not attempt to transliterate from a language unfamiliar to you. Note that the recommendations elsewhere in this chapter related to capitalization (11.18), punctuation (11.19), and word division (11.20) for languages that use the Latin alphabet apply equally to transliterated text.

11.72 **Character sets for non-Latin alphabets.** Modern word-processing software readily allows users to enter words in a number of non-Latin alphabets. For a given alphabet, there may be a variety of non-Unicode character sets available as specialized fonts, but authors who want to include such copy should generally opt for a font that includes the correct Unicode characters if at all possible (see 11.2), after consulting their publisher. See also 2.16.

11.73 **Proofreading copy in non-Latin alphabets—a warning.** Anyone unfamiliar with a language that uses a non-Latin alphabet should exercise extreme caution in proofreading even single words set in that alphabet. Grave errors can occur when similar characters are mistaken for each other. If in doubt, editors should query the author; it may be advisable to consult the Unicode number and description (see 11.2) when referring to a given character or diacritical mark.

11.74 **Diacritics—specialized versus general contexts.** Nearly all systems of transliteration require diacritics—including, in the languages discussed below, macrons, underdots, and overdots, to name just a few. Except in linguistic studies or other highly specialized works, a system using as few diacritics as are needed to aid pronunciation is easier on readers, publisher, and author. Most readers of a nonspecialized work on Hindu mythology, for example, will be more comfortable with Shiva than Śiva or with Vishnu than Viṣṇu, though many specialists would want to differentiate the *Sh* in Shiva from the *sh* in Vishnu as distinct Sanskrit letters. For nonspecialized works, the transliterated forms without diacritics that are listed in the latest editions of the Merriam-Webster dictionaries (bibliog. 3.1) are usually preferred by readers and authors alike.

11.75 **Italics versus roman for transliterated terms.** Transliterated terms (other than proper names) that have not become part of the English language are italicized. If used throughout a work, a transliterated term may be italicized on first appearance and then set in roman. Words listed in the dictionary are usually set in roman. See also 11.3–5.

The preacher pointed out the distinction between agape and eros.

but

Once the Greek words *erōs* and *agapē* had been absorbed into the English language, it became unnecessary to italicize them or to use the macrons.

Arabic

11.76 **Arabic transliteration.** There is no universally accepted form for transliterating Arabic. One very detailed system may be found in the *ALA-LC Romanization Tables* (bibliog. 5). Another system is followed by the *International Journal of Middle East Studies* (bibliog. 5). Having selected a system, an author should stick to it with as few exceptions as possible. In the following examples, only the hamza (ʾ) and the ʿayn (ʿ) are used (see 11.77). Letters with underdots and some of the other special characters used in transliteration from Arabic are included in table 11.2. (The Arabic alphabet may be found in the alphabet table in *Merriam-Webster's Collegiate Dictionary* [bibliog. 3.1], among other sources.)

TABLE 11.2. Special characters (and Unicode numbers) for transliterated Arabic, Hebrew, Japanese, and South Asian languages

Character (and Unicode number)	Description	Languages that use it
ʹ (02B9)	modifier letter prime (see 11.92)	Arabic, Hebrew
ʿ (02BF)	ʿayn *or* ʿayin (modifier letter left half ring)	Arabic, Hebrew
ʾ (02BE)	alif (hamza) *or* ʾalef (modifier letter right half ring)	Arabic, Hebrew
Ā (0100), ā (0101)	A/a with macron	Arabic, Hebrew, Japanese, South Asian languages
Ǎ (01CD), ǎ (01CE)	A/a with caron (haček)	Hebrew
Á (00C1), á (00E1)	A/a with acute	Arabic
Ḍ (1E0C), ḍ (1E0D)	D/d with dot below	Arabic, South Asian languages
Ē (0112), ē (0113)	E/e with macron	Hebrew, Japanese, South Asian languages
Ě (011A), ě (011B)	E/e with caron (haček)	Hebrew
ə (0259)	small schwa	Hebrew
Ḥ (1E24), ḥ (1E25)	H/h with dot below	Arabic, Hebrew, South Asian languages
Ī (012A), ī (012B)	I/i with macron	Arabic, Hebrew, Japanese, South Asian languages
Ḳ (1E32), ḳ (1E33)	K/k with dot below	Arabic, Hebrew
Ḷ (1E36), ḷ (1E37)	L/l with dot below[1]	South Asian languages
Ḹ (1E38), ḹ (1E39)	L/l with dot below and macron	South Asian languages
Ṁ (1E40) ṁ (1E41)	M/m with dot above	South Asian languages
Ṃ (1E42), ṃ (1E43)	M/m with dot below	South Asian languages
Ñ (00D1) ñ (00F1)	N/n with tilde	South Asian languages
N̄ (004E+0304), n̄ (006E+0304)	N/n with macron (combining character)	South Asian languages
Ṅ (1E44), ṅ (1E45)	N/n with dot above	South Asian languages
Ṇ (1E46), ṇ (1E47)	N/n with dot below	South Asian languages
Ō (014C), ō (014D)	O/o with macron	Hebrew, Japanese, South Asian languages
Ǒ (01D1), ǒ (01D2)	O/o with caron (haček)	Hebrew
Ṛ (1E5A), ṛ (1E5B)	R/r with dot below[2]	South Asian languages
Ṝ (1E5C), ṝ (1E5D)	R/r with dot below and macron	South Asian languages
Ś (015A), ś (015B)	S/s with acute	Hebrew, South Asian languages
Š (0160), š (0161)	S/s with caron (haček)	Hebrew
Ṣ (1E62), ṣ (1E63)	S/s with dot below	Arabic, South Asian languages
Ṭ (1E6C), ṭ (1E6D)	T/t with dot below	Arabic, Hebrew, South Asian languages
Ū (016A), ū (016B)	U/u with macron	Arabic, Hebrew, Japanese, South Asian languages
Ṿ (1E7E), ṿ (1E7F)	V/v with dot below	Hebrew
Ẏ (1E8E) ẏ (1E8F)	Y/y with dot above	South Asian languages
Ẓ (1E92), ẓ (1E93)	Z/z with dot below	Arabic

[1] Variations of L/l with a combining ring below (U+0325) rather than a dot below may also be required.
[2] As with L/l, R/r variations may require a combining ring below (U+0325) rather than a dot.

11.77 **The hamza and the ʿayn.** The hamza (ʾ) and the ʿayn (ʿ) frequently appear in transliterated Arabic words and names. Writers using hamzas or ʿayns must on every occurrence make it clear, by coding or by careful instructions to the editor or typesetter, which of the two marks is intended. It should be noted that the Arabic characters are not the same as the ones used for transliteration; see table 11.2 for the preferred Unicode characters for hamza and ʿayn in transliteration. The hamza is sometimes represented—especially in nonspecialized works—by an apostrophe, as in Qur'an, and the ʿayn by a single opening quotation mark ('ayn). (Since an ʿayn often occurs at the beginning of a word, a quotation mark must be used with caution.) Most transliteration systems drop the hamza when it occurs at the beginning of a word (anzala *not* ʾanzala). See also 6.115, 6.117.

11.78 **Arabic spelling.** Isolated references in text to well-known persons or places should employ the forms familiar to English-speaking readers.

Avicenna (*not* Ibn Sina)
Damascus (*not* Dimashq)
Mecca (*not* Makka *or* Makkah)

11.79 **The Arabic definite article.** Though there is considerable variation across publications, Chicago recommends joining the Arabic definite article, *al*, to a noun with a hyphen.

al-Islam al-Nafud Bahr al-Safi al-Qaeda (*or* al-Qaida)

In speech the sound of the *l* in *al* is assimilated into the sounds *d*, *n*, *r*, *s*, *sh*, *t*, and *z*. Where rendering the *sound* of the Arabic is important (for example, when transliterating poetry), the assimilations are often shown, as in the examples below. In most other situations, the article-noun combination is written without indication of the elision, as above.

an-Nafud Bahr as-Safi

Some authors drop the *a* in *al* and replace it with an apostrophe when it occurs after a long syllable (Abū 'l-Muhallab). Some also drop the *a* when it occurs connected with a particle (wa 'l-layl). Others do not replace the dropped *a* with anything (Abū l-Muhallab; wa l-layl).

11.80 **Arabic capitalization.** Since the Arabic alphabet does not distinguish between capital and lowercase letter forms, practice in capitalizing transliterated Arabic varies widely. Chicago recommends the practice outlined in 11.6: capitalize only the first word and any proper nouns. This practice applies to titles of works as well as to names of journals and organizations. Note that *al*, like *the*, is capitalized only at the beginning of a sentence or a title. See also 11.9.

ʿAbd al-Rahman al-Jabarti, *ʿAjaʾib al-athar fi al-tarajim wa al-akhbar* (The marvelous remains in biography and history)

For citing and alphabetizing Arabic personal names, see 8.14, 16.75.

11.81 **Arabic word division.** Breaking transliterated Arabic words or names at the ends of lines should be avoided wherever possible. If necessary, a break may be made after *al* or *Ibn*. A break may be made after two letters if the second has an underdot (e.g., *iṭ-baq*). Breaks must never be made between the digraphs *dh*, *gh*, *kh*, *sh*, or *th* unless both letters have underdots. Nor should breaks be made before or after a hamza. Aside from these niceties, the rules governing English word division may be followed (see 7.36–47). It should be noted, however, that untransliterated (or unromanized) Arabic is read from right to left; if a line break occurs within an untransliterated Arabic phrase, the words must still be read right to left on each line. For an example of this in Hebrew, see 11.96.

Chinese and Japanese

11.82 **Chinese romanization.** The Hanyu Pinyin romanization system, introduced in the 1950s, has largely supplanted both the Wade-Giles system and the place-name spellings of the *Postal Atlas of China* (last updated in the 1930s), making Pinyin the standard system for romanizing Chinese. Representing sounds of Chinese more explicitly, Pinyin has been widely accepted as the system for teaching Chinese as a second language. As of 2000, the Library of Congress issued new romanization guidelines reflecting the conversion of its entire online catalog records for the Chinese collection to comply with Pinyin. Although a few authors, long familiar with Wade-Giles or other older systems (or Tongyong Pinyin, a more recent system still used by some in Taiwan), have not switched to Pinyin in their writings, Chicago joins librarians in urging that Pinyin now be used in all writing about China or the Chinese language. (In some contexts it may be helpful to the reader to add the Wade-Giles spelling of a name or term in parentheses following the first use of the Pinyin spelling.) The *ALA-LC Romanization Tables* (bibliog. 5) available online from the Library of Congress should be used with caution by anyone unfamiliar with Chinese.

11.83 **Exceptions to Pinyin.** Even where Pinyin is adopted, certain place-names, personal names, and other proper nouns long familiar in their older forms may be presented that way in English texts. Or, for greater consistency, the old spelling may be added in parentheses after the Pinyin version. If in doubt, consult the latest edition of *Merriam-Webster's Collegiate Dictionary* (bibliog. 3.1); names not listed there in older forms should be presented in Pinyin. Editors who wish to alter spellings should do so in consultation with the author.

11.84 **Apostrophes, hyphens, and tone marks in Chinese romanization.** Pinyin spellings often differ markedly from Wade-Giles and other older spellings. Personal names are usually spelled without apostrophes or hyphens, but an apostrophe is sometimes used when syllables are run together (as in Xi'an to distinguish it from Xian), even in contexts where tone marks are used (e.g., Xī'ān). The Pinyin romanization system of the Library of Congress does not include tone marks, nor are they included in many English-language publications. However, tone marks may be appropriate in certain contexts (e.g., textbooks for learning Chinese).

11.85 **Some common Chinese names.** Some names frequently encountered are listed below.

DYNASTIES		PERSONAL NAMES	
Wade-Giles	*Pinyin*	*Wade-Giles*	*Pinyin*
Chou	Zhou	Fang Li-chih	Fang Lizhi
Ch'in	Qin	Hua Kuo-feng	Hua Guofeng
Ch'ing	Qing	Lin Piao	Lin Biao
Sung	Song	Lu Hsün	Lu Xun
T'ang	Tang	Mao Tse-tung	Mao Zedong
Yüan	Yuan	Teng Hsiao-p'ing	Deng Xiaoping

The names Sun Yat-sen and Chiang Kai-shek, among a few others, usually retain the old spellings.

GEOGRAPHICAL NAMES		
Wade-Giles	*Postal atlas*	*Pinyin*
Kuang-tung	Kwangtung	Guangdong
Pei-ching (Pei-p'ing)	Peking (Peiping)	Beijing
Shang-hai	Shanghai	Shanghai
Su-chou	Soochow	Suzhou
Ta-lien	Dairen	Dalian

11.86 **Japanese romanization.** The Japanese language in its usual written form is a mixture of Chinese characters (called *kanji* in Japanese) and two *kana* syllabaries. (A syllabary is a series of written characters, each used to represent a syllable.) Since romanized Japanese, *rōmaji*, was introduced into Japan in the sixteenth century, a number of systems of romanization have been developed. The one in most common use since the early part of the Meiji period (1868–1912) is the modified Hepburn (or *hyōjun*) system. This system is used in *Kenkyūsha's New Japanese-English Dictionary* (bibliog. 3.2) and most other Japanese-English dictionaries (and is the basis of the Japanese romanization tables available online from the Library of Congress); outside Japan, it is also used almost exclusively, notably in Asian collections in libraries throughout the world.

11.87 **Modified Hepburn system.** In the modified Hepburn system, an apostrophe is placed after a syllabic *n* that is followed by a vowel or *y*: *Gen'e*, *San'yo*. A macron is used over a long vowel (usually an *o* or a *u*, though some systems allow for macrons over *a*, *i*, and *e*) in all Japanese words except well-known place-names (e.g., Tokyo, Hokkaido, Kobe) and words such as *shogun* and *daimyo* that have entered the English language and are thus not italicized. (When the pronunciation of such names or words is important to readers, however, macrons may be used: Tōkyō, Hokkaidō, Kōbe, shōgun, daimyō.) Hyphens should be used sparingly: *Meiji jidai-shi* (or *jidaishi*) *no shinkenkyū*. *Shinjuku-ku* (or *Shinjukuku*) *no meisho*.

11.88 **Chinese and Japanese—capitalization and italics.** Although capital letters do not exist in Japanese or Chinese, they are introduced in romanized versions of these languages where they would normally be used in English (see chapter 8). Personal names and place-names are capitalized. In hyphenated names, only the first element is capitalized in romanized Chinese, though both elements may be capitalized in Japanese. Common nouns and other words used in an English sentence are lowercased and italicized (see 11.3, 11.5). Names of institutions, schools of thought, religions, and so forth are capitalized if set in roman, lowercased if set in italics.

Donglin Academy; the Donglin movement

Buddhism, Taoism, feng shui [see 7.54], and other forms . . .

Under the Ming dynasty the postal service was administered by the Board of War (*bingbu*) through a central office in Beijing (*huitong guan*).

The heirs of the Seiyūkai and Minseitō are the Liberal and Progressive Parties of Japan.

It was Genrō Saionji (the *genrō* were the elder statesmen of Japan) who said . . . (note that *genrō* is both singular and plural)

11.89 **Titles of Japanese and Chinese works.** As in English, titles of books and periodicals are italicized, and titles of articles are set in roman and enclosed in quotation marks (see 8.156–201). The first word of a romanized title is always capitalized, as are many proper nouns (especially in Japanese).

Chen Shiqi, *Mingdai guan shougongye de yanjiu* [Studies on government-operated handicrafts during the Ming dynasty], . . .

Hua Linfu, "Qingdai yilai Sanxia diqu shuihan zaihai de chubu yanjiu" [A preliminary study of floods and droughts in the Three Gorges region since the Qing dynasty], *Zhongguo shehui kexue* 1 (1999): 168–79.

Okamoto Yoshitomo, *Jūrokuseiki Nichi-Ō kōtsūshi no kenkyū* [Study of the intercourse between Japan and Europe during the sixteenth century], . . .

Akiyama Kenzō, "Goresu wa Ryūkyūjin de aru" [The Gores are Ryūkyūans], *Shigaku-Zasshi* (or *Shigaku Zasshi*) . . .

11.90 **Inclusion of Chinese and Japanese characters.** Chinese and Japanese characters, immediately following the romanized version of the item they represent, are sometimes necessary to help readers identify references cited or terms used. They are largely confined to bibliographies and glossaries. Where needed in running text, they may be enclosed in parentheses. The advent of Unicode has made it easier for authors to include words in non-Latin alphabets in their manuscripts, but publishers need to be alerted of the need for special characters in case particular fonts are needed for publication (see 11.2).

Harootunian, Harry, and Sakai Naoki. "Nihon kenkyū to bunka kenkyū" 日本研究と文化研究. *Shisō* 思想 7 (July 1997): 4–53.

Hua Linfu 華林甫. "Qingdai yilai Sanxia diqu shuihan zaihai de chubu yanjiu" 清代以來三峽地區水旱災害的初步研究 [A preliminary study of floods and droughts in the Three Gorges region since the Qing dynasty]. *Zhongguo shehui kexue* 中國社會科學 1 (1999): 168–79.

That year the first assembly of the national Diet was held and the Imperial Rescript on Education (*kyōiku chokugo* 教育勅語) was issued.

Hebrew

11.91 **Hebrew transliteration systems.** There are several acceptable romanization systems for Hebrew, including the one in the *ALA-LC Romaniza-*

tion Tables (see bibliog. 5). Any such system may be used, but it is the author's responsibility to use it consistently in a given work. (The Hebrew alphabet may be found in the alphabet table in *Merriam-Webster's Collegiate Dictionary* [bibliog. 3.1], among other sources.)

11.92 **Diacritics in transliterated Hebrew.** In transliterated Hebrew, the following accents and characters are sometimes needed (though usually only in specialist materials): underdots (Ḥḥ, Ḳḳ, Ṭṭ, Ṿṿ); macrons (Āā, Ēē, Īī, Ōō, Ūū); acute accents (Śś); hačeks, or carons (Ǎǎ, Ěě, Ǒǒ, Šš); and superscript schwa (ᵊ). The ʾalef and the ʿayin may be represented in the same way as the Arabic hamza and ʿayn (see 11.77 and table 11.2). In some systems, a prime may also be needed (to separate two distinct consonant sounds that might be mistaken for a digraph).

11.93 **Hebrew prefixes.** In Hebrew, several prepositions, conjunctions, and articles appear as prefixes. Some authors use apostrophes or hyphens after these prefixes in romanized text, and some do not. (In Hebrew no such marker is used.) Either approach is acceptable if used consistently.

11.94 **Hebrew capitalization and italics.** The Hebrew alphabet has no capital letters, and there is no universally used system for capitalizing romanized Hebrew. Writers may follow normal English usage—capitalizing proper names, book titles, and so forth (see 11.6, 11.18). Some writers eschew capitalization altogether. As always, the author must ensure internal consistency. For italics in romanized Hebrew, the normal English usage may also be followed (see 11.8).

11.95 **Hebrew word division.** For romanized Hebrew, or Hebrew words incorporated into English, the principles set forth in 7.36–47 may be followed. When a double consonant occurs at the point of division, one consonant goes with each division.

Rosh Ha-shana   Yom Kip-pur

11.96 **Unromanized Hebrew phrases.** Hebrew is read from right to left. In English sentences that contain an unromanized Hebrew phrase, the Hebrew order is maintained within the sentence. (Modern operating systems can often handle a mix of left-right and right-left input in the same context.)

The first phrase in Lamentations is איכה ישבה בדד (How she sits in solitude!).

If a line break occurs within a Hebrew phrase, the words must still be read right to left on each line. Thus, if the Hebrew phrase in the example above had to be broken, the Hebrew words would appear to be in a different order.

The first phrase in Lamentations is איכה ישבה
  בדד (How she sits in solitude!).

or

The first phrase in Lamentations is איכה
  ישבה בדד (How she sits in solitude!).

As a safeguard, the author should highlight all the words in Hebrew phrases and furnish detailed instructions on how to implement line breaks.

11.97 **A note on Hebrew vowels.** Most Hebrew vowels are not letters; they are marks attached to the letters, most of which are consonants. In Hebrew texts the vowel marks (as well as dots that modify the pronunciation of consonants) rarely appear. Among texts in which the marks do appear are prayer books, printed Bibles, and poetry.

Russian

11.98 **Russian transliteration.** Of the many systems for transliterating Russian, the most important are summarized in table 11.3. Journals of Slavic studies generally prefer a "linguistic" system that makes free use of diacritics and ligatures. In works intended for a general audience, however, diacritics and ligatures should be avoided. For general use, Chicago recommends the system of the United States Board on Geographic Names. Regardless of the system followed, the spellings for names listed in the Merriam-Webster dictionaries (bibliog. 3.1) should prevail.

Catherine the Great
Chekhov
Dnieper River
Moscow
Nizhniy (*or* Nizhni) Novgorod
Tchaikovsky

11.99 **Russian capitalization.** Capitalization conventions in Cyrillic are much like those of French and should be preserved in transliteration. Pronouns, days of the week, months, and most proper adjectives are lowercased. Geographic designations are capitalized when they apply to formal institutions or political units but otherwise lowercased.

Tverskaya guberniya
tverskoye zemstvo
Moskovskiy universitet
russkiy kompozitor

TABLE 11.3. Russian alphabet (and Unicode numbers) and romanization

Basic Russian (Cyrillic) alphabet (and Unicode numbers)				
Upright	Cursive[1]	US Board on Geographic Names	Library of Congress	Linguistic system[2]
А (0410), а (0430)	*А, а*	a		
Б (0411), б (0431)	*Б, б*	b		
В (0412), в (0432)	*В, в*	v		
Г (0413), г (0433)	*Г, г*	g		
Д (0414), д (0434)	*Д, д*	d		
Е (0415), е (0435)	*Е, е*	ye,[3] e	e	e
Ё (0401), ё[4] (0451)	*Ё, ё*	yë,[3] ë (00EB)	ë	e, ë
Ж (0416), ж (0436)	*Ж, ж*	zh		ž
З (0417), з (0437)	*З, з*	z		
И (0418), и (0438)	*И, и*	i		
Й (0419), й (0439)	*Й, й*	y	ĭ (012D)	j
К (041A), к (043A)	*К, к*	k		
Л (041B), л (043B)	*Л, л*	l		
М (041C), м (043C)	*М, м*	m		
Н (041D), н (043D)	*Н, н*	n		
О (041E), о (043E)	*О, о*	o		
П (041F), п (043F)	*П, п*	p		
Р (0420), р (0440)	*Р, р*	r		
С (0421), с (0441)	*С, с*	s		
Т (0422), т (0442)	*Т, т*	t		
У (0423), у (0443)	*У, у*	u		
Ф (0424), ф (0444)	*Ф, ф*	f		
Х (0425), х (0445)	*Х, х*	kh		x
Ц (0426), ц (0446)	*Ц, ц*	ts	t͡s[5]	c
Ч (0427), ч (0447)	*Ч, ч*	ch		č
Ш (0428), ш (0448)	*Ш, ш*	sh		š
Щ (0429), щ (0449)	*Щ, щ*	shch		šč
Ъ (042A), ъ[6] (044A)	*Ъ, ъ*	” (201D)[7]	ʺ (02BA)[8]	ʺ (02BA)[8]
Ы (042B), ы[6] (044B)	*Ы, ы*	y		
Ь (042C), ь[6] (044C)	*Ь, ь*	’ (2019)[9]	ʹ (02B9)[10]	ʹ (02B9)[10]
Э (042D), э (044D)	*Э, э*	e	ė (0117)	è (00E8)
Ю (042E), ю (044E)	*Ю, ю*	yu	i͡u[5]	ju
Я (042F), я (044F)	*Я, я*	ya	i͡a[5]	ja

NOTE: The Library of Congress and linguistic systems employ the same characters as the US Board system except where noted.

[1] The Unicode numbers are the same for the upright and cursive characters; the differences in appearance depend on the italic version of a given typeface.

[2] The term *linguistic* describes a system generally preferred by journals of Slavic studies (see 11.98).

[3] Initially and after a vowel or *ъ* or *ь*.

[4] Not considered a separate letter; usually represented in Russian by *e*.

[5] Character tie, sometimes omitted, may be produced by using the combining double inverted breve (U+0361).

[6] Does not occur initially.

[7] Right double quotation mark.

[8] Modifier letter double prime (hard sign).

[9] Right single quotation mark.

[10] Modifier letter prime (soft sign).

11.100 **Titles of Russian works.** Only the first word and any proper nouns are capitalized in titles.

N. A. Kurakin, *Lenin i Trotskiy*

O. I. Skorokhodova, *Kak ya vosprinimayu i predstavlyayu okruzhayushchiy mir* [How I perceive and imagine the external world]

Note that in the original Cyrillic, titles are set in ordinary type; the Cyrillic *kursiv* is used more sparingly than our italic and never for book titles. In transliterations, however, italic should be used.

11.101 **Russian quotations and dialogue.** Russian generally resembles French in its use of guillemets (« ») for dialogue and quoted material and of dashes for dialogue (see 11.29, 11.31).

«Bozhe, bozhe, bozhe!» govorit Boris.

—S kem ya rabotayu?
—S tovarishchem.
—Kak my rabotayem?
—S interesom.

To set off a quotation within a speech, guillemets may be used, as in French. For an example, see 11.31.

11.102 **Russian ellipses.** Ellipses are used as in French (see 11.32) to indicate interruptions or breaks in thought.

Ya . . . vy . . . my tol'ko chto priyekhali.

In Russian, an exclamation point or a question mark often takes the place of one of the dots; this convention may be regularized to three dots in English publications.

Mitya! . . . Gde vy byli? . . .

11.103 **Russian uses of the dash.** A dash is sometimes inserted, with a space on either side, between subject and complement when the equivalent of *is* or *are* is omitted.

Moskva — stolitsa Rossii.

Similarly, a dash, preceded and followed by a space, is used in place of a verb omitted because it would be identical to the preceding verb.

Ivan i Sonya poyedut v Moskvu poyezdom, Lev i Lyuba — avtobusom.

11.104 **Russian word division—general.** Transliterated Russian should be divided according to the rules governing word division in the Cyrillic original. The guidelines in this section are adapted from the transliteration system of the United States Board on Geographic Names.

11.105 **Combinations not to be divided in Cyrillic transliteration.** Combinations representing single Cyrillic letters—*ch*, *kh*, *sh*, *shch*, *ts*, *ya*, *ye*, *yë*, *yu*, *zh*—should never be divided, nor should combinations of a vowel plus short *i* (or yod, transliterated *y*): *ay*, *ey*, *yey*, and so on.

11.106 **Division between Russian consonants.** Words may be divided between single consonants or between a consonant and a consonant combination.

ubor-ku chudes-nym mol-cha sred-stvo mor-skoy

The following consonant combinations are not normally divided: *bl*, *br*, *dr*, *dv*, *fl*, *fr*, *gl*, *gr*, *kl*, *kr*, *ml*, *pl*, *pr*, *sk*, *skr*, *skv*, *st*, *str*, *stv*, *tr*, *tv*, *vl*, *vr*, *zhd*. They may, however, be divided if they fall across the boundary of a prefix and a root or other such units (e.g., ob-lech', ras-kol).

11.107 **Division of Russian words after prefixes or between parts.** Words may be divided after a prefix, but generally the prefix itself should not be divided.

bes-poryadok pere-stroyka za-dat' pred-lozhit' pro-vesti obo-gnat'

Compound words should be divided between parts.

radio-priyëmnik gor-sovet kino-teatr

11.108 **Division of Russian words after vowel or diphthong.** Words may be divided after a vowel or a diphthong before a single (Cyrillic) consonant.

Si-bir' voy-na Gorba-chev da-zhe

Division after a vowel may also be made before a consonant combination.

puteshe-stvennik khi-trit' pro-stak ru-brika

South Asian Languages

11.109 **South Asian special characters.** Transliteration of the principal South Asian languages may require the following special characters (see also table 11.2):

Āā, Ḍḍ, Ēē, Ḥḥ, Īī, Ḷḷ, Ḹḹ, Ṁṁ, Ṃṃ, Ṇṇ, Ṅṅ, N̄n̄, Ññ, Ōō, Ṛṛ, Ṝṝ, Ṣṣ, Śś, Ṭṭ, Ūū, Ẏẏ

Many writers using South Asian languages, however, employ a simplified style that does not use diacritics at all—for example, substituting *sh* for various *s*'s, ignoring subscript dots for dental consonants, and omitting macrons altogether.

Classical Greek

11.110 **Transliterating Greek.** Isolated Greek words and phrases in works not focusing on ancient Greece are usually transliterated. Table 11.4 shows the Greek alphabet (with Unicode numbers) and corresponding letters of the Latin alphabet. In transliteration, all Greek accents are omitted. The macron is used to distinguish the long vowels eta (*ē*) and omega (*ō*) from the short vowels epsilon (*e*) and omicron (*o*). The iota subscript is transliterated by an *i* on the line, following the vowel it is associated with (ἀνθρώπῳ, *anthrōpōi*). The rough breathing is transliterated by *h*, which precedes a vowel or diphthong and follows the letter *r* (as in the English word *rhythm*). The smooth breathing is ignored, since it represents merely the absence of the *h* sound. If a diaeresis appears in the Greek, it also appears in transliteration. Transliterated Greek words or phrases are usually italicized unless the same words occur frequently, in which case they may be italicized at first mention and then set in roman.

11.111 **Typesetting Greek.** Authors who need to present Greek should use a Unicode-enabled font if at all possible (see 11.2). Publishers need to make sure that a Greek font is available for publication; Greek may need to be set in a slightly different size to make it visually match the surrounding type. Greek is normally not set in italics. Extra white space must occasionally be added where more than one diacritic appears over a vowel.

TABLE 11.4. Greek alphabet (and Unicode numbers) and romanization

Name of letter	Greek alphabet (and Unicode numbers)	Transliteration
alpha	Α (0391), α (03B1)	a
beta	Β (0392), β (03B2)	b
gamma	Γ (0393), γ[1] (03B3)	g
delta	Δ (0394), δ[2] (03B4)	d
epsilon	Ε (0395), ε (03B5)	e
zeta	Ζ (0396), ζ (03B6)	z
eta	Η (0397), η (03B7)	ē (0113)
theta	Θ (0398), θ[3] (03B8)	th
iota	Ι (0399), ι (03B9)	i
kappa	Κ (039A), κ (03BA)	k
lambda	Λ (039B), λ (03BB)	l
mu	Μ (039C), μ (03BC)	m
nu	Ν (039D), ν (03BD)	n
xi	Ξ (039E), ξ (03BE)	x
omicron	Ο (039F), ο (03BF)	o
pi	Π (03A0), π (03C0)	p
rho	Ρ (03A1), ρ (03C1)	r; *initially*, rh; *double*, rrh
sigma	Σ (03A3), σ (03C3), ς[4] (03C2)	s
tau	Τ (03A4), τ (03C4)	t
upsilon	Υ (03A5), υ (03C5)	u; *often* y, *exc. after* a, e, ē, i
phi	Φ (03A6), φ[5] (03C6)	ph
chi	Χ (03A7), χ (03C7)	kh, ch
psi	Ψ (03A8), ψ (03C8)	ps
omega	Ω (03A9), ω (03C9)	ō (014D)

[1] Note that γγ becomes ng, and γκ becomes nk.
[2] Sometimes incorrectly appears as ∂ (U+2202, partial differential).
[3] Also ϑ (U+03D1). [4] Final letter. [5] Also ϕ (U+03D5).

Breathings and Accents

11.112 **Greek breathing marks.** When Greek is set in the Greek alphabet, every initial vowel or diphthong or rho must be marked with a breathing, either rough (῾, dasia) or smooth (᾿, psili). The breathing mark is placed over the initial lowercase vowel (or the second vowel of a diphthong). It is positioned to the left of capital letters. Note that a single quotation mark cannot function as a breathing because it is the wrong size and does not sit close enough to the letter.

αὖτε ἕτεραι Ἕλλην ἥβη Ἶρις ὑπέχω ὠκύς ῥᾴδιος

11.113 **Greek accent marks.** There are three Greek accent marks: acute, or oxia (´); circumflex, or perispomeni, either tilde-shaped or rounded (˜ or ˆ),

depending on the typeface; and grave, or varia (`). Accents in Greek occur only over vowels. The circumflex occurs only on the two final syllables of a word. The grave accent occurs only on the last syllable. Like breathings, accents are placed over lowercase vowels, over the second vowel of a diphthong, and to the left of capital vowels. A diaeresis is used to indicate that two successive vowels do not form a diphthong but are voiced separately (as in French *naïf*).

11.114 **Unaccented Greek words.** With two exceptions, all Greek words are marked with accents—usually one, occasionally two (see below). The first exception is a group of monosyllabic words called proclitics, which are closely connected with the words following them. The proclitics are the forms of the definite article ὁ, ἡ, οἱ, αἱ; the prepositions εἰς, ἐν, ἐκ (ἐξ); the conjunctions εἰ, ὡς; and the adverb οὐ (οὐκ, οὐχ). The second exception is a group called enclitics, short words pronounced as if part of the word preceding them. Enclitics usually lose their accents (Ἀρταξερξῆς τε), and in certain circumstances the word preceding them gains a second accent (φοβεῖταί τις).

11.115 **Greek vowels.** Vowels complete with breathing marks and accents, in all combinations, are an integral part of every Greek font used in publishing. Each font, for example, should be able to provide, for lowercase eta, η, ή, ῆ, ὴ, ἠ, ἡ, ἤ, ἢ, ἥ, ἣ, ἦ, ἧ, and, for uppercase eta, Η, Ἠ, Ἡ, Ἤ, Ἢ, Ἥ, Ἣ, Ἦ, Ἧ. Additional symbols are needed for scholarly works treating ancient manuscripts or papyri. Consult the latest Unicode character charts for Greek alphabets.

Punctuation and Numbers

11.116 **Greek punctuation.** In Greek the period and comma are the same as in English; the colon and semicolon are both represented by a midlevel dot (·); the question mark is represented by a semicolon. The apostrophe (which looks almost like a smooth breathing mark) is used as an elision mark when the final vowel of one word is elided before a second word beginning with a vowel. In English texts, quoted words or passages in the Greek alphabet, of whatever length, should not be enclosed in quotation marks.

11.117 **Greek numbers.** Numbers, when not written out, are represented in ordinary Greek text by the letters of the alphabet, supplemented by three additional, obsolete Greek letters—stigma, koppa, and sampi: ϛʹ = 6, ϙʹ = 90, ϡʹ = 900. The diacritical mark resembling a prime (and defined for

TABLE 11.5. Greek numerals

1	αʹ	13	ιγʹ	30	λʹ	600	χʹ
2	βʹ	14	ιδʹ	40	μʹ	700	ψʹ
3	γʹ	15	ιεʹ	50	νʹ	800	ωʹ
4	δʹ	16	ιϛʹ	60	ξʹ	900	ϡʹ[3]
5	εʹ	17	ιζʹ	70	οʹ	1,000	͵α
6	ϛʹ[1]	18	ιηʹ	80	πʹ	2,000	͵β
7	ζʹ	19	ιθʹ	90	ϙʹ[2]	3,000	͵γ
8	ηʹ	20	κʹ	100	ρʹ	4,000	͵δ
9	θʹ	21	καʹ	200	σʹ	10,000	͵ι
10	ιʹ	22	κβʹ	300	τʹ	100,000	͵ρ
11	ιαʹ	23	κγʹ	400	υʹ		
12	ιβʹ	24	κδʹ	500	φʹ		

[1] Stigma (U+03DB); also represented with digamma (U+03DD): ϝʹ.
[2] Archaic koppa (U+03D9); also represented with koppa (U+03DF): ϟʹ.
[3] Sampi (U+03E1); formerly disigma (double sigma).

Unicode as the Greek numeral sign, U+0374) distinguishes the letters as numerals and is added to such a letter standing alone or to the last sign in a series. For example, ριαʹ means 111. For thousands, the foregoing letters are used with a different diacritical mark (the Greek lower numeral sign, U+0375): ͵α = 1,000, ͵αριαʹ = 1,111, ͵βσκβʹ = 2,222. See table 11.5.

Word Division

11.118 **Greek word division—consecutive vowels.** Diphthongs (αι, αυ, ει, ευ, ηυ, οι, ου, υι, ωυ) are never divided. But two consecutive vowels that do not form a diphthong are divided.

θε-ά-ο-μαι υἱ-ός παύ-ε-τε νε-ώς

11.119 **Greek word division—single consonants.** When a single consonant occurs between two vowels, the word is divided before the consonant.

φω-νή κε-φα-λίς μέ-γα δέ-δω-κεν μή-τηρ

11.120 **Greek word division—two or more consonants.** If a consonant is doubled, or if a mute is followed by its corresponding aspirate (πφ, βφ, κχ, γχ, τθ, δθ), the word is divided after the first consonant.

θά-λασ-σα　　συγ-χαί-ρω

If the combination of two or more consonants begins with a liquid (λ, ρ) or a nasal (μ, ν), division is made after the liquid or nasal.

ἔμ-προ-σθεν　　(*but before* μν: μέ-μνημαι)

All other combinations of two or more consonants *follow* the division.

πρᾶ-γμα	τέ-χνη	βα-θμός	αἰ-σχρός
βι-βλί-ον	δά-κτυ-λος	σκῆ-πτρον	βά-κτρον

11.121 **Greek word division—compounds.** Compound words are divided between parts; within each part the rules detailed elsewhere in this section apply. The commonest type of compound word begins with a preposition or a prefix.

ἀμφ-	ἀφ-	ὑπ-	ἐξ-έβαλον
ἀν-	ἐφ-	ὑφ-	καθ-ίστημι
ἀπ-	κατ-		δύσ-μορφος

Old English and Middle English

11.122 **Special characters in Old and Middle English.** Several Old English or Middle English letters not used in modern English occur in both lowercase and capital forms (see also table 11.1).

Ð ð　edh or eth
Þ þ　thorn

Both edh and thorn represent voiced or unvoiced *th*, as in *them* or *three*.

Ȝ ȝ　Yogh; occurs in Old English representing *g* as in *good*, *y* as in *year*, or *gh* as in *light* and *thought*. Yogh sometimes occurs in Middle English representing *y* as in *year* and *gh* as in *light* and *thought*, but normally not *g* as in *good*.
Æ æ　Ligature; should *not* be printed as two letters in Old English names and text (Ælfric).

Authors should use the correct Unicode characters for the ligature and for edh, thorn, and yogh, and should provide their publisher with a list of these and any other special characters (see 11.2). For the long *s* (ſ), see 13.7.

11.123 **Ampersand and wynn.** In Old English and Middle English texts a sort of stylized seven (the Tironian *et*) may be found for *and*, but the modern ampersand may be substituted for this. In Old English texts Ƿ or ƿ (wynn) is found for *w*; the modern *w* is often substituted for this.

11.124 **Old English vowels.** Modern editors of Old English sometimes distinguish between long and short vowels and diphthongs by means of a macron over the long versions (e.g., *ā*, *ǣ*, *ē*, *ēa*, *ēo*, *ī*, *īo*, *ō*, *ū*, *ȳ*). Note that, with the exception of the *æ* ligature, diphthongs are usually marked with a macron over only the first vowel.

American Sign Language (ASL)

11.125 **Signed languages.** The visual-gestural languages used by deaf people in different parts of the world are called signed languages. Signed languages are quite different from spoken languages (although there may be regional effects of language contact), and a particular signed language may or may not share the same national or geographic boundaries as spoken languages in the same locations. The individual elements of these languages are known as signs.

11.126 **Components of signs.** Signs have five major articulatory components—handshape, location, orientation, movement, and (in some cases) distinctive nonmanual signals.

11.127 **Writing ASL.** Many formal systems for writing signed languages exist; however, none has been adopted for widespread use by deaf signers. This section offers an overview of some of the most frequently employed conventions for written transcription of signing. For additional resources, see Charlotte Baker-Shenk and Dennis Cokely, *American Sign Language: A Teacher's Resource Text on Grammar and Culture*; and Clayton Valli, Ceil Lucas, Kristin J. Mulrooney, and Miako Villanueva, *Linguistics of American Sign Language: An Introduction* (bibliog. 5).

11.128 **Glosses in ASL.** The written-language transcription of a sign is called a *gloss*. Glosses are words from the spoken language written in small capital letters: WOMAN, SCHOOL, CAT. (Alternatively, regular capital letters may be used.) When two or more written words are used to gloss a single sign, the glosses are separated by hyphens. The translation is enclosed in double quotation marks.

The sign for "a car drove by" is written as VEHICLE-DRIVE-BY.

One obvious limitation of the use of glosses from the spoken/written language to represent signs is that there is no one-to-one correspondence between the words or signs in any two languages.

11.129 **Compound signs.** Some combinations of signs have taken on a meaning separate from the meaning of the individual signs. Various typographical conventions are used to indicate these compounds, including a "close-up" mark or a plus sign. Depending on the transcription system, the sign for "parents" might be glossed as follows:

MOTHER⁀FATHER *or* MOTHER+FATHER

11.130 **Fingerspelling.** For proper nouns and other words borrowed from the spoken language, the signer may fingerspell the word, using the handshapes from a manual alphabet. (There are numerous fingerspelling alphabets used by different signed languages, among them the American Manual Alphabet.) Fingerspelled words may be transcribed in any of the following ways:

fs-JOHN *or* J-O-H-N *or* j-o-h-n

11.131 **Lexicalized signs.** Over time, some fingerspelled words have taken on the quality of distinct signs, either by omission of some of the individual letter signs or by a change in the orientation or movement of the letter signs. These lexicalized signs are represented by the "pound" symbol (#): #WHAT, #BACK, #DO.

11.132 **Handshapes.** Most of the handshapes of American Sign Language are described by the corresponding alphabetic or numerical handshape or a variation thereof. For example, APPLE is made with an X handshape; CREATE is made with a 4 handshape; ANY is made with an Open A handshape; YELL is made with a Bent 5 handshape. Handshapes without a clear relative in the fingerspelling or number system are labeled idiosyncratically according to the transcription system in use. For example, SARCASTIC is made with the HORNS handshape; AIRPLANE is made with the ILY handshape. Handshapes for signed languages that do not use the American Manual Alphabet are often described in relation to the ASL handshapes.

11.133 **Transcriptions of signed sentences.** Signed sentences are written as a sequence of glosses, often with the spoken/written-language translation underneath in italics or quotation marks or both. (For examples, see 11.134, 11.135.) Punctuation is generally omitted from sentence transcriptions (though not from the translations). Some writers, however, add question marks and exclamation points, and a comma may be used to indicate a short pause in the sentence.

11.134 **Pronouns, possessives, and reference.** Pronouns are commonly transcribed either as IX (since these are frequently produced with the "index" finger) or as PRO. Either of these is followed by indication of person and sometimes number. A similar convention is used with the possessive marker, sometimes glossed as POSS. There are varying conventions about how to indicate person and number. Thus, a third-person singular pronoun in ASL (equivalent to English "he," "she," or "it") might be glossed as IX$_{3p}$, IX-3p, or PRO.3. A second-person plural pronoun could be glossed as IX$_{2p\text{-}pl}$. Subscript indices are often used to show signs articulated in the same location or to indicate coreferential noun phrases. The following example indicates that *he* and *his* refer back to the same person:

IX$_{3pi}$ LOSE POSS$_{3pi}$ HOUSE
He lost his house.

11.135 **Nonmanual signals.** Nonmanual gestures may be labeled based on anatomical behavior or grammatical interpretive function. These gestures, indicated by various abbreviations and terms, are typeset in a smaller font followed by a half-point rule above the ASL sentence. For example, the label *whq* is commonly used to refer to the facial expression that marks questions involving "who," "what," "when," "where," "how," or "why." This expression consists of a cluster of features that include furrowed brows and slightly squinted eyes. In the example below, *whq* occurs over the entire question (i.e., the expression is articulated simultaneously with all of the manual signs over which the line extends). In the same example, the label *t* indicates a topic marker that occurs simultaneously with the sign YESTERDAY. Correct alignment is critical to an accurate transcription.

t ___________ *whq* ___________
YESTERDAY, fs-JOHN SEE WHO
Whom did John see yesterday?

12 · Mathematics in Type

Overview

12.1 **Additional resources for math.** This chapter is mainly intended to provide guidance to authors and editors working in the sciences who have occasional need to compose or edit mathematical expressions. Those who work extensively with mathematics should consult Ellen Swanson's *Mathematics into Type*, among the other sources listed in bibliog. 2.4.

12.2 **Tools for math.** Many authors in mathematics and related quantitative fields prepare their manuscripts in LaTeX, a freely available, device-independent document markup and preparation system developed in the 1980s. In LaTeX, which is designed to work with the TeX typesetting system developed by Donald Knuth, a properly coded manuscript will generate equation numbers, cross-references, and many other elements automatically. Manuscript editors working with LaTeX documents (even on paper) should have some understanding of how the markup works to avoid, for example, marking unnecessary changes or instructions and to know when a particular change can be indicated globally. A good place to start for more information is the LaTeX website. Manuscripts that include only the occasional in-line or displayed expression, on the other hand, are usually prepared using a word processor's equation editor. For the role of MathML, a markup language that complements HTML by describing the content and structure of mathematical notation for publication in electronic formats, consult the latest version of the standard from the World Wide Web Consortium.[1] For marking mathematical copy on paper manuscripts, see 12.61–68.

Style of Mathematical Expressions

General Usage

12.3 **Standards for mathematical copy.** The author and editor should give careful attention to matters of style, usage, sense, meaning, clarity, accuracy, and consistency. Authors should use correct terminology and

1. MathML, together with alternative text, can enhance accessibility for readers who use text-to-speech and related tools. Publishers are encouraged to consult the guidelines offered by the Web Accessibility Initiative (WAI) of the World Wide Web Consortium (W3C) and, for EPUB (a standard format for e-books), the Accessibility Guidelines available from the International Digital Publishing Forum.

notation and should carefully follow the conventions of their special fields. In most cases, an author's preferences should prevail, though editors should query any apparent typographical or grammatical violations. As a general rule, mathematical copy, including displayed expressions, should "read" as clearly and grammatically as any other kind of copy. The signs for simple mathematical operations and relations have direct verbal translations: $a < b$ reads "a is less than b"; $a > b$ reads "a is greater than b"; $a + b = c$ reads "a plus b equals c." The translation is not always straightforward, however, as is the case with $df(x)/dx$, which means "the derivative of the function f of x with respect to x" and is not the quotient of two numbers $df(x)$ and dx. Moreover, mathematical notation is often abbreviated: the pair of inequalities $a < b$ and $b < c$ is usually written $a < b < c$. In mathematics it is also standard to read terms with indices, such as x_i ("x sub i"), as plural or singular depending on the context (e.g., "for a unique x_i" and "for all the x_i" are both grammatically correct). Use this convention wherever possible to avoid ugly mixtures of italic mathematics and roman "s" in forming a plural.

12.4 **Consistency of mathematical notation.** The letters and other symbols used to denote mathematical objects should be consistent and unambiguous: the same symbol should denote the same thing whenever it occurs and not be used for more than one thing. Typographical distinctions should also be made consistently; for example, if uppercase italic letters A, B, and C are used to denote sets and lowercase italic letters x, y, and z to denote the elements of sets, then a, b, and c should not be used for sets at another place without good reason.

12.5 **Words versus mathematical symbols in text.** In general, mathematical symbols may be used in text in lieu of words, and such statements as "$x \geq 0$" should not be rewritten as "x is greater than or equal to zero." Nonetheless, symbols should not be used as a shorthand for words if the result is awkward or ungrammatical. In the phrase

the vectors $r_1, \ldots, r_n, \neq 0$,

the condition "$\neq 0$" is better expressed in words:

the nonzero vectors $r_1, \ldots, r_n$

or

the vectors $r_1, \ldots, r_n$, all nonzero,

depending on the emphasis desired. Moreover, logical symbols should generally not appear in text:

> $\exists$ a minimum value of the function f on the interval $[a, b]$

should be replaced by

> there exists a minimum value of the function f on the interval $[a, b]$

or

> the function f has a minimum value on the interval $[a, b]$.

See also 12.7.

12.6 **Concise mathematical expression.** Mathematical symbols should not be used superfluously. For example, in the first statement the symbol n is extraneous, as are the parentheses in the second statement:

> There is no integer n between 0 and 1.
> This quantity is bounded above by the sum $(a + b)$.

As a general rule, no letter standing for a mathematical object should be used only once. Symbols that appear to be redundant may be qualified later in the same discussion, however, and editors should never delete a symbol without explicit instruction from the author.

12.7 **Sentence beginning with a mathematical symbol.** Mathematical symbols should not begin a sentence, especially if the preceding sentence ended with a symbol, since it may be difficult to tell where one sentence ends and another begins. For example, it is difficult to read

> Assume that $x \in S$. S is countable.

If a sentence starting with a symbol cannot easily be rephrased, the appropriate term for the symbol can be inserted in apposition at the beginning of the sentence:

> Assume that $x \in S$. The set S is countable.

If the sentences are closely related, a semicolon may be used to connect them:

A function f is even if $f(-x) = f(x)$; f is odd if $f(-x) = -f(x)$.

12.8 **Adjacent mathematical symbols.** Mathematical symbols in adjacent mathematical expressions should be separated by words or punctuation (or both), for the reasons discussed in 12.7:

Suppose that $a = bq + r$, where $0 \leq r < b$.

Signs and Symbols

12.9 **Mathematical characters.** The smallest units of mathematical writing are mathematical signs and symbols, which include letters and numbers. Table 12.1 lists some of the standard mathematical characters and their verbal translations. Unicode numbers are included, where applicable (see also 11.2), as are the LaTeX commands for producing each character. Old-style figures [like this: 1938] should be avoided in mathematical contexts because their height and position relative to the baseline is inconsistent and because, in some typefaces, a zero might be mistaken for an oh; lining figures [like this: 1938] should be used instead (see also 3.86, item 4).

12.10 **Diacritical and other marks in mathematical notation.** Ordinary italic letters are used to represent various kinds of mathematical objects. The set of distinct symbols can be greatly extended by the use of diacritics (including accents), such as $\hat{a}$, $\tilde{a}$, $\bar{a}$, $\check{a}$, $\dot{a}$, $\ddot{a}$, $\breve{a}$, and $\vec{a}$. (Note that when an *i* or a *j* appears with a diacritical mark—e.g., with an overbar or a circumflex—the dotless *i* or *j* should be used.) Double diacritics may also be used; for example, $\bar{\bar{a}}$, and $\bar{\dot{a}}$. Marks over or beneath several letters or groups of letters—for example, overlines, underlines, overbraces, and underbraces—are frequently encountered in mathematics, as are other types of stacked expressions.

12.11 **Italic letters and kerning in mathematical expressions.** Contiguous italic letters that represent separate objects must never be kerned. To this end fonts intended for mathematics are typically designed so that italic letters are less slanted than they might otherwise be (and, therefore, unlikely to crowd or overlap other typeset elements). Contiguous letters that form an abbreviation—for example, "Aut" for "automorphism group"—should be set roman; see also 12.17.

12.12 **Letters and fonts in mathematical notation.** The number of symbols can be extended by using letters from other alphabets, most often the

TABLE 12.1. Common mathematical signs and symbols (with Unicode numbers and LaTeX commands)

Sign/symbol	Name	Unicode	LaTeX
OPERATIONS			
$+$	Plus sign	002B	+
$-$	Minus sign	2212	-
$\times$	Multiplication sign	00D7	\times
$\cdot$	Dot operator (multiplication)	22C5	\cdot
$\div$	Division sign	00F7	\div
$/$	Division slash	2215	/[a]
$\circ$	Ring operator (composition)	2218	\circ
$\cup$	Union	222A	\cup
$\cap$	Intersection	2229	\cap
$\pm$	Plus or minus	00B1	\pm
$\mp$	Minus or plus	2213	\mp
$\ast$	Asterisk operator (convolution)	2217	\ast
$\circledast$	Circled asterisk operator (convolution)	229B	\circledast
$\oplus$	Circled plus (direct sum, various)	2295	\oplus
$\ominus$	Circled minus (various)	2296	\ominus
$\otimes$	Circled times (various)	2297	\otimes
$\odot$	Circled dot operator (various)	2299	\odot
$:$	Ratio	2236	:
$\amalg$	Coproduct or amalgamation	2210	\amalg
RELATIONS			
$=$	Equals sign	003D	=
$\neq$	Not equal to	2260	\neq
$\approx$	Almost equal to, asymptotic to	2248	\approx
$\cong$	Approximately equal to, isomorphic to	2245	\approxeq
$<$	Less than	003C	<
$\ll$	Much less than	226A	\ll
$>$	Greater than	003E	>
$\gg$	Much greater than	226B	\gg
$\leq$	Less than or equal to	2264	\leq
$\geq$	Greater than or equal to	2265	\geq
$\equiv$	Identical to, congruent to	2261	\equiv
$\not\equiv$	Not identical to, not congruent to	2262	\nequiv
$\mid$	Divides, divisible by	2223	\divides
$\sim$	Tilde operator (similar to, asymptotically equal to)	223C	\sim
$\coloneqq$	Colon equals (assignment)	2254	\coloneqq
$\in$	Element of	2208	\in
$\notin$	Not an element of	2209	\notin
$\subset$	Subset of	2282	\subset
$\subseteq$	Subset of or equal to	2286	\subseteq
$\supset$	Superset of	2283	\supset
$\supseteq$	Superset of or equal to	2287	\supseteq
$\propto$	Proportional to	221D	\propto
$\doteq$	Approaches the limit, definition	2250	\doteq
$\rightarrow$	Tends to, maps to	2192	\rightarrow

TABLE 12.1. *(continued)*

Sign/symbol	Name	Unicode	LaTeX
←	Maps from	2190	\leftarrow
↦	Maps to	21A6	\mapsto
↪	Maps into	21AA	\hookrightarrow
↩	Maps into	21A9	\hookleftarrow
OPERATORS			
∑	Summation	2211	\sum
∏	Product	220F	\prod
∫	Integral	222B	\int
∮	Contour integral	222E	\oint
LOGIC			
∧	And, conjunction	2227	\wedge
∨	Or, disjunction	2228	\vee
¬	Not sign (negation)	00AC	\neg
⇒	Implies	21D2	\implies
→	Implies	2192	\rightarrow
⇔	If and only if	21D4	\iff
↔	If and only if	2194	\leftrightarrow
∃	There exists (existential quantifier)	2203	\exists
∀	For all (universal quantifier)	2200	\forall
⊦	Assertion	22A6	\vdash
∴	Hence, therefore	2234	\therefore
∵	Because	2235	\because
RADIAL UNITS			
′	Minute (prime)	2032	\prime
″	Second (double prime)	2033	\second
°	Degree	00B0	\degree
CONSTANTS			
π	Pi (≈3.14159265)	03C0	\pi
e	Base of natural logarithms (≈2.71828183)	0065	e
GEOMETRY			
⊥	Perpendicular to (up tack)	22A5	\perp
∥	Parallel to	2225	\parallel
∦	Not parallel to	2226	\nparallel
∠	Angle	2220	\angle
∢	Spherical angle	2222	\sphericalangle
≚	Equiangular to	225A	\veedoublebar
MISCELLANEOUS			
i	Square root of −1	0069	i
′	Prime	2032	\prime
″	Double prime	2033	\second
‴	Triple prime	2034	\third
√	Square root, radical	221A	\sqrt
∛	Cube root	221B	\sqrt[3]

(continued)

TABLE 12.1. *(continued)*

Sign/symbol	Name	Unicode	LaTeX
!	Factorial	0021	!
‼	Double factorial	203C	!!
∅	Empty set, null set	2205	\varnothing[b]
∞	Infinity	221E	\infty
∂	Partial differential	2202	\partial
Δ	Increment, Laplace operator	2206	\triangle
∇	Nabla, del; also Laplace operator (with superscript 2)	2207	\nabla
□	d'Alembert operator (white square)	25A1	\square

NOTE: Though there are generic characters that appear similar to the ones listed in the table (e.g., asterisk [002A] for asterisk operator), the mathematical versions are preferred because they encode correct intersymbol spacing.
[a] LaTeX also defines \slash, which permits a line break after the slash.
[b] Also \emptyset.

Greek alphabet, and by representing letters from the Latin alphabet in other fonts. Examples of characters from four fonts commonly used in mathematics include the following:

Greek	*Script*	*Boldface italic*	*Boldface Greek*
ΑΒΓΔαβγδ	$\mathcal{ABCD}abcd$	***ABCDabcd***	**ΑΒΓΔαβγδ**

Lowercase script characters are often not available for a given typeface, though they have been defined for the mathematical alphabets in Unicode (see also 11.2). See also 12.65 for marking fonts on paper manuscripts.

12.13 **List of unusual mathematical characters.** Special characters specific to mathematics will generally not be available in all typefaces. Even some of the more common characters may need to be checked for availability or inadvertent substitution (e.g., letter *a* for Greek alpha, α). For electronic publication formats, special fonts may need to be embedded (and licensed accordingly). It may be advisable, therefore, to prepare a list of unusual mathematical signs, symbols, and special characters used in the manuscript, before editing begins. This is preferably done by the author but may be done by the editor. In preparing an electronic manuscript, the author should make a list of any special, nonstandard fonts. A copy should be given to the publisher, who will check to make sure the necessary characters are available for the intended publication formats. If some are not, the author may be asked to use more accessible forms; if that is impossible, the typesetter must be asked to obtain or generate the characters needed.

12.14 **Special mathematical symbols.** Many mathematical symbols have a reserved meaning: π stands for the number 3.14159265 . . . , e for the number 2.71828182 . . . , and i for the square root of −1. The symbols $\forall$, $\exists$, $\in$, $\subset$, and $\emptyset$ are used in all mathematical disciplines. Double-struck (blackboard) symbols are reserved for familiar systems of numbers: $\mathbb{N}$ for the natural numbers, $\mathbb{Z}$ for the integers ($\mathbb{Z}^+$ is the same as $\mathbb{N}$), $\mathbb{Q}$ for the rational numbers, $\mathbb{R}$ for the real numbers, and $\mathbb{C}$ for the complex numbers.

12.15 **Signs for binary operations and relations.** *Binary operations* act as conjunctions to combine two mathematical expressions. Examples of binary operation signs are + (plus sign), − (minus sign), · (multiplication dot), × (multiplication cross), ÷ (division sign), / (solidus or slash), and ∘ (composition sign). *Binary relations* act as verbs and express a relationship between two mathematical expressions. Examples of relation signs are = (equals), ≠ (does not equal), > (is greater than), and < (is less than).

12.16 **Basic spacing in mathematics.** Mathematics isn't simply read left to right in a machine-like manner, and one should be able to see the parts of an equation if it is properly set. Good mathematical spacing helps to indicate grouping: things that are more closely related should be set more tightly than things that are less closely related. Such spacing will vary according to the elements being set. In simple expressions, however, absolute spacing may be called for. Signs for binary operations (i.e., conjunctions); symbols of integration, summation, or union; and signs for binary relations (i.e., verbs) are preceded and followed by medium spaces (i.e., one-fourth of an em space):

$$x^n + y^n = z^n, \qquad X \cup \emptyset = X, \qquad (a \circ b) \circ c = a \circ (b \circ c).$$

No space follows a binary operation or relation sign when it is modifying a symbol (i.e., used as an adjective):

$$-1, \qquad +\infty, \qquad \times 5, \qquad >7.$$

In subscripts anvd superscripts, no space precedes or follows operation or relation signs:

$$x^{a+b}, \qquad y^{c-2}.$$

TABLE 12.2. Standard abbreviated notations in mathematical copy

sin	Sine	sn	Elliptic function, sn
cos	Cosine	cn	Elliptic function, cn
		dn	Elliptic function, dn
tan	Tangent	tg	Tangent[a]
cot	Cotangent	ctg	Cotangent[a]
sec	Secant	csc	Cosecant
sinh	Hyperbolic sine	cosh	Hyperbolic cosine
tanh	Hyperbolic tangent	coth	Hyperbolic cotangent
$\sin^{-1}$	Inverse sine	arcsin	Inverse sine
log	Common logarithm ($\log_{10}$)	ln	Natural logarithm
lg	Binary logarithm ($\log_2$)	$\log_e$	Natural logarithm, alternate form
sgn	Sign	arg	Argument
det or Det	Determinant	Tr	Trace (also Sp, or *spur*)
Re, $\Re$	Real part	Im, $\Im$	Imaginary part
curl	Curl; vector operator, same as $\nabla \times$	div	Divergence; vector operator, same as $\nabla \cdot$
prob or Pr	Probability	mod	Modulo (as in $a \bmod b$)
inf	Infimum; greatest lower bound	sup	Supremum; least upper bound
isom	Isomorphism	Hom	Homeomorphism
min	Minimum	max	Maximum
gcd	Greatest common divisor	lcm	Least common multiple
dex	Decimal exponent; from $10^{-1.5}$ to 10^{-3} is 1.5 dex	norm	Norm; norm $(a) = \|\|a\|\|$
dim or Dim	Dimension	ker	Kernel
wrt	With respect to[b]	iff	If and only if[b]
Var or var	Variance	Cov or cov	Covariance

[a] Frequently used by non-North American authors.
[b] Used in informal notation.

Commas used between coordinate points or in lists (see 12.19) should be followed by a medium space. See also 6.120.

12.17 **Mathematical functions.** For a list of abbreviated functions, see table 12.2. These abbreviations are followed by a thin space (about one-fifth of an em space) unless the argument is enclosed in delimiters, or fences (see 12.26), in which case they are usually closed up to the opening delimiter:

$$\ln 2\pi, \qquad \sin(x + y), \qquad \min(x_1, x_2).$$

Limits are set as subscripts to the right of the abbreviation in text and below the abbreviation in display:

$$\lim_{x\to a} f(x), \quad \lim\limits_{x\to a} f(x),$$

$$\max_{a_i\in S}(a_i), \quad \max\limits_{a_i\in S}(a_i).$$

Punctuation

12.18 **Mathematical expressions and punctuation.** Mathematical expressions, whether run in with the text or displayed on a separate line, are grammatically part of the text in which they appear. Thus, expressions must be edited not only for correct presentation of the mathematical characters but also for correct grammar in the sentence. For example, if several expressions appear in a single display, they should be separated by commas or semicolons. For example,

$$\begin{aligned} x_1 + x_2 + x_3 &= 3, \\ x_1x_2 + x_2x_3 + x_3x_1 &= 6, \\ x_1x_2x_3 &= -1. \end{aligned}$$

Consecutive lines of a single multiline expression, however, should not be punctuated:

$$\begin{aligned} (|a + b|)^2 = (a + b)^2 &= a^2 + 2ab + b^2 \\ &\le a^2 + 2|a||b| + b^2 \\ &= |a|^2 + 2|a||b| + |b|^2 \\ &= (|a| + |b|)^2. \end{aligned}$$

Expressions must carry ending punctuation if they end a sentence. All ending punctuation and the commas and semicolons separating expressions should be aligned horizontally on the baseline, even when preceded by constructs such as subscripts, superscripts, or fractions.

12.19 **Elided lists in mathematical expressions.** In elided lists, commas should come after each term in the list and after the ellipsis points if the list has a final term. For example,

$$y = 0, 1, 2, \ldots \quad \text{not} \quad y = 0, 1, 2 \ldots;$$

$$x_1, x_2, \ldots, x_n \quad \text{not} \quad x_1, x_2, \ldots\ x_n.$$

The ellipsis points should be on the baseline when the terms of the list are separated by commas. Use a medium space after each comma (see also 12.16).

12.20 **Elided operations and relations.** In elided sums or elided relations, the ellipsis points should be vertically centered between the operation or relation signs. For example,

$$x_1 + x_2 + \cdots + x_n \quad \text{not} \quad x_1 + x_2 + \ldots + x_n;$$

$$a_1 < a_2 < \cdots < a_n \quad \text{not} \quad a_1 < a_2 < \ldots < a_n.$$

Multiplication is often signified by the juxtaposition of the factors without a multiplication sign between them. That is,

$$abc \quad \text{means} \quad a \cdot b \cdot c.$$

When the multiplication sign is not explicit, the elided product may be denoted with ellipsis points either on the baseline or vertically centered:

$$a_1a_2\ldots a_n \quad \text{or} \quad a_1a_2\cdots a_n.$$

The second alternative is commonly used in displays with built-up factors:

$$\phi(n) = n\left(1 - \frac{1}{p_1}\right)\left(1 - \frac{1}{p_2}\right)\cdots\left(1 - \frac{1}{p_k}\right).$$

If the multiplication dot is present, then ellipsis points should be on the baseline and not centered. For example,

$$a_1 \cdot a_2 \cdot \ldots \cdot a_n \quad \text{not} \quad a_1 \cdot a_2 \cdot \cdots \cdot a_n.$$

If the multiplication cross is present, then ellipsis points should be centered. For example,

$$a_1 \times a_2 \times \cdots \times a_n.$$

Multiplication signs are always used when the factors need to be separated:

$$1 \times 2 \times \cdots \times 10.$$

In some contexts (such as for numbers) the use of the multiplication cross rather than the dot is a matter of preference, but in many other contexts (such as for vectors) multiplication dots and crosses have different meanings and cannot be used interchangeably.

Mathematical Expressions in Display

12.21 **Displaying mathematical expressions.** Mathematical expressions should be *displayed*—that is, set on a separate line clear of text—if they are important to the exposition, if they are referenced, or if they are difficult to read or typeset in the body of the text. If different mathematical expressions are displayed on the same line, the expressions should be separated by spacing, together with words or punctuation:

If $a = b$, then for all real numbers x,

$$a + x = b + x, \qquad ax = bx, \qquad -a = -b.$$

If different mathematical expressions are displayed on separate consecutive lines, regardless of whether there is an intervening word between two of the equations, each expression can usually be center aligned, as in the first example in 12.18. Some groups of displayed expressions will be easier to read if they are aligned on an equals sign or other relational sign:

If $a = b$, then for all real numbers x,

$$\begin{aligned} a + x &= b + x, \\ ax &= bx, \\ -a &= -b. \end{aligned}$$

For another example, see 12.22.

12.22 **Qualifying clauses for displayed mathematical expressions.** Qualifying clauses may be presented in several ways. If the main expression is displayed, the qualifying clause may also be displayed (separated from the expression by an em space or more):

If f is a constant function, then

$$f'(a) = 0 \quad \text{for all } a \in \mathbb{R}.$$

The qualifying clause may instead appear in the text, following the displayed main expression:

Suppose that the prime factorization of the integer a is given by

$$a = p_1^{k_1} \cdots p_r^{k_r},$$

where the p_i are distinct prime numbers and $k_i > 0$.

Or it may precede the displayed main expression:

For all real numbers a and b,

$$|a + b| \leq |a| + |b|.$$

And qualifying clauses may themselves include displayed expressions:

Suppose that assumptions 1 and 2 hold. Then a competitive equilibrium satisfies the following three differential equations:

$$\frac{\dot{c}(t)}{c(t)} = \frac{1}{\theta}[(1-\alpha_1)\gamma\eta(t)^{1/\varepsilon}\lambda(t)^{\alpha_1}\kappa(t)^{-\alpha_1}\chi(t)^{-\alpha_1} - \delta - \rho] - \frac{m_1}{\alpha_1},$$

$$\frac{\dot{\chi}(t)}{\chi(t)} = \lambda(t)^{\alpha_1}\kappa(t)^{1-\alpha_1}\chi(t)^{-\alpha_1}\eta(t) - \chi(t)^{-1}c(t) - \delta - n - \frac{m_1}{\alpha_1},$$

$$\frac{\dot{\kappa}(t)}{\kappa(t)} = \frac{[1-\kappa(t)]\{\Delta[\dot{\chi}(t)/\chi(t)] + m_2 - (\alpha_2/\alpha_1)m_1\}}{(1-\varepsilon)^{-1} + \Delta[\kappa(t) - \lambda(t)]},$$

where

$$\eta(t) \equiv \gamma^{\varepsilon/(\varepsilon-1)}\left\{1 + \left(\frac{1-\alpha_1}{1-\alpha_2}\right)\left[\frac{1-\kappa(t)}{\kappa(t)}\right]\right\}^{\varepsilon/(\varepsilon-1)},$$

with initial conditions $\chi(0)$ and $\kappa(0)$, and also satisfies the transversality condition

$$\lim_{t\to\infty} \exp\left\{-\left[\rho - \frac{(1-\theta)m_1}{\alpha_1} - n\right]t\right\}\chi(t) = 0.$$

12.23 **Breaking displayed mathematical expressions.** Even in displayed form, some long expressions will not fit on one line. In such cases, displayed expressions may be broken before a relation or operation sign. Such signs include the following:

Operation signs (conjunctions): $+ - \times \div \pm \cup \cap$
Relation signs (verbs): $= \neq > < \geq \leq \rightarrow \supset \subset \in \cong \equiv$

See table 12.1 for a more complete list. In displayed expressions, runover lines are aligned on the relation signs, which should be followed by thick spaces (i.e., one-third of an em space):

$$\begin{aligned} h(x) &= (x-\alpha)(x-\beta)(x-\gamma) \\ &= x^3 - (\alpha+\beta+\gamma)x^2 + (\alpha\beta+\alpha\gamma+\beta\gamma)x - \alpha\beta\gamma. \end{aligned}$$

If a runover line begins with an operation sign, the operation sign should be lined up with the first character to the right of the relation sign in the line above it, followed by a medium space (one-fourth of an em space):

$$\begin{aligned} \frac{\pi}{4} = {} & \frac{1}{2} - \frac{1}{3\times 2^3} + \frac{1}{5\times 2^5} - \frac{1}{7\times 2^7} + \frac{1}{9\times 2^9} - \frac{1}{11\times 2^{11}} + \cdots \\ & + \frac{1}{3} - \frac{1}{3\times 3^3} + \frac{1}{5\times 3^5} - \frac{1}{7\times 3^7} + \frac{1}{9\times 3^9} - \cdots \\ & + \frac{1}{4} - \frac{1}{3\times 4^3} + \frac{1}{5\times 4^5} - \frac{1}{7\times 4^7} + \cdots. \end{aligned}$$

For additional rules on breaking expressions, consult Ellen Swanson, *Mathematics into Type* (bibliog. 2.4).

Numeration

12.24 **Numbering displayed mathematical expressions.** Mathematical expressions that are referred to elsewhere in the text should be numbered or otherwise labeled. All numbered mathematical expressions must be displayed. Displayed expressions are usually centered on the line (without regard to the expression number or label). The number or label, enclosed in parentheses to prevent misreading, is usually put at the right margin, but it may be placed at the left margin.

Hence it is apparent that

$$1^3 + 2^3 + \cdots + n^3 = (1 + 2 + \cdots + n)^2. \tag{1.1}$$

In cross-references, display numbers or labels are enclosed in parentheses to match the marginal enumerations:

Recalling equation (1.1), we may conclude that . . .
or
Recalling (1.1), we may conclude that . . .

A range of numbered equations is referred to by giving the first and last numbers, joined by an en dash:

From equations (2)–(5) we obtain . . .

12.25 **Methods of numeration for mathematical expressions.** Displayed mathematical expressions may be numbered or labeled, as may definitions, theorems, lemmas, and other formal parts of the exposition. A simple numbering system offers a convenient and space-saving method of cross-reference. In texts with many displayed equations, double or triple numeration is usually preferred. In this system, the displayed expressions in each chapter are labeled with the chapter number first, followed by the section number (if any), followed by the statement number, starting with number 1 (1.1.1, 1.1.2, . . . , 1.2.1, 1.2.2, . . . , etc.). If, on the other hand, single numeration is used (e.g., in a text with relatively few displayed equations), the displays are still usually numbered starting over with 1 in each chapter. In a work with many such numbered statements, it is helpful to the reader to number them together, in a single sequence, but apart from displayed equations (e.g., definition 4.1, lemma 4.2, lemma 4.3, proposition 4.4, corollary 4.5).

Delimiters

12.26 **Common delimiters in mathematics.** Three sorts of symbols are commonly used to group mathematical expressions: parentheses (), brackets [ ], and braces {}. They are used in pairs, and their normal order is {[()]}. When necessary, the sequence of delimiters can be extended by large parentheses, brackets, and braces as follows:

$$\Bigg\{\Bigg[\Bigg(\Big\{\Big[\Big(\quad\Big)\Big]\Big\}\Bigg)\Bigg]\Bigg\}$$

In text, the braces are sometimes omitted from this sequence. Angle brackets, vertical bars, and double vertical bars carry special mathematical significance and should not be used to supplement the sequence of common delimiters.

12.27 **Functional notation.** In functional notation, nested pairs of parentheses are used instead of brackets or braces to indicate grouping:

$$(f \circ g \circ h)(x) = f(g(h(x))).$$

12.28 **Set notation.** Braces are used to delimit the elements of a set, and other delimiters should not be substituted. For example,

$$\{a_1, a_2, \ldots, a_n\}$$

denotes the set consisting of *n* objects $a_1, a_2, \ldots, a_n$, and

$$\{x : x \in D\}$$

denotes the set of all elements *x* in a set *D*. In the second example (called "set-builder" notation), the condition that defines the set follows the colon. A vertical bar is sometimes used instead of the colon to delimit the condition.

12.29 **Ordered set notation.** In ordered set notation, parentheses are used as delimiters. For example,

$$(a, b)$$

denotes the ordered pair of objects *a* and *b*, where *a* is the first element in the pair and *b* is the second element. More generally,

$$(a_1, a_2, \ldots, a_n)$$

denotes the ordered *n*-tuple of objects a_1, a_2, . . . , a_n. This notation is standard, and other delimiters should not be substituted.

12.30 **Interval notation.** In interval notation, parentheses are used to delimit an open interval—that is, one that does not include its endpoints; for example, (a, b) denotes the set of all real numbers between *a* and *b*, not including either *a* or *b*. Brackets are used to delimit a closed interval—that is, an interval that includes its endpoints. The notation $(a, b]$ signifies the interval not including *a* but including *b*, while $[a, b)$ denotes the interval including *a* but not including *b*. Parentheses and brackets in interval notation should not be replaced with other delimiters. (According to an alternative convention, $]a, b[$ denotes an open interval, $[a, b[$ an interval that includes *a* but not *b*, etc. This should not be changed if the author has used it consistently.)

12.31 **Delimiters denoting inner product.** Parentheses are sometimes used to denote the inner product of two vectors: $(\boldsymbol{u}, \boldsymbol{w})$. Angle brackets are also used as notation for the inner product: $\langle \boldsymbol{u}, \boldsymbol{w} \rangle$. See also 12.52–55.

12.32 **Binomial coefficients.** The notation $\binom{n}{k}$, "n choose k," is called the binomial coefficient and stands for the number of ways k objects can be chosen from among a collection of n objects. It is defined by

$$\binom{n}{k} = \frac{n!}{k!(n-k)!},$$

where n and k are positive integers and the notation ! stands for the factorial function,

$$n! = n \times (n-1) \times \cdots \times 1.$$

12.33 **Vertical bars in mathematical notation.** Vertical bars serve several special purposes. The modulus or absolute value of x is denoted $|x|$. The notation $|\boldsymbol{u}|$ is used for the "length" of a vector $\boldsymbol{u}$, also sometimes called the norm of $\boldsymbol{u}$ and written with a double vertical bar, $||\boldsymbol{u}||$. Vertical bars are used to denote the cardinal number of a set. The notation $|A|$ can signify the determinant of a matrix A, which is also denoted $\det A$.

12.34 **A single vertical bar in mathematical notation.** A single vertical bar with limits is used to denote the evaluation of a formula at a particular value of one of its variables. For example,

$$\int_0^{\pi/2} \sin x \, dx = -\cos x \Big|_{x=0}^{x=\pi/2} = -\cos \pi/2 - (-\cos 0) = 1.$$

12.35 **Cases in mathematical expressions.** Displayed mathematical expressions that present a choice between alternatives, or cases, may be grouped using a single brace and are punctuated as follows:

$$|a| = \begin{cases} a, & a \geq 0; \\ -a, & a < 0. \end{cases}$$

Another acceptable style is

$$f(x) = \begin{cases} 1 & \text{if } x \geq 0, \\ 0 & \text{otherwise.} \end{cases}$$

As a general rule, each alternative is equivalent to a clause in ordinary language and should be punctuated as such. If the alternatives are very long, they may be stated as separate equations:

$$I(t) = Ae^{\Gamma_1(t-t_p)}\{1 + \varepsilon_1 \cos[2\pi f(t - t_p)]\}$$
$$+ B\{1 + \varepsilon_2 \cos[2\pi f(t - t_p)]\}, \quad t \leq t_p, \tag{1a}$$

$$I(t) = Ae^{-\Gamma_2(t-t_p)}\{1 + \varepsilon_1 \cos[2\pi f(t - t_p)]\}$$
$$+ B\{1 + \varepsilon_2 \cos[2\pi f(t - t_p)]\}, \quad t > t_p. \tag{1b}$$

Subscripts and Superscripts

12.36 **Simple mathematical subscripts and superscripts.** Inferior and superior indices, exponents, and other subscript and superscript symbols occur frequently in mathematical copy. Examples are

$$x_1, \quad x^2, \quad 2^x, \quad x', \quad x_{ij}y_{jk}, \quad x^{ab}, \quad a^x b^y, \quad x''_{12}.$$

Multiple indices are written without commas between them unless there is a possibility of confusion: x_{ij} instead of $x_{i,j}$, but $x_{1,2}$ if there is a possibility of confusing the subscripts "1,2" and "12." Abbreviations or words that serve as labels in subscripts or superscripts are usually set in roman type:

$$x_{\mathrm{min}}, \quad u_{\mathrm{av}}.$$

12.37 **Complex mathematical subscripts and superscripts.** Subscripts and superscripts may themselves have subscripts and superscripts. For example,

$$x_{a_k}, \quad x_{a_k^2}, \quad 2^{x^2}, \quad 2^{x_i^2}$$

Mathematical expressions may occur as subformulas in the superior or inferior positions. For example,

$$x^{a+b}, \quad a^{-x}b^{(y-z)^2}, \quad a_{2n}^{x'y'}, \quad 2^{\sqrt{n}}$$

12.38 **Alignment of mathematical subscripts and superscripts.** Subscripts and superscripts may be stacked

$$x_i^n, \quad x_{ij}^{mn}$$

or staggered

$$X^{ab}{}_{cd},\quad X_{ij}{}^{kl}.$$

Because there are standard conventions for raising and lowering indices in some branches of mathematics, especially in tensor calculus, the relative position between superior and inferior indices should not be changed. See also 12.54.

Summations and Integrals

12.39 **Summation sign.** The summation sign Σ is used to stand for a sum of a finite or infinite sequence of terms. For example, the sums

$$a_1 + a_2 + \cdots + a_n \quad \text{and} \quad a_1 + a_2 + \cdots$$

may be written

$$\sum_{i=1}^{n} a_i \quad \text{and} \quad \sum_{i=1}^{\infty} a_i,$$

respectively. The variable i in the expressions above is called the index of summation. The subformulas below and above the summation sign are called the limits of summation and indicate where the summation begins and, if it is finite, ends. Summation limits are sometimes omitted if it is clear from the context what the limits are; for example, if all vectors are stated to be of size n and all matrices are of size $n \times n$, it is acceptable to write

$$y_i = \sum_j a_{ij} x_j.$$

When a summation sign occurs in text, its limits are placed to the right of the summation sign to avoid spreading the lines of text: $\sum_{i=1}^{n} a_i$.

12.40 **Product sign.** Product notation follows similar conventions. The products

$$a_1 \cdot a_2 \cdot \ldots \cdot a_n \quad \text{and} \quad a_1 \cdot a_2 \cdot \ldots$$

may be written

$$\prod_{i=1}^{n} a_i \quad \text{and} \quad \prod_{i=1}^{\infty} a_i,$$

respectively, and in text the limits are placed to the right of the product symbol to avoid spreading lines: $\prod_{i=1}^{n} a_i$.

12.41 **Integral sign.** The integral sign $\int$ is used to denote two sorts of integrals, called definite and indefinite. A definite integral is the integral of a function *f* on an interval $[a, b]$. This integral is denoted

$$\int_a^b f(x)\,dx.$$

The numbers *a* and *b* are called the lower and upper limits of integration, and *dx* is called the element of integration or the differential. (The *d* in some notations is not italicized; editors can usually follow an author's preference on this matter.) The limits of integration are usually placed to the right of the integral sign in both text and display. The indefinite integral is denoted

$$\int f \quad \text{or} \quad \int f(x)\,dx,$$

without limits of integration. For a function of two variables, it is common to denote an integral over both variables by a double integral sign:

$$\iint\limits_D f(x, y)\,dx\,dy.$$

Here *D* is called the set of integration.

12.42 **Spacing around differentials.** Thin spaces (about one-fifth of an em space) are placed before and after differentials:

$$dV = r^2 \sin\theta\,dr\,d\theta\,d\phi.$$

Differential expressions appearing in derivatives must be closed up to the slash:

$$dx/dt.$$

Radicals

12.43 **Radical signs.** The radical sign √ is used to denote the square root. A horizontal bar extends from the top of the radical sign to the end of the radicand:

$$\sqrt{2},\ \sqrt{\sin^2 x + \cos^2 x}.$$

In display, the radical sign extends vertically to accommodate a built-up radicand:

$$\sqrt{\frac{\ln n}{n}}.$$

The radical sign may be used to denote cube and higher-order roots. For these roots, a superscript-sized number or letter is nested within the radical sign:

$$\sqrt[3]{5}, \quad \sqrt[n]{n!}.$$

12.44 **Radical signs in text.** Radical signs can be used in text if the radicand is a simple expression: $a = m + n\sqrt{3}$. If the radicand is more complex or if the text design uses tight leading, radical signs can give the page a crowded look or interfere with descending letters in the line above. One remedy is to substitute the appropriate exponent, using delimiters to indicate the extent of the radicand. For example,

$$\sqrt{a^2 + b^2}$$

may be replaced by

$$(a^2 + b^2)^{1/2}.$$

Fractions

12.45 **Fractions in text.** Fractions are set in text with a slash to separate the numerator and denominator:

$$1/2, \quad 2/3, \quad 1/10, \quad 97/100, \quad \pi/2, \quad 11/5, \quad a/b.$$

Some common numerical fractions may be set as case fractions (text-sized fractions with a horizontal bar):

$$\tfrac{1}{2}, \ \tfrac{2}{3}, \ \tfrac{1}{10}.$$

Fractions should be enclosed in parentheses if they are followed by a mathematical symbol or expression:

$$(a/b)x.$$

For simple algebraic fractions in text, the slash should be used rather than the horizontal fraction bar. For example,

$$(ax + b)/(cx + d) \quad \text{not} \quad \tfrac{ax+b}{cx+d}.$$

The slash connects only the two groups of symbols immediately adjacent to it. Thus, $a + b/c$ means

$$a + \frac{b}{c} \quad \text{not} \quad \frac{a+b}{c},$$

which should be written $(a + b)/c$.

12.46 **Fractions in display.** In displayed mathematical expressions, all fractions should be built up unless they are part of a numerator or denominator or in a subscript or superscript:

$$\left| x^2 \sin \frac{1}{x} \right| < \frac{1}{10} \quad \text{not} \quad |x^2 \sin \tfrac{1}{x}| < \tfrac{1}{10}.$$

Fractions that include summation, product, or integral signs should always be displayed. For example:

$$\frac{\int_0^{\pi/2} \sin^{2n} x \, dx}{\int_0^{\pi/2} \sin^{2n+1} x \, dx}.$$

If there are no built-up fractions in the display, common numerical fractions may be set as case fractions:

$$|a - b| < \tfrac{1}{10}.$$

12.47 **Fractions in subscripts and superscripts.** Fractions in subscripts and superscripts should always use the slash, both in text and in display:

$$x^{a/b}, \quad y_{3/2}.$$

12.48 **Multiple and multilevel fractions.** If a mathematical expression contains more than one fraction, it should be displayed, and the horizontal bar should be used for the principal fraction sign:

$$\frac{ax+b}{cx+d} = \frac{px+q}{rx+s}.$$

Fractions should preferably be limited to two levels:

$$\frac{(a/b)+c}{(p/q)+r} \quad \text{not} \quad \frac{\frac{a}{b}+c}{\frac{p}{q}+r}.$$

Continued fractions—that is, expressions of the form $a_1 + 1/b_1$, where $b_1 = a_2 + 1/b_2$, $b_2 = a_3 + 1/b_3$, and so on—are displayed:

$$a_1 + \cfrac{1}{a_2 + \cfrac{1}{a_3 + \cfrac{1}{a_4 + \cdots}}}.$$

12.49 **Rewriting fractions using exponents.** There are times when it is desirable to represent the denominator of a fraction without using a fraction rule or a slash. This may be done by using delimiters followed by the exponent −1:

$$ab(cd)^{-1} \quad \text{instead of} \quad \frac{ab}{cd}.$$

If there is already an exponent in the denominator, it can be changed to its negative:

$$ab(cd)^{-2} \quad \text{instead of} \quad \frac{ab}{(cd)^2}.$$

If an exponential expression, particularly in text, is very complex, it may be rewritten in a simpler form. An exponential term such as

$$e^{(2\pi i \Sigma n_j)/\sqrt{x^2+y^2}}$$

can be rewritten using the abbreviation *exp*:

$$\exp\left[\left(2\pi i \sum n_j\right)/(x^2 + y^2)^{1/2}\right]$$

Matrices and Determinants

12.50 **Matrices.** Matrices are arrays of terms displayed in rectangular arrangements of rows and columns and enclosed on the left and right by either large brackets or parentheses:

$$\begin{bmatrix} a_{11} & a_{12} & \cdots & a_{1n} \\ a_{21} & a_{22} & \cdots & a_{2n} \\ \vdots & \vdots & & \vdots \\ a_{m1} & a_{m2} & \cdots & a_{mn} \end{bmatrix} \quad \text{or} \quad \begin{pmatrix} a_{11} & a_{12} & \cdots & a_{1n} \\ a_{21} & a_{22} & \cdots & a_{2n} \\ \vdots & \vdots & & \vdots \\ a_{m1} & a_{m2} & \cdots & a_{mn} \end{pmatrix}.$$

The horizontal lists of entries are called the rows of the matrix, and the vertical lists the columns. A matrix with m rows and n columns is called an $m \times n$ matrix. A matrix consisting of a single row is called a row matrix or a row vector; a matrix consisting of a single column is a column matrix or a column vector. For example,

$$[a \quad b \quad c] \quad \text{and} \quad \begin{bmatrix} a \\ b \\ c \end{bmatrix}$$

are row and column matrices, respectively. The transpose of a matrix A, often denoted A^{T}, is the matrix obtained by interchanging the rows and columns of A. For example,

$$\begin{pmatrix} a_{11} & a_{21} & \cdots & a_{m1} \\ a_{12} & a_{22} & \cdots & a_{m2} \\ \vdots & \vdots & & \vdots \\ a_{1n} & a_{2n} & \cdots & a_{mn} \end{pmatrix}$$

is the transpose of the $m \times n$ matrix given above. Column matrices such as

$$\begin{bmatrix} a \\ b \\ c \end{bmatrix}$$

may be represented in text as $(a, b, c)^{\mathrm{T}}$, col. (a, b, c), or the column vector (a, b, c), and a $2 \times n$ (for small n) matrix may be set, for example, as $\left(\begin{smallmatrix} a & c \\ b & d \end{smallmatrix}\right)$. Most matrices are displayed, however. In-line matrices cannot be broken on the line, and display matrices cannot be broken across the column or page. Authors should avoid using matrix notation for multiline equations.

12.51 **Determinants.** If A is a square matrix, the determinant of A, denoted $|A|$ or $\det A$, is a function that assigns a specific number to the matrix A. If A is an $n \times n$ matrix, the determinant of A is represented by

$$\begin{vmatrix} a_{11} & a_{12} & \cdots & a_{1n} \\ a_{21} & a_{22} & \cdots & a_{2n} \\ \vdots & \vdots & & \vdots \\ a_{n1} & a_{n2} & \cdots & a_{nn} \end{vmatrix}.$$

Vertical bars are used to distinguish the determinant of A from the matrix A. The Jacobian matrix has a standard notation:

$$J = \frac{\partial(f_1, f_2, \ldots, f_n)}{\partial(x_1, x_2, \ldots, x_n)}.$$

Its determinant (usually referred to as the Jacobian) is denoted as

$$\left|\frac{\partial(f_1, f_2, \ldots, f_n)}{\partial(x_1, x_2, \ldots, x_n)}\right|.$$

Scalars, Vectors, and Tensors

12.52 **Scalars, vectors, and tensors defined.** Three basic quantities often encountered in scientific mathematical material are scalars, vectors, and tensors. Scalars, usually denoted by lowercase italic or Greek letters, are ordinary numbers and are treated as such. Vectors are quantities that have direction as well as magnitude, and they are often denoted by boldface letters or by an arrow diacritic to distinguish them from scalars:

$$\boldsymbol{r} \text{ or } \vec{r}.$$

Because authors do not always follow these conventions, editors should be prepared to query. A vector may be written as the sum of its components:

$$\boldsymbol{r} = \sum_i r_i \hat{e}^i$$

The circumflex over the $\boldsymbol{e}$ is used to denote a vector of length 1, called a unit vector. Tensors are multidimensional quantities that extend the vector concept. A scalar is a tensor of rank 0, and a vector is a tensor of rank 1.

12.53 **Vector and tensor multiplication.** Vector and tensor multiplication employs a special notation that is relatively easy to identify in text. The inner or dot product of two vectors $\boldsymbol{u}$ and $\boldsymbol{w}$ is denoted $\boldsymbol{u} \cdot \boldsymbol{w}$; the dot product is signified by the boldface multiplication dot. The vector or cross product of two vectors $\boldsymbol{u}$ and $\boldsymbol{w}$ is denoted $\boldsymbol{u} \times \boldsymbol{w}$; the cross product is signified by the boldface multiplication cross. The multiplication dot and multiplication cross are not interchangeable for vectors as they are for ordinary multiplication. The standard notation for the tensor product of tensors

T and S is $T \otimes S$. Index notation for vectors and tensors usually takes the following form:

$$S = S_{jk}\mathbf{e}^j\mathbf{e}^k,$$

$$T^{i\cdots m}_{k\cdots l} = A^{i\cdots m}_{k\cdots n}B^n_l,$$

$$b^i = a^i_j c^j.$$

Note the correspondence of the indices in these expressions (see 12.38 for discussion of index positioning). The Einstein convention has been used here, which implies summation over the repeated index. Thus

$$c_k = \sum_j a^j b_{jk} \quad \text{is the same as} \quad c_k = a^j b_{jk}$$

unless otherwise stated.

12.54 **Additional tensor notation.** Two additional special notations are used to differentiate tensors. One is $A^i{}_{,j}$, where the subscript comma indicates a coordinate (or "ordinary") derivative. The other is $A^i{}_{;j}$, where the subscript semicolon indicates the covariant derivative. See also 12.38.

12.55 **Dirac notation.** A special form of the inner product, used especially in physics, is the Dirac bracket notation,

$$\langle a|b\rangle,$$

which can also be used in combination with operators, as in $\langle a|\boldsymbol{T}|b\rangle$ (which is not the same as $\langle a\boldsymbol{T}b\rangle$) or $\langle \boldsymbol{T}a|b\rangle$. The combinations $\langle a|$ and $|b\rangle$ are also used to denote dual vectors and vectors, respectively.

Definitions, Theorems, and Other Formal Statements

12.56 **Formal mathematical statements in text.** For definitions, theorems, propositions, corollaries, lemmas, axioms, and rules (collectively called "enunciations"), it is common practice to distinguish the head from the text—for example, by setting the head in caps and small caps (as in the examples here) or in bold or italic. Numbers for these statements, unlike those for equations, are not enclosed in parentheses, and in cross-references the numbers are also not enclosed.

DEFINITION. A *permutation* is a one-to-one transformation of a finite set into itself.

(In a definition, the term being defined is set in italic type in order to distinguish it from the rest of the text.)

> THEOREM 1. The order of a finite group is a multiple of the order of each of its subgroups.
>
> COROLLARY. If p and q are distinct prime numbers and a is an integer not divisible by either p or q, then
>
> $$a^{(p-1)(q-1)} \equiv 1(\text{mod } pq).$$
>
> LEMMA 2. The product of two primitive polynomials is itself primitive.
>
> AXIOM. Every set of nonnegative integers that contains at least one element contains a smallest element.
>
> RULE 4.4. The length of a vertical segment joining two points is given by the difference of the ordinates of the upper and lower points.

Proofs, examples, remarks, demonstrations, and solutions are usually treated in a similar manner.

> PROOF. Let $A = B$. Hence $C = D$.
>
> SOLUTION. If $y = 0$, then $x = 5$.

Proofs of theorems often end with the abbreviation *QED* or a special symbol, □ or ■.

Probability and Statistics

12.57 **Probability and statistics—additional resources.** The fields of probability and statistics are used by many disciplines beyond those of math and science. As a result of these cross-disciplinary applications, the conventions for probability and statistics are not nearly as well established as they are for many of the other concepts covered in this chapter. Those looking for more comprehensive treatment beyond the brief coverage offered here should consult the *AMA Manual of Style* or *Scientific Style and Format* (bibliog. 1.1).

12.58 **Probability.** The notation $\Pr(A)$ or $P(A)$ is used to denote the probability of an event A. The sample space—that is, the set of all possible outcomes of a given experiment—is usually denoted Ω. An event A is a subset of the sample space: $A \subseteq \Omega$. The elements of the sample space are usually denoted ω. The conditional probability of event A relative to event B—that is, the probability that event *A* occurs given that event *B* has occurred—is written

$$\Pr(A \mid B) \quad \text{or} \quad P(A \mid B).$$

Variance is denoted Var(*X*) and covariance is denoted Cov(*X*, *Y*). Both the variance and the covariance functions may be expressed with lowercase letters.

12.59 **Means and standard deviations.** The population mean is often given a special symbol in statistics, $\mu(X)$. The sample mean is denoted by $\bar{x}$. In evaluating an expression, be careful not to substitute angle brackets, $\langle X \rangle$, for an overbar, $\bar{x}$. They can mean very different things. The population standard deviation (the most common measure of dispersion) is denoted by σ (Greek lowercase sigma), and the sample standard deviation is more commonly denoted by *s*; sd or SD may be used to distinguish it from se or SE, for standard error. The arithmetic mean is most frequently written in physical sciences literature as $\langle A \rangle$ or $\bar{A}$ and the cumulant as $\langle\langle A \rangle\rangle$. Several abbreviations are used in stochastic theory and probability theory without special definition: a.e., almost everywhere; a.c., almost certainly; a.s., almost surely. See table 12.3 for statistical notation.

TABLE 12.3. Statistical notation

GREEK ALPHABET			
α	Probability of rejecting a true null hypothesis (type I error)	$\mu(X)$	Mean of the population
		Σ	Sum of
		σ	Population standard deviation
β	Probability of accepting a false null hypothesis (type II error)	σ^2	Population variance
		χ^2	Value for the chi-squared distribution
κ	Cumulant; also kappa statistic		
LATIN ALPHABET			
df, DF, dof	Degrees of freedom	*s*, sd, SD	Sample standard deviation
F	*F*-ratio	se, SE	Standard error
H	Value from the Kruskal-Wallis test	sem, SEM	Standard error of the mean
		t	Value from Student's *t*-test
H_0	Null hypothesis	*T*	Value from the Wilcoxon matched-pairs signed-rank test
ln	Natural logarithm		
log	Logarithm to base 10		
mse, MSE	Mean squared error	*U*	Value from the Mann-Whitney test
p, *P*, Pr	Probability		
r_P	Pearson correlation coefficient	W_s	Value from the Wilcoxon rank sum test
r_S	Value from the Spearman rank-order test	*z*	Value from the normal distribution

12.60 **Uncertainties.** Uncertainties in quantities are usually written with a plus or minus sign (±): 2.501 ± 0.002 or, if there is an exponent, $(6.157 \pm 0.07) \times 10^5$ or $10^{4.3\pm0.3}$. However, there are cases in which the bounds rather than the range are given, and these may be unequal; hence,

> . . . where $D/H = 1.65^{+0.11}_{-0.08} \times 10^{-5}$. . . .

Uncertainties may also be specified as se for standard error, 1 σ (or a larger multiple) or sd for standard deviation. Finally, separation into random and systematic uncertainties is written as

$$71.0 \pm 5.0 \text{ (random)} \pm 2.5 \text{ (sys)}$$

or $71.0^{+5.0}_{-4.8}$ (random) $^{+2.1}_{-1.8}$ (sys) for asymmetric bounds. When such expressions occur in an exponent, it is preferable to write a separate expression for the exponent (see 12.49).

Preparation and Editing of Paper Manuscripts

12.61 **Format of paper manuscripts for mathematics.** Manuscripts for mathematical articles and books should be printed out one-sided and double-spaced, on 8½ × 11–inch white paper, with 1¼-inch margins for text and 2-inch margins for display work. The print quality should be 300 dots per inch or better. If handwritten equations or symbols are to be inserted in the printout, allow generous space for them. Since the editor will need to provide instructions to the typesetter, there should be ample margins.

12.62 **Setting mathematics from the author's hard copy.** In the event that the publisher cannot use the electronic files prepared by the author, and to the extent that a manuscript shows all the necessary characters, symbols, and signs as they should appear, the typesetter may simply be instructed to follow the author's hard copy. Any unusual characters not achieved in the manuscript must be marked or identified. Authors should supply the highest-quality printout possible.

12.63 **Marking italic type for mathematics.** The editor of a mathematical text should either underline all copy that is to be set in italics or give general instructions to the typesetter to set all Latin single-letter mathematical objects in italics unless they are marked otherwise. The general instructions to the typesetter should also specify italic type for such letters used in subscripts or superscripts. If italics have been used in the manuscript, the editor can instruct the typesetter to follow the copy.

12.64 **Marking common mathematical abbreviations.** Abbreviations for common functions, geometric points, units of measurement, and chemical elements, which are set in roman type, should be marked as roman by the editor only where ambiguity could occur. For a list of some frequently used abbreviations, see table 12.2.

12.65 **Marking single mathematical letters in other type styles.** Special marking must be used when single letters representing mathematical objects are to be set in any typeface other than italics. A mathematical text may require the use of some roman letters, usually to indicate properties different from those expressed by the same letters in italics. Underlining is the standard method of indicating italics, but it can be used instead, with instructions to the typesetter, to indicate letters that are to be in roman. If, however, the editor does not use general instructions but underlines all letters to be set italic, then letters not underlined will be set, as implied, in roman type. Double underlining is used to indicate small capitals. Wavy underlining is used for boldface. Color codes are often used to indicate other typefaces. For example, red underlining or circling can be used for Fraktur, blue for script, green for sans serif, and so forth. The general instructions to the typesetter must clearly explain the marking and coding system used. If a photocopy must be made of the edited manuscript for estimating by the typesetter or for querying the author, avoid color coding.

12.66 **Mathematical fonts to mark on a paper manuscript.** Boldface, script, Fraktur, and sans serif are frequently used in mathematical expressions and should be indicated on a paper manuscript as suggested in 12.65.

Boldface	*Script*	*Fraktur*	*Sans serif*
ABCD	$\mathcal{ABCD}$	$\mathfrak{ABCD}$	ABCD

Double-struck, or blackboard, characters are often used for special mathematical symbols—for example, $\mathbb{N}$, $\mathbb{Z}$, $\mathbb{Q}$, $\mathbb{R}$, $\mathbb{C}$ (see also 12.14). These should be clearly indicated on the manuscript.

12.67 **Marking mathematical subscripts and superscripts.** As long as inferior and superior characters have been marked in a few places by the symbols $\vee$ and $\wedge$ (see examples below), and new characters or symbols are identified when they first appear, a typesetter should have no difficulty interpreting the manuscript. If the spatial relationship of terms is not clearly shown in a typed or handwritten expression, the terms should be marked to avoid ambiguity. For example, given the copy

$$X^k_{t1},$$

it may not be clear from the manuscript whether this means

$$X^k_{t1} \quad \text{or} \quad X^k_{t^1} \quad \text{or} \quad X^k_{t_1}.$$

The expression should therefore be marked in one of the following ways for complete clarity:

$$X^{\overset{k}{\vee}}_{\underset{t1}{\wedge}} \quad \text{or} \quad X^{\overset{k}{\vee}}_{\underset{t^{1}_{\vee}}{\wedge}} \quad \text{or} \quad X^{\overset{k}{\vee}}_{\underset{t_{1}^{\wedge}}{\wedge}}.$$

The examples above show the subscripts and superscripts aligned, or stacked. See 12.38 for discussion and examples of staggered subscripts and superscripts.

12.68 **Examples of marked mathematical copy.** Figure 12.1 shows a page of a paper manuscript as marked initially by the author and then by the editor before being sent to the typesetter. The author's marks merely identify ambiguous symbols. Figure 12.2 shows that same page set in type. Figure 12.3 shows the LaTeX source code that would generate the first part of figure 12.2. Signs and symbols that could be misread by the typesetter should be clearly identified on a paper manuscript by marginal notations or in a separate list. For lists of symbols and special characters commonly used in mathematics, see table 12.1. Illegible handwriting and unidentifiable signs and symbols can reduce composition speed and result in time-consuming and costly corrections. Certain letters, numbers, and symbols can easily be misread, especially when Greek, Fraktur, script, and sans serif letters are handwritten rather than typed. Some of the characters that cause the most difficulty are shown in table 12.4.

[Opr.: Letter symbols in ital. unless marked]

Therefore $F_x^n \subset G \cap B_n$ and $F_x^n \cap B_m = \emptyset$ for $n \neq m$, since $b \in G$. [null set] ["element of"]

The temperature function is

$$u(x, t) = \frac{2}{L} \sum_{1}^{\infty} \exp\left(-\frac{u^2 \pi^2 kt}{L^2}\right) \sin \frac{n\pi x}{L} \int_0^L f(x') \sin \frac{n\pi x'}{L}\, dx'. \quad (3.1)$$

An $m \times n$ matrix $\underset{\sim}{A}$ over a field F is a rectangular array of mn elements $a_j^{\,i}$ in F, arranged in m rows and n columns:

$$\underset{\sim}{A} = \begin{bmatrix} a_1^{\,1} & a_2^{\,1} & \cdots & a_n^{\,1} \\ a_1^{\,2} & a_2^{\,2} & \cdots & a_n^{\,2} \\ \cdot & \cdot & \cdots & \cdot \\ a_1^{\,m} & a_2^{\,m} & \cdots & a_n^{\,m} \end{bmatrix}.$$

The modulus of the correlation coefficient of X_1 and X_2 is ["greater than"]

$$\rho = |\langle x_1, x_2 \rangle| / \|x_1\| \, \|x_2\| \quad \text{for } \|x_l\| > 0, \qquad l = 1, 2.$$

[rho] [angle brackets] [ell] [ell]

Hence

$$\frac{\partial F}{\partial x} = \lim_{\Delta x \to 0} \frac{\Delta F}{\Delta x} = \lim_{\Delta x \to 0} \frac{1}{\Delta x} \left\{ \int_{a,b}^{x+\Delta x, y} P\, dx + Q\, dy - \int_{a,b}^{x,y} P\, dx + Q\, dy \right\} + P + Q.$$

From equation (2.4), where $M = [(a + b - 1)/(k + 1)]$, we obtain

$$\alpha_\nu(a + b) = (-1)^\nu \sum{}' \frac{(i_1 + \cdots + i_M)!}{i_1! \cdots i_M!} \prod_{h=1}^{M} (-1)^{i_h} \binom{a + b - kh - 1}{h}^{i_h},$$

[alpha] [lc Gr. nu]

the sum being extended over all sets $(i_1, \cdots, i_M)$.

To summarize our findings:

$$v^*(z, t_n) \gtrsim H_{\delta_1} [v(x) + o(1)] - 2\eta \geqslant v(z) + o(1) + \eta^{1/2} O(1).$$

[lc Gr. eta] [lc oh] [lc oh] [cap oh]

FIGURE 12.1. An example of typewritten and hand-marked mathematical copy. (Note that this page is not intended to make mathematical sense but is merely meant to illustrate some of the issues that may arise in preparing mathematical copy.)

Therefore $F_x{}^n \subset G \cap B_n$ and $F_x{}^n \cap B_m = \emptyset$ for $n \neq m$, since $b \in G$. The temperature function is

$$u(x,t) = \frac{2}{L}\sum_{1}^{\infty} \exp\left(-\frac{u^2\pi^2 kt}{L^2}\right) \sin\frac{n\pi x}{L}$$

$$\times \int_0^L f(x') \sin\frac{n\pi x'}{L} dx'. \quad (3.1)$$

An $m \times n$ matrix $\mathbf{A}$ over a field F is a rectangular array of mn elements $a_j{}^i$ in F, arranged in m rows and n columns:

$$\mathbf{A} = \begin{bmatrix} a_1{}^1 & a_2{}^1 & \dots & a_n{}^1 \\ a_1{}^2 & a_2{}^2 & \dots & a_n{}^2 \\ \cdot & \cdot & \dots & \cdot \\ a_1{}^m & a_2{}^m & \dots & a_n{}^m \end{bmatrix}.$$

The modulus of the correlation coefficient of X_1 and X_2 is

$$\rho = |\langle X_1, X_2\rangle| / \|X_1\|\ \|X_2\| \quad \text{for} \quad \|X_l\| > 0,\ l = 1, 2.$$

Hence

$$\frac{\partial F}{\partial x} = \lim_{\Delta x \to 0} \frac{\Delta F}{\Delta x} = \lim_{\Delta x \to 0} \frac{1}{\Delta x}\left\{ \int_{a,b}^{x+\Delta x, y} P\,dx + Q\,dy \right.$$

$$\left. - \int_{a,b}^{x,y} P\,dx + Q\,dy \right\} + P + Q.$$

From equation (2.4), where $M = [(a + b - 1)/(k + 1)]$, we obtain

$$a_\nu(a+b) = (-1)^\nu \sum{}' \frac{(i_1 + \cdots + i_M)!}{i_1! \cdots i_M!}$$

$$\times \prod_{h=1}^{M} (-1)^{i_h} \left(\frac{a + b - kh - 1}{h}\right)^{i_h},$$

the sum being extended over all sets $(i_1, \ldots, i_M)$.

To summarize our findings:

$$v^*(z, t_n) \geq H_{\delta_1}[v(x) + o(1)] - 2\eta \geq v(z) + o(1) + \eta^{1/2} O(1).$$

FIGURE 12.2. The page of manuscript shown in figure 12.1 set in type.

```
\noindent Therefore $F_{x}{}^n\subset G\cap B_n$
and $F_{x}{}^n\cap B_m=\O$ for $n\ne m$,
since $b\in G$. The temperature function is
\begin{multline}
u(x,t)=\frac{2}{L}\sum_1^\infty \exp
\left(-\frac{u^2\pi^2 kt}{L^2}\right)\sin
\frac{n\pi x}{L}\\
\times \int\nolimits_0^L f(x')\sin
\frac{n\pi x'}{L}dx'.
\end{multline}
An $m\times n$ matrix {\bf A} over a field $F$
is a rectangular array of $mn$~ele\-ments~$a_{j}{}^i$ in $F$,
arranged  in $m$ rows and $n$ columns:
\begin{align*}
{\bf A}=\left[
{\arraycolsep5pt\begin{array}{@{}cccc@{}}
a_{1}{}^1 &a_{2}{}^1 &\ldots &a_{n}{}^1\\[4pt]
a_{1}{}^2 &a_{2}{}^2 &\ldots &a_{n}{}^2\\[4pt]
.&.&\ldots  &.\\[4pt]
a_{1}{}^m &a_{2}{}^m &\ldots &a_{n}{}^m\\
\end{array}}
\right].
\end{align*}
The modulus of the correlation coefficient of
$X_1$ and $X_2$ is
\begin{align*}
\rho=|\langle X_1,\ X_2\rangle|/\|X_1\|\ \|X_2\|
\quad{\rm for}\quad \|X_1\|>0,\ l=1,2.
\end{align*}
```

FIGURE 12.3. LaTeX source listing that would generate a portion of the mathematical copy shown in figure 12.2.

TABLE 12.4. Potentially ambiguous mathematical symbols

Symbols set in type[a]	Marginal notation to operator[b]	Remarks and suggestions for manuscript preparation
a	lc "aye"	
α	lc Gr. alpha	
∝	proportional to	Leave medium space before and after ∝ and all binary operation signs (=, ≤, ∈, ∩, ⊂, etc.).
∞	infinity	
B	cap "bee"	
β	lc Gr. beta	
χ	lc Gr. chi	
X	cap "ex"	
x	lc "ex"	
×	"times" or "mult"	Leave medium space before and after × and all other operation signs (+, −, ÷, etc.). Do not add space when such signs as −, +, or ± are used to modify symbols or expressions (−3, ±1, etc.). Do not add space when operations appear as subscripts or superscripts.
δ	lc Gr. delta	
∂	partial differential	Simpler to use printer's term "round dee."
d	lc "dee"	
ε	lc Gr. epsilon	
∈	"element of"	
η	lc Gr. eta	
n	lc "en"	
γ	lc Gr. gamma	
τ	lc Gr. tau	
r	lc "ar"	
t	lc "tee"	
ι	lc Gr. iota	Avoid using ι and *i* together because of similarity in print.
i	lc "eye"	
κ	lc Gr. kappa	
k	lc "kay"	
Κ	cap Gr. kappa	
K	cap "kay"	
l	lc "el"	In some fonts, l and 1 look identical; note "el" but leave numeral unmarked; ℓ should not be used if *l* is available.
ℓ	script "el"	
1	numeral 1	

TABLE 12.4. *(continued)*

Symbols set in type[a]	Marginal notation to operator[b]	Remarks and suggestions for manuscript preparation
ν	lc Gr. nu	Avoid using ν and v together because of similarity in print.
v	lc "vee"	
O	cap "oh"	Asymptotic upper bounds $O(x)$ and $o(x)$ may occur together.
o	lc "oh"	
0	zero	
Ο	cap Gr. omicron	
ο	lc Gr. omicron	
°	degree sign	
Λ	cap Gr. lambda	
∧	wedge	
ϕ, φ	lc Gr. phi	Preference for form φ should be specified by author; ϕ more commonly used.
∅	empty or null set	
∏	product	
Π	cap Gr. pi	
π	lc Gr. pi	
ρ	lc Gr. rho	
p	lc "pee"	
∑	summation	
Σ	cap Gr. sigma	
θ, ϑ	lc Gr. theta	Preference for form ϑ should be specified by author; θ more commonly used.
Θ	cap Gr. theta	
U	cap "you"	
∪	union symbol	
υ	lc Gr. upsilon	
μ	lc Gr. mu	
ν	lc Gr. nu	
u	lc "you"	
ω	lc Gr. omega	
ϖ	round lc Gr. pi	
w	lc "double-u"	
Z	cap "zee"	
z	lc "zee"	
2	numeral 2	

(continued)

TABLE 12.4. *(continued)*

Symbols set in type[a]	Marginal notation to operator[b]	Remarks and suggestions for manuscript preparation
′	prime	Use apostrophe for prime if no prime available.
^{1}	superscript 1	In handwritten formulas, take care to distinguish prime from superscript 1 and comma from subscript 1.
,	comma	
$_{1}$	subscript 1	
—	em dash	Use two hyphens for em dash; no space on either side (except in LaTeX, where a double hyphen produces an en dash).
−	minus sign	To indicate subtraction, leave medium space on each side of sign; omit space after sign if negative quantity is represented.
–	en dash	
·	multiplication dot	Use centered period for multiplication dot, allowing medium space on each side; do not show space around a center dot in a chemical formula ($CO_3 \cdot H_2$).

NOTE: Symbols and letters that are commonly mistaken for each other are arranged in groups.

[a] Latin letters in mathematical expressions will automatically be set in italics unless marked otherwise.

[b] Only if symbols, letters, or numbers are badly written or rendered in the manuscript is it necessary to identify them for the typesetter.

13 · Quotations and Dialogue

Overview

13.1 **Scope of this chapter—and where else to look.** This chapter offers recommendations for incorporating words quoted from other sources—and, to a lesser degree, for presenting speech and other forms of dialogue—in text. For the use of quotation marks for purposes other than direct quotation, see the discussions throughout 7.48–69. For quotation marks with titles of works, see the discussions in 8.156–201. For citing the sources of quotations, discussed only peripherally here, see chapters 14 and 15. For formatting block quotations in a manuscript, see 2.19, 2.20; for the manuscript editor's responsibilities regarding quoted material, see 2.61. For quotation marks in relation to surrounding text and punctuation, see 6.6, 6.9–11. For quotations of material from languages other than English, see 11.11–17.

13.2 **Quotations and modern scholarship.** Scholarship has always depended at least in part on the words and ideas of others. Incorporating those words and ideas is central to the act of writing and publishing. The choice between quoting, on the one hand, and merely copying, on the other, can mean the difference between properly acknowledging and crediting the ideas of others and falsely representing them as your own, thus making the conventions outlined in this chapter and in chapters 14 and 15 essential to modern scholarship. These conventions extend beyond scholarship to encompass journalism and other categories of nonfiction.

13.3 **Giving credit and seeking permission.** Whether quoting, paraphrasing, or using others' words or ideas to advance their own arguments, authors should give explicit credit to the source of those words or ideas. This credit often takes the form of a formal citation incorporated into a note or parenthetical reference. For a full discussion of documentation, see chapters 14 and 15. In addition, written permission may be needed, especially for direct quotations, as follows: for more than a line or two of a poem or a song lyric in copyright; for prose quotations of, say, more than three paragraphs or for many short passages from a work in copyright; or for any excerpt from certain unpublished materials (letters, email messages, interviews, and so forth). For more information about permissions, consult chapter 4, especially 4.75–94.

13.4 **When to paraphrase rather than quote.** Authors drawing on the work of others to illustrate their arguments should first decide whether direct quotation or paraphrase will be more effective. Too many quotations with too little commentary can pose a distraction, and readers may choose to skip over long or frequent quotations. In some cases, authors who notice an error in a passage they wish to quote should paraphrase the original, eliminating the error. For "silent correction," see 13.7 (item 6); for *sic*, see 13.61.

13.5 **When quotation and attribution is unnecessary.** Commonly known or readily verifiable facts can be stated without quotation or attribution unless the wording is taken directly from another source. Authors, of course, must be absolutely sure of any unattributed facts, and editors should flag anything that seems suspicious (see 13.6). Likewise, proverbs and other familiar expressions can usually be reproduced without quotation or attribution. Of the following statements, only the last—a direct quotation—requires quotation marks and attribution (as well as a source citation, either in the text or in a note; see 13.64–72).

Until July 20, 1969, no one had set foot on the moon.
The chemical symbol for gold, Au, derives from the Latin word *aurum*.
Ithaca, New York, is located at the southern end of Cayuga Lake.
No one can convince the young that practice makes perfect.
If reading maketh a full man, Henry is half-empty.
but
It was Shakespeare's contemporary Francis Bacon who wrote that "reading maketh a ful man, conference a ready man, and writing an exact man."

For the treatment of unconventional spellings in quoted material (as in the quotation from Bacon), see 13.7, item 6.

13.6 **Ensuring accuracy of quotations.** It is impossible to overemphasize the importance of meticulous accuracy in quoting from the works of others. Authors should check every direct quotation against the original or, if the original is unavailable, against a careful transcription of the passage. This should be done *before* the manuscript is submitted to the publisher. Manuscript editors can help by spot-checking quotations against available resources to get an idea of how accurate the transcriptions are and by querying apparent errors; they may not, however, have ready access to an author's sources, nor is it typically assumed to be an editor's responsibility to confirm the accuracy of quotations. Moreover, it takes far less time for authors to accurately transcribe quotations during the writing stage than for authors or editors to go back to the original sources once a work is submitted for publication. See also 2.33, 2.136.

Permissible Changes to Quotations

13.7 **Permissible changes to punctuation, capitalization, and spelling.** Although in a direct quotation the wording should be reproduced exactly, the following changes are generally permissible to make a passage fit into the syntax and typography of the surrounding text. See also 13.8.

1. Single quotation marks may be changed to double, and double to single (see 13.30); punctuation relative to quotation marks should be adjusted accordingly (see 6.9). "Smart" quotation marks and apostrophes may be imposed (see 6.115, 6.117), and guillemets and other types of quotation marks from languages other than English may be changed to regular double or single quotation marks (see 11.11).
2. En dashes or hyphens used as em dashes may be changed to em dashes, with any space before or after the dash or hyphen eliminated as needed (see 6.85–92). Hyphens may be changed to en dashes in number ranges or other contexts where an en dash may be appropriate (for use of the en dash, see 6.78–84).
3. The initial letter may be changed to a capital or a lowercase letter (see 13.18–21).
4. At the end of the quotation, a period or other mark of punctuation in the original may be omitted or changed to a period or comma as required by the surrounding text; a question mark or exclamation point may be retained if it continues to apply to the word or words as quoted. For punctuation with ellipses, see 13.50–58.
5. Original note reference marks (and the notes to which they refer) may be omitted unless omission would affect the meaning of the quotation. If an original note is included, the quotation may best be set off as a block quotation (see 13.9), with the note in smaller type at the end, or the note may be summarized in the accompanying text. Note references added to a quotation must be distinguished from any note references in the original (see also 14.51). On the other hand, parenthetical text references in the original should be retained; if a parenthetical text reference is added to the original, it must be placed in square brackets (see 13.59–63).
6. Obvious typographic errors may be corrected silently (without comment or *sic*; see 13.61), unless the passage quoted is from an older work or a manuscript or other unpublished source where idiosyncrasies of spelling are generally preserved. If spelling and punctuation are modernized or altered for clarity, readers must be so informed in a note, in a preface, or elsewhere.
7. In quoting from early printed documents, the archaic long *s* (ſ, Unicode character U+017F), used to represent a lowercase *s* at the beginning or in the middle but never at the end of a word ("Such goodneſs of your juſtice, that our ſoul . . ."), may be changed to a modern *s*. Similarly, a title like *Vanitie and*

Vncertaintie may be changed to *Vanitie and Uncertaintie*, but writers or editors without a strong background in classical or Renaissance studies should generally be wary of changing *u* to *v*, *i* to *j*, or vice versa. See also 11.56, 11.122–23.

13.8 **Permissible changes to typography and layout.** The following elements of typography and layout may be changed to assimilate a quotation to the surrounding text (see also 13.7):

1. The typeface or font should be changed to agree with the surrounding text.
2. Words in full capitals in the original may be set in small caps, if that is the preferred style for the surrounding text. (See also 10.8.)
3. In drama or dialogue, names of speakers may be moved from a centered position to flush left.
4. Underlined words in a quoted manuscript may be printed as italics, unless the underlining itself is considered integral to the source or otherwise worthy of reproducing.
5. In quoting correspondence, such matters as paragraph indents and the position of the salutation and signature may be adjusted.

For paragraph indents in block quotations, see 13.22. For reproducing poetry extracts, see 13.25–29. For permissible changes to titles of books, articles, poems, and other works, see 8.165.

Quotations in Relation to Text

Run In or Set Off

13.9 **Run-in and block quotations defined.** Quoted text may be either run in to the surrounding text and enclosed in quotation marks, "like this," or set off as a block quotation, or extract. Block quotations, which are not enclosed in quotation marks, always start a new line. They are further distinguished from the surrounding text by being indented (from the left and sometimes from the right) or set in smaller type or a different font from the text. These matters are normally decided by the publisher's designer or by journal style. Authors preparing block quotations in their manuscripts can simply indent them from the left margin (see 2.19, 2.20). See also 13.22–24. For poetry, see 13.25–29.

13.10 **Choosing between run-in and block quotations.** In deciding whether to run in or set off a quotation, length is usually the deciding factor. In general, a short quotation, especially one that is not a full sentence, should be run in. A hundred words or more can generally be set off as a block quotation. Other criteria apply, however. A quotation of two or more paragraphs is best set off (see 13.22–24), as are quoted correspondence (if salutations, signatures, and such are included), lists (see 2.21), and any material that requires special formatting. If many quotations of varying length occur close together, running them all in may make for easier reading. But where quotations are being compared or otherwise used as entities in themselves, it may be better to set them all as block quotations, however short. For setting off poetry, see 13.25–29.

Assimilation into the Surrounding Text

13.11 **Logical and grammatical assimilation of quoted text.** In incorporating fragmentary quotations into a text, phrase the surrounding sentence in such a way that the quoted words fit into it logically and grammatically—as if there were no quotation marks—and quoting only as much of the original as is necessary. For the incorporation of full sentences (as in the last part of the example below), see 13.13–17.

> The narrator's constant references to "malicious code and obsolete data" detract from a more fundamental issue—that we are dumping "the burden of human history" onto computer hard drives. It is this vision of the future that is most alarming: "If (when?) we run out of sources of electricity," she asks, "will we forget who we are?"

13.12 **Integrating tenses and pronouns from quoted text.** In quoting verbatim, writers need to integrate tenses and pronouns into the new context.

> [*Original*] Mr. Moll took particular pains to say to you, gentlemen, that these eleven people here are guilty of murder; he calls this a cold-blooded, deliberate and premeditated murder.

> [*As quoted*] According to Darrow, Moll had told the jury that the eleven defendants were "guilty of murder" and had described the murder as "cold-blooded, deliberate and premeditated."

Occasional adjustments to the original may be bracketed. This device should be used sparingly, however.

> Mr. Graham has resolutely ducked the issue, saying he won't play the game of rumormongering, even though he has "learned from [his] mistakes."

Quotations and Punctuation

13.13 **Punctuation relative to closing quotation marks.** For a full discussion of the use of periods, commas, and other marks of punctuation relative to closing quotation marks, see 6.9–11. See also 13.7, item 4. The rest of this section is primarily concerned with punctuation relative to the beginning of quoted material.

13.14 **Comma to introduce a quotation.** When it is simply a matter of identifying a speaker, a comma is used after *said*, *replied*, *asked*, and similar verbs to introduce a quotation. Such usage is more traditional than logical, recognizing the syntactical independence of the quoted material from the surrounding text (even as the surrounding text often becomes dependent on the quoted material). A colon, though never wrong in such instances, should be used sparingly (see 13.16).

> Garrett replied, "I hope you are not referring to me."

> Fish writes, "What [the students] did was move the words out of a context (the faculty club door) in which they had a literal and obvious meaning into another context (my classroom) in which the meaning was no less obvious and literal and yet was different."

When the sentence is inverted and the quotation comes first (a common arrangement), a comma is usually required at the end of the quotation unless the quotation ends with a question mark or an exclamation point. See also 6.9, 6.10.

> "I hope you are not referring to me," Garrett replied.

When the quotation is interrupted, two commas are required.

> "I hope," Garrett replied, "you are not referring to me."

When the quotation is subordinated to or otherwise integrated into the surrounding text, no comma is needed (see also 13.15, 13.19).

> Fish observed that "what [the students] did was move the words out of a context . . ."

See also 6.40, 6.42.

13.15 **No comma to introduce a quotation.** Many writers mistakenly use a comma to introduce any direct quotation, regardless of its relationship to the surrounding text. But when a quotation introduced midsentence forms a syntactical part of the surrounding sentence, no comma or other mark of punctuation is needed to introduce it, though punctuation may be required for other reasons.

Donovan made a slight bow and said he was "very glad."

One of the protesters scrawled "Long live opera!" in huge red letters.

According to one critic, Copland's style could be called "American urban pastoral, with a touch of jazz and more than a hint of Stravinsky."

She said she would "prefer not to comment."

but

Copland's style—"American urban pastoral, with a touch of jazz and more than a hint of Stravinsky"—owes a debt to several genres and more than one continent.

She said that she would, in short, "prefer not to comment."

She said, "I prefer not to comment." (See 13.14.)

See also 6.41.

13.16 **Colon to introduce a quotation.** When a quotation is introduced by an independent clause (i.e., a grammatically complete sentence), a colon should be used. Such introductions may include a formal introductory phrase such as *the following* or *as follows* (see also 6.64).

The role of the author has been variously described. Henry Fielding, at the beginning of his *History of Tom Jones*, defines it as follows: "An author ought to consider himself, not as a gentleman who gives a private or eleemosynary treat, but rather as one who keeps a public ordinary, at which all persons are welcome for their money."

Faraday's conclusion was alarming: "Without significant intervention, your home town will have gone the way of Atlantis by century's end."

A colon may also be used in place of a comma to introduce a quotation. Such a colon, never wrong, should be used consistently—for example, to introduce quotations of more than one sentence or, occasionally, to add emphasis. See also 13.14.

> Garrett replied: "I hope you are not referring to me. Because if you are . . ."

13.17 **Period rather than colon to introduce a block quotation.** Unless introduced by *as follows* or other wording that requires a colon (see 6.64), a block quotation may be preceded by a period rather than a colon. Such usage should be applied consistently. See also 13.22–24.

> He then took a clearly hostile position toward Poland, having characterized it as a Fascist state that oppressed the Ukrainians, the Belorussians, and others.
>
>> Under present conditions, suppression of that state will mean that there will be one less Fascist state. It will not be a bad thing if Poland suffers a defeat and thus enables us to include new territories and new populations in the socialist system.

Initial Capital or Lowercase Letter

13.18 **Changing capitalization to suit syntax—an overview.** Aside from proper nouns and some of the words derived from them (see 8.1), most words are normally lowercased unless they begin a sentence (or, often, a line of poetry). To suit this requirement, the first word in a quoted passage must often be adjusted to conform to the surrounding text. In most types of works, this adjustment may be done silently, as such capitalization does not normally affect the significance of the quoted matter, which is assumed to have been taken from another context (see 13.7, item 3). In some types of works, however, it may be obligatory to indicate the change by bracketing the initial quoted letter; for examples of this practice, appropriate to legal writing and some types of textual commentary, see 13.21.

13.19 **Initial capital or lowercase—run-in quotations.** When a quotation introduced midsentence forms a syntactical part of the sentence (see also 13.15), it begins with a lowercase letter even if the original begins with a capital.

> Benjamin Franklin admonishes us to "plough deep while sluggards sleep."

> With another aphorism he reminded his readers that "experience keeps a dear school, but fools will learn in no other"—an observation as true today as then.

When the quotation has a more remote syntactic relation to the rest of the sentence, the initial letter remains capitalized.

As Franklin advised, "Plough deep while sluggards sleep."

His aphorism "Experience keeps a dear school, but fools will learn in no other" is a cogent warning to people of all ages. (See also 6.41.)

On the other hand, for a quotation that is only a part of a sentence in the original but forms a complete sentence as quoted, a lowercase letter may be changed to a capital if appropriate. In the example that follows, "those" begins midsentence in the original (see 13.20).

Aristotle put it this way: "Those who are eminent in virtue usually do not stir up insurrections, always a minority."
but
Aristotle believed that "those who are eminent in virtue usually do not stir up insurrections, always a minority."

13.20 **Initial capital or lowercase—block quotations.** The consideration of whether to lowercase a capital letter beginning a block quotation is exactly the same as it is for run-in quotations (see 13.19): the initial letter of a block quotation that is capitalized in the original may be lowercased if the syntax demands it. In the following example, the quotation from Aristotle in the Jowett translation (Modern Library) begins in the original with a capital letter and a paragraph indent. See also 13.22.

In discussing the reasons for political disturbances, Aristotle observes that

> revolutions also break out when opposite parties, e.g. the rich and the people, are equally balanced, and there is little or no middle class; for, if either party were manifestly superior, the other would not risk an attack upon them. And, for this reason, those who are eminent in virtue usually do not stir up insurrections, always a minority. Such are the beginnings and causes of the disturbances and revolutions to which every form of government is liable. (*Politics* 5.4)

On the other hand, the capital should be retained—or a lowercase letter should be changed to a capital—if the syntax requires it. See also 13.16.

In discussing the reasons for political disturbances, Aristotle makes the following observations:

> Revolutions also break out when opposite parties, e.g. the rich and the people, are equally balanced, and there is little or no middle class; . . .

13.21 **Brackets to indicate a change in capitalization.** In some legal writing, close textual analysis or commentary, and other contexts, it is considered obligatory to indicate any change in capitalization by brackets. Although this practice is unnecessary in most writing, in contexts where it is considered appropriate it should be employed consistently throughout a work.

> According to article 6, section 6, she is given the power "[t]o extend or renew any existing indebtedness."

> "[R]eal estates may be conveyed by lease and release, or bargain and sale," according to section 2 of the Northwest Ordinance.

> Let us compare Aristotle's contention that "[i]nferiors revolt in order that they may be equal, and equals that they may be superior" (*Politics* 5.2), with his later observation that "[r]evolutions also break out when opposite parties, e.g. the rich and the people, are equally balanced" (5.4).

Block Quotations

13.22 **Block quotations of more than one paragraph.** Quoted material of more than a paragraph, even if very brief, is best set off as a block quotation. (For a less desirable alternative, see 13.32.) A multiparagraph block quotation should generally reflect the paragraph breaks of the original. But if the first paragraph quoted includes the beginning of that paragraph, it need not start with a first-line paragraph indent. Subsequent paragraphs in the quotation should be indicated either by first-line paragraph indents or (less desirably) by extra line space between the paragraphs (see also 13.24). The following example, from Jane Austen's *Pride and Prejudice*, includes four full paragraphs:

> He began to wish to know more of her, and as a step towards conversing with her himself, attended to her conversation with others. His doing so drew her notice. It was at Sir William Lucas's, where a large party were assembled.
>
> "What does Mr. Darcy mean," said she to Charlotte, "by listening to my conversation with Colonel Forster?"
>
> "That is a question which Mr. Darcy only can answer."
>
> "But if he does it any more I shall certainly let him know that I see what he

> is about. He has a very satirical eye, and if I do not begin by being impertinent myself, I shall soon grow afraid of him."

If the first part of the opening paragraph were to be omitted, it would still begin flush left. For ellipses at the beginning of paragraphs, see 13.56.

13.23 **Block quotations beginning in text.** A long quotation may begin with a few words run in to the text. This device should be used only when text intervenes between the quoted matter in the text and its continuation.

> "There is no safe trusting to dictionaries and definitions," observed Charles Lamb.
>
> > We should more willingly fall in with this popular language, if we did not find *brutality* sometimes awkwardly coupled with *valour* in the same vocabulary. The comic writers . . . have contributed not a little to mislead us upon this point. To see a hectoring fellow exposed and beaten upon the stage, has something in it wonderfully diverting. ("Popular Fallacies," *Essays of Elia*, 277)
>
> "In short," says Crane, summarizing Gordon's philosophy,
>
> > there has been "almost a continual improvement" in all branches of human knowledge; . . .

A permissible alternative is to set off the entire quotation, enclosing the intervening words of text in brackets.

> There is no safe trusting to dictionaries and definitions [observed Charles Lamb]. We should more willingly . . .

13.24 **Text following a block quotation or extract.** If the text following a block quotation or extract (whether prose or poetry) is a continuation of the paragraph that introduces the quotation or extract, it begins flush left. If, on the other hand, the resuming text constitutes a new paragraph, it receives a paragraph indent. The decision in each case is usually made by the author or, failing that, may be left to the editor (see 2.19, 2.20). In works where each new paragraph is to appear flush left, distinguished only by extra line space, such a distinction may have to be ignored (or it can be signaled by imposing more line space before new paragraphs than before continued text).

Poetry Extracts

13.25 **Setting off poetry.** In a published work, two or more lines of verse are best set off as an extract. (In a note, set off three or more; see 14.38.) A poetry extract, if isolated, is often visually centered on the page between the left and right margins (usually relative to the longest line), but if two or more stanzas of the same poem appear on the same page, a uniform indent from the left may work better (see 13.26). A half line to a full line of space should appear between stanzas. Within each piece or stanza, the indentation pattern of the original should be reproduced (but indents should be distinguished from runover lines; see 13.27). For placement of the source, see 13.71. For advice on formatting poetry extracts in a manuscript, see 2.20.

                              Sure there was wine
                  Before my sighs did drie it: there was corn
                    Before my tears did drown it.
             Is the yeare onely lost to me?
                    Have I no bayes to crown it?
        No flowers, no garlands gay? all blasted?
                              All wasted?
                        (George Herbert, "The Collar")

If the quotation does not begin with a full line, space approximating the omitted part should be left.

                                        there was corn
                    Before my tears did drown it.

For text that follows an extract, see 13.24.

13.26 **Uniform indents for poetry.** Where all or most poetry extracts consist of blank verse (as in studies of Shakespeare) or are very long, uniform indents from the left margin usually work best (e.g., a left indent that matches the one, if any, used for prose extracts).

I have full cause of weeping, but this heart
Shall break into a hundred thousand flaws
Or ere I'll weep. O Fool! I shall go mad.

13.27 **Long lines and runovers in poetry.** Runover lines (the remainder of lines too long to appear as a single line) are usually indented one em from the line above, as in the following quotation from Walt Whitman's "Song of Myself":

My tongue, every atom of my blood, form'd from this
    soil, this air,
Born here of parents born here from parents the same,
    and their parents the same,
I, now thirty-seven years old in perfect health begin,
Hoping to cease not till death.

Runover lines, although indented, should be distinct from new lines deliberately indented by the poet (as in the Herbert poem quoted in 13.25). Generally, a unique and uniform indent for runovers will be enough to accomplish this. See also 2.20.

13.28 **Quotation marks in poems.** Quotation marks at the start of a line can usually be aligned with the other lines in the excerpt.

He holds him with his skinny hand.
"There was a ship," quoth he.
"Hold off! unhand me, grey-beard loon!"
Eftsoons his hand dropt he.

Some publishers prefer instead to place quotation marks at the start of a line of poetry outside the alignment of the poem, with lines left-aligned as if the quotation marks were not there. This practice, not followed by Chicago, may be impractical in certain electronic publication formats.

13.29 **Run-in poetry quotations.** If space or context in the text or in a note requires that two or more lines be run in, the lines are separated by a slash, with one space on either side (in printed works, a thin space to an en space).

Andrew Marvell's praise of John Milton, "Thou has not missed one thought that could be fit, / And all that was improper does omit" ("On *Paradise Lost*"), might well serve as our motto.

For running in more than one stanza (to be avoided if at all possible), see 13.34.

Quotation Marks

Double or Single Quotation Marks

13.30 **Quotations and "quotes within quotes."** Quoted words, phrases, and sentences run into the text are enclosed in double quotation marks. Single quotation marks enclose quotations within quotations; double marks, quotations within these; and so on. (The practice in the United Kingdom and elsewhere is often the reverse: single marks are used first, then double, and so on.) When the material quoted consists entirely of a quotation within a quotation, only one set of quotation marks need be employed (usually double quotation marks). For permissible changes from single to double quotation marks and vice versa, see 13.7 (item 1); see also 13.63. For dialogue, see 13.39.

> "Don't be absurd!" said Henry. "To say that 'I mean what I say' is the same as 'I say what I mean' is to be as confused as Alice at the Mad Hatter's tea party. You remember what the Hatter said to her: 'Not the same thing a bit! Why you might just as well say that "I see what I eat" is the same thing as "I eat what I see"!'"

Note carefully not only the placement of the single and double closing quotation marks but also that of the exclamation points in relation to those marks in the example above. Exclamation points, like question marks, are placed just within the set of quotation marks ending the element to which such terminal punctuation belongs. See also 6.9–11.

13.31 **Quotation marks in block quotations.** Although material set off as a block quotation is not enclosed in quotation marks, quoted matter *within* the block quotation is enclosed in double quotation marks—in other words, treated as it would be in otherwise unquoted text (see 13.30). An author or editor who changes a run-in quotation to a block quotation must delete the opening and closing quotation marks and change any internal ones. The following examples illustrate the same material first in run-in form and then as a block quotation:

> The narrator then breaks in: "Imagine Bart's surprise, dear reader, when Emma turned to him and said, contemptuously, 'What "promise"?'"

> The narrator then breaks in:
>
> > Imagine Bart's surprise, dear reader, when Emma turned to him and said, contemptuously, "What 'promise'?"

Similarly, converting a block quotation to a run-in quotation requires adding and altering quotation marks. For interpolations that include quoted matter, see 13.63.

Quotations of More than One Paragraph

13.32 **Quotation marks across paragraphs.** Quoted material of more than one paragraph should be presented as a block quotation if at all possible (see 13.10). If for some reason such a passage must be run in to the surrounding text, a quotation mark is needed at the beginning of the quotation and at the beginning of *each* new paragraph but at the end of only the *final* paragraph. (Note that each successive paragraph must begin on a new line, as in the original.) The same practice is followed in dialogue when one speaker's remarks extend over more than one paragraph (see 13.39). See also 13.33.

13.33 **Quotations within quotations across paragraphs.** Quoted material that contains an interior quotation that runs for more than one paragraph (as in extended dialogue from one speaker quoted in a work of fiction) should be presented as a block quotation if it all possible; original quotation marks should be preserved, except as described in 13.7. If for some reason such a passage must be run in to the surrounding text, quotation marks should be used as described in 13.32, with the following exceptions: a single quotation mark appears at the beginning and at the end of the interior quotation as a whole, and both double and single marks appear before each new paragraph belonging to the interior quotation. See also 13.30.

13.34 **Quoting more than one stanza of poetry.** A poetry quotation that spans more than one stanza should be presented as an extract, if at all possible (see 13.25). If it must be run in to the text (set off by opening and closing quotation marks), two slashes (//), with a space before and after, should appear between stanzas. For the use of the slash between run-in lines of poetry, see 13.29.

13.35 **Quoting letters in their entirety.** A letter quoted in its entirety should be set off as a block quotation. In the undesirable event that it must be run in, it should carry an opening quotation mark before the first line (including the salutation) and before each new paragraph (each of which must begin on a new line, as in the original). A closing quotation mark appears only after the last line (often the signature). See also 13.32.

Quotation Marks Omitted

13.36 **Epigraphs.** Quotation marks are not used around epigraphs (quotations used as ornaments preceding a text, usually to set the tone for what follows, rather than as illustration or documentation). Like block quotations, epigraphs receive a distinctive typographic treatment—often being set in a smaller typeface and indented from the right or left, and sometimes italicized. Treatment of sources, which are usually set on a separate line, also varies, though more than one epigraph used in the same work should receive consistent treatment. For more on sources, see 13.70–72. See also 1.37.

Oh, what a tangled web we weave,
When first we practice to deceive!
—Sir Walter Scott

It is a truth universally acknowledged, that a single man in possession of a good fortune, must be in want of a wife.
Jane Austen, *Pride and Prejudice*

13.37 **Decorative initials ("drop caps" and raised initials).** When the first word of a chapter or section opens with a large raised or dropped initial letter, and this letter belongs to the beginning of a run-in quotation, the opening quotation mark is often omitted.

OF THE MAKING OF MANY BOOKS there is no end," declared an ancient Hebrew sage, who had himself magnificently aggravated the situation he was decrying.

If the opening quotation mark is included, it should appear in the same size and with the same vertical alignment as the regular text.

13.38 **Maxims, questions, and the like.** Maxims, mottoes, rules, and other familiar expressions, sometimes enclosed in quotation marks, are discussed in 6.41 and 7.62. Questions that do not require quotation marks are discussed in 6.42 and 6.69.

Speech, Dialogue, and Conversation

13.39 **Direct discourse.** Direct discourse or dialogue is traditionally enclosed in quotation marks. A change in speaker is usually indicated by a new paragraph, as in the following excerpt from *Huckleberry Finn*:

> "Ransomed? What's that?"
>
> "I don't know. But that's what they do. I've seen it in books; and so of course that's what we've got to do."
>
> "But how can we do it if we don't know what it is?"
>
> "Why, blame it all, we've *got* to do it. Don't I tell you it's in the books? Do you want to go to doing different from what's in the books, and get things all muddled up?"

If one speech (usually a particularly long one) occupies more than a paragraph, opening quotation marks are needed at the beginning of each new paragraph, with a closing quotation mark placed at the end of only the *final* paragraph (see also 13.32).

13.40 **Single-word speech.** Words such as *yes*, *no*, *where*, *how*, and *why*, when used singly, are not enclosed in quotation marks except in direct discourse. See also 6.69.

> Ezra always answered yes; he could never say no to a friend.
> Please stop asking why.
> *but*
> "Yes," he replied weakly.
> Again she repeated, "Why?"

13.41 **Faltering speech or incomplete thoughts.** An ellipsis may be used to suggest faltering or fragmented speech accompanied by confusion or insecurity. In the examples below, note the relative positions of the ellipses and other punctuation. (For the use of ellipses to indicate editorial omissions, see 13.50–58.)

> "I . . . I . . . that is, we . . . yes, *we* have made an awful blunder!"
> "The ship . . . oh my God! . . . it's sinking!" cried Henrietta.
> "But . . . but . . . ," said Tom.

Interruptions or abrupt changes in thought are usually indicated by em dashes. See 6.87.

13.42 **Alternatives to quotation marks.** In some languages, em dashes are used to present dialogue; for examples, see 11.31, 11.47, 11.64, 11.101. For the use of guillemets (« »), see 11.29, 11.41, 11.47, 11.63, 11.101.

13.43 **Unspoken discourse.** Thought, imagined dialogue, and other internal discourse (also called interior discourse) may be enclosed in quotation marks or not, according to the context or the writer's preference. If a thought begins midsentence, it normally begins with a capital letter (as in the third example). See also 6.42.

> "I don't care if we have offended Morgenstern," thought Vera. "Besides," she told herself, "they're all fools."

> Why, we wondered, did we choose this route?

> She thought, If there's an app for that, I'll need to program it myself.

The following passage from James Joyce's *Ulysses* illustrates interior monologue and stream of consciousness without need of quotation marks:

> Reading two pages apiece of seven books every night, eh? I was young. You bowed to yourself in the mirror, stepping forward to applause earnestly, striking face. Hurray for the Goddamned idiot! Hray! No-one saw: tell no-one. Books you were going to write with letters for titles. Have you read his F?

13.44 **Numerals in direct discourse.** In quoting directly from spoken sources (e.g., interviews, speeches, or dialogue from a film or a play), or when writing direct discourse for a drama or a work of fiction, numbers that might otherwise be rendered as numerals can often be spelled out. This practice requires editorial discretion. Years can usually be rendered as numerals, as can trade names that include numerals. And for dialogue that includes more than a few large numbers, it may be more practical to use numerals. See also 9.2, 9.7.

> Jarred's answer was a mix of rage and humiliation: "For the last time, I do not have seven hundred thirty-seven dollars and eleven cents! I don't even have a quarter for the parking meter, for that matter."

> Like most proofreaders, she is a perfectionist. "I'm never happy with a mere ninety-nine and forty-four one-hundredths percent."

but

"Do you prefer shopping at 7-Eleven or Circle K?"

"I didn't get around to reading *Nineteen Eighty-Four* until 1985," he finally admitted.

"My mobile number is 555-0133."

13.45 **Indirect discourse.** Indirect discourse, which paraphrases dialogue, takes no quotation marks. See also 6.42.

Tom told Huck they had to do it that way because the books said so.
Very well, you say, but is there no choice?

Drama, Discussions and Interviews, and Field Notes

13.46 **Drama.** In plays, the speaker's name is usually set in a font distinct from the dialogue—caps and small caps, for example, or all small caps. The dialogue is not enclosed in quotation marks and is usually set with hanging indents (a style often used for bibliographies and indexes and illustrated in the following examples; see also 2.11).

R. ROISTER DOISTER. Except I have her to my wife, I shall run mad.
M. MERYGREEKE. Nay, "unwise" perhaps, but I warrant you for "mad."

Stage directions are usually italicized.

ALGERNON. That is quite a different matter. She is my aunt. (*Takes plate from below.*) Have some bread and butter. The bread and butter is for Gwendolen. Gwendolen is devoted to bread and butter.

JACK, *advancing to table and helping himself.* And very good bread and butter it is too.

13.47 **Shared lines and runover lines in verse drama.** In quoted excerpts from drama in verse, a single line of verse shared between two speakers in a play should be presented such that the second line continues where the first has left off (as in the example below, where the line begun by Barnardo is finished by Marcellus). Runover lines may be indicated as in poetry, by an indent of one em or more from the line above (see also 13.27).

BARNARDO.
    It would be spoke to.
MARCELLUS. Speak to it, Horatio.
HORATIO.
    What art thou that usurp'st this time of night,
    Together with that fair and warlike form
    In which the majesty of buried Denmark
    Did sometimes march? By heaven, I charge thee,
        speak.

13.48 **Discussions and interviews.** The transcription of a discussion or an interview is treated in much the same way as drama (see 13.46). Interjections such as "laughter" are italicized and enclosed in brackets (rather than parentheses, as in drama; see also 13.59–63). Paragraph indents are usually preferred to hanging indents (though hanging indents, which allow easier identification of the speaker, may work better if several speakers' names appear and the comments are relatively brief). Although speakers' names are usually followed by a period, a colon may be used instead. To save space, names may be abbreviated after their first appearance.

INTERVIEWER. You weren't thinking that this technology would be something you could use to connect to the Office of Tibet in New York or to different Tibet support groups in Europe?

RESPONDENT. No. Nobody seemed to have anything to do with GreenNet in the Tibet world at that time. That came much later. That's not really right. I specifically wasn't interested in connecting to the community of Tibet martyrs and fellow sufferers [*laughs*] and the emotional pathological there-but-for-the-grace-of-god-go-I people.

An author's previously unpublished transcriptions of interviews or discussions can usually be edited for such matters as capitalization, spelling, and minor grammatical slips or elisions. If an author has imposed more significant alterations, these should be explained in a note, a preface, or elsewhere. See also 4.77. Previously published transcriptions should be quoted as they appear in the original source.

13.49 **Case studies and ethnographic field notes.** An author's transcriptions of unpublished ethnographic field notes or material from case studies (the author's own or those of a colleague or assistant) pose a special case. Unlike quotations from published sources or transcriptions of interviews, such material need not be presented verbatim—whether presented as quotations or woven into the text. Rather, it should be edited for consistency—with related material and with the surrounding text—in matters of spelling, capitalization, punctuation, treatment of numbers, and so forth. And even if the author is in possession of signed releases, any otherwise anonymous subjects or informants should generally be presented under pseudonyms; a note should be appended to the text to indicate that this is the case. Whereas modifications intended to maintain participants' anonymity are acceptable, authors must take care to ensure that any changes do not lead to misrepresentation. Editors should query authors if it is not clear that appropriate provisions have been made. See also 4.77.

Ellipses

13.50 **Ellipses defined.** An *ellipsis* is a series of three dots used to signal the omission of a word, phrase, line, paragraph, or more from a quoted passage. Such omissions are made of material that is considered irrelevant to the discussion at hand (or, occasionally, to adjust for the grammar of the surrounding text). Chicago style is to use three spaced periods (but see 13.53) rather than another device such as asterisks. These dots (which are sometimes referred to as suspension points) may also be used to indicate faltering speech or incomplete thoughts (see 13.41). The dots in an ellipsis must always appear together on the same line (through the use of nonbreaking spaces; see 6.121), along with any punctuation that immediately follows; if an ellipsis appears at the beginning of a new line, any punctuation that immediately precedes it (including a period) will appear at the end of the line above. If they prefer, authors may prepare their manuscripts using their word processor's nonbreaking three-dot ellipsis character (Unicode 2026), usually with a space on either side; editors following Chicago style will replace these with spaced periods. For bracketed ellipses, see 13.58. See also 11.2.

13.51 **Danger of skewing meaning with ellipses.** Since quotations from another source have been separated from their original context, particular care needs to be exercised when eliding text to ensure that the sense of the original is not lost or misrepresented. A deletion must not result in a statement alien to the original material. And in general, ellipses should not be used to join two statements that are far apart in the original. Accuracy of sense and emphasis must accompany accuracy of transcription.

13.52 **When not to use an ellipsis.** Ellipses are normally *not* used (1) before the first word of a quotation, even if the beginning of the original sentence has been omitted; or (2) after the last word of a quotation, even if the end of the original sentence has been omitted, unless the sentence as quoted is deliberately incomplete (see 13.55).

13.53 **Ellipses with periods.** A period is added *before* an ellipsis to indicate the omission of the end of a sentence, unless the sentence is deliberately incomplete (see 13.55). Similarly, a period at the end of a sentence in the original is retained before an ellipsis indicating the omission of material immediately following the period. What precedes and, normally, what follows the four dots should be grammatically complete sentences as quoted, even if part of either sentence has been omitted. A complete passage from Emerson's essay "Politics" reads:

> The spirit of our American radicalism is destructive and aimless: it is not loving; it has no ulterior and divine ends; but is destructive only out of hatred and selfishness. On the other side, the conservative party, composed of the most moderate, able, and cultivated part of the population, is timid, and merely defensive of property. It vindicates no right, it aspires to no real good, it brands no crime, it proposes no generous policy, it does not build, nor write, nor cherish the arts, nor foster religion, nor establish schools, nor encourage science, nor emancipate the slave, nor befriend the poor, or the Indian, or the immigrant. From neither party, when in power, has the world any benefit to expect in science, art, or humanity, at all commensurate with the resources of the nation.

The passage might be shortened as follows:

> The spirit of our American radicalism is destructive and aimless. . . . On the other side, the conservative party . . . is timid, and merely defensive of property. . . . It does not build, nor write, nor cherish the arts, nor foster religion, nor establish schools.

Note that the first word after an ellipsis is capitalized if it begins a new grammatical sentence. Some types of works require that such changes to capitalization be bracketed; see 13.21. See also 13.58.

13.54 **Ellipses with other punctuation.** Other punctuation appearing in the original text—a comma, a colon, a semicolon, a question mark, or an exclamation point—may precede or follow an ellipsis (except when a period precedes the ellipsis; see 13.53). Whether to include the additional mark of punctuation depends on whether keeping it aids comprehension or is required for the grammar of the sentence. Placement of the other punctuation depends on whether the omission precedes or follows the mark; when the omission precedes it, a nonbreaking space should be used between the ellipsis and the mark of punctuation to prevent the mark from carrying over to the beginning of a new line (see 13.50). Note that this before-or-after distinction is usually *not* made with periods, where—without the aid of brackets (see 13.58)—it is likely to go unnoticed (see 13.53).

> It does not build, . . . nor cherish the arts, nor foster religion.

> As to *Endymion*, was it a poem . . . to be treated contemptuously by those who had celebrated, with various degrees of complacency and panegyric, *Paris*, and *Woman*, and *A Syrian Tale* . . . ? Are these the men who . . . presumed to draw a parallel between the Rev. Mr. Milman and Lord Byron?

> When a species . . . increases inordinately in numbers in a small tract, epidemics . . . often ensue: and here we have a limiting check independent of the struggle for life. But even some of these so-called epidemics appear to be due to parasitic worms . . . : and here comes in a sort of struggle between the parasite and its prey.

13.55 **Ellipses at the ends of deliberately incomplete sentences.** An ellipsis alone (i.e., three dots with no additional period) is used at the end of a quoted sentence that is deliberately left grammatically incomplete.

> Everyone knows that the Declaration of Independence begins with the sentence "When, in the course of human events . . ." But how many people can recite more than the first few lines of the document?

> Have you had a chance to look at the example beginning "The spirit of our American radicalism . . ."?

Note that no space intervenes between a final ellipsis point and a closing quotation mark.

13.56 **Ellipses for the omission of whole or partial paragraphs.** The omission of one or more paragraphs within a quotation is indicated by a period followed by an ellipsis at the end of the paragraph preceding the omitted part (see also 13.53). (If that paragraph ends with an incomplete sentence, only the three-dot ellipsis is used; see 13.55.) If the first part of a paragraph is omitted within a quotation, a paragraph indent and an ellipsis appear before the first quoted word. It is thus possible to use an ellipsis both at the end of one paragraph and at the beginning of the next, as illustrated in the following excerpt from Alexander Pope's "Letter to a Noble Lord":

> I should be obliged indeed to lessen this respect, if all the nobility . . . are but so many hereditary fools, if the privilege of lords be to want brains, if noblemen can hardly write or read. . . .
>
> Were it the mere excess of your Lordship's wit, that carried you thus triumphantly over all the bounds of decency, I might consider your Lordship on your Pegasus, as a sprightly hunter on a mettled horse. . . .
>
> . . . Unrivalled as you are, in making a figure, and in making a speech, methinks, my Lord, you may well give up the poor talent of making a distich.

13.57 **Ellipses in poetry and verse drama.** Omission of the end of a line of verse is indicated by a period followed by an ellipsis if what precedes them is a complete grammatical sentence (see 13.53); otherwise, only the three-dot ellipsis is used (as in the Poe example; see also 13.55). The omission of a full line or of several consecutive lines within a quoted poem or drama in verse is indicated by one line of widely spaced dots approximately the length of the line above (or of the missing line, if that is determinable). See also 13.25–29.

> Type of the antique Rome! Rich reliquary
> Of lofty contemplation . . .
> (Edgar Allan Poe, "The Coliseum")

> She would dwell on such dead themes, not as one who remembers,
> But rather as one who sees.
> . . . .
> Past things retold were to her as things existent,
> Things present but as a tale.
> (Thomas Hardy, "One We Knew")

> This royal throne of kings, this sceptred isle,
> . . . .
> This blessed plot, this earth, this realm, this England.
> (*Richard II*, 2.1.40–50)

13.58 **Bracketed ellipses.** Especially in languages that make liberal use of ellipses for faltering speech or incomplete thoughts, it is a common practice to bracket ellipses that are inserted to indicate an omission in quoted text (see, e.g., 11.32; see also 11.19). In an English context where ellipses are needed for a quotation that includes ellipses in the original text, the latter may be explained at each instance in a note (e.g., "ellipsis in original"; see also 13.62); for more than a few such instances, authors may choose instead to bracket their own ellipses, but only after explaining such a decision in a note, a preface, or elsewhere. The rules for bracketed ellipses are the same as the rules outlined in the rest of this section, with one exception—a period is placed before or after the ellipsis depending on its placement in the original. Compare the passage that follows to the passages in 13.53.

> The spirit of our American radicalism is destructive and aimless [. . .]. On the other side, the conservative party [. . .] is timid, and merely defensive of property. [. . .] It does not build, nor write, nor cherish the arts, nor foster religion, nor establish schools.

Note that a space appears before an opening bracket; a space appears after a closing bracket except when a period, comma, or other mark of punctuation follows. Within brackets, the sequence is bracket-period-space-period-space-period-bracket. Nonbreaking spaces are needed only for the two spaces between the periods within the brackets (see also 6.121). Bracketed ellipses may also be used in source citations to shorten very long titles; see 14.97.

Interpolations and Clarifications

13.59 **Missing or illegible words.** In reproducing or quoting from a document in which certain words are missing or illegible, an author may use ellipses (see 13.50–58), a bracketed comment or guess (sometimes followed by a question mark), or both. If ellipses alone are used (useful for a passage with more than a few lacunae), their function as a stand-in for missing or illegible words must be explained in the text or in a note. If a bracketed gloss comes from a different source, the source must be cited in a note or elsewhere. See also 6.99.

> If you will assure me of your . . . [illegible], I shall dedicate my life to your endeavor.

> She marched out the door, headed for the [president's?] office.

A 2-em dash (see 6.93), sometimes in combination with an interpolated guess, may also be used for missing material. As with ellipses, this device should be used consistently and should be explained (in prefatory material or a note).

I have great marvel that ye will so soon incline to every man his device and [counsel and ——] specially in matters of small impor[tance ——] yea, and as [it is] reported [unto me——] causes as meseemeth th[a——] nothing to [——]ne gentlewomen.

13.60 **Bracketed clarifications.** Insertions may be made in quoted material to clarify an ambiguity, to provide a missing word or letters (see 13.59), to correct an error, or, in a translation, to give the original word or phrase where the English fails to convey the exact sense. Such interpolations, which should be kept to a minimum lest they irritate or distract readers, are enclosed in brackets (never in parentheses). See also 6.99, 13.12.

Marcellus, doubtless in anxious suspense, asks Barnardo, "What, has this thing [the ghost of Hamlet's father] appear'd again tonight?"

"Well," said she, "if Mr. L[owell] won't go, then neither will I."

Saha once remarked of Nehru that "his position in this country can be described by a phrase which Americans use with respect to Abraham Lincoln [read: George Washington], 'first in war, first in peace.'"

13.61 **"Sic."** Literally meaning "so," "thus," "in this manner," and traditionally set in italics, *sic* may be inserted in brackets following a word misspelled or wrongly used in the original. This device should be used only where it is relevant to call attention to such matters (and especially where readers might otherwise assume the mistake is in the transcription rather than the original) or where paraphrase or silent correction is inappropriate (see 13.4, 13.7, item 6).

In September 1862, J. W. Chaffin, president of the Miami Conference of Wesleyan Methodist Connection, urged Lincoln that "the confiscation law past [*sic*] at the last session of Congress should be faithfully executed" and that "to neglect this national righteousness" would prove "disastrous to the American people."

Sic should *not* be used merely to call attention to unconventional spellings, which should be explained (if at all) in a note or in prefatory material. Similarly, where material with many errors and variant spellings (such as a collection of informal letters) is reproduced as written, a prefatory comment or a note to that effect will make a succession of *sic*s unnecessary.

13.62 **"Italics added."** An author wishing to call particular attention to a word or phrase in quoted material may italicize it but must tell readers what has been done, by means of such formulas as "italics mine," "italics added," "emphasis added," or "emphasis mine." Occasionally it may be important to point out that italics in a quotation were indeed in the original. Here the usual phrase is "italics in the original" or, for example, "De Quincey's italics." This information appears either in parentheses following the quotation or in a source note to the quotation. If there are italics in the original of the passage quoted, the information is best enclosed in brackets and placed directly after the added italics. Consistency in method throughout a work is essential.

> You have watched the conduct of Ireland in the difficult circumstances of the last nine months, and that conduct I do not hesitate to risk saying on your behalf has evoked in every breast a responsive voice of sympathy, and an increased conviction that we may deal freely *and yet deal prudently* with our fellow-subjects beyond the Channel. Such is your conviction. (William Ewart Gladstone, October 1891; italics added)

> In reality not one didactic poet has ever yet attempted to use any parts or processes of the particular art which he made his theme, unless in so far as they seemed susceptible of poetic treatment, and only *because* they seemed so. Look at the poem of *Cyder* by Philips, of the *Fleece* by Dyer, or (which is a still weightier example) at the *Georgics* of Virgil,—does any of these poets show the least anxiety for the *correctness of your principles* [my italics], or the delicacy of your manipulations, in the worshipful arts they affect to teach? (Thomas De Quincey, "Essay on Pope")

13.63 **Interpolations requiring quotation marks.** Occasionally a bracketed or parenthetical interpolation that includes quotation marks appears in material already enclosed in quotation marks. In such cases, the double/single rule (see 13.30) does not apply; the quotation marks within the brackets may remain double.

> "Do you mean that a double-headed calf ["two-headed calf" in an earlier version] has greater value than two normal calves? That a freak of nature, even though it cannot survive, is to be more highly treasured for its rarity than run-of-the-mill creatures are for their potential use?"

Attributing Quotations in Text

13.64 **Use of parentheses with in-text citations.** If the source of a direct quotation is not given in a note, it is usually placed in the text in parentheses. Although the source normally follows a quotation, it may come earlier if it fits more smoothly into the introductory text (as in the second example in 13.65). The examples in this section focus on full and short forms of parenthetical citation that may be needed in shorter works with no notes or bibliography or to provide in-text citations to a frequently quoted work. The advice in this section on placement relative to surrounding text is intended to supplement the system of notes and bibliography covered in chapter 14. For author-date references, see chapter 15.

13.65 **Full in-text citation.** An entire source may be given in parentheses immediately following a quotation (as in the first example below), or some of the data may be worked into the text (as in the second example), with details confined to parentheses. See also 6.101. For more on the proper form for full citations, see 14.23.

> "If an astronaut falls into a black hole, its mass will increase, but eventually the energy equivalent of that extra mass will be returned to the universe in the form of radiation. Thus, in a sense, the astronaut will be 'recycled'" (Stephen W. Hawking, *A Brief History of Time: From the Big Bang to Black Holes* [New York: Bantam Books, 1988], 112).

> In their introduction to *Democracy in America* (University of Chicago Press, 1999), translators Harvey Mansfield and Delba Winthrop write that Tocqueville "shows that the people are sovereign, whether through the Constitution or despite it, and he warns of the tyranny of the majority" (xvii).

13.66 **Shortened citations or "ibid." with subsequent in-text citations.** If a second passage from the same source is quoted close to the first and there is no intervening quotation from a different source, the author's name or *ibid.* (set in roman) may be used in the second parenthetical reference (e.g., "Hawking, 114" *or* "ibid., 114"). In a departure from previous editions of this manual, Chicago now prefers the first form as being the less ambiguous option, though *ibid.* may be appropriate if used consistently. Avoid overusing either form: for more than the occasional repeated reference to the same source—as in an extended discussion of a work of fiction—only a parenthetical page number is necessary. Whichever form is used, if a quotation from another source has intervened, a shortened reference that includes the title may be necessary (e.g., "Hawking, *Brief History of Time*, 114"). For more on shortened citations, see 14.29–36; for the use of shortened citations versus *ibid.* in notes, see 14.34.

13.67 **Frequent reference to a single source cited in a note.** In a work containing notes, the full citation of a source may be given in a note at first mention, with subsequent citations made parenthetically in the text.

This method is especially suited to literary studies that use frequent quotations from a single source. In a study of *Much Ado about Nothing*, for example, the note would list the edition and include wording such as "Text references are to act, scene, and line of this edition." A parenthetical reference to act 3, scene 4, lines 46–47, would then appear as in the example below. In references to a work of fiction, page numbers alone may be given.

"Ye light o' love with your heels! then, if your husband have stables enough, you'll see he shall lack no barns," says Beatrice (3.4.46–47).

Where a number of such sources (or different editions of a single source) are used in the same work, the title (or edition) may need to be indicated in the parenthetical references; it may be advisable to devise an abbreviation for each and to include a list of the abbreviations at the beginning or end of the work (see 14.59, 14.60). See also 14.246, 14.253, 14.48.

Sources Following Run-In Quotations

13.68 **Punctuation following source of run-in quotation.** After a run-in quotation, the source is usually given after the closing quotation mark, followed by the rest of the surrounding sentence (including any comma, semicolon, colon, or dash; but see 13.69) or the final punctuation of that sentence.

With his "Nothing will come of nothing; speak again" (1.1.92), Lear tries to draw from his youngest daughter an expression of filial devotion.

It has been more than a century since Henry Adams said: "Fifty years ago, science took for granted that the rate of acceleration could not last. The world forgets quickly, but even today the habit remains of founding statistics on the faith that consumption will continue nearly stationary" (*Education*, 493).

Has it been more than a century since Henry Adams observed that "fifty years ago, science took for granted that the rate of acceleration could not last" (*Education*, 493)?

A parenthetical reference need not immediately follow the quotation as long as it is clear what it belongs to. For examples, see 13.65 (second example), 13.67. See also 15.26.

13.69 **Punctuation preceding source of run-in quotation.** When a quotation comes at the end of a sentence and is itself a question or an exclamation, that punctuation is retained within the quotation marks, and a period is still added after the closing parentheses. (Compare the third example in 13.68.)

And finally, in the frenzy of grief that kills him, Lear rails, "Why should a dog, a horse, a rat, have life, / And thou no breath at all?" (5.3.306–7).

Sources Following Block Quotations and Poetry Extracts

13.70 **Parenthetical source following a block quotation.** The source of a block quotation is given in parentheses at the end of the quotation and in the same type size. The opening parenthesis appears *after* the final punctuation mark of the quoted material. No period either precedes or follows the closing parenthesis. See also 6.101, 15.26.

If you happen to be fishing, and you get a strike, and whatever it is starts off with the preliminaries of a vigorous fight; and by and by, looking down over the side through the glassy water, you see a rosy golden gleam, the mere specter of a fish, shining below in the clear depths; and when you look again a sort of glory of golden light flashes and dazzles as it circles nearer beneath and around and under the boat; . . . and you land a slim and graceful and impossibly beautiful three-foot goldfish, whose fierce and vivid yellow is touched around the edges with a violent red—when all these things happen to you, fortunate but bewildered fisherman, then you may know you have been fishing in the Galapagos Islands and have taken a Golden Grouper. (Gifford Pinchot, *To the South Seas* [Philadelphia: John Winston, 1930], 123)

Shortened references are treated in the same way as full ones. If a qualifier such as *line*, *vol.*, or *p.* is required at the beginning of the shortened reference (a *p.* may often be omitted, especially with repeated references), it should be lowercased as with sources to run-in quotations.

At last the fish came into sight—at first a mere gleam in the water, and then his full side. This was not even a distant cousin to the fish I thought I was fighting, but something else again entirely. (p. 142) *or* (142)

13.71 **Parenthetical citations with poetry extracts.** In order not to interfere with a poem's layout and overall presentation, parenthetical citations following poetry extracts are dropped to the line below the last line of the quotation. They may be centered on the last letter of the longest line of the quotation or set flush with the left margin of the poem; an additional line space may be added. Other positions are also possible (as in the examples in 13.25 and 13.72), as long as consistency and clarity are preserved.

Now more than ever seems it rich to die,
To cease upon the midnight with no pain,
While thou art pouring forth thy soul abroad
    In such an ecstasy!
(Keats, "Ode to a Nightingale," stanza 6)

13.72 **Shortened references to poetry extracts.** Shortened references to poetry are treated the same way as full ones. A quotation from Edmund Spenser's *The Faerie Queene*, once the reader knows that reference is to book, canto, and stanza, might appear as follows:

Who will not mercie unto others shew,
How can he mercy ever hope to have?
(6.1.42)

III · Source Citations and Indexes

14 · Notes and Bibliography

Source Citations: An Overview

14.1 **The purpose of source citations.** Ethics, copyright laws, and courtesy to readers require authors to identify the sources of direct quotations or paraphrases and of any facts or opinions not generally known or easily checked (see 13.1–6). Conventions for citing sources vary according to scholarly discipline, the preferences of publishers and authors, and the needs of a particular work. Regardless of the convention being followed, source citations must always provide sufficient information either to lead readers directly to the sources consulted or, for materials that may not be readily available, to enable readers to positively identify them, regardless of whether the sources are published or unpublished or in printed or electronic form.

14.2 **Chicago's two systems of source citation.** This chapter describes the first of Chicago's two systems of source citation, which uses notes, whether footnotes or endnotes or both, usually together with a bibliography. The notes allow space for unusual types of sources as well as for commentary on the sources cited, making this system extremely flexible. Because of this flexibility, the notes and bibliography system is preferred by many writers in literature, history, and the arts. Chicago's other system—which uses parenthetical author-date references and a corresponding reference list as described in chapter 15—is nearly identical in content but differs in form. The author-date system is preferred for many publications in the sciences and social sciences but may be adapted for any work, sometimes with the addition of footnotes or endnotes. For journals, the choice between systems is likely to have been made long ago; anyone writing for a journal should consult the specific journal's instructions to authors (and see 14.3).

14.3 **Other systems of source citation.** Among other well-known systems are those of the Modern Language Association (MLA) and the American Psychological Association (APA), both of which use in-text citations (described in chapter 15), and that of the American Medical Association (AMA). The AMA uses a numbered list of references cited in the text by reference number; the text numbers appear as superior figures like note reference numbers. Guidelines and examples for these three systems are to be found in the manuals of those associations. *Scientific Style and Format*, published by the Council of Science Editors (CSE) in cooperation with the University of Chicago Press, also furnishes useful guidelines on both the author-date system and numbered references (see bibliog. 1.1 for these and other style manuals). Many journals and serials—including some of those published by the University of Chicago Press—either follow one of these styles or have their own styles, often based on or similar to the systems mentioned here and in 14.2. For legal and public documents, Chicago recommends *The Bluebook*, published by the Harvard Law Review Association; see 14.269–305.

14.4 **Flexibility and consistency.** As long as a consistent style is maintained within any one work, logical and defensible variations on the style illustrated in this chapter and in chapter 15 are acceptable if agreed to by author and publisher. Such flexibility, however, is rarely possible in journal publication, which calls for adherence to the established style of the journal in question. See also 14.3.

14.5 **Citation management tools.** It is rarely necessary to create a source citation from scratch; even most printed resources will be listed with library catalogs or other online resources. From there, it is easy enough to copy and paste relevant data or to extract them using a number of available tools. Citation management applications such as EndNote or Zotero allow users to build libraries of reference data based directly on their research. These data can be used to place notes or in-text references in a manuscript or to generate bibliographies or reference lists—all formatted according to any number of citation styles (including both of Chicago's). The results, however, are only as good as the data that generate them and the software used to format them. A few caveats:

- Double-check your data. As you build your library of source data, check each field against the actual source as soon as you acquire the data for it. Make sure authors' names, titles of works, dates, and so forth are accurate and that they are entered in the appropriate fields. Check also for missing or redundant data. (It is okay, however, to collect more data than you will use in your citations.) You will need to do this whether you entered the data yourself or exported the citation from a library catalog or other resource.
- Double-check your citations. Once a source citation has been inserted in your manuscript, make sure it is correctly formatted according to the recommendations in this chapter or chapter 15. Things to look for include errant punctuation or capitalization and missing or superfluous data. Enter corrections in the citation management application (or adjust its settings, as applicable) and double-check the results in the manuscript.
- Make sure your citations are backed up. Some applications will let you back up your data automatically. It is usually a good idea also to keep local copies as a safeguard. Such backups are helpful not only for ongoing research but also in the event your manuscript must be resubmitted for any reason.

Citation management tools work best for citing recently published books and journal articles and other common publication formats. The variety of sources typically cited in a scholarly work, on the other hand, usually precludes an acceptable result from software alone. Authors are therefore strongly encouraged to review their citations for consistency, accuracy, and completeness before submitting their final manuscripts (editors, in turn, should be aware of how the software works in order to help identify any potential pitfalls). Note also that your publisher may require that such citations be presented as ordinary text, stripped of any of the underlying codes such as fields or hyperlinks used in creating or organizing them. Authors should double-check citations *after* this conversion to ordinary text and fix any problems both in the text and in the citation data; authors are also advised to save a backup copy of the penultimate version of the manuscript, with codes intact, in case the citations need to be regenerated for any reason. See also 2.22.

Sources Consulted Online

14.6 **Electronic resource identifiers.** Authors citing sources consulted online should generally include a uniform resource locator, or URL,[1] as the final element in a citation that includes all the components described throughout this chapter and in chapter 15. A URL has the potential to lead readers directly to the source cited, and authors are encouraged to include them as part of their source citations (but see 14.11). Many journal publishers, especially in the sciences, create links to sources cited in their articles as a matter of course—a process that authors facilitate when they include electronic resource identifiers with their source citations. Book publishers, on the other hand, may require URLs only in citations of sources that may otherwise be difficult to locate. Authors are therefore advised to consult their publishers early in the publication process. The information in this section—together with the examples of URLs throughout this chapter—is intended to provide guidance for those authors and publishers who wish to include them as part of their research or publications or both. See also 14.7. For citing other types of electronic formats, see 14.159, 14.163, 14.263, 14.265.

14.7 **Uniform resource locators (URLs).** A uniform resource locator, or URL—for example, http://www.chicagomanualofstyle.org/—is designed to

1. For more information about URLs, consult the website of the World Wide Web Consortium. See also 14.7.

lead a reader directly to an internet source. Note that it is never sufficient to provide only a URL; as far as they can be determined, the full facts of publication should always be recorded first. Readers should be able to judge the nature and authority of any source from the full facts of publication as detailed throughout this chapter and chapter 15. Moreover, the source to which a URL points is apt to move to a different location or to disappear altogether. For this reason, it is important to choose the version of the URL that is most likely to continue to point to the source cited. For DOIs, see 14.8. For other options, see 14.9, 14.10, 14.11. For URL syntax, see 14.17 and 14.18. For examples of URLs in source citations, see 14.23 (under "Journal Article") and throughout this chapter and chapter 15.

14.8 **Digital Object Identifiers (DOIs).** One of a number of standards addressing the need for more reliable resource identifiers is that of the Digital Object Identifier (DOI).[2] A DOI is a unique and permanent string assigned to a piece of intellectual property such as a journal article or book (or a component thereof), in any medium in which it is published. (The term "digital" refers to the identifier and not necessarily to the object.) A DOI forms a persistent URL starting with https://doi.org/ followed by a prefix (such as 10.1086) assigned by a DOI registration agency such as Crossref and then a suffix assigned by the publisher. For example, https://doi.org/10.1086/679716 identifies the article entitled "Scott's Editing: History, Polyphony, Authority," by Robert Mayer, published in the May 2015 issue of *Modern Philology*. This URL will, at a minimum, redirect the user to the latest version of a page with information that identifies the content and includes up-to-date information about its location or availability (from the publisher or other content owner). DOIs are often listed with a source in the form of "DOI:" followed by the prefix and suffix; in their source citations, authors should append this DOI to https://doi.org/ to form a URL as described above. (To find a DOI link or its target, the string starting with the prefix can be entered into the metadata search tool available from Crossref or the DOI resolver provided by the International DOI Foundation.) DOIs are an implementation of the Handle System, which also provides for URLs that begin with https://hdl.handle.net/ and function in much the same way as DOI-based URLs. Authors should prefer a DOI- or Handle-based URL whenever one is available. Examples are included throughout the section on journals (14.168–87) and at 14.161 and 14.234.

---

2. For more information about DOIs, consult the websites of the International DOI Foundation and Crossref.

14.9 **Permalinks and the like.** URLs are usually recorded by copying the version of the URL that appears with the source in a web browser's address bar (or sometimes through a sharing option) as the current link for the reference. Some internet resources list another version of the URL along with the resource itself intended for citing or sharing the link. In the absence of a DOI or the like (see 14.8), these URLs—often labeled as persistent URLs, permalinks, stable URLs, or the like—should generally be preferred. As with any URL, they should be tested to make sure they lead where intended. When a URL points to a location that requires a subscription to a commercial database (e.g., through a library), it may be better to name the database instead (see 14.11).

14.10 **Short forms for URLs.** A very long URL—one that runs to as much as a line or more of text, especially if it contains a lot of punctuation or other syntax readable mainly by computers—can often be shortened simply by finding a better version of the link. If the source offers a DOI (see 14.8), use that; otherwise, determine whether a permalink or the like is available (see 14.9). If not, it is still often possible to find a better version of the URL, sometimes by relinking to the source using the available tools for navigation. For example, a search for the 1913 novel *Pollyanna* in the Google Books database may yield a URL that looks like this:

https://books.google.com/books?id=bF81AAAAMAAJ&pg=PA226#v=onepage&q&f=false

That URL, the result of a search for a specific passage, points to a corresponding page in the book (p. 226). The URL for the main page for the book looks like this (and should be preferred, assuming a page reference is included as part of the full citation):

https://books.google.com/books?id=bF81AAAAMAAJ

Alternatively, it is usually acceptable for such formally published resources simply to list the domain name (e.g., https://books.google.com/) or the name of the database (e.g., Google Books); interested readers should be able to search for and find the cited source based on the full facts of publication. On the other hand, shortened versions of a URL provided by third-party services (and intended primarily for use with social media) should never be used. Not only are such services prone to disappear, but the original URL identifies the domain name and other elements that may be important to the citation. Publishers, however, may choose to make an exception, especially for DOIs. (Short forms for DOIs are available through a service from the International DOI Foundation.)

14.11 **Library and other bibliographic databases.** For a source consulted via a library or other commercial bibliographic database and available only through a subscription or library account, it may be best to name the database in lieu of a URL. Even a URL recommended for such a source (see 14.9) may lead a nonsubscriber to a login page with no information about the source itself. If in doubt, test the URL while logged out of the library or database; a URL that leads to information about the source, if not full access to it, is safe to use. A URL based on a DOI, which will always direct readers to information about the source, if not full access to it, should be preferred where available (see 14.8). For more information and examples, see 14.161 (books), 14.175 (journals), 14.215 (theses and dissertations).

14.12 **Access dates.** An access date—that is, the self-reported date on which an author consulted a source—is of limited value: previous versions will often be unavailable to readers; authors typically consult a source any number of times over the course of days or months; and the accuracy of such dates, once recorded, cannot readily be verified by editors or publishers. Chicago does not therefore require access dates in its published citations of electronic sources unless no date of publication or revision can be determined from the source (see also 14.13). Because some publishers in some disciplines—in particular, research-intensive fields such as science and medicine—*do* require access dates, authors should check with their publishers early on, and it never hurts to record dates of access during research (citation management software will do this automatically). (Students may be required to include access dates in their papers.) For examples, see 14.176, 14.207, and 14.233. For access dates in author-date format, see 15.50.

14.13 **"Last modified" and other revision dates.** Some electronic documents will include a date on each page or screen indicating the last time the document was modified or revised. There are no accepted standards for this practice, and for formally published material the date of publication is generally more important. A revision date should be included, however, if it is presented as the de facto date of publication or is otherwise the only available date. Such dates may be particularly useful for citing wikis and other frequently updated works. For examples, see 14.207, 14.233, 14.234.

14.14 **Authority and permanence.** Much as they do for printed publications, authors must weigh the authority of any electronic sources they choose to cite. Electronic content presented without formal ties to a publisher or sponsoring body has the authority equivalent to that of unpublished or self-published material in other media. Moreover, such content is far more likely to change without notice—or disappear altogether—than formally published materials. On the other hand, self-published material from an authority on a given subject can usually be relied on. Authors should note that *anything* posted on the internet is "published" in the sense of copyright and must be treated as such for the purposes of complete citation and clearance of permissions, if relevant (see 4.2, 4.64–69).

14.15 **Preserving a permanent record.** As part of their research, and in addition to recording accurate and complete source citations as described throughout this chapter and chapter 15, authors are strongly encouraged to keep a copy of any source that is not formally published, as a hedge against potential challenges to the research or data before, during, or after publication. Such a source might include a post on a social-networking site or app, a page from the website of a banking institution, or a version of an article on a news site reporting an ongoing crisis—any source that may be difficult to track down at a later date in exactly the form in which it was consulted. (Examples of sources that would *not* be subject to this recommendation would include an article in a journal or a magazine or any book cataloged by the Library of Congress or other national registry.) Copies may be kept in the form of printouts or as digital files (e.g., as PDFs or screen captures), or by means of a permanent link creation service such as Perma.cc.

14.16 **Publications available in more than one medium.** In many cases the contents of the print and electronic forms of the same publication are intended to be identical. Moreover, publishers are encouraged to note explicitly any differences between the two (see 1.78). In practice, because there is always the potential for differences, intentional or otherwise, authors should cite the version consulted. Chicago recommends including a URL to indicate that a work was consulted online. For practical purposes, alternate electronic formats offered by a single publisher from the same URL—for example, PDF and HTML versions of the journal article mentioned in 14.8—do *not* need to be indicated in the citation. Moreover, a DOI-based URL technically points to each medium in which a work is published. (Though a print source may list a DOI, authors need not record it as part of their research unless their publisher or discipline requires it.) For items designed to be read apart from any website, the application, format, device, or medium should be specified, depending on what might be required to consult a particular version. See also 14.6.

14.17 **URLs and other such elements in relation to surrounding text.** URLs, email addresses, and the like are unique strings that contain no spaces.

URLs should be presented in full, beginning with the protocol (usually *http*, for *hypertext transfer protocol*, or *https*, a version of the protocol that adds support for enhanced security mechanisms). Even if it follows a period, the first letter of the protocol (e.g., the *h* in *http*) is not capitalized. (In running text, avoid beginning a sentence with a URL.) The capitalization of the remaining components varies; because some resource identifiers are case sensitive, they should not be edited for style. A "trailing slash" (/), the last character in a URL pointing to a directory, is part of the URL. Other punctuation marks that follow a URL or other such identifier will readily be perceived as belonging to the surrounding text; sentences or citations that include a URL or the like should therefore be punctuated normally. Though angle brackets or other "wrappers" are standard with email addresses or URLs in some applications, these are unnecessary in the context of notes and bibliographies or in running text (see also 6.8).

14.18 **URLs and line breaks.** In a printed work, if a URL has to be broken at the end of a line, the break should be made *after* a colon or a double slash (//); *before* a single slash (/), a tilde (~), a period, a comma, a hyphen, an underline (_), a question mark, a number sign, or a percent symbol; or *before or after* an equals sign or an ampersand. Such breaks help to signal that the URL has been carried over to the next line. A hyphen should never be added to a URL to denote a line break, nor should a hyphen that is part of a URL appear at the end of a line. If a particularly long element must be broken to avoid a seriously loose or tight line, it can be broken between words or syllables according to the guidelines for word division offered in 7.36–47. Editors, proofreaders, and compositors should use their discretion in applying these recommendations, aiming for a balance between readability and aesthetics.

http://press-pubs.uchicago
.edu/founders/

http://www.jstor.org/stable
/2921689

http://www.themillions.com/2015/04/to-fall-in
-love-with-a-reader-do-this.html

http://content.time.com/time/magazine/article/0,9171
,920400,00.html

http://www.scien
tificstyleandformat.org/

It is generally unnecessary to specify breaks for URLs in electronic publication formats with reflowable text, and authors should avoid forcing them to break in their manuscripts (see 2.13).

Basic Format, with Examples and Variations

14.19 **Notes and bibliography—an overview.** In the system favored by many writers in the humanities, bibliographic citations are provided in notes, preferably supplemented by a bibliography. The notes, whether footnotes or endnotes, are usually numbered and correspond to superscript note reference numbers in the text (but see 14.53); in electronic formats, notes and note numbers are usually linked. Notes are styled much like running text, with authors' names in normal order and the elements separated by commas or parentheses.

1. Stuart Shea, *Wrigley Field: The Long Life and Contentious Times of the Friendly Confines* (Chicago: University of Chicago Press, 2014), 51–52.

If the bibliography includes all works cited in the notes, the notes need not duplicate the source information in full because readers can consult the bibliography for publication details and other information. In works with no bibliography or only a selected list, full details must be given in a note at first mention of any work cited; subsequent citations need only include a short form.

2. Shea, *Wrigley Field*, 138.

In bibliographies, where entries are listed alphabetically, the name of the first author is inverted, and the main elements are separated by periods.

Shea, Stuart. *Wrigley Field: The Long Life and Contentious Times of the Friendly Confines*. Chicago: University of Chicago Press, 2014.

For examples of the difference in format between note citations and bibliography entries, see 14.23. For a detailed discussion of notes, see 14.24–60. For shortened references, see 14.29–36. For a detailed discussion of bibliographies, see 14.61–71.

14.20 **Basic structure of a note.** A footnote or an endnote generally lists the author, title, and facts of publication, in that order. Elements are separated by commas; the facts of publication are enclosed in parentheses. Authors' names are presented in standard order (first name first). Titles are capitalized headline-style (see 8.159), unless they are in another language (see 11.6). Titles of larger works (e.g., books and journals) are italicized; titles of smaller works (e.g., chapters, articles) or unpublished works are presented in roman and enclosed in quotation marks (see

8.163). Such terms as *editor/edited by*, *translator/translated by*, *volume*, and *edition* are abbreviated.

14.21 **Basic structure of a bibliography entry.** In a bibliography entry the elements are separated by periods rather than by commas; the facts of publication are not enclosed in parentheses; and the first-listed author's name, according to which the entry is alphabetized in the bibliography, is usually inverted (last name first). A bibliography entry starts with a capital letter unless the first word would normally be lowercased (as in a last name that begins with a lowercase particle; see 8.5). As in a note, titles are capitalized headline-style unless they are in another language; titles of larger works (e.g., books and journals) are italicized; and titles of smaller works (e.g., chapters, articles) or unpublished works are presented in roman and enclosed in quotation marks. Noun forms such as *editor*, *translator*, *volume*, and *edition* are abbreviated, but verb forms such as *edited by* and *translated by*—abbreviated in a note—are spelled out in a bibliography. Compare 14.20.

14.22 **Page numbers and other locators.** In notes, where reference is usually to a particular passage in a book or journal, only the page numbers pertaining to that passage are given. In bibliographies, no page numbers are given for books cited as a whole; for easier location of journal articles or chapters or other sections of a book, the beginning and ending page numbers of the entire article or chapter are given. Electronic sources do not always include page numbers (and some that do include them repaginate according to user-defined text size). For such unpaginated works, it may be appropriate in a note to include a chapter or paragraph number (if available), a section heading, or a descriptive phrase that follows the organizational divisions of the work. In citations especially of shorter electronic works presented as a single, searchable document, such locators may be unnecessary. See also 14.160.

14.23 **Notes and bibliography—examples and variations.** The examples that follow provide an overview of the notes and bibliography style, featuring books and journal articles as models. Each example includes a numbered note and a corresponding bibliography entry. Each example also includes a shortened form of the note, suitable for subsequent citations of a source already cited in full; in practice, in works that include a bibliography that lists in full all sources cited, it is acceptable to use the shortened form in the notes even at first mention. For advice on constructing short forms for notes, see 14.29–36. For many more examples, consult the sections dealing with specific types of sources throughout this chapter.

Book with Single Author or Editor

For a book with a single author, invert the name in the bibliography but not in the notes. Punctuate and capitalize as shown. Note the shortened form in the second note. Note also that page numbers are included in a note but not in a bibliography entry, unless the entry is for a chapter (see "Chapter in an Edited Book," below). The first note cites two consecutive pages; the second note cites two nonconsecutive pages. See also 14.148.

1. Cheryl Strayed, *Wild: From Lost to Found on the Pacific Crest Trail* (New York: Alfred A. Knopf, 2012), 87–88.

2. Strayed, *Wild*, 261, 265.

Strayed, Cheryl. *Wild: From Lost to Found on the Pacific Crest Trail*. New York: Alfred A. Knopf, 2012.

A book with an editor in place of an author includes the abbreviation *ed.* (*editor*; for more than one editor, use *eds.*). Note that the shortened form does not include *ed.*

1. Meghan Daum, ed., *Selfish, Shallow, and Self-Absorbed: Sixteen Writers on the Decision Not to Have Kids* (New York: Picador, 2015), 32.

2. Daum, *Selfish*, 134–35.

Daum, Meghan, ed. *Selfish, Shallow, and Self-Absorbed: Sixteen Writers on the Decision Not to Have Kids*. New York: Picador, 2015.

Book with Multiple Authors

For a book with two authors, note that only the first-listed name is inverted in the bibliography entry.

1. Brian Grazer and Charles Fishman, *A Curious Mind: The Secret to a Bigger Life* (New York: Simon & Schuster, 2015), 188.

2. Grazer and Fishman, *Curious Mind*, 190.

Grazer, Brian, and Charles Fishman. *A Curious Mind: The Secret to a Bigger Life*. New York: Simon & Schuster, 2015.

For a book with three authors, adapt as follows:

1. Alexander Berkman, Henry Bauer, and Carl Nold, *Prison Blossoms: Anarchist Voices from . . .*

2. Berkman, Bauer, and Nold, *Prison Blossoms . . .*

Berkman, Alexander, Henry Bauer, and Carl Nold. *Prison Blossoms: Anarchist Voices from . . .*

For a book with four or more authors, list all the authors in the bibliography entry. Word order and punctuation are the same as for two or three authors. In the note, however, cite only the name of the first-listed author, followed by *et al.* See also 14.76.

1. Claire Haček et al., *Mediated Lives: Reflections on Wearable Technologies . . .*

2. Haček et al., *Mediated Lives . . .*

Book with Author plus Editor or Translator

In a book with an editor or translator in addition to the author, *ed.* or *trans.* in the note becomes *Edited by* or *Translated by* in the bibliography entry. See also 14.104.

1. Gabriel García Márquez, *Love in the Time of Cholera*, trans. Edith Grossman (London: Cape, 1988), 242–55.

2. García Márquez, *Cholera*, 33.

García Márquez, Gabriel. *Love in the Time of Cholera*. Translated by Edith Grossman. London: Cape, 1988.

Chapter in an Edited Book

When citing a chapter or similar part of an edited book, include the chapter author; the chapter title, in quotation marks; and the editor. Precede the title of the book with *in*. Note the location of the page range for the chapter in the bibliography entry. See also 14.106–12.

1. Glenn Gould, "Streisand as Schwarzkopf," in *The Glenn Gould Reader*, ed. Tim Page (New York: Vintage Books, 1984), 310.

2. Gould, "Streisand as Schwarzkopf," 309.

Gould, Glenn. "Streisand as Schwarzkopf." In *The Glenn Gould Reader*, edited by Tim Page, 308–11. New York: Vintage Books, 1984.

Journal Article

Citations of journals typically include the volume and issue number and date of publication. The volume number follows the italicized journal title in roman and with no intervening punctuation. A specific page reference is included in the notes; the page range for an article is included in the bibliography. In the full citation, page numbers are preceded by a colon. Authors should record the full information for the issue, including issue number, even if a journal is paginated consecutively across a volume or if the month or season appears with the year.

1. Benjamin Bagley, "Loving Someone in Particular," *Ethics* 125, no. 2 (January 2015): 484–85.
2. Bagley, "Loving Someone in Particular," 501.

Bagley, Benjamin. "Loving Someone in Particular." *Ethics* 125, no. 2 (January 2015): 477–507.

The URL in the following example indicates that the article was consulted online; in this case, it is based on a DOI and is preferred to the URL that appears with the article (see 14.7, 14.8). Some publishers will use the URL as the basis of a link to the cited resource. Shortened citations for subsequent references to an online source need not repeat the URL. For access dates (not shown here), see 14.176.

1. Jui-Ch'i Liu, "Beholding the Feminine Sublime: Lee Miller's War Photography," *Signs* 40, no. 2 (Winter 2015): 311, https://doi.org/10.1086/678242.
2. Liu, "Beholding the Feminine Sublime," 312.

Liu, Jui-Ch'i. "Beholding the Feminine Sublime: Lee Miller's War Photography." *Signs* 40, no. 2 (Winter 2015): 308–19. https://doi.org/10.1086/678242.

Notes

Note Numbers

14.24 **Numbers in text versus numbers in notes.** Note reference numbers in text are set as superior (superscript) numbers. In the notes themselves, they are normally full size, not raised, and followed by a period. (In manuscripts, superscript numbers in both places—the typical default setting in the note-making feature of a word processor—are perfectly acceptable.)

"Crushed thirty feet upwards, the waters flashed for an instant like heaps of fountains, then brokenly sank in a shower of flakes, leaving the circling surface creamed like new milk round the marble trunk of the whale."[1]

1. Herman Melville, *Moby-Dick; or, The Whale* (New York: Harper & Brothers, 1851), 627.

If a symbol rather than a number is used (see 14.25), the symbol appears as a superscript in the text but not in the note, where it is *not* followed by a period but may be followed by a space, as long as this is done consistently. (In some typefaces, symbols may become difficult to read as superscripts; in such cases, they may be set on the line, full size, in the text as well as the notes.)

14.25 **Sequencing of note numbers and symbols.** Notes, whether footnotes or endnotes, should be numbered consecutively, beginning with 1, throughout each article and for each new chapter—not throughout an entire book unless the text has no internal divisions. Where only a handful of footnotes appear in an entire book or, perhaps, just one in an article, symbols may be used instead of numbers (see also 14.24). Usually an asterisk is enough, but if more than one note is needed on the same page, the sequence is * † ‡. For using a combination of numbers and symbols for two sets of notes, see 14.49–51. For notes to tables and other nontextual matter, which are usually handled independently of the notes to the text, see 3.76–80.

14.26 **Placement of note number.** A note number should generally be placed at the end of a sentence or at the end of a clause. The number normally follows a quotation (whether it is run in to the text or set as an extract). Relative to other punctuation, the number follows any punctuation mark except for the dash, which it precedes.

"This," wrote George Templeton Strong, "is what our tailors can do."[1]

It was the hour of "national paths" toward socialism;[9] but that expression, which turned out to be temporary, was more an incantation than a discovery.

The bias was apparent in the Shotwell series[3]—and it must be remembered that Shotwell was a student of Robinson's.

Though a note number normally follows a closing parenthesis, it may on rare occasion be more appropriate to place the number inside the closing parenthesis—if, for example, the note applies to a specific term within the parentheses.

(In an earlier book he had said quite the opposite.)[2]

Men and their unions, as they entered industrial work, negotiated two things: young women would be laid off once they married (the commonly acknowledged "marriage bar"[1]), and men would be paid a "family wage."

14.27 **Note numbers with chapter and article titles and subheads.** In books, a note number should never appear within or at the end of a chapter title. A note that applies to an entire chapter should be unnumbered and is preferably placed at the foot of the first page of the chapter, preceding any numbered notes (see 14.52–55). (In the case of an electronic format that does not support footnotes as such, an unnumbered note might appear immediately after, or be linked from, the chapter title.) Some journal publishers place an asterisk at the end of the article title for notes that apply to an article as a whole and reserve numbered references for other notes. Note references appearing with a subhead within a book chapter or an article should be numbered along with the rest of the notes, though some editors will prefer to move such references into the text that follows the subhead.

14.28 **Multiple citations and multiple note references.** More than one note reference should never appear in the same place (such as[5,6]); however, a single note can contain more than one citation or comment (see 14.57). Nor can a note number reappear out of sequence; the substance of a note that applies to more than one location must be repeated under a new note number. To avoid such repetition, especially for a longer discursive note, a cross-reference may be used—though these must be checked carefully before publication. (See also 14.29–36.)

18. See note 3 above.

Some systems of numbered references used by publications in the sciences not only allow multiple reference numbers in the same location but also allow numbers to reappear out of sequence for repeated notes; for more details, consult *Scientific Style and Format* (bibliog. 1.1).

Shortened Citations

14.29 **When to use shortened citations.** To reduce the bulk of documentation in works that use footnotes or endnotes, subsequent citations of sources already given in full—either in a previous note or in a bibliography that provides complete bibliographic data—should be shortened whenever possible. (In a work without a bibliography, it is preferable to repeat the full citation the first time it appears in each new chapter.) The short form, as distinct from an abbreviation, should include enough information to remind readers of the full title or to lead them to the appropriate entry in the bibliography. (Some short forms are not covered here: for citing different chapters in the same work, see 14.108; for letters, see 14.111; for legal citations, see 14.275. Other short forms may be patterned on the examples in this section.)

14.30 **Basic structure of the short form.** The most common short form consists of the last name of the author and the main title of the work cited, usually shortened if more than four words, as in examples 4–6 below. For more on authors' names, see 14.32. For more on short titles, see 14.33. For more on journal articles, see 14.185.

1. Samuel A. Morley, *Poverty and Inequality in Latin America: The Impact of Adjustment and Recovery* (Baltimore: Johns Hopkins University Press, 1995), 24–25.

2. Regina M. Schwartz, "Nationals and Nationalism: Adultery in the House of David," *Critical Inquiry* 19, no. 1 (1992): 131–32.

3. Ernest Kaiser, "The Literature of Harlem," in *Harlem: A Community in Transition*, ed. J. H. Clarke (New York: Citadel Press, 1964).

4. Morley, *Poverty and Inequality*, 43.

5. Schwartz, "Nationals and Nationalism," 138.

6. Kaiser, "Literature of Harlem," 189–90.

14.31 **Cross-reference to full citation.** When references to a particular source are far apart, readers encountering the short form may be helped by a cross-reference to the original note—especially in the absence of a full bibliography. These cross-references must be checked carefully before the work is published.

1. Miller, *Quest*, 81 (see chap. 1, n. 4).

It may be better simply to repeat the full details for a source at its first appearance in the notes to each new chapter, an approach recommended by Chicago for works that lack a full bibliography.

14.32 **Short form for authors' names.** Only the last name of the author, or of the editor or translator if given first in the full reference, is needed in the short form. Full names or initials are included only when authors with the same last name must be distinguished from one another. Such abbreviations as *ed.* or *trans.* following a name in the full reference are omitted in subsequent references. If a work has two or three authors, give the last name of each; for more than three, the last name of the first author followed by *et al.*

1. Kathryn Petras and Ross Petras, eds., *Very Bad Poetry* . . .

2. Joseph A. Bellizzi, H. F. Kruckeberg, J. R. Hamilton, and W. S. Martin, "Consumer Perceptions of National, Private, and Generic Brands," . . .

3. Petras and Petras, *Very Bad Poetry* . . .

4. Bellizzi et al., "Consumer Perceptions," . . .

14.33 **Short form for titles of works.** The short title contains the key word or words from the main title. An initial *A* or *The* is usually omitted. The order of the words should not be changed (for example, *Daily Notes of a Trip around the World* should be shortened not to *World Trip* but to *Daily Notes* or *Around the World*). Titles of four words or fewer are seldom shortened. The short title is italicized or set in roman and quotation marks according to the way the full title appears.

The War Journal of Major Damon "Rocky" Gause
(Short title) *War Journal*

"A Brief Account of the Reconstruction of Aristotle's *Protrepticus*"
(Short title) "Aristotle's *Protrepticus*"

Kriegstagebuch des Oberkommandos der Wehrmacht, 1940–1945
(Short title) *Kriegstagebuch*

In short titles in languages other than English, no word should be omitted that governs the case ending of a word included in the short title. If in doubt, ask someone who knows the language.

14.34 **Shortened citations versus "ibid."** The abbreviation *ibid.* (from *ibidem*, "in the same place") usually refers to a single work cited in the note immediately preceding. In a departure from previous editions, Chicago discourages the use of *ibid.* in favor of shortened citations as described elsewhere in this section; to avoid repetition, the title of a work just cited may be omitted. Shortened citations generally take up less than a line, meaning that *ibid.* saves no space, and in electronic formats that link to one note at a time, *ibid.* risks confusing the reader. In the following examples, shortened citations are used for the first reference, as in a work with a full bibliography (see 14.29). The short forms now preferred by Chicago are followed by the same examples using *ibid.* Note that either abbreviated form (author only or *ibid.*) is appropriate only when it refers to the last item cited; where this is not the case, or where the previous note cites more than one source, the fuller form of the shortened citation must be repeated. Note also that with the preferred short form, a page reference must be repeated even if it is the same as the last-cited location (as in note 3); with *ibid.*, an identical page location is not repeated. The word *ibid.*, italicized here only because it is a word used as a word (see 7.63), is capitalized at the beginning of a note and followed by a period.

1. Morrison, *Beloved*, 3.		
2. Morrison, 18.	*or*	2. Ibid., 18.
3. Morrison, 18.	*or*	3. Ibid.
4. Morrison, 24–26.	*or*	4. Ibid., 24–26.
5. Morrison, *Song of Solomon*, 401–2.		
6. Morrison, 433.	*or*	6. Ibid., 433.
7. Díaz, *Oscar Wao*, 37–38.		
8. Morrison, *Song of Solomon*, 403.		
9. Díaz, *Oscar Wao*, 152.		
10. Díaz, 201–2.	*or*	10. Ibid., 201–2.
11. Morrison, *Song of Solomon*, 240; *Beloved*, 32.		
12. Morrison, *Beloved*, 33.		

An author-only reference (or *ibid.*) may also be used within one note in successive references to the same work.

13. Morris Birkbeck, "The Illinois Prairies and Settlers," in *Prairie State: Impressions of Illinois, 1673–1967, by Travelers and Other Observers*, ed. Paul M. Angle (Chicago: University of Chicago Press, 1968), 62. "The soil of the Big-prairie, which is of no great extent notwithstanding its name, is a rich, cool sand; that is to say, one of the most desirable description" (Birkbeck, 63 [*or* ibid., 63]).

To avoid a succession of repeated notes for the same works, the content of notes 2–4, 6, and 8–12 in the examples above might instead be placed parenthetically in the text in place of the note references, but only if the works under discussion are clear from the text (see also 13.66).

14.35 **"Idem."** When several works by the same person are cited successively in the same note, *idem* ("the same," sometimes abbreviated to *id.*) has sometimes been used in place of the author's name. Except in legal references, where the abbreviation *id.* is used in place of *ibid.*, the term is rarely used anymore. Chicago discourages the use of *idem*, recommending instead that the author's last name be repeated. See also 14.34.

14.36 **"Op. cit." and "loc. cit."** *Op. cit.* (*opere citato*, "in the work cited") and *loc. cit.* (*loco citato*, "in the place cited"), used with an author's last name and standing in place of a previously cited title, have rightly fallen into disuse. Consider a reader's frustration on meeting, for example, "Wells, op. cit., 10" in note 95 and having to search back to note 2 for the full source or, worse still, finding that *two* works by Wells have been cited. Chicago disallows both *op. cit.* and *loc. cit.* and instead uses the short-title form described in 14.33.

Commentary and Quotations in Notes

14.37 **Citations plus commentary in a note.** When a note contains not only the source of a fact or quotation in the text but related substantive material as well, the source comes first. A period usually separates the citation from the commentary. Such comments as "emphasis mine" are usually put in parentheses. See also 13.62.

1. Shakespeare, *Julius Caesar*, act 3, sc. 1. Caesar's claim of constancy should be taken with a grain of salt.

2. Little, "Norms of Collegiality," 330 (my italics).

14.38 **Quotation within a note.** When a note includes a quotation, the source normally follows the terminal punctuation of the quotation. The entire source need not be put in parentheses, which involves changing existing parentheses to brackets (see 6.101) and creating unnecessary clutter.

1. One estimate of the size of the reading public at this time was that of Sydney Smith: "Readers are fourfold in number compared with what they were before the beginning of the French war. . . . There are four or five hundred thousand readers more than there were thirty years ago, among the lower orders." *Letters*, ed. Nowell C. Smith (New York: Oxford University Press, 1953), 1:341, 343.

Long quotations should be set off as extracts in notes as they would be in text (see 13.10). In notes, more than three lines of poetry should be set off (but see 13.25; see also 13.29).

14.39 **Substantive notes.** Substantive, or discursive, notes may merely amplify the text and include no sources. Such notes may augment any system of source citation, including the author-date system (see chapter 15). When a source is needed, it is treated as in the example in 14.38 or, if brief and already cited in full, may appear parenthetically, as in the following example:

1. Ernst Cassirer takes important notice of this in *Language and Myth* (59–62) and offers a searching analysis of man's regard for things on which his power of inspirited action may crucially depend.

14.40 **Paragraphing within long notes.** To avoid page makeup problems, very long footnotes should be avoided (see 14.44). No such bar exists for endnotes, however, and very long endnotes should be broken into multiple paragraphs as an aid to reading. Authors and editors should first consider, however, whether such a note would be more effective if shortened or at least partially incorporated into the text. See also 14.45.

14.41 **Footnotes that break across pages in a printed work.** When a footnote begins on one page and continues on the next, the break should be made in midsentence lest readers miss the end of the note; a short rule appears above the continued part (see fig. 14.1). This advice applies only to the published form of a work (and is something that is generally imposed at the typesetting stage). At the manuscript stage, authors and editors should let the note-making feature in their word-processing software determine any such breaks.

14.42 **"See" and "cf."** Notes are often used to invite readers to consult further resources. When doing so, authors should keep in mind the distinction between *see* and *cf.*, using *cf.* only to mean "compare" or "see, by way of comparison." Neither term is italicized in notes (though *see* is italicized in indexes; see 16.22).

1. For further discussion of this problem, see Jones, *Conflict*, 49.
2. Others disagree with my position; cf. Fisher and Ury, *Getting to Yes*, 101–3.

Footnotes versus Endnotes

14.43 **Footnotes and endnotes—an overview.** As their name suggests, footnotes appear at the foot of a page. In a journal, endnotes appear at the end of an article; in a book, at the end of a chapter or, more commonly, at the back of the book. In multiauthor books, where the notes may differ in kind and length, and where chapters may be offered separately, they are usually placed at the end of the chapter to which they pertain. (The decision of where to place the notes is generally made by the publisher.) In electronic formats, notes are often linked to the text, and the distinction between footnotes and endnotes may not apply. At the manuscript stage, authors can work with whichever form seems most convenient, though notes should be inserted with a word processor's note-making function the Advancement of Science in 1874 Stoney had already suggested that "[n]ature presents us in the phenomenon of electrolysis, with a single definite quantity of electricity which is independent of the particular bodies acted on."[2] In 1891 he proposed, "[I]t will be convenient to call [these elementary charges] *electrons*."[3] Stoney's electrons were permanently attached to atoms; that is, they could "not be removed from the atom," and each of them was "associated in the chemical atom with each bond." Furthermore, their oscillation within molecules gave rise to "electro-magnetic stresses in the surrounding aether."[4]

Even though Stoney coined the term "electron," the representation associated with that term had several ancestors.[5] Key aspects of that representation, most notably the notion of the atomicity of charge, considerably preceded his proposal. In the period between 1838 and 1851 a British natural philosopher, Richard Laming, conjectured "the existence of sub-atomic, unit-charged particles and pictured the atom as made up of a material core surrounded by an 'electrosphere' of concentric shells of electrical particles."[6] On the Continent several physicists had made similar suggestions. Those physicists attempted to explain electromagnetic phenomena by action-at-a-distance forces between electrical particles. As an example of the Continental approach to electrodynamics consider Wilhelm Weber's electrical theory of matter and ether.[7] Weber's theory originated in 1846 and continued to evolve till the time of his death (1891). According to the initial version of that theory, electricity consisted of two electrical fluids (positive and negative). The interactions of these fluids were governed by inverse square forces, which were functions of

---

the Electron (Dublin: Royal Dublin Society, 1993), 5–28. The introduction of a new term is an event that can be easily identified and, thus, provides a convenient starting point for a biographical narrative whose subject is the corresponding representation. The appearance of a new term also signals the birth of a novel concept, whose identity has not yet solidified. Thus, it is not surprising that in its subsequent development the concept may merge with other related concepts. As we will see below, this is what happened in the case of the electron.

2. Stoney's paper was first published in 1881. See G. J. Stoney, "On the Physical Units of Nature," *Scientific Proceedings of the Royal Dublin Society*, new series, 3 (1881–1883): 54.

3. Stoney, "On the Cause of Double Lines," 583.

4. Ibid.

5. Note that the biographical approach can also come to grips with the "prehistory" of the electron's representation.

6. Kragh, "Concept and Controversy: Jean Becquerel and the Positive Electron," *Centaurus*, 32 (1989): 205.

7. For an extended discussion of Weber's program see M. N. Wise, "German Concepts of Force, Energy, and the Electromagnetic Ether, 1845–1880," in *Conceptions of Ether: Studies in the History of Ether Theories, 1740–1900*, G. N. Cantor and M. J. S. Hodge (eds.) (Cambridge: Cambridge Univ. Press, 1981), 269–307, esp. 276–83.

FIGURE 14.1. A page of text with footnotes; the first note is continued from the previous page (with a short rule above it). See 14.41.

to facilitate automatic renumbering when notes are added or deleted (see also 2.22). For footnotes to tables, see 2.31, 3.76–80. For notes in previously published material, see 2.45.

14.44 **Footnotes—pros and cons.** Readers of printed works usually prefer footnotes for ease of reference. This is especially true where the notes are closely integrated into the text and make interesting reading, or if immediate knowledge of the sources is essential to readers. The limiting factor in printed works is page makeup—it can be difficult or impossible to fit a close succession of long footnotes onto the pages they pertain to, especially in an illustrated work (a basic requirement for all footnotes is that they at least begin on the page on which they are referenced). There is also the matter of appearance; a page consisting almost exclusively of footnotes is daunting for many readers. For some remedies, see 14.56–60.

14.45 **Endnotes—pros and cons.** Endnotes, which pose no page makeup challenges beyond those of ordinary text, obviate many of the disadvantages of footnotes in printed works (see 14.44). Because of this flexibility, and because pages free of footnotes are less intimidating to many readers, publishers' marketing and sales staff may recommend endnotes in books directed to general as well as scholarly or professional readers. Nonetheless, because general readers may be disappointed to find a third or more of a book devoted to endnotes, authors still need to aim for a healthy balance between text and notes (i.e., by resisting the temptation to include an excessive number of discursive notes). The main problem with endnotes is that of finding a particular note. This difficulty (usually not encountered in electronic texts, where text and notes are linked) can be ameliorated by informative running heads (see 14.47).

14.46 **Endnote placement.** Endnotes to each chapter of a book are often best grouped in the end matter, following the text and any appendixes and preceding the bibliography if there is one (see 1.4). The main heading is simply "Notes," and the group of notes to each chapter is introduced by a subhead bearing the chapter number or title or both (see fig. 14.2). In a book that has a different author for each chapter, or whose chapters may be offered separately, endnotes normally appear at the end of each chapter. In a journal, they appear at the end of each article. In the latter two cases, a subhead "Notes" usually appears between text and notes (see fig. 14.3).

14.47 **Running heads for endnotes.** Where endnotes are gathered at the back of a printed book and occupy more than two or three pages, running introduction, over the course of my fieldwork, Eastwood's unemployment rate was 13 percent—three times as much as the rest of Chicago. Thirty-four percent of residents between eighteen and twenty-four years of age lacked a high school diploma or GED, and 70 percent of the population never finished high school.

43. In the 1945 introduction to *Black Metropolis*, Richard Wright framed the problems of African Americans living in Chicago in terms of this lack of "fulfillment." St. Clair Drake and Horace R. Clayton, *Black Metropolis: A Study of Negro Life in a Northern City* (New York: Harcourt, Brace, 1945).

Chapter Three

1. The analysis of rap lyrics and poems in *Renegade Dreams* is indebted to Steven Caton's approach in *Peaks of Yemen I Summon*. Similarly to the ethnographic context that Caton describes, I see rap music as both a creation of art and a political and social act—an act that depends in large measure on the charisma and spontaneity of the artist. In Eastwood, as in Yemeni society, the poet/rapper has the power to motivate his or her audience. But, as we will see, this power is linked to a discourse of authenticity. That is, in order for that poet/rapper's power to be realized, he or she must be viewed by the audience as authentic. Steven Caton, *Peaks of Yemen I Summon: Poetry as Cultural Practice in a North Yemeni Tribe* (Berkeley: University of California Press, 1990). See also John Jackson, *Harlemworld: Doing Race and Class in Contemporary Black America* (Chicago: University of Chicago Press, 2003); John Jackson, *Real Black: Adventures in Racial Sincerity* (Chicago: University of Chicago Press, 2005); and Marcyliena Morgan, *The Real Hiphop: Battling for Knowledge, Power, and Respect in the LA Underground* (Durham, NC: Duke University Press, 2009).

2. For Jay-Z as a corporate mogul, see Jay-Z, *Decoded* (New York: Spiegel & Grau, 2010); and Mark Healy, "Jay-Z: Renaissance Mogul," *GQ Magazine* (2006): 286–358. For hip hop moguls in general, see Lisa DePaulo, "50 Cent: Big Shot," *GQ Magazine* (2005): 289–360; Paul Gilroy, "All about the Benjamins: Multicultural Blackness—Corporate, Commercial, and Oppositional," in *Between Camps: Nations, Cultures and the Allure of Race* (New York: Routledge Press, 2004); Ice-T, *Ice: A Memoir of Gangster Redemption* (New York: Ballantine, 2011), 1–13, 89–179; Keith Negus, "The Business of Rap: Between the Street and the Executive Suite," in *That's the Joint!: The Hip-Hop Studies Reader*, ed. Mark Anthony Neal and Murray Forman (New York: Routledge, 2004); Imani Perry,

FIGURE 14.2. A page of endnotes, with a subhead introducing the notes to a new chapter and a running head showing the text pages on which the notes are referenced. See 14.46, 14.47.

ture Reviews Neuroscience, and *NeuroImage*. Members of the Lindquist team of researchers have published in *Science*[64] and the *Annual Review of Psychology*[65] as well as in new journals such as *Emotion*, *Emotion Review*, and *Social Cognitive and Affective Neuroscience*. This last journal, founded in 2006, already ranks twelfth in impact factor among all psychological journals. If the basic emotions view is "still entrenched," as Pessoa notes, it is perhaps more a question of an older generation and perhaps also of the beliefs of neuroscience experts who do not themselves work on affect and are therefore not up to date on developments in affect research.[66]

Thus, humanists with the epistemological commitments and training associated with interpretive method and with ethnographic, cultural, and literary readings must recognize that their own research and critical reflection on their own methods align them closely with the points of view of that stream of research, or those streams of research, that has supported various versions of appraisal theory, emotion regulation theory, and nonmodular understandings of neural functioning. We run the risk of placing ourselves in performative contradiction if we step back and view the modern science of emotion strictly as historians.

NOTES

1. Nicole Eustace, Eugenia Lean, Julie Livingston, Jan Plamper, William M. Reddy, and Barbara H. Rosenwein, "*AHR* Conversation: The Historical Study of Emotions," *American Historical Review* 117.5 (December 2012): 1487–1531, 1502.
2. For this use of *incommensurability*, see, e.g., Antony S. R. Manstead and Agneta H. Fischer, "Beyond the Universality-Specificity Dichotomy," *Cognition and Emotion* 16 (2002): 1–9.
3. See, e.g., Jacques Derrida, *De la grammatologie* (Paris: Minuit, 1967); and Michel Foucault, *L'archéologie du savoir* (Paris: Gallimard, 1969).
4. To mention just two classic texts that affirmed the primacy of the cognitive or symbolic dimension of culture, see E. E. Evans-Pritchard, *The Nuer: A Description of the Modes of Livelihood and Political Institutions of a Nilotic People* (Oxford: Oxford University Press, 1940); and Clifford Geertz, "Person, Time, and Conduct in Bali," in *The Interpretation of Culture* (New York: Basic, 1973), 360–411.
5. On this work, there is a large corpus of scholarly discussion. For starting points, see Sarah Grace Heller, "Light as Glamor: The Luminescent Ideal of Beauty in the 'Roman de la Rose,'" *Speculum* 76 (2001): 934–59; and C. S. Lewis, *The Allegory of Love* (Oxford: Oxford University Press, 1936), 112–56.

FIGURE 14.3. Chapter endnotes (first page of notes only), prefaced by the subhead "Notes." See 14.46.

heads (both verso and recto) showing the page numbers to which the notes pertain are a boon to readers (see 1.15). (In electronic formats without fixed pages, such running heads will not apply; instead, the notes may be linked to the text as an aid to navigation.) To determine what page numbers to use in the running head for a particular page of notes, find the numbers of the first and last notes beginning on that page (disregarding a runover from a previous page) and locate the references to these notes in the main text. The numbers of the first and last pages on which these references appear in text are the numbers to use in the running head: for example, "Notes to Pages 123–125." The last number is *not* abbreviated; compare 9.61. (If, as occasionally happens, only one note appears on a page, use the singular: e.g., "Note to Page 23.") Since these running heads can be completed only when page proofs are available, the corrections are considered "alterations" (see 2.135), and the cost may be charged to the publisher. (Another option, less useful for readers but cheaper for the publisher, is to include running heads that simply read "Notes to Chapter One," "Notes to Chapter Two," and so on; since readers are often unaware of the number of the chapter they are reading, chapter numbers must also appear in the running heads of the text itself.) When notes appear at the ends of chapters, note-related running heads are rarely necessary.

14.48 **Special considerations for endnotes.** Whereas footnote citations, because they appear so close to the text, can omit certain elements mentioned in the text, omitting them in endnotes risks irritating readers, who have to go back and forth. For example, an author or a title mentioned in the text need not be repeated in the footnote citation, though it is often helpful to do so. In an endnote, however, the author (or at least the author's last name, unless it is obvious) and title should be repeated, since at least some readers may have forgotten whether the note number was 93 or 94 by the time they find it at the back of the work. It is particularly annoying to arrive at the right place in the endnotes only to find another *ibid.* (see also 14.34). Such frustration can be further prevented by consolidating some of the endnote references, using the devices illustrated in the examples below.

1. This and the preceding four quotations are all from *Hamlet*, act 1, sc. 4.

2. Mary Norris, *Between You & Me: Confessions of a Comma Queen* (New York: W. W. Norton, 2015), 65. Further citations of this work are given in the text.

The device in the second example should be used only if the source is clear from the text, without reference to the endnotes. See also 13.67.

Two Sets of Notes

14.49 **Endnotes plus footnotes.** In a heavily documented work it is occasionally helpful to separate substantive notes from source citations. In such a case, the citation notes should be numbered and appear as endnotes. The substantive notes, indicated by asterisks and other symbols, appear as footnotes. The first footnote on each printed page is referenced by an asterisk. If more than one footnote begins on a page, the sequence of symbols is * † ‡. Should more than three such notes appear on the same page, the symbols are doubled for the fourth to the sixth notes: ** †† ‡‡. (In certain electronic formats where pagination is fluid and there is no distinction between footnotes and endnotes, such a system may need to be adapted.) See also 3.79, 14.24.

14.50 **Footnotes plus author-date citations.** The rather cumbersome practice described in 14.49 may be avoided by the use of author-date citations for sources (see 14.2 and chapter 15) and numbered footnotes or endnotes for the substantive comments. Moreover, the numbered notes can themselves contain parenthetical author-date citations when necessary, adding to the flexibility of such a system. See also 15.31.

14.51 **Editor's or translator's notes plus author's notes.** In an edited or translated work that includes notes by the original author, any additional notes furnished by the editor or translator must be distinguished from the others. Most commonly, the added notes are interspersed and consecutively numbered with the original notes but distinguished from them either by appending "—Ed." or "—Trans." at the end of the note (following the period or other final punctuation) or by enclosing the entire note, except the number, in square brackets. (An editor's or translator's comment can also be added as needed in square brackets within an original note; see 6.99.)

> 1. Millicent Cliff was Norton Westermont's first cousin, although to the very last she denied it.—Ed.
>
> *or*
>
> 2. [The original reads *gesungen*; presumably *gesunken* is meant.]

Alternatively, if there are only a few added notes, these can be referenced by asterisks and other symbols and appear as footnotes; the original notes, numbered, then appear below them, as footnotes (see fig. 14.4), or are treated as endnotes (see 14.49).

Each county has a court of justice,[10] a sheriff to execute the decrees of tribunals, a prison to hold criminals.

There are needs that are felt in a nearly equal manner by all the townships of the county; it was natural that a central authority be charged with providing for them. In Massachusetts this authority resides in the hands of a certain number of magistrates whom the governor of the state designates with the advice[11] of his council.[12]

The administrators of the county have only a limited and exceptional power that applies only to a very few cases that are foreseen in advance. The state and the township suffice in the ordinary course of things. These administrators do nothing but prepare the budget of the county; the legislature votes it.[13] There is no assembly that directly or indirectly represents the county.

The county therefore has, to tell the truth, no political existence.

In most of the American constitutions one remarks a double tendency that brings legislators to divide executive power and concentrate legislative power. The New England township by itself has a principle of existence that they do not strip from it; but one would have to create that life fictitiously in the county, and the utility of doing so has not been felt: all the townships united have only one single representation, the state, center of all national* powers; outside township and national action one can say that there are only individual forces.

*Here "national" refers to the states.

10. See the law of February 14, 1821, *Laws of Massachusetts*, 1:551 [2:551–56].

11. See the law of February 20, 1819, *Laws of Massachusetts*, 2:494.

12. The governor's council is an elected body.

13. See the law of November 2, 1791 [November 2, 1781], *Laws of Massachusetts*, 1:61.

FIGURE 14.4. Translator's footnote referenced by an asterisk, followed by author's numbered footnotes. At the foot of the page, notes referenced by symbols always precede numbered notes, regardless of the order in which the symbols and numbers appear in the text. See 14.51.

Special Types of Notes

14.52 **Unnumbered notes.** Footnotes without numbers or symbols always precede any numbered notes on the same page. They most often appear on the opening page of a chapter or other main division of a work. In a work with endnotes in which an unnumbered footnote is not an option, an unnumbered endnote—to be used with caution because it is easily missed—should appear immediately before note 1 to the relevant chapter. An example of such a note would be a note applying to a book epigraph (see 1.37), which would precede the endnotes to the first chapter and appear under a heading "Epigraph." Notes to chapter epigraphs can be handled similarly. Source notes, biographical notes, and other notes pertaining to an entire chapter or section—which often appear as unnumbered footnotes—are treated in 14.54 and 14.55. In the case of an electronic format that does not support footnotes as such, an unnumbered note might appear immediately after, or be linked from, the element to which it pertains.

14.53 **Notes keyed to text by line or page numbers.** In some works—translations and editions of the classics, for example, or books intended for a more general audience—it may be desirable to omit note numbers in the text. Any necessary notes may then be keyed to the text by line or page number, or both, usually followed by the word or phrase being annotated. (Line numbers are used as locators only if line numbers appear in the text.) Such notes may appear as footnotes or endnotes. Notes keyed to words or phrases in the text are a nicety usually applied by the publisher; unless instructed otherwise, authors should insert numbered notes in their manuscripts as described in 2.22. The annotated word or phrase may be distinguished from the annotation typographically (e.g., with italics or boldface) and separated from it by a colon or the use of brackets or other devices. Quotation marks, if used at all, should be reserved for words that are themselves direct quotations in the text. See figures 14.5, 14.6. In electronic formats, the annotated word or phrase may be linked directly to and from its appearance in the main text.

14.54 **Source notes for previously published material.** In anthologies and other collections of previously published material, or in largely new publications that contain one or more previously published chapters, the source of each reprinted piece may be given in an unnumbered footnote on the first printed page of the chapter, preceding any numbered footnotes. If the other notes are endnotes, the source note should remain a footnote if possible (and some copyright holders may request such a placement). (In certain electronic formats that do not support footnotes as such, a source note may need to be linked from, or appear immediately after, the chapter title.) For material still in copyright, the note should include the original title, publisher or journal, publication date, page numbers or other locators, and—very important—mention of permission from the copyright owner to reprint. It may also include a copyright notice if requested. Some permissions grantors demand particular language in the source note. For exercising discretion versus acceding literally to the grantor's request, see 3.32, which deals with illustrations but applies equally to text. In many cases, wording can be adjusted for

O sweete soule Phillis w'haue liu'd and lou'd for a great while,
(If that a man may keepe any mortal ioy for a great while)
Like louing Turtles and Turtledoues for a great while:
One loue, one liking, one sence, one soule for a great while,
Therfore one deaths wound, one graue, one funeral only
Should haue ioyned in one both loue and louer Amintas.
O good God what a griefe is this that death to remember?
For such grace, gesture, face, feature, beautie, behauiour,
Neuer afore was seene, is neuer againe to be lookt for.
O frowning fortune, ô death and desteny dismal:
Thus be the poplar trees that spred their tops to the heauens,
Of their flouring leaues despoil'd in an houre, in a moment:
Thus be the sweete violets that gaue such grace to the garden,
Of their purpled roabe despoyld in an houre, in a moment.
O how oft did I roare and crie with an horrible howling,
When for want of breath Phillis lay feintily gasping?
O how oft did I wish that Phœbus would fro my Phillis
Driue this feuer away: or send his sonne from Olympus,
Who, when lady Venus by a chaunce was prickt with a bramble,
Healed her hand with his oyles, and fine knacks kept for a purpose.
Or that I could perceiue Podalyrius order in healing,
Or that I could obtaine Medæas exquisite ointments,
And baths most precious, which old men freshly renewed.
Or that I were as wise, as was that craftie Prometheus,
Who made pictures liue with fire that he stole from Olympus.
Thus did I cal and crie, but no body came to Amintas,
Then did I raile and raue, but nought did I get by my railing, [C_4^v]
Whilst that I cald and cry'd, and rag'd, and rau'd as a mad man,

45 for] *omit* C E
49 Therfore] Thefore A
58 roabe] roabes B C D E
59 roare and crie] cry, and roare D
62 this] that D
64 his] *omit* E purpose.] purpose: C E; purpose? D
70 Amintas,] Amintas. C E; Amintas: D

FIGURE 14.5. Footnotes keyed to line numbers—a device best used with verse. (With prose, the notes cannot be numbered until the text has been typeset.) See 14.53.

consistency as long as proper credit is given. The following examples show various acceptable forms. See also 4.102.

Reprinted with permission from Steven Shapin, *The Scientific Revolution* (Chicago: University of Chicago Press, 1996), 15–64.

P. O'Sullivan is left to himself he will tell the whole truth about his contract with Dr. Cronin. It is not believed that O'Sullivan actually participated in the murder. He was merely an accomplice before the fact." *Chicago Tribune*, "Explaining That Ice Contract," Dec. 18, 1889.

186n6 ***Irish American papers generally praised the verdict:*** *Chicago Citizen*, "The Cronin Verdict," Dec. 21, 1889; *Chicago Herald*, "What Is Said in New York," Dec. 17, 1889.

187n1 ***The London Times, still smarting:*** *Times* (London), "The Cronin Murder Trial," Dec. 17, 1889.

187n2 ***Another London paper:*** Quoted in *New York Times*, "English View of It," "Dissatisfied with the Result," Dec. 17, 1889; *Chicago Herald*, "Press Opinion of the Verdict," Dec. 17, 1889.

187n3 ***The London* Graphic:** London *Graphic*, Dec. 23, 1889 quoted in *Chicago Tribune*, Jan. 10, 1890.

188 ***Speaking "as a citizen":*** Quoted in *Chicago Daily News*, "Four Men Guilty," Dec. 16, 1889. McConnell may have been pleased that no death sentences were passed, for he had been part of the clemency movement that followed the Haymarket trial. Later, however, he conceded that "the hanging of these men did do away with the hysteria which had pervaded the body of the people." He concluded, "And, aside from the injustice of such an occurrence, perhaps it did not matter who was hanged provided the public was satisfied." McConnell, "The Chicago Bomb Case," *Harper's Monthly* (1934), quoted in Carl Smith, *Urban Disorder and the Shape of Belief: The Great Chicago Fire, the Haymarket Bomb and the Model Town of Pullman* (Chicago: University of Chicago Press, 1995), 344n46.

190n1 ***Culver, a devout Methodist:*** *Chicago Daily Inter Ocean*, "Juryman Culver," Dec. 17, 1889; *Chicago Tribune*, "Juror Culver," Dec. 17, 1889; "Cronin Jurors Explain," Dec. 29, 1889.

190n2 ***The newspapers had little interest:*** *Chicago Daily Inter Ocean*, "Through Pat Grant's Eyes," Dec. 17, 1889; *New York Times*, "The Cronin Verdict," Dec. 18, 1889.

190n3 ***Kunze was released:*** Louis Epstean put up Kunze's $5,000 bail and paid him £100 a week for a season of ten weeks to appear at the Stanhope and Epstean Dime Museum. *Chicago Times*, "Motion for a New Trial," Dec. 17, 1889; *Los Angeles Herald*, "He Will Pose as a Dime Museum Freak," Jan. 19, 1890. In 1900 Kunze was arrested in Milwaukee and later returned to Joliet Prison—he had been convicted of swindling and had skipped town while on parole.

190n4 ***Coughlin, Burke, and O'Sullivan were handcuffed:*** *Chicago Citizen*, "The Cronin Prisoners," Jan. 18, 1890; *Chicago Tribune*, "They Start for Joliet Prison," Jan. 15, 1890; Bailie, *Cronin Case*, 425.

CHAPTER TEN

191n1 ***Looking back on the events:*** John Devoy, "The Story of Clan na Gael," *Gaelic American* (New York), Jan. 31, 1925.

191n2 ***The reputation of the Chicago police:*** Michael Whalen (Coughlin's partner) had been suspended from the force when Coughlin was arrested, but was later cleared of any involvement. However, in his trial testimony Whalen said that despite his innocence he was formally discharged from the force on August 31, 1889. Others dismissed included Detective Michael J. Crowe, Patrol Sergeant John Stift, and Patrolmen Michael Ahern, Daniel Cunningham, and Redmond McDonald. Cunningham, a long-serving detective, had given information to the defense. Ahern spent much of his time criticizing the prosecution while neglecting his patrol duty. *Chicago Times*, "Whalen Also Suspended," May 26, 1889; Testimony of Michael Whalen, *People of the State of Illinois v. Coughlin et al.*, Supreme Court of Illinois, Illinois State Archives, 7:2617–29; *Chicago*

FIGURE 14.6. Endnotes keyed to page numbers, with key phrases in bold and italics. Though unnumbered in the text, notes that share the same page have been numbered in the endnotes to facilitate reference to individual notes. See 14.53, 14.157.

If an article or chapter is reprinted under a different title:

Originally published as "Manet in His Generation: The Face of Painting in the 1860s," *Critical Inquiry* 19, no. 1 (1992): 22–69, © 1992 by The University of Chicago. All rights reserved. Reprinted by permission.

If an article or chapter has been revised:

Originally published in a slightly different form in *The Metropolis in Modern Life*, ed. Robert Moore Fisher (New York: Doubleday, 1955), 125–48. Reprinted by permission of the author and the publisher.

If a work is in the public domain (such as government publications):

Reprinted from Ambler Thompson and Barry N. Taylor, *Guide for the Use of the International System of Units (SI)* (Gaithersburg, MD: National Institute of Standards and Technology, 2008), 38–39.

14.55 **Biographical notes and acknowledgments.** In journals or multiauthor works, a brief biographical note on the author or authors may appear as an unnumbered note on the first page of each article or chapter. Alternatively, some publications put such notes at the end of the article or chapter (an approach that is sometimes also used for electronic formats that do not support the placement of unnumbered footnotes). Such identifying notes are unnecessary when the work includes a list of contributors with their affiliations. (See also 1.64, 1.66.)

Philip Ball is a freelance writer who lives in London. His many books include *Curiosity: How Science Became Interested in Everything* and *Serving the Reich: The Struggle for the Soul of Physics under Hitler*, both also published by the University of Chicago Press.

Similarly, special acknowledgments may be given in an unnumbered note, sometimes appended to the biographical information.

The authors gratefully acknowledge the assistance of Janni R. Blazer of the Chain and Fob Archive in the preparation of this chapter.

Michael Saler is professor of history at the University of California, Davis. For their comments and assistance the author would like to thank . . .

Remedies for Excessive Annotation

14.56 **Avoiding overlong notes.** Lengthy, discursive notes—especially footnotes—should be reduced or integrated into the text (see 14.44). Notes presented as endnotes can generally accommodate lengthier commentary, but this should be limited in a judicious manner (see 14.45). Complicated tabular material, lists, and other entities not part of the text should be put in an appendix rather than in the footnotes (see 1.59). A parenthetical note in the text might read, for example, "For a list of institutions involved, see appendix A."

14.57 **Several citations in one note.** The number of note references in a sentence or a paragraph can sometimes be reduced by grouping several citations in a single note. The citations are separated by semicolons and must appear in the same order as the text material (whether works, quotations, or whatever) to which they pertain. Take care to avoid any ambiguity as to what is documenting what.

Text:

Only when we gather the work of several scholars—Walter Sutton's explications of some of Whitman's shorter poems; Paul Fussell's careful study of structure in "Cradle"; S. K. Coffman's close readings of "Crossing Brooklyn Ferry" and "Passage to India"; and the attempts of Thomas I. Rountree and John Lovell, dealing with "Song of Myself" and "Passage to India," respectively, to elucidate the strategy in "indirection"—do we begin to get a sense of both the extent and the specificity of Whitman's forms.[1]

Note:

1. Sutton, "The Analysis of Free Verse Form, Illustrated by a Reading of Whitman," *Journal of Aesthetics and Art Criticism* 18, no. 2 (December 1959): 241–54; Fussell, "Whitman's Curious Warble: Reminiscence and Reconciliation," in *The Presence of Walt Whitman*, ed. R. W. B. Lewis (New York: Columbia University Press, 1962), 28–51; Coffman, "'Crossing Brooklyn Ferry': A Note on the Catalog Technique in Whitman's Poetry," *Modern Philology* 51, no. 4 (May 1954): 225–32; Coffman, "Form and Meaning in Whitman's 'Passage to India,'" *PMLA* 70, no. 3 (June 1955): 337–49; Rountree, "Whitman's Indirect Expression and Its Application to 'Song of Myself,'" *PMLA* 73, no. 5 (December 1958): 549–55; and Lovell, "Appreciating Whitman: 'Passage to India,'" *Modern Language Quarterly* 21, no. 2 (June 1960): 131–41.

In the example above, authors' given names are omitted in the note because they appear in the text. For inclusion of names in endnotes versus footnotes, see 14.48.

14.58 **Citing sources in the text rather than in the notes.** Another way to reduce the number of notes is to cite sources (usually in parentheses) in the text. This approach can work well for a string of consecutive citations that refer to the same source (with or without the use of *ibid.*; see 14.34). For discussion and examples, see 13.64–72.

14.59 **Abbreviations for frequently cited works.** If necessary, a frequently mentioned work may be cited either parenthetically in text or in subsequent notes by means of an abbreviation, with the full citation provided in a note at first mention. (This practice is more helpful with footnotes than with endnotes.) See also 13.67, 14.60, 14.29–36.

1. François Furet, *The Passing of an Illusion: The Idea of Communism in the Twentieth Century*, trans. Deborah Furet (Chicago: University of Chicago Press, 1999), 368 (hereafter cited in text as *PI*).

(Subsequent text references) "In this sense, the Second World War completed what the First had begun—the domination of the great political religions over European public opinion," Furet points out (*PI*, 360). But he goes on to argue . . .

An abbreviation differs from a short title (see 14.33) in that words may be abbreviated and the word order changed. In the following example, the author's name need not be repeated unless it is relevant to the citation.

2. Nathaniel B. Shurtleff, ed., *Records of the Governor and Company of the Massachusetts Bay in New England (1628–86)*, 5 vols. (Boston, 1853–54), 1:126 (hereafter cited as *Mass. Records*).

3. *Mass. Records*, 2:330.

14.60 **List of abbreviations.** Where many abbreviations of titles, manuscript collections, personal names, or other entities are used in a work—say, ten or more—they are best listed alphabetically in a separate section. In a book, the list may appear in the front matter (if footnotes are used) or in the end matter preceding the endnotes (if these are used). It is usually headed "Abbreviations" and should be included in the table of contents (see 1.4, 1.44). Where only a few abbreviations are used, these are occasionally listed as the first section of the endnotes (see fig. 14.7) or at the head of the bibliography. Titles that are italicized in the notes or

Notes

In citing works in the notes, short titles have generally been used. Works frequently cited have been identified by the following abbreviations:

Ac. Sc.	Archives de l'Académie des sciences.
A.P.	*Archives parlementaires de 1787 à 1860, première série (1787 à 1799)*. Edited by M. J. Mavidal and M. E. Laurent. 2nd ed. 82 vols. Paris, 1879–1913.
Best.	Theodore Besterman, ed. *Voltaire's Correspondence*. 107 vols. Geneva, 1953–65.
B. Inst.	Bibliothèque de l'Institut de France.
B.N., nouv. acqu.	Bibliothèque nationale. Fonds français, nouvelles acquisitions.
Corresp. inéd.	Charles Henry, ed. *Correspondance inédite de Condorcet et de Turgot (1770–1779)*. Paris, 1883.
HMAS	*Histoire de l'Académie royale des sciences. Avec les mémoires de mathématique et de physique . . . tirés des registres de cette académie (1699–1790)*. 92 vols. Paris, 1702–97. Each volume comprises two separately paginated parts, referred to as *Hist.* and *Mém.*, respectively.
Inéd. Lespinasse	Charles Henry, ed. *Lettres inédites de Mlle de Lespinasse*. Paris, 1887.
O.C.	A. Condorcet-O'Connor and F. Arago, eds. *Oeuvres de Condorcet*. 12 vols. Paris, 1847–49.

Preface

1. Peter Gay. *The Enlightenment: An Interpretation*, 2 vols. (New York, 1966–69), 2:319. I have suggested some criticisms of Gay's treatment of this theme in a review of the second volume of his work, *American Historical Review* 85 (1970): 1410–14.

2. Georges Gusdorf, *Introduction aux sciences humaines: Essai critique sur leurs origines et leur développement* (Strasbourg, 1960), 105–331.

FIGURE 14.7. A short list of abbreviations preceding endnotes. See 14.60.

bibliography should be italicized in their abbreviated form in the list of abbreviations and elsewhere.

Bibliographies

Overview

14.61 **Relationship of bibliographies to notes.** Although not all annotated works require a bibliography, since full details can be given in the notes, an alphabetical bibliography serves a number of purposes. Specifically, a full bibliography that includes all the sources cited in the text, in addition to providing an overview of the sources and therefore an indication of the scope of an author's research, can serve as a convenient key to shortened forms of the notes (see 14.19, 14.29). In some types of electronic publication formats, a full bibliography can streamline the process of creating links to works cited (which, in turn, enables publishers of those cited works to identify and create "cited by" links).

14.62 **Format and placement of bibliography.** A bibliography arranged in a single alphabetical list is the most common and usually the most reader-friendly form for a work with or without notes to the text. All sources to be included—books, articles, dissertations, and so on—are alphabetically arranged in a single list by the last names of the authors (or, if no author or editor is given, by the title or, failing that, by a descriptive phrase). A bibliography is normally placed at the end, preceding the index. In a multiauthor book or a textbook (or in a book offered in the form of separate chapters), each chapter may be followed by a brief bibliography. For an illustration, see figure 14.8; for the arrangement of entries, see 14.65–66. For division into sections, see 14.63.

14.63 **Dividing a bibliography into sections.** A bibliography may occasionally be divided into sections—but only if doing so would make the reader's job significantly easier. It may be appropriate to subdivide a bibliography (1) when it includes manuscript sources, archival collections, or other materials that do not fit into a straight alphabetical list; (2) when readers need to see at a glance the distinction between different kinds of works—for example, in a study of one writer, between works by the writer and those about him or her; or (3) when the bibliography is intended primarily as a guide to further reading (as in this manual). When divisions are necessary, a headnote should appear at the beginning of the bibliography, and each section should be introduced by an explanatory subhead (see fig. 14.9). No source should be listed in more than one section. For alphabetizing, see 14.65–66.

14.64 **Kinds of bibliographies.** Though Chicago generally recommends a full bibliography for book-length works, any of the bibliography categories listed here may be suited to a particular type of work. For author-date reference lists, see 15.10–16.

1. **Full bibliography.** A full bibliography includes all works cited, whether in text or in notes, other than personal communications (see 14.214). Some particularly relevant works the author has consulted may also be listed, even if not mentioned in the text. The usual heading is Bibliography, though Works Cited or Literature Cited may be used if no additional works are included.
2. **Selected bibliography.** If, for whatever reason, the author does not wish to list all works cited, the title must so indicate: Selected Bibliography may be

"About *Biology of Sex Differences*: Aims & Scope." Biology of Sex Differences. Accessed 10 February 2013. http://www.bsd-journal.com/about#aimsscope.

Accelerated Cure Project. "Analysis of Genetic Mutations or Alleles on the X or Y Chromosome as Possible Causes of Multiple Sclerosis." October 2006. http://www.acceleratedcure.org/sites/default/files/curemap/phase2-genetics-xy-chromosomes.pdf.

Albury, W. R. "Politics and Rhetoric in the Sociobiology Debate." *Social Studies of Science* 10 (1980): 519–36.

Alien 3. Directed by David Fincher. Los Angeles: Twentieth Century Fox, 1992.

Allen, Garland E. "The Historical Development of the 'Time Law of Intersexuality' and Its Philosophical Implications." In *Richard Goldschmidt: Controversial Geneticist and Creative Biologist: A Critical Review of His Contributions*, edited by Leonie K. Piternick, 41–48. Boston: Birkhauser, 1980.

———. "Thomas Hunt Morgan and the Problem of Sex Determination, 1903–1910." *Proceedings of the American Philosophical Society* 110, no. 1 (1966): 48–57.

Amos-Landgraf, J. M., et al. "X Chromosome-Inactivation Patterns of 1,005 Phenotypically Unaffected Females." *American Journal of Human Genetics* 79, no. 3 (2006): 493–99.

Angier, Natalie. "For Motherly X Chromosome, Gender Is Only the Beginning." *New York Times*, 1 May 2007, 1.

———. "Scientists Say Gene on Y Chromosome Makes a Man a Man." *New York Times*, 19 July 1990, 1.

———. *Woman: An Intimate Geography*. Boston: Houghton Mifflin, 1999.

Annandale, E., and A. Hammarstrom. "Constructing the 'Gender-Specific Body': A Critical Discourse Analysis of Publications in the Field of Gender-Specific Medicine." *Health (London)* 15, no. 6 (2011): 571–87.

FIGURE 14.8. The first page of a bibliography for a book. See 14.62, 14.67–71.

SELECTED BIBLIOGRAPHY

I list here only the writings that have been of use in the making of this book. This bibliography is by no means a complete record of all the works and sources I have consulted. It indicates the substance and range of reading upon which I have formed my ideas, and I intend it to serve as a convenience for those who wish to pursue the study of humor, comic literature, the history of comic processes, the British novel, and the particular writers and fictions that are the subjects of this inquiry. (Unless there is a standard edition or only one widely available edition of the complete works of the novelists I study, I have not listed their complete works.)

1. THE THEORY, PSYCHOLOGY, AND HISTORY OF THE COMIC

Auden, W. H. "Notes on the Comic." In *Comedy: Meaning and Form,* edited by Robert Corrigan, 61–72. San Francisco: Chandler, 1965.

Bakhtin, Mikhail. *Rabelais and His World.* Translated from the Russian by Helene Iswolsky. Cambridge, MA: MIT Press, 1968.

. . . .

2. JANE AUSTEN AND *EMMA*

Austen, Jane. *The Novels of Jane Austen.* Edited by R. W. Chapman. 5 vols. 3rd ed. London: Oxford University Press, 1932–34.

———. *Jane Austen's Letters to Her Sister Cassandra and Others.* Edited by R. W. Chapman. 2nd ed. London: Oxford University Press, 1952.

———. *Minor Works.* Edited by R. W. Chapman. Vol. 6 of *The Novels of Jane Austen.* London: Oxford University Press, 1954.

———. *"Emma": An Authoritative Text, Backgrounds, Reviews, and Criticism.* Edited by Stephen M. Parrish. Includes commentary and criticism by Sir Walter Scott, George Henry Lewes, Richard Simpson, Henry James, A. C. Bradley, Reginald Ferrar, Virginia Woolf, E. M. Forster, Mary Lascelles, Arnold Kettle, Wayne Booth, G. Armour Craig, A. Walton Litz, W. A. Craik, and W. J. Harvey. New York: W. W. Norton, 1972.

FIGURE 14.9. The opening page of a bibliography divided into sections, with an author's note explaining the principle of selection. See 14.63, 14.64.

used (and is preferred over Select Bibliography) or, if the list is quite short, Suggested Readings or Further Readings. A headnote should explain the principles of selection. See figure 14.9.

3. **Annotated bibliography.** Generally more convenient for readers than a bibliographic essay (see next item) is an annotated bibliography. Annotations may simply follow the publication details (sometimes in brackets if only a few entries are annotated), or they may start a new line (and are often indented from the left margin). See figure 14.10.
4. **Bibliographic essay.** Less formal than an annotated bibliography is a bibliographic essay, in which the author treats the literature discursively. Because

14

Annotated Bibliography of Further Reading

The following is a partial list of the anthologies of poetry and the handbooks, articles, and books about poetry and prosody that I have found useful in writing, teaching, and thinking about poetry. After each entry I have added a brief description of its most appealing features. You will notice a preference for the work of poets about poetry. Poets who are articulate about the craft of verse are among the best expositors.[1]

I. Anthologies

Allen, Donald M., ed. *The New American Poetry.* New York: Grove Press, 1960.

Concentrates on the postwar period from 1945 to 1960 and presents the work of poets who identified themselves with antiformalist movements or waves, often associated with fugitive publications and little magazines (*Yugen, Neon, Kulchur, Big Table,* etc.): the most prominent groups were the Black Mountain school (Olson, Duncan) and the experimental city poets from New York (like Frank O'Hara, LeRoi Jones, and Gilbert Sorrentino) and San Francisco (the "Beats" Kerouac, Corso, Ginsberg). John Ashbery, James Schuyler, Denise Levertov, and Gary Snyder are also represented. An anthology that awakened many readers and would-be writers to another sort of pos-

1. W. H. Auden is exemplary, even in his eccentricity. (See my discussion of some of the many volumes edited by him.) Another poet, F. T. Prince, has looked closely at Milton's prosody in a way that sheds light on prosody in general; see *The Italian Element in Milton's Verse* (1954). Poets John Frederick Nims and J. V. Cunningham are also acute when they write about verse; and I have already mentioned Charles O. Hartman and Timothy Steele in connection with meter and rhythm (see chapter 8 on accentual-syllabic meter).

FIGURE 14.10. Part of the first section of an annotated bibliography. See 14.64.

1. The "Great Tradition" in the History of Science

Those setting out to acquaint themselves with the identity of the Scientific Revolution, and with its major actors, themes, problems, achievements, and conceptual resources, can draw on a distinguished body of what now is commonly called "traditional" scholarship. If indeed it *is* traditional, that is because this literature typically manifested robust confidence that there was a coherent and specifiable body of early modern culture rightly called revolutionary, that this culture marked a clear break between "old" and "new," that it had an "essence," and that this essence could be captured through accounts of the rise of mechanism and materialism, the mathematization of natural philosophy, the emergence of a full-blooded experimentalism, and for many, though not all, traditional writers, the identification of an effective "method" for producing authentic science.

Among the outstanding achievements of this type of scholarship are the early work of E. A. Burtt, *The Metaphysical Foundations of Modern Physical Science* (New York: Doubleday Anchor, 1954; orig. publ. 1924); A. C. Crombie, *Augustine to Galileo: The History of Science, A.D. 400–1650* (London: Falcon, 1952); A. Rupert Hall, *The Scientific Revolution, 1500–1800: The Formation of the Modern Scientific Attitude,* 2nd ed. (Boston: Beacon Press, 1966; orig. publ. 1954); Hall, *From Galileo to Newton, 1630–1720* (London: Collins, 1963); Marie Boas [Hall], *The Scientific Renaissance, 1450–1630*

FIGURE 14.11. Part of the first section of a bibliographic essay. See 14.64.

works treated in this way are not alphabetized, subject divisions may be made freely (see 14.63). Such an essay may be particularly suited to certain types of archival sources that do not easily lend themselves to an alphabetical list. It may be included in addition to a bibliography, in which case it should come first. If works discussed in the essay are listed in the bibliography, they may be given in shortened form (as in notes). If there is no bibliography, the essay must include full facts of publication, whether or not the titles also appear in the notes. For an illustration, see figure 14.11.

5. **List of works by one author.** A list of works by one author, usually titled Published Works [of Author's Name] or Writings [of Author's Name], is most often arranged chronologically. If several titles are listed for each year, the dates may appear as subheads.

Arrangement of Entries

14.65 **Alphabetical order for bibliography entries.** The rules for alphabetizing index entries (see 16.56–93) apply also to a bibliography, with the modifications described in this section and, where appropriate, in 14.67–71. As for index entries, Chicago recommends the letter-by-letter system but will accept the word-by-word system, which is closer to what some word processors produce. Under the letter-by-letter system, an entry for "Fernández, Angelines" would precede an entry for "Fernán Gómez, Fernando"; under the word-by-word system, the opposite order would prevail. Note that word processors, though they can provide a significant head start, will generally not produce a perfectly sorted list for either system. In addition to correcting any software-based errors and variations, authors may need to make adjustments for any entries beginning with a 3-em dash (but see 14.67).

14.66 **Arrangement of bibliography entries with more than one author.** A single-author entry precedes a multiauthor entry beginning with the same name. Only the name of the first author is inverted.

Kogan, Herman. *The First Century: The Chicago Bar Association, 1874–1974*. Chicago: Rand McNally, 1974.

Kogan, Herman, and Lloyd Wendt. *Chicago: A Pictorial History*. New York: Dutton, 1958.

Successive entries by two or more authors in which only the first author's name is the same are alphabetized according to the coauthors' last names (regardless of the number of coauthors).

Brooks, Daniel R., and Deborah A. McLennan. *The Nature of Diversity: An Evolutionary Voyage of Discovery*. Chicago: University of Chicago Press, 2002.

Brooks, Daniel R., and E. O. Wiley. *Evolution as Entropy*. 2nd ed. Chicago: University of Chicago Press, 1986.

The 3-Em Dash for Repeated Names in a Bibliography

14.67 **The 3-em dash in bibliographies—some caveats.** The advice in this section, which explains how to use the 3-em dash to stand in for repeated bibliography entries under the same name, is aimed primarily at publishers and editors. Authors usually should not use the 3-em dash for repeated names in their manuscripts. Among other potential pitfalls, 3-em dashes do not work in computerized sorts (i.e., *all* entries with 3-em dashes will line up in one place). Moreover, an incorrectly applied dash may obscure an important detail—for example, the abbreviation *ed.* or *trans.* Publishers, too, may decide not to use 3-em dashes: 3-em dashes make it impractical to present an entry outside the context of the list and can hide entries from bibliographic databases, both of which are concerns for electronic publication formats. Where 3-em dashes are not used, simply repeat the authors' names and sort the entries as described throughout this section. See also 6.94.

14.68 **The 3-em dash for one repeated name.** For successive entries by the same author, editor, translator, or compiler, a 3-em dash (followed by a period or comma, depending on the presence of an abbreviation such as *ed.*) replaces the name after the first appearance (but see 14.67). Alphabetization is by title of work (abbreviations such as *ed.* or *trans.*, which must always be included, do not influence the order of entries). See also 14.71.

Judt, Tony. *A Grand Illusion? An Essay on Europe*. New York: Hill and Wang, 1996.
———. *Reappraisals: Reflections on the Forgotten Twentieth Century*. New York: Penguin Press, 2008.
———, ed. *Resistance and Revolution in Mediterranean Europe, 1939–1948*. New York: Routledge, 1989.
Squire, Larry R. "The Hippocampus and the Neuropsychology of Memory." In *Neurobiology of the Hippocampus*, edited by W. Seifert, 491–511. New York: Oxford University Press, 1983.
———. *Memory and Brain*. New York: Oxford University Press, 1987.

14.69 **The 3-em dash for more than one repeated name.** The 3-em dash can stand for the same two or more authors (or editors or translators, etc.) as in the previous entry, provided they are listed in the same order and no author appears for one source but not for the other. Note that the second-listed work is *authored* by (rather than *edited* by) Marty and Appleby; abbreviations for editor, translator, and so forth cannot be replaced by the 3-em dash and must always be listed explicitly. See also 14.67.

Marty, Martin E., and R. Scott Appleby, eds. *Fundamentalisms Comprehended*. Chicago: University of Chicago Press, 1995.
———. *The Glory and the Power: The Fundamentalist Challenge to the Modern World*. Boston: Beacon Press, 1992.

but

Comaroff, Jean, and John Comaroff, eds. *Modernity and Its Malcontents: Ritual and Power in Postcolonial Africa*. Chicago: University of Chicago Press, 1993.
Comaroff, John, and Jean Comaroff. *Of Revelation and Revolution*. 2 vols. Chicago: University of Chicago Press, 1991–97.

never

Author 1, Author 2, Author 3. *Title* . . .
———, Author 4, ———. *Title* . . .

14.70 **The 3-em dash for an institutional name.** The 3-em dash may also be used for institutional or corporate authors. Note that identical titles must be repeated. See also 14.67.

Unicode Consortium. *The Unicode Standard*. Version 5.0. Edited by Julie D. Allen et al. Upper Saddle River, NJ: Addison-Wesley, 2007.

———. *The Unicode Standard*. Version 7.0.0. Edited by Julie D. Allen et al. Mountain View, CA: Unicode Consortium, 2014. http://www.unicode.org/versions/Unicode7.0.0/.

14.71 **Alphabetical order for titles by the same author.** In a bibliography (as opposed to a reference list; see 15.18), titles by the same author are normally listed alphabetically. An initial *the*, *a*, or *an* is ignored in the alphabetizing. Note that *all* works by the same person (or by the same persons in the same order)—whether that person is editor, author, translator, or compiler—appear together, regardless of the added abbreviation.

Díaz, Junot. *The Brief Wondrous Life of Oscar Wao*. New York: Riverhead Books, 2007.

———. *Drown*. New York: Riverhead Books, 1996.

———. *This Is How You Lose Her*. New York: Riverhead Books, 2012.

Monmonier, Mark. *Coast Lines: How Mapmakers Frame the World and Chart Environmental Change*. Chicago: University of Chicago Press, 2008.

———. *From Squaw Tit to Whorehouse Meadow: How Maps Name, Claim, and Inflame*. Chicago: University of Chicago Press, 2006.

Mulvany, Nancy C. *Indexing Books*. 2nd ed. Chicago: University of Chicago Press, 2005.

———, ed. *Indexing, Providing Access to Information—Looking Back, Looking Ahead: Proceedings of the 25th Annual Meeting of the American Society of Indexers*. Port Aransas, TX: American Society of Indexers, 1993.

———. "Software Tools for Indexing: What We Need." *Indexer* 17 (October 1990): 108–13.

On the other hand, a bibliography of works by a single author (Writings of Author Name) is usually arranged chronologically. (For an example, see section 2 in fig. 14.9.) Two or more titles published in any one year are arranged alphabetically. See also 14.67.

Author's Name

14.72 **Author's name—overview and related discussions.** This section, on the correct form for the name of the author in source citations, applies to most of the resource types discussed in this chapter. (The examples mainly show books and journal articles.) For personal names in index entries, which are inverted in the same manner as in bibliographies and reference lists, see 16.71–74, 16.75–87.

14.73 **Form of author's name.** Authors' names are normally given as they appear with the source itself—that is, on the title page of a book or other stand-alone work or at the head of a journal article or the like. Certain adjustments, however, may be made to assist correct identification (but see 15.12). First names may be given in full in place of initials (but see 14.74). If an author uses his or her given name in one cited work and initials in another (e.g., "Mary L. Jones" versus "M. L. Jones"), the same form, preferably the fuller one, should be used in references to that author for both works. To help differentiate similar names, middle initials may be given where known. Degrees and affiliations following names on a title page are omitted.

14.74 **Authors preferring initials.** For authors who always use initials, full names should not be supplied—for example, T. S. Eliot, M. F. K. Fisher, O. Henry (pseud.), P. D. James, C. S. Lewis, J. D. Salinger, H. G. Wells. Note that space is added between initials. (Exceptions may be made for special cases like H.D.—the pen name for Hilda Doolittle.) In some instances, a cross-reference may be appropriate (see 14.81). See also 10.12. Very rarely, a portion of an author's given name omitted in the source is supplied in brackets in a bibliography entry. This practice should be limited to authors who may be known by both forms: for example, R. S. Crane may be listed as R[onald] S. Crane. See also 15.33.

14.75 **One author.** In a note, the author's name is given in the normal order. In a bibliography, where names are arranged alphabetically, it is usually inverted (last name first). See also 14.23.

1. David Shields, *How Literature Saved My Life* (New York: Alfred A. Knopf, 2013), 33.

2. Wendy Hui Kyong Chun, "On Hypo-real Models or Global Climate Change: A Challenge for the Humanities," *Critical Inquiry* 41, no. 3 (Spring 2015): 677.

3. Jeffrey Q. McCune Jr., *Sexual Discretion: Black Masculinity and the Politics of Passing* (Chicago: University of Chicago Press, 2014), 5.

4. Shields, *Literature*, 100–101.

5. Chun, "Hypo-real Models," 681.

6. McCune, *Sexual Discretion*, 105–11.

Chun, Wendy Hui Kyong. "On Hypo-real Models or Global Climate Change: A Challenge for the Humanities." *Critical Inquiry* 41, no. 3 (Spring 2015): 675–703.

McCune, Jeffrey Q., Jr. *Sexual Discretion: Black Masculinity and the Politics of Passing*. Chicago: University of Chicago Press, 2014.

Shields, David. *How Literature Saved My Life*. New York: Alfred A. Knopf, 2013.

14.76 **Two or more authors (or editors).** Two or three authors (or editors) of the same work are listed in the order in which they appear with the source. In a bibliography, only the first author's name is inverted, and a comma must appear both before and after the first author's given name or initials. Use the conjunction *and* (not an ampersand).

1. Kathryn Sorrells and Sachi Sekimoto, eds., *Globalizing Intercultural Communication: A Reader* (Thousand Oaks, CA: SAGE, 2015), xvi.

2. Steven D. Levitt and Stephen J. Dubner, *Freakonomics: A Rogue Economist Explores the Hidden Side of Everything* (New York: William Morrow, 2005), 20–21.

3. Kate D. L. Umbers, Matthew R. E. Symonds, and Hanna Kokko, "The Mothematics of Female Pheromone Signaling: Strategies for Aging Virgins," *American Naturalist* 185, no. 3 (March 2015): 422.

4. Sorrells and Sekimoto, *Globalizing Intercultural Communication*, xx–xxi.

Levitt, Steven D., and Stephen J. Dubner. *Freakonomics: A Rogue Economist Explores the Hidden Side of Everything*. New York: William Morrow, 2005.

Sorrells, Kathryn, and Sachi Sekimoto, eds. *Globalizing Intercultural Communication: A Reader*. Thousand Oaks, CA: SAGE, 2015.

Umbers, Kate D. L., Matthew R. E. Symonds, and Hanna Kokko. "The Mothematics of Female Pheromone Signaling: Strategies for Aging Virgins." *American Naturalist* 185, no. 3 (March 2015): 417–32.

For works by or edited by four to ten persons, all names are usually given in the bibliography. Word order and punctuation are the same as for two or three authors. In a note, only the name of the first author is included, followed by *et al.* with no intervening comma.

5. Natalia V. Gmuca et al., "The Fat and the Furriest: Morphological Changes in Harp Seal Fur with Ontogeny," *Physiological and Biochemical Zoology* 88, no. 2 (March/April 2015): 158.

6. Gmuca et al., "Harp Seal Fur," 160.

Gmuca, Natalia V., Linnea E. Pearson, Jennifer M. Burns, and Heather E. M. Liwanag. "The Fat and the Furriest: Morphological Changes in Harp Seal Fur with Ontogeny." *Physiological and Biochemical Zoology* 88, no. 2 (March/April 2015): 158–66.

For works with more than ten authors—more common in the natural sciences—Chicago recommends the policy followed by the *American Naturalist* (see bibliog. 5): only the first seven should be listed in the bibliography, followed by *et al.* (Where space is limited, the policy of the American Medical Association may be followed: up to six authors' names are listed; if there are more than six, only the first three are listed, followed by *et al.*)

14.77 **Two or more authors (or editors) with same family name.** When two or more authors (or editors) share the same family name (and are credited as such in the source), the name is repeated (even if the family name is not repeated in the source itself).

1. Christopher Kendris and Theodore Kendris, *501 Spanish Verbs*, 7th ed. (Hauppauge, NY: Barron's Educational Series, 2010), 14.
2. Kendris and Kendris, *501 Spanish Verbs*, 27–28.

14.78 **Author's name in title.** When the name of the author appears in the title or subtitle of a cited work (such as an autobiography), the note citation may begin with the title (i.e., assuming the authorship is clear either from the title or in the text). The bibliography entry, however, should begin with the author's name, even though it is repeated in the title. See also 14.103.

1. *Autobiography of Benjamin Franklin*, ed. John Bigelow (Philadelphia: J. B. Lippincott, 1868), 233.
2. *Autobiography of Benjamin Franklin*, 234.

Franklin, Benjamin. *Autobiography of Benjamin Franklin*. Edited by John Bigelow. Philadelphia: J. B. Lippincott, 1868.

14.79 **No listed author (anonymous works).** If the author or editor is unknown, the note or bibliography entry should normally begin with the title. An initial article is ignored in alphabetizing. (For pseudonyms, see 14.80.)

1. *A True and Sincere Declaration of the Purpose and Ends of the Plantation Begun in Virginia, of the Degrees Which It Hath Received, and Means by Which It Hath Been Advanced* (London, 1610).
2. *Stanze in lode della donna brutta* (Florence, 1547).

Stanze in lode della donna brutta. Florence, 1547.

A True and Sincere Declaration of the Purpose and Ends of the Plantation Begun in Virginia, of the Degrees Which It Hath Received, and Means by Which It Hath Been Advanced. London, 1610.

Although the use of *Anonymous* is generally to be avoided for works with no attribution, it may stand in place of the author's name in a bibliography in which several anonymous works need to be grouped. In such an instance, *Anonymous* or *Anon.* (set in roman) appears at the first entry, and 3-em dashes may be used thereafter (but see 14.67). (The dashes do not necessarily imply the same anonymous author.)

Anonymous. *Stanze in lode della donna brutta*. Florence, 1547.

———. *A True and Sincere Declaration . . .*

If, on the other hand, a work is explicitly attributed to "Anonymous" (e.g., on the title page or at the head of the work), it should be cited accordingly.

Anonymous. "Our Family Secrets." *Annals of Internal Medicine* 163, no. 4 (August 2015): 321. https://doi.org/10.7326/M14-2168.

If the authorship is known or guessed at but was omitted on the title page, the name is included in brackets (with a question mark for cases of uncertainty). (Note that in the Hawkes example, both New York and Tea Party are hyphenated in the original source.)

1. [Samuel Horsley], *On the Prosodies of the Greek and Latin Languages* (London, 1796).

2. [James Hawkes?], *A Retrospect of the Boston Tea-Party, with a Memoir of George R. T. Hewes*, by a Citizen of New-York (New-York, 1834).

[Hawkes, James?]. *A Retrospect of the Boston Tea-Party, with a Memoir of George R. T. Hewes*. By a Citizen of New-York. New-York, 1834.

[Horsley, Samuel]. *On the Prosodies of the Greek and Latin Languages*. London, 1796.

14.80 **Pseudonyms.** If a work is attributed to an invented or descriptive name, and the author's real name is not known, *pseud.* (roman, in brackets) may follow the name, especially if it might not be immediately clear to readers that the name is false (as in the first two examples below). (An initial *The* or *A* may be omitted. In a text citation, or in a shortened form in a note, *pseud.* is usually omitted.)

AK Muckraker [pseud.]. "Palin Is Back at Work." *Mudflats: Tiptoeing through the Muck of Alaskan Politics* (blog), December 5, 2008. https://mudflats.wordpress.com/2008/12/05/palin-is-back-at-work/.
Centinel [pseud.]. Letters. In *The Complete Anti-Federalist*, edited by Herbert J. Storing. Chicago: University of Chicago Press, 1981.
Cotton Manufacturer. *An Inquiry into the Causes of the Present Long-Continued Depression in the Cotton Trade, with Suggestions for Its Improvement*. Bury, UK, 1869.

A widely used pseudonym is generally treated as if it were the author's real name.

Eliot, George. *Middlemarch*. Norton Critical Editions. New York: Norton, 1977.
Twain, Mark. *The Prince and the Pauper: A Tale for Young People of All Ages*. New York: Harper & Brothers, 1899.

The real name, if of interest to readers, may follow the pseudonym in brackets. See also 14.81.

Jay-Z [Shawn Carter]. *Decoded*. New York: Spiegel & Grau, 2010.
Le Carré, John [David John Moore Cornwell]. *The Quest for Karla*. New York: Alfred A. Knopf, 1982.
Stendhal [Marie-Henri Beyle]. *The Charterhouse of Parma*. Trans. C. K. Scott-Moncrieff. New York: Boni and Liveright, 1925.

If the author's real name is better known than the pseudonym, the real name should be used. If needed, the pseudonym may be included in brackets, followed by *pseud.*

Brontë, Charlotte. *Jane Eyre*. London, 1847.
or
Brontë, Charlotte [Currer Bell, pseud.]. *Jane Eyre*. London, 1847.

For examples of screen names, see 14.208 and 14.209.

14.81 **Cross-references for pseudonyms.** In some cases, a cross-reference from a real name to a pseudonym, or vice versa, may be desired. Italicize words like *See*.

Carter, Shawn. *See* Jay-Z.

If a bibliography includes two or more works published by the same author but under different pseudonyms, all may be listed under the real name followed by the appropriate pseudonym in brackets, with cross-references under the pseudonyms (see also 14.68). Alternatively, they may be listed under the pseudonyms, with a cross-reference at the real name to each pseudonym.

Ashe, Gordon. *See* Creasey, John.

Creasey, John [Gordon Ashe, pseud.]. *A Blast of Trumpets*. New York: Holt, Rinehart and Winston, 1976.

——— [Anthony Morton, pseud.]. *Hide the Baron*. New York: Walker, 1978.

——— [Jeremy York, pseud.]. *Death to My Killer*. New York: Macmillan, 1966.

Morton, Anthony. *See* Creasey, John.

York, Jeremy. *See* Creasey, John.

or

Ashe, Gordon [John Creasey]. *A Blast of Trumpets*. New York: Holt, Rinehart and Winston, 1976.

Creasey, John. *See* Ashe, Gordon; Morton, Anthony; York, Jeremy.

14.82 **Alternative real names.** When a writer has published under different forms of his or her name, each work should be listed under the name that appears with the work—unless the difference is merely the use of initials versus full names (see 14.73). Cross-references are occasionally used (whether or not the 3-em dash is used; see also 14.67).

Doniger, Wendy. *The Bedtrick: Tales of Sex and Masquerade*. Chicago: University of Chicago Press, 2000.

———. *See also* O'Flaherty, Wendy Doniger.

If a person discussed in the text publishes under a name not used in the text, a cross-reference may be useful.

Overstone, Lord. *See* Loyd, Samuel Jones.

14.83 **Authors known by a given name.** Authors generally known only by their given names (i.e., and not by any surname) or by a mononym (other than a mononymous pseudonym) are listed and alphabetized by those names. Such titles as "King" or "Saint" or identifiers by place (e.g., "of Hippo" or "of England") are omitted, as are any alternative or fuller versions of the name, unless needed for reasons of disambiguation.

Augustine. *On Christian Doctrine*. Translated by D. W. Robertson Jr. Indianapolis: Bobbs-Merrill, 1958.

Elizabeth I. *Collected Works*. Edited by Leah S. Marcus, Janel Mueller, and Mary Beth Rose. Chicago: University of Chicago Press, 2000.

Virgil. *The Aeneid*. Translated by Robert Fitzgerald. New York: Vintage Books, 1990.

For pseudonyms, see 14.80. See also 14.246.

14.84 **Organization as author.** If a publication issued by an organization, association, or corporation carries no personal author's name on the title page, the organization is listed as author in a bibliography, even if it is also given as publisher. (But cf. 14.79.)

International Organization for Standardization. *Information and Documentation—Rules for the Abbreviation of Title Words and Titles of Publications*. ISO 4. Paris: ISO, 1997.

University of Chicago Press. *The Chicago Manual of Style*. 17th ed. Chicago: University of Chicago Press, 2017.

Title of Work

14.85 **Additional discussion of titles.** This section discusses the correct form for a title of a work in source citations and applies to most of the resource types discussed in this chapter. The examples mainly show titles of books (in italics) and journal articles (in quotation marks). For a detailed discussion of titles of works in terms of capitalization, punctuation, wording, and relationship to surrounding text, see 8.156–201. Most of the advice there applies equally to source citations.

14.86 **Italics versus quotation marks for titles of cited works.** In source citations as in running text, italics are used for the titles of books and journals. Italics are also used for the titles of newspapers and blogs, movies and video games, paintings, and other types of works. Quotation marks are generally reserved for the titles of subsections of larger works—including chapter and article titles and the titles of poems in a collection. For some types of works—for example, a book series or a website—neither italics nor quotation marks are used. For titles within titles, see 14.94. The examples below cite an article in a journal (first example) and a book (second example). For books, see 14.100–163; for journals, see 14.168–87. Other types of sources are treated in the remainder of this chapter and in chapter 15.

Jhang, Ji Hoon, and John G. Lynch Jr. "Pardon the Interruption: Goal Proximity, Perceived Spare Time, and Impatience." *Journal of Consumer Research* 41, no. 5 (February 2015): 1267–83.

Sandberg, Sheryl. *Lean In: Women, Work, and the Will to Lead.* New York: Alfred A. Knopf, 2013.

14.87 **Capitalization of titles of cited works.** As in running text, English-language titles of works are capitalized headline-style in source citations. In headline style, the first and last words of title and subtitle and all other major words are capitalized. For a more detailed definition and many more examples, see 8.159. For hyphenated compounds in headline style, see 8.161.

Quiet: The Power of Introverts in a World That Can't Stop Talking
"Shooting an Elephant"

For titles in other languages, which are usually capitalized sentence-style, see 14.98.

14.88 **Some permissible changes to titles of cited works.** The spelling, hyphenation, and punctuation in the original title should be preserved, with the following exceptions: words in full capitals on the original title page (except for initialisms or acronyms) should be set in upper- and lowercase; headline-style capitalization should be applied (but see 14.98); and, subject to editorial discretion, an ampersand may be changed to *and*. Numbers should remain spelled out or given as numerals according to the original (*Twelfth Century* or *12th Century*) unless there is a good reason to make them consistent (but *12th* may be changed to *12th*). In some cases, punctuation separating the main title from a subtitle may be adjusted (see 14.89, 14.90, 14.91). For more on permissible changes to titles, including the addition of colons and commas (including serial commas), see 8.165. For older titles, see 14.97.

14.89 **Subtitles in cited works and the use of the colon.** A colon is used to separate the main title from the subtitle (even if no colon appears in the source itself). A space follows the colon. In italicized titles, the colon is also italicized. The subtitle, like the title, always begins with a capital letter. See also 8.164, 8.165.

Gladwell, Malcolm. *David and Goliath: Underdogs, Misfits, and the Art of Battling Giants.* New York: Little, Brown, 2013.

Although in European bibliographic style a period often separates title from subtitle, English-language publications need not follow that convention for non-English titles. See also 14.98.

Fausts Himmelfahrt: Zur letzten Szene der Tragödie

14.90 **Two subtitles in a cited work.** If, as occasionally happens, there are two subtitles in the original (an awkward contingency), a colon normally precedes the first and a semicolon the second. The second subtitle also begins with a capital.

Sereny, Gitta. *Cries Unheard: Why Children Kill; The Story of Mary Bell.* New York: Metropolitan Books / Henry Holt, 1999.

Note that an em dash is usually considered part of a title or subtitle.

William C. David. *Crucible of Command: Ulysses S. Grant and Robert E. Lee—the War They Fought, the Peace They Forged.* Boston: Da Capo Press, 2014.

14.91 **Use of "or" with double titles.** Old-fashioned double titles (or titles and subtitles) connected by *or* have traditionally been separated by a semicolon (or sometimes a colon), with a comma following *or*, or more simply by a single comma preceding *or*. (Various other combinations have also been used.) When referring to such titles, prefer the punctuation on the title page or at the head of the original source. In the absence of such punctuation (e.g., when the title is distinguished from the subtitle by typography alone), or when the original source is not available to consult, use the simpler form shown in the first example. This departure from earlier editions recognizes the importance of balancing editorial expediency with fidelity to original sources. The second example preserves the usage on the original title pages of the American and British editions of Melville's classic novel (and assumes one of those editions, or a later edition that preserves such punctuation, was in fact consulted). The third example (of a modern film) preserves the colon of the original title sequence but adds a comma to separate the main title from the secondary title (distinguished only graphically in the original). In all cases, the first word of the subtitle (following *or*) should be capitalized. See also 14.87, 14.88.

The Tempest, or The Enchanted Island
but
Moby-Dick; or, The Whale
Dr. Strangelove, or: How I Learned to Stop Worrying and Love the Bomb

14.92 **"And other stories" and such.** Such tags as *and other stories* or *and other poems*, often seen with titles of books, are treated as part of the main title but usually separated from the title story, poem, essay, or whatever by a comma, even when such comma does not appear on the title page. The first part of the title is *not* enclosed in quotation marks (but see 14.94).

1. Norman Maclean, *A River Runs through It, and Other Stories* (Chicago: University of Chicago Press, 1976), 104.

When the main title ends with a question mark or exclamation point, the comma is omitted. See also 14.96.

2. Herrlee Glessner Creel, *What Is Taoism? and Other Studies in Chinese Cultural History* (Chicago: University of Chicago Press, 1970), 34.

14.93 **Dates in titles of cited works.** When not introduced by a preposition (e.g., "from 1920 to 1945"), dates in a title or subtitle are set off by commas, even if differentiated only by type style or a new line on the title page or at the head of the work. If a colon has been used in the original, however, it should be retained (but see 14.90). (Note that commas should *not* be added to non-English titles before dates; see 11.7.)

Beiser, Frederick C. *After Hegel: German Philosophy, 1840–1900*. Princeton, NJ: Princeton University Press, 2014.

14.94 **Quoted titles and other terms within cited titles of works.** Titles of long or short works appearing within an italicized title are enclosed in quotation marks, regardless of how such titles would appear alone (but see 14.95).

1. Steven D. Levitt and Stephen J. Dubner, *Think Like a Freak: The Authors of "Freakonomics" Offer to Retrain Your Brain* (New York: William Morrow, 2014).

2. Roland McHugh, *Annotations to "Finnegans Wake"* (Baltimore: Johns Hopkins University Press, 1980).

Quotation marks within an italicized title do not, of course, always denote another title.

3. Henry Louis Gates Jr. and Kwame Anthony Appiah, eds., *"Race," Writing, and Difference* (Chicago: University of Chicago Press, 1986).

A term normally quoted is enclosed in single quotation marks when it appears within a title in quotation marks (see 13.30; see also 6.11). Retain both double and single quotation marks, if any, in short citations. See also 8.165, 8.177.

4. Judith Lewis, "'Tis a Misfortune to Be a Great Ladie': Maternal Mortality in the British Aristocracy, 1558–1959," *Journal of British Studies* 37, no. 1 (1998): 28–29.

5. Lewis, "''Tis a Misfortune,'" 32.

Lewis, Judith Lewis. "'Tis a Misfortune to Be a Great Ladie': Maternal Mortality in the British Aristocracy, 1558–1959." *Journal of British Studies* 37, no. 1 (1998): 26–53.

14.95 **Italicized titles and other terms within cited titles of works.** When terms normally italicized in running text, such as species names or names of ships or words in another language (but *not* titles of works, which take quotation marks; see 14.94), appear within an italicized title, they are set in roman ("reverse italics"; see 8.173). When, however, such a term makes up the entire title, it should be italicized.

Stafford, Edward Peary. *The Big E: The Story of the USS* Enterprise. New York: Random House, 1962.
Van Wagenen, Gertrude, and Miriam E. Simpson. *Postnatal Development of the Ovary in* Homo sapiens *and* Macaca mulatta *and Induction of Ovulation in the Macaque*. New Haven, CT: Yale University Press, 1973.
Weigel, Detlef, and Jane Glazebrook. Arabidopsis: *A Laboratory Manual*. Cold Spring Harbor, NY: Cold Spring Harbor Laboratory Press, 2002.
but
Hume, Christine. *Musca domestica*. Boston: Beacon Press, 2000.

Italicized terms (including titles of works) within an article or a chapter title or any other title set in roman type remain in italics. For the capitalization of non-English titles (as in the example from *Modern Philology*), see 14.98; for species names, see 8.159.

1. Gang Zhou et al., "Induction of Maggot Antimicrobial Peptides and Treatment Effect in *Salmonella pullorum*-Infected Chickens," *Journal of Applied Poultry Research* 23, no. 3 (September 2014): 380.
2. Andrew Ford, "The Purpose of Aristotle's *Poetics*," *Classical Philology* 110, no. 1 (January 2015): 8–9.
3. Jacob Sider Jost, "Bergotte's Other Patch of Yellow: A Fragment of Heraclitus in Proust's *La prisonnière*," *Modern Philology* 112, no. 4 (May 2015): 714.
4. Zhou et al., "*Salmonella pullorum*-Infected Chickens," 381.
5. Ford, "Aristotle's *Poetics*," 20.
6. Sider Jost, "Proust's *La prisonnière*," 717–18.

14.96 **Question marks or exclamation points in titles of cited works.** When a main title ends with a question mark or an exclamation point, no colon is added before any subtitle. When the question mark or exclamation point is followed by a closing quotation mark, however, retain a colon before the subtitle (see fifth and sixth examples below). Any punctuation other than a period required by the surrounding text, note, or bibliography entry should be retained (as in example notes 3, 7–8, and 10–12; see also 6.125).

1. Yogi Berra, *What Time Is It? You Mean Now? Advice for Life from the Zennest Master of Them All*, with Dave Kaplan (New York: Simon & Schuster, 2002), 63.

2. Alison Oram, *Her Husband Was a Woman! Women's Gender-Crossing and British Popular Culture* (London: Routledge, 2007), 183.

3. Michael Tessler et al., "Diversity and Distribution of Stream Bryophytes: Does pH Matter?," *Freshwater Science* 33, no. 3 (September 2014): 778.

4. C. Daniel Batson, "How Social Is the Animal? The Human Capacity for Caring," *American Psychologist* 45 (March 1990): 336.

5. Edward Buscombe, *"Injuns!": Native Americans in the Movies* (London: Reaktion, 2006), 12.

6. Daniel Bertrand Monk, "'Welcome to Crisis!': Notes for a Pictorial History of the Pictorial Histories of the Arab Israeli War of June 1967," *Grey Room* 7 (Spring 2002): 139, http://www.jstor.org/stable/1262596.

7. Berra, *What Time Is It?*, 55–56.

8. Oram, *Her Husband Was a Woman!*, 184.

9. Tessler et al., "Diversity and Distribution," 780.

10. Batson, "How Social Is the Animal?," 337.

11. Buscombe, *"Injuns!,"* 114–15.

12. Monk, "'Welcome to Crisis!,'" 140.

When a title ending with a question mark or an exclamation mark would normally be followed by a period, the period is omitted (see also 6.124).

Hornby, Nick. *Vous descendez?* Translated by Nicolas Richard. Paris: Plon, 2005.

Tessler, Michael, Kam M. Truhn, Meghan Bliss-Moreau, and John D. Wehr. "Diversity and Distribution of Stream Bryophytes: Does pH Matter?" *Freshwater Science* 33, no. 3 (September 2014): 778–87.

14.97 **Older titles and very long titles.** Titles of works published in the eighteenth century or earlier may retain their original punctuation, spelling, and capitalization (except for whole words in capital letters, which should be given an initial capital only). Very long titles may be shortened in a bibliography or a note; indicate such omissions by the use of bracketed ellipses. As they do for the place-name London in the second example (for which the place of publication was known but did not appear with the source), the brackets signal that the ellipsis has been supplied by the author and is not part of the original title (see also 13.58). At the end of a title, the bracketed ellipsis should be followed by a period.

Escalante, Bernardino. *A Discourse of the Navigation which the Portugales doe make to the Realmes and Provinces of the East Partes of the Worlde* [. . .]. Translated by John Frampton. London, 1579.

Ray, John. *Observations Topographical, Moral, and Physiological: Made in a Journey Through part of the Low-Countries, Germany, Italy, and France: with A Catalogue of Plants not Native of England* [. . .] *Whereunto is added A Brief Account of Francis Willughby, Esq., his Voyage through a great part of Spain.* [London], 1673.

14.98 **Non-English titles of cited works.** Sentence-style capitalization is strongly recommended for non-English titles (see 8.158). Capitalize the first word of a title or subtitle and any word that would be capitalized in the original language (e.g., *Wahrheit*, *Sowjetunion*, and *Inquisición* in examples 2 and 3 and *Gâtine*, *Société*, and *l'Ouest* in example 7). Writers or editors unfamiliar with the usage of the language concerned, however, should not attempt to alter capitalization without expert help (in a pinch, a library-catalog entry may come in helpful). For the use of English forms for place-names, see 14.131.

1. Danielle Maisonneuve, Jean-François Lamarche, and Yves St-Amand, *Les relations publiques dans une société en mouvance* (Sainte-Foy, QC: Presses de l'Université du Québec, 1998).

2. Gabriele Krone-Schmalz, *In Wahrheit sind wir stärker: Frauenalltag in der Sowjetunion* (Frankfurt am Main: Fischer Taschenbuch Verlag, 1992).

3. Daniel Muñoz Sempere, *La Inquisición española como tema literario: Política, historia y ficción en la crisis del antiguo régimen* (Woodbridge, UK: Tamesis, 2008).

4. G. Martellotti et al., *La letteratura italiana: Storia e testi*, vol. 7 (Milan: Riccardo Ricciardi, 1955).

5. Ljiljana Piletić Stojanović, ed., *Gutfreund i češki kubizam* (Belgrade: Muzej savremene umetnosti, 1971).

6. Dinda L. Gorlée, "¡Eureka! La traducción como un descubrimiento pragmático," *Anuario filosófico* 29, no. 3 (1996): 1403.

7. Marcel Garaud, "Recherches sur les défrichements dans la Gâtine poitevine aux XIe et XIIe siècles," *Bulletin de la Société des antiquaires de l'Ouest*, 4th ser., 9 (1967): 11–27.

Note that, with non-English journal titles (as with any title in a language other than English), an initial definite article (*Le*, *Der*, etc.) should be retained, since it may govern the inflection of the following word (see also 8.170). Months and the equivalents of such abbreviations as *no.* or *pt.* are usually given in English (but see 14.102). For a full discussion of non-English titles of works, see 11.6–10.

14.99 **Translated titles of cited works.** If an English translation of a title is needed, it follows the original title and is enclosed in brackets, without italics or quotation marks. It is capitalized sentence-style regardless of the bibliographic style followed. (In running text, parentheses are used instead of brackets; see 11.9.)

1. Henryk Wereszycki, *Koniec sojuszu trzech cesarzy* [The end of the Three Emperors' League] (Warsaw: PWN, 1977); includes a summary in German.

2. W. Kern, "Waar verzamelde Pigafetta zijn Maleise woorden?" [Where did Pigafetta collect his Malaysian words?], *Tijdschrift voor Indische taal-, land- en volkenkunde* 78 (1938): 272.

Kern, W. "Waar verzamelde Pigafetta zijn Maleise woorden?" [Where did Pigafetta collect his Malaysian words?]. *Tijdschrift voor Indische taal-, land- en volkenkunde* 78 (1938): 271–73.

Pirumova, Natalia Mikhailovna. *Zemskoe liberal'noe dvizhenie: Sotsial'nye korni i evoliutsiia do nachala XX veka* [The zemstvo liberal movement: Its social roots and evolution to the beginning of the twentieth century]. Moscow: Izdatel'stvo "Nauka," 1977.

If a title is given only in English translation, however, the original language must be specified.

3. N. M. Pirumova, *The Zemstvo Liberal Movement: Its Social Roots and Evolution to the Beginning of the Twentieth Century* [in Russian] (Moscow: Izdatel'stvo "Nauka," 1977).

Chu Ching and Long Zhi. "The Vicissitudes of the Giant Panda, *Ailuropoda melanoleuca* (David)." [In Chinese.] *Acta Zoologica Sinica* 29, no. 1 (1983): 93–104.

A published translation is normally treated as illustrated in 14.104 or 14.183. If, for some reason, both the original and the translation need to be cited, both may be listed. For books, either of the following forms may be used, depending on whether the original or the translation is of greater interest to readers:

Furet, François. *Le passé d'une illusion*. Paris: Éditions Robert Laffont, 1995. Translated by Deborah Furet as *The Passing of an Illusion* (Chicago: University of Chicago Press, 1999).

or

Furet, François. *The Passing of an Illusion*. Translated by Deborah Furet. Chicago:

University of Chicago Press, 1999. Originally published as *Le passé d'une illusion* (Paris: Éditions Robert Laffont, 1995).

For other types of sources, adapt the relevant example as needed.

Books

14.100 **Elements to include when citing a book.** A reference to a book must include enough information to lead interested readers to the source. Most references contain at least some information not strictly needed for that purpose but potentially helpful nonetheless. The elements listed below are included, where applicable, in full notes and bibliography entries. The order in which they appear will vary slightly according to type of book, and certain elements are sometimes omitted; such variation will be noted and illustrated in the course of this section. (For author-date style reference list entries, which vary only in the placement of the date of publication, see chapter 15.)

1. Author: full name of author(s) or editor(s) or, if no author or editor is listed, name of institution standing in their place; see also 14.72–84
2. Title: full title of the book, including subtitle if there is one; see also 14.85–99
3. Editor, compiler, or translator, if any, if listed on title page in addition to author
4. Edition, if not the first
5. Volume: total number of volumes if multivolume work is referred to as a whole; individual number if single volume of multivolume work is cited, and title of individual volume if applicable
6. Series title if applicable, and volume number within series if series is numbered
7. Facts of publication: city, publisher, and date
8. Page number or numbers if applicable
9. For books consulted online, a URL (or DOI-based URL); for other types of electronic books, the application, format, device, or medium consulted; see also 14.6–18

14.101 **Form of author's name and title of book in source citations.** An author's name and the title of a book should generally be cited according to how it appears on the title page. In a bibliography entry, the first-listed author's name is normally inverted.

1. Atul Gawande, *Being Mortal: Medicine and What Matters in the End* (London: Profile Books, 2014), 79–80.

2. Gawande, *Being Mortal*, 191.

Gawande, Atul. *Being Mortal: Medicine and What Matters in the End*. London: Profile Books, 2014.

For additional considerations and many more examples, see 14.72–84 and 14.85–99.

14.102 **Non-English bibliographic terms and abbreviations.** When books in a language other than English are cited in an English-language work, terms used for volume, edition, and so on may be translated—but only if the author or editor has a firm grasp of bibliographic terms in the other language. It is often wiser to leave them in the original. "Ausgabe in einem Band," for example, may be rendered as "one-volume edition" or simply left untranslated. Moreover, abbreviations such as "Bd." and "t." (German and French/Spanish equivalents of *vol.*, respectively) that are likely to have been recorded that way in a library catalog may best be left in that form. If in doubt, check a major catalog such as that of the Library of Congress or WorldCat.

Editors, Translators, Compilers, or Cowriters

14.103 **Editor in place of author.** When no author appears on the title page, a work is listed by the name(s) of the editor(s), compiler(s), or translator(s). In full note citations and in bibliographies, the abbreviation *ed.* or *eds.*, *comp.* or *comps.*, or *trans.* follows the name, preceded by a comma. In shortened note citations and text citations, the abbreviation is omitted.

1. Jennifer Egan, ed., *The Best American Short Stories, 2014* (Boston: Houghton Mifflin Harcourt, 2014), 100.
2. Harold Schechter and Kurt Brown, comps., *Killer Verse: Poems of Murder and Mayhem* (London: Everyman Paperback Classics, 2011), 33.
3. Theodore Silverstein, trans., *Sir Gawain and the Green Knight* (Chicago: University of Chicago Press, 1974), 34.
4. Egan, *Best American Short Stories*, 301–2.
5. Schechter and Brown, *Killer Verse*, 54–56.
6. Silverstein, *Sir Gawain*, 38.

Egan, Jennifer, ed. *The Best American Short Stories, 2014*. Boston: Houghton Mifflin Harcourt, 2014.

Schechter, Harold, and Kurt Brown, comps. *Killer Verse: Poems of Murder and Mayhem*. London: Everyman Paperback Classics, 2011.

Silverstein, Theodore, trans. *Sir Gawain and the Green Knight*. Chicago: University of Chicago Press, 1974.

On the other hand, certain well-known reference works may be listed by title rather than by editor; for an example, see 14.232.

14.104 **Editor or translator in addition to author.** The edited, compiled, or translated work of one author is normally listed with the author's name appearing first and the name(s) of the editor(s), compiler(s), or translator(s) appearing after the title, preceded by *edited by* or *ed.*, *compiled by* or *comp.*, or *translated by* or *trans.* Note that the plural forms *eds.* and *comps.* are never used in this position. Note also that *edited by* and the like are usually spelled out in bibliographies but abbreviated in notes. If a translator as well as an editor is listed, the names should appear in the same order as on the title page of the original. When the title page carries such phrases as "Edited with an Introduction and Notes by" or "Translated with a Foreword by," the bibliographic or note reference can usually be simplified to "Edited by" or "Translated by." See also 14.78, 14.107, 14.99.

1. Yves Bonnefoy, *New and Selected Poems*, ed. John Naughton and Anthony Rudolf (Chicago: University of Chicago Press, 1995).

2. Rigoberta Menchú, *Crossing Borders*, trans. and ed. Ann Wright (New York: Verso, 1999).

3. *Four Farces by Georges Feydeau*, trans. Norman R. Shapiro (Chicago: University of Chicago Press, 1970).

4. Theodor W. Adorno and Walter Benjamin, *The Complete Correspondence, 1928–1940*, ed. Henri Lonitz, trans. Nicholas Walker (Cambridge, MA: Harvard University Press, 1999).

Adorno, Theodor W., and Walter Benjamin. *The Complete Correspondence, 1928–1940*. Edited by Henri Lonitz. Translated by Nicholas Walker. Cambridge, MA: Harvard University Press, 1999.

Bonnefoy, Yves. *New and Selected Poems*. Edited by John Naughton and Anthony Rudolf. Chicago: University of Chicago Press, 1995.

Feydeau, Georges. *Four Farces by Georges Feydeau*. Translated by Norman R. Shapiro. Chicago: University of Chicago Press, 1970.

Menchú, Rigoberta. *Crossing Borders*. Translated and edited by Ann Wright. New York: Verso, 1999.

Occasionally, when an editor or a translator is more important to a discussion than the original author, a book may be listed under the editor's name.

Eliot, T. S., ed. *Literary Essays*. By Ezra Pound. New York: New Directions, 1953.

14.105 **Other contributors listed on the title page.** The title page may list the names of people other than an author, editor, compiler, or translator. Such names may be included in a full note or a bibliography entry if they are considered to be a significant factor in a reader's assessment of the book. For ghostwritten books, *with* is usually sufficient. For other contributions, descriptions should accurately convey the information on the title page. Authors of forewords or introductions to books by other authors may be included if they are considered sufficiently important to mention.

Chaucer Life-Records. Edited by Martin M. Crow and Clair C. Olson from materials compiled by John M. Manly and Edith Rickert, with the assistance of Lilian J. Redstone et al. London: Oxford University Press, 1966.

Conway, Tim. *What's So Funny? My Hilarious Life*. With Jane Scovell and with a foreword by Carol Burnett. New York: Howard Books, 2013.

Cullen, John B. *Old Times in the Faulkner Country*. In collaboration with Floyd C. Watkins. Chapel Hill: University of North Carolina Press, 1961.

Hayek, F. A. *The Road to Serfdom*. With a new introduction by Milton Friedman. Chicago: University of Chicago Press, 1994.

Prather, Marla. *Alexander Calder, 1898–1976*. With contributions by Arnauld Pierre and Alexander S. C. Rower. New Haven, CT: Yale University Press, 1998.

Schellinger, Paul, ed. *Encyclopedia of the Novel*. With the assistance of Christopher Hudson and Marijke Rijsberman. 2 vols. Chicago: Fitzroy Dearborn, 1998.

Williams, Joseph M. *Style: Toward Clarity and Grace*. With two chapters coauthored by Gregory G. Colomb. Chicago: University of Chicago Press, 1995.

For specific citation of a foreword or an introduction, see 14.110.

Chapters or Other Parts of a Book

14.106 **Chapter in a single-author book.** When a specific chapter (or other titled part of a book) is cited in the notes, the author's name is followed by the title of the chapter (or other part), followed by *in*, followed by the title of the book. The chapter title is enclosed in quotation marks. Either the inclusive page numbers (see 9.61) or the chapter or part number is usually given also, though a note may instead list the page or pages cited. In the bibliography, either the chapter or the book may be listed first. For a multiauthor work, see 14.107. See also 14.153.

1. Kate Andersen Brower, "Backstairs Gossip and Mischief," in *The Residence: Inside the Private World of the White House* (New York: Harper, 2015), 211.

2. John Samples, "The Origins of Modern Campaign Finance Law," chap. 7 in *The Fallacy of Campaign Finance Reform* (Chicago: University of Chicago Press, 2006).

3. Samples, "Campaign Finance Law," 30–31.

Brower, Kate Andersen. "Backstairs Gossip and Mischief." In *The Residence: Inside the Private World of the White House*, 207–22. New York: Harper, 2015.

Samples, John. "The Origins of Modern Campaign Finance Law." Chap. 7 in *The Fallacy of Campaign Finance Reform*. Chicago: University of Chicago Press, 2006.

or

Samples, John. *The Fallacy of Campaign Finance Reform*. Chicago: University of Chicago Press, 2006. See esp. chap. 7, "The Origins of Modern Campaign Finance Law."

For chapters originally published as articles in a journal, see 14.181.

14.107 **Contribution to a multiauthor book.** When one contribution to a multiauthor book is cited, the contributor's name comes first, followed by the title of the contribution in roman, followed by *in* (also roman), followed by the title of the book in italics, followed by the name(s) of the editor(s). In a bibliography entry, the inclusive page numbers are usually given also (as in the second example below). In notes and bibliographies, the contribution title is enclosed in quotation marks. For several contributions to the same book, see 14.108.

1. Ruth A. Miller, "Posthuman," in *Critical Terms for the Study of Gender*, ed. Catharine R. Stimpson and Gilbert Herdt (Chicago: University of Chicago Press, 2014), 325.

Ellet, Elizabeth F. L. "By Rail and Stage to Galena." In *Prairie State: Impressions of Illinois, 1673–1967, by Travelers and Other Observers*, edited by Paul M. Angle, 271–79. Chicago: University of Chicago Press, 1968.

14.108 **Several contributions to the same multiauthor book.** If two or more contributions to the same multiauthor book are cited, the book itself, as well as the specific contributions, may be listed in the bibliography. The entries for the individual contributions may then cross-refer to the book's editor, thus avoiding clutter. In notes, details of the book may be given the first time it is mentioned, with subsequent references in shortened form (see also 14.31).

1. William H. Keating, "Fort Dearborn and Chicago," in *Prairie State: Impressions of Illinois, 1673–1967, by Travelers and Other Observers*, ed. Paul M. Angle (Chicago: University of Chicago Press, 1967), 84–87.

2. Sara Clarke Lippincott, "Chicago," in Angle, *Prairie State*, 362–70.

Draper, Joan E. "Paris by the Lake: Sources of Burnham's Plan of Chicago." In Zukowsky, *Chicago Architecture*, 107–19.

Harrington, Elaine. "International Influences on Henry Hobson Richardson's Glessner House." In Zukowsky, *Chicago Architecture*, 189–207.

Zukowsky, John, ed. *Chicago Architecture, 1872–1922: Birth of a Metropolis*. Munich: Prestel-Verlag in association with the Art Institute of Chicago, 1987.

14.109 **Book-length work within a book.** If the cited part of a book would normally be italicized if published alone, it too may be italicized rather than placed in quotation marks. See also 8.163, 8.183.

1. Thomas Bernhard, *A Party for Boris*, in *Histrionics: Three Plays*, trans. Peter K. Jansen and Kenneth Northcott (Chicago: University of Chicago Press, 1990).

Updike, John. *Rabbit, Run*. In *Rabbit Angstrom: A Tetralogy*. New York: Everyman's Library, 1995.

14.110 **Introductions, prefaces, afterwords, and the like.** If the reference is to a generic title such as *introduction*, *preface*, or *afterword*, that term (lowercased unless following a period) is added before the title of the book. See also 8.179.

1. Toni Morrison, foreword to *Song of Solomon* (New York: Vintage International, 2004).

If the author of the introduction or other part is someone other than the main author of a book, that author comes first, and the author of the book follows the title. In a bibliography entry, include the page number range for the part cited, as shown in the second example below.

2. Christopher Hitchens, introduction to *Civilization and Its Discontents*, by Sigmund Freud, trans. and ed. James Strachey (New York: W. W. Norton, 2010).

Mansfield, Harvey, and Delba Winthrop. Introduction to *Democracy in America*, by Alexis de Tocqueville, xvii–lxxxvi. Translated and edited by Harvey Mansfield and Delba Winthrop. Chicago: University of Chicago Press, 2000.

For including information about a foreword or other contributions to a book cited as a whole, see 14.105.

14.111 **Letters in published collections.** A reference to a letter (or memorandum or similar communication) in a published collection begins with the names of the sender and the recipient, in that order, followed by a date and sometimes the place where the communication was prepared. Words such as *letter*, *postcard*, *email*, and the like are usually unnecessary, but other forms, such as reports or memorandums, should be specified. The title of the collection is given in the usual form for a book. If not clear in the text or otherwise, a short form for the collection may be needed if correspondents differ from those listed in the first full citation (as shown in note 4). For unpublished communications, see 14.214; see also 14.228.

1. Adams to Charles Milnes Gaskell, Baden, September 22, 1867, in *Letters of Henry Adams, 1858–1891*, ed. Worthington Chauncey Ford (Boston: Houghton Mifflin, 1930), 133–34.

2. White to Harold Ross, memorandum, May 2, 1946, in *Letters of E. B. White*, ed. Dorothy Lobrano Guth (New York: Harper & Row, 1976), 273.

3. Adams to Gaskell, London, March 30, 1868, 141.

4. Adams to John Hay, Washington, October 26, 1884, in Ford, *Letters*, 361.

Adams, Henry. *Letters of Henry Adams, 1858–1891*. Edited by Worthington Chauncey Ford. Boston: Houghton Mifflin, 1930.

White, E. B. *Letters of E. B. White*. Edited by Dorothy Lobrano Guth. New York: Harper & Row, 1976.

When it is necessary to include a single letter in a bibliography, it is listed under the writer's name only.

Jackson, Paulina. Paulina Jackson to John Pepys Junior, October 3, 1676. In *The Letters of Samuel Pepys and His Family Circle*, edited by Helen Truesdell Heath, no. 42. Oxford: Clarendon Press, 1955.

14.112 **Online-only supplement to a book.** To cite an online-only supplement or enhancement to a book, include a title or a description for the content and a URL (see 14.6) in addition to the publication details for the book. Specify file format if applicable.

1. Steven J. Luck, "Electrodes and Skin Potentials" (PDF), online supplement to chap. 5 of *An Introduction to the Event-Related Potential Technique*, 2nd ed.

(Cambridge, MA: MIT Press, 2014), http://mitpress.mit.edu/books/introduction-event-related-potential-technique-0.

Edition

14.113 **Editions other than the first.** When an edition other than the first is used or cited, the number or description of the edition follows the title in the listing. An edition number usually appears on the title page and is repeated, along with the date of the edition, on the copyright page. Such wording as *Second Edition, Revised and Enlarged* is abbreviated in notes and bibliographies simply as *2nd ed.*; *Revised Edition* (with no number) is abbreviated as *rev. ed.* Other terms are similarly abbreviated. (Any information about volumes follows the edition number; for an example, see 14.232.) For the use of the word *edition* and Chicago's preferences, see 1.26. For inclusion of the original date of an older work cited in a modern edition, see 14.114.

1. Amy Einsohn, *The Copyeditor's Handbook: A Guide for Book Publishing and Corporate Communications, with Exercises and Answer Keys*, 3rd ed. (Berkeley: University of California Press, 2011), 401–2.

2. Kathryn Parker Boudett, Elizabeth A. City, and Richard J. Murnane, eds., *Data Wise: A Step-by-Step Guide to Using Assessment Results to Improve Teaching and Learning*, rev. ed. (Cambridge, MA: Harvard Education Press, 2013), 101.

3. Elizabeth Barrett Browning, *Aurora Leigh: Authoritative Text, Backgrounds and Contexts, Criticism*, ed. Margaret Reynolds, Norton Critical Editions (New York: W. W. Norton, 1996). All subsequent citations refer to this edition.

Strunk, William, Jr., and E. B. White. *The Elements of Style*. 4th ed. New York: Allyn and Bacon, 2000.

14.114 **Reprint editions and modern editions.** Books may be reissued in paperback by the original publisher or in paper or hardcover by another company. In bibliographic listings, if the original publication details—particularly the date—are relevant, include them. If page numbers are mentioned, specify the edition cited unless pagination is the same. The availability of a different format (e.g., paperback or an electronic version), the addition of new material, or other such matters can be added as needed. Modern editions of Greek, Latin, and medieval classics are discussed in 14.242–52; modern editions of English classics in 14.253–54; electronic book formats in 14.159–63.

1. Ernest Gowers, *The Complete Plain Words*, 3rd ed. (London: H.M. Stationery Office, 1986; Harmondsworth, UK: Penguin Books, 1987), 26. Citations refer to the Penguin edition.

2. Jacques Barzun, *Simple and Direct: A Rhetoric for Writers*, rev. ed. (1985; repr., Chicago: University of Chicago Press, 1994), 152–53.

Bahadur, Gaiutra. *Coolie Woman: The Odyssey of Indenture*. Chicago: University of Chicago Press, 2014. First published 2013 by C. Hurst (London).

Emerson, Ralph Waldo. *Nature*. 1836. Facsimile of the first edition, with an introduction by Jaroslav Pelikan. Boston: Beacon Press, 1985.

Fitzgerald, F. Scott. *The Great Gatsby*. New York: Scribner, 1925. Reprinted with preface and notes by Matthew J. Bruccoli. New York: Collier Books, 1992. Page references are to the 1992 edition.

National Reconnaissance Office. *The KH-4B Camera System*. Washington, DC: National Photographic Interpretation Center, 1967. Now declassified and also available online, http://www.fas.org/irp/imint/docs/kh-4_camera_system.htm.

Schweitzer, Albert. *J. S. Bach*. Translated by Ernest Newman. 2 vols. 1911. Reprint, New York: Dover, 1966.

14.115 **Microform editions.** Works consulted in microform editions (i.e., copies of printed matter reproduced for storage at a smaller size, usually on film, and read using a specialized viewer) should be cited according to the format of the original publication (e.g., book, newspaper article, or dissertation). In addition, specify the format actually consulted (e.g., microfiche or microfilm) after the facts of publication. In the first example below, the page number refers to the printed text; the other locator indicates the fiche (i.e., sheet) and frame numbers, and the letter indicates the row. Such locators will vary according to the resource.

1. Beatrice Farwell, *French Popular Lithographic Imagery, 1815–1870*, vol. 12, *Lithography in Art and Commerce* (Chicago: University of Chicago Press, 1997), microfiche, p. 67, 3C12.

Tauber, Abraham. "Spelling Reform in the United States." PhD diss., Columbia University, 1958. Microfilm.

Multivolume Works

14.116 **Volume numbers and page numbers.** In source citations, volume numbers are always given in arabic numerals, even if in the original work they appear in roman numerals or are spelled out. If the volume number is immediately followed by a page number, the abbreviation *vol.* is omitted and a colon separates the volume number from the page number with no intervening space. See the examples throughout this section. See also 14.177.

14.117 **Citing a multivolume work as a whole.** When a multivolume work is cited as a whole, the total number of volumes is given after the title of the work (or, if an editor as well as an author is mentioned, after the editor's name). If the volumes have been published over several years, the dates of the first and last volumes are given, separated by an en dash (see 9.64). See also 14.78.

1. Aristotle, *Complete Works of Aristotle: The Revised Oxford Translation*, ed. J. Barnes, 2 vols., Bollingen Series (Princeton, NJ: Princeton University Press, 1983).

Byrne, Muriel St. Clare, ed. *The Lisle Letters*. 6 vols. Chicago: University of Chicago Press, 1981.

Grene, David, and Richmond Lattimore, eds. *The Complete Greek Tragedies*. 3rd ed., edited by Mark Griffith and Glenn W. Most. 9 vols. (unnumbered). Chicago: University of Chicago Press, 2013.

James, Henry. *The Complete Tales of Henry James*. Edited by Leon Edel. 12 vols. London: Rupert Hart-Davis, 1962–64.

14.118 **Citing a particular volume in a note.** If a particular volume of a multivolume work is cited, the volume number and the individual volume title, if there is one, are given in addition to the general title. If volumes have been published in different years, only the date of the cited volume is given.

1. Muriel St. Clare Byrne, ed., *The Lisle Letters* (Chicago: University of Chicago Press, 1981), 4:243.

2. *The Complete Tales of Henry James*, ed. Leon Edel, vol. 5, *1883–1884* (London: Rupert Hart-Davis, 1963), 32–33.

3. Byrne, *Lisle Letters*, 4:245.

4. *Complete Tales of Henry James*, 5:34.

The different treatment of the volume numbers in the examples above is prescribed by logic: all six volumes of the Byrne work appeared in 1981 under the same title, whereas volume 5 of the James tales carries an additional title with a publication date not shared by all volumes in the set. The shortened form, however, need not refer to the title of the individual volume. Information about the total number of volumes (as in a work without a corresponding bibliography) may be added as follows:

1. Muriel St. Clare Byrne, ed., *The Lisle Letters*, 6 vols. . . .
2. *The Complete Tales of Henry James*, ed. Leon Edel, vol. 5 of 12, . . .

See also 14.122.

14.119 **Citing a particular volume in a bibliography.** If only one volume of a multivolume work is of interest to readers, it may be listed alone in a bibliography in either of the following ways:

Carson, Clayborne, ed. *The Papers of Martin Luther King, Jr.* Vol. 7, *To Save the Soul of America, January 1961–August 1962*, edited by Tenisha Armstrong. Berkeley: University of California Press, 2014.

or

Armstrong, Tenisha, ed. *To Save the Soul of America, January 1961–August 1962.* Vol. 7 of *The Papers of Martin Luther King, Jr.*, edited by Clayborne Carson. Berkeley: University of California Press, 1992–.

If they are different, the editor(s) for the series as a whole and for the individual volume should both be listed (see also 14.122). The publication date (or date range; see 14.117) should normally correspond to the last-mentioned title. See also 14.121, 14.144.

14.120 **Chapters and other parts of individual volumes.** Specific parts of individual volumes of multivolume books are cited in the same way as parts of single-volume books (see 14.106–12). In a note that refers to the entire chapter, a chapter number, if available, may replace page numbers (e.g., "vol. 3, chap. 9").

1. Chen Jian, "China and the Cold War after Mao," in *The Cambridge History of the Cold War*, ed. Melvyn P. Leffler and Odd Arne Westad (Cambridge: Cambridge University Press, 2010), 3:180.
2. Unpublished letter to the editor of the *Afro-American* (Washington, DC), in *The Papers of Martin Luther King, Jr.*, ed. Clayborne Carson, vol. 7, *To Save the Soul of America, January 1961–August 1962*, ed. Tenisha Armstrong (Berkeley: University of California Press, 2014), 169–71.

Jian, Chen. "China and the Cold War after Mao." In *Endings*, ed. Melvyn P. Leffler and Odd Arne Westad, 181–200. Vol. 3 of *The Cambridge History of the Cold War*. Cambridge: Cambridge University Press, 2010.

See also 14.107, 14.122.

14.121 **One volume in two or more books.** Occasionally, if it is very long, a single volume of a multivolume work may be published as two or more physical books. The reference must then include book as well as volume number.

1. Donald Lach, *Asia in the Making of Europe*, vol. 2, bk. 3, *The Scholarly Disciplines* (Chicago: University of Chicago Press, 1977), 351.

Harley, J. B., and David Woodward, eds. *The History of Cartography*. Vol. 2, bk. 2, *Cartography in the Traditional East and Southeast Asian Societies*. Chicago: University of Chicago Press, 1994.

or

Harley, J. B., and David Woodward, eds. *Cartography in the Traditional East and Southeast Asian Societies*. Vol. 2, bk. 2, of *The History of Cartography*. Chicago: University of Chicago Press, 1987–.

14.122 **Authors and editors of multivolume works.** Some multivolume works have both a general editor and individual editors or authors for each volume (and, as in the third example, additional editors for new editions). When individual volumes are cited, the editor's (or translator's) name follows that part for which he or she is responsible.

1. Herbert Barrows, *Reading the Short Story*, vol. 1 of *An Introduction to Literature*, ed. Gordon N. Ray (Boston: Houghton Mifflin, 1959).

2. *The Variorum Edition of the Poetry of John Donne*, ed. Gary A. Stringer, vol. 6, *The "Anniversaries" and the "Epicedes and Obsequies,"* ed. Gary A. Stringer and Ted-Larry Pebworth (Bloomington: Indiana University Press, 1995).

3. *Orestes*, trans. William Arrowsmith, in *Euripides IV*, unnumbered vol. 6 of *The Complete Greek Tragedies*, ed. David Grene and Richmond Lattimore, 3rd ed., ed. Mark Griffith and Glenn W. Most (Chicago: University of Chicago Press, 2013).

Note the different capitalization and punctuation of *edited by* in the following alternative versions, analogous to the treatment of a chapter in a multiauthor book (see 14.107). (Certain multivolume works may, for bibliographic purposes, more conveniently be treated as series; see 14.124.)

Donne, John. *The Variorum Edition of the Poetry of John Donne*. Edited by Gary A. Stringer. Vol. 6, *"The Anniversaries" and the "Epicedes and Obsequies,"* edited by Gary A. Stringer and Ted-Larry Pebworth. Bloomington: Indiana University Press, 1995.

or

Donne, John. *The "Anniversaries" and the "Epicedes and Obsequies."* Edited by Gary A. Stringer and Ted-Larry Pebworth. Vol. 6 of *The Variorum Edition of the Poetry of John Donne*, edited by Gary A. Stringer. Bloomington: Indiana University Press, 1995.

Ray, Gordon N., ed. *An Introduction to Literature*. Vol. 1, *Reading the Short Story*, by Herbert Barrows. Boston: Houghton Mifflin, 1959.

or

Barrows, Herbert. *Reading the Short Story*. Vol. 1 of *An Introduction to Literature*, edited by Gordon N. Ray. Boston: Houghton Mifflin, 1959.

Series

14.123 **Series titles, numbers, and editors.** Including a series title in a citation often helps readers decide whether to pursue a reference. But if books belonging to a series can be located without the series title, it may be omitted to save space (especially in a footnote). If the series title is included, it is capitalized headline-style, but it is neither italicized nor put in quotation marks or parentheses. Some series are numbered; many are not. The number (if any) follows the series title with no intervening comma unless *vol.* or *no.* is used. These abbreviations may be omitted, however, unless both are needed in a single reference (see fourth example below), or unless a series editor or other notation intervenes (see 14.124, third example). For a non-English series title, use sentence style (see 11.6 and second example below).

1. Sean Hsiang-lin Lei, *Neither Donkey nor Horse: Medicine in the Struggle over China's Modernity*, Studies of the Weatherhead East Asian Institute (Chicago: University of Chicago Press, 2014).

Martin, Jean-Pierre. *L'autre vie d'Orwell*. Collection l'un et l'autre. Paris: Gallimard, 2013.

Mazrim, Robert F. *At Home in the Illinois Country: French Colonial Domestic Site Archaeology in the Midwest, 1730–1800*. Studies in Illinois Archaeology 9. Urbana: Illinois State Archaeological Survey, 2011.

Wauchope, Robert. *A Tentative Sequence of Pre-Classic Ceramics in Middle America*. Middle American Research Records, vol. 1, no. 14. New Orleans: Tulane University, 1950.

The name of the series editor is usually omitted. When included, it follows the series title.

Allen, Judith A. *The Feminism of Charlotte Perkins Gilman: Sexualities, Histories, Progressivism*. Women in Culture and Society, edited by Catharine R. Stimpson. Chicago: University of Chicago Press, 2009.

14.124 **Series or multivolume work?** Certain types of series may lend themselves to being cited as a whole. In such cases, the series may be treated as a multivolume work, with the title of the series in italics.

Boyer, John W., and Julius Kirshner, eds. *Readings in Western Civilization*. 9 vols. Chicago: University of Chicago Press, 1986–87.

Grene, David, and Richmond Lattimore, eds. *The Complete Greek Tragedies*. 3rd ed., edited by Mark Griffith and Glenn W. Most. 9 vols. (unnumbered). Chicago: University of Chicago Press, 2013.

Usually, however, it is preferable to cite individual titles in the series, as described in 14.123; the series title then appears in roman.

Cochrane, Eric W., Charles K. Gray, and Mark Kishlansky. *Early Modern Europe: Crisis of Authority*. Readings in Western Civilization, edited by John W. Boyer and Julius Kirshner, vol. 6. Chicago: University of Chicago Press, 1987.

Euripides. *Orestes*. Translated by William Arrowsmith. In *Euripides IV*, edited by David Grene and Richmond Lattimore. 3rd ed., edited by Mark Griffith and Glenn W. Most. The Complete Greek Tragedies. Chicago: University of Chicago Press, 2013.

14.125 **Multivolume work within a series.** If a book within a series consists of more than one volume, the number of volumes or the volume number (if reference is to a particular volume) follows the book title.

Ferrer Benimeli, José Antonio. *Masonería, iglesia e ilustración*. Vol. 1, *Las bases de un conflicto (1700–1739)*. Vol. 2, *Inquisición: Procesos históricos (1739–1750)*. Publicaciones de la Fundación Universitaria Española, Monografías 17. Madrid, 1976.

14.126 **"Old series" and "new series."** Some numbered series have gone on so long that, as with certain long-lived journals, numbering has started over again, preceded by *n.s.* (new series), *2nd ser.* (second series), or some similar notation, usually enclosed in commas. (A change of publisher may also be the occasion for a change in series designation.) Books in the old series may be identified by *o.s.*, *1st ser.*, or whatever complements the notation for the new series.

1. Charles R. Boxer, ed. *South China in the Sixteenth Century*, Hakluyt Society Publications, 2nd ser., vol. 106 (London: Hakluyt, 1953).

Palmatary, Helen C. *The Pottery of Marajó Island, Brazil*. Transactions of the American Philosophical Society, n.s., 39, pt. 3. Philadelphia: American Philosophical Society, 1950.

Facts of Publication

14.127 **Place, publisher, and date.** Traditionally, the facts of publication for books include the place (city), the publisher, and the date (year). These elements are put in parentheses in a note but not in a bibliography. A colon appears between place and publisher. In a note or a bibliography, the date follows the publisher, preceded by a comma. See also 14.23.

1. Virginia Woolf, *To the Lighthouse* (London: Hogarth Press, 1927).

Thomas, Matthew. *We Are Not Ourselves*. New York: Simon & Schuster, 2014.

PLACE OF PUBLICATION

14.128 **Place and date only, for books published before 1900.** For books published before 1900, it is acceptable to omit publishers' names and to include only the place and date of publication. A comma, not a colon, follows the place. See also 14.132, 14.137.

1. Oliver Goldsmith, *The Vicar of Wakefield* (Salisbury, 1766).

Cervantes Saavedra, Miguel de. *El ingenioso hidalgo Don Quixote de la Mancha*. 2 vols. Madrid, 1605–15.

14.129 **Place of publication—city.** The place to be included is the one that usually appears on the title page but sometimes on the copyright page of the book cited—the city where the publisher's main editorial offices are located. Where two or more cities are given ("Chicago and London," for example, appears on the title page of the print edition of this manual), only the first is normally included in the citation.

Berkeley: University of California Press
Los Angeles: Getty Publications
New York: Macmillan
New York: Oxford University Press
Oxford: Clarendon Press

14.130 **When to specify state, province, or country of publication.** If the city of publication may be unknown to readers or may be confused with another city of the same name, the abbreviation of the state, province, or (sometimes) country is usually added. *Washington* is traditionally followed by

DC, but other major cities, such as Los Angeles and Baltimore, need no state abbreviation. (For countries not easily abbreviated, spell out the name.) Chicago's preference is for the two-letter postal codes (IL, MA, etc.), but some publishers prefer the conventional state abbreviations (Ill., Mass., etc.). See 10.4, 10.27. For Canadian provinces and territories, see 10.28.

Cambridge, MA: Harvard University Press
Cambridge, MA: MIT Press
Cheshire, CT: Graphics Press
Englewood Cliffs, NJ: Prentice Hall
Harmondsworth, UK: Penguin Books
Ithaca, NY: Cornell University Press
New Haven, CT: Yale University Press
Princeton, NJ: Princeton University Press
Reading, MA: Perseus Books
Washington, DC: Smithsonian Institution Press
Waterloo, ON: Wilfrid Laurier University Press
but
Cambridge: Cambridge University Press

When the publisher's name includes the state name, the abbreviation is not needed.

Chapel Hill: University of North Carolina Press

14.131 **City names in languages other than English.** Current, commonly used English names for cities such as those listed here are usually preferred whenever such forms exist. If in doubt about what form to use, record the name of the city as it appears with the source. (Names for cities such as Beijing or Mumbai that were once commonly known under older forms can usually be recorded as they appear in the source. See also 11.83.)

Belgrade (*not* Beograd)
Cologne (*not* Köln)
Mexico City (*not* México)
Milan (*not* Milano)
Munich (*not* München)
Prague (*not* Praha)
Rome (*not* Roma)
The Hague (*not* den Haag)
Turin (*not* Torino)
Vienna (*not* Wien)

14.132 **No place of publication.** When the place of publication is not known, the abbreviation *n.p.* (or *N.p.* if following a period) may be used before the publisher's name. If the place can be surmised, it may be given with a question mark, in brackets. See also 14.128.

(n.p.: Windsor, 1910)
([Lake Bluff, IL?]: Vliet & Edwards, 1890)

It is common for more recent books published through commercial self-publishing platforms not to list a place of publication. In such cases, the place of publication can usually be omitted; for examples, see 14.137.

PUBLISHER'S NAME

14.133 **Preferred form of publisher's name.** The publisher's name may be given either in full (e.g., as printed on the title page of the book) or in a somewhat abbreviated form. The shorter forms are preferred in most bibliographies (see 14.134). The form should, however, reflect the publisher's name at the date of publication, not the current name if the name has changed. Most publishers' names at the time of publication can be double-checked through any number of reputable sources, including the catalogs of the Library of Congress, WorldCat, and the *Books in Print* resources available through R. R. Bowker (see bibliog. 4.5). For reprint and other editions, see 14.113–15.

14.134 **Abbreviations and omissible parts of a publisher's name.** In notes and bibliography, an initial *The* is omitted from a publisher's name, as are such abbreviations as *Inc.*, *Ltd.*, or *S.A.* following a name. *Co.*, *& Co.*, *Publishing Co.*, and the like are also omitted, even if *Company* is spelled out. Such corporate features of a publisher's name—often subject to many changes over the years—are far less important in leading a reader to the source consulted than the publication date, and attempting to include them will invariably lead to inconsistencies. A given name or initials preceding a family name, however, may be retained, as may terms such as *Sons*, *Brothers*, and so forth. *Books* is usually retained (Basic Books, Riverhead Books). The word *Press* can sometimes be omitted (for example, Pergamon Press and Ecco Press can be abbreviated to Pergamon and Ecco, but Free Press and New Press—whose names might be confusing without *Press*—must be given in full). *Press* should not be omitted from the name of a university press because the university itself may issue publications independent of its press. The word *University* may be abbreviated to *Univ.* if done consistently.

Houghton Mifflin *not* Houghton Mifflin Co.
Little, Brown *not* Little, Brown & Co.
Macmillan *not* Macmillan Publishing Co.
W. W. Norton *not* W. W. Norton & Company

Note that there is no comma in Houghton Mifflin, but there is one in Little, Brown. Likewise, Harcourt, Brace has a comma, but Harcourt Brace Jovanovich does not. If in doubt, consult one of the sources mentioned in 14.133.

14.135 **"And" or ampersand in publisher's name.** Either *and* or *&* may be used in a publisher's name, regardless of how it is rendered on the title page. It is advisable to stick to one or the other throughout a bibliography. If the publisher's name is not in English, the equivalent of *and* must be used unless an ampersand is used instead.

Duncker und Humblot *or* Duncker & Humblot
Harper and Row *or* Harper & Row

In publisher names that form a series, the serial comma is usually omitted before an ampersand but not before *and* (see also 6.21). An exception may be made for Farrar, Straus and Giroux, which is generally so written (i.e., with an *and* but not with a serial comma).

14.136 **Non-English publishers' names.** No part of a publisher's name in a language other than English should be translated, even if the city has been given in its English form (see 14.131).

Mexico City: Fondo de Cultura Económica, 2010
Munich: Delphin Verlag, 2015
Paris: Presses Universitaires de France, 2011

Note that abbreviations corresponding to *Inc.* or *Ltd.* (German *GmbH*, for example) are omitted (see 14.134). Capitalization of a publisher's name should follow the original unless the name appears in full capitals there; in that case, it should be capitalized headline-style; if in doubt about the correct capitalization, consult one of the sources mentioned in 14.133.

14.137 **Self-published or privately published books.** Books published by the author should be cited according to information available on the title page or copyright page or otherwise known. Unless the work has been published under a publisher or imprint name (in which case it can be cited as described elsewhere in this section), such language as "self-published" (abbreviated as "self-pub." in a note but not in a bibliography entry) or "printed by the author" is usually appropriate. For works distributed through a commercial self-publishing platform, the name of the platform or distributor may be added. It is common for self-published books not to list a place of publication on the title page or copyright page; unless a place is listed or otherwise known, it can usually be omitted (see also 14.132). For e-books, add the name of the application or device required to read the book or the name of the file format, or both (see also 14.159).

1. Vasiliy Karavaev, *GOA: Confession of the Psychedelic Oyster* (self-pub., 2015), iBooks.

2. Frank Landis, *Hot Earth Dreams: What If Severe Climate Change Happens, and Humans Survive?* (self-pub., Smashwords, 2015), EPUB.

Rai, Alisha. *Serving Pleasure*. Self-published, CreateSpace, 2015.

Shumaker, O. W. *Anna's Bear: 5 Days of Moral Conflict and Pursuit, Nazi Germany, 1939*. Self-published, Amazon Digital Services, 2014. Kindle.

Older self-published works are more likely to list a city of publication or printing (see also 14.128).

Albin, Eleazar. *A Natural History of Birds: Illustrated with a Hundred and One Copper Plates, Engraven from the Life*. London: printed by the author, 1738.

14.138 **Parent companies, imprints, and such.** When a parent company's name appears on the title page in addition to the publisher's name or imprint, it is usually sufficient to cite the latter (but see 14.139). For example, the title page of a 1995 edition of *Old New York: Four Novellas*, by Edith Wharton, bears the imprint "Scribner Paperback Fiction"; below that appears "Published by Simon & Schuster." (The cities listed are New York, London, Toronto, and Sydney.) The spine carries "Scribner Paperback Fiction" (but not Simon & Schuster). The copyright page gives an address for Simon & Schuster and further explains that (for the time being) Scribner Paperback Fiction is a trademark of Macmillan Library Reference USA. Such complex arrangements are common in book publishing. Cite the work as follows:

Wharton, Edith. *Old New York: Four Novellas*. New York: Scribner Paperback Fiction, 1995.

If it is not clear which name to list, check with one of the catalogs listed in 14.133 to see which publisher is listed there, being careful to find the entry in the catalog that matches the facts of publication for the item in question. If this is not possible, or if it remains unclear which name to list, include both, separated by a slash (/) with a space on either side.

14.139 **Special academic imprints and joint imprints.** Some academic publishers issue certain books through a special publishing division or under a special imprint or as part of a publishing consortium (or joint imprint). In such instances the imprint arrangement may be specified. If the wording is not clear on the title page, copyright page, or elsewhere, consult one of the resources mentioned in 14.133.

Buell, Lawrence. *Emerson.* Cambridge, MA: Belknap Press of Harvard University Press, 2003.

Spivack, Kathleen. *With Robert Lowell and His Circle: Sylvia Plath, Anne Sexton, Elizabeth Bishop, Stanley Kunitz, and Others.* Boston: Northeastern University Press, an imprint of University Press of New England, 2012.

Taylor, Judith M. *Visions of Loveliness: Great Flower Breeders of the Past.* Athens: Swallow Press, an imprint of Ohio University Press, 2014.

Note that in the Taylor example, the state would need to be specified (i.e., Athens, OH) if the citation were to include Swallow Press but not the parent company. See also 14.141.

14.140 **Copublication.** When books are published simultaneously (or almost so) by two publishers, usually in different countries, only one publisher need be listed—the one that is more relevant to the users of the citation. For example, if a book copublished by a British and an American publisher is listed in the bibliography of an American publication, only the American publication details need be given. If for some reason (e.g., as a matter of historical interest) information is included for both publishers, a semicolon should be used as a separator. (Occasionally, the dates of publication will be different; in such cases, record both.) For reprints, see 14.114.

Lévi-Strauss, Claude. *The Savage Mind.* Chicago: University of Chicago Press; London: Weidenfeld and Nicolson, 1962.

Some copublications occur between a publisher and another institution such as a museum. These can usually be handled in the same way (but for exhibition catalogs, see 14.236).

14.141 **Distributed books.** For a book published by one company and distributed by another, the name on the title page should be used. Since distribution agreements are sometimes impermanent, the distributor's name is best omitted unless essential to users of a bibliography.

Willke, Helmut. *Smart Governance: Governing the Global Knowledge Society*. Frankfurt am Main: Campus Verlag, 2007. Distributed by University of Chicago Press.

Wording on the title page such as "Published by arrangement with . . . ," if it is of particular interest, may be included in a similar manner. For books distributed by a retail self-publishing platform, see 14.137.

DATE OF PUBLICATION

14.142 **Publication date—general.** For books, only the year, not the month or day, is included in the publication date. The date is found on the title page or, more commonly, on the copyright page. It is usually the same as the copyright date. If two or more copyright dates appear in a book, the first being those of earlier editions or versions, the most recent indicates the publication date. Chicago's books normally carry both copyright date and publication date on the copyright page. For any edition other than the first, both the edition and the date of that edition must be included in a listing (see 14.113–15).

1. *The Chicago Manual of Style*, 17th ed. (Chicago: University of Chicago Press, 2017), 6.56; cf. 16th ed. (2010), 6.54.

Turabian, Kate L. *A Manual for Writers of Term Papers, Theses, and Dissertations*. 8th ed. Revised by Wayne C. Booth, Gregory G. Colomb, Joseph M. Williams, and the University of Chicago Press Staff. Chicago: University of Chicago Press, 2013.

14.143 **New impressions and renewal of copyright.** The publication date must not be confused with the date of a subsequent printing or a renewal of copyright. Such statements on the copyright page as "53rd impression" or "Copyright renewed 1980" should be disregarded. For new editions as opposed to new impressions, see 1.26; for reprints, see 14.114.

14.144 **Multivolume works published over more than one year.** When an entire multivolume, multiyear work is cited, the range of dates is given (see 6.78). If the work has not yet been completed, the date of the first volume is followed by an en dash (with no space between the en dash and the punctuation that follows; see 6.79). See also 9.64. If a single volume is cited, only the date of that volume need appear. See also 14.116–22.

1. *The Collected Works of F. A. Hayek*, ed. Bruce Caldwell, vol. 17, *The Constitution of Liberty: The Definitive Edition*, ed. Ronald Hamowy (Chicago: University of Chicago Press, 2011), 329.

Hayek, F. A. *The Constitution of Liberty: The Definitive Edition*. Edited by Ronald Hamowy. Vol. 17 of *The Collected Works of F. A. Hayek*, edited by Bruce Caldwell. Chicago: University of Chicago Press, 1988–.

Tillich, Paul. *Systematic Theology*. 3 vols. Chicago: University of Chicago Press, 1951–63.

14.145 **No date of publication.** When the publication date of a printed work cannot be ascertained, the abbreviation *n.d.* takes the place of the year in the publication details. A guessed-at date may either be substituted (in brackets) or added. See also 14.132.

Boston, n.d.
Edinburgh, [1750?] *or* Edinburgh, n.d., ca. 1750

A work for which no publisher, place, or date can be determined or reasonably guessed at should be included in a bibliography only if accompanied by the location where a copy can be found (e.g., "Two copies in the Special Collections Department of the University of Chicago Library"). For the use of *n.d.* in author-date citations, see 15.44.

14.146 **Forthcoming publications.** When a book is under contract with a publisher and is already titled, but the date of publication is not yet known, *forthcoming* is used in place of the date. Although *in press* is sometimes used (strictly speaking for a printed work that has already been typeset and paginated), Chicago recommends the more inclusive term, which can also be used for nonprint media, for any work under contract. If page numbers are available, they may be given. Books not under contract are treated as unpublished manuscripts (see 14.215–20).

1. Jane Q. Author, *Book Title* (Place: Publisher, forthcoming).
2. John J. Writer, *Another Book Title* (Place: Publisher, forthcoming), 345–46.

Contributor, Anna. "Contribution." In *Edited Volume*, edited by Ellen Editor. Place: Publisher, forthcoming.

When a publication that cites a forthcoming title is reprinted, the citation need not be updated. For a revised edition, on the other hand, the citation can be updated to provide the final facts of publication, but only after direct quotations and other details have been checked for accuracy against the published source.

Page, Volume, and Other Locating Information

14.147 **Arabic versus roman numerals.** As the examples throughout this chapter (and chapter 15) suggest, arabic numerals should be used wherever possible in source citations—for volumes, chapters, and other divisions—regardless of the way the numerals appear in the works cited, with the notable exception of pages numbered with roman numerals in the original (usually lowercased, in the front matter of a book). Occasional exceptions are made, for example, in certain legal contexts (see 14.280).

1. See the article "Feathers," in *Johnson's Universal Cyclopaedia*, rev. ed. (New York: A. J. Johnson, 1886), vol. 3.

2. Jerome Kagan, "Introduction to the Tenth-Anniversary Edition," in *The Nature of the Child* (New York: Basic Books, 1994), xxii–xxiv.

Any number in a title of a work should generally be left as is (see also 14.88).

14.148 **Citing a range of page numbers or other specific locators.** For Chicago's preferred style in expressing a range of consecutive pages, paragraphs, or similar numbered divisions, see 9.61. First and last numbers should be used rather than first number plus *ff.* (but see 14.149).

1. *Chicago Manual of Style*, 17th ed. (Chicago: University of Chicago Press, 2017), 14.147–58.

2. Dave Eggers, *The Circle* (New York: Alfred A. Knopf, 2013), 215–16.

See the rest of this chapter for many more examples in context. References to nonconsecutive pages or other locations in the same work are separated by commas.

3. Eggers, *Circle*, 220, 222.

For author-date style, see 15.23.

14.149 **Page references with "ff." and "passim."** Only when referring to a section for which no final number can usefully be given should *ff.* ("and the following pages, paragraphs, etc.") be resorted to. Instead of the singular *f.*, the subsequent number should be used (e.g., "140–41" *not* "140f."). Similarly, *passim* ("here and there") is to be discouraged unless it follows a stated range of pages within which there are more than three or four precise references ("324–32 passim"). When used, *ff.* has no space between it and the preceding number and is followed by a period; *passim*, being a complete word, takes no period. Neither is italicized. (For *passim* in indexes, see 16.12.)

14.150 **Abbreviations for "page," "volume," and so on.** In source citations, the words *page*, *volume*, and the like are usually abbreviated and often simply omitted (see 14.151). The most commonly used abbreviations are *p.* (pl. *pp.*), *vol.*, *pt.*, *chap.*, *bk.*, *sec.*, *n.* (pl. *nn.*), *no.*, *app.*, and *fig.*; for these and others, see chapter 10, especially 10.42. Unless following a period, all are lowercased, and none is italicized (except in the rare case where it forms part of an italicized book title). All the abbreviations mentioned in this paragraph, except for *p.* and *n.*, form their plurals by adding *s*.

A Cry of Absence, chap. 6
A Dance to the Music of Time, 4 vols.

14.151 **When to omit "p." and "pp."** When a number or a range of numbers clearly denotes the pages in a book, *p.* or *pp.* may be omitted; the numbers alone, preceded by a comma, are sufficient. Where the presence of other numerals threatens ambiguity, *p.* or *pp.* may be added for clarity. (And if an author has used *p.* and *pp.* consistently throughout a work, there is no need to delete them.) See also 14.152, 14.156.

Charlotte's Web, 75–76
but
Complete Poems of Michelangelo, p. 89, lines 135–36

14.152 **When to omit "vol."** When a volume number is followed immediately by a page number, neither *vol.* nor *p.* or *pp.* is needed. The numbers alone are used, separated by a colon but no space. A comma usually precedes the volume number, except with periodicals (see 14.171) and certain types of classical references (see 14.242–52). For more on volume numbers, see 14.116–22. For citing a particular volume, with and without the abbreviation *vol.*, see 14.118.

The Complete Tales of Henry James, 10:122

14.153 **Page and chapter numbers.** Page numbers, needed for specific references in notes and parenthetical text citations, are usually unnecessary in bibliographies except when the piece cited is a part within a whole (see 14.106–12; for journal articles, see 14.174). If the chapter or other section number is given, page numbers may be omitted. The total page count of a book is not included in source citations. (Total page counts do, however, appear in headings to book reviews, catalog entries, and the like. For book review headings, see 1.98.)

1. Claire Kehrwald Cook, "Mismanaged Numbers and References," in *Line by Line: How to Edit Your Own Writing* (Boston: Houghton Mifflin, 1985), 81.

2. Nuala O'Faolain, *Are You Somebody? The Accidental Memoir of a Dublin Woman* (New York: Holt, 1996), chap. 17.

14.154 **Signed signatures.** Some books printed before 1800 did not carry page numbers, but each signature (a group of consecutive pages) bore a letter, numeral, or other symbol (its "signature") to help the binder gather them in correct sequence. In citing pages in books of this kind, the signature symbol is given first, then the number of the leaf within the signature, and finally *r* (*recto*, the front of the leaf) or *v* (*verso*, the back of the leaf). Thus, for example, G6v identifies one page, G6r–7v a range of four pages.

14.155 **Numbered leaves, or folios.** Some early books had leaf numbers rather than page numbers. Such leaves were typically numbered only on the front, or recto, side. A page citation therefore consists of the number on the leaf plus *r* (recto) or *v* (verso)—for example, 176r, 231v, or 232r–v. Such leaves are sometimes referred to as folios (e.g., folio 176r). For books or parts of books with no discernible numbers at all, pages can sometimes be counted and the result placed in square brackets. See also 14.154, 14.225.

14.156 **Line numbers.** The abbreviations *l.* (line) and *ll.* (lines) can too easily be confused with the numerals 1 and 11 and so should be avoided. *Line* or *lines* should be used or, where it has been made clear that reference is to lines, simply omitted (see 13.67).

1. Ogden Nash, "Song for Ditherers," lines 1–4.

14.157 **Citing numbered notes.** Notes are cited with the abbreviation *n* or *nn*. The usage recommended here is also used for indexes (see 16.111, 16.112, 16.113). If the note cited is the only footnote on a particular page or is an unnumbered footnote, the page number is followed by *n* alone.

1. Anthony Grafton, *The Footnote: A Curious History* (Cambridge, MA: Harvard University Press, 1997), 72n, 80n.

If there are other notes on the same page as the note cited, a number must be added. In this case the page number is followed by *n* or (if two or more consecutive notes are cited) *nn*, followed by the note number (or numbers or, in rare cases, an asterisk or other symbol). No intervening space or punctuation is required.

2. Dwight Bolinger, *Language: The Loaded Weapon* (London: Longman, 1980), 192n23, 192n30, 199n14, 201nn16–17.

3. Richard Rorty, *Philosophical Papers* (New York: Cambridge University Press, 1991), 1:15n29.

14.158 **Citing illustrations and tables.** The abbreviation *fig.* may be used for *figure*, but *table*, *map*, *plate*, and other illustration forms are spelled out. The page number, if given, precedes the illustration number, with a comma between them.

1. Jean-Paul Chavas, David Hummels, and Brian D. Wright, eds., *The Economics of Food Price Volatility* (Chicago: University of Chicago Press, 2014), 167, table 4.4.

To cite art in collections and other stand-alone works, see 14.235–37.

Electronic Books

14.159 **Books requiring a specific application or device (e-books).** Many books are published in print and as a downloadable file in one or more electronic formats. Because of the potential for differences, authors must indicate which format was consulted. E-book formats include EPUB, PDF, and many others (see 1.118). To account for differences in the ways these formats are adapted for publication, it is often more helpful to specify the name of the application (or, in some cases, the device) used to read or acquire the book than to name the specific file format (which may not be readily apparent). Like a URL for books consulted online (see 14.161), this information should be the *last* part of a full citation that follows the recommendations for citing books as detailed elsewhere in this section. The following examples show how to list different versions of the same book, formatted as a bibliography entry, starting with the print version and followed by versions acquired from a variety of different sources, from Apple to Google, for use with their branded applications or devices.

Begley, Adam. *Updike*. New York: Harper, 2014.
Begley, Adam. *Updike*. New York: Harper, 2014. iBooks.
Begley, Adam. *Updike*. New York: Harper, 2014. Kindle.
Begley, Adam. *Updike*. New York: Harper, 2014. NOOK.
Begley, Adam. *Updike*. New York: Harper, 2014. Google Play Books.

In some cases, a file format will be specified at the time a book is acquired (e.g., EPUB or PDF). In such cases, include the name of the format together with the application or device required to view or acquire the file, if any.

Borel, Brooke. *Infested: How the Bed Bug Infiltrated Our Bedrooms and Took Over the World*. Chicago: University of Chicago Press, 2015. Adobe Digital Editions EPUB.

Many e-books constitute a reprint of an earlier printed edition published before any e-book format was available (see also 1.23). In such cases, a citation should feature the original publication data (typically included in the title page and copyright information for the e-book), followed by information about the e-book. For example, to cite a Kindle version of Philip Roth's *Goodbye, Columbus* based on the 1989 30th anniversary edition of Roth's book (first published in 1959), it is sufficient to include publication details about the 1989 edition only (but see 14.114).

Roth, Philip. *Goodbye, Columbus, and Five Short Stories*. 30th anniversary ed. Boston: Houghton Mifflin, 1989. Kindle.

In a note, information about the e-book follows any page or other locator information. For examples, see 14.160. For self-published books, see 14.137.

14.160 **Page or location numbers in electronic formats.** Many e-books and other electronic formats feature reflowable or scrollable text and therefore do not have fixed pages. Depending on the application or device, "page" or other location numbers displayed along with the text in reflowable e-book formats may vary according to user-defined text size, making any reference to such numbers unhelpful to others wishing to consult the same text. Even where such numbers are invariable, they will be helpful only to those who consult the same e-book format. In such cases, it is often best to cite a chapter number or a section heading or other such milepost in lieu of a page or location number. (If paragraphs are numbered, as in this manual, cite those.)

1. Adam Begley, *Updike* (New York: Harper, 2014), chap. 2, iBooks.
2. Begley, *Updike*, chap. 9.

If a location number needs to be cited or referred to for any reason, include both the specific location and the total number of locations, using the terminology in the application. This will allow readers using other formats (including formats for which location numbers are variable) to calculate an approximate position in the book. (See also 14.137.)

3. Mary Ann Noe, *Ivory Trenches: Adventures of an English Teacher* (self-pub., Amazon Digital Services, 2016), loc. 444 of 3023, Kindle.

Some publishers include data about page numbers in their e-book formats that correspond to a print version—a practice that is especially helpful for orienting readers of e-book formats in terms of the printed book (see 1.123). (Such page numbers are not to be confused with the so-called pages in certain e-book formats representing screens of text.) Note, however, that such page numbers tend to be approximate: a single page in a printed book typically corresponds to two or more screens of text in an e-book format (usually without any indication in the latter of the precise location of the page breaks). If possible, such page numbers should be checked against—and cited to—the printed version.

14.161 **Books consulted online.** When citing the online version of a book, add a URL as part of the citation (but see below). The URL should be the *last* part of a full citation based on the principles outlined throughout this section on citing books. Note the reference to chapter in lieu of page number(s) for the source in notes 1 and 3, which lacks fixed page numbers (see 14.160). In those notes, the URLs are based on the DOIs for the chapters rather than the DOI for the work as a whole (as in the bibliography entry). See also 14.7, 14.8.

1. Mark Evan Bonds, *Absolute Music: The History of an Idea* (New York: Oxford University Press, 2014), chap. 3, https://doi.org/10.1093/acprof:oso/9780199343638.003.0004.
2. Karen Lystra, *Dangerous Intimacy: The Untold Story of Mark Twain's Final Years* (Berkeley: University of California Press, 2004), 59, http://ark.cdlib.org/ark:/13030/kt8779q6kr/.
3. Bonds, *Absolute Music*, chap. 11, https://doi.org/10.1093/acprof:oso/9780199343638.003.0012.
4. Lystra, *Dangerous Intimacy*, 60–61.

Bonds, Mark Evan. *Absolute Music: The History of an Idea*. New York: Oxford University Press, 2014. https://doi.org/10.1093/acprof:oso/9780199343638.001.0001.

Lystra, Karen. *Dangerous Intimacy: The Untold Story of Mark Twain's Final Years*. Berkeley: University of California Press, 2004. http://ark.cdlib.org/ark:/13030/kt8779q6kr/.

Especially for in-copyright books consulted through a commercial library database, a suitable URL may not be available. Even suggested links listed with the source may work only for subscribers or those with access to a particular library. (A URL based on a DOI, on the other hand, will always direct readers to information about the source, if not full access to it.) In such cases, list the name of the commercial database rather than the URL.

Borel, Brooke. *Infested: How the Bed Bug Infiltrated Our Bedrooms and Took Over the World*. Chicago: University of Chicago Press, 2015. EBSCOhost.

14.162 **Freely available electronic editions of older works.** Books and other documents that have fallen out of copyright are often freely available online. When possible, prefer scanned pages to reflowable text for the purposes of source citation. In the James examples below, the Project Gutenberg text is apparently based on the 1909 New York edition of *The Ambassadors*—and is available in a number of reflowable formats, including HTML and EPUB. But the scanned pages from Google Books of an actual copy of the 1909 edition (published in two volumes) are preferable. Not only is the Google Books version more authoritative (in part because the original title and copyright pages are included) but it also facilitates citations to fixed page numbers (see 14.160; see also 14.118).

1. Henry James, *The Ambassadors* (New York, 1909; Project Gutenberg, 2008), bk. 6, chap. 1, http://www.gutenberg.org/ebooks/432.

or, better,

2. Henry James, *The Ambassadors*, 2 vols. (New York: Charles Scribner's Sons, 1909), 1:243, https://books.google.com/books?id=WYlUAAAAYAAJ.

The Melville examples below further demonstrate the importance of finding and citing publication details about the original. The citations are for the same passage of text (see 14.24)—first, as it appears in a scanned copy of the first American edition, and next, as it appears in a similarly prepared copy of the first British edition (published in three volumes). The URL gives interested readers a chance to consult the same resources, but the citation does not depend on it (because the originals have been sufficiently identified).

3. Herman Melville, *Moby-Dick; or, The Whale* (New York: Harper & Brothers, 1851), 627, http://mel.hofstra.edu/moby-dick-the-whale-proofs.html.

4. Herman Melville, *Moby-Dick; or, The Whale*, 3 vols. (London: Richard Bentley, 1851), 3:302, http://mel.hofstra.edu/moby-dick-the-whale-proofs.html.

A bibliography entry would not include page references.

Melville, Herman. *Moby-Dick; or, The Whale*. New York: Harper & Brothers, 1851. http://mel.hofstra.edu/moby-dick-the-whale-proofs.html.

See also 14.10, 14.114.

14.163 **Books on CD-ROM and other fixed media.** In the increasingly rare case of a citation for a book on CD-ROM or other fixed media, indicate the medium after the full facts of publication, including any page or other locator information in a note.

1. *The Chicago Manual of Style*, 15th ed. (Chicago: University of Chicago Press, 2003), 1.4, CD-ROM.

Hicks, Rodney J. *Nuclear Medicine: From the Center of Our Universe*. Victoria, Austral.: ICE T Multimedia, 1996. CD-ROM.

Periodicals

14.164 **"Periodicals" defined.** In this manual, *periodical* refers to scholarly and professional journals, popular magazines, and newspapers. Periodicals are far more likely than books to be consulted online. Except for the addition of a URL (preferably based on a DOI) or, in some cases, the name of a bibliographic database, the citation of a periodical consulted online is the same as the one recommended for printed periodicals. (Some publishers may also require an access date; see 14.12.) See examples of such information, and special considerations, under specific types of periodicals. See also 14.6–18.

14.165 **Information to be included.** Citations of periodicals require some or all of the following data:

1. Full name(s) of author or authors
2. Title and subtitle of article or column

3. Title of periodical
4. Issue information (volume, issue number, date, etc.)
5. Page reference (where appropriate)
6. For periodicals consulted online, a URL or, in some cases, the name of the database used to consult the resource (see 14.6–18)

Indispensable for newspapers and most magazines is the specific date (month, day, and year). For journals, the volume and year plus the month or issue number are usually cited. Additional data make location easier.

14.166 **Journals versus magazines.** A *journal* is a scholarly or professional periodical available mainly by subscription (e.g., *Library Quarterly*, *New England Journal of Medicine*). Journals are normally cited by volume and date (see 14.171). A *magazine* is a weekly or monthly (or sometimes daily) periodical—professionally produced, sometimes specialized, but more accessible to general readers—that is available in individual issues at libraries or bookstores or newsstands or offered online, with or without a subscription (e.g., *Scientific American*, the *New Yorker*). Magazines are normally cited by date alone (see 14.188). If in doubt whether a particular periodical is better treated as a journal or as a magazine, use journal form if the volume number is easily located, magazine form if it is not.

14.167 **Basic structure of a periodical citation.** In notes, commas appear between author; title of article (in quotation marks); title of magazine, newspaper, or journal (in italics); and, for sources consulted online, URL or database name. In bibliographies, periods replace these commas. Note that *in* is *not* used between the article title and the journal title. (*In* is used only with chapters or other parts of books; see 14.106, 14.107.) Punctuation relative to any volume and issue number and for dates and page numbers depends on periodical type. In bibliography entries, the first and last pages of an article are given (for inclusive numbers, see 9.61). In notes and text citations, only specific pages need be cited (unless the article as a whole is referred to). In some electronic formats, page numbers will be unavailable (see 14.22). For examples, see 14.23, 14.168–87 (journals), 14.188–90 (magazines), and 14.191–200 (newspapers).

Journals

14.168 **Journal article—author's name.** Authors' names are normally given as they appear at the heads of their articles. Adjustments can be made, however, as indicated in 14.73. For the treatment of two or more authors, see 14.76. For additional considerations related to names of authors, see 14.72–84.

14.169 **Journal article—title.** Titles of articles are set in roman (except for individual words or phrases that require italics, such as species names or book titles; see 14.95); they are usually capitalized headline-style and put in quotation marks. As with a book, title and subtitle are separated by a colon. For examples, see 14.23 and the paragraphs below. For shortened forms of article titles, see 14.185. For additional considerations related to titles of works, see 14.85–99.

14.170 **Title of journal.** Titles of journals are italicized and capitalized headline-style. They are usually given in full—except for the omission of an initial *The*—in notes and bibliographies (e.g., *Journal of Business*). With journals and magazines with non-English titles, an initial article should be retained (e.g., *Der Spiegel*). See also 8.170. Occasionally an initialism, such as *PMLA*, is the official title and is never spelled out. In some disciplines, especially in science and medicine, journal titles are routinely abbreviated (e.g., *Plant Syst Evol*), unless they consist of only one word (e.g., *Science*, *Mind*); see 15.46. Chicago recommends giving titles in full unless a particular publisher or discipline requires otherwise.

14.171 **Journal volume, issue, and date.** Most journal citations include volume, issue number or month, and year. The volume number, set in roman, follows the title without intervening punctuation; arabic numerals are used even if the journal itself uses roman numerals. The issue number follows the volume number, separated by a comma and preceded by *no.* The issue number should be recorded even if pagination is continuous throughout a volume or when a month or season precedes the year. The year, sometimes preceded by an exact date, a month, or a season, appears in parentheses after the volume and issue data. Seasons, though not capitalized in running text (see 8.88), are capitalized in source citations. Months may be abbreviated or spelled in full (as here); seasons are best spelled out (see also 10.39).

1. Margaret Lock, "Comprehending the Body in the Era of the Epigenome," *Current Anthropology* 56, no. 2 (April 2015): 155, https://doi.org/10.1086/680350.

2. Sharon R. Wesoky, "Bringing the *Jia* Back into *Guojia*: Engendering Chinese Intellectual Politics," *Signs* 40, no. 3 (Spring 2015): 651, https://doi.org/10.1086/679524.

3. David G. Harper, "Bringing Accommodation into Focus: The Several Discoveries of the Ciliary Muscle," *JAMA Ophthalmology* 132, no. 5 (May 2014): 645, https://doi.org/10.1001/jamaophthalmol.2013.5525.

Harper, David G. "Bringing Accommodation into Focus: The Several Discoveries of the Ciliary Muscle." *JAMA Ophthalmology* 132, no. 5 (2014): 645–48. https://doi.org/10.1001/jamaophthalmol.2013.5525.

Lock, Margaret Lock. "Comprehending the Body in the Era of the Epigenome." *Current Anthropology* 56, no. 2 (April 2015): 151–77. https://doi.org/10.1086/680350.

Wesoky, Sharon R. "Bringing the *Jia* Back into *Guojia*: Engendering Chinese Intellectual Politics." *Signs* 40, no. 3 (Spring 2015): 647–66. https://doi.org/10.1086/679524.

Where more than one issue number is included, follow the usage in the journal itself, using either plural *nos.* or singular *no.* (always lowercase) and separating the digits by a slash, a hyphen (use an en dash in the published version; see 6.78), or the like. Where a span of months or seasons is given, follow the usage of the journal (but use an en dash rather than a hyphen in the published version—e.g., September–December).

4. Ismael Galván and Francisco Solano, "Melanin Chemistry and the Ecology of Stress," *Physiological and Biochemical Zoology* 88, no. 3 (May/June 2015): 353, https://doi.org/10.1086/680362.

5. Lina Perkins Wilder, "'My Exion Is Entered': Anatomy, Costume, and Theatrical Knowledge in *2 Henry IV*," *Renaissance Drama* 41, no. 1/2 (Fall 2013): 60, https://doi.org/10.1086/673907.

When a journal uses issue numbers only, without volume numbers, a comma follows the journal title.

6. J. M. Beattie, "The Pattern of Crime in England, 1660–1800," *Past and Present*, no. 62 (February 1974): 52, http://www.jstor.org/stable/650463.

When only a date is available, treat the resource like a magazine (see 14.188).

14.172 **Forthcoming journal articles.** If an article has been accepted for publication by a journal but has not yet appeared, *forthcoming* stands in place of the year and the page numbers. Any article not yet accepted should be treated as an unpublished manuscript (see 14.218). See also 14.173.

1. Margaret M. Author, "Article Title," *Journal Title* 98 (forthcoming).

Author, Margaret M. "Article Title." *Journal Title* 98 (forthcoming).

If an article is published by a journal electronically ahead of the official publication date, use the posted publication date. In such cases, page numbers or volume and issue information, or both, may not yet be available (but see 14.174).

Jubb, Robert. "The Real Value of Equality." *Journal of Politics* 77, no. 3. Published ahead of print, April 14, 2015. https://doi.org/10.1086/681262.

14.173 **Journal article preprints.** Not having been subject to peer review, preprints are treated as unpublished material. See also 1.113.

Huang, Zhiqi. "Revisiting the Cosmological Bias Due to Local Gravitational Redshifts." Preprint, submitted April 24, 2015. http://arxiv.org/abs/1504.06600v1.

14.174 **Journal page references.** In citing a particular passage in a journal article, only the page or pages concerned are given. In references to the article as a whole (as in a bibliography), first and last pages are given.

1. Donald Maletz, "Tocqueville's Tangents to Democracy," *American Political Thought* 4, no. 4 (Fall 2015): 615.

Gold, Ann Grodzins. "Grains of Truth: Shifting Hierarchies of Food and Grace in Three Rajasthani Tales." *History of Religions* 38, no. 2 (1998): 150–71.

To facilitate online publication schedules, some journals have adopted a continuous publishing model in which each article is assigned a unique ID and is considered final the moment it is published online; any subsequent print version is reproduced without any changes. Articles that include a PDF version are all paginated starting at 1 and can be cited in the notes accordingly. In a note, cited page numbers precede the article ID (e0124310 in the example below). In a bibliography, do not include the page range for an article published in this way.

2. Priyamvada Paudyal et al., "Obtaining Self-Samples to Diagnose Curable Sexually Transmitted Infections: A Systematic Review of Patients' Experiences," *PLoS ONE* 10, no. 4 (2015): 2–3, e0124310. https://doi.org/10.1371/journal.pone.0124310.

Paudyal, Priyamvada, Carrie Llewellyn, Jason Lau, Mohammad Mahmud, and Helen Smith. "Obtaining Self-Samples to Diagnose Curable Sexually Transmitted Infections: A Systematic Review of Patients' Experiences," *PLoS ONE* 10, no. 4 (2015): e0124310. https://doi.org/10.1371/journal.pone.0124310.

Most electronic journals provide page numbers. Where this is not the case, another type of locator such as a subheading may become appropriate in a note. None, however, is required. See also 14.22.

3. Jamison, Shelly, "I(nternet) Do(mains): The New Rules of Selection," *Culture Critique* 3, no. 5 (2009), under "Park Avenue Revisited."

14.175 **Journal articles consulted online.** Most people find journal articles through a library or other bibliographic database. To facilitate discovery by other readers (and linking in publications), information about the online resource should be added to the end of a citation. Many of the examples in this section include a URL. A URL based on a DOI (appended to https://doi.org/), if it is available, is preferable to the URL that appears in your browser's address bar when viewing the article (or the abstract). In the absence of a DOI, choose the form of the URL offered along with the article, if any. For articles offered online in more than one format (e.g., PDF or HTML), there is usually no need to specify which format was cited. (If an article was consulted in print, there is no need to include a URL.)

1. Frank P. Whitney, "The Six-Year High School in Cleveland," *School Review* 37, no. 4 (April 1929): 268, http://www.jstor.org/stable/1078814.

2. Miriam Schoenfield, "Moral Vagueness Is Ontic Vagueness," *Ethics* 126, no. 2 (2016): 260–61, https://doi.org/10.1086/683541.

Sometimes a suitable URL will not be available. Even suggested links listed with the source may work only for subscribers or those with access to a particular library. (A URL based on a DOI, on the other hand, will always direct readers to information about the source, if not full access to it.) In such cases, list the name of the commercial database rather than the URL.

3. Zina Giannopoulou, "Prisoners of Plot in José Saramago's *The Cave*," *Philosophy and Literature* 38, no. 2 (2014): 335, Project MUSE.

See also 14.6–18.

14.176 **Access dates for journal articles.** Access dates are not required by Chicago in citations of formally published electronic sources, for the reasons discussed in 14.12. Some publishers and some disciplines, however, may require them. When they are included, they should immediately precede the URL (or database information), separated from the surrounding citation by commas in a note and periods in a bibliography entry.

1. Charlotte F. Narr and Amy C. Krist, "Host Diet Alters Trematode Replication and Elemental Composition," *Freshwater Science* 34, no. 1 (March 2015): 81, accessed August 1, 2017, https://doi.org/10.1086/679411.

3. Narr and Krist, "Host Diet," 88–89.

Narr, Charlotte F., and Amy C. Krist, "Host Diet Alters Trematode Replication and Elemental Composition." *Freshwater Science* 34, no. 1 (March 2015): 81–91. Accessed August 1, 2017. https://doi.org/10.1086/679411.

14.177 **Article page numbers in relation to volume or issue numbers.** When page numbers immediately follow a volume number, separated only by a colon (as in a shortened citation; see 14.185), no space follows the colon. But when parenthetical information intervenes, a space follows the colon. (This rule applies to other types of volumes as well; see, e.g., 14.116.)

Social Networks 14:213–29
Critical Inquiry 1, no. 3 (Winter 1975): 479–96

When, as occasionally happens, the page number follows an issue number, a comma—not a colon—should be used.

Diogenes, no. 25, 84–117.

14.178 **Journal special issues.** A journal issue (occasionally a double issue) devoted to a single theme is known as a special issue. It carries the normal volume and issue number (or numbers if a double issue). Such an issue may have an editor and a title of its own. An article within the issue is cited as in the first example; a special issue as a whole may be cited as in the second example.

1. Miwako Tezuka, "Jikken Kōbō and Takiguchi Shūzō: The New Deal Collectivism of 1950s Japan," in "Collectivism in Twentieth-Century Japanese Art," ed. Reiko Tomii and Midori Yoshimoto, special issue, *Positions: Asia Critique* 21, no. 2 (Spring 2013): 351–81, https://doi.org/10.1215/10679847-2018283.

Tomii, Reiko, and Midori Yoshimoto, eds. "Collectivism in Twentieth-Century Japanese Art." Special issue, *Positions: Asia Critique* 21, no. 2 (Spring 2013).

14.179 **Journal supplements.** A journal supplement, unlike a special issue (see 14.178), is numbered separately from the regular issues of the journal. Like a special issue, however, it may have a title and author or editor of its own.

Agha, Asif. "Tropes of Branding in Forms of Life." In "The Semiotic Corporation," edited by Kyung-Nan Koh and Greg Urban. Supplement, *Signs and Society* 3, no. S1 (2015): S174–94. https://doi.org/10.1086/679004.

14.180 **Articles published in installments.** Articles published in parts over two or more issues may be listed separately or in the same entry, depending on whether the part or the whole is cited.

1. George C. Brown, ed., "A Swedish Traveler in Early Wisconsin: The Observations of Fredrika Bremer," pt. 1, *Wisconsin Magazine of History* 61 (Summer 1978): 312.

2. Brown, "Swedish Traveler," pt. 2, *Wisconsin Magazine of History* 62 (Autumn 1978): 50.

Brown, George C., ed. "A Swedish Traveler in Early Wisconsin: The Observations of Fredrika Bremer." Pts. 1 and 2. *Wisconsin Magazine of History* 61 (Summer 1978): 300–318; 62 (Autumn 1978): 41–56.

14.181 **Article appearing in two publications.** Chapters in books have sometimes begun their lives as journal articles, or vice versa. Revisions are often made along the way. The version actually consulted should be cited in a note or text citation, but annotation such as the following, if of specific interest to readers, may follow the citation. See also 14.54.

Previously published as "Article Title," *Journal Title* 20, no. 3 (2016): 345–62.

A slightly revised version appears in *Book Title*, ed. E. Editor (Place: Publisher, 2017), 15–30.

14.182 **Place where journal is published.** If a journal might be confused with another with a similar title, or if it might not be known to the users of a bibliography, add the name of the place or institution where it is published in parentheses after the journal title.

1. Diane-Dinh Kim Luu, "Diethylstilbestrol and Media Coverage of the 'Morning After' Pill," *Lost in Thought: Undergraduate Research Journal* (Indiana University South Bend) 2 (1999): 65–70.

Garrett, Marvin P. "Language and Design in *Pippa Passes*." *Victorian Poetry* (West Virginia University) 13, no. 1 (1975): 47–60.

14.183 **Translated or edited article.** A translated or edited article follows essentially the same style as a translated or edited book (see 14.104).

1. Arthur Q. Author, "Article Title," trans. Tim Z. Translator, *Journal Title* . . .

Author, Arthur Q. "Article Title." Edited by Edward A. Editor. *Journal Title* . . .

14.184 **New series for journal volumes.** New series in journal volumes are identified by *n.s.* (new series), *2nd ser.*, and so forth, as they are for books (see 14.126). Note the comma between the series identifier and the volume number.

1. "Letter of Jonathan Sewall," *Proceedings of the Massachusetts Historical Society*, 2nd ser., 10 (January 1896): 414.

Moraes, G. M. "St. Francis Xavier, Apostolic Nuncio, 1542–52." *Journal of the Bombay Branch of the Royal Asiatic Society*, n.s., 26 (1950): 279–313.

14.185 **Short titles for articles.** In subsequent references to journal articles, the author's last name and the main title of the article (often shortened) are most commonly used. In the absence of a full bibliography, however, the journal title, volume number, and page number(s) may prove more helpful guides to the source.

1. Daniel Rosenblum, "Unintended Consequences of Women's Inheritance Rights on Female Mortality in India," *Economic Development and Cultural Change* 63, no. 2 (January 2015): 223, https://doi.org/10.1086/679059.

2. Rosenblum, "Female Mortality in India," 225.

or

3. Rosenblum, *Economic Development and Cultural Change* 63:225.

The page numbering for *Economic Development and Cultural Change* is continuous throughout a single volume. Where that is not the case, the short form should include the issue number in addition to the volume number (i.e., "63 (2): 225").

14.186 **Abstracts.** An abstract is treated like a journal article, but the word *abstract* must be added.

Matute, Daniel R. "Noisy Neighbors Can Hamper the Evolution of Reproductive Isolation by Reinforcing Selection." Abstract. *American Naturalist* 185, no. 2 (February 2015): 253–69. https://doi.org/10.1086/679504.

14.187 **Electronic supplements or enhancements to journal articles.** Components of journal articles with a printed counterpart that are offered only online—including supplementary data or supporting information, sometimes also referred to as enhancements—can usually be cited according to how they are referred to in the journal. File formats for multimedia content should be indicated if relevant.

1. "Ghost Dancing Music," Naraya no. 2, MP3 audio, cited in Richard W. Stoffle et al., "Ghost Dancing the Grand Canyon," *Current Anthropology* 41, no. 1 (2000), https://doi.org/10.1086/300101.

2. Gemma L. Cole and John A. Endler, "Variable Environmental Effects on a Multicomponent Sexually Selected Trait," *American Naturalist* 185, no. 4 (April 2015): table A.3 (online only), https://doi.org/10.1086/680022.

3. M. Suárez-Rodríguez and C. Macías Garcia, "There Is No Such a Thing as a Free Cigarette: Lining Nests with Discarded Butts Brings Short-Term Benefits, but Causes Toxic Damage," *Journal of Evolutionary Biology* 27, no. 12 (December 2014): 2719–26, https://doi.org/10.1111/jeb.12531, data deposited at Dryad Digital Repository, https://doi.org/10.5061/dryad.4t5rt.

Song, Aiping, Linxiao Wang, Sumei Chen, Jiafu Jiang, Zhiyong Guan, Peiling Li, and Fadi Chen. Target gene sequences (file name: "Dataset S1.seq"). In "Identification of Nitrogen Starvation-Responsive MicroRNAs in *Chrysanthemum nankingense*." *Plant Physiology and Biochemistry* 91 (June 2015): 41–48. https://doi.org/10.1016/j.plaphy.2015.04.003.

See also 14.159, 14.257, 14.261–68.

Magazines

14.188 **Basic citation format for magazine articles.** Many of the guidelines for citing journals apply to magazines also (and see 14.166). Titles of magazine articles are treated like titles of journal articles: they are capitalized headline-style, set in roman, and placed in quotation marks (see 14.169); as with the titles of journals, an initial *The* in the title of the magazine is usually dropped, and the title is set in italics (see 14.170). Weekly or monthly (or bimonthly) magazines, even if numbered by volume and issue, are usually cited by date only. The date, being an essential element in the citation, is not enclosed in parentheses. While a specific page number may be cited in a note, the inclusive page numbers of an article may be omitted, since they are often widely separated by extraneous material. When page numbers are included, a comma rather than a colon separates them from the date of issue.

1. Beth Saulnier, "From Vine to Wine," *Cornell Alumni Magazine*, September/October 2008, 48.

2. Jill Lepore, "The Man Who Broke the Music Business," *New Yorker*, April 27, 2015, 59.

Walker, Mandy. "Secrets to Stress-Free Flying." *Consumer Reports*, October 2016.

See also 14.190 and the guidelines for newspapers (14.191–99).

14.189 **Magazine articles consulted online.** For magazine articles consulted online, include a URL at the end of a citation or, if no suitable URL is available, the name of the database (see also 14.175). Specific page numbers usually will not be available but may be cited if they are (see also 14.22). See also 14.6–18.

1. Karl Vick, "Cuba on the Cusp," *Time*, March 26, 2015, http://time.com/3759629/cuba-us-policy/.

2. Henry William Hanemann, "French as She Is Now Spoken," *Life*, August 26, 1926, 5, ProQuest.

Magazine articles offered for download using a specific app should cite the name of the application or device used to acquire or read the article.

3. Adam Gopnik, "Trollope Trending," *New Yorker* (iPhone app), May 4, 2015.

14.190 **Magazine departments.** Titles of regular departments in a magazine are capitalized headline-style but not put in quotation marks.

1. Patricia Marx, "Big Skyline," Talk of the Town, *New Yorker*, April 27, 2015, http://www.newyorker.com/magazine/2015/04/27/big-skyline.

2. Debra Klein, Focus on Travel, *Newsweek*, April 17, 2000.

Wallraff, Barbara. Word Fugitives. *Atlantic Monthly*, July/August 2008.

A department without a named author is best cited by the title of the magazine.

Gourmet. Kitchen Notebook. May 2000.

Newspapers

14.191 **Basic citation format for newspaper articles.** The name of the author (if known) and the headline or column heading in a daily newspaper are cited much like the corresponding elements in magazines (see 14.188–90). The month (often abbreviated), day, and year are the indispensable elements. Because a newspaper's issue of any given day may include several editions, and items may be moved or eliminated in various editions, page numbers may usually be omitted (for an example of a page number in a citation, see 14.197). In a note or bibliographic entry, it may be useful to add "final edition," "Midwest edition," or some such identifier. If the paper is published in several sections, the section number (e.g., sec. 1) or title (e.g., Nation) may be given. To cite an article consulted online, include the URL or, if no suitable URL is available, the name of the database (see also 14.175).

1. Editorial, *Philadelphia Inquirer*, July 30, 1990.

2. Mike Royko, "Next Time, Dan, Take Aim at Arnold," *Chicago Tribune*, September 23, 1992.

3. Christopher Lehmann-Haupt, "Robert Giroux, Editor, Publisher and Nurturer of Literary Giants, Is Dead at 94," *New York Times*, September 6, 2008, New York edition.

4. "Pushcarts Evolve to Trendy Kiosks," *Lake Forester* (Lake Forest, IL), March 23, 2000.

5. David G. Savage, "Stanford Student Goes to Supreme Court to Fight for Her Moms," *Los Angeles Times*, April 27, 2015, Nation, http://www.latimes.com/nation/la-na-gay-marriage-children-20150424-story.html.

6. John Myers, "Invasive Faucet Snails Confirmed in Twin Ports Harbor," *Duluth (MN) News-Tribune*, September 26, 2014, EBSCOhost.

Because news sites may update certain stories as they unfold, it may be appropriate to include a time stamp for an article that includes one. List the time as posted with the article; if the time zone is not included, it may need to be determined from context (e.g., EST in the example below). A copy of the article should be retained as cited (see 14.15). See also 10.41.

7. Jason Samenow, "Blizzard Warning: High Winds, About Two Feet of Snow Forecast for D.C. Area," *Washington Post*, January 21, 2016, 3:55 p.m. EST, https://www.washingtonpost.com/news/capital-weather-gang/wp/2016/01/21/blizzard-warning-high-winds-around-two-feet-of-snow-forecast-for-d-c-area/.

For blogs, which are cited similarly to online newspapers, see 14.205–10.

14.192 **Newspaper headlines.** Since headlines are often grammatical sentences, sentence-style capitalization is preferred in the headlines of many newspapers. In source citations, however, Chicago recommends headline style for citing headlines in notes and bibliographies for the sake of consistency with other titles. See also 8.158, 8.159.

"Justices Limit Visiting Rights of Grandparents in Divided Case"

Headlines presented entirely in full capitals in the original are usually converted to upper- and lowercase in a citation (but see 7.52).

14.193 **Titles of newspapers.** An initial *The* is omitted from the title of a newspaper (see 8.170). A city name, if not part of the title of a local newspaper, should be added. The name of the state or, in the case of Canada, province may be added in parentheses if needed (usually in abbreviated form; see 10.27, 10.28). In some cases, the city or state can be added and italicized as part of the official title; if in doubt, add the information, in parentheses and roman type, *after* the italicized title of the newspaper.

Chicago Tribune
Guardian (Manchester)
Hackensack (NJ) Record
Oregonian (Portland, OR)
Ottawa (IL) Daily Times
Saint Paul (Alberta or *AB) Journal*
Times (London)

For such well-known national papers as the *Wall Street Journal* or the *Christian Science Monitor*, no city name is added. In some cases, however, a newspaper will need to be identified by nation.

Times (UK)
Guardian (UK edition)
Guardian (US edition)
but
International New York Times

14.194 **Non-English titles of newspapers.** Names of cities not part of the titles of newspapers published in languages other than English may be added in roman and parentheses after the title (see also 14.131). An initial *The*, omitted for English-language papers, is retained in titles of non-English-language papers if the article is part of the title (see 14.98). Titles of newspapers are treated in many languages more like the names of institutions than like the titles of books and other works; in general, the capitalization of the source (in the masthead or elsewhere) can be used. If in doubt, however, prefer sentence style (see 11.6). (Titles in all capitals should be rendered in sentence style.)

Al-Akhbar (Beirut)
Al-Akhbar (Cairo)
El País (Madrid)
Frankfurter Zeitung
Il Messaggero (Rome)
La Crónica de Hoy (Mexico City)
Mladá fronta dnes (Prague)
Wen Hui Bao (Shanghai)

14.195 **Regular columns or features.** Regular columns or features may carry headlines as well as column titles. Like the names of sections (see 14.191), these should appear in roman, capitalized but without quotation marks, when they are included in a citation.

1. Marc Jaffe, "Finding Love in Seesawing Libidos," Modern Love, *New York Times*, March 6, 2015, http://www.nytimes.com/2015/03/08/style/finding-equilibrium-in-seesawing-libidos.html.

Editorials and the like may be described generically.

2. "Junk Science at the F.B.I.," editorial, *New York Times*, April 27, 2015, http://www.nytimes.com/2015/04/27/opinion/junk-science-at-the-fbi.html.

14.196 **Letters to the editor and readers' comments.** Published letters to the editor, like editorials (see 14.195), are treated generically, usually without headlines.

1. John Q. Public, letter to the editor, *Los Angeles Times*, September 7, 2008.

Readers' comments are treated like the comments for a blog post (see 14.208; see also 14.209). In a note, list names as they are recorded with the comment; any other identifying information can usually be included in parentheses. A direct link to the comment may be included if available; otherwise, link to the article. Replies can be cited in reference to the cited comment, using a short form for the latter (with the help of a cross-reference to the relevant note, if necessary; see 14.31).

2. Chris (California), April 29, 2015, comment on Sheryl Gay Stolberg and Richard Pérez-Peña, "Baltimore Police Cite Presence of Minors in Defending Response to Unrest," *New York Times*, April 28, 2015, http://www.nytimes.com/2015/04/29/us/baltimore-riots.html#permid=14810877.

3. Lizzy (St. Louis, MO), reply to Chris, April 29, 2015.

14.197 **Weekend supplements, magazines, and the like.** Articles from Sunday supplements or other special sections are treated in the same way as magazine articles—that is, cited by date. They are usually dealt with in notes or parenthetical references rather than in bibliographies. Citations of print editions may include a specific page reference (see 14.188).

1. Rachel Kaadzi Ghansah, "What Toni Morrison Saw," *New York Times Magazine*, April 12, 2015, 48.

14.198 **Citing a newspaper article in text rather than in a bibliography.** Newspapers are more commonly cited in notes or parenthetical references than in bibliographies. A list of works cited need not list newspaper items if these have been documented in the text. No corresponding entry in a bibliography would be needed for the following citation (nor would it be necessary in such a case to include information about edition or, for an article consulted online, a URL):

The *New York Times*, in advance of the 2015 NFL season, published a report that the Green Bay Packers would host the Chicago Bears on Thanksgiving Evening, "a renewal of the N.F.L.'s longest-running rivalry," during which the Packers were planning to retire Brett Favre's jersey ("Patriots-Steelers to Open N.F.L. Season," Associated Press, April 22, 2015). Favre, a three-time NFL MVP, is mentioned without further attribution.

If a bibliography entry were needed, it would appear as follows (see also 14.200):

Associated Press. "Patriots-Steelers to Open N.F.L. Season." *New York Times*, April 22, 2015. http://www.nytimes.com/2015/04/22/sports/football/patriots-steelers-to-open-nfl-season.html.

14.199 **Unsigned newspaper articles.** Unsigned newspaper articles or features are best dealt with in text or notes. But if a bibliography entry should be needed, the title of the newspaper stands in place of the author.

1. "In Texas, Ad Heats Up Race for Governor," *New York Times*, July 30, 2002.

New York Times. "In Texas, Ad Heats Up Race for Governor." July 30, 2002.

14.200 **News services and news releases.** Names of news services, unlike titles of newspapers, are capitalized but not italicized.

the Associated Press (AP)
United Press International (UPI)

1. Associated Press, "Texas A&M Galveston Professor Fails Entire Class, Quits Course," *Dallas Morning News*, April 28, 2015, http://www.dallasnews.com/news/education/headlines/20150428-texas-am-galveston-professor-fails-entire-class-quits-course.ece.

A news release (also called a press release) is treated similarly.

2. Federal Emergency Management Agency, "FEMA Awards $2,781,435 Grant to DuPage County," news release no. RV-NR-2015-006, March 19, 2015, https://www.fema.gov/news-release/2015/03/19/fema-awards-2781435-grant-dupage-county.

Reviews

14.201 **Basic citation format for reviews.** In citations of reviews of publications, performances, and the like, the elements are given in the following order:

1. Name of reviewer if the review is signed
2. Title of the review, if any (a headline should be included only if needed for locating the review)
3. The words *review of*, followed by the name of the work reviewed and its author (or composer, or director, or whomever) or sponsor (network, studio, label, etc.)
4. Location and date (in the case of a performance)
5. The listing of the periodical in which the review appeared

If a review is included in a bibliography, it is alphabetized by the name of the reviewer or, if unattributed, by the title of the periodical (see 14.204).

14.202 **Book reviews.** Cite book reviews by author of the review and include book title and author(s) or editor(s). Follow applicable guidelines for citing periodicals.

1. Ben Ratliff, review of *The Mystery of Samba: Popular Music and National Identity in Brazil*, by Hermano Vianna, ed. and trans. John Charles Chasteen, *Lingua Franca* 9 (April 1999): B13–B14.

2. David Kamp, "Deconstructing Dinner," review of *The Omnivore's Dilemma: A Natural History of Four Meals*, by Michael Pollan, *New York Times*, April 23, 2006, Sunday Book Review, http://www.nytimes.com/2006/04/23/books/review/23kamp.html.

Brehm, William C. Review of *Strike for America: Chicago Teachers against Austerity*, by Micah Uetricht. *Comparative Education Review* 59, no. 1 (February 2015): 177–79. https://doi.org/10.1086/679296.

14.203 **Reviews of plays, movies, television programs, concerts, and the like.** Reviews of plays, concerts, movies, and the like may include the name of a director in addition to any author, producer, sponsor, or performer, as applicable.

1. Ben Brantley, review of *Our Lady of Sligo*, by Sebastian Barry, directed by Max Stafford-Clark, Irish Repertory Theater, New York, *New York Times*, April 21, 2000, Weekend section.

2. Emily Nussbaum, "Button-Pusher," review of *Black Mirror*, Channel 4 (UK), created by Charlie Brooker, *New Yorker*, January 5, 2015, http://www.newyorker.com/magazine/2015/01/05/button-pusher.

3. Manohla Dargis, "She's the Droid of His Dreams," review of *Ex Machina*, directed by Alex Garland, *New York Times*, April 10, 2015, New York edition.

4. Nussbaum, review of *Black Mirror*.

Kozinn, Allan. Review of concert performance by Timothy Fain (violin) and Steven Beck (piano), 92nd Street Y, New York. *New York Times*, April 21, 2000, Weekend section.

14.204 **Unsigned reviews.** Unsigned reviews are treated similarly to unsigned articles (see 14.199). If such a review must appear in the bibliography, it is listed under the title of the periodical.

1. Unsigned review of *Geschichten der romanischen und germanischen Völker*, by Leopold von Ranke, *Ergänzungsblätter zur Allgemeinen Literatur-Zeitung*, February 1828, nos. 23–24.

Ergänzungsblätter zur Allgemeinen Literatur-Zeitung. Unsigned review of *Geschichten der romanischen und germanischen Völker*, by Leopold von Ranke. February 1828, nos. 23–24.

Websites, Blogs, and Social Media

14.205 **Websites, blogs, and social media defined.** For the purposes of this discussion, *website* refers to the collection of pages (*web pages*) made publicly available via the internet at a specific location on the World Wide Web by an individual or an organization. A *blog* (from *weblog*) is a web-based forum that consists of posted entries organized by date or topic (and often also titled or signed, or both) and usually accompanied by readers' comments. *Social media* (or *social networking*) refers to any internet-based forum for public communication shared by means of a dedicated platform or service. A website can host or consist of a blog or social media content, and blogs overlap with social media (not to mention online periodicals), blurring the distinctions between the terms. All three can include multimedia content (see 14.267–68). Social media can also consist of privately shared content, which is normally cited like other forms of personal communication (see 14.214).

14.206 **Titles for websites, blogs, and social media.** Titles of websites are generally set in roman without quotation marks and capitalized headline-style. In a departure from the recommendations in the previous edition, the title of a website that is analogous to a traditionally printed work but does not have (and never had) a printed counterpart can be treated like the titles of other websites, subject to editorial discretion. For example, Wikipedia can be treated as a website rather than as a conventional encyclopedia, with roman rather than italics for the title. (When in doubt, opt for roman.) Titled sections or pages of a website are usually placed in quotation marks. The titles of blogs—like those of journals and other periodicals—can usually be set in italics; titles of blog posts (analogous to articles in a periodical) are placed in quotation marks. (The distinction between a blog and a website is often unclear; when in doubt, treat the title like that of a website.) Many websites do not have titles per se; these can be identified in terms of the entity responsible for the site (and cited accordingly). For additional examples, see 8.191–92.

the website for the University of Chicago; the "Alumni & Friends" page
the website of the *New York Times*; the *New York Times* online
The Chicago Manual of Style Online; "Chicago Style Q&A"
Wikipedia; Wikipedia's "Let It Be" entry; Wikipedia's entry on the Beatles' album *Let It Be*
Google; Google Maps; the "Google Maps Help Center"
Dot Earth (blog); "Can Future Global Warming Matter Today?," by Andrew C. Revkin, posted August 23, 2016

Social media content is usually untitled. If needed for the purposes of citation, the text of a post itself (either in part or as a whole) can stand in as title. For examples, see 14.209.

14.207 **Citing web pages and websites.** To cite original website content other than the types of formally published sources discussed elsewhere in this chapter, include as much of the following as can be determined: the title or description of the specific page (if cited); the title or description of the site as a whole (see 14.206); the owner or sponsor of the site; and a URL. The word *website* (or *web page*) may be added (in parentheses) after the title or description of the site if the nature of the source may otherwise be unclear. Also include a publication date or date of revision or modification (see 14.13); if no such date can be determined, include an access date (see 14.12). For frequently updated resources, a time stamp may be included (as in the Wikipedia example, which records the time as it was listed with the source; see also 9.39). Citations of website content can often be limited to the notes; in works with no notes, they may be included in the bibliography (cited by the owner or sponsor of the site).

1. "Apps for Office Sample Pack," Office Dev Center, Microsoft Corporation, updated October 20, 2015, https://code.msdn.microsoft.com/office/Apps-for-Office-code-d04762b7.

2. "Privacy Policy," Privacy & Terms, Google, last modified March 25, 2016, http://www.google.com/policies/privacy/.

3. "Balkan Romani," Endangered Languages, Alliance for Linguistic Diversity, accessed April 6, 2016, http://www.endangeredlanguages.com/lang/5342.

4. "Wikipedia: Manual of Style," Wikimedia Foundation, last modified April 7, 2016, 23:58, http://en.wikipedia.org/wiki/Wikipedia:Manual_of_Style.

5. City of Ithaca, New York (website), CivicPlus Content Management System, accessed April 6, 2016, http://www.cityofithaca.org/.

Microsoft Corporation. "Apps for Office Sample Pack." Office Dev Center. Updated October 20, 2015. https://code.msdn.microsoft.com/office/Apps-for-Office-code-d04762b7.

If a site ceases to exist before publication, or if the information cited is modified or deleted, this information should be included in the text or note.

As of April 1, 2015, the city was forecasting a completion date of "late summer [2015]" for the renovations (a projection that had been removed from the city's website by July 15, 2015).

6. "Biography," on Pete Townshend's official website, accessed December 15, 2001, http://www.petetownshend.co.uk/petet_bio.html (site discontinued).

Such dates, together with the URL, give interested readers a chance to find the information through the Internet Archive or other means. At the same time, authors should retain a copy of any source that is likely to change or disappear (see 14.15).

14.208 **Citing blog posts and blogs.** Blog posts are cited like online newspaper articles (see 14.191–200). Citations include the author of the post; the title of the post, in quotation marks; the title of the blog, in italics (see 14.206); the date of the post; and a URL. The word *blog* may be added (in parentheses) after the title of the blog (unless the word *blog* is part of the title). Blogs that are part of a larger publication should also include the name of that publication. Citations of blog posts, like those of newspaper articles, can often be relegated to the text or notes (see also 14.198); if a bibliography entry is needed, it should be listed under the author of the post.

1. Deb Amlen, "One Who Gives a Hoot," *Wordplay* (blog), *New York Times*, January 26, 2015, http://wordplay.blogs.nytimes.com/2015/01/26/one-who-gives-a-hoot/.

2. William Germano, "Futurist Shock," *Lingua Franca* (blog), *Chronicle of Higher Education*, February 15, 2017, http://www.chronicle.com/blogs/linguafranca/2017/02/15/futurist-shock/.

Germano, William. "Futurist Shock." *Lingua Franca* (blog). *Chronicle of Higher Education*, February 15, 2017. http://www. chronicle.com/blogs/linguafranca/2017/02/15/futurist-shock/.

If it is necessary to cite an entire blog, list it in a bibliography under the name of the editor (if any) or the title of the blog.

Amlen, Deb, ed. *Wordplay* (blog). *New York Times*. http://wordplay.blogs.nytimes.com/.

Lingua Franca (blog). *The Chronicle of Higher Education*. http://www.chronicle.com/blogs/linguafranca/.

Comments can usually be cited in the text, in reference to the related post. If the comment is cited in a note, list the name of the commenter and the date of the comment, followed by the information for the related post. Use a shortened form to refer to a post that has been fully cited elsewhere (see 14.29–36). A URL for the comment is usually unnecessary but may be listed if available. For obviously fictitious names, there is usually no need to add *pseud.* (if known, the identity can be given in the text or in the citation, following the screen name in square brackets; see 14.80). A name in all lowercase can usually be capitalized (see 8.4).

3. Viv (Jerusalem, Isr.), January 27, 2015, comment on Amlen, "Hoot."

4. Jim, February 16, 2017, comment on Germano, "Futurist Shock," http://www.chronicle.com/blogs/linguafranca/2017/02/15/futurist-shock/#comment-3158909472.

5. Stephanos C, February 21, 2017, reply to Jim, http://www.chronicle.com/blogs/linguafranca/2017/02/15/futurist-shock/#comment-3167173570.

14.209 **Citing social media content.** Cite publicly available content shared via social media according to the general guidelines and examples in this paragraph. Private content, including direct messages, is considered a form of personal communication and should be cited as described in 14.214. For a citation in a note or bibliography entry, include the following elements:

1. The author of the post. List the real name (of the person, group, or institution), if known, followed by a screen name, if any, in parentheses. If only a screen name is known, use the screen name in place of the author's name.
2. In place of a title, the text of the post. Quote as much as the first 160 characters, including spaces (the maximum length of a typical text message), capitalized as in the original. (If the post has been quoted in the text, it need not be repeated in a note.)
3. The type of post. List the name of the social media service and include a description if relevant (*photo*, *video*, etc.).
4. The date, including month, day, and year. Time stamps are usually unnecessary but may be included to differentiate a post or comment from others on the same day.
5. A URL. A URL for a specific item can often be found via the date stamp.

Comments are cited in reference to the related post, in a shortened form if fully cited elsewhere (see 14.29–36). A URL for the comment itself is optional but may be added if available. See also 14.208. Citations of social media content can often be limited to the text, as in the first example; if it is important to provide a link, include a note. A frequently cited account or an extensive thread related to a single subject or post may be included in a bibliography.

Conan O'Brien's tweet was characteristically deadpan: "In honor of Earth Day, I'm recycling my tweets" (@ConanOBrien, April 22, 2015).

1. Junot Díaz, "Always surprises my students when I tell them that the 'real' medieval was more diverse than the fake ones most of us consume," Facebook, February 24, 2016, https://www.facebook.com/junotdiaz.writer/posts/972495572815454.

2. Conan O'Brien (@ConanOBrien), "In honor of Earth Day, I'm recycling my tweets," Twitter, April 22, 2015, 11:10 a.m., https://twitter.com/ConanOBrien/status/590940792967016448.

3. Chicago Manual of Style, "Is the world ready for singular they? We thought so back in 1993," Facebook, April 17, 2015, https://www.facebook.com/ChicagoManual/posts/10152906193679151.

4. Pete Souza (@petesouza), "President Obama bids farewell to President Xi

of China at the conclusion of the Nuclear Security Summit," Instagram photo, April 1, 2016, https://www.instagram.com/p/BDrmfXTtNCt/.

5. Kristaps Licis, "But what is the surprise here?," February 24, 2016, comment on Díaz, "Always surprises," https://www.facebook.com/junotdiaz.writer/posts/972495572815454?comment_id=972558569475821.

6. Michele Truty, "We do need a gender-neutral pronoun," April 17, 2015, comment on Chicago Manual of Style, "singular they," https://www.facebook.com/ChicagoManual/posts/10152906193679151?comment_id=10152906356479151.

7. Souza, "President Obama."

Chicago Manual of Style. "Is the world ready for singular they? We thought so back in 1993." Facebook, April 17, 2015. https://www.facebook.com/ChicagoManual/posts/10152906193679151.

Because social media content is subject to editing and deletion, authors are advised to retain a copy of anything they cite (see 14.15). For additional considerations, see 14.6–18.

14.210 **Electronic mailing lists and forums.** Content posted to electronic mailing lists or forums can be cited much like other types of social media (see 14.209). Include the name of the correspondent, the title of the subject or thread (in quotation marks and capitalized as in the original), the title of the list or forum (followed by *list* or *forum* or the like, if not part of the title), the title of any host site (see also 14.206), the date of the message or post, and a URL. (Posts on private forums or lists can be cited like personal communications; see 14.214.)

1. John Powell, "Pattern matching," Grapevine digest mailing list archives, Electric Editors, April 23, 1998, http://www.electriceditors.net/grapevine/archives.php.

2. Caroline Braun, reply to "How did the 'cool kids' from high school turn out?," Quora, August 9, 2016, https://www.quora.com/How-did-the-cool-kids-from-high-school-turn-out/.

Interviews and Personal Communications

14.211 **Unpublished interviews.** Unpublished interviews are best cited in text or in notes, though they occasionally appear in bibliographies. Citations should include the names of both the person interviewed and the interviewer; brief identifying information, if appropriate; the place or date of the interview (or both, if known); and, if a transcript or recording is available, where it may be found. Permission to quote may be needed; see chapter 4.

1. Andrew Macmillan (principal adviser, Investment Center Division, FAO), in discussion with the author, September 1998.

2. Benjamin Spock, interview by Milton J. E. Senn, November 20, 1974, interview 67A, transcript, Senn Oral History Collection, National Library of Medicine, Bethesda, MD.

3. Macmillan, discussion; Spock, interview.

14.212 **Unattributed interviews.** An interview with a person who prefers to remain anonymous or whose name the author does not wish to reveal may be cited in whatever form is appropriate in context. The absence of a name should be explained (e.g., "All interviews were conducted in confidentiality, and the names of interviewees are withheld by mutual agreement").

1. Interview with health-care worker, July 31, 2017.

14.213 **Published or broadcast interviews.** An interview that has been published or broadcast or made available online can usually be treated like an article or other item in a periodical. Interviews consulted online should include a URL or similar identifier (see 14.6–18). See also 14.264, 14.267.

1. Lydia Davis, "The Art of Fiction No. 227," interview by Andrea Aguilar and Johanne Fronth-Nygren, *Paris Review*, no. 212 (Spring 2015): 172, EBSCOhost.

2. McGeorge Bundy, interview by Robert MacNeil, *MacNeil/Lehrer NewsHour*, PBS, February 7, 1990.

3. Russell Crowe, interview by Charlie Rose, *Charlie Rose*, April 23, 2015, http://www.charlierose.com/watch/60551640.

Bellour, Raymond. "Alternation, Segmentation, Hypnosis: Interview with Raymond Bellour." By Janet Bergstrom. *Camera Obscura*, nos. 3–4 (Summer 1979): 89–94.

14.214 **Personal communications.** References to conversations (whether face-to-face or by telephone) or to letters, email or text messages, or direct or private messages shared through social media and received by the author are usually run in to the text or given in a note. They are rarely listed in a bibliography. Most such information can be referred to simply as a conversation, message, or the like; the medium may be mentioned if relevant.

In a conversation with the author on January 6, 2009, lobbyist John Q. Advocate admitted that . . .

Though inconclusive, a fifteen-second video shared with the author via Instagram by the subject's family did suggest significant dementia.

1. Jane E. Correspondent, email message to author, April 23, 2017.
2. Facebook direct message to author, April 30, 2017.

An email address or the like belonging to an individual should be omitted. Should it be needed in a specific context, it must be cited only with the permission of its owner. See also 13.3.

Papers, Contracts, and Reports

14.215 **Theses and dissertations.** Titles of theses and dissertations appear in quotation marks—not in italics; otherwise, they are cited like books. The kind of thesis, the academic institution, and the date follow the title. Like the publication data of a book, these are enclosed in parentheses in a note but not in a bibliography. If the document was consulted online, include a URL or, for documents retrieved from a commercial database, the name of the database and, in parentheses, any identification number supplied or recommended by the database. For dissertations issued on microfilm, see 14.115. To cite an abstract (as in the notes), simply add the word "abstract" after the title (see also 14.186).

1. Ilya Vedrashko, "Advertising in Computer Games" (master's thesis, MIT, 2006), 59, http://hdl.handle.net/1721.1/39144.
2. Melanie Subacus, "*Duae Patriae*: Cicero and Political Cosmopolitanism in Rome," abstract (PhD diss., New York University, 2015), v, http://pqdtopen.proquest.com/pubnum/3685917.html.
3. Vedrashko, "Advertising in Computer Games," 61–62.

Choi, Mihwa. "Contesting *Imaginaires* in Death Rituals during the Northern Song Dynasty." PhD diss., University of Chicago, 2008. ProQuest (AAT 3300426).

14.216 **Unpublished manuscripts.** Titles of unpublished manuscripts, like the titles of other unpublished works, appear in quotation marks. (For manuscripts under contract but not yet published, see 14.146.) Include the words *unpublished manuscript* and the date of the version consulted, if known; for electronic files, a last-saved or last-modified date may be appropriate. End the citation with an indication of format.

1. Lane Redburn, "Touch-Sensitive Interiors: A Behavioral Analysis" (unpublished manuscript, May 5, 2017), LaTeX and GIF files.

Balderdash, Pat. "Presbyopia and Screen Size: A Relational Analysis." Unpublished manuscript, last modified May 5, 2017. Microsoft Word file.

14.217 **Lectures and papers or posters presented at meetings.** The sponsorship, location, and date of the meeting at which a speech was given or a paper, slides, or poster presented follow the title. This information is put in parentheses in a note but not in a bibliography. If the information is available online, include a URL.

1. David G. Harper, "The Several Discoveries of the Ciliary Muscle" (PowerPoint presentation, 25th Anniversary of the Cogan Ophthalmic History Society, Bethesda, MD, March 31, 2012).

2. Viviana Hong, "Censorship in Children's Literature during Argentina's Dirty War (1976–1983)" (lecture, University of Chicago, Chicago, IL, April 30, 2015).

Rohde, Hannah, Roger Levy, and Andrew Kehler. "Implicit Causality Biases Influence Relative Clause Attachment." Poster presented at the 21st CUNY Conference on Human Sentence Processing, Chapel Hill, NC, March 2008. http://idiom.ucsd.edu/~rlevy/papers/cuny2008/rohde-levy-kehler-2008-cuny.pdf.

Teplin, Linda A., Gary M. McClelland, Karen M. Abram, and Jason J. Washburn. "Early Violent Death in Delinquent Youth: A Prospective Longitudinal Study." Paper presented at the Annual Meeting of the American Psychology-Law Society, La Jolla, CA, March 2005.

A paper included in the published proceedings of a meeting may be treated like a chapter in a book (see 14.120). If published in a journal, it is treated as an article (see 14.168–87).

14.218 **Working papers and the like.** Working papers and similar documents, sometimes produced in advance of publication on a particular topic, can be treated in much the same way as a dissertation or thesis (14.215) or a lecture, paper, or other presentation (14.217).

1. Deborah D. Lucki and Richard W. Pollay, "Content Analyses of Advertising: A Review of the Literature" (working paper, History of Advertising Archives, Faculty of Commerce, University of British Columbia, Vancouver, 1980).

Bronfenbrenner, Kate, and Dorian Warren. "The Empirical Case for Streamlining the NLRB Certification Process: The Role of Date of Unfair Labor Practice Occurrence." ISERP Working Papers Series 2011.01, Columbia University, New York, NY, June 2011. http://hdl.handle.net/10022/AC:P:10603.

In the second example above the term *working paper* is part of a formal series title, therefore capitalized (see 14.123–26). Unless the item is available online, it is sometimes useful to add *photocopy* or otherwise indicate the form in which an unpublished document may be consulted.

Alarcón, Salvador Florencio de. "Compendio de las noticias correspondientes a el real y minas San Francisco de Aziz de Río Chico . . . de 20 de octobre [1771]." Photocopy, Department of Geography, University of California, Berkeley.

For journal article preprints, see 14.173.

14.219 **Private contracts, wills, and such.** Private documents are occasionally cited in notes but rarely in bibliographies. More appropriately they are referred to in text (e.g., "Marcy T. Feldspar, in her will dated January 20, 1976, directed . . .") or in notes. Capitalization is usually a matter of editorial discretion.

1. Samuel Henshaw, will dated June 5, 1806, proved July 5, 1809, no. 46, box 70, Hampshire County Registry of Probate, Northampton, MA.

2. Agreement to teach in the Editing Program of the Graham School, University of Chicago, signed by Héloïse Abelard, June 1, 2017.

14.220 **Pamphlets, reports, and the like.** Pamphlets, corporate reports, brochures, and other freestanding publications are treated essentially as books. Data on author and publisher may not fit the normal pattern, but sufficient information should be given to identify the document.

1. Hazel V. Clark, *Mesopotamia: Between Two Rivers* (Mesopotamia, OH: Trumbull County Historical Society, 1957).

2. *Lifestyles in Retirement*, Library Series (New York: TIAA-CREF, 1996).

3. McDonald's Corporation, *2014 Annual Report*, March 2015, http://www.aboutmcdonalds.com/mcd/investors/annual_reports.html.

Material obtained through loose-leaf services can be handled similarly.

4. *Standard Federal Tax Reporter*, 1996 ed., vol. 4 (Chicago: Commerce Clearing House, 1996), ¶ 2,620.

Manuscript Collections

14.221 **Overview and additional resources.** The 1987 edition of the *Guide to the National Archives of the United States* offers the following advice: "The most convenient citation for archives is one similar to that used for personal papers and other historical manuscripts. Full identification of most unpublished material usually requires giving the title and date of the item, series title (if applicable), name of the collection, and name of the depository. Except for placing the cited item first [in a note], there is no general agreement on the sequence of the remaining elements in the citation. . . . Whatever sequence is adopted, however, should be used consistently throughout the same work" (761). This advice has been extended by the leaflet *Citing Records in the National Archives of the United States* (available from the National Archives and Records Administration; see bibliog. 4.5), which includes advice on citing textual and nontextual records, including electronic records and digitized resources. Citations of collections consulted online (to date, a relative rarity for this type of material) will usually take the same form as citations of physical collections, aside from the addition of a URL or database name (see 14.6–18).

14.222 **Note forms versus bibliography entries.** In a note, the main element of a manuscript citation is usually a specific item (a letter, a memorandum, or whatever) and is thus cited first. In a bibliography, the main element is usually either the collection in which the specific item may be found, the author(s) of the items in the collection, or the depository for the collection. (Entries beginning with the name of the collection or the last name of the author—which sometimes overlap—tend to be easiest to locate in a bibliography.)

1. James Oglethorpe to the Trustees, 13 January 1733, Phillipps Collection of Egmont Manuscripts, 14200:13, University of Georgia Library.
2. Alvin Johnson, memorandum, 1937, file 36, Horace Kallen Papers, YIVO Institute for Jewish Research, New York.
3. Revere's Waste and Memoranda Book (vol. 1, 1761–83; vol. 2, 1783–97), Revere Family Papers, Massachusetts Historical Society, Boston.

Egmont Manuscripts. Phillipps Collection. University of Georgia Library.
Kallen, Horace. Papers. YIVO Institute for Jewish Research, New York.
Revere Family Papers. Massachusetts Historical Society, Boston.

Specific items are not included in a bibliography unless only one item from a collection is cited. For more examples, see 14.229, 14.230.

14.223 **Specific versus generic titles for manuscript collections.** In notes and bibliographies, quotation marks are used only for specific titles (e.g., "Canoeing through Northern Minnesota"), but not for generic names such as *report* or *minutes*. Generic names of this kind are capitalized if part of a formal heading actually appearing on the manuscript, lowercased if merely descriptive. Compare 14.229, example notes 7–10.

14.224 **Dates for manuscript collections.** Names of months may be spelled out or abbreviated, as long as done consistently (see 10.39). If there are many references to specific dates, as in a collection of letters or diaries, the day-month-year form (8 May 1945), used in some of the examples below, will reduce clutter, though the American month-day-year style used throughout this manual may be preferred instead (May 8, 1945). See also 6.38, 9.31.

14.225 **Folios, page numbers, and such for manuscript collections.** Older manuscripts are usually numbered by signatures only or by leaves (sometimes called folios) rather than by page (see 14.154, 14.155). More recent ones usually carry page numbers (and some older manuscripts have been paginated in the modern era); if needed, the abbreviations *p.* and *pp.* should be used to avoid ambiguity. Leaves introduced at the beginning or end of a manuscript when rebound (e.g., by a modern library or publisher) are not usually counted in the numbering. Some manuscript collections have identifying series or file numbers, which may be included in a citation.

14.226 **"Papers" and "manuscripts."** In titles of manuscript collections, the terms *papers* and *manuscripts* are synonymous. Both are acceptable, as are the abbreviations *MS* and (pl.) *MSS*. If it is necessary to distinguish a typescript or computer printout from a handwritten document, the abbreviation *TS* may be used. See also 10.42.

14.227 **Location of depositories.** The location (city and state) of such well-known depositories as major university libraries is rarely necessary (see examples in 14.229).

University of Chicago Library   Oberlin College Library

14.228 **Collections of letters and the like.** A note citation of a letter starts with the name of the letter writer, followed by *to*, followed by the name of the recipient. Given names may be omitted if the identities of sender and recipient are clear from the text. (Identifying material may be added if appropriate; see 14.211.) The word *letter* is usually omitted—that is, understood—but other forms of communication (telegram, memorandum) are specified. If such other forms occur frequently in the same collection, it may be helpful to specify letters also. For capitalization and the use of quotation marks, see 14.223. For date form, see 14.224. See also 14.111, 14.214, 14.231.

14.229 **Examples of note forms for manuscript collections.** See also 14.222, 14.223.

1. George Creel to Colonel House, 25 September 1918, Edward M. House Papers, Yale University Library.

2. James Oglethorpe to the Trustees, 13 January 1733, Phillipps Collection of Egmont Manuscripts, 14200:13, University of Georgia Library (hereafter cited as Egmont MSS).

3. Burton to Merriam, telegram, 26 January 1923, box 26, folder 17, Charles E. Merriam Papers, Special Collections Research Center, University of Chicago Library.

4. Minutes of the Committee for Improving the Condition of the Free Blacks, Pennsylvania Abolition Society, 1790–1803, Papers of the Pennsylvania Society for the Abolition of Slavery, Historical Society of Pennsylvania, Philadelphia (hereafter cited as Minutes, Pennsylvania Society).

5. Hiram Johnson to John Callan O'Laughlin, 13 and 16 July 1916, 28 November 1916, O'Laughlin Papers, Theodore Roosevelt Collection, Harvard College Library.

6. Memorandum by Alvin Johnson, 1937, file 36, Horace Kallen Papers, YIVO Institute for Jewish Research, New York.

7. Undated correspondence between French Strother and Edward Lowry, container 1-G/961 600, Herbert Hoover Presidential Library, West Branch, IA.

8. Memorandum, "Concerning a Court of Arbitration," n.d., Philander C. Knox Papers, Manuscripts Division, Library of Congress.

9. Joseph Purcell, "A Map of the Southern Indian District of North America" [ca. 1772], MS 228, Ayer Collection, Newberry Library, Chicago.

10. Louis Agassiz, report to the Committee of Overseers . . . [28 December 1859], Overseers Reports, Professional Series, vol. 2, Harvard University Archives.

11. Gilbert McMicken to Alexander Morris, 29 November 1881, Glasgow (Scotland), Document 1359, fol. 1r, Alexander Morris Papers, MG-12-84, Provincial Archives of Manitoba, Winnipeg.

12. Daily Expenses, July 1787, images 7–8, George Washington Papers, Series 5: Financial Papers, 1750–96, Library of Congress, Washington, DC, http://memory.loc.gov/ammem/gwhtml/gwseries5.html.

The content of subsequent citations of other items in a cited manuscript collection (short forms) will vary according to the proximity of the earlier notes, the use of abbreviations, and other factors. Absolute consistency may occasionally be sacrificed to readers' convenience.

13. R. S. Baker to House, 1 November 1919, House Papers.
14. Thomas Causton to his wife, 12 March 1733, Egmont MSS, 14200:53.
15. Minutes, 15 April 1795, Pennsylvania Society.

14.230 **Examples of bibliography entries for manuscript collections.** The style of the first six examples below is appropriate if more than one item from a collection is cited in the text or notes. Entries are usually listed under the name of the collection or under the author(s) of the items contained therein. See also 14.222.

Egmont Manuscripts. Phillipps Collection. University of Georgia Library.

Merriam, Charles E. Papers. Special Collections Research Center, University of Chicago Library.

Pennsylvania Society for the Abolition of Slavery. Papers. Historical Society of Pennsylvania, Philadelphia.

Strother, French, and Edward Lowry. Undated correspondence. Herbert Hoover Presidential Library, West Branch, IA.

Washington, George. Papers. Series 5: Financial Papers, 1750–96. Library of Congress, Washington, DC. http://memory.loc.gov/ammem/gwhtml/gwseries5.html.

Women's Organization for National Prohibition Reform. Papers. Alice Belin du Pont files, Pierre S. du Pont Papers. Eleutherian Mills Historical Library, Wilmington, DE.

If only one item from a collection has been mentioned in text or in a note and is considered important enough to include in a bibliography, the entry will begin with the item.

Dinkel, Joseph. Description of Louis Agassiz written at the request of Elizabeth Cary Agassiz, n.d. Louis Agassiz Papers. Houghton Library, Harvard University.

14.231 **Letters and the like in private collections.** Letters, memorandums, and such that have not been archived may be cited like other unpublished material. Information on the depository is replaced by such wording as "in the author's possession" or "private collection," and the location is not mentioned.

Special Types of References

Reference Works

14.232 **Reference works consulted in physical formats.** Well-known reference books, such as major dictionaries and encyclopedias, are normally cited in notes rather than in bibliographies. They are also more likely than many resources to be consulted online (see 14.233). If a physical edition is cited, not only the edition number (if not the first) but also the date the volume or set was issued must be specified. References to an alphabetically arranged work cite the item (not the volume or page number) preceded by *s.v.* (*sub verbo*, "under the word"; pl. *s.vv.*).

1. *Encyclopaedia Britannica*, 15th ed. (1980), s.v. "salvation."
2. *Oxford English Dictionary*, 2nd ed. (CD-ROM, version 4.0, 2009), s.v. "hoot(e)nanny, hootananny."
3. *Dictionary of American Biography* (1937), s.v. "Wadsworth, Jeremiah."

Most other reference works, however, are more appropriately listed with full publication details like any other book resource. (For examples of how to cite individual entries by author, see 14.234.)

4. *The Times Style and Usage Guide*, comp. Tim Austin (London: Times Books, 2003), s.vv. "police ranks," "postal addresses."
5. *MLA Style Manual and Guide to Scholarly Publishing*, 3rd ed. (New York: Modern Language Association of America, 2008), 6.8.2.

Diccionario de historia de Venezuela. 2nd ed. 4 vols. Caracas: Fundación Polar, 1997.

Garner, Bryan A. *Garner's Modern English Usage*. 4th ed. New York: Oxford University Press, 2016.

14.233 **Reference works consulted online.** Online reference works can be cited much like their printed antecedents; they are normally cited in the notes rather than in bibliographies (see 14.232). For continually updated resources, an edition number will usually be unnecessary. Instead, include a posted publication or revision date for the cited entry; if none is available, supply an access date. Time stamps may be included for frequently updated resources (as in the Wikipedia example, which records the time as it was included with the entry; see also 9.39). Include a URL as the last element of citation; if the entry lists a recommended form for the URL, use that version. See also 14.6–18. The facts of publication are often omitted, but signed entries may include the name of the author. Note that names in entries are not always inverted as in printed editions; follow the usage in the source (cf. example notes 1 and 2). For the use of italics versus roman in titles like Wikipedia, see 14.206.

1. *Encyclopaedia Britannica Online*, Academic ed., s.v. "Arturo Toscanini," accessed April 6, 2016, http://academic.eb.com/EBchecked/topic/600338/Arturo-Toscanini.

2. Grove Music Online, s.v. "Toscanini, Arturo," by David Cairns, accessed April 6, 2016, http://www.oxfordmusiconline.com/subscriber/article/grove/music/28197.

3. Wikipedia, s.v. "Stevie Nicks," last modified April 2, 2016, 18:30, http://en.wikipedia.org/wiki/Stevie_Nicks.

4. *Merriam-Webster*, s.v. "app (*n.*)," accessed April 6, 2016, http://www.merriam-webster.com/dictionary/app.

14.234 **Citing individual reference entries by author.** For certain reference works—particularly those with substantial, authored entries—it may be appropriate to cite individual entries by author, much like contributions to a multiauthor book (see 14.107). Such citations may be included in a bibliography.

Isaacson, Melissa. "Bulls." In *Encyclopedia of Chicago*, edited by Janice L. Reiff, Ann Durkin Keating, and James R. Grossman. Chicago Historical Society, 2005. http://www.encyclopedia.chicagohistory.org/pages/184.html.

Masolo, Dismas. "African Sage Philosophy." In *Stanford Encyclopedia of Philosophy*. Stanford University, 1997–. Article published February 14, 2006; last modified February 22, 2016. http://plato.stanford.edu/archives/spr2016/entries/african-sage/.

Middleton, Richard. "Lennon, John Ono (1940–1980)." In *Oxford Dictionary of National Biography*. Oxford University Press, 2004; online ed., 2011. https://doi.org/10.1093/ref:odnb/31351.

Artwork and Illustrations

14.235 **Citing paintings, photographs, and sculpture.** Information about paintings, photographs, sculptures, or other works of art can usually be presented in the text rather than in a note or bibliography. If a note or bibliography entry is needed, list the artist, a title (in italics), and a date of creation or completion, followed by information about the medium and the location of the work. For works consulted online, add a URL.

1. Salvador Dalí, *The Persistence of Memory*, 1931, oil on canvas, 9½ × 13″ (24.1 × 33 cm), Museum of Modern Art, New York, http://www.moma.org/collection/works/79018.

2. Dorothea Lange, *Black Maria, Oakland*, 1957, printed 1965, gelatin silver print, 39.3 × 37 cm, Art Institute, Chicago, http://www.artic.edu/aic/collections/artwork/220174.

McCurry, Steve. *Afghan Girl*. December 1984. Photograph. *National Geographic*, cover, June 1985.

Picasso, Pablo. *Bull's Head*. Spring 1942. Bicycle saddle and handlebars, 33.5 × 43.5 × 19 cm. Musée Picasso Paris.

To cite a work of art included as a numbered illustration in another publication, see 14.158.

14.236 **Citing exhibition catalogs.** An exhibition catalog is often published as a book and is treated as such.

Witkovsky, Matthew S., ed. *Sarah Charlesworth: Stills*. Chicago: Art Institute of Chicago, 2014. Published in conjunction with an exhibition of the same title, organized by and presented at the Art Institute of Chicago, September 18, 2014–January 4, 2015.

or, if space is tight,

Witkovsky, Matthew S., ed. *Sarah Charlesworth: Stills*. Chicago: Art Institute of Chicago, 2014. Exhibition catalog.

A brochure—the kind often available to visitors to an exhibition—may be treated similarly.

14.237 **Citing maps.** Information about maps can usually be presented in the text rather than in a note or bibliography. If a note or bibliography entry is needed, list the cartographer (if known) and the title of the map (in italics) or a description (in roman), followed by the scale and size (if known) and publication details or location of the map (see also 8.199, 14.235). Undated maps consulted online should include an access or revision date (see also 14.12, 14.13).

1. Samuel de Champlain, cartographer, *Carte geographique de la Nouvelle Franse*, 1612, 43 × 76 cm, in *The History of Cartography*, vol. 3, *Cartography in the European Renaissance* (Chicago: University of Chicago Press, 2007), fig. 51.3.

2. *Yu ji tu* [Map of the tracks of Yu], AD 1136, Forest of Stone Steles Museum,

Xi'an, China, stone rubbing, 1933?, 84 × 82 cm, Library of Congress, http://www.loc.gov/item/gm71005080/.

3. Satellite view of Chicago, Google Earth, accessed April 2, 2016, https://www.google.com/maps/@41.7682665,-87.723154,93759m/data=!3m1!1e3.

US Geological Survey. *California: Yosemite Quadrangle*. 1909; repr., 1951. 30-minute series quadrangle, 1:125,000 scale. National Map, Historic Topographic Map Collection. http://nationalmap.gov/.

See also 14.158.

Scriptural References

14.238 **Biblical references—additional resource.** Any writer or editor working extensively with biblical material should consult the latest edition of *The SBL Handbook of Style* (bibliog. 1.1), which offers excellent advice and numerous abbreviations.

14.239 **Bible chapter and verse.** References to the Jewish or Christian scriptures usually appear in text citations or notes rather than in bibliographies. Parenthetical or note references to the Bible should include book (in roman and usually abbreviated), chapter, and verse—never a page number. A colon is used between chapter and verse. Note that the traditional abbreviations use periods but the shorter forms do not. For guidance on when to abbreviate and when not to, see 10.44. For full forms and abbreviations, see 10.45, 10.46, 10.47.

Traditional abbreviations:

1. 1 Thess. 4:11, 5:2–5, 5:14.
2. Heb. 13:8, 13:12.
3. Gen. 25:19–36:43.

Shorter abbreviations:

4. 2 Sm 11:1–17, 11:26–27; 1 Chr 10:13–14.
5. Jo 5:9–12; Mt 26:2–5.

14.240 **Versions of the Bible.** Since books and numbering are not identical in different versions, it is essential to identify which version is being cited. For a work intended for general readers, the version should be spelled out, at least on first occurrence. For specialists, abbreviations may be used throughout. For abbreviations of versions, see 10.48.

1. 2 Kings 11:8 (New Revised Standard Version).
2. 1 Cor. 6:1–10 (NRSV).

14.241 **Other sacred works.** References to the sacred and revered works of other religious traditions may, according to context, be treated in a manner similar to those of biblical or classical works. Citations of transliterated texts should indicate the name of the version or translator. The Koran (or Qur'an) is set in roman, and citations of its sections use arabic numerals and colons (e.g., Koran 19:17–21). Such collective terms as the Vedas or the Upanishads are normally capitalized and set in roman, but particular parts are italicized (e.g., the *Rig-Veda* or the *Brihad-Aranyaka Upanishad*). For authoritative usage, consult *History of Religions*, an international journal for comparative historical studies (bibliog. 5).

Classical Greek and Latin References

14.242 **Where to cite classical references.** Classical primary source references are ordinarily given in text or notes. They are included in a bibliography only when the reference is to information or annotation supplied by a modern author (see 14.246, 14.251).

The eighty days of inactivity reported by Thucydides (8.44.4) for the Peloponnesian fleet at Rhodes, terminating before the end of Thucydides's winter (8.60.2–3), suggests . . .

14.243 **Identifying numbers in classical references.** The numbers identifying the various parts of classical works—books, sections, lines, and so on—remain the same in all editions, whether in the original language or in translation. (In poetry, line content may vary slightly from the original in some translations.) Arabic numerals are used. Where letters also are used, they are usually lowercased but may be capitalized if the source being cited uses capitals. Page numbers are omitted except in references to introductions, notes, and the like supplied by a modern editor or to specific translations. See also 14.245, 14.250.

1. Ovid, *Amores* 1.7.27.
2. Aristotle, *Metaphysics* 3.2.996b5–8; Plato, *Republic* 360e–361b.

14.244 **Abbreviations in classical references.** Abbreviations of authors' names as well as of works, collections, and so forth are used extensively in classical references. The most widely accepted standard for abbreviations is the list included in *The Oxford Classical Dictionary* (bibliog. 5). When abbreviations are used, these rather than *ibid.* should be used in succeeding references to the same work. (Abbreviations are best avoided when only two letters are omitted, and they must not be used when more than one writer could be meant—Hipponax or Hipparchus, Aristotle or Aristophanes.)

1. Thuc. 2.40.2–3.
2. Pindar, *Isthm.* 7.43–45.

14.245 **Punctuation in classical references.** Place a comma between the name of a classical author (abbreviated or not) and the title of a work. No punctuation intervenes, however, between title and identifying number (or between author and number when the author is standing in for the title). Numerical divisions are separated by periods with no space following each period. Commas are used between two or more references to the same source, semicolons between references to different sources, and en dashes between continuing numbers. If such abbreviations as *bk.* or *sec.* are needed for clarity, commas separate the different elements.

1. Aristophanes, *Frogs* 1019–30.
2. Cic., *Verr.* 1.3.21, 2.3.120; Caes., *B Gall.* 6.19; Tac., *Germ.* 10.2–3.
3. Hdt. 7.1.2.
4. Sappho, *Invocation to Aphrodite*, st. 1, lines 1–6.

14.246 **Citing specific editions of classical references.** Details of the edition used, along with translator (if any) and the facts of publication, should be either specified the first time a classical work is cited or given elsewhere in the scholarly apparatus. If several editions are used, the edition (or an abbreviation) should accompany each citation. Although many classicists will recognize a well-known edition merely from the last name of the editor or translator, a full citation, at least in the bibliography, should be furnished as a courtesy.

1. Epictetus, *Dissertationes*, ed. Heinrich Schenkl (Stuttgart: Teubner, 1916).
2. Herodotus, *The History*, trans. David Grene (Chicago: University of Chicago Press, 1987).
3. Solon (Edmonds's numbering) 36.20–27.

14.247 **Titles of classical works and collections.** Titles of works and published collections are italicized whether given in full or abbreviated (see 14.244). Latin and transliterated Greek titles are capitalized sentence-style (see 8.158, 11.6, 11.54).

1. Cato's uses of *pater familias* in *Agr.* (2.1, 2.7, 3.1, 3.2) are exclusively in reference to estate management. For the *diligens pater familias* in Columella, see *Rust.* 1.1.3, 1.2.1, 5.6.37, 9.1.6, 12.21.6.

2. *Scholia graeca in Homeri Odysseam*, ed. Wilhelm Dindorf (Oxford, 1855; repr. 1962).

3. *Patrologiae cursus completus, series graeca* (Paris: Migne, 1857–66).

14.248 **Superscripts in classical references.** In classical references, a superior figure is sometimes used immediately after the title of a work (or its abbreviation), and preceding any other punctuation, to indicate the number of the edition.

1. Stolz-Schmalz, *Lat. Gram.*^{5} (rev. Leumann-Hoffmann; Munich, 1928), 390–91.

2. *Ausgewählte Komödien des T. M. Plautus*^{2}, vol. 2 (1883).

In former practice, the letters accompanying numerals in citations of classical works (see 14.243) sometimes appeared as superscripts (e.g., 3.2.996^{b}5–8).

14.249 **Collections of inscriptions.** Arabic numerals are used in references to volumes in collections of inscriptions. Periods follow the volume and inscription numbers, and further subdivisions are treated as in other classical references.

1. *IG* 2^{2}.3274. [= *Inscriptiones graecae*, vol. 2, 2nd ed., inscription no. 3274]

2. *IG Rom.* 3.739.9–10. [*IG Rom.* = *Inscriptiones graecae ad res romanas pertinentes*]

3. *POxy.* 1485. [= *Oxyrhynchus papyri*, document no. 1485]

Some collections are cited only by the name of the editor. Since the editor's name here stands in place of a title, no comma is needed.

4. Dessau 6964.23–29. [= H. Dessau, ed., *Inscriptiones latinae selectae*]

14.250 **Fragments of classical texts.** Fragments of classical texts (some only recently discovered) are not uniformly numbered. They are published in collections, and the numbering is usually unique to a particular edition. Two numbers separated by a period usually indicate fragment and line. The editor's name, often abbreviated in subsequent references, must therefore follow the number.

1. Empedocles, frag. 115 Diels-Kranz.
2. Anacreon, frag. 2.10 Diehl.
3. Hesiod, frag. 239.1 Merkelbach and West.
4. Anacreon, frag. 5.2 D.
5. Hesiod, frag. 220 M.-W.

In citations of two or more editions of the same set of fragments, either parentheses or an equals sign may be used.

6. Pindar, frag. 133 Bergk (frag. 127 Bowra).
or
7. Pindar, frag. 133 Bergk = 127 Bowra.

14.251 **Modern editions of the classics.** When Greek, Latin, or medieval classics are cited by page number, the edition must be specified, and the normal rules for citing books are followed. See also 14.246.

1. Propertius, *Elegies*, ed. and trans. G. P. Goold, Loeb Classical Library 18 (Cambridge, MA: Harvard University Press, 1990), 45.

Aristotle. *Complete Works of Aristotle: The Revised Oxford Translation.* Edited by J. Barnes. 2 vols. Bollingen Series. Princeton, NJ: Princeton University Press, 1983.

Maimonides. *The Code of Maimonides, Book 5: The Book of Holiness.* Edited by Leon Nemoy. Translated by Louis I. Rabinowitz and Philip Grossman. New Haven, CT: Yale University Press, 1965.

14.252 **Medieval references.** The form for classical references may equally well be applied to medieval works.

1. Augustine, *De civitate Dei* 20.2.
2. Augustine, *The City of God*, trans. John Healey (New York: Dutton, 1931), 20.2.
3. *Beowulf*, lines 2401–7.
4. Abelard, *Epistle 17 to Heloïse* (Migne, *PL* 180.375c–378a).
5. *Sir Gawain and the Green Knight*, trans. Theodore Silverstein (Chicago: University of Chicago Press, 1974), pt. 3, p. 57.

Classic English Poems and Plays

14.253 **Citing editions of classic English poems and plays.** Classic English poems and plays can often be cited by book, canto, and stanza; stanza and line; act, scene, and line; or similar divisions. Publication facts can then be omitted. For frequently cited works—especially those of Shakespeare, where variations can occur in wording, line numbering, and even scene division—the edition is normally specified in the first note reference or in the bibliography. The edition must be mentioned if page numbers are cited (see 14.251).

1. Chaucer, "Wife of Bath's Prologue," *Canterbury Tales*, frag. 3, lines 105–14.
2. Spenser, *The Faerie Queene*, bk. 2, canto 8, st. 14.
3. Milton, *Paradise Lost*, bk. 1, lines 83–86.
4. *King Lear*, ed. David Bevington et al. (New York: Bantam Books, 2005), 3.2.49–60. References are to act, scene, and line.

Dryden, John. *Dramatic Essays*. Everyman's Library. New York: Dutton, 1912.

Shakespeare, William. *Hamlet*. Edited by Ann Thompson and Neil Taylor. Arden Shakespeare, 3rd ser. London: Thomson Learning, 2006.

14.254 **Short forms for citing classic English poems and plays.** A citation may be shortened by omitting *act*, *line*, and the like, as long as the system used has been explained. Arabic numerals are used, separated by periods. In immediately succeeding references, it is usually safer to repeat all the numbers. The author's name may be omitted if clear from the text. For citing sources in text, see 13.67.

1. Pope, *Rape of the Lock*, 3.28–29.
2. *Lear* (Bevington), 4.1.1–9, 4.1.18–24.
3. "Wife of Bath's Prologue," 115–16.

Musical Scores

14.255 **Published scores.** Published musical scores are treated in much the same way as books.

1. Giuseppe Verdi, *Il corsaro* (*melodramma tragico* in three acts), libretto by Francesco Maria Piave, ed. Elizabeth Hudson, 2 vols., *The Works of Giuseppe Verdi*, ser. 1, *Operas* (Chicago: University of Chicago Press; Milan: G. Ricordi, 1998).

Mozart, Wolfgang Amadeus. *Sonatas and Fantasies for the Piano*. Prepared from the autographs and earliest printed sources by Nathan Broder. Rev. ed. Bryn Mawr, PA: Theodore Presser, 1960.
Schubert, Franz. "Das Wandern (Wandering)," *Die schöne Müllerin (The Maid of the Mill)*. In *First Vocal Album* (for high voice). New York: G. Schirmer, 1895.

In the last example above, the words and titles are given in both German and English in the score itself. See also 14.99.

14.256 **Unpublished scores.** Unpublished scores are treated in the same way as other unpublished material in manuscript collections (see 14.221–31).

1. Ralph Shapey, "Partita for Violin and Thirteen Players," score, 1966, Special Collections, Joseph Regenstein Library, University of Chicago.

Scientific Databases

14.257 **Citing data from a scientific database.** In the sciences especially, it has become customary to cite data from a database by listing, at a minimum, the name of the database, a descriptive phrase or record locator (such as a data marker or accession number) indicating the part of the database being cited or explaining the nature of the reference, an access date, and a URL. In bibliographies, list under the name of the database. See also 14.6–18.

1. NASA/IPAC Extragalactic Database (object name IRAS F00400+4059; accessed April 6, 2016), http://ned.ipac.caltech.edu/.
2. GenBank (for RP11-322N14 BAC [accession number AC087526.3]; accessed April 6, 2016), http://www.ncbi.nlm.nih.gov/nuccore/19683167.

GenBank (for RP11-322N14 BAC [accession number AC087526.3]; accessed April 6, 2016). http://www.ncbi.nlm.nih.gov/nuccore/19683167.
NASA/IPAC Extragalactic Database (object name IRAS F00400+4059; accessed April 6, 2016). http://ned.ipac.caltech.edu/.

To cite supplementary data for a journal article, see 14.187.

Patents and Standards

14.258 **Patents.** Patents are cited under the names of the creators and dated by the year of filing.

Iizuka, Masanori, and Hideki Tanaka. Cement admixture. US Patent 4,586,960, filed June 26, 1984, and issued May 6, 1986.

14.259 **Standards.** To cite a standard published by a specific industry group or by a national or international standards organization, include the name of the organization, the title of the standard (in italics), an edition or other identifying number or label, and publication information. Standards consulted online should include a URL. In the notes, standards can be cited by title; in a bibliography entry, list under the group or organization, even if that entity is also the publisher.

1. *Bibliographic References*, ANSI/NISO Z39.29-2005 (Bethesda, MD: National Information Standards Organization, approved June 9, 2005; reaffirmed May 13, 2010), 3.2.2.

2. *Extensible Markup Language (XML) 1.0*, 5th ed., ed. Tim Bray, Jean Paoli, C. M. Sperberg-McQueen, Eve Maler, and François Yergeau (W3C, November 26, 2008), http://www.w3.org/TR/2008/REC-xml-20081126/.

National Information Standards Organization. *Bibliographic References*. ANSI/NISO Z39.29-2005. Bethesda, MD: NISO, approved June 9, 2005; reaffirmed May 13, 2010.

Worldwide Web Consortium (W3C). *Extensible Markup Language (XML) 1.0*. 5th ed. Edited by Tim Bray, Jean Paoli, C. M. Sperberg-McQueen, Eve Maler, and François Yergeau. W3C, November 26, 2008. http://www.w3.org/TR/2008/REC-xml-20081126/.

Citations Taken from Secondary Sources

14.260 **Citations taken from secondary sources.** To cite a source from a secondary source ("quoted in . . .") is generally to be discouraged, since authors are expected to have examined the works they cite. If an original source is unavailable, however, both the original and the secondary source must be listed.

1. Louis Zukofsky, "Sincerity and Objectification," *Poetry* 37 (February 1931): 269, quoted in Bonnie Costello, *Marianne Moore: Imaginary Possessions* (Cambridge, MA: Harvard University Press, 1981), 78.

Audiovisual Recordings and Other Multimedia

14.261 **Multimedia—elements of the citation.** The citation for recordings and other multimedia content usually includes some or all of the following elements:

1. The name of the composer, writer, performer, or other person primarily responsible for the content. Include designations such as *vocalist*, *conductor*, or *director* as appropriate.
2. The title of the work, in italics or quotation marks, as applicable (see 8.197).
3. Information about the work, including the names of additional contributors and the date and location of the recording, production, or performance.
4. Information about the publisher, including date of publication.
5. Information about the medium or format (e.g., LP, DVD, MP3, AVI). Supplementary information, such as the number of discs in an album and the duration of the recording, as applicable, may also be given.
6. Any additional information that might be relevant to the citation.
7. For sources consulted online, a URL (see 14.6–18).

The order of these elements—and which ones are included—will depend not only on the nature of the source but also on whether a part or the whole is cited and whether a particular contributor is the focus of the citation.

14.262 **Discographies, filmographies, and the like.** Discographies, filmographies, and the like are specialized bibliographies that list (and sometimes annotate) materials such as audio recordings, video recordings, and multimedia packages. The examples in this section are modeled on notes and bibliography entries but would be appropriately presented as a separate list, either preceding the bibliography or as an appendix (see also 14.63). For advice on music discographies, consult Suzanne E. Thorin and Carole Franklin Vidali, *The Acquisition and Cataloging of Music and Sound Recordings* (bibliog. 5). For an example, see figure 14.12.

Recordings and Live Performances

14.263 **Musical recordings.** For the typographic treatment of musical compositions in running text, see 8.193–97. Those guidelines, however, do not necessarily apply to recordings when listed in a note or a bibliography. *Symphony* or *sonata*, for example, is capitalized when part of the title of a recording. A citation may begin with a title in a note; in a bibliography

ANNOTATED DISCOGRAPHY

This brief discography primarily lists commercial records readily available in the United States which have selections that pertain to genres, styles, instruments, and ensemble types that I have discussed in the book.

Huayno Music of Peru, vol. 1 (1949–1989), Arhoolie (CD 320), edited with notes by John Cohen (1989). This recording includes reissues of Peruvian recordings of the type that I have called the "commercial wayno style" (or "urban-country" style) from the 1950s and 1960s in Lima. Selections 1 (Jilguero del Huascarán) and 3 (Pastorita Huaracina) are by particularly important "country music" stars from Ancash; selection 2 is by a Junín orquesta with harp, violin, saxes, and clarinets.

Kingdom of the Sun: Peru's Inca Heritage, Nonesuch (H-72029), recorded by David Lewiston (n.d.). This recording includes an excellent example of a sikumoreno ensemble (side 1, band 4) of the type heard in the city of Puno and in the Province of Chucuito, Puno. It also includes a wayno that I refer to in chapter 9, "Adios pueblo de Ayacucho" (side 1, band 1), played in Ayacuchano style, and waynos from other regions. Side 2, band 2 is a good example of a kena solo.

Music of Peru, Folkways (FE 4415), notes by Harry Tschopik, Jr. (1950 [1959]). The recordings on side 1, bands 1 and 3, and side 2, band 1, demonstrate the ensemble sound approximating early estudiantinas (especially side 1, band 3); the bass support provided by the guitars is particularly typical. Wayno (huayno) and marinera genres are included.

Música Andina del Perú, Patronato Popular y Porvenir Pro Música Clásica (write: Proyecto de Preservación de la Música Tradicional Andina, Pontificia Universidad Católica del Perú, Instituto Riva Agüero, Jr., Camaná 459-Lima 1, for this and other recordings from Junín, Cajamarca, and Arequipa), edited with notes by Raúl Romero (1987). This excellent survey of highland Peruvian music includes examples of charango music from Cusco (side 1, band 1); the unison pitu style from Cusco (side 3, band 8—this style is quite different from the sound of pitu ensembles in Conima); the music for the Puneño traje de luz dance, "La Diablada," performed by a brass band (side 3, band 9); chiriguano panpipe music from Huancané (side 3, band 10); and choquela (chokela) music from Puno (side 3, band 11), a tradition previously performed in Conima.

315

FIGURE 14.12. The first page of a discography. See 14.262.

entry, list by author, performer, or other primary contributor. If the conductor or performer is the focus of the recording or is more relevant to the discussion than the composer, either one may be listed first. For the date, include the date of the recording or the copyright date or published date included with the recording, or both. If a date or other information cannot be determined from the recording (a common problem with older recordings and with music files downloaded out of context), consult a library catalog or other resource; citations without such information are generally unacceptable. If no date can be found, use "n.d." (for *no date*). Recordings on LP or disc typically include acquisition numbers, which follow the name of the publisher with no intervening comma. For streaming audio formats and downloads, list the service or the file format, as applicable.

1. *The Fireside Treasury of Folk Songs*, vol. 1, orchestra and chorus dir. Mitch Miller, Golden Record A198:17A–B, 1958, 33⅓ rpm.

2. New York Trumpet Ensemble, with Edward Carroll (trumpet) and Edward Brewer (organ), *Art of the Trumpet*, recorded at the Madeira Festival, June 1–2, 1981, Vox/Turnabout PVT 7183, 1982, compact disc.

3. Richard Strauss, *Don Quixote*, with Emanuel Feuermann (violoncello) and the Philadelphia Orchestra, conducted by Eugene Ormandy, recorded February 24, 1940, Biddulph LAB 042, 1991, compact disc.

4. Billie Holiday, vocalist, "I'm a Fool to Want You," by Joel Herron, Frank Sinatra, and Jack Wolf, recorded February 20, 1958, with Ray Ellis, track 1 on *Lady in Satin*, Columbia CL 1157, 33⅓ rpm.

5. "Umbrella," featuring Jay-Z, MP3 audio, track 1 on Rihanna, *Good Girl Gone Bad*, Island Def Jam, 2007.

or

6. "Umbrella," featuring Jay-Z, Spotify, track 1 on Rihanna, *Good Girl Gone Bad*, Island Def Jam, 2007.

Mozart, Wolfgang Amadeus. *Don Giovanni*. Orchestra and Chorus of the Royal Opera House, Covent Garden. Sir Colin Davis. With Ingvar Wixell, Luigi Roni, Martina Arroyo, Stuart Burrows, Kiri Te Kanawa, et al. Recorded May 1973. Philips 422 541-2, 1991, 3 compact discs.

Pink Floyd. *Atom Heart Mother*. Capitol CDP 7 46381 2, 1990, compact disc. Originally released in 1970.

Rubinstein, Artur, pianist. *The Chopin Collection*. Recorded 1946, 1958–67. RCA Victor / BMG 60822-2-RG, 1991, 11 compact discs.

Weingartner, Felix von, conductor. *150 Jahre Wiener Philharmoniker*. Recorded in 1936. Preiser Records PR90113 (mono), 1992, compact disc. Includes Beethoven's Symphony no. 3 in E-flat Major and Symphony no. 8 in F Major.

Musical recordings are usually listed in a separate discography (see fig. 14.12) rather than in a bibliography. If included in a bibliography, they are best grouped under an appropriate subhead (see 14.63).

14.264 **Recorded readings, lectures, audiobooks, and the like.** Recordings of drama, prose or poetry readings, lectures, and the like are treated much the same as musical recordings (see 14.263). Facts of publication, where needed, follow the style for print media. See also 14.267–68.

1. Dylan Thomas, *Under Milk Wood*, performed by Dylan Thomas et al., Caedmon TC-2005, 1953, 33⅓ rpm, 2 LPs.

2. Harry S. Truman, "First Speech to Congress," April 16, 1945, Miller Center of Public Affairs, University of Virginia, transcript and Adobe Flash audio, 18:13, http://millercenter.org/president/speeches/speech-3339.

3. Calvin Coolidge, "Equal Rights" (speech), ca. 1920, in "American Leaders Speak: Recordings from World War I and the 1920 Election, 1918–1920," Library of Congress, copy of an undated 78 rpm disc, RealAudio and WAV formats, 3:45, http://memory.loc.gov/ammem/nfhtml/.

4. Eleanor Roosevelt, "Is America Facing World Leadership?," convocation speech, Ball State Teacher's College, May 6, 1959, Muncie, IN, radio broadcast, reel-to-reel tape, MPEG copy, 1:12:49, http://libx.bsu.edu/cdm/singleitem/collection/ElRoos/id/1.

Auden, W. H. *Selected Poems*. Read by the author. Spoken Arts 7137, 1991. Audiocassette.

Strayed, Cheryl. *Wild: From Lost to Found on the Pacific Crest Trail*. Read by Bernadette Dunne. New York: Random House Audio, 2012. Audible audio ed., 13 hr., 6 min.

14.265 **Video and film recordings.** Citations of video and film recordings, like citations of sound recordings, will vary according to the nature of the material (television show, movie, etc.). Any facts relevant to identifying the item should be included. Indexed scenes are treated as chapters and cited by title or by number. Ancillary material, such as critical commentary, is cited by author and title. Note that in the *Monty Python* example, the citation is of material original to the 2001 edition, so the original release date of the film (1975) is omitted. See also 14.267–68.

1. *American Crime Story: The People v. O. J. Simpson*, episode 6, "Marcia, Marcia, Marcia," directed by Ryan Murphy, written by D. V. DeVincentis, featuring Sterling K. Brown, Kenneth Choi, and Sarah Paulson, aired March 8, 2016, on FX, https://www.amazon.com/dp/B01ARVPCOA/.

2. "Crop Duster Attack," *North by Northwest*, directed by Alfred Hitchcock (1959; Burbank, CA: Warner Home Video, 2000), DVD.

3. Louis J. Mihalyi, *Landscapes of Zambia, Central Africa* (Santa Barbara, CA: Visual Education, 1975), 35 mm slides, 40 frames.

4. *The Greek and Roman World* (Chicago: Society for Visual Education, 1977), filmstrip, 44 min.

Cleese, John, Terry Gilliam, Eric Idle, Terry Jones, and Michael Palin. "Commentaries." Disc 2. *Monty Python and the Holy Grail*, special ed. DVD. Directed by Terry Gilliam and Terry Jones. Culver City, CA: Columbia Tristar Home Entertainment, 2001.

Cuarón, Alfonso, dir. *Gravity*. 2013; Burbank, CA: Warner Bros. Pictures, 2014. Blu-ray Disc, 1080p HD.

Handel, George Frideric. *Messiah*. Atlanta Symphony Orchestra and Chamber Chorus, Robert Shaw. Performed December 19, 1987. Ansonia Station, NY: Video Artists International, 1988. Videocassette (VHS), 141 min.

Mayberry, Russ, dir. *The Brady Bunch*. Season 3, episode 10, "Her Sister's Shadow." Aired November 19, 1971, on ABC. https://www.hulu.com/the-brady-bunch.

14.266 **Live performances.** Live performances, unlike recordings, cannot be consulted as such by readers. For that reason, it is generally sufficient to mention details in the text or in the notes rather than in a bibliography. In addition to specifying the name and location of the venue and the date of the performance, include as much information as needed to identify the performance according to the guidelines outlined in 14.261. For the use of italics and quotation marks and other considerations for titles of works, see 8.156–201.

In a performance of Lin-Manuel Miranda's *Hamilton* at the Richard Rodgers Theatre in New York on February 2, 2016, . . .

1. *Hamilton*, music and lyrics by Lin-Manuel Miranda, dir. Thomas Kail, chor. Andy Blakenbuehler, Richard Rodgers Theatre, New York, NY, February 2, 2016.

To cite a recording of a live performance, consult the relevant examples at 14.263, 14.264, and 14.265.

Online Multimedia and Apps

14.267 **Videos, podcasts, and other online multimedia.** Cite online multimedia according to the recommendations throughout this section; include a URL as the final element of the citation (see also 14.261). If no date can be determined from the source, include the date the material was last accessed. (See also 14.6–18.) If the material is a recording of a speech or other performance, or if it is a digital version of a published source, include information about the original performance or source. Whether to list information about the original or the digitized copy first will depend on the information available and is usually up to the author. Copies of sources that are under copyright and which have been posted without ties to any publisher or sponsor should be cited with caution. For multimedia designed to run in a web browser, a file format does not need to be mentioned; if a downloadable file was consulted (as in example notes 1 and 3), specify format. See also 14.264, 14.187.

1. A. E. Weed, *At the Foot of the Flatiron* (American Mutoscope and Biograph Co., 1903), 35 mm film, from Library of Congress, *The Life of a City: Early Films of New York, 1898–1906*, MPEG video, 2:19 at 15 fps, http://www.loc.gov/item/00694378.

2. "Lang Lang: *The Chopin Album*," interview by Jeff Spurgeon, Artists at Google, October 15, 2012, video, 54:47, October 18, 2012, featuring performances of Nocturne in E-flat Major, op. 55, no. 2; Etude in F Minor, op. 25, no. 2; Etude in E Major, op. 10, no. 3; and "Grande valse brillante" in E-flat Major, op. 18, https://youtu.be/1d8xv1HHKtI.

3. Mike Danforth and Ian Chillag, "F-Bombs, Chicken, and Exclamation Points," April 21, 2015, in *How to Do Everything*, produced by Gillian Donovan, podcast, MP3 audio, 18:46, http://www.npr.org/podcasts/510303/how-to-do-everything.

Brown, Evan. "The 10 Commandments of Typography." Infographic. DesignMantic, April 11, 2014. http://www.designmantic.com/blog/infographics/ten-commandments-of-typography/.

Kessler, Aaron M. "The Driverless Now." Produced by Poh Si Teng and Jessica Naudziunas. *New York Times*, May 2, 2015. Video, 2:01. http://www.nytimes.com/video/business/100000003662208/the-driverless-now.html.

Lyiscott, Jamila. "3 Ways to Speak English." Filmed February 2014 in New York, NY. TED video, 4:29. https://www.ted.com/talks/jamila_lyiscott_3_ways_to_speak_english.

To cite comments, adapt the recommendations for citing comments on blog posts or social media (see 14.208, 14.209).

4. Frithjof Meyer, comment on "Lang Lang," March 2015.

14.268 **Multimedia app content.** Multimedia apps include video games, interactive books and encyclopedias, and other content designed to function as a stand-alone application for use on a computer or other device. To cite, list relevant information as described throughout this section on recordings and multimedia and elsewhere. Include any version number and information about the device or operating system required to run the app. In the next-to-last example, the publishing information for *Gems* *and Gemstones* is in parentheses because such annotations are styled like notes. See also 8.190.

1. *Gems and Jewels*, iPad ed., v. 1.01 (Touchpress, 2011), adapted from Lance Grande and Allison Augustyn, *Gems and Gemstones: Timeless Natural Beauty of the Mineral World* (Chicago: University of Chicago Press, 2009).

2. *Angry Birds Transformers*, v. 1.4.25 (Rovio Entertainment, 2014), Android 4.0 or later, soundtrack by Vince DiCola and Kenny Meriedeth.

Grande, Lance, and Allison Augustyn. *Gems and Jewels*. iPad ed., v. 1.01. Touchpress, 2011. Adapted from Lance Grande and Allison Augustyn, *Gems and Gemstones: Timeless Natural Beauty of the Mineral World* (Chicago: University of Chicago Press, 2009).

Rovio Entertainment. *Angry Birds Transformers*. V. 1.4.25. Rovio Entertainment, 2014. Android 4.0 or later. Soundtrack by Vince DiCola and Kenny Meriedeth.

Legal and Public Documents

14.269 **Recommended stylebooks.** Citations in predominantly legal works generally follow one of two guides: (1) *The Bluebook: A Uniform System of Citation*, published by the Harvard Law Review Association; or (2) the *ALWD Guide to Legal Citation*, prepared and published by the Association of Legal Writing Directors and Coleen M. Barger (see bibliog. 1.1). *The Bluebook* is the most widely used citation guide; its conventions predominate in law reviews. The *ALWD Guide* differs in some elements and aims to be somewhat simpler. Chicago recommends using one of these systems for citing legal and public documents—including cases, constitutions, statutes, and other government documents—even in works with a predominantly nonlegal subject matter. This approach recognizes the ubiquity of these citation formats in legal publications, commercial databases, and government archives. Any editor working extensively with legal and public documents should have one of these manuals on hand. Most of the examples in this section are based on *The Bluebook* (exceptions are made for secondary sources and certain unpublished government documents; see 14.291, 14.292). *The Bluebook* and the *ALWD Guide* are used in the United States. For citation guides used in Canada, see 14.293; for those used in the United Kingdom, see 14.297.

14.270 **Legal and public documents online.** *The Bluebook* includes specific guidelines for citing sources consulted online. In general, for citations of cases, constitutions and statutes, and like materials, print sources are preferred, but online versions authenticated by a government entity or considered to be the official version (or an exact copy thereof) can be treated as if they were print. (If a URL is required, it may be appended as the last element of the citation; for an example, see 14.276.) Citations of sources consulted through commercial databases such as Westlaw or LexisNexis should include the database name and any applicable identification number (or, in the case of constitutions and statutes, information about the currency of the database). For examples, see 14.276. To cite books, periodicals, and other types of nonlegal sources consulted online, Chicago's recommendations can usually be followed (see 14.6–18).

14.271 **Note form for legal-style citations.** Legal publications use notes for documentation and rarely include bibliographies. The examples in this section, based on the recommendations in *The Bluebook*, are accordingly given in note form only. Any work so cited need not be listed in a bibliography (but see 14.291). Works using the author-date style (chapter 15) and citing only a handful of legal and public documents may limit those citations to the text, using citation sentences and clauses that include the same information as footnotes, as suggested in *The Bluebook*; those with more than a very few legal-style citations, however, may need to supplement the author-date system with footnotes or endnotes. See 15.58–59.

14.272 **Typefaces in legal-style citations.** In *Bluebook* style, italics are used for titles of articles and chapters (a major difference from nonlegal usage), uncommon words or phrases in languages other than English (but not such well-known terms as *de facto* or *habeas corpus*), certain introductory signals indicating a cross-reference (such as *See*), case history (such as *aff'd*; see 14.278), and procedural phrases (such as *In re*). Italics are also used for case names in textual sentences, whether in the running text or in the notes. All other material, including case names in citations, appears in roman. (See 14.276.) In addition, formal *Bluebook* style specifies caps and small caps for constitutions, the titles of books and their authors, and the names of periodicals and websites. The examples in this section use a simpler style advocated by some law reviews, substituting upper- and lowercase roman type for caps and small caps. Note, however, that the examples in this section are limited to legal and public documents (but see 14.291). Though *Bluebook*-style citations to books, articles, and other types of secondary sources may be appropriate in works with predominantly legal subject matter, these are not covered here.

14.273 **Page numbers and other locators in legal-style citations.** In *Bluebook* style, for most sources the first page number is cited, following the name of the source and usually with no intervening punctuation; references to specific page numbers follow the first page number, separated by a comma. Some types of sources are cited by section (§) or paragraph (¶) number; references to specific pages within such sections follow a comma and *at* (in roman type).

14.274 **Abbreviations in legal-style citations.** *The Bluebook* specifies abbreviations for the names of reporters, cases, courts, and legislative documents, as well as journals and compilation services. It also includes guidelines for abbreviating certain terms commonly used in legal citations. Most abbreviations in *The Bluebook* use periods or apostrophes, but exceptions are made for abbreviations of organizational names such as NBC or FDA. In citations (but not in running text), *Bluebook* style specifies *2d* and *3d* rather than *2nd* and *3rd* for ordinals and capitalizes abbreviations like *No.* and *Sess.* Works that otherwise follow Chicago style—which differs on some of these points (see, e.g., 10.4)—should, for legal citations, follow *Bluebook* style, as shown in the examples in this section. The following example cites a decision by the United States Court of Appeals for the Seventh Circuit, reported in volume 206 of the *Federal Reporter*, third series, beginning on page 752, with the citation specifically referring to footnote 1 on that page (see also 14.278).

1. NLRB v. Somerville Constr. Co., 206 F.3d 752, 752 n.1 (7th Cir. 2000).

In running text, most terms should be spelled out—including terms such as *chapter*, *part*, *article*, *section*, *paragraph*, and so forth (but, in case names, not *v.* or common abbreviations such as *Co.*, *Inc.*, or *Gov't*). For more specific recommendations, consult *The Bluebook*. See also 8.80, 8.82.

14.275 **Short forms for legal-style citations.** *The Bluebook* allows certain short forms for subsequent citations to the same source. Short forms include case names reduced to the name of only one party (usually the plaintiff or the nongovernmental party); statutes and legislative documents identified only by name or document and section numbers; treaties identified only by name (or sometimes a short form thereof); and the use of *id.* (in italics). Cases are the most readily shortened forms; examples are included in the section that treats them (14.276–79). Works that cite only a few legal documents may be better off using the full form for each citation. See also 14.29–36.

Cases and Court Decisions

14.276 **Cases or court decisions—basic elements.** Full case names in citations, including the abbreviation *v.*, are set in roman in notes; short forms in subsequent citations are italicized (as are full case names mentioned in textual sentences; see example 3). Full citations include volume number (arabic), abbreviated name of the reporter(s), the ordinal series number of the reporter (if applicable), the abbreviated name of the court (if not indicated by the reporter) and the date together in parentheses, and other relevant information (see 14.279). A single page number designates the opening page of a decision; an additional number designates an actual page cited. In a shortened citation, *at* is used to cite a particular page (example 3); absence of *at* implies reference to the decision as a whole (example 4). See also 14.272, 14.275.

1. United States v. Christmas, 222 F.3d 141, 145 (4th Cir. 2000).
2. Profit Sharing Plan v. Mbank Dallas, N.A., 683 F. Supp. 592 (N.D. Tex. 1988).
3. *Christmas*, 222 F.3d at 145. The court also noted that under *United States v. Sokolow*, 490 U.S. 1, 7 (1989), police may briefly detain a person without probable cause if the officer believes criminal activity "may be afoot." *Christmas*, 222 F.3d at 143; *see also* Terry v. Ohio, 392 U.S. 1 (1968).
4. *Profit Sharing Plan*, 683 F. Supp. 592.

Cases consulted online should normally be cited to the appropriate reporter(s). Though rarely used in *Bluebook*-style citations, a URL that points directly to an official resource may be appended as shown here (see also 14.6).

5. State v. Griffin, 211 W. Va. 508, 566 S.E.2d 645 (2002), http://www.courtswv.gov/supreme-court/docs/spring2002/30433.htm.

When a commercial electronic database is cited, include the docket number, name of the database, and any identifying date and number supplied by the database. References to page or screen numbers are preceded by an asterisk. Short forms may include only the database identifier.

6. Family Serv. Ass'n v. Wells Twp., No. 14-4020, 2015 U.S. App. LEXIS 6174 (6th Cir. Apr. 16, 2015).
7. *In re* D.S., No. 13-0888, 2014 WL 1495489 (Iowa Ct. App. Apr. 16, 2014).
8. *Family Serv. Ass'n*, 2015 U.S. App. LEXIS 6174, at *5.
9. *D.S.*, 2014 WL 1495489, at *1.

See also 14.270.

14.277 **United States Supreme Court decisions.** All Supreme Court decisions are published in the *United States Reports* (abbreviated U.S.) and are preferably cited to that reporter. Cases not yet published therein may be cited to the *Supreme Court Reporter* (S. Ct.), which publishes decisions more quickly. Because the court's name is indicated by the reporter, it is not repeated before the date.

1. Citizens United v. Federal Election Comm'n, 558 U.S. 310 (2010).
2. Obergefell v. Hodges, 135 S. Ct. 2584 (2015).
3. *Citizens United*, 558 U.S. at 322.

14.278 **Lower federal-court decisions.** Lower federal-court decisions are usually cited to the *Federal Reporter* (F.) or to the *Federal Supplement* (F. Supp.). Relevant case history should be included.

1. United States v. Dennis, 183 F. 201 (2d Cir. 1950).
2. Locke v. Shore, 682 F. Supp. 2d 1283 (N.D. Fla. 2010), *aff'd*, 634 F.3d 1185 (11th Cir. 2011).
3. Eaton v. IBM Corp., 925 F. Supp. 487 (S.D. Tex. 1996).
4. *Dennis*, 183 F. at 202.
5. *Locke*, 682 F. Supp. 2d at 1292.

For the use of spaces relative to ordinals, see 14.279.

14.279 **State- and local-court decisions.** Decisions of state and local courts are cited much like federal-court decisions. If both the official and the commercial reporters are cited, they are separated by a comma. If the court's name is identified unambiguously by the reporter, it is not repeated before the date. If a case was decided in a lower court, the abbreviated court name appears before the date (as in example 4). Note that a space is used before an ordinal that follows an abbreviated reporter name consisting of two or more letters—"Cal. 2d" (*California Reports*, second series)—but not with initialisms like "A." in "A.2d" (*Atlantic Reporter*, second series) or "N.Y.S." in "N.Y.S.2d" (*New York Supplement*, second series). Some state courts have adopted a public domain citation format for more recent cases; consult *The Bluebook* for guidance.

1. Williams v. Davis, 27 Cal. 2d 746 (1946).
2. *Id.* at 747.
3. Henningsen v. Bloomfield Motors, Inc., 32 N.J. 358, 161 A.2d 69 (1960).
4. Kendig v. Kendig, 981 N.Y.S.2d 411 (App. Div. 2014).
5. *Williams*, 27 Cal. 2d 746.

If it is important to avoid *id.* (as in an electronic format where individual notes may be presented out of context), use a shortened citation form instead. The short form for note 2, above, would be "*Williams*, 27 Cal. 2d at 747." See also 14.34, 14.35.

Constitutions

14.280 **Constitutions.** In citations to constitutions, the article and amendment numbers appear in roman numerals; other subdivision numbers are in arabic. (For nonlegal style see 9.28.) In *Bluebook* style the name of the constitution is capitalized; other abbreviations are lowercased.

1. U.S. Const. art. I, § 4, cl. 2.
2. U.S. Const. amend. XIV, § 2.
3. Ariz. Const. art. VII, § 5.
4. Ark. Const. of 1868, art. III, § 2 (superseded 1874).

Legislative and Executive Documents

14.281 **Legislative documents—abbreviations.** Abbreviations for federal legislative documents include "Cong." (Congress), "H." (House), "S." (Senate), and other standard abbreviations for such terms as *document*, *session*, and *resolution*. Unless it is not clear from the context, "U.S." may be omitted (and, for House and Senate documents published as of 1907, the session number can generally be omitted). For lists of abbreviations and many examples, consult *The Bluebook*. See also 14.274.

14.282 **Laws and statutes.** Bills or joint resolutions that have been signed into law—"public laws," or statutes—are first published separately, as slip laws, and then collected in the annual bound volumes of the *United States Statutes at Large* (abbreviated in legal style as "Stat."), where they are referred to as session laws. Later they are incorporated into the *United States Code* (U.S.C.).

1. Homeland Security Act of 2002, Pub. L. No. 107-296, 116 Stat. 2135 (2012).
2. Homeland Security Act of 2002, 6 U.S.C. § 101 (2012).

14.283 **Bills and resolutions.** Congressional bills (proposed laws) and resolutions are published in pamphlet form (slip bills). In citations, bills or resolutions originating in the House of Representatives are abbreviated "H.R." or "H.R. Res.," and those originating in the Senate, "S." or "S.

Res." The title of the bill (if there is one) is followed by the bill number, the number of the Congress, a section number (if relevant), and the year of publication in parentheses. Authors wishing to cite a bill that has been enacted should cite it as a statute (see 14.282).

1. Safe and Accurate Food Labeling Act of 2015, H.R. 1599, 114th Cong. (2015).

14.284 **Hearings.** Records of testimony given before congressional committees are usually published with titles, which should be cited in full and set in italics. The relevant committee should be listed as part of the title. Note that *Before*—which Chicago would normally lowercase in a title (see 8.159)—is capitalized according to *Bluebook* style, which capitalizes prepositions of more than four letters. (This style need not be followed in a book that otherwise follows Chicago style.) Include the number of the Congress, the page number cited (if any), the year in parentheses, and the speaker's name, title, and affiliation in parentheses.

1. *Homeland Security Act of 2002: Hearings on H.R. 5005, Day 3, Before the Select Comm. on Homeland Security*, 107th Cong. 203 (2002) (statement of David Walker, Comptroller General of the United States).

14.285 **Congressional reports and documents.** In *Bluebook* style, numbered reports and documents are cited by the number of the Congress, which is joined to the document number by a hyphen. House and Senate reports are abbreviated "H.R. Rep." or "S. Rep."; documents are abbreviated "H.R. Doc." or "S. Doc." A specific page reference, if needed, is added following *at*. The year of the report or document is placed in parentheses. Additional information (e.g., to indicate a conference report) follows the year, in parentheses. If not mentioned in text, a title and author (if any) may be included in the citation.

1. Select Comm. on Homeland Security, Homeland Security Act of 2002, H.R. Rep. No. 107-609, pt. 1 (2002).
2. H.R. Rep. No. 113-564, at 54 (2014) (Conf. Rep.).
3. S. Doc. No. 77-148, at 2–5 (1941).

14.286 **Congressional debates since 1873.** Since 1873, congressional debates have been published by the government in the *Congressional Record*. Daily issues are bound in paper biweekly and in permanent volumes (divided into parts) yearly. Since material may be added, deleted, or modified when the final volumes are prepared, pagination will vary among the different editions. Whenever possible, citation should be made to the permanent volumes. Note that, following *Bluebook* style, italics are not used for the name of the publication. The page number (preceded by "H" or "S," for House or Senate, in the daily edition) is followed by the date, which is placed in parentheses. If the identity of a speaker is necessary, include it in parentheses.

1. 147 Cong. Rec. 19,000 (2001).

2. 161 Cong. Rec. S4335 (daily ed. June 22, 2015) (statement of Sen. Hatch).

14.287 **Records of congressional debates before 1873.** Until 1873, congressional debates were privately printed in *Annals of the Congress of the United States* (covering the years 1789–1824; also known by other names), *Register of Debates* (1824–37), and *Congressional Globe* (1833–73). In citing the date, refer to the year of publication rather than the year in which the debate occurred. Note that the *Globe* is normally cited by number and session of Congress (and page number), whereas the *Annals* and *Debates* are cited by volume number. As with citations to the *Congressional Record*, the titles are abbreviated and not italicized.

1. Cong. Globe, 34th Cong., 3d Sess. 149 (1856).

2. 42 Annals of Cong. 1697 (1824).

3. 3 Reg. Deb. 388 (1829).

14.288 **State laws and municipal ordinances.** The titles of state codes (compilations) for laws and municipal ordinances are set in roman type. A name is included in parentheses where necessary to indicate the version of a code cited. The date following a code (or the version of a code) indicates the year the current code was published. Form of citation will vary by state. The date a specific law was passed may be included in parentheses at the end of the citation. For an exhaustive treatment of state-by-state variations, consult *The Bluebook*.

1. Ohio Rev. Code Ann. § 3305.08 (West 2003).

2. An Act Guaranteeing Governmental Independence, Ky. Rev. Stat. Ann. § 520.020 (LexisNexis 1985) (passed Jan. 3, 1974).

14.289 **Presidential documents.** Presidential proclamations, executive orders, vetoes, addresses, and the like are published in the *Weekly Compilation of Presidential Documents* (Weekly Comp. Pres. Doc.) and in the *Public Papers of the Presidents of the United States* (Pub. Papers). Proclamations and executive orders are also carried in the daily *Federal Register* (Fed. Reg.) and then published in title 3 of the *Code of Federal Regulations* (C.F.R.). Some executive orders and proclamations appear in the *United States Code*; include a citation if therein (see example 3).

1. Proclamation No. 8214, 73 Fed. Reg. 1439 (Jan. 8, 2008).

2. Exec. Order No. 11,609, 3 C.F.R. 586 (1971–75).

3. Exec. Order No. 13,653, 3 C.F.R. 330 (2013), *reprinted as amended in* 42 U.S.C. § 4321 app. (2012).

For more examples, consult *The Bluebook.*

14.290 **Treaties.** The texts of treaties signed before 1950 are published in *United States Statutes at Large*; the unofficial citation is to the *Treaty Series* (T.S.) or the *Executive Agreement Series* (E.A.S.), each of which assigns a number to a treaty covered. Those signed in 1950 and later appear in *United States Treaties and Other International Agreements* (U.S.T., 1950–) or *Treaties and Other International Acts Series* (T.I.A.S., 1945–), which also assigns a number. Treaties involving more than two nations may be found in the *United Nations Treaty Series* (U.N.T.S., 1946–) or, from 1920 to 1946, in the *League of Nations Treaty Series* (L.N.T.S., 1920–46). These and other sources are listed in *The Bluebook.* Titles of treaties are set in roman and capitalized headline-style (recall that *The Bluebook* capitalizes prepositions of more than four letters). Country names are generally abbreviated (see also 14.274). An exact date indicates the date of signing and is therefore preferable to a year alone, which may differ from the year the treaty was published in one of the works above. Page numbers are given where relevant.

1. Treaty Banning Nuclear Weapon Tests in the Atmosphere, in Outer Space and Under Water, U.S.-U.K.-U.S.S.R., Aug. 5, 1963, 14 U.S.T. 1313.

2. Convention Concerning Military Service, Den.-It., July 15, 1954, 250 T.I.A.S. 3516, at 45.

14.291 **Secondary sources and freestanding publications.** When citing secondary sources and other freestanding publications, Chicago rather than *Bluebook* style can usually be followed. Such materials include not just books and articles but also legislative documents, pamphlets, and reports. For subsequent citations or citations of individual documents, shortened forms may be devised as needed (as in example notes 2 and 4; see also 14.59). The following examples are not meant to be exhaustive. Those who are required to follow *Bluebook* style should consult that manual, whose recommendations differ.

1. *The Federalist Papers*, ed. Lawrence Goldman (Oxford: Oxford University Press, 2008).

2. *Federalist*, no. 42 (James Madison).

3. *Journals of the Continental Congress, 1774–1789*, ed. Worthington C. Ford et al. (Washington, DC, 1904–37), 15:1341.

4. *JCC* 25:863.

5. *Public Papers of the Presidents of the United States: Herbert Hoover, 1929–1933*, 4 vols. (Washington, DC: Government Printing Office, 1974–77), 1:134.

6. Martha L. Minow, "Making History or Making Peace: When Prosecutions Should Give Way to Truth Commissions and Peace Negotiations," *Journal of Human Rights* 7, no. 2 (2008): 174–75.

7. *Median Gross Rent by Counties of the United States, 1970*, prepared by the Geography Division in cooperation with the Housing Division, Bureau of the Census (Washington, DC, 1975).

8. Ralph I. Straus, *Expanding Private Investment for Free World Economic Growth*, special report prepared at the request of the Department of State, April 1959, 12.

9. Illinois General Assembly, Law Revision Commission, *Report to the 80th General Assembly of the State of Illinois* (Chicago, 1977), 14–18.

Though the legal-style citations discussed elsewhere in this section are usually limited to the notes (see 14.271), the secondary sources or free-standing works discussed here may be included in a bibliography (see also 14.61).

Continental Congress. *Journals of the Continental Congress, 1774–1789*. Edited by Worthington C. Ford et al. 34 vols. Washington, DC, 1904–37.

14.292 **Unpublished government documents.** For general guidelines and many examples that can be adapted to government documents, see 14.221–31. Most unpublished documents of the federal government are housed in the National Archives and Records Administration in Washington, DC, or in one of its branches. All, including films, photographs, and sound recordings as well as written materials, are cited by record group (RG) number. A list of the record groups and their numbers is given in the *Guide to the National Archives of the United States*, augmented by the leaflet *Citing Records in the National Archives of the United States* (available from the National Archives; see bibliog. 4.5), which includes advice on citing its electronic records and digitized resources. Names of specific documents are given in quotation marks.

1. Senate Committee on the Judiciary, "Lobbying," file 71A-F15, RG 46, National Archives.

2. National Archives Branch Depository, Suitland, MD, Records of the National Commission on Law Observance and Enforcement, RG 10.

Canada

14.293 **Canadian reference works.** The major reference work for citing Canadian public documents and legal cases in a Canadian context is the *Canadian Guide to Uniform Legal Citation*, edited and published (in English and French) by the Carswell/McGill Law Journal (see bibliog. 1.1). Also valuable are Douglass T. MacEllven, Michael J. McGuire, Neil A. Campbell, and John N. Davis, *Legal Research Handbook* (bibliog. 5); *Canadian Almanac and Directory* (bibliog. 4.4); and Gerald L. Gall, F. Pearl Eliadis, and France Allard, *The Canadian Legal System* (bibliog. 5). Authors citing more than a few Canadian legal or public documents should consult one of these works. Additional resources may be found online through Lexum. For citing the occasional example in a US context, *The Bluebook* (see 14.269) provides some recommendations and examples.

14.294 **Canadian legal cases.** The following examples illustrate *Bluebook* style. The basic elements are similar to those used in US law citations; the date is enclosed in square brackets, followed by the volume number if pertinent, the abbreviated name of the reporter, and the page number. Canadian Supreme Court cases since 1876 are cited to *Supreme Court Reports* (S.C.R.). Federal Court cases are cited to *Federal Courts Reports* (F.C., 1971–2003; F.C.R., 2004–) or *Exchequer Court Reports* (Ex. C.R., 1875–1971). Cases not found in any of these sources are cited to *Dominion Law Reports* (D.L.R.). Cite the year of the decision in parentheses if it is different from the reporter year. Include the volume number of the reporter if applicable. Add "Can." and the abbreviated court name in parentheses if not clear from the context. For citing other reporters, including those covering the provinces and territories, consult *The Bluebook.*

1. Egan v. Canada, [1995] 2 S.C.R. 513.
2. American Cyanamid Co. v. Novopharm Ltd., [1972] F.C. 739 (Can. C.A.).
3. Canada v. CBC/Radio-Canada (2012), [2014] 1 F.C.R. 142.

Since 1998, many cases have been assigned neutral citations to facilitate immediate publication online. A neutral citation should appear first, ahead of any parallel citation to an official reporter. In the following example, "SCC" (no periods) refers to the Supreme Court of Canada.

4. Robertson v. Thomson Corp., 2006 SCC 43, [2006] 2 S.C.R. 363 (Can.).

14.295 **Canadian statutes.** Federal statutes appeared through 1985 in the *Revised Statutes of Canada* (R.S.C.), a consolidation that was published every fifteen to thirty years; federal statutes enacted since then are cited as session laws in the annual *Statutes of Canada* (S.C.). (Current consolidated federal statutes are available online from the Justice Laws Consolidated Acts collection.) Citation elements are similar to US statutes: the name of the act, the abbreviated name of the compilation, publication date, chapter number (in *R.S.C.*, the chapter number includes the initial letter of the name of the act), and section number if applicable. Add "Can." in parentheses if it is not clear from the context. Statutes for the provinces and territories are cited similarly; consult *The Bluebook* for guidance.

1. Companies' Creditors Arrangement Act, R.S.C. 1985, c. C-36, s. 5 (Can.).
2. Canada Elections Act, S.C. 2000, c. 9.

14.296 **Unpublished Canadian government documents.** Library and Archives Canada (LAC) houses the unpublished records of the federal government, both individually written and institutional, as well as historically significant documents from the private sector. The guide to the entire LAC collections is available online, as are the archives for each province and territory. For citing unpublished materials, see the guidelines and examples in 14.221–31.

United Kingdom

14.297 **UK reference works.** The catalogs of the National Archives (the official archive for England, Wales, and the central UK government), available online, extend to the documents of the former Public Record Office, the Historical Manuscripts Commission, the Office of Public Sector Information, and Her Majesty's Stationery Office (HMSO), among others. The UK Parliament also makes its catalogs available online. Printed guides include the *Guide to the Contents of the Public Record Office*; Frank Rodgers, *A Guide to British Government Publications*; and John E. Pemberton, ed., *The Bibliographic Control of Official Publications* (all in bibliog. 4.5). For citing UK legal and public documents in a US context, *The Bluebook* (see 14.269) provides an overview.

14.298 **UK legal cases.** In *Bluebook* style, the basic elements in citations to UK legal cases are similar to those used in US law citations: the name of the case, in roman (cases involving the Crown use the abbreviation "R" for Rex or Regina); the date, which is enclosed in parentheses when the volumes of the reporter are numbered cumulatively, or in square brackets when the year is essential to locating the case (there is either no volume number or the volumes for each year are numbered anew, not cumulatively); the abbreviated name of the reporter; and the opening page of the decision. If the court is not apparent from the name of the reporter, or if the jurisdiction is not clear from the context, include either or both, as necessary, in parentheses. Until recently, the courts of highest appeal in the United Kingdom (except for criminal cases in Scotland) were the House of Lords (H.L.) and the Judicial Committee of the Privy Council (P.C.). In 2005 the Supreme Court of the United Kingdom was established. In 2009 it assumed the appellate jurisdiction of the House of Lords and the devolution jurisdiction of the Judicial Committee of the Privy Council. Most cases are cited to the applicable report in the *Law Reports*, among these the Appeal Cases (A.C.), Queen's (King's) Bench (Q.B., K.B.), Chancery (Ch.), Family (Fam.), and Probate (P.) reports. For other reports applicable to cases dating back to AD 1094, consult *The Bluebook*.

1. R v. Dudley and Stephens, (1884) 14 Q.B.D. 273 (D.C.).

2. Regal (Hastings) Ltd. v. Gulliver, [1967] 2 A.C. 134 (H.L.) (appeal taken from Eng.).

Cases heard since 2001 are assigned a neutral citation to allow for immediate online publishing. A neutral citation should appear first, ahead of any parallel citation to an official reporter. In the following example, "UKSC" (no periods) refers to the Supreme Court of the United Kingdom.

3. HJ (Iran) v. Sec'y of State for the Home Dep't, [2010] UKSC 31, [2011] 1 A.C. 596 (appeal taken from Eng. & Wales C.A.).

14.299 **UK parliamentary publications.** Parliamentary publications include all materials issued by both houses of Parliament, the House of Commons (H.C.) and the House of Lords (H.L.): journals of both houses (sometimes abbreviated *CJ* and *LJ*); votes and proceedings; debates; bills, reports, and papers; and statutes.

14.300 **UK statutes.** The Acts of Parliament are identified by title (in roman), year (also include the regnal year for statutes enacted before 1963), and chapter number (c. for chapter; arabic numeral for national number, lowercase roman for local). Monarchs' names in regnal-year citations are abbreviated as follows: Ann., Car. (Charles), Edw., Eliz., Geo., Hen., Jac. (James), Phil. & M., Rich., Vict., Will., W. & M. The year precedes the name; the monarch's ordinal, if any, follows it (15 Geo. 6), both in arabic numerals. An ampersand is used between regnal years and between names of dual monarchs (1 & 2 W. & M.). *The Bluebook* advises including the jurisdiction in parentheses if it is not clear from the context.

1. Act of Settlement, 1701, 12 & 13 Will. 3, c. 2.
2. Consolidated Fund Act, 1963, c. 1 (Eng.).
3. Manchester Corporation Act, 1967, c. xl.

Early statutory material for the United Kingdom is compiled in *The Statutes of the Realm* (1235–1714) and *Acts and Ordinances of the Interregnum* (1642–60); additional material through 1800 has been published in various versions of *The Statutes at Large*. Later acts have been published as Public General Acts. For more information, see Legislation.gov.uk, a database of UK legislation published by the National Archives.

14.301 **Publication of UK parliamentary debates.** Before 1909, debates from both houses were published together; since then they have been published in separate series.

Hansard Parliamentary Debates, 1st series (1803–20)
Hansard Parliamentary Debates, 2d series (1820–30)
Hansard Parliamentary Debates, 3d series (1830–91)
Parliamentary Debates, 4th series (1892–1908)
Parliamentary Debates, Commons, 5th series (1909–81)
Parliamentary Debates, Commons, 6th series (1981–)
Parliamentary Debates, Lords, 5th series (1909–)

In *Bluebook* style, cite the volume number and series and include the year and column number. In example 3, H.C. is included to indicate the House of Commons series. (In the first two examples, no such indication is necessary.)

1. 249 Parl. Deb. (3d ser.) (1879) cols. 611–27.
2. 13 Parl. Deb. (4th ser.) (1893) col. 1273.
3. 407 Parl. Deb. H.C. (5th ser.) (1944–45) cols. 425–46.

Although no longer the official name, *Hansard* (less often, *Hansard's*) is still sometimes used in citations to all series of parliamentary debates. Such usage is best avoided, however.

14.302 **UK command papers.** Command papers are so called because they originate outside Parliament and are ostensibly presented to Parliament "by command of Her [His] Majesty." The different abbreviations for "command" indicate the series and must not be altered. No *s* is added to the plural (Cmnd. 3834, 3835).

C. (1st series) 1 to C. (1st series) 4222 (1833–69)
C. (2d series) 1 to C. (2d series) 9550 (1870–99)
Cd. 1 to Cd. 9239 (1900–1918)
Cmd. 1 to Cmd. 9889 (1919–56)
Cmnd. 1–9927 (1956–86)
Cm. 1– (1986–)

A command paper may consist of a pamphlet or several volumes. If not clear from the context, the author of the report is included. Dates may include a month or just a year.

1. HM Treasury, The Basle Facility and the Sterling Area, 1968, Cmnd. 3787, at 15–16.

2. First Interim Report of the Committee on Currency and Foreign Exchanges after the War, 1918, Cd. 9182.

3. Review Body on Doctors' and Dentists' Remuneration, Thirteenth Report, 1983, Cmnd. 8878.

14.303 **Unpublished UK government documents.** For general guidelines and many examples, which can be adapted to government documents, see 14.221–31. The main depositories for unpublished government documents in the United Kingdom are the National Archives (NA) and the British Library (BL), both in London. Their catalogs are available online through the websites of the National Archives and the British Library. (The British Library is a division of the British Museum; before it was called the British Library, citations to documents housed therein used the abbreviation BM.) References usually include such classifications as Admiralty (Adm.), Chancery (C), Colonial Office (CO), Exchequer (E), Foreign Office (FO), or State Papers (SP) as well as the collection and volume numbers and, where relevant, the folio or page number(s). Among important collections in the British Library are the Cotton Manuscripts (with subdivisions named after Roman emperors, e.g., Cotton MSS, Caligula [Calig.] D.VII), the Harleian Manuscripts, the Sloane Manuscripts, and the Additional Manuscripts (Add. or Addit.).

1. Patent Rolls, 3 Rich. 2, pt. 1, m. 12d, NA (Calendar of Patent Rolls, 1377–1381, 470).

2. Hodgson to Halifax, 22 Feb. 1752, NA, CO 137:48.

3. Clarendon to Lumley, 16 Jan. 1869, NA, FO Belgium/133, no. 6.

4. [Henry Elsynge], "The moderne forme of the Parliaments of England," BL, Add. MSS 26645.

5. Minutes of the General Court, 17 Apr. 1733, 3:21, BL, Add. MSS 25545.

6. Letter of a Bristol Man, BL, Add. MSS 33029:152–55.

International Entities

14.304 **Intergovernmental bodies.** *The Bluebook* outlines the main reporters for international courts (such as the International Court of Justice), commissions, and tribunals. Also included are abbreviations for intergovernmental bodies such as the United Nations (and its principal organs), the European Union, and those devoted to specific areas such as human rights, trade, and health. The basic elements of citations to international law cases are similar to those used in US law citations (see 14.276–79); for examples, consult *The Bluebook*. (In addition to intergovernmental bodies, *The Bluebook* covers about three dozen jurisdictions outside the United States.) For treaties, see 14.290.

14.305 **United Nations documents.** The United Nations makes many of its documents available online (in English)—including those published by the General Assembly and the Security Council and dating back to the first General Assembly in 1946. *The Bluebook* provides guidance primarily for citing documents in the Official Records, but it considers the website of the United Nations an acceptable alternative. In general, list by the authorizing body (and the author or editor where appropriate), the topic or title of the paper, the document number or code (if any), and the date. Series and publication numbers, place of publication, and a page reference may also be included. For documents consulted online, include a URL as the final element in the citation (see 14.6–18).

1. UN Security Council, Resolution 2222, Protection of Civilians in Armed Conflict, S/RES/2222, ¶ 5 (May 27, 2015), http://www.un.org/en/sc/documents/resolutions/2015.shtml.

2. UN General Assembly, Resolution 67/18, Education for Democracy, A/RES/67/18 (Nov. 28, 2012), http://www.un.org/en/ga/67/resolutions.shtml.

3. S/RES/2222, ¶ 16.

15 · Author-Date References

Overview

15.1 **The scope of this chapter.** This chapter describes the second of Chicago's two systems of source citation, which uses parenthetical author-date references and a corresponding reference list. Because this system is similar in many respects to the notes and bibliography system discussed in chapter 14, much of the information from that chapter is not repeated here. For an introduction to source citations in general, including a discussion of systems other than the two recommended by Chicago, readers are encouraged to consult the overview in chapter 14 (14.1–18).

15.2 **Author-date references versus notes and bibliography.** Most of the recommendations in chapter 14 for how to style names of authors, titles of works, and other components in notes and bibliographies are identical for the author-date system described in this chapter. The author-date system differs primarily in its use of parenthetical text citations rather than citations in numbered notes and, in the bibliography (called a reference list in author-date style), the placement for the year of publication. For the use of notes with the author-date system, see 15.31.

15.3 **Notes and bibliography entries as models for author-date references.** Most of the examples in chapter 14 are readily adapted to the author-date citation style—in almost all cases by a different ordering or arrangement of elements. Most reference list entries are identical to entries in a bibliography except for the position of the year of publication, which in a reference list follows the author's name. Unlike bibliography entries (see 14.64), each entry in the reference list must correspond to a work cited in the text. Text citations differ from citations in notes by presenting only the author's last name and the year of publication, followed by a page number or other locator, if any. This chapter, by focusing on these and other differences, will show how to adapt any of the examples in chapter 14 to the author-date system.

15.4 **Sources consulted online.** For a detailed discussion of URLs and DOIs, access dates and revision dates, and other considerations for citing sources consulted online, see 14.6–18. Most types of sources consulted online can be cited by adding a URL (or, in some cases, the name of the bibliographic database) after the full facts of publication. For examples in the author-date style, see 15.9, under "Journal Article," and throughout 15.46–49 and 15.50–52. For more examples, see 14.161, 14.162, and throughout the discussions on periodicals (14.164–204) and elsewhere in chapter 14. For examples of access dates in author-date format, see 15.50.

Basic Format, with Examples and Variations

15.5 **The author-date system—overview.** The author-date system is used by many in the physical, natural, and social sciences and is recommended by Chicago for works in those areas. Sources are cited in the text, usually in parentheses, by the author's last (family) name, the publication date of the work cited, and a page number if needed. Full details appear in the reference list—usually titled "References" or "Works Cited"—in which the year of publication appears immediately after the author's name (see fig. 15.1). This arrangement makes it easy to follow a text citation to the corresponding full source in the reference list. (In electronic formats, text citations may be linked to their corresponding reference list entries.)

Text citations:

Like many other cultural fields, the video game industry is one that rewards novelty, especially when it is packaged in terms that are recognizable to consumers and critics (Lampel, Lant, and Shamsie 2000; Hutter 2011). . . . But the forefront of the industry finds continuous experimentation with the singular challenge of video gaming: how to create a convincing form of narrative storytelling that is nonetheless animated, perhaps uniquely so, by the actions of the users (Bissell 2011).

Reference list entries:

Bissell, Tom. 2011. *Extra Lives: Why Video Games Matter*. New York: Vintage Books.

Hutter, Michael. 2011. "Infinite Surprises: Value in the Creative Industries." In *The Worth of Goods: Valuation and Pricing in the Economy*, edited by Jens Beckert and Patrick Aspers, 201–20. New York: Oxford University Press.

Lampel, Joseph, Theresa Lant, and Jamal Shamsie. 2000. "Balancing Act: Learning from Organizing Practices in Cultural Industries." *Organization Science* 11 (3): 263–69.

For more examples of text citations and reference list entries, see 15.9. For a detailed discussion of reference lists, see 15.10–16 and 15.17–20. For text citations, see 15.21–31.

United States and the Secularization Thesis

is not sensible when, as in some of our data, cohort replacement and intracohort change work in opposite directions. In our data, cohort replacement always pushes aggregate religiosity down, but in some cases intracohort change pushes it up, although never by enough to offset the force of cohort replacement. In these instances, the cohort replacement component can be interpreted as an estimate of how much aggregate religiosity would have declined because of cohort replacement were it not for intracohort change in the other direction.

The graphical and linear decomposition methods provide distinct and complementary descriptions. In the graphical approach, multiple birth years (usually 10) are collapsed into a single cohort, and the three-survey moving averages provide a degree of smoothing within each cohort, but otherwise the points plotted show the full complexity of change between and within cohorts. By contrast, the statistical decomposition is based on raw values for each individual year of birth and survey year, from which the regression produces smooth trends.

REFERENCES

Baker, Joseph O'Brian, and Buster Smith. 2009. "None Too Simple: Examining Issues of Religious Nonbelief and Nonbelonging in the United States." *Journal for the Scientific Study of Religion* 48 (4): 719–33.

Bell, Andrew, and Kelvyn Jones. 2014. "Another 'Futile Quest'? A Simulation Study of Yang and Land's Hierarchical Age-Period-Cohort Model." *Demographic Research* 30: 333–60.

Berger, Peter, Grace Davie, and Effie Fokas. 2008. *Religious America, Secular Europe? A Theme and Variations*. Burlington, Vt.: Ashgate.

Bongaarts, John, and Tomáš Sobotka. 2012. "A Demographic Explanation for the Recent Rise in European Fertility." *Population and Development Review* 38 (1): 83–120.

Brenner, Philip S. 2011. "Exceptional Behavior or Exceptional Identity? Overreporting of Church Attendance in the U.S." *Public Opinion Quarterly* 75 (1): 19–41.

———. 2012. "Identity as a Determinant of the Overreporting of Church Attendance in Canada." *Journal for the Scientific Study of Religion* 51 (2): 377–85.

Bruce, Steve. 2011. *Secularization: In Defence of an Unfashionable Theory*. Oxford: Oxford University Press.

Chaves, Mark. 1989. "Secularization *and* Religious Revival: Evidence from U.S. Church Attendance Rates, 1972–1986." *Journal for the Scientific Study of Religion* 28 (4): 464–77.

———. 1991. "Family Structure and Protestant Church Attendance: The Sociological Basis of Cohort and Age Effects." *Journal for the Scientific Study of Religion* 30 (4): 501–14.

———. 2011. *American Religion: Contemporary Trends*. Princeton, N.J.: Princeton University Press.

Crockett, Alasdair, and David Voas. 2006. "Generations of Decline: Religious Change in Twentieth-Century Britain." *Journal for the Scientific Study of Religion* 45 (4): 567–84.

De Graaf, Nan Dirk. 2013. "Secularization: Theoretical Controversies Generating Empirical Research." Pp. 321–54 in *Handbook of Rational Choice Social Research*, edited by Rafael Wittek, Tom A. B. Snijders, and Victor Nee. Stanford, Calif.: Stanford University Press.

1553

FIGURE 15.1. Part of a reference list for a journal article in the social sciences. See 15.5, 15.6, 15.10–16.

15.6 **Basic structure of a reference list entry.** In a reference list entry, the year of publication is the second element, following the author's name. Otherwise, a reference list entry is structured like an entry in a bibliography (see 14.21): the elements are separated by periods, and the first-listed author's name, according to which the entry is alphabetized in the reference list, is usually inverted (last name first). Titles are capitalized headline-style unless they are in a language other than English (see 8.159, 11.6); titles of larger works such as books and journals are italicized; and titles of smaller works such as journal articles are presented in roman and enclosed in quotation marks (see 8.163, 14.86). Noun forms such as *editor*, *translator*, *volume*, and *edition* are abbreviated, but verb forms such as *edited by* and *translated by* are spelled out.

15.7 **Basic structure of an in-text citation.** In the author-date system, a citation in the text usually appears in parentheses and includes only the first two elements in a reference list—the author and the year of publication (hence the name of the system), with no intervening punctuation. A page number or other locator may be added, following a comma. Terms such as *editor* or *translator*, abbreviated in a reference list, are omitted from a text citation. In a parenthetical reference to two or more works, a semicolon usually separates each work from the next (but see 15.30).

15.8 **Page numbers and other locators.** In text citations, where reference is usually to a particular passage in a book or journal, only the page numbers pertaining to that passage are given. In reference lists, no page numbers are given for books; for easier location of journal articles or chapters or other sections of a book, the beginning and ending page numbers of the entire article or chapter are given. See also 15.23.

15.9 **Author-date references—examples and variations.** The examples that follow provide an overview of the author-date system, featuring books and journal articles as models. Each example includes a reference list entry and a corresponding text citation. For the sake of consistency, text citations are presented in parentheses, though they do not always appear that way in practice (see 15.28). For more examples, consult the sections dealing with specific types of works throughout this chapter.

Book with Single Author or Editor

For a book with a single author, invert the name in the reference list; in the text, include only the last name. Punctuate and capitalize as shown. To cite a specific passage, a page number or range is included in a text citation, separated from the year by a comma (a comma is also used between nonconsecutive page references). Page numbers are not included in a reference list unless the entry is for a chapter (see "Chapter in an Edited Book," below). See also 9.60–64.

Strayed, Cheryl. 2012. *Wild: From Lost to Found on the Pacific Crest Trail.* New York: Alfred A. Knopf.

(Strayed 2012, 87–88)
(Strayed 2012, 261, 265)

A book with an editor in place of an author includes the abbreviation *ed.* (*editor*; for more than one editor, use *eds.*). Note that the text citation does not include *ed.*

Daum, Meghan, ed. 2015. *Selfish, Shallow, and Self-Absorbed: Sixteen Writers on the Decision Not to Have Kids.* New York: Picador.

(Daum 2015, 32)

Book with Multiple Authors

For a book with two authors, only the first-listed name is inverted in the reference list.

Grazer, Brian, and Charles Fishman. 2015. *A Curious Mind: The Secret to a Bigger Life.* New York: Simon & Schuster.

(Grazer and Fishman 2015, 188)

For a book with three authors, adapt as follows:

Berkman, Alexander, Henry Bauer, and Carl Nold. 2011. *Prison Blossoms: Anarchist Voices from . . .*

(Berkman, Bauer, and Nold 2011, 7–10)

For a book with four or more authors, include all the authors in the reference list entry (see also 14.76). Word order and punctuation are the same as for two or three authors. In the text, however, cite only the last name of the first-listed author, followed by *et al.* (see also 15.29).

(Haček et al. 2015, 384)

Book with Author plus Editor or Translator

In the reference list, do not abbreviate *Edited by* or *Translated by*. See also 14.104.

García Márquez, Gabriel. 1988. *Love in the Time of Cholera*. Translated by Edith Grossman. London: Cape.

(García Márquez 1988, 242–55)

Chapter in an Edited Book

In citations of a chapter or similar part of an edited book, include the chapter author; the chapter title, in quotation marks; and the editor. Precede the title of the book with *In*. Note the location of the page range for the chapter in the reference list entry. See also 14.106–12.

Gould, Glenn. 1984. "Streisand as Schwarzkopf." In *The Glenn Gould Reader*, edited by Tim Page, 308–11. New York: Vintage Books.

(Gould 1984, 310)

Journal Article

Citations of journals typically include the volume and issue number and date of publication. The volume number follows the italicized journal title in roman and with no intervening punctuation. A specific page reference is included in the text; the page range for an article is included in the reference list, preceded by a colon. Authors should record the full information for the issue, including issue number, even if a journal is paginated consecutively across a volume or if the month or season appears with the year.

Bagley, Benjamin. 2015. "Loving Someone in Particular." *Ethics* 125, no. 2 (January): 477–507.

(Bagley 2015, 484–85)

The URL in the following example indicates that the article was consulted online; in this case, it is based on a DOI and is preferred to the URL that appears with the article (see 14.7, 14.8). Some publishers will use the URL as the basis of a link to the cited resource. For access dates (not shown here), see 14.176.

Liu, Jui-Ch'i. 2015. "Beholding the Feminine Sublime: Lee Miller's War Photography." *Signs* 40, no. 2 (Winter): 308–19. https://doi.org/10.1086/678242.

(Liu 2015, 312)

For the use of parentheses with issue numbers (as for a journal for which the month or season is unavailable or otherwise not listed), see 15.47. For the use of a colon with volume numbers (as for a journal for which only volume and year are listed), see 15.48.

Reference Lists and Text Citations

Reference Lists

15.10 **Function and placement of reference lists.** In the author-date system, the reference list is the prime vehicle for documentation. The text citations (see 15.21–31) are merely pointers to the full list. A reference list, like other types of bibliographies (see 14.64), is normally placed at the end of a work, preceding the index, if there is one. In a multiauthor book or a textbook (or any book to be offered in the form of individual chapters), each chapter is usually followed by its own reference list, in which case the list is preceded by a subhead such as References or Literature Cited. Journal articles are always treated this way.

15.11 **Alphabetical arrangement of reference list entries.** A reference list is arranged alphabetically (except in a numbered reference system; see 14.3) and should generally not be divided into sections. (Types of sources that are not readily adapted to author-date style are often better cited in notes; see, for example, 15.58–59.) All sources are listed by the last names of the authors (or, if no author or editor is given, by the title or, failing that, a descriptive phrase). Rules for alphabetizing an index (see 16.56–93) apply also to a reference list, with the modifications described in 14.66 and 15.17–20. For an illustration, see figure 15.1.

15.12 **Authors' names in reference list entries.** In a reference list as in a bibliography, record the authors' names as they appear on the title page or at the head of an article or chapter, with the exceptions noted in 14.72–84. Some publications, especially in the natural sciences, use initials rather than full given names (see 15.33). Where this practice is followed, an exception should be made where two authors share the same initials and last name. For text citations, see 15.22.

15.13 **Titles in reference list entries.** Titles and subtitles of books, articles, and other works in reference lists should be treated according to the rules set forth in 14.85–99 and exemplified throughout chapter 14. It is recognized, however, that some publications—particularly journals in the natural sciences—generally prefer sentence-style capitalization for titles (see 8.158), tend not to use quotation marks or italics, and abbreviate journal titles (see 15.46).

15.14 **Placement of dates in reference list entries.** Because the text citations consist of the last name of the author or authors (or that of the editor or translator) and the year of publication, the year in the reference list appears directly after the name, not with the publication details. (When the date of publication includes month and day, the year may be repeated to avoid any confusion; for an example, see 15.49.) This arrangement facilitates easy lookup of reference list entries.

Pager, Devah, and David S. Pedulla. 2015. "Race, Self-Selection, and the Job Search Process." *American Journal of Sociology* 120, no. 4 (January): 1005–54. https://doi.org/10.1086/681072.

Unger, Roberto Mangabeira, and Lee Smolin. 2014. *The Singular Universe and the Reality of Time: A Proposal in Natural Philosophy*. Cambridge: Cambridge University Press.

For *n.d.* and the use of access dates for sources consulted online, see 15.44 and 15.50. See also 15.55.

15.15 **Abbreviations in reference list entries.** In reference lists, spell out such phrases as *edited by* or *translated by*, which are capitalized if following a period. On the other hand, noun forms such as *editor* (*ed.*) and *translator* (*trans.*) are always abbreviated, as are such standard bibliographic terms as *volume* (*vol.*), number (*no.*), and so forth. Abbreviations may be used with greater frequency as long as they are used consistently. For example, *University* may be abbreviated to *Univ.*, and months given with journal citations may be abbreviated (see 10.39). See also 15.33, 15.46.

15.16 **Single author versus several authors—reference list order.** As in a bibliography (chapter 14), a single-author entry in a reference list precedes a multiauthor entry beginning with the same name. Only the first author's name is inverted. Successive entries by two or more authors in which only the first author's name is the same are alphabetized according to the coauthors' last names (regardless of how many coauthors there are).

Lamont, Michèle. 2012. "Toward a Comparative Sociology of Valuation and Evaluation." *Annual Review of Sociology* 38 (August): 201–22. https://doi.org/10.1146/annurev-soc-070308-120022.

Lamont, Michèle, and Nicolas Duvoux. 2014. "How Neo-liberalism Has Transformed France's Symbolic Boundaries?" *French Politics, Culture & Society* 32, no. 2 (Summer): 57–75. https://doi.org/10.3167/fpcs.2014.320208.

Lamont, Michèle, Jason Kaufman, and Michael Moody. 2000. "The Best of the Brightest: Definitions of the Ideal Self among Prize-Winning Students." *Sociological Forum* 15, no. 2 (June): 187–224. http://www.jstor.org/stable/684814.

Lamont, Michèle, and Ann Swidler. 2014. "Methodological Pluralism and the Possibilities and Limits of Interviewing." *Qualitative Sociology* 37, no. 2 (June): 153–71. https://doi.org/10.1007/s11133-014-9274-z.

The 3-Em Dash for Repeated Names in a Reference List

15.17 **The 3-em dash in reference lists—some caveats.** The advice in this section, which explains how to use the 3-em dash to stand in for repeated reference list entries under the same name, is aimed primarily at publishers and editors. Authors usually should not use the 3-em dash for repeated names in their manuscripts. Among other potential pitfalls, 3-em dashes do not work in computerized sorts (i.e., all entries with 3-em dashes will line up in one place). Moreover, an incorrectly applied dash may obscure an important detail—for example, the abbreviation *ed.* or *trans.* Publishers, too, may decide not to apply 3-em dashes: 3-em dashes make it impractical to present entries outside the context of the list (e.g., in a pop-up box or when linking directly from in-text citation to reference list entry) and can hide entries from bibliographic databases, both of which are concerns for electronic publication formats. Where 3-em dashes are not used, simply repeat author name(s) and sort the entries as described throughout this section. See also 6.94.

15.18 **Chronological order for repeated names in a reference list.** For successive entries by the same author(s), translator(s), editor(s), or compiler(s), a 3-em dash replaces the name(s) after the first appearance (but see 15.17). The entries are arranged chronologically by year of publication in ascending order, *not* alphabetized by title (as in a bibliography; see 14.71). Undated works designated *n.d.* or *forthcoming* follow all dated works (see 15.44–45).

Schuman, Howard, and Jacqueline Scott. 1987. "Problems in the Use of Survey Questions to Measure Public Opinion." *Science* 236 (4804): 957–59. https://doi.org/10.1126/science.236.4804.957.

———. 1989. "Generations and Collective Memories." *American Sociological Review* 54, no. 3 (June): 359–81. http://www.jstor.org/stable/2095611.

Note that the 3-em dash *cannot* stand in for the same two or more authors as in the previous entry if they appear in a different order. The following two entries are alphabetized as if they are by two different sets of authors (i.e., "Jean" comes before "John"):

Comaroff, Jean, and John Comaroff, eds. 1993. *Modernity and Its Malcontents: Ritual and Power in Postcolonial Africa*. Chicago: University of Chicago Press.

Comaroff, John, and Jean Comaroff. 1991–97. *Of Revelation and Revolution*. 2 vols. Chicago: University of Chicago Press.

15.19 **The 3-em dash with edited, translated, or compiled works.** The 3-em dash replaces the preceding name or names only, not an added *ed.*, *trans.*, *comp.*, or whatever. The chronological order is maintained, regardless of the added abbreviation.

Woodward, David. 1977. *The All-American Map: Wax Engraving and Its Influence on Cartography*. Chicago: University of Chicago Press.

———, ed. 1987. *Art and Cartography: Six Historical Essays*. Chicago: University of Chicago Press.

———. 1996. *Catalogue of Watermarks in Italian Printed Maps, ca. 1540–1600*. Chicago: University of Chicago Press.

Woodward is the author of the first and third items, editor of the second.

15.20 **Reference list entries with same author(s), same year.** Two or more works by the same author in the same year must be differentiated by the addition of *a*, *b*, and so forth (regardless of whether they were authored, edited, compiled, or translated) and are listed alphabetically by title. Text citations consist of author and year plus letter.

Fogel, Robert William. 2004a. *The Escape from Hunger and Premature Death, 1700–2100: Europe, America, and the Third World*. New York: Cambridge University Press.

———. 2004b. "Technophysio Evolution and the Measurement of Economic Growth." *Journal of Evolutionary Economics* 14, no. 2 (June): 217–21. https://doi.org/10.1007/s00191-004-0188-x.

(Fogel 2004b, 218)
(Fogel 2004a, 45–46)

When works by the same two or more authors list their names in a different order, then *a*, *b*, and so forth cannot be used. See 15.18.

Text Citations

15.21 **Agreement of text citation and reference list entry.** For each author-date citation in the text, there must be a corresponding entry in the reference list under the same name and date. It is the author's responsibility to ensure such agreement as well as the accuracy of the reference (see 2.32). Among other things, specific page references to a journal article, when given in a text citation, must fall within the range of pages given for the article in the reference list entry. Manuscript editors can help authors by cross-checking text citations and reference lists and rectifying or querying any discrepancies or omissions (see 2.63).

15.22 **Text citations—basic form.** An author-date citation in running text or at the end of a block quotation usually consists of the last (family) name of the author, followed by the year of publication of the work in question. In this context, *author* may refer not only to one or more authors or an institution but also to one or more editors, translators, or compilers. No punctuation appears between author and date. Abbreviations such as *ed.* or *trans.* are omitted. See also 15.23.

Text citations:

(Hetherington and Rudolph 2015)   (Grove 2015)

References:

Grove, John. "Calhoun and Conservative Reform." 2015. *American Political Thought* 4, no. 2 (March): 203–27. https://doi.org/10.1086/680389.

Hetherington, Marc J., and Thomas J. Rudolph. 2015. *Why Washington Won't Work: Polarization, Political Trust, and the Governing Crisis.* Chicago: University of Chicago Press.

To refer to two or more sources in the same text citation, separate the sources with semicolons (but see 15.30).

(Hetherington and Rudolph 2015; Grove 2015)

Where two or more works by different authors with the same last name are listed in a reference list, the text citation must include an initial (or two initials or a given name if necessary).

Text citations:

(C. Doershuk 2017)   (J. Doershuk 2016)

References:

Doershuk, Carl. 2017. . . .   Doershuk, John. 2016. . . .

15.23 **Page and volume numbers or other specific locators in text citations.** When a specific page, section, equation, or other division of the work is cited, it follows the date, preceded by a comma. When a volume as a whole is referred to, without a page number, *vol.* is used. For volume plus page, only a colon is needed. The *n* in the Fischer and Siple example below indicates "note" (see 14.157). The last example shows one strategy for citing a specific location (e.g., a section heading) in a work that contains no page or section numbers or other numerical signposts—the case for some electronic formats (see 14.160).

(Piaget 1980, 74)
(LaFree 2010, 413, 417–18)
(Claussen 2015, para. 2.15) *or* (Claussen 2015, ¶ 2.15)
(Johnson 1979, sec. 24) *or* (Johnson 1979, § 24)
(Fowler and Hoyle 1965, eq. 87)
(Hsu 2017, chap. 4)
(García 1987, vol. 2)
(García 1987, 2:345)
(Barnes 1998, 2:354–55, 3:29)
(Fischer and Siple 1990, 212n3)
(Hellman 2017, under "The Battleground")

Some journals omit page numbers in citations of other journal articles except when citing a direct quotation.

15.24 **Additional material in text citations.** The parentheses that enclose a text citation may also include a comment, separated from the citation by a semicolon (see also 15.30).

(Mandolan 2017; *t*-tests are used here)

15.25 **Text citations in relation to surrounding text and punctuation.** Except at the end of block quotations (see 15.26), author-date citations are usually placed just before a mark of punctuation though need not be if the sentence would otherwise not require it. See also 15.28.

> Recent literature has examined long-run price drifts following initial public offerings (Ritter 1991; Loughran and Ritter 1995), stock splits (Ikenberry, Rankine, and Stice 1996), seasoned equity offerings (Loughran and Ritter 1995), and equity repurchases (Ikenberry, Lakonishok, and Vermaelen 1995).
> *but*
> There is evidence, for example, that the negative outcomes associated with family structure instability are more pronounced for young children as compared with older children (Sigle-Rushton and McLanahan 2004) and for boys as compared with girls (Cooper et al. 2011).

Where the author's name appears in the text, it need not be repeated in the parenthetical citation. Note that the date should immediately follow the author's name, even if the name is used in the possessive. This usage serves the logic and economy of the author-date style. (For a reference to a person rather than the work, it may be appropriate to include the given name on first mention.)

> Fiorina et al. (2005) and Fischer and Hout (2006) reach more or less the same conclusions. In contrast, Abramowitz and Saunders (2005) suggest that the mass public is deeply divided between red states and blue states and between churchgoers and secular voters.

> Tufte's (2001) excellent book on chart design warns against a common error.

15.26 **Text citations in relation to direct quotations.** Although a source citation normally follows a direct quotation, it may precede the quotation—especially if such a placement allows the date to appear with the author's name.

> As Edward Tufte points out, "A graphical element may carry data information and also perform a design function usually left to non-data-ink" (2001, 139).
> *or*
> As Edward Tufte (2001, 139) points out, "A graphical element may carry data information and also perform a design function usually left to non-data-ink."

When the source of a block quotation is given in parentheses at the end of the quotation, the opening parenthesis appears *after* the final punctuation mark of the quoted material. No period either precedes or follows the closing parenthesis.

> If you happen to be fishing, and you get a strike, and whatever it is starts off with the preliminaries of a vigorous fight; and by and by, looking down over the side through the glassy water, you see a rosy golden gleam, the mere specter of a fish, shining below in the clear depths; and when you look again a sort of glory of golden light flashes and dazzles as it circles nearer beneath and around and under the boat; . . . and you land a slim and graceful and impossibly beautiful three-foot goldfish, whose fierce and vivid yellow is touched around the edges with a violent red—when all these things happen to you, fortunate but bewildered fisherman, then you may know you have been fishing in the Galapagos Islands and have taken a Golden Grouper. (Pinchot 1930, 123)

See also 13.70–72.

15.27 **Several references to the same source.** When the same page (or page range) in the same source is cited more than once in one paragraph, the parenthetical citation can be placed after the last reference or at the end of the paragraph (but preceding the final period). When referring to different pages in the same source, however, include a full parenthetical citation at the first reference; subsequent citations need only include page numbers.

> Complexion figures prominently in Morgan's descriptions. When Jasper compliments his mother's choice of car (a twelve-cylinder Mediterranean roadster with leather and wood-grained interior), "his cheeks blotch indignantly, painted by jealousy and rage" (Chaston 2000, 47). On the other hand, his mother's mask never changes, her "even-tanned good looks" (56), "burnished visage" (101), and "air-brushed confidence" (211) providing the foil to the drama in her midst.

15.28 **Syntactic considerations with text citations.** An author-date citation is a form of bibliographic shorthand that corresponds to a fully cited work; it does not refer to a person. Note how, in the examples in 15.25 and 15.26, the wording distinguishes between authors and works. A locution such as "in Smith 2009," though technically proper, is usually best avoided except as part of a parenthetical citation. To help readers identify the source citation, prefer "in Smith (2009)" or, for example, "in Smith's (1999) study." Note that square brackets should be used in parenthetical text references that require additional parentheses, as in the second example (see 6.101).

There are at least three works that satisfy the criteria outlined in Smith's (1999) study (see Rowen 2006; Bettelthorp 2004a; Choi 2008).

These processes have, in turn, affected the way many Latin Americans are treated in the United States (see, e.g., Haviland [2003, 767] on how US courts disregard the existence of indigenous languages and "reluctantly" make allowance only for Spanish in translation services).

15.29 **Text citations of works with more than three authors.** For more than three authors (or in some science publications, more than two), only the name of the first author is used, followed by *et al.* (and others). Note that *et al.* is not italicized in text citations.

(Schonen et al. 2017)
According to the data collected by Schonen et al. (2017), . . .

If a reference list includes another work of the same date that would also be abbreviated as "Schonen et al." but whose coauthors are different persons or listed in a different order, the text citations must distinguish between them. In such cases, the first two authors (or the first three) should be cited, followed by *et al.*

(Schonen, Baker, et al. 2017) (Schonen, Brooks, et al. 2017)

Alternatively, a shortened title, enclosed in commas, may be added. In the following examples, *et al.* refers to different coauthors, so *a*, *b*, and so on cannot be used (see 15.20):

(Schonen et al., "Tilting at Windmills," 2017)
(Schonen et al., "Gasoline Farmers," 2017)

For treatment of multiple authors in a bibliography or reference list, see 14.76, 15.9 (under "Book with Multiple Authors"), 15.16.

15.30 **Multiple text references.** Two or more references in a single parenthetical citation are separated by semicolons. The order in which they are given may depend on what is being cited, and in what order, or it may reflect the relative importance of the items cited. If neither criterion applies, alphabetical or chronological order may be appropriate. Unless the order is prescribed by a particular journal style, the decision is the author's.

(Armstrong and Malacinski 1989; Beigl 1989; Pickett and White 1985)

Additional works by the same author(s) are cited by date only, separated by commas except where page numbers are required.

(Whittaker 1967, 1975; Wiens 1989a, 1989b)
(Wong 1999, 328; 2000, 475; García 1998, 67)

Additional references prefaced by "see also" follow any other references (see also 15.24).

(Guest et al. 2006; see also Stolle et al. 2008; Rahn et al. 2009)

15.31 **Author-date system with notes.** Where footnotes or endnotes are used to supplement the author-date system, source citations within notes are treated in the same way as in text (see fig. 15.2).

1. James Wilson has noted that "no politician ever lost votes by denouncing the bureaucracy" (1989, 235). Yet little is actually ever done to bring major reforms to the system.

For the use of notes with legal-style citations, see 15.58. For more on footnotes and endnotes, see 14.24–60.

Turning to the econometric evidence, I present some estimates of changes in expected retirement ages drawn from the Bank of Italy panel of household-level data. The methodology adopted is a "difference-in-difference" estimator and draws heavily on the work of Attanasio and Brugiavini (1997) described above. In particular, the basic identifying assumption is that the 1992 reform is the only relevant change (as far as differential labor supply decisions are concerned), and I therefore exploit the reform to measure behavioral responses before and after the event. The first difference is the time difference, the second that between groups. Groups in the population are assumed to be exogenously determined, and, given the availability of panel data, I can control for individuals' characteristics throughout (Venti and Wise 1995). It is worth recalling at this stage that the Amato reform of 1992 has gradually postponed the normal retirement age but has not tackled the early retirement option, apart from restricting eligibility requirements in the public sector.[47]

47. The normal retirement age gradually moves from sixty to sixty-five for men. The early retirement option is available (Hoy 1996), but public-sector employees need thirty-five years of contributions to become eligible in place of the previous twenty years (fifteen for married women). In the public sector, normal retirement age has been sixty-five throughout.

FIGURE 15.2. A sample of text with both parenthetical text citations and a footnote. See 15.31.

Author-Date References: Special Cases

15.32 **Items not necessarily covered in chapter 14.** The majority of examples in chapter 14 can be adapted to the author-date system simply by moving the year of publication to follow the author's name (see 15.3). This section focuses on special cases not necessarily covered there or for which a suitable author-date form may not be apparent.

Author's Name

15.33 **Publications preferring initials for authors' names.** The reference lists in some publications, especially journals in the natural sciences, always use initials instead of given names. When periods are used, space appears between them (Wells, H. G.); when periods are omitted, as in some journals' styles, no comma intervenes between last name and initials, and no space appears between the initials (Wells HG). Chicago recommends using the form of the name as it appears with the source unless otherwise required.

15.34 **Author-date format for anonymous works (no listed author).** If the author, editor, translator, or the like for the work is unknown, the reference list entry should normally begin with the title. An initial article is ignored in alphabetizing. Text citations may refer to a short form of the title but must include the first word (other than an initial article). See also 15.37, 15.39, 15.49, 14.79.

Stanze in lode della donna brutta. 1547. Florence.

A True and Sincere Declaration of the Purpose and Ends of the Plantation Begun in Virginia, of the Degrees Which It Hath Received, and Means by Which It Hath Been Advanced. 1610. London.

(*True and Sincere Declaration* 1610)
(*Stanze in lode della donna brutta* 1547) *or* (*Stanze* 1547)

As in notes and bibliographies, bracket a name in reference lists and text citations if the authorship is known or guessed at but was omitted on the title page (use a question mark to indicate uncertainty). (Note that in the Hawkes example, both New York and Tea Party are hyphenated in the original source.)

[Hawkes, James?]. 1834. *A Retrospect of the Boston Tea-Party, with a Memoir of George R. T. Hewes*. By a Citizen of New-York. New-York.

[Horsley, Samuel]. 1796. *On the Prosodies of the Greek and Latin Languages.* London.

([Horsley] 1796) ([Hawkes?] 1834)

Works explicitly attributed to "Anonymous" (e.g., on the title page or at the head of the work) should be cited accordingly.

Anonymous. 2015. "Our Family Secrets." *Annals of Internal Medicine* 163, no. 4 (August): 321. https://doi.org/10.7326/M14-2168.

(Anonymous 2015)

15.35 **Pseudonyms in author-date references.** Pseudonyms are indicated in reference lists in exactly the same manner as they are in bibliographies (see 14.80, 14.81). Text citations should refer to the first-listed name and will omit the indication *pseud.*

Centinel [pseud.]. 1981. Letters. In *The Complete Anti-Federalist*, edited by Herbert J. Storing. Chicago: University of Chicago Press.

Stendhal [Marie-Henri Beyle]. 1925. *The Charterhouse of Parma.* Translated by C. K. Scott-Moncrieff. New York: Boni and Liveright.

(Stendhal 1925) (Centinel 1981)

See also 14.82. For examples of screen names in author-date references, see 15.52.

15.36 **Editor in place of author in text citations.** For works listed by editor(s) or compiler(s) or translator(s) in a reference list, abbreviations such as *ed.* or *eds.*, *comp.* or *comps.*, or *trans.* following the name are omitted in text citations.

Silverstein, Theodore, trans. 1974. *Sir Gawain and the Green Knight.* Chicago: University of Chicago Press.

Soltes, Ori Z., ed. 1999. *Georgia: Art and Civilization through the Ages.* London: Philip Wilson.

(Silverstein 1974) (Soltes 1999)

15.37 **Organization as author in author-date references.** If a publication issued by an organization, association, or corporation carries no personal author's name on the title page, the organization may be listed as author in the reference list, even if it is also given as publisher. To facilitate shorter parenthetical text citations, the organization may be listed under an abbreviation, in which case the entry must be alphabetized under that abbreviation (rather than the spelled-out name) in the reference list.

ISO (International Organization for Standardization). 1997. *Information and Documentation—Rules for the Abbreviation of Title Words and Titles of Publications*. ISO 4:1997. Paris: ISO.

NISO (National Information Standards Organization). 2010. *Bibliographic References*. ANSI/NISO Z39.29-2005. Bethesda, MD: NISO, approved June 9, 2005; reaffirmed May 13, 2010.

(NISO 2010) (ISO 1997)

See also 15.55, 14.259.

Title of Work

15.38 **Publications preferring sentence-style capitalization for titles.** Especially in the natural sciences, many publications that use a version of the author-date style prefer sentence-style capitalization for cited titles (except, usually, the titles of journals, which are often abbreviated; see 15.46). In sentence style, only the first word in a title or a subtitle and any proper names are capitalized (see 8.158). Some publications do not capitalize the first word in a subtitle unless it is a proper noun. Works that prefer this style also may not use quotation marks for chapter or article titles or italics for titles of books (and sometimes journals). (Such usage is normally limited to reference lists; in the text, the use of headline-style capitalization, quotation marks, and italics for titles is the norm for English-language publications.) Though Chicago recommends headline style and the use of quotation marks or italics in both its systems of documentation, these forms can be readily adapted to other, sparer systems.

15.39 **Citing author-date sources by title.** Works for which no author is credited or can be determined (including any organization or publisher as author; see 15.37, 15.49) are listed by title in a reference list entry. In the text, a short version of the title (up to four words) may be used. Unlike short forms for titles in notes and bibliography style (see 14.33), short forms for in-text references must include the first word of the title (aside from any article) to facilitate alphabetical lookup. For examples, see 15.34.

Books

EDITION, VOLUME, OR COLLECTION

15.40 **Reprint editions and modern editions—more than one date.** When citing a reprint or modern edition in the author-date system, it is sometimes desirable to include the original date of publication. Whether or not any information about the original publication is included, the original date is listed first, in parentheses. If the pagination of the original edition does not match that of the reprint, indicate the edition cited.

Austen, Jane. (1813) 2003. *Pride and Prejudice*. London: T. Egerton. Reprint, New York: Penguin Classics. Citations refer to the Penguin edition.

Darwin, Charles. (1859) 1964. *On the Origin of Species*. Facsimile of the first edition, with an introduction by Ernest Mayr. Cambridge, MA: Harvard University Press.

Maitland, Frederic W. (1898) 1998. *Roman Canon Law in the Church of England*. Reprint, Union, NJ: Lawbook Exchange.

The parentheses are rendered as square brackets in the in-text citation (see 6.101).

(Austen [1813] 2003)   (Darwin [1859] 1964)   (Maitland [1898] 1998)

For more than one work by the same author, the first date determines placement in the reference list (see 15.18).

Maitland, Frederic W. (1898) 1998. *Roman Canon Law in the Church of England*. Reprint, Union, NJ: Lawbook Exchange.

———. (1909) 1926. *Equity, Also the Forms of Action at Common Law: Two Courses of Lectures*. Edited by A. H. Chaytor and W. J. Whittaker. Reprint, Cambridge: Cambridge University Press.

When the original date is less important to the discussion, use the date of the modern source. The date of original publication may be included at the end of the reference list entry but need not be.

Trollope, Anthony. 1977. *The Claverings*. With a new introduction by Norman Donaldson. New York: Dover. First published 1866–67.

———. 1983. *He Knew He Was Right*. 2 vols. in one. New York: Dover. First published 1869.

(Trollope 1977)   (Trollope 1983)

15.41 **Multivolume works published over more than one year.** When a multivolume, multiyear work is included as an entry in the reference list (as in the Tillich example below), the range of dates for the work as a whole follows the author's name. The corresponding text citation should include a volume number with any references to specific page numbers or to cite a specific volume (see also 15.23). When an individual volume is listed (as in the Hayek example), the date for that volume should follow the name of the author; information about the work as a whole follows information about the individual volume. If the work has not yet been completed, the date of the first volume is followed by an en dash (with no space between the en dash and the punctuation that follows). Text citations of volumes listed individually in the reference list do *not* include the volume number, even with references to specific page numbers. See also 14.116–22. For en dashes with numbers, see 6.78, 6.79, 9.64.

Hayek, F. A. 2011. *The Constitution of Liberty: The Definitive Edition*. Edited by Ronald Hamowy. Vol. 17 of *The Collected Works of F. A. Hayek*, edited by Bruce Caldwell. Chicago: University of Chicago Press, 1988–.

Tillich, Paul. 1951–63. *Systematic Theology*. 3 vols. Chicago: University of Chicago Press.

(Tillich 1951–63, 1:133)   (Tillich 1951–63, vol. 2)   (Hayek 2011, 329)

15.42 **Cross-references to multiauthor books in reference lists.** To avoid repeating information, individual contributions to an edited volume may include cross-references to an entry for the volume as a whole. Note that cross-references to other titles in the reference list take the form of text citations but without any parentheses.

Draper, Joan E. 1987. "Paris by the Lake: Sources of Burnham's Plan of Chicago." In Zukowsky 1987, 107–19.

Harrington, Elaine. 1987. "International Influences on Henry Hobson Richardson's Glessner House." In Zukowsky 1987, 189–207.

Zukowsky, John, ed. 1987. *Chicago Architecture, 1872–1922: Birth of a Metropolis*. Munich: Prestel-Verlag in association with the Art Institute of Chicago.

This approach is best used only if more than a few individual contributions to the same volume are cited or if the volume itself is also cited in the text. Otherwise, include full publication details in the entry for each individual contribution. See also 14.107.

Draper, Joan E. 1987. "Paris by the Lake: Sources of Burnham's Plan of Chicago." In *Chicago Architecture, 1872–1922: Birth of a Metropolis*, edited by John

Zukowsky, 107–19. Munich: Prestel-Verlag in association with the Art Institute of Chicago.

15.43 **Author-date style for letters in published collections.** In the author-date system, letters in published collections should be cited by the date of the collection. The dates of individual correspondence should be woven into the text. The material in the examples at 14.111 could be cited as follows:

Adams, Henry. 1930. *Letters of Henry Adams, 1858–1891.* Edited by Worthington Chauncey Ford. Boston: Houghton Mifflin.
White, E. B. 1976. *Letters of E. B. White.* Edited by Dorothy Lobrano Guth. New York: Harper & Row.

In a letter to Charles Milnes Gaskell from London, March 30, 1868 (Adams 1930, 141), Adams wrote . . .

White (1976, 273) sent Ross an interoffice memo on May 2, 1946, pointing out that . . .

FACTS OF PUBLICATION

15.44 **No date of publication in author-date references.** When the publication date of a book or other work cannot be ascertained, the abbreviation *n.d.* takes the place of the year in the reference list entry and text citations. Though it follows a period in the reference list, *n.d.* remains lowercased to avoid conflation with the author's name; in text citations, it is preceded by a comma. A guessed-at date may be substituted (in brackets, with a question mark to indicate uncertainty). See also 14.132, 15.18.

Nano, Jasmine L. [1750?]. *Title of Work* . . .
———. n.d. *Title of Another Work* . . .

(Nano [1750?])   (Nano, n.d.)

For the use of *n.d.* for website content cited by access date, see 15.50. See also 15.54.

15.45 **"Forthcoming" in author-date references.** Like *n.d.* (see 15.44), *forthcoming* can stand in place of the date in author-date references. It should be reserved for books under contract with a publisher and already titled but for which the date of publication is not yet known. If page numbers are available, they should be given as needed. Books not under contract are treated as unpublished manuscripts (see 14.216). In text citations, *forthcoming* is preceded by a comma. See also 14.146.

Faraday, Carry. Forthcoming. "Protean Photography." In *Seven Trips beyond the Asteroid Belt*, edited by James Oring. Cape Canaveral, FL: Launch Press.

(Faraday, forthcoming)

Periodicals

15.46 **Publications preferring abbreviations for journal titles.** In many publications in the sciences, journal titles are abbreviated (often with periods omitted) unless they consist of only one word. ISO 4, a standard developed by the International Organization for Standardization, is the main authority for abbreviations of words in serial titles (bibliog. 4.7). Standard abbreviations for scientific journals may also be found in *BIOSIS Serial Sources* and through the NLM Catalog, a service of the US National Library of Medicine, among other resources (bibliog. 4.5). For more detailed information, including lists of additional resources, see the latest edition of *Scientific Style and Format* or the *AMA Manual of Style* (bibliog. 1.1).

15.47 **Parentheses or comma with issue number.** Though authors are encouraged to record all available data for their manuscripts (see 15.9, under "Journal Article"), sometimes only a volume and issue number will be available (and in some cases, it may be a publisher's preferred style not to record a month or season). When that is the case, the issue number is placed in parentheses. When only an issue number is used, it is set off by commas and not enclosed in parentheses. Compare 15.48.

Glass, Jennifer, and Philip Levchak. 2014. "Red States, Blue States, and Divorce: Understanding the Impact of Conservative Protestantism on Regional Variation in Divorce Rates." *American Journal of Sociology* 119 (4): 1002–46. https://doi.org/10.1086/674703.

Meyerovitch, Eva. 1959. "The Gnostic Manuscripts of Upper Egypt." *Diogenes*, no. 25, 84–117.

15.48 **Colon with volume number.** Authors are encouraged to record all available data for their manuscripts (see 15.9, under "Journal Article"). Sometimes, however, there is no issue number, or it may be intentionally omitted (usually according to a publisher's preferred style), either for a reference to a journal that is paginated continuously throughout a volume or when a month or season is included. When there is no issue number, and where no month or season is recorded, the page number reference follows the volume number, separated by a colon and with no intervening space. If the month or season is included, it is enclosed in parentheses, and a space follows the colon. Compare 15.47.

Gunderson, Alex R., and Manuel Leal. 2015. "Patterns of Thermal Constraint on Ectotherm Activity." *American Naturalist* 185:653–64. https://doi.org/10.1086/680849.

but

Gunderson, Alex R., and Manuel Leal. 2015. "Patterns of Thermal Constraint on Ectotherm Activity." *American Naturalist* 185 (May): 653–64. https://doi.org/10.1086/680849.

15.49 **Newspapers and magazines in reference lists.** It is usually sufficient to cite newspaper and magazines articles entirely within the text—a strategy that is identical in form in both systems of citation. See 14.198. If a reference list entry is needed, repeat the year of publication with the month and day to avoid any confusion.

Kauffman, Stanley. 1989. Review of *A Dry White Season* (film), directed by Euzhan Palcy. *New Republic*, October 9, 1989, 24–25.

Meikle, James. 2015. "Nearly 75% of Men and 65% of Women in UK to Be Overweight by 2030—Study." *Guardian* (UK edition), May 5, 2015. http://www.theguardian.com/society/2015/may/05/obesity-crisis-projections-uk-2030-men-women.

If a newspaper article is unsigned, the title of the newspaper stands in place of the author.

New York Times. 2002. "In Texas, Ad Heats Up Race for Governor." July 30, 2002.

(*New York Times* 2002)

See also 15.34, 15.37.

Websites, Blogs, and Social Media

15.50 **Websites and access dates in author-date format.** Chicago requires an access date in citations of websites and other sources consulted online only if no date of publication or revision can be determined from the source (see 14.12). In those cases—that is, when only an access date is used—record *n.d.* as the date of publication in the reference list entry and for the in-text citation. To avoid conflation with the name of the author, *n.d.* is always lowercase (see also 15.44).

Alliance for Linguistic Diversity. n.d. "Balkan Romani." Endangered Languages. Accessed April 6, 2016. http://www.endangeredlanguages.com/lang/5342.
CivicPlus Content Management System. n.d. City of Ithaca, New York (website). Accessed April 6, 2016. http://www.cityofithaca.org/.

(Alliance for Linguistic Diversity, n.d.) (CivicPlus, n.d.)

For sources that include a date of publication or revision, use the year of publication in the reference list entry. Repeat the year with the month and day to avoid any confusion.

Google. 2016. "Privacy Policy." Privacy & Terms. Last modified March 25, 2016. http://www.google.com/policies/privacy/.

(Google 2016)

See also 15.37.

15.51 **Citing blogs in author-date format.** Blogs and blog posts are cited in author-date format by adapting the recommendations outlined in 14.208. It is often sufficient to cite blog posts, like newspaper and magazine articles, entirely within the text (see 15.49). If a reference list entry is needed, repeat the year of publication with the month and day to avoid any confusion.

Germano, William. 2014. "Futurist Shock." *Lingua Franca* (blog), *Chronicle of Higher Education*. February 15, 2017. http://www.chronicle.com/blogs/lingua franca/2017/02/15/futurist-shock/.

(Germano 2017)

Comments are not included in reference lists; instead, they should be cited in the text, in reference to the related post.

A comment on Germano (2017) from WordObsessed (on March 15, 2017) insisted that . . .

References to an entire blog should likewise be made in the text rather than in a reference list. The URL can be listed in parentheses.

Lingua Franca, a blog published by the *Chronicle of Higher Education* (http://www.chronicle.com/blogs/linguafranca/) . . .

For the use of screen names in author-date format, see 15.52.

15.52 **Citing social media content in author-date format.** Social media content can be cited in author-date format by adapting the recommendations outlined and exemplified in 14.209. Like citations for text messages and other personal communications (see 15.53), citations of social media content can often be limited to the text. A frequently cited account or an extensive thread related to a single subject or post, however, may be included in a reference list. In the reference list, include the real name and a screen name, if both are available. In the text, cite the name under which the entry is listed (usually the real name unless only a screen name is available). Repeat the year with the month and day in the reference list to avoid any confusion. See also 15.35.

Chicago Manual of Style. 2015. "Is the world ready for singular they? We thought so back in 1993." Facebook, April 17, 2015. https://www.facebook.com/ChicagoManual/posts/10152906193679151.

Díaz, Junot. 2016. "Always surprises my students when I tell them that the 'real' medieval was more diverse than the fake ones most of us consume." Facebook, February 24, 2016. https://www.facebook.com/junotdiaz.writer/posts/972495572815454.

O'Brien, Conan (@ConanOBrien). 2015. "In honor of Earth Day, I'm recycling my tweets." Twitter, April 22, 2015, 11:10 a.m. https://twitter.com/ConanOBrien/status/590940792967016448.

Souza, Pete (@petesouza). 2016. "President Obama bids farewell to President Xi of China at the conclusion of the Nuclear Security Summit." Instagram photo, April 1, 2016. https://www.instagram.com/p/BDrmfXTtNCt/.

(Chicago Manual of Style 2015)
(Díaz 2016)
(O'Brien 2015)
(Souza 2016)

Comments are cited only in the text, in reference to the related post.

Michele Truty agreed, saying that "we do need a gender-neutral pronoun" (April 17, 2015, comment on Chicago Manual of Style 2015).

Direct or private messages shared through social media and received by the author are cited as personal communications (see 15.53).

Interviews and Personal Communications

15.53 **Unpublished interviews and personal communications.** In a parenthetical citation, the terms *personal communication* (or *pers. comm.*), *unpublished data*, and the like may be used after the name(s) of the person(s) concerned, following a comma. If the medium is important and not mentioned in the text, it may be incorporated into the parenthetical reference. Reference list entries are unneeded, though each person cited must be fully identified elsewhere in the text. Initials may be used for first names. Unless it is mentioned in the text, a date should be added in parentheses, following a comma. The abbreviation *et al.* should be avoided in such citations.

(Julie Cantor, pers. comm.)
(Jonathan Lee, Facebook direct message to author, May 5, 2017)
(Brenda Hasbrouck, text message to author, May 5, 2017)
(A. P. Møller, unpublished data; C. R. Brown and M. B. Brown, unpublished data)

Manuscript Collections

15.54 **Manuscript collections in author-date format.** When citing manuscript collections in author-date format, it is unnecessary to use *n.d.* (no date) in place of the date. Dates of individual items should be mentioned in the text, when applicable.

Egmont Manuscripts. Phillipps Collection. University of Georgia Library.
Kallen, Horace. Papers. YIVO Institute for Jewish Research, New York.

Oglethorpe wrote to the trustees on January 13, 1733 (Egmont Manuscripts), to say . . .

Alvin Johnson, in a memorandum prepared sometime in 1937 (Kallen Papers, file 36), observed that . . .

If only one item from a collection has been mentioned in the text, however, the entry may begin with the writer's name (if known). In such a case, the use of *n.d.* may be appropriate. See also 15.44.

Dinkel, Joseph. n.d. Description of Louis Agassiz written at the request of Elizabeth Cary Agassiz. Agassiz Papers. Houghton Library, Harvard University.

(Dinkel, n.d.)

Patents and Standards

15.55 **Patents or other documents cited by more than one date.** Cite patents and other documents that include more than one date as follows (note that the year of issue is repeated to avoid ambiguity):

Iizuka, Masanori, and Hideki Tanaka. 1986. Cement admixture. US Patent 4,586,960, filed June 26, 1984, and issued May 6, 1986.

For examples of standards cited in author-date format, see 15.37.

Citations Taken from Secondary Sources

15.56 **"Quoted in" in author-date references.** To cite a source from a secondary source ("quoted in . . .") is generally to be discouraged, since authors are expected to have examined the works they cite. If an original source is unavailable, however, mention the original author and date in the text, and cite the secondary source in the reference list entry.

Costello, Bonnie. 1981. *Marianne Moore: Imaginary Possessions*. Cambridge, MA: Harvard University Press.

In Louis Zukofsky's "Sincerity and Objectification," from the February 1931 issue of *Poetry* magazine (quoted in Costello 1981) . . .

Audiovisual Recordings and Other Multimedia

15.57 **Citing recordings and multimedia in author-date format.** Audiovisual recordings and other multimedia can be cited in author-date format by adapting the recommendations and examples outlined and exemplified in 14.261–68. (In many cases, however, it will be more appropriate to list such materials in running text and group them in a separate section or discography; see 14.262.) Older sources on outdated media are more likely to be consulted in the form of a digital copy; though authors should cite the format consulted, it is generally useful to give information about the original source, if available. Moreover, the date of the original recording should be privileged in the citation. Whom to list as "author" depends on the focus of the citation and is a matter of authorial discretion.

Coolidge, Calvin. [1920?]. "Equal Rights" (speech). In "American Leaders Speak: Recordings from World War I and the 1920 Election, 1918–1920." Library of Congress. Copy of an undated 78 rpm disc, RealAudio and WAV formats, 3:45. http://memory.loc.gov/ammem/nfhtml/.

Grande, Lance, and Allison Augustyn. 2011. *Gems and Jewels.* iPad ed., v. 1.01. Touchpress. Adapted from Lance Grande and Allison Augustyn, *Gems and Gemstones: Timeless Natural Beauty of the Mineral World* (Chicago: University of Chicago Press, 2009).

Holiday, Billie, vocalist. 1958. "I'm a Fool to Want You." By Joel Herron, Frank Sinatra, and Jack Wolf. Recorded February 20, 1958, with Ray Ellis. Track 1 on *Lady in Satin.* Columbia CL 1157, 33⅓ rpm.

Lyiscott, Jamila. 2014. "3 Ways to Speak English." Filmed February 2014 in New York, NY. TED video, 4:29. https://www.ted.com/talks/jamila_lyiscott_3_ways_to_speak_english.

Pink Floyd. 1970. *Atom Heart Mother.* Capitol CDP 7 46381 2, 1990, compact disc.

Rihanna [Robin Fenty], vocalist. 2007. "Umbrella." Featuring Jay-Z. MP3 audio. Track 1 on Rihanna, *Good Girl Gone Bad.* Island Def Jam.

Rovio Entertainment. 2014. *Angry Birds Transformers.* V. 1.4.25. Rovio Entertainment. Android 4.0 or later. Soundtrack by Vince DiCola and Kenny Meriedeth.

Strayed, Cheryl. 2012. *Wild: From Lost to Found on the Pacific Crest Trail.* Read by Bernadette Dunne. New York: Random House Audio. Audible audio ed., 13 hr., 6 min.

Weingartner, Felix von, conductor. 1936. *150 Jahre Wiener Philharmoniker.* Preiser Records PR90113 (mono), 1992, compact disc. Includes Beethoven's Symphony no. 3 in E-flat Major and Symphony no. 8 in F Major.

(Coolidge [1920?])
(Grande and Augustyn 2011)
(Holiday 1958)
(Lyiscott 2014)
(Pink Floyd 1970, track 2)
(Rihanna 2007)
(Rovio Entertainment 2014)
(Strayed 2012)
(Weingartner 1936)

Live performances, which cannot be consulted as such by readers, are generally not cited in a reference list. Instead, incorporate the details about the performance into the text. See also 14.266.

In a performance of Lin-Manuel Miranda's *Hamilton* at the Richard Rodgers Theatre in New York on February 2, 2016, . . .

Legal and Public Documents

15.58 **Using notes for legal and public documents.** Legal publications use notes for documentation and few include bibliographies. Any work using the author-date style that needs to do more than mention the occasional source in the text should therefore use supplementary footnotes or endnotes; see 15.31. This advice does not extend to documents that are collected in secondary sources or published as freestanding works (see 14.291), since these are readily adaptable to the author-date system (see 15.3). For a full discussion of legal and public documents, including examples, see 14.269–305.

15.59 **Citing legal and public documents in text.** Works with only a handful of citations to legal and public documents may be able to limit these to the text, using the forms detailed in 14.269–305. Note that in legal style, parentheses within parentheses are used (see also 6.97).

> In *NLRB v. Somerville Construction Co.* (206 F.3d 752 (7th Cir. 2000)), the court ruled that . . .

> In the *Congressional Record* for that day (147 Cong. Rec. 19,000 (2001)), Senator Burns is quoted as saying that . . .

In order to avoid such awkward constructions in the text, however, Chicago advises using notes for citations to legal and public documents whenever possible (see 14.271).

16 · Indexes

Overview

16.1 **The back-of-the-book index as model.** This chapter offers basic guidelines for preparing and editing an alphabetically arranged index to a book-length work. Much of the advice—modeled on the requirements for a book with fixed page numbers or other locators (see 16.12)—applies also to indexes for electronic formats that lack such mileposts (see 16.13). General principles of indexing are covered, as are the specifics of Chicago's preferred style in matters of typography, alphabetizing, and the like.

16.2 **Why index?** In this age of searchable text, the need for an index made with human input is sometimes questioned. But a good index can do what a plain search cannot: it gathers all the substantive terms and subjects of the work, sorts them alphabetically, provides cross-references to and from related terms, and includes specific page numbers or other locators or, for electronic formats, direct links to the text. This painstaking intellectual labor serves readers of any longer work, whether it is searchable or not. For searchable texts, an index provides insurance against fruitless queries and unintended results. In a word, a good index makes the text more accessible.

16.3 **Who should index a work?** The ideal indexer sees the work as a whole, understands the emphasis of the various parts and their relation to the whole, and knows—or guesses—what readers of the particular work are likely to look for and what headings they will think of. The indexer should be widely read, scrupulous in handling detail, analytically minded, well acquainted with publishing practices, and capable of meeting almost impossible deadlines. Although authors know better than anyone else their subject matter and the audience to whom the work is addressed, not all can look at their work through the eyes of a potential reader. Nor do many authors have the technical skills, let alone the time, necessary to prepare a good index that meets the publisher's deadline. Some authors produce excellent indexes. Others would do better to enlist the aid of a professional indexer.

16.4 **The indexer and deadlines.** Most book indexes have to be made between the time page proofs are issued and the time they are returned to the typesetter—usually about four weeks. (For an illustration of how indexing fits into the overall publishing process for books, see 2.2.) An author preparing his or her own index will have to proofread as well as index the work in that short time span. Good indexing requires reflection; the indexer needs to stop frequently and decide whether the right choices have been made. A professional indexer, familiar with the publisher's requirements, may be better equipped for such reflection. For journals that publish a volume index (see 1.110), the indexer may have several months to prepare a preliminary index, adding entries as new issues of the journal arrive. The final issue in the volume is typically indexed from page proofs, however, and the indexer may have as little as a week to work on the last issue and prepare the final draft of the index.

16.5 **The role of software in indexing.** A concordance—or a complete list of terms (typically minus articles, prepositions, and other irrelevant elements) and their page locations or frequency of use—can be produced automatically. But a concordance is not the same as an index. Most indexes of the type described in this chapter are produced from scratch, typically from paginated page proofs, either electronic or hard copy, generated by a page-layout program. Word processors are typically used in entering and editing terms and locators in a separate document and can provide rudimentary help in the process of sorting entries and managing cross-references. Dedicated word processors for indexers can automate many of the formatting and cross-referencing tasks particular to indexing and are a good investment especially for professional indexers (see 16.104). See also 16.7, 16.13.

16.6 **Single versus multiple indexes.** A single, comprehensive index—one that includes concepts and names of persons and other subjects—is recommended for most works. Certain publications, however, such as journals and lengthy scientific works that cite numerous authors of other studies, may include an index of named authors (see 16.115) in addition to a subject index. An anthology may include an author-and-title index, and a collection of poetry or hymns may have an index of first lines as well as an index of titles. It is generally an advantage if two or more indexes appearing in one work are visually distinct from one another so that users know immediately where they are. In a biological work, for example, the headings in the index of names will all be in roman type and will begin with capital letters, and there will be no subentries, whereas most of the headings in the general subject index will begin lowercase and many subentries will appear; and if there is a taxonomic index, many headings will be in italics. Separate running heads should be used, indicating the title of each index (e.g., Index of Names, Index of Subjects).

16.7 **Embedded indexes.** An embedded index consists of key terms anchored with underlying codes to particular points in the text of an electronic publication. These terms can facilitate a reader's queries to a search engine in much the same way that a good subject index gathers keywords under subject headings to increase the chances that a reader will be led only to the relevant areas of a text. For example, a search for the word "because" in a properly coded online encyclopedia might lead to those passages that discuss the Beatles' *Abbey Road* song "Because" rather than to every instance of the omnipresent conjunction. The principles of selection for embedded indexes are similar to those for traditional back-of-the-book indexes. Many journal publishers, especially in the sciences, rely on standard keyword vocabularies and have largely done away with traditional indexes. On the other hand, many book publishers anchor their back-of-the-book index entries to the electronic files that drive publication in print and other formats in order to facilitate hyperlinked indexes for e-book formats (see also 16.13).

16.8 **Resources for indexers.** For greatly expanded coverage of the present guidelines, along with alternative methods, consult the second edition of Nancy Mulvany's *Indexing Books* (bibliog. 2.5). Anyone likely to prepare a number of indexes should acquire that work. For further reference, see Hans H. Wellisch, *Indexing from A to Z*, and Linda K. Fetters, *Handbook of Indexing Techniques* (bibliog. 2.5).

Components of an Index

Main Headings, Subentries, and Locators

16.9 **Main headings for index entries.** The main heading of an index entry is normally a noun or noun phrase—the name of a person, a place, an object, or an abstraction. An adjective alone should almost never constitute a heading; it should rather be paired with a noun to form a noun phrase. A noun phrase is sometimes inverted to allow the keyword—the word a reader is most likely to look under—to appear first. The heading is typically followed by page (or paragraph) numbers (see 16.12) and sometimes a cross-reference (see 16.15–23). For capitalization, see 16.11.

agricultural collectivization, 143–46, 198
Aron, Raymond, 312–14
Bloomsbury group, 269
Brest-Litovsk, Treaty of, 61, 76, 85
Cold War, 396–437
Communist Party (American), 425
Communist Party (British), 268
imperialism, American, 393, 403
police, Soviet secret. *See* Soviet secret police
war communism, 90, 95, 125
World War I, 34–61
Yalta conference, 348, 398

16.10 **Index subentries.** An entry that requires more than five or six locators (page or paragraph numbers) is usually broken up into subentries to spare readers unnecessary excursions. A subentry, like an entry, consists of a heading (usually referred to as a subheading), page references, and, rarely, cross-references. Subheadings often form a grammatical relationship with the main heading, whereby heading and subheading combine into a single phrase, as in the first example below. Other subheadings form divisions or units within the larger category of the heading, as in the second example. Both kinds can be used within one index. See also 16.127. For sub-subentries, see 16.27, 16.28.

capitalism: and American pro-Sovietism, 273, 274; bourgeoisie as symbol of, 4, 13; as creation of society, 7; Khrushchev on burying, 480; student protests against, 491, 493

Native American peoples: Ahualucos, 140–41; Chichimecs, 67–68; Huastecs, 154; Toltecs, 128–36; Zapotecs, 168–72

16.11 **Initial lowercase letters in main headings and subheadings.** The first word of a main heading is normally capitalized only if capitalized in text—a proper noun (as in the second example in 16.10), a genus name, the title of a work, and so on. Traditionally, all main headings in an index were capitalized. Chicago recommends this practice only where the subentries are so numerous that capitalized main headings make for easier navigation. Indexes in the sciences, however, should generally avoid initial capitals because the distinction between capitalized and lowercased terms in the text may be crucial. Subheadings are always lowercased unless the keyword is capitalized in text (like "Khrushchev" in the first example in 16.10 and all the subentries in the second example).

16.12 **Locators in indexes.** In a printed work or PDF, locators are usually page numbers, though they can also be paragraph numbers (as in this manual), section numbers, or the like. When discussion of a subject continues for more than a page, paragraph, or section, the first and last numbers (inclusive numbers) are given: 34–36 (if pages), 10.36–41 (if paragraphs), and so on (see 16.14). The abbreviations *ff.* or *et seq.* should never be used in an index. Scattered references to a subject over several pages or sections are usually indicated by separate locators (34, 35, 36; *or* 8.18, 8.20, 8.21). Though the term *passim* has often been used to indicate scattered references over a number of not necessarily sequential pages or sections (e.g., 78–88 passim), individual locators are preferred. For use of the en dash, see 6.78.

16.13 **Linked indexes for e-books and other electronic formats.** At a minimum, indexes destined for e-book formats should be linked to the text. Page number data for a printed format can provide the basis of such links, and publishers are encouraged to include this data in their electronic publication formats. In formats with reflowable text, however, the actual place in the text may be several screens beyond the location of the first "page." For this reason, index entries are best linked directly to the passage of text to which they refer. (In works like this manual, links can be made directly to numbered paragraphs.) This approach, though it requires considerable intervention on the part of the publisher or indexer, produces a better experience for the reader. A detailed specification for indexes using EPUB, a standard format for e-books, is available from the International Digital Publishing Forum.

16.14 **Inclusive numbers in indexes.** Publishers vary in their preferences for the form of inclusive numbers (also known as continuing numbers). Although the simplest and most foolproof system is to give the full form of numbers everywhere (e.g., 234–235), Chicago prefers its traditional system (presented below), which is efficient and unambiguous. The system is followed in all examples in this chapter. Whichever form is used in the text should be used in the index as well.

First number	*Second number*	*Examples*
Less than 100	Use all digits	3–10 71–72 96–117
100 or multiples of 100	Use all digits	100–104 1100–1113
101 through 109, 201 through 209, etc.	Use changed part only	101–8 808–33 1103–4
110 through 199, 210 through 299, etc.	Use two digits unless more are needed to include all changed parts	321–28 498–532 1087–89 1496–500 11564–615 12991–3001

Roman numerals are always given in full—for example, xxv–xxviii, cvi–cix. In an index that refers to section numbers, the same principles apply as for page numbers (e.g., 16.9–14, 16.141–45). For use of the en dash between numerals, see 6.78; see also 9.60.

Cross-References

16.15 **Cross-references in indexes—general principles.** Cross-references are of two main kinds—*see* references and *see also* references. Each is treated differently according to whether it refers to a main heading or to a subheading. *See* and *see also* are set in italics (but see 16.22). In electronic publication formats, cross-references should link to the terms to which they refer. Cross-references should be used with discretion; an overabundance, besides irritating the reader, may signal the need for consolidation of entries.

16.16 **"See" references and "double posting."** *See* references direct a reader from, for example, an informal term to a technical one, a pseudonym to a real name, an inverted term to a noninverted one. They are also used for variant spellings, synonyms, aliases, abbreviations, and so on. The choice of the term under which the full entry appears depends largely on where readers are most likely to look. *See* references should therefore be given only where the indexer believes many readers might otherwise miss the full entry. Further, the indexer and anyone editing an index must make certain that no *see* reference merely leads to another *see* reference (a "blind cross-reference"). If, on the other hand, the entry to which the *see* reference refers is about the same length as the *see* reference itself, it is often more useful to omit the *see* reference and simply give the page numbers under both headings. Such duplication (or "double posting") will save readers a trip.

FBI (Federal Bureau of Investigation),
  145–48
Federal Bureau of Investigation,
  145–48
rather than
Federal Bureau of Investigation. *See*
  FBI

See also 16.46.

16.17 **"See" references following a main heading.** When a *see* reference follows a main heading, as it usually does, it is preceded by a period and *See* is capitalized. If two or more *see* references are needed, they are arranged in alphabetical order and separated by semicolons. They reflect the capitalization and word order of the main heading.

adolescence. *See* teenagers; youth
American Communist Party. *See* Communist Party (American)
baking soda. *See* sodium bicarbonate
Clemens, Samuel. *See* Twain, Mark
Den Haag ('s Gravenhage). *See* Hague, The
Lunt, Mrs. Alfred. *See* Fontanne, Lynn
Mormons. *See* Latter-day Saints, Church of Jesus Christ of
Roman Catholic Church. *See* Catholicism
The Hague. *See* Hague, The
Turwyn. *See* Terouenne
universities. *See* Harvard University; Princeton University; University of Chicago
van Gogh, Vincent. *See* Gogh, Vincent van
Virgin Queen. *See* Elizabeth I

16.18 **"See" references following a subheading.** When a *see* reference follows a subheading, it is put in parentheses and *see* is lowercased.

statistical material, 16, 17, 89; as online supplement (*see* supplements, online); proofreading, 183

This usage applies to both run-in and indented indexes, and to sub-subentries. See 16.27, 16.28.

16.19 **"See" references to a subheading.** Most *see* references are to a main entry, as in the examples in 16.17. When a cross-reference directs readers to a subentry under another main heading, *see under* may be used.

lace making. *See under* Bruges
Pride and Prejudice. See under Austen, Jane

An alternative, to be used when a *see under* reference might fail to direct readers to the right spot, is to drop the word *under* and add the wording of the subheading, following a colon. (Although a comma is sometimes used, a colon is preferred.) The wording of the cross-reference must correspond to that of the relevant subheading so that readers can find it quickly.

lace making. *See* Bruges: lace making
Pride and Prejudice. See Austen, Jane: *Pride and Prejudice*

16.20 **"See also" references.** *See also* references are placed at the end of an entry when *additional* information can be found in another entry. In run-in indexes, they follow a period; in indented indexes, they appear on a separate line (see 16.26). *See* is capitalized, and both words are in italics. If the cross-reference is to a subentry under another main heading, the words *see also under* may be used. If two or more *see also* references are needed, they are arranged in alphabetical order and separated by semicolons. As with *see* references, *see also* references must never lead to a *see* reference.

copyright, 95–100. *See also* permission
 to reprint; source notes
Maya: art of, 236–43; cities of, 178;
 present day, 267. *See also under*
 Yucatán

If *see also under* does not work in a particular context—for example, when one of the *see also* references is to a main entry and another to a subentry—the word *under* should be dropped and the wording of the subentry added after a colon.

Maya: art of, 236–43; cities of, 178. *See
 also* Mexican art; Yucatán: Maya

When a *see also* reference comes at the end of a subentry—a rare occurrence, and somewhat distracting—it is put in parentheses and *see* is lowercased.

equality: as bourgeois ideal, 5–6, 7;
 contractual quality, 13; in democracy's definition, 24 (*see also* democracy); League of the Rights of Man
 debate on, 234–35

16.21 **Correspondence between cross-references and headings.** All cross-referenced headings (and subheadings, if used) should generally be cited in full, with capitalization, inversion, and punctuation exactly as in the heading referred to. But a long heading may occasionally be shortened if no confusion results. For example, in an index with frequent references to Beethoven, "*See also* Beethoven, Ludwig van" could be shortened to "*See also* Beethoven" if done consistently.

16.22 **Italics for "see," "see also," and so forth.** The words *see*, *see under*, and *see also* are normally italicized. But if what follows (e.g., a book title or a word in another language) is in italics, the words are preferably set in roman to distinguish them from the rest of the cross-reference. This is not necessary when they follow italics.

Austen, Jane. See *Pride and Prejudice*
but
Pride and Prejudice. See Austen, Jane

16.23 **Generic cross-references.** Both *see* and *see also* references may include generic references; that is, they may refer to a type of heading rather than to several specific headings. The entire cross-reference is then set in italics.

public buildings. *See names of individual buildings*
sacred writings, 345–46, 390–401, 455–65. *See also specific titles*

When generic cross-references accompany specific cross-references, the former are placed last, even if out of alphabetical order. The conjunction *and* is normally used, following a semicolon (even if the generic cross-reference follows only one other cross-reference).

dogs, 35–42. *See also* American Kennel Club; shelters; *and individual breed names*

Run-In versus Indented Indexes

16.24 **Flush-and-hang formatting for indexes.** Indexes are generally formatted in flush-and-hang (or hanging-indent) style. The first line of each entry, the main heading, is set flush left, and any following lines are indented. When there are subentries, a choice must be made between run-in and indented styles (see 16.25, 16.26). In print publications (and electronic works modeled on the printed page), indexes are usually set in multiple columns. In manuscripts, however, columns should not be used (see 16.131).

16.25 **Run-in style for indexes.** In run-in style, the subentries follow the main entry and one another without starting a new line. They are separated by semicolons. If the main heading is immediately followed by subentries, it is separated from them by a colon (see first example below). If it is immediately followed by locators, these are preceded by a comma and followed by a semicolon (see second example below). Further examples of run-in entries may be seen in 16.10, 16.20, 16.141.

coordinate systems: Cartesian, 14; distance within, 154–55; time dilation and, 108–14. *See also* inertial systems; moving systems

Sabba da Castiglione, Monsignor, 209, 337; on cosmetics, 190; on whether to marry, 210–11; on wives' proper behavior, 230–40, 350

Chicago and many other publishers generally prefer run-in style because it requires less space. It works best, however, when there is only one level of subentry (but see 16.27). For the examples above in indented style, see 16.26.

16.26 **Indented style for indexes.** In indented style (also known as stacked style), each subentry begins a new line and is indented (usually one em). No colon appears before the first subheading, and subentries are not separated by semicolons. Runover lines must therefore be further indented (usually two ems) to distinguish them clearly from subentries; whether runover lines belong to the main entry or to subentries, their indentation should be the same. (Indentation is always measured from the left margin, not from the first word in the line above.) *See also* cross-references belonging to the entry as a whole appear at the end of the list of subentries (as shown in the first example below). A *see* or *see also* reference belonging to a specific subentry is placed in parentheses at the end of the subentry, as in run-in indexes (see 16.18, 16.20). See also 16.23.

coordinate systems
  Cartesian, 14
  distance within, 154–55
  time dilation and, 108–14
  See also inertial systems; moving systems

Sabba da Castiglione, Monsignor, 209, 337
  on cosmetics, 190
  on whether to marry, 210–11
  on wives' proper behavior, 230–40, 350

Indented style is usually preferred in scientific works and reference works (such as this manual). It is particularly useful where sub-subentries are required (see 16.28).

16.27 **Sub-subentries in run-in indexes.** If more than a handful of sub-subentries are needed in an index, the indented format rather than the run-in type should be chosen. A very few, however, can be accommodated in a run-in index or, better, avoided by repeating a keyword (see example A). If repetition will not work, subentries requiring sub-subentries can be indented, each starting a new line but preceded by an em dash flush with the margin; the sub-subentries are then run in (see example B). Em dashes are *not* used where only one level of subentry is needed.

Example A (run-in index: sub-subentries avoided)

Inuits: language, 18; pottery, 432–37;
  tradition of, in Alaska, 123; tradition
  of, in California, 127

Example B (run-in index: subentries requiring sub-subentries indented with em dash, sub-subentries run in)

Argos: cremation at, 302; and Danaos
  of Egypt, 108; Middle Helladic, 77;
  shaft graves at, 84
Arkadia, 4; Early Helladic, 26, 40;
  Mycenaean, 269, 306
armor and weapons
—attack weapons (general): Early
  Helladic and Cycladic, 33; Mycenaean, 225, 255, 258–60; from shaft
  graves, 89, 98–100; from tholos
  tombs, 128, 131, 133
—body armor: cuirass, 135–36, 147,
  152, 244, 258, 260, 311; greaves,
  135, 179, 260; helmets, 101, 135
—bow and arrow, 14, 99, 101, 166, 276
Asine: Early Helladic, 29, 36; Middle
  Helladic, 74; Mycenaean town and
  trade, 233, 258, 263; tombs at, 300

16.28 **Sub-subentries in indented indexes.** In an indented index, sub-subentries are best run in (see example A below). If, in a particular index, running them in makes the index hard to use, they have to be indented more deeply than the subentries (example B). When the first method is used, runover lines need not be indented more than the standard two ems, already a fairly deep indentation. When the second is used, runover lines have to be indented three ems, which may result in some very short lines. See also 16.142, 16.143.

Example A (indented index: run-in sub-subentries)

nutritional analysis of bamboo, 72–81
  digestible energy, 94–96, 213–14,
    222
  inorganic constituents: minerals,
    81, 83–85, 89; silica (*see* silica
    levels in bamboo); total ash, 73,
    79, 80, 91, 269, 270
  methods used, 72–73
  organic constituents, 73–79, 269,
    270; amino acids, 75–76, 86, 89;
    amino acids compared with other
    foods, 77; cellulose, 73, 78, 269,
    270; crude protein, 73–75, 80,
    89–91, 213, 269, 270; standard
    proximate analysis of, 78–80;
    vitamin C, 78, 79

Example B (indented index: sub-subentries indented)

nutritional analysis of bamboo, 72–81
  digestible energy, 94–96, 213–14, 222
  inorganic constituents
    minerals, 81, 83–85, 89
    silica (*see* silica levels in bamboo)
    total ash, 73, 79, 80, 91, 269, 270
  methods used, 72–73
  organic constituents, 73–79, 269, 270
    amino acids, 75–76, 86, 89
    amino acids compared with other foods, 77
    cellulose, 73, 78, 269, 270
    crude protein, 73–75, 80, 89–91, 213, 269, 270
  standard proximate analysis of, 78–80
  vitamin C, 78, 79

If sub-sub-subentries are required (which heaven forbid!), style B must be used, and they must be run in.

General Principles of Indexing

16.29 **Style and usage in the index relative to the work.** Each index is a tool for one particular work. By the time the index is prepared, the style used in the work has long been determined, and the index must reflect that style. If British spelling has been used throughout the text, it must be used in the index. Shakspere in the text calls for Shakspere in the index. Hernando Cortez should not be indexed as Cortés. Older geographical terms should not be altered to their present form (Constantinople to Istanbul, Siam to Thailand, etc.). The use of accents and other diacritical marks must be observed exactly as in the text (Schönberg *not* Schoenberg). Only in the rare instance in which readers might not find information sought should a cross-reference be given. Any terms italicized or enclosed in quotation marks in the text should be treated similarly in the index. If inclusive numbers are given in full in the text (see 16.14; see also 9.62), that style should be used in the index.

16.30 **Choosing indexing terms.** The wording for all headings should be concise and logical. As far as possible, terms should be chosen according to the author's usage. If, for example, the author of a philosophical work uses *essence* to mean *being*, the main entry should be under *essence*, possibly with a cross-reference from *being*. If the terms are used interchangeably, the indexer may either choose one (in this case a cross-reference is imperative) or list both (see 16.16). An indexer relatively unfamiliar with the subject matter may find it useful to ask the author for a brief list of terms that must appear in the index, though such terms will usually suggest themselves as the indexer proceeds through the proofs. Common sense is the best guide. For journals, terms may have been established in advance, either by a predetermined list of keywords within the discipline or by previous journal indexes (see 1.111). See also 16.21.

16.31 **Terms that should not be indexed.** Although proper names are an important element in most indexes, there are times when they should be ignored. In a work on the history of the automobile in the United States, for example, an author might write, "After World War II small sports cars like the British MG, often owned by returning veterans, began to make their appearance in college towns like Northampton, Massachusetts, and Ann Arbor, Michigan." An indexer should resist the temptation to index these place-names; the two towns mentioned have nothing to do with the theme of the work. The MG sports car, on the other hand, should be indexed, given the subject of the work. Similarly, names or terms that occur in passing references and scene-setting elements that are not essential to the theme of a work need not be indexed. (An exception might be made if certain readers of a publication would be likely to look for their own names in the index. Occasional vanity entries are not forbidden.)

Indexing Proper Names and Variants

16.32 **Choosing between variant names.** When proper names appear in the text in more than one form, or in an incomplete form, the indexer must decide which form to use for the main entry and which for the cross-reference (if any) and occasionally must furnish identifying information not given in the text. Few indexes need to provide the kind of detail found in biographical or geographical dictionaries, though reference works of that kind will help in decision-making.

16.33 **Indexing familiar forms of personal names.** The full form of personal names should be indexed as they have become widely known. (Any variant spelling preferred in the text, however, must likewise be preferred in the index; see 16.29.) Note that brackets are used in the following examples to distinguish Chicago's editorial glosses from parenthetical tags such as those in some of the examples elsewhere in this section, which would actually appear in a published index.

Cervantes, Miguel de [*not* Cervantes Saavedra, Miguel de]
Fisher, M. F. K. [*not* Fisher, Mary Frances Kennedy]
London, Jack [*not* London, John Griffith]
Poe, Edgar Allan [*not* Poe, E. A., *or* Poe, Edgar A.]

But in a work devoted to, say, M. F. K. Fisher or Cervantes, the full form of the name should appear in the index.

16.34 **Indexing pseudonyms or stage names.** Persons who have used pseudonyms or other professional names are usually listed under their real names. If the pseudonym has become a household word, however, it should be used as the main entry, with the real name in parentheses if it is relevant to the work; a cross-reference is seldom necessary.

Æ. *See* Russell, George William
Ouida. *See* Ramée, Marie Louise de la
Ramée, Marie Louise de la (pseud. Ouida)
Russell, George William (pseud. Æ)
but
Molière (Jean-Baptiste Poquelin)
Monroe, Marilyn (Norma Jean Baker)
Rihanna (Robyn Rihanna Fenty)
Twain, Mark (Samuel Langhorne Clemens)
Voltaire (François-Marie Arouet)

16.35 **Indexing persons with the same name.** Persons with the same name should be distinguished by a middle initial (if either has one) or by a parenthetical tag.

Campbell, James
Campbell, James B.
Field, David Dudley (clergyman)
Field, David Dudley (lawyer)
Pitt, William (the elder)
Pitt, William (the younger)

In works that include many persons with the same last name (often a family name), parenthetical identifications are useful. For example, in *Two Lucky People*, by Milton Friedman and Rose D. Friedman (University of Chicago Press, 1998), the following identifications appear:

Friedman, David (son of MF and RDF)
Friedman, Helen (sister of MF)
Friedman, Janet (daughter of MF and RDF)
Friedman, Milton (MF)
Friedman, Rose Director (RDF)
Friedman, Sarah Ethel Landau (mother of MF)

16.36 **Indexing married women's names.** A married woman who is known variously by her birth name or by her married name, depending on context, should be indexed by her birth name unless the married name is the more familiar. A married woman who uses both birth and married names together is usually indexed by her married name (unless the two names are hyphenated). Parenthetical clarifications or cross-references may be supplied as necessary.

Marinoff, Fania (Mrs. Carl Van Vechten)
Sutherland, Joan (Mrs. Richard Bonynge)
Van Vechten, Fania. *See* Marinoff, Fania
but
Besant, Annie (née Wood)
Browning, Elizabeth Barrett
Clinton, Hillary Rodham

16.37 **Indexing monarchs, popes, and the like.** Monarchs, popes, and others who are known by their official names, often including a roman numeral, should be indexed under the official name. Identifying tags may be omitted or expanded as appropriate in a particular work.

Anne, Queen
Benedict XVI (pope)
Elizabeth II (queen)

16.38 **Indexing princes, dukes, and other titled persons.** Princes and princesses are usually indexed under their given names. Dukes, earls, and the like are indexed under the title. A cross-reference may be needed where a title differs from a family name.

Charles, Prince of Wales
Cooper, Anthony Ashley. *See* Shaftesbury, 7th Earl of
Shaftesbury, 7th Earl of (Anthony Ashley Cooper)
William, Prince

Unless necessary for identification, the titles *Lord* and *Lady* are best omitted from an index, since their use with given names is far from simple. *Sir* and *Dame*, while easier to cope with, are also unnecessary in most indexes. Brackets are used here to denote Chicago's editorial glosses (see 16.33).

Churchill, Winston [*or* Churchill, Sir Winston]
Hess, Myra [*or* Hess, Dame Myra]
Thatcher, Margaret [even if referred to as Lady Thatcher in text]

But in a work dealing with the nobility, or a historical work such as *The Lisle Letters* (University of Chicago Press, 1981), from which the following examples are taken, titles may be an appropriate or needed element in index entries. The last two examples illustrate distinctions for which expert advice may be needed.

Arundell, Sir John
Audley, Thomas Lord
Grey, Lady Jane ["Lady Jane Grey" in text]
Whethill, Elizabeth (Muston), Lady ["Lady Whethill" in text]

16.39 **Clerical titles in index entries.** Like titles of nobility, such abbreviations as *Rev.* or *Msgr.* should be used only when necessary for identification (see 16.38).

Councell, George E. (rector of the Church of the Holy Spirit)
Cranmer, Thomas (archbishop of Canterbury)
Jaki, Rev. Stanley S.
Manniere, Msgr. Charles L.

16.40 **Academic titles and degrees in index entries.** Academic titles such as *Prof.* and *Dr.*, used before a name, are not retained in indexing, nor are abbreviations of degrees such as *PhD* or *MD*.

16.41 **"Jr.," "Sr.," "III," and the like in index entries.** Abbreviations such as *Jr.* are retained in indexing but are placed after the given name and preceded by a comma (see also 6.43).

King, Martin Luther, Jr.
Stevenson, Adlai E., III

16.42 **Indexing saints.** Saints are indexed under their given names unless another name is equally well or better known. Parenthetical identifications or cross-references (as well as discretion) may be needed. See also 16.74.

Aquinas. *See* Thomas Aquinas, Saint
Borromeo, Saint Charles
Catherine of Siena, Saint
Chrysostom, Saint John
Thomas, Saint (the apostle)
Thomas Aquinas, Saint

16.43 **Indexing persons whose full names are unknown.** Persons referred to in the work by first or last names only should be parenthetically identified if the full name is unavailable.

John (Smith's shipmate on *Stella*)
Thaxter (family physician)

16.44 **Indexing incomplete names or names alluded to in text.** Even if only an epithet or a shortened form of a name is used in the text, the index should give the full form.

Text	*Index*
the lake	Michigan, Lake
the bay	San Francisco Bay
the Village	Greenwich Village
the Great Emancipator	Lincoln, Abraham

16.45 **Indexing confusing names.** When the same name is used of more than one entity, identifying tags should be provided.

New York (city) *or* New York City
New York (state) *or* New York State

16.46 **Indexing abbreviations.** Organizations that are widely known under their abbreviations should be indexed and alphabetized according to the abbreviations. Parenthetical glosses, cross-references, or both should be added if the abbreviations, however familiar to the indexer, may not be known to all readers of the particular work. Lesser-known organizations are better indexed under the full name, with a cross-reference from the abbreviation if it is used frequently in the work. See also 16.16.

EEC (European Economic Community)
MLA. *See* Modern Language Association
NATO

Indexing Titles of Publications and Other Works

16.47 **Typographic treatment for indexed titles of works.** Titles of newspapers, books, journals, stories, poems, artwork, musical compositions, and such should be treated typographically as they appear in text—whether italicized, set in roman and enclosed in quotation marks, or simply capitalized (see also 8.156–201).

16.48 **Indexing newspaper titles.** English-language newspapers should be indexed as they are generally known, whether or not the city of publication appears on the masthead. The name is italicized, as in text, and *The* is omitted. If necessary, a city of publication may be added in parentheses following the title.

New York Times
Times (London)
Wall Street Journal
Chicago Sun-Times
Christian Science Monitor
Cleveland Plain Dealer

For newspapers published in languages other than English, any article (*Le*, *Die*, etc.) normally follows the name, separated by a comma (but see 16.52). The city of publication may be added parenthetically, following the title.

Akhbar, Al- (Cairo)
Monde, Le (Paris)
Prensa, La (Buenos Aires)
Süddeutsche Zeitung, Die

16.49 **Indexing magazine and journal titles.** Magazines and journals are indexed in the same way as newspapers (see 16.48). *The* is omitted in English-language publications, but the article is included, following the name, for non-English ones (but see 16.52).

JAMA (*Journal of the American Medical Association*)
New England Journal of Medicine
Spiegel, Der
Time

16.50 **Indexing authored titles of works.** A published work, a musical composition, or a piece of art that merits its own main entry should also be indexed under the name of its creator, often as a subentry. The main heading is followed by the creator's name in parentheses (except in an index in which all titles cited have the same creator).

Look Homeward, Angel (Wolfe), 34–37
Wolfe, Thomas: childhood, 6–8; early literary influences on, 7–10; *Look Homeward, Angel*, 34–37; and Maxwell Perkins, 30–41

Several works by a single creator are sometimes treated as subentries under a new main heading, following a main entry on the creator. This device is best employed when many works as well as many topics are listed. Separate main entries may also be included for the works.

Mozart, Wolfgang Amadeus, 49–51, 55–56; early musical compositions of, 67–72, 74–80; to Italy with father, 85–92; Salzburg appointment, 93–95; in Vienna, 98–105

Mozart, Wolfgang Amadeus, works of: *La clemenza di Tito*, 114; *Don Giovanni*, 115; *Idomeneo*, 105–6; *Jupiter* Symphony, 107; *The Magic Flute*, 111–13; *The Marriage of Figaro*, 109–12

16.51 **Indexing English-language titles beginning with an article.** In titles beginning with *A*, *An*, or *The*, the article is traditionally placed at the end of the title, following a comma, when the title forms a main heading. When such a title occurs as a subheading, it appears in its normal position in a run-in index, where inversion would be clumsy and unnecessary, but is inverted in an indented index for easier alphabetic scanning.

Professor and the Madman, The (Winchester), 209–11
Winchester, Simon: *Pacific*, 190–95; *The Professor and the Madman*, 209–11; *The River at the Center of the World*, 211–15

Winchester, Simon
  Pacific, 190–95
  Professor and the Madman, The, 209–11
  River at the Center of the World, The, 211–15

See also 16.56.

16.52 **Indexing non-English titles beginning with an article.** Since initial articles in non-English titles sometimes modify the following word, they are usually retained in an index. In publications intended for a general audience, especially those that mention only a few such titles, it is acceptable to list the titles in the index exactly as they appear in the text, without inversion and alphabetized according to the article.

Eine kleine Nachtmusik (Mozart), 23
La bohème (Puccini), 211

In a more specialized work, or any work intended for readers who are likely to be well versed in the languages of any non-English titles mentioned in the text, the titles may be inverted as they are in English (see 16.51). According to this practice, the articles follow the rest of the title in main headings but remain, as in English titles, in their normal position in run-in subheadings. In both positions, the articles are ignored in alphabetizing.

bohème, La (Puccini), 211
clemenza de Tito, La (Mozart), 22
kleine Nachtmusik, Eine (Mozart), 23

Mozart, Wolfgang Amadeus: *La clemenza de Tito*, 22; *Eine kleine Nachtmusik*, 23
trovatore, Il (Verdi), 323
but
"Un deux trois" (Luboff), 47 [alphabetize under *U*]

An indexer unfamiliar with the language of a title should make sure that the article is indeed an article and not a number (see last example above). French *un* and *une* and German *ein* and *eine*, for example, can mean *one* as well as *a*. See also 11.6–10.

16.53 **Indexing titles beginning with a preposition.** Unlike articles, prepositions beginning a title always remain in their original position and are never dropped, whether in English or non-English titles—nor are they ignored in alphabetizing.

For Whom the Bell Tolls
Por quién doblan las campanas

16.54 **Indexing titles ending with a question mark or exclamation point.** A question mark or exclamation point at the end of an indexed title should be followed by a comma wherever a comma is called for by the syntax of the heading. See also 16.94, 6.125.

Carver, Raymond, 23–27, 101, 143–44; "Are You a Doctor?," 25; *Will You Please Be Quiet, Please?*, 25–27, 143. *See also* Iowa Writers' Workshop

16.55 **Subtitles in index entries.** Subtitles of books or articles are omitted both in main headings and in subheadings unless essential for identification.

Alphabetizing

16.56 **Alphabetizing main headings—the basic rule.** To exploit the virtues of alphabetizing and thus ease the way for readers, the first word in a main heading should always determine the location of the entry. This principle occasionally entails inversion of the main heading. Thus, for example, *A Tale of Two Cities* is inverted as *Tale of Two Cities, A* and alphabetized under *T*, where readers would be inclined to look first. See also 16.9, 16.51, 16.52. For subentries, see 16.68–70.

16.57 **Computerized sorting.** Few computerized sorting options—and none of the standard options available with ordinary word processors—can perfectly conform to either system of alphabetization as described here. Those using a word processor to create their indexes will have to edit the finished product for the glitches and inconsistencies that invariably remain. Because word processors tend to produce a variation on the word-by-word system, it may be easier to opt for that system rather than imposing letter-by-letter (see 16.58). Some dedicated indexing programs, on the other hand, have been specially programmed to sort according to the letter-by-letter or word-by-word system in conformance with the detailed guidelines presented in this section. See also 16.104, 16.67.

Letter by Letter or Word by Word?

16.58 **Two systems of alphabetizing—an overview.** The two principal modes of alphabetizing—or sorting—indexes are the *letter-by-letter* and the *word-by-word* systems. A choice between the two should be made before indexing begins, though occasionally an indexer will find, as indexing progresses, that a change from one to the other is appropriate. (Such a change would of course need to be applied to the entire index.) Dictionaries are arranged letter by letter, library catalogs word by word (though online catalogs can usually be sorted by other criteria, such as format, date, availability, or relevance to a search). Chicago, most university presses, and many other publishers have traditionally preferred the letter-by-letter system but will normally not impose it on a well-prepared index that has been arranged word by word. In an index with many open compounds starting with the same word, the word-by-word system may be easier for users. Both systems have their advantages and disadvantages, and few users are confused by either. Most people simply scan an alphabetic block until they find what they are looking for. The indexer must understand both systems, however, and the following paragraphs offer guidelines for each. For a fuller discussion, consult Nancy Mulvany, *Indexing Books* (bibliog. 2.5).

16.59 **The letter-by-letter system.** In the letter-by-letter system, alphabetizing continues up to the first parenthesis or comma; it then starts again after the punctuation point. Spaces and all other punctuation marks are ignored. The order of precedence is one word, word followed by a parenthesis, word followed by a comma, then (ignoring spaces and other punctuation) word followed by a number, and word followed by letters. The index to this manual, in accordance with Chicago's traditional preference, is arranged letter by letter.

16.60 **The word-by-word system.** In the word-by-word system, alphabetizing continues only up to the end of the first word (counting an abbreviation or a hyphenated compound as one word), using subsequent words only when additional headings begin with the same word. As in the letter-by-letter system, alphabetizing continues up to the first parenthesis or comma; it then starts again after the punctuation point. The order of precedence is one word, word followed by a parenthesis, word followed by a comma, word followed by a space, then (ignoring other punctuation) word followed by a number, and word followed by letters.

16.61 **The two systems compared.** In both systems a parenthesis or comma (in that order) interrupts the alphabetizing, and other punctuation marks (hyphens, slashes, quotation marks, periods, etc.) are ignored. The columns below illustrate the similarities and differences between the systems.

Letter by letter	*Word by word*
NEW (Neighbors Ever Watchful)	N. Ewing & Sons
NEW (Now End War)	NEW (Neighbors Ever Watchful)
New, Arthur	NEW (Now End War)
New, Zoe	New, Arthur
new-12 compound	New, Zoe
newborn	New Deal
newcomer	new economics
New Deal	New England
new economics	new math
newel	New Thorndale
New England	new town
"new-fangled notions"	New Year's Day
Newfoundland	new-12 compound
N. Ewing & Sons	newborn
newlyweds	newcomer
new math	newel
new/old continuum	"new-fangled notions"
news, lamentable	Newfoundland
News, Networks, and the Arts	newlyweds
newsboy	new/old continuum
news conference	news, lamentable
newsletter	*News, Networks, and the Arts*

News of the World (Queen)	news conference
news release	*News of the World* (Queen)
newt	news release
NEWT (Northern Estuary Wind Tunnel)	newsboy
New Thorndale	newsletter
new town	newt
New Year's Day	NEWT (Northern Estuary Wind Tunnel)

General Rules of Alphabetizing

16.62 **Alphabetizing items with the same name.** When a person, a place, and a thing have the same name, they are arranged in normal alphabetical order.

hoe, garden	London, England
Hoe, Robert	London, Jack

Common sense must be exercised. If Amy London and Carolyn Hoe were to appear in the same index as illustrated above, adjustments in the other entries would be needed.

garden hoe	London (England)
hoe. *See* garden hoe	London, Amy
Hoe, Carolyn	London, Jack
Hoe, Robert	

16.63 **Alphabetizing initials versus spelled-out names.** Initials used in place of a given name come before any spelled-out name beginning with the same letter.

Oppenheimer, J. Robert	Oppenheimer, K. T.
Oppenheimer, James N.	Oppenheimer, Katharine S.

16.64 **Alphabetizing abbreviations.** Acronyms, initialisms, and most abbreviations are alphabetized as they appear, not according to their spelled-out versions, and are interspersed alphabetically among entries. See also 16.46, 16.74.

faculty clubs	NATO
FBI	North Pole
Feely, John	NOW (National Organization for Women)
LBJ. *See* Johnson, Lyndon B.	

Two exceptions: an ampersand (&) may be treated as if spelled out, and an at sign (@), which normally can be treated like the letter *a*, may be ignored as part of a screen name.

16.65 **Alphabetizing headings beginning with numerals.** Isolated entries beginning with numerals are alphabetized as though spelled out. (For numerals occurring in the middle of a heading, see 16.61, 16.66.)

1984 (Orwell) [*alphabetized as* nineteen eighty-four]
125th Street [*alphabetized as* one hundred twenty-fifth street]
10 Downing Street [*alphabetized as* ten downing street]

If many numerals occur in an index, they may be listed together in numerical order at the beginning of the index, before the *A*s.

16.66 **Alphabetizing similar headings containing numerals.** When two or more similar headings with numerals occur together, they are ordered numerically, regardless of how they would be spelled out.

Henry III	L7	section 9
Henry IV	L44	section 44
Henry V	L50	section 77

The *L* entries above would be placed at the beginning of the *L* section. See also 16.61.

16.67 **Alphabetizing accented letters.** Words beginning with or including accented letters are alphabetized as though they were unaccented. (Note that this rule is intended for English-language indexes that include some non-English words. The alphabetizing practices of other languages are not relevant in such instances.)

Ubeda	Schoenberg
Über den Gipfel	Schomberg
Ubina	Schönborn

This system, more than adequate for most English-language indexes, may need to be supplemented by more comprehensive systems for indexes that contain many terms in other languages. The Unicode Consortium has developed extensive specifications and recommendations for sorting (or collating) the characters used in many of the world's languages. For more information, refer to the latest version of the *Unicode*

Collation Algorithm, published by the Unicode Consortium (bibliog. 5). See also 11.2.

Subentries

16.68 **Alphabetical order of subentries.** Introductory articles, prepositions, and conjunctions are disregarded in alphabetizing subentries (but see 16.53), whether the subentries are run in or indented. To preserve the alphabetic logic of the keywords, avoid substantive introductory words at the beginnings of subheadings (e.g., "*relations* with," "*views* on").

Churchill, Winston: as anti-Fascist,
369; on Curzon line, 348, 379; and
de Gaulle, 544n4

In indented style, where alphabetizing functions more visually, it may be better to dispense with such introductory words or to invert the headings, amplifying them as needed. The subheadings from the first example could be edited for an indented index as follows:

Churchill, Winston
anti-Fascism of, 369
Curzon line, views on, 348, 379
de Gaulle, relations with, 544n4

16.69 **Numerical order of subentries.** Occasional subentries demand numerical order even if others in the same index (but not the same entry) are alphabetized.

Daley, Richard J. (mayor): third term,
205; fourth term, 206–7
flora, alpine: at 1,000-meter level,
46, 130–35; at 1,500-meter level,
146–54; at 2,000-meter level, 49,
164–74

16.70 **Chronological order of subentries.** In a run-in index, the subentries for the subject of a biography may be arranged chronologically rather than alphabetically so as to provide a quick summary of the subject's career and to avoid, for example, a subheading "death of" near the beginning of the entry. This system should be used with caution, however, and only when the biographical and chronological logic is obvious from the subentries.

Personal Names

16.71 **Indexing names with particles.** In alphabetizing family names containing particles, the indexer must consider the individual's personal preference (if known) as well as traditional and national usages. The biographical entries in Merriam-Webster's dictionaries (bibliog. 3.1) are authoritative for well-known persons long deceased; library catalogs and encyclopedias are far broader in scope. Cross-references are often advisable (see 16.17). Note the wide variations in the following list of actual names arranged alphabetically as they might appear in an index. See also 8.5, 16.75, 16.84.

Beauvoir, Simone de
Ben-Gurion, David
Costa, Uriel da
da Cunha, Euclides
D'Amato, Alfonse
de Gaulle, Charles
di Leonardo, Micaela
Keere, Pieter van den
La Fontaine, Jean de
Leonardo da Vinci
Medici, Lorenzo de'
Van Rensselaer, Stephen

Charles de Gaulle is a good example of the opportunity for occasional editorial discretion: *Webster's* and the Library of Congress, for example, list the French statesman under "Gaulle"; the entry in *American Heritage* is under "de Gaulle"—the usage normally preferred by Chicago.

16.72 **Indexing compound names.** Compound family names, with or without hyphens, are usually alphabetized according to the first element (but see 16.36). See also 8.6, 8.11, 16.83, 16.84.

Lloyd George, David
Mies van der Rohe, Ludwig
Sackville-West, Victoria
Teilhard de Chardin, Pierre

16.73 **Indexing names with "Mac," "Mc," or "O'."** Names beginning with *Mac* or *Mc* are alphabetized letter by letter, as they appear.

Macalister, Donald
MacAlister, Paul
Macauley, Catharine
Macmillan, Harold
Madison, James
McAllister, Ward
McAuley, Catherine
McMillan, Edwin M.

Names beginning with *O'* are alphabetized as if the apostrophe were missing.

Onassis, Aristotle
O'Neill, Eugene
Ongaro, Francesco dall'

16.74 **Indexing names with "Saint."** A family name in the form of a saint's name is alphabetized letter by letter as the name is spelled, whether *Saint*, *San*, *St.*, or however. A cross-reference may be useful if *Saint* and *St.* are far apart in an index. See also 16.42, 16.93.

Sainte-Beuve, Charles-Augustin
Saint-Gaudens, Augustus
Saint-Saëns, Camille
San Martin, José de
St. Denis, Ruth
St. Laurent, Louis Stephen

Non-English Personal Names

16.75 **Indexing Arabic names.** Modern Arabic names consisting of one or more given names followed by a surname present no problem.

Himsi, Ahmad Hamid
Sadat, Anwar

Arabic surnames prefixed by *al* or *el* (the) are alphabetized under the element following the particle; the article is treated like *de* in many French names.

Hakim, Tawfiq al-
Jamal, Muhammad Hamid al-

Names beginning with *Abu*, *Abd*, and *Ibn*, elements as integral to the names as *Mc* or *Fitz*, are alphabetized under those elements.

Abu Zafar Nadvi, Syed
Ibn Saud, Abdul Aziz

Context and readership may suggest cross-references. For example, in an index to a work likely to have readers unfamiliar with Arabic names, a cross-reference may be useful (i.e., "al-Farabi. *See* Farabi, al-").

16.76 **Indexing Burmese names.** Burmese persons are usually known by a given name of one or more elements and should be indexed under the first element. If the name is preceded in text by a term of respect (*U*, *Daw*, etc.), that term either is omitted or follows in the index.

Aung San Suu Kyi [alphabetize under *A*]
Thant, U [alphabetize under *T*]

16.77 **Indexing Chinese names.** Chinese names should be indexed as spelled in the work, whether in the Pinyin or the Wade-Giles system. Cross-references are needed only if alternative forms are used in the text. Since the family name precedes the given name in Chinese usage, names are not inverted in the index, and no comma is used.

Li Bai [Pinyin; alphabetize under *L*]
Mao Tse-tung [Wade-Giles; alphabetize under *M*]

Persons of Chinese ancestry or origin who have adopted the Western practice of giving the family name last are indexed with inversion and a comma.

Kung, H. H. Tsou, Tang

16.78 **Indexing Hungarian names.** In Hungarian practice the family name precedes the given name—for example, Bartók Béla, Molnár Ferenc. In English contexts, however, such names are usually inverted; in an index they are therefore reinverted, with a comma added.

Bartók, Béla Molnár, Ferenc

Family names beginning with an initial should be indexed under the initial (see also 8.13).

É. Kiss, Katalin

16.79 **Indexing Indian names.** Modern Indian names generally appear with the family name last and are indexed accordingly. As with all names, the personal preference of the individual as well as usage should be observed.

Gandhi, Mohandas Karamchand
Krishna Menon, V. K.
Narayan, R. K.

16.80 **Indexing Indonesian names.** Usage varies. Some Indonesians (especially Javanese) use only a single, given name. Others use more than one name; even though the given name comes first, these are often indexed like Chinese names, with no inversion or punctuation (see third and fourth examples). Indonesians with Muslim names and certain others whose names may include a title or an honorific are indexed by the final element, with inversion. The indexer must therefore ascertain how a person's full name is referred to in text and which part of the name is used for a short reference.

Habibi, B. J.
Hatta, Mohammed
Marzuki Darusman
Pramoedya Ananta Toer
Suharto
Sukarno
Suryokusumo, Wiyono

16.81 **Indexing Japanese names.** In Japanese usage the family name precedes the given name; names are therefore not inverted in the index, and no comma is used. If the name is westernized, as it often is by authors writing in English, the family name comes last. The indexer must therefore make certain which practice is followed in the text so that the family name always appears first in the index.

Tajima Yumiko [alphabetize under *T*]
Yoshida Shigeru [alphabetize under *Y*]
but
Kurosawa, Noriaki [referred to in text as Noriaki Kurosawa]

16.82 **Indexing Korean names.** In Korean usage the family name precedes the given name, and this is how it is usually presented even in English-language contexts. Persons of Korean origin living in the West, however, often invert this order. The indexer must therefore make certain which practice is followed in the text so that the family name appears first, with or without inversion, in the index.

Kim Dae-jung [alphabetize under *K*]
Oh Jung-hee [alphabetize under *O*]
but
Lee, Chang-rae [referred to in text as Chang-rae Lee]

16.83 **Indexing Portuguese names.** The Portuguese, unlike the Spanish (see 16.84), index surnames by the last element. This does not include the designations *Filho* (son), *Neto* (grandson), and *Júnior*, which always follow the second family name.

Câmara Júnior, José Mattoso
Jucá Filho, Cândido
Martins, Luciana de Lima
Silva Neto, Serafim da
Vasconcellos, J. Leite de

Where both Portuguese and Spanish names appear in the same context, cross-references may be necessary.

16.84 **Indexing Spanish names.** In Spain and in some Latin American countries a double family name is often used, of which the first element is the father's family name and the second the mother's birth name (*her* father's family name). The two names are sometimes joined by *y* (and). Such compound names are alphabetized under the first element. Cross-references will often be needed, especially if the person is generally known under the second element or if the indexer is uncertain where to place the main entry. *Webster's* is a good guide for persons listed there. Where many Spanish names appear, an indexer not conversant with Spanish or Latin American culture should seek help.

García Lorca, Federico
Lorca, Federico García. *See* García Lorca, Federico
Ortega y Gasset, José
Sánchez Mendoza, Juana

When the particle *de* appears in a Spanish name, the family name, under which the person is indexed, may be either the preceding or the following name (depending in part on how a person is known). If it is not clear from the text and the name is not in *Webster's* or otherwise widely known, a cross-reference will be needed.

Balboa, Vasco Núñez de
Esquivel de Sánchez, María
Fernández de Navarrete, Juan
Fernández de Oviedo, Gonzalo

Traditionally, a married woman replaced her mother's family name with her husband's (first) family name, sometimes preceded by *de*. Her name should be alphabetized, however, by the first family name (her father's).

Mendoza de Peña, María Carmen [woman's name after marriage]
Mendoza Salinas, María Carmen [woman's name before marriage]
Peña Montalvo, Juan Alberto [husband's name]

In telephone directories and elsewhere, some women appear under the husband's family name, but this is not a recommended bibliographic or indexing practice. Many modern women in Spanish-speaking countries no longer take the husband's family name. See also 8.11.

16.85 **Indexing Thai names.** Although family names are used in Thailand, Thais are normally known by their given names, which come first, as in English names. The name is often alphabetized under the first name, but practice varies. Seek expert help.

Sarit Thanarat [*or* Thanarat, Sarit]
Sivaraksa, Sulak [*or* Sulak Sivaraksa]
Supachai Panitchpakdi

16.86 **Indexing Vietnamese names.** Vietnamese names consist of three elements, the family name being the first. Since Vietnamese persons are usually referred to by the last part of their given names (Premier Diem, General Giap), they are best indexed under that form.

Diem, Ngo Dinh [*cross-reference under* Ngo Dinh Diem]
Giap, Vo Nguyen [*cross-reference under* Vo Nguyen Giap]

16.87 **Indexing other Asian names.** Throughout Asia, many names derive from Arabic, Chinese, the European languages, and other languages, regardless of where the bearers of the names were born. In the Philippines, for example, names follow a Western order, giving precedence to the family name, though the names themselves may be derived from local languages. In some parts of Asia, titles denoting status form part of a name as it appears in written work and must be dealt with appropriately. When the standard reference works do not supply an answer, query the author.

Names of Organizations and Businesses

16.88 **Omission of article in indexed names of organizations.** In indexing organizations whose names begin with *the* (which would be lowercased in running text), the article is omitted.

Beatles (band)
Unicode Consortium
University of Chicago

16.89 **Indexing personal names as corporate names.** When used as names of businesses or other organizations, full personal names are not inverted, and the corporate name is alphabetized under the first name or initials. An organization widely known by the family name, however, should be indexed under that name. In both instances, cross-references may be appropriate.

A. G. Edwards & Sons, Inc. [alphabetize under *A*]
Penney, J. C. *See* J. C. Penney Company, Inc.
Saphir, Kurt. *See* Kurt Saphir Pianos, Inc.
but
John G. Shedd Aquarium. *See* Shedd Aquarium

A personal name and the name of that person's company should be indexed separately.

Morgan, Junius S., 39, 42–44; J. S. Morgan & Company, 45–48
J. S. Morgan & Company, 45–48. *See also* Morgan, Junius S.

Names of Places

16.90 **Indexing names beginning with "Mount," "Lake," and such.** Proper names of mountains, lakes, and so forth that begin with a generic name are usually inverted and alphabetized under the nongeneric name.

Geneva, Lake
Japan, Sea of
McKinley, Mount

Names of cities or towns beginning with topographic elements, as well as islands known as "Isle of . . . ," are alphabetized under the first element.

Isle of Pines
Isle of Wight
Lake Geneva, WI
Mount Vernon, NY
Valley Forge

16.91 **Indexing names beginning with the definite article.** Aside from a very few cities such as The Hague (unless the Dutch form *Den Haag* is used; see 16.92) or The Dalles, where *The* is part of the formal name and thus capitalized, an initial *the* used informally with place-names is omitted in indexing. See also 8.45.

Bronx	Netherlands
Hague, The	Ozarks
Loop (Chicago's downtown)	Philippines

16.92 **Indexing names beginning with non-English definite articles.** Names of places beginning with definite articles such as *El*, *Le*, *La*, and the like, whether in English- or non-English-speaking countries, are alphabetized according to the article.

Den Haag	La Mancha
El Dorado	Le Havre
El Paso	Les Baux-de-Provence
La Crosse	Los Alamos

16.93 **Indexing names of places beginning with "Saint."** Names of places beginning with *Saint*, *Sainte*, *St.*, or *Ste.* should be indexed as they appear in the text—that is, abbreviated only if abbreviated in text. Like personal names, they are alphabetized as they appear. Cross-references may be appropriate (e.g., "Saint. *See* St.," or vice versa). Note that French hyphenates place-names with *Saint*. See also 10.30, 11.26.

Saint-Cloud (in France)	Ste. Genevieve
Sainte-Foy	St. Louis
Saint-Luc	St. Vincent Island
St. Cloud (in Florida)	

Punctuating Indexes: A Summary

16.94 **Comma in index entries.** In both run-in and indented indexes, when a main heading is followed immediately by locators (usually page or paragraph numbers; see 16.12), a comma appears before the first locator. Commas appear between locators. Commas are also used when a heading is an inversion or when a main heading is qualified, without subentries. The second example illustrates three uses of the comma. For the role of commas in alphabetizing, see 16.61.

lighthouses, early history of, 40–42
Sabba da Castiglione, Monsignor, 209,
  337; on cosmetics, 190, 195, 198

16.95 **Colon in index entries.** In a run-in index, when a main heading is followed immediately by subentries, a colon appears before the first subheading. In an indented index, no punctuation is used after the main heading. A colon is also used in a cross-reference to a subentry. See also 16.20.

Maya: art of, 236–43; cities of, 178. *See also* Yucatán: Maya

Maya
  art of, 236–43
  cities of, 178
  See also Yucatán: Maya

16.96 **Semicolon in index entries.** When subentries or sub-subentries are run in, they are separated by semicolons. Cross-references, if more than one, are also separated by semicolons.

astronomy: Galileo's works on, 20–21, 22–23, 24; skills needed in, 548–49. *See also* Brahe, Tycho; comets; Flamsteed, John

16.97 **Period in index entries.** In a run-in index a period is used only before *See* (or *See under*) or *See also* (or *See also under*). In an indented index a period is used only before *See*. When a *see* or *see also* reference in parentheses follows a subheading or a subentry in either a run-in or an indented index, no period is used. No period follows the final word of any entry. For examples, see 16.17, 16.20, 16.19, 16.143.

16.98 **Parentheses in index headings.** Parentheses enclose identification or supplementary information. For the role of parentheses in alphabetizing, see 16.61.

Charles I (king of England)
Charles I (king of Portugal)
Of Human Bondage (Maugham)

16.99 **Em dash in index entries.** For use of the em dash in run-in indexes that require occasional sub-subentries, see example B in 16.27.

16.100 **En dash in index entries.** The en dash is used for page ranges and all other inclusive locators (e.g., "dogs, 135–42"). For abbreviating inclusive numbers in indexes, see 16.14. See also 6.78, the index to this manual, and examples throughout this chapter.

The Mechanics of Indexing

Before Indexing Begins: Tools and Decisions

16.101 **Schedule for indexing.** Anyone making an index for the first time should know that the task is intensive and time-consuming. An index for a three-hundred-page book could take as much as three weeks' work or more. See also 16.4.

16.102 **Indexing from page proofs.** For a printed work, the indexer must have in hand a clean and complete set of proofs (usually showing final pagination) before beginning to index. A PDF version is generally more helpful than a printout because it can be used to search for specific terms (and can be printed out as needed; see also 16.105). For a journal volume, the work may begin when the first issue to be indexed has been paginated, and it may continue for several months, until page proofs for the final issue in the volume have been generated. For electronic formats, where index entries are linked to their location in the text, additional considerations may apply (see 16.13). See also 16.108, 16.117–25.

16.103 **Publisher's indexing preferences.** Before beginning work, the indexer should know the publisher's preferences in such matters as alphabetizing, run-in or indented style, inclusive numbers, handling of numeric headings, and the like (all matters dealt with in earlier sections of this chapter). For a journal volume index, the style is likely to be well established, and the indexer must follow that style. If the publisher requests an index of a particular length, the indexer should adjust the normal editing time accordingly. See also 16.131.

16.104 **Indexing tools.** The dedicated indexing programs used by many professional indexers automate such tasks as cross-referencing and the collation of entries and subentries and include special options for alphabetizing—for example, to exclude certain words or characters and to conform to either the letter-by-letter or word-by-word system (see 16.58). Such programs, however, tend to require more learning time than most authors can afford (see 16.4). Fortunately, an index can be prepared according to the guidelines in this chapter by simply entering terms and locators into a separate document using an ordinary word processor—though cross-references and alphabetizing, in particular, will need to be checked manually throughout the process (see 16.57; see also 16.5). For the latest information about tools for indexing, consult the website of the American Society for Indexing.

16.105 **Using the electronic files to index.** Publishers' policies vary as to whether they can agree to supply indexers with page proofs in electronic form. A searchable PDF file can be helpful in double-checking that additional instances of particular terms have not been overlooked. Some indexers may prefer also to annotate and refer to the PDF rather than a paper copy as they create the index. It should be noted, however, that an index cannot be automatically "generated" from a PDF file and that there is no substitute for rereading the whole work. See also 16.5, 16.13, 16.119.

16.106 **Formatting index entries.** Consult with the publisher up front to determine whether a run-in or indented index is required (see 16.24–28) and whether there are any other specific requirements. Format the manuscript accordingly, using a flush-and-hang style (see 16.24). See also 16.131.

16.107 **Indexing the old-fashioned way.** Before the advent of word processors (and their cutting-and-pasting and sorting functions), indexers used to handwrite or type preliminary entries and subentries on 3″ × 5″ index cards, then alphabetize and edit the cards, and finally type the index, while further refining it, on 8½″ × 11″ sheets. For details, consult Nancy Mulvany, *Indexing Books* (bibliog. 2.5), or the thirteenth or fourteenth edition of this manual (no longer in print but available in large libraries). The procedures described in the following sections can be adapted to the index-card method.

When to Begin

16.108 **Preliminary indexing work.** Although some planning can be done at the manuscript stage, most indexes are prepared as soon as a work is in final, paginated form, or "page proofs." It is crucial, in fact, that indexing not begin until pagination is final. For indexes in which the locators are paragraph or section numbers rather than page numbers, however (or where entries will be linked to specific locations in the text for electronic formats), earlier iterations of the final or near-final manuscript can often be used to get a head start. Authors who are not preparing their own indexes may compile a list of important terms for the indexer, but doing much more is likely to cause duplication or backtracking.

What Parts of the Work to Index

16.109 **Indexing the text, front matter, and back matter.** The entire text of a book or journal article, including substantive content in notes (see 16.110), should be indexed. Much of the front matter, however, is not indexable—title page, dedication, epigraphs, lists of illustrations and tables, and acknowledgments. A preface, or a foreword by someone other than the author of the work, may be indexed if it concerns the subject of the work and not simply how the work came to be written. Substantive material in an introduction, whether in the front matter or, more commonly, in the body of the work, is always indexed (for introduction versus preface, see 1.43). Book appendixes should be indexed if they contain information that supplements the text, but not if they merely reproduce documents that are discussed in the text (the full text of a treaty, for example, or a questionnaire). Appendixes to journal articles are indexed as part of the articles. Glossaries, bibliographies, and other such lists are usually not indexed.

16.110 **Indexing footnotes and endnotes.** Notes, whether footnotes or endnotes, should be indexed only if they continue or amplify discussion in the text (substantive notes). Notes that merely contain source citations documenting statements in the text (reference notes) need not be indexed.

16.111 **Endnote locators in index entries.** Endnotes in printed works are referred to by page, the letter *n* (for *note*), and—extremely important—the note number, with no internal space (334n14). If two or more consecutive notes are referred to, two *n*'s and an en dash are used (e.g., 334nn14–16). Nonconsecutive notes on the same page are treated separately (334n14, 334n16, 334n19). If an index entry refers to numbered notes from more than one chapter that occur on the same page in the endnotes, it can be helpful to include the chapter number in parentheses after the note number, especially if two notes share the same number or where the notes might otherwise appear to be out of order.

birds, 334n2 (chap. 8), 334n2 (chap. 9), 335n9
cats, 212n18 (chap. 1), 212n2 (chap. 2), 218n25

16.112 **Footnote locators in index entries.** Footnotes in a printed work are generally referred to in the same way as endnotes. When a footnote is the only one on the page, however, the note number (or symbol, if numbers are not used) may be omitted (156n). Note numbers should never be omitted when several notes appear on the same page. (If symbols are used, use the symbol: e.g., 156n*, 173n*, 173n†.) If there is indexable material in a text passage and in a related footnote, only the page number need be given. But if the text and the footnote materials are not connected, both text and note should be cited (156, 156n, 278, 278n30).

16.113 **Indexing notes spanning more than one printed page.** For endnotes or footnotes that continue onto another page, normally only the first page number is given. But if the reference is specifically to a part of a note that appears on the second page, the second page number should be used. Referring to a succession of notes, however, may require inclusive page numbers (e.g., 234–35nn19–23).

16.114 **Indexing parenthetical text citations.** Documentation given as parenthetical author-date citations in text is not normally indexed unless the citation documents an otherwise unattributed statement in the text (see 16.110). Any author discussed in text should be indexed. In some fields it is customary to index every author *named* in the text; check with the publisher on the degree of inclusiveness required. See also 16.115.

16.115 **Indexing authors' names for an author index.** Author indexes are more common in disciplines that use a variation of the author-date system (see chapter 15). Since most authors are cited in text by last name and date only, full names must be sought in the reference list. Occasional discrepancies between text and reference list, not caught in editing, have to be sorted out or queried, adding to the time it takes to create an author index. Is L. W. Dinero, cited on page 345, the same person as Lauren Dinero, discussed on page 456? If so, should she be indexed as Dinero, Lauren W.? (Answer: only if all or most authors are indexed with full first names—a situation that may be determined by the reference list.) Where a work by two or more authors is cited in text, the indexer must determine whether each author named requires a separate entry. Should Jones, Smith, and Black share one index entry, or should three entries appear? And what about Jones et al.? Chicago recommends the following procedure: Make separate entries for each author whose name appears in text. Do not index those unfortunates whose names are concealed under *et al.* in text.

Text citations	*Index entries*
(Jones, Smith, and Black 1999)	Black, M. X., 366
(Sánchez et al. 2001)	Cruz, M. M., 435
(Sánchez, Cruz, et al. 2002)	Jones, E. J., 366
	Sánchez, J. G., 435, 657
	Smith, R. A., 366

16.116 **Indexing illustrations, tables, charts, and such.** Illustrative matter may be indexed if it is of particular importance to the discussion, especially when such items are not listed in or after the table of contents. References to illustrations may be set in italics (or boldface, if preferred); a headnote should then be inserted at the beginning of the index (see 16.141 for an example). Such references usually follow in page order.

reptilian brain, 199, 201–3, *202*, 341,
477, 477–81

Alternatively, references to tables may be denoted by *t*, to figures by *f*, plates by *pl*, or whatever works (all set in roman, with no space following the page number). Add an appropriate headnote (e.g., "The letter *t* following a page number denotes a table"). If the number of an illustration is essential, it is safer to use *table*, *fig.*, and so on, with no comma following the page number.

authors and printers, 69, 208t, 209t,
210f
titi monkeys, 88 table 5, 89–90, 122–
25, 122 fig. 7

Marking Proofs and Preparing Entries

16.117 **Beginning to highlight and enter terms.** After a perusal of the table of contents and the work as a whole, an indexer should begin highlighting terms to be used as main headings or subheadings. This is normally done by hand-marking a set of proofs (either on paper or PDF). Inexperienced indexers are advised to mark the proofs—at least in the early stages—with the same kind of detail as is illustrated in figure 16.1. Most indexers prefer to mark one section (or chapter or journal issue) at a time and—using a word processor or dedicated indexing software (see 16.104)—to enter and alphabetize the marked terms in that section before going on to the next section. The notes belonging to the section, even if endnotes, should be checked and, if necessary, indexed at the same time (see 16.110). As the indexer becomes more skilled in marking the proofs, less underlining and fewer marginal notes may suffice.

16.118 **Deciding how many terms to mark.** The number of terms to mark on any one page obviously depends on the kind of work being indexed. As a very rough guide, an average of five references per text page in a book will yield a modest index (one-fiftieth the length of the text), whereas

54 ❧ CHAPTER THREE

those who find the hurting of others fun, no arguments against it can fully succeed, and the history of efforts to explain why "human nature" includes such impulses and what we might do to combat them could fill a library: books on the history of Satan and the Fall, on the cosmogonies of other cultures, on our genetic inheritance, including recently the structure of our brains, on sadism and why it is terrible or defensible. And so on. I'll just hope that here we can all agree that to hurt or harm for the fun of it is self-evidently not a loving choice.[1]

One embarrassing qualification: we amateurish amateurs do often inflict pain on others. We just don't do it on purpose.

Work and Play, Work as Play : as play —56 : work as —56

To celebrate playing for the love of it risks downgrading the work we do that we love. In fact we amateurs are often tempted to talk snobbishly about those who cannot claim that what they do they do for the love of it. As Bliss Perry put the danger: "[T]he prejudice which the amateurs feels toward the professionals, the more or less veiled hostility between the man who does something for love which another man does for money, is one of those instinctive reactions—like the vague alarm of some wild creature in the woods—which give a hint of danger." : loving one's

The words "professional" and "work" are almost as ambiguous as the word "love." Some work is fun, some gruesome. Winston Churchill loved his work—but needed to escape it regularly. I hated most of the farm work I did as an adolescent, and escaped it as soon as possible. : of one's work I hated having to dig ditches eight hours a day for twenty-five cents an hour. Yet working as a teacher and a scholar, I have loved most of my duties—even the drudgery parts. A member of the Chicago Symphony Orchestra told me that he hates his work—his playing—and is eager for retirement. Politicians celebrate work as what will save welfare recipients from degradation; for them, to require people to work, even if they're underpaid and even if the job is awful, is a virtuous act. : work celebrated by

Such a mishmash of implied definitions makes it impossible to place work in any simple opposition to play or pleasure. In *Homo Ludens* Johan Huizinga occasionally writes as if the whole point of life were to have fun by *escaping*

1. A fine discussion of the dangers threatened by "doing things for the love of the doing" is given by Roger Shattuck in *Forbidden Knowledge*. Shattuck argues that the art-for-art's-sake movement, with its many echoes of Walter Pater's celebration of "burning" with a "hard, gemlike flame" and living for the "highest quality" of a given moment, risks moving us toward "worship of pure experience without restraint of any kind." The temptations of sadistic ecstasies lurk in the wings. As I shall insist again and again, to make sense out of a title like *For the Love of It* requires careful distinction among diverse "loves," many of them potentially harmful.

FIGURE 16.1. Sample page of proof from Wayne Booth's *For the Love of It*, marked up for indexing. See 16.117–25.

fifteen or more will yield a fairly long index (about one-twentieth the length of the text or more). If the publisher has budgeted for a strictly limited number of pages, the indexer should work accordingly. Remember that it is always easier to drop entries than to add them; err on the side of inclusiveness. See also 16.30, 16.31, 16.103, 16.109–16.

16.119 **How to mark index entries.** To visualize the method advocated here, suppose you are indexing a chapter from Wayne Booth's *For the Love of It* (University of Chicago Press, 1999), a consideration of work and play and work as play (see fig. 16.1). You have read through the chapter once and now have to go back and select headings and subheadings for indexing this particular section (of which only the first paragraphs are shown here). You decide that the whole section (pp. 54–56) will have to be indexed under both *work* and *play*, so you mark the section head as shown. (On the marked proofs, a colon separates a proposed principal heading from a proposed subheading.) Going down the page, you underline *Bliss Perry* (which will of course be inverted—Perry, Bliss—as a heading; similarly for the other personal names). You also underline *amateur* and *professional* (modifying them to the plural). In the second paragraph, you underline *work* and *love*, with proposed subheads, and *Churchill* (noting the first name in the margin). You decide to index *Chicago Symphony Orchestra*—which in another work might be tangential but here ties in with the book's major subtheme of musical performance and appreciation—and also mark *politicians*, with proposed subhead. You underline *Huizinga* (adding "Johan" in the margin) and the work *Homo Ludens*, which might also be a subheading under "Huizinga, Johan." In the note, you mark two names (supplying a first name for Pater), one title, and one additional term (see also 16.110).

16.120 **Planning index subentries.** For each term marked, you should make an effort to write in a modification—a word or phrase that narrows the application of the heading, hence a potential subentry. Although some such modifications may eventually be dropped, they should be kept on hand in case they are needed. Otherwise you may end up with some headings that are followed by nothing but a long string of numbers, which makes for an all but useless index entry. The modifications can be altered and added to as the indexing proceeds.

16.121 **Recording inclusive numbers for index terms.** If a text discussion extends over more than one page, section, or paragraph, both beginning and ending numbers—which will depend on what locator system is being used (see 16.12)—must be recorded. See also 16.14.

16.122 **Typing and modifying index entries.** Most entries at this stage will include three elements: a heading, a modification (or provisional subentry), and a locator (page or paragraph number). While typing, you will probably modify some of the headings and add, delete, or alter subheadings and locators (a process that may at the same time entail changes to cross-references and to alphabetical order). After typing each entry, read it carefully against the page proofs—in particular, checking that the page numbers or other locators are correct. You are unlikely to have time to read your final index manuscript against the marked-up proofs, though you should certainly retain the proofs for reference until the work has been published. See also 16.106.

16.123 **Alphabetizing entries as part of the indexing process.** Many indexers alphabetize as they type; others let their software do it, intervening as necessary. By this time the indexer should have decided whether to use the letter-by-letter or the word-by-word system (see 16.58–61). If the system chosen proves unsatisfactory for the particular work as the index proceeds, a switch can be made if the publisher agrees. See also 16.57.

16.124 **Final check of indexed proofs.** After typing all the entries, read quickly through the marked-up proofs once again to see whether anything indexable has been omitted. You may find some unmarked items that seemed peripheral at the time but now, in the light of themes developed in later chapters, declare themselves to be significant. Or you may have missed major items. Now is the time to remedy all omissions.

16.125 **Noting errors during indexing.** Although not engaged to proofread, the indexer has to read carefully and usually finds a number of typographical errors and minor inconsistencies. If indexing a book (rather than a journal volume, most of which will already have been published), keep track of all such errors and send a list to the publisher (who will be very grateful) when, or before, submitting the index.

Editing and Refining the Entries

16.126 **Refining the terms for main headings.** The assembled entries must now be edited to a coherent whole. You have to make a final choice among synonymous or closely related terms—*agriculture*, *farming*, or *crop raising*; *clothing*, *costume*, or *dress*; *life*, *existence*, or *being*—and, if you think necessary, prepare suitable cross-references to reflect those choices. For journals, the terms may have been established in the indexes for previous volumes and should be retained.

16.127 **Main entries versus subentries.** You also have to decide whether certain items are best treated as main entries or as subentries under another heading. Where will readers look first? In a work dealing with schools of various kinds, such terms as *kindergarten*, *elementary school*, *middle school*, and *public school* should constitute separate entries; in a work in which those terms appear but are not the primary subject matter, they may be better treated as subentries under *school*. An index with relatively few main entries but masses of subentries is unhelpful as a search tool. Furthermore, in an indented index an excessively long string of subentries may begin to look like a set of main entries, so that users lose their way alphabetically. Promote subentries to main entries and use the alphabet to its best advantage.

16.128 **When to furnish subentries.** Main headings unmodified by subentries should not be followed by more than five or six locators. If, for example, the draft index of a work on health care includes an entry like the first example below, it should be broken up into a number of subentries, such as those in the second example, to lead readers quickly to the information sought. The extra space needed is a small price to pay for their convenience.

hospitals, 17, 22, 23, 24, 25, 28, 29–31, 33, 35, 36, 38, 42, 91–92, 94, 95, 96, 98, 101, 111–14, 197

hospitals: administration of, 22, 96; and demand for patient services, 23, 91–92; efficiency of, 17, 29–31, 33, 111–14; finances of, 28, 33, 36, 38, 42, 95, 112; and length of patient stay, 35, 94, 98, 101, 197; quality control in, 22–25, 31

16.129 **How to phrase subheadings.** Subheadings should be as concise and informative as possible and begin with a keyword likely to be sought. *A*, *an*, and *the* are omitted whenever possible. Example A below, *not* to be emulated, shows poorly worded and rambling subheadings. Example B shows greatly improved subentries that conserve space. Note the page references immediately following the main entry; when a main entry has one or more subentries, such undifferentiated locators should normally be reserved for definitive or extended discussions of the term (some indexers will prefer to add *defined* or a similar subhead). Example C adds sub-subentries, making for quicker reference but requiring more space (see 16.27, 16.28). For arrangement of subentries, see 16.68–70.

Example A (*not* to be emulated)

house renovation
  balancing heating system, 65
  building permit required, 7
  called "rehabbing," 8
  correcting overloaded electrical circuits, 136
  how wallboard is finished, 140–44
  installing ready-made fireplace, 191–205
  painting outside of house adds value, 11
  plumbing permit required, 7
  removing paint from doors and woodwork, 156–58
  repairing dripping faucets, 99–100
  replacing clogged water pipes, 125–28
  replacing old wiring, 129–34
  separate chimney required for fireplace, 192
  straightening sagging joists, 40–42
  termite damage to sills a problem, 25
  three ways to deal with broken plaster, 160–62
  violations of electrical code corrected, 135
  what is involved in, 5

Example B (improvement with fairly inclusive subentries)

house renovation, 5, 8
  electrical repairs, 129–34, 135, 136
  fireplace, installing, 191–205
  heating system, balancing, 65
  legal requirements, 7, 135, 192
  painting and decorating, 11, 156–58
  plaster repair, 160–62
  plumbing repairs, 99–100, 125–28
  structural problems, 25, 40–42
  wallboard, finishing, 140–44

Example C (improvement with sub-subentries)

house renovation, 5, 8
  electrical repairs: circuit overload, 136; code violations, 135; old wiring, 129–34
  heating system: balancing, 65; fireplace installation, 191–205
  legal requirements: electrical code, 135; permits, 7; separate chimney for fireplace, 192
  painting and decorating: painting exterior, 11; stripping woodwork, 156–58
  plumbing repairs: clogged water pipes, 125–28; dripping faucets, 99–100
  structural problems: sagging joists, 40–42; termite damage, 25
  wall and ceiling repairs: broken plaster, 160–62; wallboard, finishing, 140–44

If it looks as though an index is going to require a great many sub-subentries, the indexer should check with the publisher before proceeding.

16.130 **Checking cross-references against edited index headings.** As a final or near-final step in editing the index, make sure that all cross-references match the edited headings. See also 16.15–23.

Submitting the Index

16.131 **Index submission format.** Having carefully proofread the draft and checked alphabetical order and all cross-references, punctuation, and capitalization to ensure consistency—and having produced an index of the required length, if one has been specified—you will now send the final draft to the publisher. If the publisher requires a printout, allow margins of at least one inch both left and right, and leave the text unjustified. Do not format the index in columns. Use hard returns only at the end of each entry and, for an indented-style index (see 16.26), at the end of each subentry. Use single line spacing, and apply hanging indents using your software's indentation feature (see 16.24; see also 2.11). Do not impose end-of-line hyphenation (see 2.13). If there is more than one index, give each an appropriate title (Author Index, Subject Index, etc.) and save each in a separate file. To avert disaster, keep a copy of the final draft that you send to the publisher, as well as your marked-up proofs, until the work has been published. Send the publisher a list of any errors you have found (see 16.125).

Editing an Index Compiled by Someone Else

16.132 **What to do with a very bad index.** Editing a well-prepared index can be a pleasure. Little work should be needed. A poorly prepared one, however, presents serious problems. As an editor, you cannot remake a really bad index. If an index cannot be repaired, you have two choices: omit it or have a new one made by another indexer (at additional cost).

16.133 **Index-editing checklist.** Editing an index requires some or all of the following steps, not necessarily in the order given here. Note that it is not necessary to check every heading and every locator against the work—which would take forever—but it is necessary to read the index carefully and to refer to the latest version of the page proofs from time to time.

1. Check headings—in both the main entries and subentries—for alphabetical order.
2. Check the spelling, capitalization, and font (i.e., italics or roman) of each heading, consulting the page proofs if in doubt.

3. Check punctuation—commas, colons, semicolons, en dashes, etc.—for proper style and consistency (see 16.94–100).
4. Check cross-references to make sure they go somewhere and that headings match (see 16.21). Make sure they are needed; if only a few locators are involved, substitute these for the *see* reference (see 16.16). Ensure that the placement of all cross-references within entries is consistent.
5. Add cross-references you believe are necessary.
6. Check to make sure there are no false locators such as "193–93" or "12102" (and figure out whether these may be the product of a typo) and make sure the locators to each main heading and subheading are in ascending order.
7. Check subentries for consistency of order, whether alphabetical or chronological. See 16.68–70.
8. If some entries seem overanalyzed (many subentries with only one locator or, worse, with the same locator), try to combine some of them if it can be done without sacrificing their usefulness. If subheadings are more elaborately worded than necessary, try to simplify them.
9. If awkward or unnecessary sub-subentries appear, correct them by adding appropriate repeated subentries or by adjusting punctuation (see 16.27, 16.28).
10. Look for long strings of unanalyzed locators and break them up, if possible, with subentries (see 16.10, 16.129).
11. Evaluate the accuracy of locators by a random check of five to ten entries. If more than one error shows up, consult the author or the indexer; every locator may have to be rechecked.
12. If the index needs trimming, delete any entries (and cross-references thereto) that you know from your work on the book are trivial, such as references to persons or places used only as examples of something. But be careful. You may offend someone or let yourself in for a lot of work. A handful of unnecessary entries, if they are very short, will not mar an otherwise good index.

16.134 **Instructions for typesetting the index.** At this stage the publisher will have prepared specifications for typesetting the index, and few further instructions are needed. To avoid problems, a brief note such as the following (for an indented index to a book) may be prefixed to the index manuscript after consulting the detailed specifications:

> Set two columns, flush and hang, ragged right; indent subentries one em; indent runovers two ems; preserve en dashes between continuing numbers; leave one line space between alphabetical blocks. Set headnote across both columns. See publisher's design specifications for size and measure.

For an example of a headnote, see 16.141.

Typographical Considerations for Indexes

16.135 **Type size and column width for indexes.** In print works, indexes are usually set in smaller type than the body of the work, often two sizes smaller. That is, if the body copy is set in ten-on-twelve-point type, and the extracts, bibliography, and appendixes in nine-on-eleven, the index will probably be set in eight-on-ten. Indexes are usually set in two columns; with a type page twenty-seven picas wide, the index columns will each be thirteen picas, with a one-pica space between them. In large-format print works, however, the index may be set in three or even four columns.

16.136 **Ragged right-hand margin for indexes.** For very short lines, such as those in an index, justifying the text usually results in either gaping word spaces or excessive hyphenation, making for difficult reading. Chicago therefore sets all indexes without justification ("ragged right").

16.137 **Indenting index entries.** All runover lines are indented, whether the subentries are run in or indented. In indexes with indented subentries (see 16.26), runover lines have to be indented more deeply than the subentries; all runovers, whether from a main entry or a subentry (or even a sub-subentry, should these too be indented), should be indented equally from the left margin. Thus, in an indented index the subentries may be indented one em, the sub-subentries two ems, and the runovers for all entries three ems. (For avoiding sub-subentries, see 16.27, 16.28.) All these matters, however, must be determined before type is set.

16.138 **Fixing bad breaks in indexes.** The final, typeset index should be checked for bad breaks. A line consisting of only one or two page numbers should not be left at the top of a column, for example. A single line at the end of an alphabetic section (followed by a blank line) should not head a column, nor should a single line at the beginning of an alphabetic section remain at the foot of a column. Blemishes like these are eliminated by rebreaking entries or transposing lines from one column to another, by adding to the white space between alphabetic sections, and sometimes by lengthening or shortening all columns on facing pages by one line.

16.139 **Adding "continued" lines in an index.** If an entry breaks at the foot of the last column on a right-hand page (a recto) and resumes at the top of the following left-hand page (a verso), the main heading should be repeated, followed by the word *continued* in parentheses, above the carried-over part of the index.

In an indented index with indented sub-subentries it may be necessary to repeat a subentry if the subentry has been broken.

16.140 **Making typographic distinctions in index entries.** A complicated index can sometimes be made easier to read by using different type styles or fonts. If, for example, names of writers need to be distinguished from names of literary characters, one or the other might be set in caps and small caps. Page references to illustrations might be in italic type (see 16.116) and references to the principal treatment of a subject in boldface. If devices of this kind are used, a headnote to the index must furnish a key (see 16.141, 16.143).

Examples of Indexes

16.141 **A run-in index with italicized references to figures and tables.** Run-in indexes are the most economical of the five formats exemplified in this section. Note the italic page references and the headnote explaining their use. Boldface could also be used for that purpose (see 16.143). For more examples and further discussion, see 16.25, 16.27, 16.94–100. See also 16.68, 16.140.

Page numbers in italics refer to figures and tables.

If occasional sub-subentries are required in a run-in index, you may resort to the style illustrated in 16.27, example B, using em dashes.

16.142 **An indented index with run-in sub-subentries.** For further examples and discussion, see 16.28. See also 16.68.

16.143 **An indented index with indented sub-subentries and highlighted definitions.** Note the deep indentation for runover lines (see 16.137). A boldface page number indicates that the term is defined on that page (explained in a headnote at the beginning of the index). Italics could also be used for that purpose (see 16.141). For further discussion and examples, see 16.28. See also 16.68, 16.140.

Page numbers for definitions are in boldface.

If occasional sub-sub-subentries are essential (they should be avoided if at all possible), they must be run in to the sub-subentries in the same way as sub-subentries are run in at 16.28, example A.

16.144 **An index of first lines.** Unless all the poems, hymns, or songs indexed have very short lines, indexes of this kind are often set full measure (rather than in multiple columns) for easier reading. Letter-by-letter alphabetizing is normally used. Note that lines beginning with *A*, *An*, or *The* are alphabetized under *A* or *T*.

After so long an absence, 295
A handful of red sand, from the hot clime, 108
An old man in a lodge within a park, 315
Beautiful valley! through whose verdant meads, 325
From this high portal, where upsprings, 630
O'er all the hill-tops, 617
Of Prometheus, how undaunted, 185
O hemlock tree! O hemlock tree! how faithful are thy branches, 614
There is no flock, however watched and tended, 107
The young Endymion sleeps Endymion's sleep, 316

16.145 **An index with authors, titles, and first lines combined.** To distinguish the elements, authors' names may be set in caps and small caps, titles of poems in italics, and first lines in roman type, sentence style, without quotation marks. If needed, a headnote to this effect could be furnished. Letter-by-letter alphabetizing should be used.

Cermak, it was, who entertained so great astonishment, 819
Certain she was that tigers fathered him, 724
CHESTERVILLE, NORA M., 212
Come, you whose loves are dead, 394
Coming Homeward Out of Spain, 73
Commemorate me before you leave me, Charlotte, 292
Complaint of a Lover Rebuked, 29
COMPTON, WILBER C., 96
Confound you, Marilyn, confound you, 459

In a general index, poem titles would be set in roman and enclosed in quotation marks, as in text or notes (see 8.181, 8.182).

Glossary

This glossary focuses on key terms related to the typography, design, and production of works published in both print and electronic formats. Many of these terms are too specialized to be treated in the text of the *Manual*; for terms not covered here that may be defined within the text of the *Manual*, consult the index.

AA. An abbreviation for *author's alteration.* See also **alteration.**

adhesive binding. A method of binding that employs glue instead of stitching to hold the pages or signatures together and is widely used for journals and paperback books. Three types of adhesive binding are currently used: perfect binding, notch binding, and burst binding. Contrast **case binding; flexibinding.**

alteration. A change from the manuscript copy introduced in proof, as distinguished from a *correction* made to eliminate a typesetter's or printer's error. See also **AA; DA; EA.**

app. An abbreviation for *application.* Now commonly used to refer to any computer program, *app* can be used more narrowly to refer to an interactive version of a publication such as a dictionary or other reference work.

arabic numerals. The familiar digits used in arithmetical computation. In many type fonts, arabic numerals are available in two basic forms: *lining*, or *aligning* (1 2 3 4 5 6 7 8 9 0), and *old style* (1 2 3 4 5 6 7 8 9 0), abbreviated *OS* and characterized by ascenders and descenders. Contrast **roman numerals.**

artwork. Illustrative material (photographs, drawings, maps, and so forth) intended for reproduction.

ascender. The portion of a lowercase letter that extends above the *x-height*, as in *b* and *d*. Contrast **descender**; see also **arabic numerals.**

ASCII file. See **plain-text file.**

back margin. The inner margin of a page; that is, the margin along the binding side of the page. See also **gutter.**

baseline. In type, an imaginary common line that all capital letters, x-heights, and lining arabic numerals rest on.

beta testing. The final checking of a website or other application before it is released. Such testing is ideally carried out under normal operating conditions by users who are not directly involved in developing the application.

binding. (1) A covering for the pages of a publication, using such materials as leather, cloth, and paper. (2) The process by which such a covering is attached. See also **adhesive binding; case binding; flexibinding.**

bitmap. A digital representation of an image consisting of an array of pixels, in rows and columns, that can be saved to a file. Each pixel in the grid of the bitmap contains information about the color value of its position, which is used, for example, to display an image on a monitor or print it to a page. Contrast **vector graphic**.

blanket. In offset printing, the resilient rubber covering of the blanket cylinder, which receives the ink impression from the plate cylinder and offsets it onto the paper.

bleed. To run an illustration or other ink coverage beyond the edge of a sheet of paper before it is trimmed. Also used as a noun, to refer to the area beyond the trim.

blind embossing. See **embossing**.

blind folio. See **folio**.

blind stamping. See **stamping**.

block quotation. Quoted material set off typographically from the text. Also called *extract*. Contrast **run in**.

bluelines. An abbreviation for *blueline proof*; also called *blues* or (in Europe and Asia) *ozalids*. A type of photographic proof generated by a printing firm. Though this method of producing proofs is no longer widely used, the term is now sometimes used to refer to the final proof produced from a typesetter's electronic files. See also **digital proof**.

boards. Stiffening material used in binding to form the foundation of the cover; formerly wood, now generally a paper product such as binder's board (the finest quality), pasted board (often used in case binding), or chipboard (low quality). Redboard is used for flexible bindings. The bare board is sheathed in (or sometimes affixed with) one of a variety of cover materials.

body text. The running text of a work, as distinguished from the display text used for chapter openings, subheads, and so forth.

boldface. Type that has a darker and heavier appearance than standard type (as in the entries in this list of key terms).

broadside. Designed to be read or viewed normally when the publication is turned ninety degrees. In University of Chicago Press practice, the *left* side of a broadside table or illustration is at the *bottom* of the page. Because most publications are taller than they are wide, broadside images are usually landscape. See also **landscape**.

bulk. The thickness of paper measured in number of pages per inch; also used loosely to indicate the thickness of a publication, excluding the cover.

burst binding. A type of adhesive binding in which the untrimmed spine is perforated and force-fed with glue.

caps. An abbreviation for *capital letters*. See also **small caps**.

case. A hard cover or binding made by a case-making machine or by hand and usually printed, stamped, or labeled before being glued to the gathered endpapers that are attached to the signatures. A case that is covered entirely by one type of material is a one-piece case; a case in which the spine is covered by one type of material and the front and back cover boards by another (often in a different color) is a three-piece case.

case binding. A method of encasing a book in a rigid cover, or *case*. The gathered signatures can be Smyth sewn or side sewn together or adhesive-bound; endpapers are glued to the first and last signatures; a hinge of heavy gauze (the *super*) is glued to the spine of the sewn signatures; and the case is secured to the book by being glued to the flaps of the super and to both endpapers. Contrast **adhesive binding; flexibinding**.

castoff. An estimate of the space, or number of printed pages, that a manuscript will occupy when typeset.

catchword. In very old books, a word or part of a word printed below the last line of text to signal the word on the following page. Also called *catchphrase*.

character. A letter, numeral, symbol, or mark of punctuation.

character count. An approximate measure of the length of a manuscript made by multiplying the number of characters and spaces in an average line by the number of lines in the manuscript. The "character count" feature of many word-processing programs can provide a precise total.

character encoding. A set of machine-readable numbers or other elements—or *code points*—that correspond to a set of alphanumeric characters and symbols such that they can be interpreted by a computer. See also **Unicode**.

character reference. A plain-text placeholder defined for a markup language such as SGML, HTML, or XML and used to refer to a special character that is unavailable in a particular character encoding or from a particular input device such as a keyboard.

clothbound. Bound with a rigid cover, usually cloth wrapped around boards. Contrast **paperback**.

CMYK. An abbreviation for the basic colors used in process color printing—cyan (C), magenta (M), and yellow (Y), plus black (K)—to approximate all the colors in the spectrum. See also **RGB**.

code. See **tag**.

colophon. A statement, usually at the back of a publication (as in this manual), about the materials, processes, and individuals or companies involved in its preparation, production, and manufacturing. The term is also used to refer to a publisher's logo as it often appears on the title page and spine of a book. See also **imprint**.

color printing. See **process color printing**.

color proof. A form of proof used to check the accuracy of color reproduction before printing. Also called *prepress proof*.

color separation. (1) The analysis of color copy for reproduction in terms of the three process colors (plus black) to be used in printing; separation is achieved by shooting through filters or by electronic scanning. (2) A film negative or positive, or a digital file, so produced for preparation of the printing plate. See also **process color printing**.

comp. An abbreviation for *comprehensive layout*, as for a dust jacket, and also for *composition* or *compositor*.

compositor. See **typesetter**.

computer-to-plate (CTP) technology. A process in which print-ready electronic files are imposed directly onto offset printing plates, thus eliminating the need for an intermediate stage involving film.

continuous tone. An image, such as a photograph, with gradations of tone from dark to light, in contrast to an image formed of pure blacks and whites, such as a pen-and-ink drawing. See also **halftone**.

contract proof. An image proof that shows the tonal range, color, and quality that the printer is contractually obligated to match on press.

cover. The two hinged parts of a binding, front and back, and the center panel, or *spine*, that joins them; also the three surfaces making up the covers in this sense, when used to carry printed matter. See also **dust jacket**.

crop. To cut down an illustration, such as a photograph, to improve the appearance of the image by removing extraneous areas.

CSS. An abbreviation for *cascading style sheets*. A style sheet language used to define the presentation of a document marked up in HTML or another formal markup language.

cyan. A greenish blue, one of the three primary colors (plus black) used in process color printing. See also **CMYK**.

DA. An abbreviation for *designer's alteration*. See also **alteration**.

descender. The portion of a lowercase letter that extends below the x-height, as in *g* and *p*. Contrast **ascender**; see also **arabic numerals**.

die. See **stamping**.

digital printing. A type of printing in which the transfer of electronic images to paper is accomplished with ink-jet or laser printers. Contrast **offset printing**; see also **print on demand**.

digital proof. A type of proof generated directly from electronic files and typically output on a laser printer. See also **bluelines**.

display type. Type used for title pages, chapter openings, subheads, and so on, usually distinguished from the type used for body text by a different, often larger font. See also **body text**.

DOI. An abbreviation for *Digital Object Identifier*, a unique alphanumeric string (e.g., 10.1086/597483) assigned to a publication or other unit of intellectual property. A DOI appended to https://doi.org/ provides a means of looking up the current location(s) of such an object on the internet. See also **ISBN; ISSN**.

dots per inch (DPI). See **resolution**.

DRM. An abbreviation for *digital rights management*. Refers to a system designed to protect copyrighted electronic works from unauthorized use, copying, or distribution.

drop cap. An uppercase character set in a type size larger than the text and "dropped," or nested, into lines of text, usually as the first character in the opening paragraph of a chapter or other section of text.

drop folio. See **folio.**

DTD. An abbreviation for *document type definition*. In a markup language such as XML, a set of rules about the structure of a document that dictate the relationships among different tags and allowable text or elements within specified tags. Also called *schema*. See also **tag.**

dust jacket. Also called *jacket*. A protective wrapping, usually made of paper, for a clothbound book; its *flaps*, which fold around the front and back covers, usually carry promotional copy. See also **cover.**

EA. An abbreviation for *editor's alteration*. See also **alteration.**

e-book. An abbreviation for *electronic book*. See also **EPUB.**

ECF. An abbreviation for *elemental chlorine-free*. Refers to paper bleached with a chlorine derivative that releases hazardous substances, including dioxin, into the environment. Contrast **PCF; TCF.**

edition. (1) A publication in its original form, or any subsequent reissue of the publication in which its content is significantly revised. (2) More informally, a term used to refer to each format in which a publication appears (for example, a book published in both cloth and paperback bindings, or a journal published in both electronic and print forms). However, the designation *second edition* would not be applied to the secondary format, or to a second or subsequent *impression* of the publication, in the absence of significant content changes. See also **impression; reprint.**

em. A unit of type measurement equal to the point size of the type in question; for example, a six-point em is six points wide. See also **point.**

embossing. Forming an image in relief (that is, a raised image) on a surface such as a case or a paper cover or dust jacket. If the process does not involve metallic leaf or ink, it is called *blind embossing*. See also **stamping.**

em dash. A short typographical rule measuring the width of an em.

en. A unit of type measurement half the size of an em.

en dash. A short typographical rule measuring the width of an en.

endpapers. Folded sheets pasted or, rarely, sewn to the first and last signatures of a book; the free leaves are then pasted to the inside of the front and back covers to secure the book within the covers. Sometimes endpapers feature printed text or illustrations. Also called *endsheets*.

EPS. An abbreviation for *encapsulated PostScript*. A type of file used to encode graphics so they can be embedded in a larger PostScript file.

EPUB. An abbreviation for *electronic publication*. An international standard format for packaging and encoding content for distribution as a single file based on XHTML and CSS together with compatible formats and technologies. EPUB can be used as an open format for electronic books, or e-books, or in conjunction with commercial products that employ systems of digital rights management. See also **CSS; DRM; XHTML.**

extract. See **block quotation.**

F&Gs. See **folded-and-gathered sheets.**

figure. An illustration printed with the text (hence also called a *text figure*), as distinguished from a plate, which is printed separately. More generally, *figure* is used to refer to any illustration in a published work, including charts (but not tables).

file. A block of digital information with a unique name and location in a computer system or storage medium that can be accessed and manipulated by users of the system or by the system itself. Programs, documents, and images are all examples of data stored in files.

flaps. See **dust jacket.**

flexibinding. Also called *limp binding.* A method of binding in which the pages or signatures are sewn together and the lightweight cover (sometimes with flaps) is then affixed, as in adhesive binding. The result is a publication that is lighter and less bulky than a casebound book but sturdier and more flexible than an adhesive-bound paperback. Contrast **adhesive binding; case binding.**

flush. Even, as with typeset margins. Lines that are set *flush left* are aligned vertically along the left-hand margin; lines set *flush right* are aligned along the right-hand margin. See also **justified; ragged right.**

flush-and-hang style. A copy-setting style in which the first line of each paragraph begins flush left and subsequent, or runover, lines are indented (as in this glossary). Also referred to as *hanging indent.*

folded-and-gathered sheets. Also called *F&Gs* or *sheets.* The collection of all printed signatures in a publication, folded into imposed page sequence and gathered for binding. See also **imposition; signature.**

folio. A page number, often placed at the outside of the running head at the top of the page. If it is placed consistently at the bottom of the page, the number is a *foot folio*; if it is placed at the bottom of the page on display pages only, it is a *drop folio.* A folio counted in numbering pages but not printed (as on the title page) is a *blind folio*; any folio printed is an *expressed folio.* Sometimes also used to refer to the page, or leaf, itself.

font. A complete assortment of a given size and style of type, usually including capitals, small capitals, and lowercase together with numerals, punctuation marks, ligatures, and the commonly used symbols and accents. The italic of a typeface is considered a part of the equipment of a font of type but is often spoken of as a separate font. Often used as a synonym for **typeface.**

foot folio. See **folio.**

four-color process. See **process color printing.**

FTP. An abbreviation for *file transfer protocol*. The protocol, or set of instructions and syntax, for moving files between computers on the internet.

gallery. A section of illustrations grouped on consecutive pages rather than scattered throughout the text.

galley proof. Proof showing typeset material but without final pagination. The term, an anachronism, once referred to the long, narrow columns of type, or "galleys," prepared by a printer before pages were composed, by hand. See also **page proof**.

GIF. An abbreviation for *graphic interchange format*. A file format for compressing and storing bitmapped graphics that contain line art or text for viewing onscreen. Contrast **JPEG**; see also **PNG**.

gutter. The two inner margins (back margins) of facing pages of a book or journal.

hairline rule. A very thin rule—whose width is variously defined as one-quarter point, one-half point, or one-fifth of an em.

hairspace. See **thin space**.

halftone. An image formed by breaking up a continuous-tone image, such as a photograph, into a pattern of dots of varying sizes. When printed, the dots, though clearly visible through a magnifying glass, merge to give an illusion of continuous tone to the naked eye.

halftone screen. A grid used in the halftone process to break an image up into dots. The fineness of the screen is denoted in terms of lines per inch, as in *a 133-line screen*.

hanging indent. See **flush-and-hang style**.

hard copy. A paper copy of text, artwork, or other material, as opposed to a copy that has been stored in digital form.

hardcover binding. See **case binding**.

head margin. The top margin of a page.

HTML. An abbreviation for *hypertext markup language*. A specific set of tags used to describe the structure of hypertext documents that make up most web pages. Web browsers interpret these tags to display text and graphics. HTML is an application of SGML.

HTTP. An abbreviation for *hypertext transfer protocol*. The protocol, or set of instructions and syntax, for exchanging web pages and related content on the internet and for enabling links between such content. HTTPS (the *S* stands for *secure*) is a version of the protocol that adds support for encryption and related security mechanisms.

hypertext. The organization of digital information into associations connected by links. In a hypertext environment, objects such as text and images can contain links to other objects in the same file or in external files, which users can choose to follow. See also **HTML**; **HTTP**.

imposition. The process of arranging the pages for a printed book in such a manner that, when folded, they will appear in the correct order and sequence and in the correct orientation. See also **computer-to-plate (CTP) technology; folded-and-gathered sheets.**

impression. (1) The inked image on the paper created during a single cycle of a press; the speed of a sheet-fed printing press is given in terms of impressions per hour. (2) A single printing of a publication; that is, all the copies printed at a given time. See **edition; reprint.**

imprint. The name of a publisher or a division of a publisher, often as it appears on the title page of a book, sometimes together with a location and a date. See also **colophon.**

indent. To set a line of type so that it begins or ends inside the normal margin. In *paragraph* indentation the first line is indented from the left margin and the following lines are set full measure. In *hanging* indentation (also referred to as *flush and hang*) the first line is set full measure and the following lines are indented. See also **flush-and-hang style.**

internet. A global, public network of computers and computer networks that communicate using TCP/IP (transmission control protocol/internet protocol).

ISBN. An abbreviation for International Standard Book Number. Publishers usually assign an ISBN to each book in each format (e.g., cloth, paperback, or e-book format) under a system maintained by the International ISBN Agency and administered in the United States by R. R. Bowker. The ISBN uniquely identifies the book, thus facilitating order fulfillment and inventory tracking. See also **DOI; ISSN.**

ISSN. An abbreviation for International Standard Serial Number. An ISSN is a unique eight-digit number that identifies a titled journal or other periodical through a database of numbers maintained by the ISSN International Centre. Books that are part of a monograph series may also be assigned an ISSN in addition to an ISBN. See also **DOI; ISBN.**

issue. Used primarily to refer to journals or other periodical publications, typically to indicate the publication's sequence within a larger volume. Although the issue is often designated by a numeral, other means of identification (such as a month or season) may be used instead of or in addition to issue number. See also **volume.**

italic. A slanted type style suggestive of cursive writing (*like this*). Contrast **roman.**

jacket. See **dust jacket.**

JPEG. An abbreviation for *Joint Photographic Experts Group*. A file format commonly used to compress and store bitmapped graphics that contain photographic and other continuous-tone images for viewing on-screen. Contrast **GIF; PNG.**

justified. Spaced out to a specified measure, as with printed lines, so that left and right margins are aligned. Contrast **ragged right.**

kern. The part of a letter that extends beyond the edge of the type body and overlaps the adjacent character, as the *j* in *adjacent* or the *T* in *To*.

kerning. The selective adjustment of space between particular characters (called "letterspacing") to improve appearance or ease of reading.

landscape. Having a greater dimension in width than in length (or height), as with an image or a document. Contrast **portrait**; see also **broadside**.

layout. A designer's plan of how the published material, including illustrative content, should appear.

leading. Also called *line spacing*. The visual space between lines of type, usually measured in points from baseline to baseline. This word, derived from the element *lead*, rhymes with "heading."

letterspacing. See **kerning**.

ligature. A single character formed by joining two characters, such as *œ*, *fi*, or *ff*. Older, more decorative forms (such as *ct*—a *c* joined to a *t* by a loop) are known as *quaint characters*.

line art. Copy for reproduction that contains only solid blacks and whites, such as a pen-and-ink drawing. Contrast **continuous tone**.

line spacing. See **leading**.

lining numbers. See under **arabic numerals**.

lowercase. The uncapitalized letters of a font. Contrast **uppercase**.

macro. From *macroinstruction*. A sequence of operations that is defined for reuse in a computer program. In word processing, a macro can be used to perform complex or repetitive tasks.

makeup. Arrangement of type lines and illustrations into page form.

margin. The white space surrounding the printed area of a page, including the back, or gutter, margin; the head, or top, margin; the fore edge, or outside, margin; and the tail, foot, or bottom, margin. Contrast **type page**.

markup. (1) A sequence of characters, often called *tags* or *codes*, that indicate the logical structure of a manuscript or provide instructions for formatting it. (2) The insertion of such tags in an electronic manuscript; also, traditionally, pencil markup on a paper manuscript.

MathML. An application of XML for tagging mathematical expressions.

measure. The length of the line (usually in picas) in which type is set. *Full measure* refers to copy set the full width of the type page. *Narrow measure* refers to a block of copy (such as a long quotation) indented from one or both margins to distinguish it from surrounding full-measure copy, or to copy set in short lines for multicolumn makeup.

metadata. A form of structured resource description; literally, data about data. The metadata for a given publication may include, among other things, copyright information, an ISBN or ISSN, a volume or issue number, the title and creator of the work, and a description. Metadata is typically recorded using a standard syntax based on a markup language such as XML.

notch binding. A type of adhesive binding in which the untrimmed spine is notched and force-fed with glue.

OCR. An abbreviation for *optical character recognition*. A technology that converts images of text (as from a scan of a printed page) into character data that can be manipulated like any other digital text.

offprint. An article, chapter, or other excerpt from a larger work issued as a separate unit. When offered electronically, sometimes called *digital offprint*.

offset printing. Also called *offset lithography*. The most common type of printing for large print runs of books and journals. The pages to be printed are transferred through computer-to-plate technology to a thin, flexible metal plate, curved to fit one of the revolving cylinders of a printing press. The image on this plate is then transferred to, or *offset* onto, the paper by means of a rubber blanket on another cylinder. Contrast **digital printing**.

old-style numbers. See under **arabic numerals**.

opacity. The measurement of transparency of paper. The higher a paper's opacity, the less tendency there is for text and images printed on one side of a sheet to show through to the other side.

orphan. The first line of a paragraph stranded at the bottom of a page or column. An orphan can be avoided by changes in wording or spacing to the text that precedes it. Contrast **widow**.

page proof. Proof showing typeset material that has been paginated to reflect the placement of text, illustrations, and other design elements. Some publications may require one or more stages of *revised page proof* for checking corrections.

paperback. Bound with a cover stock rather than a cloth-and-board cover. Also called *paperbound*. Contrast **clothbound**.

pattern matching. In word processing, a search or search-and-replace operation that uses a formal syntax to find every instance of a specified string of text or "pattern" and, conditionally, replace it with a different string. Such patterns are known in some contexts as *regular expressions*.

PCF. An abbreviation for *process chlorine-free*. Refers to recycled papers bleached without using chlorine or chlorine derivatives beyond what may have been used originally to produce the recovered wastepaper. Contrast **ECF**; see also **TCF**.

PDF. An abbreviation for *portable document format*. An Adobe Systems file format—and now a formal, open standard (ISO 32000-1)—for stable, device-independent delivery of electronic documents. Preserving such elements as fonts, layout, and pagination, PDF is used not only as the basis for many printed publications but also as a format for electronic publications, including many journal articles and e-books. See also **PostScript (PS)**.

PE. An abbreviation for *printer's error*. See also **printer's error (PE)**.

perfect binding. A type of adhesive binding that involves mechanically roughening off about an eighth of an inch from the spine of the folded-and-gathered sheets. This treatment produces a surface of intermingled fibers to which an adhesive is applied, and a cover (usually paper) is wrapped around the pages. Note that the design of a perfect-bound book should account for the fact that part of the inside margin will be lost in the binding process.

pica. A unit of type measurement equal to twelve points (approximately one-sixth of an inch).

pixel. See **resolution.**

plain-text file. An informal term for a file that contains data encoded using only letters, numerals, punctuation marks, spaces, returns, line breaks, and tabs with no additional formatting or special characters. Plain-text files are often referred to as ASCII files, although newer encoding schemes may be used, and other kinds of data (such as XML) can also be stored as plain-text files.

plate. (1) An image-bearing surface that, when inked, will produce one whole page or several pages of printed matter at a time. (2) A printed illustration, usually of high quality and produced on special paper, pasted or bound into a publication; when so printed, plates are numbered separately from other illustrations.

PNG. An abbreviation for *portable network graphic*. A file format for compressing and storing bitmapped graphics that contain line art or text for viewing onscreen. Contrast **JPEG**; see also **GIF**.

point. (1) The basic unit of type measurement—0.01384 (approximately one seventy-second) of an inch. (2) A unit used in measuring paper products employed in printing and binding—0.001 inches.

portable document format. See **PDF**.

portrait. Having a greater dimension in length (or height) than in width, as with an image or a document. Contrast **landscape**.

PostScript (PS). An Adobe Systems programming language used to describe pages (in terms of trim size, font, placement of graphics, and so forth) and to tell output devices how to render the data. Portable Document Format (PDF), a descendant of PostScript, is somewhat more flexible. See also **PDF**.

prepress. The processes undertaken by a printing firm between the receipt of the electronic files and any other materials from the publisher (or its typesetter) and the printing of the publication.

prepress proof. See **color proof**.

preprint. Part of a book or journal printed and distributed or posted online before publication for promotional purposes or, in time-sensitive fields such as science and medicine, to mitigate the delay of publication schedules and peer review.

press sheet. Also called *printed sheet* or *running sheet*. In offset printing, a large sheet of paper that emerges from the press with pages printed on both sides, each from a single plate. The sheet must then be folded so that the pages fall into proper sequence. See also **signature**.

presswork. The actual printing of a publication, as distinguished from composition, which precedes it, and binding, which follows.

printer's error (PE). An error made by the typesetter (or *compositor*), as distinguished from an *alteration* made in proof by the author, editor, or designer.

print on demand (POD). An application of digital printing that allows one or more copies of a book or other publication to be printed and bound at the time it is ordered. See also **digital printing**.

process color printing. The halftone reproduction of full-color artwork or photographs using several plates (usually four), each printing a different color. Each plate is made with a halftone screen. *Process colors* are cyan, magenta, and yellow, plus black (CMYK). See also **halftone screen.**

proof. The printed or electronic copy made from electronic files, plates, negatives, or positives and used to examine and correct a work's text, illustrations, and design elements before final printing. A publication may involve several stages of proof; see **bluelines; color proof; digital proof; galley proof; page proof.**

protocol. A standard set of instructions and syntax that define the rules by which documents are shared between computers over a network. See also **FTP; HTTP; internet.**

PS. See **PostScript (PS).**

ragged right. Set with an uneven right-hand margin, as with printed lines. Contrast **justified.**

recto. The front side of a leaf; in a book or journal, a right-hand page. To *start recto* is to begin on a recto page, as a preface or an index normally does. Contrast **verso.**

redline. In word processing, a document in which changes (additions and deletions) are shown, or "tracked," by the application of text attributes such as strikethrough, underlining, boldface, or color. Often used as a verb: *to redline*. Also called *legal blackline*.

reprint. A publication in its second or subsequent printing, or *impression*. A reprint may include corrections or new material or both and may be published in a format different from the original printing (for example, as a paperback rather than a clothbound book, or as an e-book). The extent of the changes usually determines whether the reprint is considered a new *edition* of the publication. See also **edition; impression.**

resolution. (1) The number of pixels per unit of measure used to form an image. In the United States, image resolution is calculated per inch; the more pixels per inch, the higher the quality of the image. (2) The number of actual dots per unit of measure at which an image or page is output, usually by a printer or an image-setting device. In the United States, output resolution is usually expressed per inch; the more dots per inch, the higher the quality of the output.

RGB. An abbreviation for the additive color model that uses red (R), green (G), and blue (B) pixels to render color images on displays for computers and other devices. RGB images are converted to CMYK for printing.

roman. The primary type style (like this), as distinguished from italic (*like this*).

roman numerals. Numerals formed from traditional combinations of roman letters, either capitals (I, II, III, IV, etc.) or lowercase (i, ii, iii, iv, etc.). Contrast **arabic numerals.**

run in. (1) To merge a paragraph or line with the preceding one. (2) To set quoted matter continuously with text rather than setting it off as a block quotation.

running heads. Copy set at the top of a page, often containing the title of the publication or chapter, chapter number, or other information. Such copy is sometimes placed at the bottom of the pages, in which case it is referred to as *running feet*.

runover. (1) The continuation of a heading, figure legend, or similar copy onto an additional line. (2) In flush-and-hang material, all lines after the first line of a particular item. (3) Text that is longer than intended, running onto another page, or reset material that is longer than the material it was meant to replace.

saddle stitching. Also called *saddle wiring*. A method of binding that involves inserting thread or staples through the folds of gathered sheets, as in pamphlets and magazines.

sans serif. A typeface with no serifs (like this). Contrast **serif.**

Scalable Vector Graphics (SVG). See **vector graphic.**

scale. To calculate (after cropping) the proportions and finish size of an illustration and the amount of reduction or enlargement needed to achieve this size. In electronic formats, illustrations and other elements are often scaled to adjust to a particular screen size or other parameters.

scan. To produce a digital bitmap of an image (text or graphics) using a device that senses alternating patterns of light and dark and of color. The resolution and scaling percentage of the desired output should be considered before the image is scanned.

schema. See **DTD.**

screen. A halftone screen; also the dot pattern in the printed image produced by such a screen.

serif. A short, light line projecting from the top or bottom of a main stroke of a letter; originally, in handwritten letters, a beginning or finishing stroke of the pen. Contrast **sans serif.**

sewing. The process of stitching signatures together as part of binding. See also **side sewing; Smyth sewing.**

SGML. An abbreviation for *standard generalized markup language*, an international standard for constructing sets of tags. SGML is not a specific set of tags but a system for defining *vocabularies of tags* (the names of the tags and what they mean) and using them to encode documents. See also **tag; XML.**

sheet-fed press. A printing press using paper in sheet form. Contrast **web-fed press.**

sidehead. A subhead that (1) lies partly outside the margin of the text and is set on a line of its own; (2) lies wholly outside the text margin; or (3) begins a paragraph and is continuous with the text. A subhead of the third sort is sometimes called a *run-in sidehead*. See also **run in**.

side sewing. In binding, a method of sewing that involves stitching the signatures from the side, close to the spine, before attaching the case. Libraries typically rebind books in this manner. A side-sewn book is more durable than a Smyth-sewn book but will not open flat. See also **Smyth sewing**.

signature. A press sheet as folded, ready for binding. A signature is usually thirty-two pages but may be only sixteen, eight, or even four pages if the paper stock is very heavy, or sixty-four pages if the paper is thin enough to permit additional folding. The size of the press also affects the size of the signature. See also **folded-and-gathered sheets; press sheet**.

small caps. An abbreviation for *small capitals*. Capital letters set at the x-height of a font (LIKE THIS), usually for display.

Smyth sewing. A method of sewing that involves stitching the signatures individually through the fold before binding them. A Smyth-sewn book has the advantage of lying flat when open, unlike a side-sewn or perfect-bound book. See also **perfect binding; side sewing**.

spec. An abbreviation for *specification* (plural *specs* or *spex*)—as in *design specs*.

spine. The "back" of a bound publication; that is, the center panel of the binding, hinged on each side to the two covers, front and back, and visible when the book or other item is shelved. Typically the title of the publication is printed on the spine. Also called the *backbone*.

spread. Two facing pages, a verso and a recto.

stamping. Imprinting the spine of a case and sometimes the front cover with hard metal dies. Stamping may involve ink, foil, or other coloring material; if it does not, it is called *blind stamping*. See also **embossing**.

stub. The left-hand column of a table. See also **table**.

style sheet. (1) A set of programming instructions that, in conjunction with a markup language such as XML or HTML, determine how a document is presented on a screen, on a printed page, or in another medium such as speech. (2) A record of terms kept by a manuscript editor to document particular usages for a specific manuscript. See also **CSS**.

subhead. A heading, or title, for a section within a chapter or an article. Subheads are usually set in type differing in some way from that of the text; for example, in boldface, all capitals, caps and small caps, or upper- and lowercase italic. See also **sidehead**.

subscript. A small numeral, letter, fraction, or symbol that prints partly below the baseline, usually in mathematical material or chemical formulas.

superscript. A small numeral, letter, fraction, or symbol that prints partly above the x-height, often in mathematical or tabular material or to indicate a footnote or endnote.

table. A more or less complex list presented as an array of vertical columns and horizontal rows.

tag. (1) In SGML and languages derived from SGML, a generic marker used to specify and (when paired) delimit an element in the structure of a document. The process of adding tags to a manuscript is known as *tagging* or *markup*. (2) More informally, a synonym for *code*. See also **markup; SGML; XML.**

TCF. An abbreviation for *totally chlorine-free*. Refers to paper bleached without using chlorine or chlorine derivatives. Contrast **ECF**; see also **PCF**.

thin space. A very small space, defined as one-fifth (or sometimes one-sixth) of an em, added between characters. A similar space, known as a hair space, is even smaller than a thin space.

thumbnail. A miniature rendition of a page or an image. In electronic publications, a thumbnail is often used to indicate a link to a larger electronic object.

TIFF. An abbreviation for *tagged image file format*. A file format developed by Aldus and Microsoft and used to store bitmapped graphics, including scanned line art, halftones, and color images.

trim size. The dimensions, usually in inches, of a full page in a printed publication, including the margins.

typeface. A collection of fonts with common design or style characteristics. A typeface may include roman, italic, boldface, condensed, and other fonts. The various typefaces are designated by name: Baskerville, Caslon, and Times Roman, for example. See also **font**.

type page. The area of a typeset page occupied by the type image, from the running head to the last line of type on the page or the folio, whichever is lower, and from the inside margin to the outside margin, including any area occupied by sideheads.

typesetter. A person, firm, facility, or machine that prepares books, articles, or other documents for publication. The term, now somewhat of an anachronism, has its origins in the composing—or "setting"—of individual pieces of type, by hand, and binding them together to make individual pages. Also called *compositor*.

type styles. See **boldface; italic; roman.**

Unicode. A system of character encoding developed by the Unicode Consortium and incorporated into the ISO standard for universal multiple-octet coded characters (ISO/IEC 10646). See also **character encoding**.

unjustified. See **ragged right**.

uppercase. The capital letters of a font. Contrast **lowercase**.

URL. An abbreviation for *uniform resource locator*, or the address used to locate a document on the internet (e.g., http://www.press.uchicago.edu/).

vector graphic. A digital representation of an image defined by shapes such as lines and curves rather than by pixels. Line art is typically created, edited, and scaled as a vector graphic. Scalable Vector Graphics (SVG) is a standard that defines vector graphics for XML. Because SVG images are both searchable and resolution independent, they are a preferred format for websites and mobile devices. Contrast **bitmap**.

verso. The back side of a leaf; in a book or journal, a left-hand page. Contrast **recto**.

volume. Used to refer (a) to a book or a specific, usually numbered, book in a series or (b) to a series of issues of a journal or other periodical publication. See also **issue**.

web browser. A computer program designed to access information on the internet or on a local network. See also **HTML**; **web page**.

web-fed press. A printing press using paper in roll form. Contrast **sheet-fed press**.

web page. A virtual document delivered via the World Wide Web and viewed in a web browser.

website. A collection of closely related and hyperlinked web pages maintained by an individual or organization.

widow. A short, paragraph-ending line appearing at the top of a page. Widows should be avoided when possible by changes in wording or spacing that either remove the line or lengthen it. Contrast **orphan**.

wiki. A website designed to allow visitors to edit and contribute content.

World Wide Web. Also called *the web*. The internet's most widely used information-retrieval service. The World Wide Web uses hypertext transfer protocol (HTTP) to allow users to request and retrieve documents (web pages and multimedia objects) from other computers on the internet.

x-height. In type, a vertical dimension equal to the height of the lowercase letters (such as *x*) without ascenders or descenders.

XHTML. An application of XML for producing HTML that conforms to the rules established for a particular XML-based document. See also **EPUB; HTML.**

XML. An abbreviation for *extensible markup language*. A subset of the SGML standard, used for structuring documents and data on the internet and for publication in a variety of electronic formats. See also **SGML**.

XSL. An abbreviation for *extensible style sheet language*. A family of style sheet languages used to define the presentation of XML documents and their conversion, or transformation, into other formats such as HTML (using XSLT, extensible style sheet language transformations).

Bibliography

The works listed here offer a starting point for writers, editors, and others involved in publishing who would like more information about topics covered in this manual. The list includes all the works cited in the text as further resources along with other useful references. Although some make recommendations that diverge from those of this manual, they reflect the specific demands of different disciplines and the evolving traditions of writing, editing, and publishing. As with all reference sources, readers should carefully evaluate their suitability for a given purpose.

1 Works on Writing and Editing

1.1 Style

The ACS Style Guide: Effective Communication of Scientific Information. 3rd ed. Edited by Anne M. Coghill and Lorrin R. Garson. Washington, DC: American Chemical Society, 2006. https://doi.org/10.1021/bk-2006-STYG.

ALWD Guide to Legal Citation. 5th ed. Edited by the Association of Legal Writing Directors and Coleen M. Barger. New York: Wolters Kluwer Law & Business, 2014.

AMA Manual of Style: A Guide for Authors and Editors. 10th ed. Edited by Cheryl Iverson. New York: Oxford University Press, 2007. Also available at http://www.amamanualofstyle.com/.

American Institute of Physics. Author Resource Center. AIP Publishing. http://publishing.aip.org/authors.

Apple Style Guide. Apple, April 2013. https://help.apple.com/asg/mac/2013/ASG_2013.pdf.

The Associated Press Stylebook and Briefing on Media Law. Updated annually. New York: Associated Press. Also available at https://www.apstylebook.com/.

Australian Guide to Legal Citation. 3rd ed. Melbourne University Law Review Association, in collaboration with Melbourne Journal of International Law. Melbourne, 2010. https://www.law.unimelb.edu.au/files/dmfile/FinalOnlinePDF-2012Reprint.pdf.

Berkshire Manual of Style for International Publishing. Great Barrington, MA: Berkshire Publishing, 2011.

The Bluebook: A Uniform System of Citation. 20th ed. Cambridge, MA: Harvard Law Review Association, 2015. Also available at https://www.legalbluebook.com/.

Canadian Guide to Uniform Legal Citation. 7th ed. In English and French. Toronto: Carswell/McGill Law Journal, 2010.

Catholic News Service. *CNS Stylebook on Religion: Reference Guide and Usage Manual*. 4th ed. Washington, DC: Catholic News Service, 2012.

CSE Manual. See *Scientific Style and Format.*

Editing Canadian English. 3rd ed. Editors' Association of Canada. Toronto: Editors Canada, 2015. https://editingcanadianenglish.ca/.

Garner, Bryan A. *The Elements of Legal Style*. 2nd ed. New York: Oxford University Press, 2002.

Holoman, D. Kern. *Writing about Music: A Style Sheet*. 2nd ed. Berkeley: University of California Press, 2008.

International Organization for Standardization. *Information and Documentation—Guidelines for Bibliographic References and Citations to Information Resources.* 3rd ed. ISO 690. Paris: ISO, 2010. In English and French. https://www.iso.org/obp/ui/#iso:std:43320.

Journal of Clinical Microbiology. *Instructions to Authors*. Washington, DC: American Society for Microbiology. Revised May 2015. http://jcm.asm.org/site/misc/journal-ita_org.xhtml.

Lipson, Charles. *Cite Right: A Quick Guide to Citation Styles—MLA, APA, Chicago, the Sciences, Professions, and More*. 2nd ed. Chicago: University of Chicago Press, 2011.

The Maroonbook: The University of Chicago Manual of Legal Citation. Anniversary ed. Edited by the University of Chicago Law Review. 2015. https://lawreview.uchicago.edu/page/maroonbook.

MHRA Style Guide: A Handbook for Authors, Editors, and Writers of Theses. 3rd ed. London: Modern Humanities Research Association, 2013. Also available at http://www.mhra.org.uk/.

Microsoft Manual of Style. 4th ed. Redmond, WA: Microsoft Press, 2012.

MLA Handbook. 8th ed. New York: Modern Language Association of America, 2016.

MLA Style Manual and Guide to Scholarly Publishing. 3rd ed. New York: Modern Language Association of America, 2008.

New Oxford Style Manual. 2nd ed. New York: Oxford University Press, 2012. Combines *New Hart's Rules* and *New Oxford Dictionary for Writers and Editors*.

The New York Public Library Writer's Guide to Style and Usage. New York: HarperCollins, 1994.

The New York Times Manual of Style and Usage. Rev. ed. Edited by Allan M. Siegal and William G. Connolly. New York: Three Rivers Press, 1999.

Publication Manual of the American Psychological Association. 6th ed. Washington, DC: American Psychological Association, 2009. Also available at http://www.apastyle.org/asc/.

Reporting on Religion 2: A Stylebook on Religion's Best Beat. Edited by Diane Connolly and Debra L. Mason. Westerville, OH: Religion Newswriters, 2007. Also available at http://religionstylebook.com/.

Sabin, William A. *The Gregg Reference Manual: A Manual of Style, Grammar, Usage, and Formatting*. 11th ed. New York: McGraw-Hill, 2011. Also available at http://www.mhhe.com/business/buscom/gregg/.

Sampsel, Laurie J. *Music Research: A Handbook*. 2nd ed. New York: Oxford University Press, 2012.

The SBL Handbook of Style: For Biblical Studies and Related Disciplines. 2nd ed. Edited by Billie Jean Collins. Atlanta, GA: SBL Press, 2014.

Scientific Style and Format: The CSE Manual for Authors, Editors, and Publishers. 8th ed. Compiled by the Style Manual Committee of the Council of Science Editors. Chicago: Council of Science Editors in cooperation with the University of Chicago Press, 2014. Also available at http://www.scientificstyleandformat.org/.

Strunk, William, Jr., and E. B. White. *The Elements of Style*. 4th ed. Boston: Allyn and Bacon, 2000.

Style Manual for Political Science. Rev. ed. Washington, DC: American Political Science Association Committee on Publications, 2006. http://www.apsanet.org/files/APSAStyleManual2006.pdf.

The Times Style and Usage Guide. Rev. ed. Compiled by Tim Austin. London: Times Books, 2003.

Turabian, Kate L. *A Manual for Writers of Research Papers, Theses, and Dissertations: Chicago Style for Students and Researchers*. 9th ed. Revised by Wayne C. Booth, Gregory G. Colomb, Joseph M. Williams, and University of Chicago Press editorial staff. Chicago: University of Chicago Press, 2018.

———. *Student's Guide to Writing College Papers*. 5th ed. Revised by Gregory G. Colomb, Joseph M. Williams, and the University of Chicago Press editorial staff. Chicago: University of Chicago Press, 2018.

US Geological Survey. *Suggestions to Authors of the Reports of the United States Geological Survey*. 7th ed. Revised and edited by Wallace R. Hansen. Washington, DC: Government Printing Office, 1991. Also available at http://www.nwrc.usgs.gov/lib/lib_sta.htm.

US Government Publishing Office. *GPO Style Manual: An Official Guide to the Form and Style of Federal Government Publishing*. 31st ed. Washington, DC: Government Publishing Office, 2016. https://www.govinfo.gov/gpo-style-manual.

Walker, Janice R., and Todd Taylor. *The Columbia Guide to Online Style*. 2nd ed. New York: Columbia University Press, 2006.

The Wall Street Journal Guide to Business Style and Usage. Edited by Paul R. Martin. London: Free Press, 2002.

Words into Type. 3rd ed. Based on studies by Marjorie E. Skillin, Robert M. Gay, and other authorities. Englewood Cliffs, NJ: Prentice Hall, 1974.

The Yahoo! Style Guide: The Ultimate Sourcebook for Writing, Editing, and Creating Content for the Digital World. Edited by Chris Barr. New York: Yahoo! / St. Martin's Griffin, 2010.

1.2 *Grammar and Usage*

Aitchison, James. *Cassell Dictionary of English Grammar*. 2nd ed. London: Cassell, 2001.

Baron, Dennis. *Grammar and Gender*. New Haven, CT: Yale University Press, 1986.

Bernstein, Theodore M. *The Careful Writer: A Modern Guide to English Usage*. New York: Atheneum, 1965.

———. *Miss Thistlebottom's Hobgoblins: The Careful Writer's Guide to the Taboos, Bugbears, and Outmoded Rules of English Usage*. New York: Farrar, Straus and Giroux, 1971.

Burchfield, Robert W. *Unlocking the English Language*. New York: Hill and Wang, 1991.

Ebbitt, Wilma R., and David R. Ebbitt. *Index to English*. 8th ed. New York: Oxford University Press, 1990.

Follett, Wilson. *Modern American Usage: A Guide*. Revised by Erik Wensberg. New York: Hill and Wang, 1998.

Fowler, H. W. *A Dictionary of Modern English Usage*. 2nd ed. Revised and edited by Sir Ernest Gowers. Oxford: Oxford University Press, 1965.

Fowler's Modern English Usage. 4th ed. Edited by Jeremy Butterfield. New York: Oxford University Press, 2015.

Garner, Bryan A. *The Chicago Guide to Grammar, Usage, and Punctuation*. Chicago: University of Chicago Press, 2016.

———. *Garner's Modern English Usage*. 4th ed. New York: Oxford University Press, 2016.

Gordon, Karen Elizabeth. *The Deluxe Transitive Vampire: The Ultimate Handbook of Grammar for the Innocent, the Eager, and the Doomed*. Rev. ed. New York: Pantheon, 1993.

———. *The New Well-Tempered Sentence: A Punctuation Handbook for the Innocent, the Eager, and the Doomed*. Rev. ed. Boston: Houghton Mifflin, 1993.

Gowers, Ernest. *Plain Words: A Guide to the Use of English*. Revised and updated by Rebecca Gowers. London: Penguin Books, 2015.

Greenbaum, Sydney. *Oxford English Grammar*. New York: Oxford University Press, 1996.

Hale, Constance. *Sin and Syntax: How to Craft Wickedly Effective Prose*. Rev. ed. New York: Three Rivers Press, 2013.

Johnson, Edward D. *The Handbook of Good English*. New York: Pocket Books, 1991.

Maggio, Rosalie. *How to Say It: Choice Words, Phrases, Sentences, and Paragraphs for Every Situation*. 3rd ed. New York: Prentice Hall, 2009.

Merriam-Webster's Dictionary of English Usage. Springfield, MA: Merriam-Webster, 1994.

O'Conner, Patricia T. *Woe Is I: The Grammarphobe's Guide to Better English in Plain English*. 3rd ed. New York: Riverhead Books, 2009.

The Oxford Dictionary of English Grammar. Edited by Sylvia Chalker and Edmund Weiner. New York: Oxford University Press, 1998.

Shertzer, Margaret. *The Elements of Grammar*. New York: MacMillan, 1996.

Trask, R. L. *Language: The Basics*. 2nd ed. New York: Routledge, 1999.

Trimble, John R. *Writing with Style: Conversations on the Art of Writing*. 3rd ed. Boston: Pearson, 2010.

Wallraff, Barbara. *Word Court: Wherein Verbal Virtue Is Rewarded, Crimes against the Language Are Punished, and Poetic Justice Is Done*. New York: Harcourt, 2000.

Walsh, Bill. *Lapsing into a Comma: A Curmudgeon's Guide to the Many Things That Can Go Wrong in Print—and How to Avoid Them*. Chicago: Contemporary Books, 2000.

Williams, Joseph M., and Joseph Bizup. *Style: Lessons in Clarity and Grace*. 12th ed. Boston: Pearson, 2016.

Wilson, Kenneth G. *The Columbia Guide to Standard American English*. New York: Columbia University Press, 1993.

Zinsser, William. *On Writing Well: The Classic Guide to Writing Nonfiction*. 30th anniversary ed. New York: HarperCollins, 2006.

1.3 Research and Writing

Abbott, Andrew. *Digital Paper: A Manual for Research and Writing with Library and Internet Materials*. Chicago: University of Chicago Press, 2014.

Becker, Howard S. *Writing for Social Scientists: How to Start and Finish Your Thesis, Book, or Article*. 2nd ed. Chicago: University of Chicago Press, 2007.

Belcher, Wendy Laura. *Writing Your Journal Article in 12 Weeks: A Guide to Academic Publishing Success*. 2nd ed. Chicago: University of Chicago Press, forthcoming.

Bell, Susan. *The Artful Edit: On the Practice of Editing Yourself*. New York: W. W. Norton, 2007.

Booth, Wayne C., Gregory G. Colomb, Joseph M. Williams, Joseph Bizup, and William T. FitzGerald. *The Craft of Research*. 4th ed. Chicago: University of Chicago Press, 2016.

Cook, Claire Kehrwald. *Line by Line: How to Edit Your Own Writing*. Boston: Modern Language Association / Houghton Mifflin, 1985.

Gastel, Barbara, and Robert A. Day. *How to Write and Publish a Scientific Paper*. 8th ed. Santa Barbara, CA: Greenwood, 2016.

Gerard, Philip. *The Art of Creative Research: A Field Guide for Writers*. Chicago: University of Chicago Press, 2017.

Germano, William. *From Dissertation to Book*. 2nd ed. Chicago: University of Chicago Press, 2013.

Ghodsee, Kristen. *From Notes to Narrative: Writing Ethnographies That Everyone Can Read*. Chicago: University of Chicago Press, 2016.

Graff, Gerald, and Cathy Birkenstein. *"They Say / I Say": The Moves That Matter in Academic Writing*. 3rd ed. New York: W. W. Norton, 2014.

Greene, Anne E. *Writing Science in Plain English*. Chicago: University of Chicago Press, 2013.

Harman, Eleanor, Ian Montagnes, Siobhan McMenemy, and Chris Bucci, eds. *The Thesis and the Book: A Guide for First-Time Academic Authors*. 2nd ed. Toronto: University of Toronto Press, 2003.

Hart, Jack. *Storycraft: The Complete Guide to Writing Narrative Nonfiction*. Chicago: University of Chicago Press, 2011.

———. *A Writer's Coach: The Complete Guide to Writing Strategies That Work*. New York: Anchor Books, 2007.

Jensen, Joli. *Write No Matter What: Advice for Academics*. Chicago: University of Chicago Press, 2017.

Kidder, Tracy, and Richard Todd. *Good Prose: The Art of Nonfiction*. New York: Random House, 2013.

Lanham, Richard A. *Revising Prose*. 5th ed. New York: Pearson Longman, 2007.

Lerner, Betsy. *The Forest for the Trees: An Editor's Advice to Writers*. Rev. ed. New York: Riverhead Books, 2010.

Lipson, Charles. *How to Write a BA Thesis: A Practical Guide from Your First Ideas to Your Finished Paper*. Chicago: University of Chicago Press, 2005.

Luey, Beth, ed. *Revising Your Dissertation: Advice from Leading Editors*. Updated ed. Berkeley: University of California Press, 2007.

McCloskey, Deirdre. *Economical Writing*. 3rd ed. Chicago: University of Chicago Press, forthcoming.

McMillan, Victoria E. *Writing Papers in the Biological Sciences*. 5th ed. Boston: Bedford / St. Martin's, 2006.

Miller, Jane E. *The Chicago Guide to Writing about Multivariate Analysis*. 2nd ed. Chicago: University of Chicago Press, 2013.

———. *The Chicago Guide to Writing about Numbers*. 2nd ed. Chicago: University of Chicago Press, 2015.

Montgomery, Scott L. *The Chicago Guide to Communicating Science*. 2nd ed. Chicago: University of Chicago Press, 2017.

Pinker, Steven. *The Sense of Style: The Thinking Person's Guide to Writing in the 21st Century*. New York: Viking, 2014.

Pyne, Stephen J. *Voice and Vision: A Guide to Writing History and Other Serious Nonfiction*. Cambridge, MA: Harvard University Press, 2009.

Stein, Arlene, and Jessie Daniels. *Going Public: A Guide for Social Scientists*. Chicago: University of Chicago Press, 2017.

Sword, Helen. *Stylish Academic Writing*. Cambridge, MA: Harvard University Press, 2012.

———. *The Writer's Diet: A Guide to Fit Prose*. Chicago: University of Chicago Press, 2016.

Zeiger, Mimi. *Essentials of Writing Biomedical Research Papers*. 2nd ed. New York: McGraw-Hill, 2000.

2 Works on Publishing

2.1 Manuscript Editing and Proofreading

Anderson, Laura. *McGraw-Hill's Proofreading Handbook*. 2nd ed. New York: McGraw-Hill, 2006.

Borel, Brooke. *The Chicago Guide to Fact-Checking*. Chicago: University of Chicago Press, 2016.

Butcher, Judith, Caroline Drake, and Maureen Leach. *Butcher's Copy-Editing: The Cambridge Handbook for Editors, Copy-Editors, and Proofreaders*. 4th ed. New York: Cambridge University Press, 2006.

Copyediting: Language in the Digital Age. Bimonthly newsletter published by McMurry, Inc. Also available at http://www.copyediting.com/.

Einsohn, Amy. *The Copyeditor's Handbook: A Guide for Book Publishing and Corporate Communications; With Exercises and Answer Keys*. 3rd ed. Berkeley: University of California Press, 2011.

Judd, Karen. *Copyediting: A Practical Guide*. 3rd ed. Menlo Park, CA: Crisp Learning, 2001.

Lyon, Jack M. *Microsoft Word for Publishing Professionals*. West Valley City, UT: Editorium, 2008.

Norris, Mary. *Between You & Me: Confessions of a Comma Queen*. New York: W. W. Norton, 2015.

Norton, Scott. *Developmental Editing: A Handbook for Freelancers, Authors, and Publishers*. Chicago: University of Chicago Press, 2009.

Saller, Carol Fisher. *The Subversive Copy Editor: Advice from Chicago (or, How to Negotiate Good Relationships with Your Writers, Your Colleagues, and Yourself)*. 2nd ed. Chicago: University of Chicago Press, 2016.

Stainton, Elsie Myers. *The Fine Art of Copyediting*. 2nd ed. New York: Columbia University Press, 2002.

University of Chicago Press Editorial Staff. *But Can I Start a Sentence with "But"? Advice from the Chicago Style Q&A*. With a foreword by Carol Fisher Saller. Chicago: University of Chicago Press, 2016.

2.2 Illustrations

Briscoe, Mary Helen. *Preparing Scientific Illustrations: A Guide to Better Posters, Presentations, and Publications*. 2nd ed. New York: Springer-Verlag, 1996. https://doi.org/10.1007/978-1-4612-3986-4.

Monmonier, Mark. *Mapping It Out: Expository Cartography for the Humanities and Social Sciences*. Chicago: University of Chicago Press, 1993.

Ross, Ted. *The Art of Music Engraving and Processing: A Complete Manual, Reference, and Text Book on Preparing Music for Reproduction and Print*. Miami: Hansen Books, 1970.

Swan, Ann. *Botanical Portraits with Colored Pencils*. Hauppauge, NY: Barron's Educational Series, 2010.

Tufte, Edward R. *Envisioning Information*. Cheshire, CT: Graphics Press, 1990.

———. *The Visual Display of Quantitative Information*. 2nd ed. Cheshire, CT: Graphics Press, 2001.

———. *Visual Explanations: Images and Quantities, Evidence and Narrative*. Cheshire, CT: Graphics Press, 1997.

Zweifel, Frances W. *A Handbook of Biological Illustration*. 2nd ed. Chicago: University of Chicago Press, 1988.

2.3 Rights and Permissions

Aufderheide, Patricia, and Peter Jaszi. *Reclaiming Fair Use: How to Put Balance Back in Copyright*. Chicago: University of Chicago Press, 2011.

Bielstein, Susan M. *Permissions, a Survival Guide: Blunt Talk about Art as Intellectual Property*. Chicago: University of Chicago Press, 2006.

Crews, Kenneth D. *Copyright and Your Dissertation or Thesis: Ownership, Fair Use, and Your Rights and Responsibilities*. ProQuest, 2013. http://media2.proquest.com/documents/copyright_dissthesis_ownership.pdf.

Fischer, Mark A., E. Gabriel Perle, and John Taylor Williams. *Perle, Williams & Fischer on Publishing Law*. 4th ed. New York: Aspen, 2013. Annual loose-leaf updates.

Fishman, Stephen. *The Copyright Handbook: What Every Writer Needs to Know*. Berkeley, CA: Nolo, 2011.

Goldstein, Paul. *Goldstein on Copyright*. 3rd ed. New York: Aspen, 2005. Loose-leaf updates.

Kaufman, Roy S. *Publishing Forms and Contracts*. New York: Oxford University Press, 2008.

Nimmer, Melville, and Paul Edward Gellner, eds. *International Copyright Law and Practice*. Newark, NJ: LexisNexis Matthew Bender, 2004. Loose-leaf updates.

Nimmer, Melville, Paul Marcus, David A. Myers, and David Nimmer. *Cases and*

Materials on Copyright and Other Aspects of Entertainment Litigation, Including Unfair Competition, Defamation, Privacy. 8th ed. New Providence, NJ: LexisNexis, 2012.

Nimmer, Melville, and David Nimmer. *Nimmer on Copyright*. Rev. ed. 11 vols. Newark, NJ: LexisNexis Matthew Bender, 2005. Loose-leaf updates.

Patry, William F. *The Fair Use Privilege in Copyright Law*. 2nd ed. Washington, DC: Bureau of National Affairs, 1995.

———. *Moral Panics and the Copyright Wars*. New York: Oxford University Press, 2009.

———. *Patry on Copyright*. 8 vols. St. Paul, MN: Thomson/West, 2007–. Loose-leaf updates.

Strong, William S. *The Copyright Book: A Practical Guide*. 6th ed. Cambridge, MA: MIT Press, 2014.

Suber, Peter. *Open Access*. Cambridge, MA: MIT Press, 2012. http://cyber.law.harvard.edu/hoap/Open_Access_(the_book).

2.4 Mathematics

American Mathematical Society. Author Resource Center. AMS. http://www.ams.org/publications/authors/. Includes access to Swanson, *Mathematics into Type*.

Gowers, Timothy, ed. *The Princeton Companion to Mathematics*. Princeton, NJ: Princeton University Press, 2008.

Higham, Nicholas J. *Handbook of Writing for the Mathematical Sciences*. 2nd ed. Philadelphia: Society for Industrial and Applied Mathematics, 1998.

The International System of Units (SI). 8th ed. Sèvres: Bureau International des Poids et Mesures, 2006; updated 2014. http://www.bipm.org/en/si/si_brochure/.

Knuth, Donald E. *The TeXbook*. Boston: Addison-Wesley, 2000.

Kopka, Helmut, and Patrick W. Daly. *Guide to LaTeX*. 11th ed. Boston: Addison-Wesley, 2010.

Lamport, Leslie. *LaTeX: A Document Preparation System; User's Guide and Reference Manual*. 2nd ed. Reading, MA: Addison-Wesley, 1999.

Mittelbach, Frank, et al. *The LaTeX Companions: A Complete Guide and Reference for Preparing, Illustrating, and Publishing Technical Documents*. 3rd ed. Boston: Addison-Wesley, 2007.

Paulos, John Allen. *Innumeracy: Mathematical Illiteracy and Its Consequences*. 1st pbk. ed. New York: Hill and Wang, 2001.

Spivak, Michael. *The Joy of TeX: A Gourmet Guide to Typesetting with the AMS-TeX Macro Package*. 2nd ed. Providence, RI: American Mathematical Society, 1990.

Swanson, Ellen. *Mathematics into Type*. Updated edition by Arlene O'Sean and Antoinette Schleyer. Providence, RI: American Mathematical Society, 1999.

Thompson, Ambler, and Barry N. Taylor. *Guide for the Use of the International System of Units (SI)*. Gaithersburg, MD: National Institute of Standards and Technology, 2008. http://www.nist.gov/pml/pubs/sp811/.

2.5 Indexing

Ament, Kurt. *Indexing: A Nuts-and-Bolts Guide for Technical Writers*. Norwich, NY: William Andrew, 2001.

Booth, Pat F. *Indexing: The Manual of Good Practice*. Munich: K. G. Saur, 2001.

Browne, Glenda, and Jon Jermey. *The Indexing Companion*. Melbourne: Cambridge University Press, 2007.

Cleveland, Donald B., and Ana D. Cleveland. *Introduction to Indexing and Abstracting*. 4th ed. Santa Barbara, CA: Libraries Unlimited, 2013.

Fetters, Linda K. *Handbook of Indexing Techniques: A Guide for Beginning Indexers*. 5th ed. Medford, NJ: Information Today, 2013.

Mulvany, Nancy. *Indexing Books*. 2nd ed. Chicago: University of Chicago Press, 2005.

Stauber, D. Mi. *Facing the Text: Content and Structure in Book Indexing*. Eugene, OR: Cedar Row Press, 2004.

Wellisch, Hans H. *Indexing from A to Z*. 2nd ed. New York: H. W. Wilson, 1995.

2.6 Design

Bringhurst, Robert. *The Elements of Typographic Style*. 4th ed. Seattle: Hartley and Marks, 2013.

Chappell, Warren, and Robert Bringhurst. *A Short History of the Printed Word*. 2nd ed. Point Roberts, WA: Hartley and Marks, 1999.

Craig, James, and Irene Korol Scala. *Designing with Type: The Essential Guide to Typography*. 5th ed. New York: Watson-Guptill, 2006.

Dowding, Geoffrey. *Finer Points in the Spacing and Arrangement of Type*. Rev. ed. Point Roberts, WA: Hartley and Marks, 1995.

Duckett, Jon. *HTML and CSS: Design and Build Websites*. Indianapolis: Wiley, 2011.

Gill, Eric. *An Essay on Typography*. Boston: David R. Godine, 1988.

Hendel, Richard. *Aspects of Contemporary Book Design*. Iowa City: University of Iowa Press, 2013.

———. *On Book Design*. New Haven, CT: Yale University Press, 1998.

Hochuli, Jost, and Robin Kinross. *Designing Books: Practice and Theory*. Rev. ed. London: Hyphen Press, 2003.

Johnston, Edward. *Writing and Illuminating and Lettering*. 1946; repr., New York: Dover, 1995.

Lupton, Ellen. *Thinking with Type: A Critical Guide for Designers, Writers, Editors, and Students*. 2nd ed. New York: Princeton Architectural Press, 2010.

McLean, Ruari. *The Thames and Hudson Manual of Typography*. New York: Thames and Hudson, 1992.

Tschichold, Jan. *The Form of the Book: Essays on the Morality of Good Design*. Point Roberts, WA: Hartley and Marks, 1995.

———. *The New Typography*. New ed. Translated by Ruari McLean. With a foreword by Richard Hendel and an introduction by Robin Kinross. Berkeley: University of California Press, 2006.

2.7 Production

Beach, Mark, and Eric Kenly. *Getting It Printed*. 4th ed. Cincinnati: HOW Design Books, 2004.

Berger, Sidney E. *Rare Books and Special Collections*. Chicago: American Library Association, 2014.

Book Industry Study Group. *BISG Quick Start Guide to Accessible Publishing*. BISG, March 2016. https://www.bisg.org/publications/bisg-quick-start-guide-accessible-publishing.

The Bookman's Glossary. 6th ed. Edited by Jean Peters. New York: R. R. Bowker, 1983.

The Columbia Guide to Digital Publishing. Edited by William E. Kasdorf. New York: Columbia University Press, 2003.

Eckersley, Richard, Richard Angstadt, Charles M. Ellertson, Richard Hendel, Naomi B. Pascal, and Anita Walker Scott. *Glossary of Typesetting Terms*. Chicago: University of Chicago Press, 1994.

EPUB 3 Overview: Recommended Specification. Edited by Garth Conboy, Matt Garrish, Markus Gylling, William McCoy, Murata Makoto, and Daniel Weck. International Digital Publishing Forum, June 26, 2014. http://www.idpf.org/epub/301/spec/epub-overview-20140626.html.

Extensible Markup Language (XML). V. 1.1, 2nd ed. Edited by Tim Bray, Jean Paoli, C. M. Sperberg-McQueen, Eve Maler, François Yergeau, and John Cowan. W3C recommendation, August 16, 2006. http://www.w3.org/TR/2006/REC-xml11-20060816.

Friedl, Jeffrey E. F. *Mastering Regular Expressions*. 3rd ed. Sebastopol, CA: O'Reilly, 2006.

Glaister, Geoffrey Ashall. *Encyclopedia of the Book*. 2nd ed. New Castle, DE: Oak Knoll Press, 2001.

Johnson, Arthur W. *The Thames and Hudson Manual of Bookbinding*. London: Thames and Hudson, 1981.

Kinross, Robin, Jaap van Triest, and Karel Martens, eds. *Karel Martens: Printed Matter*. 2nd ed. London: Hyphen Press, 2002.

Lawler, Brian P. *Official Adobe Print Publishing Guide: The Essential Resource for Design, Production, and Prepress*. 2nd ed. Berkeley, CA: Adobe Press, 2005.

Lee, Marshall. *Bookmaking: Editing, Design, Production*. 3rd ed. New York: Norton, 2004.

National Information Standards Organization. *Journal Article Versions (JAV): Recommendations of the NISO/ALPSP JAV Technical Working Group*. Proposed standard NISO RP-8. In partnership with the Association of Learned and Professional Society Publishers. April 2008. Available at http://www.niso.org/publications/rp/RP-8-2008.pdf.

Pocket Pal: A Graphic Arts Production Handbook. 20th ed. Memphis, TN: International Paper, 2007.

Register, Renée, and Thad McIlroy. *The Metadata Handbook: A Book Publisher's Guide to Creating and Distributing Metadata for Print and Ebooks*. 2nd ed. Columbus, OH: DataCurate, 2015. http://themetadatahandbook.com/.

Rogondino, Michael, and Pat Rogondino. *Process Color Manual: 24,000 CMYK Combinations for Design, Prepress, and Printing*. San Francisco: Chronicle Books, 2000.

Unicode Consortium. *The Unicode Standard*. Version 9.0.0. Mountain View, CA: Unicode Consortium, July 2016. http://www.unicode.org/versions/Unicode9.0.0/.

XML. See *Extensible Markup Language*.

XML.com. Textuality Services and O'Reilly Media. https://www.xml.com/.

2.8 The Publishing Industry

Benson, Philippa J., and Susan C. Silver. *What Editors Want: An Author's Guide to Scientific Journal Publishing*. Chicago: University of Chicago Press, 2012.

Brewer, Robert Lee, ed. *2015 Guide to Self-Publishing*. Cincinnati, OH: Writer's Digest Books, 2014.

Coker, Mark. *The Secrets to Ebook Publishing Success*. 2014 ed. Smashwords Guides, bk. 3. Los Gatos, CA: Smashwords, 2012. EPUB, Kindle, PDF.

Friedman, Jane. *The Business of Being a Writer*. Chicago: University of Chicago Press, 2018.

Germano, William. *Getting It Published: A Guide for Scholars and Anyone Else Serious about Serious Books*. 3rd ed. Chicago: University of Chicago Press, 2016.

Ginna, Peter, ed. *What Editors Do: The Art, Craft, and Business of Book Editing*. Chicago: University of Chicago Press, 2017.

Greco, Albert N. *The Book Publishing Industry*. 2nd ed. Mahwah, NJ: Lawrence Erlbaum, 2005.

ILMP (International Literary Market Place). Medford, NJ: Information Today. Published annually. Also available at http://books.infotoday.com/directories/ilmp.shtml.

Journal of Electronic Publishing. Published quarterly by Michigan Publishing, University of Michigan Library. http://www.journalofelectronicpublishing.org/.

Journal of Scholarly Publishing. Published quarterly by the University of Toronto Press. Also available at https://www.utpjournals.com/Journal-of-Scholarly-Publishing.html/.

Kurowski, Travis, Wayne Miller, and Kevin Prufer, eds. *Literary Publishing in the Twenty-First Century*. Minneapolis: Milkweed Editions, 2016.

LMP (Literary Market Place). Medford, NJ: Information Today. Published annually. Also available at http://books.infotoday.com/directories/lmp.shtml.

Luey, Beth. *Handbook for Academic Authors*. 5th ed. New York: Cambridge University Press, 2009.

Rabiner, Susan, and Alfred Fortunato. *Thinking Like Your Editor: How to Write Great Serious Nonfiction—and Get It Published*. New York: W. W. Norton, 2002.

Striphas, Ted. *The Late Age of Print: Everyday Book Culture from Consumerism to Control*. New York: Columbia University Press, 2009.

Suzanne, Claudia. *This Business of Books: A Complete Overview of the Industry from Concept through Sales*. 4th ed. Tustin, CA: WC Publishing, 2003.

Thompson, John B. *Merchants of Culture: The Publishing Business in the Twenty-First Century*. 2nd ed. New York: Plume, 2012.

3 Dictionaries

3.1 English Dictionaries

American Heritage Dictionary of the English Language. 5th ed. Boston: Houghton Mifflin Harcourt, 2011. Also available at https://www.ahdictionary.com/.

Barber, Katherine, ed. *Canadian Oxford Dictionary*. 2nd ed. Oxford: Oxford University Press, 2004. https://doi.org/10.1093/acref/9780195418163.001.0001.

Merriam-Webster's Collegiate Dictionary. 11th ed. Springfield, MA: Merriam-Webster, 2003. Continually updated at https://www.merriam-webster.com/.

Merriam-Webster Unabridged. See *Webster's Third New International Dictionary of the English Language, Unabridged*.

Moore, Bruce, ed. *Australian Oxford Dictionary*. 2nd ed. Oxford: Oxford University Press, 2004. https://doi.org/10.1093/acref/9780195517965.001.0001.

New Oxford American Dictionary. 3rd ed. Edited by Angus Stevenson and Christine A. Lindberg. New York: Oxford University Press, 2010. https://doi.org/10.1093/acref/9780195392883.001.0001.

Oxford English Dictionary. 2nd ed. 20 vols. Oxford: Oxford University Press, 1989. Continually updated at http://www.oed.com/.

Roget's II: The New Thesaurus. 3rd ed. Boston: Houghton Mifflin, 1995.

Roget's 21st Century Thesaurus in Dictionary Form. 3rd ed. Edited by Barbara Ann Kipfer. New York: Bantam Dell, 2005.

Shorter Oxford English Dictionary. 6th ed. 2 vols. New York: Oxford University Press, 2007.

Webster's New World College Dictionary. 4th ed. Cleveland: Webster's New World, 2001.

Webster's Third New International Dictionary of the English Language, Unabridged. Springfield, MA: Merriam-Webster, 1993. Continually updated, as *Merriam-Webster Unabridged*, at https://unabridged.merriam-webster.com/.

Wiktionary: The Free Dictionary. San Francisco: Wikimedia Foundation. https://www.wiktionary.org/.

3.2 Bilingual Dictionaries

ABC Chinese-English Comprehensive Dictionary. Edited by John DeFrancis. Honolulu: University of Hawai'i Press, 2003.

Cassell's Italian Dictionary. Compiled by Piero Rebora, Francis M. Guercio, and Arthur L. Hayward. New York: John Wiley, 1994.

Kenkyūsha's New Japanese-English Dictionary. 5th ed. Tokyo: Kenkyūsha, 2003.

Larousse Unabridged French Dictionary: French-English, English-French. Edited by Faye Carney. Paris: Larousse, 2010.

Minjung's Essence English-Korean Dictionary. 11th ed. Elizabeth, NJ: Hollym International Corp., 2015.

Oxford Arabic Dictionary: Arabic-English, English-Arabic. Edited by Tressy Arts. Oxford: Oxford University Press, 2014.

Oxford German Dictionary: German-English, English-German. 3rd ed. Edited by Werner Scholze-Stubenrecht, J. B. Sykes, M. Clark, and O. Thyen. Oxford: Oxford University Press, 2008.

Oxford-Hachette French Dictionary. 4th ed. Edited by Marie-Hélène Corréard et al. Oxford: Oxford University Press, 2007.

Oxford Latin Dictionary. 2nd ed. Edited by P. G. W. Glare. 2 vols. Oxford: Oxford University Press, 2012.

Oxford-Paravia Italian Dictionary. 3rd ed. Oxford: Oxford University Press, 2010.

Oxford Russian Dictionary. 4th ed. Edited by Marcus Wheeler, Boris Unbegaun, Paul Falla, and Della Thompson. Oxford: Oxford University Press, 2007.

Oxford Spanish Dictionary. 4th ed. Edited by Beatriz Galimberti Jarman and Roy Russell. Oxford: Oxford University Press, 2008.

The University of Chicago Spanish-English Dictionary. 6th ed. Edited by David Pharies. Chicago: University of Chicago Press, 2012.

3.3 Medical and Scientific Dictionaries

Clapham, Christopher, and James Nicholson. *Concise Dictionary of Mathematics*. 4th ed. New York: Oxford University Press, 2009.

A Dictionary of Biology. 6th ed. Edited by Elizabeth A. Martin and Robert Hine.

Oxford: Oxford University Press, 2010. https://doi.org/10.1093/acref/9780199204625.001.0001.

A Dictionary of Chemistry. 6th ed. Edited by John Daintith. Oxford: Oxford University Press, 2008. https://doi.org/10.1093/acref/9780199204632.001.0001.

A Dictionary of Mechanical Engineering. Edited by Tony Atkins and Marcel Escudier. Oxford: Oxford University Press, 2013. https://doi.org/10.1093/acref/9780199587438.001.0001.

A Dictionary of Physics. 6th ed. Edited by John Daintith. Oxford: Oxford University Press, 2009. https://doi.org/10.1093/acref/9780199233991.001.0001.

Dorland's Illustrated Medical Dictionary. 32nd ed. Philadelphia: Elsevier Saunders, 2012.

Oxford Dictionary of Science. 6th ed. Edited by Elizabeth A. Martin. New York: Oxford University Press, 2010.

Stedman's Medical Dictionary. 28th ed. Baltimore: Lippincott Williams & Wilkins, 2006. Also available at http://stedmansonline.com/.

USP Dictionary of USAN and International Drug Names. Rockville, MD: US Pharmacopeial Convention. Revised annually. Available at http://www.usp.org/store/products-services/usp-dictionary.

4 General Reference Works

4.1 Biography

American Men and Women of Science. 32nd ed. 8 vols. Farmington Hills, MI: Gale, 2014.

American National Biography Online. New York: Oxford University Press, 2000–. Updated semiannually. http://www.anb.org/.

Burke's Peerage, Baronetage, and Knightage. 107th ed. Multiple vols. London: Burke's Peerage, 1826–. Also available, with additional related resources, at http://www.burkespeerage.com/.

Canadian Who's Who. Toronto: University of Toronto Press. Published annually, with semiannual supplements. Also available at http://canadianwhoswho.ca/.

Chambers Biographical Dictionary. 9th ed. London: Chambers Harrap, 2011.

Concise Dictionary of National Biography: From Earliest Times to 1985. 3 vols. Oxford: Oxford University Press, 1992.

Dictionary of American Biography. 11 vols. New York: Scribner's, 1995. Supplements. Succeeded by *American National Biography*.

Dictionary of Canadian Biography. 14 vols. Toronto: University of Toronto / Université Laval, 1966–. Supplements. Continued, with updates, at http://www.biographi.ca/.

A Dictionary of Scientists. Oxford: Oxford University Press, 1999. Published online 2003. https://doi.org/10.1093/acref/9780192800862.001.0001.

Directory of American Scholars. 10th ed. 6 vols. Detroit: Gale Group, 1942–.

The International Who's Who. London: Europa / Routledge, 1935–. Published annually. Also available at http://www.worldwhoswho.com/.

Marquis Who's Who on the Web. New Providence, NJ: Marquis Who's Who. Continually updated. http://www.marquiswhoswho.com/.

Merriam-Webster's Biographical Dictionary. Springfield, MA: Merriam-Webster, 1995. Continued by the biographical entries in *Merriam-Webster's Collegiate Dictionary* and *Merriam-Webster Unabridged* (bibliog. 3.1).

New York Times. Obituaries. https://www.nytimes.com/section/obituaries/. Also available from ProQuest Historical Newspapers.

Oxford Dictionary of National Biography. 60 vols. Prepared under various editors. New York: Oxford University Press, 1885–2004. Also available at http://www.oxforddnb.com/.

Thomson, David. *The New Biographical Dictionary of Film*. 6th ed. Knopf, 2014.

Who's Who. London: Bloomsbury, 1849–. Published annually.

Who's Who in America. New Providence, NJ: Marquis Who's Who, 1899–. Published biennially. See also *Marquis Who's Who on the Web*.

4.2 *Geography*

Canadian Geographical Names. Geographical Names Board of Canada, Natural Resources Canada. Continually updated. http://www.nrcan.gc.ca/earth-sciences/geography/place-names/10786.

Columbia Gazetteer of the World. 2nd ed. Edited by Saul B. Cohen. New York: Columbia University Press, 2008. Online ed., http://www.columbiagazetteer.org/.

Getty Thesaurus of Geographic Names Online. Getty Research Institute. Los Angeles: J. Paul Getty Trust. Continually updated. http://www.getty.edu/research/tools/vocabularies/tgn/.

Mayhew, Susan. *A Dictionary of Geography*. 4th ed. Oxford: Oxford University Press, 2009. https://doi.org/10.1093/acref/9780199231805.001.0001.

Merriam-Webster's Geographical Dictionary. 3rd ed. Springfield, MA: Merriam-Webster, 1997. Continued by the geographical entries in *Merriam-Webster's Collegiate Dictionary* and *Merriam-Webster Unabridged* (bibliog. 3.1).

NGA GEOnet Names Server (GNS). Washington, DC: National Geospatial-Intelligence Agency. Continually updated. http://geonames.nga.mil/gns/html/.

Oxford Atlas of the World. New York: Oxford University Press, 1992–. Updated annually.

The Times Comprehensive Atlas of the World. 14th ed. London: Times Books, 2014.

United States Board on Geographic Names. US Department of the Interior and US Geological Survey. Continually updated. https://geonames.usgs.gov/.

The World Factbook. Washington, DC: Central Intelligence Agency. Continually updated. https://www.cia.gov/library/publications/the-world-factbook/.

4.3 *Encyclopedias*

The Canadian Encyclopedia. Historica Canada. http://www.thecanadianencyclopedia.ca/.

Columbia Encyclopedia. 6th ed. New York: Columbia University Press, 2000.

Encyclopedia Americana. 30 vols. Danbury, CT: Scholastic Library, 2006. Also available from Grolier Online.

The New Encyclopaedia Britannica. 15th ed. 32 vols. Chicago: Encyclopaedia Britannica, 2010. Final print version. Continued online, as *Encyclopaedia Britannica*, at https://www.britannica.com/.

Wikipedia: The Free Encyclopedia. San Francisco: Wikimedia Foundation. https://www.wikipedia.org/.

4.4 *Almanacs and Yearbooks*

Canadian Almanac and Directory. Toronto: Grey House, 1847–. Published annually.

The Europa World of Learning. London: Europa / Routledge, 1947–. Published annually. Also available at http://www.worldoflearning.com/.

Europa World Year Book. London: Europa / Routledge, 1926–. Published annually. Also available at http://www.europaworld.com/pub/.

The Statesman's Yearbook. Basingstoke: Palgrave Macmillan, 1864–. Published annually. Also available at http://www.statesmansyearbook.com/.

Whitaker's Almanack. London: J. Whitaker & Sons / Stationery Office / Bloomsbury, 1868–. Published annually.

World Almanac and Book of Facts. New York: World Almanac Books, 1868–. Published annually.

4.5 *Guides to Books, Periodicals, and Other Sources*

ABI/Inform Complete. Ann Arbor, MI: ProQuest. http://www.proquest.com/products-services/abi_inform_complete.html.

Anglo-American Cataloguing Rules. See *RDA: Resource Description and Access*.

Ashley, Lowell E. *Cataloging Musical Moving Image Material: A Guide to the Bibliographical Control of Videorecordings and Films of Musical Performances and Other Music-Related Moving Image Material*. Canton, MA: Music Library Association, 1996.

Australian and New Zealand Books in Print. Melbourne: D. W. Thorpe, 1958–2003.

Bibliographic Index. New York: H. W. Wilson, 1937–2011.

BIOSIS Serial Sources. Philadelphia: Thomson Reuters, 2012.

Book Review Digest. New York: H. W. Wilson, 1903–. Published monthly, except for February and July, with annual cumulations. Also available, as *Book Review Digest Plus*, at https://www.ebscohost.com/wilson.

Book Review Index. Detroit: Gale Research Company, 1965–. Published monthly, with quarterly and annual cumulations. Also available as *Book Review Index Online*.

Books in Print. New York: R. R. Bowker. Published annually. Also available at http://www.booksinprint.com/.

British Books in Print. London: J. Whitaker; New York: R. R. Bowker. From 1988 to 2003 titled *Whitaker's Books in Print*; before 1988 variously titled *British Books in Print* or *The Reference Catalogue of Current Literature*. Continued by *Books in Print*, global edition.

Canadian Books in Print. Toronto: University of Toronto Press. Published annually through 2006. Continued by *Books in Print*, global edition.

Catalog of U.S. Government Publications. Washington, DC: Government Publishing Office. https://catalog.gpo.gov/.

Citing Records in the National Archives of the United States. General Information Leaflet 17. Washington, DC: National Archives and Records Administration, 2010. https://www.archives.gov/publications/general-info-leaflets/17-citing-records.html.

Dissertation Abstracts International. Ann Arbor, MI: University Microfilms International. Published monthly with annual cumulations.

Guide to Reference. 12th ed. Edited by Bob Kieft. Chicago: American Library Association, 2008. Ceased updating as of 2016. http://www.guidetoreference.org/.

Guide to the Contents of the Public Record Office. 3 vols. London: Her Majesty's Stationery Office, 1963–68.

Guide to U.S. Government Publications. Edited by Donna Batten. Formerly known as *Andriot*. Detroit: Gale Research Company. Updated annually.

Humanities Index. New York: H. W. Wilson. Published quarterly with annual cumulations. Continued by *Humanities Index International* at EBSCOhost.

Index Islamicus. Leiden: Brill. Published quarterly with quinquennial cumulations. Also available at http://bibliographies.brillonline.com/browse/index-islamicus.

Library of Congress Subject Headings. Washington, DC: Library of Congress Cataloging Distribution Service. Published annually. Now available online only, from http://www.loc.gov/aba/.

Livres disponibles [French books in print]. 8 vols. Paris: Cercle de la librairie, 1977–2004.

The New Walford Guide to Reference Resources. 9th ed. 3 vols. London: Facet, 2005–15.

New York Times Index. New York: New York Times Company. Annual cumulations. Available from ProQuest Historical Newspapers.

NLM Catalog: Journals Referenced in the NCBI Databases. Bethesda, MD: National Center for Biotechnology Information, US National Library of Medicine. https://www.ncbi.nlm.nih.gov/nlmcatalog/journals.

O'Gorman, Jack, ed. *Reference Sources for Small and Medium-Sized Libraries.* 8th ed. Chicago: American Library Association, 2014.

PAIS International in Print. New York: Public Affairs Information Service. Published monthly, with every fourth issue being cumulative. Continued by PAIS International, ProQuest.

Pemberton, John E., ed. *The Bibliographic Control of Official Publications.* New York: Pergamon, 1982. Also available at http://www.sciencedirect.com/science/book/9780080274195.

PubMed. Bethesda, MD: US National Library of Medicine. https://www.ncbi.nlm.nih.gov/pubmed/.

RDA: Resource Description and Access. Chicago: American Library Association; Ottawa: Canadian Library Association; London: Chartered Institute of Library and Information Professionals, 2010. Updated annually. Available at http://www.rdatoolkit.org/.

Reader's Guide to Periodical Literature. New York: H. W. Wilson. Published quarterly, with annual cumulations. Also available from EBSCOhost.

Rodgers, Frank. *A Guide to British Government Publications.* New York: H. W. Wilson, 1980.

Schmeckebier, Laurence F., and Roy B. Eastin. *Government Publications and Their Use.* 2nd ed. Washington, DC: Brookings Institution, 1969.

Science Citation Index. Philadelphia: Institute for Scientific Information. Published bimonthly with annual cumulations. Continued by Thomson Reuters Web of Science.

Social Sciences Index. New York: H. W. Wilson. Published quarterly with annual cumulations. Also available from EBSCOhost.

UKOP: Catalogue of United Kingdom Official Publications. London: Chadwyck-Healey. Continually updated. http://www.ukop.co.uk/.

Ulrich's International Periodicals Directory. New York: R. R. Bowker. Published annually. Supplemented quarterly by *Ulrich's Update.* Continued by Ulrichsweb Global Serials Directory, from ProQuest, http://ulrichsweb.serialssolutions.com/.

Verzeichnis Lieferbarer Bücher [German books in print]. Frankfurt am Main: Verlag der Buchhändler-Vereinigung. Published annually. Also available at http://www.vlb.de/.

Web of Science. See *Science Citation Index.*

Whitaker's Books in Print. See *British Books in Print.*

4.6 *Quotations and Trivia*

Bartlett, John. *Bartlett's Familiar Quotations: A Collection of Passages, Phrases, and Proverbs Traced to Their Sources in Ancient and Modern Literature.* 18th ed. Edited by Geoffrey O'Brien. New York: Little, Brown, 2012.

Crystal, David, and Hilary Crystal. *Words on Words: Quotations about Language and Languages.* Chicago: University of Chicago Press, 2000.

The Oxford Dictionary of Quotations. 8th ed. Edited by Elizabeth Knowles. Oxford: Oxford University Press, 2014. https://doi.org/10.1093/acref/9780199668700.001.0001.

Schott, Ben. *Schott's Original Miscellany.* 1st US ed. New York: Bloomsbury, 2003.

Shapiro, Fred R., ed. *Yale Book of Quotations.* New Haven, CT: Yale University Press, 2006.

4.7 *Abbreviations*

Abbreviations.com. STANDS4 Network. Continually updated. http://www.abbreviations.com/.

Acronyms, Initialisms & Abbreviations Dictionary: A Guide to Acronyms, Abbreviations, Contractions, Alphabetic Symbols, and Similar Condensed Appellations. 49th ed. 11 vols. Edited by Kristin Mallegg. Farmington Hills, MI: Gale, 2015.

Davis, Neil M. *Medical Abbreviations: 32,000 Conveniences at the Expense of Communication and Safety.* 15th ed. Warminster, PA: Neil M. Davis Associates, 2011.

Department of Defense Dictionary of Military and Associated Terms. Joint Publication 1-02. Washington, DC: Joint Chiefs of Staff. Updated monthly. http://www.dtic.mil/doctrine/dod_dictionary/.

Dorland's Dictionary of Medical Acronyms and Abbreviations. 7th ed. Philadelphia: Saunders, 2015.

International Organization for Standardization. *Information and Documentation—Rules for the Abbreviation of Title Words and Titles of Publications.* ISO 4. Paris: ISO, 1997.

Molloy, Mike. Acronym Finder. Continually updated. http://www.acronymfinder.com/.

Vance, Burt. *A Dictionary of Abbreviations.* Online only. Oxford University Press, 2011. https://doi.org/10.1093/acref/9780199698295.001.0001.

Webster's Guide to Abbreviations. Springfield, MA: Merriam-Webster, 1985. Superseded by the entries for abbreviations in *Merriam-Webster's Collegiate Dictionary* and *Merriam-Webster Unabridged* (bibliog. 3.1).

5 Miscellaneous Works Cited in Text

ALA-LC Romanization Tables: Transliteration Schemes for Non-Roman Scripts. Compiled and edited by Randall K. Barry. Washington, DC: Library of Congress, 1997. Updated at http://www.loc.gov/catdir/cpso/roman.html.

American Naturalist. Journal published monthly by the University of Chicago Press for the American Society of Naturalists. http://www.journals.uchicago.edu/toc/an/current.

Baker-Shenk, Charlotte, and Dennis Cokely. *American Sign Language: A Teacher's Resource Text on Grammar and Culture.* Washington, DC: Gallaudet University Press, 1991.

Daniels, Peter T., and William Bright, eds. *The World's Writing Systems.* New York: Oxford University Press, 1996.

Duden: Die deutsche Rechtschreibung. 26th ed. Der Duden in zwölf Bänden, vol. 1. Mannheim: Dudenverlag, 2013.

Gall, Gerald L., F. Pearl Eliadis, and France Allard. *The Canadian Legal System.* 5th ed. Scarborough, ON: Carswell, 2004.

Grevisse, Maurice. *Le bon usage: Grammaire française.* 15th ed. Edited by André Goosse. Paris: Duculot, 2011. Also available at http://www.lebonusage.com/.

HGNC. Database of human gene names. HUGO Gene Nomenclature Committee. http://www.genenames.org/.

History of Religions. Journal published quarterly by the University of Chicago Press. http://www.journals.uchicago.edu/toc/hr/current.

Horticulture. Magazine published ten times a year by F+W Publications.

International Code of Nomenclature for Algae, Fungi, and Plants (Melbourne Code). Prepared and edited by John McNeill et al. Regnum Vegetabile 154. Königstein, Germany: Koeltz Scientific Books, 2012. Also available at http://www.iapt-taxon.org/nomen/.

International Code of Zoological Nomenclature. 4th ed. London: International Trust for Zoological Nomenclature, 1999. Also available at http://www.iczn.org/iczn/index.jsp.

International Journal of Middle East Studies. Journal published quarterly by Cambridge University Press for the Middle East Studies Association of North America.

International Telecommunication Union. *Notation for National and International Telephone Numbers, E-Mail Addresses and Web Addresses.* ITU-T Recommendation E.123, February 2, 2001. http://www.itu.int/rec/T-REC-E.123-200102-I/en.

Lesina, Roberto. *Il nuovo manuale di stile.* 2nd ed. Bologna: Zanichelli, 2009.

MacEllven, Douglass T., Michael J. McGuire, Neil A. Campbell, and John N. Davis. *Legal Research Handbook.* 6th ed. Markham, ON: LexisNexis Canada, 2013.

Mouse Genome Database. Mouse Genome Informatics. http://www.informatics.jax.org/.

The New Grove Dictionary of Music and Musicians. 2nd ed. 29 vols. Edited by Stanley Sadie. New York: Grove, 2001. Also available at http://www.oxfordmusiconline.com/.

The Oxford Classical Dictionary. 4th ed. Edited by Simon Hornblower, Anthony Spawforth, and Esther Eidinow. Oxford: Oxford University Press, 2012. https://doi.org/10.1093/acref/9780199545568.001.0001.

Physical Review Letters. Published weekly by the American Physical Society. http://journals.aps.org/prl/.

Pullum, Geoffrey K., and William A. Ladusaw. *Phonetic Symbol Guide*. 2nd ed. Chicago: University of Chicago Press, 1996.

Real Academia Española and Asociación de Academias de la Lengua Española. *Diccionario panhispánico de dudas*. Madrid: RAE / ASALE, 2005. Also available at http://www.rae.es/.

———. *Ortografía de la lengua española*. Madrid: RAE / ASALE, 2010. Also available at http://www.rae.es/.

Thorin, Suzanne E., and Carole Franklin Vidali. *The Acquisition and Cataloging of Music and Sound Recordings: A Glossary*. Canton, MA: Music Library Association, 1984.

Unicode Collation Algorithm. Unicode Technical Standard no. 10. Version 9.0.0. Edited by Mark Davis, Ken Whistler, and Markus Scherer. Unicode Consortium, May 18, 2016. http://unicode.org/reports/tr10/tr10-34.html.

Valli, Clayton, Ceil Lucas, Kristin J. Mulrooney, and Miako Villanueva. *Linguistics of American Sign Language: An Introduction*. 5th ed. Washington, DC: Gallaudet University Press, 2011.

Wertheim, Eric. *The Naval Institute Guide to Combat Fleets of the World: Their Ships, Aircraft, and Systems*. 16th ed. Annapolis, MD: Naval Institute Press, 2013.

Zurick, Timothy. *Army Dictionary and Desk Reference*. 4th ed. Mechanicsburg, PA: Stackpole Books, 2010.

Index

References are to paragraph numbers except where specified as table, figure (fig.), or page number (p.). Page numbers in the online edition link directly to terms in the glossary.

The Chicago Manual of Style

Designed by Matt Avery
Typeset by Graphic Composition, Inc., Bogart, Georgia
Book printed and bound by Edwards Brothers Malloy, Ann Arbor, Michigan
Jacket printed by Phoenix Color, Hagerstown, Maryland

Composed in Lyon, designed by Kai Bernau, and Atlas Grotesk, designed by Kai Bernau, Susana Carvalho, and Christian Schwartz
Printed on 50# Glatfelter Offset
Bound in Arrestox Linen

DISTRIBUTED BY THE CHICAGO DISTRIBUTION CENTER

X Y & Z 1 2 3

D E F G H I J K

T U V W X Y &

0 A B C D E F

P Q R S T U V

6 7 8 9 0 A B C

M N O P Q R S

1 2 3 4 5 6 7 8 9

H I J K L M N O

X Y & Z 1 2 3